Cultures in Contact

A book in the series

Comparative and International
Working-Class History

General Editors: Andrew Gordon, Harvard University

Daniel James, Indiana University

Alexander Keyssar, Harvard University

CULTURES
IN
CONTACT

World Migrations in the Second Millennium

Dirk Hoerder

Duke University Press   *Durham & London 2002*

© 2002 Duke University Press All rights reserved
Printed in the United States of America on acid-free paper ∞
Typeset in Trump Mediaeval by Tseng Information Systems, Inc.
Library of Congress Cataloging-in-Publication Data appear
on the last printed page of this book.

Contents

Maps and Figures

FIGURES

Acknowledgments and Dedication

As a student I was fortunate to experience the fascinating 1960s and 1970s when new questions were asked, when the "underdogs" or "working classes" were placed in the center of attention. Like other eager young men I later realized that women had gotten lost in men's historiography. Throughout my academic career women in scholarship have persistently asked questions and improved my approaches to a gendered world, the women among my student assistants changed generic masculine language to gender-neutral wording without bothering to ask. Edward Said's critique of orientalism and the concept of imaginary ethnography as well as studies of how the West was viewed by Others have helped me to understand processes of knowledge production. I have benefited greatly from all of them.

I have read widely for this research, but my languages are limited to German, English, and French. Friends and colleagues have on occasion helped with Spanish, Portuguese, Italian, Swedish, and Dutch. Scholars from some countries, who customarily provide English or French abstracts with their publications, have facilitated my access to other national discourses, as did my colleagues in the internationally cooperative Labor Migration Project. In particular, I am grateful to my colleagues at Duke University who provided a stimulating intellectual environment. Toronto colleagues—Canadians of Italian, Ukrainian, and other origins—welcomed me whenever I did research in that delightful city. My study of Canadian immigrant autobiographies has supplemented the global perspective taken here. I am indebted to my students at York University, the University of Toronto, and Duke University, for lively discussions, and to those in Bremen, who shared their own migratory experiences with me.

I am indebted to the University of Bremen for agreeing to a leave of absence and to the Deutsche Forschungsgemeinschaft and the Canada Council who supported parts of it. Its scope notwithstanding, no major grants and research staff have supported the project—some of its limitations derive from the fact that it was a single-person undertaking. But no individual works in a void. Marion Schulz, Camilla Sledz, Gabriele Intemann, Deborah Allen, and others helped with the bibliographical searches. Paul Betz's copyediting, Irina Schmitt's, and Annika McPherson's proofreading were a major help. I could test my approaches by lectures at several North

American and European universities and discuss my findings at the meetings of the Social Science History Association.

Differentiated arguments of studies cited often had to be reduced to a few lines. Dates, even in standard works, often varied slightly from one to the next. I have caught some such inconsistencies but others may have escaped my notice. Several colleagues read whole chapters or provided comments on my understanding of distant cultures and migration systems: Nancy Green and Jack Veugelers, Lewis H. Siegelbaum and Donna R. Gabaccia, Steve Hochstadt, and many others named in the annotations at appropriate places. Martin Klein, Sucheta Mazumdar, Martin Franzbach, Gabriele Scardellato, Robert E. Johnson, and Leslie Page Moch read particular chapters and saved me from many errors, as did two anonymous reviewers and the series editors. All of them have questioned assumptions, improved interpretations, and provided encouragement when the vast subject matter threatened to overwhelm me. I am deeply grateful to all of them—and take sole responsibility for any errors remaining.

In particular I am indebted to my wife, Christiane Harzig, an accomplished migration historian in her own right, for many stimulating discussions. Our daughter Anna usually bore my mental life in the past with patience. Once, after another lengthy trip to give papers and do research, she greeted me with that piercing look of hers. "If this continues, I am going to emigrate. (*Pause*) And I am going to write emigrant letters—*then* you have something to do research on. (*Another pause*) But I am going to copy parts of them from other emigrants' books. And (*intensification of the piercing look*) then you are lost!" I dedicate this book to both of them.

Contexts: An Introductory Note to Readers

Migration, once defined as a crossing of borders between states, is now understood as a social process and appears as a basic condition of human societies. It begins with departure out of parental households and ranges as far as transcontinental or transoceanic moves—a geographic scope that might be one and the same move of a man or a woman. On the other hand, marriage migration from one village to the next could involve more demands for adaptation than a move from a society to an ethnic enclave a continent away. Dislocation by famine or war could end in death, foraging nearby or afar, or in long-distance migration. In the medieval and early modern periods merchant travel, military service abroad, political exile, and student mobility could and did provide information for others who then migrated permanently. In this survey no restrictive definition of mobility and migration has been adopted, though distinctions are outlined.

The comprehensive approach chosen here—the connection of economic region, social world, polity, and family of departure via intervening inducements and obstacles to a recharting of life-courses after arrival—demands both analysis of the whole of the societies and of human agency of particular men and women. From the point of view of individuals, societies consist of regional economies and cultures and, after migration, of religious, craft, or ethnic networks. I have tried to indicate ranges of options voluntary migrants felt they had as well as the constraints faced by forced migrants.

As to numbers of migrants, it was impossible to aggregate "pluralist" and contradictory information into one set of data. Sometimes individuals were counted, sometimes heads of families; often statistics did not distinguish gross from net migration. States, or rather state administrators, had specific interests to inflate or deflate migration statistics and generally lacked adequate systems of collecting data. Some migrants avoided being counted; others were counted repeatedly; sometimes nonmigrants wanted to be counted. In a state-centered approach, units of counting vary in size from China to Luxembourg or, like the Habsburg Empire or the Southeast Asian states, changed boundaries over the course of history. I refer to estimates and to the revision of estimates, sometimes voicing skepticism of high estimates.

Any work of this scope, unless a synthesis in a few deft strokes, creates difficulties in organization. I have opted for an integrated chronological, topical, and spatial perspective. To help readers interested in one particular region of the world or in one particular topic navigate their way through this study, references at the end of specific sections provide guidance to chapters or parts of chapters that continue the regional or topical discussions. For example, the migration history of Russia/the Soviet Union/the Commonwealth of Independent States begins as part of European urbanization and regional agricultural settlement (chap. 12), separates into a distinct system (chap. 13), then becomes one of several forced labor systems (chap. 17), and opens up again after 1989 (chap 19.9). Similarly, forced labor appears in the Mediterranean system of slavery; expands into Asian bondage, African human pawnship, and European indenture; continues into African slavery and Asian "coolie" labor; and extends into twentieth-century German, Russian, and Japanese forced labor. I have frequently pointed to similarities between migration processes in different cultures—reservoirs for cheap labor, for example, like Polish territories for the economy of Germany and Mexican people for the economy of the United States. Such comparisons are but heuristic devices to understand distant, "foreign," developments within familiar frameworks. They do not adequately reflect differences between specific migratory movements.

Conventional designations for pre–nineteenth-century states, like "France" and "Britain" or "India" and "China," impose statist concepts on diversities of regional cultures without even common languages. For lack of better terms, this study, too, has to rely on such defective terminology. Similarly, conventional designations for social regimes are misleading. Serfdom, for example, suggests sedentary ways of life under lordly control. How did enserfed families react when soil was exhausted, when children needed land, or when an epidemic killed off most of their neighbors? Were peasants not agents, if constrained ones, of their own lives? The same question has been asked about slaves in the Americas and about carters and boatmen in China. About one-half of the populations living at any particular time in history change residence by marriage migration. Many migrate to perceived opportunities and to shape their own and their children's lives—provided the emotional cost in ruptured relationships does not increase beyond expected material advantage. Quantifiers would have difficulties in approaching these multiple scales, but each and every migrant weighs his or her or the family's options and arrives at a sum total, a chart for their life-course decisions.

One colleague in migration research in exasperation reduced the data for his graphs and maps because otherwise they would have looked like a bowl of spaghetti. Human movement might as well be compared to the grains in a sack of rice. In a way, both spaghetti and sacks of rice would be easy to study; migrants, by contrast, have minds of their own and plans for their futures. Myriads of moves across space result from the will of men and women to fashion lives. The survival of forced migrants depended on their will to reconstruct their identities and attempt to regain some control over their values, emotions, and relationships. In contrast, throughout history rulers and administrators, plantation owners and capitalists, theorists of race and population planners have reduced human mobility to schemes facilitating their policies and reduced women and men and children to human material. Their constructs were—and are—of pitiful simplicity when compared to the complex choices of a South American Native family faced with armed Spanish and Portuguese newcomers, or those of a Chinese peasant family with insufficient land, or those of a Turkish family caught up in twentieth-century labor migrations. In many of the grand schemes of states and political economies, grains of rice were treated with more care than human beings.

My own cultural world, the Euro–North American one, has shaped my perspective. It has helped me to transcend national histories and to integrate the multiple migrations of particular ethnic groups into the Atlantic Migration System. But as an attempt to provide a synthesis of migrations worldwide, of cultural interaction and conflict, the Atlantic perspective proved to be confining. It did not equip me to deal with cultural intricacies of the Indic World or the cultures of sub-Saharan Africa. In writing this book, I have changed terminologies and viewpoints from one draft to the next in order to move away from Atlanto-centric perspectives. I hope that this global approach will provoke further critical discussion, that my arguments will be expanded and revised by scholars whose background is culturally different.

Exploration of many cultures involves a great number of contrasting and conflicting perspectives (map 1.1). Where is east, where west? America is a western culture viewed from Europe, an eastern one viewed across the Pacific. Maps contain ambiguities, and cartography has been Eurocentric for centuries. According to Harley and Woodward, "Recognition of the ideological, religious, and symbolic aspects of maps, particularly when linked with a more traditional appreciation of maps for political and practical purposes, greatly enhances the claim that cartography can be regarded as a graphic language in its own right." Early maps have been called "imagined evocations of space"—but is a late-twentieth-century Western map of seventeenth-century Indian Ocean and East Asian trade that merely charts routes of European colonizer shipping more than a self-serving image, an instrument of power? And which chronology do we follow? When in the Latin Christian Era the year 2000 began, Coptic Christians still lived in 1716, and the Jewish world had entered they year 5760. The Tamil calendar pegs the count at 2029; the Buddhist one at 2543, the Sikh one at 301. Or should time be counted not by religions but by arrival in a territory? Then the first people in Australia might count the year 42,000.[1]

Who is the Other? Medieval "heretics" like twentieth-century C.E. "draft-dodgers" espouse different ethical principles, political beliefs, and emotional worlds than those with the power to define and to shape received discourse. An emigrant in one culture is an immigrant at the end of his or her voyage—and perhaps a vagrant in between. An innocuous statement, such as "the farmer sold his grain," may disguise family labor and migrations.

It is impossible to refashion the whole terminology, chronology, and conceptualization of migration, but I attempt to use it cautiously. Different human ways of living—whether in small groups (tribes), within limited cultural territories (ethnicities), or in large entities (states, nations, empires), or of continental or transcontinental dimensions (civilizations)—are equally valid cultural expressions. Amerindian retreat is as much a migration as Euro-American expansion, and both are connected by power relations. National cultures, a very recent phenomenon in the history and material life of societies, are in constant evolution and transformation. "Race" and "color of skin" are social constructs whose connotations vary over time and across cultures; the White/Colored dichotomy posits that White is no color; designations like the "Indian" or "Negro problem" are White discursive strategies to hide the problem of White racism. Usage of terms also changes over time and from one culture to the other. "Whites" are also called Caucasians, but the peoples of the Caucasus region are not necessarily considered White in the present. Europeans and Americans of European origin think of themselves as White; the U.S. census defines the peoples of North Africa and southwestern Asia as White. On the other hand, Anglo-Saxon and Nordic racist thought of the late nineteenth century considered East Europeans, South Europeans, the Irish, and Jews not to be White. Such constructions are numerous, and there are as many shades of white as of any other color.

In this study, I deal with men and women leaving their homes or, to use a different emphasis, striking out into new directions. They lived under constructs of color and culture but wanted to evaluate losses, options, and chances according to their own terms of reference. I attempt to focus on their lives, cultural expressions, and initiatives, not merely on "streams," "flows," or "waves" of migrant masses.

1

Worlds in Motion, Cultures in Contact

Historians study men and, less so until recently, women who left archives rather than traces in the sand. Thus migrants have been shortchanged in historiography though human mobility, the agency of men and women, continuously changed societies and redefined parameters of action. My first goal is to describe and analyze migration from the local level to the continent-wide and global. My second goal is to discuss interaction resulting from migration. Warrior migrants aggressively destroy existing societies. Peasant and labor migrants aim at becoming part of the host societies. In intermediate stops and at the end of their journeys they have to earn their living and establish new communities. They fall in love and beget and give birth to children, fuse their cultural traditions with exigencies of the new surroundings, and develop new subsistence bases. Third, I focus on the self-changing societies into which migrants enter. They do not undermine stable cultures. In fact, societies throttled by stability face the departure of men and women who look for opportunities more challenging and promising for their life-courses.

1.1 People on the Move: Changes over Ten Centuries

This inquiry begins with a Mediterranean-outward approach and traces connections to East Asia and sub-Saharan Africa. Equally valid perspectives would start from China or the Gulf of Persia–Indic World. In Europe migrations of whole peoples— Visigoth, Teutonic, Slavic—ended in the eleventh century with permanent settlement, and gender relations probably changed at this time.[1] In Central Asia and Africa people's migrations continued for several more centuries. Historic migrations in other civilizations were summarized retrospectively when in the sixteenth century European colonizers began to trade with peoples along the coasts of all oceans. The colonizers' construct of a White versus Colored dichotomy between themselves and Others hid processes of ethnogenesis in which colonial creole peoples emerged. It assumed cultural hierarchies and posited racial superiorities where the dichotomy was one of power and the differences were cultural.

Onto such mixed peoples nineteenth-century Europe-centered gatekeepers imposed constructs of ethnoculturally homogeneous nations—though among Chinese sages concepts of superiority existed to which Japanese propagandists juxtaposed their people's valor. For centuries peoples from the three continents of Asia, Africa, and Europe interacted from the Levant to the South Seas. The cultures of the Indian Ocean or of the Americas, not yet named, influenced each other and changed over time. Mediterranean, Chinese, and Indian traders formed mixed societies along the coasts of the globe. Slaves were forced to migrate; peasant people migrated voluntarily. All intermarried or consorted with resident peoples. Genetically "pure" or culturally self-contained peoples are merely myths, and continuities from times immemorial are but ephemeral self-constructions of ethnic identities. Ethnic pluralism and multiculturalism, the catchwords of the 1990s, have been societal practice throughout history.

Migration, cultural interaction, and change have been constituent features of human life, of construction of societies, of commercial exchange. Views of the Self and the Other often were (and are) self-serving. The Central Asian and Islamic "Turks" were said to threaten Christian Europe at a time when Latin Christians destroyed the Byzantine Christian World and annihilated dissenters. When under seventeenth-century Islamic Ottoman rule different peoples and creeds coexisted, if only in hierarchical relationships, the Christian powers of the "Holy Roman Empire" and beyond destroyed one-third of West Central Europe's people in warfare over religious persuasions and power. In the present, when Third World refugees are said to flood industrialized societies, First World capital penetrates the remotest corners of the globe and uproots local people. Who is perceived as a stranger, as the Other, depends on power relationships, on contemporary gatekeepers and retrospective historiographers.

Five periods of migration and cultural change may be discerned. In the first, the multi-civilizational Mediterranean and Black Sea World of Latin and Byzantine Christendom, of Sunni and Shiite Islam, and of Jewish communities included western Asia, southern Europe, and northern Africa. Caravan traders on trans-Saharan routes connected the world of the Eastern Mediterranean to Black Africa. Trans-Asian routes, interrupted by Mongol expansion at the end of the thirteenth century, were reestablished during the *pax mongolica*. The Mediterranean World's core shifted from the intercultural Alexandria-to-Constantinople crescent to Urban Italy in Latin Christendom. Transalpine Europe remained distant until the fifteenth century, though merchants traveled northward over the mountain passes and via fairs to Bruges in the Urban Netherlands. The endless feudal wars in the north, however, induced merchants from Urban Italy to explore a westward circum-Iberian route with their galleys. A separate northern "common market," the fourteenth-century Baltic-centered Hanseatic Federation, lost its position to the North Sea–oriented Dutch within a century. After 1500 trade and the commercial core shifted to the urban segments of the Atlantic seaboard, the Iberian and Dutch societies. In the eastern Mediterranean, the emerging Ottoman Empire realigned Muslim states, both Turkoman and Arab. Genoese merchants traded with Islamic Arab merchants and through them with India. Trade zones surpassed state boundaries, while commercial links and the mobility of producers connected civilizations—but were also forces of conflict and competition.

The Mediterranean slave system brought Central Asian, North African, and Black African men and women to southern Europe and European ones to North Africa. Christian crusaders mobilized masses, but achieved no unity. Latin, Byzantine, Coptic, Nestorian, and other denominations interacted with the various Judaic, Islamic, Indic-Hinduist, and Buddhist East Asian denominations. Frankish settlers in Palestine converted to Arab-Islamic culture; Norman peoples settled along the Atlantic coast and in Sicily; peasant migrations made Central Europe a zone of interspersed Slavic and Germanic settlement. Towns and cities across the world depended on continuous in-migration to even maintain population levels. The fourteenth-century climatic change and plagues, in which one-third of the Eurasian peoples died, formed the major caesura; recovery of population size and previous levels of economic activity took a century and a half. In transalpine Europe, wars, struggles between ruling families and their political apparatuses, and doctrinal rigidity of religious gatekeepers influenced migratory patterns. Only after the Peace of Westphalia in 1648 did a new state system and new migrations evolve.

By the fifteenth century, "Europe" became a concept, and Latin Christianity had externalized Others, Jews in particular. The Islamic World had been unified by the house of Osman from the Balkans and the Black Sea through its Anatolian core into North Africa and the Gulf of Hormuz. New bureaucratic rationalities competed with hereditary privileges in empires and religions. The Christian and Islamic civilizations' "time of troubles" from the 1570 to the 1650s dislocated men and women.[2] Throughout the period, the construction of Others in ethnic or religious terms amalgamated the many into larger categories, such as the Huns, Turks, Franks, and Germans. On a cognitive level this process provided simple recognizable structures for the perplexing multiplicity of peoples. On the level of social relations it provided boundaries and permitted in-group solidarity. On the level of power relationships it denigrated the Other.

A second period, beginning as early as the mid-fifteenth century, brought merchants and soldiers from the Western Mediterranean to societies of other large and elaborate civilizations. The societies of Western Africa had been part of Arab-Mediterranean trade and had developed their own patterns of migration and cultural exchange. The civilizations of the Americas were characterized by labor migrations and dislocation by war. In the Indic World the merchants of the trade emporia moved and settled from East Africa to Siam, from cities of the Gujarat to southern China. The arrival of Europeans, though involving at first only a trickle of migrants, overwhelmed populations in the Americas by pathogens and destruction, wrought havoc in African societies by the transatlantic slave trade, and established small coastal enclaves in Asia. Migration and settlement in Asia or Africa had as a corollary intermarriage, consorting, or rape. Children of mixed cultural background were born; new peoples came into being. After contact with the Europeans, peaceful migrations and military conquest resulted in re-formation of peoples; modern peoples created and recreated themselves: Spanish-Italian-Native in Argentina, Dutch-African-English-Indian in the Cape Colony, and Native-Chinese-Other on the Malayan peninsula. In Europe, on the other hand, the Iberian states expelled Jews and Moriscos who reestablished their trade connections from North Africa and Amsterdam. The feudal orders discouraged commercial enterprise and physical labor.

An intercivilizational comparative approach to migrations suggests fundamental similarities. Across the globe administrators and mercenaries, clerics and pilgrims, merchants and traders, peasants and laborers, vagrants and marginal people moved, were sent to distant locations, or departed from adverse living conditions. Wherever rulers or religious leaders built palaces, fortifications, or temples and cathedrals, immigrant artisans and artists settled. Migrant laborers built roads and bridges in China and in the Andes. Architects of the Taj Mahal, the cathedral of Chartres, and Tenochtitlán needed skilled workmen from elsewhere, and women came to feed them. Regardless of culture, women dominated in the production of textiles and clothing, and service jobs were taken by migrating single women. Warrior segments of peoples penetrated into the territories of others, settled, killed, intermingled, and adjusted to the new social and natural environments. Such migrations involved a search for "frontiers" of opportunity; all—including the belatedly constructed prototype, the settlement of the North American West—also involved the expulsion of previously settled peoples. Frontier societies are characterized by the absence of political structures, of powerful capital and rigid class structures, and of corporatist domination. Opportunities to gain access to local resources were comparatively large. Each change in relative economic power engendered important migratory movements on all levels of social life.[3]

Within this global framework, migrations were unique to each society, depending on economic practices, social structures, and power relationships, as well as on the right to relocate, gender hierarchies, and children's position. Intersocietally they depended on investment strategies and exploitative relationships. Capital flows from the cores provided just the initial impetus. The newcomers traded and transported enslaved and temporarily indentured laborers in ever larger numbers to plantation economies. Labor created wealth depending on soil fertility, mineral resources, or climate. Profits from the labor of colonized populations or immigrant settlers were remitted to stockowners in the cores. These reverse transfers impoverished and mobilized laboring men and women in the peripheries and changed demand for labor in the metropoles.

Emigrants from Europe headed in two directions. The many from the peasant strata moved to colonies of agrarian settlement in temperate climates; the few with capital and power or their representatives moved to tropical territories. Self-serving assumptions that local populations, whether in the Caribbean or in Asia, would labor for the European foreigners came to naught, and European underclasses could not be mobilized easily for distant labor. Settlers in temperate zones chose to advance cost of travel to laboring men and women who bound themselves to work off the debt. Plantation owners in the tropical economies chose to rely on labor bound into lifetime hereditary slavery by force. Religion and color of skin served as criteria to hierarchize and exploit people.

In a third period, industrialization and concentration of production in the Atlantic cores demanded a reallocation of labor from the agrarian to the urban sector. Artisans and skilled workers migrated with their families. Unskilled rural laboring people migrated to repetitive factory work. Imagined or real opportunities in Britain, the United States ("America"), European Russia, or the Germanies became more easily accessible by railroads and iron-hulled steamships. Those impoverished to a degree that they could not even afford low-cost ocean travel had to stay—or to move locally and intraregionally on foot. The producing classes of mercantilist states became the surplus populations of the new industrial order in liberal states, an internationally mobile proletariat. Migration in a Russo-Siberian System remained distinct to the end of the nineteenth century.

In Asia under colonialism, the Chinese trader diaspora connected with the foreigners' enclaves, and local populations either were mobilized against their will and transported to distant plantations or were immobilized to produce export crops locally. The first system of forced mass migration, African chattel slavery in the Americas, was replaced by a second system, contractual, often slavelike work of men and women from Asia. Like European serfs, African slaves and Asian coolies in day-to-day resistance and in reproductive culture from sundown to sunup strove for at least partially self-directed lives within the structural constraints. Indentured Asian laborers had some choice in deciding whether to return home, reindenture, or form independent immigrant communities. The internally diverse and well-organized Indian community in Southeast Africa's Natal, for example, was as much an immigrant community as comparable communities in North American cities.

In the nineteenth century, the separate colonial systems of particular states became an integrated imperial world order. Europe's fast-growing population spread across the world as settlers, and the capitalists of Europe jointly with their North American descendants established a tight grip on global resources. Whenever capital was to be made profitable, racialized and gendered laborers were recruited by experiment and calculation to tap the cheapest supply. The power relationship between classes and between core and colonies determined who was moved where or who had the possibility to move on his or her own initiative. High returns on capital were matched by low returns on labor. Color of skin other than White assigned people to low-paying, highly controlled work, as did female sex, caste, and class. For voluntary migrant workers, internationalized segments of labor markets provided options. East Elbian agricultural laborers, for example, chose between Berlin and Chicago, while South Indian Tamils did so between Ceylon, other Asian destinations, and East Africa. But they tended to move along specific migration paths and to rely on networks established by fellow villagers, fellow workers, or kinspeople abroad. The

Pacific Migration System began to supplement the Atlantic System until its slow-down by exclusion of Asians from North American states. This period lasted to 1914–18 in the Euro-American World and to 1937 in Asia.

The fourth period, the decades of the first half of the twentieth century, is characterized by vast refugee migrations in Europe, accelerated migrations in Asia, and stagnation of the Atlantic Migration System (but with initial steps toward a North and Central American Migration Region). During the Age of Bourgeois Revolution, political exiles and refugees crossed borders, and economically active burghers and educated citizens constructed folk cultures into national identities and demanded cultural homogenization, whether it be, for example, Magyarization or Americanization. People excluded from self-styled nations as minorities began to emigrate, and migrants to allegedly homogeneous cultures became aliens expected to acculturate. Adaptation, an interaction over generations, was enforced under the rule of democratic nationalism.

The two North American states, which closed their borders to Asian immigrants in the 1880s, took divergent approaches to East and South Europeans after 1917. The United States curtailed their immigration on grounds of racial inferiority, while Canada, still in search of immigrants, ranked East European families as sturdy agriculturalists. When economic power shifted from Western Europe to the United States, and when the unrestricted speculation ended in the depression of the 1930s, transatlantic migration fell to low levels. Within the United States a mass migration of African Americans from the southern sharecropping and plantation economies replenished the labor reservoir of the northern industrial sectors. French-Canadians moved to the northeast, Mexican *braceros* to the southwest.

In Europe and northern Asia, the Russo-Siberian System increasingly involved rural-to-urban migrations and under Stalinism forced labor. Nazi Germany imported forced laborers and resettled ethnic populations. After both wars, tens of millions of people fled or were expelled, in many instances reversing migratory directions of previous centuries.

Latin America as well as northern and sub-Saharan Africa, experienced internal rural-to-urban migrations. Caribbean inter-island migrations expanded northward to the cities of the United States and Canada. In Africa, still under colonial rule, self-mobilization increased. It was not the oft-cited economists' construct, the "invisible hand of the market," that reallocated labor, but rather the interests of families to monetarize income, diversify economic activities, weigh new opportunities.

Within Asia, the contract labor system lasted to the 1930s. In China recruitment expanded from the southern to the northern provinces, while in India populations remained more sedentary, though interrural migrations and moves to mines and factories increased. Millions of Chinese peasants migrated to Manchuria, one of the large colonizing ventures on the northern frontier of agriculture. Japan began its imperialist expansion by sending colonists to Korea, Manchukuo, and China. The end of World War II and the independence of colonized lands also brought religious strife and mass flight.

Across their possessions, the colonizer powers had envisioned some type of Anglicization or Francoization. Conversion was temporarily achieved through "colonial auxiliaries," through merchant brokers like Indian passenger migrants or Overseas Chinese, and through the concept of one global British citizenship or culturally French *négritude*. But educational migrants from colonial elites to universities of the cores developed human and social capital that, combined with indigenous cultural resources, came to challenge and replace White administrators and rule. When power relationships changed, migratory directions reversed toward Europe. Independence often involved massive population shifts, in particular the flight of colonial auxiliaries, whether from Algeria, Burma, or Indonesia.

Finally, in the decades since the 1950s new patterns emerged: transpacific migration, return migration from former colonies, multiple labor migrations, and refugee generation as well as distinct regional labor migration systems in the developing world.

In the postcolonial period, Third World migrants entered the metropoles in increasing numbers. The internationalized non-White underclasses began to migrate into social spaces that internationalized white-colored middle classes had reserved for themselves. Monochrome White societies had changed into multicolored ones by the mid-1960s when European "mother countries" or "fatherlands" imposed restrictions—at a time when in North America racist immigration quotas were lifted. In the United States, Asian and Pacific Islander in-migration grew from 13 percent of the total during the 1960s to more than one half since the early eighties. In Canada, too, they eclipsed European-origin migrants. The transpacific moves occurred concomitant with larger internal South, Southeast, and East Asian migrations.

While the North American continent became part of both the Atlantic and Pacific economic spheres, the transatlantic migratory connection disintegrated. In its place, two separate south-north migration systems involved men and women from the Caribbean-Mexican region to North America and from the Mediterranean—once again including North Africa—to transalpine Europe. The rising economic power of oil-producing Arab states resulted in a third labor migration system of Egyptian and Palestinian migrant men, Southeast Asian women for domestic work, and experts from Europe and North America. In Asia, India and China experienced huge internal migrations. From the Southeast Asian economies, women decided to migrate to the service sectors of North America and the "Middle East," the British term for the cultures of the eastern Mediterranean and the Gulf of Hormuz. Fast developing economies, for example on the Asian side of the Pacific Rim, attracted migrants. But Japan attempted to prevent immigration of men and women of other cultures, while European states sought to impede the acculturation of guest-worker immigrants.

At the turn to the twenty-first century, the division of the globe into a North Atlantic core (First World), a separate and formerly closed socialist region (Second World), and a peripheral Third World, is being replaced by a realignment of centers of investment and patterns of migration. New regional and intercontinental migration systems emerge that no longer resemble those of previous centuries.

These global migrations are unique in character but not new in kind. Medieval migrations encompassed the then-known world, colonial migrations much of the globe, and the proletarian free and bound mass migrations the whole globe. Late-twentieth-century migrations are distinguished from earlier ones by their absolute volume, if not necessarily by ratio of migrants per thousand of population. Rapid moves back and forth between societies of origin and receiving societies and tele-communication between movers and persisters enable migrants to function across cultural space, to obtain a transnational or transcultural social competence. The new migration systems result from disparities between capitalist and decolonized worlds and from migrant decision making in the context of internationalized segmented labor markets in structures of "global apartheid."[4]

The *longue durée* approach to migration challenges traditional interpretations. First, migration was ubiquitous and ever-present. Attention to institutions, politics, and settled cultures focused on residents, neglected migrants. Second, it illustrates how resident populations interact with migrants culturally, intermarry, or fight. Much of the migrants' input into cultures and social systems over time appears neither as "foreign" nor as deliberately constructed, since, once adopted, innovations become part of the Self and are considered indigenous. For the next generation they appear as local traditions.

1.2   Changing Paradigms and New Approaches

Into the 1960s, migration history in Europe and North America pursued an Atlanto-centric approach emphasizing the westward flow of agrarian settlers and neglecting moves of workers and of women, return migration and multiple crossings. The image of free migrations into a democratic society, the United States, fit the Euro-American worldview of the times. Transpacific and interperiphery moves, migration-inducing global power relationships, and migration-inducing global investment strategies received little attention, nor were a few early studies calling for new approaches or dealing with Asian contract labor and Latin American migrations better received. The substantial research on forced migrations from Africa remained separate as part of the history of slavery; seminal studies of migration in other continents, Latin America, for example, remained part of regional history. The study of human migrations was predominantly White history. No comparative approaches to migration history emerged.[5] As regards cultural interaction in receiving societies, the Chicago School of sociology's concepts of the early twentieth century and Milton Gordon's 1964 model of "assimilation" in the United States framed research. A revision of such monocultural models of society based on Anglo-French dualism in Canada and published in the late 1940s could not overcome the mainstream approaches.[6] Only in the mid-1990s did Anthony Richmond's new synthesis of theoretical perspectives and approaches provide a framework that would have been needed decades earlier to create a more nuanced and comprehensive approach to migration.[7]

A review of recent theoretical approaches in migration research, in particular of nineteenth- and twentieth-century labor migration, revealed the inadequacy of *neo-classical economics* and historians' discussions of general push and pull factors. Both restrict themselves to geographic differences in supply and demand of labor and resources as indicated by variables on the macrolevel of societies, states, or regions.[8] The more informative economic microtheory differentiates between nominal, real, and expected wage levels as compared to standards of living.[9] Since most migrants arrive with little or no means and need immediate access to labor markets, job availability rather than wage differentials was the most important factor of attraction. Downswings of migration volume occur when recessions cut jobs—with a time lag due to information transmission and the need to reflect on and reconsider departure plans. A parallel macrolevel *political ideology approach* postulated the pull of the freedom of "America," even though frontier society opportunities existed throughout history. Again, only microlevel studies comparing constraints and opportunities in particular regions of origin with those in the particular receiving regions can yield results. Nineteenth-century political refugees chose among France, Switzerland, Great Britain, and the United States. Twentieth-century students from particular colonies chose particular universities of the metropoles.[10]

In the terminology of the *new economics of migration*, "families, households, or other culturally defined units of production, consumption and child-rearing are the appropriate units of analysis."[11] Migration provides access to scarce resources, such as jobs, wages, capital for small-scale business, and consumption choices. Migrants from peasant societies intend to enlarge landholdings or plan to increase their social standing in the society of origin by ostentatious consumption. When mechanization renders skills obsolete and undercuts the ability to feed families, skilled workers may migrate to distant economies that still rely on human skill. Women move because of better access to labor markets and less constraining gender roles. Increasingly marginal agrarian incomes may result in the reallocation of family labor: tending of farms is left to women and children, while seasonal or multi-annual labor migration is assigned to adult and adolescent males. Migration permits risk diversification since potentially poor harvests or underemployment may be balanced by wage income from abroad and poor wages by food production on the farm.

Segmented labor market theory explains mesolevel processes of insertion into host societies. Since migrant recruitment occurs through informal channels of friends or kin, informants provide access to jobs only within the segment known to them. Specific recruitment policies, too, are intended to fill labor shortages in undersupplied segments. Migrants concentrate in low-level segments of the labor market shunned by residents. In advanced industrial societies they also concentrate in well-paying and stable factory jobs if native-born workers object to conveyor belt routines. Conflict occurs when immigrant and resident workers compete for one segment of the labor market and differ in the price for their labor—in other words, when the newcomers undercut established wage scales. Conflict may also occur when migrants introduce innovation into stagnant sectors of the receiving society's economy.[12]

The *world systems approach* and *dependency theories*, which have mistakenly posited a single Euro- or Atlantocentric model of capitalist development, analyze un-equal power relationships. First, capital investments in colonial areas induce mobili-zation of plantation or mining labor by wage incentive, administrative compulsion, or military force. Second, the theory helps us understand the interrelatedness of migra-tions, as when Manchester's cloth manufacture competed with factories in New En-gland, Bombay, and Łódź, and was connected to cotton plantations in the U.S. South, Egypt, and Uganda. All were destinations of labor migrants with different standards of living and wage levels. Third, global approaches avoid the limitations of bilateral migration studies by emphasizing multidirectional moves and returns. Fourth, world systems, viewed not as channeling investment (capital penetration) to lesser devel-oped countries (LDCs) but as extracting capital out of less powerful states/economies by unequal terms of trade, help explain the present-day mass out-migration from those countries. The theory does not explain, however, who of a targeted reservoir of labor migrates or is selected by his or her community to migrate.[13]

Social and human capital approaches to migration link the microlevel of indi-viduals and families to the mesolevel of economic regions and global migration op-tions. Human agency as well as the larger context is reflected in new paradigms of migration and in sophisticated conceptualizations of parameters of mobility.

New Paradigms

In the 1960s, societal recognition of the validity of ethnic cultures, the impact of newly independent Third World countries, and economic growth in Asia resulted in changed immigration regulations and in new research. Canadian interdisciplinary ap-proaches, U.S. social history of ethnicity, new countrywide studies in Europe, South Asian emigration research, and concepts of immigrant culture as well as of global capital transfers replaced the narrow emphasis on allegedly uprooted Europeans in North America. Studies of Asian contract labor emphasized community formation. Studies of migration in Africa under and after colonialism reassessed voluntary and involuntary mobility and reintroduced human agency into slave migrations. Migra-tion studies, however, emerged as part of regional history rather than as a global ap-proach to population mobility. A plurality of national scholarly discourses and a new multisided international research agenda emerged. In the Netherlands and Sweden, for example, multiethnic in-migration provided a stimulus to reconceptualization; in Natal and India a new self-awareness changed the image of passive coolies to active migrant men and immigrant families.[14]

With regard to the northern hemisphere, the notion of a one-way flow of agrarian settlers to an imagined "America" was expanded to the concept of two nineteenth-century intercontinental migration systems, the Russo-Siberian System and the System of the Atlantic Economies. Collaborative projects combined expertise on cul-ture of origin and receiving culture.[15] The new paradigm incorporated the impor-tance of internal European and North American migrations as well as the choice among three overseas destinations, Anglo-America, Latin America, or Europe (that

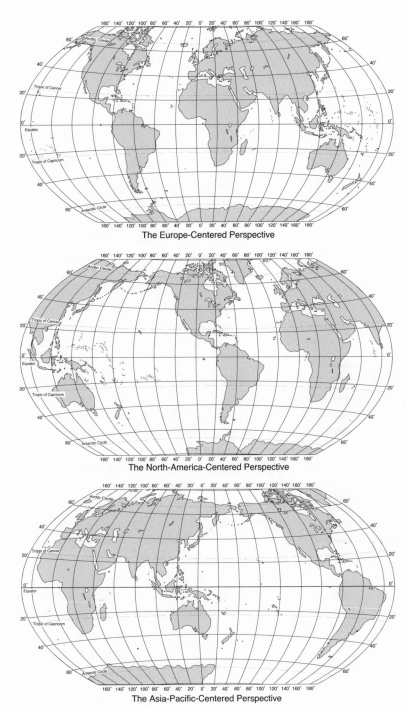

The Europe-Centered Perspective

The North-America-Centered Perspective

The Asia-Pacific-Centered Perspective

Scale at the Equator 1: 140 000 000

1.1   Perspectives: Euro-, American-, Asian-Centeredness

is, returning home). The comparative approach to frontier societies and postmigration insertion reduced the postulated exceptionalism of the United States to one case of several. Canada, Brazil, Argentina, and—outside the Western Hemisphere— Siberia, Australia, and perhaps South Africa were frontier societies in the nineteenth century.[16]

Coolie migration and Asian exclusion were reconceptualized as an Asian and Pacific Migration System, expanding the focus with concepts of economic spheres, with studies of interaction of bound and free migrants, and with analyses of labor markets and racializations. Reasons for emigration in the sending regions of India and South China were analyzed: British-imposed taxation and landholding patterns, the caste system, traditional Indian merchant migrations; imperial Chinese maladministration and revolts, overpopulation and natural disasters as well as colonial penetration. Of particular innovative impact were studies of international labor demand and of the interaction between passengers and coolies, or free and unfree migrants, in receiving societies.[17]

The emphasis on the nineteenth-century industrializing (White) world was challenged by research on (Colored) interperiphery mobility. The vast majority of Asian contract laborers moved between colonial worlds. Internal migrations in Africa and Latin America depended on local conditions as well as on interference from the cores. Labor migration to plantation economies contrasted with migration in the service of imperial administrations. Again, similarities to other migrations emerged: centers of investment and income attracted laborers and servants; women moved more often in short-distance migrations, men over larger distances. Family formation after migration involved additional moves, whether a return to the place of origin, the sequential migration of partners, or joint migration after marriage.[18]

As regards class, labor historians influenced by the English New Left history of working-class culture and moral economies came to recognize the multiethnic or international composition of working-classes and reconceptualized the nineteenth-century proletarian mass migration.[19] Castles, Cohen, Sassen-Koob, and Potts pointed to changes in the distribution of labor between developed and lesser developed regions and to capital flows. Questioning the assumption of both liberal and Marxist economic theory that in capitalist economies free wage labor replaces any form of indenture, serfdom, or slavery, they suggest that forced and free labor continue to co-exist, depending on which power relationships obtain and the state of development of the means of production ("labor regimes"). Guerin-Gonzales and Strikwerda among others have added studies of labor militancy among migrants in peripheral economies. As a result of worldwide movements of workers from a particular ethnic group, global diasporas of, for example, Chinese, Italians, Poles, and Palestinians have come into being.[20]

Research on ethnicity lost its antiquarian character resulting in self-laudatory histories of group achievements. Questions about the construction of nations and races surfaced after European countries received migrants from their former colonies and after scholars in the newly independent states began to approach the subject.

Attention-craving talking heads of the early 1990s blamed U.S. pluralism or Canadian multiculturalism for disuniting the societies; right-wing politicians in Europe garnered votes by demanding exclusion of non-White immigrants. In India local "sons of the soil" opposed immigrant settlers.[21] The numerous publications on national culture, on the Self and the Other, and "us" versus "aliens" cannot be reviewed here. Much of the antimigration argument still assumes nationality and the nation-state to be permanent determinants of collective identities while overlooking alternative models of identity formation and multiple identities in immigrant and multiethnic states of the past and present. The connections between ethnicity and nationalism have been best outlined by A. D. Smith in his continualist approach; of comparable value are the studies of the constructions of national consciousness and nationalism by Hobsbawm and Ranger.[22]

Gender-specific role assignment and access to migration options demand gendered research approaches. In the past, women had less access to resources to defray migration costs or were restrained from traveling on their own. Once in command of independent incomes, women developed migration chains of their own. The conceptualization of family economies by Tilly and Scott had a major impact on migration research, women scholars being at the forefront of incorporating the new theory. Simon and Brettell argue that structural constraints of world political economies result in shared experiences of immigrant women, regardless of their culture of origin. Sikh women, Colombian and Algerian domestics, Vietnamese and Turkish female laborers, Soviet Jewish women as part of family migrations, and, to take a final example, Portuguese women in Germany, Canada, or the United States share experiences of wage and unpaid labor, of family migration and re-formation, and of gender hierarchies. Female-first migrations from Southeast Asia into domestic service leave men and children to cope on their own and with the help of kin. When married women subsequently bring in their husbands, complex negotiations about gender hierarchies occur, since women are both breadwinners and guides to the ways of the receiving society.[23]

Generational aspects in processes of acculturation emerge from the experience unique to women of giving birth in a situation of potential or real cultural conflict. Under the social construction of child-rearing as women's sphere, the experience of the second-generation immigrants is patterned by women. Life-cycle research indicates that average age of marriage changes after migration, often inching upward, thus giving women more independence and both partners more time to accumulate savings. In some migrant contexts, freedom from parental constraints and dependence on land inheritance brought down marriage age. Household formation no longer depended on parental dowries or bride prices but rather on earning capacities and strategies of the two partners. Lastly, the care for old people, in particular for parents, was left to nonmigrating sisters or brothers. Migration increases the dependency ratio and thus social expenditures in regions of departure while reducing it in societies of arrival. Immigrant women's high participation rates in labor markets and the change in their life-cycles—due to having fewer children and living a considerable geographic distance from elderly relatives—result in new attitudes toward the gender-specific division of labor and in new strategies of family formation in the second generation.

Parameters of Mobility and Migration

What distance has to be covered, what cultural boundaries have to be crossed, and what decisions have to be made to define a "move" as a "migration"? A woman, crossing parish boundaries to marry and become part of her husband's family—a process of insertion and acceptance—may be considered a migrant. Crossing of village boundaries in nineteenth-century settings involved complexities not found on international borders. Short-distance marriage migration, which—disregarding celibacy—involves half of the population, is part of societal patterns of mobility. A Swedish peasant, interviewed by a researcher, lamented that he had never left his village and had not seen the church whose steeple was visible in the distance—but added as an afterthought "except for my years in America." Income-generating migration across continents and oceans may lead from one small community of compatriots to another without noticeable change.

Conceptually, local moves are distinguished from migration within political borders or economic regions and from long-distance cross-border migration. However, cultural change or moves between economic regimes and stages rather than arbitrary political borders determine demands for adjustment of immigrants. A nineteenth-century Polish family crossing the border between the Russian and German empires remained within their ethnocultural context, whereas Polish men and women moving within Prussia from eastern, ethnically Polish territories to western mining areas did move into a different culture and from an agricultural-village economy to an industrial-urban one. Twelfth-century Arab merchants sailing from Hormuz to Southeast Asia found communities of other Arab merchants along the way, as did Chinese moving in the Southeast Asian diaspora. Geographical distance is relative. For migrant Italians around 1900, crossing the Atlantic to work seasonally in the Argentinean wheat harvest involved less mental and cultural distance, less change in work patterns, and less cost than a train ride across to Alps to the East Elbian wheat fields. Mental distances and mental maps have to be taken into account.

Migration has a beginning and an end. Permanent mobility constitutes a way of life in itself, itinerancy with the next destination in view, peregrination with an ulterior goal. Travels are temporary visits in a distant culture for specific purposes. Migration may occur in stages with stops along the route for lengthy periods of time. It may be circular, bringing migrants back to their homes. Absence may be limited seasonally to a few months each year, to a few years, or extend for working life. Emigration constitutes an intentionally permanent move that, however, may be followed by secondary or return migrations when conditions at the destination become unsatisfactory. European religious dissenters or Indian merchants of the diaspora moved again when opportunities declined. Migration may be unintentionally permanent when migrants who plan to return "next year" finally die in the receiving society; or it may be involuntarily permanent when exiles may not return because of hostile, even life-threatening regimes "at home." Migration involves a continuum from travel to lifetime emigration.

Migration may be voluntary, coerced, or forced. Any decision to migrate is "free" only within both the macrolevel constraints in the society of origin and the legal limitations of receiving societies, and given the ability to defray the "opportunity cost" of the move. On the microlevel of individuals, migrants have been considered autonomous in taking the decision to leave, or have been assumed to act under ethnocultural or age-specific *Wanderlust*, or have been ranked on a scale that contrasts personalities ready to explore friendly expanses with others clinging to the known and traditional. Emphasizing individuals in local contexts, Samuel Baily compares out-migrations from different Italian villages with each other and the varying destinations chosen and presents a complex analysis of individual, family, and village economic factors influencing migrants' choices. Letter series and oral testimony show how families, spread across continents, keep relations intact and discuss the advantages and disadvantages of their moves in terms of both economic security and emotional benefits or losses. "Free" decisions are made within networks, information flows, and perceived socioeconomic options and constraints.[24]

Unfree migrations indicate particularly pronounced unequal power relationships. Forced migrations, whether African slavery or wartime labor in Europe, severely constrain the agency of captured men and women. Day-to-day resistance and flight occurred under threat of violent punishment or even of physical annihilation. Survival, however, depended on a re-creation of cultural specifics distinct from those of the masters.[25] Coerced migrations rigorously limit choice upon departure but permit some decision making upon arrival. Refugees, for example, attempt to choose a country of destination within the constraints of distance and admission regulations. They have to enter segmented labor markets in the receiving society to ensure survival unless permanent camp-existence or reliance on transfer payments is intended or politically enforced.

The study of migration and acculturation has to incorporate the different forms of mobility. Returning travelers, pilgrims, and soldiers provide information on destinations for migrants. Experience in voyaging facilitates migratory moves. Itinerancy, vagrancy, and seasonal mobility undercut notions of sedentary lives rooted in the land or localized traditions.

1.3 Migrants as Actors and a Systems Approach

On the basis of the new paradigms and the sophisticated approaches, I propose a human-centered approach to migration that includes the societal frame of reference. As agents of their own lives, men, women, and their children look not only for material security but for emotional-spiritual-intellectual security as well. Hermits excepted, few find the latter without the former. Thus, securing basic subsistence is the first goal—with other medium-range goals in mind. The Florentine *catasto* (land register) distinguished between "heads" and "mouths"—and perhaps "hearts" might be added. What is acceptable at minimum depends on the reference group and the moment in history. Women and men migrate when conditions at potential destinations seem better to a degree that the opportunity costs—loss of relationships, fear of change and the unknown, the actual fare—are lower than hoped-for benefits. Departure decisions are made in the structural framework of political, social, and economic constraints of the society of origin as experienced in the particular home region. Who out of a large pool of potential migrants leaves is negotiated within the context of family economy, kin relations, sibling sequence, friendship ties—unless persons are exiled by institutions, ostracized by communities, or forced into flight by human-made or natural disasters.

One method of understanding particular cultural frames of reference is comparative research. First, culturally different immigrant groups may be compared to each other in gendered analyses on the levels of sociocultural and economic background, migration experiences, and acculturation processes. Second, societies of origin and of destination may be compared to each other as regards continuity as well as reorientation and disruption. Third, emigration needs to be compared to other options like internal migration. In all of these approaches, class, gender, and ethnicity are beginning to be integrated with demographic and life-cycle approaches in an overarching *systems approach.*

Migration Systems: A Comprehensive Theoretical Perspective

A comprehensive study of migration systems should address individual men's and women's departure, travel, and reinsertion, along with the multiple directions and different goals involved.[26] A migration system, on the level of empirical observation of geographical space, is a cluster of moves between a region of origin and a receiving region that continues over a period of time and is distinct from nonclustered multidirectional migrations. Gross and net quantity of migration flows, continuity over time, ratio per 1,000 population, may be measured on this level. On the macrolevel, migration systems connect two distinct societies, each characterized by degree of industrialization and urbanization, by political structures and current policies, by specific educational, value, and belief systems, by ethnic composition and demographic factors (age structure, marriage patterns, dependency ratio), and by traditions of internal, medium-distance, and long-distance migrations. On this level, general push-and-pull factors and statewide admission regulations are analyzed.

Decision making about migration occurs on a mesolevel of regional economies, where stagnation or growth and differential access to resources may diverge from statewide patterns. The regional socioeconomic frame influences life-chances and options for life-projects more directly than larger frameworks. On this level, motivations and migrant characteristics are analyzed. Likewise, insertion into the new society takes place on the mesolevel of particular regional settings, of particular labor market segments, or, for children, of regional school systems. Interests, values, and customs are analyzed in this context.

On the microlevel of individual human capital, the propensity to migrate in psychological terms and the capabilities of acquiring social capital are actuated. Actual decisions are taken on the local level of kinship, village, and neighborhood economies. The many factors of mesolevel economics and social norms enter into individual decision making as subjectively weighed factors, meant to satisfy the material and nonmaterial interests of those who remain as well as of those who leave.[27]

Since, first and foremost, voluntary (and coerced) migrants have to be able to establish an economic base at the destination (survival economy), migration systems connect areas having a relative surplus of labor, skills, and capital or lack of resources (such as land) with areas with a relative demand for labor, skills, or resources. It is not, however, "objective" data on these factors but their reflection in the minds of migrants that explain decisions to move. At least some segments of the receiving area have to be internationalized and be connected via information flows to recruitment areas. Changes of the parameters, like higher wages or better working conditions, the mobilization of untapped labor resources, or changes of entry and retirement age may meet demand for jobs in the society of departure or for workers in the society of destination. Division of feudal landholdings, for example, may provide land resources and reduce among the landless the need to emigrate. At present the massive dislocation of people with little access to societal structures of decision making by infrastructural improvements occur at a rate of 10 million individuals a year according to World Bank estimates. Other solutions are available. Within existing power hierarchies such solutions are considered more costly by power elites than the migration alternative.[28]

Migration systems are self-regulating processes in the framework of macrolevel constraints and are flexible enough to react to individual interests, regional fluctuations in supply and demand, and larger economic cycles. Information flows may be started by active recruitment from the top down or come about by prior contacts from the bottom up. In classic labor and settlement migration systems, the information flow regulates quantity of arrivals; any recession or rise in land prices brings forth letters, oral information, or, in modern times, telecommunication, announcing to prospective migrants that chances are poor or, during phases of expansion, that economic insertion is easily possible. Where a particular state exerts domination over areas of labor supply, systems of forced labor in-migration may be established. Similarly, internally repressive states may become refugee-generating areas.

Acculturation and job searches are mediated by earlier immigrants, who congregate in ethnic communities. With social differentiation in the immigrant/ethnic communities, additional segments of the labor market or other resources are tapped; a labor market internal to the community develops. State governments, industrial sectors, or particular employers may influence the system by exit and entry regulations or active recruitment. Because of microlevel interests, macrolevel regulations may be circumvented by illegal or, from the viewpoint of migrants, clandestine migrations.

The initial entry into new surroundings is usually not a conscious move into a framework of different societal institutions, into capitalist economic conditions, or into a polity of democratic character. Rather it is a move into one particular labor market segment, into one particular area with cheap land, into a society in which trade or other entrepreneurial options are larger than at the place of departure. Migrants' experiences in internationalized labor markets and internationally accessible agricultural land suggest that men and women function in similar work environments even if the surrounding culture differs. The initial period of settling in often demands quick adaptation, including the shedding of many old-country habits. Among rural immigrants in urban environments, a surprising loss of traditional customs has been brought about by the need to earn a living in industry. Only after such change by force of circumstance and after the establishment of an economic basis does the process of acculturation become self-determined; ethnic enclaves may cushion host-society pressures.[29]

Whether in urban or rural environments, the process of settling in—of acculturation—occurs on a very localized level by reliance on the labor power of a single person or a single family. Immigrant letters show that the establishment of a survival economy and its broadening precedes the extension of emotional ties. When friends or relatives are brought in by prepaid tickets, the first to arrive are those whose labor power is needed most. Wage-working males usually bring over other single men to strengthen the pool of persons with earning capacity in labor markets to which they have access. Women are brought in in small numbers, each to care for several men as a boarding-house keeper or cook. Single self-supporting women in domestic service bring over other women for whom they provide access to jobs and who thus can support themselves immediately. On farms, or, rather, on land that is to become agricultural, families settle because the division of labor in agriculture makes the presence of both sexes imperative (unless, of course, the division of labor is changed). Migration thus involves a trajectory from family economy and neighborhood networks via reliance on individual human capital in a variety of makeshift living circumstances to the reestablishment of social capital in long-term strategies of family formation and entry into networks that provide resource leverage.

The process of insertion into the receiving society reaches a new level when a viable basis of income-generation has been reached. Then children or, more rarely, elderly parents may be brought over to join the family and community. Immigrant parents structure local socioeconomic environments to achieve survival for themselves and better futures for their daughters and sons. In the process, immigrant societies emerge as ethnic enclaves or new social formations, and the departure and host societies are changed by loss or gain of human capital. The immediacy of the need for material survival implies that after temporary separation of spouses and parents from children by sequential migration, the reconstituted family has no "free" time for an adjustment of family relations, for reflection on new circumstances. Work and emotional relationships have to be resumed on the spot, have to function immediately. They cannot be re-created deliberately and slowly. A transfer of traditional gender roles and child-parent relationships occurs with no questioning of the old-country practices at first. Changes are mandated by new exigencies and occur over time and involve self-directed adjustments in the new worlds.

The *systems approach to migration* thus combines analysis of the position of a society of origin in the global order, its structures, the regional specifics, selection and self-selection of migrants from a reservoir of potential leavers and persisters, the process of migration itself, and—within the receiving society's structures—the insertion into partly internationalized labor markets, the formation of ethnic enclaves or of transcultural networks, and the interaction with new social values and norms. Examples range from medieval journeymen migrations in Central Europe to migrations of industrial and service labor to oil-producing states since the 1970s, from the Atlantic Migration System to the Asian Migration System. Examples of self-regulation include the slowdown of migration during the Great Depression of the 1930s and of agriculturalists' migrations when land resources become scarce and expensive.

The analysis of the continuity of life-course planning is better suited to the interpretation of migration and acculturation than an emphasis on the disruptive aspects of cultural change. In this model, the political is reduced to a distant framework, though some scholars—Aristide Zolberg, for example—argue for a more determining role of the state. Blanket concepts like modernization theory or industrialization and urbanization as mobility-inducing factors have been abandoned as too vague or positively misleading. Even the concept of demographic transition and overpopulation as push factors, once considered statistically sound, have been reassessed in view of the fact that only a small percentage of all European migration was directed overseas.[30] The level on which individual life-courses and families interact with social systems is the mesolevel of regional economies, ethnic territories marked by particular dialects, communities of shared values, religions, and patterns of everyday life.[31]

The Mesolevel Approach to Migrant Decision Making

The mesolevel is the arena where potential migrants receive their socialization, have to come to terms with larger socioeconomic forces, and live, act, and feel as community and family members, where migrants act out aspirations and values and pursue customs or choose innovative strategies.[32] This level comprises, first, family economies as well as kin and friendship networks, in which information is digested, decisions are made, and the interests of group members are weighed and, ideally, are balanced. Such negotiating processes depend on power hierarchies between genders and generations. Their goal is not equilibrium or equal rights and benefits but rather a compromise between individual interests satisfying the local moral economy within the framework of socially allocated status and gendered and intergenerational power relations. Second, in regional economies potential migrants have to find a way to earn a living. There they look for jobs, expect to become independent of their families of birth, and, usually, establish their own families. Thus family strategies and regional job markets are closely entwined. Family and individual goals are not restricted to purely economic income maximization but include a search for "independence" and human dignity within specific norms and values.[33]

Third, information flows concerning potential destinations connect mesolevel economic regions because earlier migrants act as informants. Historically, oral reports from insiders in a circle of acquaintances—letters from emigrant fellow-villagers or traveling traders—had a much more powerful effect on stimulating migration than recruitment by "outsiders" like government agents or labor recruiters. Realistic information through letters, however, was evaluated within the mental parameters of the culture of origin—for example, within an image of a mythical "America" or of other destinations.[34]

The concept of family economies, along with the inclusion of nonmeasurable emotional and spiritual factors in the negotiating process, avoids the reductionist approach to wage differentials and permits a comprehensive approach to decision-influencing factors. Family economies combine the income-generating capabilities of all family members with reproductive needs—such as care for dependants, whether children or elderly—and consumption patterns so as to achieve the best possible results according to traditional norms. Allocation of resources depends on the stage of the family life-cycle and individual life-courses as well as on gender and generational power hierarchies. The allocation of time, labor power, and the skills of all members has to be negotiated in terms of the maximization of benefits for each: of income or leisure, child-care or out-work, education or wagework for children, traditional networking or individualist separation from the community.[35]

Viewed from the bottom up, this *holistic material-emotional approach* considers individuals as making conscious choices about perceived opportunities. Decisions about life-courses, levels of subsistence, and aspirations for betterment involve a conglomerate of traditional cultural norms and practices, of actual emotional and spiritual needs, and of economic rationales. Immigrant women workers have wanted "bread and roses, too"—community beyond cash. A methodological problem results: loss of relationships, sadness, and homesickness, which involves childhood memories and network-deprivation (such as happiness and social contacts), cannot be measured by one scale as wages may be.

As to those who stay behind, the departure of beloved ones involves emotional loss: in the case of aging parents the absence of work-sharing younger family members; in the case of women and children increased workloads and often control by other male family or community members. Economic gains achieved by migrants and transferred back to the locality of origin influence status among neighbors. Loss of status may arise from working conditions or societal demands and different cultural norms in the host society that induce migrants, male or female, to transform themselves to a degree as to become unacceptable to fellow-villagers and nonmigrating kin. The estrangement is illustrated by families not recognizing their returning kin or by return migrants, disenchanted with "home," departing for a second time and permanently.

The intricate connection between economic and emotional factors is shown in the timing of decisions to leave. Both—economic slumps in material status at home or in the receiving society with the resulting decrease in earning opportunities and emotional "slumps" in family relations—influence the timing of departures. The macroeconomic aspect is well known: recessions in receiving countries are followed by a downturn of in-migration, whereas recessions in departure societies do not cause immediate upswings in out-migration because of emotional ties that bind. Similarly, changes in intrafamilial relationships—such as the death of a parent, especially a mother, or the arrival of a new parent by remarriage, especially a stepmother—cause increased out-migration. At a time when emotional relationships within a family unit have to be rearranged, latent migratory potential is actuated, and departure is easier.[36]

The *holistic material-emotional approach* also helps us understand acculturation processes. Migrants, whether moving for commercial, agricultural, or wagework purposes, have to come to terms with the receiving society to the degree that they can fulfill their goals. Quick insertion (assimilation), often demanded by receiving societies, may thus be in the interest of newcomers. A temporary loss of cultural self-expression is expected to lead to improved lifestyles. If, however, pursuit of future economic well-being becomes ever more costly in terms of loss of quality of life, goal achievement by migration may appear to be overpriced to the degree that benefits are negligible. Departures will be postponed; migrants will return; patterns of mobility may be adjusted.[37] After migration, the cultural and structural experiences of the region of origin serve as self-organizing concepts in migrant communities (*natio, Landsmannschaften*). Unequal power relationships, structural constraints, and the reorganization of networks are part of mesolevel activity.

On the experienced mesolevel, migrants develop both their human and their social capital and evaluate the emotional, material, and spiritual benefits accruing to themselves and their immediate kin in terms of projected life-courses. These life-course projects add up to local and global migrations over the centuries.

I

The Judeo-Christian-Islamic Mediterranean
and Eurasian Worlds to the 1500s

The eleventh-century Afro-Eurasian world consisted of seven civilizations linked by traveling merchants and their clerks, carters, servants or slaves, and concubines or, less often, wives. Those of the "Americas"—a later designation—remained separate. The Chinese, Indic, Muslim, and Byzantine civilizations extended over large contiguous territories. While the fifth, Latin Christendom, clung to the western Mediterranean and peripheral transalpine Europe, the sixth, Jewish one had lost its original center in Judea but remained a culturally and economically vibrant diaspora. The seventh, the cultures of sub-Saharan Africa, was connected by trade routes (map 2.1). Merchants, intellectuals, and religious thinkers of the civilizations interacted, as did the little people along the trade routes spanning the globe and in the vast cultural borderlands in which civilizations overlapped (chap. 2.1–2).

In the Mediterranean world of northern Africa, southern Europe, and western Asia centered on the Mediterranean, several types of large-scale and long-distance migrations were specific to particular regions and periods. Slavery in the Mediterranean involved men and, over time, mainly women, from North Africa, West Central Asia, and sub-Saharan Africa. Norman raiders and state-builders from Scandinavia migrated southwestward to the shores of the Atlantic and as far as Sicily, southeastward to Slavic territories and Byzantium. The migrant men joined with local women to form new societies of mixed cultural background. Muslim armies established a sophisticated society with Jewish-Christian-Islamic transcultural centers on the Iberian Peninsula. Christian raiders, called crusaders, moved across central and southeastern Europe to Palestine, often accompanied by large numbers of women. Migration as well as crusading brought western European settlers and military personnel into the territories of Slavic peoples (chap. 2.3).

A perspective from the eastern core of the Eurasian World, from China or Southeast Asia, would emphasize other large-scale and long-distance migrations specific to regions and periods: Mongol expansion and state-building, Manchu penetration, southward settlement of Han Chinese, internal Hakka migrations, development of the Chinese diaspora into Southeast Asia. A perspective from South Asia would focus

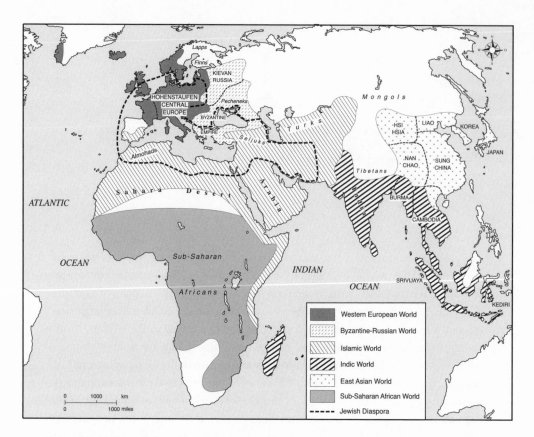

2.1 Cultural Regions, 12th Century

on the vast commercial linkages along the coasts of the Indian Ocean, the cosmopolitan elites at courts, the Islam-Hindu interaction.

Other migrations of the Mediterranean World, similar across societies, continued from the eleventh to the sixteenth century and beyond. The upper levels of dynastic societies—cosmopolitan elites, itinerant administrators, and their uprooted mercenaries—traveled across the continent. At the bottom level, rural families migrated when land became scarce or were moved by lords according to economic interests or the exigencies of noble culture. The urban worlds of commerce and production attracted journeymen and maids from the adjoining countryside, and urban elites circulated between towns. Skilled craftsmen migrated over large distances to building and mining projects. Finally, large numbers of wayfarers roamed countrysides, and towns and pilgrims and clerics moved across Europe and as far as Jerusalem (chap. 3).

Across Asia and Europe the mid-fourteenth-century plagues severely depleted local populations, forced families to reassemble in viable communities, and created a caesura in population movements (chap. 2.4). By that time, warfaring Iberian Christians had expelled Muslims and persecuted Jews. Latin warfare against Byzantine Christendom became Catholic-Lutheran warfare after 1517 and generated large refugee migrations. Doctrinal homogeneity demanded by the papal court led to flight or physical annihilation (chap. 4). In the eastern Mediterranean, the Muslim Ottoman Empire's multiethnic and multireligious society included both free and unfree migrations (chap. 5.1). The cultural and economic center of Europe shifted northward, in particular to the Urban Netherlands and their seaborne trade (chap. 5.2). The shift from eastern Mediterranean to Portuguese exploration of trade and slaving along the western Atlantic coast of Africa and of Spain across the Atlantic wrought havoc among settled peoples and opened new perspectives for migration (chap. 5.3).

2

Antecedents: Migration and Population Changes
in the Mediterranean-Asian Worlds

Two approaches, cultural and economic, help conceptualize peaceful or conflictual interaction in Mediterranean-Asian Worlds. According to Jerry H. Bentley, inter-civilizational contact led to "conversion," to cross-cultural exchange through voluntary association, through political, social, or economic pressure, or through assimilation. Janet Abu-Lughod has extended and differentiated the economic world-systems approach of Immanuel Wallerstein. With 1250, a period of "increased economic integration and cultural efflorescence," as a starting point, a global perspective permits an understanding of economic linkages, but regionalized approaches can do justice to distinct developments—for example, in the Islamic World of the Indian Ocean or the Animist World of pastoral and mining cultures in sub-Saharan Africa. Analyses based on commodity and capital flows need to be supplemented by examining the moves of men and women along the trade routes, of families or individuals to colonization projects, of enslaved, bound, or free laborers. Neither the conversion nor the world-systems approach fully integrates the world of dynastic or clerical politics or the decision making of common men and women.

The perspective taken here starts from distinct civilizations and economic systems, connected by webs of commerce and separated by cultural, often religious, practices. Systems evolve over long periods of time (*longue durée*), but the processes involved emerge from the myriad of decisions made by simple people within their short lifetimes. All such decisions depended on personal interests and power relationships between groups; all linked material and emotional interests as well as the economic and the ideological spheres. They were made in the framework of religious-cultural structures that explain the norms, values, and customs involved and of trading systems driven by merchant and consumer interests. Cultures and commerce influenced each other; the material, spiritual, and emotional aspects of everyday life influenced travel, migration, and processes of acculturation.

It has been assumed that shifts in culture and trade did not influence the life of rural men, women, and children, whether in the Euphrates or Rhone valleys. The mobility of the upper strata has been juxtaposed to village-bound peasants and urban underclasses. Such binary models of society cannot do justice to the relations between multiple social strata, the mobility between regions, and the creation of cultures. The worlds of material life, commerce, and worldwide financial transactions, to borrow from Braudel, have to be linked with negotiated emotional lives in families and in rural and urban neighborhoods.[1]

2.1   The Afro-Eurasian World

The Byzantine–Arabic–West Asian core of transcontinental trade, religious contact, and intellectual exchange comprised the region from Baghdad and Trebizond to the shores of the Persian Gulf and the Black Sea and to Constantinople, Cyprus, and Alexandria, with connections extending to the cities of Amalfi and Venice. Transalpine passes reached from Urban Italy into northern Europe; trans-Saharan caravan routes connected Black Africa; and eastern transoceanic human migration was "one of the enduring consequences of the harnessing of the monsoons."

Arab learning drew on Indic and Chinese knowledge. Science and philosophy were fostered in Abbasid Baghdad in the "House of Knowledge" (from the ninth to the eleventh century), in Cairo's "House of Science" established in 995, and in Umayyad Córdoba from the reign of 'Abd ar-Raḥmān III (r. 912–61). In Baghdad scholars had translated Greek, Syriac, Persian, and Sanskrit texts into Arabic. Hindu numerals and calculation methods, adopted in the Arab World, came to Europe via Venetian merchant houses and Iberian scholars. Aristotle's main work was preserved in Arabic only; Christian scholars arriving with the crusaders cooperated in translations from Arabic to Latin. Arab science included astronomy, medicine, optics, and chemistry. Research results were applied in healing, summarized in an encyclopedia of natural history, and used for new technologies. Westernized names of Arab scholars indicate their impact on Europe.

Arab culture and commerce as well as settlers from the desert peninsula and the arid northern littoral of the Persian Gulf reached "the little ports and fishing villages along the [East African] coast, and it was the continuing trickle of newcomers who, along with the visiting merchants, assured and reinforced the Islamic-mindedness of coastal society." For them East Africa was "a fertile, well-watered land of economic opportunity and a place of salvation from drought, famine, overpopulation, and war." Settlers from as far away as Tashkent reached Mogadishu (Muqdisho) in the thirteenth century, men "who quickly married into the local families or took slave concubines, thereby obliterating any tendencies toward racial separatism." On the Indic subcontinent immigrants of Turkish, Afghan, Persian, and Arab origin formed new elites and engaged in a long process of conversion and interaction with Hindu culture, to which rural populations remained faithful. New immigrants arrived about 1330, when the sultan decided to fill administrative and judicial positions with men from afar. Patronage and gifts attracted many including the famous traveler Abū 'Abd Allāh ibn Baṭṭūṭah.[2]

Commerce, according to Abu-Lughod, involved eight trading circuits, to which those of the Baltic–North Sea area and of the sub-Saharan region have to be added

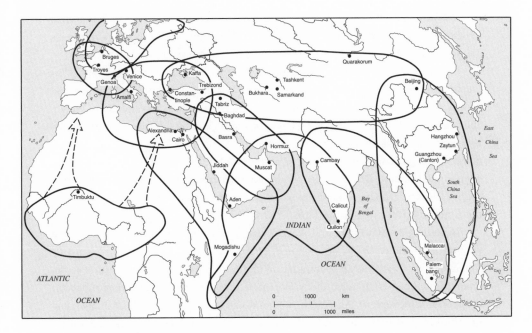

2.2 Circuits of the 13th-Century World System

(map 2.2). Shifts in continental long-distance trade, changes in the relative importance of centers of production, and variations in power relationships affected the amount of food available to small agrarian or artisanal producer families at the expanding and contracting ends of the exchanges. When warfare between Hanseatic, Danish, and pirate fleets in the Baltic Sea reduced fish exports from the famous markets of Scania (Skåne), the poor in a radius of a thousand kilometers (600 miles) saw local herring prices increase up to tenfold. Changes in production and political disruptions in the South German cloth-producing towns by the early fifteenth century increased demand for cotton and promoted "large increases in Syrian cotton cultivation." If resources became insufficient, some—if not all—members of a family had to migrate. Other families expanded production and hired men and women from abroad. Basic foods, like cereals and seasonings (such as salt and sugar), spread among the common people living along the major trade routes and into valleys and hinterlands. Foodways adapted, if slowly. Consumption of spices, a core element of the intercontinental trade, on the other hand, was limited to households of better-placed families. The Slavic regions east of the Elbe and north of the Danube rivers were touched but lightly by Mediterranean commerce until the Military Orders expelled from Palestine migrated to the Baltic littoral. Trade networks extended as far east as Kiev.[3]

Commercial activities and dynastic states interacted, of which three aspects merit emphasis. First, merchants struggled to limit the acts of autocratic rulers, administrators, or local lords, and to foster adherence to the *pacta sunt servanda* principle. Trade could not be conducted without binding agreements. Second, warfare among political rulers interrupted long-term interaction, drained resources, and increased the traders' transaction costs. Third, rural and urban laboring populations had to be integrated into their respective political subsystems, so that massive resources did not have to be allocated for their control and repression.

In a sensitive discussion of terminology, concepts, and periodization, Abu-Lughod has argued that theoretical consistency cannot do justice to complex historical processes. Into the overarching economic approaches of Wallerstein, Weber, and Marx, she incorporated gradual changes and regionally differing developments. Demographic factors need to be considered, too. While population growth is a gradual process involving the reproductive activities of millions of actors of both sexes, population disasters, whether natural or men-made (rather than "man-made"), bring about cataclysmic change: the plagues of 1348–51, the transfer of Eurasian germs into the Americas after 1492, or the Thirty Years' War of 1618–48.

According to Abu-Lughod, linkages between the world trading centers led to a long-term slowdown in the development of less powerful and dependent segments. The rise of the West was an accumulation of profits from worldwide resources—derived from nature, labor, technology, and intellectual activity—rather than the result of superior achievement. Aggressive conquest and colonization made exchange relationships increasingly unequal; in long-distance trade, plunder replaced exchange.

Communication across the vast expanse from north Africa via the southern belt of the Eurasian continent to China rested on a shared understanding of the value of coins (whether gold, silver, or copper), on mercantile linguae francae (Italian, Arabic, Greek, Hebrew, and medieval variants of Latin and Mandarin Chinese), and on the exchange of ideas and the conversion of spiritual norms.

> Distances, as measured in time, were calculated in weeks and months at best, but it took years to traverse the entire circuit. And yet, goods were transferred, prices set, exchange rates agreed upon, contracts entered into, credit—on funds or on goods located elsewhere—extended, partnerships formed, and, obviously, records kept and agreements honored.

Along the routes, the many labored for their livelihood: hundreds of thousands of sailors and transport workers and the women who supported them or worked in agriculture, the numerous families of miners and artisans, and the masses of domestics and spinners who provided the productive labor and did the reproductive work in households and inns. World systems driven by capitalist accumulation and top-level economic interest (Wallerstein, Frank) but divided into distinct spheres by states, cultures, and mercantile trading circuits (Abu-Lughod) function as a result of the life-course decisions of myriads of individuals. Routes became cultural highways, spaces of synthesis and plural identities.[4]

2.2   Over Continents and Oceans: Cross-Cultural Encounters

A web of coastal shipping connected the Mediterranean and China, the African east coast, India, and the Southeast Asian islands. With the twelfth-century increase in trade a network of transcontinental land routes, some dating from the Roman period, was reestablished or newly developed. Postmasters, merchants, clerks, and scholars of North African–Arab, Spanish-Jewish, or Italian-Christian background wrote intercontinental travel guides. Commodities, labor, and bullion were moved along these routes. They served political and cultural interchanges between empires as well as the spiritual quests of pilgrims, and they became the arenas where images of the Self and the Other developed (see maps 2.3 and 2.4).[5]

Along the trans-Asian "silk routes," travel, supported by numerous relay stations, was facilitated by the cosmopolitan attitudes of thirteenth-century Mongol rulers and by the *pax mongolorum* after Genghis Khan united the different realms.[6] In northern Africa—Ifriqiya was the Arabic name for Tunis—the trans-Saharan caravan routes to Timbuktu or Agadès expanded in response to the increased demand for gold; new wells were dug; and oases relay stations enlarged. Land-route travel was time-consuming. Camels, the ubiquitous means of transport and travel, could travel about 40 kilometers (25 miles) per day. They were vastly superior to oxen, more resilient and stronger than packhorses, and able to negotiate routes that no carts could travel.[7] In Europe, the Latin Church supported the expansion of routes and the building of hostels to encourage pilgrimages.

Around 900 C.E., ibn Khordādbeh, postmaster of the Arab province of al-Jibāl in Persia, compiled his eight-volume *Book of the Roads and Countries* as a guide for the postal system. He described roads and sea routes as far as Korea, giving detailed directions, distances, weather conditions, and road security. More than four centuries later, c.1335, the Florentine Francesco Balducci Pegolotti, operating out of the Genoese trading center of Kaffa, wrote a handbook for the China trade. His *Della Practica della Mercatura*, circulating in manuscript copies and printed in 1766, described the trip to Beijing with resting places and dangerous stretches and advised which food to carry, where to exchange money or to hire guides, and when to engage interpreters for Turkish dialects. He listed weights and measures used in Genoa, Tana, and Cathay, as well as the packing methods and the quality of the goods. A Catalan manual for trade in Africa was compiled and copied by those interested, and— informed by Jewish coreligionists and Arab scholars—Abraham Cresques mapped Africa in his *Catalan Atlas* of 1375.[8]

From 1160 to 1173, Benjamin, rabbi of Tudela in Aragon, set out to explore commercial possibilities, to take a census of Jewish people worldwide, and to find places of refuge for Spanish Jews in case of Muslim persecution. Via Rome, Cyprus, Jerusalem, and Damascus, he reached Baghdad's community of 40,000 Jews. On the island of Kish in the Gulf of Hormuz some 500 Jews and merchants from India, Persia, and Yemen exchanged silks and spices, cotton and hemp, foods and woods. Through Persia's Jewish communities of Isfahan and Shiraz, with more than 10,000 members each, Benjamin of Tudela traveled to the Malabar Coast of India, where Arab and Chinese merchants met. He continued to Ethiopia and Egypt and returned to Paris via Russia, Bohemia, and Germany.[9]

For commercial connections and cultural exchange, the Venetian Polo family

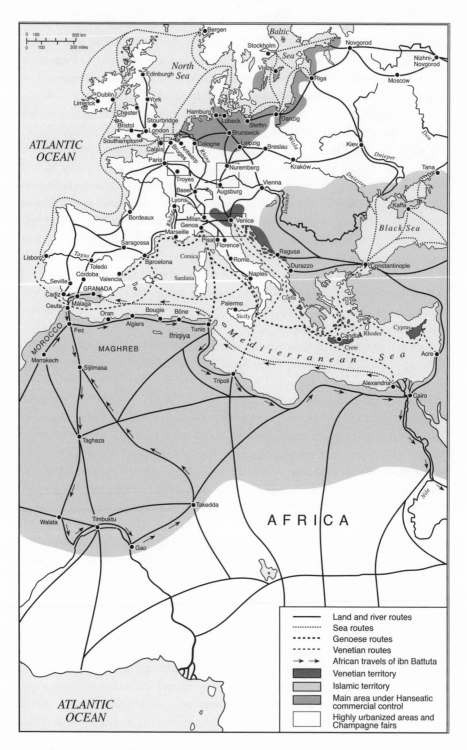

2.3   Afro-Eurasian Trade Routes, 12th–15th Centuries I

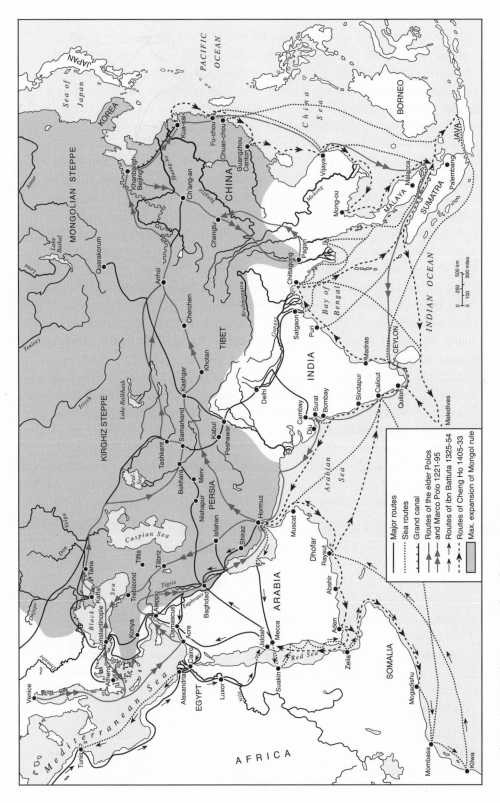

2.4 Afro-Eurasian Trade Routes, 12th–15th Centuries II

provides an example. The brothers Nicolò and Maffeo voyaged to China from 1255 to 1266. On his return, Nicolò learned that his wife had died and that their son Marco had been raised by his sister, Flora. In 1271, accompanied by the seventeen-year-old Marco, the two brothers set out via Acre to Khanbalik, meaning "city of the king" (later Beijing). Mongol rulers had subdued Song China and established "a truly cosmopolitan society": soldiers and traders came from Central Asian peoples, and some of the administrators, merchants, missionaries, and diplomats were from Europe. Foreign religions were tolerated, and Muslim merchants resided in their own quarters in port towns. The thousand-mile Grand Canal, linking Kin-sai (later Hangzhou) to Beijing, was built—how many workers were mobilized? By the early 1300s, eastward journeys "were relatively commonplace, and the trade between East and West considerable." For the European imagination, Marco Polo, who returned only in 1295 via Java, Sumatra, India, and Arabia, remains the epitome of a traveler, although Jewish merchants and, even more so, their Arab counterparts covered greater distances and left a large body of travel narratives, the *rihla* literature.[10]

In a "fundamentally political campaign to establish alliances" with Mongol rulers, the popes from 1245 onward sent missionaries to strengthen the cultural dimension; other missionaries traveled to India and Southeast Asia. William of Rubrouck (Willem van Ruysbroeck), a Franciscan in the Mongols' cosmopolitan capital Qaraqorum (Karakorum) in 1253–55, met Alans (ancestors of modern Ossetians)— some 30,000 of whom served as armorers and bodyguards—Georgians, Armenians, Persians, Turks, as well as Chinese. He met Slavs, Hungarians and Greeks, Germans, Frenchmen, including a sculptor, and one or more Englishmen. Roman Catholics, Nestorians, and Buddhists lived in the capital and in Mongol-ruled China; Jews, Christian Armenians, and Muslims in Guangzhou (Canton), South China's main trading center. A few women were part of the migrations—for example, a wealthy Armenian lady and an Italian merchant's daughter.[11] A Chinese author described the intercultural patterns of living:

> By the time of the [Kublai Khan] the land within the Four Seas had become the territory of one family, civilization had spread everywhere, and no more barriers existed. For people in search of fame and wealth in north and south, a journey of a thousand *li* [about 600 kilometers] was like a trip next door, while a journey of ten thousand *li* constituted just a neighborly jaunt. Hence, among people of the Western Regions who served at court, or who studied in our south-land, many forgot the region of their birth, and took delight in living among our rivers and lakes. As they settled down in China for a long time, some became advanced in years, their families grew, and being far from home, they had no desire to be buried in their fatherland. Brotherhood among peoples has certainly reached a new plane.[12]

Under the Song dynasty (960–1279), Chinese merchants and missionaries in turn traveled westward; their sailors used the compass centuries before European mariners. They traded along the African coast from Somalia to Madagascar, and their relations with local women resulted in what Teobaldo Filesi called "a fine crop of half-caste children." In the middle of the thirteenth century, a Uighurian monk of the Nestorian Church traveled via Baghdad and Constantinople to Armenia, Italy, Paris, and Germany. The high point of outward contacts was reached with the seven voyages of the grand eunuch Cheng Ho, starting in 1405, to India, Ceylon, and Aden. Chinese ships could accommodate up to 1,000 passengers with their provisions, and each of Cheng Ho's fleets carried 27,000 or more men. When the imperial court ordered a stop to the explorations in 1435, citing both costs and unwanted cultural imports, private ventures by merchants continued, and a Chinese diaspora emerged in Southeast Asia before the arrival of the Portuguese from the west.[13]

In North Africa during the mid-1250s, Islamic rulers in Tunis permitted Latin religious orders to open a school to teach Arabic to their itinerant preachers. Travelers, merchants, and missionaries came from Europe, while Ethiopian and other African envoys traveled to Venice. The Arab-Jewish geographer Ibrāhīm ibn Ya'qūb in the mid-tenth century C.E. (or mid-fourth century Muslim Era [M.E.]) had journeyed around Europe from Ireland to Poland, and from Saxony to Sicily, and his report was cited for centuries thereafter. The legal scholar Abū 'Abd Allāh ibn Baṭṭūṭah (1304–68), after voyaging to Anatolia, Arabia, and Asia, traveled to the sub-Saharan salt mines of Taghaza in 1351–54 C.E. En route in Sijilmasa, he lodged with a family whose kinsman he had met in China. Travel on the difficult desert stretch from Tasarahla (Bir al-Ksaib) to Walata was as well organized as on Mongol routes and Latin pilgrim roads. One man traveled ahead to find lodgings, and a group from Walata met the caravan with fresh supplies of water. At Gao (Kawkaw), a large city and former Songhai capital, ibn Baṭṭūṭah observed the usual salt exchange but also the exchange of cowry shells, suggesting that the trading network extended to the east coast. Like other traveling men, ibn Baṭṭūṭah, who married several times, was accompanied by a wife over long stretches of his trips and—following the customs of Chinese merchants—by slave girls on his way to China. While travel was considered dangerous and wearisome for men, his consorts also traveled when pregnant and gave birth to children en route.[14]

In the Mediterranean, the main centers of exchange were Islamic Alexandria and Byzantine Constantinople. The finery of the Byzantine court encouraged artisanal virtuosity and attracted immigrants. These highly skilled craftsmen were, in turn, called to distant cities and capitals. Venetians, Amalfians, Pisans, and Genoese lived in distinct quarters. Natural riches, highly developed urban production, and internal migration between cities made the Eastern Christian civilization self-sufficient. Nevertheless, its products and its position in the center of shipping routes made Constantinople by 1200 the hub of trading networks extending to Novgorod and Kiev, to Trebizond, and to Persia and Egypt. Genoese merchants used their colony in Kaffa on the Crimean Peninsula to wrest trade with Kievan Rus and Central Asian merchants from their Byzantine competitors. Via Samarkand they connected to Chinese merchants and carters (see chap. 7.1).[15]

Alexandria linked the Muslim World westward to Tunisia, Sicily, al-Andalus, and onward to Atlantic Morocco, Seville, and Lisbon. The empires of Mali and Ghana sent caravans with gold and silver to Tunis. Northbound routes to Trebizond connected Arab and Asian traders. Eastward ones followed southern pilgrim routes into the Arab peninsula or those through Persia to Samarkand, the connecting point to Turkestan and to China. Via Shiraz and Kirman (Kermān), Alexandria's traders reached the Indic subcontinent. Indian merchants were particularly active in the islands of Southeast Asia. Arab and Indic merchants established quarters in Chinese port cities, and Jewish families from Persia and India traded cotton. The first Indian tea plantations supplied the increasing demand of China.[16]

The numerous travel accounts, their information and distortions, achieved lasting impact. Friar Odorico da Pordenone's account of his Asia-bound travels from 1324 to 1328 survived in about seventy manuscript copies; it was later printed, used as a source by Sir John Mandeville (1377), and reprinted in Richard Hakluyt's *Voyages* of 1589.[17] In their writings, the travelers' selections, categories, and prejudices transformed cultural contact into a published "imaginary ethnography," whereby observers could project preconceived notions onto Others and then report them as empirical evidence. The reported size of precious stones and of quantities of gold as well as accounts about nakedness and cannibalism among some distant peoples testify to the construction of the Other as the primitive, but with a penchant for the spectacular. Descriptions of distant peoples, who are both enormously rich as well as incredibly depraved, serve as invitations for civilizing "missions," which leave souls presumably saved, bodies dead, and riches in the hands of "explorer-missionaries."[18]

Within the Latin World, the *Guide du Pèlerin* for the route to Santiago de Compostela provides evidence for the juxtaposition of the Self and the Other. According to the author, probably a twelfth-century monk, the people in his fertile home province of Poitou were vigorous. In neighboring Bordelais, however, the speech was rough and the land desolate. Further removed, the inhabitants of Gascony, "light in words, talkative, mockers, debauchees, drunkards, gourmands, badly dressed in rags and unprovided with money," were not fully redeemed by their willingness to help pilgrims. Fredric Jameson has described such narration as a "process of transformation" whereby unexplored landscapes and their inhabitants are "worked over" until they can be "dissolved and assimilated by the older value systems" of the writers, be it those of Poitou, of the Bible, or of a Latin-European culture. The alien has to undergo a process of "neutralization," while the new and unknown has to be inserted into the frame of the known, into the cultural beliefs of observing traveler-writers and their readers. Such "neutralization" is not unidirectional, from the Latin West outward; accounts by travelers from the East attest to the universality of the process.[19]

Through this near-global network of commercial connections, a wide variety of luxury items and bulk goods (such as lumber and iron) were moved, slaves transported, and laborers mobilized. Foodstuffs like wheat and olive oil from northern Africa, wine from Syria, tuna from the Atlantic coast, sugar from Spain, Sicily, Syria and beyond, entered the European trading networks and influenced dietary habits. Horses, whether Arabian steeds or Turkestan ponies, were provided for the luxury market, as were Persian Gulf pearls and Red Sea corals, dyes, and perfumes. Traders in Baghdad markets exchanged furs, honey, and wax from Russian territories; spices, gems, and iron from the Indic world; and gold and ivory from East Africa. Alexandrian artisans worked with Iberian lumber. Slave traders marketed East African men and women through Arab networks, Slavic or Turkish ones through the Italian enclaves on the Black Sea.[20] How many hands had handled a package of spices en route from the South Sea to a European household? How many women cooked and washed for the transport laborers in homes, inns, or caravan relays?

Guidebooks for intercontinental trade made "no reference to Europe, the exports of which were too few and too insignificant to deserve mention, though possibly some of them may have been included in the list for Byzantium." Viewed from wealthy economies, northern Europe appeared as undersupplied, even as depraved. To people in the Songhai Empire and Ghana, it was obvious that gold was always lacking north of the Sahara. Chinese merchants and travelers were appalled at European barbarism. From the eleventh century onward, however, merchants from Italian cities began to compete with Muslim and Jewish ones. They quickly adopted Jewish-Arab-Indic accounting techniques and maritime knowledge. Syrian merchants and pedlars who had traveled as far as France were replaced by Italians. Urban Italy provided an interface between Europe north of the Alps and the Arabic and Asian Worlds.[21]

From the eleventh to the sixteenth century, Latin Europe's position in the trade networks changed for several reasons.[22] Christian forces established themselves in the major cities of the Iberian Peninsula and reduced interaction with Islam, and Venice used the Fourth Crusade in 1204 to reduce the influence of Byzantine Christendom. When Mongol expansion temporarily severed overland trade to Asia, it continued as seaborne trade through Alexandria mediated by Arab merchants. A realignment of Muslim states, both Turkish and Arab, into the Ottoman Empire and Mamluk Egypt, changed power relations. The papal interdiction against trade with the Mamluks (1359) slowed down European trade with Asia, but many Christian merchants maintained their contacts. Constantinople, by then an impoverished and depopulated city, was captured by Ottoman troops in 1453 (see chap. 5.1).[23]

Commerce followed spatial patterns separate from political entities and divided Europe into four trade zones. "Urban Italy," that is, the cities of the northern Italian plain as well as Amalfi, Naples, and Palermo in the south, had control of the Mediterranean—albeit divided among themselves—and interacted with Byzantine and Arab merchants. Second, around the Baltic Sea, the loose federation of Hanseatic cities emerged between 1150 and 1250, controlled trade from the thirteenth to the fifteenth century, and reached out to London and Novgorod and southward along the Rhine to Cologne. On Europe's western margin, London and the English Midlands began to enter the trading networks. The third zone consisted of a string of fairs from Urban Italy via Geneva and Lyon to Saint-Denis by the eleventh and Champagne by the twelfth and thirteenth centuries, and to Bruges and the emerging Urban Netherlands after the middle of the fourteenth century. Incessant fighting among dynasties—for example, the Hundred Years' War of 1338 to 1453—marginalized entire regions north of the Alps for long periods of time because transaction costs for commerce became prohibitive. In the late fourteenth century, a fourth center, the merchant-capitalist houses of the Fugger and Welser families in Augsburg and Nuremberg (with about 20,000 inhabitants) extended their trade and credit network into Hungary and Spain. "These regions developed the most advanced marketing systems, low cost transportation and effective public administration." Such trade, which has been labeled "international" even though neither nations nor dynastic economies existed, linked the four zones into trans-European networks.[24]

The eleventh-century royal market in the city of Léon on the northern Iberian Peninsula illustrates the nature of local and trans-European mercantile interaction. Craftspeople and provisioners came from the neighboring townships, each of which specialized in a particular artisanal product or type of food. They sold their wares next to medium-distance traders bringing Toro wine, Zamora oil, salt from Castile, and cider from Asturia and jostled for space with long-distance merchants from Muslim Iberia and from Byzantium.[25] In the exchange between local, transregional, and intercontinental trade, credit practices evolved, and coins became known and accepted over large distances, with their denominations growing larger. Learning from Arab culture, Lombard and Jewish merchants replaced Roman numerals with figures that had been adapted by Arabs from Indic culture and developed a banking system that encompassed Europe. These new financial transactions signaled the advent of a different economy in Europe: the replacement of feudal rule and manorial agriculture by commercial capitalism.

2.3   Pre-Plague Migrations in Mediterranean and Transalpine Europe

From the tenth to the thirteenth century, seven major migrations in the Mediterranean World and transalpine Europe involved dispersal, colonization, or state-building.[26] Migrations of dispersal were 1) forced, as in the case of Mediterranean slavery, or 2) mainly voluntary, as in the case of Jews in this period. Jewish migration, which even in flight involved family units and a shared culture, created transcontinentally linked communities. Slaves, torn as individuals out of many cultures, recreated at best fragments of their cultures of origin. Migrations that involved state-building included—most significantly—3) the Islamic expansion into Sicily, southern Italy, and Spain; 4) Norman societies from Brittany via England to Sicily as well as eastward into Slavic territories; and 5) the warrior-pilgrims of the crusades turned settlers (1099–1187). Two more migrations involved colonization by 6) West Central Europeans in Slavic-settled territories east of the Elbe River in the ninth century and from about 1125 to c.1410 and by 7) Christian families from further north in the Iberian Peninsula (see map 2.5). In addition, incursions from the east, first by Magyars from the trans-Danubian plains in the tenth century and then by Mongols in the thirteenth century, left no permanent traces in West Central Europe except for images

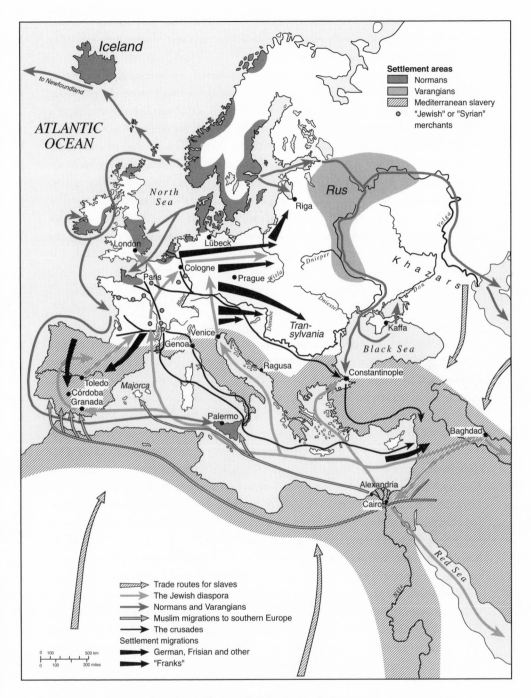

Settlement areas
- Normans
- Varangians
- Mediterranean slavery
- "Jewish" or "Syrian" merchants

Trade routes for slaves
- The Jewish diaspora
- Normans and Varangians
- Muslim migrations to southern Europe
- The crusades

Settlement migrations
- German, Frisian and other
- "Franks"

Iceland

to Newfoundland

ATLANTIC
OCEAN

North
Sea

London

Lübeck

Riga

Rus

Paris

Cologne

Prague

Volga

Dnieper

Khazars

Rhine

Wisła

Dniester

Don

Venice

Transylvania

Kaffa

Genoa

Ragusa

Black Sea

Toledo

Majorca

Córdoba

Granada

Constantinople

Palermo

Baghdad

Alexandria

Cairo

Red Sea

Danube

0 100   500 km
0 100   300 miles

2.5   Migrations of Dispersal, State-Building, and Colonization before 1347

of bloodthirsty eastern nomad horsemen. Mongols did destroy the Baghdad-centered Muslim culture, sacking the city in 1258 and 1393, but they could not conquer the Muslim Ottoman state in Anatolia.

Demography and inheritance practices contributed to migration for purposes of military aggression and expansion. Younger sons of the nobility, especially the lower nobility, were sent off to conquer new territories—thus ridding the home society of a particularly unruly element and families of competitors for inheritances. Accompanied by smaller or larger numbers of armed knights they "crusaded" in Palestine, the Iberian Peninsula, and Polish-Prussian territories; later they "conquered" the Aztec and Inca states. Younger sons and daughters of the peasantry colonized unsettled areas within their states or estates of origin or settled in the eastern marches and in Castile. Younger sons of merchants moved to distant shores to establish trade connections. None of these colonies and settlements lasted unless women were part of the move and the newcomers formed communities to replace soldier-migrants lording it over local populations.

Mediterranean Slavery

In the Mediterranean region, Islamic, Jewish, Byzantine, and Latin Christian peoples all practiced state slavery (administrative, military, or fiscal) and private slavery (productive, commercial, or domestic). Neither type was collective by ethnic group or color of skin. Rather, individuals were enslaved by raiders (as captives of wars) or as a result of poverty-induced sale by relatives or through self-sale. Captives could be ransomed. Thus European rulers freed sailors or officers captured in war by Muslims. They often relied on Jewish intermediaries because of their intercivilizational familial connections. The three major slave-trading routes extended from the German-Slavic borderlands, conquered by ninth-century German rulers, to Muslim Córdoba; from the Black Sea region to the Mediterranean; and from south Russia to Egypt in the thirteenth century.

By the eleventh century, "productive" slavery in agriculture, the crafts, or mining had come to an end in Mesopotamia, but in southern Italy, Sicily, and Spain, agricultural work, especially sugar cultivation, was still performed by enslaved men. State slavery, which continued in the Ottoman and Arab-Muslim World, most often involved military service. The professional slave soldiers of Muslim armies, especially in Almohad Morocco and Hafsid Tunis, were supplemented by Christian mercenaries drawn mainly from Spain. Starting in the ninth century, the Abbasid caliphate used Turkish slave mamluks (from the Arabic *mamlūk*, "to own," but in historical usage applied to white, that is, Turkish or Central Asian male slaves). In twelfth-century Egypt, armies consisted of free Berbers as cavalry, of Mamluk horsemen, and of Black Sudanese foot soldiers. By 1250 the Mamluks had risen to the status of a political class and formed the ruling slave oligarchy in Egypt and Syria for 250 years. Later, janissaries—elite troops levied from subdued populations—held elevated positions in the Ottoman Empire (see chap. 5.1). In Europe, municipalities or rulers filled the treasury by renting state slaves as workers to private individuals (fiscal slavery). Domestic slavery continued in all of these societies.[27]

Catchment areas included the Caucasus region, Arab North Africa, sub-Saharan Black Africa, and any Christian-Muslim war zone. In the course of the struggle over the Iberian Peninsula, each power treated the other's territories as a reservoir of slaves. East European and Asian slaves from the areas between the Volga and Dnieper (Dnepr) Rivers[28] and from Central Asia, according to Verlinden, included seventy different ethnicities. Men and women of Greek-Byzantine, Caucasian and Crimean, Russian, Bulgarian, Gypsy, or Turkish background were traded as far as the Maghreb and Iberia. African slaves included "Blacks" from the East African coast and Central Africa as well as Berbers and Arabs. The Islamization of the Sudan and Guinea around 1100 connected these areas to the trade routes.[29] After the devastations of the plague, Slavic and Tatar peoples sold children into slavery to ensure their survival.

Genoese merchants, through their trading colony at Kaffa, controlled the slave trade in the eastern Mediterranean, while the East and Central African trade was in the hands of Arab merchants. Slaves were retailed in practically all ports of the Mediterranean. After the emergence of the Ottoman Empire, the eastern supply was used mainly within its borders, though small numbers of Slavic women continued to be traded through Adriatic ports. The North African supply system remained operative, but the volume of trade declined in the twelfth century. A new Atlantic system of slavery emerged after 1440, when Portuguese and, later, Spanish traders began to carry West African slaves to the Lisbon and Seville slave markets and introduced them into the labor regimes of the Atlantic plantation islands (see chap. 5.3).

In Europe, slave societies reached from the Iberian Peninsula via the Italian to the Balkan Peninsula. In Andalusia, the Muslim conquerors of the eighth century had introduced African slaves of many ethnicities as well as West Asian ones from as far away as Persia. They remained in bondage after the Christian conquest and were supplemented by captured Muslims and further, albeit reduced, imports from the North African slave markets. Christian armies resorted to mass enslavement of Muslims after the capture of the island of Majorca in 1229, during the captive-taking at Lucera in 1300, and after the fall of Granada in 1470–92. The case of Lucera, in the kingdom of Naples, furnishes an example of the willfulness and economic interest of rulers. In 1269 the city's Arab-Muslim population surrendered to Charles of Anjou. Intending to place a Christian colony in the town, the king invited people from Provence to settle. When for lack of financial or material support only a few families accepted the offer, Charles, in need of money and laborers, captured the Muslim townspeople in 1300. At first, he compelled them to work as agriculturists on royal domains; he then sold into slavery about 9,800 surviving men, women, and children.[30]

In terms of social integration and gender roles, the demise of productive slavery improved the lot of slave men. Rewards rather than threats of punishment were used as an inducement to work. Flight was uncommon, except on the part of free-moving sailor-slaves. In cities with uncontrolled hinterlands like Ragusa (Dubrovnik), half of the fugitives were male, even though men accounted for only 10 percent of the local slave population. Male slaves in homes hardly did menial domestic work. Most were carefully selected, educated, and treated as sons or business partners. Many could do business on their own and accumulate property. Some, in particular in the Jewish diaspora, acted as agents in distant cities. Slaves were increasingly sought for household chores—for what society considered women's work. Thus slave status became feminized, and around 1300 women outnumbered men by two to one in slave markets. In 1460, 97 percent of Genoese slaves were female. Accordingly, prices paid for women were higher than those for men.

In Mediterranean commercial centers, varying over time, slaves accounted for 5 to 15 percent of the populations and formed a "vital section of the working population." Women, who often had to care for their dependent children, were considered more tractable than men. Control was exerted by curfews and by prohibitions against congregating. Forceful sexual exploitation by Christian masters, although canonically condemned and punishable, was frequent. In Ragusa, however, slave women could sue aggressors in the courts.[31]

Domestic slavery was specific to the evolution of urban economies and patrician lifestyles. Gender differentiation and "personalized" care changed labor from general domestic service to nursing and attending to a single person at a time. As a consequence, slaves held positions of trust and emotional attachment. They advanced from a marginal position to being an integrated part of family life. In wills, they could be manumitted or were bequeathed to other family members under provisions that prohibited sale. In the Jewish world, manumission implied full membership in the religious community and the right to marry. The conversion of slaves was common in the Cairo Jewish community and among Christian slave owners on the Iberian Peninsula.

As illustrated by Circassian or North African slave women in Genoa, where 5,000 slaves lived in a population estimated at 60,000 in 1380, "social integration" and "intercultural contact" often involved consensual concubinage with a male of the household. As a rule, children of such unions were adopted and endowed by the fathers. In Siena, fathers had to assume the cost of birth of their children by slave women. On the other hand, the semi-familial position notwithstanding, in the fifteenth century about 10 percent of the Genoese slave population was traded annually. In Ragusa, slaves were trained and then sold in Venice for higher prices. The presence of slaves was, "for the towns of the owners, a factor of diversity and enrichment."[32]

The Jewish Diaspora

By the eighth century, some 90 percent of the Jews who had been expelled from Judea in the Roman period lived in the Arab Umayyad and Abbasid caliphates (661–c.1100), where they could move freely. Baghdad became the religio-cultural center.[33] From forced and voluntary migrations a thriving diaspora emerged, an early globalization of one ethnoreligious group. The socioeconomic structures of the Arab states fostered urbanization of Jewish lifestyles. Jointly with Arabs, Jewish merchants became the leading force in long-distance and intercontinental trade until Christian crusaders in Jerusalem and Mongol horsemen in Baghdad wrought havoc in their communities. Once the disintegrating eastern Arab empires no longer provided protection, the communities of the Iberian Peninsula became the core of the Jewish diaspora.[34]

Pluralist Muslim societies, in contrast to Latin Christendom, accorded religious minorities a position as "protected persons" who paid a special poll tax but otherwise were left to administer their own affairs. The dispersed Jewish communities achieved intra- as well as intercommunal cohesion by codification of Judaic law in the Mishnah, by recording the evolution of legal-religious doctrine in the Talmud, and by means of their common language. They migrated in family or neighborhood groups and thus, at their destinations, could form stable communities much faster than, for example, the temporary, single-gender merchant migrants from Urban Italy.[35] The rabbinical *responsa* literature gave advice about travel and about relations with host societies—about acculturation in modern terms. According to advice given in 1301, immigrants should "closely observe the established burghers" so that "their sons and daughters will behave like" the resident gentiles.[36]

Emanating from eleventh-century Cairo, Jewish and Arab merchant connections spanned the seas and reached Arabia, the East African coast, India, and China. The Radhanite community established itself in the southern ports of France and linked the trade of the Rhone River to Arab lands. Craftsmen migrated to expanding economies or circulated through Muslim villages as itinerant artisans. Others were transferred by the caliphate's authorities to where they were needed, while still others were forced to flee from mistreatment. The thriving Cairo community attracted the troubled and unfortunate in search of support. Scholars migrated across the Mediterranean World in search of learning or better positions or simply to earn a living. Women moved with their husbands or traveled on their own between segments of geographically extended families. They undertook pilgrimages and conducted business. Single immigrant men often married women from the host community to gain access to their social and economic relations. Sons were sent to distant relatives for training purposes, and families intent on extending their trade connections exchanged sons and daughters in "mercantile marriages" to form relationships of trust in the interlinked Jewish Mediterranean society.[37]

Under Muslim rule, Iberian Jewry had entered a "golden age" as early as the eighth century. But beginning in the mid-1140s, when the North African Almohads, styling themselves defenders of the purity of Islam, invaded and killed Jews and "impure" Muslims alike, thousands were forced to flee.[38] After these interruptions and the Christian advance from the north, the age of tolerance continued in Toledo, the central city of Castile, under Alfonso VI and VII (r. 1072–1157). A cooperation of scholars from the three religions and civilizations in Christian Toledo and Muslim Córdoba continued the learned traditions of Baghdad and provided translations of Greco-Arab philosophy into languages of the Western World. Jews recolonized depopulated areas as landowners, assumed leading positions at courts, and occasionally served as military commanders. Some anti-Semitic expressions notwithstanding, Jews were offered protection in the kingdom of Aragon in 1247 and held an esteemed position in the Iberian multifaith societies until the mass rioting of 1348.[39]

In western Europe, Jews migrated during the tenth and eleventh centuries into the Rhine valley, where they established communities in Cologne, Mainz, and Frankfurt/Main. Jews from France migrated in small numbers to England after 1066. In the thirteenth century others moved into Poland and Lithuania, where a Polish prince granted them a charter in 1264. Here, too, Jewish migrants concentrated in towns, but they also participated in rural colonization and forest clearances. Among the Central European Ashkenazim, Yiddish (based on medieval German) replaced Hebrew in everyday transactions and became the transcontinental language of the lower classes. Feudalism forced Jewish families into small-town or urban economies by prohibiting them from owning land, though exceptions existed, especially in Slavic territories.

Jewish society supported neither a warrior group nor a sanctified, distinct clergy. Its power structure was based neither on land nor on physical prowess or military strength. Community self-organization facilitated reestablishment or adaptation in the course of migrations. Divided into a wealthy group of leaders, a middling section, and impoverished people at the bottom, communities also replicated socioeconomic hierarchies after each migration or flight. Family "networking" was part of everyday life and permitted long-distance connections without a political superstructure. This Mediterranean period was followed by the "dark ages" of persecution and murder across Europe (see chap. 4.2).[40]

Norman Societies

From the ninth to the twelfth century, Scandinavian "norsemen" migrated as "Viking" raiders[41] and "Norman" occupation forces southwestward to England and beyond and as "Varangians" or "Rus" southeastward via the Baltic Sea into eastern Europe (hence the name Russia). Norman nobles, some discontented with a reorganization of their home societies, settled as invaders and state-builders along the borders of Europe: in mid-tenth-century northwestern France ("Normandy"), in England and Wales after 1066, and in Sicily and southern Italy from 1103 to 1194. All imposed their rule over local populations and merged with or replaced local nobilities. Chain migrations of adventurers and settlers who intermarried locally and accepted local languages established new populations. As rulers they improved political structures by reforming traditional systems of taxation and administration and reducing the burdens of the peasantry.

From England, invaded by perhaps 6,000 warriors with their families, Norman culture penetrated into Wales and Ireland and reached the Scottish nobility. The introduction of primogeniture and the intermarriage of the conqueror families' younger sons and daughters with nonaristocratic families achieved a fusion of newcomer and native cultures.[42]

Sicily, under Muslim control from 827 on, was a Norman stopover along the way to the Holy Land until, in 1072, they took control, established the kingdom of Sicily, and conquered southern Italy, then part of the Byzantine Empire. Byzantine, Arab-Islamic, and Scandinavian interaction and cultural conversion transformed local practices. Sicilian Muslims and Christians had lived intermingled. Contrary to papal orders, the new rulers did not convert Muslims, but they achieved partial Christianization through the extensive immigration of settlers. Palermo, with a population of 300,000, was home to Arabs and Berbers, Greeks and Lombards, Jews, Persians, Turks, and Black Africans. Foreign sailors and merchants resided in the city's "Slav Quarter." King Roger II forced Greek weavers and embroiderers to migrate to Palermo, where they introduced the cultivation of silk worms, which then spread to northern Italy.

Sicily's agriculture had benefited from Muslim improvements on Roman irrigation techniques through the application of Persian expertise. They introduced sugarcane cultivation from the Levant. When after 1150 the oppression of Muslims increased, many emigrated to North Africa. After the rebellion of 1222–24, some 16,000 were deported to Lucera in southern Italy.[43] Immigrants from French Normandy and Lombardy filled their places. Like Muslim Iberia, though on a smaller scale, Sicilian culture achieved a fusion of Islamic, Latin Christian, and Jewish elements, with additional input from Byzantine Christianity. The chancery was bilingual, conducting affairs in Arabic and Latin, with some documents drawn up in Greek. The courts of the Norman King Roger II (r. 1103–54) and of Frederick II of Hohenstaufen (r. 1212–50) were centers of intellectual exchange. Frederick, born of a Norman mother and a German father and educated in Sicily—then the Italian section of the "Holy Roman Empire"—founded the University of Naples and the medical school of Salerno. He married Constance of Aragon, who provided additional cultural input through her retinue of Aragonese knights, court ladies, and troubadours. The next dynasty however, the French Angevins, had different goals. To transform Sicily and Naples into the nucleus of a new and powerful Byzantine empire, they imposed harsh fiscal demands. Exploitation brought the coexistence of cultures, the *convivencia*, to a sudden stop. In a bloody conflict, erupting reportedly after some Angevin soldiers insulted a young married Sicilian woman, many of the French administrators were killed in 1282.[44]

Crusaders and "Frankish" Settlement in Palestine

Inspired by the Cluniac revival, more than a hundred groups of men and women voyaged as pilgrims to the Holy Land in the eleventh century.[45] The crusades proper (1096–1291) mobilized more and sometimes emptied entire villages. Who were the crusaders and in what numbers did they move across the continent? In the First Crusade of 1096–99, described as an "aimless mass migration . . . accompanied by pillage and anti-Semitic" acts, perhaps 42,000—or as many as 130,000 according to other sources—set out. In 1201 Venice contracted to ship 4,500 knights, 9,000 squires, and 20,000 foot soldiers. Papal envoys recruited children, shepherds, and others from Normandy and the Dutch provinces to the Rhine valley for the so-called popular crusades from 1212 to 1230. After their arrival in Palestine, the men and women who came from the whole of western Europe were called "Franks" and thus homogenized by ascription.[46]

During the trip east, cultural interaction including conflict involved all social levels. The 100,000 men who are said to have sailed from Regensburg in southern Germany down the Danube passed through numerous cultures.[47] During the first crusade, some 30,000 warrior-pilgrims had to be fed and accommodated in Constantinople, where they met Italian merchants, Turkish sailors, and Russian traders. Antiforeigner riots repeatedly erupted. In 1204 Venice first used the crusading troops to sack Constantinople and thus rid itself of an economic rival; it then requested that the pope call on "the inhabitants of the West, of all ranks and both sexes" to repopulate the city.[48]

Some noblemen's wives and daughters joined the crusades and carried arms; tens of thousands of wives, nuns, servants, and prostitutes followed the treks. Many more were left behind. Widows of French pilgrims founded a convent, and English ones were assaulted by men who coveted the property of their deceased husbands. In intergenerational terms, younger sons and minor nobility from the overpopulated feudal system hoped to acquire income and wealth. Chronicles of the time reveal particular cultural constructions of sexuality and gender roles as well as of sexuality and the Other. During the siege of Antioch in 1097–98, the city's Muslim defenders expelled the male Christian inhabitants as potential allies of the invaders but offered protection for the women and children left behind. On the Christian side, thousands of women accompanying the besieging army were sent away, not for their protection but because of the spiritual leaders' deep aversion to sexuality. Military defeats were attributed to sexual licentiousness. Arab and Turkish soldiers were portrayed as lusting after (beautiful) Christian women, but a distinctly irritated Christian chronicler had to note that Latin soldiers lusted after Byzantine women and, for that matter, boys.[49]

As the Venetian sacking of Constantinople indicates, crusades were fueled by motives other than religious ones. For example, the Military Orders, once protective organizations for pilgrims, became corporate military establishments. They accumulated fabulous riches, at first by bequests, then through regular incomes, and finally by seizing lands of the "infidels." Some of the orders initiated a process of ethnicization; thus the multiethnic Teutonic Order "Germanized" itself and no longer admitted men of other backgrounds.[50]

In 1099 Jerusalem was overwhelmed and sacked by Christian warriors. They massacred Muslims, torched the synagogue where the city's entire Jewish population had taken refuge, and expelled their non-Latin coreligionists. To revitalize the city, King Baldwin I (r. 1100–1118) encouraged survivors to stay and invited Maronite Syrian Christians, "with their wives and children, flocks and herds, and all their households" from villages across the Jordan. They were not granted equal status with conquering Christians. To repopulate the countryside, settlers arrived from southern France and, in smaller numbers, from the Italian and Iberian peninsulas, a total of about 140,000 in a resident population of perhaps half a million.[51]

The crusader states from 1099 to 1187 accommodated diverse cultures in a hierarchy of power and status. Some scholars see this "as evidence of the creation of a Franco-Syrian nation" and emphasize intermarriage and friendly relations. Others stress conflict and suggest that intermarriage meant that male victors took women as spoils of war. In municipal courts, a Frankish magistrate sat with two Frankish and four Syrian jurors. Interaction between the cultures increased 1) when the warrior-pilgrims and their children adopted local lifestyles; 2) when second-generation, locally born Christian ethnics began to outnumber the immigrants; and 3) when learned clerics delved into Arab knowledge to create a new intercultural scholarship based on Arab transmission of lost Greek texts. Interaction and acculturation could also increase the potential for conflict, as when Europeans modified their weapons to incorporate Arab and Turkish methods of warfare. The diversity and quantity of newcomers, some of whom came from as far as Norway and Russia, caused Jerusalem's native-born inhabitants to complain about the "strangers."[52]

The Latin bishop of Acre castigated second- and third-generation Franks for acculturating. They indulged, so he wrote, "in baths, fine clothes, sex and magical practices, which they find more important than fighting. Furthermore, they make alliance with the Arabs, accept their ideas, and are soft and effeminate." A chronicler of the kingdom of Jerusalem noted that a mere three decades after arrival of the Franks, "God turned the West into the East; for we who were easterners are now become Orientals: he who was a Roman or a Frank has become in this land a Galilean or a Palestinian, he who was from Rheims or Chartres has been made into a Tyrian or Antiochene." For the newcomers, the process of orientalization meant to aspire to a higher culture than their own culture of origin.[53]

A brief glance at Muslim pilgrims in Mecca reveals throngs of people as diverse as those in Jerusalem. "Turks of Azerbaijan walked with Malinke of the Western Sudan, Berbers of the Atlas with Indians of Gujerat . . . the adherents of the four main legal schools, plus Shi'is, Zaydis, 'Ibadis, and other sectarians, prayed together." Ibn Baṭṭūṭah spent three years in Mecca, as a scholar-sojourner or pilgrim-in-residence, living off alms and with the support of learned patrons.[54]

With the success of Turkish armies and rulers from Kurdistan under Ṣalāḥ ad-Dīn Yusūf ibn Ayyūb (Saladin) and their reconquest of Jerusalem in 1187, Christian military men and entrepreneurs left for new frontiers. The Orders first relocated to Mediterranean islands, then either to Iberia or to the Baltic for expansionist crusades against Muslims or Slavic and Baltic peoples. Italian merchant-entrepreneurs, who supplied most of Europe with sugar produced by slave labor, relocated their plantations first to Cyprus, Crete, and Aegean islands, and, after the successful twelfth-century Iberian crusades, to Andalusia. Transit trade and "residence in the Holy Land brought European men [and women] into contact with Oriental produce and dramatically increased demand for spices, scented woods, dyes, silk and porcelain in France and Italy," from which the greater part of the immigrants came. The mass itinerancy of the crusades and the high rates of return among survivors caused a "demonstration effect" that spread their new food habits at home. "In a sense, the East invaded Europe through the stomach." The introduction of spices and condiments, such as lemon, sugar, syrup, sherbet, coffee, jasmine, and saffron, "altered the aristocratic—and later popular—cuisine of Western Europe dramatically." Medicinal drugs, including camphor, laudanum, balm, aloe, and alum, were imported. As crusades and missionary activities decreased and immigration came to an end, the Turko-Muslim rulers kept the Holy City open to Christian pilgrimages (see chap. 3.4).[55]

Muslims in al-Andalus

Muslim merchants had traded in Europe for centuries: Syrians regularly attended French fairs, and a Pisan monk complained about "Turks and Lybians and Parths and Chaldeans" at Italian markets. Muslim slaves were part of all southern European societies, and free Muslims had formed communities along the northern littoral of the Mediterranean. The geographic proximity of Europe and North Africa is striking. Sicily reaches further south than the northern coast of Tunis, and only a narrow strait separates the Iberian Peninsula from Morocco. From the eighth to the sixteenth century, Muslims ruled several Mediterranean islands, enclaves on the sea's northern shores, and in three larger territories of Europe. From the Volga to Crimea, the thirteenth-century incursions of Mongol peoples left Muslim populations behind. In the Balkans, Turkoman Muslims settled under Ottoman rule in the fourteenth century (chap. 5.1). In al-Andalus in the Iberian Peninsula, Muslim rule extended from 711 C.E. (92 M.E.) to the eleventh century and in Granada to 1492 (897), and Muslims lived under Christian rulers until their expulsion in 1614.[56]

Enjoined by the Koran to respect adherence to the other monotheistic "religions of the Book" (Bible and Talmud), Muslims coexisted with Jews and Christians. Scholars of the three faiths cooperated closely, and merchants adhering to the different faiths did business with each other. In periods of conflict, however, mass conversions could be forced on conquered populations, as in the case of the late Byzantine Empire. In peacetime, voluntary conversion did take place, as in the area from Syria to Mesopotamia. Arab conquest—aside from the ravages of war—left local populations intact.

In 711 and 712 (92 and 93), Muslim armies, totaling 25,000 men, invaded the Iberian Peninsula and defeated the Christianized Visigothic forces. Resident Jews, who had been subjected to forced baptism from 612 on, welcomed the Muslims as liberators, and some Christian lords joined forces with them. Jews opened the gates of Granada and Toledo to the armies, which in accordance with Islamic law saved the inhabitants from plunder and death. Of the 300,000 prisoners taken, one-tenth belonged to the caliph and were marched to Damascus by land. Intermittent fighting with Christians and struggles between Muslim sects brought other armies and large numbers of mercenary Berbers to al-Andalus in subsequent centuries.[57]

Christians fled or migrated northward to Christian lands, from Catalonia to neighboring Valencia, or to the islands of Majorca, Sicily, and Sardinia, or as far as Greece. Muslim soldiers settled down: at first, Berbers mainly in mountainous areas,

Arabs mainly in the cities. The 12,000 "Syrian" soldiers of 742 (124) were assigned vacated lands according to regional origin: those from Damascus in Elvira (Granada); Jordanian men in the district of Rayya (Málaga); those from Palestine in Sidonia (Medina Sidonia); those from Hamus in Seville; those from Qasnarin in Jaén; those from Egypt in Beja; and the remainder in Todmir (Murcia). Among the newcomers, conflicts about the spoils divided early from later arriving ones, and migrants of common ethnicity formed generational cohorts based on time of arrival. In times of peace, Islamic migrants came as urban craftsmen or transplanted their highly developed agricultural techniques. With the exception of minor Norman settlements along the lower Guadalquivir River, little immigration of other peoples occurred. By 1100 (c.500), Muslims outnumbered Christians because of immigration, conversion, and natural growth. Thereafter, the balance reversed owing to warfare and immigration of Christians from the north.[58]

A process of conquest and peaceful intermingling created a mosaic of ethnoreligious groups. The newcomers—Libyans, Syrians, Persians, and Copts from Egypt as well as slave soldiers—came to be called *moros* (Moors), a term derived from the Roman *mauro* for inhabitants of Mauritania. In Christian usage the term implied inferior social status. Jews lived in self-contained communities. The mixed ethnoreligious groups were called *mozárabes*, Christians living under Muslim rule, and *mudéjars*, Muslims living under Christian rule. *Moriscos* were converts from Islam to Christianity and their descendants; *muladís* converts from Christianity to Islam. All usually lived in distinct neighborhoods, practiced their religions, and organized their administrative and legal procedures according to their own traditions. Either from conviction or because of economic considerations, Christians converted to Islam. Converts did not have to pay the poll tax imposed on non-Muslim peoples, but they were often derided as *renegados* (traitors) by their former coreligionists. Over time these terms have served to marginalize groups as well as to distinguish them for analytical purposes.[59]

Dynastic and religious conflict continued between and within religions. Conquered Muslims were enserfed by Christian lords or sent into domestic slavery, as were Christians during Muslim advances. Imported slaves might convert after conquest to gain freedom. Sub-Saharan Black slave bodyguards were labeled as "dumb ones" because they did not speak Arabic. (Similarly, Slavic people called their German neighbors *nemec*, "mute," because they could not talk to them.) Like other Muslim rulers, 'Abd ar-Rahmān III (r. 912–961; 300–350) developed a nonethnic administration, the *clientela* of some 15,000 persons, with slaves from the Black Sea region as well as purchased Frankish, German, Lombard, and Calabrian children. Once they were educated, they staffed high civil and military posts or served as harem eunuchs and palace guards.[60]

Because of well-developed connections to other Islamic lands, because of revolt and fighting, and because of raids by Christian or Muslim forces, there were numerous voluntary, compelled, and forced migrations. When a more intolerant version of Islam became predominant, many *mozárabes* fled to Christian-ruled areas north of the Douro (Duero) and the Ebro. After an uprising, 15,000 *muladís* with their families were expelled[61] and left for Fez (Fès), Alexandria, and eastern Mediterranean islands. When construction workers were needed in Fez, several thousand peasant families from al-Andalus augmented the number of local craftsmen. Although of the same religion, they practiced a different culture and lived in separate quarters, each centered on a mosque.

Córdoba, as capital of the Umayyad dynasty, housed a population of perhaps 500,000 by the tenth century.[62] It was home to schools of medicine, mathematics, philosophy, and poetry, rivaling Baghdad and Byzantium as a center of learning and literature. Among the scholars invited to teach at the university, bi- or multilingualism was the rule. On the material level, the basis for interchange and accumulation of knowledge was the production of paper, a technology that had been developed in China, carried to Samarkand, and adopted in Arab Mesopotamia by the 750s. Migrating craftsmen had spread the technology to Cairo. Córdoba's large paper mills supplied other parts of Europe with the expensive commodity by the twelfth century. Printing, known in tenth-century Egypt, did not spread to Europe; it only served to disseminate knowledge after it was reinvented by Gutenberg in the mid-fifteenth century.

About 13,000 weavers, many of them North African immigrants, plied their trade in Córdoba, and a leather industry, working fine "cordovan" and "moroccan" materials, earned high renown at European courts. Musicians and slave women from the East came to play and sing at the court. Slaves of Slavic origin alone numbered 14,000. Craftsmen from Byzantium decorated the interiors of mosques and the royal palace. Streets were paved and some were illuminated at night by torches. The building and ornamental styles of immigrant Byzantine, Arab, and North African craftsmen combined with those of local artisans to form the Hispano-Muslim architectural tradition.[63]

Intermarriage between religions and ethnicities involved all strata. Women of the palace, including sultans' wives and mothers, came from many ethnicities, among them Basques and Visigoths. Many were educated and some wrote poetry at a time when women in the rest of Europe could hardly aspire to learn to read and write. In the early period of conquest, when the invaders' sex ratio was imbalanced, Muslim soldiers had to look for local wives if they wanted to marry. Perhaps the erotic implications of the Other, the exotic, contributed to the integration of peoples. If contemporary reports did not merely reflect ascription and envy, men from the south considered blond northern women attractive while northerners had a liking for women with dark hair. The sources do not reveal women's preferences. By 1100 differences between groups had decreased, but relative concentration of particular groups varied widely across the peninsula. Most third-generation immigrants were bilingual, whether of Arab or Spanish-Christian origin, and a creole language, a spoken Romance dialect written with Arab script, developed.[64]

Muslim Iberia was an "urban" society in 1000 C.E. compared not only to Christian Iberia, with its single city of León, but also to the rest of Europe. Thereafter, as Muslim power, lifestyles, and high culture began to decline, Christian crusading armies started to attack. On the ideological battleground, Christian scholars describe this warfare as *reconquista* (reconquest). The pre-Muslim population, however, had consisted of Visigothic rulers and a population mix of Visigoths, earlier Roman invaders and their slaves, imported slaves, and the native peoples. The postconquest population may have stood at six to seven million before the plagues (Harvey), with over one million Muslims, perhaps 300,000 Jews, and perhaps 300,000 Muslims and *mozárabes* in Granada.[65]

The two centuries of conquest were characterized by both atrocious warfare and tolerant coexistence. Toledo fell as early as 1085 (478); Córdoba and Seville as late as 1236 (633) and 1248 (646). Christian victory in the decisive battle of Tolosa in 1212 (609) brought an intensification of religious exclusiveness and a new dogmatism in the construction of the Other. Rather than being resettled or sold into slavery, a large number of Muslims were slaughtered on the insistence of churchmen. Islamic men from among the Berber peoples, called on to support Muslim rulers, fought Jews and Christians and, in a new spirit of intolerance, also their urbane Arab coreligionists.[66] Men of the Latin Church forced conversion and slavery on Muslims and broke agreements in the name of their faith, but, as yet, they had not achieved control. For example, Alfonso VI of Castile, *el rey de los dos cultos* (the king of the two faiths), granted liberty, the right to property, legal self-administration, protection from new taxation, and freedom of worship to Muslims, including Christian converts.[67]

At the court of Alfonso the Wise in twelfth-century Toledo, translations from Arabic and Greek into Hebrew and Latin were undertaken. This cultural mediation, the "Renaissance of the twelfth century," is exemplified by the career of the leading Muslim scholar, ibn Rushd (c.1126–98), often known by his Westernized name Averroës, who became master of the Christian scholars. The cooperation was continued as Latin-language Christian/Arabic/Jewish–inspired scholarship in the realm of the Plantagenet kings of England from the mid-twelfth to the thirteenth century. Adelard of Bath had lived in Toledo and had translated Al-Khwarizmi's astronomical and trigonometric tables into Latin, a work continued in England by Robert of Chester with a translation of his algebra.[68]

In Granada, which remained an independent Islamic state from 1238 until 1492 (636 to 897), many of the remaining Christians sought refuge in the mountains, fled to the north, or—viewed as potential supporters of Christian invaders—were transported to North Africa. In reverse direction, Muslims filtered southward from Christian societies to practice their religion without restraints, and Granada flourished under this influx of competent agricultural and craft families. The resulting gradual Arabicization of the intercultural society involved abandoning the local Romance language and a "positive affirmation of identity: to dress, eat, sleep, wash, speak, sing, pray, and be, in quite distinctive ways."[69]

The Christian armies were as multiethnic as the Muslim ones, consisting of Castilians, Aragonese, Leonese, Galicians, Asturians, Navarrese, and Basques, as well as of Franks, Germans, and Italians. Some came as mercenaries, others from conviction—but all in search of plunder. As in all Mediterranean "crusading," they invaded societies rich both in agricultural and urban craftsmanship and introduced militarization as well as the vagabondage and mendicancy of soldiers without employment.[70] Immediately after conquest, Muslim populations were expelled or sold into slavery if they had resisted. Others left for North Africa. The "immense" transfers of population from conquered cities, like Jaén, Córdoba, and Seville, depleted urban crafts and unskilled labor. While many North African Muslim rulers did not welcome these refugees, who were different in culture and custom, Moroccan and Tunisian towns saw great economic benefits from the influx of artisans. In some towns, the refugees' descendants continued their special industries in the twentieth century.

Muslims who surrendered to Christian armies could pursue their callings and pay taxes as subjects. Following Muslim examples, the *leyes de moros* offered protection as long as religion was not practiced in public. Even under duress, some stayed and lived unobtrusive lives because their skills were in demand. Treatment varied by social and political status. Muslim dignitaries and learned men might receive permission to stay and move freely. When Valencia was taken in 1238, the Muslim ruler and nobility received safe conduct. Most of the free Muslim population and their slaves decided to remain and became the only Islamic group in Christian Spain to continue the use of Arabic. Contravening Church policies, some Christian nobles encouraged Muslim immigration and the creation of new settlements to overcome shortages of rural labor and to tap the skills of Muslim craftsmen.[71] Though revolts against the new rulers occurred, most Muslims (*mudéjars*) remaining elsewhere adapted language, customs, and religious practices to a "new Islam" in which the Koran was translated into the vernacular. "Islamic Spain in the mid-thirteenth century . . . emerges as . . . a number of strongly differentiated groups, each with a distinct past and without institutions, even religious ones, which would have enabled them to envisage united action." For them, "survival was no mean achievement."[72]

To settle the frontier, vacated or not, Christians moved southward and mingled with the remaining Muslims, Mozarabs, and Jews in "kaleidoscopic variations at different times and in different areas." Christian society became as differentiated as Muslim society had been. To repopulate their territories rulers granted favors to settlers, a "whirlwind of liberties,"[73] as MacKay called it: tax exemption; exemption from levies and special dues; marriage-like cohabitation without the blessings of the Church—provided the woman had not been captured by force. Consequently, feudal bondage, typical of northwestern Europe, did not emerge at this time. French and Flemish settlers arrived, as did the Hospitallers' Order after it had been chased out of Palestine. By the fourteenth century all had become one population. In Portugal, Christian settlement reached the Tagus (Tejo) River in the second half of the twelfth century and the Algarve in the thirteenth. At first, this migration relieved population pressures in the north, but later the frontier opportunities came to be seen by administrators as an unwelcome population drain. Immigrants also filled towns. About 24,000 men, women, and children moved to Seville after the flight of its previous inhabitants, which included the loss of about 16,000 highly skilled handloom weavers who had produced brocades, muslins, and velvets. Merchants, especially Italian ones, were settled in privileged positions as *francos* in suburbs (see chap. 5.3). Others, the Genoese in particular, invested in land.[74]

Intra-Christian cultural exchange increased when Santiago de Compostela became one of the three main pilgrim destinations (chap. 3.4), but interfaith hostility resulted in the expulsion of the Jews in 1492 (chap. 4.2) and of the Moriscos in 1609–14 (chap. 4.1). New population change was brought about by slave imports from sub-Saharan Africa and by sizable emigrations to the Americas (chap. 5.3).

Settlement in the "Wendish" Slavic Territories

Another agrarian frontier emerged in the northeast of Europe from the ninth to thirteenth century and, according to a nineteenth-century interpretation, attracted "Germans" into thinly settled Slavic lands. Migrations were more complex, however, as was the ethnic composition of the migrants. On the level of power, the interests of the Latin Church and the so-called Holy Roman Empire combined to send missionaries and military commanders eastward. Large-scale revolts of Slavic peoples of the region in 983 and 1066 prevented a consolidation of rule. On the level of migrants and their culture, the east-west moves included many ethnicities and the Flemish from the North Sea coast in particular. At first, Flemish settlers were recruited to drain bogs in much of the northern German lands. In a second phase, German and Flemish settlers moved further east into areas between the Elbe and Oder Rivers in the ninth century. The migrants came to be summarily called "Germans" and the many resident Slavic groups "Wends." Contemporaries, aware of cultural borderlands and interaction in the region, named the northeastern, immigrant-founded German-language towns of the Hanseatic League the "Wendish quarter."[75]

The growing agrarian population of the many Germanic ethnic groups could find subsistence by internal colonization or migration into towns until the early twelfth century. From mid-twelfth to the early fourteenth century, several factors attracted men and women of many strata into East Central Europe. Slavic rulers struggling with neighboring ones appealed for military help to German lords. Colonizing activities of the Cistercians reached these territories. Apart from the early phases, the emperors of the Central European "Holy Roman Empire" were involved only marginally—they were busy in the Italian peninsula and Sicily, then lost power in the latter thirteenth century. The main actors were the military men expelled from the Holy Land. The Teutonic Knights, a German-language order only after 1198, relocated first to Venice and then to Transylvania. "Teutonic" in name and membership, the Order was trans-European in practice with regulations drafted according to Sicilian models under the influence of Emperor Frederick II of 1226. The Polish duke Conrad of Masovia invited them to fight against the "Saracens of the North," the Baltic peoples. Armed with a papal decree in addition to swords, it subdued the Baltic Prussians (1231–88) and established an expansionist (immigrant) military regime. In another twist of the construction of ethnicities, territories, and states, the later state of Prussia and the label "Prussians" for Germans thus derive from a people of Baltic ethnicity. The Knights ruled for a century until defeated at the battle of Tannenberg in 1410. Later, unpaid mercenaries sold the Order's remaining possessions to the Polish king.[76]

From the 1150s to the 1340s, settlers in the northeastern territories came from areas of origin that stretched from Brittany to the lands along the Elbe River; among them were "Gallici" and Flemish, Saxons and other Germanic ethnicities. In the northeast they moved into bogs and other lands difficult to cultivate or into lands settled by Baltic and Slavic agriculturalists under the rule of the Order. At first, migrants came from densely populated Rhenish and Flemish areas. The latter, experts in draining lowlands, were usually settled under their own *ius flandricum* and were joined by Hollanders and Zeelanders. Danes migrated under the political alliance between rulers of Mecklenburg and the Nordic states.[77]

In the northeast, immigrant families—often with many children whose labor was needed for clearance, drainage, and other work—settled the Wendish areas, which much later became part of eastern Germany, and then moved into Polish and, finally, Lithuanian territories. In the center, newcomers moved into western parts of Hungary; in the south, Austrian territories were settled. Further southeast, Transylvania was colonized by men and women from the Moselle area, from Luxembourg, Flanders, and Lower Saxony. Their statute of 1224 privileged them as the "Saxon Nation of Hungary." Along the Danube, the designations "Saxon" or "Swabian" (rather than "German") became the generic names for immigrants from the west. Except for deaths incurred during warfare, local populations remained intact, and over time newcomers and resident inhabitants mixed. Some migrant groups established closed colonies, like those in Transylvania, where each ethnic group restricted itself to endogamous marriage. To the present day, the Slavic Sorbs of Lusatia (the Lausitz) remain as a separate ethnic group among German or Germanized peoples.[78]

Under commissions from local or conquering rulers, locators recruited, guided, and settled migrants in return for territories or rights over the peasants. Thousands of villages and hundreds of towns were founded. Attractive positions secured by contract induced landless sons of peasants with their wives and children to come and servile families to flee their lords. The privileged position is comparable to settlement processes on the Iberian frontier. Over time, new and old settlers became indistinguishable. Meanwhile, artisans and traders, merchants, and patricians moved into existing towns or founded new ones, like Riga in 1201. They introduced variants of Germanic urban law, often falsely labeled generically as *ius teutonicum*. Rather than of imperial significance or German character, it was territorial law tailored to mercantile and patrician needs, most commonly following that of the city of Magdeburg. This migration was supported by the Wendish cities of the Hanseatic League, in particular the young town of Lübeck, itself founded only in 1158 by Rhenish and Westphalian migrants. The urban migrants were granted the status of free persons by local rulers who needed nonservile, revenue-producing citizens because serfs produced only for their lords. Urban political structures, long-distance trade, and artisanal production followed customs of German towns and German became the urban and commercial lingua franca. This process separated the inserted urban populations from both local peasants and long-settled nobles.[79]

The Polish, Bohemian, and Hungarian territorial states remained separate political entities; only Hungary temporarily belonged to the "Holy Roman Empire." After the migrations, predominantly German-settled areas reached beyond the Oder River to Riga in the northeast. Bohemia and Moravia remained Czech, and Lower Austria became a German ethnic territory. But most areas, including those west of the Oder, had mixed populations. In both Poland-Lithuania and Russia, town populations were "islands" of German-speaking burghers of West and West Central European background. Thus, in most of East Central Europe, rural and urban populations, as well as lords and peasants, were ethnically different. The migrations had reflected population growth. The poor harvests of the early fourteenth century and the mid-century plagues depleted the reservoir of migrants, and the movement came to a sudden stop when the European population collapsed and large colonized areas reverted to wasteland.

2.4 Population Growth and Decline

Agricultural expansion and population increase occurred in parallel. Rapid population growth, which began in tenth-century northern Italy and shortly after in central, western, and northern Europe, peaked in the "long" century from 1150/1200 to 1300. While population tripled in these regions, it grew more slowly in eastern Europe. Family-reconstitution approaches show migration, at least over short distances, to be ubiquitous.[80] Europe's population accounted for about one-seventh of the world total and engaged in the large outward-bound migrations of crusaders and of settlers to Iberian, southern French, and eastern territories.[81] Among nonmigrating populations, increasing density augmented endemic strife between peasants and nobles. The latter opposed clearances in order to preserve their hunting privileges; peasants in need of arable land gradually pushed the forests back.

The thirteenth-century expansion of commerce resulted in urban growth. On average, 7–8 percent of the European population lived in cities, a much higher share of which were in Urban Europe—Northern Italy, the Netherlands, and Muslim al-Andalus—with lower rates in northern and eastern Europe. By 1300 twenty-two Italian communities counted more than 20,000 inhabitants, while in transalpine Europe only Paris, London, Cologne, and Prague did so. By 1600 the two Mediterranean peninsulas—the Italian and the Iberian—"supported over 17 percent of their total population in cities of at least 5,000 inhabitants." Because of disease and unsanitary living conditions, cities could not reproduce their own populations, creating an "urban graveyard effect," and thus were dependent on constant in-migration. The growth of cities meant the growth of migration.[82]

Young women moving to service positions accounted for a large percentage of this rural-to-urban migration, which often was circular because many returned to the countryside to marry and rear children (see chap. 3.3). Recent research indicates that couples exerted some control, either legitimate or illegitimate, over their reproductive capacity. Across different cultures, for example, breast-feeding played an important role in spacing births and assuring survival of infants.[83] In general, patterns of family formation, rather than mortality crises, were the centerpiece of demographic developments. Between leaving the family of birth and forming a family for procreation, a stage of mobility placed adolescents and young adults in other families in service or training positions. Consequently, the age of marriage increased.

One can discern four different patterns of family formation and thus four patterns of demand for land and jobs by the next generation. The first two can be found in eastern Europe (roughly in the area of Orthodox Christianity) and northwestern Europe: late marriages (the average age for women being between twenty-three and twenty-seven years, and higher for men), widespread celibacy, and dependent, single, live-in work by young adults. In northwestern Europe, marriages were contracted only after subsistence was assured, whether with a dowry or with inherited land. This model of nuclear families was supplemented by a third pattern, a southern one, of stem families in which one son married, becoming the head of a more extended household (southern France, southern Germany, and the *zadruga* in Croatia). A fourth pattern of nuclear families with early marriage predominated in southern Spain and southern Italy. Reduction of the number of children seems to have followed real-wage indices with a delay of one generation. Gendered patterns of migration emerged from higher death rates of women in the age group between twenty and forty because of childbirth and hard work. Their low position improved in the thirteenth century, and they increasingly participated in pilgrimages when adoration of the Virgin Mary began. Women's position and their ability to migrate deteriorated as a result of the "growing patrilinearity of inheritance practices in Italy and France" and the slow ousting of women from artisanal trades.[84]

After three centuries of population growth and consequent mobility, the climate deteriorated during the so-called Little Ice Age, approximately from 1300 to 1500. In the winters of 1303 and 1306–7 the Baltic Sea froze over, and populations that had expanded into hilly and mountainous areas suffered from the cold. The wet years of 1315–16 and after brought on famine and dysentery. The seed-yield ratio for major food crops declined by more than 50 percent. Hunger induced large cityward migrations in search of stored grain or other foods, but concentrations of people increased the spread of contagious diseases. In Bruges during a few months in 1316, 3,000 men, women, and children died. Mortality rates were lower where distribution networks for agrarian produce were better.[85]

Famine in a one year often brought food shortages in following years, whether

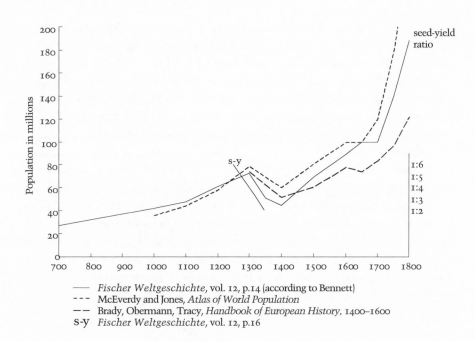

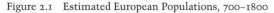

——— Fischer Weltgeschichte, vol. 12, p.14 (according to Bennett)
- - - McEverdy and Jones, *Atlas of World Population*
— — Brady, Obermann, Tracy, *Handbook of European History, 1400–1600*
s-y *Fischer Weltgeschichte*, vol. 12, p.16

Figure 2.1   Estimated European Populations, 700–1800

due to the consumption of seed grain or to a weakening that reduced the capability
for field labor. Severe undernourishment or inadequate diets cause lack of motivation and general passivity—the "laziness" that lords ascribed to their peasantry. Any
famine or its threat sent people to regions better off or presumed to be so. Hunger hit
all family members, and thus all had to move. Permanent malnutrition, on the other
hand, reduced the ability to decide to move and to act on such decisions.[86]

In this unstable situation, the plagues hit. Carried by rats and fleas, the epidemic
arrived from Asia in Crimea and the Levant in 1346 and 1347, or, according to other
interpretations, it was endemic in local rodent populations and erupted when famine had weakened immune systems. It carried away on average about one-third of the
western European population in 1348–49—in dry regions fewer, in some as much as
50 percent. Further epidemics caused the loss of another 20 percent by 1385, and a few
more percent in the next decades (measured by death rates not adjusted for births).
In much of Europe, hilly and other marginal regions, as well as entire villages, were
deserted for a century or longer. Survivors migrated to re-form population clusters
and viable economic units. Lords tried to relocate their subjects or to attract replace-
ments so as to secure income at least from part of their holdings. Between 1400 and
1460 the population remained stable. The dryer areas, Spain and Asia Minor in particular, were less affected, which laid the population basis for the expansion of future
Habsburg Spain and the Ottoman Empire (fig. 2.1).[87]

Several major changes caused a restructuring of power relationships, patterns of migration, and economic interaction. The impact of the plagues was felt in the whole

of Eurasia. It disrupted Chinese society and economy in 1325, then again in 1345. When the Mongol Empire collapsed and the tolerant Mongol rulers and their dependant peoples departed from China, some Eastern Christians left with them. Others blended into Chinese society. After 1368 the new Ming dynasty further reduced foreign contacts. At the same time, trade routes were disrupted by the nomadic invasions of Mongols from Asia into Europe under Timur the Lame (1336–1405) and of Berber peoples into Arab coastal regions. The Byzantine civilization, weakened by the Venetian attack of 1204, faced the emerging Turko-Muslim Ottoman Empire. Throughout the period, European populations were, or had to be mobile for many reasons (chap. 3). The increasingly doctrinaire Latin Church forced non-Christians as well as dissenting Christians to flee (chap. 4). The emergence of the Ottoman Empire in the southeast and the Atlantic forays of the Portuguese and of Habsburg Spain in the southwest brought about new forms of migration (chap. 5). Common people had to react to the economic, political, and religio-ideological developments in shaping their lives. Those who wanted to move could face encouragement from above or had to overcome restrictions placed on them by the powerful.

3

Continuities: Mobility and Migration from the Eleventh to the Sixteenth Century

The medieval and early modern periods, once said to be characterized by peasants bound to the soil, were in fact times of high mobility. In a transcendental sense and as a topos of medieval literature and thought, men and women were on a road through life: "*Viator* is man on his way. The word implies direction, dedication, movement, and disregard of frontiers."[1] Elites moved across the continent; administrators traveled from estate to estate; and mercenaries from many ethnic backgrounds left destruction in their paths. Merchants traded across Europe and between civilizations. The colonization of land necessitated migrations of rural families; the populating of towns required migrations of unmarried rural women and men. Specific obligations and customs determined both the type of mobility and the selection of those who could be mobile. Pilgrims left for a few weeks; merchants often moved for years at a time; noble families permanently removed younger children into distant religious or military service. Wherever demand occurred for *men*power only, men had to decide whether to migrate on their own and live celibate, or bring in wives and children, or mix with women of the local population. Each course influenced the gendered division of reproductive work that might be shifted to lower-class servants or subjected colonial populations. Children born after migration, whether of immigrant or local women, wives or concubines, became part of the local populations.[2]

In Western Christendom traveling was considered worldly suffering and the upkeep of roads and bridges became a religious duty. Monasteries assumed responsibility for stretches of roads, the Church might "pay" laborers merely by remittance of penance for sins allegedly committed. Municipalities engaged in difficult construction projects brought in experts from abroad. A French cleric, for example, supervised the building of London Bridge around 1200. Court officials intending to travel ordered roads to be improved, and the Church, intending to mobilize pilgrims, had roads, signposts, and networks of hostels built.

The frequency with which travelers appear in the literature and the arts of medieval times suggests that they held a central place in society or at least in people's minds. Lodging places served as information exchanges at a time when news traveled, at least among common people, only by word of mouth. Accounts of extraordinary

events spread exceedingly fast. In an inn a trader from Flanders might talk with peasants from the village, pilgrims might relate—and inflate—their experiences, small
traders praised the goods they carried, sometimes spices, raisins, and wines from far
away, destined for a nearby manor.[3]

Communication across language barriers, necessary even to buy one's daily food,
was eased by "self-service" from street vendors of both sexes who spread their wares
in public spaces, visible for pick-and-pay with no spoken words needed. Curiosity,
rather than hostility, determined attitudes toward Others.

3.1   Itinerancy at the Top of Dynastic Society

European nobilities from different cultural backgrounds intermingled freely through
marriage and long-distance geographical mobility. Men in religious hierarchies were
recruited from many ethnicities. Status rather than ethnicity defined a person. Since
administrative institutions did not extend over a realm, itinerant officials collected
taxes or held court. Warfare necessitated concentrations of armed men and auxiliaries.

Cosmopolitan Nobles and Their Households

Nobles moved across space to conduct political negotiations, to wage war, to arrange
marriages, or simply to gain subsistence. No local agrarian economy could feed a
whole court over a long time. During their two hundred years of rule (1056–1254) over
the Central European and Italian ("Holy Roman") Empire, the Welf and Hohenstaufen
families intermarried with some fourteen dynasties ranging from England in the
west, to Aragon and Castile in the southwest, Byzantium in the southeast, and Kiev
in the east. Since marriages implied rule over family-held territories, women represented dynastic interests and were political actors. Where female lineage and inheritance had been institutionalized, noninheriting princes relocated to the possessions
of their brides. Weddings, tournaments, and other festivities brought visiting noble
families with attendants from abroad. In England, where early fourteenth-century
noble households contained between a few dozen and more than 200 servants, most
of the staff relocated with every change of residence. Such households became more
sedentary when administrators resided on their lord's estates and the new market
economy made possible provisioning by purchase.[4]

In many parts of Europe, the nobility was not of the same ethnic culture as the
middle classes (if extant) or peasant populations. Immigrant nobilities imposed themselves, as in the case of the German knights on Baltic peoples after 1200 or Austrian
nobles on the seventeenth-century Bohemian people. The nobility, cosmopolitan and
driven by a certain predatory bent, amassed lands by dispossessing others. Territorial units were family concerns, liable to corporate raiding, to use a late-twentieth-
century term.

The welding together of disparate territories into dynastic entities involved complex cultural mergers at all social levels. In the region that was to become modern France the Capetian house from 987 to 1328 ruled over regions as culturally diverse as Flanders in the north and Provence in the south. It intermarried with nobility from Kiev, Holland, Brabant, Castile, Aragon, Navarre, Merano, and sent sons or daughters to Flanders, Brabant, England, Antioch, and Sicily. The kings granted charters to colonizers (*hôtes*) to settle wastelands, and founded *villes neuves* in the north and *bastides* (fortified towns) in the south. Common people, in family groups or singly, moved into new settlements or expanding towns. Recruiters for the crusades toured the area intermittently and sent tens of thousands to Asia Minor. English Plantagenet rulers coveting continental lands came with alien troops from the British Isles, with rented Levantine warships, and with mercenaries from all over Europe. After these "English" were victorious, Parisian administrators accepted them as lords because rulers had more in common among themselves than with the people over whom they ruled. Cohabitation occurred without the loss of distinctiveness on either side. In the middle stratum of Capetian society, the Champagne fairs attracted merchants from the entire continent; scholars from many parts of Europe taught at the University of Paris; and monks from the Abbey of Cluny in Aquitaine migrated into northern France, Lorraine, and other parts of western Europe. Artists from Flanders settled in Paris and at the court of Burgundy and introduced new materials and decorative styles. Renaissance culture, carried by migrating artists and scholars, radiated outward from Paris.[5]

On the Italian peninsula, to cite a second example, cultural influences and migrations encompassed an even broader spectrum. In the south, Muslim rulers and agriculturalists arrived from North Africa merged with immigrant Scandinavian nobles and negotiated with the Byzantine administrators of Apulia and Calabria. In the center, German and French popes and their advisers inserted themselves as heads of the Latin Church and consorted with immigrant courtesans. In the north, the German-Sicilian Hohenstaufen dynasty held sway. Rule within any of the Mediterranean civilizations implied temporary moves or permanent migrations, and the resultant intermingling could be cooperative and creative or conflict-ridden and destructive.

Itinerant Administrators

In urban Europe administrations were already centrally located. But in agrarian Europe, often of low population density, rulers and administrators moved through the country, partly because of inadequate trade and transport networks to provision them, partly to ensure administrative and judicial control over their subjects. With their large retinues, they traveled over considerable distances and came in touch with many cultures. Maximilian I of Habsburg (1459–1519) spoke German as a child, was educated in Latin, and spoke French with his wife; he addressed his subjects in Wendish and Bohemian and conducted diplomatic and military affairs in Flemish, Spanish, Italian, and English. In a single year (1299–1300) Edward I of England changed residence seventy-five times or every five days on average. (When the allegedly shiftless underclasses engaged in such itinerancy, it was called "vagrancy.") With the king moved half a dozen or more high officials and a multitude of archers, servants, valets, and grooms. To reduce the retinue—as modern readers aware of gender roles might guess—their wives were ordered to stay at home. At each stop the train was met by all those who were locally involved in administrative and legal proceedings. Thieves and harlots joined in. Edward III (r. 1327–77), with a retinue of a thousand people, spent two years in the Low Countries and on the Rhine. Middle-level officials, royal judges and sheriffs, as well as rent collectors traveled semiannually or quarterly to assess duties or hold court (hence the modern term "circuit judge").[6]

Traveling men of the Church, notwithstanding papal interdictions, used these public appearances for ostentatious displays of wealth. The bishop of Hereford was accompanied by about forty armed squires, by *valleti*—clerks, carters, porters, falconers, grooms, messengers—by kitchen servants and a baker, and, lastly, by boys and pages. Men from the hierarchy made formal ecclesiastical visitations to religious houses in their jurisdiction. Exchanges of personnel between monasteries entailed voyages; friars and nuns of the mendicant orders worked and begged as they went on their way. Gender became an issue when bishops commanded nuns, who cared for the sick and poor, to observe strict enclosure.[7]

Itinerant administrators caused apprehension among local people, who had to provide accommodation and food. The official purveyors of the English king had the right to requisition food from a distance of ten leagues (about 30 miles or 50 kilometers) in circumference around the travel route. Often they did not pay for what they took, and imposters never did. Carts and horses were appropriated by the intruders, and at harvest time, in particular, this could have a lasting impact on the amount of grain a peasant family could store for its own consumption. Monasteries provided nightly shelter for free to traveling nobles and clerics, to wealthy benefactors and poor people. People in the money economy—whether they were merchants, small landowners, or lowly carters—used inns and paid for food and lodging.

In the sedentary administrations of Urban Italy permanent migration replenished officialdom. Between 1343 and 1382, 65 percent of all public notaries in Genoa came from families that had recently migrated to the city. Of the 171 notaries active in 1382, at least eleven had practiced their profession overseas, while another eleven had been abroad in other capacities. Surnames like "de . . ." and "Oltremarini" indicate migration; "Negri" and "Moro" signal influence from Muslim Africa. The upper and middle strata of European society were highly mobile.[8]

Warfaring Mercenaries

Men in military service added a further element to medieval mobility and came into contact with alien ways of life. In war they dislocated civilians. Back at their hearths, they could provide information about different worlds or, to phrase it more cautiously, tell stories. The city-states of Urban Italy could not draw on local populations to draft men; nor did their mercantile ethos accept the idleness and costs of unproductive military establishments. They hired mercenaries from elsewhere. Enterprising leaders and groups of men offered themselves on contract (Italian: *condotta*), as *condottieri*. Throughout Europe footmen replaced knights, that is, cavalry. They used new weapons and came with regionally varying skills: English archers and crossbowmen, Swiss pikemen, Flemish burgher forces, and, later, Italian gunfighters or exiled Albanian and Greek *stradioti* on light horse (from Italian, *strada:* street). Mercenaries hired on for pay under "military enterprisers" received wages only as long as work was available. By 1300 rulers of territorial states began to raise armies from all subjects fit to bear arms, mobilizing men and camp-following women regardless of social rank. This democratization of warfare implied increasing geographic mobility, which was frequently involuntary and without self-determined destinations. Soldiers often settled wherever they were disabled or discharged and became part of the respective local population.[9]

Since specialists needed training and since long-term drafting of peasants damaged the food supply of a state, professional mercenary armies and seaborne privateers organized themselves into companies of 100 to 250 fighters known as *routiers* or *Haufen*. The leaders, frequently from the lower nobility, often had been dislocated by economic necessity, resulting from their position in the sibling sequence, or by political conditions. Their low-ranking followers were indebted peasants, marginalized rurals, sentenced criminals pardoned for military service, relapsed religious men, and petty thieves driven by need—thus the French saying that a mercenary is a man "qui doit mourir pour avoir de vivre" ("who has to die in order to have something to live on"). Peasants enlisted as mercenaries in the wake of others who had destroyed their homes.

Among this *men*power were women of standing, allowed by regional feudal customs the right to succession, who took the role of armed ladies or commanded *condottieri* companies. A few became heroines and symbols like Jeanne d'Arc. Some wives accompanied their soldier-husbands, and large numbers of unmarried women from the lower strata moved with the troops as cooks, servants, provisioners, and prostitutes. In 1646 a Bavarian corps of 480 footmen was followed by seventy-four servants, three sutlers, 314 women and children, and 160 horses. The accompanying cavalry corps of 481 combatants, was followed by 236 servants, nine sutlers, 102 women and children, and 912 horses. All had to be housed and fed wherever they passed.[10]

The itinerant military professionals came from regions of population surplus. The mountainous cantons of central Switzerland were a reservoir of pikemen. In the fifteenth century, 50,000 adolescents and young men left the valleys, and from the sixteenth to the eighteenth century the centennial average climbed to 250,000 (map 3.1). In France, three peripheral upland or poor-soil regions furnished the mass of men: Provence, the Pyrenean valleys, and the densely populated provinces of Brabant, Flanders, and Hainaut. Scotland and the Germanies furnished *Landsknechte*, and aristocratic Italian families nurtured *condottieri* leaders, a largely trans-European "class of contractors on a purely commercial basis." Mercenaries sold their services across religions and civilizations. Russians fought in Byzantine armies, Christians

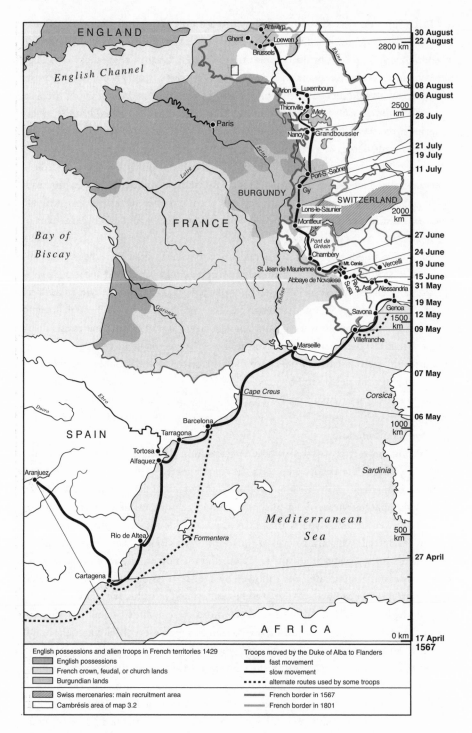

ENGLAND

English Channel

Antwerp
Ghent   Loewen
Brussels

Rhine

30 August
22 August
2800 km

Paris

Arlon   Luxembourg
Thionville
Metz
Nancy   Grandboussier

Seine

08 August
06 August
2500 km
28 July

BURGUNDY

Loire

Port-S.-Saône
Gy

SWITZERLAND

Lons-le-Saunier
Montfleur

21 July
19 July
11 July
2000 km

FRANCE

Bay of
Biscay

Pont de
Grésin
Chambéry

Mt. Cenis   Vercelli

St. Jean de Maurienne
Abbaye de Novalese

Dora
Susa

Asti   Alessandria

27 June
24 June
19 June
15 June
31 May

Rhône

Genoa

Savona
1500 km

19 May
12 May
09 May

Garonne

Marseille

Villefranche

07 May

Cape Creus

Corsica

06 May
1000 km

Duero

Ebro

SPAIN

Barcelona
Tarragona
Tortosa
Alfaquez

Sardinia

Aranjuez

Rio de Altea   Formentera

Mediterranean
Sea

500 km

27 April

Cartagena

AFRICA

0 km

17 April
1567

English possessions and alien troops in French territories 1429
  English possessions
  French crown, feudal, or church lands
  Burgundian lands

  Swiss mercenaries: main recruitment area
  Cambrésis area of map 3.2

Troops moved by the Duke of Alba to Flanders
  fast movement
  slow movement
  alternate routes used by some troops

  French border in 1567
  French border in 1801

3.1   Warfaring Mercenaries and Armies

in Moroccan service, Saracen archers in southern Italian forces, and English ones in Persian armies. When out of employment, these multiethnic groups or monoethnic "nations" of ruffians pillaged among the indigenous population wherever they happened to find themselves. Local people came to associate brutal conduct with a particular ethnic origin. An Englishman, according to an Italian saying, is the devil in person; *Landsknechte* of diverse German dialects were held in disrepute in most of Central Europe. Did this type of intermittent hostile interaction lead to permanent ethnicization of negative experiences?[11]

In the fifteenth century, mercenary bands were replaced by standing armies and military lifestyles became more sedentary. Rulers encouraged immigration of alien military artisans. In London, German armorers, Milanese founders, French masters, and a Moravian specialist settled near the armories. In Sweden, a French entrepreneur produced arms with an immigrant labor force. Wherever troops were to be ferried across the sea—whether it was the Channel, the Baltic, or the Mediterranean—large numbers of artisans from many origins were needed to build the hulks. Armies still consisted of culturally mixed components. During early sixteenth-century English rulers' campaigns in France, combatants of Welsh, English, Cornish, Irish, Manx, and Scotch extraction fought together, and up to one-third of the men were "Spaniards, Gascons, Portingals, Italians, Arbannoises, Greeks, Turks, Tartars, Almains, Germans, Burgundians, [and] Flemings." During the wars of the first half of the seventeenth century, Sweden, which had retained the *levée en masse*, integrated Irishmen and Scots into the units and reinforced its army by levies on allies and occupied territories. Temporarily, less than one-tenth of Gustavus's 140,000 men were Swedes. The Spanish army of Flanders in the century after 1567 consisted of six different ethnicities, the Spanish soldiers themselves usually coming from garrisons in Italy.[12]

To summarize, in the sphere of empowered classes, of midlevel administrators, or mercenaries, we observe a world in motion. Diverse ethnicities intermarried, fought, ruled over, or plundered culturally alien populations. Large-scale war could induce high levels of rural mortality and resettlement. At the end of the Hundred Years' War in the 1450s, major parts of France had to be resettled; after the Thirty Years' War in 1648, about one-third of the population in war-torn Central Europe was dead. Repopulation involved large migrations.

3.2 Migrations of Rural People and Servants

Depending on the region, between 65 and 95 percent of the European population were agriculturalists; the rate fell to 55 percent only in a few exceptionally urbanized areas. Serfdom reigned in most of the English, French, and German territories until, by the thirteenth and fourteenth centuries, services were commuted into cash payments and, finally, emancipation was achieved. From the early sixteenth century on, territorial lords, further to the east, succeeded in reimposing conditions of serf-

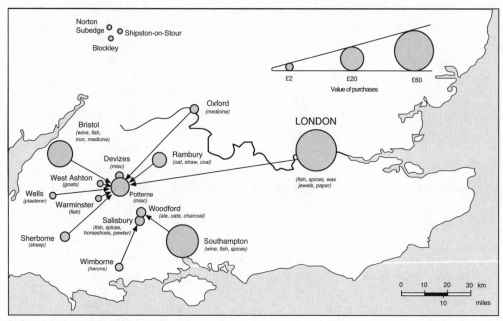

Purchases (valued) by the Bishop of Salisbury, 1406 - 07

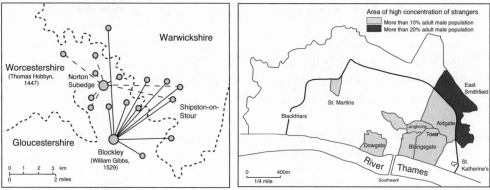

Peasant Debts, 15th and 16th Centuries

The Distribution of London's Foreign Population in 1550

3.2   Peasant Mobility and Market Connections

dom.[13] Common people—whether they were peasant families, rural laborers, small-town servants, or wayfarers at the very bottom of society—gained an inkling of worlds other than their own through tales told by pilgrims or spice-carrying pedlars and by watching passing travelers from among the high and mighty (map 3.2).

The image of a sedentary Europe has its roots in the top-down political history of territorial nobles and their serfs. Economic, demographic, or life-cycle approaches provide more analytical insights. Lords temporal or spiritual competed for revenues from freehold peasants, serfs, or the numerous grades in between. The "labor supply had often to be reapportioned between old and new cultivated land," between more and less powerful lords. Each peasant family with more than two surviving chil-

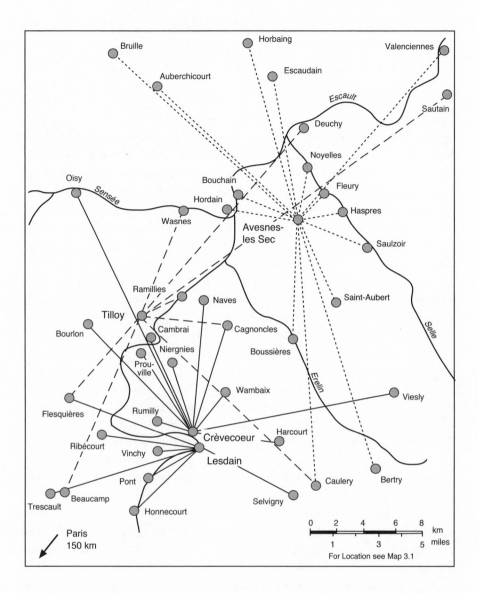

dren needed additional land for the next generation. Young rural families sought land to become independent of parental constraints. In regions devastated by wars, new people and population growth were needed before the 1340s necessitated cultivation of additional land. After the mid-fourteenth-century demographic crisis, formerly cultivated marginal upland areas reverted to animal husbandry; the importance of regional fairs increased over the large trans-European ones; and local fairs redistributed the produce of pastoral regions toward the grain-growing lowlands. Over the next two centuries, regional moves by middlemen intensified again and reachieved long-distance dimensions. In the interstices of agriculture and commerce, of transhumance and trade, merchants and drivers annually moved up to 60,000 head of cattle from Scotland to England in the sixteenth century and much larger numbers from Denmark and East Central Europe toward Hamburg and the Dutch cities (see chap. 12.2).[14]

Migration and Relocation in Agriculture

A peasant with his family was valuable property. Churches and knights competed for their labor and had to acquire from princes with surplus populations the *licentia populandi* for their estates. To attract immigrants, the legal status of peasants was codified and extended to their descendants. Both serfs and free men came. Some were accorded heritable tenures under rent arrangements; others took on leases for only a few years. From about 1050 onward, organized settlement began in northern France, Flanders, and the Low Countries. From there, enterprising peasants moved to marshes in Lower Saxony, Saxony, and northern Wendish areas. In 1112 the Cistercian Order made colonization its mission, and a mere forty years later some 330 cloisters extended from the hills of Wales and the English moors via French nobles' lands to the Hohenstaufens' Slavic territories. This success induced secular lords to reduce forest lands in favor of settlements. In the Black Forest and Alpine regions, more land at higher elevations far from towns or markets was cultivated. Local or regional markets that developed in conjunction with the towns permitted crop sales and thus cash yields.

While short- or medium-distance settlement moves remained the rule, by the twelfth century the need for colonists extended over large distances. In the French lands immigrant *hospes* brought in new peasant households; to populate Normandy, settlers were recruited from as far away as Scandinavia. In the East Mark and along the Danube, Slavic inhabitants from Alpine valleys and free settlers from southern German territories came; later, Flemish or other locators divided lands, recruited settlers, and often installed themselves as village leaders (*Schultheißen*). In the Spanish March, locals and people from neighboring territories settled. The Hungarian king invited German and Flemish families into Transylvania. And in Palestine, conquered territories were filled with long-distance migrants. All intermingled in marriage and adapted themselves to the indigenous languages and customs.[15]

Because of the need to invest in labor to achieve good crops on a long-term basis, the more independent peasants played a particularly important role. Along the Rhine, the compelled obligations of both *corvée* and tithe were reduced, so that peasant families "would till the land more willingly." Arbitrariness, on the other hand, induced or forced many peasants to sell their ancestral holdings and to migrate to other lands (*"multos vendere patrimonium et ad peregrinas migrare terras compulit"*). Peasants constantly struggled for permission to clear forests or did so without asking, while lords clung to social ideology—that is, their claims to the rights of the hunt in large forests. Lords also feared that partially exhausted lands might not be properly cared for if villagers saw the prospect of moving to newly cleared soil.

The Cistercians' practice of colonization, the largest of all such contemporary undertakings, served as a model. They attracted families from among landless peasants and war-ravaged territories, subjects of arbitrary lords, and offspring of their own settlers elsewhere. Placed in a contractual relationship, immigrants received house and yard, a small plot of arable land, and a lease for land to be cleared. In return, they paid a fixed share of their annual harvests. Though bound to perform some duties for the monastery, settlers were independent villagers who did not have to provide regular labor on the manorial demesne, which was the larger economic unit. Larger planned villages (*bourgs*) with market rights were settled under similar contractual relations.

In France, Louis VI (r. 1108–37) imitated the Cistercian Order. The immigrant peasants of his *villes neuves* were free from imposts and military service, as were settlers under the Spanish *fueros* (governmental decrees) and *cartas de población* (charters to populate/to settle). Close to seigneurial estates, however, even if newly settled or recently resettled, servitude remained the rule or was reimposed. Peasant cottars, ranking between serfs and freeholders, settled marginal estate lands without secure tenure and provided the hired labor in peak seasons, as did the *conversi*, lay servants, and laborers of the Cistercians. The manifold differences in status provided options to move away or to negotiate better terms. In England, villeins owing services and payments to the manor lived in close proximity to free farmers settled on the land by lords after the devastations of the Norman invasions. "Individual peasants' enterprise" was common among Scandinavian immigrants and local men and women. Secular and spiritual lords became increasingly interested in cash yields and thus preferred more active peasants. Those who were unproductive were forced off the land.[16]

Peasant families who struggled for more land also struggled for less obligatory labor. Having to sacrifice cultivation of their own crops for those on manorial lands posed the issue squarely since the family's food supply was at stake. In the interests of both lords and peasants, more and more dues, whether in labor or in kind, were commuted into cash payments, sometimes known as quit-rents. Cash, which could be dispensed according to personal preference, increased available options. None of these developments occurred uniformly and at the same time throughout Europe, and the same lord might employ different types of labor depending on the local traditions, supply of peasant populations, and interests. Lifetime service was gradually replaced by leases for a fixed number of years. These leases might mean improved conditions for the leaseholder upon renegotiation, but they might also lead to dispossession and forced mobility. Lords who turned to sheep- or cattle-raising in pursuit of higher profits ejected the tillers of the soil. By 1300 half of English peasant households depended on the seasonal wagework of out-migrating men. Figures for the French countryside were similar. In his *Utopia* (1516), Sir Thomas More described landlords as "greedy individuals" who chase off "men and women, husbands and wives, widows and orphans, mothers and tiny children, together with all their employees." These then became wayfaring families, persecuted by authorities for vagrancy.[17]

In northern Italy, rural households multiplied with population growth and landholdings became fragmented. In improvement and colonization projects woods and fens were reclaimed; canals, dikes, and irrigation works were built; and settlements appeared on the upper slopes of Alpine valleys ("highland emigration"). In the urban sphere, the size of towns increased phenomenally—some reached 100,000 by about 1300—because of their draw to rural in-migrants, whose *inurbamento* was by choice. Milan's two great canals were built between 1177 and 1229. Where rural depopulation endangered urban food supplies, restrictions were placed on out-migration, but on the whole, restraints were few, and agricultural workers from Liguria migrated to Corsica and as far as Palestine.[18]

In late medieval times, towns and cities in the east-central and eastern parts of Europe attracted rural immigrants to a degree that in emigrant villages the contraction of households became the pattern. In historic Hungary, from 1300 on, formerly enserfed peasants could move if they paid a lump sum (*terragium*) to their lord. If they were refused permission to leave, peasants had themselves abducted by the lord with whom they wanted to settle or were abducted by lords who needed their labor. This migration to more powerful lords or into market towns was undertaken to improve familial living conditions. Peasant brides could transport their dowry to the groom's holding free of duties. Widows who remarried, however, had to leave working-age sons with the original lord, and young boys could move with the mother but had to return as adults. Ruthless exploitation of peasant families by the nobility and extreme increases in taxation—up to 500 percent during the struggle of King Matthias Corvinus (r. 1458–90) against the Ottoman advance—led to flight as well as to revolt in 1514. The ruling elites suppressed the revolt and, in its aftermath, the freedom to move.

In all of Europe, as Dyer has observed for England, "serfs moved about a great deal, in contradiction of the supposed restrictions on the unfree." Lords "often sought to prevent migration and preserve the village, but sometimes removed the inhabitants from a decayed place." However, by their expansion of holdings or their neglect of soils, "but above all by their emigration and immigration," peasants "were often the decisive force behind the decline, continuation or desertion of a settlement." Both lords and peasants weighed the benefits of better soil, closer markets, and cheaper lands. Depending on power relationships, competition between upper-class families, and the supply of peasants and laborers, men and women in the medieval economy were not simply tied by custom and law. Rather, they evaluated options, weighed opportunity costs, negotiated socioeconomic improvements at home or through migrating, and otherwise made decisions.[19]

The calculation of economic interests to achieve an acceptable standard of living for a family, or to profit from cheap labor, resulted in a phase of intensive struggle between classes from the second half of the fourteenth to the first quarter of the sixteenth century. In peasant uprisings, the lowly tried to improve their position by active intervention, but the final outcome—which was dependent on many factors— usually was a reintroduction of higher rents, more service, and stricter regulation of servile status. In the east of Germany, and in the Baltic, Slavic, and Hungarian territories in particular, rigorous measures were taken by the nobility to prevent out-migration, retrieve escaped serfs from cities, and punish escapees harshly. By mid-sixteenth century the "second serfdom" was in place. It was to last until the 1850s when men and women again left—but this time to cross the Atlantic.[20]

Laborers and Servants

Landless rural men and women hired themselves out by the year to farmers or migrated to towns and cities, some temporarily, others permanently. The saying "*Stadt-luft macht frei*" (town air imparts liberty) referred to fugitive serfs who gained their freedom unless claimed within a year and a day by their lord.

In historic Hungary, migrants to Buda (the capital) and Pest (the bourgeois and lower-class town) came from the immediate rural neighborhood and from smaller towns within a distance of no more than two days of travel by foot (20–35 kilometers), as well as from southern trans-Danubia, a rural area with no cities. Peasant sons who wanted to learn a trade had to migrate to the cities, and obtaining their lord's permission to leave might require a pledge to return after apprenticeship. Just under half of the in-migrants originated in more distant parts of the country. Overall, 52 percent of the migrants in the case of Buda and 43 percent in the case of Pest came from towns and smaller market centers; the longer the distance traveled, the higher the ratio of men and women of urban origins. Given urban-rural ethnic differences, in-migration often changed the ethnic composition of towns. Thus Székesfehérvár, with a Walloon immigrant population in the thirteenth century, had a Magyar population by the fifteenth century. While immigrant men and women from the countryside found spouses among other local migrants, brides or grooms among the bourgeoisie often came from distant towns.[21]

All over Europe, the position of the rural and urban wage-earning populations changed dramatically after the mid-fourteenth-century population decline. The imbalance between supply and demand for laborers and servants led to intensive struggles with noble and bourgeois masters who harnessed the coercive power of the state in their interests. In England, for example, refusal of work, migration to areas with higher wages, and demands for wage increases became widespread. In June 1349, even before Parliament could meet after the first plague outbreak, a royal ordinance on which the Statute of Labourers of 1351 was to be based, attempted complete conscription of labor.

> Any man or woman, in our realm of England, of whatever condition, either free or servile, sound in body and under the age of sixty years, living not by merchandise nor practising a definite craft, nor having personally wherewith to live, nor possessing land which he would cultivate, nor being somebody else's servant, if he is requested to serve in a service congruent to his status, shall be bound to serve the one that shall thus request him.[22]

He/she was forbidden to leave the home district or to receive wages higher than pre-plague subsistence wages, notwithstanding a substantial rise in prices for daily necessities.

In the next half-century, the struggle between classes continued. The English House of Commons ascribed all calls for improvement to the "malice of servants" demanding "outrageous" or "excessive" wages. Laboring men and women demanded payment in cash rather than in kind, as well as day labor rather than the customary contracts for a full year, and they were ready to migrate. "As soon as their masters challenge them with bad service or offer to pay them for their service according to the form of the said statutes, they flee and run away suddenly out of their service and out of their own district, . . . [to] strange places unknown to their said masters."[23] Individually, landlords did hire laborers at higher wages to save their harvests; collectively, they sought to regain control by passing vagrancy laws. When perhaps 100,000 marched on London during the great peasant uprising of 1381, captured rebels testified to the role of wayfarers in spreading the news.

Since migration meant resistance, authorities attempted to immobilize laboring people. In 1387 a London ordinance prohibited the employment of apprentices unless they swore that they had been born free. By 1388 traveling men and women of lower status, including students on their way home, needed written permission to be in transit from a "good man" assigned to this duty in each district or borough.[24] Regulations restricting mobility were imposed across Europe. In Sweden and Norway, men and women without fixed abode, and later all poorer social elements, were required to accept any labor or service offered. The French *Grand Ordonnance* of 1352, like similar Italian laws, was intended to keep labor "in place" geographically, socially, and economically. The northern German urban *Knechteordnungen* were imposed in 1354; Tyrolean regulations of 1349 and 1352 required artisans, day laborers, and women and men in servile positions to work at pre-plague wage levels. While they were prohibited from leaving, laborers and craftsmen from elsewhere were invited to come, provided they would work for the wages offered. In the course of the century after the plague, authorities reimposed their control.[25]

Wayfaring Men and Women

In the view of their social superiors, men and women from the lower orders needed masters. While neither the destructiveness of warring nobles nor the dislocation caused by enclosure was discussed, "masterless" people were considered dangerous to the structure of society. The Franciscans' conceptual connection between poverty and saintliness came to be rejected: the poor were desanctified. In Tudor England, paternalistic social attitudes were replaced by a new commercialism; in Venice, regulations against beggars were tightened.[26] An English "Acte for the punishment of vacabondes" summarized the wide array of persons who were deemed suspect:

> all ydle persones goinge aboute in any contrey of the said Realme, using subtyll craftye and unlawfull games or playes, and some of them fayninge themselves to have knowledge in phisnomye, palmestrye, . . . and all fencers, bearwardens, comon players in interludes and minstrels not belonging to

any baron of this realme . . . all juglers, pedlars, tynkers, and petye chap-
men . . . and all scollers of the Universityes of Oxford or Cambridge yt goe
about begginge . . . and all shipmen pretendinge losses by sea.

The post-plague statutes and antimigration ordinances became the poor laws of 1495
to 1610 and in the nineteenth century were adapted to cover industrial workers.[27]

Vagrancy became a theme in contemporary literature. François Villon, banished
from Paris in 1463, composed his famous "vagrants' songs." Langland's *Piers Plow-
man* described the wayfaring of laborers, and Chaucer's *Canterbury Tales* that of pilgrims.

The drifting population included off-duty soldiers, often draftees who had been
forced to leave their calling, their families, and their regional home culture. In one
typical case in the Germanies, a woman deserted by her husband had made a single
move away from her hometown and worked as a nurse. Then she met a discharged
wayfaring *Landsknecht* who had lost his moorings. She followed him and repeatedly
found herself positions as a servant. But whenever she wanted to return to settled
life, her companion turned rough and "out of fear" she moved on with him—until
finally both were arrested. Impoverished casual laborers; men and women with marital problems or a history of sexual misconduct or abuse, or of violent behavior toward
others; women with children out of wedlock; sexually exploited female servants—all
left their hometowns or were forced to leave. Rebellious peasants, and many other
types of rebels, also left.[28]

In fourteenth-century Europe, poverty was structural rather than the result of
particular catastrophes, like famines, epidemics, or wars. Vagrancy "was the product
of profound social dislocations—a huge and growing poverty problem, disastrous economic and demographic shifts and massive migration."[29] Enclosure caused the dislocation of peasants; agrarian work became more casual; the aristocracy reduced its
number of servants; the apprenticeship system lost its encompassing grip; and irregular patterns of employment sent laborers onto the road. Recent research for the
period 1560 to 1640 indicates that 20 to 30 percent of the English population was impoverished, and the rate occasionally reached peaks of 50 percent. About half of the
vagrants were single males; somewhat above one-quarter were single females; and
couples, often with children, accounted for the rest. Most commonly, they had been
or were laborers, servants, or cloth-workers. Many moved in search of labor, but some
did so merely out of curiosity. Though these people changed where they were staying
almost daily, inns became in effect their permanent homes.[30]

For pedlars, tinkers, and similar traders, itinerancy was essential to their livelihood. While some carried imported goods, most sold products of their own crafts.
Hawking their goods, they moved over large distances, whereas others, such as fish-
mongers, traded regularly over shorter routes. Women too "hawked" their skills and
hired themselves out as wet nurses. Also on the road were the salesmen of health
or—as others would have it—death: tooth drawers, herbalists, and apothecaries, all
of whom were often said to be from foreign lands. Many were quacks, intent on gain,

but wise women or healing men practiced locally where their skills were known. All carried news, and apprehensive authorities again and again attempted to regulate routes and to confine wanderers to specific areas.[31]

While pedlars traveled with their wares, traders in entertainment—like minstrels, tumblers, jugglers, and singers—owned nothing but their skills and perhaps an instrument or a performing bear. Some came from distant lands, like the Italian juggler whose presence was recorded in fifteenth-century Nuremburg. Musicians, including troubadours who were in the upper echelons of itinerant entertainers, were invited to perform at weddings of a noble family's offspring or during tournaments. They fell into disgrace when their songs were deemed subversive, as happened to Welsh minstrels accused by the English of fomenting rebellion. Their satirical songs challenged proud nobles and pontificating churchmen.[32]

A wide variety of men and women were forced onto the roads even though they had not committed a shameful offense and lacked an itinerant trade. The numerous retainers and servants of the wealthy were often dismissed at the death of their patrons or masters. With no marketable skills, they quickly drifted into poverty and often became vagrants. Others took to the road because of unrest, or poverty, or desire to see new places, as did the students of Oxford and Cambridge. Debtors might don the pilgrims' cloak and prostitutes often came from far away and continued to travel far distances. Perambulating monks, in search of sustenance, were little different from petty rogues. The poor were often driven out of their niches and haunts (*"la chasse aux pauvres"*) and ordered to depart, only to wander to a different town to beg. Along with a few Gypsy men, women, and children, outlaws (portrayed in legend as residing in forests and giving to the poor) also are to be counted among the mobile population. Most vagrants wandered in the vicinity of their districts of origin, though some did reach the far corners of kingdoms. Unlike pilgrims, they did not move about to reach specific destinations, but they did have to forage along the way.[33]

To summarize, rural populations, though partly enserfed (*Leibeigene*) or dependent (*Hörige*), migrated either legally or without permission to obtain better living conditions. Servants moved in order to accept new contracts annually, for a number of years, or on a permanent basis. Laborers increased their bargaining power by increasing their mobility. Most rural-to-urban migrants covered only short distances of at most a week's travel. Rural families were formed and re-formed by birth and death, by "in-migration" or "out-migration" of brides at marriage, by entry and exit of servants, and by the arrival and departure of relatives, including offspring. Remarriage often implied the arrival not only of a new spouse but also of children from previous unions. Mobility varied, however, from region to region. In France, rural populations were relatively sedentary after the repopulation at the end of the Hundred Years' War, but urban ones were highly mobile. In the case of Scandinavia, on the other hand, one research team commented: "Nowhere have we found the immobility often associated with the preindustrial, agrarian society, nowhere we could discover mental horizons coinciding with parish or town borders."[34]

All urban strata were highly mobile, and urban population growth, often interrupted by wars, famines, and epidemics, was never linear. Few families could be traced for more than three generations in the same town or city. Ouges, in Burgundy, lost 30 percent of its households in the first three quarters of the fourteenth century, grew and stabilized during twenty-five years of peace, and then lost almost four-fifths of its households in three decades of war.

Rather than one-time disasters, however, poor urban sanitary conditions were the most serious threat to individuals' lives and population growth. Diseases carried off so many that cities required constant in-migration to keep their population levels stable. In fact, many would have vanished without rural immigration. In Hungary's capital only one or two children (on average 1.4) survived per family. Lower-class urban in-migration came from surrounding areas with long-term migrational ties to the city or from distant places with economic ties. The connections provided information about options—though perhaps mercifully not about death rates.

By the mid-fourteenth century, four Italian cities—Milan, Venice, Naples, and Florence—reached a population of almost 100,000; Genoa, Bologna, and Rome, as well as Paris and Ghent in the north, grew to about 50,000 inhabitants. The populations of Cologne, Bruges, Brussels, and London grew to levels between 35,000 and 50,000, as did the Iberian cities of Córdoba, Granada, Barcelona, and Seville, which had experienced massive population loss after the end of Muslim rule. By the sixteenth century, Urban Italy had lost its preeminence owing to the shift of trading to the Atlantic coast, and the Urban Netherlands achieved primacy in trade and in the (bourgeois) arts. They attracted migrants from many origins. Central Europe by contrast, had lost its role. The "Holy Roman Empire" (*Romanum Imperium* since 962, *Sacrum Imperium* since 1157), a culturally disparate and geographically extended conglomerate of states and fiefs, had passed its apogee after the death of Frederick II of Hohenstaufen in 1250. Thereafter, petty dynasties divided the empire off the political map. But the region's cities were the basis of the urban migrations into eastern Europe, and the southern German urban core, as well as the northern Hanseatic cities, remained influential.

Family strategies were part of the rise of the cities and of the urban bourgeoisie as a class. Italian urban nobles sent their children into commerce; Dutch burghers refrained from ostentatious consumption. Both hired cheap soldiers from abroad and reinvested profits. Commercial expansion could be achieved by establishing marital relations with partner firms elsewhere, and thus transaction costs remained low. By contrast, territorial nobilities supported children unproductively in military service or sent them to monasteries. Journeymen artisans—in particular, masons—crisscrossed Europe and remained unmarried for duration of their migrations.[35]

By the twelfth century, a web of commercial connections and roads connected European cities (see map 2.3). The main axis led from Urban Italy via a string of fairs, in particular in Champagne, to the Dutch cities. From the Rhine valley, with Cologne as its central city, an eastward route stretched via fairs at Frankfurt/Main and Leipzig to Kraków, from which all East Central European markets could be reached.[36] Merchants settled temporarily in distant ports and market towns or installed in those places reliable clerks who were conversant with local customs. In the crusader states, such settlements "constituted entire sections of cities including small orchards and cultivated plots." In North African ports, however, European merchants supported only small "advanced operational bases." Connections from Urban Italy to northwestern Europe expanded on the initiative of Lombard merchants and, in 1229, Venice established a *fondaco dei tedeschi* for incoming German merchants near a Jewish traders' quarter and the *curia slavorum* for Dalmatian, Ragusan, and other southeastern merchants. Around 1500, about 300 merchants from Nuremberg, Augsburg, and Strasbourg lived in the *fondaco* with their staffs. A proud thirteenth-century Genoese poet noted, "So many are the Genoese, so scattered worldwide—that they build other Genoas wherever they reside."[37]

Merchant enclaves in distant towns could be limited to a single large building, such as the *fondaco* (from Arabic, *funduq*), or they might comprise several streets or an entire quarter. Their quasi-extraterritorial status was either granted by charter or simply acquiesced to. In some cultures, host society officials would seal off the zone for the night by locking it from the outside. Inside, self-supporting and self-contained mercantile communities transacted their own business, followed their own religion, lived according to the laws of their home city, and elected their own officers. Local magistrates would step in to adjudicate only conflicts with merchants from the host society or other cultures. Such enclaves reached their peak in the early fourteenth century and attracted immigrant craftsmen, sailors, and laborers.[38]

Traders—in particular, young men intent on gaining experience and capital—came by circular migration and stayed for a few months or several years. Dante recorded the sorrow of wives left behind "because of France" and other *oltremonte* or *oltremare* destinations. Merchants residing far from home, however, often sent for their wives, formed families, and acculturated to local customs. In the world of merchant cosmopolitanism, they joined local elites, and over time a locally born second generation formed the core of the community. Intermarriage and acculturation might, however, imply loss of broker functions and of chartered status.

Since "Italian" merchants—a label affixed by host societies—originated in independent city-states, they developed no uniform pattern of colony organization. Venetians excluded outsiders from their colonies, while the Genoese in their Black Sea colonies readily granted political and mercantile status to in-migrating Latins, Greeks, Armenians, Turks, and Jews. Commercial enclaves and colonies could become more powerful than the host society. Venice captured mines and agricultural fiefs and colonized entire Mediterranean islands with the aid of local serfs or hired labor. In the Levant, Venetian entrepreneurs forced suppliers into mass production or copied their techniques and shifted production to Italy, sometimes re-exporting the products, such as textiles, to the former areas of production. Each shift of production implied both the downsizing and expansion of labor forces by migration or the re-distribution of work by gender and age. In Urban Italy itself, migrating laborers were attracted to larger establishments, *botteghe* (large workshops), but most tasks were farmed out to resident small-town craft families, mobility being limited to carters.[39]

Hanseatic merchants established enclaves only in Novgorod in the east, Bergen in the north, and Bruges and London in the west. These *Kontore* (business offices) or *Höfe* (staple yards) were administered by councils elected by the three constituent Rhenish, Wendish, and Baltic-Livonian regions. They accommodated a German-language population of artisans, most of whom came only for a season or a few years, and very few traveled with wives and children. This male-only lifestyle and its culture of drinking separated the sojourners from local populations and sometimes led to brawls. Only in the herring markets of southern Sweden did the merchants have women with them to help pack and salt the tens of thousands of barrels of fish. From the *Kontore* outward, Norwegian merchants traded to the Faeroes, Iceland, and Greenland, while German merchants reached eastward to Riga and the towns of the Teutonic Order. They made connections to the Mediterranean via Bruges or Cologne.[40]

Along the northwesterly Lombardy-to-Flanders route, merchants from Italian cities mingled with Jewish, Dutch, and German traders. All had to pay safe-conduct fees to regional rulers. To maintain trade as one of their sources of income, the counts of Champagne decided to give three months' notice when the withdrawal of protection was planned, so that merchants could depart with their wares in time. By the mid-thirteenth century, merchants organized locally to form *universitates mercatorum* for self-administration. New regional groups kept on emerging in particular niches of commerce.[41]

The northwesterly route had its equivalent in northeasterly ones via Constantinople and the Black Sea up the Dnieper and Don Rivers into Russia. Along the Danube River, Greek, Jewish, Hungarian, and German merchants reached Bohemia via Vienna and Urban South Germany via Regensburg. In the early fourteenth century, Constantinople accommodated colonies from Marseille, Montpellier, Narbonne, Barcelona, Ancona, Florence, and Ragusa (Dubrovnik), as well as merchants from London and the Germanies. The local Byzantine or ethnically Greek merchants lost their preeminent position to the Genoese in the city's suburb of Pera, who had arrived in secondary migrations from Genoa's Crimean colony of Kaffa and conducted fifteen times as much trade as the city itself (see chap. 5.1).[42]

On the Iberian Peninsula, merchants from Genoa, Piacenza, Pisa, Lucca, Como, and Marseille opened branch houses in Seville, as did Portuguese, English, French, and German traders. "Special streets and a new *barrio* (suburb) were set apart for the privileged foreign traders." By the 1270s Genoese galleys traveled from Majorcan ports to the Atlantic and northward along the coasts to London and the Urban Netherlands. Thereafter, economic power was concentrated in the Atlantic overseas empires.[43]

Commerce necessitated credit arrangements, and with the merchants came moneylenders from Chieri, near Turin, and from Cahors in southern France—or they could be Jews, whose insecure status relegated them to backward areas. They exerted financial influence over local populations, and, in times of financial contraction, debtor-creditor relationships became ethnicized. The generic term "Lombards" for money changers is evidence of how widely perceived Italians were as dealers in currency, and anti-Semitic violence underscored the bigotry concerning Jews as creditors. In the fourteenth and fifteenth centuries, the Florentine Medicis and the southern German Fuggers and Welsers joined the financiers as early capitalist families.

When goods were moved, men had to travel. Merchants became more and more sedentary and hired servants locally from among immigrants from the nearby countryside. For their trade they hired specialized carriers, often Tuscans for Italian houses or men from the Dauphiné for Marseille merchants. In seaborne trade, crews of Italian galleys numbered from 175 to 200, and occasionally up to 300. Some, like French Huguenots, were slaves who had been captured during the religious wars. Many, some of them conscripted, came from fishing and sailor families of the Ligurian coast. Immigrant seafarers and laborers from Dalmatia, Albania, or from as far as Hungary, were hired on as oarsmen. Reaching London, the galley crews met with local dockworkers, brawled and drank together. Some deserted or fell ill, and for the return trip Germans and Flemings were hired. Overland routes, traveled by express mercantile couriers, clerical or princely messengers, and multitudes of carters, permitted a fanning out in many directions. Because initial investment was lower than in seaborne trade, families with lesser fortunes could participate; because of retail peddling, poorer people could buy or at least view goods brought from abroad.[44]

England and East Central Europe joined the transcontinental connections late. When the English court expelled the "foreign" financiers in 1290, new foreigners—in-migrating Italians—replaced the Jews. Overseas trade, too, was mostly in the hands of migrants. Englishmen handled 35 percent of wool exports; Italians 24 percent; and Flemish and other merchants the remainder. The English merchants of London recruited themselves from the city, from the so-called Home Counties, and, over time, from all English territories. Some Welsh and Irish people joined. Widows of English provincial merchants migrated to London to marry urban men. Of the foreigners, mainly Italians and a few Frenchmen, and, in small trade, Germans and Flemings, many were admitted to citizenship, often after they had married English wives. But violence also occurred. A scene in *Sir Thomas More*, ascribed to Shakespeare, mentions the "wretched strangers, their babies at their back, with their poor luggage plodding to th' ports and coasts for transportation" after violence against foreign journeymen in 1517. The London "merchant class," as Sylvia Thrupp put it, became a "melting-pot."[45]

The Hungarian capital provides an example of migration and marriage in an area where urban development began comparatively late. Buda's upper classes selected brides from connected mercantile towns. Between Vienna and Buda, an exchange of marriage partners occurred; others came from as far away as St. Gall (Switzerland), Nuremberg, Breslau/Wroclaw, and Kraków; a few still came from the cultures of origin of earlier immigrants, Wallonia and the Germanies. For smaller towns, the radius of the marriage market was smaller but the percentage of immigrant partners not necessarily lower. Burgher elites of some Hungarian cities intermarried with local nobility, and brides emigrated from the latter's country seats. State boundaries were irrelevant for the selection of spouses.[46]

City or dynastic policies determined the framework for migration. While England relied on immigrants, and Italian towns on colony-bound emigrants, the city-state of Ragusa decided to avoid population growth. Magistrates monitored immigration closely and, to achieve commercial growth and expansion nevertheless, permitted women to participate in a variety of spheres.[47] Thus the Europe of merchant families—along with the supporting trades of carriers, dockworkers, and producers—was a world in which the local and the distant came into close contact.

Marriage and Mobility among the Common People

Short-distance migration replenished urban reservoirs of female servants and laborers and male unskilled workers. In-migrants tended to be young, and women, in particular, often planned to return to their home village for marriage. Other women came at an older age, as widows, to make use of urban amenities if they could afford them or to make use of urban almsgiving if they were impoverished. Urban capital and rural labor interacted closely. Although the connection with out-work and cottage production is well known, it should be noted that agricultural producers in the vicinity of cities were also linked to urban markets. Landowning burghers from the city of Florence granted loans to their sharecropping families to tie them to the land. This attempt to prevent them from migrating to better conditions could, however, induce them to flee intolerable debt payments in times of dearth.[48]

Free in-migrants in Urban Italy—who might interact with urban slaves from Central Asia or North Africa—established settlement patterns based on ties to their village of origin, making urban neighborhoods "the physical extensions of particular villages." From Genoa, where newcomers could acquire citizenship easily, they sent gifts, and they continued to own land and visited kin in their community of origin. In Florence, journeymen artisans came mainly from the local population, though—in contrast to other Italian cities—no restrictions were placed on foreign craftsmen. When immigrant men married upward, the close relations mandated by the patricians' clientele system counteracted the migrants' kinship systems. Patrician families encouraged downward-marriage of daughters because the clientele relation kept the dowry within the family.[49]

According to Braudel, migration into particular cities in the Mediterranean World was characterized by the predominance of one or two major ethno-religious groups: Corsicans in Marseille; Andalusian Moriscos in Seville; Christians and Berbers at Algiers; and African slaves in Lisbon. In Venice, migrants from neighboring towns joined those from more distant territories of the Venetian realm: Albanians, Greeks, Persians, and Turks, to name only a few. As Braudel put it, "These indispensable immigrants were not always unskilled laborers or men of little aptitude. They often brought with them new techniques that were as indispensable as their persons to urban life." To escape urban congestion, nobles and bourgeois alike would move in the reverse directions and leave the towns seasonally in search of fresh air, vineyards, and fields. Their servant women and men accompanied them. Like the immigrants who returned home from multi-annual stays in cities, they transferred urban lifestyles into the countryside.[50]

The small Hungarian town of Pécs, with a population of about 5,000 in 1620, provides an example of multiple ethnic and cultural conversions, interactions, or conflicts over time. By the year 1000, the town's population was Magyar. Its eleventh-century cathedral reflected the influence of Italian master-builders and of French sculptors. Immigrant stonecutters opened a workshop. The first bishop was of French origin, and German immigrants arrived at about the same time. In the sixteenth century, when Turkish troops arrived and stayed for 150 years, the town's character became "oriental"—Muslim and Ottoman—and the original population was pushed to the fringes of the settlement. Greek merchants, Bosnian tanners, Serbian marauders, Tatar troops, and Jewish residents were listed in chronicles. Ottoman administrators worked out compromises when different Christian denominations clashed over the use of a church.[51]

Among urban families—as was true of their rural counterparts—migration and temporary mobility contributed to a constant recombination of households. "The co-residential household (and indeed the entire population of the city) was extremely fluid. Servants were hired and dismissed; sons departed and returned." Babies were placed with wet nurses, and some never returned. Daughters who were not to marry were sent to convents at an early age. Others moved off into patrilocal marriages. Daughters of poorer parents had to leave for service work to earn their dowry, and, in some cultures, they received in lieu of wages a dowry upon marriage.[52]

Wayfarers reached the towns and cities as a fluctuating population of impoverished men, women, and children. The records of the almshouse in Toulouse reveal high rates of in-migration. In Basel, most of the out-of-town poor came from neighboring regions, though a few had migrated over large distances. In thirteenth- and fourteenth-century European cities, 35 to 40 percent of the inhabitants were poor: about half of them were laboring poor with no reserves; up to one-quarter were smallholders whose condition was precariously marginal; and the last quarter depended on alms. The wages of French laborers were insufficient to feed a family in the first half of the fourteenth century. By taking loans in the pre-harvest months at usurious interest rates from foreign moneylenders, French peasants often lost their land. Itinerancy and reliance on urban alms were often the only course left to these families. In the German states, the fifteenth-century shift from individual to municipal almsgiving involved new screening processes to select the "worthy poor," to confine others to workhouses, and to discredit beggary. One official's *Liber Vagantorum*, a manual used to classify vagrants, was reprinted thirty-two times from 1510 to 1530. In the mid-sixteenth century, Italian cities opened asylums for prostitutes and shelters for orphans, poor girls, widows, and women with marital troubles. Venice passed a law according to which beggars could be sent back to their home village.[53]

Urban women had a place in shopkeeping, in artisanal workshops as vendors of their husbands' products, and in markets as purveyors of agricultural produce and other goods. But they hardly left town; itinerant pedlars were mainly male. Resident women shared acculturation experiences as marriage partners of in-migrating men.

Traveling Journeymen and Out-of-Town Maids

In contrast to merchants who became more sedentary, journeyman artisans became increasingly mobile during the fourteenth century, whether out of curiosity, or out of a desire for training or economic betterment, or to achieve independence. "Running off" was also a means of protest to remind masters and town officials that the urban economy could function only when the producers were accorded a legitimate position in society. Like migrating free or servile agrarians, journeymen were economically informed actors in their own lives. Employers increased wages, albeit grudgingly, to assure themselves of a labor supply. The structural prerequisites for these movements were the existence of connected urban labor markets and deferred marriage. Migrations involved apprentices, journeymen, and masters. An apprenticeship often required, to begin with, a move from village to town. Young rural women were trained in urban households or provided cheap labor.[54]

Both apprentices and maids accepted live-in service positions. Social convention then as now deemed women's work—the preparation of food, sewing of garments, raising of children—to be less skilled than work done in craftshops.[55] Live-in arrangements, important for economic considerations, also involved emotional relationships. Masters and their wives often sent sons into apprenticeship in trades accorded greater social prestige or placed them in clerical institutions, and they may have filled the resulting gap in their families with the "substitute sonship" of their own apprentices. Journeymen's lore, on the other hand, frequently stressed negative aspects like control over their behavior, long working hours, or the poor quality or limited amount of food served. The sexual allusions in male songs concerning masters' wives and daughters involved an economic component: to marry a master's daughter meant to establish oneself in business. A gendered approach to these relations will have to inquire why maids were not suitable marriage partners for sons but instead became—like female slaves in Italy—the objects of the sexual desires of the males in a household. In contrast to the integration of children born to Genoese slave women, elsewhere in Europe a child from a master-servant sexual relationship was the sole responsibility of the mother, who usually lost her live-in job and thus a "home" for the newborn.[56]

In most trades, masters employed no more than one or two journeymen; so the number of independent workshops was high, as were possibilities for marriage and shared work with spouses. Many societies permitted widows to manage the family's workshop. In 1444, 11 percent of the Strasbourg guilds' members were women. Wage schedules promulgated by city authorities, however, fixed women's wages at half those of men's. The wage gap was similar in Basel. In Cologne's silk crafts, women masters accepted female apprentices. They came from cities and towns up to seventy kilometers distant—or more if travel could be by boat—some even from as far away as Antwerp or Lübeck. When labor markets contracted, women were marginalized in production but remained active in selling the shop's products. In general, "during the sixteenth century restrictions placed upon women working and living outside the patriarchal household increased." Artisanal couples who practiced their trade together sometimes were forced into transiency or out-migration to nonguild rural locations by hostile, all-male journeymen associations.[57]

Whereas for maids the live-in situation continued over the centuries, journeymen might hire themselves out temporarily as soldiers since the pay was better and since local campaigns were short and not necessarily dangerous. Self-employed rural artisans who practiced their crafts without guilds moved between seasonal work in agriculture and urban work in winter—though urban guilds were able over time to exclude rural migrants. Masters unable to establish themselves continued to migrate, while settled masters sent their sons to be apprenticed in other towns. Long-distance migrations not related to a person's craft were undertaken occasionally in response to specific opportunities. Large numbers of German artisans worked in the Scanian herring fisheries in the 1320s and in Italy in the 1380s. Guilds increasingly mandated and regulated multi-annual medium- and long-distance migrations as part of journeymen's training. Migrations became obligatory in the German-language areas of Central Europe from the late sixteenth century onward, and to the west the *tour de France* (a journeyman's traveling apprenticeship) was put into practice. In the Germanies the practice lasted to the 1800s.[58] The journeymen developed ritualized forms of circular migration that included protective communities in the towns of destination—as in the case of Flemish and Brabantine weavers in fourteenth-century London, York, and Florence. Local guilds or *compagnonnages* ritually greeted arriving journeymen to gain information from the newcomer, to provide him with a job, and to prevent him from going to a master who paid poorly. When no job was available, work was offered for a limited period of time, commonly two weeks, to provide the means for the next leg of the trip. In hostels, the landlord and boardinghouse "mother" acted as surrogate parents. Mendicant orders, especially the Franciscans, whose lifestyle and travel experience resembled those of journeymen culture, provided religious services.[59]

Gender relations were reflected in the sexual conduct of journeymen as well as in their songs. Given the high incidence of migration, many lived in temporary unions while others frequented prostitutes. The latter were not yet as marginalized as they would become in later periods, and in medieval Latin a prostitute was called a *meretrix*, someone who earns a living and "merits" pay. One scholar referred to "the meretricious arts" of upper-class courtesans and thus placed sex work on a par with the "useful arts" of artisans. Many were migrants, too, in fifteenth-century southern France, for example, from war-disrupted northern regions.[60] Journeymen's songs reflected the traditional topos of disrupted relationships and the sadness felt upon separation from parents, brothers and sisters, and—most often—"my love."[61] Occasionally a consolation was added: another woman would be waiting at the end of a journey, while the woman left behind would find consolation with an incoming journeyman. English sailors' songs provided a variant: loved women who were to be left behind donned men's clothes and joined their sweethearts on board ship.[62]

Distances traveled could be substantial. In towns of the Upper Rhine valley of the 1440s, 40 percent of the journeymen had moved 51–150 kilometers (three to six days of travel) and another 30 percent some 151–300 kilometers (a maximum of two weeks). Midsized cities attracted migrants from distances of two to fourteen days of travel, while larger cities had a greater power of attraction over greater distances. Migrants who moved more than 300 kilometers came from the Baltic territories as well as Poland, Bohemia, and Austria—probably from among German-language urban groups. German became an artisanal lingua franca, and migrating journeymen established colonies outside the contiguous German-language territories. In addition to distance and size of town, trade characteristics determined migration patterns. Men whose crafts required specialized urban training moved over large distances, while men in more common crafts, learned in villages, moved over shorter distances (map 3.3). Maids generally came from the environs of cities, areas from which few men came.[63]

Outside of the German-language migration circuits, "the artisan community in the sixteenth century was made up of many races, rarely native to the area." Florentine crafts employed workmen from Flanders and Brabant in the fourteenth century, and in Verona in 1561 not one of the master craftsmen who manufactured black cloth was a native. The armory in Brescia "was continually expanding and contracting according to circumstances, losing its workers to neighboring towns, then recovering them. . . . Over long distances and short, a mobile labour force was constantly responding to variations in demand." The same was true for English armories.[64] In the Upper Rhenish borderland between German and French culture, the issue of cross-cultural interaction and competition came to the fore when town regulations began to exclude "Frenchmen, Savoyards, and Lotharingians" from jobs. Local women may not have shared this attitude. Male authorities promulgated the exclusion of foreigners because they "cunningly and secretly" had married daughters or widows of established burghers, and, so they lamented, no women were left for the sons of local patricians. Adding a dramatic pitch, they noted that these couples "increased" (reproduced) and that local young men soon would have to move away.[65]

From the sixteenth century on, the migrations of journeymen expanded to Paris and London; Scandinavian journeymen crisscrossed Europe; and German-language artisans and French workers migrated to Sweden. Many settled far from where they had been born or trained. Women's migrations remained short in distance, but marriage often linked women to men who were from distant regions but close in status.

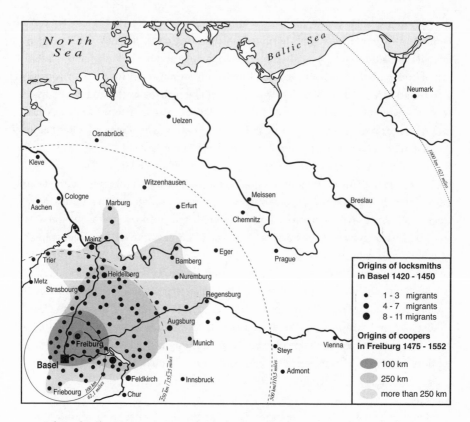

3.3   Selected 15th-Century Artisans' Migrations

Masons' Lodges and Miners' Migrations

In two highly skilled trades, masonry and mining, trained men often had to be recruited from elsewhere for large projects. The expansion of mining in late-ninth-
century Europe and the mining boom from 1460 to 1520 required experienced manpower well informed about technological advances in other locations. The building
of cathedrals and abbeys, as well as of castles and fortifications, took off in the
twelfth century in an assertion of religious and secular power. Such undertakings
required large numbers of masons, supporting laborers, and men in related trades,
such as carpenters, smiths, plumbers, glaziers, and plasterers. The most highly skilled
masons, the hewers who shaped the stone blocks, were called "freemasons." In times
of labor shortages, women were sometimes employed in unskilled jobs on construction sites.[66]

Originally, master masons were also architects. But when buildings became more
complex, specialization developed and individuals with particular architectural and
ornamental skills had to be brought in from distant places. Navvies and carriers
usually came from local populations. For religious projects they often labored on a
voluntary, unpaid basis. Skilled construction workers typically were from other lands.

The central element of the Gothic style, the pointed arch, was Arabic in origin and was probably introduced by men returning from crusades. Château Gaillard, built in Normandy in 1196, required 400 masons and 1,200 workers and incorporated features of Palestinian castles. Stained glass windows had to be imported from specialized workshops over large distances. Master masons carried the Gothic style eastward into Poland, and migrating Byzantine masters carried their style into Russia.[67]

The building trades were connected by far-reaching and fast communication networks. When, for example, the tower of a church in Ulm in southern Germany was in danger of falling in 1493, 117 masons arrived within a week for urgent repair work. Networks spanned the continent: Lombard masons worked in Catalonia in 1175, French ones in Uppsala, Sweden, in 1287. Trans-European religious orders relied on the same architects and masters whether building in France or in Hungary. The thirteenth-century architect Villard de Honnecourt worked in Cambrai, Laon, Reims, Meaux, and Chartres—but also in Hungary. German stonemasons at large construction sites organized themselves into lodges or *Hütten* and shared hostel accommodations. They erected a workshop, a *Bauhütte*, to prepare stone and thus work —and income from wages—could be extended into the colder months of the year. A lodge at Xanten, in the Dutch-German borderlands, included migrants from French Flanders, Holland, Antwerp and Brussels, and Westphalian and Rhenish cities, and they all worked alongside local helpers. In 1459 these migrants met supraregional regulations for the honor of the trade, good craftsmanship, and pious behavior.[68]

Long-distance miners' migrations benefited, in a way, from the short-distance movements of agriculturalists up mountainsides brought about by population increases. The resulting accidental discoveries of surface veins of ores and the increasing demand for silver, salt, coal, and stone combined to create an expanding demand for labor. Metals, minerals, and salt entered the long-distance trade networks. (Gold continued to be supplied from south of the Sahara.) The most significant Central European silver mining was concentrated in the German Harz Mountains and later in the environs of the Bohemian town of Kuttenberg (Kutná Hora). From there skilled men migrated toward the eastern Alps, the Vosges and Jura mountain ranges, and southwestern France and to the nearer new mining towns of Bohemia and Slovakia. English tin mines and the Swedish Bergslagen district also attracted men. To increase their revenues, the abbess Hildegard of Bingen (1098–1179) and a duchess of Brunswig, both well informed about mining and processing technologies, encouraged investment and immigration. Lords offered to miners privileges similar to those granted to agrarian colonists and freemasons: freedom of the person, freedom of movement, and freedom to prospect for ores.

When mining operations promised long-term employment, immigrants brought their families. Surface bodies of ore, however, often were quickly exhausted, and families faced further migration. Few written sources refer to women as working in mines, but fifteenth-century illustrations show women and children working above ground sorting and breaking up ore. Like journeymen artisans, miners left en masse when lords or absentee urban capitalists imposed poor working conditions. Involuntary departures came in the wake of disasters that shut down mines. Experts and investor migrants transferred technology and capital. In Sweden, King Valdemar (r. 1250–75) favored the settlement of German miners; as a result, German capital and merchants followed and achieved a dominant position in the latter thirteenth century. In 1444 an English master miner moved to Saxony, and in 1528 an Augsburg merchant had immigrant German miners prospect for ores in England, Wales, and Ireland. English mining capital recruited Central European miners in the 1560s.[69]

Mining and smelting operations induced migrations of men and families who were involved in associated supportive trades. Charcoal had to be burned and hauled to a smelting site, and metal bars had to be carried to markets. Finnish peasants and charcoal burners migrated to the mining communities in central Sweden. How many men and horses were needed to distribute the 2,000 tons of iron produced annually in early fourteenth-century Styria? New mining towns attracted merchants, shop-keepers, artisans, independent women, miners' wives, and domestics. While German-speaking miners predominated in most locations, the composition of the labor force was often multiethnic. In thirteenth-century Kuttenberg, German and Bohemian miners seem to have lived in separate quarters. They worked under regulations writ-ten in Latin by Italian legal experts. The exhaustion of surface beds, together with the fourteenth-century population decline, slowed down production. Mining became a part-time occupation of rural people, and professional miners had to supplement their incomes by agriculture.

Mass migrations of miners responded to politics and war. Skilled mine laborers were drafted to under*mine* fortifications during wars. When, owing to Ottoman ex-pansion, the Byzantine-Genoese alum mines in Phocaea were abandoned, 3,000 miners lost their jobs; but 6,000 were hired within a short time when alum was dis-covered in Central Italy. In general, however, Ottoman rule left mining communities intact and allowed self-regulation according to existing customs.[70] During the boom from the 1460s to the 1520s, sparked by the advent of new technologies and increased demand, about 100,000 miners worked in the Habsburgs' Austrian and Spanish pos-sessions; when the dynasty with support of southern German capitalists incorporated Latin America into its realm, some of those workers were sent to colonial mines. Together with enslaved migrant workers of subjugated peoples, they vastly increased silver production after 1546. The resulting fall in prices forced European mining fami-lies into unemployment and poverty. Then the Thirty Years' War brought mining to a standstill in most of Central Europe.[71]

3.4 Pilgrims' and Clerics' Wanderings Stimulated by Devotion and Curiosity

The institutions and the faithful of the Latin Church took part in medieval mobility. The administration of its trans-European realm made it necessary for functionar-ies to travel (chap. 3.1). In order to enter a convent or a monastery, an individual by definition had to leave the family, either voluntarily or perforce when parents placed in these institutions of celibacy daughters who were not to marry or sons who were not to inherit. The proselytizing among "infidels" necessitated long-distance moves by missionaries and encounters with cultures as distant as Buddhist China (see chap. 2.2). In the warrior-pilgrimages of the crusades, hundreds of thousands moved across European and Levantine cultures. The Christian persecution of "heretics" as well as of Muslims and Jews caused mass flight and resettlement (see chaps. 2.3 and 4). Travel to places of spiritual contemplation, faith healing, and penitence was common to many religions.[72] In Latin Christendom the "golden age" of pilgrimage from the eleventh to the fourteenth century ended in decline and internal criticism with the Reformation begun in 1517.

The decision to undertake a pilgrimage ideally reflected a pious desire to pray at a particular shrine. In other cases it was a journey of penitence imposed by authorities or—viewed from another perspective—a removal of an offender from the community. A pilgrimage could also be an escape, an entertainment, or a trip inspired by curiosity. The pious and the penitent who could afford the cost sent deputized "professional pilgrims." Victor Turner defined pilgrimages as a three-stage social process from a ritualized departure to a second, "liminal stage" (from Latin, *limen*: threshold) of traveling and worship during which the structures of ordinary society were replaced by an egalitarian *communitas*. Transformed, the pilgrims returned to reenter their home communities. These temporary peregrinations involved identity formation, self-definition, and community integration, and they reflected life itself, the *vita peregrina*, the physical and spiritual migration between birth and death.[73] Men and women of all social classes traveled. Though the all-male Church authorities warned women not to participate, the ratio of women ranged between 33 and 50 percent.[74]

Among the three destinations of the *peregrinationes maiores*, Jerusalem ranked first until renewed Muslim rule after 1187 required fees and negotiations for safe-conduct. Thereafter, Rome with its tombs of the apostles Peter and Paul emerged as a new center. The city received a boost in 1300 when Pope Boniface VIII granted the first plenary indulgence to all pilgrims going to Rome. The tomb of St. James at Santiago de Compostela in Spain, the third shrine of trans-European importance, was the destination of roughly 18,000 English pilgrims alone each year in the sixteenth century (map 3.4). Canterbury in England attracted only limited numbers of continental pilgrims. *Peregrinationes minores* were middle-distance moves to secondary centers. When the Church began to support cults of particular saints and revitalized women's roles in the worship of Mary, the number of sacred places expanded; *Wallfahrten*, lasting only one or a few days, mobilized hundreds of thousands. Such short-distance pilgrimages permitted more and poorer people to participate, and they kept the pilgrims' offerings within the reach of the local clergy.[75]

Relics that could attract pilgrims were in great demand, and the Latin crusaders, by sacking Byzantine Constantinople in 1204, provided the market with a new supply. In an early form of advertising, local clerics compiled lists of miracles associated with "their" shrine to attract more of the faithful. Holy cities prospered from "esteem income" because of their magnetic power to draw pilgrims from traditional networks

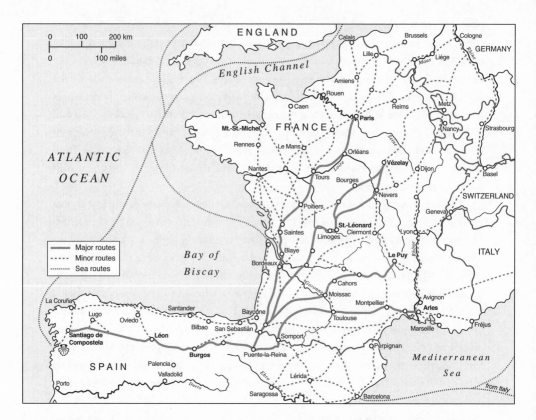

3.4 Long-Distance Pilgrimage to Santiago de Compostela, 15th and 16th Centuries

and, on a more mundane level, because they could draw upon an existing network of roads and commercial connections. To accommodate the significant numbers of pilgrims, infrastructures were improved; along the route of the Islamic hajj to Mecca, water cisterns, watchtowers, and milestones were installed. The Latin Church commanded peaceable passage for pilgrims, as it did for merchants on their travels to fairs.[76]

The volume of pilgrim traffic was sizable. After 1300, between 300 and 500 men and women annually left from Venice for Jerusalem. Pilgrimages to Rome, whose population was estimated at 50,000 in 1500, seem to have been inflated in Church records: 30,000 were said to have arrived daily in 1300, the year of Boniface VIII's indulgence. Nevertheless, during the fourteenth century probably more than 100,000 came annually. From England each year, about 3,000 pilgrims left for Rome and Santiago de Compostela in the 1430s—or about 90,000 men and women in the span of one generation of thirty years, which equaled roughly 3 percent of the total English population.[77]

Many features of pilgrimages, aside from their spiritual aims, resemble the mass voyaging of nineteenth-century emigrants or even twentieth-century package tours for tourists.[78] From Marseille, Genoa, or Venice, where pilgrims destined for Jerusalem collected, a return trip took approximately four months. A Dominican friar, Felix Fabri, who traveled in 1480 and 1483 by way of Venice, described the booking of his passage.[79] In the square before St. Mark's Church, "stood two costly banners, raised aloft on tall spears, white, and ensigned with a red cross." They indicated the booking office. Venice's authorities had entrusted two senators with "the care of pilgrims," and their servants "stood beside the banners, and each invited the pilgrims to sail with their master." The pilgrims quickly realized that promises to depart within a day or two were patently untrue. A waiting period of four weeks was in store. A contract regulated the duties of the captain and set forth food allowances. Pilgrims like Fabri had to buy their own bedding, which they could resell after the trip. For better food, they might take a live chicken in a cage; and for the leg of the trip from Jerusalem to the Jordan, they were told to pack "wyne, water, harde eggys and chese" since there were no sellers along the way.[80] The captains used the voyage for commerce, stored goods in the pilgrims' cabins, and prolonged the trip by unscheduled stops. In Jerusalem, hostels catering to specific creeds or ethnicities provided mass accommodations; stores sold rosaries, crosses, boxes that contained holy earth, and other souvenirs. A pilgrimage to Jerusalem became so highly valued that by the twelfth century the biography of Charlemagne (742–814), the epitome of medieval Christian kings, was embellished with a fictitious pilgrimage.[81]

Friar Fabri's narrative throws light on why historians know so little about female pilgrims. In the account of his first trip, he does not mention women on board until the men became seasick and women took care of them. In telling of his second trip, he complains bitterly about a woman ever curious about, in his opinion, useless things. Busy sightseeing in Crete, she missed the galley, but she arranged for other transportation and rejoined her party five days later. In the Holy Land, women emerge from his account in their usual roles: the House of Italian Ladies took care of pilgrims' needs. Religious women, such as the mystic Margery Kempe (c.1373–c.1439), also visited Jerusalem. She had been a brewer, had given birth to fourteen children, and became a vocal prophet. She traveled to English shrines, the Holy Land (1414–18), Santiago de Compostela (1417–18), and Norway and Danzig (1433–34).[82]

Voyagers to the Holy Land "brought back with them, in addition to a vast number of holy relics, an appreciation for the peculiar products of that region—jewels, silks, perfumes, and spices." A German merchant observed cotton-growing on Aegean islands, salt production on Cyprus, and strange birds and animals on Rhodes. His view of the all-powerful Church changed. Not only were Christian pilgrims forced to accept protection from the "infidels" in Palestine, but in Jerusalem the several Christian denominations prayed separately and fought each other. In ports, he was surprised by the "diverse creeds and folk from many countries."[83]

The second-most important destination, Rome, also had to provide a large number of accommodations for clerics on business. The fourth Lateran Council in 1215, for example, was attended by 400 bishops as well as 800 abbots and priors. Each was accompanied by his retinue of clerks and servants. If the 1,200 officials traveled with ten attendants each—a very conservative estimate—some 13,000 persons needed housing.⁸⁴ Pilgrims, arriving after a trip of five to nine weeks one-way from England and a week less from France, stayed for several days to complete their religious duties and to satisfy their sightseeing interests. They were warned to beware of "strange folk," learned to change money, and were away from home for about three months. Seemingly prohibitive costs did not deter ordinary people: three-quarters of the English hostel's guests were cobblers, weavers, brewers, tanners, and rustics. Hostels housed pilgrims and clerical immigrants according to their ethnicity: Franks, Frisians, Lombards, Irish, Anglo-Saxons. They were often connected to churches or study centers (*scholae*).⁸⁵ Confession could be made in any of several languages, and guidebooks were available for religious and secular sights. "Rome-faring" became so common a feature of life that everyday language came to reflect the phenomenon: the verb "to roam" entered the English language, and the surnames *Römer* and *Romée* evolved in German and French.

Rome was the only city in Europe with a surplus of men, including resident, immigrant, and sojourning clerics, as well as foreign diplomats at the papal court. Consequently, prostitutes migrated to Rome from as far away as Spain. Most were of lower- or lower-middle-class origins. But the social scale ranged from girls prostituted by mothers to support a destitute family to women with entrepreneurial talents and sparkling intellectual capacities. Confined in the institutions of religion, men were not only deprived of sexual relations with women but also of the entire sphere of female culture. Courtesans—from the Italian term *cortigiana* (court lady)—were educated, conversant about many things, had musical talents, and moved among the well-born. Next to marriage or cloister, consorting with the men of the Church thus provided a third option for women to chart a life-course and to earn an independent income as in domestic or artisanal labor. Many were highly esteemed and later married. On the other hand, clerical zealots saw nothing but prostitutes in the streets of Rome. In 1528 one of them counted 39,000—among a population of 55,000.⁸⁶

The spontaneous growth of pilgrimages to local shrines after 1300 involved hundreds at each site each year, thousands in the case of larger ones. In an attempt to regain control over mobility, the Church admonished monks, "Your cell is your Jerusalem," and exhorted laypersons, "Those who wander much are but little hallowed." Away from home and outside of social constraints, the threshold that pilgrims passed did not necessarily lead to the kingdom of God, for their conduct was often secular or even bawdy. A variant of the religious peregrination can be seen in the impulsive moves of men and women acting on some type of inspiration or fear. "Dancers," "flagellants," and other itinerant fanatics crossed through French, Italian, and German territories from the thirteenth to the fifteenth century. The frequent appearance of pilgrims and other travelers in medieval literature, sculpture, and illustrations testifies to their importance in the construction of a world beyond the local.

Many lesser clergy traveled widely and frequently. Often mentioned but hardly ever welcomed were those known as pardoners, who made a business out of selling Church pardons. More important were the friars and nuns of the mendicant orders, who tried to bring the opulent and corrupt Church into line with the lives of the poor and who combined ardent preaching with social work. Travel was a function of the size of a particular order and its regional or continent-wide extension. From the tenth to the twelfth century, Benedictines, in particular, had gone forth to Christianize Danes, Swedes, and Norwegians in the north and Hungarians, Slavs, and Baltic peoples in the east. Missionary activists among conquered Muslim populations in the Iberian Peninsula interacted with merchants and the Military Orders or cooperated with colonizers. In the marshlands along the North Sea coast, the archbishop of Bremen in 1106 contracted to bring in Dutch settlers and to establish parishes. Missionaries in the Holy Land lost their support with the demise of the crusader states but could minister to the newly established Italian merchant communities and act as interpreters.[87]

As written and printed information increased, the importance of mobility for obtaining knowledge about distant lands, other cultures, new craft technologies, and options for migration declined. Merchants used written guidebooks, and master artisans consulted trade manuals about patterns and technologies. Although the aristocracy remained trans-European and the men of the Church mobile, a new exclusionist approach to religious ideology and spirituality in the Latin Church's realm led to mass flight. By contrast, the Muslim World, which became the realm of the Ottoman Empire, purposefully developed patterns of coexistence and state-enforced migration for economic development (chap. 4). The link between people, a state's economy, and policies related to migration developed in Europe only under mercantilism (chap. 5).

4

The End of Intercivilizational Contact and

the Economics of Religious Expulsions

Among the faithful of the three "religions of the Book"—Judaism, Christianity, and Islam—spirituality involved pilgrimages that often covered large distances. The Latin Christian Church's centralized structures necessitated traveling and migration for administrative and missionary purposes. Cultural coexistence or interaction in borderlands between civilizations or in Mediterranean interfaith societies characterized the everyday conduct of men and women of different creeds who lived side by side in separate quarters according to their own customs, values, and laws. States did not impose uniformity but permitted corporate groups to regulate their own affairs, sometimes under "protective" payments to a ruler, often without overt fees in view of contributions to the economy and tax income. In Muslim Iberia and within the Muslim Ottoman Empire, coexistence regulated by the Koran became the rule—as it was in the whole of the Mediterranean World.

Groups of fanatics—often, as in the case of the Berbers, of different ethnicity —from time to time interrupted such coexistence. "Purifying" military invasions forced the faithful to flee or even killed off the allegedly nonpure. In Christendom, the eleventh-century Latin papacy embarked on a course of ever more rigorous affirmation of its superiority and its exclusion of pluralism. Venetian rulers seized the opportunity to profit from the Church's absolutism by transporting crusaders and using them to destroy their Byzantine competitors of the Orthodox faith. On the other hand, Christian merchants did not submit to papal interdictions against trade with Muslims, as ordered, for example, in 1291.

Whereas Pope Sylvester II (c.945–1003), who was of French origin and studied mathematics, still spoke Arabic, the narrow-minded eleventh-century men of the Latin Church first reduced Muslims and Jews to subaltern positions, then expelled Muslims and had Jews harassed, expelled, or killed. In time, exponents of alternative Christian interpretations and reform movements were branded as heretics and persecuted. The inflexibility and corruption of the Church and the great monastic orders as well as the inflammatory preaching by particular prelates and priests drove groups of the faithful into mass flight before the final split of the Reformation.[1] The expulsion or killing of Muslims, Jews, and "heretics" left economies impaired. It permitted self-styled true believers to seize businesses, craftshops, and landholdings of the religious Others. But long-term damage to the economic life often was so drastic that expelled Jews were asked to return or Muslims were tolerated. In such cases, their religious rites were restricted to private life. Similarly, strong Christian reform groups like the Huguenots could negotiate safe positions within a Catholic society.

4.1   The End of Coexistence: Expulsion of Muslims

In the mid-thirteenth century, the major Christian states on the Iberian Peninsula— Aragon, Castile, and Portugal—had reduced Muslim territories to the caliphate of Granada. They tolerated and relied on Muslim populations by granting them freedom of religion and the security of their property if they capitulated (see chap. 2.3). Urban Muslims, without whom regional economies would have collapsed, were ordered to vacate a city's center and to resettle in the margins. Small-town and rural families of Muslim craftsmen and agriculturalists were still offered favorable terms of settlement because of their skills and because only they had the expertise to keep the complex irrigation systems for horticulture, viticulture, and agriculture functioning. Christians and Muslims continued to interact in everyday life and shared customs like weddings or burial rites.[2]

The Christian invaders, hoping for booty and quick riches, denigrated industrious labor. Industriousness became a character trait of subaltern peoples. In the middle strata of society, a warrior class rather than a commercial one set the tone. Men of the Church strove to terminate coexistence despite common economic interests, social integration, and centuries of interaction and acculturation. Archbishops urged political rulers to expel all Muslims—for example, in Tarragona in 1337. In Valencia, in the 1440s, dates for departure were fixed and then withdrawn—resulting in a type of psychological uprooting. Municipal authorities imposed economic restrictions, such as on the sale of land to Muslims. Since Muslims continued to own irrigated lands that provided high yields, their expulsion would permit Christian lords to seize such assets.

New restrictive decrees of 1380 turned separate quarters into segregated ones. Christian authorities demarcated Muslim *morerías* (Moorish quarters), as they had *juderías* before, and forced people to move into their confines within eight days or forfeit all property. Coexistence and interaction were too deeply engrained, however, to end suddenly. Moorish masters and Christian masons jointly built churches at the invitation of Christian clerics. Muslims served in the armies of their Christian rulers and Christians in those of Muslim rulers. For over a century, monarchs were "too sagacious to obey" (Lea) the requests of the churchmen. In 1480, however, the Catholic rulers of Castile and Aragon, Ferdinand and Isabella, rigorously imposed further restrictions and began a war of aggression against Granada in 1482.

To prevent Muslim-Christian unions through marriage and to assert Christian men's claims, Christian women were enjoined not to enter *morerías*. In the 1490s, regulation of sexuality and control of women expanded into the sphere of giving birth

and creating life. Christian women were prohibited from employing Muslim midwives. Moreover, medieval dress codes that determined the outward signs of status by
gender, age, family, and class, were amended to denote religion and ethnicity, neither
of which was easily visible by mere physical appearance.[3]

In 1492 Granada was conquered by Christian crusaders from France, England,
Ireland, the Germanies, Poland and, as usual, Switzerland, who received plenary in-
dulgences for fighting the infidels. The Naṣrid ruler and 6,000 followers left for North
Africa. Emigrant families were allowed to take with them the proceeds from the sale
of their possessions. Muslims who capitulated and chose to stay were offered protection of their lives and property as well as self-administration and freedom of worship.
But in-migrating Christians were forbidden to join the religio-occupational guilds of
Muslim craftsmen. "The Capitulations if fully and loyally implemented would have
set up a state which was truly neutral as between Islam and Christianity." But the
Church intervened with forced baptisms and sexual violation: "I saw all the noble
ladies, widows and married, subjected to mockery, and I saw more than three hundred maidens sold at public auction." Men were imprisoned in chains and left to lan-
guish in their own excrement. Traditional Muslim dress and customs were outlawed.
The Muslims' first rebellion against this destruction of self-respect (1499–1501) was
crushed, and thereafter Islam was no longer a public religion in Granada.[4]

In 1502 Muslims from the kingdom of Castile and León were forced to "choose"
between emigration via distant ports on the Bay of Biscay or "voluntary" baptism.
Only in Aragon did they remain protected. In recognition of the lengthy process
of cultural change and the emergence of new identities, the authorities of Valencia granted Muslims a forty-year period of grace—in return for a payment of 50,000
ducats. But once again, the Church and its Inquisition (established in 1478) intervened. Orders to learn Spanish within three years and to abstain from the use of Arabic even in private life, together with the burning of Arabic books, destroyed cultural
independence. Prohibitive taxes on Granada silks and the confiscation of property
undercut Muslim economic life. From the 1550s onward prohibitions against visiting
bathhouses, a practice now labeled and condemned as a Muslim (or a Jewish) rite, up-
set the religious aspects of everyday life and affected general cleanliness. The Inquisition, which levied a "protective tax" from Muslims, nevertheless imposed Christian
lifestyles upon them. When Christian nobles protected Muslim laborers and agriculturalists whose labor and expertise they needed, the Inquisition moved to punish
them, too. In need of a functioning economy and a labor force itself, the Church prohibited Moriscos from emigrating, which would have been their only alternative to
forced conversion. After a second unsuccessful revolt in former Granadian territories, more than 150,000 Muslims were deported to Castilian villages, and perhaps
30,000 of them died during the winter march to their new locations.[5] Christian colonists were invited to settle the vacated lands, and the proceeds from land sales went
to the Crown. The sixteenth century became a period of particularly large and involuntary population movements.

Three hundred years after the end of the Christian conquest and a century after the fall of Granada, new immigrants and Old Christians had repopulated the peninsula, and land became a scarce commodity. Surviving Moriscos often still held the better-tilled and irrigated lands. Because of larger family sizes, their numbers increased faster than did the Christian population. Thus, in a final move, the Moriscos were expelled from Spain between 1609 and 1614. In Valencia, where they lived closely intermingled with the Christian population (map 4.1), they were given a mere three days to board ships; elsewhere they were allowed a few weeks and given permission to take with them their movable possessions. Valencia lost one-third of its population, and other areas less. Those expelled had to pay their own fare to North Africa. In Portugal, where some Muslims had remained as slaves after the expulsion of 1497, their presence was prohibited in Lisbon in 1621 and in the rest of Portugal in 1641. Estimates range from some 270,000 or 300,000 to perhaps even half a million men, women, and children who were deported. Damage "to the agriculture and productive industry of Spain, resulting from the exile of so large a body of its most efficient workers" was lasting. Venetian envoys repeatedly remarked upon the "aversion to labor, which was contemptuously regarded as dishonoring" among the Christian population. Who was to labor became the major issue in Iberian transatlantic colonial conquest.[6]

North African societies received a boost from the refugees' skills. In thirteenth-century (seventh-century M.E.) Tunis, the bulk of the inhabitants originated from Andalusia, and Sicilian immigrants lived in Algiers, Tunis, and Kairouan. In 1530 the Ottoman admiral Khayr ad-Dīn Pasha, of Greek origin, evacuated Muslims from Spain. From 1600 to 1610, 30,000 Moriscos arrived from Agde, Languedoc, alone. The roughly 48,000 Andalusian refugees in Tunis developed new suburbs and villages. They considered themselves superior to local people, did not intermarry, and remained linguistically separate by continuing to speak Spanish and Catalan. They made agricultural improvements and built irrigation canals—and even brought in Dutch engineers for advice. The city's Council of Ten had eight members of Andalusian descent. But the refugees faced hostility from local people and persecution because their Hispanic religio-cultural practices were considered heretical.[7]

4.2 Continuing Persecution: Anti-Jewish Pogroms and Expulsions

The Latin Church circumscribed the socioeconomic and political position of Jews ever more narrowly by the papal decrees of 1078 and conciliar pronouncements of 1179 and 1215. In the Mediterranean World, the deeply engrained integration of civilizations, commercial enterprises, and scholarly work at first reduced the impact of these limitations. In the different Northwest European World, however, the crusaders could be utilized for pogroms after 1096; states expelled entire Jewish communities from the late thirteenth century onward; and during the fourteenth-century plagues, persecutions assumed continent-wide dimensions. Mass flight transferred substantial parts of the Sephardic Jews to the Ottoman Empire and of the Ashkenazim to

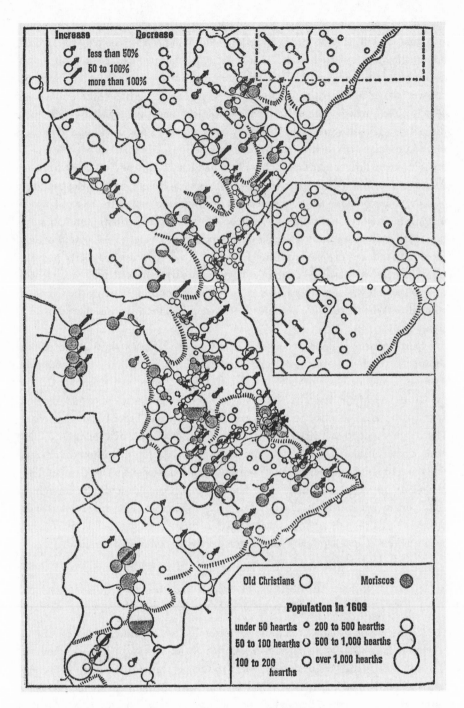

Increase | Decrease
less than 50%
50 to 100%
more than 100%

Old Christians ◯   Moriscos ⬤

Population in 1609
under 50 hearths   200 to 500 hearths
50 to 100 hearths   500 to 1,000 hearths
100 to 200 hearths   over 1,000 hearths

4.1　Moriscos and Christians in Valencia between 1565 and 1609

Polish-Lithuanian territories (map 4.2). The so-called Gypsies were persecuted and killed, too (see chap. 5).[8]

Rulers, magistrates, and clerics defined and restricted the position of Jews. The Church decreed that Jews should not hold important offices in Christian states and that no Jew should be placed in a position superior to any Christian. The doctrine of Jews as "serfs of the king," which prohibited them from carrying weapons even for self-defense, placed them in need of protective legislation or of contractual relationships. They had to pay in either case, and, accordingly, they were placed under the authority of the treasury in some states—as were fiscal slaves. On the municipal level, the "right of settlement" doctrine gave towns jurisdiction over the admission of newcomers. Privileged groups received encouragement and grants; less privileged ones had to pay for permission to settle; others were excluded altogether. The imposition of badges on Jews, as had happened to Muslims in Castile, perverted the tradition of visibly denoting status and life-cycle position to intentionally visible marginalization. The badge of distinction became a badge of infamy.

In economic life, guilds by definition were religious institutions to which non-Christian men or women could not be admitted. Access by Jews to urban occupations was restricted. In Western Europe, Jews could not own land, which had earlier been possible for them in Eastern Europe and the Iberian Peninsula. The Christian— and Muslim—prohibition against interest-bearing credit transactions created a demand for financiers. Specific Christian ethnoregional groups—in particular, the migrating Lombards, Cahorsians, and people of Chieri—who traditionally were engaged in finance, continued to practice their trade. But men—and occasionally women—of Jewish faith became the principal financial agents in Europe, whether lending small sums to peasants or giving huge advances to courts. The debate about usury placed Jewish creditors in a precarious position, and their expulsion or murder might serve the interests of all debtors, including the monarch who authorized such brutal measures. Western European Jewry, once a culture that encompassed a complete range of economic activities, was reduced to trading, from poor pedlar to prestigious merchant, and to money lending, from pawnbroker to banker.[9]

The arena of anti-Jewish propaganda encompassed the essential elements of life, both material and spiritual. Jewish women were said to suckle pigs, and whole communities of Jews were portrayed as being bent on murdering Christian children. They were accused of "clipping coins," that is, scratching silver off the edges, and thus cheating the poor out of food. They were charged with desecration of the host.

In northwestern Europe, those who had "taken the cross" in 1096 massacred thousands of Ashkenazi men, women, and children along their route from the Rhine valley eastward. Sporadic but recurrent violence served to terrorize Jewish communities; devastating pogroms were conducted in Norwich, England in 1144, in Frankfurt/Main in 1241, and in Roettigen, Bavaria, in 1298, to name only a few places. Each persecution ended in the flight of at least some of the survivors. State-organized mass persecution began with the expulsion of Jews from England in 1290, an exclusion that lasted until the second half of the seventeenth century. Most of the esti-

4.2 Jewish Expulsions, 11th-15th Centuries, and Gypsy Migrations, 9th-15th Centuries

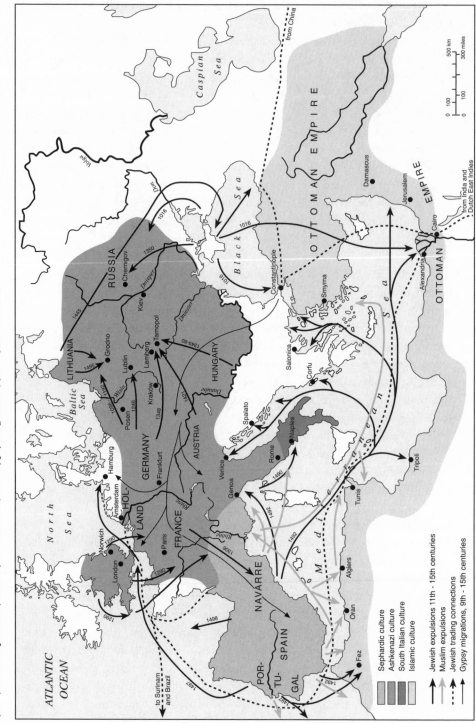

Sephardic culture
Ashkenazi culture
South Italian culture
Islamic culture

Jewish expulsions 11th - 15th centuries
Muslim expulsions
Jewish trading connections
Gypsy migrations, 9th - 15th centuries

mated 16,000 refugees headed for France. There, tolerant conditions had deteriorated since 1230, and a mass expulsion occurred in 1306. Although Jews were invited back in 1315, few responded—and all were expelled again in 1394.[10] In southern Italy and Sicily, Frederick II (1194–1250) had invited Jewish craftsmen and agricultural experts to settle. But from 1290 to 1293 the Jewish communities in the kingdom of Naples were destroyed, and expulsions from northern Urban Italy began at the same time. The terror of local pogroms intensified during the "dreadful half century" from 1298 to 1348 and set the stage for the plague-related massacres that destroyed 350 Jewish communities in German territories alone and ranged from Christian Spain to Poland-Lithuania. Refugee or returnee communities often consisted mainly of widows and children, with only a few surviving adult males. Widows worked as washerwomen and in making garments, and some were even admitted to crafts.[11]

The economics of state-imposed expulsion varied. The timing might coincide with a decline of the importance of Jewish financiers and moneylenders. It might also mirror ethno-religious competition, such as when Lombards entered the money-lending market, though French rulers also expelled the Lombards at one point. Newly emerging groups of bureaucrats from within the ruling ethnicity, as in England, might enter tax collection and state finances. Socioeconomic conflict was involved when Jewish—or any other—moneylenders unintentionally strengthened one group—for example, smallholders at a time when powerful landlords pursued a policy of enclosure. Thus the expulsion of credit-giving (Jewish) financiers—and the subsequent unavailability of money for loans—would force impoverished smallholders to depart. While the persecuted Jewish diaspora created a memory of expulsion, the smallholders "disappeared" into the ranks of vagrants, the urban poor, and the agricultural proletariat. By force of circumstance, the Jewish diaspora—in particular in Poland-Lithuania—provided shelter to Jewish exiles from England, but the descendants of displaced English smallholders found opportunities in distant communities only after emigration to North America began.

The migration of Ashkenazi Jews to Polish lands had begun as early as the first crusades, though some turned to Ottoman-ruled Balkan and Greek cities. Polish rulers from 1264 onward granted to the immigrant Ashkenazim privileges, autonomy, and freedom of commerce to further economic development in their respective realms. Mass in-migration from the second half of the fourteenth century, however, and competition with resident urban merchants and artisans—themselves descendants of earlier German-language immigrants—caused conflict and segregation into ghettos. Their religion's emphasis on written texts and schooling made Jews the most highly educated group in East Central Europe. In cities like Kraków Jews mingled with Italian Renaissance architects, German and Flemish artists, and scholars from many ethnocultural backgrounds. During the religiously tolerant "Golden Age of Poland" under the last Jagiellonian kings, community self-administration received lasting sanction in 1551, and East Central Europe became a center of Jewish culture for two centuries. But the Ashkenazim's position as middlemen between the enserfed rural population and urban markets made them both a particularly important and vulnerable group: restrictions on permanent settlement and purchase of real estate were secured in Kiev by Christian merchants starting in 1503; massacres occurred during the 1648 Cossack Uprising; the status of Jews was diminished to subservience when Kiev was annexed to Russia in 1667; and, finally there was the Russian Orthodox Christian Church's virulent anti-Semitism (see chaps. 12.1 and 13.5).

In the thirteenth-century Iberian societies, Jews retained their positions in high offices and, contrary to canonical law, were permitted to build synagogues. But their role as tax collectors and the ostentatious display of wealth by the Jewish elite negatively affected their interaction with Christian populations. Inflammatory sermons by both lowly monks and high-placed clerics increased the Christians' propensity for violence. After the massacre of several thousand Jews in Seville in 1391, the surviving women and children were sold into slavery. Hunger riots as well as attacks against brigands, French merchants, and nobles spread from Córdoba, via Madrid, to Aragon and pointed to the broad social discontent.[12]

In Castile, forced conversion or high ransom payments were imposed on Jews beginning in the fourteenth century. Highly educated *conversos*, also known by the more derogatory term *marranos* (pigs), stayed on in their high offices, and they and the Spanish nobility intermarried. The Inquisition persecuted Jews, Muslims, and *conversos* alike. Among the converted, some continued to practice their former religion secretly; others were simply accused of doing so; many of these so-called *judaizers* were burned alive in autos-da-fé. In the 1480s, many cities confined Jews to separate quarters, then the diocesan authorities of Seville, Córdoba, and Cadiz expelled them altogether. Tens of thousands were forced to depart. Even though Jewish financiers had supported the policies of Ferdinand and Isabella and had financed their campaigns against the Muslims of Granada, under clerical pressure the Catholic monarchs decreed on 30 March 1492 that all Jews were to leave within three months. Estimates of refugees vary from 41,000 *families* to 800,000 *persons*; most recent scholarship counts between 150,000 and 165,000 emigrants, an additional 50,000 baptized ones, and another 20,000 who died during the flight. Perhaps two-thirds of the Spanish Jews went to Portugal, only to be faced with forced baptism and expulsion in 1496–97.[13]

Iberian Jewry dispersed throughout the Mediterranean World. In Muslim North Africa, communities in Fez, Sétif, and Tunis, as well as in Cairo and Alexandria, were divided into ethnic quarters according to the regional origins of the refugees. Other Jews settled in Palestine and Syria, where they differed from local coreligionists because of their less strict observance of religious injunctions and, as a consequence, met with prejudices and hostility. In the Ottoman Empire, towns with existing Jewish communities along the coasts of the Aegean Sea proved particularly attractive. Sultan Bāyezīd II (c.1447–1512) reportedly commented after the arrival of some 90,000 refugees: "You call Ferdinand a wise king, he who impoverishes his country and enriches our own." They received encouragement and, if impoverished, help (see chap. 5.1). Next to Poland-Lithuania, the Ottoman Empire became the second center of Jewish culture and commerce. Both societies suffered from the disintegration of the political structures of the host states at the end of the seventeenth century.[14]

The Europe of Latin Christendom thus lost some of its most active populations in the economic arena and interrupted its interaction with Jewish culture and scholarship. Eight centuries of Iberian *convivencia* (coexistence) ended in the late fifteenth century. Only Lombardy and the kingdom of Naples accepted some of the refugees, and a group of Portuguese Jews converged in Amsterdam. Their thriving mercantile community assumed a position in the Dutch economy that lasted until the German occupation in World War II. To the present, this kind of coexistence with either Jews or Muslims has not resumed.

Developments in fifteenth-century Spain initiated a type of exclusion that was to become a dominant aspect in the construction of the Other. The Inquisition buttressed its struggle for control over all aspects of life by a new concept of *limpieza de sangre* (purity of Christian blood). Pure lineage or ascribed "race" became a prerequisite for entering military orders, administrative positions, and university teaching. Ironically, under these rules, the "Catholic Monarchs"—descended from *converso* families among others—could not have been crowned. At the bottom of Spanish society, labeling in terms of sexuality and religion also became common. A casual laborer in 1647 had this version of "unclean" lineage: "I worked for Martín for six months, and he still has not paid me the money owed to me. He is a cuckold, and he is also a secret Jew, and his wife is the bastard daughter of a Moor."[15] Proof of blood lineage became a tool for the Inquisition and Old Christians in their power struggles with other ranking groups in society. Since intermarriage over generations had made ethnic lineage a category impossible to define, *limpieza* became a mechanism of control and rapacity rather than being, in modern terms, a racist theory. As the certifying institution, the Inquisition was moved "not by zeal for the faith and the salvation of souls, but by lust for wealth," according to a papal comment of 1482. In a way, it continued the Christian conquerors' strategy of amassing booty. But, in regard to the future, it helped to expel middle-class elements of society characterized by Otherness. The concept of *limpieza* also suggests new constructions of race at a time when contacts with people of Africa and the Americas intensified. No longer did Mediterranean merchants pursue business and profit intercivilizationally regardless of color of skin and religion. Politicians and planters came to covet heathen territories and Black or Brown labor forces.[16]

4.3   Internecine Strife: Christians against Christians

Expulsion, flight, and emigration, as well as mutilation and massacre, were also part of Latin Christendom's internal history. From the tenth century onward, monastic reform orders and so-called heretical movements spread their ideas. Adherents of the latter were persecuted and fled. Adherents of the former migrated across the continent in proselytizing missions. English Lollards and Bohemian Hussites in the fourteenth and fifteenth centuries linked economic exploitation with religious dissent, and many had to flee. With the early-sixteenth-century reformations and subsequent counter-reformations, English Puritans, Dutch Protestants, and French Huguenots fled in large numbers across Europe and, from the 1620s on, to North America. European states offered refuge because of the economic potential of middle-class artisans, manufacturers, and merchants. In North America, William Penn settled dissenters both for spiritual reasons and to populate his colony. Religious refugees became economic migrants when they crossed state borders (map 4.3).

Alternative approaches to religion involved poorer social strata, rural as well as urban, whose means did not enable them to emigrate. Itinerant preachers and non-enclosed religious women ministered to them. The emphasis on personal religious experience increased women's roles in religion, and as a result persecutions became gendered. Women could hardly emigrate on their own, and the labeling of unconventionally religious women as witches in a papal edict of 1484 resulted in the killing of perhaps as many as one million in a mania that lasted into the eighteenth century. The migratory consequences for religious movements appealing to the poor are difficult to ascertain. Did some peasants emigrate after their revolts had been quelled, and did some women move to societies with less persecution?

On the other hand, ethnic characteristics of domination and economic status were clearly related to previous migrations and expressed in terms of religion: in Spain, a "French" queen and archbishop nullified edicts of tolerance; an "Italian" queen ordered the persecution of Huguenots in France; a "foreign" clergy was criticized in England; a self-styled "German nation" within the multiethnic "Holy Roman Empire" protested against "Welsche"—that is, Italian, French, and other foreign clergy—and accused them of practicing simony, selling indulgences, and generally corrupt behavior. The ethnicization of Others of high standing had implications for lowly Others of the same cultural origin. Persecution would follow ascribed ethnicity rather than status.[17]

The migrations of adherents of the larger dissenting movements have been frequently studied. An internal crusade between 1208 and 1229 destroyed in southern France the Albigensians, who incorporated Bulgarian-Eastern Church traditions but were mainly a movement of the lower classes, and the Waldensians, named after a Lyons merchant. The survivors who emigrated carried their ideas to northern Italy and Central Europe.[18]

Reformers turned to vernacular languages and translated the Latin Bible, thus democratizing worship. The first English-language Bible of the Oxford preacher John Wycliffe (c.1330–84) influenced the late fourteenth-century mass reform movement of the Lollards before it was driven underground. Bohemian students who had moved to English universities when Richard II and Anne of Bohemia-Luxembourg married in 1382, carried Wycliffe's teachings back to Bohemia, as did some of the nobles who had accompanied the new English queen.

In Bohemia, the Czech Hussites rose against the German-language Church, urban middle classes, and rulers. Jan Hus (c.1369–1415), a teacher at the University of Prague and popular as a preacher in the vernacular Czech language, was called to

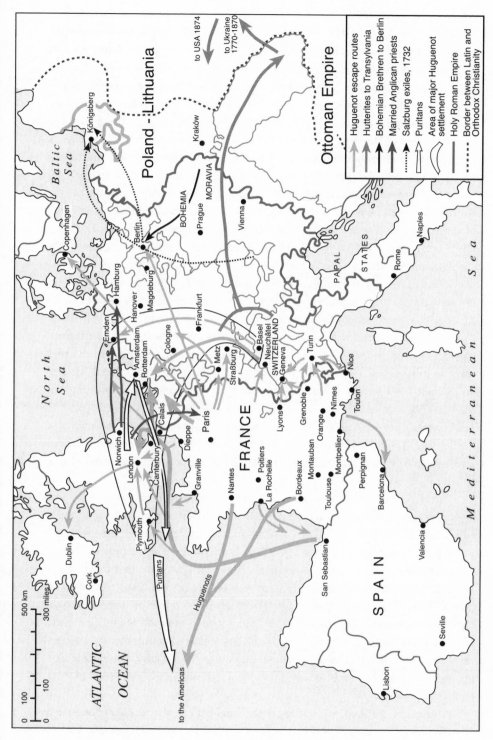

4·3 Christian Flight and Migrations

defend his views at the Council of Constance after Prague's German-language professors seceded and migrated to Leipzig in 1409. Hus, despite a promise of safe conduct, was burned at the stake. From 1420 to 1433 religious wars devastated much of Bohemia. Emigrant Hussites joined with Waldensian and Catharist migrants, and in 1467 one group formed itself into the Bohemian Brethren, who numbered perhaps 100,000 by 1500. When coerced into emigration from the 1540s on, mostly single families left; but in some cases entire communities of Bohemain Brethren moved to Silesia, Poland, or Hungary. Others settled in Saxony, on the lands of Count Zinzendorf (his estate Herrnhut among other places), and in Berlin. "We left, myself and my wife. I carried our little daughter Catherine in a wicker basket on my back. We walked at night and hid during the day for six nights. . . . Once my daughter fell out of the basket over my head—for some time we could not find her in the snow." After 1620 the Habsburg counter-reformation and re-Germanization forced more to leave. While wholesale expulsion was not possible since as much as three-quarters of the population sympathized with the Brethren, war and emigration reduced Bohemia's population from 1.7 to 0.9 million in the next four decades. Emigration continued to the early eighteenth century, and subsequently some communities moved to North America. They carried with them new ideas about living industrious lives to please God, concepts that came to be known as the "Protestant Ethic" of the middle classes.[19]

Criticism of the Latin Church culminated in the Reformation in Saxony (Luther, 1517), in Zurich and Geneva (Zwingli and Calvin), and in Scotland (Knox).[20] Except for Zwingli, these reformers had to flee prosecution at least once in their lives.[21] The reformers, in turn, forced dissidents in their own ranks to flee. Labeled "sects" or "enthusiasts," the Anabaptists, the Hutterites, the Mennonites and Amish, and the Baptists and Quakers met with relentless persecution. The survivors, after migrations across principalities and continents, settled in Bohemia, Prussia, Russia, and, finally, North America.[22]

The large Protestant movements[23] of the Germanies, of England and its Irish colony, of France, and of the Netherlands experienced forced migrations that proved to have a lasting impact. Refugees with economic skills were settled in the receiving polities in privileged positions and consequently might face hostility from local populations. Priests or pastors were imprisoned and were compelled either to convert or to leave. Dutch Catholics paid bribes, soon termed "recognition fees," to officials for nonenforcement of the exclusion laws. These payments might be compared to the tax on non-Muslims in the Islamic states. Subjects had to accept the religion of the respective territorial ruler. This implied mass conversion each time a ruler converted or when a new ruler of a different denomination took over. Emigration to neighboring territories as an alternative was granted as a right in 1648 in the Treaty of Westphalia.[24]

In England, Parliament confirmed the establishment of the Anglican state-church in 1534. From 1534 to 1539, the extensive properties of the Catholic Church were sold to the landed gentry and urban bourgeoisie in the greatest transfer of property in modern English history. The dissolution of the monasteries forced monks and nuns to re-migrate to their families or to emigrate. Married Anglican priests and bishops depended on the position taken by a particular queen or king toward reform and marriage. They were forced to flee to the continent or to send away their wives and children, were recalled, fled again, or were granted leave to emigrate before penalties on marriage were reimposed. Exiles established churches in German and Swiss towns and settled permanently. Reformers from the continent, followed by their wives and children, sought refuge in England. The secret Catholic Church in England trained and ordained its priests abroad, while English women who wanted to serve as nuns or lay sisters migrated to the continent. Lay "English Ladies" refused enclosure and gave refuge to Irish, French, German, Hungarian, and Italian sisters who had been denied separate orders or nonenclosure by the male Catholic hierarchy.[25]

In Ireland, the anti-Catholic measures taken by the English crown were part of the colonial expropriation of "the Natives." The English rulers confiscated Church properties, settled immigrants, and distributed land to favorites. The Anglo-Irish ("Old English"), the New English, and the Ulster Scots emerged as cultural or ethnic groups. Soldiers of the conquest who were settled in Ireland by the authorities provided information for other settlers. The suppression of the last great Irish rebellion in 1602, and the flight of the Catholic earls five years later, made available additional landholdings for Protestant immigrants. Ulster Plantation received tens of thousands of Scottish and English Protestants. By the late seventeenth century, three-fourths of Irish agricultural land was in the hands of English, Scottish, and Anglo-Irish immigrant Protestants. Their descendants, together with impoverished Irish peasants, migrated to the North American colonies from the eighteenth century onward, and the twentieth-century Protestant-Catholic class conflicts in Northern Ireland originated in these colonial-religious migrations of the early seventeenth century.[26]

Sizable dissenting groups in England wanted to purify further the new Anglican Church. These "Puritans"—fragmented into Separatists, Presbyterians, and Congregationalists—voluntarily or under persecution emigrated first to Dutch cities and then to North America. The Pilgrim "fathers"—together with mothers, children, and servants—founded Plymouth Plantation in 1620 and the Massachusetts Bay Colony settlements in the 1630s. They laid the basis for one of the important regional cultures in North America—just as Muslim refugees did in North Africa and Jewish refugees did in Poland-Lithuania. The Plymouth migrants had first moved to Amsterdam in 1608 and then to Leiden a year later. They enjoyed religious freedom in Holland but were excluded from the guilds. They feared the loss of contact with English language and culture, especially for their children. Just over a decade after settlement in Massachusetts, a doctrinal split and a conflict over gender roles again propelled Roger Williams, Anne Hutchinson, and others to emigrate. The religious migrations bound for North America were financed by merchant adventurers, who expected returns on their investments.[27]

In France, the Huguenots pursued religious reformation and acted as a political party under the ambitious Guise family. In the negotiations with the crown and in religious civil wars, women played important religious-diplomatic as well as warmongering roles. During the second war, Huguenot pastors were ordered to leave the country. Several thousand, perhaps as many as 20,000 Huguenots of both sexes and all ages, were massacred on 24 August 1572, the night of St. Bartholomew. The 1598 Edict of Nantes granted toleration and integration into French political and cultural life. The resumption of the wars in 1628 and the revocation of the edict in 1685, however, forced 200,000 men, women, and children to emigrate to Swiss cantons, Dutch provinces, England, and Ireland, as well as to German-Protestant principalities, Brandenburg-Prussia in particular.[28] Earlier migrations had taken Huguenots into Alsace, especially Strasbourg, and later they would migrate either directly or via England to North America. Some could carry their movable possessions, but others lost everything.[29] In times when departure from France was prohibited, those who were caught while trying to escape were often sent into galley-slavery, which brought them into contact with enslaved Turkish prisoners. Huguenots, in turn, also occasionally expelled Catholics from territories that they controlled. Some of these refugees settled in Seville.[30]

Huguenots were the largest group of refugees within Christendom, and their migrations provided sizable input to receiving economies. The community of Canterbury, where refugees arrived in three waves from the 1540s to the beginning of the eighteenth century, can serve as an example of community composition, economic activities, and religious pressures from the host society. Registers for the period from 1590 to 1644 list more than 2,100 English-born residents and about 1,350 foreign-born ones from Flanders (41.8 percent), Nainaut (Henegouwen) (13 percent), Artois (8.1 percent), and other Dutch provinces. Thus the community was internally heterogeneous in terms of origin and language and by generation. The "Walloon parish," like other "foreign churches" in Canterbury received a charter that granted permission for innovative economic activities in textile making ("in Flanders fashion") while it prohibited competition with local textile crafts. It also regulated the social and political position of the community. In the 1640s the dogmatic Anglican archbishop William Laud succeeded in restricting the charter's freedom-of-religion clause to the foreign-born immigrant generation. After vigorous protest, the community gave in and second-generation immigrants began to attend Anglican services. Some, however, emigrated again. On the whole, the refugees were well regarded for improving English manufactures.[31]

The Netherlands, sections of which had successively come under Spanish-Habsburg rule from 1477 to 1543, consisted of the French-speaking ethnically Walloon areas in the south and the northern Dutch provinces with their powerful cities. During the war of independence from 1568 to 1648, thousands of northern Dutch Protestants fled the Catholic-Spanish multiethnic mercenary armies to Frankfurt/Main and Hamburg, other Protestant German towns, and London. Within the Dutch provinces, an estimated 60,000 to 80,000 fled northward to escape Spanish-Catholic persecution between 1500 and 1600. Many more left because of subsequent economic stagnation. They spoke French or dialects that differed from those of the northern Dutch. The Protestant Urban Netherlands, relying on the skills, expertise, and manpower of the immigrants, became the strongest mercantile and manufacturing center of Europe during the so-called Dutch golden age of the seventeenth century (see chap. 12.3).[32]

Following Luther's reformist declaration in 1517, the news of his challenge spread fast. His residence in the town of Wittenberg became a center of attraction for clerics from Italy, France, Portugal, Britain, Scotland, Poland, Hungary, and Finland, as well as from South Slav and Balkan peoples. A century later, the warfare related to Latin Christendom's reform and fragmentation ended with the Thirty Years' War of 1618-48: mercenaries of many ethnic backgrounds crisscrossed Central Europe, one-third of the population was killed or died as a consequence of the warfare, hundreds of thousands fled re-Catholicization. Religious expulsion and flight continued for another century or more (see chap. 12.4). In Russia, Tsarina Elizabeth Petrovna (1709–62) ended religious toleration and imposed conversion on both Muslims and Jews. In the West, the repopulation policies of mercantilist rulers marked the next half-century.

5

Ottoman Society, Europe, and the
Beginnings of Colonial Contact

A variety of cultural, political, and social developments, some of which had been discernible for some time, began to change the European and Islamic Worlds from 1400 on. In the southeast, the Ottoman Empire expanded and formalized structures of ethnic coexistence that had been informally practiced in the Mediterranean World. In the northwest, dynastic fragmentation was supplemented by a concept of *universitas*, a European unity. Scholarly migrations that spanned the continent forged a sense of a European culture. In Nuremberg, scholars and merchants combined to write a chronicle of the world, that is, their known world of commerce and urban life across the globe. After ten years, the magnum opus, the *Schedelsche Weltchronik*, was published in Latin in 1493—the compiler, printer, and illustrators all lived on one street. In neighboring Augsburg, the famous Albrecht Dürer in 1508 portrayed an "Ethiopian" who worked in one of the mercantile houses as a clerk. As the core of worldwide commerce, urban society developed in spurts. The concentration of political life in capitals, sedentary courts, and growing administrations changed the role of the state; in economic life, state-chartered companies of merchant adventurers replaced the networks of large commercial regions extending over multiple polities. From the southwest, from the Iberian Peninsula outward, the old type of interaction by commerce and cultural exchange (brokerage) was reshaped into trading patterns based on power. State-supported merchants penetrated lesser-developed regions as well as highly developed but less powerful ones.

To some extent, northeastern Europe became part of the new *universitas*. Kraków had long been a city of commercial and cultural exchange, and from Prague, as an intellectual center, ideas radiated outward. The region's urban constitutional structures continued to reflect those of German towns, but the growth of serfdom and the powerful position of the nobility retarded the emergence of bourgeois societies and commercial outreach. The "local parasitism of a military class" (McNeill) prevented the self-articulation of peasant and artisanal interests. Further east, the Muscovy Empire developed commercial connections to northern Europe through the Baltic Sea and continued the previous connection to the Mediterranean World via the Black Sea.[1]

By the time of the Renaissance, Latin Christendom had disengaged itself from other civilizations and constructed Islamic culture as the Other, to be fought in its political form, the Ottoman Empire. The Ottoman sultans, in turn, adopted Sunni orthodoxy and persecuted heresies. As a result, Islamic scholars no longer sought an exchange of ideas and knowledge. Jewish culture, segregated into Eastern Europe, flowered until it succumbed to economic decline. Cultural contacts with Africa and Asia were reduced to the importation of slaves and spices respectively. The curiosity that had been part of twelfth-century exchanges gave way to the profit motive and the desire for domination.

The construction of the Other came to include a new life-threatening aspect when the ethno-religiously distinct Gypsies,[2] who presumably moved out of north-western India when Arab rulers imposed themselves in the ninth and tenth centuries, reached the Balkans in the eleventh and western Europe in the fifteenth century. Few in number and working in itinerant crafts and as entertainers, they influenced neither politics nor commerce nor scholarship. The gatekeepers of European identity developed a new and deadly approach toward this tiny minority. Gypsies and those labeled as such came to be seen as Others who were to be denied the right to existence. While Gypsies could be killed with impunity, Jews were persecuted but remained part of economic and cultural life, and Africans were enslaved but remained part of the labor force.[3]

5.1 Ethnic Coexistence in Ottoman Society

Patterns of stratified coexistence of different ethnosocial groups had been developed by the Normans along the shores of the Atlantic, by the crusader migrants in Palestine, and by merchants in their Baltic *Kontore*, Mediterranean *funduqs*, or Black Sea colonies. Merchants' colonies and Jewish communities administered their own internal affairs. Recognition and acceptance of differences without attempts to proselytize were fundamental to all forms of coexistence. In the Turko-Arab-Islamic World, the Ottoman state codified coexistence at a time when the Latin Church exorcised peaceful ethnoreligious relations from its realm.

Asia Minor, hellenized under Greek rule and christianized by Byzantine emperors, had been the scene of both manifold involuntary population transfers and voluntary migrations involving numerous peoples: Christian refugees from Arab lands; Greek Cypriots; demobilized soldiers of Frankish, Russian, English, Norman, German, Bulgaric, Saracen, or Albanian background; as well as Kurdish, Georgian, Syrian, and Armenian peoples.[4] Eastern Christians' contacts with nomadic Turkish peoples from Central Asia began in the eleventh century when Seljuq armies advanced into Palestine and Turkoman people migrated into Anatolia. Turkish armies, originally there at the invitation of the Byzantine emperor, conquered most of Anatolia. These nomadic newcomers settled, and out of their principalities the Ottoman Empire emerged.[5]

Victorious in battle, the Ottoman state lost the ideological war unleashed by the

Latin Church and by feudal lords in response to their class's annihilation by the conquerors. To finance the war against "the Turks," common Christian people were required to pay a "Turk tax." Thus, "the Turk" seemed to reduce the standard of living of everyman and everywoman. Western scholarship, subservient to the feudal-Christian view, has described "the Turks" as destructive of Christian European civilization.[6] Edward Said has demonstrated how occidental intellectuals constructed "the Orient" as a reflection of the European world. Travelers and observers departed (and continue to depart) with an "internally structured archive" that conditioned (and still conditions) their experiences and perceptions. The term "Turk" had no precise meaning among Western Europeans when they first heard about them through captivity narratives (as later American colonists learned about "Indians"): Turks were characterized by cruelty and cupidity, drunkenness and gluttony; by pride and showmanship combined with cowardice; by trickery and roguery; and, of course, by lascivious conduct. Ottoman society did not ransom its captured subjects except for a few high-ranking persons, and thus no counternarratives of captivity in Christian states appeared. Ottoman prisoners of war of many ethnicities were used in Christian states as slaves, servants, and workers. In literature, they appear as subservient, private slaves who serve as go-betweens bearing love letters, a role that imparted to them a romantic-exotic "Oriental" touch. Occidental authors of fiction confused the Mediterranean Others, Turks and Moriscos, with each other.

In popular songs of protest, however, the negative stereotype could be turned on its head to point out to local authorities that they were worse:

> You who've killed us with your noose,
> With red-hot irons and like abuse,
> Who've left us hungry here to die
> Or frightened, to the Turk to fly.

This skit was sung on the streets of Naples in the 1580s during a food shortage when any protest was suppressed.[7]

Migration and the Peoples of the Empire

While "the Turk" spread in Europe's fiction, the actual Ottoman Empire did advance westward. The empire established a foothold in the Balkans—a Turkish term meaning "wooded mountains"—in the 1350s and conquered Serbian, Bosnian, and Bulgarian territories from the 1370s to the 1440s. The ethnic composition of local populations changed substantially with the arrival of Turks as slave soldiers in Muslim armies. In 1526 most of historic Hungary came under Ottoman rule after the battle of Mohács; Transylvania's three "nations"—the Magyars (the main group of modern-day Hungarians), Szeklers, and Germans—with the Romanians, who were not designated as a nation, were formed into a vassal state in 1540. But Vienna, twice the target of Ottoman sieges, was successfully defended by multiethnic mercenaries. Hungary remained part of the Ottoman realm for one and a half centuries, and the Balkans for more than four, but no major shifts of local populations occurred. Peasants from war-devastated areas, however, migrated to other villages to join viable communities; those assigned to Ottoman warriors escaped to lands of the imperial fisc, where conditions were decidedly better.

To the east, the Italian colonies in the eastern Mediterranean and along the coasts of the Black Sea lost their independence after 1463, and Kaffa was captured in 1475. To the south, the empire expanded to the Persian border and to Algiers. It defeated the rival Mamluk empire of Syria and Egypt in 1516–17 (map 5.1).[8]

To incorporate conquered populations for the benefit of the empire, Ottoman authorities used *sürgün* or forced migration: to establish an ethnic Turkish presence among, for example, peoples in the Balkans; or to resettle rebellious peoples in regions where control was easier. Also, to assure the obedience of those left in their traditional territories, parts of a population could be resettled in or near Istanbul, or their rulers' sons might be placed at the imperial court as hostages. The state thus avoided both the cost of a permanent occupation force and the imposition of military units on local populations. In addition, merchants, artisans, and other subjects could be ordered to resettle in places where their services were needed by the imperial administration. Magistrates selected families from among experienced craftsmen and traders who might later ask relatives to join them. Thus *sürgün* migration could be advantageous to those involuntarily involved because of the superior opportunities at their destination.[9]

During wars of expansion, inhabitants of towns who surrendered without siege could continue their lives and economic activities unmolested. On the other hand, inhabitants of towns that had resisted by force of arms were ordered to leave or were enslaved. Their movable possessions fell into the hands of pillaging soldiers, and their houses and gardens were given to in-migrants recruited from Anatolia or to Jewish refugees escaping pogrom-prone Christian Europe. Moriscos arrived in sizable numbers.[10]

Although territorial expansion of the empire was conceived of as a holy war to extend the realm of Islam, non-Islamic populations were granted the status of protected subjects (*dhimmis* or *zimmis*). The institution of the *millet* permitted self-administration of ethnic and ethno-religious groups under a leadership acceptable to the Ottoman rulers. Such leaders could be drawn from hereditary elites who sent sons to Istanbul as hostages. More often, however, traditional spiritual leaders replaced secular rulers as spokespersons. In other cases, after physical elimination of an indigenous nobility, Turkish warlords (*gâzî*) and tax collectors with their cavalry (*sipâhî*) became administrators of newly created tax districts (*timars*).

Spiritual elites, freed from sharing power with temporal lords, supported the sultan, and so did the common people, who could continue their traditional customs and beliefs unmolested. Two features, however, were special to non-Muslims. They had to pay a special tax, the *haraç*, and Christians were subject to the *devsirme*, a levy

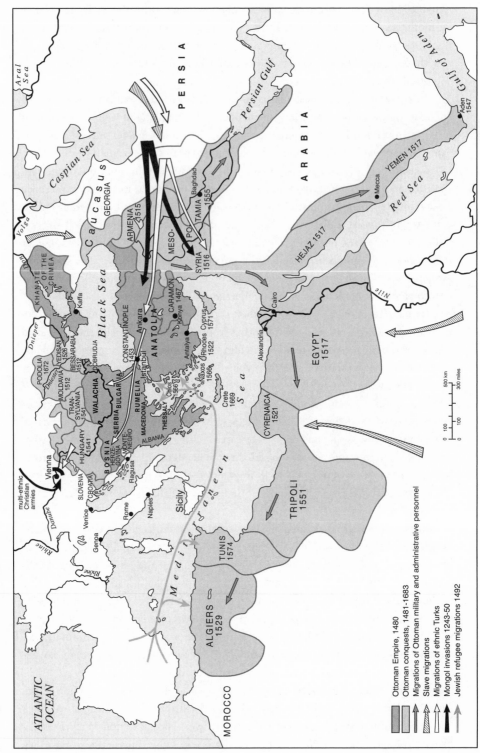

5.1   Migration and the Ottoman Empire, 1300–1683

of boys for state service. A third feature, specific dress codes for Jews and Christians including a prohibition on wearing finery and silk, was often evaded, and wealthy Jews disregarded it.

Christians were split into numerous groups that feuded over doctrines concerning the nature of Christ and observed widely varying rituals. For Greek-Byzantine and Russian-Orthodox Christians, Ottoman rule was a liberating experience after their oppression by the Latin Church and its crusaders. Latin Christians, on the other hand, looked to Rome for liberation and in turn were regarded as rebellious and potential supporters of invasion forces. Other eastern Christians—the Nestorian or Monophysite Copts in Egypt, Jacobites in Syria, Armenian believers, or the Maronites in Lebanon—had been regarded as schismatics by both the Papal and the Greek Churches. Under the Ottoman rulers, they led independent and protected lives.[11]

The legal position of Jews was superior to that in any state of Christian Europe. They were free to practice their religion and to take up any profession. Consequently, they, too, remained loyal to the system and rose high in the sixteenth-century political elite. They received a grant of land at Lake Tiberias in Galilee to settle Italian-Jewish refugees. Islamic prohibitions notwithstanding, Jews did build new synagogues. Ashkenazi and Sephardic Jews, as well as Romaniote Greek-speaking ones from former Byzantine areas, formed a lively and internally heterogeneous community that was augmented by Jews who had been liberated from Christian rule whenever new territories were conquered. Jewish craftsmen and merchants were invited to settle or, through *sürgün*, were settled wherever needed. Bursa and Edirne housed particularly large Jewish communities, as did most port towns. Given the persecution of Hispanic Jewry—perhaps more than 100,000 were offered asylum— the pogroms all over Western Europe, and the disintegration of the Arab caliphates, the Ottoman Empire became a center of Jewish culture and economic life, equal to the Ashkenazi community in Polish-Lithuanian territories. When Baghdad was conquered in 1534, the remnants of the Arab-Jewish community there were also incorporated.[12]

Faced with Venetian mercantile and Latin religious hostility, Constantinople had dwindled to between 30,000 and 40,000 inhabitants of Greek-Byzantine and Italian origin. Some "Franks"—that is, English, Dutch, Venetians, and French—remained in the city or its suburb, Pera. Once Constantinople was conquered in 1453 and renamed Istanbul, the policy of repopulating the city after the centuries of decline began with the sultan inviting Christian inhabitants who had fled to return and resettle in their dwellings. Along with Greeks and Armenians, Genoese and Venetian merchants came and settled all over town, while Jews originally lived in their traditional quarter. Second, the sultan provided some Christian prisoners of war with housing and allowed them to ransom themselves with their earnings. Third, governors of Anatolian and Rumelian provinces had to send 4,000 families to the city, where they were provided with homes and work. Fourth, over the next few decades, families from newly conquered cities were ordered to migrate to Istanbul. Once established, these involuntary migrants often served as hosts for friends and former neighbors who followed them through voluntary migration. New populations were settled to help provision Istanbul. Later, the Dobrudja region on the western coast of the Black Sea was revitalized by hundreds of newly founded villages, the repopulation of port towns, and the construction of granaries to supply the capital. About one million ethnic Turks lived as agriculturalists in the Balkans and Dobrudja. Thirty thousand peasants, mainly Serbians, were settled in villages near the capital to produce food.

In 1477, twenty-five years after its liberation or conquest, Istanbul counted some 100,000 inhabitants. A majority of them were Muslims; about one-third were Greek Orthodox Christians; and 15 percent were Jewish. The rest were Armenians, Greeks from Karaman, non-Muslims from Kaffa, Gypsies, and other Europeans. Egyptian artisans came as specialists for tile making and ceramics production. In-migration swelled the population to 400,000 in the first half of the sixteenth century, and the population nearly doubled again before the century's end, making Istanbul the largest city in Europe, a rank that Muslim cities in Iberia had held in earlier centuries. Problems of provisioning and maintaining the water supply provoked decrees to restrict immigration to the capital.[13]

Anatolia and the Ottoman Balkans were crisscrossed by a network of roads. These included the old eastbound merchant routes, pilgrim routes to Mecca, as well as newly constructed trade links. Within this network, hostels and bridges were built, and caravanseries were opened. Turkoman nomads and soldier-farmers were brought in to guard and maintain them and to cultivate neighboring rural areas. In addition, semireligious fraternities, dervishes (religious men similar to Christian monks), and immigrants built hospices for their own purposes and organized themselves into chartered *zâviyes* to secure the safety of travelers and to provide them with accommodation. Towns developed around such government-sponsored or privately initiated nuclei. Such chartered lodging places were the origin of most fourteenth- and fifteenth-century villages in Anatolia and the Balkans. The sultan used the *zâviye* institution to resettle villages destroyed during the sixteenth-century Persian wars.

For transport along the routes, camels, horses, or mules were hired from eastern Turkish or southern Arab nomads. Their drivers moved with them, as did carters. In the 1521 campaign against Belgrade, 30,000 camels were needed, and 10,000 wagons carried provisions from the fertile regions of the Lower Danube. The volume of trade had increased massively when the *pax mongolica* permitted resumption of the China trade, and Bursa became the main exchange. Italian merchants traded their imports for Chinese porcelain, and Arab merchants carried goods from India. Over time, Ottoman subjects, Armenians from Kaffa, Jews, Greeks, and Muslim Turks replaced the Italian merchants. Thus trade with Asia, which according to Christian European contemporary propaganda and historiography had been cut off by the sultans, continued in full bloom.[14]

The Nonethnic Structures of a Multiethnic Empire

The Ottoman rulers often annihilated conquered nobilities and abolished feudal dues and compulsory labor. The resultant changes could be dramatic. Serbian peasants, for example, who had labored two days a week for their Serbian lords, worked as tax-paying Ottoman subjects a mere three days a year for their new lords. Thus, agrarian populations often saw the new rulers as liberators. According to Inalcik,

> The protective administration of the Islamic state, with its religious laws and guarantees of tolerance, succeeded the terrifying raids of the *gâzîs* [nomadic warlords]. Furthermore, the protection of the peasantry as a source of tax revenue was a traditional policy of the near-eastern state. . . . The Otto-man Empire was thus to become a true "Frontier Empire," a cosmopolitan state, treating all creeds and races [ethnicities] as one, which was to unite the Orthodox Christian Balkans and Muslim Anatolia in a single state.

While most affairs were regulated by community magistrates, the centralized admin-istration was represented locally by *kadis* before whom lords and peasants were equal. For two centuries, until about 1600, this structure could and did mediate conflicts and check abuses by the powerful.[15]

Towns were divided administratively into quarters and these in turn into cultur-ally distinct districts (*malhalle*) centered on a mosque, synagogue, or church. Reli-gious institutions were responsible for the inhabitants' social and cultural welfare. As head of the district, the imam, rabbi, or priest was supported by secular officials. Immigrants settled close to co-ethno-religionists, sometimes outside a town's fortifi-cations. Intermarriage between Muslims and non-Muslims was permitted; and while non-Muslim brides of Muslim men did not have to convert, their children had to be raised as Muslims. Ethno-religious groups often specialized in particular crafts, and so even in work-life contact was limited to members of a person's reference group. They interacted through guilds (*esnâfil*) and in the marketplace.

On the top level of the empire, nonethnic elites and a nonethnic, artificial lan-guage—*lingua nullius*—prevented the emergence of a hegemonic ethnic group. In pre-Ottoman Islam, the Arabic language had served as the religious and mercantile lingua franca from the eastern Mediterranean to the borders of Persia, while in every-day usage ethnic languages were retained. In the Ottoman period, the Turkish lan-guage became the lingua franca for commerce and local administration from Anatolia to central Asia. To avoid ethnolinguistic hegemony, both the central institutions and the high culture of Istanbul used a *lingua nullius*, the Turkish/Arabic/high-literary-Persian Osmanlica. But decrees and literary works were also translated into every-day Turkish. European scholars and artists migrated to the sultans' court during the apogee of Ottoman culture, under Mehmed II (r. 1451–81).[16]

To prevent ethnicization and nepotism in civil and military service, the sons of Muslim Turks (the ethnicity of the ruling class) were excluded from public office. Instead, a non-ethnospecific palace elite of men and women was created for bureau-cratic, military, and reproductive functions. A special male caste of state "slaves" (*kul*) was drawn from captives of war, of whom one-fifth belonged to the sultan by law, and from slaves purchased in the open market. An estimated 20,000 came annually to Istanbul in the seventeenth century. Originally, captives of war became foot soldiers, later they formed the empire's elite corps—the janissaries. Free Muslims formed the cavalry (sipâhîs). The most important source of manpower for the palace from the late fourteenth century onward, however, was the *devsirme*, a levy of children from non-Turkish Christian populations. Urban families, and rural or small-town ones with only one son, were exempted. At irregular intervals, fathers with their male children had to appear before imperial officials who selected boys fit for service and sent them to Istanbul. Because of the opportunity for upward mobility, some families, especially poor ones, sent sons voluntarily, and others, including Muslims, tried to bribe officials to have their children accepted for state slavery. Over the two hundred years during which the *devsirme* functioned, about 200,000 boys were levied.[17]

Male "slave" children were converted to Islam and received several years of education. After a second, merit-based selection, they continued training according to their special aptitudes for the palace, the bureaucracy, or the army. They filled positions up to the highest ranks, including those of viziers and grand vizier (ministers and prime minister). Thus state offices were filled by de-ethnicized men from the protected peoples who were bound to the sultan but free to accumulate property and follow their talents. They might be called "professional Ottomans." The mobility of converts had no parallel in other contemporary societies. In Spain, for example, the position of Jewish *conversos* was precarious; Latin Christian monasteries offered educational opportunities only for young male Christians of modest background.[18]

The women of the palace (women's quarters, or harem) were selected from female war captives, from the slave markets, or from across the empire. They, too, were educated and trained to acquire skills and to refine their tastes. The de-ethnicized women prepared for a variety of service roles, held property, and could involve themselves in charitable and cultural affairs—for example, by endowing foundations. Many became wives of pages and administrators.[19] Islamic law permitted a sultan up to four wives, as well as concubines, and these were selected from among the women of the palace. For instance, Roxelana, the wife of Suleiman I (r. 1520–66), had been a Russian captive. This policy freed the Ottoman dynasty from entering into marriage contracts with other dynasties and from any resulting property and power transactions. Birth control was practiced to limit the number of such de-ethnicized children competing for positions. To reduce intergenerational conflicts, princes remained in the imperial household and under its control. Women could wield considerable political power, especially as mother of the reigning sultan (vâlide sultan), and the mother of the first son of a sultan held a particularly honored position. Their public roles increased after the end of their childbearing years, when they contributed to public displays of authority and of power and wealth.[20]

Legally, Muslims could not be enslaved, so most slaves came from other ethnoreligious groups. Often, they were converted and manumitted. In Muslim households, a Muslim slave concubine who had borne a child enjoyed a legally and socially enhanced position. She could not be sold or alienated from the household and became free upon the master-father's death. If the father wanted to marry her, he had to manumit her first. The children enjoyed equal rights with those of free mothers. The main exchange for slaves was the Antalya market, where captives from both Asia and Africa were sold. Through Kaffa, slaves from the north were procured at an annual rate of 25,000 by the middle of the sixteenth century. Ottoman slavery was a continuation of the Mediterranean system (see chap. 2.3). Slaves could buy their freedom, acted as commercial agents for their owners, and were frequently manumitted. The slave elite shaped Ottoman cultural life, since tutors of the sultans and of educated families, as well as artists and architects, were drawn from their number. As a loosely bound service elite, their status was the diametrical opposite of the status of slave labor forces in European colonies.

In the sixteenth century, the population of the empire increased by about 40 percent in rural areas and twice that much among urban people. In Anatolia, rich tax collectors established large landholdings. They made the transition to commercial agriculture and displaced parts of the peasantry. Both developments resulted in increasing numbers of landless youths who joined itinerant groups or resorted to brigandage. The Turkish term *levend* came to denote both a landless person and a brigand. The government transported Anatolian peasants and landless people to Cyprus after its conquest in 1570–71. Others fled on their own to the Caucasus region. Migration to overpopulated cities was prohibited, but many moved nevertheless. Toward the end of the sixteenth century, landless young men were recruited as salaried troops. Consequently, the elite janissaries were no longer the only force equipped with firearms. When discharged without pay, the ex-soldiers roamed the Anatolian countryside, as bands of discharged mercenaries had done in Europe for centuries.[21]

After about 1400, the empire influenced European, Islamic, Persian, and Indian affairs for three centuries. At the time of the early-sixteenth-century Reformation, Ottoman diplomats suggested alliances to Protestant powers, but the negotiations ended inconclusively. Military reverses began in 1683, and by 1699 the rising Habsburg-Austrian empire had extended its rule over Hungary and initiated a settlement policy for its northern Balkan territories (chap. 12.2). Ottoman society, before its decline in the eighteenth century, incorporated pluralist structures that permitted the retention of culture, marketplace interaction as well as intermarrige, and a de-ethnicization of political structures and high culture. Migration, even the involuntary *sürgün*, provided opportunities to individuals and families and served regional or imperial economic interests.

5.2 Many-Cultured Renaissance Europe

Viewed from the Mediterranean perspective of Islamic or Jewish culture, Latin Christian Europe north of the Pyrenees and the Alps was a backward, uncouth area. Only in the fourteenth century did *l'Europe désenclavante* (Bennassar and Chaunu) move out of this marginalized position. The process, which involved both boundary construction against neighboring civilizations and self-definition, was based on economic growth and required a reshaping of the relations between dynastic rulers and their polities. Migrant intellectuals played an important role in this innovation.

Scholars' and Artists' Trans-European Migrations

The memory of the intercivilizational achievements of Islamic, Jewish, Asian, and European scholars, merchants, and artisans that had shaped European life came to be hidden through the Latin Church's "doctrinal mind-washing" (Burman), which under the Inquisition culminated in an "appalling ignorance."[22] While courtiers and merchants became more sedentary, the intellectual segment of the elite remained mobile. Scholars had to wander from one center of learning to another. Universities, still few and far between in the twelfth and thirteenth centuries, emerged as a network of learning by the fourteenth century (map 5.2). With Latin as the lingua franca and a similar organization of studies from university to university, a trans-European *peregrinatio academica* could develop. A community (*universitas*) of the learned emerged and formulated various systems of philosophy based on treatises by Greek and Roman scholars (hence the renaissance or rebirth of classical antiquity).

The dense network of universities resulted in a regionalization of catchment areas for students, most of whom came by internal migration. At four universities in southern France, 13.5 percent of the 6,200 students in the last quarter of the fourteenth century came from territories outside "France," particularly from neighboring Iberian states. Once originating mainly from patrician families of larger cities, students increasingly came from smaller towns. Poor students, dependent on work or alms, may have migrated over longer distances to study in a busy town where jobs and alms could be found more easily. Noble students traveled with servants or hired local ones. Universities were all-male communities, but at least one woman in men's clothing migrated across Poland to study at the university in Kraków. The percentage of "foreign" students grew. At the university of Leiden, founded in 1575, 41 percent of the 2,725 students in its first quarter-century came from outside the United Provinces, but by the mid-seventeenth century, 52 percent came from as far away as Hungary, Germany, Poland, the Ottoman Empire, and the British Isles.[23]

Some sovereigns tried to restrict the mobility of university teachers to prevent salary increases—much like the mid-fourteenth-century attempts of municipalities to control artisans' wages. Group migrations of teachers and students resulted from academic and economic crises. Doctrinal differences between scholars or among students could result in withdrawal and migration to a university considered more congenial or in the expulsion of the "dissidents." Tensions and fighting between students and townspeople could also lead to expulsion, and expensive provisions and housing could impel a mass departure by those seeking to negotiate better living conditions. Another reason for moving on was conflict between teachers and students organized by regional origin who—to use modern terminology—constructed "out-

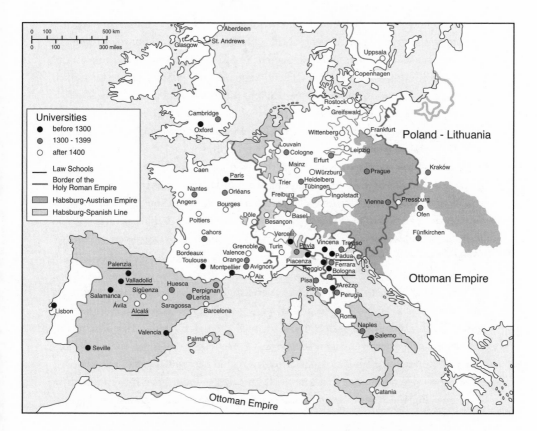

5.2 Europe: Universities, 13th–15th Centuries, and Major Political Regions, 1550

groups" through ethnic ascription. The pursuit of universal knowledge could easily become particularized.[24]

Like academics, artists migrated to and between cultural centers. Dependent on wealthy patrons, their destinations changed with the changing fortunes of dynasties. In the twelfth century, St. Albans became a European artistic center; continental craftsmen, especially French ones, traveled to the English cathedral town in great numbers. Beginning in the fourteenth century, Urban and Papal Italy attracted visitors, while at the same time Italian artists, architects, and intellectuals migrated to courts, building sites, and other places of anticipated opportunity all over Europe and the Ottoman Empire. Next in number to Italians, Flemings from the Urban Netherlands were found in many places. From the third urban culture, the Hispanic one, few artists or craftsmen migrated northward—rather, as Muslims and Jews, they were being expelled southward.

Artists' migrations increased in the fifteenth and sixteenth centuries. About a quarter of the Italian migrants headed for France; somewhat more than 50 percent traveled elsewhere in Europe, and the remaining 25 percent went to other continents.

In late fifteenth-century Kraków, Italian scholars taught law, and Italian stonecutters worked on the cathedral. Others provided sculptures and artwork for the Kremlin in Moscow, and still others found employment in Spain. Migration and ethnic ascription could be complex. Domenikos Theotokopoulos from Crete (1541–1614) studied in Italy before becoming the famous "Spanish" artist known as El Greco ("the Greek"). The migrations of scholars, artists, master craftsmen, and other experts were often related to each other or sequential. Art and architectural history is full of references to Italian schools, French influences, and Flemish draperies. Dutch painters in turn migrated to Italy, and Dutch paintings were sold to patrons in Italy starting in the first half of the fifteenth century. Building a castle, decorating its interior, and filling it with art and learning required many different specialists. Their relationship is reflected in the designation of useful, mechanical, decorative, and liberal arts. Mining technology and waterworks in medieval and early modern parlance were "*Künste*," literally meaning works of art, and "art-isans," those who implemented such technologies, also migrated.[25]

Following in the footsteps of pilgrims and students, English gentlemen travelers moved to the continent for educational purposes. From the late sixteenth century onward, many went to Paris or Bologna to study. Others, traveling with servants for excitement and dissipation, evoked a negative response. In England, they were considered "Italianated": atheistic, morally corrupt, and deceitful. On the positive side, those who traveled in search of humanist knowledge could hope for remunerative positions after their return because states needed fewer soldiers and more administrators.[26]

The Medieval and Early Modern Concept of "Natio"

The migrations and commercial connections of trans-European scholars have been called "international," and research on nineteenth-century nation-states has attempted to trace modern polities to the consolidation of the English and French states. However, the medieval Latin term *natio* merely referred to a common regional and cultural origin. Italian merchants in London were divided into four *nationes* by city of origin. They acted jointly only when the need arose, as when they threatened to depart for Winchester after the London anti-alien riot of 1457. Italian merchants at the Champagne fairs, on the other hand, formed a *universitas mercatorum*, a corporate group.

In institutions of learning and in the councils of the Church, corporate organization was by *natio*, often in a fourfold division into English, French, Italian, and German, with borders that were "somewhat fanciful or highly inconsistent." Once divisions had been established, in-migrating men from new cultural groups were allocated to one of the existing *nationes*. At the University of Paris, one *natio* consisted of scholars just from the Isle de France, another combined all English and German scholars. In general, the Italian *natio* was a Mediterranean group that included Iberian scholars and clerics, while the German *natio*, often a catch-all category, could include Bohemians, Scandinavians, and Netherlanders. Any *natio* encompassed diverse peoples who had more in common among themselves than with other *nationes* but who nevertheless had to use Latin for their lingua franca.[27]

The concept of *natio* reflected the heterogeneity of polities. Dynastic states like "France" and "England"—that is, units smaller than empires and larger than dukedoms—incorporated many independent realms and principalities. Any particular monarch owned only some territories and claimed overlordship in others. Most of the French and English princes, dukes, and barons, "also held lands and had interests outside the kingdom," which demanded policies to hold the diverse parts together. The Italian peninsula included Lombardy, the many competing city-states of Urban Italy, Venice and its possessions, the Papal States, the kingdom of Naples, and others. The term "absolute monarchy" suggests uniformity, but everyday monarchical administration consisted of negotiations with local nobilities and urban patriciates to reconcile divergent local customs and to bind the multiple corporate parts to loyalty to the ruling dynasty or the particular monarch.[28]

Similarly, there was no apparent "national" homogeneity of the populations within dynastic units. England's "Natives" accommodated Norman immigrants and Cistercian monks, German and Italian merchants, and clerics from the Italian peninsula and elsewhere. Below this level of the trans-European elite were the regional cultures, including the Welsh, Scottish, and Cornish cultures, in addition to the English. The mix was compounded by migrating Irish people and the Anglicization of Ireland. When the Dutch-born King William III (r. 1689–1702) was attacked in a poem titled "The Foreigner," Daniel Defoe responded with his satire "The True-Born Englishman":[29]

> These are the heroes that despise the Dutch,
> And rail at new-come foreigners so much;
> Forgetting that themselves are all derived
> From the most scoundrel race that ever lived. . . .
> The Pict and painted Briton, treach'rous Scot,
> By hunger, theft, and rapine, hither brought;
> Norwegian pirates, buccaneering Danes,
> Whose red-hair'd offspring everywhere remains:
> Who, joined with Norman French, compound the breed
> From whence your true-born Englishmen proceed. . . .
> From whence a mongrel half-bred race there came
> With neither name nor nation, speech or fame . . .
> A true-born Englishman's a contradiction,
> In speech an irony, in fact a fiction.
> The Eternal Refuge of the Vagabond . . .
> Dutch, Walloons, Flemings, Irishmen, and Scots
> Vaudois, Valtolins, and Huguenots . . .
> French Cooks, Scotch Pedlars, and Italian Whores

Were all madelars, or Lords Progenitors . . .
Whose Children will, when riper Years they see, . . .
Call themselves English, Foreigners Despise.

In the French case, the Albigensian Crusade of 1208–13 had destroyed early on the distinct culture of the southeastern region, but Bretons, Basques, and Corsicans remained ethnocultural minorities. A recent study commenting on the "purity" of the French nation ("Le 'Melting Pot' de la Gaule du Haut Moyen Âge") found an originating Gallo-Roman group augmented by Germanic immigrants (Goths, Franks, and Allemanic and Burgundian people), by Bretons from the Celtic islands, by Gascons from the Pyrenees, and by Normans out of Scandinavia. Other peoples in French territories included Jews, a few Syrians and Greeks, and small groups from Saxony, Iberia, and Ireland. Strong regional cultures and allegiances emerged—Burgundy, Normandy, Aquitaine, Gascony, and Flanders, to name only a few. Immigrants quickly became part of the regional cultures, but from region to region the dialects and languages remained heterogeneous.[30]

Along the shores of the Mediterranean, it was common for men and women of different ethnicities to marry, thus blending Spanish, Italian, Greek, Arab, Berber, Jewish, and Byzantine extractions. In East Central Europe, immigrants from German and Flemish territories mixed with Slavic and Baltic peoples. The Germanies proper, as well as France, were crisscrossed by mercenary bands, traveling merchants and carters, clergymen and pilgrims, maids, prostitutes, and journeymen artisans. All of them left children, settled, moved again, intermarried, and interacted. Constructions of genetically "pure" European peoples, separate from neighboring North Africans or Palestinians, have no basis in the reality of medieval life.

These composite cultures were reflected in languages from many linguistic and social traditions. No common "high" languages were spoken by all social classes, and regional dialects were not necessarily understandable to each other. In England, Franco-Norman came to dominate. It was not until three centuries later, in the 1370s, that vernacular English became "official" and was used in grammar schools, and in 1399 Parliament was opened by a speech in English for the first time. Of the foreign terms in the English language, 55 percent came from French in the 1460s. A French "national" style based on Parisian French began to take form in the sixteenth century among the educated and in political usage. Among the common people, local dialects continued to be spoken in the early twentieth century.[31]

From Dynastic to Territorial State: Centralization versus Localism

The "high" culture of trans-European scholars and the homogenization of elite groups, who often took a syncretic approach to differences, reflect a process of "conversion" or acculturation. The high aristocracy of Renaissance Europe remained an amalgamated European class. When Francis II of France (r. 1559–60) married Mary, Queen of Scots, she arrived with a considerable retinue of Scottish followers. Charles I of Spain, who had Spanish parents and was educated in Flanders, came to the Iberian Peninsula as Emperor Charles V of the Central European ("Holy Roman") Empire with a retinue of Flemish followers, whose disdain for Spanish hierarchies ranked among the causes for the Comuneros Uprising of the cities.

Centralization under powerful monarchs or urban patriciates occurred only in parts of Europe. Territorial states—politically and economically viable structures that outlasted individual rulers and dynasties—emerged where rulers, male or female, bound the potentially divisive nobility to the center and supplemented it with a bureaucracy or integrated it with parts of the bourgeoisie. This process might involve a relocation of nobles to the capital and the creation of universities to train administrators, thus occasioning student travel. Where the nobility remained dominant, as in Spain and Portugal, or where too many disparate units were tied together, as in the Central European Empire, such development was retarded.

Commercial interests and their agents benefited from territory-wide, uniform laws and—like governmental administrators, merchants, and manufacturers—began to act on a statewide basis, thus ending their supraregional cooperation. The combination of dynastic and commercial interests culminated in the political economy of mercantilism. A capitalized political core in western and southwestern Europe became more strongly connected to less powerful and geographically remote areas. Individual "adventurers," like robber barons of earlier times, shipped out as pirates, buccaneers, or entrepreneurs, hoping to receive support from the state and/or the crown. This private pursuit of warfare for pecuniary profit resembled what the lesser feudal nobility had done to gain territory. Most merchants, however, organized themselves in companies to spread risks and to pool capital, connections, and experience. In 1555 the English Association of Merchant Adventurers, or Muscovy Company, was chartered for trade with Russia. The English East India Company, chartered in 1600, began trading with Persia via Surat in 1616. Dutch and French merchants followed the same patterns for expanding long-distance trade.

The northern Italian city-states consolidated their rule over the adjoining countryside in the late fourteenth century. The towns of Holland and Zeeland revolted against rule by the Spanish Habsburgs in 1557 and with other provinces formed the Union of Utrecht in 1579. Urban rule permitted commercial outreach. On the Iberian Peninsula, the dynastic units of Castile and Aragon were joined by marriage to form the future Spain, which like Portugal became a dynastic territorial state. Both lacked a commercial bourgeoisie and thus remained dependent on the Urban Netherlands and the merchants there, including the Jews whom they had expelled.

In the Germanies of the sixteenth century, no centralization could be imposed. The principalities and petty dynasties emphasized their position by "conspicuous consumption," whether embodied in the splendor of Renaissance castles or in an expanding court apparatus that served as a source "of social power and dominance" but was unproductive. While reforming dynasties became sedentary, the imperial overextension and resulting itinerancy of the Habsburgs brought on "the insufficiencies of a bureaucratic" rule. Charles V thought of his forty-year reign as "a long voyage," during which he traveled nine times to his German possessions, six times to his Spanish ones, seven times to Italy, ten times to the Netherlands, and was twice in England and in Africa—this at a time when itinerant rule had become anachronistic (map 5.2).

In East Central Europe, no centralized monarchies emerged either. In Poland, only the nobility (the *szlachta*) formed the "nation" since the peasants were their property. In these areas, the economies remained geared to maximum profits for manors and courts, and states lacked tax-paying subjects. As a consequence, neither small nor large rulers invested in infrastructural improvements, and they failed to calculate the economic capabilities of their subjects. The region was to become a reservoir for migrant labor.

Trained administrators—recruited in some states from the nobility, in others from an emerging bourgeoisie—became "professional statists," who were similar to the service elite of "professional Ottomans" in the southeast. They might lose their positions as a result of dynastic or war-related changes, or they might switch loyalties and remain in office. As an interested part of the educated elite, administrators would become an important component of societal driving forces in the nineteenth-century development of national consciousnesses and nation-states. As true of the Church, only males could take part in the administration of the state. Venality and the inheritance of offices affected both marriage regulations and reproductive rules. Male legalists remolded family networks, reduced the inheritance rights of refractory children, and changed the rules of marital separation. Under French law, for example, wives charged with adultery were deemed unfit to hold offices inherited from their families; the accusing husbands took them over, instead. In the case of secret, out-of-marriage pregnancies, well-placed and articulate women reacted by entering into alliances with midwives, and if unjustly accused they responded with public pamphleteering. "Disgraced" women from the lower classes had to emigrate.[32]

The masses of the people, on the other hand, had local or regional ties and spoke "vernacular" languages or dialects. Among the rural classes, according to a study of the Hohenlohe lands in southern Germany, in- and out-migration occurred under both a moral economy of mutual obligations and an "un-Christian" market economy that favored the strong. To survive locally and avoid out-migration, peasants articulated their interests. When ordered in 1597 to convert subsistence grain lands into vineyards for marketable crops, they refused. "They fear [a local official reported] that they could not feed their children." Peasants rebelled, as in the Peasants' War of 1524–25 and the wave of lesser revolts from 1560 to 1660. While the regional economy expanded from 1450 to 1560 and grew rapidly from the 1560s to the 1640s, it became increasingly connected to markets in which prices and not mutual obligations counted. From 1570 to 1683 peasants in the Hohenlohe's Langenburg district experienced twenty-five years of famine. Even when supplies were insufficient locally, merchants from distant areas—whether from northern Italy or from Dutch cities—combed the district for supplies. Those who were only marginally self-sufficient suffered, and to buy grain for food they had to supplement their incomes through cash earned from temporary labor migration or work in rural crafts. If they lacked cash for taxes, they might be dispossessed and forced onto the road. Others would then move in from elsewhere to take their chance on the same plots of land. In 1588 a villager pleaded with the lord to whom he was in debt "to take pity on my wife and small, helpless children until I get some money and not to drive me away, but out of mercy, to let me stay." According to Robisheaux, "The making of Germany's rural proletarians after 1560 took place in a climate of hunger, fear, and desperation." Only those with some means left could migrate purposefully, for most social descent led to permanent wayfaring. Southwestern Germany, where division of inheritance among all children of a deceased parent was the rule, became an area of mass emigration from the seventeenth century onward.[33]

The cooperation of merchant companies and state bureaucracies and the conceptualization of mercantilist policies meant that mercantile and state geographical units became congruent. In general, the emigration of persons with particular skills or with taxpaying capability was restricted, while men and women from afar, like skilled religious refugees, might be encouraged to immigrate to increase a state's economic potential. *Ubi populus, ibi obulus*—loosely translated as "where there are people, there is money for the ruler"—became "where there are people, production and commerce may flourish." Since no homogeneous national populations had even been conceptualized, monarchs settled migrants under special regulations, either chartered as traders for specific periods of time or granted permanent privileges, as in the case of skilled artisans. The elite's concepts of the state and the migration decisions of small people influenced each other. Boundaries were more likely to be drawn by professional statists than by bureaucrats of the religious institutions, and regional, "ethnic" popular cultures had little impact on such boundaries. The generic designations "Germans" for western Europeans in Russia or "Franks" for northwestern Europeans on the Iberian Peninsula or "Wends" for all Slavic peoples came to be replaced by uniform territorial designations like France or Spain, whose culturally diverse inhabitants then became French or Spanish.

5.3 From the Iberian Peninsula to Sub-Saharan Africa and across the Atlantic

Europe, the poor neighbor of Asia, continued to import African gold, the one product its trading partners in Asia were interested in. From a European economic perspective, gold-rich Africa and luxury-goods-producing Asia were targets for profitable conquest; from an ideological perspective, a crusading spirit was part of Iberian religiosity;[34] from a political perspective, the quest for dominance in trade was part of a power struggle between dynastic-mercantilist states. Having neither goods nor culture to export and a faith that stood in competition with other equally valid belief systems, Europe compensated for its weakness by engaging in a mission to convert heathens and, more significantly, by bringing to bear its superior firepower.[35]

The Portuguese crown was favorable to merchant undertakings but faced an obstacle to internal development—a rocky and barren countryside. Unable to compete with Arab, Ottoman, and Urban Italian Mediterranean traders, its political-mercantile entrepreneurs began to search for a passage around Africa to Asia. The prevailing winds and currents in the Atlantic favored Portugal's ports; Prince Henry, called "the Navigator," and the military zeal of a nobility in search of a cause gave impetus to the mercantile project. The quest for a new access route to West Africa involved few economic risks because prices had risen phenomenally in the trans-Saharan gold trade from 1300 to the early fifteenth century and direct trade was certain to yield enormous profits. Castile and Aragon (united by marriage after 1479) did not offer costly competition because of internal struggles. Only after the destruction of Granada (1483–92) did the Spanish urban and landowning elites shift their attention from the Mediterranean to the Atlantic, from internal to overseas colonization. The multiethnic composition of their society, which had evolved from coexistence to assimilation by force and to expulsion, may have influenced Spanish attitudes toward "Natives" in overseas colonization. The coastal forts and trading stations of the Portuguese, on the other hand, more closely resembled the traditional colonies and *funduqs* along the coasts of the Mediterranean and the Black Sea.

Portuguese fishermen had sailed far into the Atlantic in search of tuna and cod. They reached Madeira (1419), the Canaries (1419), the Azores (1431), and the Cape Verde Islands (1445). Entrepreneurs introduced the cultivation of sugar cane, grapes, and grain. In the Cape Verde Island, the native Guanches were killed or else enslaved and then transported to the Iberian Peninsula; Flemish agriculturalists and traders were settled on the Azores.[36] Portugal, which seized the port of Ceuta from Morocco in 1415, was barred from additional North African conquest by Arab resistance. But the major obstacle to a further southward advance was psychological: the contemporary conviction that the (flat) world ended at Cape Bojador. When it was finally rounded in 1434, trade proved disappointing until gold from the upper Senegal River, the upper Niger River, and the "Gold Coast" (today's Ghana) began to enter the bartering system. This exchange improved both the bargaining power of Black African rulers, who could chose between selling to Arab or Portuguese merchants, and Portugal's economic position in Europe. To divert the gold trade from trans-Saharan routes into their own networks, the Portuguese in 1481 sent carpenters and stonemasons as well as their ubiquitous soldiers to construct Fort "El Mina" (the mine). Within a decade after the arrival of the Portuguese, the sub-Saharan Afro-Atlantic slave trade began (map 5.3).[37]

African Slavery in Europe

Mediterranean slavery (see chap. 2.3) had become marginal when a few Black people from the Canary Islands were brought to Portugal and when investors and royal officials formed a company for African slaving in the 1440s. A century later, Black Africans had totally replaced Arab "Moors" as slaves. Portugal's monopoly, challenged unsuccessfully by Seville traders in the 1470s, lasted for almost 150 years until Dutch and British traders inserted themselves.[38] Slaves were either captured by small con-

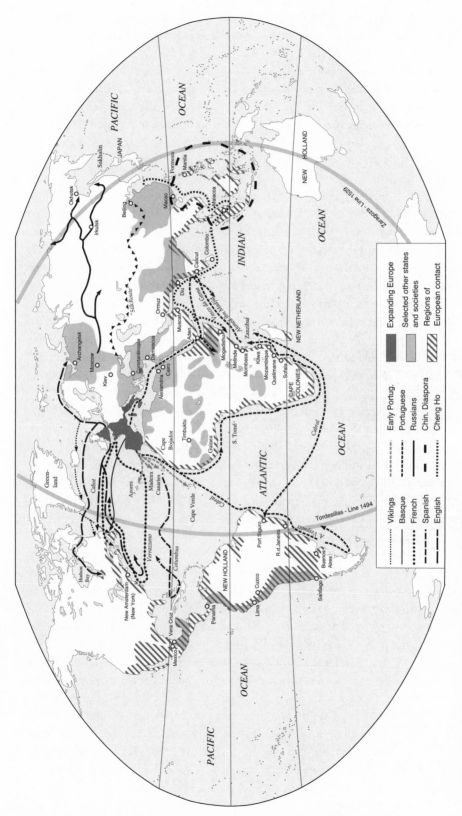

5.3 "Europe Finds the Larger World," 15th to Early 16th Centuries

tingents of Portuguese or bought from Muslim or African traders; local men served as interpreters or seamen. Most were sold in the slave markets of Lisbon and Seville. By one estimate, some 48,800 Africans were transported as slaves to Europe between 1451 and 1600; another estimate places the figure at 150,000 even before 1500, not counting the Africans who were killed or who died on the voyage. In the period 1519–20, men and women, imported at a ratio of 58 to 42, were considered to be of equal value, as suggested by their prices. The imports declined after the mid-1500s and almost ceased after 1600 because of the competitive demand from the Americas and an increased domestic reservoir of labor. Surplus slaves were resold to Spain (see chap. 6).[39]

Afro-European slavery changed the patterns of exploitation, work, and manumission that had evolved in Mediterranean slavery. Under the new system, slaves first became an item of prestige for wealthy urban families. Investor-bought male slaves were a second type; they were hired out for any available employment, though rarely in agriculture. Since most guilds refused to admit slaves as members, they were reduced to being the most poorly rewarded labor. These slaves had to turn over part of their earnings to the investor, but they could keep the rest and even purchase their own freedom. The third and harshest condition was that of royal slaves, who were assigned to public projects, mines, or galleys. Ethnic stereotypes came to label African slaves as docile and easily converted and Arab and Berber ones as malicious. Branding was common, and the brutal punishments meted out to slaves became a theme in literature.[40]

As to whether slave imports deprived Portuguese of their jobs and lowered wages or offset the labor shortages caused by the emigration of Portuguese men, a differentiated analysis finds overpopulation in the north but underpopulation and harsh landlord-imposed working conditions in the south. The out-migration of southern laborers to Lisbon and other cities was often not in step with labor markets and thus ended in emigration. "Slaves were imported to do the jobs the emigrants had refused to do" because of the conditions of employment. After 1500, some freedpersons of African descent migrated to the Americas.

With a population of about one million at the end of the fifteenth century, Portugal had the highest concentration of Black people of any European society, but even so slaves accounted for only 1 to 2 percent of the population in the north, 5 percent in the south, and 10 percent in Lisbon. Manumitted and self-freed Africans amounted to 1 percent of the total. Spanish slaves, about 100,000 in a population of nine million, were concentrated in the city of Seville. In 1564, some 7 percent of the inhabitants were slaves, including some of white color, and free Blacks also lived there. In the larger archbishopric of Seville, their representation declined to about 3 percent. Some White people expressed fear of being overwhelmed by dark-skinned ones. A visiting Flemish humanist noted in 1535: "Captive blacks and Moors perform all tasks; Portugal is so crowded with these people that I believe that in Lisbon there are more men and women slaves than free Portuguese . . . in Évora I thought that I had come to some city of evil demons: everywhere there were so many blacks whom I so loathe."

Shaping this opinion were projections of fear and constructions of the "Normal" and the Other rather than the actual urban concentration of slaves.[41]

African people developed their own everyday culture. They formed charitable associations, even though freedmen and -women labored under restrictions, especially with regard to contact with enslaved coethnics. Marriage with Portuguese and Spanish men and women was permitted, and the children of those marriages were called mulattos or, if they were very dark, *loros* or *loras*. Trained and educated through their own efforts or by wealthy owners, some formerly enslaved men and women, often children of mixed marriages, were highly esteemed for literary and other achievements. Over time, they "mingled with their free neighbors, . . . lost their ethnic identity," and became indistinguishable by color of skin, culture, or social position. But by the early 1600s male legislators prohibited Portuguese women from developing relations with slave men or admitting them into their houses. Men were not stigmatized for sexual relations with slave women.[42]

Expansion to Sub-Saharan Africa and Asia

Further Iberian expansion benefited from the rediscovery of Ptolemy's *Geography*, from thirteenth-century travelers' accounts, and from the knowledge of Jewish merchants collected in the *Catalan Atlas* (see chap. 2.1). The Portuguese state became heavily involved in financing expeditions because costs could not be borne by individual merchants and chartered companies had yet to be organized. Political support was also needed in distant ports where no previous colonies of compatriots existed and because new territories could be claimed for the crown, with the conversion of souls left to the Church. Urban Italy, whose city-states lacked power and whose galley technology was unsuited to ocean travel, could not involve itself in such ventures. Rather, the cities contributed out-migrating seafaring experts and profited from the distribution of commodities that were unloaded in Lisbon and Seville. Genoese, Flemish, and German merchants migrated to Iberian opportunities.[43]

Expansion necessitated trans-European and, briefly, intercivilizational technological exchange. Hanseatic cogs and Mediterranean galleys were combined in the Iberian caravel; transport carracks with an original carrying capacity of 400 tons were developed to a capacity of 1,000 tons after 1500. The Arab lateen (triangular) sail improved rigging and Asian and Arab navigatory aids, including the floating magnetic needle and the astrolabe, helped captains to establish their position by measuring the elevation of sun and stars. Knowledgeable East African Arab pilots led European sailors to what they considered their own discoveries. In 1498 Vasco da Gama, after rounding the African Cape, was surprised to find a flourishing town at Quelimane, Mozambique, that was connected through coastal trade to Madagascar and Arabia, and, by ocean trade, to India. He hired Ahmed ibn Madjid, who with his knowledge of the monsoon winds and with his Indo-Arabic sea charts guided the ships and crews from the port of Malindi to Calicut in southwest India. Although the Portuguese had taken eighty years to master the African coast from Ceuta to the Cape of Good Hope, they needed a mere fifteen years to reach China because they could rely on Arab, Indian, and Chinese experience. Exploration of the new routes was once again an achievement of Euro-Jewish-Arab-Asian science and experience, but in view of the Latin Church's hostility to such interactions they were not publicly admitted. Also, because by this time Europeans controlled the print media, news about the contributions of Others failed to be disseminated.

Subsequent to Portuguese intrusions, patterns of mobility and migration changed for African peoples. While the population drain of the forced transatlantic slave migrations had not yet begun, trade intensified, followed new routes, and involved new commodities like ivory and *malagueta* pepper. When the Portuguese learned about the gold mines of Zimbabwe, they quickly abandoned peaceful trade and conquered the mines. The thousands of miners fled, however, and the mines remained closed because no experienced labor force could be tapped locally or transported from Europe.

At ports along the eastern Indian Ocean, which were divided into ethno-commercial trade emporia (see map 2.2), the Vijayanagar state in southern India and the Mogul empire in northern India (as well as the Chinese Ming dynasty further east) attempted to block the advancing Portuguese. Because of their superior armament, the Portuguese established themselves at strategic locations—Mozambique and Mombasa on the East African coast in 1498, Hormuz and Goa in 1510 and 1515, Malacca (Melaka) on the Malay Peninsula in 1511, Macao in China in 1557, and finally Nagasaki, Japan (1570). Most of these trading cities were characterized by ethnic diversity. In Calicut, merchants from the Malabar Coast traded with Bengalese, Deccans, Chetti, Arabs, Persians, Turks, Somalians, and Maghrebians. The merchant community of Malacca included Gujarati Muslims and Tamil Hindus; Javanese, Luzonese, and Chinese merchants lived in particular quarters where they retained their customs and maintained trade with particular regions. Intermarriage with local women was widespread, and the Portuguese adopted the pattern.

In order to divert the trade in goods from India and the Malay Peninsula via the Cape of Good Hope to Lisbon, Portuguese fleets attempted to cut off supplies to Arab merchants at Red Sea ports who traded with Ottoman and Urban Italian merchants. By 1500, when the price of pepper in Lisbon fell to only one-fifth of what it was in Venice, the Egyptian-Venetian trade was ruined. The Ottoman sultans had encouraged the transit trade, from Asia to Western Europe via the Ottoman realm, and by supplying the newly immigrated English had doubled their trade revenues. The Portuguese, however, introduced a system of passes for non-Portuguese shipping in order to impose their rule, collect taxes, and oust competitors. The rulers of the South Asian states had not merged mercantile and political interests and lacked maritime aspirations; they therefore accepted the Portuguese as intermediaries handling trade, for example, with Arab merchants at Hormuz.[44]

Only a small number of Portuguese migrated eastward, including sailors involved in the trade between Asian ports, missionaries and Jesuits, and a few administrators. Their settlements never totaled more than 12,000–14,000 male adults, including clerics of other European backgrounds, who considered themselves Portuguese. An Arab author from the Malabar Coast described the newcomers:

> A race of devils among the tribes of mankind arrived in Malabar, dirty in their customs, enemies of Allah and his prophet. They were called Franks; they worshipped wooden images of gods, knelt before images of stone. The shape of their bodies and the look on their faces showed them to be despicable. Their eyes were blue like those of the ghosts of the desert; they pissed like dogs, and they forced people to abandon their religion. . . . Cheating and misleading, they came disguised as merchants. They wanted pepper and ginger for themselves and left for others nothing but coconuts.[45]

The text reveals how self-styled superiors were viewed by those who had no reason to consider themselves inferior. It proceeds to describe the change in mercantile dealings from transcontinental trust to deception backed by guns.

Except for the transfer of profits, Europe remained marginal to Asia's trade. Eighty-five percent of the spice trade remained within Asia, and of the ginger and pepper from Sumatra and southwestern India, cinnamon from Ceylon, nutmeg and mace from the Banda islands, and cloves from the Moluccas, only 14 percent was sold to Europe and 1 percent to America.[46] Within Europe, the Portuguese and Spanish were marginalized by new patterns of capital accumulation, investment, and commercial relationships over long distances. Travel to and from Asian destinations entailed large amounts of time: six months from Lisbon to Goa, eighteen months or more from there to Macao and back. The better-financed Dutch merchants, organized as the Dutch East India Company in 1602, assumed control over many Portuguese trading posts after the 1590s. The contempt for both commerce and the merchant class expressed by the Iberian states and their nobilities resulted in their losing control over profits from the distribution of imports even while they still dominated the exploitative trade with Asia. Spices arriving at Lisbon were sold through the Spanish-Habsburg Netherlands. And after independence from Spain, Dutch mercantile houses—including expelled Iberian Jews—continued to reap the profits. The skewed relationship between economic and political power is highlighted by the fact that the taxes paid by the Dutch to the Spanish-Habsburg crown in the period 1477–1568 were seven times as high as the revenues derived from the legendary South American silver fleets.

Early Contact with the Americas

One of many navigators from stagnating Urban Italy, who migrated to Portugal in search of work, married a Portuguese woman and visited European courts. Finally, he found support for his projected venture in Spain: with three ships Cristóbal Colón (Columbus) set out to find a westward passage to the Indies. First, it is worth recalling that his largest ship was only forty meters in length and manned by 100 sailors. More than half a century earlier, the Chinese commander Cheng Ho had crossed the Indian

Ocean, and his largest ship, at 140 meters in length, was able to accommodate about 1,000 sailors, soldiers, and servants (see map 2.3). Second, it merits attention that— just as da Gama had the help of an Arab pilot—one El Pietro Negro, who was probably of African origin, served as a pilot on Columbus's ship. Third, it should be noted that Basque fishermen had supplied the masses of pilgrims in Santiago de Compostela with cod from a source they never betrayed to competitors, which was probably the banks of Newfoundland. And, of course, the "New World" had been a Norse/Viking settlement site reached via the Greenland trade route centuries earlier.[47]

In 1492 Columbus reached the "Indies"—the Caribbean "West Indies" as it turned out. Another Italian migrant, Giovanni Caboto, licensed by the British crown under the name of John Cabot, seems to have reached northern American shores in 1497. Two years later, in 1499, the Portuguese arrived on the Brazilian coast almost by accident. Wanting to avoid costly competition, Portugal and Spain had asked the pope to divide the expected new "discoveries" (or booty) between them. Without either party realizing it, the resulting demarcation line of 1493–94 made the future Brazil part of the Portuguese realm.[48] While a circum-African trip to Asia took many months, the Iberia-Brazil route took no more than three or four weeks. Westbound ships surpassed in number the eastbound ones going to Asia as early as the 1520s. From 1504 to 1650, about 10,600 Seville-registered ships alone crossed the Atlantic. The multiethnic merchant communities in Lisbon and Seville—the Seville Genoese, in particular—were instrumental in the expansion. Iberian trading houses served as training posts for transoceanic ventures. Merchants who engaged in the Muscovy and East India trade came from English firms with strong Iberian connections and experience.[49]

The trends in migration history and demography in the post-conquest Americas were the opposite of what occurred in Asia. Whereas in the African-Asian expansion climate and sickness caused the European intruders to suffer heavy losses, in the Americas it was the settled populations that suffered because they lacked immunity from the intruders' germs. Then the *conquistadores* embarked on the destruction of cultures in a rapacious quest for gold rather than for dominance in trade. In Asia, the Europeans had to negotiate with merchants; in America, they needed common laborers. As in the Christian conquest of the Iberian Peninsula, the mentalities of the advance parties were characterized by a spirit of looting, a desire to acquire land, and the search for a frontier for male warring and adventure.

While the arrival of European pathogens led to population collapse in the Americas, population development in Europe began to show strong growth. Contributing to this development were dietary changes due to foods that Europeans came to know in Central and South America. This conversion of material life reached the everyday patterns of consumption of common people within a century (see chap. 11.2).

The outward reach of Europe resulted in centuries of self-laudatory publications, still epitomized in the term "New World." Eberhard Schmitt, one of the foremost authorities on European expansion, has deconstructed the traditional interpretation from an intercivilizational perspective. Columbus's "plan was not original: his calculations and argumentation were simplistic or plain wrong; his search for gold and spices was obsessive. His belief that he was an instrument of providence makes twentieth-century observers shudder. . . . His one-dimensionality made him the perfect symbol for the entry of the Occident into world history."[50] He never admitted to himself that his West Indies were not India. A quarter-century later, in 1519, Ferdinand Magellan, a Portuguese in the service of the Spanish crown, circumnavigated the southern tip of the Americas, only to refuse to acknowledge that the Pacific Ocean was larger than anticipated. His crew almost perished because not enough food was taken on board.

A first result of the fifteenth-century expansion was the development of a worldwide web of colonial migrations from Europe outward. Second, within colonial areas during the sixteenth century two patterns emerged: flight from the invaders and forced, compelled, or free labor migrations to the centers of investment. Plantation-agriculture demanded the in-migration of labor forces, whether voluntary or not, while the import of foodstuffs to the metropoles necessitated the adaptation of labor requirements at home (see chaps. 6–9). Third, with support from African rulers, Arab, European, and Euro-American traders forced on African populations the mass migration of slave labor to the Americas (chap. 10). As a consequence of the hierarchized interaction, worldviews and foodways changed, and new peoples came into existence (chap. 11).

II

Other Worlds and European Colonialism
to the Eighteenth Century

From the 1470s to the mid-sixteenth century, Europe experienced prosperity, economic expansion, and population growth. Portugal's early outreach to Africa and Asia involved only coastal trading posts, which meant that the cultures and states on which they bordered remained intact. In the Indic World, the seventeenth-century Dutch intrusion marked the change from the domination of trade to the annexation of territories. Native peoples became subaltern groups in empires centered in Europe. Other continents then became prey to European merchant-adventurers and crown-supported explorer-exploiters with small complements of sailors, soldiers, factors, and servants. Four regional patterns of interaction with Native peoples emerged.

In sub-Saharan Africa, the European powers expanded the indigenous practices of enslavement by engaging in the mass exportation of men, women, and children to the Americas; a new type of bondage resulted: chattel slavery. Material goods and bullion were also exported. Most of the actual enslavement, like most of the mining and production, was left to the African elites and their states. Trans-Saharan Afro-Muslim traders connected these economies to the Mediterranean and, across the savannah, from Senegambia to Ethiopia. Other traders linked the Slave Coast to Central Africa. Because the European states had limited means, coastal trading posts were cost-efficient and effective. The domination of transcontinental commerce would have required large armies to subdue and rule societies. After 1450, a South Atlantic ocean-driven trading system developed. Free and slave migrations intensified (chap. 6.3); northbound and eastbound slave trade continued (chap. 6.4); and slavery in Africa expanded (chap. 6.5). Societies based on slave labor emerged in the Americas (chap. 10).

In Asia, transcultural maritime commerce ("the trade emporia") had been conducted in the three regions of the Indian Ocean, between the Southeast Asian islands, and in the South and East China Seas for millennia. Parallel, land-centered tribute and independent commercial trade linked regions, but involved cultural exchange only on a more limited, bilateral scale. This long-distance trade did supply even common people, for example, with salt. Short-distance supply to villages increased mobility and contacts but remained internal to local cultures. South, East, Southeast Asia and Japan also experienced vast settlement migrations as well as attempts at military conquest. When Chinese imperial overseas trade was cut off in 1435, the merchant community scattered into a diaspora and continued to pursue trade from elsewhere. The Portuguese arrival "was not a pacific movement, but an acquisitive and predatory drive for commodities and profits to be made on the rich products of the outer world" (Andrews). In superseding Portuguese control over traditional commercial ports and maritime trade emporia, the Dutch in the latter 1600s began to acquire plantations; in the eighteenth century the English went further and built an empire. Spanish and French acquisitions, however, remained limited. The European intrusion into Asian lands did not deplete the population base as it had in Africa because of the slave trade, but the agents of the European powers and European freebooters eager for profit were bent on exploiting the cheap labor that they saw as available to them (chap. 7). Plantation societies created out of forced labor signaled a new phase of migration and enforced "conversion" to the demands of European capital.

In the Americas, territories were conquered, states destroyed, and societies depopulated. Climatic conditions and precontact social organization resulted in two distinct migratory patterns. In the tropical zones, the European invaders, who were unwilling to work for themselves, faced resistance among surviving local populations on whom they tried to impose unfree toil, which led to the mass importation of slaves from tropical Africa (chap. 8). In the moderate zones, the settlement-migration of European peasant families and large landowners pushed surviving native peoples back (chap. 9). In the nineteenth century, free mass migrations provided mobile labor (chap. 14).

In the seventeenth and eighteenth centuries, these patterns of forced and free migration and settlement merged on a global scale. Farmers settled in South Africa, Australia, and elsewhere. Plantation economies based on slave labor emerged in the whole of the "southern hemisphere," a Euro–North American construct beginning far north of the equator along a line incorporating societies south of the Mediterranean, the Himalayas, and from the North American plantations south of the Chesapeake.

In the Mediterranean and Indian Ocean regions, the tradition of recognizing "resident aliens as communities entitled to autonomy from the direct control of local authorities" (Curtin) was abruptly reversed by the Europeans who came to conquer and deprive resident peoples and elites alike of their autonomy. With regional variations, merchants of previous centuries had been granted chartered status at the Champagne fairs and in London, in the Hanseatic zone and the Kiev and Muscovy states. In host societies, traders lived separately to preserve their cultural integrity. Without such barriers, they would "disappear" as a result of intermarriage and acculturation and would lose competitive advantage as cross-cultural brokers. In sub-Saharan Africa, the same goals were achieved by intermarriage or multiple marriages: trading men moved between bases managed by women. In some societies, new peoples of mixed culture acted as brokers, or separate towns kept merchants apart from local people. Languages were pidginized to permit cross-cultural communication; in West Africa, for example, Krio emerged as the lingua franca. In the Indian Ocean trade, when it was at its peak before Vasco da Gama led the Portuguese there,

Swahili was well developed. It became the lingua franca in much of East Africa's interior in the nineteenth and twentieth centuries, while along the coast the respective local languages remained in use.

In the Atlantic World, two parallel migration systems developed from southwestern Europe to Central and South America (chap. 8) and from northwestern Europe to North America (chap. 9). Accordingly, two cultural spheres developed in the Americas, one Latin and one mainly Anglo. In the Caribbean, departure states and cultures of origin interacted through buccaneering and the acquisition of neighboring islands. In North America's southern belt, the two cultural and economic systems interacted in the seaboard's plantation economy and in the south-central and southwestern hybrid Mexican-American culture. In the early nineteenth century, the Latin states became politically independent but remained economically dependent on capitalist cores. From the mid-1840s onward, the United States exerted a more or less direct overlordship in parts of Latin America. Toward the end of the century, the two migration processes merged, with the Italian diaspora, in particular, encompassing both Americas. A South Atlantic Slave Migration System mediated by European and North American traders connected Africa with the Americas and for centuries brought more men and women to the Americas than the free or indentured migrations of Europeans.

In the Pacific, the Spanish established a trade connection from New Spain/Mexico to the Philippines. The small amount of migration along this route was the first stage of the Pacific Migration System (chaps. 8.5, 15.5). Wherever demand for labor arose, resident populations were forced to labor for the colonizers' export economies, or distant populations were forced into mass migrations, including slave migrations, to destinations where capital from the core needed workers (chaps. 10, 15). In all of the free, coerced, and forced migrations, Europeans entered local or regional power arrangements and had to accommodate their goals to their means and to the cultural practices of other civilizations. For a long time, their beliefs in empire remained chimeras—exaggerated views of their own power.

6

Africa and the Slave Migration Systems

Intercontinental and intercivilizational migration and trading systems incorporated North Africa as an integral part of the Mediterranean World and East Africa as part of the Indian Ocean World, while they also linked sub-Saharan economies. Culturally, the societies were divided into Islamic sub-Saharan and East Africa, an Animist Atlantic Africa, and the Bantu-speaking world further south. African migrations up to the sixteenth century may be grouped into four partly overlapping categories: 1) westward from Arabia via Egypt to Morocco, 2) up the Nile valley and either further south along the Great Lakes in East Central Africa or westward into the savannah, 3) from the Fulbe region on the Atlantic coast westward into the savannah, and 4) colonizing migrations further south. Most migration was driven by the search of ecological niches or, in the savannah, for additional pasture.[1] Others involved political displacement, the mobility of traders and artisans, and, at the bottom of social hierarchies, the transfer of women and children, in particular, under pawnship and slave arrangements.

Egypt was connected to the Baghdad Arab caliphate and its successor states until the thirteenth century, when it came under the rule of the Mamluk Circassian slave dynasties; in the sixteenth century it was incorporated into the Ottoman Empire. In Morocco, Vandals from Europe and Arab immigrants from the east mixed with Berber peoples from the Atlas Mountains. This Muslim population penetrated northward into Europe (see chap. 2.3), while in the south the barrier of the Sahara was crossed by three major caravan routes to Ghana and Mali in the west, to Songhai on the upper Niger River, and to Kanem in the center. Along these routes and western coastal lowlands, Islam had reached the sub-Saharan peoples. Religious conversion was entwined with gendered power and property relationships: the spiritual and the material interacted. In matrilinear and mixed matri- and patrilinear societies, conversion to Islam involved a shift of inheritance patterns through the male line alone. Sub-Saharan African peoples, when adopting Islam, Africanized it.

Along the Mediterranean, Sulami and Hilali Bedouin people, perhaps a quarter of a million, migrated westward to Tripolitania after 1050. Further west, Sanhaja Berbers and the Almoravid sect established a state. Subsequent migrations were impelled by dynastic struggles and by intolerant warrior-monks emerging from monastery-type garrisons (*ribats*). Pilgrimages to Mecca involved hundreds of thousands of the faithful. Mamluk Egypt imported slave soldiers from the north and slaves for mine labor from the south. As few as 10,000 Mamluks ruled over some four to five million Egyptians in the early 1300s. Although the heavily taxed peasant families (*fellahin*) were prohibited from leaving their land for the cities, they were expelled when unable to pay taxes. Labor duties for landlords and public works involved temporary labor migrations. In the fifteenth century, Portuguese and French merchants or aggressors established coastal enclaves in Morocco and Tunisia.

During the time that the Portuguese, and subsequently other Europeans, expanded their maritime interests, the fourfold sociospatial division of the continent remained intact: the Mediterranean North with connections to the Strait of Hormuz; the West African gold, iron, and trading economy in the Sudanic belt, separated from the south by the equatorial forest belt; the East African economy connected northward to Egypt and Arabia and southward to the mines of the upper Zambezi region but most intensively to the trade emporia of the Indian Ocean. In the three coastal belts increasingly sendentary societies centered on large cities and developed complex political structures. In the fourth region, the interior, pastoral people's migrations continued and endemic diseases served to prevent the entry of foreigners. Below the equatorial forest, three smaller west-east belts—the inhabited space of Angola, the forbidding Kalahari Desert, and the Khoi cultures of the Cape—remained distant from the world economy. Large interior regions were accessible via the Niger, Benue, Zambezi, and Nile Rivers and, because of settlement patterns, to a lesser degree via the Congo.[2]

6.1   Migration and the Mixing of Peoples in Sub-Saharan Africa to the Sixteenth Century

Sub-Saharan Africa was settled, in linguistic terms, by peoples of Afro-Asiatic, Nilo-Saharan, Niger-Congo, and Khoisan origin. Definitions and terminology vary. The Niger-Congo *Bantu* ("people," plural of *muntu:* person) lived as farmers, cattle-raisers, or copper- and iron-working artisans. They had spread from the lands along the Niger River southward across the forest belt. Among dispersed settling peoples resident in the area at the time of Bantu arrival, their villages became cultural centers, their language preponderant. Intermarriage created new peoples, and "cross-cultural borrowing" led to new lifestyles (map 6.1).

In the vast region from the Nile to the Great Lakes, migrations of whole peoples and cultures continued southward, while slaves and cultural influences also moved northward. From the eleventh to the eighteenth century, this mobility led to the Arabization of Nilotic Sudan. Among others, Juhaynah Arabs moved from Mamluk Egypt to the Nubian segment of the Nile because of increasing population density; Madai and Kalenjin pastoralists moved to the Kenyan highlands; Baquarra Arabs moved from the White Nile westward into the sub-Saharan agricultural zone. In-migration

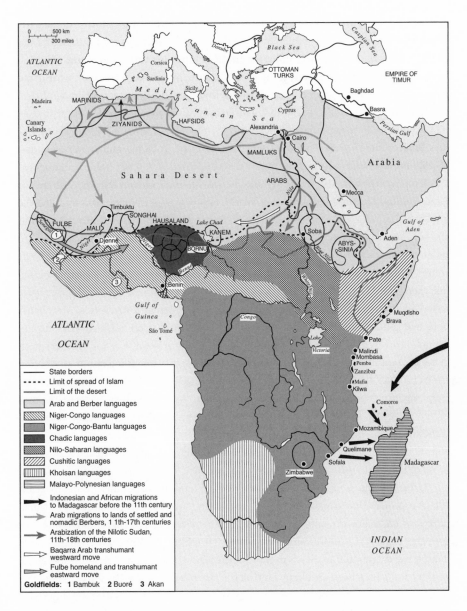

6.1 African Peoples in 1400

from the north induced southward mobility among the cultures of the Tana River region. In the sixteenth century, Arab peoples from the Red Sea coasts moved inland to the south of Khartoum. Flight from warfare between the Muslim and Christian rulers of Adal and Abyssinia resulted in minor migrations. Agriculturalists who migrated went in search of sustenance and only rarely attempted to take land by force. As migrants settled down and intermarried, peoples formed and re-formed. Local languages continued; newcomers' languages were adopted; mixed languages emerged. When cattle-raisers and tillers of the soil intermingled, hierarchical relationships usually developed. Improved food supply and population increase brought on further migrations. Among the states of the Sudanic belt, from tenth-century Ghana, through Mali in the thirteenth and fourteenth centuries, to sixteenth-century Songhai, wars of expansion, raids, and internal divisions caused flight, captivity migration, and political exile. Bornu, for example, was founded by Sefawa rulers and their followers after they had been in exile from Kanem for a century.[3]

Trade routes conveyed slaves and free, cultural patterns and material goods, metals in particular, to neighboring or distant societies. Islamic traders connected the western Bambuk and Bouré goldfields near historic Ghana and the Ashanti or Akan goldfield to the Mediterranean World, and from there Venetians extended the gold trade to Asia. By 1300 the Bantu Shona people of Zimbabwe began to exploit the gold-bearing deposits of the southern African plateau. From Zimbabwe north to what later came to be called Lake Victoria, iron metallurgy had its center, and export routes radiated out. In the center, Katanga copper-mining peoples engaged in long-distance trade. The trading networks of the west and west-central social space were based on artisanal production and local and regional demand structures. Merchants obtained goods from regionally concentrated goldsmiths, iron-working artisans and artists—as well as other metallurgists—potters of many societies, and weavers with gendered patterns of production. Agricultural products were traded regionally, sometimes by river fleets, while the caffeine-containing kola nuts, some spices, and salt from Saharan deposits entered long-distance trade. Agriculturalists and artisans generated surpluses sufficient to support nonproducing nobilities and magistrates and Muslim-African long-distance traders. In the markets, local women jostled with merchants from far away. As in medieval Europe, small amounts of imports from other areas of the world were traded next to local produce (chap. 3.3).

Urban cultures, like that of Djenné, needed food imports, supported a mercantile bourgeoisie that consumed luxury goods, and attracted large numbers of transport workers as porters, camel drivers, and pirogue sailors. Northeast of Djenné, salt caravans of 10,000 or more camels arrived in Timbuktu. An important Saharan trade center, the cosmopolitan city "attracted countless ethnic groups" including Songhai, Arabic, and Tamashagh speakers. During the sixteenth century, Timbuktu's scholar-notables taught some 4,000–5,000 in-migrating students (in a population of perhaps 50,000) and made the city a center of the book trade.[4]

East African coastal societies engaged in and were shaped by transoceanic commercial migrations and exchanges.[5] Resident peoples faced competition from merchants from Daybul, the northwestern Indian port settled by Arab invaders in 711. The impact of their oceanwide trading community may be compared to the impact of the Normans in England in 1066 (Davidson). Newcomers to Zanzibar originally came from the Persian Gulf littoral. Around 1200 or earlier, peoples called Shirazi (from Shiraz, Persia) arrived along the eastern coasts, but—instead of being Persians—they were presumably Africans from the north who intermingled with earlier "Syrian" merchants. When doctrinal differences divided the Islamic religion, the East African

Shiites fled southward and Islamic proselytizing brought Arab newcomers.[6] In 1415 Malindi, a seaport in what is now southeastern Kenya, sent an ambassador to the imperial court of China, and in the 1420s and 1430s, the Chinese fleets of Cheng Ho touched East Africa. Like the Comoros, Madagascar had been settled by long-distance migrants: Muslim Indonesians along the east coast, Bantu along the west coast. While some of the early inhabitants moved inland, others intermarried, leading to the emergence of the Antalaot and Iharanian peoples, who spoke a Malayo-Polynesian language. The present-day Malagasy population developed out of this intermingling.[7]

Changes in long-distance demand and supply altered local cultures and migration patterns. When Arab, Indian, and sometimes Chinese merchants sought ever increasing amounts of ivory in exchange for Indian cottons and manufactured goods, the need to safeguard long-distance trade gave new importance to leadership among East African peoples. Links between traders and chiefs were often strengthened by intermarriage. When locals intermarried with sailors and other newcomers from Arabia and India, the Swahili culture emerged (from Arabic *sahil:* coast), which was Muslim in religion and culture and African in language and ethnic heritage. Through ties of marriage and affection, local women opened the way for newcomers to establish themselves. Parallel to such cultural conversion was the exclusion of captives from the interior, who were exported to the Baghdad caliphate as production slaves for the salt mines at Basra and the plantations along the Strait of Hormuz.

By 1400, as a result of such trade mobility and migrations, thirty-seven trading towns extended from Muqdisho (Mogadishu) to Sofala in the south. The major ones, like Malindi, Mombasa, and Kilwa, could perhaps be compared with Venice and Genoa. Kilwa, like Venice, expanded its control over neighboring coastal regions though never over inland peoples. Locally minted coins and cowrie shells from the Maldive Islands served as currency. In 1331 ibn Baṭṭuṭāh described the people as "devout, chaste, and virtuous" and thought that its large mosques made Kilwa "one of the most beautiful and well-constructed towns in the world."[8] While the ocean trade was in Arab hands, African merchants developed connections to the inland societies and to the mines of the Zimbabwe culture of 1200–1450 C.E., which used coerced labor for mining, including girls for particularly narrow shafts. Zimbabwe's rulers and armies consisted of immigrants, but its workers were local peoples; when the veins were exhausted by the mid-fifteenth century, emigration ensued. The coastal urban societies were hierarchically structured, with a Muslim elite in control of political and commercial life, a mainly African population of artisans, mariners, and craftsmen in bead- and cotton-production, and a slave population from the interior, usually non-Muslim in culture. People traveled great distances and came from far away.

In fifteenth-century West Africa, immigrant Fulbe people assimilated most of the pastoralists of the savannah. Europeans had only a light impact on the region. When the Portuguese reached Benin in the early 1480s, "they found it the powerful capital of a considerable empire," with ramparts, entry gates, a large palace, and wide streets. A Dutch visitor compared the capital to cities in the Netherlands but saw it as more spacious. Raw iron, finished utensils, and the artwork of the iron-masters was sold in the market. The ruler entrusted trade with Europeans to particular agents. But the Portuguese onslaught and wars with neighboring feudal states brought about Benin's decline. At the mouth of the Congo River, the Kongo kingdom's economy of craft production, agricultural surpluses, and interregional trade was disrupted after the 1480s by the Portuguese demand for slaves. Portuguese immigrants settled the island of Madeira (which by 1550 had 20,000 inhabitants, including 3,000 slaves), populated the Azores, and established the Cape Verde Islands as a port of call on the long-distance voyages to the Cape of Good Hope, Brazil, and the Spanish Indies. São Tomé was colonized by forcing young Portuguese-Jewish men and women to emigrate there, and about half of 4,000 inhabitants were resident agricultural slaves. In addition, thousands of slaves debarked while in transit for export to the Americas. Previously, Islamic traders had begun a cross-Saharan slave trade; within Africa, slavery became an "assimilative institution" that changed population composition by adding people to kin groups, villages, or societies.

In Central Africa's interior, migrations continued and dispersed new cultural techniques from pottery to iron utensils for agriculture, hunting, and fishing. Whereas a limited number of brokers and their carriers could mediate the spread of artifacts, the diffusion of the Bantu languages required "intimate, long-term contact between speakers." North of the Zambezi River, several regional kingdoms emerged: the Luba and Lunda kingdoms near Lake Kisale and others south of Lake Malawi (Lake Nyasa). According to oral traditions, immigrant hunting men who founded the new states married the daughters of local rulers. Luba chiefs competing unsuccessfully for power probably were among the migrants who asserted their rule over the Lunda and other peoples. South of the Zambezi, cattle-raising societies were male-dominated. The animals provided the wealth to buy brides. Because women tilled the land, the wealthier a man was, the more worker-brides he could purchase. All cattle-based societies were susceptible to overgrazing and droughts, and whole regions had to be abandoned, like the Toutswe sites in eastern Botswana. Iliffe interprets all of the pre-sixteenth-century migrations as colonizing endeavors.[9]

From their islands and West African coastal bases, the Portuguese or "Franks" under Vasco da Gama rounded the Cape of Good Hope in 1498. From the Iberian Peninsula, others, impressed by legends about African Christian kings and their riches, pursued a Mediterranean route and migrated to Abyssinia. The rulers of this last of the East African Christian kingdoms claimed descent from King Solomon and the Queen of Sheba, thus asserting their legitimacy by invoking their migratory experiences. Through both routes, the Portuguese reached East African towns like Mediterranean traders before them. This world, new to them, had been described two and a half centuries earlier by a Chinese customs official and another century earlier by the geographer al-Idrīsī. A chronicler in Kilwa noted that the Portuguese "were corrupt and dishonest persons who had only come to spy out the land in order to seize it." But trade competition and dynastic disputes between the cities prevented any common action. A plan to destroy da Gama's ships came to naught, and at Malindi he was supplied for the leg to India with a pilot and provisions, which, according to the Kilwa Chronicle, were put under a curse. In the coastal towns, the Portuguese saw "many handsome houses of stone and mortar several storeys high, with many windows and flat roofs." The streets were "well laid out" and the trade was voluminous and profitable. Indian merchants and their wives displayed their wealth, and trading families connected inland agriculturalists, ivory hunters, and miners with the Indian subcontinent. It was a "cosmopolitan world."[10]

6.2   Merchant Communities and Ethnogenesis

By 1600, African populations amounted to an estimated 5–6 million in the North, 12–13 million in Egypt and the Nile states, 24 million in the region north of the Kalahari Desert, and 13 million in East and Central Africa. Those south of the Sahara formed the population base for the slave trade that increased rapidly after the 1630s. Around 1700 Portuguese and Ottoman traders began to sell firearms to Africans to increase the supply of slaves and of ivory. Intra-African political and military mobilization involved mercenaries and intercultural conflict. Moroccan rulers, for example, marched troops into the sub-Saharan states in the late sixteenth century, and Bornu rulers hired Turkish mercenaries. Christian Abyssinia—with weak Portuguese support—succumbed to the attacks of neighboring Muslim rulers who had Ottoman help. The pastoralist Oromo or Galla people moved into southern Abyssinia. At first young men expanded grazing grounds; then families or clans followed. They collected taxes from the residents, devastated the highlands, and became Abyssinian mercenaries.

In transoceanic communication, Lisbon remained on the top of the power and commercial hierarchy into the mid-seventeenth century, with Goa as its regional center for the Indian Ocean. But Indian metropolitan centers remained strong, supplying merchants, bankers, and capital to East African towns. Arab traders established a Surat-based commercial operation that extended from northwestern India to Oman. Further south, a Zambezi-Goa trade connection competed with one that linked Kilwa to Oman (maps 6.2, 6.3).[11]

In the increasing internal African trade, several distinct types of merchant communities emerged as a result of migration and ethnogenesis. In many African societies, the sphere of religion and commerce was separate from the sphere of politics and the military. "Merchant clerics," in contrast to European "merchant warriors," could travel and establish contacts easily (Curtin). Soninke merchants developed a doctrine of pacifism to emphasize their neutrality. Some trading groups, like the Kongolese Nzabi, formed stateless societies, bound together by fictitious kinship, ritualized comradeship, or contractual partnership. In Islamic societies, too, religious and trading activities merged: "Muslim" and "trader" were often synonymous. Spread by Arab traders, Islam was first embraced by merchants in a belt from Senegal to Zanzibar (and further on to the Philippines) and accommodated Muslims regardless

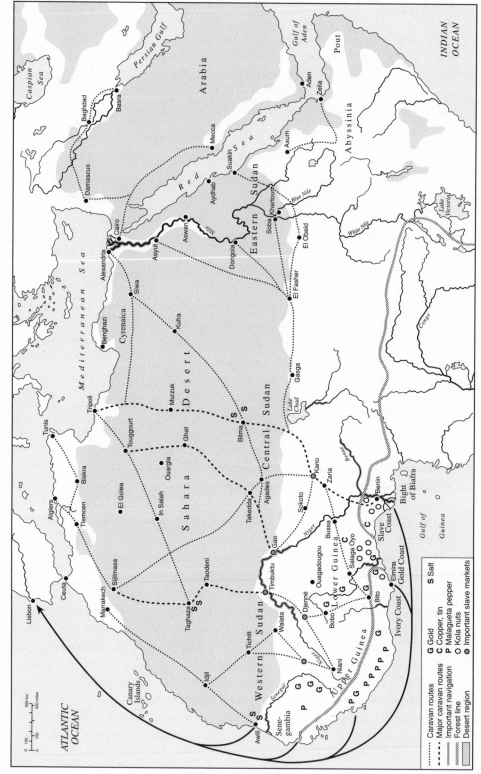

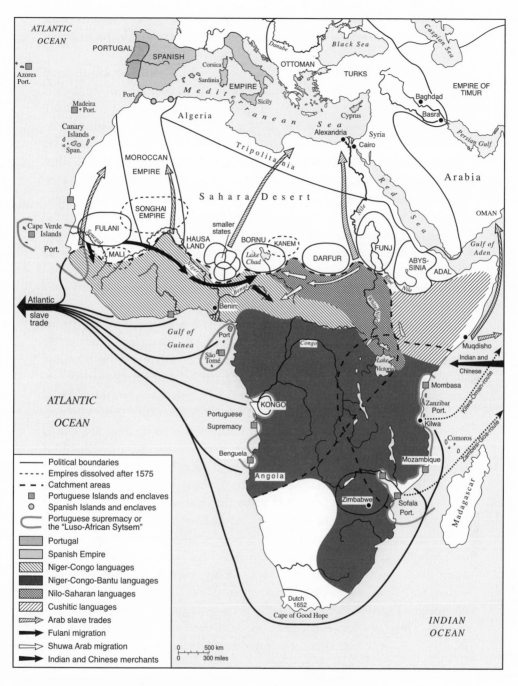

6.3   African Trade and Migration around 1600

of creed, Sunni or Shia.[12] Such patterns stood in contrast with Mediterranean *funduqs* and recent Portuguese *feitorias*, in which merchants lived in segregated extraterritorial, self-governing quarters.

The Ibadi, who followed the Kharajite version of Islam, were a northern group of traders. Persecuted by Algerian Sunni regimes, they took refuge in the oasis of Ouargla and, after 1000 C.E., in the Mzab valley of Algeria. There they established a date-farming agricultural base and migrated to Mediterranean cities to enter the retail trade. Algeria's Ottoman rulers granted them—like Black African and European Christian merchants—the right to self-administration. This ethnic clustering lasted for centuries until, after the French colonial conquest of Algeria in the 1830s, their service as cultural brokers was no longer required. The Mzabis adapted by developing new patterns of migration. Families from the five Mzab towns sent selected sons off as labor migrants but encouraged them to marry before leaving—and kept the wives at home. The male urban communities were tightly regulated by religious leaders of the home community, who sought to preserve the traditional puritanical ways of life and the Berber language. This separation from the societies of the host towns prevented acculturation as late as the mid-twentieth century.[13]

In the Hausa-speaking region, separate towns or in-town quarters (*zongos*) were assigned to merchants or established by them. In Kumasi, the capital of Ashanti, the ethnic trading community numbered 60,000 in the mid-tenth century. Merchants of different ethnocultural background occupied separate but neighboring quarters. Ethnicity, social status, and experience determined who traveled and who became settled landlord-brokers in the trading circuits and diasporic settlements. Those who were on the move belonged to particular *asalis*, endogamous groups of a common, usually distant place of origin. Three particularly important *asali* groups, including two of servile origin, originating from peoples north of Hausaland, separated from their kin and culturally became Hausa. Such mobility established a common savannah trading culture from Cape Verde to Lake Chad. Along the kola-nut route to the Volta River basin (today's Ghana), such ethnic islands survived into the twentieth century.[14]

In East Africa, multiethnic nomad groups—the Zimba, for example—wrought havoc by ravaging coastal towns in the later sixteenth century. Some of the towns sought alliances with Ottoman envoys, but no support was forthcoming. A standoff between the Portuguese and the Ottoman empires slowed down trade along the Strait of Hormuz and Red Sea routes. This conflict permitted local Arab rulers, after 1650, to keep Oman free from domination and to establish overlordship in several East African cities. They sent Arab administrator-migrants to these commercial centers.

The Portuguese impact on the nonfortified East African towns was demoralizing; they "wrecked and looted and burned with a destructiveness previously unknown in Africa." In 1505 two Franciscan priests set down a cross in Kilwa, and—after the ships' commander prayed—the town was pillaged and set on fire. In Mombasa "neither man nor women, young or old, nor child however small [remained], all who had failed to escape had been killed and burned." Towns whose merchants and rulers continued to trade independently were sacked repeatedly, and urban populations were forced into

flight. To provide strongholds for their fleets, Portuguese commanders fortified Sofala, Mozambique Island, Kilwa, and Mombasa. But forced by circumstances, including a lack of settlers and women migrants, the Portuguese then merged indigenous
cultural patterns with their own heritage. As other traders before them had done,
Portuguese merchants intermarried locally. Crew members, left behind as brokers
when their ships departed, joined with African brokers to establish contacts with the
interior. By permission of the Portuguese crown, they built private fortified trading
posts (*prazos*). Goanese came from Portugal's enclave in India, and Afro-Portuguese
and Afro-Indian children were born and matured. Some "Portuguese" were "simply
Africans who chose to accept a Portuguese identity." "The *prazos* became cross-
cultural communities, gradually more African than European." Thus the Portuguese
left no lasting cultural impact. The Swahili language, under Arab influence written
in Arabic script, merely absorbed some sixty new words from Portuguese (such as the
names for playing cards, as noted by Davidson). The architecture remained African,
and Swahili culture recovered from the initial disruption. The Portuguese could "ruin
the older patterns of commerce but [were] too weak to create a viable alternative."
Ironically, "Portugal's most important contribution" may have been "to increase Africanization of coastal culture by reducing contact with Arabia."[15]

6.3   Changes: The Atlantic Slave Trade to the Nineteenth Century

While Asia became the supplier of luxury goods and the Americas the supplier of
plantation products, Africa supplied enslaved workers.[16] Slavery and debt bondage,
so-called rights-in-persons, were indigenous to many African societies. In payment
of a debt, men or women pawned themselves or, more commonly, children or other
relatives (mainly female) to the creditor. A pawn's labor covered the interest but not
the principal. Pawned persons usually stayed close to their family of origin, but they
moved when the creditor moved. The borderline between debt bondage and slavery
was fluid, and pawns might be sold into slavery. Pawning served social and familial
functions in enabling creditors to acquire wives (by paying parents' debts in return for
a daughter) and to acquire concubines and thus additional children and labor power;
it also gave male debtors and creditors increased control over wives. As it came to
an end, the practice was feminized and generally limited to adult women and female
children. Pawnship continued into the twentieth century and grew in importance
during the depression of the 1930s.[17]

Enslavement through warfare and raids (the more common practice) involved a
high loss of human life and left behind destroyed villages, where those who had escaped capture faced starvation. The populations of whole villages were moved during warfare or forced to provide food for elites and armies. Slavery in African societies placed captives in new social relations: its oppressive aspects notwithstanding,
it was assimilative or integrative. After the end of productive slavery, the societies
of the Arab and Indian Ocean World limited slavery to service, either domestic or in

commerce or government. In rights-in-person (Islamic or Animist) slavery, the captives joined families or institutions and were considered human beings of limited legal status. By contrast, in chattel (Christian) slavery in the Atlantic trade, men and women became things (chattel), first on the islands in the Mediterranean and off the African coast and then on the vast estates of the Americas (and a few islands in the Indian Ocean). Rights-in-person slavery valued women because of their labor and childbearing capabilities. Under the regime of Atlantic chattel slavery, men were preferred.

Within Africa slavery was practiced less along the east coast than at the Horn or in the savannah. But for two millennia traders had sold slaves from East Africa northward (chap. 6.4). The region was, at first, hardly touched by the Atlantic trade, except for the Portuguese export of Africans from Malindi and Mozambique, some of whom even reached Mexico before 1600. Slavery on European-owned plantations began particularly early in Mauritius, where the native African and Afro-Indian population was insufficient for sugarcane cultivation introduced by French settlers, who arrived in 1714. By 1767, Mauritius had a slave population of 15,000, which grew to 49,000 in 1807. Developments in Réunion were similar. The economic regime on the European-ruled Indian Ocean islands was an extension of the São Tomé and Atlantic island models.

When the demand of the Atlantic plantation complex (Curtin) was added to the internal and eastern demand for slaves from the 1440s to the 1880s, millions of men and women, especially of young age, and children were wrenched from their villages and families. "Alone, a person was nobody. The self was defined in relationships to others. One was a son, a daughter, a parent, or a grandparent, and had a place, large or small, in the village. What one was or was known to be rested on others." Each indidivual experienced something akin to what Olaudah Equiano, aged eleven, and his sister remembered as a traumatic rupture. Born into a wealthy family in Benin in 1745, he was playing at home while the adults worked in the fields or were otherwise occupied. Suddenly, even though lookouts were present, two men and a woman climbed the wall of the compound, seized the two children, and carried them off. Bound and gagged, they traveled for two days and then were separated despite their tears and entreaties. Olaudah was sold from trader to trader and finally transported by canoe. The Atlantic crossing was as new and fearsome to him as it was to European emigrants who traveled by their own free will. Slaves from the far reaches of the Lunda empire might travel a distance of 1,000 miles (1,650 kilometers); enslaved co-ethnics sent east from the same regions might traverse 700 miles (1,150 kilometers) to the coast.[18] In West Africa, the slave trade and raids by neighboring peoples on each other assumed much larger proportions when the Euro-American demand for enslaved labor grew. The traditional social core of the system, rights-in-person, was transformed into the economic rationale of commodification of human beings (see chap. 5.3). Capitalized initially from the European core, the plantation system in the Spanish, Dutch, English, and French Caribbean, in Brazil after the 1530s, and in North America after the 1630s developed an insatiable demand for slave labor to produce sugar and profits for the core. Just as salt, indispensable to human survival, was to spawn the French Revolution when the government raised the *gabelle* (the tax on salt), so sugar became seemingly indispensable as a major flavoring item and exacted the heavy toll on human lives that incited slave rebellions, most notably the one in St. Domingue. Across the globe, daily food consumption, patterns of trade, and the exploitation of unfree labor were intricately linked.

In the first half of the seventeenth century, West African slaving exported approximately 10,000 men and women annually to the Americas. The trade more than doubled over the next half-century, assumed massive proportions in the eighteenth century, and—the prohibition of the slave trade notwithstanding—declined only slowly in the first half of the nineteenth century, but did so precipitously thereafter.[19] Refined by Lovejoy, Curtin's "census," in fact an estimate of the Atlantic slave trade, revised the traditional assumption that some 15 million Africans were deported. Of the 11.7 million who were carried off, 9.8 million arrived in the Americas, the others having perished during the voyage. To gauge the total human toll, one has to add to the mortality figures the deaths incurred by the raids and by the marches in coffles to the coast. According to Curtin, from 1450 to 1600, 125,000 slaves came to the Americas; 1.3 million in the next century (average annual arrivals increasing from 7,500 to 24,100); 6 million in the period 1701–1810 (about 40,000 annually before 1740, approximately 60,000 thereafter); and another 1.9 million from the legal end of the trade to 1870 (40,000 annually until 1850). The figures include East Africans traded by the Portuguese around the Cape. After the legal prohibition of the trade by the European powers between 1807 and 1815, the pent-up demand following the Napoleonic wars, the sugar boom in Cuba, and the coffee boom in Brazil fueled a large "contraband" trade. Over the whole period, about one-third of the forced migrants were women (map 6.4).[20]

All three stages of enslavement—capture and transport to the coastal dungeons, the ocean voyage, and the "seasoning period" after arrival—had repercussions for the societies involved. African societies and states adapted to the slave trade; profits from the Atlantic passage accumulated in the Portuguese, British, French, Dutch, and other mercantile centers and influenced commercial relations and labor migrations; and the receiving societies changed economically, demographically, and culturally.

In territorial terms, the Euro-commercial powers remained limited to the coastal trading stations, a few zones of Portuguese supremacy, and the tiny Dutch Cape Colony. The ideology of Christian superiority and European supremacy as expressed in the higher levels of occidental discourse was hardly reflected in day-to-day dealings in the African trading posts. Europeans had to negotiate privileges from regional and local states and paid tributes, fees, and duties; only on occasion did they rely on guns. Traders, except during the initial decades, were not about to embark slave-hunting expeditions of their own and tapped, instead, into existing African practices of enslavement. This was cost-effective since Europeans had neither sufficient manpower nor a knowledge of the interior and of local customs and practices of warfare. In the 1490s, Portuguese missionaries, teachers, and craftsmen briefly stopped the

6.4 From Many Peoples to Generic Chattel Slaves

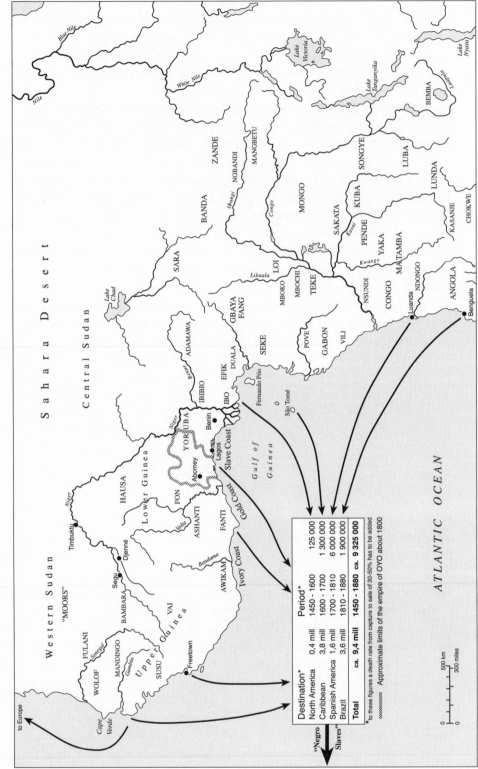

Destination*	Period*			
		1450 - 1600	125 000
North America	0,4 mill	1600 - 1700	1 300 000
Caribbean	3,8 mill	1700 - 1810	6 000 000
Spanish America	1,6 mill	1810 - 1880	1 900 000
Brazil	3,6 mill		
Total	ca. 9,4 mill	1450 - 1880	ca. 9 325 000

*to these figures a death rate from capture to sale of 30-50% has to be added
ooooooooo Approximate limits of the empire of OYO about 1800

slave trade with the Kongo kingdom, where the ruler had accepted Christianity. But profit motives overrode spirituality—slaving was quickly resumed.

The European gunpowder empires spawned local gunpowder states to supply them with forced labor. African political and social structures adapted to the commerce. The fifteenth-century African states of the savannah were replaced as trade centers by a coastal belt of states negotiating with the Europeans, an inland belt of intermediate trading societies, and a slave-generating interior. Along the Bight of Benin, demand permitted the kingdoms of, first, Benin, then Dahomey, and finally Oyo, to become important slave-trading states. Further to the south, the Kasanje and Matamba states became intermediaries for the Angola coast. Societies and polities became hierarchically layered into weak supplying societies, male-warrior raiding societies, independent trading networks, and slave-selling states. To participate in the trade, African states needed an "appropriate political and commercial organization." With substantial regional variations, this involved "a combination of military power, economic resources and institutional adaptation sufficient to carry European trade goods into the interior" and to guard slaves on the return trip. Interior societies—whether they were states or mercantile "houses" and "families"—had to increase both their slaving raids and their ability to move the captives. Thus the goods-conveying non-state networks of particular ethno-religious groups were increasingly supplemented with and, by the eighteenth century, supplanted by state-backed armed networks financed by duties or tributes to kings or their local representatives. To take one early example, toward the end of the seventeenth century the Wolof Kajoor state increased the number of its slave warriors, and militarization increased in the region of the upper Senegal River after the French established a trading post. By the early eighteenth century, the Bambara state of Segu had been turned into "an enormous machine to produce slaves,"[21] and a British report of 1721 noted that African kings "commit great depredations inland."

At first, men and women from coastal peoples were enslaved: for example, Fulani, Mandinka, Wolof from Senegambia and Ibo, Ibibio, Efik, and Moko ethnics from the Bight of Benin and the Niger delta. The rivalry between the Yoruba and Aja peoples produced captives. By the eighteenth century, slaves came from the distant interior Luba and Lunda state, whose wars of expansion resulted in large numbers of captives. Over time, the populations of all states and peoples from Dahomey to the Kongo kingdom to Angola were reduced in order to supply men, women, and children, though slaving decreased in the north and intensified in the Portuguese south. Demand in the Americas for particular skills influenced the composition of the catchment areas: educated urban slaves, miners from the goldfields, skilled cattle- and horsemen. The emphasis on plantation work and on the image of "dumb Negroes" has eclipsed this aspect of slavery. The interaction of captives of different nations and the intensification of long-distance trade involved the emergence of linguae francae—Yoruba, for example.[22]

European supremacy hurt or benefited social strata in West African states in highly differentiated ways. Communal elements receded in the face of hierarchical structures. Pawnship and war captivity as traditional ways of bondage were replaced by slave-producing warfare, raids, and judicial processes adapted to conviction and sale (from which the judges-kings profited), sale by powerful relatives or superiors, and, finally, sale for debts or as protection from starvation during famines.

Out of a West African population estimated at around 25 million in 1700, about 40,000 men and women were deported annually or nearly half a million in a dozen years. Further south, from the Congo to Angola's hinterlands exports were higher during the peak years. This population loss occurred at a time when populations in Europe, Asia, and the Americas began to increase rapidly. The captives, in the most reproductive segment of their life-cycle, were segregated into a westward flow of men across the Atlantic, while most captured women stayed within African slaveholding societies. Planters' demands for a male labor force resulted in imbalanced sex ratios. Patrick Manning has argued that the slave trade limited population growth in West Africa up to 1750, caused population decline from 1750 to 1850, and kept the population stagnant on the continent as a whole. Others, Martin Klein, for example, have suggested considerably higher depletion rates, attributable to high losses due to warfare, the difficulties of noncaptured survivors in sustaining themselves in destroyed villages, "wastage" in transit, and reduced reproduction rates. The latter argument sees 150 years of population decline before 1850, stagnation thereafter, and, with European territorial acquisitions, the last third of the nineteenth century becoming the bloodiest period in African history.[23]

Authors reluctant to concede the damage done to individuals and societies have suggested that the region, with a population density similar to Europe, could not have supported larger numbers of people; that the Atlantic connection through imports of new food crops improved standards of living in the slave-producing regions; and that in a "civilizing" process tribal or regionally confined societies were induced to develop and strengthen a "unitary, territorial political authority" akin to elaborate European political structures and nation-building. Such apologetic conjectures overlook the fact that individuals, local groups, and whole societies have numerous options to react to change and to problems resulting from population growth. Population reduction in West Africa was imposed by unequal power relationships between Europe and Africa and between social classes in African societies. Weaker, segmented societies were wiped out in the process; community solidarity decreased; and gender relations changed. Elected chiefs became autocratic.[24]

The African intermediary states no longer acted as cultural brokers, as merchants in the past had done. Those conveying slaves to the coast had no conception of a plantation system. Only at the coastal depots did Europeans become involved in person as merchants and shippers. Later, some European traders settled in the interior. To gain a share of the trade or to control it, they developed close relations with the respective rulers and often intermarried. Such men came from many European nations: Irishmen with little capital, Englishmen who married into locally important families, Dutchmen with far-reaching connections, men of Euro-African background who built a power base by having several wives, numerous children, and more slaves.

In the coastal slave exchanges, captives were thrown into dungeons or penned up in open-air barracoons. Costs had to be low. Thus food was poor and often insufficient; the sorting, consigning, and processing were done with no regard for the commodity ("human cattle"), as long as it was not damaged or permitted to deteriorate beyond salability. "When we treat concerning buying them," the commodified human beings were ordered to strip down regardless of sex and age and, naked, were examined as to health and ability to labor, "even to the smallest member without the least distinction or modesty."[25] When the commodity did deteriorate, as Olaudah Equiano did by refusing to eat, it—he or she—was tied down and flogged. If the deterioration progressed beyond recovery, however, the commodity was dropped by the wayside or thrown overboard. A certain amount of spoilage was part of the calculation, but such spoilage was not meant to reduce profitability of the trade.

Chattel slavery irrevocably destroyed the networks of kinship and neighborhood. Elders were not honored: since they could not work, they were discarded or left to die. Men and women who had defined their social identities in relationships became items in the marketplace. Communication with other commodified captives might depend on sign language because of the linguistic variations among ethnic groups. Survival required new forms of communication and, since the new world was alien, the total adaptation of behavior. Intentionally deprived of their identities, slaves were made into nonpersons.

On the ships, African people of many ethnicities and European sailors, often also of many cultural backgrounds, mingled. The slave ships became a "meeting place of geographically remote disease environments" (Sheridan). Slaves were tightly packed on the ships—an experience the colonized Irish shared to some degree during their trips for seasonal work in England and in the Quebec-bound famine-era "coffin ships." The fettered slaves were left to wallow in their own excrement, although they were exercised regularly. The food was poor and inadequate. Equiano related that the sailors threw unused fresh fish overboard rather than feed the starving cargo. Since ships were not capable of carrying sufficient amounts of drinking water, dehydration aggravated ill health. Sailors wanting sex used the female cargo. Illness, utter desperation, and death characterized the "middle passage" across the hot equatorial waters. Suicide to escape humiliation and destruction of identity was common. The punishment of any infractions, including the refusal to eat and the attempt to kill oneself was brutal, as was the punishment meted out to the ships' free sailors. A British act of 1788 limited transport to three slaves for every two tons of a ship, but this still involved intermediate decks often spaced at no more than two feet in height. On the individual level, providing linguistic or sexual services to the Europeans might ensure physical survival—unless fellow-sufferers reacted with lethal violence. Such compromises did not ensure self-determination: interpreters and sexual partners were often sold like all others. Given the desperate regime of the profit motive, a desperate slave effort at self-liberation ("mutiny") was a rationale for ensuring identity.

The voyage could take just three weeks from the westernmost African ports to the easternmost coast of Brazil, but it could extend to three months from Angola to Virginia or last longer from Mozambique around the Cape. Of those surviving the ordeal in the period from 1451 to 1870, the largest share went to Brazil, followed by the British Caribbean, the French Caribbean, and Spanish America. Minor shares went to the Dutch and Danish Caribbean, to the British North American colonies/United States and, finally, to the Atlantic islands and Europe.[26]

The 9.8 million enslaved men and women and the millions of indentured laborers and free migrants entered stratified labor markets for slave, redemptioner, or free labor. The degrees of agency and the ratios in power relationships differed, as did death rates. Some planters adopted a "seasoning" period of several years of light tasks and health care. Others immediately sent new slaves to the particularly hard labor of forest clearing. According to contemporary planters' reports, one-quarter to one-half of the newly arrived slaves died in the first few years even on—from the owners' point of view—well-managed plantations. In much of the Atlantic World of societal regimes based on slave labor, the economic rationale physically entered the bodies of individual human beings, providing some with lives of affluence and ample food, such as the burghers depicted by the Dutch school of painters, and others with suffering, lashings, and death. Healthy workers received marks of distinction: red-hot irons were used to brand them with the company logo. Commodified labor forces in the Americas had to reconstruct personal identities and collective communities before regaining even a small amount of agency in their lives. Even then, their lives and their community solidarity remained conditional on the pleasure of their owners.

In global economic terms, African intermediaries, whether whole states or specific elite groups, provided European merchants with labor power capable of producing wealth while receiving in exchange goods for consumption or, in the case of guns, instruments for looting others. In the sales-process, the use value of persons under the rights-in-persons regime was replaced by exchange value of commodified human beings. Some economists have rejected Eric Williams's argument that the profits from slave labor significantly contributed to English industrialization. Except for the merchants of Bristol and Liverpool, whose annual profits were sustained at just under 10 percent of the investment, most slave merchants reaped low returns on their capital. The notion of the extremely profitable nature of the slave trade thus has had to be scaled back to the profitability of particular voyages in particular trading connections. However, econometric calculation often overlooks the obvious. The classic view that African slaves provided the labor for the plantation economies and European planters the capital is true only for the initial phase. Thereafter slave labor created value that permitted the system to expand. Regardless of whether English or other capitalists were able to reap large or small profits, the sale and productivity of slave labor massively changed African societies and built societies across the Americas. The economic connections ranged widely: U.S. shipyards constructed the fast slave ships that in the nineteenth-century illegal trade could outrun any vessel of the British navy, and merchants of all the European powers traded slave-produced sugar and coffee across the Atlantic. The plantation complex involved a forced labor regime, including control over the workers outside of working hours, labor forces that were not self-sustaining, large-scale capitalist agricultural mass production for export, imports of food and clothing, control over production and the society as well as over global investments from a distant core society. The multidirectional slave trade was one of the most important factors in the complex procedures of capital accumulation in the Atlantic core. According to Curtin, "The economic model for enslavement is one of burglary, not of production. In economic terms, the value of the slave is not a real cost but an 'opportunity cost.'"[27]

In the globally connected system, many profited. "At the height of the eighteenth-century commerce, gunsmiths in Birmingham alone were exporting muskets to Africa at the rate of between 100,000 and 150,000 a year, and it was common talk that one Birmingham gun rated one Negro slave." International commercial relations and trade in human beings, in other words, encouraged men to migrate to Birmingham or local residents to enter the trade of gunsmith or join the international labor market for sailors (see chap. 7.4 for the Dutch example). Thus whole sections of the European population were involved: owners of shares in slave ships, suppliers of commodities for the triangular (or more complex) trade, and consumers of slave-produced sugar.[28]

6.4   Continuities: Slavery in the Islamic and Asian Worlds

A twelfth-century Chinese source noted the presence in China of slaves from East Africa, commenting that they are easily captured and "have no longing for home." Africans, both free and enslaved, reached the Southeast and East Asian societies as sailors. Rulers in those regions imported captive Africans to demonstrate status. At South Asian courts, Black slaves could serve household or political functions. In Egypt and the Ottoman Empire, African slaves manned armies and rose to power. Like most authors into the 1960s, Davidson concluded that "along the East Coast [of Africa], so far as all known records indicate, slaving remained a minor aspect of trade or one that was altogether absent." Since then, research has shown that Islamic Arabs were "master slavers," who traded slaves longer and in larger numbers than Europeans.[29]

The trade across the Sahara, the Red Sea, and the Indian Ocean, which lasted from 650 to 1900 C.E., carried the largest number of captives to North Africa and Arabia, the smallest number to India, and negligible numbers further east. Before 1500 C.E. annual departure rates probably amounted to between 1,000 and 6,000. The Koran sanctioned the enslavement of non-Muslims, in making "non-belief" rather than origin or color of skin the basis for slavery. The borderlines between believers and nonbelievers were fluid, however. For raiders and traders, profit was the same regardless of whether the captive was pagan or Muslim. Although according to doctrine only capture in religious war (jihad) and birth to a slave mother and slave father could result in slave status, in practice raiding served the same purpose.

Productive slavery of men had been common only in the irrigation areas of southern Mesopotamia/Persia/Iraq. Slaves were used on Basra plantations since the ninth century and on the smaller estates along the Persian Gulf. For Basra, "this key metropole of Indian Ocean commerce," as Gordon puts it, "slaving helped to build a capitalistic world system in the sense that Wallerstein attributes exclusively to the Atlantic-centered European hegemony." Since 1200 highly skilled slaves worked as pearl divers in the Persian Gulf. In this dangerous trade, in which the accident rate was high and life expectancy short, only small numbers found income. Free and slave divers worked together.[30]

In general, bondage in the East involved state or domestic service. Arabic rulers sought slave soldiers for particular military undertakings, for standing armies, or for service as palace guards. Slave soldiers often came from a wide variety of regions and cultural origins: they could be Africans, Turks, or Circassians. Tribute to rulers might be paid in slaves. In administrative service, slaves could rise to high positions, as at Indian courts (see chap. 7.1), in the Ottoman Empire (see chap. 5.1), or in Egypt. In merchant "families," male and female slaves became a kind of nonrelated kin varying in position from servants in the house and business yard to sailors on the dhows of the Arab coastal trade or to educated clerks. They might be paddlers of canoes in inland trade or crew members in Indian Ocean shipping. They might guard other slaves or be used as carriers in head porterage. Domestic slaves remained a luxury of the upper social strata; this predominantly female servant labor force was integrated into wealthy families, the retinue of princes and princesses, and the courts of rulers. Dependency relationships placed restrictions on sale. Slavery was part of everyday social existence rather than a segregated aspect of life.

The impossibility of slaves' returning to their places of origin and the relatively benign nature of the system, enjoined by the Koran, legitimized the system to such a degree that flight and revolt were rare and no abolition movement developed.[31] With regional variations, slaves and freemen had the same relationship to Allah. They could marry with their master's permission, and slave women marrying freemen were to receive a dowry from their master. Slave women could not be separated from their young children. Harsh punishments were prohibited. In a contractual labor arrangement (mukataba), slaves kept part of their incomes and, if successful, could in turn own slaves, become substantial property owners, and purchase their freedom. Under Islamic law, manumission signified a slave owner's atonement for transgressions and sins. It was also a sign of wealth and benevolence and often part of an owner's last will and testament.

After the end of productive slavery, the vast majority of the slaves were women and children. The Koran permitted men—if they could pay the bride-price and provide support—up to four wives, and slave women could be supported at a lower status as concubines. Children of masters/free fathers assumed his status and were of equal standing with the children of free wives. Their slave mothers assumed special status and could no longer be sold or alienated by the master-husband. Like male state slaves of different origins (African, Turkish, or Slavic), African, Georgian, and Circassian slave women might intermingle in the same household or court. The latter came from the regions that also supplied Istanbul, Ragusa, and Italian cities. Ethnic ascriptions emerged: societal views of beauty caused young Abyssinian—Galla—women to be valued above women from other African peoples and Circassian women above others from the Caucasus catchment area.

The restriction of women to a female space, the harem, and the prohibition of contact with other men resulted in the neutering of male slave attendants. Such eunuchs were castrated upon capture or, if born in slavery, as young boys—a practice that involved high mortality rates. They became part of the family of the court and could rise to influential positions and property ownership. Enslaved wives and concubines of rich men could draw on a retinue of enslaved female servants, their number being a sign of status. Women, men, and children torn out of their lineage by the act of enslavement could and usually did socialize into the lineage of their masters, if only perhaps for lack of an alternative.[32]

While the Eastern trade involved smaller numbers than the Atlantic one, those reaching the thinly settled Arab peninsula and North Africa accounted for a comparatively large segment of the population. In the Americas, slaves usually married other slaves, though many slave men were unable to marry because of the paucity of women, and their children were thus of African origin and of slave status. In the Orient, by contrast, the children resulting from the intermingling of free and slave parentage and of Arab, Persian, Indian, and African origins were of "mixed ancestry" and often free in status.[33]

In some African Muslim societies, in particular among the Omanis but also in Western Sudan, slavery assumed a character between state and Euro-Atlantic chattel slavery. When the capitalist mode of production penetrated East Africa, the sea-oriented Omani rulers of Zanzibar established a plantation regime with slave labor from the African interior to produce cloves for export. Among the island's Shirazi population, the middle class profited from the commerce, but the plantation economy marginalized peasants. The rulers became powerful intermediaries between the African catchment basins and the Middle Eastern centers of demand. They sold slaves to Arabia and to the Portuguese. Before 1750, 1,000–2,000 slaves were traded annually; after 1750, trade expanded rapidly, and the catchment basin extended across Central Africa to the Kongo (Zaire) River. Even though slaves sold through Portuguese-held ports of the African East Coast were traded as far as Brazil, the Eastern and Atlantic Systems remained distinct.[34]

From 1700 to 1900, according to Austen, the trans-Saharan trade supplied Egypt from Nilotic Sudan with an estimated 0.8 million and Libya, Tunisia, Algeria, and Morocco from Western Sudan with about 0.95 million. The East African coastal trade may have involved 1.2 million along the Red Sea coast and 1.1 million along the Swahili coast. Of those enslaved, some 5 percent remained at the desert edge for local use, and 20 percent died en route. In the nineteenth century, the volume increased four- to sixfold. "Multiple and overlapping networks—rising, declining, and sometimes flourishing again" over a millennium and a half—explain the many-faceted Eastern System, which contrasts sharply with the single system that bound Africa to the Americas.[36]

6.5   The Transformation of Slavery in Atlantic and Muslim Africa

The intensification of forced outbound sales and migrations and the nineteenth-century intrusion of plantation economies into Western Sudan changed traditional pawnship and enslavement practices in the several distinct regions of Africa. Since control was easier where slaves had no relatives and no knowledge of local geography and customs, enslavement within Africa also meant forced migration and sale, even though transport outside the continent was not the objective. The "transformations" to which Lovejoy refers in the title of his study of slavery involved more than the two outside influences, the economic rationales of Muslim commerce and Christian capitalism. The active involvement of African states in the enslavement process and the resulting transformation of political and social structures into male warrior societies intensified. Political fragmentation and natural disasters, such as drought and famine, also played a role. Most deeply affected were gender relations and family economies in the three periods of internal African slavery: 1350–1600, 1600–1800, and the nineteenth century.[37]

During the first period, internal slavery entailed, first, a loss of status and self-agency and, then, reinsertion into society with the acceptance of subservient status and laboring at the command of owners. Such marginalization involved new bonds in the double sense of "bonding" and "bondage." Individual captives, who in most societies could not be sold, developed life-course strategies within the limitations of their subservient position. Slave children remained enslaved, but—socialized into a new kin group and society—they were less distinguishable from their free counterparts than their uprooted parents were.[38]

In the second period, at a time when wage labor increased in Europe, slavery expanded and took on new forms in Africa. The process of marching or transporting slaves to collection points at coastal ports or the desert's edge involved multiple sales, and "for each transaction there was always the choice of whether to keep the slave or sell him or her again." Refractory, rebellious slaves were sold to distant places, often overseas, thus decreasing the potential for resistance. In terms of gender, the Atlantic slave trade complemented internal slavery. In the export trade, men dominated by a ratio of two to one. In the Sudanic and savannah trading area, in which the sales of women were predominant, surplus captured men were often killed. Keeping a slave meant an increase in a warrior society's subsistence base. Merchant houses, too, expanded from families and kin groups to containing ever larger numbers of slaves.

On the level of families, the intensification of slavery and increased wealth permitted payment of the bride-price for several wives. This in turn increased the number of female and child workers who contributed to the wealth of the head of a family.

Women were considered more valuable than men because they, like children, were easier to capture, to move about, and to control at the intended destination. Traditionally responsible for agricultural labor in most African societies, they made the better workers, and by giving birth they could further enlarge a family's labor force.

Political elites with an initial advantage of power and/or wealth passed the opportunity costs of enslavement entailed by the Atlantic trade to their subalterns, and they improved their economic position by increasing the number of bound laborers attached to themselves. Similarly, merchants increased their enslaved personnel, often granting a certain autonomy in the interest of effective long-distance trade relationships. For Muslim clerics, status came to be based on a retinue of slave laborers. This "made possible the creation of an alternative elite not dependent on commerce and with limited links to the rulers." In concert with the European slaving powers, these three elites—spiritual, commercial, and political—prevented the development of antislavery movements in Africa, though perceptive observers noted the damaging consequences of the trade early on. Rulers who initiated trading relationships by giving household servants to Portuguese men complained as early as 1526 that too many people were being carried off. In the 1670s reform-minded rulers began to advocate antislavery positions. Another half-century later, a king of Dahomey offered Europeans land to establish plantations in order to stop the exportation of people.[39]

Like the medieval dynasts in Europe, the new type of leaders, whose power was based on slave raiding or trading, combined political power with the accumulation of wealth. While the slave merchant elites in Europe (and, to a lesser degree, in the Americas) accumulated capital for further investment, the new African elites—like Europe's feudal nobility—accumulated wealth for status and warfare. Although the European nobility succumbed to merchants' economic power and to state centralization, African traders could not gain ascendancy over political rulers. In the hierarchy of imperial political economies and the transoceanic export trade, only Christian-European and Islamic-Arab merchants amassed capital on a large scale. The new African elites did not invest in their societies, and inter-society violence prevented even modest internal growth—a trend that resembled the decline of European regions ravaged by dynastic warfare, as occurred in the Hundred Years' War. The increasing reliance on slaves as workers resembled the Iberians' disdain for manual labor when they could rely on enslaved Muslims. Such "use-value" societies sought loyalties and displays of wealth in order to control public discourses of power and status, whereas in the capitalist world exchange-value dominated the political economies.

In the third period of the Eastern System, production slavery was introduced into the agriculture of Western Sudan, and slaveholding increased to such a degree that in some districts the slave population outnumbered the free in the late nineteenth century. By about 1900, slaves averaged 18 percent in a population of four million in the Haut-Sénégal-Niger districts and in the Guinea districts 35 percent in a population of 1.4 million. Low procreation rates meant that slave populations constantly had to be replenished by further raids. While slavery was incidental to societies in which less than 10 percent of the population was enslaved, it became a central aspect of the societal regime when more than one-third of the population was enslaved. In such regimes, the merchant broker had been replaced by the soldier, "who lived as a parasite off the turmoil" and off booty, of which women as forced agricultural laborers were the most important type. U.S. scholars have discussed slavery in the U.S. South in terms of a "loss of manhood," and some wish to argue that the same applies to the African cultures in which the process of enslavement began. In Africa, however, it was a redefinition of manhood toward aggressiveness and dominance outside of traditional relationships. The debate about slavery's cultural effect might better be conducted in terms of the loss of personal societal identities and of the supremacy of power and profit over moral economies and interpersonal relationships. The changed relationships and power hierarchies involved both genders: "Most slave owners were male, but a large percentage of the users were female, and the distinction between ownership and usage rights is important."[40]

After the end of the contraband trade (see chap. 10.5), capture declined to almost zero and manumission increased. But internal slave trading, once "a marginal feature of society," continued to be "vital to production."[41] Thus Africa's migration history had begun with long-lasting migrations of peoples and then continued with migrations connected to state formation and stabilization from the twelfth to the sixteenth century. From the late seventeenth century on, capture, forced migration, and export resulted in the disintegration of traditional political-societal structures and reduced Africa's role among world powers beyond the experience of any other colonial territory (see chap. 17.2).

Parallel to the bound exodus, migrations of peoples and the re-formation of ethnic groups continued throughout the seventeenth century and into the nineteenth century in the Great Lakes region and toward the southern tip of the continent. The cattle-breeding Masai aggressively moved into what is today southern Kenya and Tanzania after 1500 and headed further south in the eighteenth century. They came to control the caravan routes from and into the interior and derived protection payments from their position. Other southward migrating people included the Luo and some Somali peoples. Only in the nineteenth century were these pastoralists' and agriculturalists' migrations directly influenced by the intrusion of Europeans (see chaps. 9.5, 16.1). In parts of West Africa, a prolonged drought from the late sixteenth into the seventeenth century and wars between dynasties weakened indigenous societies. Migration and state-building became less self-determined than in previous centuries.

Across Africa, the transatlantic exchange introduced new food plants and changed diets. Maize and manioc permitted population increase, which then led to expansion and further migrations. Across the Europe-centered political economies of the Americas, the labor of the forced migrants contributed to capital accumulation. Forced migration resulted in the emergence of an African diaspora and the culture of the Black Atlantic.

7

Trade-Posts and Colonies in the World

of the Indian Ocean

The maritime trade emporia of the world of the Indian Ocean, the Persian Gulf, and the eastern Mediterranean, like the economic zones in medieval Europe, functioned separately from political rule. So did the trans-Asian caravan routes, which, however, could be interrupted by warfare and political turmoil (see map 2.2). In the trade emporia's "age of partnership" (Das Gupta), commercial exchange was mediated by brokers and based on trust. The four major cultural regions remained distinct throughout the centuries.[1] South Asian merchants were the most important traders in the Indian Ocean, and Indic influences penetrated the second region, Southeast Asia, from 650 to 1250 (map 7.1). Chinese developments were land-based with westward connections across Central Asia, though in the sixteenth and seventeenth centuries traders from China began to trade in Southeast Asia. Japanese merchants, on the other hand, remained largely confined to their home islands, forming only a few distant migrant enclaves. Viewed from a global perspective, capitalist developments in the Asian economies occurred distinct from but in contact with Europe. It was only when European state-supported merchants assumed a more dominant role that the worlds of the Indian Ocean and the South China Sea lost their cohesion—even though they retained their vitality (map 7.2).[2]

7.1 Migrations of Peoples and Merchants
before European Contact

Cultural conversion and large-scale migrations were part of most Asian societies. Since the eighth century, internal migrations and state-building had been influenced from the outside by Arab-Islamic merchant migrations and conquests by Turkish and Mongol peoples from Asia's interior. When Islam reached the territories of today's Iran, Afghanistan, and Pakistan, slave dynasties of Turkish background formed the Ghaznavid Empire. Other Turkish people from central Asia, pushed westward under the Tang dynasty in the seventh century, appeared in European history as opponents of the crusader states in the eleventh century and became the founders of the Ottoman Empire. By 1050 C.E., the Arab geographer al-Bīrūnī, fluent in Sanskrit, compiled

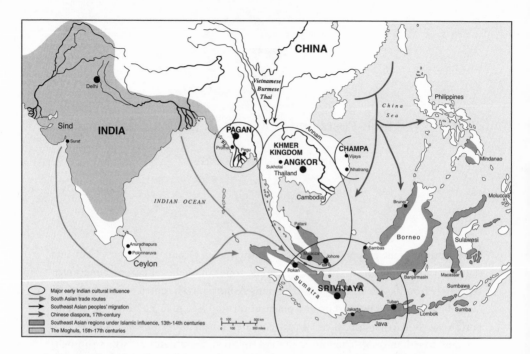

7.1   Indian Hindu and Arab Muslim Contact to Southeast Asia, 10th–17th Centuries

a *Book of India*, and in the mid-twelfth century, al-Idrīsī was sent by Roger II of Sicily to collect information on the eastern world (see chap. 2.2).[3]

From 1200 C.E. onward, a voluntary or conflictual convergence of East and West, of Arab and Mongol expansion, effected far-reaching cultural and political changes. In military conquest, Mongol rulers massacred or enslaved many peoples. Persian, Mesopotamian, and Afghan scholars, writers, artists, and artisans emigrated or fled to Indian states. Like Baghdad and Córdoba in earlier times, Lucknow in the upper Ganges valley became an intercultural intellectual center. In exile the scholars created a synthesis of Indian and Persian forms of literature and architecture and spread the Persian language. Crafts diversified with the migration of Zoroastrian skilled artisans from Persia to India. At this time, the Gypsies or Romani presumably began their westward migration through Egypt to Europe (see chaps. 5, 12.1). When Mongol rulers came to accept the Islamic faith, they incorporated Muslim populations and facilitated travel and commerce as well as cultural exchange. They attracted poets, musicians, and men of learning from a variety of cultural origins (see chap. 2.2). The mid-fourteenth-century plagues disrupted all of these societies.[4]

In the three Islamic empires from Anatolia to South Asia—the Ottoman realm, the Safavid dynasty's Persia, and Mughal India—which reached their peak in the sixteenth century, artists from many origins and slaves from Africa served at the courts. In South Asia, where invading Islamic dynasties and armies established the Delhi sultanate in 1206, which lasted to 1526 in the north and to 1605 in the south, populations were mixed religiously and ethnically; the ruling group was of Turk-

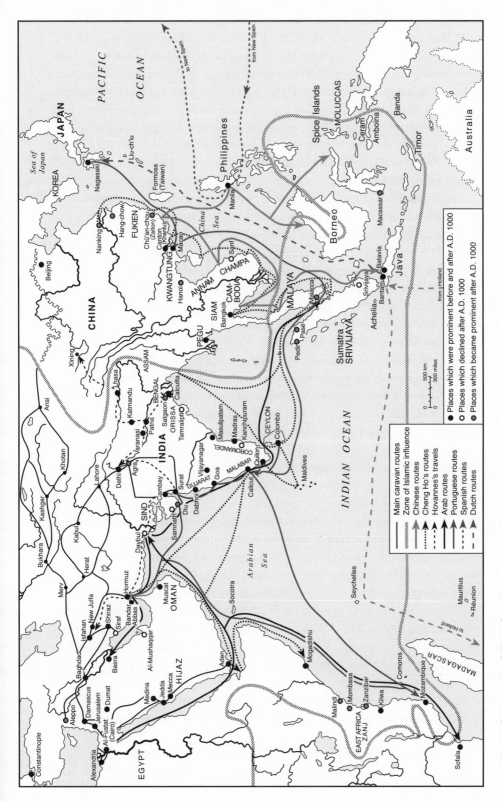

7.2   The Trade Emporia of the Indian Ocean, 1000–1600

ish origin. The elites and urbane sections of the subsequent Mughal Empire (1526–1858) blended Indic, Persian, and Turkish culture. Proselytizing members of Muslim Sufi orders moved about from the eleventh to the sixteenth century and then were forcibly dispersed because of their unwillingness to acquiesce to the sultanate's policies. The southward migration of yeomen-warriors from Vijayanagar established Telugu-speakers among native Tamil-speakers. In the Brahmaputra valley of early-thirteenth-century Assam, a Shan people from upper Burma, the Ahoms, established themselves. The mobility of common people remained limited; while the fusion of high cultures hardly touched them, in-migration of new rulers, expansion, and religious conversion did.

Wherever Turkic or Afghan power held sway, the spread of the comparatively egalitarian Islamic faith challenged hierarchically ordered, caste-rooted Hindu societies. So did indigenous anti-caste social movements. Castes rose in rank or constructed themselves as being above previously ruling castes. Converts to Islam often came from castes or segments of the population with low status. When Muslim men married Hindu women, the children were raised Islamic (a late-nineteenth-century British census listed "Hindu Mohammedans"). Religious toleration included abolishment of the tax on non-Muslims for more than a century after 1564.[5] Communities of Jews and Armenians, Arabs and Chinese, Muslims and Christians, Hindu and Jain traders from the Gujarat, Turks and Parsees, Abyssinians and people from the western Malabar Coast lived in commercial centers, such as multicultural Patna (map 7.3).[6]

In Southeast Asia, Burmese, Vietnamese, and Thai peoples migrated southward into the areas they now inhabit. In the Mataram Empire on Java, the peaceful coexistence of Buddhists and Hindus was destroyed by a devastating eruption of the Merapi volcano in the tenth century, and the survivors migrated from central to eastern Java. Under the Buddhist Srivijaya Empire, ruling the coasts of the Malay Straits from the seventh to the thirteenth century, South and East Asian merchants exchanged goods; Persian and Arab traders arrived with Mediterranean merchandise; and produce from the Indonesian islands was traded. The Arab merchants introduced Islam into the region. Javanese trading missions to the Chinese Imperial Court may have met papal envoys there (see chap. 2.2). In the fourteenth century, refugees from warfare on the Malay Peninsula, Java, and other islands, founded the city of Tumasik (later, Singapore). Chinese settled in Palembang on Sumatra, where merchants from southern India came to buy pepper; in the thirteenth and fourteenth centuries, they were largely supplanted by Gujarati and Bengali traders. At the turn of the fifteenth century, Chinese mercantile influence increased east of the Malay Peninsula. After the demise of the Srivijaya Empire, powerful non-state-based groups or "pirates"—including Japanese fugitives, Chinese outlaws, and escaped African slaves from Portuguese Macao and other Malay and island towns—rendered trade unsafe until the strengthened Japanese state imposed order in the 1570s. They presaged the "trade and plunder" principles of European buccaneers.[7]

In the sixteenth century, when migration within and between Indonesian islands was extensive, the port of Malacca achieved commercial predominance. The Celates,

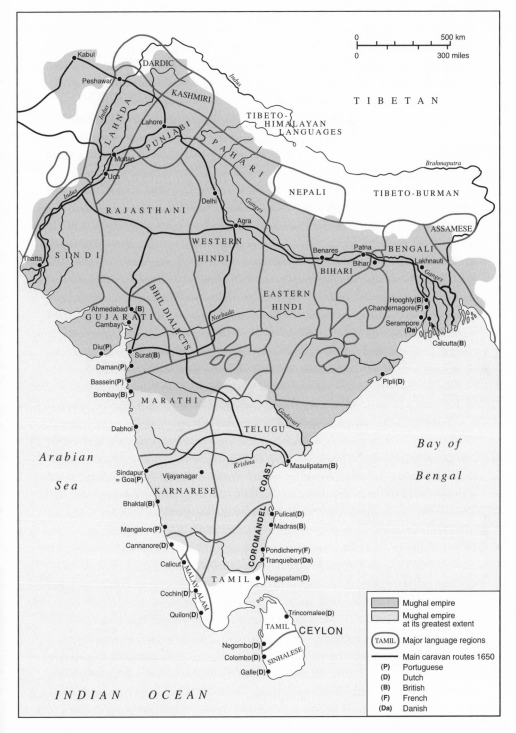

7.3   Cultures of the Indian Subcontinent

a coastal people, provided boats, seamen, and maritime expertise. The sultan's officials chose among the foreign merchants, who were divided into four groups, overseers or port captains (*shabandars*) to govern them. They paid relatively light duties and special taxes. The senior group, Gujarati merchants, numbered as many as 1,000, with up to 5,000 transient sailors. The second group consisted of Klings from the Coromandel Coast, Bengalis, Peguans, and Pasèans. The third group included merchants from Java, the Molluccas, the Banda Islands, Palembang, Borneo, and the Philippines, and the fourth group was made up of Chinese and people from the Ryúkyú Islands. Malay became the lingua franca of the archipelago, and Malacca in the era of the sultans provided "a cosmopolitan environment, . . . a melting pot of peoples."

In the smaller ports of Pasè and Pidië merchants from several of the South Asian ports, Siam, and the Malay Peninsula called. Islam spread through the islands, and fourteenth-century Chinese merchants traded directly with several of the islands. Chinese craft products, Indian cloths, and local food were traded, and rulers entered agreements with foreign merchants. Sailors and merchants may have stayed for extended periods of time. The Bandanese intermarried with Malays, Chinese, and Javanese. Malay and Javanese merchants crisscrossed the seas. The rulers, some of whom reportedly were of Chinese ancestry, hired soldiers to expand their reach, subjugated neighboring peoples, and sold slaves along the trade routes. Skilled shipwrights built junks of large size, and captains drew charts of the inter-island sea-lanes. The result was a spiritually pluralist and—in terms of material goods—cosmopolitan society.[8]

Further into the Pacific, in the world of the many islands, people voyaged in double canoes. James Cook, during his three voyages (1768–79), on Tahiti met Tupaia, who navigated him to distant islands and knew of perhaps as many as 130 islands. Missionaries and explorers were astonished at the Tahitians' "extensive and multidirectional knowledge." A Spanish captain took a man by the name of Pukuro to Lima and realized that Polynesians could navigate by the stars, the winds, and the swell of the sea with the same precision achieved by "the most expert navigator of civilised nations"; in addition, they "prognosticated the weather" without fail, a feat no European cosmographer ever achieved. When they came to know the compass, they did not bother to use it. However, other peoples—the Marquesans and Tongans, for example—had a more limited knowledge. Voyaging was done for purposes of trade, war, and collecting food. Inter-island migrations followed upon internal civil strife and economic disruption—both frequent occurrences.[9]

China's involvement in the Indian Ocean trade, extending to East African towns, originated from the southern provinces. At first, long-distance trade was mediated by colonies of foreign merchants—120,000 were said to live in Canton (Guangzhou) in 878 C.E.—but after the turn of the eleventh century local merchants and shipbuilders increasingly participated. Their trading diasporas along the sea-lanes consisted at first of sojourners, whose length of stay depended on the eight-month monsoons, then of permanent residents. Long-term "head guests"—for example, in Siam under the Ayuthaya dynasty (1350–1767)—expected deference from short-term co-residents. Before returning home, they often put in their place younger "new guests," to whom they advanced the cost of passage, thus binding them financially. Chain migrations established kinship communities. When the Ming dynasty curtailed overseas trade after 1435, merchants formed permanent diasporic communities in Malacca, Manila, and Batavia to trade with all of the Southeast Asian World, known as *Nanyang* in Chinese (map 7.4).

Within China, artisans producing luxury goods migrated to courts and residences of the wealthy, and urban men and women went to distant cities; pedlars moved across the countryside, and servants traveled to the new residences of their masters. Administrators from the capital assumed posts in distant provinces, and—to prevent the abuse of family influence—an enforced circulation of elites sent administrators away from their home provinces. Recurring natural calamities, such as droughts, floods, famines, or extended periods of malnutrition (for example, during the seventeenth-century "little ice age"), caused short-term mass migrations and long-term population displacement. In a culture wedded to human porterage, large numbers of haulers, porters, and barge-pullers moved about. In agriculture, the building of irrigation systems demanded workers from distant places. In times of subsistence or debt crises, female children could be sold to free a family from one mouth to feed and to ensure the child's survival. Natural catastrophes or menmade disasters like war and maladministration also uprooted adult men, who roamed the countryside and pillaged from peasants. When a peasant family's winter supplies were stolen, they in turn had to forage far and wide.

Six major migrations of resettlement were orchestrated by the Ming government in the late fourteenth century to areas devastated by northern wars. Some 150,000 households of landless tenants from southern Jiangsu/Kiangsu and northern Chekiang/Zhejiang were sent to the Feng-yang area along the Huai River in northern Anhui. Peasants from southern Shanxi/Shansi were sent to the low plains of Hebei/Hopei, Shandong/Shantung, and Henan/Honan. To strengthen northern defenses, 70,000 Chinese and Mongol households were relocated to the north of Beijing/Peiping. In 1421, when the capital was moved from Nanjing to Beijing, peasants involved in market gardening and artisans migrated. Some 45,000 gentry households were removed from their seats of power and brought under closer surveillance. Soldiers along much of the northern border were settled in military colonization schemes during the fifteenth century. Migrations not induced by the government also occurred.[10]

In the early seventeenth century, rebellion and ethno-dynastic conflict mobilized millions. Peasant rebels, disloyal provincial bureaucrats, and Jürchen people (Manchus) from the north dismantled Ming rule. Hundreds of thousands of soldiers sacked northern towns, uprooting urban populations and peasant families by expulsion, military conscription, or slave-like contract labor. After 1644, the new Manchu Qing (Ch'ing) dynasty attracted people for resettlement of the war-devastated regions. In an effort to merge the conquering and conquered peoples, the government quartered Jürchen soldiers with Chinese families. After massive ethnic conflict, Chinese and Jürchen were separated into distinct urban quarters. In Beijing the Chinese

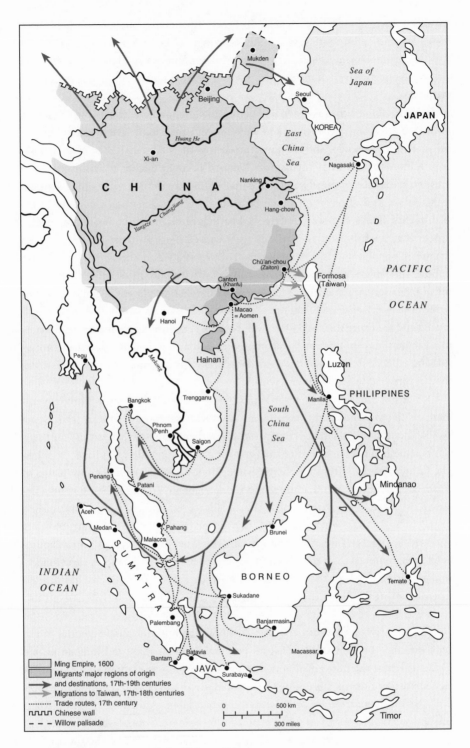

Sea of
Japan

JAPAN

Mukden

Beijing

KOREA

Seoul

Huang He

East
China
Sea

Xi-an

Nagasaki

C H I N A

Nanking

Hang-chow

D

PACIFIC

Yangtze = Changjiang

Chū'an-chou
(Zaiton)

OCEAN

Canton
(Khanfu)

Formosa
(Taiwan)

Macao
= Aomen

Hanoi

Hainan

Luzon

Pegu

Mekong

PHILIPPINES

Bangkok

Trengganu

Manila

Phnom
Penh

South
China
Sea

Saigon

Penang

Patani

Mindanao

Aceh

Medan

Pahang

Malacca

Brunei

INDIAN

OCEAN

S U M A T R A

B O R N E O

Temate

Sukadane

Palembang

Banjarmasin

Bantam

Batavia

Macassar

JAVA

Surabaya

Timor

	Ming Empire, 1600
	Migrants' major regions of origin
→	and destinations, 17th–19th centuries
→	Migrations to Taiwan, 17th–18th centuries
····	Trade routes, 17th century
⊓⊔⊓⊔	Chinese wall
– – –	Willow palisade

0   500 km

0   300 miles

7.4   Chinese Migrations and the Chinese Diaspora

were relocated to the southern part of the city, and fertile lands around the capital were confiscated for use by some 40,000 loyal soldier-settlers. Dislocated farmers pillaged the countryside, however, and wealthy Chinese landlords used the turmoil to increase their own holdings. The Jürchen, unused to farming, resettled Chinese agriculturalists as serflike dependents. Resistance by deposed Chinese elite families involved women as military leaders and as refugees. Reportedly, to prevent intermarriage visual separation was achieved by a ban on Manchu women binding their feet—this made them ugly from Chinese men's point of view. However, the "bound-feet, bound-mouth" stereotype was a Western construct supported by Chinese historiography of the early 1900s. In many regional cultures of China, women never bound their feet. The lives of slave and laboring women, as well as of farm women and servants, differed in practice from Confucian norms of subservience. Seventeenth-century itinerant female "teachers of the inner chambers" spread knowledge and literacy, and in highly developed provinces, like Jiangsu, women migrated to work in silk industries and other types of urban labor.[11]

The higher ranks of the Qing administration and scholarship were staffed by double appointments of Manchu and Chinese; Mongols also served as regional administrators. Thus a multiethnic elite emerged with a bilingual element at the very top. At the apex of the ethnic hierarchy were the Manchu, followed by educated Chinese and Mongols; at the bottom were the common Han Chinese. Cultural change was imposed on all: changed hairstyles were reflected in the popular saying "keep your hair and lose your head, or change your hair and keep your head." Since the Chinese accounted for the vast majority of the population and of the lower administrators, Chinese remained the standard language, and over time the Manchu were absorbed.

As in the past, vast agrarian migrations characterized the seventeenth and later centuries. First, the Hakkas or "guest people" had migrated southward, replacing the indigenous population in five major migrations from the fourth century C.E. to Qing rule. Displaced by northern invasions, they had come to settle as far south as the southernmost provinces; from there, they were to join the nineteenth-century overseas migration. For two hundred years after 1653, depopulated Sichuan/Szechwan was an immigration region for voluntary migrants from neighboring Hupeh/Hubei and Shaanxi/Shensi provinces. Second, the Yangtze Highlands were developed mostly by migrants from Hubei and Hunan. At the beginning of the eighteenth century, poor people, often unmarried men, from the southeastern coastal provinces began to settle the hills and mountains as "shack people." They cut the forests: after a few high-yield years the topsoil was washed away, and a century-long process of soil erosion began. Displaced local non-Chinese Miao rebelled but were subdued by military expeditions. Third, the Han River drainage areas of Gansu/Kansu, Shaanxi, Hubei, and Henan/Honan provinces were settled. Subsistence farming depleted soils. In late-eighteenth-century southern Shaanxi, the population consisted of Natives (10 percent) and of immigrants from Hubei, Anhui, and Jiangsu (50 percent), from Jiangxi/Kiangsi, Shanxi, Henan, Sichuan, and Guangsi/Kwangsi (30 percent), and from eight other provinces (10 percent). Mobility was to increase after the mid-nineteenth century (see chap. 15.4–5).[12]

Settlement migration and military conquest interacted on the margins of the empire, involving the islands of Hainan and Formosa/Taiwan (1683); Mongolia, Tibet, and Kashgaria (1751–59); and suzerainty over Burma (1765–69). The "New Territories" in the west were occupied by garrisons of soldier-settlers, 20,000 men with about 100,000 dependents. In the north, Russians explored the Amur (1643–46), and the two empires negotiated border treaties in 1689 and 1727—in part because the Chinese government feared an alliance of Russia and the powerful warriors from the nomadic Zunghar (Dzungar) tribes. In Central Asia, the migration of peoples continued into the 1700s because of imperial Chinese expansion and Mongol contraction and because of nomadic lifestyles under harsh natural circumstances (see chap. 13.1). Chinese traders and laborers migrated in limited numbers into adjoining Russian territories. In the mid-seventeenth century, Taiwan (called by the Portuguese Ilha Formosa: the beautiful island) was ruled by the Dutch East India Company (1624–62) and received more than 100,000 refugees from Qing rule. The life of the leader of the flight to Taiwan, Zheng Chenggong, also known as Koxinga to Europeans, illustrates cultural interaction. The son of a Chinese father and a Japanese mother, he was in contact with fugitive Black slaves, visiting merchants from Nagasaki and Macao, and Dutch colonization personnel. When captured by Qing forces and garrisoned by 8,000 soldiers, Taiwan became a rough frontier society. The Native peoples resisted and remained distinct in mountainous areas. In the course of the warfare, coastal mainland populations, suspected of supporting the rebels, were removed and resettled.[13]

Islam became part of life in China, while Nestorian Christianity declined; and the Jesuits, whose impact had hardly reached beyond the court, were expelled when they began to expound papal dogmatism in 1705–06. Buddhism developed a specifically Chinese character. Coastal mercantile communities remained cosmopolitan with clandestine but intense connections to the diaspora and to merchants in Nagasaki, Japan. In the west, the spread of Lamaism involved invasions, expulsion, and flight, as well as peaceful conversion. China was "a polyglot society, an efficient melting pot which worked remarkably well over the centuries in creating a multicultural civilization."[14]

The population of 150 million in 1573 declined through the period of Manchu conquest and internal troubles by as much as one-third in the mid-seventeenth century and then started to climb rapidly to 181 million in 1751 and to 300 million in 1790. At the beginning of the eighteenth century, the imperial court emancipated the bound and outcast groups at the bottom of society, such as the wedding and funeral musicians in Shaanxi and Shanxi provinces, the hereditary servants of Anhui, boatmen, oyster gatherers, pearl fishers of the coastal regions, and others. Economic macroregions emerged, of which the middle Yangtze region, in particular, received a massive in-migration of people who retained their original agrarian way of life. Along the Yangtze and Han Rivers people moved into upland areas, and in southern Manchuria they moved into forested lands. The distant contacts with the

Americas brought the sweet and ordinary species of potato, maize, and other new food crops to China. The opium poppy began its spread, as yet without European involvement. Northward settler migrations into Mongolia and Manchuria began in the mid-seventeenth century but until the 1850s remained small (chap. 18.1).[15]

Emigration before the nineteenth century involved miners, merchants, artisans, and pilgrims, mostly from the Han River delta. Miners sailed to southern Thailand and the Malay Peninsula to work in the tin lodes there and to Borneo to extract gold. Northward migration toward Russian territories remained small. This first period of the establishment of "Overseas Chinese" lasted from the fifteenth century to 1850. European colonial powers relied on them as middlemen until nineteenth-century imperialism changed power relationships.[16]

Japan interacted with neighboring peoples through cultural affinity to China and military exploits in Korea. Mongols invaded Japan first in 1274 and then in 1281 with 150,000 soldiers and Korean and Chinese sailors. When Emperor Hideyoshi sent some 200,000 men to wreak destruction on Korea in 1592, he probably did so to rid his reign of troublesome warriors. Japanese merchants began to trade overseas in the Kamakura Period (1185–1333). In the following Ashikaga Period, foreign trade grew, religious trade guilds appeared, and crafts and industries were encouraged. After a century of contact with European merchants from the 1540s to the 1640s, the intolerant Jesuits were expelled first, followed by Western merchants. Japanese merchants, who ranked fourth and last in the social hierarchy, below peasants and artisans, were forbidden to go abroad in 1636, and the government renounced participation in the trade emporia. Foreign trade was handled by Chinese and Koreans and a few remaining Dutch merchants through Nagasaki. Some exiled Chinese scholars lived in Japanese cultural centers toward the end of the seventeenth century. In the Tokugawa Period (1600–1868), Edo (later, Tokyo) was founded and experienced phenomenal inmigration and growth. As in medieval Europe, nobles left hostages at the court and had to spend part of their lives there. In the eighteenth century, rural-to-urban migrations of peasant families increased. During the 225 years in which contacts with foreigners were limited, the government nevertheless imported Western writings, such as Galileo's, through Dutch intermediaries. The information thus acquired helped spur the takeoff after 1853.[17]

The types of migration in Asia, internal or across borderlands, resembled those of other continents. First, in cosmopolitan administrations highly qualified foreigners assumed influential positions. In Mughal India, Deccanis and Africans and their joint offspring, the Muwallads (freedmen through conversion or kinship affiliation), resented the preferment of recent immigrants. Antiforeigner violence erupted. Second, men earned their living as mercenaries wherever opportunity arose: Chinese soldiers in Ceylonese armies (latter thirteenth century), European and Ottoman artillery men in India (fourteenth century), mounted archers of Turkish, Mongol, Persian, and Arab background in the Delhi sultanate (1420s).[18] Third, artisans in luxury trades migrated to courts, small or large. A relocation of a court, a rise of a center of trade, a new shrine, set men and their families in motion, as did construction of a new capital or of temple and tomb complexes.[19] Towns interacted with the countryside, and their demand for food meant intensified agriculture, which in turn increased demand for labor. When urban service trades developed, in-migration filled the demand. Across Asia, famines sent populations into flight and compelled survivors to migrate far and wide, from the Gujarat in the 1630s, for example. Victims of famines might be sold or might sell themselves and their children into slavery to survive. In the trading circuits, an interruption of the regular pattern of the monsoons might prevent the annual fleet from sailing and provisions from arriving. The resulting financial crises and yearlong shortages of supplies caused population dislocation.[20]

Of the four cultural regions, only southern China spawned a large emigration movement (see chap. 2.2). After the 1620s, some Japanese migrated to the Philippines, Cambodia, and Siam, but only two decades later the Tokugawa reduced migration. After the Chinese imperial court curtailed overseas trade in 1435, merchants, artisans, and laborers who resided temporarily along the sea-lanes became a permanent diaspora. In the next centuries, the "Overseas Chinese" formed a network from Canton to the Southeast Asian islands with settlements in Manila, Bantam, and Malacca. Men from these colonies involuntarily spread further when the Dutch kidnapped Chinese for labor in Batavia and other colonies. A second Chinese network involved the "western ocean" between China, Japan, and Korea. A third diaspora of about 10,000 Chinese emerged in the "eastern ocean" in response to being invited by Siamese rulers to assume positions as foreign traders under royal monopoly in the seventeenth century. In the capital of Ayutthaya, the Chinese and western Muslims were permitted to live within the city walls in quarters of their own, often in richly adorned houses. Other foreigners—Portuguese, Javanese, Malays, Makassarese, and Pegu (coastal Burmese)—lived outside the walls, each group administered by a chief of its own choosing. A French report described the city as a magnificent and bustling port with camps and villages of the different trading nations between the city walls and the rice fields from which the urban population was supplied. The East India Company sent a British representative and a Greek one as well. By the eighteenth century, Bangkok's shipyards provided the region with Chinese-style junks.[21]

The Portuguese reached these worlds from Hormuz and Goa in the sixteenth century: Malacca in 1511, Macao in China in 1557, and finally Nagasaki. While China permitted a permanent settlement of Portuguese, the Dutch secured only tributary status a century later, in 1656–67. Gungzhou/Canton and, until 1760, Fujian, were designated as the only ports for external commerce. In Japan, the government designated the fishing village of Nagasaki as an enclave for merchants and missionaries when the Portuguese arrived. Spanish traders came in 1602, then Dutch and English ones. Relations remained tense in many enclaves (see chap. 5.3), and the Japanese government expelled the Westerners in the mid-seventeenth century.[22]

An emphasis on European penetration of the Indic world—on silks, porcelains, and other luxury trade items—hides the fact that the bulk of even the maritime trade remained local or regional. A Eurocentric construction also overlooks the sixteenth-century Ottoman-Egyptian-Arab axis and its connections to both Venice and India.[23]

In the Indic trade system, like the Mediterranean one, merchants linked through family relations or relied on intermediaries usually of the same ethnic, religious, or cultural background. Within particular ports, security of person and property, mechanisms for enforcing contracts, and facilities for anchorage, warehousing, banking, and accommodation were available to traders regardless of cultural background. The trade emporia were based on political neutrality and open markets.[24]

7.2 Parsees, Jews, Armenians, and Other Traders

While the Chinese merchant diaspora was linked by sea, the Indian subcontinent and Central Asia hosted nonterritorial groups that were trader ethnicities, especially Parsees, Jews, and Armenians. In the eighth century, the Parsees, followers of the Zoroastrian faith in Persia, fled the Muslim advance rather than convert to Islam. They settled in Gujarat, adopted the Gujarati language, and took advantage of economic and educational opportunities whenever offered. As merchants and artisans they spread across several of the trade emporia. When the British came, they learned English and served as middlemen between the new masters and the Hindu population.

The Jewish communities dated from the decline of the Baghdad caliphate and the city's destruction by Mongols in 1258. The refugees became known as Baghdadi, Babylonian Arab-speaking Jews.[25] Of the several groups, the Bene Israel had migrated even earlier. They probably reached western India in the sixth century C.E. and lost contact with the rest of the Jewish diaspora. They acculturated and served as mercenaries in Indian—and later British—armies, and sought educational opportunities in Bombay. A second group, the Cochin Jews of the Malabar Coast, traded as far as northern Europe. A third group settled in Bombay and Calcutta in the eighteenth century. The Iberian rulers had expelled Jews in the 1490s, just before Portuguese ships arrived in the Indian Ocean and seven decades before the Spanish arrived in the Philippines. While the Iberian states thus lost long-distance trading experts, refugee Portuguese Jews in Amsterdam reconnected with their Asian coreligionists, diverting the lucrative distribution of Asian imports to the Netherlands.[26]

Armenian merchants, unarmed like their Jewish counterparts and thus able to avoid the overhead costs of a military establishment, bought protection when necessary. Theirs had been a century-long history of displacement. At the time of the crusades, the Armenian state of Cilicia had bordered the northeastern Mediterranean, with Aleppo as its major entrepôt. After the Muslim-Turkish assumption of power, the autocephalous Christian Armenians fled to a region between the Caspian and the Black Seas and dispersed across Mediterranean Europe. They operated in niches and interstices between state-backed merchants or the emporia of the region, trading with eastern Nestorians and Ethiopian Christians. Although Crimean Armenians adopted the local Tatar language and codified it in Armenian script, they retained their religious and ethnic identity. When involuntary migration under Ottoman rule reconnected them to communities still using the Armenian language, they had to relearn the ancestral language. Others established themselves, parallel to Jews, as important mercantile groups in the Ottoman Empire's consecutive capitals, Bursa, Adrianople, and Istanbul. As Christians, they sometimes benefited and sometimes suffered from competition between Sunni Osmans and Shiite Safavids. During the Ottoman-Persian wars, some were involuntarily resettled in New Julfa, a mercantile town adjoining Persia's capital, Isfahan.[27]

Armenians traded along the eastward silk route, supplied the Genoese west-bound seaborne trade, and moved northward along the Volga route, reaching the Baltic Sea and trading with merchant sojourners from the German Hansa. A fourteenth- and fifteenth-century northwestward route extended via Danubian and Polish lands to the fairs of Nuremburg and Bruges, and in 1660s Amsterdam Armenian merchants settled alongside Turks and a few Hindus and interacted with Russian, English, and Jewish traders.[28] When Turkish and Arabian coffee was introduced into Europe, migrating Armenians established themselves as coffeehouse keepers in France where philo-Armenians began a vogue of cultural imitation (map 7.5).

The extent of the Armenian networks is illustrated by a New Julfa merchant, Hovhannes Joughayetsi, who, in 1682, traveled via Bandar 'Abbās (near Hormuz) and Surat to Agra in the upper Ganges valley (map 7.2). After a brief return to Surat in 1684, he spent the next year in and near Agra, then moved to Tibet and lived for six years in Lhasa and traded with Chinese merchants. In 1693 he returned to Patna in the central Ganges valley, crossed through Bengal, and ended his journal in Calcutta. Along these routes, merchants of ethnically different diasporas conveyed goods and interacted with dozens or hundreds of carters, hostel-keepers, interpreters, and money changers. For protection and community, such travelers connected to local self-organized "nations," as many-cultured as in Europe. In Lhasa, for example, Armenians and Kashmiri formed one "nation" to settle disputes internally and to negotiate with local authorities.[29]

Local merchants in India, as elsewhere, were many-cultured, too: Kerala trade was dominated by Gujarati from the north and Chetti from the Coromandel Coast, both of Hindu faith; by Muslim Persian and Arab visitors; as well as by local "Mappila," twelfth-century transients who had settled. As in Africa, merchants entered into temporary and multiple marriages, with families in different ports: "The new social group was Muslim in religion, Arabian in some aspects of culture, but Indian by descent."[30]

7.3   Portuguese Trade-Posts, Spanish Manila, Chinese Merchants

Portuguese, as the first newcomers from Europe, arrived in Asia by coastal routes known to peoples from the West African littoral and, beyond the Cape of Good Hope, to Indo-Arab seafarers (see chap. 5.3). Others came as mercenaries or traders via Mediterranean routes. One Pero da Covilha visited Kilwa and settled and married in Christian Ethiopia. Alien to the trade emporia consensus, without goods to exchange, and

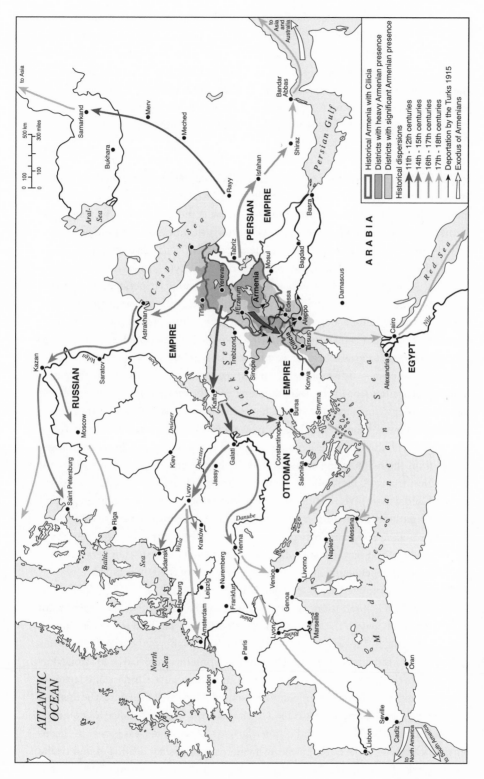

7.5   The Armenian Diaspora, 11th–20th Centuries

unable to hold large territories, the Portuguese relied on their one strength, the ruthless use of power, and limited themselves to trade-posts and minuscule territorial enclaves. Traditional patterns of intercivilizational contact—whether early Mediterranean, in the region of the Black or Red Seas, or Indic—underwent fundamental change. Owing to their power, Europeans could turn their negative balance of trade into a positive one by using African gold and Peruvian silver as a commodity for exchange. They rose from marginality to superiority by dictating the terms of trade.[31]

From their enclaves, the representatives of the European powers and joint-stock companies negotiated with local and regional rulers. Compromises had to be worked out that did not increase the costs of coercion beyond the income from domination. From their strategically placed ports, the Portuguese enforced a pass-system and payment of duties on all other merchants for—to use a modern cliché—gangster-type "protection services." Conscious of both their own weakness and the importance of establishing their superiority as a principle, they gave free passes to merchants from powerful states. The English geographer Richard Hakluyt (1552–1616) commented: "Some seeke authoritie and places of commandement, others experience by seeing of the worlde, the most part worldly and transitorie gaine, and that often times by dishonest and unlawfull meanes, the fewest number the glorie of God and the saving of the soules of the poore and blinded infidels." Like the Frankish crusaders and Iberian *conquistadores*, Europeans in Asia wanted wealth without having to work for it.[32]

The trade-posts—or "factories" (from Portuguese *feitorias*)—set up under treaties with regional rulers since 1500, were different from the self-governed enclosed Mediterranean *funduqs* or Hanseatic *Höfe*. They were extraterritorial enclaves that served as bases of power, though small in compass. Even in Goa, their main enclave in the Indic World, the Portuguese remained a minority. Gujarati Hindus and Jains and people from the neighboring areas formed the largest group. Ethiopian Christians, Indian Nestorians, Armenians, and Muslims (from the vicinity, East Africa, Persia, and Arabia) did most of the business. In Portuguese Hormuz at about 1600, 40 percent of the population was Muslim, 27 percent Hindu, 17 percent Portuguese Christians, 10 percent Indian and Indo-Portuguese Christian, and 7 percent Jewish. Merchants, sailors, soldiers, and servants stayed and intermarried. Luso-Asians or "Black Portuguese" traded independently and formed communities of their own and partnerships with local—for example, Javanese—merchants.[33]

The Spanish conquest, in contrast, began from the east, across the Pacific from New Spain/Mexico with the occupation of the harbor of Manila in the Philippines in 1571 (see chap. 8.4). The population consisted of descendants of the original Negritos and immigrant Indonesian peoples. The latter's commercial role had been strong during the era of the Indonesian Srivijaya Empire and Sung China. Chinese and Japanese craftsmen and Arab-Islamic merchants had settled. Like the Portuguese, the Spanish constructed a socioeconomic world in which their lack of merchandise for commercial exchange did not show. Their bullion transport from Mexico was part of the economy "of a needy western Europe seeking means of exchange for dealing in high-value luxury goods within an already established inter-Asian exchange nexus."[34] Similar to the Portuguese in their quest for control, the Spanish monopolized the transpacific galleon trade. They too had no intention of working. "Since their daily bread was ensured with so little effort, the Spaniards did not care to engage in agriculture, retail trade or mining, much less did they care to engage in industry." This retrospective scholarly opinion was also held by contemporary Euro-Spanish visitors who considered the Manila-Spanish slothful and saw them as malicious swindlers and gamblers who abhorred nothing so much as physical work. They "even refused to teach the natives, whom they groundlessly believed indolent, the trades and crafts they taught in New Spain." They relied in all respects on the Chinese, "who did not need to be taught anything for they already knew the various crafts and in many cases were more skilful at them than the best Spanish craftsmen." When warriors from Formosa captured Spanish ships for their own profit, the Spanish labeled them "pirates." The definition of legitimacy—and of piracy, too—is a question of power, including power over historiographical discourse.[35]

The Chinese community in Manila, numbering a mere 150 at the time of Spanish intrusion, grew quickly. Merchants from Fujian and the diaspora took advantage of the opportunities opened by the silver imports from Peru. They supplied the Manila-Spanish through their extensive junk trade in silks and other expensive goods destined for the Mexican-Spanish upper classes. Chinese artisans, market gardeners, and fishermen settled in Manila, as did a few Japanese. While the Euro-Spanish and Mexican-Spanish community numbered fewer than 1,000 by 1600, the 20,000 Chinese formed the second-largest overseas community after the Siam-Chinese. The Natives' economy, however, was limited to supplying the growing urban populations with food. The resulting cash influx, spent on Chinese imports, changed local lifestyles. Since both the Spanish and the Chinese communities were almost exclusively male, intermarriage or informal unions with Native women brought forth a "Mestizo" population.

Incapable of cultural mediation, the Spanish briefly attempted to convert the Chinese to Catholicism but quickly settled into stereotyping the "sangley" as inferior and despicable. At first, they instituted segregation similar to that imposed on minorities on the Iberian Peninsula—though, in contradistinction to the "Moors" and Jews, the Manila-Chinese formed the majority of the inhabitants. To assure Spanish control, the Chinese were forced to settle in Parián, a walled ghettolike quarter within the reach of the guns of the Spanish fort. High taxes, special levies of money and forced labor, as well as enslavement created massive discontent.[36] A second, bloody, level of repression was reached when the Manila-Chinese rebelled, or when visiting Chinese imperial officials or Manchu adventurers raised fears among the Spanish. The whole Chinese population of 20,000 was massacred in 1603 and two-thirds or more of the population of 30,000 in 1639. Before a further massacre in 1662, many could flee. Thereafter a third period was characterized by expulsions. The Spanish limited the Chinese to 6,000 residents, expelled them in 1686, then called them back and expelled them again. The expulsions, like those of Jews and Moriscos from the Iberian Peninsula, meant serious economic disruption. Like European Jews, who lacked the protection of a state, the Overseas Chinese had no means of defense. After 1766, a fourth policy encouraged Chinese to immigrate, settle, and intermarry with Catholicized *indias*.

With increasing numbers, Spanish and Chinese settled in other towns of the islands, and little Pariáns, Pariancillos, sprang up. In the mixed society, the Hispanicized "Indio" culture, to use the Spanish term, ranked lowest, while Chinese and Spanish competed for elite status, since both groups considered themselves as originating in a high culture. When the island of Luzon was transformed from a trading center to a colony, the Chinese-Philippine Mestizo population assumed economic leadership. As middlemen and financiers, they provided local people with credit and in cases of default seized their land; from their urban-based economy, they expanded to landholder status. By 1850, when the Spanish restricted Chinese immigrant activities again, it was the mixed local community that gained rather than the marginalized European elite.[37]

In the cultures of the Indic World, Europeans remained a tiny minority. When the Mughal Empire's population amounted to perhaps 100 million, an estimated 2,400 men left Portugal annually for "India" in the first quarter of the sixteenth century; then the numbers fell to between 1,000 and 1,500. Net migration after deductions for deaths and return voyages amounted to about 77,000 in almost a century. In 1590, only 14,000 European-born Portuguese lived in Asia. (By comparison, emigration to the Atlantic islands and Brazil involved 3,000–5,000 annually out of a population of one million.) Except for a few wives and daughters of the elite and a few prostitutes, no Portuguese female migration to Asia took place. From local unions, a Luso-Asian group emerged.[38]

Christianization had little if any impact. In 1542 the Jesuit Francis Xavier migrated to become "apostle to the Indies." In Kerala he found an active Christian community of the Syrian Christian Church. Allessandro Valignano (1555–1639), his co-Jesuit of the Nagasaki mission, expounded the interrelatedness of profit and power: Christianized Japanese could not be exploited to the limits. "If we could govern these places with true Japanese severity, killing whenever necessary, they would be much more useful to us than they are now." In fact, the converted Christians were protected as subjects of the Japanese emperor. Valignano constructed his vision of exploitation, which was of European origin, as a Japanese character trait. Christianization in the Protestant variant, as propagated by the Dutch, also never overcame the "love of gain." During the 200 years of colonization, a mere 1,000 *predikanten* (some with families) came. The English East India Company (EIC) supported fewer men of the Church; only the Spanish and Portuguese in the Americas sent more. When power and profit were at stake, the Protestant Dutch aligned themselves with Muslim Moluccans against Catholic Portuguese; and Christian shipowners vied for the lucrative traffic of Muslims pilgrims from Batavia to Mecca. Some officials commented on the duplicity: "The conversion of the so-called [European immigrant] Christians in the colony must be undertaken before there is any hope of converting the heathen."[39]

The European enclaves faced well-organized states and empires. Up to the eighteenth century, the Mughal Empire maintained the respect of the colonial powers: "There is a virtual dichotomy between the historical currents that swept across India from the Mughal power centers of Delhi or Agra, on the one hand, and those that merely lapped its shores, emanating from the headquarters of distant trading companies in Europe." Like Urban Italy and the Urban Netherlands in Europe, the urban-centered trade emporia of the Asian ports were much more effective and influential than the enclaves of warrior-merchants from Portugal and Spain.[40]

7.4   Slavery and Eurasian Society under
Dutch Colonial Rule

Portugal faced vigorous competition from Dutch, British, Danish, and French merchants from the 1590s onward. The Dutch established themselves in Sumatra and Java in 1596 and 1602 and made Batavia (later, Jakarta) their headquarters. They captured Portuguese Malacca in 1641 and established trading stations in Siam, where they had to compete with Japanese hired as warriors and Chinese engaged in trade. Having regained their independence from Habsburg rule, the Dutch expanded trade with the Levant and South America and wrested control over trade-posts from the Portuguese. The Spanish and Portuguese model of state-sponsored and state-regulated mercantile ventures was replaced by a model of commercial capital pooled into large state-chartered companies. The first of these, the London-based Muscovy Company founded in 1555, operated in the northern fur trade. Most companies, however, traded with and later ruled societies in the south: the Dutch East India Company (*Vereenigde Oost-Indische Compagnie*, VOC) founded in 1602, the EIC (1600), and the Royal African Company (1672), as well as the French *Compagnie des Indes Orientales* (1664). Their emergence marked the change from royal monopoly to a bureaucratic economic organization based on larger financial networks. Family-organized political dynasties and incorporated capital pools cooperated. Although the widows of merchants had been able to continue the family business, they were excluded from the new corporations. The companies, which "had the legal right to raise armies and navies, to fight wars, and make peace within their zone," became territorial powers with control over laboring populations in Asia after the mid-eighteenth century (see chap. 15). But, even then, the Europeans "remained an alien body on the fringe of Asian society."[41]

While some of the VOC's directors argued that profits depended on a flourishing Native trade, its governor-general of the Indies, Jan P. Coen (1587–1629) demanded "good warships" to monopolize the spice trade to Europe and control the inter-Asian trade. His quest for power was helped along by the disintegration of the Indonesian dynastic states. In his grandiose scheme, Dutch settler families would establish a population base by colonizing Amboina (Ambon), the Banda Islands, and Jacatra or Bantam. He also wanted to attract immigrants from Madagascar, Burma, and China, whom he considered industrious. Military strength was to be bolstered by thousands of Japanese mercenaries. Thus, with a small number of troops, Coen set out to destroy European competition in the Spice Islands. Unsuccessful in dislodging the English and the Spanish, he turned against the peoples of the Banda Islands, who resisted his attempts to monopolize the marketing of their mace and nutmeg. The islanders were crushed, executed, killed by starvation, or sold into slavery to Java. Their land was to be settled by Dutch colonizers and worked with slave labor imported from elsewhere. Few Dutch families came, but Native populations were transferred at will. After quelling an uprising in western Ceram (1651), the voc transferred 12,000 inhabitants to Amboina and Manipa. When military expeditions destroyed their spice cultivation, the people of Ceram and other islands had to flee the devastated regions. By the 1630s, spice production had declined to one-fourth of the pre-Dutch level. The indigenous populations, too, had declined; but since they were not traded, no statistics exist. Even Dutch commentators noted that in the Moluccans insufficient food imports threw inhabitants back on subsistence agriculture and thus prevented them from picking cloves. Inter-island food exchange and trade was interrupted; refugees were generated faster than plantations.[42]

A monocultural community formation of European colonizers would have meant that women migrated in numbers equal to men. But women were reluctant to do so, at least to destinations in tropical climates. In view of the risks, those who did migrate were of an adventurous character. Rather than credit their pluck, men who left accounts or wrote histories charged them—like female pilgrims in Europe—with loose morals. Sailors of outbound vessels did smuggle streetwalking women on board; wives of ranking administrators were brought out to play their role in the public pomp and ritual of colonial rule; and other women did migrate on their own. Most community formation by colonizers relied on intermarriage with indigenous women. They were expected to convert to Christianity, which upper-class women were not willing to do. Regardless of class, few parents consented to a daughter marrying a Dutchman—Dutch drinking habits and frequenting of taverns were publicly visible and decried even by Dutch observers. Native female partners of European men, positioned in imperial exploitation and sexual hierarchies, were constructed as dissolute, lustful, and designing. It is fair to assume that men and women formed partnerships within power hierarchies according to deliberate strategies. Given the reticence of Native women, intermarriage was mostly with "Eurasian"—that is, Indo-Portuguese—women. "Far from forming a 'New Netherlands' in the tropics, [Dutch settlements] became increasingly removed from cultural influences of the homeland." The "homeland," in fact, barred mixed couples from return by excluding "colored" wives from the Netherlands.

Former voc employees accumulated property and set up shop as independent craftsmen, traders, moneylenders, or tavernkeepers. They formed families with Native wives, concubines, or slaves, and mid-seventeenth-century advocates of intermarriage demanded schooling for mixed children, who, as was assumed, in a few generations would differ little from "pure" Netherlanders. It seems that European sperm, like European gunpowder, was considered dominant. But assumptions of European superiority had little bearing on the socialization of children of mixed couples or of European couples with slave nannies. In view of the size of the indigenous population and assignment of child-care to the Native mothers or to slaves, children grew up in Asian cultural environments rather than European ones. Everyday languages were Malay and Portuguese rather than Dutch.[43]

In Batavia—a city that was as cosmopolitan as Malacca, Manila, and Goa in its heyday from 1700 to 1730—the headquarters of the VOC attracted Chinese craftsmen and market-gardeners. The population more than doubled to over 68,000 from 1680 to 1690. In 1720 Batavia's population consisted of 2,000 Europeans, mainly Dutch merchants (2.2 percent of the total population), 1,100 Eurasians, 11,700 Chinese, 9,000 non-Indonesian Asians of Portuguese culture (*mardijkers*), 600 Indo-Arab Muslims, 5,600 immigrants from a dozen islands, 3,500 Malays, 27,600 Javanese and Balinese, and 29,000 slaves of varying ethnic origins including Africans. By 1790 the three largest groups in a population of 135,000 were the 44,700 Javanese/Balinese, the 37,700 Chinese, and the 25,000 slaves. Of the company's 6,000 or more paid employees, most were soldiers recruited in Asia. Because of the shortage of Dutch men, Batavia's garrison of 143 soldiers in 1622 included Germans, Swiss, Englishmen, Scots, Irishmen, Danes, Flemings, Walloons, and others. Moluccan garrisons included men from German port towns as well as from the remote Shetlands. As was true of the medieval *Landsknechte*, Swiss and German men predominated (see chap. 3.1). Few European merchants immigrated since they could not compete with Chinese or local merchants and their well-established trading networks. A Eurasian culture emerged and was cherished. European and Euro-mixed men and women could afford luxury and cheap or enslaved attendants. They would never have attained such a life in the Netherlands, nor could they have maintained it if they returned home. Their Batavian culture was an amalgam of Indonesian, Chinese, Portuguese, and Dutch practices.[44]

7.5 Colonizing Cores, Global Reach, and the British Shift to Territorial Rule

While no replicas of Dutch or other European societies emerged in the colonies, the colonial project did change home societies. Developments were inextricably entwined, and no boundaries separated colonizer from colonized except in construction and racist ideology. In the case of the Dutch, the VOC's expansionist activities required, to begin with, considerable numbers of men as sailors, soldiers, and administrators, enlisted for terms of six years, but also families for settlement. The small Dutch society at home became an immigration society (see chap. 12.3). Internal European migration brought artisans from many countries and religious refugees to Amsterdam and the VOC's recruiting offices. Women to be sent out for purposes of marriage came from Antwerp, the Germanies, and as far away as Norway. Some stayed and married in the Dutch towns. Returnees settled as immigrants in the Netherlands or in their countries of origin. They brought new patterns of consumption and expectations about servants with them.[45]

From 1600 to 1800 the voc employed more than one million European migrant laborers. A decision of the voc's board not to hire Norwegians, "Easterlings," Frenchmen, Englishmen, or Scots was quickly abandoned. Annually, thousands of sailors were needed for the Asian trade, perhaps 1,000 for the Guinea trade, just under 2,000 for the West Indies, not counting the North Sea fisheries and Arctic whale-fishing industry. By the end of the seventeenth century, the voc employed some 30,000 men, about half of whom were sailors. Wars and deaths in the tropics depleted the labor force. On Asian voyages less than one-third of the soldiers survived; for sailors the survival and return rate stood at about 60 percent. One reason to brave the high mortality rates was the hope for gain beyond wages since the voc's sailors were permitted to carry a small amount of merchandise back to Europe and to trade on their own account. Self-determined in-migration to the Netherlands became insufficient, and the voc sent recruiting parties to port cities along the littoral of the North Sea.[46]

As a transit station for migrants from much of Europe and an immigration society, the Urban Netherlands developed from its colonial profits a bourgeois high culture that influenced European painting and consumption styles. The merchants' patronage encouraged a school of painters to reflect the bourgeoisie's values rather than those of the nobility. The painters were familiar with Japanese prints, Mughal miniatures, and Chinese drawings. Similarly, in the mid-nineteenth century, the British imperial government would send out photographers to capture images of its possessions and their natural beauties and monuments—but hardly ever of the Native peoples. The empire was to be brought home to be viewed by the gentry and the middle classes (see chap. 11.1).[47]

The end of Dutch preponderance in Europe after the Treaty of Utrecht in 1713 brought a swift decline to its metropolitan economy. At the beginning of the seventeenth century, the East India Company had gained the upper hand over the voc. In India, which was to become the cornerstone of the British Empire, the EIC acquired Bombay in 1661; Calcutta was founded in 1690; and as late as 1796 the EIC took Ceylon from the Dutch. Expansion occurred in constant struggle and warfare with the Mughal Empire and, later, the Maratha rulers. In the northwest, the Sikhs, a religiously defined group with Muslim and Hindu elements, established their own state in the Deccan.

After the Portuguese trade-posts and Dutch control over plantation districts waned, the EIC and subsequently the British government aimed at territorial rule over the subcontinent. But merchants migrating from the core still relied on local, diasporic, or long-distance Asian merchants, who had the advantage of greater purchasing power, larger populations, and more extensive hinterlands. Bankers, cross-cultural brokers, guides, and advisers, or, in some ports, professional mediators—such as the *dubash* in Madras and the *banian* in Bengal—all were part of the Asian multiethnic and multilingual merchant communities and the interlocking trade diasporas. Parsee shipyard owners and Indian craftsmen built the British fleet, while Indian *lascars* (sailors) and East Africans manned the vessels. Not until the half-century between 1740 and 1790 did full control in the eastern seas shift to the Europeans.

The collapse of Mughal India and the aggressive policies of the Marathas weakened the South Asian societies internally. In Surat, Maratha incursions resulted in the emigration of peasants and the lands falling waste. Reformers could not stem the tide, and economic decline wrought havoc among the producing populations. At the same time, the rapacity of the EIC's employees, encouraged by the example of the Company's chief administrator in Bengal, Robert Clive, increased. After 1773–74, Parliament limited the EIC's powers and abolished its monopoly rights in 1813 in India and in 1833 in China.

Under the Company's rule, Bengali merchants were ruined; ever higher taxes were extorted from the indigenous populations; and large "indemnities" were imposed on Native rulers who resisted the intruders. As the cost of coercion increased, the EIC, which had paid a dividend of 7–10 percent on its capital annually in the first half of the eighteenth century, ran deficits. After the mid-1700s, it had to raise additional capital in Britain rather than reinvest Asian profits. It needed a parliamentary bailout to become profitable again, paying annual dividends of 8 percent after 1801. While solving the EIC's debt crisis, the British Empire lost most of its colonies in North America, a development that changed migratory patterns in the Western Hemisphere (see chap. 9).

The British government sent Lord Cornwallis to India to serve as governor-general, from 1786 to 1793. In North America, in 1781, he had had to surrender to settlers of European origin who were not willing to accept an inferior status in the empire. In India's colonial administration, too, reform was urgently needed, but Cornwallis, "believing that Indians were hopelessly corrupt, . . . excluded them from posts paying more than £500 a year." Thus the colonizers projected their own ineptitude and greed onto the colonized.

In India, Cornwallis cemented British rule, and a successor of his in the 1850s suppressed a large-scale revolt. Because power influences discourse, the American colonist rebellion became known as a "war of independence" whereas the Indian one was called "the mutiny." At the turn of the nineteenth century, the British Empire consolidated its colonies globally. Wherever the British invested the capital earned from their colonies, skilled and unskilled immigrant workers from the neighboring countryside or more distant trade circuits found work. After the early nineteenth century, when the African slave trade was prohibited, control of huge reservoirs of human beings in Asia permitted the recruitment and export of laborers to wherever the imperial economy demanded manpower (see chap. 15). In personal relations, the British also switched to a new pattern—higher levels of racist segregation. When British men in the colonies fathered children, they repudiated them and did not integrate themselves into a multiracial society as Dutch men had done, albeit against avowed VOC policy.[48]

According to Lionel Frost, "In 1500, Europe was a peripheral economic power: it had only three of the world's twenty largest cities (the rest were in Asia, the Middle East, or Africa). By the nineteenth century, a world economy had emerged which was centered on an increasingly urbanized and industrialized Europe. Thirteen of the world's twenty largest cities in 1850 were in Europe, or across the Atlantic in areas which had been colonized by Europeans."[49] Via the globalization of colonial rule, rule over colonial enclaves developed into nineteenth-century imperialism (see chap. 16).

8

Latin America: Population Collapse

and Resettlement

The coming of the Europeans, which left the mass of the Asian peoples almost unperturbed and at first increased the enslavement of human beings in Africa only slightly, caused unprecedented demographic disaster in the Americas. Nevertheless, colonial migration and cultural patterns both interrupted and continued precontact moves. Cuzco remained a center of attraction while pre-Columbian migrations from northern Mexico to the Central Valley ended. Three major migratory developments demand attention. From 1500 to 1800, perhaps two to three million Europeans immigrated; millions of people from the First Nations moved or were moved after the mid-1500s, in particular to the mining centers in north central Mexico and to Peru's seventeenth-century Potosí; and about seven million Africans were brought in. Four areas in the "new world" may be discerned by population patterns: the Caribbean islands, the densely populated highlands of Mesoamerica and the Central Andes, the Brazilian forests and Argentine grasslands, as well as the thinly settled northern half of the continent (map 8.1).[1]

8.1   Peoples of the Americas in 1492 —
Demographic and Cultural Collapse

The Caribbean islands or "West Indies" were the home of the Ciboney, the Arawak including the Taino, as well as the Carib (Kalinagos). Inter-island trading was not highly developed. Columbus described the Arawak in a famous passage of his journal: "They are affectionate people and without covetousness and apt for anything, which I certify to your Highnesses that I believe there is no better people or land in the world. They love their neighbours as themselves and have the sweetest speech in the world and gently, and are always smiling." He also mentioned that they used gold for personal adornment. Given European rapacity, this was to be their undoing.[2]

On the Central American mainland, migrations of whole peoples reshaped population distribution into the first half of the second millennium. Toltecs migrated southward after 800 C.E. Their agricultural and scholarly achievements, jointly with those of the Mixtec, Zapotec, and other peoples formed the base of the fourteenth-

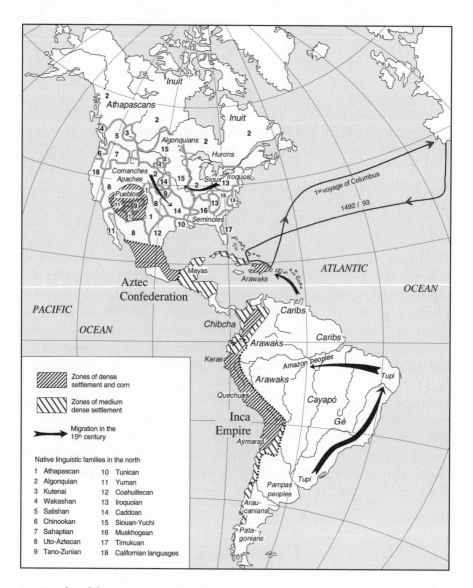

8.1   Peoples of the Americas in the 15th Century

century Aztec culture. Mayan peoples migrated into Yucatán in the ninth and tenth centuries, but they deserted their cities four hundred years later for Guatemala. The small Chibcha culture of the Bogotá plateau (Colombia) traded in salt, fruits, and gold. The Inca Empire emerged in the ninth century, incorporated neighboring peoples by conquest, and established postal and messenger systems. Its agriculture, including irrigation, was highly developed; by maintaining a large-scale storage of grains, the state protected people against the threat of famines and resulting dislocation. People were obligated to labor for the state or its theocratic ruler, and imperial administrators mobilized masses. Construction of a fortress at Cuzco involved the labor of some 40,000 workers seasonally for ten years. Road and bridge building involved additional workers; the preparation of food for storage still others; and service to Inca notables yet more men and women. The court attracted noble families from incorporated peoples to Cuzco and sent out administrators. Both involuntary resettlement of rebellious populations and voluntary rural-to-urban moves were an integral part of life in this highly developed and centralized society.[3]

Inca and Aztec societies, like those of the Iberian peninsula, depended on bound labor and the enslavement of war captives and of criminals—for example, as punishment for the theft of sacred objects and for rape. Raids on neighboring peoples served to fill labor reservoirs and, it seems, enabled the capture of high-ranking persons for sacrificial rites. Depending on the society, slaves were low-ranking servantlike members of families or were property and could be punished or killed at will. As visible signs of their status they bore brands (Nicaragua) or had their heads shaved (Yucatán). According to Spanish sources based on oral traditions of Natives, slaves were traded from Nicaragua and Yucatán to Honduras and Guatemala. The mid-fifteenth-century Totonac, for example, took slaves from many ethnicities, tearing families apart and marching captives off in yokes.[4]

In the third region of what was to become "Latin" America, the forests and eastern littoral of South America, peoples lived in regionally limited self-organized communities without state superstructures. The fourth region from the Rio Grande to the Arctic, which was to become Anglo America, contained a mosaic of distinctive cultures from nomadic hunter-gatherers to farmers to populous urban societies. Between the Atlantic seaboard and the Appalachian slopes, mostly Algonquian-speaking peoples combined agriculture with game hunting. Along the St. Lawrence River and the Great Lakes, horticulturalists, hunters, and gatherers traversed large distances by birch-bark canoe. To the south, almost from Lake Erie to the shores of the Gulf of Mexico, the peoples of the Mississippian mound-building cultures and proto-states had established themselves. In the southwest, pueblo cultures engaged in intensive agriculture. Ranching, fishing, and gathering groups extended to the California coast. Further north on the Pacific coast, a marine economy of fishers and traders with seagoing cedar canoes lived in relative abundance, sometimes raiding neighboring peoples for slaves. The Plains remained thinly settled, and the Arctic peoples were sparse (see chap. 9).[5]

Precontact population size is difficult to estimate. A 1939 projection based on the thinly settled North American cultural region yielded a low estimate of 8.4 million, while Dobyns's 1966 estimate topped 100 million. Low figures often serve apologetic purposes: the deaths of scattered heathen peoples elicit less criticism than the bleak picture ("black legend") of mass extermination. A recent opinion, cautioning that estimates may be 30 to 50 percent off, supports figures in the range of 90 to 112 million people for the whole continent, about 25 million of them in central Mexico. In a demographic disaster unparalleled in history, these populations may have declined to approximately two million within a century after contact. Whatever the actual numbers may be, historians agree that population decline amounted to about 90 percent on average, with several Caribbean populations totally wiped out by pathogens carried unwittingly by the Europeans. Death came less swiftly among the dispersed North American peoples. An unknown pathogen transmitted to the Laurentian Iroquois by a French expedition in 1600 exterminated this people. A Spanish expedition in Florida caused desolation by warfare. The political or demographic vacuum was filled by the in-migration of other Native peoples or the concentration of remaining populations, as in postplague Europe. The process of displacement, destruction, and cultural reorganization lasted until the 1880s.[6]

As a cause of genocide, the deliberate exploitation of Native peoples to the point of death ranked next to pathogens on the Caribbean islands and the Iberian military conquest of the complex cultures of Central and Andean America. About 600 men wrought bloody havoc in the Aztec Empire in 1519–21; 150 to 180 men aided by a smallpox epidemic did the same in the Inca Empire in 1533–34. The Chibcha culture succumbed in 1536–41. Within two decades, three high cultures had been wiped out. "Successful" *conquistadores* often engaged in warfare among themselves. Those who survived and kept the favor of their monarchs carried home riches and became the farsighted explorer-statesmen of historical lore—European lore.[7]

Next came immigrant men of the Church, in larger numbers and more powerful than in Asia. To protect First Peoples from their "idolatrous worship" as well as from death-bringing Euro-white and colony-born, European-ancestry Creole exploitation, Jesuits and Franciscans formed administrative units, "states," from the Paraná River to California. "Indians" were forced to migrate and resettle in these zones and to labor for their protectors. The Jesuit Order, operating globally in India, Japan, China, and Latin America, "was a child of the era of commercial capitalism, and its members did not always observe the medieval prohibition against taking interest [on their investment]. As bankers and enterprisers they made, in fact, a pioneering contribution." The welfare regulations for the Natives were totalitarian, and the protection given was sufficiently successful that embittered settlers coveting the Indians' labor fought the clerics.

The best-known mission, which will serve as an example, targeted the approximately 100,000 Guaraní Indians of the Upper Paraná River. "Paraguay," not identical with the modern state of that name, was a well-intentioned "utopian socialist" experiment according to supporters and an exercise in "theocratic communism" according to critics. It was destructive of Native values and cultures: the Order took in spirit what laymen took in economic or sexual exploitation, as Gilberto Freyre argued. While the mission kept off the armed slave-raiders from São Paulo, the Guaraní people became over time a frontier garrison for the Spanish against the Portuguese—and some later joined colonial mainstream society. In the power struggles, the corporate clerics lost to the profit-hungry settlers. Portugal expelled the Jesuits from all its dominions in 1759; Spain expelled the 2,200 Jesuits in its American colonies in 1767. Their multiethnic German, French, and Italian composition and their opulent lifestyle were held against them. Most went to Italy; but when the pope dissolved the

Order in 1773, American-born men may have returned and participated in independence movements.[8]

The frightful toll on human lives and the *conquistadores'* callousness—as well as the destruction of whole civilizations—have distracted attention from the impact of surviving Amerindians and their cultures on the immigrants. For long, historians' Eurocentric approaches contributed to the burial of memory. Peasant studies of the 1960s and 1970s had a stimulating effect. Since then research, now based on indigenous-language sources, has grown extensively. In colonial Peru, patterns of internal migration continued Inca traditions. When missionaries constructed Christian churches, they chose preconquest sacred sites. Thus the colonized attended Catholic service and their own spiritual sites. The success of missionary activities could be claimed—what went on in Natives' heads and hearts, their minds and belief-systems, was discreetly glossed over. By interaction and conversion new cultural practices emerged, as Nancy M. Farriss has sensitively sketched for the Spanish and Yucatec Maya. Cultural interaction also juxtaposed many European and more African languages with some 2,000 tongues of the First Peoples.[9]

8.2   Iberian Migration and Settlement

Iberian societies were deeply changed by emigration to the Americas and by the import of silver, produce, and plants. Now refuted is the traditional view that the Castilian lesser nobility (*hidalgos*) or at least its surplus sons made up the bulk of the migrants. At first, most migrants came from the urban middle strata; the wealthier ones were accompanied by servants of both sexes. Servants, who in contrast to English and German migrants were unindentured, remained for some time in their masters' retinues and then struck out for themselves. One-third of the emigrants came from Andalusia, with the two Castiles and Extremadura sending another 30 percent. Seville alone usually sent more migrants than all other cities combined, including in-migrants from Castile, Portugal, and other Iberian states who had lived in the city temporarily. The Seville-Andalusian dialect became the standard language in the Caribbean. Sixteenth-century emigrants

> represented nearly all ranks of society and a variety of occupations. They included distinguished officials and high ecclesiastics, secular priests and notaries hoping to find positions, artisans planning to establish themselves with their trades, peoples responding to the urging of relatives who had gone before them, and young men and women employed as servants. Emigrants were married and single, adults and children, and traveled in combinations of all kinds.[10]

Toward the century's end, however, the social composition changed. According to Boyd-Bowman, a "depressing composite picture" of the emigrants emerged: "a poverty-stricken Andalusian male aged 27½, unmarried, unskilled and probably only semi-literate, driven by hunger to make his way . . . in the employ of any man who would pay his passage"; or, a woman in her early thirties, traveling with her thirty-six-year-old husband, two young children, a manservant, and a maid. Men often deserted their families, and authorities ordered men to send for their wives or return home.[11]

Migrants, whether wealthy or poor, left a society in motion. Wealthy non-Castilian families relocated to Seville to escape the exclusion of "foreigners" from the profitable colonial trade. Spanish population decline in the late sixteenth and first half of the seventeenth century and the incorporation of Portugal (1580–1640) led to the in-migration of Portuguese craftsmen. By 1640, one-quarter of Seville's inhabitants had been born in Portugal, and in Old Castile and Extremadura a majority of skilled workers were of Portuguese origin. Portuguese also selected Spanish colonial possessions as their destination—Buenos Aires and Peru, for example. After Portugal's independence was restored in 1640, their migration slowed, and French laborers from the Auvergne arrived in Spain to benefit from the colony-enriched economy.[12]

Contemporary perceptions described emigration to the Americas as representing a loss of tens of thousands of able-bodied people from the Iberian Peninsula each year. Emigration was large in relation to the home population base, but it was small in relation to the size of the new territories. Out of a population of eight million, on average about 250,000 emigrants left for the Spanish American possessions from 1500 to 1600 (2,500 annually), about 200,000 from 1601 to 1650 (4,000 annually), and another quarter million from 1650 to 1800. Foreigners were at first excluded from immigration. Portugal's less restrictive immigration policy opened Brazil to all nationalities. It excluded non-Catholics but included exiled criminals (*degredados*) and deported prostitutes. The gold rush to Brazil's interior briefly raised immigration levels around 1700, and during the whole eighteenth century perhaps 400,000 came out of a home population of one to two million per generation.[13]

To underpin Spanish colonial society with a stable agriculture based on family labor, Bishop Las Casas began to recruit peasant families by offering free passage, free land to be held in perpetuity, financial support during the first year of residence, exemption from taxes but not tithes, some free Indian labor, and bounties for particular crops. According to the crown, tenant farmers unable to "obtain enough to sustain themselves, their wives and children without much poverty and drudgery" ought to avail themselves of the opportunity to emigrate. But regional lords of the soil, unwilling to forgo the services of their tenants, sabotaged recruitment, which ended after only two years in 1519. Migration, social structures, and power are intricately related.

The recruitment and social composition of migrants depended on regional economies and cultures of migration. Basques, mobile as fishermen and herdsmen, formed a sizeable minority of the newcomers. In Castile, the crushing of the *comunero* rebellion in 1521 or secret sympathies for the Jewish or Islamic faiths may have contributed to migration decisions. In the eighteenth century, governments in Galicia and the Canaries sponsored emigration.[14]

Women accounted for only about 6 percent of the early migrants; but in the mid-sixteenth century their share increased to one-third, and in the eighteenth century the sex ratio was balanced. Figures are, as always, difficult to ascertain. For example, when the fleet of 1604 left, fifty women had been granted a license to leave for New Spain, but six hundred were counted on board. More women than men migrated from Seville, and complete families departed from the Canaries. Gendered inheritance patterns and family economies induced colonists without sons to send for nephews to join them as heirs to business or as friars. Colonists' letters created an image of higher incomes and higher status, the latter indicated by ownership of a horse by each and every man.[15]

In the early sixteenth century Portuguese emigration began in the south, in Algarve and its port towns, and then shifted to the central regions and the Atlantic ports, especially Lisbon. By the last third of the sixteenth century, the north sent most of the emigrants. Two decisive changes in migration patterns occurred at the end of the seventeenth century. First, the early colonies—the Atlantic islands, which were more densely populated than Portugal itself—became centers of family emigration to Brazil and Mozambique. Second, diasporic moves brought men and women to agricultural and urban jobs in many parts of the world, westward as far as Hawai'i, where eastbound Asian laborers arrived at the same time. By 1800, Portuguese-origin settlers, including descendants from mixed marriages who considered themselves Portuguese, amounted to 400,000 on the Atlantic islands, 80,000–100,000 in sub-Equatorial Africa, and some 120,000 or fewer in the Asian World; in Brazil the numbers grew from 30,000 by 1600 to 100,000 by 1700 and, because of the gold rush, to 1.8 million in 1800.

In the Iberian societies, calls were occasionally sent out to wealthy colonials to return and invest their riches at home. Those who did return accommodated themselves to their hometowns without upsetting social structures or settled in the nearest larger town. Merchants, rather than return permanently, moved through extended networks of family businesses and settled where fortune or misfortune placed them. The crisis of the Spanish economy in the seventeenth century discouraged return. Officeholders returned from Portugal's colonies with their newly acquired wealth; new Christians returned from Brazil; and skilled craftsmen from state-sponsored projects to which they had been sent. For common people, however, the retransfer of savings involved numerous obstacles, and their agricultural yields and job opportunities were better in the colonies.[16]

In the process of emigration, return, and information exchange, old and new societies influenced each other. The Spanish crown had intended to establish an "ideal society" controlled by its appointed representatives and modeled on European patterns. But officials attempting to replicate Spain in America had to come to terms with different socio-geographical environments. In "the Indies," which offered career alternatives and new resources, corporate social structures proved difficult to reestablish. At home, in Andalusia, for example, departures and immigration from Portugal and France affected social hierarchies, conventions, and values.[17]

New Spain's society at first was characterized by floating populations of male vagrants and "supernumerary" young women—those who did not find a husband.

But from the seventeenth century onward more stable settlement patterns predominated. Nevertheless, changes in agricultural and mining economies, in investment patterns, and in economic and tax policies forced the upper classes to relocate and their laborers to move about in search of employment. The transient population was mainly composed of Spanish, Mulatto, and Black miners to and from ore or placer deposits. Colonial officials in this frontier society had to implement population policies that had little internal coherence and continuity.[18]

The Spanish crown, which had been reluctant to admit foreigners to the colonies, during a "liberal" period (1526–38) under Charles V leased Venezuela to the southern German Welser company. However, the miners sent by the company ceased activities by 1546. In Spain, foreigners could easily be naturalized before departure and, when in financial straits, were granted exemptions by the crown for a fee. Converted Jews, Moriscos and their descendants, "Gypsies," and those convicted by the Inquisition could not enter the Spanish Americas. Black and Mulatto freemen emigrated in small numbers. Later, Portuguese, among them women, and Italians were admitted. Other non-Spaniards came as clerics of non-national Orders, as prisoners of war, and as soldiers and sailors. One ship's sailors in Lima, in 1544, consisted of a Corsican owner, a Greek master, and a crew of Genoese, Corsican, Greek, and Slavic men. Shipbuilders and other skilled artisans often were foreigners—silversmiths and tailors, for example, came from Flemish towns. Foreign merchants, including English and French, were tolerated. In 1700, foreigners in New Spain amounted to perhaps 3 percent of the European-born in a total population of approximately three million. While Spain was a "melting pot" for immigrant Europeans, "Peruvian Spaniards remained in deepest ignorance" about the Others. "They called Irishmen Levantines, and were unable to tell a Hungarian from a Corsican." Foreigners quickly became Hispanicized, sought naturalization, married locally, and changed to Catholicism. Thus, according to Lockhart, "foreign cultural influence was nil."[19]

Most Castilian migrants chose to go to the island of Hispaniola or Española (now Haiti and the Dominican Republic), where colonial society first lost its rough edges. Adventurers preferred Peru, and settler families favored fertile lands. Toward the eighteenth century, when the emigration of unskilled men was discouraged, skilled craftsmen were in demand but accounted for only one-tenth of the Peruvian arrivals.[20] Spain's American colonies and its Atlantic trade had suffered from structural problems since the 1610s. Silver mining and minting, which peaked in the 1580s, caused inflation at home. Increasing colonial agricultural and craft production resulted in a decline of exports from the homeland. Seville merchants suffered from buccaneers in the Caribbean, from the Inquisition at home, and from high crown-imposed taxation wherever they traded. The intended ideal society had not materialized.

8.3 Early Exploitation and Enslavement in the Caribbean

On his second voyage, in 1493, Columbus transported between 1,200 and 1,500 Spanish men to Hispaniola. The settlement without women was to be the self-sufficient nucleus of Spanish power and the search for gold. In the next decades, towns were founded on other islands; placer gold was washed in riverbeds; domesticated animals, especially horses and hogs, but also cattle, sheep, and goats were imported. Labor— the digging of gold and raising of crops—was assigned to the Arawak. Following practices of the Christian conquest of the Iberian Peninsula, the Spanish used Thomas Aquinas's theory of "just wars" (set forth in his *Summa Theologiae*) against people of other faiths and against heathens. After 1513, a formal request (*requerimiento*) to submit and accept the Christian faith had to be read publicly to the Indios. If they submitted, they were to remain free; otherwise, warfare and enslavement would commence.

Whether free or enslaved, the First Peoples had to bear the cost of colonization. Tributes (*demora*), one-fifth of which was the crown's share, permitted Spanish (military) immigrants to recoup investments, accumulate wealth, and achieve status. They were levied to defray the cost of the viceregal administration, as tithes to the Church, and as traditional offerings to the caciques. The crown kept grants of rights-to-soil and rights-in-person separate. Estates (*estancias*) required a second grant, *encomienda*, which implied jurisdiction over the inhabitants of one or more villages or parts of a village and a right to tribute and labor services (from Spanish *encomendar:* to consign to someone's charge). Colonial governors apportioned conquered settlements of Indios among persons of rank and other deserving newcomers. Thus, formally, Indios were not tied to the soil, although their mobility was restricted. Labor services (*servicios personales*) involved involuntary mobility and encompassed any type of labor from agriculture to mining, from porterage to construction, as well as household work. This labor regime transferred aspects of European serfdom to the Americas. By law only *indios útiles*—men between the ages of seventeen and fifty-four (eighteen and fifty in some sources)—were granted for labor service. In practice, women and children, too, had to labor for the *encomendero.* Such grants of services ended—in the written laws—after 1549. Thus, for *estancia* labor and the collection of tributes, Indios were immobilized; for labor distant from their settlements, they were forced to migrate (see chap. 10.1).[21]

The Arawak's system of locally shifting field (*conuco*) cultivation and kitchen gardens—along with hunting, fishing, and gathering—had provided them with ample food, and riverbeds provided gold for body adornment. The conquerors requisitioned their labor for six to eight months per year and forced men and women to migrate to placer mining. At the same time, workloads on the *conucos* expanded to raise food for the immigrants and their families and servants. The Spanish population on Hispaniola rose to 8,000–10,000 in 1509, while the Arawak died at an exponential rate, perhaps three million in the first fifteen years of the Spanish presence. Some 60,000 survived by 1508. With each death and each new arrival from Spain, more demands were placed on the surviving men and women. Many fled into the mountains or committed suicide. When Charles V ended Arawak serfdom, a smallpox epidemic killed the last survivors.

In response to the labor shortage, the Iberian-Spanish crown in 1509 authorized raids on "useless" islands—those with no gold and Spanish settlement—with the provision that captives receive wages and be supplied with necessities. However, the Caribbean-Spanish, whose raids yielded some two million islanders within a decade, considered them slaves. At first, most raids took place on Puerto Rico. Discovery of placer gold on other islands brought forth minor gold rushes. On the Bahamas (Lucayas), where no gold was found, *naborías perpetuas*—serfs not bound to land and thus legally transferable to wherever they were needed—became slaves for life. Human loss during the voyages was extreme, and the seas were said to be floating with corpses. By 1514 the islands were depopulated. Prices for one *naboría* increased from five to 150 gold pesos from 1509 to 1512. With the rapid depletion of placer gold, an increasing proportion of surviving slaves were used as house slaves, and colonists began to experiment with sugarcane cultivation. Those developments were repeated in Jamaica after 1509, in Cuba after 1511, in the Lesser Antilles, and in the islands off the Venezuelan coast.

Wherever Europeans settled and Native peoples had been annihilated, new slave labor forces were brought in, at first from West Africa and the Canaries (map 8.2). This population transfer added yellow fever and malaria to the scourges of the Native peoples of the Americas; it also added new foods, such as the yam roots cultivated by Africans. With the depletion of human, mining, and agricultural resources, the immigrant population, still mainly male, moved to more profitable "New World" locations. *Villas* (Spanish for "towns") were abandoned, new ones established, and others revived. Some moved in search of quick profits, others to escape destitution, and all fled their own ravages upon human beings and nature. Some *encomiendas* became virtually worthless when epidemics decimated the indigenous workers; others were too distant from markets. After 1536, widows could succeed to their deceased husbands' grants but were "seldom permitted to remain single." This offered men the chance to acquire property through marriage, with "doubtless at times . . . less than desirable results for the women involved." Spanish *conquistadores* and administrators redistributed Native peoples or parts of communities to new *encomenderos* at will, thereby hurting their own economy and sending the First Peoples into further forced mobility.[22]

Spain's colonial project of re-creating Castilian society and of turning Indios into Spanish peasants bore as little relation to conditions in the Americas as Columbus's assumptions did to geography. Recognizing the failure, the Castilian government then projected a dual society after 1513: *pueblos de españoles* as settlements separate from the *pueblos de indios*. A third group, Blacks and Mulattoes, who were not tributary to the Spanish, were not permitted to reside in Indio villages. Because labor continued to be demanded from First Peoples and cultural hegemony was maintained over them, the two societies had to be spatially contiguous. Thus Indios were to resettle from their traditional villages to the vicinity of Spanish towns. This "contiguous separation," probably modeled on the separate quarters in Iberian towns, was never strictly observed.[23]

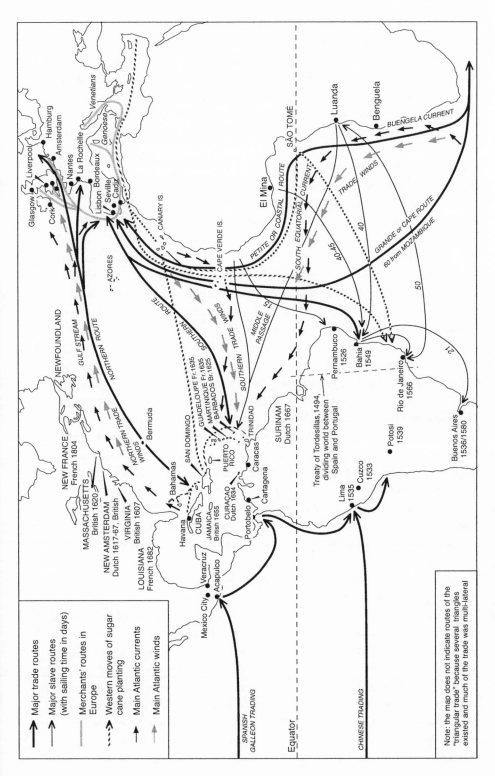

8.2 Mediterranean, Transatlantic, and Transpacific Voyaging

By the end of the 1520s, Havana had taken the place of Santo Domingo as the foremost Spanish town in the Caribbean. Raising stock, rather than digging for gold, became the main labor activity, and hides and sugar became staple products for export. While the first European boom population declined, the population of West African slave and free escapees emerged. When regular officials took over rule of the islands from the *conquistadores* in the 1530s, no native labor was left. Immigrant family units with their immigrant servants and without supporting Natives relocated to Cuba or to Florida, Mexico, and Peru. In the 1520s the mainland, *tierra firme,* became the focus of the *conquistadores'* and immigrants' greed. The forced migration of men in porterage services and to mining sites, as well as the capture of women and children for agricultural labor, separated families and prevented marriage. The decline in procreation compounded the toll exacted by epidemics, massacres, and death from overwork.

After the Iberian states occupied and looted the states and societies of the Americas, self-organized pirates—"freebooters" or "buccaneers," labeled "illegal"—along with privateers chartered by Spain's European rival states, established domains on islands deserted or not yet claimed in the Caribbean and off the Brazilian coast. As "legal" entrepreneurs, they intended to join the profit center. In 1630 English and French adventurers from Saint Barthélemy expelled the Spanish garrison of Tortuga, established "an international association for crime" (according to French historian Pierre Chaumu), and soon claimed the western third of Hispaniola, Saint Domingue. The colony came under control of the French state during the ascendancy of Jean-Baptiste Colbert's mercantilist policies. But since the island now lacked easily accessible precious metals and Native laborers, the colonists turned to agriculture with *engagés* and slaves (see chap. 10.4). Other European states' and corsair communities included Anglican English, Protestant Dutch, Huguenots, Catholic French, escaped indentured servants, and shipwrecked sailors. Men from well-placed families, who had come upon hard times, followed the tradition of military looting: eleventh-century crusading, the medieval robber barons' local hustling, and now seaborne buccaneering. Pirates and English, French, and Dutch state-sent occupation forces fought the Spanish; the Carib on the southern islands, who fiercely resisted the intrusions; and each other. But "in order to maximize profits from their colonies, . . . [all] copied current practices in the Spanish and Portuguese empires."[24]

The colonies of the Netherlands in the Americas were as multicultural as Dutch society itself. They included the island colonies of Tobago (1632–54), Curaçao (1634), the Virgin Islands and St. Martin (1648), as well as the mainland ones of New Amsterdam (Guiana) and Surinam (1667) and, in the north, New Netherland (1616–64; later, New York). Migrants, perhaps one-quarter of whom came as families, originated mainly from the province of Zeeland. Dutch-Portuguese-Jewish families emigrated to Surinam and radiated out from there. The New Netherland/New York colony, with a population of about 10,000, accommodated English and Scottish dissenters, Mennonites, Quakers, and German Lutherans. They mixed with Swedes from the Delaware colony and with refugees from the Brazilian Dutch colony.[25]

By 1770 perhaps 35,000 people of French origin lived in the French possessions, comprising Haiti, i.e., the western third of the island of Santo Domingo (1667), and Guadeloupe and Martinique (1635), as well as mainland Guiana/Cayenne (1674). British conquests included Jamaica (1655), several islands of the Lesser Antilles, and, on the mainland, the Georgetown area on the Guiana coast. By 1700 the European-origin population of 50,000 included a sizable Irish group and "owned" 150,000 African-origin slaves. Slave labor was most profitable in staple-crop production. In the first phase, tobacco was cultivated with one or a few indentured servants and some seasonal labor. Only in the second phase (1645–50) did the large sugar estates with their slave labor regime emerge. The third phase—the extension and stabilization of the sugar economy—lasted until the abolition of slavery in the British Empire. All English colonies had Black majorities by the end of the seventeenth century, and a century later the African-origin population approached 80 percent of the total. Dominating European-origin lifestyles faced majority African-origin cultures.[26]

Settlement in the tropical climate of the Caribbean and the Brazilian lowlands caused high mortality among Europeans and, at least initially, among Africans. Even new settlements in temperate regions of both Americas experienced high death rates because of poor food, lack of adaptation to the environment, and lack of doctors or medically experienced women. This raises the issue of why men (and few women) continued to move to the tropical belt. Profits were high for those who lived to reap them, and potentially free migrants, perhaps like freebooters, did not calculate death as an outcome. Indentured servants who came from a different class and had little expectation of fabulous riches, shunned the high-mortality regions if they had a choice of destination. For two centuries, the Caribbean plantation economies, through the export of sugar and other staples and the generation of capital, had a much more important impact on their respective European home economies than the economically marginal colonies of New France and New England in the north. But the latter, with articulate clerics, college-educated intellectuals, and a religious earnestness in large segments of the populations, were to dominate discourse when they became independent in 1776 or acquired cultural autonomy, as Quebec did in 1774. Mythic "America"—with its ideology of the pursuit of happiness—reflected the idea of a country of the free rather than the reality of a slave economy with extreme mortality and racially mixed but not legally sanctioned unions.

8.4 The First Transpacific Migration System

Spain and New Spain, which had to avoid the Portuguese-controlled Asia-bound routes via the African Cape, sent ships from Acapulco across the Pacific after 1532. The conquest of the Philippines began in 1565, and Manila was settled in 1571.[27] The city, supplied by the Chinese junk trade, became Spain's Asian entrepôt (see chap. 7.3). The trade was financed by silver dug from the Peruvian mines by the forced labor of "Indios" (see chap. 10.1); the Asian goods were produced by Manila-Chinese craftsmen. Following Iberian traditions of enslavement of prisoners of war (see chaps. 2.3

and 5.3), the Spanish enslaved native Filipino, Chinese, and some Japanese men and women and, from the 1570s to 1597, transported several thousand to Mexico and Peru. When the Iberian-Spanish government limited the Manila-Acapulco trade to two galleons annually in 1593 and abolished Asian slavery in the empire, smuggling increased and the first Pacific System did not decline. Other Chinese migrated of their own free will, expanding the patterns of mobility of the Indian Ocean trade emporia and the Chinese diaspora to Latin America. Merchants established businesses; artisans were encouraged to cross the Pacific; laborers joined the communities. With skills surpassing those of Europeans and superior technologies, Chinese ship carpenters could construct ships that were up to ten times larger than Columbus's; they built the Spanish galleons in Manila and in Acapulco.

The slave transports, the continued Spanish and Chinese transpacific trade, and Chinese traditions of diaspora-formation account for the Asian-origin population of Lima, Peru (1.5 percent in 1600), for the Chinese colony in Mexico City in 1635, and—probably—for Acapulco's designation as "ciudad de los Chinos." The migrants originally came from the Philippines, Portuguese Macao, and coastal towns of southern China. During the eighteenth century, immigrants from Asia and their Hispanicized or Indianized descendants lived along the coasts of Peru and Mexico. Since few women went along, intermarriage prevented the emergence of lasting ethnocultural enclaves.

With the decline of the transpacific connection in the second half of the seventeenth century, fewer migrants reached the American Pacific coast. Migration ended with the galleon trade in 1815. However, in the 1780s the British East India Company, reaching from its Asian entrepôts for the northwestern coast of America, sent ships across the Pacific to Vancouver Island. The crews consisted of Chinese sailors, and Chinese craftsmen were recruited to construct forts and ships in the North American colony. Some of these Chinese settled and intermarried locally; but through the two centuries before the emergence of the second Pacific Migration System (see chap. 15.5) only a few individuals from Asia reached the Americas. Filipinos migrated to the Mississippi River delta and formed a lasting colony in the eighteenth century. Major Chinese migration was destined for the Hawai'ian Islands.[28]

8.5   Ethnogenesis in Latin America

New Latin American peoples emerged from the surviving First Nations, the enslaved African newcomers, and the European immigrants. Though still strongly Native in culture on the mainland, they were mainly African in culture on the islands. Power resided with European origin and Whiteness (map 8.3). The eighteenth-century societies consisted of the four Spanish viceroyalties (New Spain, New Granada, Peru, and Río de La Plata), Portuguese Brazil (incorporating after 1654 Dutch Brazil), Dutch Surinam, French Cayenne, and British Guiana, as well as the Caribbean colonies. By 1760, New Spain counted 3.75 million inhabitants, 60 percent of whom were Indians. Colonial Whites and *castas* (African slaves and free persons), and a few Asians accounted

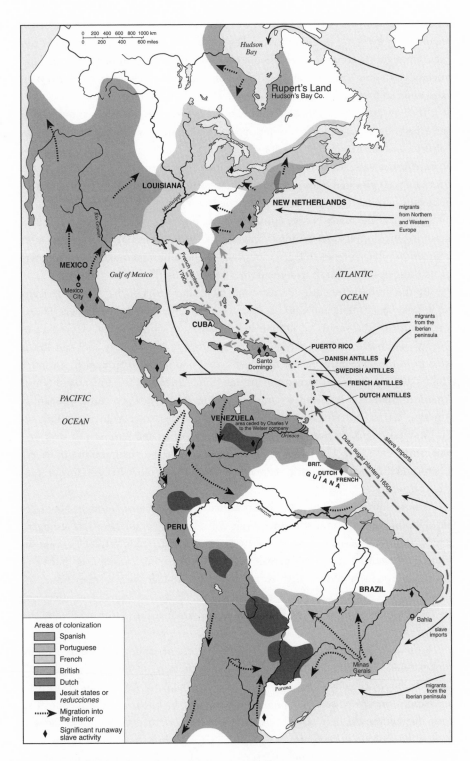

8.3 Zones of Cultural Conflict and Contact, 18th Century

Within the figure, the following labels appear:

0 200 400 600 800 1000 km
0   200   400   600 miles

Hudson
Bay

Rupert's Land
Hudson's Bay Co.

LOUISIANA

Mississippi

NEW NETHERLANDS

migrants
from Northern
and Western
Europe

Rio Grande

MEXICO

Gulf of Mexico

Mexico
City

ATLANTIC

OCEAN

French planters
1790s

CUBA

migrants
from the
Iberian
peninsula

PUERTO RICO

Santo
Domingo

DANISH ANTILLES

SWEDISH ANTILLES

FRENCH ANTILLES

DUTCH ANTILLES

PACIFIC

OCEAN

VENEZUELA
area ceded by Charles V
to the Welser company

Orinoco

slave imports

BRIT.
DUTCH
GUIANA
FRENCH

Dutch sugar planters 1650s

Amazon

PERU

BRAZIL

Bahia

slave
imports

Minas
Gerais

Paraná

migrants
from the
Iberian peninsula

Areas of colonization

Spanish

Portuguese

French

British

Dutch

Jesuit states or
reducciones

Migration into
the interior

Significant runaway
slave activity

for almost 40 percent. Only 1 percent was Spanish-born. Brazil's Portuguese-origin population grew to 1.8 million in 1800. The Iberian-born, "pure" Spanish and Portuguese immigrants, it has to be recalled, were descendants of peninsular Natives, immigrant Germanic Visigoths and—in lesser numbers—Vandals, Muslim North Africans, and conquering "Franks."

The new power elite relied on the old to collect tributes, including human labor and First Peoples' caciques and other upper-class families, whose children were acculturated to the new power relationships in which the Spaniards threatened uncooperative ones with autos-da-fé. Like postcontact African rulers, such families could continue their elevated roles or enhance their positions by collaborating. Daughters of cacique families, "princesses," were married to or married Spanish men. The common people of the many Native cultural groups, however, clung to their traditional lifestyles. Involuntary and voluntary migrations, the intermarriage of survivors after population collapse, Spanish legislation, and European immigrant attitudes homogenized these peoples at least to some degree into "Indios."[29]

By the mid-seventeenth century more than four-fifths of the Afro-Americans came from Senegambia and Guinea, sent via Cape Verde–based slave traders. Thereafter, much of the supply of human beings was sent from Angola. According to Curtin's estimates, 125,000 slaves arrived in Spanish America (75,000) and Brazil (50,000) in the sixteenth century and over 1.3 million in the seventeenth century.[30] From 1500 to 1810, total forced migrations from Africa to the Central and South American mainland involved 2.5 million people. About 950,000 came to Spanish America; slaves in Portuguese Brazil numbered perhaps 200,000 in 1700. With regard to total migration from the Old Worlds, both Africa and Europe, just over one half came from Africa. Life in the tropical lowlands, harsh working conditions everywhere, and imbalanced sex ratios explain frightfully high mortality and low procreation rates.[31]

Among European migrants, the initial male predominance "brought about genetic mixing and cultural adjustments of considerable complexity," according to Borah, with non-Iberians leaving "relatively little demographic residue" except on some Caribbean islands. The Spanish Inquisition's concept of *limpieza* (purity of blood) did not carry weight with regard to sexual contact with women from "inferior" peoples, whether by rape, concubinage, which was widespread, or affectionate relations. The concept's aim, boundary construction against Others, failed in the Americas.

Postconquest peoples thus emerged in a process of ethnogenesis out of many backgrounds. Medieval Mediterranean Iberian traditions of dividing people into status groups by religion and origin were transferred to Latin America in the form of legislation concerning complex hierarchies arranged by birth, caste, and color. The basic distinction was between *peninsulares*, Spanish or Portuguese born in Europe, and *criollos* born in the colonies of European-origin parents. As *gente de razón*, both stood above all others, the *castas*. One consequence of separation by caste and socially unacceptable intercourse had to be borne by children: in one São Paulo parish, for example, 23 percent of all free children born between 1741 and 1845 were illegitimate and 16 percent were foundlings. Because of their special status as well as their origins from many European peoples, Catholic "ecclesiatics" were sometimes listed separately.

The construction of groups was flexible. In theory, "Spaniards"—*Españoles, gente de razón,* or *gente decente*—comprised only "pure-bred" *peninsulares* and colony-born *criollos,* "apart from a handful of hispanised caciques" and Indian princesses whose "race" followed that of their husbands. "Not all whites belonged to the respectable classes, but all the respectable were white"—by self-definition (Brading). Thus, in practice, this category could comprise all men and women of some European descent and those practicing a European culture. The second tier, categorized by partners in procreation, was constructed as *mulattos,* children of White and Black parents, and *mestizos,* of White and Native parentage. Gendered discourse had White men decide to consort with Indian or Black women, but women, of course, pursued their own strategies, including improvement of their social position. The descent classification was extended across generations, *quadroon* or *quinterón.* On the bottom level stood the "Indios" and "Negroes," both divided into free and unfree, as well as *zambos,* children of African and Indian parents, but the terms varied regionally. For all practical purposes, by the eighteenth century new peoples of multiple ethnic backgrounds and different shades of light or dark had emerged. Men and women born in Europe always were a minuscule minority holding the majority of social, economic, and political assets.[32]

Arab-inspired urban traditions of the Iberian Peninsula reemerged in the Spanish colonies. European-origin "Whites" gravitated to the cities, as did Indios (in view of the harsh rural labor requirements). In 1697 Giovanni Careri, a merchant from Naples, Italy, considered Mexico City equal to Italian towns. With nearly 100,000 inhabitants, it was the largest city in the Americas: half of its inhabitants were Spanish-Americans, under 10 percent Indios, the others Mestizos, Blacks, and Mulattoes.[33] On New Spain's thinly settled northern frontier (today's northern Mexico and southwestern United States), colonists were to situate new towns on a hill—the peninsular Muslim and Christian logic of urban defense. Street layout by grid pattern began from a central plaza bounded by official buildings and a cathedral. This center provided room for rituals of power and status. To ensure economic viability and tax income, Native laborers were to be requisitioned from the vicinity. To ensure social order, single residents were to be encouraged to marry and vagrants put to work or deported. Actual developments on the frontier were different. Negroes and Mulattoes could be declared free, but—like Jews in Europe—they were prohibited from carrying weapons and—like non-Muslims in the Ottoman Empire—subject to paying a special tax. Land grants, given to persons of standing only, inhibited individual prospecting and entrepreneurship.[34]

Up to 1640, the southern frontiers, Chile and the La Plata region, received less than 4 percent of Spanish immigrants. Cattle roaming the open grassland (called *pampa* after a Native group called Pampa) attracted cow-killers and traders in hides.

Gauchos formed a group of "trans-frontiersmen," as did the *llaneros* in the Orinoco valley of New Granada (Venezuela), the *vaqueros* of northern Mexico, and the cowboys of the North American Plains. Contrary to Euro-American white male daredevil images, the herders included Black and Indian men and some women. Out of unions with or abuse of Native women, the grasslands or *pampa* segment of the Argentine people emerged.[35]

Portuguese- or Luso-Brazilian society, with fewer visible riches, after more than a century of migration consisted of a mere 50,000 Portuguese-Brazilians with some 120,000 slaves, half of them Amerindians, the others Africans. In port cities, vagrants and prisoners but also artisans, whose skills were needed on board ship, were press-ganged into service, an involuntary mobility from which many never returned. Euro-Brazilian and mestizo armed *bandeirantes* (from Portuguese *bandeira:* flag) penetrated the interior in search of gold, but, finding Indians, they became slavers. Some of them settled and intermarried, as did *Paulista* men, who moved to the interior from the plateau west of São Paulo and adopted the Tupí language. Their ethnoculturally mixed trading posts often became the nuclei for later cities. Discovery of alluvial gold deposits and diamonds in the Minas Gerais in the 1690s and early 1700s caused large-scale, predominantly male immigration and the importation of slaves. When, after the mid-seventeenth century, the deposits seemed exhausted, out-migration reduced the slave population by 20 percent within two decades. Then a shift from an export-driven mining economy to a diversified agricultural economy supplying internal markets opened new opportunities, and the population stabilized by natural reproduction rather than by in-migration. The slave community's increasingly balanced sex ratio permitted family formation. Slaves were still imported into Tejuco for diamond production, but farming families migrated to particular expanding agricultural areas like the Rio das Mortes. Spatial mobility, including that of free Afro-Brazilians and Mulattoes, remained high.

By the early nineteenth century, Brazil had the largest free "colored" population of any slave society in the Americas, even though the plantation economy, in particular slave-labor-based coffee production, was expanding. Slave estates, small or large, were embedded in a free labor economy. The lives and work of the free colored men and women resembled those of the Luso-Brazilians. They could enter most occupations, developed social organizations, and could and did own slaves. Luso-Brazilians, however, were generally wealthier and more likely to own slaves. Elite membership was limited to the many shades of white, from pure white to light-colored. At the time of the first national census in 1872, 1.5 million Afro-Brazilians (15.3 percent) remained enslaved in a population of 10.1 million. Abolition was to come in 1888. The rest of the society was of mixed and white origin in a ratio of six to four. Since categories are constructions, some statistics designated only slaves as "Black." In all Latin societies, castes notwithstanding, people mixed more often than in the rigidly segregationist Anglo-Caribbean and U.S. societies.[36]

8.6   Internal Migrations in the Colonial Societies

The visibility of transatlantic emigration and the self-centeredness of European scholarship have retarded research on internal migrations in Latin America, the Caribbean, and North America.[37] In the first half of the seventeenth century, the migratory drift was from longer-settled Mexico southward to the Andean Peruvian frontier of opportunities, to peripheral areas of Venezuela, and to the La Plata plains. Many movements are comparable to those of Europe and Asia—for example, the mobility of students and of novices who chartered careers for themselves in distant convents. Rural-urban and urban-urban migrations were similar in intention but different in composition because of the factor of skin color. Some migratory traditions continued from the Inca period, others were specific to colonial society. Indios migrated permanently to the towns; Black people moved between towns; and Euro-Latin Americans circulated much like urban elites in Europe.[38]

The Indios' pasturing of llamas and alpacas involved transhumance similar to the Spanish *mesta*. Those who were resettled or kidnapped from their home *ayllus* (or village and its social organization) to live under tutelage of Christian Orders in *congregaciones* and *reducciones* collectively paid tribute, functioned as labor reservoirs, and were meant to be homogenized into a Catholic Latin–Native culture. But in the Christian hamlets, the involuntary migrants split into separate quarters by regional or local origin. As laborers, Native and Black Latin Americans had to migrate to work in valleys and coastal lands on plantations and estates (*haciendas, ranchos*) or to towns for domestic service. They "resisted acculturation either by flight or by re-grouping within pueblos around pre-conquest affiliations." First Peoples migrated "from adversity" rather than "to opportunity," leaving the rural sphere to escape the obligatory labor service, the worst of which was mine labor in the highlands (see chap. 10.1). They attempted to improve their lot within the structures of Spanish-American rule.[39]

Black Latin Americans' migrations depended on status (free or slave) and cultural origin. Men and women served as urban domestics; urban Black craftsmen were sometimes able to purchase their freedom. Sugar and cotton plantations in west coast valleys were worked by African-origin slaves, as were placer mines. Panning for gold in valleys required large numbers of workers to dig canals to divert rivers from their natural course. Unfree migrant labor was housed in temporary shelters rather than permanent settlements. Because of the high risks, the increasingly costly Africans were not used in high-altitude mining.[40]

European-origin people, including Flemings, Germans, Neapolitans, Genoese, Greeks, and their Euro-Latin-Native offspring migrated to economic regions of sustained growth or in search of riches. Commerce, stock raising, and plantations attracted settlers, merchants, and entrepreneurs. Barely profitable agriculture increased the propensity to move to cities and search for other sources of income. Mining towns, especially those involved in the extraction of silver, attracted investors and independent prospectors. Administrators with their families had to move to the places where superiors posted them. Because of ritual displays of power, wives and children often accompanied officials to participate in public functions. Women also migrated, formed unions, and were economically active on their own.[41]

Five examples will illustrate urban and rural migrations from the seventeenth century to the mature eighteenth-century societies: migrant insertion in Lima and Cuzco; marriage migration in Michoacán on the Yucatán Peninsula; drifting and purposeful migration to mining in northern Mexico; population patterns in Mexico City of the Bourbon period; and, finally, the development of Santa Maria de Buenos Aires, Argentina. In the eighteenth century, when the volume and frequency of migration increased, administrators indicated a fear of losing control over people in the dichotomy of opportunity and escape: "To be from an unknown place allowed one the opportunity or risk of defining one's own marital, racial, occupational, and social background."[42]

Seventeenth-century Lima, like larger towns across the globe, was encircled by small vegetable producers, who in this instance employed internal Indio labor migrants. Cuzco, after a devastating earthquake in 1650, experienced a period of sustained growth: some Indios were forcibly resettled to the city; most came by choice from surrounding areas; others left the *reducciones*; and tribute-conveying messengers stayed. Immigrant Indio artisans affiliated themselves with guilds, severed contacts with their home *ayllus* and with kin living some distance away, and identified with their postmigration families. Urban-to-rural migrations involved men who took temporary jobs in agriculture. Transport laborers usually received only one-way consignments and thus had to move wherever contracts took them. Wives who were deserted by out-migrating husbands sued for support. Andean society, in which women held a substantial position, stressed reciprocity. Women owned and transmitted property, migrated with families or on their own, and entered the wage labor force but were restricted to personal and domestic service or were hired as wet nurses. In the seventeenth century, 70 percent of the Indios hired had been born outside the city. Labor migrants represented "key aspects of the transformation of indigenous society under Spanish Rule."[43]

Late-colonial migration, according to Robinson's summary of the complex causes, resembled mobility to other continents. The "significant variables" were

> the availability of land and other natural resources; the opportunities of employment in a changing economic context; the need to escape from socio-economically defined hardship, especially under conditions of famine and epidemic disease; the desire to benefit from the perceived services in urban centers; the general "opening" of closed-corporate Indian communities to the cultural influences of *mestizo* society; and last, but not least, the effect on Michoacán of regional socio-economic change throughout New Spain and beyond.

Young people, "at a most important stage in the lifecycle," migrated when ready to establish their own households just before or after marriage. "Social status and economic opportunity" made such migration an indicator of socioeconomic change. In long- and densely settled regions, out-migration involved attempts to retain rather than improve standing. The smaller the village and thus the pool of partners, the higher was the migration rate: 90 percent as compared to 20 percent in the urban society of Valladolid. "Miscegenation and spatial mobility" or ethnogenesis were related to agricultural change, beginning industrialization, and "an increasingly mobile workforce." Migration to perceived opportunities initiated "a systematic process of social change"; in late-colonial New Spain, "to move was to attempt to progress." However, in declining regions like Central Highland Ecuador from 1778 to 1825, out-migration was intended to avoid impoverishment.[44]

Northern Mexican mining had attracted a labor force of perhaps 11,000 free and drafted Indians as well as Black slaves when the seventeenth-century depression caused many to depart. Mobility was related to status: mine owners and families of rank were unable to liquidate their assets quickly, whereas low-ranking men and women, for whom relocation was less costly in terms of self-assumed identities and societally assigned position, moved more easily. Then the eighteenth-century mining boom attracted investors and skilled miners, who were "free, well-paid, geographically mobile" laborers, often working in partnership with owners. In some regions a surplus of trained miners moved with their families to new lodes or expanding established mines. New discoveries attracted and sustained populations of 10,000 to 20,000 persons within a few years, including shopkeepers, service personnel, and transport workers. Near Mexico City, miners were mostly Indians; further north in Guanajuato, Zacatecas, and Sombrerete, they were mainly Mulattoes and Mestizos. Mobility decreased when frontier towns reached stability. In Guanajuato of the 1790s, more than three-quarters of the male inhabitants had been born locally; only the merchant class continued its pattern of mobility. When labor struggles juxtaposed capitalists and miners and turned profit-sharing to wage labor, miners' families—like their early modern European counterparts—resumed migration. Some of the Central American mining and refining technology was imported via the migration of experts from the Iberian Peninsula and the Germanies.

Mexico City's immigrant population consisted of merchants, northern Spanish peasants, Basques, and Montañeses from Santander. In Iberia, the last two of those groups had a long history of out-migration, the men from Santander moving to Andalusia to take up innkeeping. Ethnic organizations reflected continued regional premigration loyalties and administrative recognition of group self-definition. Cloth production attracted migrants to Puebla and involved mule drivers who brought the raw material from Veracruz and Oaxaca and carried the finished cloth to Mexico City. Mexico's population almost doubled from the mid-1700s to 6.1 million in 1810, of whom on average 60 percent were Indians, 22 percent were *castas* (Mestizos and Mulattoes), and 18 percent self-described "Spaniards." The struggle for independence of 1808 pitted the resident Creoles against immigrant Españioles who arrogated the best positions to themselves. In the course of the struggle, however, the lower classes stood pitted against the "Whites."[45]

In Buenos Aires, founded in 1536 and resettled in 1580, in-migration changed opportunity structures for the previous residents when the city expanded rapidly in the eighteenth century. The lower precontact population density of the La Plata region as compared to that of Mexico explains different color ratios: 80 percent were classified as White in 1744, 17 percent as Negro and Mulatto, and 3 percent as Indian and Mestizo. From 1744 to 1810, the population grew from 10,000 to 42,500 with a near-balanced sex ratio and a color ratio of 66:33:1. Whereas among White heads of households 57.5 percent of the men and 73.1 percent of the women had been born locally in 1744, only 30.5 percent and 53.4 percent respectively were locally born in 1810. The peninsular Spanish staffed the municipal and viceregal bureaucracies and were overrepresented among the "commercial class." The role of established families decreased under conditions of rapid growth and change "in response to fluctuating patterns of immigration and out-migration." Superstratification by innovative and flexible immigrant men reduced "the occupational opportunities and potential for social mobility available to the native-born population"; in fact, they displaced them "from the upper and middle levels of the occupational hierarchy." The shares of long-distance migrants from other parts of Spanish America and Spain increased. Few women came from Spain (2.7 percent in 1810) as compared to 31.7 percent of the men —thus the latter married into the social networks of resident women. Foreign-born men accounted for about 8 percent of the population in both periods, but foreign-born women for less than 1 percent. Among common people in 1810, 59 percent of the artisans were immigrants. Below them, more than three-fourths of the Black population were slaves, who in a process of substratification competed "with the local free population for semi-skilled and unskilled jobs." Thus "significant numbers of the free, local-born population were forced to emigrate from the city and seek opportunities in the interior or in other Spanish colonies." This explains "the popular chauvinistic, anti-Spanish sentiment" of the period of independence.[46]

At the turn of the nineteenth century, in the Age of Democratic Revolution, people conscious of their own futures shaped new political structures, sometimes in alliances regardless of color, elsewhere according to hierarchies of caste and enslavement. African-origin people, in what has been called "a Two Hundred Years' War," had rebelled, formed Maroon communities with surviving Native peoples and had attempted to join forces with European-origin indentured servants. In the wake of the weakening of Spanish and Portuguese rule under Napoleonic expansion in Europe, most of the new multicultural Latin American people, dividing themselves into different "nations," achieved independence by 1825—a struggle that involved displacement and exile (see the case of Haiti, chap. 10.4).[47]

Contrary to nationalists and advocates of Euro-White superiority, colony and state formation was not a simple European-controlled process. Like the gauchos in the La Plata region and the bandeirantes in Brazil, who established "semi-European" quasi-states, buccaneers developed their own seaborne rule, and escaped slaves set up self-governed landlocked strongholds. Buccaneers and *corsairs*, "essentially stateless persons," established quasi-governmental rule and lived off commerce and raids. Tolerated by all of Spain's seventeenth-century competitors, they looted from Spanish ships what the Spanish had looted from Indio societies. As private entrepreneurs, they saved the English and French states the trouble of deploying their navies and acquired information about the region vastly more detailed than what bureaucracies in metropolitan capitals could access. Their "trans-frontier" communities lasted to about 1700.

On the other hand, a second group of builders of self-organized societies, fugitive slaves or Maroons (from *cimarrones*, Spanish for "wild," "untamed"), had to avoid interaction. Africans absented themselves from labor for short periods of time (*petit marronage*) or left for good (*grand marronage*). Their autonomous societies in the Antilles, Brazil, Florida, and elsewhere were strategically located in inaccessible forests or mountains, becoming enclaves in the colonial structures, states within states. Their societies neither followed earlier African communal traditions nor served as models of solidarity of the downtrodden. As warrior societies on constant alert to ward off search-and-destroy missions conducted by planters or governments, they raided for slaves and women. These predominantly male societies on occasion permitted women with leadership capabilities to rise to high positions, as was the case, for example in Jamaica, where leaders combined religious roles with political ones. Like their Brazilian counterparts they sometimes negotiated treaties with the colonial governments, offering policing services against more recent fugitives. Colonial governments used their military strength—just as Russian tsars bound the free Cossacks to their imperial designs.[48]

After independence—with some Maroon communities still in existence—new patterns of migration emerged. Immigration from Europe stagnated; the importation of slaves was reduced and came to an end. Toward the close of the nineteenth century, a new mass migration from Europe began (see chap. 14.2).

In conclusion, it may be asked why the whitest parts of the Euro-immigrant population in Latin America continually emphasized their Iberian background rather than drawing strength and cultural independence from the fusion of traditions. By contrast, the North American British colonials briefly engaged in rhetoric about their rights as Englishmen, which the London government rebuffed, but then proudly emphasized their Americanness. So did most of the Mexican leaders of the independence movement who called themselves "Americanos." Americanness, however, did not include Black and Indian populations either in North or Latin America. While in the North segregation kept White and Black apart, in the South they mingled. Were the strong presence of "Indio" and African peoples under prevailing racist thought and the impact of Europe's power to define superiority reasons to deny cultural and genetic integration of peoples of three continents? Were the comparatively small number of Native peoples in North America and the near-absence of fusion reasons to make the Europeanness of Americans self-evident? While the Spanish crown in particular wanted to reestablish the Iberian model of society in New Spain, the Puritans, who came to dominate the northern discourse, separated consciously from the old society and wanted to create a better, purer, "new" England. Cultural conversion may be either proudly claimed or denied, but the choice of one or the other course is determined by interests that the gatekeepers who shape national discourses assume to exist. In Latin America, after near-genocide and stabilization new peoples created themselves.

9

Fur Empires and Colonies of Agricultural

Settlement

Settlement, in particular of North America, has been characterized for a long time as a story of hardy settler families civilizing the wilderness by hard and honest labor. This paradigm demanded that the Others—primitive but crafty, bloodthirsty, or noble savages—had to recede before the "march of progress." Spanish and Portuguese discourse had been different: Native peoples had to labor; "Indian princesses" were to be married; those who resisted had to die. At the time of conquest, all of the European powers simply and soberly sought colonies that were economically viable and sent riches to the home or core economy. Even the Puritans' missionary zeal never assumed the dimensions accorded it by their hagiographers. They were businesspeople. Private enterprise within the context of imperial policies—whether pursued by London investors, Dutch entrepreneurs, or French traders—had only one goal: to make acquisitions and investments profitable. Except for mast pines and pitch, however, the North American English contributed little of economic value. The English in Australia were in a worse situation: the continent became a receptacle for people whom contemporary administrators considered criminals. To create what in the twenty-first century is called a favorable investment climate, it was necessary to remove Native peoples who refused to cede real estate, pay taxes to the intruding state apparatuses, and work for intruding entrepreneurs, whether they were settler families or mercantile companies.

In the discourse on conquest, on the amassing of riches, or on penetrating the wilderness, maleness was redefined. Reared in an ethic that despised manual labor and glorified fighting the "Moors," the Iberian-Catholic *conquistadores* came for loot. Medieval warfare in the Iberias followed socioreligious prescriptions: no warring on holy days of any religion was to be permitted, for example, and chivalric exploits both to reduce an enemy and to conquer the admiration, heart (and, perhaps, body) of a beautiful noble lady were advocated. By the time of the conquest of the Americas, religion had become merely a pretext for total war: no restraint was put on destruction beyond the capacity even to carry off the loot, and Native women were treated solely as objects of sexual gratification. In nineteenth-century North America, noble male individuals who never married saved women from savages and guided stable families to fertile lands. Male "orphan heroes" without social relationships, whether they were civilized loners or frontier roughnecks, achieved success. The imperial strategists, however, never fell for the male lore. The French king had women ferried across the Atlantic at royal expense to help create stable societies; Catherine II of Russia ordered her Cossacks to marry and settle; the British bound single young men as servants into family units. The men migrating to the fur empires of North America and Siberia did not fall for the lore, either. They entered into halfway alliances with the cultures of the First Peoples by cooperation and informal intermarriage.[1]

9.1 Fur Empires in North America and Siberia

North America and Siberia became part of European knowledge and economic systems at the same time (map 9.1). Europe's states north of the Alps and Carpathians expanded territorially, and their merchants extended their reach financially to the northern fur-producing ecologies. Powerful groups within states began a search for distant spaces to deposit "criminals"; weaker dissenting groups searched for spaces uncontaminated by official religious doctrines. Expansion was intended to be, if not profitable, at least self-financed. Jacques Cartier, on France's behalf, explored opportunities in northern North America in 1535; Czar Ivan IV granted a patent to colonize Siberia to the merchant family Stroganov in 1558 (see chap. 13.1).

Cartier, who on his arrival found Basque vessels loading cod at the mouth of the St. Lawrence River, located areas suitable for settlement. Aside from temporary camps of fishermen and whalers, settlement began only three-quarters of a century later in Port Royal and Quebec in 1604–08. In the south, the border of Spanish intrusion and rule reached from St. Augustine (Florida, 1565) to Santa Fe (New Mexico, 1598). On the other hand, the first English colony, Roanoke (North Carolina, 1585), vanished without a trace. Only after 1607 did immigrants survive with the help of First Peoples' handouts. When the British reduced the influence of Spain and France, a belt from Florida and New Orleans across the southwest to California remained an Anglo-Hispanic cultural borderland; France's Quebec stayed French-Anglo in culture and language, and Acadia/Nova Scotia was a bilingual region.

By 1610, western Siberia to the Yenisey River was known to the Russians; three decades later, they reached middle Siberia to the Lena, and, shortly thereafter, eastern Siberia—in the course of the advance Native peoples were subjugated. By 1637, scouting parties reached the Pacific; in the mid-seventeenth century, the Amur region; and, in 1742, the northeastern tip of Siberia. Russian exploration was halted by China along the Amur River but extended to North America via Alaska.[2] From the fifteenth century onward, Siberia served as a refuge for peasants fleeing deteriorating rural living conditions, conscription during the struggle with the Mongols, and, after 1649, the codification of laws and customs regarding serfdom. Russian, other Slavic, and Tatar refugees organized themselves outside the borders of Poland-Lithuania and Russia as "kazaks" or Cossacks, meaning "free men" in Turkish-Tatarian. Tsarist governments recognized them as semi-independent groups in return for military sup-

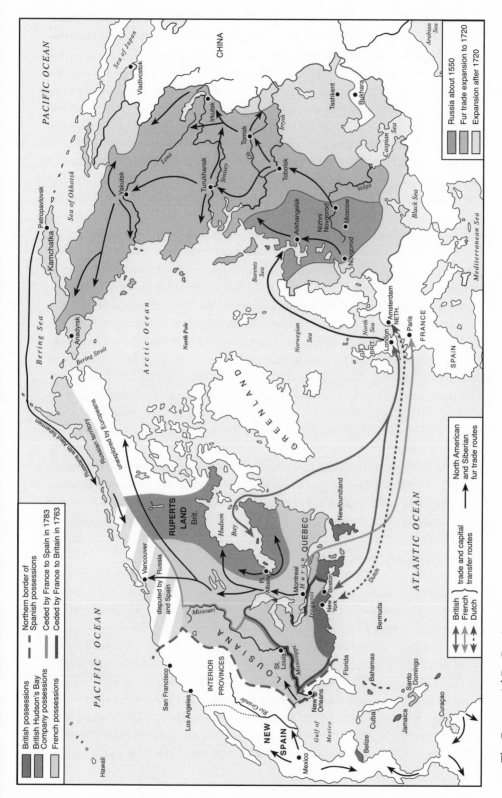

9.1 The Commercial Fur Empires

port, and both Cossacks and kazaks came to be considered ethnic groups. Subsequently, adventurers and escaped serfs came as fur hunters, traders, and merchants; settlers followed. The society also had its share of frontier criminals, prostitutes, and fugitives, who easily crossed into China if pursued. Siberia was integrated into the world economy of the fur trade by the 1640s, but migration patterns comparable to Atlantic ones emerged only in the 1800s.[3] Siberia was made a penal colony, and historical discourse has dwelled on the low quality of its human material and oppressive tsarist rule. The illiterate peasants and deportees who built Siberian society could not commit their version of the story to writing. By contrast, the highly literate British North American dissenting elites fashioned their own historiography almost from the beginnings of settlement, searching their souls for motivation and examining their success for signs of God's providence. Though both France and Great Britain shipped criminals to North America, their presence hardly entered the discourse.

From the Atlantic coast, European trappers migrated ever further inland, harvesting fur or trading for it. Unintentionally, they spread their diseases among Native peoples. Siberian Natives, on the other hand, were resistant to Eurasian pathogens. North American First Peoples, supplying European and Euro-Native traders with furs in exchange for imported goods, competed with each other. Migration, warfare, and flight resulted. The demand for beaver skins for the then-fashionable felt hats and the introduction of iron tools for hunting caused resource depletion and the extension of trapping further to the west or the east on the respective continents. French *habitants* fled the constraints of the semifeudal society of the St. Lawrence valley by moving to the Great Lakes fur economy. The Hudson River was used as a second entryway by the Dutch and the English since the 1610s. From the 1650s on, the Hudson's Bay Company opened a third, northern route, sending mainly Scots and Orkneymen as trappers. These married or consorted with Native women, and another mixed culture developed. When the men returned to Britain, the Company granted small pension-type payments to the women and children left behind. After the British takeover in 1763, Quebec-French involvement in the fur trade declined, though Montreal traders and French-Native Red River Métis continued their activities. In Siberia, too, British capital connected the fur empire to world markets.

With the rise of long-distance trade of such dimensions, English merchants had to acquire new skills. Those who had migrated to the opportunities of the Iberian transatlantic trade had learned from Genoese immigrant and local Portuguese and Sevillian merchants. As "Anglo-Iberian traders" they returned to the British Isles and transferred their experience to new markets. The Russian fur trade, for example, was from 1555 onward in the hands of an English association of merchant adventurers, the London Muscovy Company. This empire-backed company expanded southward from its entrepôt in Arkhangelsk to Astrakhan and reduced the role of the resident Armenian merchants, who lacked state backing (see chap. 7.2). Combining profits and experience, the Anglo-Iberian traders ventured in other directions, establishing connections to the Canary Islands and the Guinea coast, as well as to the Barbary ports, and provided "the first generation of Turkey merchants and some of the leading figures in the East India Company." They were a globalized merchant-capitalist elite.[4]

In the fur economies on both continents, Native peoples were first used as partners, then forced into retreat, and finally annihilated or placed in reservations in North America or incorporated into Siberia and Central Asia. While they had held an essential role in the fur trade, they were obstacles to agricultural settlement.

9.2   North America: Native Peoples and Colonization

In agricultural North America, south of the fur empire, developments differed from the Spanish and Portuguese quest for riches, which had turned into settler colonization almost inadvertently. The Jamestown, Virginia, colonists of 1607 stood halfway between both types of settlement. When expectations of an abundance of precious stones and of First Peoples' (forced) labor did not materialize, the gentlemen adventurers among the 600 first arrivals did not deign to work. Most starved; some 10 percent survived. Settlement with an ethic of hard work began with the arrival of the English dissenters and of planters who introduced cash crops (tobacco at first), as well as with the preplanned seigneurial society of the French government. As in the tropical colonies, death tolls in the temperate zone were high at first because Europeans were not prepared to cope with the environments they found themselves in. Bartering for food with Amerindian resident groups tided the newcomers over until their farm labor produced food sufficient for survival. Fertile and (from a European's viewpoint) abundant land soon permitted surpluses beyond self-sufficiency and, as a consequence, earlier marriage and larger numbers of children. While the French state attempted to replicate feudal society, the English Pilgrim fathers and mothers, after their stopover in the Netherlands, by compact established governmental structures semi-independent from Great Britain, but they retained social hierarchies between masters and servants modeled on British society.[5]

After a century and a half of settler warfare against "Indians," few First Nations remained east of the Appalachian range, though the Iroquois Federation still played a military-diplomatic role in the English-French rivalry (see chap. 8.1).[6] The White-over-Red paradigm has overshadowed conversion in the opposite direction, White into Red or Black into Red, as well as the development of Red-Black enclaves, such as those of the Florida Seminoles, who also intermarried with Cuban fishermen.[7] From the sixteenth century on, large Amerindian migrations into the North American plains and the adoption of horses, a Euro-Spanish input into their cultures, brought forth distinctive lifestyles. Ojibwa and Siouan peoples moved westward from the Great Lakes, and the Apache, Cheyenne, and Comanche peoples moved aggressively southward into territories of the sedentary pueblo peoples (see map 8.1). Native peoples who did adapt to "the White man's ways" fared no better. The Cherokee, Creek, and other peoples of the southeastern United States, though sedentary and "civilized," were deported when intruding Euro-Americans coveted their land in the

1830s. The culture and self-rule of the Métis in Canadian Manitoba similarly could not survive the settlers' onslaught of the 1870s. In the United States, wars reduced the Plains people to camp ("reservation") status by the 1880s. The deportations and the intrusion of European missionaries destroyed belief systems and cultural customs (map 9.2).[8]

9.3 Forced, Bound, and Free Migrations

From the point of view of imperial governments, the voluntary settlement of the North American colonies was slow; and, from the point of view of the settlers, labor was scarce. To speed settlement and fill the demand for labor, men and women were deported; others migrated under indentures; and religious refugees seized the opportunities (maps 9.3 and 9.4).

Deportation was a punishment for criminal offenses or in mitigation of harsher sentences; it also served as a means of ridding home governments of political dissenters or of getting rid of marginal people—such as vagrants, orphans, and the poor—whom societies were unwilling to care for. "Criminal" offenses, in contemporary thought, included social misconduct, the stealing of food out of hunger, minor offenses, or the lack of a fixed abode. Condemned offenders were sent by Portugal to its African posts from 1415 on, by Spain to Hispaniola and Africa, by the Netherlands to Batavia and the Moluccas, and by Denmark, for a brief time, to Greenland. The German states—lacking colonies—had to send offenders, under the guise of free migrants, off to wherever they could land.[9] The English vagrancy act of 1597 had authorized banishment to lands beyond the sea, but, at first, not against the will of the offender. Involuntary deportation, related to the demand for labor in the colonies, began after 1615 to Virginia, Jamaica, and Barbados. By the later eighteenth century, deportation was used to populate whole colonies: Australia received about 160,000 convicts from 1788 to the 1860s. Globalized convict labor built many of Britain's fortifications and trade establishments around the world. After having served their time, most stayed as free persons. Deportation was also a punishment for "rebels" in the colonies—for example, the approximately 140 "rebels" from the two Canadas in 1837–38 and prisoners from the Indian "mutiny" of 1857–58.[10] French authorities deported some 720 minor offenders to Quebec before the 1740s and perhaps 1,250 to Louisiana, where they accounted for 18 percent of the arrivals before 1721. Political offenders were deported from revolutionary France to the colonies, to French Guiana (Cayenne), for example. Criminals were sent after 1850 to Cayenne and the French Pacific Islands (New Caledonia). In the Russian penal system, deportation to Siberia began in the mid-seventeenth century (see chap. 13.4). The system was abolished in Britain in the 1850s and in France in the early 1930s. Approximately half a million convicts were sent out from western Europe; perhaps 1.5 million from European Russia.

Indentures provided men and women, unable to afford the cost, with passage to a colony. As Steinfeld has argued, they were the norm in English and American labor

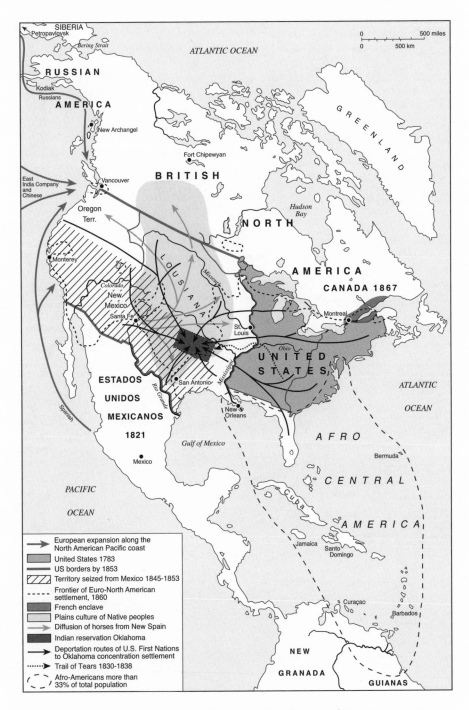

Legend:

- European expansion along the North American Pacific coast
- United States 1783
- US borders by 1853
- Territory seized from Mexico 1845-1853
- Frontier of Euro-North American settlement, 1860
- French enclave
- Plains culture of Native peoples
- Diffusion of horses from New Spain
- Indian reservation Oklahoma
- Deportation routes of U.S. First Nations to Oklahoma concentration settlement
- Trail of Tears 1830-1838
- Afro-Americans more than 33% of total population

Map labels:

SIBERIA
Petropavlovsk
Bering Strait
ATLANTIC OCEAN
0   500 miles
0   500 km

RUSSIAN
Kodiak
Russians
AMERICA
New Archangel

GREENLAND

Fort Chipewyan

East India Company and Chinese

BRITISH
Vancouver

Oregon Terr.

Hudson Bay

NORTH

Monterey

L O U I S I A N A
Missouri

AMERICA
CANADA 1867

Colorado,
New Mexico
Santa Fe

St. Louis
Montreal

Ohio

U N I T E D
S T A T E S

ATLANTIC

OCEAN

ESTADOS

UNIDOS

MEXICANOS

1821

Rio Grande
San Antonio
Mississippi
New Orleans

AFRO

Gulf of Mexico

Bermuda

Mexico

Spanish

PACIFIC

OCEAN

C E N T R A L

Cuba

A M E R I C A

Jamaica   Santo Domingo

Curaçao
Barbados

NEW

GRANADA

GUIANAS

9.2   From the Euro-Cultural Zones of 1800 to the Dispossession of First Nations, 1890

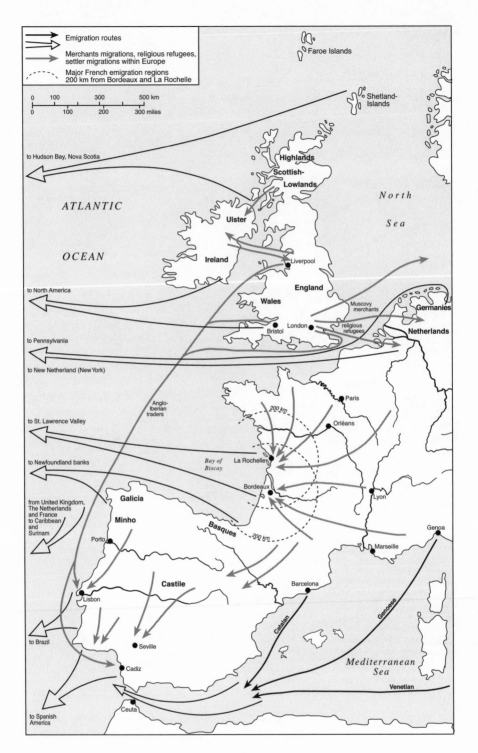

Emigration routes

Merchants migrations, religious refugees,
settler migrations within Europe

Major French emigration regions
200 km from Bordeaux and La Rochelle

Faroe Islands

Shetland-Islands

0   100   300   500 km
0   100   200   300 miles

to Hudson Bay, Nova Scotia

Highlands

Scottish-
Lowlands

North

Ulster

Sea

ATLANTIC

Ireland

Liverpool

OCEAN

England

Wales

Muscovy
merchants

Germanies

to North America

London

religious
refugees

Netherlands

Bristol

to Pennsylvania

to New Netherland (New York)

Paris

Anglo-
Iberian
traders

to St. Lawrence Valley

Orléans

200 km

*Bay of
Biscay*

La Rochelle

to Newfoundland banks

Bordeaux

Lyon

from United Kingdom,
The Netherlands
and France
to Caribbean
and
Surinam

Galicia

Minho

Basques

200 km

Genoa

Porto

Marseille

Castile

Barcelona

Catalan

Lisbon

Genoese

to Brazil

Seville

*Mediterranean
Sea*

Cadiz

Venetian

Ceuta

to Spanish
America

9.3   Origins: The Eastern Atlantic Rim, 15th–18th Centuries

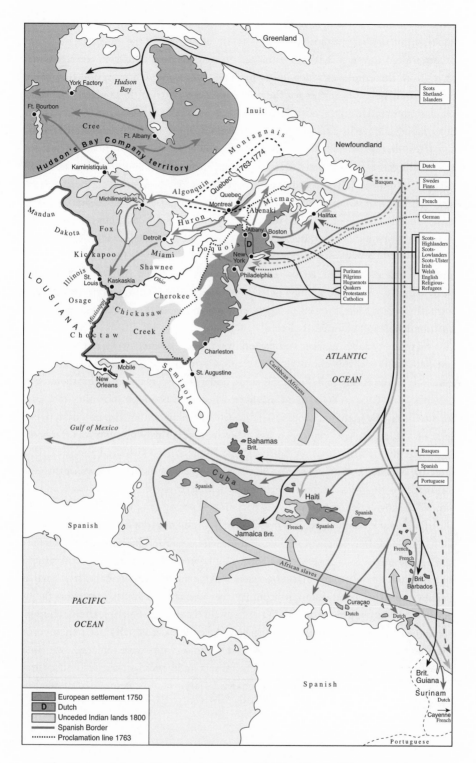

Greenland

York Factory
Hudson Bay

Ft. Bourbon
Cree
Ft. Albany
Inuit

Newfoundland

Hudson's Bay Company territory

Kaministiquia
Montagnais
1763-1774

Algonquin
Quebec
Micmac
Montreal
Abenaki
Halifax

Mandan
Michilimackinac

Dakota
Fox
Huron
Albany
Boston

Detroit
Iroquois
D

Miami
New York

Kickapoo
Shawnee
Philadelphia

LOUSIANA
Illinois
St. Louis
Kaskaskia
Ohio

Osage
Cherokee

Mississippi
Chickasaw
Creek

Choctaw

Charleston

Mobile
Seminole
St. Augustine

New Orleans

Gulf of Mexico

ATLANTIC
OCEAN

Caribbean Africans

Bahamas
Brit.

Cuba
Spanish

Haiti

Spanish
Jamaica Brit.
French
Spanish

Spanish

African slaves

French
French

Brit.
Barbados

PACIFIC
OCEAN

Curaçao
Dutch
Dutch

Spanish

Brit.
Guiana

Surinam
Dutch

Cayenne
French

Portuguese

	Scots Shetland-Islanders
Dutch	
Basques	Swedes Finns
	French
	German
	Scots-Highlanders Scots-Lowlanders Scots-Ulster Irish Welsh English Religious-Refugees

| | Puritans Pilgrims Huguenots Quakers Protestants Catholics |

Basques	
Spanish	
Portuguese	

	European settlement 1750
D	Dutch
	Unceded Indian lands 1800
——	Spanish Border
······	Proclamation line 1763

9.4   The Western Atlantic Rim: Destinations and Shifting Zones of Encounter to 1800

relations, rather than being a specific form of emigration only. Unfree labor relations had traditionally been imposed by the state. In the opinion of the powerful, the lower orders should never be without a master or mistress, and contracts were enforceable—from the employer's side only—by state intervention, a provision that made even consensual labor unfree for the duration of the contract. In England such legal regulations dated from the postplague years, and, in this tradition, the Massachusetts colonial legislature in 1641 attempted unsuccessfully to regulate downward "excessive rates" demanded by laborers. In Virginia, which was to earn profits for investors, the first migrant workers were to live under military law, be housed in barracks, and till the land collectively. As contractual service for a specified period of time, coerced, semivoluntary, or voluntary indenture resembled apprenticeship provisions in some respects and slave labor in other respects. Indenture might end in exploitation and death. In the American colonies, male and female laborers could, as a contemporary observer sourly noted, migrate elsewhere or set up independent farming. They could simply refuse to be hired. At the end of their three to seven years of service, they were—ideally—equipped to cope with the new social and natural environment, had a small starting capital for an independent life, and had been socialized to become useful members of colonial societies.[11]

An efficient labor market and postcontract independence explain why between one-half and two-thirds of all White English-, German-, and French-language immigrants to North America before 1776 came under indentures to work off the cost of passage. They tried to avoid the Caribbean because of the high mortality rate and, for survivors, the high land prices there. Most worked in staple-crop production, but later on skilled artisans came to urban labor markets. Most common was transport by merchants or ship captains, who sold the laborers for a specified period of time after arrival. Passage might also be advanced by governments, speculators, or the new joint-stock companies. Sometimes potential settler-employers hired servants and advanced the cost, or poor migrants paid part of their passage and worked off the rest. In the mid-Atlantic colonies, traders marched indentured men and women to the hinterland for sale of their terms of service, and masters could sell indentured servants for their remaining years of service to other employers. German-language indentured servants, whose only labor market consisted of German-speaking employers, called Pennsylvania the "best poor man's country" because of their ability to support themselves after their contracts ended. In the early fluid colonial societies, those who survived the high mortality rate on the Chesapeake could occasionally rise to planter or merchant status. In plantation work, bound White servants were replaced over time by African slaves (see chap. 10.5). Indentured servitude, often subsumed under rural settlement migration, was highly responsive to labor market demands. It ended in the 1820s.[12]

9.4 Across the North American Continent: Settlement Migration in Stages

Settlement migration seemingly implies stability: peasant families arrive and stay; single men clear land, form a family, and remain put. When communities increase, a church is built and institutional life organized. In farming societies across the world, however, each farming family's offspring needed more land, and thus the second generation migrated over short distances to marginal land away from the original community's center. The third generation had to move further inland or, between economic sectors, to wage labor in coastal towns. Agricultural settlement often did not imply residential stability: when sons and daughters migrated on, parents might follow; new frontiers promised higher yields. Thus each subsequent native-born generation and each subsequent cohort of arrivals settled further west in North America and further east in Siberia. "Settlement" as a process involves migration in stages by the first generation and intergenerational multidirectional mobility by later generations.[13]

French settlements along the St. Lawrence from 1664 to 1680 received 2,000 indentured servants, 1,000 soldier-settlers (including Swiss and Germans), and 1,000 women for purposes of family formation, as well as others—a combined total of below 10,000. In Louisiana, some 7,000 arrived between 1717 and 1721. Most indentured and free migrants from France, perhaps as many as 35,000, went to the West Indies. Subsequently, the people arriving included deportees: vagabonds, salt smugglers, and wayward young men rejected by their families. Settler or *engagé* recruitment was undertaken by *seigneurs*, proprietary companies, or merchants and captains from La Rochelle and Bordeaux. Since they tapped the same reservoir of young men as recruiters for the army, the competitive market responded to supply and demand. To earn their commission, recruiters might accept aged, infirm, or destitute men, Spanish-origin people, or children as settlers and soldiers and send them off to the colonies. There, in theory at least, only healthy French Catholics were accepted. Protestant foreigners could live in the colonies temporarily, while French Huguenot refugees were excluded from New France. While internal migrants in France originated mainly in the overpopulated Massif Central, emigrants often came from coastal Normandy and Britanny. Most came from regions within a radius of 200 kilometers from the port towns or from cities connected to the ports by networks of migration, trade, or communication. At a time when only 15 percent of the total French population lived in towns, more than half of the *engagés* came from towns and cities, mainly from poor families, and artisans outnumbered peasants. Women, often from orphanages, were sent under tutelage of the king as *filles du roi*. When ranking colonist men demanded the shipment of women of status, administrators lacked power to fill the order.[14] When the recruitment of indentured workers waned after 1665, the government, seeking to force the pace of settlement, ordered ships bound for the West Indies after 1698 and for New France after 1714 to carry a small number of workers. Some of such *engagés*, mostly single males, returned after their term, while others fled. When families were recruited, persistence rates increased.

French emigration from 1604 to 1763 came out of a population of approximately 20 million, and remained low. By the mid-eighteenth century, New France had only 55,000 inhabitants, Louisiana 4,000, Saint Domingue and Martinique about 12,500 each, Cayenne a mere 1,000. In eighteenth-century French-Canada, where religio-ideological aspects combined with socioeconomic rationales, each woman on average gave life to eight children. More than two-fifths of the population was under fifteen years of age. The demography of the society was colony-generated.[15]

Like the French in Quebec, the German-language immigrants in Pennsylvania lived in a culturally compact region. By 1800, a total of 75,000–100,000 migrants had arrived from southwestern German principalities, Switzerland, the Rhenish districts, Alsatia, and Westfalia. These territories, parts of which had been resettled by Swiss and other immigrants after the Thirty Years' War, supplied emigrants to the Prussian east and Habsburg Balkan territories a generation later and to southern Russia from 1763 on (see chaps. 12.2 and 13.2). About half a million left from 1700 to 1820. Uprooted by religious wars, both Catholics and Protestants migrated; Krefeld Quakers and other Palatines were offered a home by William Penn. At first, most migrated in larger family units. Later, young nuclear families and single men and women from textile-producing areas migrated through Rotterdam, where merchants prefinanced their trips, thus profiting from labor market demand and from the willingness of friends and kin to "redeem" the bound servants ("redemptioners") by paying their fare. In passages via Rotterdam, the debt was repaid by varying lengths of service; in English and Irish practice, however, the period of service was fixed, but prices varied.

Migration was an economic project: it had to be profitable to colonial proprietors, shipping companies, employers of bound labor, and the migrants themselves. "In Germany, peasants could expect to harvest three grains of wheat for every seed they sowed; in Pennsylvania a crop yield of ten to one was normal." By migrating, peasants also freed themselves from overbearing bureaucrats, whose lifestyles were financed by taxation. A mid-nineteenth-century caricature depicts a group of emaciated peasants standing in front of a comfortably seated, pot-bellied official requesting permission to emigrate. As he patronizingly questions them, "Is there then no way to keep you here?" a voice from the background comments, "If you would leave, we might stay."[16]

With regard to British migration, the category "English" stands as much in need of deconstruction as "Franks" in the Mediterranean or "Germans" in eastern Europe. This ethnically heterogeneous group was—taking into account Celtic—(formerly) linguistically diverse, included Anglican and dissenter English, Protestant and Catholic Irish, Scots, Scotch-Irish (especially of the period 1714–20), and some early Welsh (beginning in 1682). By 1700 the British Caribbean and North American possessions counted perhaps 270,000 inhabitants of British background. From 1700 to 1775, of some 260,000 British immigrants, the majority were Irish; Scots ranked second; 50,000 were English, and some were Welsh.[17] Emphasis on dissenting religions has sidetracked research. The "Great Migration" of Puritans to New England was intended to result in a culture founded on the stable "city upon a hill" from which faith would radiate outward. But religious schisms and the need for land for subsequent generations induced a "Great Reshuffling" that dispersed colonists in the region. English migrants were more often of urban artisanal than of agrarian or dissenter background. A strong family component is discernible. While the government intended to rid England of the shiftless, it was middling people who left in self-financed migrations and lower-middle-class people who came as servants. As to quantity, more White and more free migrants came to the colonies in the seventeenth than in the eighteenth century, when the ratio of European bound and African slave migrations increased. A comparison of emigrants from England to Ireland and those from England to the Chesapeake reveals that the former originated among landowning classes in straitened circumstances, who hoped to achieve rental incomes and to build mansions by exploiting Irish tenants, whereas the latter, having become planters, worked with a few indentured servants or slaves and lived in shacks.[18]

Scottish transatlantic migration grew out of migratory traditions to continental Europe dating from long before the union of Scotland with England in 1707: mercenaries went to France, Prussia, and Sweden; pedlars to Denmark and Poland; and merchants to Copenhagen and Malmö, Warsaw and Kraków, Dutch cities, and elsewhere. By 1600, there were four major destinations: Ulster, to which some 30,000 Scottish lowland farmers and others from the Hebrides, the Orkneys, and the Shetlands went; Poland, where tens of thousands arrived as merchants, small traders, and soldiers; Sweden, home for Scottish merchants as well as government-recruited soldiers; and England, which according to ethnocentric members of Parliament was "overrun" with Scots.

From 1600 to 1650, 85,000 to 115,000 left out of a population of 1–1.2 million. Between 1640 and 1660, following Cromwell's victories, Scottish prisoners were sent to American colonies, as well as to Tangier and Guinea, and after 1652 between 60,000 and 100,000 migrated to Ireland. In the eighteenth century, Scottish continental migration dwindled while migration to Ireland and England increased, often as an intermediate stage before a transatlantic move. At first, most migrants came from the Lowlands, an estimated 30,000 before 1763 from among skilled and educated social groups. From 1763 to 1775 perhaps 40,000 Scots suffering from the linen recession emigrated, including merchants, tradesmen, evangelists, and laborers. Highland emigration involved soldiers, tenant farmers at midlife with their children, and indentured servants. Harvest failures increased the propensity to migrate, as did commercial development and sheep clearances, which eroded the rationale for clan structures and resulted in the dispossession of tenants. At critical junctures, large, well-organized parties left, settled in blocs, reestablished kinship ties and hierarchies—and instigated the manufacture and distribution of Highland lore.[19]

Although Irish seventeenth- and eighteenth-century migration was multidirectional, most nineteenth-century migrants crossed the Atlantic. Poverty, population increase, and English overlordship were push factors; long-term migratory traditions were facilitating factors; and multiple opportunities served as the incentives. Irish people moved to the Amazon basin, the West Indies, Europe, and North America. Protestant Irish were employed by the English East India Company; Catholic Irish found employment in the French East India Company. As mercenaries, they migrated as far as Central Europe; as settlers and laborers, they moved beyond the confines of the British Empire. In French service, Irish mercenaries established connections to French colonies; as sailors on English vessels, they acquired knowledge about the settlement potential (and its limitations) of Canadian regions. Their mass departure, of course, has to be explained at least in part by the displacement through immigration of Protestant Scots and Anglican English people. No other western European country in the seventeenth century received as many settlers with military skills, means, and powerful backing. By the eighteenth century, Irish migrants increasingly left in families, often from segments of society that had improved their standard of living. Poverty-induced migrations of the poor into armies on the continent decreased. Only younger sons of landowners continued to migrate into military service as officers.

While the outflow increased in absolute numbers from 130,000 in the seventeenth century to 155,000 from 1701 to 1775, it remained stable or decreased per 1,000 of population, which grew rapidly from about two million in 1701 to around 4.4 million in 1791. In the Americas, Irish immigrants settled from the St. Lawrence to the La Plata. The communities in the West Indies were, however, constantly decimated by deaths. Most chose settlement along the northern Atlantic coast and in the Canadas. At the same time, seasonal migration to England and the Scottish Lowlands increased. So did internal rural-to-urban migration, tripling the populations of Dublin and Cork. As a distinct ethnic group, the Scotch-Irish remained particularly involved in emigration. The increasing early nineteenth-century emigration to North America and to England assumed the character of mass flight during the Great Hunger of the 1840s (see chap. 14.1).[20]

In addition to English-, French-, and German-language immigrants, Walloons, Dutch speakers, Swedes, and other Scandinavians came to the North American colonies. Finns, arriving with the early Swedes, introduced log-cabin construction, usually considered a quintessentially American contribution to material culture. Men and women from Minorca, Livorno, and Greece settled in Florida. Religious refugees included Pietists, Moravians, Huguenots, Mennonites, and Old Order Amish. Lutheran Palatines fled the devastations of war by first going to England; they then continued to New York to produce naval stores, as crown-invited artisans had done in previous centuries in British shipyards (see chap. 3.1). Disappointing economic conditions forced them to migrate to the Schoharie Valley, then to the Mohawk Valley, and finally to Pennsylvania. "Settlement" often involved such sequences of mobility.[21]

Immigration to colonial North America peaked between 1760 and 1775 when around 15,000 came annually. The total of just under a quarter million amounted to almost 10 percent of the population of 1775: 55,000 Protestant Irish, 40,000 Scots,

30,000 English people, 12,000 German-speakers—65,000 of them under indentures; largest in number were the 85,000 African slaves. Thus, only about two-fifths arrived "free," albeit under economic constraints. British migrants, three-quarters of them men and half under twenty-five years of age, came from metropolitan London, from provincial Yorkshire, and from the Scottish highlands. Boyd-Bowman's composite picture of the typical emigrant from Spain (see chap. 8.2) resembled that of the typical emigrant Londoner: "an impecunious young artisan or craftsman . . . [who] has found employment irregular or nonexistent, and, without prospects, still unmarried and without family . . . committed, typically to four years of bonded servitude in the colonies." Emigrants from the provinces, predominantly young families, went to Nova Scotia, New York, and North Carolina. Whenever land was filled or labor market opportunities seemed better elsewhere, settlers and former indentured servants migrated again. Whatever a migrant's ethnic origin, if he or she survived the trip and the first adjustment, chances in the colonies were considerably better than in Europe. From the seventeenth century to the time of U.S. independence, however, increasing social stratification was matched by a continuous decline in opportunities.[22]

Colonial North America developed into a mobile society as a result of interregional migration, circuits to sell redemptioners, migration from New England to Nova Scotia, the sale and forced migration of slaves, the deportation and return of Acadians, and the mass flight or emigration of Loyalists. The declaration of independence by thirteen of the North American colonies had in part its basis in migrants' demand for land as well as speculators' interests. The perceived shortage of land east of the Alleghenies had led to demands that the British government open the Ohio valley, protected by the Proclamation line as Indian territory. After the war, such lands were set aside for soldiers and officers. In 1790, the U.S. population of 3.9 million consisted of people of English origin (49 percent), African slaves and a few free Black people (20 percent), Germans and Scots (7 percent each), and people of Scotch-Irish, Irish, Dutch, French, Swedish, and Spanish origin. Internal Euro-American westward migration dislocated Amerindian peoples into involuntary westward moves.[23] The portrayal of settlement as one broad and continuous westward movement glosses over the multifaceted history of internal migration. Internal improvements—road and canal construction as well as the building of the first railroads—mobilized unskilled labor for earthworks and, after completion, facilitated travel of additional migrants. In New England, newcomers from old England introduced textile machinery. Textile mills, because of the ready access to waterpower built in places with no previous settlement, attracted farm families' daughters. Their brothers often migrated west to lands more fertile than the local hills. Since the young women could circulate between work on the parental farm and wagework, they diversified family incomes and could organize and strike when working conditions deteriorated after the depression of 1837. From the 1840s on, factory owners replaced the self-confident mill "girls" with Irish families whose famine migration made them a cheaper labor force, precluded their return home, and prevented—at first—labor militancy. The Irish were joined by Catholic French-Canadians from the St. Lawrence valley, where high numbers of children and slow industrialization hindered the development of local job opportunities.[24]

The ports of New York, Philadelphia, and Baltimore in the mid-Atlantic states (and later, on the Gulf, the ports of New Orleans and Galveston) were the urban receptacles or transit stations for the ever-increasing number of arrivals from Europe. Many stayed in the cities, at least temporarily; others moved west. Further south, the plantation economy shifted to cotton and moved from the exhausted soils along the tidewater to, first, the piedmont of the Alleghenies and, then, across the ridge to lands east of the Mississippi. Planters migrated, and with them went their slaves. Rebellious slaves were sold "down the river"—another forced migration to an even harsher labor regime. Rather than following African or Afro-Caribbean patterns, the Afro-American forced migrants transposed their plantation culture. By about 1840, agricultural land had been settled as far west as the Mississippi, and Amerindian people had been removed. The supply of agrarian migrants did not fill the demand of the new West-Central states, which undertook recruiting campaigns for settlers in Europe. As early as the 1840s, immigration was composed of, one-third each, settlers, artisans/skilled workers, and unskilled workers/agrarian laborers/domestics. High urban demand for labor induced an east- or northbound migration of supernumerary farm children to Pittsburgh or Chicago.

From 1790 to 1820, just under a quarter-million immigrants arrived; from 1820 to 1840, three-quarters of a million; from 1841 to 1850, 1.7 million; and, in the last decade before the civil war, from 1851 to 1860, 2.6 million. These are gross figures from the port statistics and may have to be reduced because of return to Europe. Because of the pervasive ideology that immigrants came to stay in the United States, departures were not even counted before 1908. Return was probably low in the era of sailing vessels; but once steamships came into use in the 1870s, the rates of return increased to one-third of the arrivals by around 1900. Rates of immigration per thousand of population grew from 1.2 in the 1820s to 9.3 in the 1850s; the foreign-born as a percentage of the total population amounted to 9.7 in 1850. By 1900, less than 5 percent of the migrants were settlers; 95 percent were mostly single male and female workers moving in sequential migrations to relatives and acquaintances. The exchange of population between the United States and Canada was sizable along the forty-ninth parallel and has only recently been studied comprehensively because Canadian immigration statistics, collected since 1852, were restricted to ocean-port arrivals. The labor migration of French-speaking Québecois families to the New England textile mills began as a trickle in the 1840s but grew fast. As the industrial sector expanded, the closing of the agricultural "frontier" was announced by the government in 1893.[25]

The settlement of the United States, a century-long project, was furthered by an elaborate but changing perception of "America." At the time of independence and the writing of the Constitution, the image reflected the ideal of free political institutions; it then evolved in relation to a discourse about free or cheap land and, toward the end of the century, to fascinating stories of a dynamic industrial society. By the end of the 1800s, however, social stratification in the United States had reached European proportions. Migrants did send home realistic descriptions of hard work and deprivations. If their letters had painted a rosy picture, kin and former neighbors would have followed, expecting to receive help in finding a job or getting settled: an autocorrective to overblown success stories. On the other hand, the expectation that life could be better in this world, the nineteenth-century secularization of hope, brought forth an image of America of almost otherworldly beatitude. To place these hopes and the volume of migration in perspective, we have to remind ourselves that Vienna was viewed as an El Dorado, Paris as a city of freedom, and the German Ruhr District and London as places providing opportunities. Regardless of the continent and their destination, migrants valued the increase in choice when wages were paid in cash rather than in kind. Often, however, they saw the facade rather than the actual working and living conditions (see chap. 14.2).[26]

The Atlantic perspective of settlement in North America has to be supplemented by a continental one (northbound from Mexico) and a Pacific one. Colonization from Spanish California to the Bering Strait was undertaken, in terms of empires, by the new Creole people from New Spain, by the British coming via the Pacific from East Asia, and by Russians from Siberia. California and the whole of the U.S. Southwest were Amerindian and Spanish-Mexican in culture before the first English-speaking immigrants arrived. This section of the continent was settled by migrants before the Jamestown settlers touched the East Coast. From the north, Russian and Siberian fur traders, entrepreneurs, and fishermen, accompanied by Aleut hunters, came but remained marginal. In 1783 they established a base on Kodiak Island, Alaska, and after 1806 they established a fort and farming communities for revictualling in San Francisco Bay. The Russian Empire withdrew from imperial competition and the cultural exchanges along the Pacific coast of the Americas, selling Alaska to the United States in 1867. In the intervening decades, the native Aleut population of 30,000 in the 1780s had succumbed to diseases; 3,000 still lived in the 1860s. The second generation of fur hunters was of mixed Russian-Aleut parentage. From Asia, Chinese skilled workers and sailors reached Vancouver Island in East India Company vessels and settled in Hawai'i (see chap. 8.4). The second phase of the Pacific Migration System brought Chinese and later Japanese settlers and workers from the mid-1840s onward (see chap. 15.5). Native peoples—California tribes, Northwest Coast Indians, Aleuts—were decimated or driven back, while some were incorporated as fishermen or laborers. The advance guard of the three imperial powers, including very few women, originated from many nationalities.

9.5   Other Settlement Colonies: The African Cape and Australia

Settlement in the Dutch and later British Cape Colony began parallel to that in North America and southern Russia and Siberia (see chap. 13). Australia and New Zealand became European settler diasporas in the eighteenth century, and in the nineteenth century Portuguese migrated to Angola and Mozambique; French Algeria received a host of different settlers; Kenya and other East African territories attracted English ones. Only a few Europeans settled in the German colonies of the late nineteenth century. In Latin America, Argentina attracted Italian immigrants, and Brazil drew Poles, Germans, and small numbers of others. In view of the climate, the thinly settled original inhabitants, and the ethnicity of the immigrants, the Cape Colony and Australia were comparable to North America. The construction of the United States as a paradigmatic frontier society reflects the nineteenth-century myth of "America" rather than a special position. Frontier societies existed across the world.

The "age of European hegemony" implied more than overlordship. It involved worldwide exploitation of native labor and, in several instances, genocide. Following the pattern of the "Indios" from Mexico to Argentina and the "Indians" of North America (whether Iroquois, Sioux, or Pueblo), indigenous peoples in South Africa (San [Bushmen] and Khoi [Hottentots]) and Australasia (Maoris and Aborigines) were displaced. Surviving peoples were relegated to the bottom rung of colonial society as a labor reservoir and for sexual exploitation. Intermarriage across color lines resulted in color hierarchies. White peoples' law designated North American and Australian aborigines wards of the government on reservations or in the outback. Among most of the original peoples, cultural destruction with physical survival was not followed by readjustment, however painful. Only in the last quarter of the twentieth century did immigrant societies, especially New Zealand, Australia, and Canada, attempt to mitigate the suffering of the descendants.[27]

The Dutch Cape Colony, located on the southern tip of Africa, became a "halfway house between Europe and Asia" from its inception in 1652 until 1869, when the Suez Canal changed routes of trade, travel, and migration (map 9.5). The "healthy, subtropical and partly fertile" land was inhabited by wandering San and Khoi peoples when the voc established a post to victual passing maritime traffic. The company did not plan settlement, but ex-soldiers, sailors, clerks, and artificers stayed and developed an economy with their own interests in view rather than those of the voc: "South Africa's frontier was initially entered by Dutch-speaking hunters, traders, and pastoralists, who moved and settled often amidst equally, if not more, powerful African communities." Since the free Khoi were unwilling and unaccustomed to labor in fields and since the Dutch newcomers, too, refused to engage in agriculture, the post's commanding officers who had to supply the voc's ships and thought globally suggested the recruitment of Chinese laborers and market-gardeners whose entrepreneurial spirit and work had satisfied company officials in Java and Taiwan. When free Chinese did not choose to migrate to the Cape, the introduction of slaves was suggested, but few were sent before the development of the slave trade with Madagascar in the 1670s. The enslavement of local Africans had been forbidden by the Company's board. Experienced free Khoi men worked as herdsmen, grooms, and drivers, and some women as domestics, but neither in agriculture.[28]

Under these circumstances, the voc decided to encourage a free-burgher model of settlement to provide for Company servants returning from its eastern colonies. When population growth lagged because many of the prospective residents intended

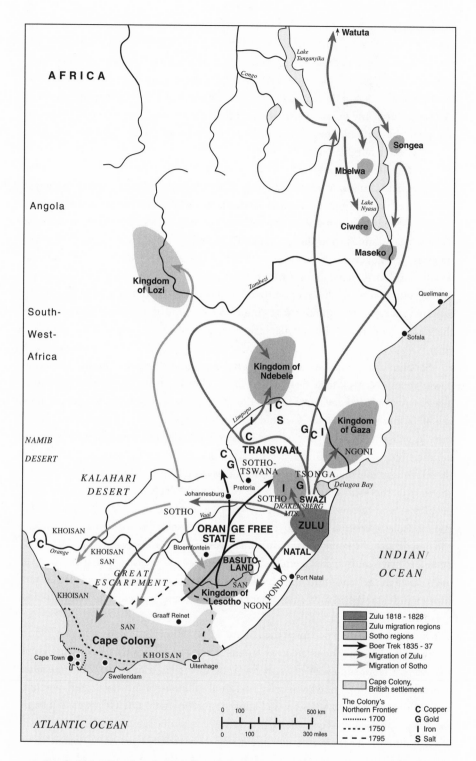

9.5   South Africa: Peoples, Cape Colony, Migrations

to embark for the Netherlands, Company-assisted passage of Huguenot refugees provided a boost in 1685. In contrast to practices in Europe, the Huguenots were not permitted to form an ethno-religious enclave. They dispersed among Dutch farmers, introduced viticulture, and assimilated. By 1780, the colony counted 11,000–12,000 free burghers, 3,000 of them in Cape Town. New immigrants, mostly men, intermarried with Dutch and French-Dutch women from earlier migrations, and thus the formation of the Afrikaner people began. Visitors were struck by gender differences: the wealthier male burghers were "lethargic," while women of the burgher class, active and intelligent, generated family income by renting rooms to officers and passengers of revictualling Indiamen and by other economic activities. Among the lower classes, men worked as artisans; women rented to sailors and soldiers, and by trading smuggled goods between upcountry farmers and ship crews they contributed more to family economies than the men. The Company rejected local demands for free trade and self-government, and tensions emerged between European-born Dutch and locally born Afrikaners, derogatorily called "Boers." The expanding and now slave-owning Boers were much better off than farmers in the Netherlands, and the colony experienced rapid growth after 1730. Independent-minded, they accepted rulings of the States-General but did so reluctantly after the end of Company rule in 1795 (see chap. 6.5).

Economic development depended on labor supply, cultural preferences, and power relationships. Stock raising, in which Khoi herdsmen took jobs, expanded quickly. Agricultural development, on the other hand, was slow because of the lack of a labor force, though farmers could hire Company-soldiers under a kind of indenture. In 1716 the Company introduced slavery and ended the recruitment of peasant families. Boer cattlemen first edged the Khoi out of their best pastures, then out of their less desirable lands. Further north, at this time, Tutsi groups established themselves over the local Hutu. States were formed and declined, and Bantu-speaking peoples moved further to the south. By the nineteenth century, the Ngoni, Kololo, and Ndebele redirected their moves northward to distance themselves from the expansion of both the Boers and the Zulus. The resulting "wars of wandering," also connected to slave raids, lasted from the 1780s to the 1830s, weakened native societies, and peaked in the 1820s *mfecane,* the time of troubles. The Zulus expanded their territories and established their rule; other peoples were annihilated or moved west- and northward.

In 1806 the British occupied the colony. Ethnocultural tensions soared when in 1827 English became the mandatory language and the abolition of slavery undercut the farmers' labor supply. The British government tried to change the colony's ethnic composition by ill-planned assisted emigration schemes. Some 5,000 men, women, and children arrived in 1819–20, and another 40,000, including Germans, did so in the next four decades. Few laborers came since exploitation of the Native peoples made it difficult for them to find work at acceptable conditions. As in Acadia (later, Nova Scotia) after the takeover from France in 1713, the British imposed Anglicization; to retain their own cultural and economic lifestyle, about 10,000 Boers moved east- and northward in the Great Trek of 1835–38. To occupy lands of the "Kaffirs," a derogatory designation for the Bantu Xhosa derived from the Arab word for non-Muslim Africans, the Boers triggered a bloody war. Others migrated to Natal, competed for land with in-migrating Zulus, and founded Transvaal. Segregation in society increased, and interracial unions declined. British and Boers kept apart from each other, and both isolated themselves from the several Native peoples of the region (see chaps. 16.1 and 18.4).[29]

Australia, like Canada and South Africa, was to be one of the white settler colonies of the British Empire, becoming self-sustaining as the result of a government-mandated mix of bound labor and wealthy farmers. Imperial authorities discouraged free migration to Australia except for farmers with capital. The shipment of "convicts" began in 1788 when the newly independent United States refused to accept them. They were to labor for the farmers and thus support themselves in this long-distance continent-wide penitentiary. Sheep raising and wool production, which became the major economic activities, integrated Australia into the world economy by the 1820s and increased the demand for labor in the 1830s. The many Aboriginal Peoples, divided into more than 350 cultural groups and spread from coast to coast, were displaced, suffered from famine, and were killed. The New Zealand Maori, after the beginning of British settlement in 1837–40, fared hardly better.[30]

Over six decades, before the system's end in 1852, some 160,000 convicts, including Black Britons, reached Australia. The gradual decline of shipments in the 1820s was related to humanitarian concerns rather than economic considerations.[31] One-sixth of the deportees were women. Though often labeled "prostitutes," the "female convicts were not part of a criminal sub-class but of a sexually-segregated working class subject to the vicissitudes of fluctuating employment levels and prices, as well as to declining economic opportunities and to less financial remuneration than their poorly paid male counterparts" (Oxley). Placing the concept of criminality in its contemporary context and subjecting deportation records to a social-history-inspired analysis, Nicholas and Shergold argue that a labor aristocracy was deported rather than the "dregs" of society. The male deportees were more literate and more skilled than the average population of London; women were young, skilled, mobile, and mainly single without children. Their offenses were minor property crimes.[32] A few hundred convicts were West Indians Blacks, who often were previous migrants to Great Britain. A few "rebels" from Canada were transported in the 1830s, as were "mutineers" from India in the late 1850s.[33]

Grand or petty schemes to populate the continent were promulgated, some by men with devious minds: first, in the 1780s and 1820s, the vast reservoirs of labor in Asia were to be tapped; second, American Loyalists of the 1780s and their Black slaves were to be brought in; third, Pacific islands were to be raided to provide the convict men with women. By 1850, when most of the colony's population was still composed of the children of deportees, immigration increased. Free men and women came; paupers arrived through programs of assisted migration. Sending off the poor was part of the British elite's concept of ridding their country of "human refuse"—men and women marginalized by "agricultural depression, cyclical downturn in the new industrial economy, and 'overpopulation.'" Those transported, often against their will, did find life chances superior to those "at home." The distance and the resulting cost, however, militated against mass transport, and migration and the numbers involved remained insufficient to fill the demand for labor.

To overcome this shortage, the Australian government developed a concept of subsidized migration, selling public land to raise funds for assisting the next cohort of migrants (and British shipping companies in the process). Agents in Britain searched the countryside for sturdy and healthy agricultural workers with only limited success, unless the pressure of economic circumstances, Highland poverty, impending famine, debt, or eviction added "motivation." The recruitment area extended to the continent because of the English dynasty's Hanoverian connection. In the 1850s emigration of impoverished miners from the German Harz was assisted. Men could sign up but had to have the consent of their wives in what was to be permanent family migration. Since administrators in Hanover (Hannover) were afraid of destitute returnees, they selected miners with good work records to provide their families with a chance to establish new lives in Australia. Free self-financed migration increased from 500 in 1830 to 10,000 in 1850. Easy access to land and profits from pastoral agriculture changed the image of a depot for convicts to one of profits to be made. Anglo-Indians came in search of investment opportunities or to retain their lifestyle after retirement, as others did in Canada.

When in 1851 gold was discovered (as in California in 1848, in British Columbia in 1858, and in New Zealand in 1861), the population more than tripled from 0.4 million in 1850 to 1.15 million in 1860. Labor demand and rising wages attracted ethnically and socially heterogeneous free migrants. Young, internationally mobile men, willing to take risks, often came from families who had benefited from industrialization. In the nineteenth century, perhaps 1.6 million migrants arrived. From 1901 to 1930, 2.77 million arrived, and 2.23 million departed, leaving a net gain of about half a million.[34]

A few laborers from British India had been recruited for British Australia by private entrepreneurs in 1837–44; a few Eurasians from India followed in 1852–54; and a few Pacific Islanders came in the late 1840s. After 1851, free Asian gold diggers arrived, as did laborers imported by Chinese merchants. Labor demand from mining, sugar estates, and other enterprises initiated further, almost exclusively male, Chinese and Pacific Islander migration (around 60,000 from each ethnicity by 1900). They came under contracts; many returned home; and, from voluntary unions or prostitution involving European women, some 2,500 Australasian children remained in the country by 1890. Economic niches were filled by experts from abroad: Afghan camel drivers were indispensable for organizing transport in the arid interior; Malay and Japanese pearl divers worked along the coasts from Queensland to Western Australia, creating on the side an export business of trepang (or sea cucumber) to China. In disregard of economic rationales, this migration was barred in 1901. While Canadian officials would discreetly talk of "preferred nations," their Australian counterparts, bluntly racist, developed a "white Australia" policy. Asian migrants, cheaper with regard to transportation costs, were in no way inferior to their European brethren. Recruitment of labor migrants in Ireland or London could not fill the demand. Thus Italian and Maltese workers came to Queensland, where because of the tropical working conditions the convict system had lasted longest. In Australia, as in parts of the Americas, the working-class diasporas of Chinese (and others) and Italians (and others) met in the labor markets. Immigration restrictions for non-White people were to last to the mid-twentieth century.

States and their governmental elites and a country's inhabitants or "subjects" frequently did not agree on social hierarchies, political institutions, and migration projects. Thus governments developed policies of convict deportation, of the coerced transport of settlers, and of sending bound labor to settlement colonies. Government-mandated shifting-about of populations also included forced migrations of unwanted people in the core and lack of labor in particular peripheral areas. Elsewhere, British imperial authorities settled British subjects—of English, Welsh, Scottish, or Irish ethnicity—to neutralize colonial subjects, who were acquired by war or peace treaty and were of a religion and an ethnicity not acceptable to Anglican or upper-class British ideologies. In worst-case scenarios, established settler populations—substantial middle-class people—were deported en masse because of assumed imperial interests. In the British North American colonies, the French-speaking Acadians were dispersed to New England and Louisiana in the 1750s. The independent—from the British point of view, recalcitrant—Dutch-African Boers were transported in 1910. Takeover of a colony somewhere in the world by a different empire in the course of core-decided imperial wars could force planters and settlers into flight, as was true of Dutch sugar planters from formerly Dutch Brazil to the Dutch Antilles in the 1650s, of Loyalists from the independent American colonies to Canada and elsewhere in the 1770s and 1780s, and of French planters from Haiti to Louisiana in the 1790s.

Compared to labor migrations in the half-century after 1860 (chap. 14), migrations of agrarian settlers account for a small part of the redistribution of peoples across the globe, but for a large part of the expulsion and flight of Native populations. By 1900, about 4 million Europeans lived in Australia and New Zealand; of Europeans in Africa, only 0.75 million were in Algeria (14 percent of 5.25 million), 1.25 million on the Cape and in Rhodesia (21 percent of 6 million), and a few tens of thousands in Mozambique and Angola. The numbers of Europeans in British East Africa and the German colonies remained insignificant.

10

Forced Labor Migration in and to

the Americas

Slavery and forced labor had been part of Inca and Aztec as well as Asian and African societies. Within European and Russian-Siberian societies, serfdom, debt peonage, the forced labor of soldiers, and hard labor in punishment for crimes existed. All of these involved lower social classes or castes, prisoners of war, or criminals; others involved raids on less powerful neighbors—whether they were states, small societies, or clans—in order to capture laborers. Colonial enslavement placed Europeans over Others, and the color White over any other color, first when the Portuguese began to transport Africans to Europe in the 1440s, and next when Dutch colonizers in the Southeast Asian islands forced peasant families to plant export crops. In 1760 the Dutch commissioner of native affairs ordered Javanese "to make obligatory yearly plantings of a specified number of [coffee] trees." This "system of forced cultivation" aggravated exactions of the Native aristocracy and was enforced by debt bondage to the VOC (chap. 7.4). In the same vein, the British in the Cape Colony in 1809 issued the "Hottentot Proclamation" to compel the Khoi families to remain in one particular district and to bind their children to their parents' employer for ten years—in an "apprenticeship" in the language of the times. French planters introduced the system to their islands in the Indian Ocean.[1]

In the Americas, the early sixteenth-century Spanish enslavement of Caribbean peoples ended with their annihilation (chap. 8.3), and the Spanish importation of slaves from different peoples resulted in cultural fusion (chap. 8.4). Among the colonizers, agricultural producers needed labor bound to the soil, while entrepreneurs in mining and mass production of export crops needed labor bound from long distances. Thus two seemingly contradictory methods to obtain labor without paying wages were used: the enforced immobility and the enforced mobility of "Indios." The next step was to import African slaves in large numbers. Finally, after the abolition of slavery and after brief experiments with free labor migrants from Europe, the labor demand was filled by voluntary and involuntary contract ("coolie") migrants from Asia (chap. 15). After the mid-nineteenth century, forced laborers were increasingly replaced by the European proletarian mass migration, which was voluntary within economic constraints (chaps. 12–14; for twentieth-century forced labor regimes, see chaps. 17.2 and 17.4).

In sixteenth-century Central and South America and in the Caribbean colonies, first, the *encomienda* system, a de facto form of slavery, tied indigenous families as labor units to *hacienda*s or appropriated them to state officials or plantation owners; second, under the *repartimiento* system Native people were forced to migrate to public work, mines, or plantations. Third, the *mita* system involved forced migration to Peruvian mines (map 10.1).

10.1 The Forced Immobility and Mobility of Native Labor in Spanish America

Almost upon arrival, Columbus considered the enslavement of the Arawak and carried several back as a gift to the Catholic monarchs, Ferdinand and Isabella. He intended to finance the westbound expeditions, including the transport of cattle and pack animals, by the eastbound transport and sale of human beings as slaves. Learned opinion in Spain was divided about the humanity and slave status of the "new" people; the bound labor of subjugated peoples of different religions had previously been part of Iberian Christian-Muslim warfare. Though Queen Isabella once ordered that all slaves transported to the Iberian Peninsula be sent home, returning Spaniards continued to import "servants." High mortality prevented the emergence of an American slave population in the Iberian societies.[2]

In the colonies, *conquistadores* and migrants financed the acquisition of lands for the crown with their own means and intended to recoup their investments quickly. Neither their own physical labor nor agriculture would provide the returns desired; looting and bound labor did. As beneficiaries of the system of temporarily bound labor they considered "Indios" to be slaves, and governors were among the most active traders because the crown's levy of one-fifth of the sale price proved lucrative. Rebellions of First Peoples, sometimes purposefully provoked, served as a pretext for further enslavement. Neither royal edicts, considered unwarranted "interference," nor legal arguments could prevail against the interests of the colonizers. Royal interdictions were reflected in price increases rather than in changed practices.[3]

After the Caribbean islands had been depleted of potential forced laborers, the continent became the catchment area in 1517. In consequence of interpositions by Bishop Bartolomé de Las Casas, by the "Protector of Indios" in New Spain, Bishop Juan de Zumárrage, and by Charles V, Indio slavery was formally abolished in the *Leyes Nuevas* in 1542; the import of African slaves had begun in the 1510s. Thereafter First Peoples became subjects of the Spanish monarchs and wards of the Catholic Church. In Mexico, the abolition of Indio slavery was completed only in 1561, and on the periphery of the colonial realm it continued to be tolerated by representatives of the crown. The *Recopilación de las leyes de los reinas de Indias* (1680), which had to renew the prohibition of slavery, exempted peoples who waged war against Span-

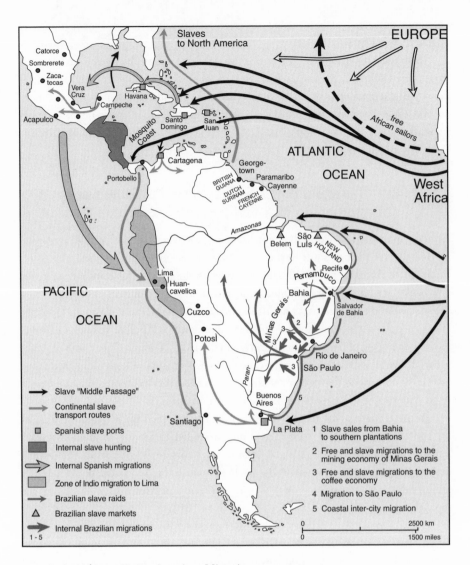

10.1 Latin–African–Native American Migrations

ish rule, such as the Caribs, Araucanians, and Midananos, as well as the Chichimec in northern Mexico, where the demand for mine labor was high. The remnants of Indio slavery lasted into the eighteenth century.[4] The labor of Indios and their interaction with bound and free workers of other cultures varied between regions. In the Caribbean, genocide precluded interaction; in Mexico and Peru, tributary and forced labor continued Aztec and Inca practices; in the cordilleras, where the terrain did not permit plantation production, the labor demand differed from that in the Caribbean, Brazil, and—later—the southern British North American colonies.[5]

Sources differ widely about the volume of the trade; given the high mortality rate, any figures are unreliable. Ranking individuals and officials owned large numbers of bound servants; Hernando Cortés, for example, had 3,000 slaves after conquest and 400 at the time of his death. How many he worked to death and replaced by new ones remains unknown. Sherman assumed a total of 150,000 slaves in central America for the period of 1524–49, one-third of whom were shipped out; MacLeod considered 200,000 for the Nicaraguan slaving period of 1532–42 alone a low figure; a guess of five million captives transported to Panama and Peru before 1548 is unrealistic in view of transport facilities. Bolland has recently argued for a figure of 0.5 million and a similar number of deaths in raiding. Regardless of the total for slavery itself, "The number forced into labor under circumstances often little better than slavery is, however, another matter" (Sherman).[6]

While "the greatest concentration of Indian population in Central America was in the highlands of Guatemala, as it is today, the centers of the most active slave trading were Honduras and Nicaragua," because of the proximity of Honduran ports to the Antilles and Nicaraguan connections to Peru. Horses, pack animals, and cattle were more valuable than Indios and were often paid for in slaves. At the time of conquest, an Indio had cost 1–3 gold pesos and a horse 500–800; by the 1530s, the capture of an escaped African slave paid a bonus of 5 pesos, of a horse or other animal 1 peso, and of an Indio or India only half a peso. Women and skilled artisans brought higher prices than unskilled men. Four trade routes developed: short-distance to Mexico, medium-distance in small numbers to northern Mexican mines and in large numbers to the plantation islands, and long-distance via Panama and down the coast to Peru. When both provinces were depopulated after a mere fifteen years, Guatemalans were enslaved and marched to Mexico or shipped to Peru and Venezuela. Numerous societies were destroyed in a holocaust of deportation and forced labor. Along Nicaragua's Mosquito Coast, African slaves were used to capture Indio slaves. To avoid enslavement and death, indigenous people fled into inaccessible woods and mountains, and so did Africans. Out of their intermarriage the Miskito population emerged.[7]

Most of the labor in the Spanish Main—Peru, Mexico, and Central America— was performed under the *encomienda* regime. Grants to ranking Spanish colonizers distributed the Native inhabitants for labor services and to provide tribute. Children under fourteen years of age and women had been exempted from slavery. The transport of Indios out of their home provinces had also been prohibited. Two economic approaches militated against each other. Most *encomenderos* and colonial administrators, who could not pass their titles to their children, exploited Natives to the extreme without regard for population decline. On the other hand, local clerics and the distant Castilian government argued for protection of the First Peoples for purposes of conversion and state-building. Involuntary migration due to assignment to distant work ran counter to the avowed goals of Christianization and Hispanicization. The Church's influence had to be exerted continuously and regularly. Unless "New Spain" was to become a depopulated wasteland, people had to survive and increase.

Since freedom of movement might enable Indios to remove themselves from Catholic Spanish influence, the laws remained ambiguous. De jure free Indios were free to move, whereas Indios who were resettled in *reducciones*—assigned to governmental or other work projects—and *encomendados* were bound to their place of settlement. Indios were free to marry according to their own choice, but it was ruled that the bride had to move to the residence of the groom and that children were tributary to the husband's *encomendero.* Up to the mid-sixteenth century, Indio slave labor involved artisanal production and mining, construction, milling, sugarcane cultivation and processing, and cattle raising. In mines, free and enslaved Indios worked alongside each other, the latter charged with the more dangerous work. Over the next centuries, the *encomienda* remained a territorially based social system characterized by the transition to a paternalistic labor regime, which was exploitative or benevolent depending on the *encomendero,* and finally to free labor after about 1700.[8]

The enslaved men, women, and children reacted by engaging in rebellion, flight, passive resistance, and suicide. With their identities shattered and bodies exploited, whole communities abandoned hope, became lethargic, and died off. Women rebelled by aborting or killing their babies to save them from life under the Catholic regime. To the Spanish, the Inca rebellion of 1535–36 emphasized the need for an imported—that is, African—labor force without local ties. Later, "Brown, White and Black chattels" were used concurrently and developed strategies of survival and of resistance.

The *repartimiento de indios* assigned free Indios to immigrant owners of the soil or to the royal treasury for work on public projects. Each village had to provide a certain number of adult male laborers for public works and to fill requests for labor by private individuals. Caciques and other officials (*cabildos*) who were exempted from labor duties selected the men under authority of a Spanish judge (*juez repartidor*). The draftees had to present themselves for work in the central square of a town no more than 10 miles (16.5 kilometers) from their villages. They were assigned to public tasks without pay or to private employers who had to pay wages. The system resulted in family disruption and abuses of the men's labor power and of the remaining women's bodies. In the first third of the seventeenth century, *repartimiento* lost its function.[9]

Mobility in Peru differed from Central American patterns. Under Inca rule, villages of subjugated peoples had been resettled as whole communities. These *mitimaes* demanded permission from the new Spanish rulers to return to their original habitations. After vacillating, the crown ordered Indios to remain where Inca or Spanish conquest and rule had deposited them: the viceroy's report on population distribution of 1570 was to be considered the basis for determining the "original" residence. Neither the Indios nor the labor markets took much note of the assigned place of residence. The census of 1683, which for the first time distinguished between *originarios* (settled since 1570) and *forasteros* (nontributary migrants and their descendants), recorded 45 percent of the male Indios as *forasteros.*[10]

Since precontact times, porters (*tamemes*, from Nahuatl *tlameme*) were the main means of transport because the wheel was unknown—and would have been unusable in mountain porterage—and because the only animal to be used for packing were llamas. The *tamemes* were a highly mobile group of workers, and the Spanish increased demand for porterage massively. Their position was worse than that of pack animals. While the latter had to be imported from Europe, men could be corralled or rented from *encomenderos* locally, wherever a person was needed or whenever another porter had died from overwork. Porters were forced to carry up to four *arrobas* (46 kilos) each and their own food. Hauls for merchants often involved 500–1,000 kilometers of trails through rugged terrain. The distance from the port of Veracruz to Santiago was immense. After the 1530s, the crown first prohibited the use of women and children as *tamemes*, then limited loads to two *arrobas*, and finally restricted forced porterage to no more than a day's journey from a conscripted man's village. Even after enforcement of these regulations, local famines occurred because of the absence of *tameme* men from their fields. The deadly continuous trips from the highlands to the lowlands were also prohibited. But forced labor migration from the cool highlands to plantation work in the tropical lowlands and back home did continue and resulted in high death rates.

The Peruvian Spanish continued the Inca use of *yanaconas*, men attached to rulers in servile functions who never returned to their communities of origin. In agricultural settings, they became serfs but could not be sold. Across the colonial realm, traveling officials loved the pomp and circumstance of large retinues as a ritualized public display of status and power. Like the Dutch in Batavia and colonizers elsewhere, wealthy Spanish men surrounded themselves with indigenous servants and mistresses; when they moved, their servants moved with them. Such servants (*naborías* first captured on Caribbean islands and then delivered in payment of tribute in Central America) encompassed all women and children exempted from enslavement and not assigned to *encomenderos* after the 1530s. They lived outside of village communities and accompanied their masters to wherever warfare, administrative duties, or economic activity sent them. Thus locally rooted people were de-ethnicized into a mobile servant class that "shared a certain degree of foreignness with the Negroes and foreign Indians." They were described as legally free but could not return to their communities of origin because the costs were prohibitive. Men without social ties except the service ties to their masters were occasionally described as particularly brutal to settled Indio populations. Later, *naborías* became personal servants; wherever their service ended, they settled, married, and became part of local populations.[11]

Next to *encomienda* and *repartimiento* systems, the *mita* involved forced labor. Demand for mine labor in Peru increased in 1545 with the discovery of the silver veins of Potosí. The new city, which counted 120,000–160,000 inhabitants in the seventeenth century, temporarily became the largest in the Americas. The *mita*, a special system of labor allocation, was instituted in 1574, three decades after the legal abolition of slavery. A vast territory from Cuzco in the north to Tarija in the south, covering 1400 kilometers in length and 400 kilometers in breadth was designated as a labor reservoir.[12] Mine owners, who needed 4,500 workers daily, organized labor in a three-week rhythm. Because of the thin air at an elevation of 4,000 meters (12,000 feet) and because of the dangerous and exhausting working conditions, the men were to rest for two weeks after each week of labor. Thus a total of 13,500 *mitayos* were needed. By 1600, 11,000–12,000 workers were reported to be working at the same time. They came in annual forced mass migrations from their villages. According to Gibson, "Local Indian officials directed the selection and organization. When the appointed day came the laborers formed a huge procession, with their families, llamas, food, and other supplies. From a distant province the journey required several months. In the seventeenth century many thousands of persons and animals were constantly wending their way to and from Potosí." *Mitayos*, bound for a year, were to be free from forced labor for six years. Mercury mines, which were highly unhealthy, were connected by elaborate transportation systems to silver mining areas, where mercury was needed in the process to reduce silver ore. Small silver mines and the mercury mines in Huancavelica could draw on as many as 620 workers from a region of up to forty miles away. The *mita de plaza* obliged adult male laborers from distances of up to ten days' journey by foot to work in Lima and other towns.

All *mita* service was onerous and disruptive to communities and families, but the Potosí *mita* was deadly. Mine administrators forced laborers to stay in the mines day and night during the working week, undercut the regulation of working hours by piecework, and had workers whipped to extract more labor. Within a century, the laboring population of the sixteen *mita*-provinces declined from 81,000 to 10,600 — an "extermination by labor," to use the terminology of a twentieth-century forced labor regime. When reduced populations could no longer fill the quotas, the rest period was reduced from six years to one. To keep up appearances, *mita* was paid labor at an annual wage of 45 pesos, but the cost of the journey and a year's residence in Potosí amounted to 100 pesos.[13]

In the Zacatecas silver mines of Central Mexico, on the other hand, free Indio mining labor numbering some 5,000 had predominated since the discovery of the deposits in 1546. The wages were low; but miners could sell some ore on their own account, and miners' wives and children worked on the *hacienda* of the mine owner. According to Bakewell, "There came Aztecs, Tlaxcalans, Cholultecans and Otomíes. Very soon Indians arrived also from Michaocán and the Pueblos de Avalos. While the lure of riches lasted there was no faltering in this stream of voluntary labourers. . . . There were certainly, from time to time, shortages of labour, caused [by a strike and] by disasters such as the epidemic of 1576 and lesser visitations of disease in later years; but the numbers were in general quickly made up again."

In settled Spanish-American societies, permanently bound labor was increasingly replaced by temporary *repartimiento*, and, over time, free labor became the rule. As early as 1600, free laborers, including *mitayos* in their time off, had received wages seven times as high as the Potosí mining wages. Under the free labor regime, city-bound migrations filled urban, mine, and plantation labor demand (chap. 8.6).[14]

10.2 The Atlantic Slave Trade and African Slavery in Spanish America

The first Africans reached the Americas as acculturated Iberians with the *conquistadores*.[15] Peninsular slaves were traded to the Spanish and Portuguese possessions in the next decades. Trade between Africa and the Americas, according to the Treaty of Tordesillas of 1494, was under Portuguese control. Lisbon merchants—and the ubiquitous Genoese—migrated to Seville when, in 1513, the Spanish government institutionalized a licensing (asiento) system to control imports and to collect fees. The Anglo-Iberian traders also became involved. Licences were granted for "pieces" (pieza, peças), units of labor that were the equivalent of a male slave in working age. Women, children, and old people were designated as fractions of one "piece."[16]

African slaves came to the Caribbean islands early in the sixteenth century, originally as house slaves and status symbols. At midcentury, the importation of them increased, but only toward the end of the century did plantation slavery assume large proportions. By governmental decree, slaves could be landed only at designated Caribbean and continental ports. As a result, a sizable contraband trade and a price differential between legally imported and smuggled slaves developed. One-third of the shipments were to consist of women. Trade to Portuguese Brazil, all of the Caribbean colonies, and North America was in private hands. With the decline of Portuguese and Spanish power, the "traffic in slaves became and remained an international affair."[17]

The two major regions of origin were the Western Sudan, from which Wolof, Mandinka, Yoruba, Songhai, and Hausa among others came via São Tomé, and the Portuguese-controlled Kongo-to-Angola region, from which Bantu ethnicities came from via the ports of Luanda and Benguela (see map 6.4). The British, French, Dutch, and Danish Caribbean imported 3.8 million slaves; 3.6 million were brought into Brazil, 1.6 million into Spanish America, and 0.4 million into British North America (Curtin).[18] While Brazil received 40 percent of the total, its share declined from 29 percent in the seventeenth to 10 percent in the eighteenth century. In view of the skewed male-female ratio, no slave population except that of British North America/the United States was able to reproduce itself. In the period in which 3.8 million Africans arrived in the Caribbean, only 0.6 million European voluntary and bound migrants came, but in 1800 2.1 million Africans and 0.9 million Europeans lived in the region (Emmer)—labor-related mortality explains this second American demographic catastrophe. Among the white but multiple-origin population, however, were descendants of slaves, whose shade of color permitted classifications other than Black, Negro, or African (map 10.2).[19]

Three major routes distributed slaves from the ports of arrival: northbound from Veracruz to Mexico, southbound from Cartagena to Lima, and across the continent from Buenos Aires to Potosí. Just as slaves were passed from merchant to merchant during their journey to the African coast, they were sold and resold in America on the way to their final destination. The voyage to Peru from Cartagena began in coastal ships to Portobelo (near Colón), continued by land to the Pacific coast, and then went by ship to Callao/Lima, which in all took some four to five months. Merchants migrated to the profitable trade cities. Portuguese Jews came—and Spanish inquisitors followed to oust them for the benefit of Spanish traders. In Venezuela, slaves were imported by the Welser Company, which administered the colony for two decades

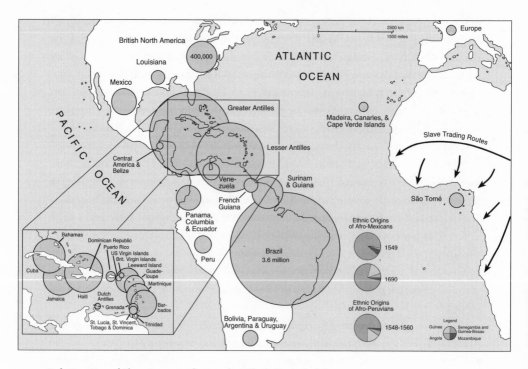

10.2   Relative Size of Slave Imports during the Whole Period of the
Atlantic Trade by Destination and Selected Ethnic Origins

after 1528, and thereafter by Caracas merchants. The Welsers were southern Germans, and the merchants were a mix of Basques, Portuguese, Jews from Portugal, second-generation Canary Islanders, Creoles from Santo Domingo, and people from the several regions of Spain. English merchants established themselves in eighteenth-century Buenos Aires. At the slaves' destinations involuntary mobility continued. Spanish-American slaves may have changed hands twenty to thirty times during their lifetimes: internal migration followed intercontinental transport. Free Blacks, in the sources often not distinguishable from slaves, either took the same routes to jobs or developed separate routes to better living conditions in small agriculture or urban work. In the second half of the colonial period, African slavery declined in the Mexican and Peruvian economies as Native populations recovered and free Mestizo laboring populations entered the market.[20]

The vast majority of the slaves worked in mining. In early gold mining—for example, in New Granada and eighteenth-century Brazil—the profits of slave labor covered the purchase price within a year. Transportation costs and the local labor supply determined labor usage. The digging of placer gold in tropical lowlands far from Indian populations involved some 60 percent of the 70,000 slaves in New Granada in 1778. In silver mining in northern Brazil and Peru's high sierra, on the other hand, Indios from the region were used, while imported and expensive Africans worked as overseers or in refining. Economic calculations were paramount: *mitayos* had to be fed by their villages, and providing food for a slave couple almost equaled the income derived from them. Furthermore, additional human labor, drawn from the Indios, could be requested at no cost, whereas commodified labor, for which the model was African, had to be bought. In 1611, 5,000 Africans lived in Potosí (3.3 percent of the population), mostly as domestic servants of mine owners, officials, and merchants. A division of labor tied to climatic zones emerged. Indios were used as labor in the sierra; Africans were put to work in the coastal valley economies.

Agricultural slaves produced cash crops—tobacco, sugar, cocoa, and cotton—for export to European and later North American markets. They also grew food supplies for local populations employed in mine labor and for the expanding cities. "An active agricultural commerce was established between the fertile lowlands and valleys of the Andean region and the densely populated mining centers" in Bolivia and Peru. In the early seventeenth century, 20,000 Africans worked in the vineyards of the coastal Peruvian Ica and Pisco valleys and in the northern Peruvian sugar-producing valleys. Subsequently, slave labor in the production of food for local consumption came to be supplemented with the debt peonage of Indios and with free local labor.

The third field of employment, urban tasks, involved many facets. Wealthy burghers owned servants for domestic chores and for the display of wealth in the home or in public; religious orders kept slaves for a wide variety of services; and businessmen used them for transport labor, especially for long-distance hauling after the prohibition on employing Indios distant from their home villages. Master craftsmen and small entrepreneurs employed slaves, in particular in construction work but also in many skilled trades. Such Africans could become highly skilled, gain their freedom, and open their own shops. Royal officials purchased slaves for public construction projects, such as fortifications, roads, and bridges. Indio communities, unwilling to provide laborers for public works, sometimes paid for slave labor instead. Descendants of the Inca nobility might also own slaves for the display of status.

In central cities, like Lima, market-gardeners came to rely mainly on chattel slaves, usually no more than forty per establishment. A firm's proprietor could sell field slaves with the land, herdsmen with the herds. The upper classes employed slaves on "a lavish scale," and women received them as part of their dowries. Small entrepreneurs bought and sold them as investments or rented them out as temporary labor. "The population of Lima in the middle of the seventeenth century was over half black. . . . Lima and Mexico City had in fact the largest concentrations of Blacks in the western hemisphere. And figures of other cities and towns in Spanish America . . . indicate substantial black populations."[21]

Legislation was created in an attempt to prevent slave mobility and resistance. Flight was one way to resist, and "vagabondage" was often involuntary. Slaves were discarded after the death of owners or when sectoral or regional economic crises made slave labor unprofitable. Such mobile slaves intermingled with free people or formed communities of fugitives (cimarrones) in hidden and fortified self-supporting villages. Freedmen and -women often settled in cities because economic opportunities there were better. Manumission was widespread and followed color and gender lines. Women were manumitted twice as often as men—they and their partners created free African-origin and mixed-origin communities, which in turn could provide support for fugitives or collect money to buy the freedom of enslaved kin and friends. Light-colored Mulattoes were manumitted more often than Black American–born Creoles, and the latter more often than African-born Blacks. Light-skinned freedmen and -women, according to contemporary Euro-Latin socio-racial assumptions, would "whiten" society.[22]

In Afro-Latin thought, considerations of color definitely ranked second to legal self-liberation gained by the purchase of freedom or by "illegal" flight. In Venezuela of the 1720s, some 20,000 *cimarrones* were said to live in *cumbes* or *quilombos* of, on occasion, several thousand inhabitants. Around 1800, slaves numbered about 60,000, and there were more than 20,000 free fugitives. As early as 1683, the Spanish crown had requested that slaveholders treat their slaves better in order to prevent flight. Missionaries were sent to the *cumbes* to pacify the inhabitants and to resettle them in legal villages. Slaves had no intention of waiting for the legislative abolition of slavery, which occurred in Venezuela four decades after independence in 1854 and in Spanish Cuba as late as 1880–86. They had a clear conception of the system of power that expropriated their labor and knew that planters stole the just rewards of their toil. They called flight "stealing oneself" (a U.S. term), and in the process of fleeing they reappropriated not only the surplus they produced but also control over their own lives. Planters, too, knew the doublethink of the system. When a slave purchased his or her own freedom, French owners called it "vendre un nègre à lui-même." Even though the ideology of slavery was all-pervasive, its actors, both the owners and the captives, understood its internal contradictions.

The Indios, on the other hand, saw even enslaved Africans as part of the forces of intrusion. By manumission or by marriage of (former) slave women to white men, Africans could enter the ranks of the colonial oppressors, and their upward mobility stabilized colonial social structures. But the mixing of peoples made society one of graded complexions rather than a White-Brown-Black division into opposing racial lines.[23]

10.3 Enslaved and Free Africans in Portuguese Brazil

In Portuguese Brazil, the coerced mobilization of Native labor, the forced migrations of African slaves, and the status of free Africans differed from the comparable set of conditions in Spanish America. As they had when they set up trade-posts in Asia and Africa, the Portuguese at first limited themselves to coastal settlements and strongholds. During the "coastal period," they tried to rely on free or enslaved First Peoples' labor. They negotiated with local Tupí-Guaraní and Tapúias for dyewoods, brazilwood in particular. When Portugal's Asian trade declined after 1530, Brazil's economic importance increased, and the introduction of sugarcane cultivation brought a clash of cultures. The subsistence-oriented Tupí neither saw the plantation system's usefulness nor savored its profitability. The Portuguese, who had little knowledge of

Tupí society and were not interested in acquiring it, attempted to recruit men for fieldwork, even though in Tupí society agriculture was the sphere of women. Brazil-Portuguese forced Tupí and inland Gé into slavery but the Iberian-Portuguese government repudiated this strategy because First Nations were needed as allies against the Dutch, French, and British, who were taking hold of the Guiana territories.

A third position was that of the Jesuits, who opposed forced labor in favor of forced settlement in the interest of systematic missionary work. From 1552 to 1759, the Jesuits' *aldeias*, "concentration villages," practiced separate settlement—as the Spanish had propagated—to force the Christian belief, acculturation, and "civilized" forms of labor on First Peoples. The Tupí fled, were decimated by famines and epidemics, forced to labor if they resisted acculturation as adults, and kidnapped as babies to be Hispanicized in separate nurseries and schools for labor. European immigrants wanted direct exploitation, and a law of 1596 granted the Jesuits—a total of 130 men—the sole right to lure Indios out of the forests and to allocate their waged labor to colonists (*bandeiras religiosas*). By the mid-seventeenth century, after the opening of the Amazon basin, they controlled fifty-four *aldeias* with about 200,000 Natives. The concentration villages prevented physical annihilation of the Tupí but assimilation brought the cultures of the Tupí and the Guaraní to an end.

After 1570, when the European-origin population had grown to 20,000–25,000 and the Native coastal population was depleted, European, Mestizo, and Indio slave hunters, who until then had traded for captives of inter-Indian strife, began *entradas* to the interior to capture "Red Gold," as native slaves were called. In 1575–76 alone, some 20,000 Indios were abducted from the hinterland of Bahia to Brazil's first capital, Salvador, and whole communities were annihilated in the process. Further south, slave catchers fanned out as far as Paraguay and Paraná. In 1609 the government prohibited enslavement, but a century and a half later still had not succeeded in enforcing the decree. In the century after 1620, 100,000–200,000 Native slaves were sold in the markets of Belém and São Luís do Maranhão.[24]

Because of the massive demand for labor, African slaves had replaced most of the Native labor by the mid-seventeenth century. Of the total slave imports to the Americas, Brazil received 42 percent in the seventeenth century, just under one-third in the eighteenth, and 60 percent in the nineteenth. Labor demand and forced or free migration followed economic cycles. The brazilwood economy based on Indio labor was followed by a sugar ("white gold") economy (1570–1670) and a gold and precious stone exporting period (1680–1770), both relying on slave labor. During the cotton and cattle period (1770–1830), African slave and European immigrant labor was employed, but surplus slaves were exported to Spanish America. In the coffee economy after 1830, the change to free labor and European immigration was completed. In the course of these changes, Brazil's economic center moved from northeastern coastal regions to Rio de Janeiro and to the mining economy of Minas Gerais, then to the south and the center, and finally to the uplands of Rio de Janeiro and São Paulo in the coffee economy. Each geographical shift implied a redirection of (forced) labor migrant flows and large-scale internal migrations of pioneer entrepreneurs and free settlers. Each expansion into the interior also involved attempts to enslave additional Natives because transport of African slaves was more costly, employment in small-scale enterprise was not profitable, and the opportunities for escape were large.

Sixteenth-century Salvador da Bahia in the northeast imported slaves from West Africa and Angola. Seventeenth-century Central African and Angolan slaves were usually sent to the sugar plantations, while West African slaves were employed in the cities as domestic slaves and rented out for casual and skilled labor. Men and women of Yoruba and Hausa background often worked on their own account and paid a share to their owners. Many could buy their freedom, and, unlike their owners, they often could read and write. Culturally, they were Muslim. In the eighteenth century, West Africans were transported to Bahia and Angolan Africans to the southern mining and coffee economies. During the early Minas Gerais mining boom, the demand for skilled miners rose—and for a time slaves with mining experience from African goldfields fetched high prices. Although African women were skilled agriculturalists, the Portuguese preferred male labor and paid higher prices for men.[25]

In Spanish America, with its multiple suppliers, the slave population was heterogeneous. But in Brazil, where slaves from one region of origin were again regionally concentrated after arrival, they engaged in a re-creation of ethnic identities. According to Nishida, "Those who came from the same African language group but from different ethnic lineages or subgroups often associated with one another under the label imposed by the slaveowners. As a group, they sought and continually created common symbols they could share among themselves. Ethnicity was thereby symbolically recreated."[26]

Slaves on northeastern sugar estates had a life expectancy of no more than six to eight years after their arrival. When the Dutch conquered Pernambuco and parts of Bahia after 1625 (Dutch Brazil), sugar production for world markets, which had made Brazil a rich and successful colony, shifted to the Spanish and French Antilles. Later, a period of drought and epidemics prevented a resurgence of the Brazilian production. The shift to the mining economy of Minas Gerais induced annual in-migrations of 2,000–4,000 Euro-Latins from 1705 to 1750 and slave migrations of almost two million during the whole century. At mid-century, several 100,000 slaves labored in mine and riverbed deposits. The Portuguese crown prohibited the immigration of European mining experts for fear of competition and intervention by their states of origin. Skilled West African miners developed innovations locally. The work was hard, and the hours were long; but since owners had to rely on slave expertise and loyalty, the sale of gold dust by slaves was accepted—and many purchased their freedom with the proceeds. Hinterland societies without policing agencies and the sizable population of free Africans made flight easy for acculturated slaves, who knew the terrain and easily blended into the local society. The next economic cycle, the coffee economy, began with slave labor on quasi-feudal latifundias (*fazendas*) west of Rio de Janeiro. Declining world market prices, soil exhaustion, and the end of the slave trade resulted in a shift to São Paulo and in the encouragement of Latin European labor migration.[27]

At the time of independence in 1822, 2.5 million of Brazil's 3.8 million inhabitants were classified as *prêto* (Black) or *pardo* (Dark, Brown, Mulatto), of whom 0.6 million were free. Unfree status reflected color hierarchies: Black was the color of almost 90 percent of the slaves but only of 15 percent of the free non-White population. Of all the slave societies in the Americas, Brazil provided the best opportunities to achieve freedom through manumission or self-purchase. Intermarriage resulted in a mixing of "races," and since West African Muslims were often educated—more so than Portuguese Christians—social ascent was possible. For centuries Africans were the mainstay of the economy, but the dark side of this pivotal role was the early death of large numbers of slaves under a work regime that could import more human beings for less cost than was necessary to maintain them in good health and raise children.

For survivors, the pervasive racism meant that the darker the skin, the lower the status in the color-coded social slots assigned by society and the more likely a life in poverty. The basic distinction between being enslaved and being free was made visible in dress: slaves were prohibited from wearing shoes. A rigorous classificatory scheme of 1834 listed at the top 1) Portuguese born in Portugal and 2) Portuguese born in Brazil. Below them stood 3) Mulattoes having White fathers and Black mothers and 4) Mamluks, the offspring of *raças branca* and Indian women. On the next level down were 5) subgroups of pure Indios, 6) civilized Indios, and 7) primitive Indios. Almost at the bottom stood 8) Brazilian-born Blacks (Creoles), 9) Christianized Blacks (Ladinos), and 10) African-born Blacks (Boçaes). And at the very bottom were 11) *bode* or Mestizos having Negro and Mulatto parents and 12) *curiboca* of Black Mestizo and Indio parentage. Color and origin determined whether slaves labored in production or in domestic service and whether they could rise socially.

The complex system permitted slaves to own slaves, and multiple color, labor, and status differentiation prevented the emergence of a common culture of the African-origin Brazilians. The slaves, divided by region of origin, accepted notions of rank. One group of slaves might negotiate with their owner to assign dangerous or disliked tasks to a lower-ranking slave ethnicity. Slave artisans might purchase other, cheaper slaves for their masters in return for their own freedom. Fugitives in self-organized communities kept slaves and engaged in slave raids. When regions became more densely settled and state institutions stronger, flight became more difficult. Under the impact of the French Revolution in 1789, resistance surged again and found expression in numerous rebellions. In everyday life, however, free Blacks oriented themselves toward the imposed hierarchies; as the saying went, "Black but with the soul of a White man."[28]

Return migration from nineteenth-century Brazil to Africa permitted the use of human capital in a socioeconomic space that allocated privileged status to the "Brazilians." After some reverse acculturation, they became cultural-commercial brokers, engaging in trade with Brazil, teaching their African-born children the Portuguese language, and organizing Catholic parishes to emphasize status. Some of these West Africa–Brazil connections endured to the end of the twentieth century.[29] In the later nineteenth century, slave labor (abolished in 1888) and internal migration no longer satisfied demand. From 1871 to 1920, more than three million Europeans reached Brazil, as "wage slaves," to use a term of the labor movement of the time (see chap. 14.2).

10.4 Slave-Based Societies in the Caribbean

In the eighteenth century the Caribbean World, the first center of Spanish power (chap. 8.3), then marginal to the *tierra firme* and Brazil, became the prototypical slave-based production environment for world-market oriented sugarcane cultivation. The plant, originally from India, had itself been carried by the migration of cultivators through ever-changing labor regimes via the eastern Mediterranean to the Muslim-Iberian World and, in the fifteenth century, to the Portuguese Atlantic islands, where plantation owners developed technical know-how and management experience with large-scale slave labor (chaps. 2.3 and 5.3). They transferred this model to the Americas, first to Spanish Santo Domingo in 1503 and a few decades later to Brazil.[30]

In Brazil, the Protestant commercially oriented Dutch established themselves in the Guianas and in Bahia (Dutch Brazil) in the 1620s; the British extended their reach to Jamaica (1655–70), and the French states extended theirs to western Hispaniola or Haiti (1697). These states—in contrast to Spain's and Portugal's practices—left colonization and political rule to government-chartered joint-stock companies, such as the Compagnie des Îles d'Amérique, the Royal African Company, the Plymouth Company, and others. The capitalist merchant entrepreneurs pursued a policy of populating the new territories with capital-owning planters and with indentured labor of many origins, from Ireland, Scotland, and the Germanies, for example. But the first staple for the metropoles, tobacco, proved to be of inferior quality, and labor shortages proved insurmountable. Those indentured servants who survived the climate left the rigorously controlled plantation labor to migrate elsewhere. They joined the buccaneers or moved to Florida (British after 1763), French Louisiana (U.S. after 1803), or elsewhere.

Thus the mid-seventeenth-century merchant financiers saw their future in producing specialized crops for world—that is, European—markets with permanently bound labor. The slaves were, however, less docile than expected: the English of Barbados exported their first sugar in 1647 and faced their first slave rebellion in 1649. The French systematized the exploitation of Africans in the Caribbean *Code Noir* of 1685. "The Atlantic world of plantation agriculture, big business, international commerce, and slavery" had come into existence. At the top level of the economic system, Europe was dominant; at the bottom level, Europeans hardly penetrated the minds of the commodified labor arriving with their own identities and lifestyles, even if damaged in the Middle Passage. Their strict and visible control mechanisms left Whites with the illusion of power over lives and cultures whose spiritual and emotional aspects remained invisible to them. Although all of the colonizing powers sought the hierarchical segregation of peoples/races/classes, the new Atlantic World was to become an amalgam of Native, African, and European cultures. The Caribbean, because of the early annihilation of the First Peoples and the size of slave populations, was to become the core of the Black Atlantic.[31]

While diverse sociopolitical structures evolved in the region, there were only two economic regimes: settler colonies and colonies of exploitation. Migrants' decisions depended on perceived opportunities. Small farm families and indentured men and women, who peopled the early French possessions, intended to live in small independent holdings and shunned plantation societies. Power relations destroyed migrants' life-course projects: planters reduced their compatriots to poverty. The settlers fled, and slaves were brought in. In 1654 the Portuguese expelled from Brazil the Dutch and Jewish settlers, who in their flight to the Antilles transferred their expertise in sugar-mill technology. In 1656 Guadeloupe was a settler colony and counted 12,000 French people and 3,000 slaves; in 1770, when it was a colony of exploitation, it counted 12,000 French people who owned 80,000 slaves.[32]

In the Spanish Caribbean, immigrants sought economic improvement and social mobility beyond the restraints of Iberian society. Officials came with their wives to serve as a family model for re-creating Spanish society. As a strategy to encourage family migration, the crown prohibited married men from staying overseas without their wives and children for more than six months. But the unintended result was an influx of unmarried young men, who formed their own local liaisons and families. Slave and free women, whether victimized or not, contributed their cultural heritage, and owing to gendered child-care patterns handed it down to the children. English imperial planners and wealthy migrants, often sons of the gentry, pursued a different model. Officials, planters, and investors remained transients, identifying with the home society, sending their children back to boarding schools, and returning home with profits. As a consequence, their cultural impact in the Caribbean was low. The Dutch, who could not afford emigration because of their small population, had even less influence on lifestyles.

But since the Dutch colonizers, usually from the burgher classes, could rely on their trans-European commercial organization, they acted as financiers, commercial middlemen, milling experts, and freighters. In St. Eustatius, which the Dutch made a free port, French, English, and Spanish merchants mingled and traded in products from the whole of the Caribbean. Of the roughly 20,000 inhabitants in 1781, 15,000 were slaves, some of whom participated in trade on their days off. Half a century later, the English sacked the island. As a result of emigration, the population declined to 400 Whites with 2,000 slaves in 1840—a thriving center had been devastated. Other island societies were equally multicultured. British Trinidad's White population of 4,400 men and women in 1811 consisted of ten nationalities: East Indians (1,700), English people (1,100), Spaniards and French people (about 600 each), Americans, Germans, Corsicans, Italians, Maltese, and Portuguese.[33]

In the framework of their imperial economies, the Dutch, French, and English colonies experienced an economic takeoff after 1700, while the Spanish lagged. Core-based investors with access to political institutions demanded long-term stability and legal frameworks that would make investments profitable. While indentured servants pursued their own interests, African labor bound for life ensured control and return on investments. Thus, with vast numbers of slaves, eighteenth-century Saint Domingue and Jamaica became the sugar colonies par excellence. Planters imported slaves rather than encouraging them to procreate. Imported labor could be exploited immediately; no costs were incurred for raising children to working age. In Jamaica of the early 1830s, it cost twice as much to rear a slave girl or boy than to import a slave. The low birthrates of African women may also be connected to traditions of extended breast-feeding and/or to deliberate birth control in view of the dismal life prospects of children.[34]

Free "persons of color" dominated the small trade—just as diasporic Chinese traders did in the Asian colonial sphere. The emergence of an African diaspora had not been part of the blueprints of any of the metropolitan societies. (In the tradition of mobility restrictions imposed on the lower classes in Europe, one English colonial governor called free persons of color "unappropriated people.") Slaves followed their own economic interests; women, in particular, played an important role in trading. White colonial legislators created a plethora of restrictions. Jamaica's Assembly prohibited slaves in 1711 from owning livestock and from engaging in small-scale trade without the written permission of their masters. St. Lucia in the 1730s, the French Antilles in the 1760s, and Cuba in 1840s followed suit. But the "world the slaveholders made" or intended to make faced the continuous challenge of "the world the slaves made."[35]

An emphasis on slave self-determination and free Afro-Caribbeans should not distract attention from the brutal, often deadly plantation labor. This was the lot of the majority of Caribbean Africans, about four-fifths of the total. In the 1830s about 80 percent of the field slaves were employed in sugar production; only in Jamaica the figure was lower. In the fields, as in the processing of cane in the rolling mill and the boiling house, and in the barreling of molasses and raw sugar for export, men and women worked side by side. A rise in social status was possible for only a few. Next in the hierarchy stood the domestic slaves and mechanics; above them were slaves working for wages as hired hands; and at the top were skilled or professionally trained slaves. With only small White populations present, few house slaves were required, and, fearful of women's cultural impact, British planters, in particular, eschewed the employment of Black nurses for child-care. In the Caribbean, as in all Euro-American slave societies, men were valued for physical strength and feared as rebels, whereas women were valued for their labor and their sexuality and feared for their "sharp tongues," their cutting comments on overseers and owners. Victorian White men's imaginations made the latter the inverse of their image of White women: "physically strong, exuding a warm animal sensuality, an inferior subspecies of the female sex."

Enslaved Africans formed families—all planter, overseer, and slave driver violence, projections, and interference notwithstanding. Capital strategies for cutting costs often forced slave populations to produce their own food on small plots of land and sew their own garments. This increase in labor burdens was matched by increased self-determination. The hours from sundown to sunup were their own, and the planters' attempts to curtail cultural and religious activities or self-provisioning and sale of surplus met with adamant opposition: the slaves defended their tiny self-carved niches of autonomy. Wherever slavery was abolished, freed families went into marginal agriculture rather than choosing to remain on the plantations; for this independence they even accepted potentially lower standards of living owing to poor soils and distance from markets.[36]

The free population of African or Mulatto lineage amounted to more than 40 percent of the total only in Curaçao (1833) and Puerto Rico (1860); it was only 16 percent in Cuba (1860) and even less in Jamaica and Barbados and in French Saint Domingue and Martinique. The decline of colonial island economies often resulted in emigration of Whites and a relative increase of the free Colored population, which, because women were manumitted more often than men, was predominantly female and urban and engaged in small independent trading. In some colonies—Saint Domingue, for example—the male planter aristocracy and free Mulatto women joined in concubinage, the latter pursuing a successful strategy to establish their group as an independent economic and political factor. Urban free Colored men, on the other hand, competed with the lowest ranks of the European-origin population as well as with slaves hiring themselves out to purchase their freedom.

Saint Domingue best exemplifies the complex sociopolitical developments and political economies of the Caribbean power strategies and plantation regimes. In 1697 the island, a stronghold of *corsairs*, changed in status to being a French colony. This implied an economic restructuring from settler colony to plantation regime. The independent French farming families were forced to leave, some 4,000 of them displaced by a dozen French planters. Around 1790, this richest of all French colonies had a population of 0.03 million Whites, 0.028 free people of color, and 0.5 million slaves. Its economy imported up to 30,000 slaves annually and employed some 15,000 sailors to ship its products to France. Metropolitan France valued such Caribbean possessions. Forced to conclude the Treaty of Paris with Britain in 1763, France had ceded all its unproductive North American continental possessions and their French-origin settlers (Quebec, Acadia, and parts of Louisiana) in return for Saint Domingue's profitable sister colonies Martinique, St. Lucia, and Guadeloupe and their populations. European sovereigns reassigned colonial populations in much the same way that Europe's noble classes had at one time sold their serfs. The political economy of feudalism had expanded to having a global reach, albeit under the new terms of mercantilism and statecraft.[37]

Unlike the situation in Saint Domingue, development in Cuba lagged under Spanish imperial control. A brief British interlude in 1762 introduced economic liberalism, but in exchange for Florida (with its Maroon communities) the island was returned to Spain in 1763. In the six months of occupation, the British abolished state monopolism and imported 10,700 slaves, five times the Spanish administration's annual quota. While about one-quarter of Cuba's 1774 population of about 170,000 were slaves, free and forced mass immigration increased the population to 705,000 in 1827, of which 41 percent (287,000) were slaves.

The diverging developments on three islands illustrate the changes brought about by the Age of Revolution, the abolition of slavery, and the new global power relationships: the Haitian revolution, the Jamaican end of slavery, and the procrastination of the Spanish on Cuba in the face of U.S. capital's intrusion.

Thanks to new concepts of human rights and of government by social contract, the Mulattoes and Negroes of Saint Domingue/Haiti cast off their yoke. The French Revolution brought the class distinctions in Saint Domingue between *grands blancs*, *petits blancs*, and *gens de couleur* to a crisis. Whites agitated against the extension of the declaration of human rights to the colonies; Mulattoes, with the support of the French *Amis des Noirs*, demanded it. First, the *grands blancs* rose against the king; then the *petits blancs* and *gens de couleur* turned against the *grands blancs*. When the French National Assembly in May 1791 placed all colonial free persons on an equal footing regardless of color, the Saint Domingue Whites responded with a massacre of free Mulattoes. To gain their freedom slaves rose up and began a rebellion in August 1791, two years before the National Assembly in France abolished slavery. Ten thousand or more planters fled, mostly to Cuba, taking some of their servants with them. The former slave Toussaint changed his last name from that of his owners, Bréda, to L'Ouverture, meaning "the opening"—a new beginning, a new deal. According to Geggus, "Such slaves who lived at the interface between white and black society needed to know the ways of both worlds. To maintain their standing in both communities, they had to be shrewd observers of human nature and skilled performers in a number of roles." Toussaint L'Ouverture forged the rebellious slaves into an army and began to establish a new economic order: "If the essence of things creole is creative adaptation, this was a truly creole army." Imperial Napoleonic France responded by sending an invasion army of 40,000, but the ex-slaves defeated the generals and their men in 1804. They also defeated British and Spanish forces. Perhaps the struggle for freedom was inspired by traditions of Native peoples of the Americas. Some of the Afro-Caribbean fighters referred to themselves as "Incas" in what may have been an echo of the Peruvian uprising of 1780. Although the victorious Haitians declared independence, the polity was wracked by antagonism between Mulattoes and Blacks, between *grands gens de couleur* and *petits noirs*. When the ex-slaves refused to continue to work on the plantations, the export economy collapsed. Their regional peasant economies did not become integrated into one national economy, and poverty remained widespread. The freedom the ex-slave families sought on their little plots deprived the state of export and tax revenues.[38]

The British Empire's emancipation of slaves in 1834–38 made Jamaica's sugar noncompetitive. The African-origin population migrated internally to form independent villages rather than to work for planters. Economic readjustment went on for decades.

Cuban Whites massacred much of the island's Afro-Caribbean leadership in 1844 to forestall independent political action by free Colored people. Cuba benefited from the Haitian and Jamaican postslavery noncompetitiveness. In 1870 it supplied 41 percent of the world's sugar production. Though slave prices almost tripled from 1830 to 1855 while world market prices for sugar fell, slaves constituted the majority of the workforce. U.S. capitalists began to invest. By 1880, when slavery was converted into six more years of apprenticeship, only 150,000 slaves were left on the island. Free Black labor refused plantation work because sufficient agricultural land permitted African-Cuban families to set up independent small farming. The Spanish government had opposed importing European labor; but, after U.S.-supported independence, immigration was permitted (see chap. 15.5).[39]

Throughout the nineteenth century, Caribbean planters discussed the end of slavery and experimented with many different European and Asian labor forces, free or indentured, but they did not convert to new labor in time. They used their influence in legislatures to designate ex-slaves "apprentices" and keep them bound for four to six years. The debates echoed the bitter discussion in England about an independent agricultural population unwilling to work according to the dictates of employers (see chap. 12.2). Free Blacks settled near plantations to take wage labor according to their own needs, formed separate inland communities, or migrated between islands to take advantage of wage differentials. On some islands, the authorities distributed land to induce laboring families to stay.

Almost frantically, planters tried to recruit Black labor. To begin with, in terms of the cost of migration, local free labor was cheapest. Voluntary inter-island and island-mainland migrations were assisted by paid passages, free ferry services, and bounties to labor-transporting ship captains. Tens of thousands moved according to wage levels, working conditions, and legal status. Over time this migration became self-sustaining. In British Guiana alone, some 40,500 voluntary migrants—most of them from Barbados—arrived before 1893. Second, the labor reservoir was enlarged. The British navy's "liberated Africans" from slave ships were disembarked in Sierra Leone or St. Helena or temporarily in Rio de Janeiro or Havana. About 40,000 liberated Africans came to the Caribbean and British Guiana before 1866. To earn their keep, they were indentured, at first for one year and later for three years. Many joined communities of free Afro-Caribbeans. Free Blacks migrated from the United States to the less racist island societies. Third, planters recruited free Africans from among the Kru of Sierra Leone; but once migrants returned and reported on working conditions, no further enlistment could be obtained. Free immigrant Portuguese, mostly Cape Verdeans, were deemed because of skin color to be part of the Black labor force.

Through intermarriage a "new polyglot society of free peoples" emerged, homogenized on each island and divided into states but developing a regional sense of identity. This society also included the descendants of contract laborers from Asia (chaps. 14.2 and 15.5).[40]

10.5 African Slavery in Anglo-America

The history of Africans in North America differed in many respects from slave experiences in Latin America. First, the numbers imported directly from Africa were small. Most arrived from the Caribbean after they had survived the seasoning period and thus underwent a second involuntary migration into yet another society and another regime of labor and race relations. Though imports increased in the eighteenth century, the share of Black people in the total U.S. population remained comparatively low: 18 percent (including 1.5 percent free) in 1790, 16 percent in 1815, and 13 percent in 1860. Only in colonial South Carolina before the 1730s did Blacks ever form a majority. Second, only in North America did the slave population grow from natural increase. Family formation and child-care were possible and considered economically acceptable by slave owners. After the end of the slave trade, planters in areas of soil exhaustion kept some slave families but sold their children when they reached working age to profitable plantations further west and south. Third, slave owners usually resided on their plantations, and a closer relationship to the slave community emerged. Under this type of harsh paternalism, slaves were not worked to death; planters assumed responsibility for food, clothing, and housing. But control, exploitation, and punishment remained the rule. Fourth, however, the brutal control exerted over free Negroes was reflected in the sharp Black-White juxtaposition and the terrorism of lynching, a combination of torture and auto-da-fé that had no equivalent in the Latin societies.[41]

Few Africans reached Canada: within the context of British Atlantic trade, an early free community emerged in Halifax; flight from the rebellious colonies brought Black Loyalists and the slaves of White Loyalists to Canada after 1774; fugitive U.S. slaves came to Upper Canada/Ontario until 1865. As a society without slavery, the cities from Windsor via Toronto and Montreal to Halifax were part of the Black Atlantic.

Slavery was concentrated in the plantation South (about 40 percent of the U.S. population in 1770), although the institution reached into the northern colonies/ states (less than 5 percent in 1770) and into the western territories. The forced migration of Africans first brought bound servants to Virginia in 1619; but while for Europeans indentured labor did not extend beyond seven years, the status of Africans ("non-Christians") was changed to servitude for life, with children following the status of the mother.[42] To communicate among each other, the transported Africans had to merge their many languages into a pidgin or lingua franca, as in the Gullah language spoken along the coast of the Carolinas. Once acculturated, some slaves rebelled, and many engaged in day-to-day resistance. Self-liberation involved flight to Florida's Maroon communities, westward to free territories and states, or northward. Perhaps 50,000 men, women, and children moved via the self-help network of the "underground railroad" to free states and to Canada. In contrast to the opportunities afforded in Brazil, the free communities in the United States were too small and too powerless to protect fugitives. While Quakers and free Black Americans demanded abolition early on, slave hunters even attempted to re-enslave free Negroes. Manumission, possible but infrequent, involved a racial ideology that sent perhaps 15,000 former slaves back to Sierra Leone and Liberia before 1860 to form viable communities without slavery as well as to missionize Africans.

The decline of tobacco, rice, and indigo cultivation, and the concomitant expansion of the cotton economy entailed the concentration of slave ownership. Though institutionally and economically the underpinning of southern society, the system involved comparatively small numbers of White owners, some 380,000 people out of a population of more than 8 million in 1860. Of these only 2,300 were large planters with more than 100 slaves. The U.S. South was part of the circum-Caribbean slave and plantation system and resembled Belize and other Latin American societies more than the U.S. northern states. The planters controlled, in addition to their slaves, the political system and shaped the prevailing ideology. The shift from the U.S. coast to the piedmont and, after 1815, west to the Mississippi and south to Louisiana involved massive internal migrations, via both the sale of individuals and the transferal of whole plantation populations. The further to the south, the harsher the exploitation became. To be sold "down the [Mississippi] river" was a form of punishment for refractory slaves.[43]

The emergence of slave communities became possible not only because of planter paternalism but more so because of natural increase and a resulting balanced sex ratio. Marriage and child-raising patterns followed African traditions within a North American framework. When the sale of individual men and women broke up families, kinship networks supported the remaining members of truncated families. Since manumission and the self-purchase of freedom remained the exception, only 320,000 free Negroes were listed in the census of 1830, mostly in urban communities.[44]

Immigration, emigration, and internal migration involved multidirectional moves. After the slave revolt in Saint Domingue, several U.S. states—in particular, South Carolina—prohibited the importation of slaves and the entry of free Negroes from the West Indies to avoid notions of human rights and self-determination from penetrating southern society. The acquisition of Florida in 1819 was intended to prevent escape to the Maroon/Native Seminole communities. Westward settlement involved slave migrations as well as conflict over the extension of slavery. Free and enslaved Afro-Americans were involved in cattle-raising in the Anglo-Spanish border zone of Texas. As in Brazil, the end of the Atlantic slave trade increased internal trading and the resulting involuntary mobility. Travelers observed the migrants in chains and commented on the system. By 1832 Virginia exported 6,000 locally born slaves annually. Increasingly, slaves were hired out for seasonal agricultural work or on an annual basis to industry. They were thus connected to urban working-class traditions—for example, in Tennessee—and a process of urbanization began. Free Africans established small agricultural communities in the Old Northwest. After emancipation and the end of the Civil War in 1865, small-scale emigration from the South began, but White racism in the North and Black community cohesion in the South prevented a mass exodus before the beginning of the twentieth century.[45]

Abolitionist impulses and the end of the slave trade did not originate mainly in Britain, as has often been argued. Though the Quakers in the United States were at one time involved in the slave trade, they demanded abolition in the 1770s. The anti-slavery *Amis des Noirs* in France played an influential role from 1788 on. Most important, Mulattoes and free Blacks in the colonies exerted pressure on the French National Assembly. The Haitian slaves' war for freedom changed the forum of debate from constitutional and human rights philosophy to front-page news. Slavery in Haiti and other French-Caribbean possessions ended in 1794; the slave trade was officially halted in the British Empire in 1807; and the other European powers declared an end to the trade after the Congress of Vienna in 1815.

U.S. abolitionist activities peaked in the 1830s and 1840s. For economic reasons—to equalize the cost of labor in the sugar-producing colonies—Britain had to press other slave-trading societies to follow its lead in emancipating slaves. Thus economic rationales and moral impulses interacted, whether in legislatures or on the high seas. In the mid-nineteenth-century Atlantic World, British naval patrols still had to enforce the ban on the trade. It became effective only in the 1860s and 1870s.

Slavery itself came to an end in the British Empire in 1834 but with "apprenticeship" imposed until 1838. It was stopped in the French colonies, where it had been reinstituted under Napoléon, in 1846 and in the Dutch possessions in 1873. In the remnants of the Spanish Empire, slavery was abolished in Cuba in 1880 with a six-year "apprenticeship" tacked on. The two most important societies and polities based, in part, on slave labor, Brazil and the United States, continued slavery until 1888 and 1863-65 respectively. Only then was total bondage replaced by Asian contract labor migrants, European free labor migrants, and internally migrating African-origin labor in the Americas. The classic exposition of new middle-class—not capitalist—economic doctrines, Adam Smith's *The Wealth of Nations* (1776), had called slavery an anachronism that would not be able to compete with free labor.[46]

Elsewhere around the globe, the other (non-chattel or rights-in-persons) forms of slavery ended in the Ottoman Empire between 1830 and 1857—at first for "white" Central Asian slaves and then for African slaves. In North Africa, where the system involved fewer numbers, slavery was abolished in Tunis in 1846. The British occupation of Egypt in 1882 and its subsequent control over Nilotic Sudan reduced the supply of Africans, but proslavery rebellions forced the British to compromise on the issue. In the societies of the eastern Mediterranean, slavery ended around 1900. In West Africa, on the other hand, the system continued to expand during the late-nineteenth-century European territorial conquests. From the sixteenth to the nineteenth century, a Black Atlantic World had developed parallel to the European Atlantic World, both inextricably entwined.

11

Migration and Conversion: Worldviews, Material

Culture, Racial Hierarchies

Expansion forced people coming into the orbit of Europe's power and influence to adapt while surrendering as little of their identity as possible; it also forced Europeans to reconstruct their view of the world. Though contact often did not involve whole societies or large regions but limited contact zones or borderlands, intercultural exchange in what European elites called colonies often involved violence. Such interposition might rely on hierarchies and exploitative practices that were traditional in the indigenous societies, whether Inca or Manchu. But from the fifteenth century on, the European states and their intellectual and economic elites globalized faster than the states and elites of other civilizations. The new economic masters transported working-age populations across the globe in order to exploit them, often leaving them to die. Those who survived the Europeans' rule fled, resisted, or subverted the masters' schemes. The Others saw the newcomers as bearers of germs, guns, and self-serving grandiloquence rather than of civilization and faith.

Three major consequences followed from migration and contact. First, Europeans had to explain the existence of the peoples of the Americas, not mentioned in the Bible, the basic text of their worldview: either these creatures were not human, or the Bible was wrong. Second, on the level of material culture, peoples across the world incorporated new foods, seasonings, and stimulants, thus changing everyday diets and lives. Third, the imbalanced sex ratio of the conquerors and colonizers and the need for laborers in plantation regimes—as well as power relationships and affectionate ties—resulted in the emergence of new peoples by cultural and genetic mixing and in a newly developed racialized hierarchy of peoples.

Economically, European hegemony involved a division of labor and of the profits of labor: the colonized worked, and the European colonizers accumulated. Culturally, the Indian-Arab-Jewish-Christian Mediterranean culture, as appropriated by Latin Christendom and labeled Occidental or Western, faced African and American challenges. Out of this contact emerged a White and a Black Atlantic, neither one a mere extension of the Old Worlds, as well as new, fused Central and South American "Indio"-Euro-African cultures. The Asian worlds remained more distant. Unequal power and capital relationships structured contacts that reached deep into the every-

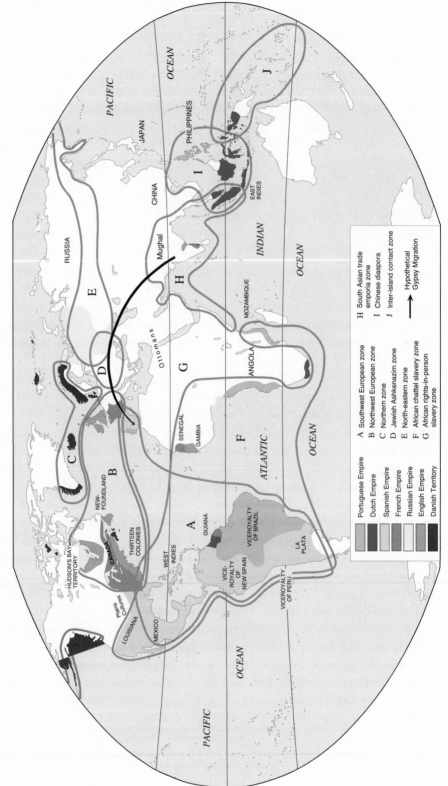

11.1   Empires with Colonies and Zones of Encounter/Borderlands, 1775

day lives and agency of people, whether in beneficial ways or in the form of identity-shattering commodification (map 11.1).

11.1 Euro-Atlantic Society Reconstructs Its Worldview

Cultural and intellectual exchange between the new worlds and the old cores did not repeat earlier patterns (see chap. 5.2). Nothing emerged that was equivalent to the Arab-Jewish-Christian universal learning based on a mutual recognition of achievements. The Portuguese, who did not talk to those who knew, "discovered" coasts and societies well known to Africans and Asians. The Iberians extended their customs, concepts and practices of slavery, patterns of noble feuding and conquest, and patterns of social hierarchies. In an "acquisitive and predatory drive for commodities and profits" involving a "looting [of] the natives," they destroyed practices of peaceful—even if hierarchical—exchange among merchants from many cultures of origin in the Indian Ocean's trade emporia.[1] Unmitigated, power-backed self-interest replaced cooperation, negotiation, and exchange. Other European powers, once they ventured outward, shared practices of domination, which were shaped by the new middle-class, state-backed capitalism rather than by the dynamics of feudalism. While the ruthless use of power was visible and horrifying, the processes of capital accumulation remained distant and invisible.

The landfall of the Spanish in the Americas did involve a discovery. Europe's intellectual elites discovered that the biblical view of the world was wrong—an unanticipated problem of major proportions. The supreme reference work for the shape of the world, for all things natural, and for divine-rights political theory did not mention the existence of peoples like the Arawak whom the surprised *conquistadores* "found," and their premature label, Indian-Asians, peeled off quickly. Under the hegemony of the Latin Church, all "facts" of nature and society "ultimately had to be made intelligible in terms of one or another component of the canon." When the peoples of the Americas burst into European view and worldviews, the canon collapsed, and guidelines for political action had to be developed from scratch: Were the newly found beings human? If so, could they be enslaved? Could "just war" be waged against them and Spanish rule affirmed? In Spain, the issues were addressed in public disputations by eminent theologians with or without American experience as well as by experts on canon or civil law. In the next century and after, trans-European political theorists—such as Hugo Grotius, Samuel von Pufendorf, John Locke, Montesquieu, and Thomas Hobbes—joined the debate. The new reference point, "the Indians" (West Indians), replaced the Bible, inspired by Semitic culture, and the texts of Greek antiquity, inspired by a "Black Athena." Empiricism in the social sciences emerged out of the factual arrival of peoples in a worldview that had no place for them. Imprisoned in their cultural assumptions, however, scholars embarked on a new Eurocentric discourse, projecting European, later also North American, virtues and vices onto Others. The empirical impetus was deflected into an "imaginary ethnography" in which Europeans emerged as civilized, the Others as primitive. The "explanation" had to jus-

tify Europe's domination, culturally and economically. God as the supreme being receded in practical importance behind Europeans as superior beings. In the process,
the trans-European lay intellectual elite gained ascendancy over the trans-European
organized clergy as interpreters of societies. In its reduced sphere, the Latin Church,
until then victorious over all critics/heretics (see chap. 4.3), faced the challenge of
Puritans and Protestants, who organized themselves in rival church structures.[2]

Three aspects of the new political theory were of particular importance: the depiction of the Others as depraved, the construction of a state of nature, and the connection between the "new" peoples and the Old World. First, the initial labeling
emerged immediately upon conquest when Columbus's original admiration for the
simplicity and hospitality of Arawak society gave way to a negative categorization
under the guise of ethnographic description. The customs of the First Peoples of the
Americas—whether foodways or sexuality, family life or political structures, agriculture or manufacture, habits of work, hierarchy or private property—were scrutinized
with European culture as the referent to determine whether the Indians were similar
human beings endowed with reason. Those arguing from economic interest for enslavement found the objects of these debates, living people, wanting in all respects:
they ate spiders, worms, raw meat, and the cannibals among them even ate their
neighbors. They practiced sodomy, incest, and homosexuality. They did not transform nature into agri-, material, or other culture. They evidenced no work discipline
and thus lacked control over their natural desires. They had no "natural" hierarchy
of men over women and children. With regard to property relationships, they neither
acknowledged the sanctity of private property nor amassed riches. In short, they were
"beastly, wild and cruel," without "obedience" and "royalty." Those who argued for
the Indians' humanity acknowledged numerous faults, but saw remedies in Christianization, work discipline, and Hispanicization (later: Europeanization). War was
justified if the Indians refused to accept the right of the Christians to civilize them.
A minority, Bartolomé de Las Casas among them, countered that European legal doctrines did not necessarily apply to other peoples and contested the Church's claim to
the power to assign lands not mentioned in the Bible to Christian rulers.[3]

Second, subsequent theorists argued that the new peoples lacked governmental
structures or knew only tyranny, as in the case of the Aztecs; that they lived in a
state of nature without private property[4] and without written law or regulations, in
which anarchy reigned and violence was the supreme arbiter. An opposing school of
thought contrasted an ideal, peaceful state of nature—before sin and expulsion from
paradise—with the shortcomings of later governmental states, including European
ones. In his *Second Treatise on Government* (1690), Locke castigated the doctrine
"that all government in the world is the product only of force and violence, and that
men live together by no other rules but that of beasts, where the strongest carries
it, and so lay a foundation for perpetual disorder and mischief, tumult, sedition, and
rebellion." He then described a state of "equality, wherein all the power and jurisdiction is reciprocal." Views of the foundation of societies had come full circle. In a way,
Locke's position reflected Columbus's initial view of Arawak society.[5]

Third, the intellectual *conquistadores* from Spain, France, and England connected their constructions of social organization and state structures of the Others as "primitive" and of themselves as civilized by linear time, through which the Others might move upward to the level of Europeans. Societies in their "infancy" had to develop according to an ulterior goal, a secular *telos*, from wild beastliness to a rule of law and protection of private property. Reason would impel human Others to leave their miserable condition and recognize orderly, state-enforced civil freedom. This process could be aided by the highly developed Europeans: Jesuits in their *reducciones* would teach religion, and *encomenderos* would inculcate the merits of work.[6]

Compared to the open exchange between earlier Christians, Muslims, and Jews, this new fixed point of reference, the European Self, if with variations, had obvious advantages for its proponents. In the Mediterranean World, Arab-Islamic and Jewish societies had been more highly developed than those of Latin (as distinct from Byzantine) Christendom. Through crusading warfare and papal pronouncements, the Latin Church was involved in dismantling the spiritual and worldly claims of its Christian competitor, Byzantium, and then juxtaposed Christians and non-Christians in a binary opposition that prevented negotiation, brokerage, and regulated coexistence as practiced by the merchants of the Mediterranean. Subsequent to the "discoveries" in 1492 and thereafter, Europeans used themselves as the measure of civilization and appointed themselves gatekeepers over the political and economic theory that governed contacts across the globe. This Self-Other dichotomy—in which Indians appeared as indolent, sexually licentious, without a gender hierarchy, and living in anarchy—involved Europeans' projections of feared and actual shortcomings of their own onto Others: with regard to bloody sacrifice, biblical texts referred to human beings offered to God; with regard to cannibalism, the Holy Communion involved a reception of the body of Jesus; with regard to women, subservience had to be secured against their repeated attempts to change their assigned position; as for sexuality, prostitutes and courtesans migrated to Rome; as for work, Spanish hidalgos and upper classes detested it, as did the first immigrants in Spanish America or Spanish Manila, in Dutch Batavia or English Virginia. In a trans-European consensus, they expected the ethnic Others to labor for them, just as social Others, the lower estates, labored at home. As for societal organization, when European explorer-exploiters came upon functioning communities from West Africa to India to the Americas, they chose not to learn new languages and acquire knowledge of Others' rules and practices—and created chaos, in Indian Ocean economic relations as well as among American populations.

The gatekeepers were belligerents in a struggle over the power to define whose interests would determine the pattern of order, who labeled whom as anarchic, despotic, ungovernable. To paraphrase Todorov, a different system of exchange, of everyday life, and of norms and spirituality, was in the view of European observers equivalent to the absence of a system, and from this supposed absence an inferior condition or even bestiality could be inferred. David Landes's exposition of Europeans' accumulation of knowledge and their concomitant ascendancy over other peoples of the world (which constituted "modernity") skirts the issue of their lack of understanding of personal relations and of their lack of tolerance for a coexistence of alternative options and overlooks the issues of power, armament, capital, and definitions of property relations.[7]

European hegemony, however, was complex. Political philosophers' concepts of the state differed from those of the perpetrators of conquest. Imperial governments, merchants and entrepreneurs in the cores, grantees of large tracts of land, and small settlers in the colonies held widely varying perspectives on the societies to be established. The interests of emigrants, the rationale of core-controlled accumulation, and the designs of political rule often contradicted each other. The French government intended its "New France" in the St. Lawrence valley to be a copy of France in Europe, complete with social hierarchies, with *seigneurs* and *habitants*. The latter, like peasants throughout history, followed their own interests and moved off by going into the fur trade. "New Spain," which was meant to replicate Iberian institutions, became the colonists' self-creation. In British America, some economically minded recipients of large tracts of land offered religious refuge to attract immigrants—for example, Catholics in Lord Baltimore's Maryland and dissenters of many persuasions in William Penn's *silvae* or woods. The Puritans, who set out to create a purified "New England," built profit-oriented mercantile communities engaged in the slave trade.[8]

In European societies, the educated bourgeoisie fashioned its views of colonial acquisitions and their inhabitants through literary works. Whereas the political philosophy of the time was trans-European and the drive for independence intercolonial, literatures were products of particular societies and particular colonizing experiences, as a comparison of Spanish and English literature demonstrates. In Spanish writings of the Golden Age, the absence of "Indios" reflects the near-genocide committed by the conquerors, and the depiction of the new world as a variant of the old mirrors the aspirations of the administrative elites. The male return migrant from Spanish America was typified as a *nouveau riche* in search of status and a suitable bride, often a braggart but always kindhearted. Returning women, beautiful and rich, appeared as desirable marriage partners. Black people, visible in Spanish society as "Negroes" and "Mulattoes" and thus more difficult to exclude from representation than Indios, might be depicted, in the case of women, as kindhearted and hardworking and, in the case of men, as roguish, but they were generally shown to be slothful and lazy if left to their own devices. Such an image may have been a continuation of earlier characterizations of "Turks," with the ethnic label changed. Individuals from the original Americans—as Indian "princes" or "princesses"—were accepted in Spanish society without reference to *limpieza de sangre*, the boundary construction that excluded Jews and Moors at home.[9]

In English and, with different emphasis, in French literature, the Other was "the Indian," heathen and always male, and "his" squaw. The heathen could be a "noble savage" but became "bloodthirsty" when not ceding his land graciously to immigrants. Literary imagination and colonial "eyewitness accounts" described cultural contact as Christianization or, in the genre of the "captivity narrative," in terms of the torture of Whites, women in particular, by Reds. Literature did not portray either the captivity of Native women in White male power relationships or the acculturation of European immigrants to Native American societies. The cultural hegemony of the cores also meant that the new colonial Euro-Creole cultures were hardly reflected in literary discourse and history of the Old Worlds.[10]

When travel to the colonies was difficult but imperial achievements were part of political rhetoric in the cores, the means of information, beyond literary reflection, extended from Richard Hakluyt's *The Principal Navigations, Voyages, Traffiques, and Discoveries of the English Nation* of 1589 to a voluminous body of travel narratives. Atlases and manuals for navigation took up where medieval cartographers had left off and informed the reading public of "foreign" ways of life, curiosities, manners, and customs. Dutch painters rendered images of Dutch investments in Spitsbergen fish processing, Swedish weapons factories, North African towns, and Surinam plantations. The voc in Amsterdam had letters cast for Asian languages in order to export them to the colonies and to develop printing under its control. After the invention of photography in the 1850s, visual reproductions of picturesque sights of the colonial empires could be admired in bourgeois homes. On the other hand, a scholarly endeavor that took other cultures seriously, such as the University of Leiden's Oriental press, remained without societal impact.[11]

Emigration necessitated a reconceptualization of mercantilist thought, of assumptions about population growth, and of the place of paupers in society. Departure for purposes of acquiring land for a monarch had been subsidized, but the emigration of economically active parts of a state's population was detrimental, internally because of the loss of tax revenues and externally because of the potentially competitive position. While the French government under Colbert forbade emigration in 1669, its flight-inducing persecution of the Huguenots in 1685 indicated that religio-ideological conformity counted for more than mercantilist doctrine. Montesquieu, in the middle of the eighteenth century, still accepted Colbert's stance: "The usual effect of colonization is to weaken the mother country without populating the new land. Men must remain where they are." On the other hand, a Spanish author, anticipating Malthusian ideas about population pressures, advocated emigration (or, alternatively, celibacy) as early as 1681.

In general, European population and economic theorists agreed that states should rid themselves of vagrants, beggars, and criminals, male or female: such burdensome classes, in the process of emigration, would transform themselves into revenue-producing colonial assets. A Spanish writer of 1742 argued that criminals condemned to penal servitude who were joined in marriage with prostitutes would produce excellent colonists. Spanish Gypsies, 12,000 in number, should be transported to colonize the Orinoco river region in Venezuela. A century and a half later, the British government was to ship off "surplus" populations. Dynasties' "subjects," human material to be used or discarded, were constructed as "misfits" at home but as contributing to the glory and the revenues of the "home" state in distant colonies. Just as the flag sometimes followed commerce, so political theorists followed elite interests.[12]

While sending out "misfits" indicated a core-colony hierarchy, the grand juxtaposition of depraved Natives and civilized Europeans diverted attention from Euro-Europeans' practice of of discriminating against colony-Europeans. European elites constructed themselves as the only culturally pure, and thus superior, relegating their emigrant cousins, the White colonials, to an intermediate, dependent status. Early immigrant groups, in turn, often considered themselves "founding peoples" who were entitled to discriminate against later arrivals, especially if they were of a different cultural background. The White and mixed-origin colonials, who acted in their own interests, much to the discomfiture of the respective companies and governments, held an important advantage over the non-White colonized. They spoke the language of the metropole and knew its systems of reference; thus they could communicate and raise demands. Creole elites of the colonial polities in the Americas enjoyed leverage "at home." Colonized populations administered by transient bureaucrats, such as those of India, could not communicate in the reference systems of the core. Thus the Age of Revolution after the 1760s came to involve not only the struggles of the fourth estate, the lower classes in Europe, but also of the new Euro-Afro-Indio American peoples in their bid for self-government. In the British colonies in North America, the colonists raised the double question: were they, constitutionally, Englishmen, Englishwomen, and English children? Were they to bail out the mismanaged East India Company? When the island English did not yield in their claim of superior status, the colonial English (and all others) separated as self-styled "Americans" in 1776. In Spanish and Portuguese Latin America, natural rights ideology and the European core's loss of power during its internal wars (1796–1815) permitted Euro-Creole polities to achieve independence by the 1820s. Caribbean-Creole slaves in French Haiti followed the same principles of individual rights and societal self-government. On the other hand, the colonized non-White peoples achieved independence only a century and a half later. The independence of "White" colonies and of "Colored" ones involved further reconstructions of European self-views among the several intellectual, political, and economic elites.[13]

11.2 Material Culture in Everyday Life

Cultural exchanges between Asian, American, European, and African peoples in the sphere of material life involved the everyday life of all classes, introducing new foodways, changing dress and consumption patterns, and providing luxury goods en masse and new medicines. Nonmigrating people were supplied with products from the plantation complex. Ever larger numbers of sailors saw other cultures, reported about their experiences, engaged in the trade of foreign goods, and produced children in liaisons with Others; laborers transported alien wares; market and shopkeeping women traded new goods. Lives changed, as did technologies. Intercontinental voyaging necessitated innovations in ship construction and utilized knowledge gathered over centuries by fishermen and coastal traders. These, in turn, sailed further into the oceans. Portuguese sailors, for example, manned the Massachusetts whaling fleet. Traditionally, sailors were skilled and "expected to be treated with respect and consulted about matters that concerned them, including the course and duration of the voyage." With the rising demand for crews, nautically unskilled sons of peasant families migrated to the large coastal centers of Europe and Southeast Asia, and on board the command lines came to function from the top down. Many of these plough-to-ship migrants who survived the hardships of life at sea settled in distant port towns and formed partnerships with local women. Those who returned might marry immigrant maids from their own rural culture who staffed the ever-increasing number of merchant and middle-class households in port towns.[14]

Medieval Mediterranean medicine had incorporated Arab, Jewish, and Eastern knowledge until, at the beginning of the modern period, narrow-minded Christian physicians rejected wisdom "from so strange a place" as the Levant or India. The healing arts came under attack: wise women were burned as witches, and the Church designated washing, and thus cleanliness, as a Jewish and Muslim practice. In the past, "during the centuries when Arab medicine had reigned supreme in Europe, Venice had been the chief emporium for the sale of drugs." In the sixteenth century, the Americas provided new drugs—sassafras, coca, aromatic balsams, the antimalarial quinine, and an untold number of other new substances. Merchants recognized the profit potential, and the southern German Fuggers granted a loan to the king of Spain in return for a monopoly on the antisyphilitic holywood lignum vitae (*Guaiacum sanctum*). Travelers, explorers, and sailors sent home unusual plants and other curiosities. A Canadian plant, for example, was delivered by a Portuguese sailor to a Paris apothecary. In 1569 the Spanish medical savant Nicolás Bautista Monardes, who had studied the Greek-Arab medical tradition, published the first magisterial work on the healing drugs from the Americas, which was translated into English, Italian, French, German, and Latin. Later, expeditions of scholars collected specimens; governments established botanical gardens; and when exploration changed to exploitation, botanists' research results became state secrets to be commercialized in plantation agriculture.[15]

As in the cases of crusader acculturation and the adoption of Muslim technology on the Iberian Peninsula, better-placed Europeans adopted whatever imports were superior or were considered superior to previously known goods. Within the Asian World, millions of pieces of porcelain were traded. When European merchants began to buy, a new trade circuit involved carriers, packers, wagoners, and sailors. To meet the demand, Chinese pottery owners increased imports of the fashionable "Mohammedan blue" coloring from Turkistan and sold their wares to Batavia. Via the Cape of Good Hope route, sailors shipped three million pieces of Chinese porcelain to Dutch ports in Europe from 1602 to 1657, and almost 200,000 pieces of Japanese porcelain in the next quarter century. Luxury goods, such as Asian porcelains and silks, changed tastes and refined artistic styles but were available to select classes only. Sensing an opportunity, seventeenth-century Delft potters began to imitate the Chinese blue-and-white style and found a ready market. In the eighteenth century, their cheap "chinoiserie" came to be considered "typically Dutch." In the process of adaptation, consumers Europeanized the origins of their new material culture.[16]

Cloth production in India and fur "harvesting" in North America and Russia changed dress codes, cottage production, and household economies, as well as the demand for and division of gendered labor across the world. According to Lemire, "India was a cornucopia of textiles, in colours, patterns, and qualities unrivalled in Europe." Fine cotton textiles, mass-imported by the Dutch and the English East India companies during the European "Indian craze" of the seventeenth century, attracted buyers "from the greatest gallants to the meanest cook-maids." To satisfy European tastes and imaginations, importing merchants created the "Indian" styles, which forced Madras workers to print Gujarat motifs mixed with Japanese ones and European patterns sent for adaptation. Indian producers invested until the British swamped the Asian markets with factory-made textiles produced by English men and women who had migrated from their villages to factory towns (see chap. 15.1).

The cottons of Peru and of New Mexico Hopi pueblos, which yielded finer fibers than plant strains of the Old Worlds, "were destined to provide the entire world's commercial crop." The plantation production of cotton expanded from colonies in the Americas to Egypt, East Africa, and India. Colonial lords extracted sisal and other fiber crops as tributes from local populations until sufficient profits permitted commercial cultivation for export markets. The lives of men and women engaged in fiber weaving and cloth production had to adapt to new materials, to new markets, and to the competition of labor elsewhere, labor often made cheap by power relations and lifestyles. New labor reservoirs, new production methods, and new regimes of control over workers had to be developed.

Colors and fashions spread from distant civilizations to Europe and from Europe outward. Alum from the eastern Mediterranean was needed to fix colors. From the Americas came the bright red of cochineal, from India, annatto, a red body paint and food color. Tropical legume trees replaced costly dyewoods, called *"brasil,"* a name given to the region where the new supply grew and where Tupí Indios were pressured into labor. At first, European merchants bought many of the new wares from local producers, whose dealings, in precolonial times, had involved mutual if unequal obligations rather than accounting practices. The new merchants, foreign to such societies based on interpersonal relationships, attached producers to distant commercial cores. Peoples in northern fur or southern slave procurement, in Indian texile production or in other occupations, accepted imported commodities in exchange for their products with no notion that they were entering into credit relationships.[17]

Regardless of continent and society, intercultural contact changed foodways of high- and low-status groups. African slaves imported roots and ways to prepare the new foods to the Americas. The potato and other food crops from the Americas nourished families from Europe to Asia. The profits to be derived from spices and flavorings initiated the European quest for the Asia trade. Soon mild stimulants—sugar, coffee, and tea from Asia, as well as cocoa from South America—also found a clientele. Intoxicating stimulants—such as tobacco, opium, and coca—fueled profits. Tobacco cultivation spread from the Caribbean and North America to the Mediterranean and Anatolia. Cigarmakers' migrations extended from Manila in the Philippines to Havana, Cuba, and from Hamburg, Germany, to Tampa, Florida. Semicultivated tropical fruits, nuts, and vegetables enriched European tables. Avocados, peppers, and many other semitropical delicacies were soon grown in Spain, and the tropicalization of Andalusia was part of a globalizing of tastes. Involuntary labor migrants, who began by producing food crops locally, were often mobilized to raise industrial crops for expanding distant populations.[18]

Since the fifteenth century, the European consumption of spices and flavorings from the Southeast Asian islands, India, and Ceylon expanded—the use of Moluccan spices, for example, increased by 500 percent from 1500 to 1620. The immense profits of merchant houses and worldwide trading connections were visible to the average consumer: in the German language, *Pfeffersack* (pepper bag) became a synonym for a wealthy merchant, and imported foods came to be called *Kolonialwaren.* Forced labor regimes lowered production costs and ever larger segments of the European and Euro-American populations could afford the spices that often made food palatable that had suffered from lack of means of preservation or refrigeration. Each increase in consumption, in turn, required a mobilization of labor, new patterns of migration, and sailors for additional ships. For example, pepper in its many varieties grew in most tropical climates and had been imported by Arab traders from India's Malabar Coast. By the 1560s, imports via Ottoman Alexandria and Beirut to Venice and Marseille, as well as via Portugal to Amsterdam, averaged 3.3 million pounds per year. By the early 1620s, when the Dutch had replaced the Portuguese traders, imports amounted to 6.7 million pounds annually. Vanilla—the dried pods of climbing wild orchids—had been gathered and prepared by local Indios. When the Totonac of the Veracruz region began to plant the vines, the French, whose rule extended far beyond the world of the Totonac, copied the process of cultivation and established vanilla plantations on the Indian Ocean island of Réunion in the 1860s. Aztec foodways became European practice via Indian Ocean labor.[19]

Mild stimulants had first reached the Europe of the crusades when Levantine cane sugar was imported. Cocoa beans, raised in orchards in Aztec southern Mexico and in Central America and consumed as *chocolatl,* were sufficiently valuable to be used as a medium of exchange in the Andes. By the mid-seventeenth century, cocoa sold in London, and mass cultivation expanded from northern South America to the Antilles and, later, to West Africa. Coffee, a fashionable drink in the Ottoman Empire, reached the European public from Arabia. The Dutch introduced coffee beans to Southeast Asia, coerced village labor to cultivate and harvest the crop, and sold Javanese coffee in Amsterdam. Transplanted to Latin America, coffee was grown on confiscated Indio lands by newly mobilized labor forces from Asia, America, and Europe.[20]

Tea illustrates the spread and impact of a mild stimulant across civilizations. Known for a long time because of its medical effects, consumption spread among the Chinese in the twelfth century and Japanese Zen Buddhists developed a tea-drinking ceremony. Indian, Armenian, Chinese, and other merchants traded it along the Darjeeling-Tibet-China "tea route," and Arab merchants introduced tea to Europe. In 1610, when Dutch East Indiamen carried their first cargo to the Netherlands, it was sold in pharmacies, and the voc subsidized enterprising doctors, who advocated tea in doses of fifty to two hundred cups daily per person as a cure-all. By 1660 the wealthy in Paris, Berlin, and London drank tea "served with the best sugar, in Japanese porcelain cups on inlaid tables, and with golden tea-spoons." By the end of the century, it reached the lower classes and was hawked in the streets. Sipping of tea in private social circles became a pastime for ladies; men, however, preferred public coffeehouses; thus socializing customs changed. When, in 1773, the British government imposed a surcharge on teas in the North American colonies in order to boost the East India Company's sagging finances, women organized a tea boycott; and men in Boston, after drinking Caribbean slave-produced rum, destroyed chests of tea. When attempting to punish the offenders, Britain faced the prospect of losing half a continent.

Twenty million pounds of dried "black" tea ready for consumption—the total European import in 1790—required 80 million pounds of fresh "green" tea leaves. Male and female pickers, under good conditions and by hard work, could pick up to 100 pounds a day: in other words, 800,000 workdays were required to meet the European demand. The transport of this quantity involved artisans in the manufacture of a quarter-million standard moisture-proof tea chests having an eighty-pound capacity. Carters carried them to ports; dockworkers loaded them; and sailors manned hundreds of ships to get them to their destinations. Twenty million pounds of tea translate—depending on customs of preparation—into 4.5 billion cups of tea. Perhaps the ageless colonizers' adage, rendered famous by Rudyard Kipling, "East is East and West is West—and never the twain shall meet" stands in need of revision: the drinking customs of the "little heathen Chinese" and "pig-tailed coolie" became a model for European elites, common people, and racists.[21]

Native peoples from the North American pueblos to the Andes showed Europeans how to cultivate plants of high nutritional value: maize (corn), sweet "potatoes," tomatoes, squash, yucca or manioc (cassava), and potatoes. By the 1570s, Seville hospitals served potatoes to their patients. Consumption spread rapidly through Europe, and potatoes became the mass staple of common people. In Prussia, the modernizing monarch had soldiers guard the new crop when peasants refused to grow the alien vegetable. In Ireland, potatoes served as a principal food of peasants impoverished by British colonial landlords and faced with rapid population growth. In China, migrations changed with the introduction of potato cultivation. Maize was grown by peoples in the Americas from the St. Lawrence valley to the plains of the La Plata. It nourished the first English colonists in the Massachusetts Bay Colony, was transplanted to Spain, and became a common crop in Europe; then Portuguese traders introduced it to Africa, India, and China. Manioc became a staple of diets in Southeast Asia.[22]

Tree harvesting and industrial crops involved changes in labor regimes, migration patterns, and production methods in colonies and cores. Colonial entrepreneurs exploited tropical hardwoods without reforestation. The British merchant marine relied on mass cutting of timber for shipbuilding, and the navy reserved a monopoly on mast pines from New England. Turpentine and rosin from American pitch pines entered European naval stores. New England lumber produced for the British Isles and for British colonies worldwide and the cutting of West African hardwoods to meet French demand were part of a process of deforestation that would change climates and send people into flight from environmental damage in the twentieth century. Rubber, first collected in Brazil by migrant Native and immigrant laborers, was later harvested in the Kongo by forced Native labor. After the British smuggled seeds to their Malayan possessions, the ubiquitous planters imported Tamil work gangs from southern India to cultivate rubber trees in an area extending from Singapore to Malacca. Well-capitalized firms replaced the planters and sent managers to run the plantation estates. Thus the planters' descendants became company employees or had to migrate again. The competing Dutch planted rubber trees on Sumatra with Javanese and Chinese laborers: "Local villages gave way to company towns." Palm oil harvested in West Africa lubricated the machinery of the industrial cores.

Wherever plant foods, industrial export crops, or range-cattle meats were mass-produced, the original peasant owners lost their land and were expelled, and local or imported native labor was exploited. Malnourishment resulted from the reduction of acreage for growing traditional subsistence foods. By the nineteenth century, the industrialization of food production included cereals, grown by immigrants with the help of seasonally migrating harvest workers in Argentina, the North American plains, and the southern Russian plains or by resident landlords with Polish migrant workers in the East Elbian plains—until mass production glutted world markets and agricultural machinery reduced demand for labor in the 1880s. Then surplus peasant and laborer families had to join new routes of global migrations (chap. 14). The millions of nineteenth-century voluntary and coerced Asian labor migrants had to be provided with rice and under British and French control, rice-producing areas expanded in Southeast Asia (chap. 15). In fields and in Rangoon mills, internal Burmese migrants prepared the crop for export to other parts of the British Empire. Around Bangkok, Thailand, canal construction linked the eastern with the northern rice-producing plains; Chinese and Thai migrants settled, and Muslim Malay and Laotian prisoners of war came as well as freed urban slaves. The third area of production, Cochin China, under French domination since 1861, produced largely for the Chinese market with Chinese merchants as intermediaries.[23]

Europe's middle and upper classes bought Chinese procelains and Indian silks; its growing populations survived only because of intercivilizational adaptation of South American basic foods. From the mid-nineteenth century onward, the ubiquitous immigrant Chinese cooks spread their ways of preparing food to the Anglo-American worlds. Although survival and cultural change depended on the achievements of all actors, White ideologies of superiority not only remained intact but also became more powerful.

Migration across time and societies had brought forth new peoples by cultural and genetic fusion within a framework of power hierarchies. In Europe, Circassian and North African slaves arrived; Syrian and Armenian traders moved across the continent; soldiers recruited from distant regions intermingled with settled populations; Jews and Christians, usually after conversion, intermarried. In Europe's colonial worlds, from the fifteenth to the nineteenth century, the massive exchange of genes and cultures among tens of millions of migrants and resident populations characterized the genesis of modern peoples. Given the power hierarchies between men and women and the sex ratios among Spanish, Chinese, British, or other emigrants, intercourse or intermarriage occurred, whether or not the societies of arrival and the women involved assented to it. Unions occurred voluntarily because of emotional attraction, regardless of what ideologues of Whiteness or other racial purity might have preached.

The trade emporia of the Indic World left vast populations untouched, but Asian migrants and African sailors moved over considerable distances; the populations of all port cities of the Indian Ocean, including East Africa, were mixed. Whether they were internal commercial, artisanal, or labor migrants, or whether they were refugees from famines or conquerors like the Manchu, migrants adapted, and their offspring became part of local society. In East Africa, children of mixed unions merged into one or the other component of local society; Southeast Asian societies incorporated Malay, Chinese, and Indian peoples, with some European participation.

Creole populations emerged in Latin America; in what came to be the United States, Black, White, and Red mixed. In two Métis cultures, French-Canadian *coureurs de bois* and Hudson's Bay Company Scots lived in stable unions with women of the First Nations, who assumed the role of cultural brokers. These societies' futures were determined by discourses of power. The French-language Métis on the Red River (part of today's Manitoba) were dispersed by land speculators using the Canadian government's tools of power. The English-language Métis of the Pacific coast constructed themselves as the White elite and founded *British* Columbia. As in all societies with a strong British ideology, the construction of Whiteness was particularly rigorous. Crèvecoeur's "new man" in Anglo-America, "that strange mixture of blood," was a mixture of Europeans. In the Age of Revolution, the "derived peoples" of the Americas explicitly defined themselves as different from the Europeans. Although in Latin America an anonymous eighteenth-century artist could depict sixteen different groups resulting from "crossbreeding," the Anglo-American construction of Whiteness—curiously inconsistent with the usual construction of "White" genes as dominant—emphasized "purity" and, under the "one drop" rule, segregated all those said to have one drop of non-White blood. Racist absolute categories skirt the question of how much white is White?[24]

Up to about 1820 approximately five Africans were brought to the Americas for each European migrant. All English Caribbean colonies had Black majorities by the end of the seventeenth century. When the slave system collapsed in the Caribbean, 90 percent of the peoples in Jamaica and Saint Domingue and approximately half of the Cuban, Puerto Rican, and other island populations were steeped in African-origin lifestyles. Three out of ten inhabitants in Buenos Aires were of African origin in 1830; one-third of the Brazilian population was in 1890. Only in the United States was the percentage lower. In the language of formal demography, the New World population of 700 million in the 1990s "include[d] roughly 100 million people of African ancestry," and "the African contribution to the Middle Eastern gene pool [was] roughly of the same proportion." African-origin people accounted for 50 percent of Bahrain's population in 1831, for more than one-third in Oman in 1835, and for less than one-third in Central Arabia (Nejd) in 1862–63. The contributions of Africans varied according to segregation: they were spread widely in Arabia, involved large segments of Latin America's peoples, but remained segregated to the extreme in the British Caribbean and the United States populations.[25]

The boundaries between White and Other were and are relatively fuzzy because of the White male usage of Colored female bodies, because of hierarchical but mutually advantageous "housekeeping" arrangements, and because of affectionate unions regardless of skin color or other distinguishing features. The Iberian Church's *limpieza de sangre* was an unenforceable postulate of a dogmatic, ideologically celibate group of men. The White-Colored dichotomy of Anglo-Atlantic cultures assumes that White is not a color. Exclusionary definitions of race and color have not been the sole prerogative of Europeans, as is shown by Chinese attitudes toward neighboring peoples, the concepts of light and dark among peoples of the South Asian subcontinent, and the hierarchization of light-skinned Arabs and black-skinned sub-Saharan Africans. As masters of the discourse, Europeans constructed themselves as models with no need for further improvement and saw lesser "Others" as susceptible to benevolent influences from Whites. Economic and political power relationships account for differences in status and explain why some learn to read and write while others are left to work with pick and shovel.

The White Euro-Christian constructs were propagated by religious or intellectual gatekeepers who were human beings corseting themselves into self-discipline and, in the case of the Latin Church, self-denial of sexuality. In his *Principal Navigations* of the late sixteenth century, Hakluyt claimed early on preeminence for the English, who "have excelled all the nations and people of the earth." Three centuries later, British administrators described "the typical African . . . [as] a happy, thriftless, excitable person, lacking self-control, discipline, and foresight," and vaunted themselves as endowed with "the ability to administer native races . . . one of the heritages of our race in which we may have just pride." The whole was "an exclusively masculine project," as Robert Miles has commented, and it remained so when White male political theorists deemed all human beings to be created equal.[26]

In eighteenth-century Euro–North American thought, scholars added their insights, or perhaps outlooks, to clerics' and administrators' pronouncements. Georges-Louis Leclerc de Buffon's fourty-four volume *Histoire naturelle* (1749–1804) ends with a classification in which the white race is held to be the norm. Deviations were to be explained by climate and/or "mild and apparently uncontagious" disease (Benjamin Rush) or the separate evolution of species (Voltaire). This quest for knowledge and systematization was self-centered, and Charles White's *Account of the Regular Gradation in Man* (1799) constructed a hierarchical "great chain of being" with "various degrees of intelligence and active powers suited to their [scientifically demonstrable] stations." White, who never traveled, based his whole scheme on hearsay from men returning from the colonies and placed Africans between Whites and apes. Like other male commentators, he showed a peculiar concern with reproductive organs and miscegenation. Across civilizations and ages, Otherness was constructed not only by skin color but also by alleged sexual characteristics and practices.

"White over Black," became the basic pattern of interpretation. Since the Bible had been disposed of as a source of knowledge, the story of the Christian God's monogenetic creation, which made human beings equal, was challenged by a theory of the polygenetic origins of human races.[27] By considering non-White races incapable of advancing toward civilization on their own, administrators and missionaries assigned themselves a civilizing raison d'être that would justify appropriate salaries. Should the "dark-skinned races" not listen, exterminating warfare might be justified against the "colored vermin." In these color hierarchies, Europeans also classified the "lesser elements" of their own people and their neighboring peoples. The instability of French governments, according to Josiah Clarke Nott, an Alabama physician and co-author of *Types of Mankind* (1854), was said to be due to "the turbulent dark men in the nation" and the peripheral labor-supplying European peoples were regarded as olive or dark and Jews as non-White. The thesis of Darwin's scholarly *Origin of Species* (1859) was recast in terms of Social Darwinism. Superiority and thus the justification of exploitation would last for a long time, since the other races had to progress from an infantile state to a mature stage, a process that "must necessarily take centuries to accomplish satisfactorily," as a British government official opined.[28]

Debates about the end of slavery had ramifications for racist thought. For Afro-Caribbean and Afro-American abolitionists, equality was at issue; for Euro-American abolitionists, however, African-origin people were human but not necessarily acceptable as fellow citizens. In the 1770s, people defined as Black amounted to 0.02 percent of the French population, 0.2 percent in Britain, between 2 percent (Massachusetts) and just under 50 percent (South Carolina) in the United States, and up to 90 percent in the Caribbean sugar islands. Governments developed a new rhetoric, inflating numbers and devising regimes of control. The French government opined: "The Negroes are multiplying every day in France. They marry Europeans, the houses of prostitutions are infected by them, the colors mix, the blood is changing." Segments of the 1830s abolitionist movement in the United States advocated return of free Blacks to Africa, where Liberia was founded for them. After the 1860s, racist pogroms occurred across the "white" worlds: anti-Black lynch mobs in the United States and anti-Jewish riots in tsarist Russia; mutilation and death in the Belgian Congo; sadistic or sexually abusive punishment of male and female laborers in Dutch Java; extermination by labor of Chinese coolies in Spanish Cuba. Racists developed ever more elaborate theories of racial superiority (Joseph-Arthur de Gobineau, 1853–55), or resorted to plain invective on the "Nigger Question" (Thomas Carlyle, 1849). The victory of Japan over Russia in 1905 was discussed in terms of "yellow" over "white."[29]

Strategies of capital accumulation in the cores benefited from racial constructions and contributed to them through labor regimes and racialized hiring practices of plantations, mines, and factories. The peoples considered inferior, whether from the European periphery, Africa, or Asia, supplied the bound and free labor forces. Race, ethnicity, and class intersected. While within White societies segments of the laboring classes were ethnicized, racialization occurred on a global scale. Within each segment, gender hierarchies placed men over women. In the eighteenth and nineteenth centuries, most European emigrants of modest means shared this ideology.

III

Intercontinental Migration Systems
to the Nineteenth Century

Although the Afro-Atlantic Slave Migration System came to an end in the 1870s, three other intercontinental systems generated mass migrations during the nineteenth century after having been limited in volume and scope: the Atlantic Economies System, the Russo-Siberian System, and the Asian Contract Labor System with its extension across the Pacific. Settlement and urbanization in Russia, part of European urbanization processes, developed into a distinct and separate system (chaps. 12 and 13). The dual Atlantic pattern—the growing Western European connection to North America and the Iberian connection to Central and South America—merged into a single system that encompassed territories from Poland and Ukraine to the Pacific coast of the Americas (chap. 14). Because of the impending end of African slavery, the mobilization of colonial labor reserves in Asia began early in the nineteenth century. Indigenous free migration systems, in particular that of the Chinese diaspora, and imperially imposed mobility, particularly in British India, were tapped by European powers—and later by the United States (chap. 15). Until its resumption in the mid-twentieth century, racist exclusion reduced but did not interrupt this migration. Atlantic migration came to a sudden stop at the beginning of World War I in 1914; from an economic point of view, however, the Great Depression (1929–39) was more important as a harbinger of changes. The two interwar decades were a period of stagnation and temporary changes (chaps. 17 and 18).

Routes changed, and the transportation revolution speeded the mobility of people and products. Construction work in itself involved vast migrations: 20,000 conscripted Egyptian *fellaheen* dug the Suez Canal, and European and Asian migrants by the tens of thousands were involved in digging the Panama Canal. Eastward to Asia, the Suez Canal cut travel time by half after 1869; westward from the Americas, the Panama railroad (1855) and the opening of the Panama Canal in 1914 facilitated travel and transport.

With the consolidation of European–North American imperialism, these migration systems supplied labor to wherever capital needed workers and provided options other than toil at home for laboring men and women. Wherever they arrived, free and bound workers developed forms of resistance and articulated their own interests.

The Russo-Siberian migrations, which supplied labor and settlers internally, interacted with the Atlantic System—through Jewish, Polish, and Ukrainian migrations—
and with the Asian-Pacific System through Chinese contract labor in eastern Siberia.
The once-central Mediterranean Sea had become a backwater to the oceans, and the
once-marginal area of Europe north of the Alps became a lively region, in which internal migration by far surpassed the transatlantic moves and the thin stream to the
colonies.

12

Europe: Internal Migrations from the
Seventeenth to the Nineteenth Century

In the seventeenth century, shifts of power between states, rivalries between empires, and further wars of religion changed patterns of migration—though some patterns did remain intact. Surplus agrarian populations moved in search of vacated fertile lands, but also of ever more marginal lands: the devastation of much of Central Europe during the Thirty Years' War (1618–48) necessitated repopulation, and the expansion of the Ottoman Empire (beginning with the battle of Mohács in 1526) and its retreat after 1699 caused population exchanges and increased checkerboard patterns of settlement in the Balkans and the south of Russia. In highly developed Urban Italy and the Urban Netherlands, processes of deindustrialization and sectoral economic change—in particular, in textiles—resulted in massive downward or upward adjustments of labor forces that were often predominantly female. Regional labor migration systems emerged. Mercantilist policies and urbanization processes mobilized large numbers of men and women, and political dissenters had to go into exile.[1]

Migrants based their decisions on opportunities said to be available elsewhere, which they assumed to be better than those in the home communities. Regionally distinctive economic developments reduced the chances for leading an independent life in some areas; in other places, they provided cheap land for farmers, seasonal employment for rural laboring men (whose wives and children maintained the home base), and better job opportunities and cash wages for urban laborers and domestics. Some governments offered newcomers freedom of religion, political liberties, or economic privileges. The Netherlands, for example, for two centuries proved "most attractive to those longing for greater prosperity, more freedom, and, in many cases, for the perfect combination of the two." This view foreshadowed the ideology of unlimited opportunities in "America." Prospective migrants expected hard work; few looked for gold in the streets. Return migrants and letters from emigrants also reduced overblown hopes to realistic expectations.[2]

12.1 Continuities and New Patterns from Medieval to Modern Migrations

In some cases, the migration patterns of the medieval and early modern period (see chaps. 2–5) continued; in other cases, they were adapted, totally changed, or brought to an end. First, mobility resulting from political rule and administration changed. Rulers and their aides and entourages had become sedentary in capital cities, but colonial expansion imposed a new mobility on administrators and soldiers across unprecedented distances (chaps. 6–8).[3] Similarly, the institutions of the Church had become sedentary, but they sent religious men and women as missionaries into the colonized realm of other religions and civilizations. The trans-European nobility, which was losing its functions while retaining its wealth, on occasion extended its marriage market. U.S. industrialist families married children to noble families of Europe to gain access to titles in exchange for providing access to capital. The nobility and, increasingly, bourgeois families might alternate between town houses and countryseats, taking their servants with them. The upper strata of European societies remained mobile but did not engage in permanent migration.

Second, the politics of war involved higher degrees of mobility as a result of military drafts and multiyear service as well as the dislocation of civilian populations. Soldiers of many ethnicities migrated to serve in the Dutch and Swedish armies; Prussian kings hired men from distant places; and Swiss peasants continued to emigrate to armed service. In the *Kriegshandwerk* (craft of war), the drilling period was a kind of apprenticeship, and soldiers' migrations may have resembled those undertaken by skilled artisans. Migrant soldiers served in the regular armies; mercenaries or legionnaires were only hired for armies in the colonies.[4] Weapons makers and military instructors also continued to migrate—for example, German specialists went to London, and English naval officers to St. Petersburg. They often served as technical innovators and, like industrial entrepreneurs, as organizers of masses of men. In imperial armies, professional soldiers of many ethnic backgrounds mingled, but common soldiers were assigned to ethnically or regionally distinct regiments. The Habsburgs' multiethnic officer corps formed a non-national elite.[5]

Draft-based army recruitment separated young men from their families and placed them in all-male institutions. In Russia, draftees served for twenty-five years (almost for life) until the law was changed in 1874; in Prussia soldiers had to colonize eastern wastelands after their enlistment; demobilized Swedish soldiers had to be housed by villages and became informants about distant regions or tellers of tall tales. Forced migration involved soldiers bought and sold to obtain specific types of men or to raise money for a prince. Of the "Hessians" sold to the British crown for use in the North American colonies, thousands stayed behind as prisoners of war and then remained voluntarily as free laborers or settlers who brought over family members. Similarly, after the Swedish army's defeat at Poltava (Ukraine) in 1709, surviving Swedish soldiers settled and married locally. Mass conscription during the French

Revolution and during Napoleonic imperialism mobilized millions. The march on Moscow in 1812 involved 0.6 million French, Italian, Dutch, Swiss, Austrian, Prussian, and other German men. The French cultural impact—exerted first by refugee members of the nobility and then by soldiers left behind—was as visible as the impact of voluntary migrants elsewhere. The multiethnic composition of armed forces was one reason for the introduction of "uni-forms," which were tailored to reflect soldiers' traditional home costumes.[6]

Third, religious migrations changed as the flight from religious persecution declined, while the withdrawal of privileges for religious minorities, in the context of the shift from negotiated subject to homogenized citizen status, induced group migrations. Old Believers in Russia, who had rebelled against reforms in 1697–98, left for Siberia; Orthodox Serbs, in 1690, fled from Ottoman rule to southern Hungary while Muslims fled from Habsburg rule; Mennonites and Doukhobors left Europe for North America. States reimposed control over powerful religious orders: the Spanish government expelled the Jesuits in 1767, and the Austrian government dissolved monasteries in the 1780s, releasing 36,000 of the secluded clerics. Increasing religious tolerance, on the one hand, could lead to riots, as when Polish Catholics expelled Greek Orthodox Catholics and Protestants after the king had granted equal status to them; or it could generate in-migration, as when the Russian trading community grew after receiving permission to build an Orthodox church in Ottoman Istanbul in the 1770s.

Fourth, the new nineteenth-century constructions of nation-states and of race could not accommodate non-national ethno-religious groups, such as Jews and Gypsies. Parallel to the decline of the Polish-Lithuanian, then Russian, Jewish community, Western European societies had again permitted Jewish settlement and granted emancipation, first in revolutionary France in 1790–91 and as late as 1867–96 in the Habsburg state. During Europe's colonial expansion, Jewish merchants intensified contacts with coreligionists in Arab lands and in Asia or founded new corresponding firms in distant places. Intercolonial migrations continued past traditions of mobility. Jews from Aleppo and Damascus, for example, migrated to Bombay. Amsterdam Jews migrated to Dutch Surinam. Within Europe, their position improved from the lack of secure legal standing (the central feature of middle-class society), via an important role in the commercial-capitalist economy, to integration into nation-states, despite lingering anti-Semitism.[7] Much smaller in number, Gypsies remained marginalized, and contemporary authorities as well as later scholarship constructed the group not as one more ethnicity but as a marginal group marked by a criminal pathology. They traveled in search of work, specializing in small repairs or other tasks of low prestige. Itinerant traders as well as ethnic Gypsies developed elaborate ways of traveling, sending advance parties to explore the demand for their skills as well as possible campgrounds. The "service nomads" showed "organizational flexibility and willingness to move and to switch occupations, which enabled them to fill gaps in the host economy."[8]

Fifth, in contrast to the insecurely positioned Gypsies and Jews, men and women from the hegemonic new middle-classes moved freely. Highly skilled experts criss-crossed Europe and, increasingly, the Atlantic World: Dutch drainage experts, Swiss dairymen and -maids, cabinetmakers from Germany, bakers from Switzerland, Italian tile-laying craftsmen. Polish and Scottish traders moved across the continent; industrialists traveled to learn about new technologies; even delegations of farmers occasionally went abroad to seek information about foreign methods of cultivation.[9] The educational migration of students declined with the increasing density of institutions of higher learning. But young men who departed from small towns to attend universities often remained in larger cities, where they found more profitable employment. In some societies, the sons of wealthy families traveled for some years in England and France—rather than in Italy as in earlier times. Upon their return, they might invite, say, English mechanics to work in their families' factories. A Leiden-educated great elector of Brandenburg, for example, recruited Dutch farmers to help cultivate the fens in his realm.[10]

Migration patterns remained gendered. In the child-rearing portion of their life-cycle, women's migration frequency was lower than that of men. As before, they moved across shorter distances, usually into domestic service and textile production. The influence of rural women on child-rearing patterns, eating habits, and other aspects of the reproductive sphere in urban middle-class households remains a neglected field of study. Also lacking are studies of the transfer of urban lifestyles by women upon their return to their home villages. As wives and sometimes as co-workers in family units, women were part of experts' migrations. Young women, in search of education, migrated to countries where universities would accept them. In the nineteenth century, they had to go into political exile.

Given the gender-specific allocation of moral liabilities, women from villages might have to flee to the anonymity of towns and cities because of pregnancy out of wedlock and similar reasons for being ostracized. Marriage migration, which once sent women to patrilocal families, was reoriented toward the establishment of independent households. In some areas of emigration, young wives were kept in the groom's family to bind the son to home, kin, and neighbors. On the other hand, distant labor markets with jobs only for men induced women to follow in sequential migration to distant marriage markets, either by their own means or with prepaid tickets as brides. Increasingly, women developed their own routes into independent wagework and accounted for two-fifths of the transatlantic labor migrations.[11]

Thus the myriads of small migrations, whether temporary or permanent, defy spatial definition. They supplemented the three major types of mobility within distinct spaces: agricultural, labor, and cityward migrations that were one-way or circular. The increasing system of border controls instituted by nation-states did not deter migrants from pursuing their goals, and the transnational labor markets defied nationalist exclusiveness.

As in earlier centuries, expanding rural populations sent young men and women to new land. The adage that peasants are rooted in the soil holds true only as long as their crops sustain them. Peasant families could till their leaseholds as their lords and the cyclical nature of the economy permitted. Changes in rural life and production expanded the social geography of villagers' lives. Landowners changed long-term tenures into renegotiable short-term leases in order to increase the flexibility and profitability of their estates, forcing tenant families to migrate and take seasonal wage-labor. Such proletarianized men and women reached their maximum earning capacities early in life; they married young and raised children in young adulthood. If they were in danger of becoming impoverished, poor-law wardens would admonish them to search for work in the region or to migrate elsewhere, leading them perhaps to drift into urban concentrations. Typically, overseers of the poor dropped off orphaned boys and girls as young as thirteen years of age in London to fend for themselves. If the poor had to be mobile, the rich could be more so. In Terling, Essex, in 1671, 40 percent of the great farmer families had lived in the village for only one generation, and none for more than two; of the yeomen and craft families, only 13.8 and 28.6 percent respectively had remained sedentary over three generations; of the laboring poor, no more than 19.3 percent stayed that long.[12] Inheritance and dowry, soil exhaustion and new agricultural techniques affected each succeeding generation's decision to stay or to leave.[13]

Among sheep- and cattle-raising peasants, one type of rural mobility continued unabated. In Mediterranean Europe, transhumance—that is, the pasturing of livestock in the mountains in summer and in coastal lowlands in winter—involved the mobility of herdsmen and their families. In northern Europe, cattle drives, for which the American West would become famous in the nineteenth century, lasted from the early modern period (see chap. 3.2) to the invention of the refrigerator car (map 12.1). Cattle were moved from Scotland to England and from Eastern Central Europe to the Germanies and the Netherlands. In the Hungarian plains, where cattle merchants of Transylvanian, Armenian, Greek, and Bulgarian background leased summer grazing lands, seasonally migrating Romanian herdsmen guarded the animals. Romanian harvest laborers came; servants met at annual hiring fairs with local lords; itinerant craftsmen plied their trades in villages too small to support specialized craftsmen. Thus the region from the Balkans through the Hungarian plains to the Polish-Lithuanian lands was crisscrossed by traders, artisans, and transport laborers, and oppressive lords sent peasant families fleeing in search of better conditions.[14]

On the Iberian Peninsula, transhumance originated with Muslim agriculturalists' introduction of merino sheep. Under Christian rule, a Castilian sheep-raisers' guild, the Mesta, monopolized the wool trade, which in 1492 was disrupted by the expulsion of the Jews. Decades elapsed before credit relations were rebuilt. By the mid-sixteenth century, 3.5 million sheep were grazed in flocks of 1,000 or more. The herdsmen and sometimes their wives and children traversed distances of 150 to 450

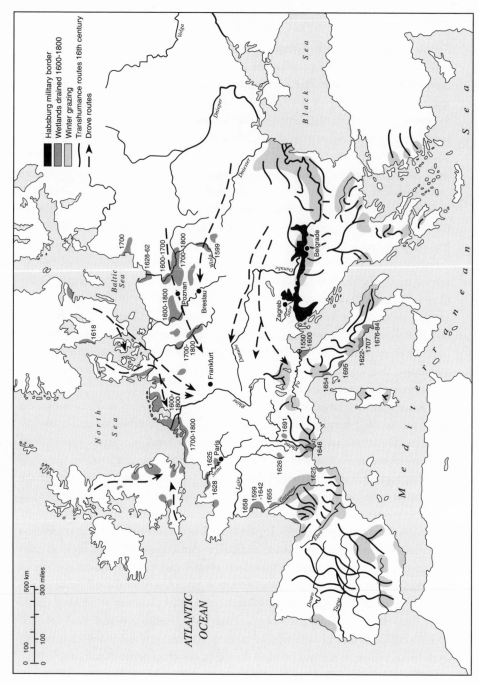

12.1   European Rural Migrations, 16th–18th Centuries

Habsburg military border
Wetlands drained 1600-1800
Winter grazing
Transhumance routes 16th century
Drove routes

miles (250–750 kilometers) in the spring and fall. Herdsmen, like teamsters, were recruited from northern Castilian highland towns, Madrid, Valladolid, Toro, Zamora, Salamanca, and Tordesillas.[15] Sheep "walks" were also common in Provence, Algeria, and in the Balkans where transient herdsmen were called "Vlachs" (also the name of an Aromanian people, who were probably of Roman, Greek, Bulgarian, and Albanian origin). The multilingual migrants seem to have influenced the area's linguistic history. They were integrated into long-distance trade. When wool markets in distant places contracted, disaster hit the Macedonian and Albanian villages. In southern France and on the Iberian Peninsula, transhumance declined in the eighteenth century, although remnants of it lasted up to the 1970s.[16]

Among tillers of the land, patterns of residence stabilized after 1600. Nevertheless, in France, Germany, and England, one-third to more than one-half of the population migrated at least once in their lifetimes in the seventeenth and eighteenth centuries. In seasonal rural-to-rural migrations (the first option), single men and women followed harvest cycles. Rural-to-urban migrations (the second option) continued unabated unless cottage production (a third option) kept people sedentary while raw materials or semifinished goods were transported to surplus labor forces. This proto-industrial regime had advantages for entrepreneurs and laborers. The initial investments for entrepreneurs were low because families engaged in cottage production provided their own looms, potter's wheels, or other tools. The laborers, not dependent on scarce cultivable land and land transferal by their parents, could marry earlier. The raising of large families was economically rational, given that children provided labor and thus income in this type of production. When production began to be concentrated in capitalized manufactures, however, the landless producer families became a surplus group, which involuntarily provided a large reservoir for internal migration and emigration.[17]

Adolescent sons and daughters of peasant families who wanted to continue to till the land chose a fourth option, the colonization of marginal soils nearby or of fertile areas farther away. In Western Europe, they cultivated uninhabitable marshes and peat bogs, terraced hillsides, or reoccupied abandoned terraces. In the Balkans, the Habsburg rulers distributed territories conquered from the Ottoman Empire to soldier-settlers and to immigrants recruited further west. In the southern Russian plains, nobles with their serfs settled from the 1760s on (chap. 13.2). In addition, the governments of France, Britain, Spain, Denmark sought settlers in limited numbers.[18]

Colonization of Marginal Lands Nearby

Young peasant couples without land moved to eke out a subsistence: in the Maritime Alps of southern France and adjoining Italy they terraced steep mountainsides; in Prussia and north of Bremen they colonized the peat bogs and river marshes; in Scandinavia they struggled with hostile northern climatic conditions.[19] Northern German fen colonization, which had been undertaken by peasant initiative as early as the

1620s, received support from the mercantilist Hanoverian-English government in the eighteenth century. Surveyors explored the region's potential for agriculture and peat digging, and the commissioner for settlement wanted settlers of medium age, in good health and industrious, with a wife used to work and several teenage children to help them in their endeavors. Two centuries later, in the 1890s, the Canadian secretary of the interior commented, "a stalwart peasant in sheep-skin coat . . . with a stout wife and a half-dozen children, is good quality" for settling the prairies. Rather than adventurous men on their own, families were needed, inasmuch as they could presumably form labor units having a settled domestic life and secure emotional bonds.

In the northern German region, families had to settle in sod huts but received grants in aid and temporary exemption from paying taxes. Owing to poor yields from agriculture and modest income from the sale of peat, men migrated to Dutch farms over summer. In retrospect, families summarized their "opportunities" as "*Den ersten sien Dot, den tweeten sien Not, den drütten sien Brot*"—death to the first generation, need to the second, bread to the third. The Dutch peat colonies (*veenkolonien*) of southern Groningen, on the other hand, had been transformed in the seventeenth century into populous, semi-industrialized villages by capitalist consortia.[20] To resettle villages devastated by plagues and wars in Brandenburg, East Prussia, and the Prussian-Lithuanian areas, the government after the 1740s recruited families and invited Protestant refugees from Salzburg. Drainage of the marshes of the Oder, Warthe (Warta), and Netze (Noteć) Rivers permitted some 300,000 or more men, women, and children to settle 60,000 homesteads in 900 new villages. Almost 20 percent of the population of Brandenburg-Prussia were immigrants or their children, who were placed in a dependent position vis-à-vis the lords of the soil. The king called the region the settlers' "America," and villages were named "Maryland," "Philadelphia," and the like. One example may illustrate the complex migrations. The French Huguenot Saint-Just family, a Saxon military officer's family, and the Moravian-origin Meilicke family separately chose the same region as destination. After a century of intermarriage, they found that land had become scarce; so some migrated further east, others to towns, and several to North America (map 12.1).[21]

Colonization of Distant Vacated Lands

Within the framework of mercantilist and military policies to populate particular regions, the Habsburg and Romanov governments recruited peasant families for the Military Border and South Russia where the Ottoman Empire had been pushed back.[22] The Austrian Habsburgs, styled the "Occident's bulwark" against the "Turks," received military support from several European dynasties—in the campaign of 1685, for example, 24,000 Hungarians, Bavarians, and Brandenburg-Prussians (in equal numbers); 5,000 Saxons and 4,500 Swabians; 11,000 men from Brunswick-Lüneburg; 14,000 from the Rhenish areas and Cologne; and 18,000 Polish soldiers. When these troops were disbanded, some settled. Others, who returned, told of the horrors of warfare and provided information about routes, agricultural conditions, and vacated farmlands. The half-century of intermittent fighting as well as flight and plagues reduced the population in some regions to about 10 percent of its level at the time of the Ottoman conquest in the early sixteenth century. In 1699 the Habsburgs became rulers of Hungary and two decades later annexed Transylvania, Serbia, and Little Walachia.

Pursuing a policy of mercantilist "populationalism," the Habsburg state liberalized and changed traditional economic restrictions. Immigrant artisans were exempted from monopolist guild regulations; vagrants were assigned to produce textiles in workhouses; and new factories hired immigrant workers. Religious freedom was granted to members of the Orthodox Church and Protestants, and Jews, hitherto excluded from immigration, were admitted to encourage commerce.[23] The German language served as the administrative lingua franca and by 1784 was the only accepted one. Elites, Bohemian and Hungarian nobility, imperial administrators, and cultural and educational structures underwent an Austrian variant of Germanization. Cultural adaptation was voluntary, but access to wealth and political influence depended on it.

From the sixteenth to the eighteenth century, the government settled the Croatian, Slavonian, and Transylvanian military borders (map 12.1) with soldier-farmers; Croatian extended families (zadruga), all males over sixteen being liable to military service; Serbian border guards (granicari); settlers from the Germanies; and refugees belonging to other ethnicities. This policy of keeping the standing army small protected the productive capacity of the population and the fiscal resources of the state. Though land was free, living conditions were harsh since immigrants had to reside wherever the fortunes or misfortunes of war had established the boundary. Thus some of the immigrants moved on to cultivable land in the Ottoman realm.

After 1689, recruitment of settlers for fertile plains was coordinated by a centralized agency (Einrichtungswerk). Vojvodina became a multiethnic territory with Serbian, Croatian, Romanian, German, and Hungarian peasants. Refugee groups came from the Ottoman Empire; the Armenian population of Wallachia sought refuge in 1672, and 30,000 Serbs came in the 1690s. From the early 1700s onward, settlers arrived from German principalities. Families received free land and three years' exemption from taxation. However, adverse frontier conditions (such as having to live in dugouts or lacking provisions) resulted in death rates as high as 40 percent among thousands of families. Like Dutch towns, the Bremen wetlands, and cities in general, the Balkans developed a reputation as a graveyard for immigrants.[24]

From 1740 to 1770, German-language immigrants introduced crop rotation, specialized in marketable crops, and encouraged commerce. Local peasants' adoption of these innovations and the absence of an extortionate nobility improved general standards of living. Swabian, Saxon, Serbian, and Romanian peasants came and were joined by Magyar and Slovak serfs who fled their masters' estates, where labor (robot) due to lords still amounted to between fifty-two and 104 days a year. From the 1740s to the 1790s, 150,000 to 200,000 arrived, and smaller numbers followed up to the 1820s. By recruiting these settlers, the Vienna government prevented the immigration of

Hungarian nobles and Magyar peasants, an ethno-political move to reduce the impact of Hungary in the politics of the empire.[25] An admission fee, imposed on German-language immigrant families after 1829, coincided with the post-1815 resumption of emigration to North America. Eastward migration from the German principalities ended, and for half a century their impoverished surplus populations accounted for the bulk of the German-origin transatlantic migrations.

Throughout its 220-year history from the peace of Karlovac to the peace of Versailles, the Habsburg Empire was a "state of many peoples." German-speaking Austrians and Hungarian-speaking Magyars formed the dominant groups, with "minorities" or lesser nationalities composed of Czechs and Slovaks, Slovenes, Croats, Serbs, Romanians, Ruthenians, Szeklers, and Transylvanian descendants of twelfth-century German-origin immigrants. "Minorities" were majorities in their traditional territories or in immigrant bloc settlements. The marketplace interaction in local languages and the overlay of administrative, commercial, and Church languages led to a multilingualism of illiterate local people, who as labor migrants after the 1880s carried these linguistic skills to the multiethnic urban immigrant quarters of the North Atlantic world.[26]

A century after the Habsburg Empire's conquest of Ottoman territories, the Russian Empire's armies reached the Black Sea and the formerly Genoese Crimean Peninsula in 1783. After conquest Cossacks and some 50,000 Tatar men fled into the Ottoman Empire. The latter left behind a population of 160,000, two-thirds of whom were women. Cossacks were permitted to return on condition that they abandon their male military communities (their "lives without women") and settle as families. A decree of 1763 opened the South Russian Plains for settlement: Russian and Ukrainian internal migrants came in larger numbers, and members of the nobility arrived with their serfs. People from the overpopulated German south and Mennonites immigrated up to the 1820s; thereafter, Russian authorities preferred Slavic settlers in order to facilitate acculturation.[27]

Authorities under Prince Potemkin (1739–91) designed a complex policy of protection, privileges, and acculturation (chap. 13.2); but when, as early as 1780, Catherine II came to inspect the colonization project, progress was still very limited. Fearing for his career, the count had one-street artificial village facades erected along the route, filling them with just-in-time shipments of cheering recent immigrants. "Potemkin villages" became proverbial and have been interpreted as bogus evidence of a nonexistent prosperity. However, in view of the actual colonization efforts, they provided a counterpoint to the "graveyard" view of migration. They reflected the administrators' projects and the migrants' dreams at the time the first deliberate steps were taken toward a better future.[28]

In other parts of Europe—for example, in eighteenth-century Spain—"retrograde agrarian systems" characterized by latifundia, absentee ownership, poverty, and depopulation resulted in involuntary mobility. Landless latifundium laborers were sent to work far from their homes, and their families were forced into vagrancy. In the 1760s and 1770s, mercantilist reformers commented critically: "The true treasure of the state is men. . . . How can we grow prosperous when he who works does not reap and he who reaps does not work?" Plans to resettle the Sierra Morena under the protection of the crown's Swiss regiments were entrusted to a Bavarian adventurer. He was to recruit 6,000 German and Flemish Catholics of both sexes, divided into equal groups of peasants and artisans. At least one-half had to be in the prime of life, and small children were to be included to serve immediate needs and provide for the future.[29] From 1766 to 1769, the profit-oriented adventurer sent some 7,800 migrants, regardless of their qualifications. The Spanish director of colonization, who (like Prince Potemkin) was planning for the future, faced difficult terrain and traffickers in human migrants. Thus progress was slow. In 1835 the privileges of the "new towns" were revoked to reduce tensions with native peasants.[30]

Enclosure and the Mobilization of Labor: The English Case

Throughout Western Europe, the higher capitalization of agriculture, new crops, and the raising of livestock decreased the chances of peasant families to derive subsistence from smallholdings. The state-supported enclosure of land in England by gentry and urban capitalists, which accelerated in the eighteenth century, can serve as an example of how poorer people were forced to depart from their villages. If they were lucky, peasant families could move into agriculture elsewhere, usually on more marginal lands. Others shifted to village industries for subsistence. Still others had to migrate to urban centers or, as indentured servants, to America. Some contemporary observers criticized the growing inequality, the depopulation of the countryside, and the destruction of the traditional rural economy. Others saw a new economic order emerge. Reducing the agrarian population to the level of the laboring poor dependent on child labor, a pamphlet of 1781 noted, would result in earlier marriages and more children—in other words, a larger labor force—and thus farmers with large holdings would be assured of laborers and maids. The Other was constructed in social terms. The lower strata who used the commons—the commoners—were a "sordid race," lazy, foreign, and dangerous. Their "beggarly independence," constructed as "idleness," was criminalized by vagrancy laws. Efforts to reduce the mobility of the poor included restrictions on teaching geography in workhouses and injunctions against exhibiting maps on school walls. Marginal but independent men and women were said to be thieves of (potential) national wealth; their impoverishment and control would thus be advantageous to the national economy, "disagreeable and painful as it may be to the tender and feeling heart."[31]

Depopulation followed on enclosure. In Northampton only one-third of the parishes were enclosed, but a mere 10 percent of the shire's population lived there. Those "set free" had either gone to uplands and fens or to the expanding cloth-producing villages. Villagers resisted pressures for out-migration and defended their subsistence by arson and rioting. Local farmers able to negotiate the structural changes or well-capitalized immigrant farmers, dependent on immediate and regular profits from crops to pay interest on mortgages and repay the principal, became part of a new market-oriented economy. Smallholding families "could best survive if they adopted their own specialized agricultures, or if their lands were solely adjuncts to trade." Farmer-weavers and commoner-shoemakers in open-field villages were no longer guaranteed subsistence in periods of high food prices, nor could farm servants save wages for a future independence. "Parliamentary enclosure caused the disappearance of the English peasantry." According to Jonas Hanway's *Virtue in Humble Life* (1774), the "political economy" of the nation—that is, enclosure—drove "people into great towns."[32]

One destination for the displaced families or their younger members was the increasingly prevalent urban middle-class household, where servants became a symbol of status, even among lowly tradesmen, while the nobility's demand for servants was declining. In the mid-fifteenth century, the earl of Warwick had been accompanied by 600 servants on going to Parliament; the less important deputy-steward in Westmoreland had a retinue of 290 maids and men-servants. Middle-class employers considered farm girls and boys industrious and virtuous in stark contrast to urban lower-class servants, who were considered unfit to raise middle-class children. The vast numbers that came into London because of higher wages drained agriculture of "hands"—heads and hearts seem to have been less in demand. Across time and place, the capital's glitter, excitement, and novelty attracted young people, who "imagine the metropolis to resemble that paradise promised to the mahometans by their prophet." Servants returning to their families or accompanying masters and mistresses into the country at the end of the London "season" motivated others to leave too. Economists commented: "Many of the very prime of the people are taken from labour, to be attendants of the Opulent."[33]

The late eighteenth-century English servant class of 110,000 men and 800,000 maids amounted to nearly 10 percent of the combined English and Welsh population of 10.4 million. In interclass cultural exchange maids adopted the dress forms of their mistresses and carried the new fashions into the countryside. Their precarious social status forced unemployed servants to return home, emigrate, or resort to petty thievery. Among female "criminals" shipped to Australia, domestics accounted for the largest share. Both sexes could go into textile production or, somewhat later, factory work. Servant mobility, once a phase in the individual life-cycle, became a lifelong experience.[34]

12.3 Regional Labor Migration Systems, 1650s to 1830s

For family migration, jobs for all were needed. Alternatively, men migrated, returning only for spring sowing and harvest work, while women and children tended the agricultural plot the rest of the time; or men and women migrated separately into noncontiguous gendered labor markets, sometimes leaving children in the care of female relatives.[35]

In the mid-1600s, three regional migration systems brought laborers and independent producers to the newly independent Urban Netherlands in the North Sea System, southward in the Franco-Spanish System, and in particular to Sweden in the Baltic Migration System (map 12.2). Improved labor market opportunities and the influx of men and women resulted in better marriage-market conditions. Thus the productive and reproductive spheres were closely linked.

The Republic of the United Provinces experienced balanced growth in many sectors of its economy. Foreign trade and colonial expansion required sailors for the navy and the merchant marine as well as soldiers (chap. 7.4); service work and textile manufacture attracted women; agriculture underwent an early process of specialization, with seasonal peaks in labor demand. The Iberian economies' lack of distribution networks for their colonial imports left this profitable commerce to Dutch merchants, and local production benefited from skilled and entrepreneurial religious refugees in the sixteenth century (chap. 4). Iberian Jews[36] and, after the 1750s, Ashkenazi Jews as well as French Huguenots came. So did, in smaller numbers, English, Czech, French, Swiss, Polish, Prussian, Austrian, and German migrants, whether Herrnhuters, Catholics, Lutherans, Greek, Comenians, Quakers, or Puritans.

Still, labor remained scarce. The native Dutch first left the lowly "trades" of soldier and "cow-keeper." Soldiers "they can hire from England, Scotland and Germany, to venture their lives for Six pence a day, whilst themselves safely and quietly follow such Trades, whereby the meanest of them gain six times as much," noted economist William Petty as early as 1671. "Danes and Polanders" were sent to work in menial labor. "By this entertaining of Strangers . . . their Country becomes more and more peopled, forasmuch as the children of such Strangers, are Hollanders and take to Trades, whilst new Strangers are admitted *ad infinitum.*"[37] A quantitative assessment based on marriage registers of several Dutch towns shows increasing in-migration after de facto independence in the 1580s. Between 1585 and 1622, one-third of Amsterdam's 105,000 inhabitants were either immigrants fleeing Habsburg Catholicization of the southern provinces or children of immigrants. One of them noted, "Here is Antwerp itself changed into Amsterdam." In the first half of the seventeenth century, 40 percent of those getting married were foreign-born; from 1680 to 1800 the ratio stood at 25 percent on average. The native-born population—including second-generation immigrants—of about two million integrated half a million immigrants, most of whom came before 1700.[38]

Because of the relative decline of the Dutch position in world systems, migration rates decreased in the eighteenth century. Impoverished working families sent children off to local or migrant labor. In the "Golden Century" after the 1590s, the "humble, distressed, and hungry common people" had apprenticed children, but employers, rather than preparing them for a trade, used them as servants almost "like slaves." As a result, they lacked the human capital necessary for self-determined migration and successful economic reinsertion. Poorhouse wardens sent children and

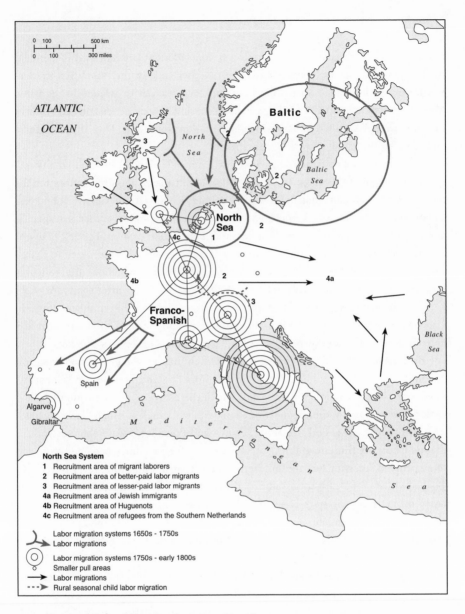

ATLANTIC

OCEAN

North
Sea

Baltic

Baltic
Sea

**North
Sea**

Franco-
Spanish

Spain

4a

Algarve

Gibraltar

Black
Sea

M e d i t e r r a n e a n

S e a

North Sea System
1   Recruitment area of migrant laborers
2   Recruitment area of better-paid labor migrants
3   Recruitment area of lesser-paid labor migrants
4a Recruitment area of Jewish immigrants
4b Recruitment area of Huguenots
4c Recruitment area of refugees from the Southern Netherlands

  Labor migration systems 1650s - 1750s
  Labor migrations
  Labor migration systems 1750s - early 1800s
  Smaller pull areas
  Labor migrations
  Rural seasonal child labor migration

12.2   European Labor Migration Systems, 1650–1850

women to textile factories, which would release them during the next economic
slump. Involuntary poverty-related mobility increased.[39]

Seasonal labor migrants seeking employment in agriculture—peat digging, hay-
ing, grain and potato harvesting—and in brick-making arrived at a rate of 30,000
annually. They left complex family work cycles and entered equally complex work
cycles of peasant families in Holland (fig. 12.1). Soldiers, navymen, and sailors staying for more than a year, often as crewmembers for the Dutch East India Company's

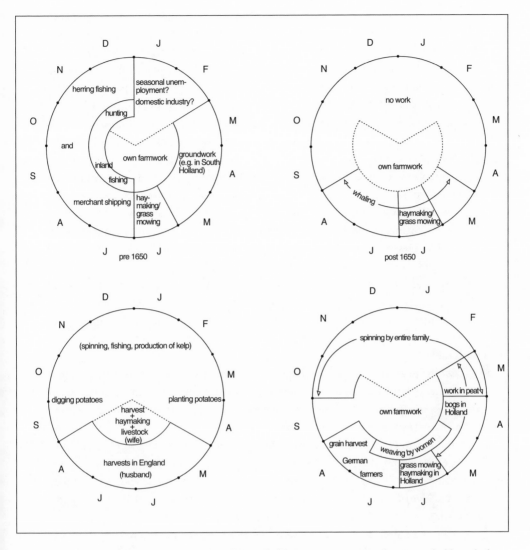

Figure 12.1 Annual Work Cycles of Irish and Westphalian Tenant Farm Worker Households and of Laborers and Small Farmers in North Holland, 17th–19th Centuries

vessels, numbered almost 1.2 million (1600–1800). Female servants came, some from as far as Norway. Seasonal migrants walked up to 300 kilometers to the coastal strip of Holland and Zeeland. Sailors and soldiers came from distances of up to 500 kilometers, and religious refugees from even further away. Given the segmentation of labor markets, little competition with "native" Dutch—often of immigrant descent—occurred.[40] The Netherlands, like any of the European colonial powers at the height of imperial activity, became a multicultured society.[41]

The second system, the Franco-Spanish one, had its origins in settler and soldier migrations during the expulsion of peoples of Muslim faith from the Iberian

Peninsula, the expulsion of whole ethno-religious groups, flight from the Inquisition (chaps. 2.3, 4.1), and in subsequent colony-bound emigration, which reduced population growth at home (chap. 8.2). Emphasis on the religious character of the expulsions veils the aspect of class. Crown and Church expelled the middle classes, Jewish merchants and financiers, Morisco and Jewish artisans and shopkeepers, intellectuals of both groups, and prosperous Morisco agriculturalists. In addition, Christian Iberians of rank considered tilling of the soil dishonorable. The elaborate Arab irrigation systems fell into disrepair, and American silver imported to Castile by the shipload caused inflation. While the Dutch core needed labor because of balanced economic growth, Spain needed immigrants because of its imbalanced population development, the skewed class structure, and religious intolerance.[42]

By shifting its European commerce to the temporarily dependent Dutch merchants, the Spanish state discouraged commercial development and capital accumulation. The preeminence of the nobility and the hidalgo class and the semifeudal opportunities in the colonies impeded the emergence of a native bourgeoisie, and the low regard for manual labor impeded the emergence of a peasantry. Immigrant or temporarily present merchants from most other European states filled the gap and became a "guest" middle class. When Spain's global position declined, many of them returned to their countries of origin, taking connections, expertise, and capital with them.[43]

On the next lower social level, guest laborers, artisans, and traders from France were attracted in large numbers between 1650 and 1750 by wages three times higher than at home. They could connect to an existing community since 10 to 20 percent of the early seventeenth-century male Catalonian population was of French origin. About 200,000 French were said to reside in Spain, some 40,000 in Madrid alone. Many came temporarily; more decided to stay, marry, and integrate; friends, kin, and neighbors came in sequential migrations. They labored in menial tasks or as skilled artisans. Spanish society, not as mixed as the Dutch one, thus included a guest middle class supported by a French-origin working class.[44]

Like the Dutch North Sea System, the third migration system was related to naval connections and hegemony. From the 1650s to the 1720s, when Sweden controlled most of the shores of the Baltic Sea and dominated vast hinterlands, its need for soldiers, workers, and middle-class experts was supplied through the Baltic Migration System. The state's efficient central administration raised and allocated large fiscal resources for internal economic improvements. Following the Dutch model, the army recruited foreign soldiers—25,000 by 1699. Government-employed mining experts explored the country's iron and copper beds, and soon the traditional immigration of German miners began to grow. The nobility, part of the polity but not agenda-setting as in Spain, embarked on the construction of castles and residences jointly with the crown and wealthy burghers. Master builders and journeymen masons, stonecutters, and sculptors came from the Germanies and from other parts of Europe. Dutch, Walloon, Jewish, French, and Scottish migrants brought capital or skills. Baltic nobles joined the Swedish aristocracy; Finnish peasants settled in central and northern Sweden. Entrepreneurs from abroad often hired masters and journeymen from their place of origin—for example, French potters for a French-owned faience-manufactory. By the 1750s, internal labor migration networks connected the surplus farming population to lumbering areas and coastal manufactures, and trans-Baltic migration declined. Stockholm, whose German element of Hanseatic times had long been Swedicized, exerted a pull on skilled and unskilled workers from Finland (part of Sweden until 1809) and the northern German states.[45]

Labor Migration Systems, 1750s to 1830s

After the mid-eighteenth century, Sweden, Spain, and the Netherlands had passed their apogees. Their relative importance in the European economy declined, and with it their attractiveness for migrants. French and British expansion followed different patterns, and, accordingly, intra-European migration patterns did not simply repeat the seventeenth-century models. Until Napoleonic imperialism wrought havoc among European states and economies, and until westbound migration across the Atlantic resumed in the 1820s, several smaller labor migration systems in Western and Southern Europe filled labor demand.

By the early 1800s, of the three previous systems only the North Sea one continued to operate. Eastern England—Lincolnshire and East Anglia as well as London—attracted 20,000 migrants annually from as far away as western Ireland, Wales, and Scotland. Paris each year attracted about 60,000 workers from the Massif Central, the Alps, and the west of France, which earlier had provided labor migrants for Spain.[46] Like Dutch cities and London, Paris attracted skilled workers and artisans from German-speaking Central Europe. Their migrations received renewed impetus when reactionary German politics forced liberal and freethinking men and women into exile after the 1830s. Migration for economic reasons, journeymen artisan's travels, and political exile merged (chap. 12.5).

In southwestern Europe, the Spanish capital, Madrid, and surrounding parts of Castile attracted 30,000 migrants annually from Galicia, the northwestern corner of the kingdom, for harvesting and for building an infrastructure. Further to the south, an Algarvian system brought migrants to Alentejo, southern Spain, and Gibraltar, an enclave more multicultured than most European cities. Along the western Mediterranean littoral, sailors, dockworkers, and artisans migrated to Marseille's busy port, and the fertile coastal region between Catalonia and Provence attracted about 35,000 migrants from the Pyrenees, the Massif Central, and the Alps. Braudel called the mountains of the Mediterranean "une fabrique d'hommes à l'usage d'autrui," a factory generating men and women who walked from their places of birth to distant labor markets.[47] In northern Italy, agriculture in the plains of the Po River was short of about 50,000 workers annually, and cities like Milan and Turin attracted additional men and women. Here, too, people came from surrounding hills. The pull of the cities, once strong (chap. 3.3), was not comparable to that of Paris or London, though Rome needed migrants in large numbers. The central Italian provinces of Tuscany and Lazio, as well as the islands of Elba and Corsica, attracted about 100,000 workers for the harvesting of grain and other crops annually (map 12.2).

Thus the annual seasonal migration to the three northern centers of production involved about 110,000 people annually and in the southern cores around 215,000. Other, minor systems with an annual intake of below 10,000 involved perhaps a further 100,000 migrants. Diffuse urban migrations have to be added. The Mediterranean systems continued medieval patterns, while the systems in western and southwestern Europe emerged in response to the shift toward the Atlantic World.[48] In a second phase after the 1820s, migrants joined the transatlantic route.

Further to the east, new patterns of labor migration began to fill traditional centers like Kraków and the expanding cities of Budapest and Warsaw. Moscow and St. Petersburg attracted ever larger numbers of seasonal and multi-annual labor migrants. In these landlocked territories, remote from the Atlantic World, islands of extractive industries and manufacturing developed in vast agricultural lands (see chap. 13). From the sixteenth to the mid-seventeenth century, refugee Protestants moved from the whole of northwestern Europe into Polish lands. Itinerant Scottish traders helped supply them. In the Balkans, Armenian traders were part of the supply networks. Albanians, who migrated as soldiers across Europe (chap. 3.1), and who at the time of the demise of the Byzantine Empire and Venetian rule had settled communities in Italy, remained highly mobile.[49]

Finally, larger interregional networks connected cities of the north and east with particular regions of emigration of artisans and producers of culture. The expansion of Sweden onto the continent, Poland's traditional connections with cultures as far as Italy and as close as Bohemia, the mediating role of the Kraków bourgeoisie (which had once even been described by the Arab and Jewish travelers and geographers), and the cultural attractiveness of some Polish nobles' courts explain the Swedish-Polish interaction. Similarly, Scotland with its surplus populations, cultural expressions, and military traditions sent migrants to the continent, and to Sweden and Poland in particular. The long-distance migrations of sailors and soldiers, artists and artisans, teachers, students, and musicians covered similar regions but did not necessarily interact.[50]

12.4   Urbanization and Migrations

Immigrants and sojourners connected particular rural regions and rural worlds in general with urban conglomerations (map 12.3). Some were distinguishable by customs and language; others merely by their dialects. From the mid-seventeenth century to the end of the bourgeois-democratic revolutions in the mid-nineteenth century, labor migrations accounted for the bulk of moves. In comparison, the intra-European migrations of agriculturalists were small and increased only with nineteenth-century overseas emigration. Men and women moved out of a need to earn a subsistence, rather than looking for betterment or social ascent. Women came to earn a dowry as a basic investment in their future family's household, and men

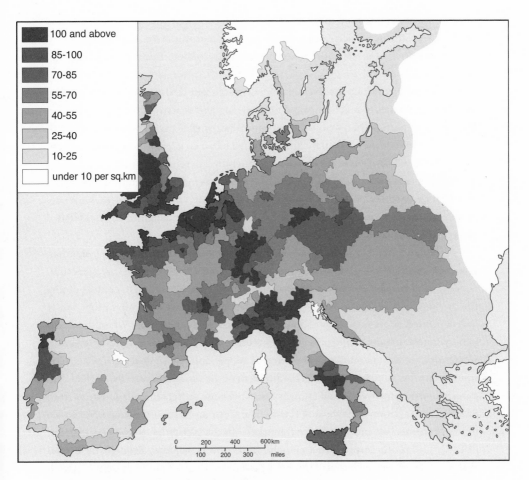

12.3 Population Density in the Early 19th Century

came in search of regular employment to feed families.[51] Models of preindustrial migration start from the countryside and postulate proletarianization because of demographic growth, new capital-intensive agriculture, and cottage industries (Tilly) or, alternatively, because of labor demands in towns and cities, especially in Urban Italy and the Urban Netherlands (De Vries). The two approaches are complementary in that they deal with the connectedness of out- and in-migration regions.[52]

Growing urban populations, whether in medieval Urban Italy, Ottoman Istanbul, or Dutch cities, needed provisions, and the surrounding agricultural countryside attracted additional laborers. By the mid-seventeenth century, London, for example, had extended the reach of its food markets to distant villages where families specialized in market gardening or developed a carrying trade; hucksters and market women were self-employed. Eighteenth-century households in the vicinity of towns or within merchants' and traders' buying circuits offered dairy and handicraft products for sale to supplement income from land or fishing. Thus they eked out an independent existence—independent of year-round or seasonal wagework. Such lifestyles, which combined marginal farming, independent cottage production, and commons pasturing, reflect and show versatility and initiative. Better-placed employers in search of a labor force interpreted such self-determination of hours and needs as indolence.

Cityward migrations involved all social strata from laborers and maids via artisans and mechanics to merchants and nobles. Huguenots arrived in urban areas, and Jews became part of the Western European urban worlds again. Men with capital, technical expertise, or particular skills migrated between geographically distant centers of demand. The circulation of elites and migration in response to economic cycles were part of urbanization processes. Family formation induced migration: the search for marriage partners by women among male urban migrants, and the search for economic security by journeymen artisans among widows or daughters of established masters.

Although migration is commonly associated with the maintenance of urban population levels (chap. 3.3) or urban growth, long-term depressions, structural changes in particular economic sectors, and the regional relocation of centers of textile production led to out-migration and urban decline. A city's net migration gain or loss depended on its relative position in commerce and production. When the flourishing Protestant copper and brass manufacturers of Aachen and its vicinity in southwestern Germany encountered problems of supply and had to deal with a Catholic ruler, many migrated to England in the first half of the 1600s. There, they worked copper imported from Sweden and Hungary, and the state protected their products from Swedish competition by imposing tariffs. The German-English producers were able to insert themselves into continental markets. In the Netherlands, the textile boom in Leiden (1638–40) resulted in 4,000 children from Liège being brought there, and Walloon drapers were accused of importing to Leiden beggars' children from Norwich in eastern England, Douai in northern France, and Kleve in western Germany. The structural decline in lace making, for example, forced skilled women and children to migrate to other cities or to villages, if production was relocated to the countryside, or left them destitute. Migrations during recessions were sometimes flight from starvation.[53]

Artisans, Merchants, and Refugees

Before religious persecutions subsided by the eighteenth century, mercantilist governments continued to welcome religious refugees. Like the circulating artisans and merchants, most of these involuntary migrants came with skills, with human capital (to use the modern term), and with the social capital of trading connections. What counted was the migrants' contribution to a state's economy rather than their religious or ethnic culture. Wesel, Emden, Kleve, (Frankfurt-)Bockenheim, and, later, Hamburg, Bremen, Nuremberg, and other cities accommodated Huguenot colonies. Large communities settled in the Palatinate and along the Lower Rhine, in Magdeburg and Halle, Frankfurt/Oder and Königsberg. Brandenburg-Prussia even sent recruiting officers to France to offset the devastating population loss of its "founding wars" and to rebuild the economy devastated by the Thirty Years' War. Royal edicts settled a small number of Jewish families expelled from Vienna in 1671 and about 20,000 Huguenots in 1685. When Berlin became a city, French Huguenot gardeners were recruited for vegetable cultivation and settled on free plots of land; the local Slavic "Wends" were placed on a par with Germans; Bohemian refugees came in the 1730s and 1740s. Some families came with considerable assets; others almost without clothing: all added human capital to local labor reserves. Immigrants opened shops, produced textiles, especially fineries like lace and silks, and skilled artisans worked in many trades.

Even Catholics were recruited when shortages of people with particular skills occurred, as in the case of gunsmiths from the southern Netherlands in 1722. Construction workers reached Berlin from Vogtland and other central German uphill areas with surplus populations. Bohemian, Saxon, Palatine, Württemberg, and Polish spinners and weavers were settled in special colonies. As prosperity increased, specialized tradesmen, such as French-Swiss clockmakers, were invited to settle. By the 1780s, one-third of Berlin's population consisted of immigrants and their descendants. Europe's cities were as multicultured as the ones in North America.[54]

Religious freedom, legal status, and liberties were negotiated in the interests of state and crown, on the one hand, and of ethno-religious immigrant groups, on the other. Mennonites, for example, were exempted from army service but had to pay a levy for a military academy. Newcomers could be exempted from the admission fees to burgher status and could receive grants or loans to establish themselves in business. Guilds had to open their ranks to immigrants. At the pleasure of the crown, some immigrant groups received chartered status separate from and above the local population. Administrations, which expected the newcomers to refine local lifestyles, played down resulting conflicts. In Berlin, residents from diverse social backgrounds joined in fact the "French" community. Over time, the non-German groups adopted the German language; intermarriage made borderlines difficult to ascertain; a person's legal status as an immigrant or "regular" subject became difficult to define. The Prussian reform legislation of 1808–09 abolished remaining privileges.[55]

From being an issue of urban population replenishment, migration developed into a statewide issue in mercantilist states like Sweden and England. In England, Parliament debated the arrival of foreign Protestants and the migration of Scots in combination with population stagnation and economic development. (The Scots were cultural Others but British subjects after the union of 1707.) The burgher status of urban in-migrants, or what might be called city-zenship, was regulated in the General Naturalization Act of 1709. Controversial debates over the citizenship of Scots indicate that no common concept of a nation existed. Contrary to states that still expelled residents for religio-ideological reasons, British theoreticians viewed people as economic assets. Criticism of the mass recruitment of 13,000 Palatine Germans in 1709 who came without urban skills outlined the limits of admission. What counted was performance, not humanitarian concerns or religious and cultural Otherness.[56]

Artisan journeymen migrations (chap. 3.3) continued to be guild-regulated, but printed trade manuals made the spread of knowledge by migration superfluous. The allocation of labor supplies conflicted with demand, and masters in conjunction with town authorities manipulated rules. In times of labor shortages, apprentices could be hired as journeymen without having to travel. In times of oversupply, masters attempted to compel increased mobility. In times of labor strife, they introduced a kind of "contract labor" (*verschriebene Gesellen, Frachtgesellen*) by recruiting "foreign" journeymen, offering them a fixed contract and paying the travel expenses. "Foreign" implied distance rather than a different ethnic or national origin.

The trans-European journeymen artisans' migrations influenced nineteenth-century migration patterns of skilled workers, machine-operating mechanics, and technical experts. Most moved within the German-language orbit, but the shortage of skilled labor in post-serfdom Eastern and southeastern Europe explains the routes taken via Prague and Warsaw to St. Petersburg or via Budapest into the Balkans and, occasionally, on to Constantinople and to Alexandria, Egypt. In the south, a hostel for migrating German bakers existed in sixteenth- and seventeenth-century Venice. In the west, migrations reached artisans' colonies in Paris and London. Journeymen expanded their political consciousness and social organization and, in the nineteenth century, interacted with political exiles. German, the lingua franca of artisans and skilled workers in Central and Eastern Europe, also became the lingua franca of the labor movement.

Ethnic belonging, real or ascribed, might influence hiring practices and the assignment of status. In Latvian Riga, wealthy guilds considered themselves "German" and admitted only ethnically German journeymen while labeling all others as "un-German" or "Latvian." Because of intermarriage and interaction over centuries, such categorization was used arbitrarily to support existing ethnic hierarchies. Many guilds, in fact, had become ethnically overwhelmingly Latvian from the mid-seventeenth century onward.[57]

The advent of mass production in manufactures (from Latin *manus:* hands, *facere:* to do) and in factories (workshops using machinery) created havoc in artisanal production and lifestyles. Migration regulations degenerated into a means for guild-masters to keep journeymen on the move. French research indicates the large volume of mobility. Around 1800, 10 percent of the French population of 28 million were laborers and domestics, who migrated over short distances, as well as skilled workers and artisans, who moved over long distances. Migration to and from Britain, on the other hand, was limited and mainly served purposes of technological exchange. Eighteenth-century Scottish production techniques for the making of tin, for example, were improved after the visit of a Scottish entrepreneur to production centers in Hanover and Saxony. In the nineteenth century, exchanges of work processes and technological innovation came to include North America.[58]

The continuity from artisans' to skilled workers' migrations may be illustrated by connections between the Germanies and England. Palatine families migrated to England under the dual impact of religious oppression at home and assistance from the English crown or manufacturers. Cutlers could set up for themselves in London if they applied for naturalization. The city's council silenced the protests of native artisans. Into the nineteenth century, sugar refiners came from northern German states to London, and swordmakers migrated from the Palatinate to northern England. To reduce imports of Bohemian glass, glassblowers were induced to come with their families to England secretly, and glass huts were set up for them near Newcastle. Immigrant Palatine needlemakers of 1567 later competed with those at home, and by 1839 a Rhenish manufacturer spied on English production processes to reimport them. In general, skilled artisans came because raw materials were easily obtainable, market facilities were better, and skills were valued more. In their wake others followed, such as teachers for their children.[59]

Although merchants continued to operate in trans-European networks, they had become sedentary. Swiss merchants were active in France in the seventeenth and eighteenth centuries, and merchants from Nuremburg settled in Posen/Poznań. Italian merchants from Alpine mountain valleys established links to Cologne in the Rhine valley; peddlers and shopkeepers, a few workers and artisans, chimney sweeps, pewterers, and a small number of servants, hostelkeepers, and caterers followed. They no longer formed colonies in the medieval sense but lived under locally varying "alien law" (*Fremdenrecht*), which could be applied restrictively when competition was feared or liberally when labor or capital was needed. Some moved back and forth between their Italian and German homes; others returned permanently after years of absence; still others, who married local women and raised children, followed the process of acculturation from immigrant to ethnic to local.[60]

Long-distance trade continued overland from India to Russia, from Russia to China, from Mediterranean Europe to Mediterranean Africa, and across the Sahara, but compared to resident merchants in urban agglomerations and small towns, the traveling traders were few in number.[61] Kraków, for example, was throughout its history a transshipment center between distant economic worlds (map 12.4). It had been part of the Hanseatic federation and was connected to Italy and the Levant. Drovers passed through; sheepskin coats were made and traded; fish sold to Russian markets. Its Jewish population in the Kasimirz quarter had far-flung business relations, as did the German, Polish, Italian, and other merchants in Kraków. Some of its magnificent buildings reflect Italian styles and Italian workmanship.[62]

In Europe, a circulation of elites involved a "transfer of young people between distant cities," with daughters and sons of merchants or artisans becoming mobile through marriage and the exchange of business partners. In seventeenth-century Nördlingen in southwestern Germany, for example, between 10 and 20 percent of the population were in-migrants from German-language cities and from abroad, most of them middle-class men and women. Only immigrants with means could become burghers. Townsmen sought immigrant brides, whereas few of the immigrant men could or did marry local women. Urban migrations followed the up- and downswings of relative economic position and economic cycles.[63]

12.4 Long-Distance Trade Routes in East Central Europe, Kraków, 1500–1800

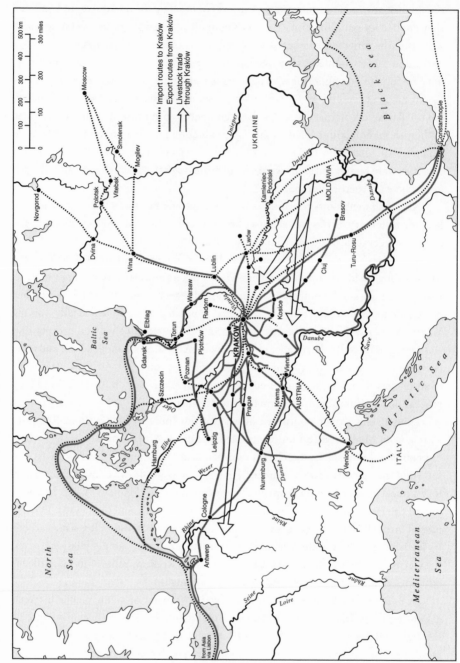

Migrations into established towns changed population composition continuously.[64] The population of Frankfurt/Main grew from 11,500 inhabitants in 1500 to 20,000 in 1600, declined by more than 3,000 till 1650, and reached 27,500 by 1700. In these two hundred years, natural increase contributed to population growth only in two decades. In 1600, several thousand migrating journeymen artisans, 3,000 middle-class Dutch Protestant in-migrants, and 2,500 Jews accounted for more than 40 percent of the inhabitants. Immigrant women working as domestics have to be added to the number. In 1762, only 15 percent of 1,870 journeymen artisans had been born in the town; most came from the nearby surroundings (32 percent) and from southern German states as well as Austria (24 percent).[65]

Towns newly founded or purposefully expanded by dynastic rulers attracted men and women from across Europe (chap. 3.3). When Cosimo de' Medici I granted duty-free port facilities to Livorno (1565) and freedom of settlement and religion (1593), Jews and Moriscos, entrepreneurs and artisans came singly or as families.[66] In the period from 1603 to 1619, Gothenburg in Sweden was founded as a colony for Dutch merchants who had long been involved in copper exports. Other immigrants and Swedes settled, and a German community emerged. Adapting the earlier concepts of separate jurisdiction for immigrant mercantile and artisanal communities, Gothenburg's first charter made Dutch and Swedish official languages and apportioned the city council seats to four Swedes, three Netherlanders, three Germans, and two Scots.[67]

Western, Southern, and West Central European cities accommodated the same populations as the surrounding countryside. East Central and Eastern European cities, like Riga, usually consisted of immigrant and inserted middle classes and patriciates, as well as "vernacular" lower classes. The modernizing policies of Tsar Peter I followed, literally, western artisanal routes. The tsar traveled in disguise to Riga, Prussia, the Netherlands, and England in 1697–98 and 1716–17. Along the way, he worked in several trades—as gunfounder, ship carpenter, and engineer—and studied navigation. As "master artisan" on the throne, he founded St. Petersburg in 1703 on the Gulf of Finland, near the former Hanseatic town of Novgorod. Building styles reflected changed European power hierarchies and concomitant changes in patterns of migration. No longer did Italian architects dominate the scene; rather, Dutch and northern German architects and engineers introduced a bourgeois baroque and built canals. Only in the case of the famous "Winter Palace" was an Italian recruited.

Two decades after its founding, the city counted 40,000 inhabitants plus seasonal workers in the summer and had become the leading port of the empire, making it the major link to Stockholm and Western Europe. Urban expansion was due to merchant colonies, which included Dutch and English, and to urban growth, the work of Finnish workers and craftsmen, of German artisans and burghers, as well as of many others. Internal in-migration was related to the city's function as the capital: conscripted navy and army personnel brought 41,000 dependents in the 1790s. Russian merchants, too, had to be pressured to move from genteel Moscow to the swamps of the new capital. The population grew to 150,000 by 1764 and to 225,000 in 1800. The tsars brought in "exotic" retainers: Black personnel for the palace came from New England's free Afro-American population, and "the great-grandfather of the Russian poet Pushkin was an African slave acquired in France by Peter I and married into a Russian noble family." An observer in 1801 described the demand for special skills, "the numerous wants of a great city" and the court. "Many thousands of industrious and ingenious foreigners have been induced to settle here"; their industry "flows . . . in beneficial streams through all the adjacent provinces," often via trade conducted by the "common Russian . . . [who] by his frugal and poor way of living, tries to save some money to become a merchant." People, money, and goods moved according to economic demand and life-course strategies regardless of external political or internal administrative borders.[68]

While St. Petersburg, as the capital, attracted a broad range of migrants, Łódź, a small rural town in Russian Poland, exemplified the growth of industrial towns at a time when the administrative planning of urban polities was superseded by unplanned capitalist growth. Planned expansion from the 1820s to the 1840s made Łódź a purely industrial textile city, and planners attracted "useful foreigners" by offering them privileges and housing in special quarters. Jews, excluded from the town, were offered residence on a neighboring private estate. From 1877 to 1914, unplanned industrialization resulted in a disastrous decline in standards of hygiene. The population grew ninefold: Polish rural immigrants who came as unskilled workers; German-speaking Saxon, Pomeranian, Silesian weavers; Jewish and Bohemian factory operatives; Swiss and Czech technicians. Capitalists, who resided in the town for only part of the year, included German, English, and French men and their entourage; the administrators and police forces were Russian. Abject poverty existed in the immediate neighborhood of fabulous residences. Working-class men and women formed mutual aid societies with friends from the same village of origin but were socialized into a multiethnic labor force rather than into Polish culture. Migrants were always more numerous than native Poles.[69]

In the west, Paris as a city with a long history of in-migration and growth reveals a picture surprisingly similar in some respects. As a capital and a commercial center, it outgrew all attempts to limit its expansion, to define boundaries: 200,000 inhabitants in 1600, 500,000 in 1700, 600,000–700,000 in 1789. On the other hand, migrants arrived in structured urban social spaces, not at a construction site as in St. Petersburg. Specific regions of origin provided migrants with specific crafts. The "geography of work" included water carriers from Auvergne, Savoyard children working as shoe-cleaners and chimney sweeps, horse-dealers and coachmen from Le Perche and Normandy, and masons from the Limousin. Textile and clothing workers came from the north, workers in the food trades from Burgundy and Normandy. In some *faubourgs* and in trades like food-processing, in-migrants accounted for almost 80 percent of the inhabitants or workers. In the eighteenth century, about 90 percent of the mainly female servants and of casual male laborers were born outside the city. Many had worked for years in relay towns along the trade and supply routes before venturing into the metropolis. Half of all servants came between the ages of fifteen and twenty-five, but almost a quarter were over thirty at the time of arrival. Servants from surrounding regions, who stayed for a few years, brought rural cultural input into urban families and carried new customs back home. Migratory interchange reduced mortality, as germs were carried back to villages and immunized later migrants before their arrival. Among migrants from abroad, German-speaking people, Jews, and Belgians (from the Habsburg Netherlands) predominated. The mercantile classes were cosmopolitan. "On the eve of the Revolution Paris was a town of subtle hierarchies and cultural brokers."[70]

Cities like Paris and St. Petersburg were also centers of the European community of learning. Since the mid-seventeenth century, academies of letters and sciences established by rulers and "patriotic" learned societies of the educated bourgeoisie supplemented the medieval university tradition (chap. 5.2). They attracted scholars and inventors, industrialists, and innovators, who were increasingly "corresponding members" rather than migrants. While governments wanted to strengthen the economic and intellectual potential of a particular country, scholars remained cosmopolitan. Of the first sixteen members of the Academy of Sciences in St. Petersburg, for example, thirteen were German, two were Swiss, and one was French.[71]

The local and the cosmopolitan, as well as the practical and the theoretical, were still closely intertwined. Students' migrations to centers of learning, artisans' migrations in quest of skills, gentlemen's travels, often with servants and tutors, in pursuit of education (and pleasure), high-ranking women's travels in the retinue of ambassadors, and industrialists' tours to inspect production methods away from home—all were part of a general quest for progress, improvement, and innovation. If we believe their accounts, these travelers—like the medieval ibn Baṭṭūṭah—seem to have done without women. But women in privileged positions participated in scientific classifying and collecting activities; others provided centers of social-intellectual exchange.[72]

In contemporary thought, the mechanical arts, the liberal arts, and the decorative arts were of equal value. But without the mechanical or "useful" arts, the liberal and decorative ones would not survive. The art-isans, artists, and art-ful researchers were engaged in a joint project. Only in the mid-nineteenth century, when the age of machinery began, did mechanics and technicians separate themselves to form technical academies. Though the goal of all such endeavors was abstract "progress" and practical "internal improvements" in mercantilist states and, subsequently, in many-cultured societies labeled nation-states, the non-national character of knowledge dictated transcultural intellectual exchange. Thus knowledge remained universal, but its application became internal to states and self-constructed nations.[73]

12.5 Bourgeois Revolution, Nation, and Political Exile

While religious flight decreased after the final expulsion of the Huguenots from France in 1685, flight into political exile, although not uncommon earlier, assumed large proportions during the Age of Democratic Revolution and in the state-driven nation-building process (nation-states) thereafter. The democratic reconceptualization of "the people" from subjects to citizens implied loyalty of all people to their state, homogenized the patchwork of cultures and territories of dynastic states into one "national" culture, and established states with a single citizenry (chap 14.3). Exile could now be imposed on whole disloyal sections of a population. "At this historical moment, émigrés in the modern sense came into existence as transnational or revolutionary figures" (Miller). The first phase of mass exile involved "counter-revolutionary" or antirepublican adherents of anciens régimes. First came the United Empire Loyalists (Tories) from the new United States; next the nobility from revolutionary France. Although the French Revolution has generally been considered the more violent, uprooting was much more common in the American Revolution: over 60,000, or 24 persons per 1,000 inhabitants, left the colonies, while a mere 5 per 1,000 (129,000) departed from France. Loyalist families with their servants and slaves fled to the remaining British colonies in the Americas (the future Canada and the West Indies) or to Britain; French nobles fled to the German principalities and Russia.[74]

A second phase followed upon the reestablishment of reactionary regimes at the Congress of Vienna in 1815. During the struggles for republican, middle-class nation-states, reformers and revolutionaries were incarcerated, deported, expelled, or compelled to flee. As a result of the several uprisings in Poland and the ones in Naples (1820) and Piedmont (1821) and the as yet unsuccessful movement for Italian unification, Switzerland, France, and Great Britain—and the cities of Geneva, Paris, and London in particular—became centers of political refugees. Later, the United States hosted refugee democrats.[75] In the 1830s, Mazzini's "Young Italy" expanded into a "Young Europe" and served as a model. A "Young Germany" and a "League of the Ostracized" (Bund der Geächteten) developed among German exiles in 1830s Paris. The largest émigré group was made up of Poles who were fighting for an independent country and democratic reconstitution of the "nobles' republic." The exiles shared experiences of alienation, and some formed transnational communities. With support from kindred groups in the receiving societies—the English Chartists, for example—a cosmopolitan approach to democratic restructuring emerged; the highly mobile exiles cooperated with reform and labor movements.[76]

Though the political sphere and revolutionary theory have been considered a male reserve, women were of considerable importance in this emigration. On the political level, they provided discussion forums, salons, or corresponded with emigrants. On the level of gendered spheres, they provided the family environment in which exiled men operated and, in the frequent cases of extreme poverty, made survival possible. They suffered alienation and defeat. "I had lost myself . . . I saw a great deal, and dreadfully vividly," wrote Natalie Herzen in 1869. Jane Carlyle introduced Mazzini to English thought. All of the pre-1848 emigrant groups established communities, raised families, and—occasionally—discussed whether women would be treated equally in the societies-to-be. Outspoken women demanded equal rights. Aware that gender roles in North America or university education in Switzerland provided opportunities, women pursued migration strategies to better their position. From North America, they described their new position in letters back home; from Switzerland, university-educated Russian women returned to struggle for improved rights in the prerevolutionary society.[77]

Many exiles returned to support the revolutionary movements of 1848–49. Their failure sent thousands of men and women of many ethnic backgrounds to North America. From among the German Forty-eighters, Mathilde Franziska Anneke established the first women's newspaper in the United States, and Carl Schurz became the U.S. secretary of the interior. Kossuth, from Hungary, attempted to rally revolutionaries for further activities in Europe. Other families of exiles migrated to homesteads, but they lacked experience to succeed. In London, some 4,400 emigrants gathered. Those who had moved to Paris had to leave after the coup d'état of 1852. These highly articulate and highly heterogeneous reformers and revolutionaries were men and women with projects but without power.[78]

The age of bourgeois-democratic revolution changed into an age of working-class self-assertion through migration and revolution. The repression of the Paris Commune of 1871, of the German socialist movement from 1878 to 1890, and of the Russian revolution of 1905 caused exile and politically motivated labor migrations. Host governments imposed restrictions when a tiny minority of "propagandists of the deed" resorted to political assassination in the 1890s. In Russia, deportation to Siberia remained a punishment for dissenters (chap. 13.4). Migrating and exiled leaders of national unions and of the Socialist Internationals after 1864 supplemented the middle classes' cosmopolitanism with a working-class internationalism. Some blended easily into labor movements of the receiving societies, in the United States in particular. Others formed parallel ethnic labor movements, which merged with mainstream ones only after a process of acculturation. After the 1870s, national governments and labor movements had to deal with international labor migrations and attempts at internationalizing class struggles (chap. 14.2).[79]

13

The Russo-Siberian Migration System

Of the three nineteenth-century migration systems, the landlocked Russian one emerged from multidirectional medieval connections. In a first phase, Russia was distant from and yet connected to Scandinavia via the Baltic as well as to the Mediterranean via the Black Sea. By the eleventh century, immigrant Normans had established themselves as the ruling Kievan group over Russian, Finnish, Baltic, and Turkoman peoples. Byzantine Greek and Jewish merchants came up the Dnieper (Dnepr) River to Kiev; Russian princes and princesses traveled to Constantinople; and the marriage of Ivan III and Zoë of Byzantium in 1472 brought Byzantine artisans and Italian architects to Moscow (chaps. 2.3 and 3.3). The multiethnic empire began to incorporate foreign elites, like the Tatar nobility, assigning them complementary functions, such as military duties and, later, administrative or commercial ones.

In a second phase, the northeast was explored and commercially connected to Western Europe. Toward the west, Russia opened its "window" to Baltic maritime trade and incorporated Central European peoples and colonizer settlements: Poles after the Great Northern War with Sweden (1700–21), and German-language Baltic urban populations and Polish peasants during the dividing-up of Poland from 1772 to 1795. Southward territorial expansion, in conflict with the Ottoman Empire, incorporated peoples of the steppe; after conquest, immigrant settlers were recruited from the Germanies, Bulgaria, and Persia (chap. 12.3), and the urbanization processes were similar to those of the Atlantic World (chap. 12.4).

In the third phase of migrations—during the nineteenth century—the Russo-Siberian Migration System was separated from the Atlantic System by a permeable border zone from Lake Peipus via Smolensk and the Dnieper to Odessa. Colonists, merchants, and technicians crossed this zone heading east, and Jews and Ukrainians left Russia for North America. Internally, labor migrants moved to four centers of industrialization, Moscow, St. Petersburg, the Urals, and the Don basin; rural migrants moved to the southern fertile plains and, eastward, to Siberia's southern fringe.

When Russia began its conquest of Siberia in the mid-sixteenth century, the Portuguese were penetrating Asian trade; half a century had passed since Spain conquered the Caribbean, and half a century later the British began settlement of North America. Siberia's First Peoples, like those in North America, became part of a fur empire (chap. 9.1). Russian hunters, like the French *coureurs de bois* from the St. Lawrence valley, penetrated deep into fur-providing territories. Agricultural settlement, on the other hand, began closer to central Russia, in "New Russia" as some of Ukrainian territories were called. Again, the developments were similar to those in North America, where "New England" and "New France" were settled early, while the trans-Allegheny west and the "Great Desert" seemed as distant and forbidding a territory as Siberia (map 13.1).

In the Caucasus Mountains and in the vast Central Asian territories from the Caspian Sea to Manchuria, the migrations of nomadic peoples continued. In the territories of Tatars, Greeks, Alans, Russians, Bulgars, Karaims, Zichians, and Kipchacs, which had been depopulated and repopulated repeatedly, five periods of ethnogenesis and suzerainty may be discerned. First, from the mid-eleventh to the beginning of the thirteenth century, a Cuman-Kipchac supremacy over the steppe existed, followed, in the second period, by the rule of the Mongols from the mid-thirteenth to the early fifteenth century. Thereafter, in the third period, the rise of the centralized Russian state and of the borderland Dnieper Cossacks began. But at the turn of the seventeenth century, marking the fourth period, war with the Polish-Lithuanian Rzeczpospolita interrupted early colonization, which resumed after Ottoman expansion into the area, marking the fifth period.[1]

Caucasian people had been captured for the medieval Mediterranean slave trade. Under thirteenth- and fourteenth-century Mongol rule, many peoples had converted to Sunni Islam, and subsequently some were incorporated into the Ottoman Empire. Thus the codification of languages into written form often followed Arabic script.[2] To the south of Russia lived Cossacks and Bashkirs, Circassians, Armenians, Ossetians, Azerbaijanis, and Georgians. After unsuccessful resistance to tsarist suzerainty, the Bashkirs, a Turkish people, settled, like the Cossacks, into the role of an advance frontier guard.

Peoples from the Caspian Sea to Mongolia remained mobile. The Kalmyk, a western Mongolian group of Tibetan Buddhist faith, arrived on the Caspian littoral in the 1630s, but in the 1770s its Torgud subgroup remigrated eastward to the Dzungarian Basin (in today's China). The Kirghiz, once described in Chinese sources as red-haired and white-skinned, intermingled with Mongolian peoples and adapted Turkish culture. Many settled near Alma Ata in the thirteenth century; smaller groups lived in China and Afghanistan. A part of this people broke off in the seventeenth century as "Kazakhs" (that is, "the separated"). Their seminomadic life, patriarchal-feudalist structures, and horse-, cattle-, and camel-raising economy were threatened

13.1 Expansion of Russia, 16th–19th Centuries

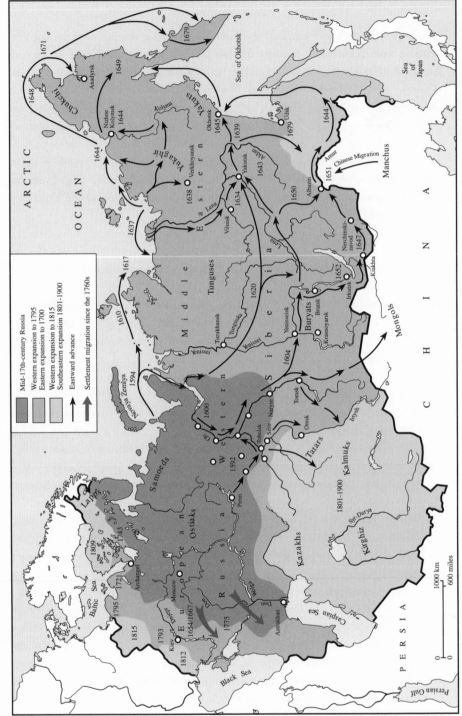

when Russian immigrant settlers occupied some of the land. Uzbeks, descendants of the Golden Horde of the fourteenth century, settled in about 1500 and formed a succession of independent states. Turkoman and other peoples completed the mix of cultures. From the twelfth to the fourteenth century, merchant caravans had crossed these territories along the "silk route" (see chap. 2.2), and later Persian merchants crossed them on their way northward via Samarkand and Tashkent to Russia (map 13.2).[3]

As a penal colony for "criminals," Siberia became after 1648 the destination of forced migrations of vagrants, beggars, and fortune-tellers, the same sort of classes that the British Empire would transport after 1788 to Australia. The categories of deportees grew: recalcitrant serfs from the 1760s onward, prostitutes, and, after 1800, Jews who failed to pay taxes for three consecutive years. Political exile, sanctioned by law in 1729 but imposed on a large scale only after the Decembrist uprising of 1825, involved populists, anarchists, critical writers, and socialists. Men—and a few women—had to trek from Tomsk for 1,000 miles (1,650 kilometers) to Irkutsk on Lake Baikal: an estimated 100,000 Polish rebels, 50,000 Russian political exiles, and 40,000 criminals by 1891. About 5,000 women, some with children, joined deported husbands. Many exiles toiled in coal or gold mines. Their spirit was celebrated in a poem by Alexander Pushkin (1799–1837). After 1900, exile all but ceased to be meted out as punishment. Throughout the period, other involuntary migrants came: officials compelled to move to the region's administrative posts; vagabonds, disinherited persons, fugitives from debts; and Old Believers fleeing persecution.[4] The ethnic Russian population of Siberia increased from 200,000 in 1700 to half a million in 1800, but the native non-Russian people still accounted for half of the total population.[5]

In the eighteenth century, non-Russian peoples in the east became fur-suppliers, military guards, or herdsmen, a division of labor that ended with the political-military incorporation of these peoples after the mid-nineteenth century. By the end of the nineteenth century, Russia had become a multiethnic empire with ethnic Russians accounting for 40–44 percent of the population and all of the East Slavic peoples for about 68 percent.

13.2   Rural Colonization and Urban Migrations, 1700–1861

Urbanization processes and agrarian settlement in the second phase of Russian migrations paralleled those of the rest of Europe. Expansion and reforms were achieved by Peter I ("the Great," r. 1682–1725) and Catherine II ("the Great," r. 1762–96). In the northeast, the Baltic Migration System (chap. 12.3) ceased to function with the end of Swedish hegemony, and Stockholm, Copenhagen, and St. Petersburg became separate centers of attraction. In the south, Russia incorporated the vast flock-grazing territories of the Bashkir, Kirghiz, and Kalmyk peoples. In the process, a Russian variant of "orientalism" (Said) constructed images of these Others that denigrated their cultures and self-determined activities.[6]

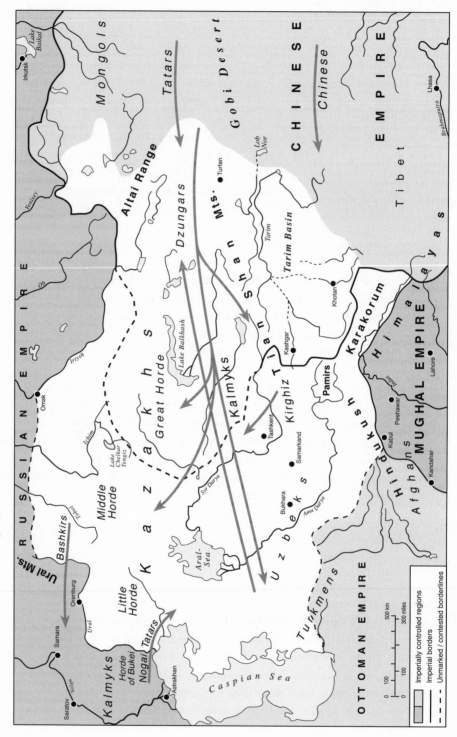

13.2　Migrations of Central Asian Peoples, 16th–18th Centuries

The Ukrainian southward migrations that had been arrested by Ottoman expansion resumed over the period 1550–1640 and reached the Black Sea by 1770. Ukrainian-settled lands had been part of Poland-Lithuania until they were transferred to Russia in 1654. From further north, peasants from Poland-Lithuania moved southward into northern Ukrainian-settled territories. The early eastward colonization by German-speaking and Flemish people (chap. 2.3) was thus followed by southeastward moves of Polish and Ukrainian peasants in Galicia and from Kiev to the Black Sea. Cities, in particular Kiev, held mercantile populations as varied as those of the Mediterranean: merchants from Novgorod, Jewish migrants from the east; Tatar traders; numerous Greek merchants, artisans, and clerics; Genoese from Crimea; Armenians.[7] Up to the mid-eighteenth century, merchants from India frequented the region's commercial centers, encouraged by the Russian government, which wanted to circumvent Ottoman and Iberian middlemen.[8]

Military requirements and mercantilist policies, as "populationist" as those of Vienna in the Balkans, resulted in state-sponsored colonization. From the 1670s to the early 1700s, an estimated 350,000 people, among them 200,000 runaway serfs, moved from Central Russia to the southern periphery. As elsewhere, the absolutist state was unable to exert absolute control and often legalized self-determined migrations ex post facto. By the 1740s, migration to Bashkiria and to the region of Ukraine called "New Russia" entered vast agricultural lands and tapped mineral and ore deposits. Until then, "settlers were sent to new areas usually because these needed population, rarely because the settlers themselves wanted or needed to be moved" (Bartlett). The scientist Mikhail Lomonosov (1711–65) suggested that single people and "whole ruined families" from war-torn Western Europe be encouraged to come.[9]

From the mid-eighteenth century onward, frontier settlers increasingly came on their own initiative: fugitive serfs, peasants, and owners of estates, as well as criminals. Serfs turned into pioneers for many reasons: heavy taxation, long military service, the suppression of dissent, or the imposition of new customs. Authorities in New Russia, in view of the shortage of settlers and laborers, were loath to apprehend and return fugitives. Similarly, slaves who escaped from the Kirghiz were not returned, although, to avoid warfare, indemnities were paid. Kalmyk and other immigrants from Asia, converted to Orthodox Christianity and were settled in Stavropol, a new town on the Volga. Religious converts also changed their ethnicity and "lost the former distinction of their nationality," as a contemporary source put it. By "Serbian military immigration" the shifting military border was defended by soldier-farmers and their families. Ethnically, these immigrants were heterogeneous: "Serb" was the generic term for soldier-migrants, just as "German" was the generic term for foreigners in Russian towns. Deported Polish servicemen, who were prisoners of war from newly conquered areas, and Prussian soldiers, whose desertion had been encouraged, began to cultivate the potentially fertile steppe lands.[10]

Like the patterns of settlement in mining areas in the Don basin or the Urals or in the new towns, rural patterns of settlement produced a multiple-origin population: Montenegrins, Albanians, Greeks, Armenians, Vlachs, Zaporog and Don Cossacks, Jews, Italians, Russian Old Believers, and Gypsies. The largest group was Ukrainian. As almost everywhere, immigrants mingled by intermarriage with native populations and with each other. When, because of the Ottoman decline, the military aspects of the settlement process subsided, a "Chancellery of Guardianship," comparable to the Habsburg *Einrichtungswerk* for Balkan settlers, surveyed land and allocated homesteads. The government upheld the inviolability of property held by the semi-nomadic Bashkirs, but—as in the case of the North American Native peoples—in the end the newcomers held the land.[11]

After 1762–63, the authorities attracted settlers from western and Central Europe, especially German-language people, for areas from the Dniester (Dnestr) to the Donets River (chap. 12.2). An edict by Catherine I, a kind of homestead law, granted 1) freedom of religion, 2) thirty to eighty *desiatinas* (eighty to 315 acres) of free land per family, 3) interest-free loans for implements, 4) exemption from taxation for ten to thirty years in agriculture and for ten years in towns, 5) self-administration, and 6) "perpetual" exemption from military service. Contrary to the interspersed settlement of the Orenburg Province, the privileged foreign settlers, including Swedes and Jews,[12] were placed in compact settlements along the Volga, in southern Ukraine, and later in Volhynia between Kiev in the east and the Bug River in the west. From the German territories about 11,000 families (41,600 individuals) came. Thus an arc of culturally heterogeneous German-language colonies, divided into Protestant, Catholic, and Mennonite groupings, stretched from the Baltic-German towns through Volhynia, southwestern Ukraine and the Crimean Black Sea-Germans to the Stavropol- (North Caucasus) Germans and Volga-Germans around Saratov.[13] About 11,000 families (41,600 individuals) came. In addition, a number of cities from St. Petersburg via Odessa to Tiflis (Tbilisi) had German communities, inserted as commercial and artisanal classes, and other immigrant urban peoples (map 13.3).[14]

The policy of settling foreigners was pursued from 1762–63 to 1804; it then was continued in amended form into the 1830s. Historians have often emphasized the role of the Westerners in introducing agricultural improvements. Contemporary Russian authorities, however, increased internal migration and the recruitment of Slavic settlers. From the 1740s to the 1770s, 0.8 million men, women, and children participated in the internal southward population shift, and from 1780 to 1850 another 3.5 million, mainly state serfs, migrated. By the mid-nineteenth century, the families that achieved high rates of natural increase supported a market-oriented rural economy exporting grain in large quantities, first through the port of Odessa and later via westward rail networks.[15]

Migration and the Growth of the Cities

Because of the anti-urban, antibourgeoisie policies of the powerful nobility, urbanization had a shifting history. The bourgeoisie, which had defended its position against

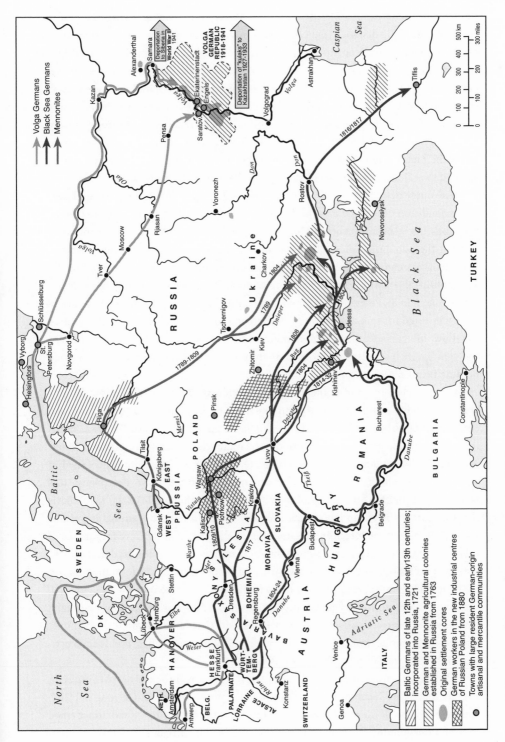

13.3   Settlement and Origin of Russian-Germans, 1763–1914

the nobility's encroachments into the fifteenth century, declined with the end of the Hanseatic long-distance trade. The tsars improved Moscow's position relative to other towns by compelling the resettlement of rich merchants from Novgorod, Pskov, and Smolensk. Like merchants from abroad, they and their employees lived in special quarters, often designated by the name of their place of origin. Moscow's growth accelerated when Tsar Peter I established close relations with the foreigners' community. A Scottish immigrant, Patrick Gordon, and a French-Swiss immigrant from Geneva, Franz Lefort, became influential political advisers. A 1702 manifesto intensified the practice of calling upon Westerners for capital, technical expertise, commercial experience, and artisanal skills, as well as for military service.

The outer town (*posad*) of many cities, with high population densities and poor living conditions, absorbed most of the lower-class permanent, multiyear, or seasonal migrants. In eighteenth-century Moscow, lodgers and serfs accounted for about one-third of the population of 200,000. During the winter, this figure doubled because more workers came and because the gentry (*dvoriane*), the social group below the high nobility (*boyars*), returned from their countryseats with their handymen and servant women. In St. Petersburg, after its first century (chap. 12.4), immigrants and temporary in-migrants remained numerous. Return migrants, the *pitershchiki*, appeared to fellow villagers as urbane. The numerous visitors to the city provided women in the vicinity with supplementary income from rented rooms. In town, these women became boardinghouse keepers.[16]

Common laborers and workers for the new industries were recruited from among *obrok*-serfs whose owners, receiving annual dues, easily granted permission for such employment (see below). With this *otkhodnichestvo* practice, legalized in 1724, feudal lords resembled labor bosses, and serfdom the industrial slavery in the United States. Most of the serf-migrants remained connected to their villages; some succeeded in buying their freedom; and some fled to the new territories. In St. Petersburg, this labor force accounted for 150,000 of the city's 450,000 inhabitants in the 1840s. Serfs lost their utility as cheap labor once industry began to require training and skills. Patterns of migration determined family life or the lack of it. The predominance of men (sex ratio 3:1) and poverty among the Russian lower classes resulted in the abandonment of infants, one-fourth to two-fifths of whom were left in foundling homes in the period 1800–50. Among the 14,000 foreigners (3.1 percent of the inhabitants), the sex ratio was almost balanced. Immigrant mechanics worked in their own independent small enterprises, and ethnicities mingled. One large building, for example, housed an Armenian priest, a German pastor, and German, English, and French artisans. Ethnic segregation was low in St. Petersburg.[17]

The incorporation of Vyborg, Riga, and Revel (Tallinn) into the Russian Empire in 1711 included the German-origin estates of Baltic cities, the Baltic-German nobility, and the Slavo-Baltic-German peasantry. Culturally, the groups remained intact since capitulations granted freedom of religion to Protestants, urban self-administration, and the restoration of noble landholdings sequestered under the preceding Swedish rule. New immigrants and long-settled ethnics quickly achieved influence at the

Russian court. Many became administrators; others were adventurers.[18] In both its private and state sectors, the economy relied on foreigners for a whole range of occupations, from free journeymen artisans to wealthy entrepreneurs. Greeks and Armenians came; Czech skilled workers and Prussian artisans immigrated; Dutch and northern German technical experts found opportunities. Administrators studied the settling of Huguenots by Western European rulers but did not implement plans for an immigrant-staffed silk manufacture.

Because the immigrant lower and inserted upper-middle classes did not "fit" into a societal structure that juxtaposed nobility and serfs, and because sections of the nobility were willing to invest rather than see foreign capitalists take the profits, contracts between the tsarist bureaucracy and immigrant investors involved time-consuming negotiations, were tenuous, and at times attracted adventurers rather than businessmen. By the mid-eighteenth century, the government began to train local labor with the help of foreign experts in order to reduce the need for immigration by adjusting the structure of Russian society. At the same time, the Russian nobility began a struggle to reduce the influence of the "Germans"—that is, the heterogeneous "foreigners"—including Baltic-Germans settled for centuries as well as recent arrivals of many cultural backgrounds. At least in Baltic cities, the German language, however, remained the lingua franca. The inserted position of "foreigners" and their economic function resembled the circumstances of mercantile and upper-class immigrants and sojourners in other societies having a powerful class of nobles. At the turn to the nineteenth century, the generic "foreigner" category was differentiated by the mass arrival of refugee French nobles, by French soldiers and officers who did not straggle back home after the defeat of Napoléon's army, and by subsequent migration. French culture influenced the Russian nobility's courts.[19]

13.3 Peasants into Proletarians: Internal Migration in Industrializing Russia after Emancipation

Nineteenth-century European Russia was an industrializing society. When, in 1842, the British ban on exporting textile machinery was lifted, textile production based on free wage-labor quickly developed in the annexed Polish territories, especially in Łódź (chap. 12.4). In 1897, at the time of the first empire-wide census, 10 percent of the adult male and just under 5 percent of the adult female population of European Russia worked in industry, as railroad workers, artisans, or servants (about seven million in a population of 93 million). The provinces of Moscow (the "Central Industrial Region") and St. Petersburg, as well as the four provinces of the southern Don basin and Urals industrial belt, with their mining and smelting industries, received the bulk of the internal labor migrants. In 1897, 74 percent of Moscow's inhabitants of one million and 70 percent of St. Petersburg's 1.25 million were migrants (map 13.4).[20]

All of the other forty-four provinces had negative migration balances. Low out-migration characterized the three Baltic provinces (subsequently Estonia and Latvia) because of the language differences and the thinly settled provinces north of St. Petersburg. The mass of the migrants came from the two core agricultural belts. In the northern one, because of the poor soils, peasants traditionally supplemented agricultural income by engaging in cottage industry. The south-central belt comprised areas with fertile soils and sufficient rain.[21] As a consequence, labor regimes differed. In the northern *obrok* system, the prevailing quitrent arrangement had monetarized peasant duties. Serfs paid their owners an annual sum out of income obtained from the sale of crops, cottage production, or labor migration. Some owners even helped them set up business or find city labor and housing close to factories. Cottage production and seasonal migration resulted in higher literacy rates and the accumulation of modest savings. In the south, labor was needed throughout the year, and, under the *barschina* system, serfs were obliged to work up to three days per week on their owners' lands. State serfs usually worked under the *obrok* system.

Later than in Prussia (1807) and Austria-Hungary (1848) but approximately at the same time that slavery ended in the United States (1863), serfdom was abolished in 1861. Emancipated peasants had to compensate their former owners by land cessions or indemnity payments and thus saw their economic independence compromised from the very beginning. Permanent land shortages and cash crises were exacerbated by a near-doubling of the population from 68.5 million in 1850 to 126 million in all of Russia in 1897. Families' adjustment of childbearing patterns to new socioeconomic circumstances achieved results only a generation later. Relative rural overpopulation resulted in migration, which was voluntary for those who desired wage incomes (and thus became proletarianized) and involuntary for those who would have preferred to remain on the land. Like the Hohenzollern territories east of the Elbe and the Danubian sections of the Habsburg monarchy, Russia was characterized by a feudal-bourgeois type of socioeconomic development that contrasted with the bourgeois-capitalist way of Western Europe and North America.[22] These three vast agrarian regions became reservoirs of labor: through internal migration for Russian industry, through seasonal migration for German agriculture and industry, and through emigration for economic sectors in other parts of Europe and North America (chap. 14).[23]

One type of coerced mobility continued: draftees in the imperial army served for twenty-five years, and their families considered them lost. Only in 1874 was military service reduced to six years; more than another three decades later, it went down to three. Similarities with labor migration were evident: the army urbanized rural recruits; officers rented out soldiers for paid work—often a type of forced labor—or used them for private chores; off-duty soldiers could also undertake paid free labor (*volnye raboty*) on their own account; soldiers' leaves to visit their home villages resembled return migration. However, since villages and families sent their least productive members into the army, the impact of returning soldiers was lower than that of labor migrants.[24]

Peasant emancipation did not make men and women "independent" in a modern sense. Each village commune (*mir*) held land collectively and reallocated this common wealth among its male "souls" annually. After emancipation, the commune was collectively responsible for payment of taxes and compensation to former owners.[25] Out-migrating men remained part of the community, and the commune-administered pass system for seasonal or multiyear absences required men to pay their share of taxes and expected them to return for spring sowing or harvest work. Seasonal migrants had to be fed in the village in winter; they also returned during slumps in employment. Later, men who renounced their rights to land could leave permanently, but, with no social security system in place, few chose this option. Of the 13 million passes granted in the decade after emancipation (1861–70), 99.6 percent were for one year or less. In the next decade, the number of passes granted tripled. In the decade from 1891 to 1900, when 71 million passes were issued, the share of the long-term absences grew fifteenfold, albeit only to 2.6 percent of the total. Since the fee for seasonal passes was lower and renewal possible, these figures do not adequately reflect duration of stay in cities.[26]

In 1897, 9.4 million men and women (11.7 and 8.0 percent of their respective shares of the population) did not reside in their province of birth. These net migration figures do not reflect gross moves: multiple migrations, migration and return before the census date, emigration, rural-urban migration within the populous Moscow and St. Petersburg provinces, or intraprovincial migration in European Russia. To spread the risk of insufficient income, many families followed the almost worldwide pattern of gender-specific allocation of labor resources to male wage labor at a distance and female farm labor at home.[27] After emancipation, out-migration continued to be correlated to soil fertility—that is, to labor regimes, patterns of work, and attitudes toward traditional agricultural life.[28]

Temporary mass migration to industrial work influenced family relations as well as peasant, worker, and gendered mentalities and the urban self-organization of male sojourners. Young men, ready to migrate, often received a passport only after having married because parents and elders saw emotional attachment as a way to tie the men's work capacity to the community. Whereas in the rural/mining contexts of the Don and Donets basins and the Urals men and women migrated jointly, more than 80 percent of the urban male migrants lived separated from their families because of gendered labor markets. The women left behind were "orphans," as one author argued.[29] Most peasant families could not afford to or did not want to "cast off agriculture completely, . . . to leave it in the hands of women to carry on some way or other is a decision the majority come to. . . . Therefore, women not only plough, plant, rake, and gather hay and grain, but often execute the social obligations of men as well" (*Zemstvo* report, from Kostroma Province, 1912).[30] Studies of rural women in Poland, Slovakia, and Croatia-Slavonia left behind by husbands who migrated to city work or to North America suggest that workloads doubled while independence remained limited because of meddling by relatives (often elderly males) in the home and farm economy. Children of such bifurcated households hardly ever saw their fathers. Women visiting their husbands in the cities had a glimpse of urban life and of male working-class standards of living, the latter probably having been no inducement to follow. When women migrated, however, they acculturated quickly to urban life and married late—in contrast to immigrant men who represented peasant culture and married early. Rural single or widowed older women, in particular, were compelled by economic need to search for jobs in the cities.[31]

Migrant men from the same village or region (*zemliaki*, fellow countrymen) settled close to each other, as did fifteenth-century migrants in Beijing or Genoa or twentieth-century newcomers in Montreal or Nairobi. Neighborhood support, shared traditions of everyday life, and festive customs eased the transition into urban life and factory work. Self-organized in *arteli*, collective units of life outside of the factory, the men cooked together or hired one woman to do the work, elected a leader, and regulated their affairs. Some also hired themselves out jointly, and men searched for work wherever networks of *zemliaki* or *artel*-fellows might direct them. High levels of geographic and job fluctuation demanded supportive communities. Thirteen percent of Moscow's inhabitants of 1882 had arrived in the preceding year. Like the village *mir*, the *artel* was a democratic as well as a constraining institution.[32]

Newcomers' mentalities changed in stages; proletarianization occurred over generations. Serfs and emancipated peasants first became seasonal labor migrants; then, with longer sojourns in the factories, they became peasant-workers still bound to the village. When ties loosened, they changed to worker-peasants; only their urban-born sons and daughters would become true urban workers, proletarians. However, as a result of the *mir* system and the bifurcated family structure, children were usually raised in the rural world, distant from the working-class environments of industrial cities. Thus their generation would begin the cycle again: each generation of workers had to be socialized anew into factory life, whether in Russia, North America, or Western Europe. Migrants who did not return to their village origins developed both craft skills and proletarian mentalities. More recent migrants substratified them. They or their children could enter skilled positions—until Taylorization and mass production reduced the demand for skilled workers.[33]

The migrants' urban working-class living conditions were frequently abominable. "The people [in Moscow] live in impossible condition: filth, stench, suffocating heat. . . . They lie down together barely a few feet apart, there is no division between sexes, and adults sleep with children. The air is saturated with the most dreadfully foul language."[34] Descriptions of 1890s New York or Berlin evoke similar images; regardless of industrial city or continent, contemporary photos and etchings resemble each other. Migration, which increased independence through cash wages and reduced the danger of pre-harvest subsistence crises, could still imply a downward slide in living conditions, sanitary ones in particular.

13.4 The Nineteenth-Century Siberian Frontier and Chinese Mongolia

Although forced and involuntary migration continued, from the seventeenth century on the vast majority of the migrants reached Siberia voluntarily as peasants in search of free land or more land or a life without servitude or government regulations.[35] Officials and nobility in the emigration areas complained about shortages of laborers and military recruits, but Siberian administrators, like their South Russian colleagues, were unwilling to apprehend and return immigrants. No policy could stop the flow, and edicts of the tsars tended to accept the ongoing process of migration "by their own will," even that of state serfs after 1822. Human initiative defied bureaucratic regulation, and peasant interests proved stronger than self-interested restrictions imposed by the nobility. Prospective migrants often organized themselves into groups and sent scouts to locate land and explore conditions. Cossacks, too, moved again and settled in Siberia.[36]

In the 1830s, Count P.-D. Kiselyov of the Ministry of State Domains called for a consistent migration policy, commissioned a land survey, and argued for the sufficient allotment of land to each male peasant "soul"—that is, to household heads and their families. In 1835 administrators who knew of peasant discontent suggested possibilities to accommodate one million peasants. But nobles and conservative bureaucrats stalled policy-making for fear of social disruption.[37] About 375,000 migrants, including exiles, arrived in Siberia from 1801 to 1850, on average a mere 7,500 annually. Still, state peasants from the central and southeastern provinces resettled in West Siberia faster than surveyors could proceed, and high birth rates among the newcomers accelerated population growth.[38]

After 1861, peasant families migrated in ever larger numbers to southern Siberian and trans-Caspian lands; the mining frontier became a magnet from the 1880s on, parallel to the Canadian West. While transcontinental railroads began to facilitate movement in the 1880s, the freedom to move after 1861 explains the mass migrations of settler-pioneers. Similarities between the United States and Imperial Russia were many.[39] The Great American Desert was considered uninhabitable; "Even in Siberia people live," a Russian proverb wryly noted. The U.S. and Canadian governments encouraged migration through homestead acts, in 1862 and 1872 respectively, as did the Russian Chancellery of Guardianship in the mid-eighteenth century and P. A. Stolypin's policies of 1906–11. Migrants settled on consolidated holdings and created social systems more equal and more dynamic than in their home villages. In the United States, Mormons fled westward; in Russia, Old Believers moved eastward; Canada received Russian Doukhobors and Mennonites. Russian migration to Siberia, however, involved almost exclusively families and political exiles, as highly educated, socially responsible men and women provided teachers and nurses to villages and towns in advance of state action.[40]

In the decades from 1880 to 1914, about 20 million men, women, and children moved from Europe to North America; in the Russo-Siberian System to the 1920s, 10 million moved eastward and southward. From 1851 to 1890, the average number of newcomers to Siberia grew from 19,000 to 42,000, and free migration more than quadrupled by 1914. After 1900, exiles accounted for only 1.7 percent of the migrants. From 1851 to 1890, 1.1 million came, and, from 1891 to 1914, 4.2 million, plus some 0.7 million unregistered migrants, or a total of approximately six million between 1851 and 1914. Of the total Siberian population of 9.4 million in 1911,

13.4   Siberia, the Russian Far East, and Alaska, 19th Century

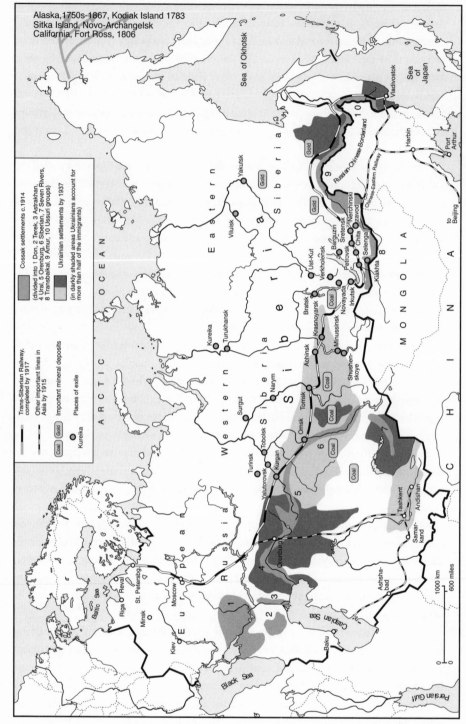

Alaska,1750s-1867, Kodiak Island 1783
Sitka Island, Novo-Archangelsk
California, Fort Ross, 1806

Trans-Siberian Railway,
completed by 1917

Other important lines in
Asia by 1915

Important mineral deposits

Places of exile

Coal   Gold

Kureika

Cossak settlements c.1914

(divided into 1 Don, 2 Terek, 3 Astrakhan,
4 Ural, 5 Orenburg, 6 Siberian, 7 Seven Rivers,
8 Transbaikal, 9 Amur, 10 Ussuri groups)

Ukrainian settlements by 1937

(in darkly shaded areas Ukrainians account for
more than half of the immigrants)

First Peoples accounted for a mere 10 percent. Immigrants and their descendants were of mainly Russian, Ukrainian, and Ruthenian ethnic origin. Ukrainian emigration to Siberia and Canada was paralleled by Russian migration to Ukrainian cities. Belorussians were involved in small numbers at most.[41] As in Canada, much of the northern territories were uninhabitable, and settlers were concentrated along a 600-kilometer-wide strip in West and Central Siberia. Settlement was easier for the estimated four million settlers in the trans-Caspian and trans-Aralian regions and in Kazakhstan.[42]

In Central and East Asia, Chinese and Russian administrators had fought over or negotiated about borders since traders and explorers had met at the Amur River in the mid-seventeenth century. Migrant Chinese laborers and small merchants originated from northern recruitment areas outside the reach of Western European colonial powers. Russian and Chinese settlers lived interspersed in separate villages. When the Chinese imperial government reduced emigration restrictions in 1858, some 200,000 crossed into the Russian Far East, often as sojourners. By 1910, 100,000 Chinese, some skilled workers or urban artisans, lived there. The Amur River became a trade artery, and many worked as navvies on the Trans-Siberian Railway alongside skilled workers from Germany and Italy in a labor force that was 25 percent foreign. Chinese merchants and artisans moved to Vladivostok; one-third of the population of Khabarovka (Khabarovsk) was Chinese. They organized themselves into self-governing guilds under headmen. In the Amur goldfields, 15 percent of the labor force was made up of Chinese contract workers in 1900, 76 percent in 1915. Like pidgin English in California, a Russo-Chinese pidgin became the lingua franca. Chinese people met with discrimination and racism, but intermarriage was widespread. The Chinese could neither register for land nor stake claims; wages were low and subject to further deductions by contractors. Some Koreans and Japanese joined the agricultural settlers and the labor force. Russian administrators, of White mentality, attempted to restrict the "yellow peril." But the region was economically dependent on the immigrants. The Russian Far East, temporarily including Alaska, became a meeting ground for Eurasian and Pacific peoples (map 13.4, fig. 13.1).[43]

Parallel to Russian settlement in Siberia, Chinese eastward migration to Inner Mongolia began in the seventeenth century and increased by the mid-nineteenth century. An imperially imposed change in chieftainships, the introduction of Lamaism, and the imposition of an annual period of residence in Beijing on chiefs or princes had reduced the power of the nomad pastoralists.[44] During the slow Mongol retreat, some groups stayed and adopted Chinese ways of life and the regional dialect of the Chinese language. Others settled in Chinese cities, and Mongol women married Chinese men. Outside of cities, seasonally arriving Chinese traders often lived with Mongol women. Elsewhere, in Chinese Turkistan, for example, Chinese men acculturated and joined Mongol communities. Traders close to the edge of settlement acquired land that they later sold to immigrant peasants. Thus nomad Mongols were slowly pushed back ever further. The caravan and carting trade was in the hands of local Muslims. Given the distances, sleeping carts provided wealthy trav-

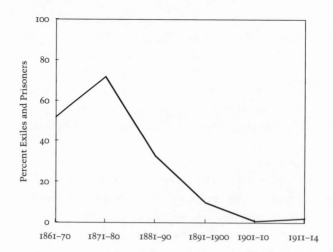

Figure 13.1   Migration to Asian Russia, 1887–1910, and Percentage of Exiles and Prisoners, 1861–1914

elers with day and night accommodation. Traders, pedlars, and artisans, almost exclusively Hebei men, were different by dialect and ethnicity from Shandong settlers and their seasonal harvest laborers. In towns such as Chahar-Hara, Mongol tents and yurts were mixed with Chinese houses; in villages Chinese and Mongol lived separate.[45]

13.5   Leaving the Orbit of the Russo-Siberian System before 1914

Next to settler migration to Siberia and internal labor migration in European Russia, a third movement carried Jews, Poles, and Baltic peoples westward into the Atlantic Migration System. Jewish and Polish migrants jointly accounted for 68 percent of Russian emigration to North America; others included Belorussians and Ukrainians (11 percent), Lithuanians (9 percent), Finns (7 percent), and Russian-Germans and Mennonites who left after their privileges were withdrawn (5 percent). Russian radicals fled to France, England, Germany, and Switzerland; women left the empire to pursue opportunities in higher education. From 1830 to 1860, only about 30,000 of the tsar's subjects left the empire and thus the Russo-Siberian Migration System. From 1860 to 1914, 4.5 million followed. Compared to labor migrants and Jewish flight, the number of political and educational émigrés was small.[46]

Polish Rebels, Russian Revolutionaries, and Women Students

In the late eighteenth century, reformers in Poland modeled their organizations on clubs in revolutionary France and discussed the recently ratified U.S. Constitution. When they proclaimed the Constitution of 1791, Russia, supported by parts of the

Polish nobility, intervened and jointly with the Hohenzollern and Habsburg empires carved up independent Poland in the third and last partition of the country in 1795. Polish military officers, as part of the intelligentsia, fled and staked their hopes on Napoléon. The emperor relied on a Polish legion in northern Italy but then transferred it to Haiti to quell the "slave insurrection"; most of the soldiers and officers perished. About 100,000 Poles joined Napoléon's march on Moscow. This ended the stage of soldiers' migrations.

Under the order imposed in 1815 by the Congress of Vienna, Polish peasants were not given ownership of their land—a cause for mass emigration later. At first, conquered Poles rebelled unsuccessfully three times: in Warsaw in 1830–31, in Kraków in 1846, and, finally, in the Congress Kingdom in 1863–64. The Russian government deported captured "rebels" to Siberia and began a Russification policy after 1830. Some 7,000–8,000 refugees headed for Paris, and for decades thereafter the "Great Emigration" dominated Polish political activity in France and England. In the wake of the uprisings, cities like Vilna (Vilnius) lost their influence as centers for ethnic culture and consciousness by being deprived of their institutions of higher learning. Young people had to migrate to universities elsewhere in Europe; the Polish underground had to rely on émigré literature and on leaflets.[47]

Emigration gave Polish Romanticism its specific features. In contrast to the monarchist aristocrats, the Left Wing was composed mainly of the intelligentsia, the poor gentry, and lower-level and noncommissioned officers. The non-noble revolutionary democrats played a more important role in the national movement than ever before and, influenced by German utopian socialism and Mazzini's Italian national idea, advocated "Communes of the Polish People." Others, like the poet Adam Mickiewicz, lamented in the *Polish Pilgrimage* (1832) the émigrés' French and bourgeois social surroundings in Paris, which were inhabited by a spirit "callously indifferent to anything except profit." The fear of materialism was echoed by migrants of many ethnicities across the Atlantic World. The Polish émigrés were to become a nucleus for late-nineteenth-century Polish labor migrants' organizations, and the exiles' descendants provided leadership to Polish miners arriving in France from Germany after 1918.[48]

Many Russian reformers and revolutionaries also left for Western Europe. After Nikolay Turgenev had been declared the first "émigré" by the government in 1825, the refugees "emerged as a kind of society-in-exile, a second Russia abroad. . . . [It] became the repository of the dreams of thousands of people who believed that a day would someday dawn when the tsarist autocracy would be abolished and replaced by a more humane system of rule."[49] Famous exiles included Alexander Herzen and his family, the anarchist Mikhail Bakunin, and the mutual-help advocate Count Peter Kropotkin. Before the 1860s, the small émigré community consisted of some 200–225 individuals. Many of the post-1860s political refugees had experienced Siberian exile or imprisonment before leaving. As described in Ivan Turgenev's famous novel *Fathers and Sons* (1862), they met in modest reading rooms, which—rather than secret cells—were the centers of activities. They smuggled their publications into Russia. Their visions were larger than life. The impoverished I. A. Kel'siev planned to write about the "Woman Question" while his wife, "thin," with "tear-stained eyes," was dying, and he envisioned revolutionary centers from London to Turkey encircling Russia. He and many others suffered from host societies' prejudices against émigrés. "They lived—survived would be a better way to put it—in a fog of bitter disappointments and unrealized hopes."[50]

The 1870s, after the emancipation of serfs, became a period of realignment. Long-time émigrés saw their visions challenged by recent arrivals and women students, the *narodniki,* who planned to educate the peasant masses and incite working-class action. The "new emigration" (Miller) followed socialist principles. Emigration increased after 1900, with Germany becoming the center for the social-democratic and liberal refugees, Paris the center of the revolutionaries, and Switzerland the turntable of ideas and personal trajectories. Other emigrants worked from Italy and Balkan countries. Militants who returned during the revolution of 1905 were soon forced into exile again. Large numbers of revolutionary Jewish workers, many of whom had to flee, increased the stream of U.S.-bound migrants. As in the case of German workers under the antisocialist law, flight, political emigration, and labor migration formed a complex whole. The several generations of antitsarist refugees of the decades from 1825 to 1914 formed the first Russian political emigration.[51]

Young women in search of education left for the West—if their families supported their quest for education and could afford their stay abroad. Some 100 women and half as many men studied in Switzerland before the tsarist government, in 1873, prohibited women from departing by threatening the "future mothers" with exclusion from charity and medical work. Many returned. But when the repression of 1882 again closed Russian universities to women—except for the one in St. Petersburg—educational migration resumed.[52] From the 1860s on, Swiss universities, except for the University of Basel, enrolled Russian women. In Zurich, their main center, they met other foreign reformers, such as the English Sophia J. Blake, who were discouraged by discrimination at home. From 1882 to 1913, the 5,000–6,000 Russian women accounted for one-third to one-half of all the foreigners enrolled.[53] In one count, of a total countrywide student body of 6,444, 2,322 were from Russia.[54] Other students from Russia also emigrated: Armenians and Baltic-Germans, Poles who boycotted Russian educational institutions, and Jews who were subject to admission quotas. Most planned to return to devote themselves to medical and charitable work in villages and, perhaps, among the urban poor. After the revolution of 1905, Russian universities again enrolled women, 44,000 in 1915. The Swiss population and, in particular, male students—but not the professors—had viewed the Russian women with a certain hostility. Mostly single and of modest circumstances, they were independent or, viewed from the other side, "immoral." Many returned to high-level political reformist or revolutionary activities; others experienced exile or imprisonment. When, in 1907, a woman student attempted to assassinate a visiting former Russian minister of the interior, Swiss public opinion took an unexpected turn. Democratic traditions overruled aversion to violence and notions of women's roles: "Gessler wasn't killed by a kiss, either." Punishment was relatively mild.[55]

The exile student communities, like those of political refugees, were character-ized by modest lifestyles—"honest poverty," as the saying has it. The one commodity available in abundance was politics—in which men cherished traditional gender roles. When the German social democrat Clara Zetkin organized a peace conference of socialist women in Bern in March 1915, a solitary male sat in a coffee shop around the corner feeling a need to instruct the five Russian Bolshevik women delegates on how to vote. He went by the name of Lenin.[56]

The Emigration of Russian-Germans and Mennonites

Emerging Russian nationalism clashed with attitudes of ethnocultural superiority among long-established settlers from Western Europe. For decades, German-language and Mennonite immigrants had adapted to their host cultures, efforts at cultural retention notwithstanding, but they remained in enclaves—hyphenated German-Russian and Russian-Mennonite ethno-religious communities.[57] The reform period of the 1860s resulted in the equalization of all inhabitants and with it the withdrawal of privileges. The oppressive regime of Alexander III (r. 1881–94) discriminated against religious dissenters, Latin Christian denominations, and all non-Russian "national minorities." The new quest for national homogeneity imposed demands for assimila-tion. As a consequence, approximately 150,000 of the discriminated left westbound for North America in semivoluntary or compelled secondary migrations from 1899 to 1914. Many more left in the 1920s, fleeing atheism and collectivism. The Canadian prairies became the receiving areas for tens of thousands, who often planned to settle in blocs similar to their rural colonies in Russia.

One example illustrates the cultural trajectories. Eduard Duesterhoeft's ances-tors had migrated to Volhynia. According to his recollections, German settlers had arrived in three periods: after 1816 from the Danzig area and the Palatinate, later from cities and towns in Poland and Germany, and again after the Polish uprisings of 1831 and 1863. Wanting to study for the ministry, he returned to Hanover, Germany, in 1913—but in 1914 World War I began: "We foreign students . . . were Russian citizens, so we had to report to the police. . . . There were German boys from Australia, . . . from Africa, from Poland, all intending to go back as pastors on completion of their studies. But, we were all forced to labour there for a few years in the institution." They used the time to improve their German. "You see, *if you are German* but come from Russia, they would correct every word you would utter, saying it was wrong" (emphasis added). In the 1920s, Duesterhoeft migrated to Canada and ended up in the dust bowl area, watching others leave.[58]

Labor Migrations and the Jewish Pale of Settlement

Russian Poles and Jews living west of the border zone between the Russo-Siberian and Atlantic Migration Systems left westbound. So did some Russians, though the 95,000 "Russian" immigrants in the United States in 1910 and the 170,000 arrivals in the

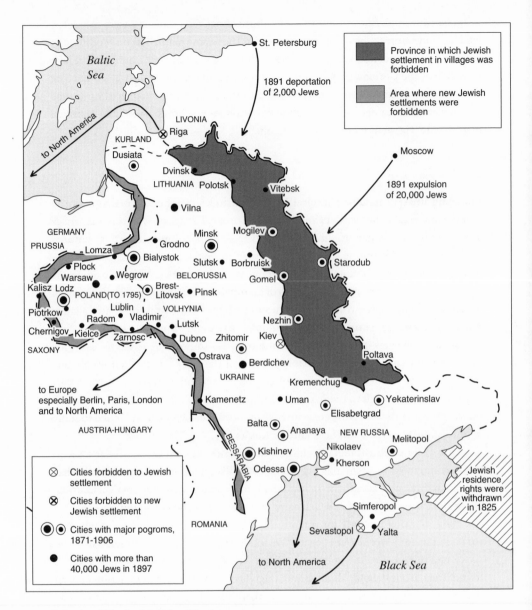

Map legend:

Province in which Jewish settlement in villages was forbidden

Area where new Jewish settlements were forbidden

⊗ Cities forbidden to Jewish settlement

⊗ Cities forbidden to new Jewish settlement

◉ ⊙ Cities with major pogroms, 1871-1906

● Cities with more than 40,000 Jews in 1897

Baltic Sea

to North America

1891 deportation of 2,000 Jews

St. Petersburg

Moscow

1891 expulsion of 20,000 Jews

LIVONIA
KURLAND
Dusiata
⊗ Riga
Dvinsk
LITHUANIA Polotsk
Vitebsk
Vilna
GERMANY
PRUSSIA
Lomza
Minsk
Mogilev ◉
Grodno
Bialystok
Plock
Slutsk Borbruisk
Starodub
Warsaw
Wegrow
BELORUSSIA
Gomel ◉
Kalisz Lodz
POLAND(TO 1795)
Brest-Litovsk Pinsk
Piotrkow
Lublin
VOLHYNIA
Chernigov
Radom Vladimir
Lutsk
Nezhin ◉
Kielce
Zarnosc
Dubno Zhitomir Kiev
SAXONY
Ostrava
Poltava
Berdichev
UKRAINE
Kremenchug
to Europe especially Berlin, Paris, London and to North America
Kamenetz Uman
Yekaterinslav
Elisabetgrad
Balta ◉
Ananaya NEW RUSSIA
Melitopol
AUSTRIA-HUNGARY
BESSARABIA
Kishinev
Nikolaev
Kherson
Jewish residence rights were withdrawn in 1825
Odessa ◉
ROMANIA
Simferopol
Sevastopol ⊗ Yalta
to North America
Black Sea

13.5   Poland and the Jewish Pale of Settlement

next decade included Carpatho-Ruthenians ("Rusyns"), Ukrainians, and other people from the empire. Most went to New York and Pennsylvania as unskilled laborers. Polish men and women, in all three partitioning empires, faced restrictions on account of their culture and language. Looking back historically, one finds that Poles had left for seasonal harvest migrations since the mid-fifteenth century. As serfs, they had followed their lords eastward and mixed with Lithuanian and Belorussian peasants. Because peasants were not defined by the nobility as part of the Polish *"natio,"* a national identity emerged only slowly, despite reform concepts propagated

326   Cultures in Contact

by the Enlightenment. A global diasporic consciousness among the large numbers of nineteenth-century Polish labor migrants worldwide stood in contrast to the localized consciousness found in the partitions.[59]

Most of the westbound migrants from the Russian Empire were Jews (see the background for this in chaps. 4.2 and 12.1). Of the world's Jewish population, an estimated three-quarters lived in Eastern Europe in the late eighteenth century (750,000–900,000); by the end of the nineteenth century their numbers had grown to 5.2 million in Russia and 2 million in other parts of East and East Central Europe. Their economic activities, more varied than in Western Europe, included trade and crafts in urban contexts, commercially mediating positions between bound agrarian populations and urban markets, and agricultural pursuits. The last partition of Poland in 1795 incorporated most of the Jewish population into Russia's Polish, Belorussian-Lithuanian, and Ukrainian territories; another 17 percent lived in the Habsburgs' Galicia (map 13.5, fig. 13.2).

In the nineteenth century, the tsarist government discriminated ever more strongly against Jews. The 1804 "Statute concerning the Jews" defined them as "urban," and in the next three years an estimated half-million persons were compelled to relocate from countryside to town. A decree of 1835 restricted them to a "Pale of Settlement," exempting only Jewish men and women in particular crafts or with high educational attainments. Jewish innkeepers lost the right to sell liquor to peasants; the emancipation of serfs deprived Jews of their functions as intermediaries. The May decrees of 1882 forced an additional half-million Jews to leave the countryside and restricted access of young Jewish men and women to higher education. In 1891, the 22,000 Jewish artisanal and trading families of St. Petersburg and Moscow were deported to the overcrowded *shtetls* and ethnic quarters of the Pale. Restrictions and social changes destroyed most of their traditional sources of livelihood and the *Luftmensch*, a person so poor as to have to live off the air, became a figure of popular tales. The culture of the *shtetl*, the small town, emerged, characterized by high literacy, religious conservatism, abject poverty, and overcrowding. In the Pale, one-fifth of the Jewish population was dependent on the charity of the community.[60]

Early marriage combined with a strong sense of family resulted in large numbers of children. As a result, the Jewish population increased more than twice as fast as the empire's population as a whole. Internal migration brought many Jewish families from the stagnating northeastern borderlands of the former Polish-Lithuanian Commonwealth to the southern provinces of Russia. For a short period, the government attracted Jewish families as settlers to agricultural regions. Even within the Pale and the developing towns of the southwest, some cities—Kiev, for example—retained the medieval "right of settlement" privilege, or more precisely a right to discriminate against Jews (*ius de non tolerandis Judaeis*). In the new and thriving port town of Odessa, on the other hand, with only 250 Jewish inhabitants in 1795 and 152,000 in 1904, a vibrant Jewish culture emerged. To small-town Jews, cityward migration seemed attractive but dangerous, providing opportunities but threatening family cohesion, and substituting materialism for religiosity. After 1871, pogroms inspired fear

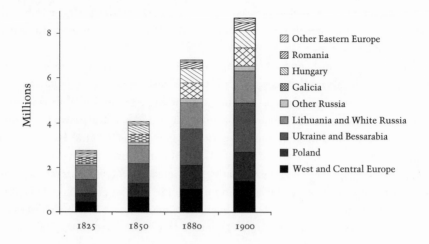

Figure 13.2   Distribution of Jewish Population in Europe, 1825–1900

in Jewish households; charges of ritual murder of Christian children were once again raised; and the bloody Kishinev pogrom of 1903, which had the tacit support of tsarist authorities, combined to induce mass emigration into the labor markets of the Atlantic economies, which transferred elements of the cultures of the *shtetl* and of Odessa to North America (Chap. 14.1).[61] World War I brought all movement to a standstill; the Revolution of 1917 changed all parameters of action.

13.6   The Soviet Union: The "Other America" or "Bolshevik Dictatorship"

Migration to and from Russia under its new socialist government of 1917 was characterized by several special features that warrant a brief and separate treatment of the postwar decade. Peasant migration to Siberia and internal migration to industrializing centers continued. As an external factor, U.S. immigration restrictions directed against people from Eastern and Southern Europe and against "radicals" reduced Atlantic migration. Both factors combined to keep the Russo-Siberian Migration System separate from migrations in the Atlantic economies.

In the immediate aftermath of revolution, civil war, and famine in 1921, the "second emigration"[62] consisted of supporters of the defeated tsarist regime. A million or more Russians fled to Western Europe and—in new directions—to the Far East, Turkey, and Syria (chap. 17.1). Others were expelled by the new Bolshevik government. The community's center was first in Berlin and after the mid-1920s shifted to Paris, where the new arrivals joined the Russian community of political refugees from tsarist oppression. Secondary centers were Prague, Belgrade, and, in the Far East, Harbin and Shanghai.[63] The emigrants came mainly from groups threatened by the restructuring of society—the nobility, military officialdom, the tsarist bureaucracy, the realm of politics, the segments of the arts patronized by the old regime, and from the bourgeoisie and intelligentsia in general. Few of the peasants and workers who had been soldiers in the monarchist White Army fled, since most could not afford exile. Emigration thus was political, military, and economic.[64] Most émigrés considered themselves "Russian," regardless of ethnicity, though some formed separate Polish, Ukrainian, Armenian, and Jewish communities or communities of other ethnic composition.

The emigration of Russians to Germany was a peculiar kind of chain migration. Dynastic connections to the Württemberg dynasty, Russian retainers at the Prussian court, trade connections to Leipzig, and prewar visits by the nobility to the spas of Wiesbaden and Baden-Baden (the latter had a Russian Orthodox church) provided the information base for emigration and colony-building after 1917. Lower-class and impoverished refugees, mostly men, had to take any work available, including the recent innovation of taxi-driving. Some married and were acculturated; others moved to France, where the war-related shortage of men and postwar economic growth resulted in demand for labor. The French government also directly recruited Russian workers in Gallipoli and Constantinople. Wealthy emigrant families that had lived royally in Germany suddenly lost their standing during inflation and currency reform, and many moved to Paris. From about 500,000, the number of Russians in Germany declined to 150,000 in 1928. Their children went to German schools and would have followed a course of integration, but by 1936 the Nazi regime discussed plans to confine Russian families to work camps. By 1937, only about 45,000 Russians remained, many of right-wing or fascist persuasion.[65]

Russian exiles have been treated in terms of a global diaspora (Raeff) or as a multi-centered and diverse group (Schlögel). The consolidation of the new Soviet state and its dynamism in the 1920s shattered hopes for return. Considerable numbers of exiles became naturalized, if offered the option. The League of Nations' refugee office estimated that no more than 355,000 remained unassimilated in 1937. With the German occupation of France in May 1940, Paris irrevocably lost its role as the center of the greater exile community. After the war, New York emerged as the new center. In the Far East, the Japanese aggression wrought havoc among exile communities, whether they were Russian or Jewish.[66]

In the 1920s and early 1930s, while Russian refugees and Western capitalist opinion began to construct the image of a "Bolshevik dictatorship" at a time when economic recovery was achieved and before the Stalinist aspects of the system became paramount, the industrializing Soviet Union attracted migrants for economic as well as political reasons. Some of the 70,000–80,000 newcomers expected to find an ideal workers' republic comparable to the ideal American republic imagined in earlier times. Margaret Bourke-White's photos of 1930–32 show the Soviet Union's promising environment, as do the "complex pictures" of the German emigrant Heinrich Vogeler. Traveling through Siberia in 1929, Otto Heller called it "another America." His description of frontier opportunities, happy pioneers, and powerful machines reflects the promise of a future that continued to attract many (chap. 17.2). In this period of new ideas and visions, a Russian emigrant in Sofia, Nikolai S. Trubetskoi, proclaimed in *Exodus to the East* that the Russians were a Eurasian people, separate from the "Romano-Germans" and similar to the "youthful" culture of America. The end of the vision of "another America" came in the 1930s with forced labor camps and in 1941 with the German invasion (chap. 17.3).[67]

14

The Proletarian Mass Migrations

in the Atlantic Economies

After the 1820s, the several regional European migration systems, circular movements, and one-directional flows (chap. 12) became an integrated hemispheric system
extending from Russia's Jewish Pale of Settlement (chap. 13) to Chicago, New Orleans,
Buenos Aires, and beyond. Migrants coming westward from the Atlantic coast, northward from Spanish America, eastward from Siberia into Alaska, and from Asia into
California and British Columbia, incorporated ever larger segments of the continent
into the Atlantic World, reducing the space of the First Nations in the process. Within
Europe, an industrialized core attracted workers from an agrarian periphery. Internal labor migrations on the North American continent balanced demand and supply
and transformed labor forces. The immigration of settlers and workers to Canada was
paralleled by the internal moves and out-migration of French-Canadians.

The emancipation of serfs, slaves, and Jews facilitated geographical mobility.
When serfdom ended between 1762 (in Savoy) and 1861 (in Russia), the former serfs
had to compensate their lords for the loss of labor and fees. Reduced landholdings and
cash payments forced emancipated—and emaciated—peasants and their children to
migrate. Slave emancipation began with self-liberation in Haiti in 1804, was achieved
in the United States in 1863–65, and in Brazil as late as 1888 (chap. 10). Like the former
serfs, the emancipated U.S. slaves did not receive the land and initial implements
they demanded ("forty acres and a mule"), and could eke out only a precarious subsistence. Economic dependency, legal restrictions, and social control by lynch mobs
sent Black Americans into mass northward migrations after 1900.[1]

Emancipation was part of the equalization of legal status in bourgeois-democratic
societies, but only fractions of the people in nineteenth-century nation-states were
politically enfranchised and had access to administrative institutions staffed by
middle-class men speaking the dominant language.[2] Political theory and practice in
the age of democratic states and of culturally homogeneous nation-states excluded
women, laboring classes, and cultural minorities. The continuing inequalities increased the reservoir of those men and women ready to migrate in search of less discrimination and fewer inequalities or better jobs and wages.

In the range of 50 to 55 million Europeans—or about one-fifth of Europe's entire population in 1800—left between 1815 and 1939 for North America (35 million), South America (eight million), and other parts of the world. Perhaps seven million returned. Internal migrations, especially rural-urban moves, involved about half or more of the total European populations by the middle of the nineteenth century. Transcontinental railroad construction facilitated long-distance moves and permitted easy access to emigration ports. After the 1870s, steamships speeded migration, facilitated return, and made seasonal cross-Atlantic moves possible.[3]

The process of equalization deprived privileged immigrant groups, such as Huguenots, Mennonites, or Russian-Germans, of their special status and sent many of the latter two groups into secondary migrations. In the Western European Jewish diaspora, continuing discrimination and the powerful impact of the nation-state ideology induced intellectuals to adopt the project. In 1896 Theodor Herzl, raised in multiethnic Budapest and living in Vienna, where about 10 percent of the population was Jewish, published his *Der Judenstaat (The Jewish State)*. The cosmopolitan Herzl, who held no geographic preferences, first suggested Argentina as the location for the state he had in mind; then, influenced by British coreligionists, he supported the land of Zion, Palestine, as the location.[4] Although the Jewish state was to achieve independence only more than half a century later, most migrants now moved within a framework of both national economies and economic dependencies. In the Americas, the independence acquired by most of the British colonies after 1776 and by most of the Spanish and Portuguese colonies by 1825 (chaps. 8 and 9) changed political and economic relationships. For about a century, the United States remained in a position of economic dependency relative to the European core, and the same type of dependency lasted longer for the Latin American states. Nevertheless, toward the end of the nineteenth century, the core increasingly encompassed not only Atlantic Europe but also the northeastern United States.[5] Transpacific connections remained of limited importance for almost another century (chaps. 15.5, 19.5).

14.1   From Subsistence to Cash: Family Economies in Crisis

In the European segment of the Atlantic World, agrarian migrations changed when rural labor became increasingly seasonal and land ever more scarce (chap. 12.2). The centralization of production forced women, children, and men from village industries to migrate and join factory labor forces. Transborder migration within Europe was particularly high for Poles and Italians. Overseas migration, per 1,000 of population, was particularly high from Norway and Ireland, but the rate from France was low. In absolute numbers over time, the several British and German peoples supplied the largest shares. Migration became a move between economic stages of development, from rural to industrial work, and between concepts of time, from agrarian "natural" time to industrial "clock" time. In the 1880s, the schedules for steamship and railway travel necessitated the worldwide standardization of time.

The proto-industrial transfer of production to sedentary cottage dwellers was reversed with the self-transfer of such working families to centralized job locations:

first manufactories, then machine-driven factories, and finally metropolitan conglomerations. Unskilled rural workers mobilized themselves for employment in local road improvement, track laying, canal digging, and river regulation. Then English navvies, German *Erdarbeiter*, and Hungarian *kubykos* began to follow construction camps that extended Europe's railways from a mere 332 kilometers in 1831 to more than 300,000 kilometers by 1876. Soon they migrated intercontinentally to dig the Panama Canal or to carve railway grades into the Rocky Mountains. English engineers and Dutch drainage experts also directed infrastructural or "internal" improvements in the colonies.[6]

The nineteenth-century mass migrations to cheap land in fertile and easy-to-till plains from South Russia to North America and from Argentina to Australia resulted in economies of scale, with new transportation circuits to facilitate the wide distribution of the products. North American immigrant farmers hired migrant laborers for the harvest. East Elbian landlords drove out their tenants, invested in machinery and converted their lands to sugar beet crops, and imported Polish seasonal laborers. The plains of South Russia were tilled by internal migrants and some in-migrating foreigners. In the 1880s, Argentina filled its plains with European immigrant colonists and Italian seasonal harvest workers. This mass production and the concomitant decline in prices in world markets caused an agricultural crisis in the 1880s, which forced millions of European small peasants off their land and, since agriculture needed no more laborers, into the industries of the Atlantic economies.

Core and Periphery: The Division of Europe

When factory-produced cloth could suddenly be bought cheaply in village or corner stores, home and subsistence producers, usually women, became dramatically aware of the futility of their labors. To supply a family with homemade cloth demanded a winter's work—but purchases of the same material required cash. The decline of world market prices for agricultural products reduced men's meager cash incomes at the same time. When cheap cloth and agricultural machinery made women's and men's work obsolete, families faced "free" time and empty tables. The spiraling demand for cash in rural family economies and the collapsing supply caused a cash crisis that forced individuals and whole populations to reorient their lifestyles, production and consumption patterns, and attitudes toward migration.[7]

Men and women who turned to urban labor markets—whether local, regional, or international in scope—often aimed at extending their peasant lifestyles, accepting temporary proletarianization as an expedient to avoid being permanently stuck in that condition. Similarly, when mechanization threatened the skills and wages of artisans and workers, many migrated to economies where their skills were still in demand. Miners and workers who had left independent peasant status only a generation or two before sometimes migrated in hopes of returning to landownership. Women's migrations often still covered shorter distances: they had less access to travel funds and faced tighter family control; they were expected to care for children and aging parents; the wages to be earned did not warrant the expense of long-distance moves. In the socially constructed division of labor, men's life-courses followed earning capacities in ever more distant labor markets, while women's remained tied to family labor and to agriculture, including dairy production. Over time, as longer lives extended the span between children becoming independent and infirm parents needing care, women, too, moved into distant labor markets. They reduced their dependence by migrating and by restructuring their life-cycle phases through later marriages.

Agricultural work patterns, according to historians of industrial work, were irregular, determined by weather and the natural cycles of sowing and harvesting. After migration, such patterns would have to be regularized according to clock time and, in the period of time and motion studies, to machine time. Immigrant workers did express bitter resentment at the tyranny of factory whistles and of the extension of "natural" daylight working hours through artificial lighting; in agriculture, tasks were substituted for each other in response to inclement weather or the season, and seasonal migration redistributed harvest labor according to supply and demand (map 14.1). Only itinerant workers experienced irregular work patterns. The early steel factories, on the other hand, were characterized by frequent breakdowns of machinery, economic cycles, and the arbitrariness of foremen. The work habits of immigrant peasants had to be irregularized (resulting in "spoiled identity"), and, with time being signaled by the one functioning piece of equipment, the factory whistle, work habits became irrational.[8]

The emphasis on the steel and iron industries in nation-states as indicators of modernization, which replaced the emphasis on textile production and food production in family economies, has narrowed the analysis of gendered divisions of labor to male factory work. Work in the home and in agriculture was hardly affected by the tons of steel produced, but imports of cheap grains produced by immigrant farmers or laborers, such as wheat in Europe or rice in Asia, wrought havoc with farm economies. Similarly, the emphasis on political borders diverted attention from connections between the local and the global. Investments in cotton plantations with slave or contract labor regimes, whether in the southern United States, Egypt, Uganda, or elsewhere, and investments in factories, whether in Manchester, Bombay, Lowell, or Łódź, demanded quick and permanent changes in the allocation of family labor, whether Irish, Dutch, or Tamil. There never was a linear pattern from primitive agriculture to modern industries, and migrants responded with myriads of back-and-forth, circular, temporary, or permanent moves.[9]

Similarly, the analytical juxtaposition of labor-exporting European (emigration) and labor-importing North American (immigration) countries is a simplification not supported by data. Within Europe, England, the Netherlands and Belgium, France, the western and central areas of Germany, Lower Austria, Bohemia, and Switzerland became labor-importing industrialized core countries. At the same time, Great Britain and the Germanies exported settlers and workers, whereas only a few workers left France, owing to an early stabilization of population levels there. England drew

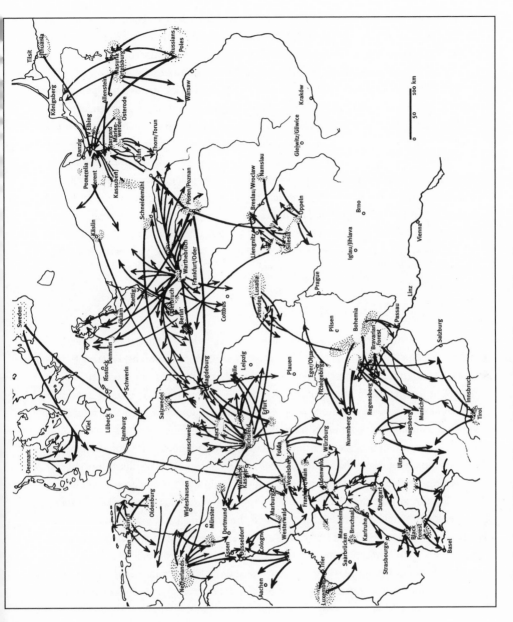

14.1 Destinations of Migrant Harvest Labor in Central Europe, 1860s–1870s

workers mainly from its Irish colony, as did Switzerland from Italy (earlier from Germany), France from most of its neighboring countries and Poland, and Germany from Poland and Italy. Belgium and sections of Austria attracted large numbers of labor migrants but experienced heavy out-migration at the same time (map 14.2).

The societies and economies of the periphery—Ireland, Portugal and Spain, Italy and southeastern Europe, the Polish and the Eastern European Jewish territories, as well as the Scandinavian countries—were relegated to supplying labor. The mass export of unskilled, mainly rural populations from Ireland to England began early and increased after 1815. In all of Europe, migration figures skyrocketed in the 1880s. The departure of young working-age adults implied that the dependency costs of raising children and caring for the old were left to the societies of origin, while in labor-importing countries the ratio of producing and tax-paying populations with low age-group-specific health-care costs increased. The division between reproductive and productive labor was also a division between labor-supplying and labor-importing societies.

Early Surplus Labor: Britain and the Germanies

The largest emigration movements came from the British Isles (English, Scotch, Welsh, and Irish peoples) and from German-speaking lands (Swabians, Palatines, Hessians, Mecklenburgers, Swiss, Austrians, and others). Both groups have often been treated as distinct from other peoples. In the British Empire, self-perception turned British newcomers into founding peoples and made other newcomers the immigrant ethnics. Notions of empire-building neglected the migrations of skilled and common laborers. German self-perception concentrated on departing peasant populations and overlooked proletarians. As for the civilizing missions assumed by older German and British research on migration, men of rank did impose cultural patterns on Others, and German and English workers abroad sometimes did show attitudes of superiority. North American scholarship accepted this line of thinking by dividing immigrants into an "old immigration" of Germans, Irish people, and Scandinavians and a post-1880s "new immigration" of Southern and Eastern Europeans. The former was assumed to have consisted of pioneer settlers, and the latter of unskilled proletarians. The late-nineteenth-century discourse on genetic differences devalued the Eastern and Southern European "races" as less than "White" and inferior to Anglo-Teutonic "stock." But as early as the 1840s two-thirds of the men and women who selected the United States as their destination went into wagework. The Irish, with the exception of Protestants going to Canada, never fit the cliché of settler migration, and large numbers of Germans and Scandinavians came as workers. Some Poles, Czechs, and Jews, on the other hand, went into agriculture as farmers. The distinction between old and new and between higher and lower quality does not hold. British migrants came from the peripheral Scottish Highlands, Wales, Cornwall, and colonial Ireland, as well as from industrialized England and Scotland. Early capitalization, enclosure, consolidation of landholdings, and market orientation of peasant production (chap.

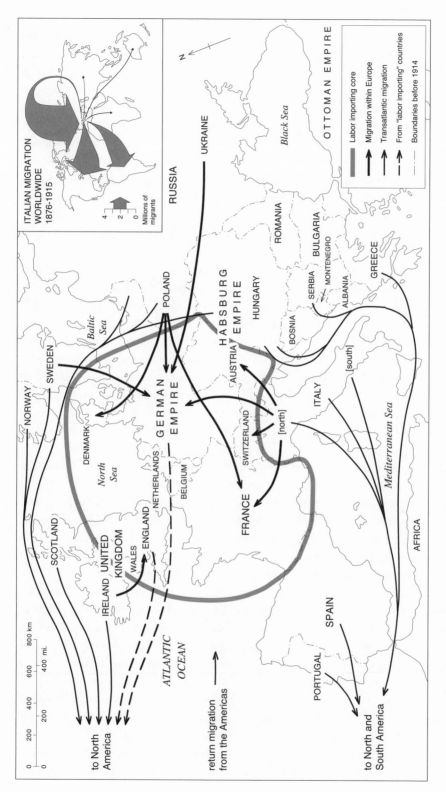

14.2 Migrations from the European Periphery to the Cores of the Atlantic Economies, 1880s–1914

ITALIAN MIGRATION
WORLDWIDE
1876-1915

Millions of
migrants

4
2
0

Labor importing core
Migration within Europe
Transatlantic migration
From "labor importing" countries
Boundaries before 1914

OTTOMAN EMPIRE

Black Sea

RUSSIA

UKRAINE

ROMANIA

BULGARIA

SERBIA
MONTENEGRO
ALBANIA
GREECE

BOSNIA

POLAND

HABSBURG
EMPIRE

HUNGARY

AUSTRIA
[south]

ITALY

[north]

Mediterranean Sea

AFRICA

Baltic
Sea

SWEDEN

NORWAY

DENMARK

GERMAN
EMPIRE

North
Sea

NETHERLANDS

BELGIUM

SWITZERLAND

FRANCE

SCOTLAND

IRELAND UNITED
KINGDOM

WALES
ENGLAND

ATLANTIC
OCEAN

to North
America

return migration
from the Americas

PORTUGAL

SPAIN

to North and
South America

0   200   400   600   800 km
0   200   400   600 mi.

12.2) sent many English and Scots into industry and caused migrations comparable to the Dutch North Sea System.[10] With regard to overseas destinations, more English than Irish ethnics departed from 1871 to 1914: 5.5 million were English and Welsh, 2.3 million were Irish, and 1.2 million were from Scotland. More than half returned, with higher return rates among people of English origin than among those of Irish extraction. Among English migrants, urban dwellers predominated; among Scots and Irish people, those of rural origins were dominant; and among people of Welsh and Cornish origin, miners and their dependents predominated. Women accounted for two out of every five migrants. The fare from Liverpool to New York was $45 in 1860 but fell to half that amount in the 1880s. After the 1890s, most migrants went to Canada and other British Dominions rather than to the United States. The temporary labor migration of single men, considered potentially destabilizing by manpower planners of the receiving societies, was a British phenomenon long before Italians or Eastern Europeans became "birds of passage."[11]

The British government's attitudes toward emigration reflected "national" economic interest as perceived by those classes who staffed the policy-making institutions. As early as 1606, a political economist had called the export of laboring people "a double commodity, in the avoidance of people here, and in making use of them there" (Bacon). To the 1930s, British population planners pursued this utilitarian approach: they prohibited the emigration of skilled workers to prevent competition for British products from abroad; they shipped off convicts to cut the costs of the penal system; under the system of indentured labor, they encouraged people without prospects to leave the British Isles; and children of the poor were shipped off from the 1880s onward. In the decades before 1914, a surplus population was to be siphoned off according to the imperialist concept of "Empire Settlement."[12] Labor unions, faced with high rates of unemployment among their members, came to share the attitude that emigration might reduce social imbalances in the home society.[13]

Migration processes in the German-language territories were similar, but industrial migrations began later. To the early nineteenth century, the east- and westward emigration of peasant families (including non-related servants) predominated. In southwestern Germany and in Lower Austria, children were traditionally hired out for distant seasonal rural labor, and young adolescents were sent off to feed themselves.[14] At first, emigrants still came from the densely populated southwestern smallhold areas, thereafter increasingly from the central principalities, and in the last third of the century from the northeastern latifundia. Many of the early smallholder migrants could reestablish themselves in agriculture, but almost none of the farm laborers could do so. In overwhelming numbers, they became wage laborers in North America—or in the industrializing centers of Germany.[15]

About six million men, women, and children from the German states emigrated from 1820 to 1929.[16] In absolute numbers, German emigration was second only to that of the United Kingdom until Italian emigration surpassed it in 1900; per thousand of population, Germany ranked tenth among European sending countries. Almost 90 percent went to the United States; others went to Argentina and Brazil. In marginal areas, women had been engaged in heavy field labor, even pulling plows where poverty precluded the use of draft animals. Their letters from North America indicated their relief at having been freed from such toil, and they counseled sisters and female friends to follow. German men, in turn, developed an image of American and German-American women spending their lives in rocking chairs. Return migration from North America was low. As elsewhere, returnees built the proverbial "America houses" in their home communities, thus indulging in "conspicuous consumption" to signify their postmigration status.[17]

Emigration from the Germanies and, after 1871, from the German Empire declined steeply after 1893. From 1878 to 1890, the antisocialist law had added political pressure to economic factors, and some skilled workers still migrated to England, Russia, the Balkans, and beyond. Internal industrialization absorbed the surplus agrarian labor; after the mid-1880s German Junkers and industrialists hired Poles for low-paying seasonal labor on the eastern latifundia and for mining jobs in the industrialized Ruhr district. Italians and western Ukrainians (Ruthenians) came; Russian Jews migrated to major cities. After 1900, Germany was, in absolute figures, second only to the United States as an importer of labor.[18]

Working-Class Diasporas from the Periphery: Irish People, Poles, Jews, and Italians

Irish, Polish, Jewish-settled, and Italian territories became part of the capitalist world's labor reservoirs in the 1880s. The working-class migrants from Europe's periphery entered receiving societies at the bottom, in contrast to the English, German, and Spanish migrants in previous centuries, who arrived as members of conquering ethnicities. Their diasporas were labeled racially inferior, olive- or dark-skinned.

In Ireland, seasonal and permanent migration to England, the Scottish Lowlands, and the European continent had long been an income-generating strategy of smallholders and the underclasses. From 1846 to 1848, the fungal potato blight destroyed much of the peasants' food base. Those fleeing the "great hunger" were at first described as "clean and industrious," but by 1847 they were debilitated by starvation. Illness decimated the human cargo of the "coffin ships" at a rate of one in six. In the decade after 1841, Ireland's total population declined by 20 percent on average, with the highest losses in rural areas. Emigration, which decreased from the mid-1850s to the 1870s, reached unparalleled heights thereafter. Between 9.5 and 15.0 per 1,000 inhabitants left annually, with departures regionally concentrated in the six western counties. From the prefamine years to 1911, Ireland's population declined from 8.0 to 4.4 million.[19]

"Exile from Erin," as the Irish emigrants described their "fate," differed from migrations of other cultural groups in that women outnumbered men by a small margin from 1871 to 1891 and by a margin of 55 to 45 from 1901 to 1910. Separate gender cultures, late marriages, and a high rate of celibacy divided men and women. The resulting low fertility brought natural population increase to a standstill from 1880 to 1914. The status of women worsened after the famine. Marriages arranged to keep dowries in families subjected young women to additional constraints; their workload was worse than that of German peasant women described above. Male recreational space and drinking culture excluded women. Male clergy, including Protestants, relegated women to subservient roles even more than in other cultures. A national educational system after 1831 helped English-speaking Irish women join Anglo-American societies more easily than women from other language groups. But, like Irish men, they had to face the deeply ingrained prejudices of their employers.[20]

Eighty-five percent of Irish postfamine emigrants went to the United States. England, Wales, and Scotland were the next most important destinations. Australia's and New Zealand's shares were surpassed by Canada's in the 1890s. Most migrants were Catholic, and some were bilingual, speaking both English and Gaelic. In England, Irish migrants became agricultural and urban laborers; in the United States, they were mostly urban workers and day laborers. Prepaid tickets were the major means of financing the passage to North America.[21]

Among Poles, Jews, and other Eastern Europeans, mass migration westward followed earlier small multidirectional flows. Under the late-nineteenth-century regime of "imperial nationalism" in the Hohenzollern, Habsburg, and Romanov realms, the respective dominant cultures, now self-styled "nations," attempted to incorporate "minorities" culturally by depriving them of educational institutions and a press in their own language, even in regions of traditional settlement. In reaction, people from such marginalized cultures placed more emphasis on their own national consciousness, and their middle classes, with the help of emigrants, demanded political self-administration. The Slovak national movement, for example, was stronger in North America than in Slovakia, where the Magyar rulers had closed off secondary education for them. Labor migration and national "awakening" interacted.

Among Poles, rural wage labor and casual urban labor increased after the emancipation of serfs in the Prussian partition (1807–50), in Austrian Galicia (1848), and in the Congress Kingdom (1864). Land shortages were dramatic. While the population grew by 117 percent from 1860 to 1914 (the European average being 70 percent), the estates of the nobility remained inviolate. In Prussia, peasants on tiny holdings were ejected, and peasants of middling status had to cede one-fifth to one-third of their land to compensate their former owners. Capitalist penetration of agriculture and mechanization proceeded rapidly, and new export crops, especially wheat and sugar beets, increased the seasonality of labor. In Galicia, holdings of under five hectares, too small for a family's subsistence, were the rule. Sons and daughters who did not inherit land migrated into wagework, as did inheriting sons in order to be able to pay off siblings. Poverty was exacerbated by the Habsburg government's policy of "calculated backwardness" with regard to fringe regions and "minority" peoples. Poles and other nondominant peoples suffered from investment patterns intended to benefit only the ruling ethnicity. Polish nobles supported the policy to keep cheap labor in agriculture.[22]

In the third annexation area, Congress Poland (after 1864, the Polish provinces of Russia), where about one-third of the rural population belonged to the landless proletariat, the population grew by 272 percent from 3.3 million in 1810 to 12.1 million in 1910. The region experienced rapid economic growth. Weavers and clothiers immigrated from Prussian Poland (1810s–20s), and skilled textile workers from Saxony (1830s–40s). Textile factories in Łódź (chap. 12.4) and metal—as well as other—industries in Warsaw attracted local rural and foreign skilled labor. Unfavorable Prussian and Russian tariff policies retarded further growth and development of an internal labor market. Immigration restrictions were imposed in the revolutionary year of 1848 because of the textile workers' militancy. From 1860 to 1914, an estimated 10 million Poles out of a population of 29 million migrated. One-fifth to one-fourth moved internally to industrializing Polish cities and centers of investment. This "impermanent" urban population returned home for harvest work or to stay over the winter. Living in Russia proper were 600,000 Polish migrants, one-third of them workers. The Polish communities in St. Petersburg numbered 60,000, in Odessa and Riga about 24,000 each, in Moscow 20,000. Some 6,000 peasants in search of land traveled as far as Siberia. Most migrated westward to the German Reich; some went to Belgian mines and Danish agriculture or became laborers in France. Small numbers went to South America and Australia, and about 20 percent to the United States. Urban workers accounted for merely 12 to 15 percent of the departures. Polish labor migrants might cross imperial borders but remain within Polish ethnic territories, or they might cross cultural boundaries but remain within political-imperial borders.[23]

The Jewish community in Russia was forced into emigration and flight because of anti-Semitic discrimination and pogroms, rapid population growth and poverty, lack of industrial jobs and access to land, and persecution of labor and political activists (chaps. 12.1, 13.5). About 2.5 million—out of a total Jewish population of 5.2 million in 1897—left between 1880 and 1914. Skilled workers and small artisans stayed mostly in European metropoles, especially Berlin, Paris, and London, where acculturated national Jewish communities felt overwhelmed by the masses. More than two million went to the United States, 200,000 to Great Britain, and a mere 60,000 to Palestine. The majority originated in the contiguous Lithuanian, East Polish, and Belorussian provinces, the areas closest to the German and Polish emigration regions as well as to the ports of departure, Hamburg and Bremen. Population increase, on the other hand, was highest in the Ukrainian provinces of the Pale, from which some migrated via Odessa.[24]

Among Italian agriculturalists, the worldwide agricultural crisis of the 1880s that glutted world markets wrought havoc. The exploitation of colonial labor and cheap transportation facilities caused further economic damage: Indian rice competed with the Piedmont production; Chinese and Japanese silks ousted Italian ones from their customary markets; French-ruled Tunisia and Algeria competed with Italy's trade in citrus fruits, figs, and oil. The Italian government hurt laborers and *contadini* by instituting tariff policies in the interest of industrialists and *latifundistas*. As a consequence, almost 14 million men and women left from 1876 to 1914, and another

4 million from 1915 to 1930. While taxation financed government expenses for the military and the bureaucracy, emigrants' remittances, largely deposited in banks, funded industrialization in the Milan/Turin/Genoa triangle.[25]

From 1876 to 1900, three-fifths of the migrants departed from northern Italy (comparable to the pattern in England); the others were from southern Italy, where lords and absentee owners refused to modernize and invest (comparable to the situation in Ireland or Galicia). In the north, the economically lagging Venetian areas lost 13 percent of their population. In addition to economic cycles (the disastrous fall season in 1904 and the economic depression in the United States of 1907–08), politics affected migration: for example, military service during the Italo-Turkish war or a dispute with Argentina about the sanitary inspection of migrants. Emigrants traveled to Western Europe (44 percent), to North America (from Montreal to New Orleans) (30 percent), and to Brazil and Argentina (22 percent). Skilled artisans followed their traditional routes to France and Germany. When offered work by East Elbian lords, Italian rural migrants compared it to seasonal work in Argentina, finding the labor conditions in Germany's eastern sectors worse and the train fare across the Alps more expensive than a transatlantic ship ticket. Those who could afford the passage to Latin America went there. Compared to conditions in the United States, the prospects were better, the language problems smaller, the cultural adjustment easier, and the potential for upward mobility higher. Brazil and Argentina, the favored destinations before 1900, as well as Venezuela and Uruguay, engaged in active recruitment and paid travel subsidies. Those with little money who were in search of quick wages went to North America, which after 1900 became the favored destination with an annual intake of up to half a million.[26] "Again the evidence reveals that the migrants were not the destitute and desperate but enterprising people able to make cooperative decisions."[27]

Economic conditions elsewhere on the European periphery induced people, regardless of their ethnic culture, to evaluate their migration options. From the Iberian Peninsula, 4.7 million left between 1871 and 1914, with Argentina, Brazil, and Cuba as the main destinations. *Golondrinas* ("swallows"), who were often from Spanish Galicia, crossed the Atlantic seasonally for harvest work, benefiting from the inverse seasons in the southern and northern hemispheres. Balkan and Greek people joined the Atlantic Migration System late. As subjects of the Ottoman Empire, their commercial relations and contacts had been centered on the eastern Mediterranean rather than on the Atlantic. In the Habsburg Empire, Slovenes, Croats, Hungarians, and Slovaks could connect to westward information networks and thus entered the Atlantic System. From the borderlands between the Russo-Siberian and Atlantic Systems, Ukrainians moved in both directions, and the Baltic peoples went westward, albeit in small numbers. The three Scandinavian peoples, as well as the Finns and Icelanders, added to the migration flows some 2.1 million men and women, more than 90 percent of whom went to North America.[28] The European working classes and surplus rural populations moved from peripheries sharing underdevelopment or lesser-developed political units to segmented internationalized labor markets in the industrialized core of the Atlantic economies.

The whole of the complex migration and acculturation processes of the Atlantic Migration System may be illustrated by one Italian village and one woman. Rosa, a foundling baby from Milan, was raised in a nearby village by foster parents. At age seven, her foster mother placed her in a silk factory in the village as a child laborer. Later, in short-distance premarriage employment she had to work in a silk factory a day's walk away, where older women trained her. Boys would migrate with their fathers over larger distances to be trained as masons or plasterers. Young men from this village went to France in medium-distance unskilled labor migration for seasonal or multiyear construction work. Rosa's foster father, as sailor, had seen America and served as an information link outward. No links upward existed: an unbridgeable chasm separated Rosa's backyard home from the "rich" in the front of the same house, who could put even a little meat into the soup. The nearby urban world was socially distant, too: villagers did not dare talk to road workers from Milan.[29]

Adult men from the village, single or married, traveled to Missouri iron mines. Some of these long-distance temporary labor migrants married before departing and took their wives with them because they "need[ed] a woman to do their washing and cooking," who thereby entered a kind of marriage migration into unpaid service work. At one time, skilled female silk workers—accompanied by a male foreman—even migrated beyond the Atlantic System to train Japanese silk workers. The villagers were part of worldwide labor markets.[30] For Rosa, mobility across continents was easier to achieve than out of her gender sphere. Married against her will by her foster mother, she was left behind when the husband departed for Missouri until he ordered her to come over with the next gang of men. Four women in this group exemplify aspirations and experiences. Rosa had to leave her infant son with her mother; earning capacity came before emotional needs. In sequential family migration, another woman with children traveled to rejoin her husband after years of separation. A third woman was to marry a man she had last seen at the age of seven. A fourth was to marry a stranger, who was even from a different region of Italy; marriage provided the ticket both to traditional respectability and to the New World. After 1900, 94 percent of all migrants to the United States were going to kin (79 percent) or friends (15 percent). Family formation and reproductive work, like wage labor, spanned continents.[31]

The very morning after Rosa and the men arrived in Missouri, the peasants began mine work, and Rosa assumed her role as keeper of her husband's boardinghouse. Newly arriving migrants with severely limited support systems had to begin work immediately ("economics of survival") and had to function within reconstituted kin relationships without delay (transfer of traditional gender roles). The internationalized labor markets created transnational communities. For some men change was dramatic: from tilling the soil to working underground. For Rosa it was equally unsettling. She had to work for twelve men. For breakfast she served coffee, a drink of the "rich" that she had never before tasted or prepared. Given the mix of her boarders, she had to "Italianize" her cooking, which was rooted in the cuisine of her home province, Lombardy. Between breakfast and lunch during her first day in Missouri, she had to buy provisions from German-speaking farmers and English-speaking store-keepers. The postmaster was friendly, which to Rosa was a surprise because in Italy men in such exalted positions would have demanded great deference. These migrants' initial adaptation had to take place in less then twenty-four hours.[32]

Labor migration, often juxtaposed to farming families' moves, frequently was an intermediate stage to postpone the radical transition to factory life. Men migrated temporarily, leaving behind wives and children; or families migrated to a homestead, and then men left to take wage labor. Such migrants between modes of production could enter distant labor markets at lower wages than urbanized proletarians because the rest of the family's agricultural labor provided subsistence for the winter months. Contrary to the modernization paradigm, labor migrants often did not intend to be-come "modern"; their aim was to preserve traditional ways of life in artisanal occu-pations or agriculture. One-third of the sojourners returned from the United States between the 1890s and the early 1920s; most intra-European migrants returned. Re-turn migrants or emigrant letters provided information about options in particular labor market segments that were far away. Subsequent migrants aimed for this par-ticular segment and location; only incidentally did they change countries. Thus the migrants' experiences do not support the postulated radical break between traditional and modern societies or between cultures. They used their individual human capi-tal as well as their social capital (the networks and resources of the community) to achieve improvement of life projects with sufficient continuity to prevent emo-tional breakdown. Success or failure also depended on power relationships in the host society and (un)equitable access to resources.

14.2   The "Proletarian Mass Migration"

The nineteenth-century "proletarian mass migration" occurred within the frame-work of major changes in labor and economic regimes. First, some socioeconomic regions trained surplus skilled workforces: England advanced technicians, Germany skilled workers, and Italian regions construction craftsmen. Skilled immigrants trained unskilled local labor forces across the Atlantic economies. From a family per-spective, married couples did not adjust the number of children downward to com-pensate for lower infant mortality and longer lifespans. Second, the technology of production changed. The homogenization of work and the simplification of com-plex production processes into ever-smaller repetitive tasks (Taylorism) permitted the hiring of unskilled workers having rural backgrounds. Third, mass production displaced workers while increasing the supply of consumer goods. The invention of the disassembly line in cattle slaughtering in 1890s Chicago created factory jobs and made some of women's work in homes redundant. The invention of the assembly line in Detroit's automobile industry in the 1910s permitted the mass production of con-sumer technology at prices affordable for lower income groups. Fourth, labor markets were internationalized. Mass production in the fields had created labor markets for slave and bound labor in plantation economies and for seasonal free migrant labor in grain and root crops. Language or culture or prior training mattered little.[33]

First moves in the receiving society depended on the migrants' "starting capital" since they were excluded from access to social resources. Between 1899 and 1910, labor migrants to the United States carried on average $21.50 per person—Jews about $12 and German-speakers about $40. The need to rely on one's own labor immediately and the flexibility required to find a job meant that only young and healthy men and women selected themselves or were chosen by their families to migrate.[34] Scarce resources also circumscribed gender spheres. Labor migrant communities could not afford a one-to-one relationship of productive to reproductive labor, and men joined in common living arrangements to cut costs, whether in Russian *arteli* or North American boardinghouses. One hired woman cooked and washed for a dozen or more men. Sometimes men took turns to do the domestic work themselves. This clustering of foreign and working-class males was seen with great concern by advocates of bourgeois respectability, of middle-class social reform. Immigrant women, on the other hand, usually did not cluster. As live-in servants, they were housed with and under the control of "respectable" families of the receiving society. They also learned new habits and customs of everyday life.

Migrants faced complex stratified and segmented labor markets. Jobs in the primary growing, capital-intensive, securely established concentrated sector offered (and still offer) relatively high wages, good working conditions, employment stability, and the potential for promotion. Only a few skilled migrants—such as German workers in Budapest or in Chicago—could reach for such jobs; most were held by native-born workers. Jobs in the secondary stagnating, exploitative, and competitive sector, are characterized by irregular employment, low pay, and hazardous or unpleasant working conditions. These were and are open to unskilled migrants, regardless of cultural origin or nationality. A tertiary marginal or ghetto sector demanded and provided high flexibility.[35]

With regard to competition with native-born workers, migrants acquired information about labor market segments from earlier migrants or through employer recruitment. Only segments commensurate with their skills or lack of skills and with their communication problems and cultural Otherness were open to them. Segments were stratified according to skills and language competency and segregated by gender, ethnicity, skin color, and, sometimes, religion. Only some segments offered internationalized access. Thus insertion into the receiving society did not result in job competition unless two culturally defined groups of workers competed for the same labor market segment but differed in the price of their labor (split labor market). Large-scale in-migration could, however, result in either an oversupply of labor or, in a positive sense, an increase in production and jobs because of growing demand.[36]

During the "proletarian mass migrations," international labor markets did not automatically produce an international class consciousness. Men and women from rural economies as well as from the cities came from proletarianized sections of their societies. They joined factory labor forces and adapted traditional forms of protest to industrial work relations, combined ethnocultural values with class-cultural ones, and organized and cooperated. When working-class organizations of the native-born considered the immigrants unorganizable or when employers pitted ethnic groups against each other, cultural exclusiveness and conflict could fragment immigrant working classes.

Internationally accessible labor market segments provided migrants with the initial basis for survival. Culture provided links to other immigrants and permitted community formation and the development of social capital. When adjusting to new labor markets, migrant working men and women had more to lose than their chains (to vary the famous phrase in Marx and Engels's *Communist Manifesto*). To avoid loss of regionally specific ethno-class or race-class cultures and thereby individual identities, they based their supportive organizations and material life on their culture of origin within the framework of the receiving society. They were wary of labor organizations of the receiving native-born working class, which reflected class practices of the new hegemonic culture. Adjustment to new societies and new labor movements involved multiple negotiations and compromises.

The shift from agrarian and artisanal production to mass production and wage labor permitted family economies to be composed and recomposed more easily because under the former regime the joint husband-wife working unit and ownership of land or the workshop militated against the migration of only one partner. Factory or service jobs for single men and women permitted them to live, work, and migrate according to their specific interests. Rural immigrant women in Stockholm, for example, combined work with nontraditional family formation. As single women, they kept their rights to property, wages, and children. Such "concubinage," stigmatized in village societies, was possible in urban surroundings. Migration was the means of achieving a new lifestyle; young people in general and women in particular could expand the boundaries of their sphere.[37]

Industrial Europe: Immigrant Societies, Multiethnic Cities

Europe's late-nineteenth-century cities housed multiethnic populations. However, unlike the cultural orientation of North America and Australia, where even British-origin people had been immigrants, the middle-class cultural gatekeepers from Europe's recently constituted nations postulated monocultural states. They educated new generations under an agenda of exclusive national culture and monopolized cultural space as historically ethnic/national soil. Thus no concepts of immigrant cities, ethnic mosaics, or pluralism developed.

Most of the labor migrations before 1914 remained internal to states or empires. At the height of the transatlantic moves, only 5 percent of all Austro-Hungarian migrants left the empire; the others moved internally, with Prague and Vienna receiving the largest share.[38] Many of the expanding manufacturing towns in Europe still resembled industrial islands in an agrarian world. They drew on working-age populations from the surrounding countryside and on distant cities for skilled workers and managerial personnel. Western European urban populations experienced the in-migration of ethnoculturally similar but economically distant peasant peoples, while in the ethnoculturally stratified Eastern European cities, ethnically distinct from the surrounding rural populations, multilingual working classes emerged. Immigrant skilled workers joined the existing German-language groups; unskilled migrants joined the underclasses speaking local languages.

By the mid-nineteenth century, most of Europe's cities housed populations that were 50 percent nonindigenous. Glasgow, for example, had colonies of Scots from smaller towns and the Highlands, a Lithuanian community, Irish migrants, and a small number of Italians. Before 1890, urban population growth was mainly achieved by net in-migration: 100 percent of the increase in St. Petersburg, 72 percent in Munich, 64 percent in Paris, 57 percent in Copenhagen, 40 percent in Leipzig. This was the more significant since young first-generation migrants also transported the higher rural marital fertility patterns to the cities.[39]

The number of immigrants and net migration gain at a specified point in time provide merely a static picture. The gross volume of migration reflects the actual degree of mobility. In mid-1850s Duisburg, Germany, the rate of in- and out-migration was 16 per 100 inhabitants per year; the birth rate was half that. By 1900, the annual rate of in- and out-migration had increased to more than 40 per 100 inhabitants. In addition, between 15 and 35 percent of the residents changed their address each year. One out of six in-migrants was a foreigner from the Netherlands, Italy, Austria-Hungary, Belgium, Denmark, and Russia. Single newcomers were sojourners; only young families stayed. In the port city of Bremen, Polish and Ruthenian men and women worked in textile factories; Italians joined them. Many of the merchant families in Bremen traced their roots to other European "nations," but shared economic interests were more important than a distinct culture of origin. In addition, about 200,000 migrants who were in transit passed through the city annually by 1900, or about 700 per working day.[40]

Four cities or regions illustrate the multiple patterns of migration and acculturation. Newcomers in the Austrian capital, Vienna, and in the German mining and smelting center known as the Ruhr District had to deal with the availability of jobs and sociocultural segregation within the framework of the Habsburg and Hohenzollern empires. The interaction of immigrant and native labor on the job and the willingness to acculturate could not overcome the cultural exclusiveness of the hegemonic group. Paris, on the other hand, accommodated internal as well as foreign migrants with a mix of centralized cultural practices and pluralist interaction. The multiethnic populations of Budapest, which had grown over time, had traditions of ethnic self-help and enjoyed the acceptance of heterogeneity, albeit a hierarchically structured one.

Because of their political linkages, the nobility's consumption patterns, and investments by the bourgeoisie, capital cities attracted large numbers of heterogeneous migrants. Vienna exerted its pull over most of the Habsburg Empire, self-defined as a "state of many peoples." Migrants came from Bohemia, Moravia, Slovakia, the Hungarian lands, Polish-Ukrainian-Jewish Galicia, and Bukovina. Greek traders, Italian merchants, and Jewish families lived in distinct quarters. Perceptive observers could see that Vienna's promise as a place of opportunity remained unfulfilled, calling it a "Potemkian city": the tantalizing facades of aristocratic and bourgeois quarters suggested riches to be made, but the harsh working conditions of the factories and the drab working-class quarters—afflicted with poverty, pneumonia, and prostitution—were invisible to migrants before their expectations, developed at a distance, clashed with reality.[41] In the two decades before 1900, Vienna's population grew by 130 percent. Men and women from the Czech lands, next to Lower Austria the most industrialized part of the monarchy, arrived in particularly large numbers. Immigrant women in service positions created "Viennese cuisine" with its Bohemian flavor and Hungarian menus. Cultural opportunities and patronage attracted intellectuals and artists. Many workers came seasonally, and ethnic associations registered a membership turnover of up to 100 percent per year, as was also true of Germany's labor unions. The proletarian migrations involved high mobility at a particular stage of the life-cycle. These were not single moves going in one direction.[42]

Improvement of socioeconomic position demanded an adoption of the Czech-Viennese, who often arrived speaking already both languages, with the German-speaking majority. Residential segregation was low within districts as a whole, but higher from street to street and highest in particular tenement blocs. Imbalanced ratios of men to women, 100 to 112 among German-speakers, 100 to 82 among Czech-speakers, led to intermarriage and cultural fusion. Although the immigrants were animated by a desire to be integrated into Viennese society, they had to face the growing nationalism of German-speaking Austrians. Within the imperial framework, the two nationalities competed for resources—political influence, industrial development, and social prestige. When nationalists enforced Germanization on the Czechs in their home base of Bohemia, as well as on the diasporic Czechs in Vienna, people migrating from Czech cultural space to the job-providing German-language center became pawns in a struggle for identities and dominance. Austria-Hungary, the state of many peoples, fell prey to the preachers of monoculturalism.[43]

In the German Ruhr District, the international linkages typical of capital cities did not exist, and the upper classes did not engage in the sort of conspicuous consumption that could generate jobs. The demand for laborers to work in coal mines and the smelting industry was met by the surrounding countryside until, after 1880, Polish workers from the Prussian annexation were recruited. As citizens, they did not face restrictions on mobility, but, as in Vienna, nationalist authorities interfered with the self-determined pace of acculturation by prohibiting the use of the Polish language in public meetings. Industry's demand for additional laborers (400,000 Poles and 50,000 Mazurians) conflicted with the government's project to forge a culturally homogeneous society. In reaction to the political-cultural restrictions, the bilingual Polish ethnics with German citizenship reverted to closed ethnic associations and increased their use of the Polish language.[44]

While the Austrian socialist party attempted to combine class and ethnicity in an everyday cooperation rather than holding forth about a postulated internationalism ("Little" or intra-Austrian International), German unions and social democracy showed little understanding of ethnicity within class. Thus Polish migrants formed their own labor union, which was rooted in Catholicism, thereby reaching out to workers inexperienced with unionization. The two imperial governments' demands for unconditional assimilation forced migrants to emphasize their "Polishness" or "Czechness" as a political and economic resource. In the middle of an acculturation process, they were forced into a secondary minority formation.[45]

Patterns of interaction were different in cities with historically multiethnic populations. Budapest's inhabitants consisted of German-speaking German and Jewish middle and upper classes from earlier migrations and of Magyar-speaking lower classes, mostly recent migrants from the region. From 1850 to 1910, when the city grew by almost 700,000 to 864,000 inhabitants and when industry increasingly relied on non-Magyar migrants, a Magyar-language Hungarian national culture emerged; resident German- and Jewish-origin middle classes as well as labor unions adopted the new culture and replaced German as their lingua franca with multilingualism. The city's Slovak, Polish, Serbian, Czech, Rumanian, and Italian workingmen and -women, under cultural pressure and economic incentives, became socially and culturally more homogeneous. Others emigrated. The enforced Magyarization and economic discrimination in peripheral areas of Hungary sent Slovaks and migrants from other targeted groups to industrial cities across Europe and North America.

Because of the middle-class demand for domestics, women accounted for much of the migration. Combined with the higher mortality of men, this resulted in a sex ratio in favor of women. Due to the low "dependency rate" specific to migrants and the high level of women in the labor force, family composition differed from other parts of the country, and women's rate of marriage was low. Whereas in the late 1860s about a quarter of Budapest's in-migrants, mainly skilled workers, had been born outside of Hungary, by 1900 the local labor supply filled the jobs in mass industrial production. Foreign in-migration declined to 9 percent of the total in 1910. Budapest's development might be labeled diversity within homogenization policies.[46]

In Paris, the traditional small immigrant communities included Polish exiles and Russian anarchists, artists from most of Europe and North America, and students from many origins (chap. 12.4). The large colony of transient German journeymen artisans lost its position when Prussia engaged in war against France in 1870–71. Visible and culturally distinct but not alien, the internal migrants included wood merchants from Auvergne, laborers from Limousin, servant women from Brittany, masons from the Creuse region, chimney sweeps from many hinterlands, prostitutes from still more, and domestics from rural areas as well. Men established fraternal organizations, and women the everyday support networks.[47] After the 1880s, Italian stonecutters and laborers became the nucleus of a permanent community. Jewish migrants from the east came with images of Paris's revolutionary past and an awareness of the early emancipation of Jews in the city. They entered a newly emerging labor market segment, the ready-made-clothing industry; thus there was no competition with French workers. Socialist and union policies coalesced with Jewish working-class radicalism. Prejudices in the hegemonic culture and occasional labor tensions could not prevail in a situation where immigrant labor was needed and where authorities did not fuel latent resentment.[48]

Turning from case studies to the national level, one finds that Britain, France, and Germany—like Switzerland, Austria, and the Netherlands—imported labor but developed contrasting policies. Britain's census of 1861 listed almost three-quarters of a million Irish-born residents; in 1911, almost 650,000 Irish, 96,000 Polish Jews, and 53,000 Germans were counted. Italians came as itinerant traders. Imperial connections explain the colonies of Indian *lascars* and of Chinese dockworkers. A long-standing African community was part of dock-life in Liverpool. Returning merchants and administrators brought nannies and servants from the colonies, and one observer grumbled that "the Asiatic and African faces" in London would be better placed in "the ethnographic galleries of the . . . British Museum." Though expansionists with regard to the world at large, many politicians were restrictionists at home. Foreigners had been expelled throughout British history and in 1793 Parliament sanctioned the practice of keeping out French revolutionaries and atheists. Immigrants from the empire's Native populations were unwanted. Socialist Russian Jews and non-White seamen and nannies were targeted in the 1905 Aliens Act and the 1919 Aliens Restriction Act.[49]

France promoted immigration, and the government praised foreigners for "filling a void" in the mid-1800s. In 1901, when about half a million French people resided abroad, over a million foreigners lived in France (2.6 percent of the population). The French-speaking Belgians were surpassed in number by Italians in 1901; Germans, Spaniards, Austro-Hungarians, Swiss, and many others had settled. Though public opinion feared a peaceful invasion, almost no antiforeigner measures passed the legislature because of the usefulness of immigrants as workers and because of the need to offset demographic decline. By a law enacted in 1889, birth on French soil conferred citizenship. The high casualty rate in World War I (1.3 million dead, 1.1 million wounded) and the implementation of an eight-hour workday in 1919 exacerbated the labor shortages. Recruitment treaties were signed with Poland and Czechoslovakia, and as many as 200,000 German-Poles from the Ruhr District migrated to French and Belgian mines because of less oppressive cultural structures.[50]

In Germany, late industrialization meant low in-migration before the 1880s, but by 1890 the annual influx amounted to 433,000. Russian and Austrian Poles came into the eastern Prussian provinces as agricultural laborers; Italians took jobs in the southern German construction industry. The 1907 census listed 340,000 Austrian-Germans, Poles, and Ruthenians from Austria-Hungary; 201,000 Russians, Baltic Germans, Poles, and Lithuanians from Russia; 126,000 Italians, 52,000 Dutch people, 27,000 Swiss, about 10,000 persons per country from Denmark and France, and lesser numbers from five other nationalities. The total increased to 1.26 million in 1910, among them 543,000 women. To enter the Reich, workers had to have a job and, beginning in 1903, a "legitimizing card," under the terms of which they agreed to be, in effect, submissive and not change jobs. With regard to Poles, most German states accepted only single workers, and women in harvest gangs could not bring with them children under the age of fourteen. Prussia forced foreign Polish agricultural laborers to leave for the winter to prevent acculturation and to cut employers' wage costs. Special restrictions applied to Lithuanian and Czech migrants in ethnically mixed border provinces. Russian Jews were subjected to restrictions after the 1905 revolution. Industrialists, who had to invest in training their foreign workers, were able to exempt Polish industrial labor from the annual return stipulation. Attempts by the Austrian, Hungarian, and Russian governments to improve the status of their migrating citizens—if only modestly—were rebuffed by German authorities. The policy was to rely on a rotating labor force, which served as a reservoir in times of labor shortages and was easily dismissable during recessions. Comparable to the situation in Switzerland, this was the extreme case of recruiting foreign labor under a policy of nonimmigration.[51]

North American Immigrant and Afro-American Migrations

The North American core extended from the Atlantic coast to Montreal and Toronto and to Chicago and St. Louis. Its periphery included the North American West, the U.S. South, and the mixed Mexican-American Southwest. From 1871 to 1920, the United States received 20 million immigrants net, and Canada 4.6 million. Before the early 1870s, immigrants brought more capital from Europe (initial capital, inheritances, gifts) than they sent back. Only thereafter did their remittances help finance Europe's development.

Throughout the nineteenth century, entrepreneurs migrated across North America—much as they had done in Europe and still did in Africa—to recently settled areas—for example, from New York to New Mexico and from Montreal to Winnipeg. In Santa Fe or El Paso, newcomers from the East connected with the long-settled Spanish-Mexicans. Migrants of many origins from New Spain founded towns in California. Along the border between Canada and the United States, a large-scale exchange of population involved textile workers in the Quebec–New England labor market, lumberjacks, craftsmen, small farmers in the Great Lakes region, and settlers in the West. Emigration from the United States involved investor-planters moving to independent Texas and Hawai'i and—after 1898—to colonized Cuba and the Philippines as well as to China and Japan.

There evolved a sequence of internal labor migrations and other types of migration depending on demand and supply and on the political regulation of labor and land: the migration of planters with their slaves away from the upper south tidewater and toward the Mississippi; short-distance moves of New England farm women to textile mills in the 1820s to 1840s; sending of slaves to industrial work, 1840s–50s; transcontinental westward moves of farmers, the depopulating of Amerindian settlements, and an eastbound counter-movement from farms to the cities; unbound

European immigrant labor in a gender ratio of 60:40—with some restrictions after 1880—up to the period 1917–24; unbound labor migration from Asia as well as the importation of bound labor; multiple rural-urban migrations; the migration of Black workers to northern cities starting in the 1910s; and a further mobilization of women for home-front work during World War I and for clerical work in the 1920s.[52]

Cultural spaces developed as a result of migration, the combination of annexation and migration, and forced migration: Anglo New England and British Canada, the French St. Lawrence valley, a German-Scandinavian and Canadian belt along the forty-ninth parallel (chap. 9.4), a Hispanic belt along the Mexican border, and an Afro-American region in the Southeast (chap. 10.5). First Nations maintained a pueblo culture in the territories of Arizona and New Mexico and a coastal culture in British Columbia (map 14.3). Westward migrations in the United States did not serve as a safety valve to defuse class conflict; rather, urbanization attracted the surplus rural population, as also happened in Europe. The "frontier" was not a line advancing across the continent but involved rural settlement, mining advances, urban investment, and colonization in California and British Columbia. A checkerboard pattern of islands of rapid development, agricultural lands, and unsettled territories emerged. Agricultural land could be acquired more cheaply than in Europe. Though more family farms were established in the early 1900s than ever before, "bonanza farms" or corporate latifundia soon displaced settler families, just as Caribbean plantation owners had displaced settlers in the eighteenth century. The out-migration of U.S. farming families accelerated during the Great Depression of the 1930s; emigration from marginal Canadian homesteads continued for half a century after 1918.[53]

The patterns of labor migration resembled those found in Europe. Unskilled male workers with rural backgrounds dug railway beds, roads, mines, and sewage ditches. A first upward step was work sheltered from the weather. As was the case in Budapest, labor market segments in U.S. factories were open to immigrants. Geographical mobility was high, from areas where low-paying entry-level jobs predominated to regions with better conditions or wages. While several unions of the American Federation of Labor built an image of stolid respectability, some workers organized after 1900 (the Industrial Workers of the World) created an idealistic vision of footloose hobos, proud tramps, and bitter strikes. The government destroyed radical organizations and deported political activists, as did the Canadian government for several decades. Involuntary return migration ensued. In some strikes, immigrant and native-born workers took opposite sides or used different strategies: native-born workers tended to rely on labor organizations, and immigrants tended to engage in spontaneous strikes. In mining towns, striking immigrants could hold out for a long time because continuing semi-agrarian ways of life, such as gardening and raising pigs, provided families with food.[54]

In the 1850s, Chicago temporarily became the western outpost of the Atlantic Migration System. Emerging out of a trading post set up by the son of a Black slave woman and a French nobleman, it appeared on the map a century after St. Petersburg in 1803, at a time when London counted two million inhabitants. Chicago had

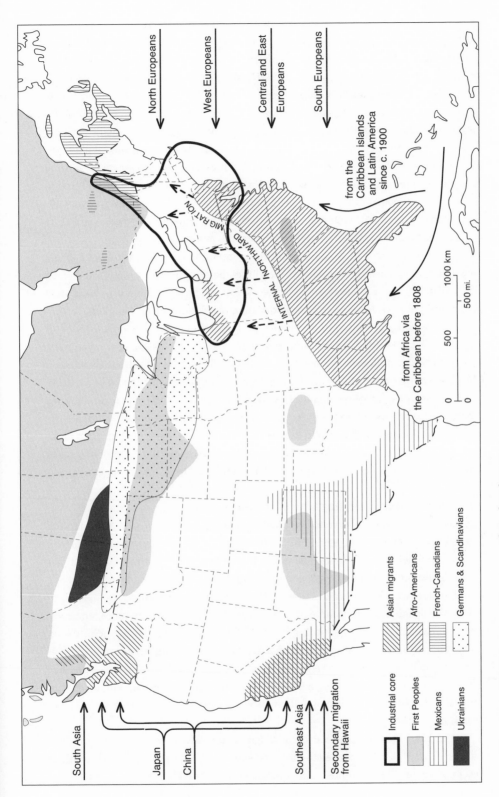

North Europeans

West Europeans

Central and East Europeans

South Europeans

from the Caribbean islands and Latin America since c. 1900

INTERNAL NORTHWARD MIGRATION

from Africa via the Caribbean before 1808

South Asia

Japan

China

Southeast Asia

Secondary migration from Hawaii

1000 km

500 mi.

500

0

0

Industrial core

First Peoples

Mexicans

Ukrainians

Asian migrants

Afro-Americans

French-Canadians

Germans & Scandinavians

14.3 Migration to North America, 1865–1924, and Bicultural Regions

four million inhabitants in less than a century. Canal construction in the 1840s and railroad construction in the 1850s brought unskilled Irish and German workers. Immigrant merchants mediated between prairie settlers and eastern markets. The city's demand for lumber and firewood gave struggling immigrant farmers the opportunity to supplement their insufficient agricultural incomes by migrating temporarily to wagework, leaving women and children on the homestead: wintertime lumbering and summertime railroad construction. This continued European smallhold peasants' patterns of accepting seasonal wagework. Germans, Irish people, Poles, and Swedes formed the largest immigrant groups; three-quarters of the population were foreign-born or had foreign-born parents. If the estimate of average return migration from the United States of one-third of all immigrants around 1900 holds true for Chicago, tens of thousands could relate the story of its phenomenal growth—and of its depressions and poverty—to prospective migrants in Europe.

Immigrant men and women, who could remember the slaughtering of a single pig as a festive occasion shared with neighbors before migration, were hired on in the expanding meat industry, in which workers from forty different ethnic cultures processed 300,000 pigs and cattle in 1900. Canned food found instant markets; it revolutionized food preparation in the home and thus affected the gendered division of labor. Chicago's second big industry, the manufacturing of agricultural machinery, also involved a multiethnic labor force and caused additional millions to migrate. Mechanization on the ever more frequently large farms reduced the labor input on large farms to harvest-time migrant labor and forced many North American families to leave bankrupt farms and move to cities. Mechanization also cut production costs to levels that made small farms in Europe unprofitable, thus sending European families into labor migration. In both industries, the harsh working conditions caused strikes and labor protests, leading to the development of multiethnic labor organizations.[55]

The complexities faced by labor migrants are exemplified by an Austrian socialist baker's family who emigrated to New York in 1910 and moved to Cleveland in 1912. On the transatlantic steamer, they were seated with a Transylvania-German woman and her two daughters. The mother had been in the United States with her husband for more than ten years, and the two girls had been raised by relatives. She had become Americanized and spoke in a mixture of Transylvania-German and English; the daughters had become Magyarized and spoke Magyar among themselves and Transylvania-German with their mother. The mother had dressed them to look like young urban women, so that upon arrival they would not appear to be "greenhorns." She herself, however, was dressed in traditional village garb, which she had probably never worn in America. During the visit to her old-world kin she had to appear to fellow villagers as one of them, not changed beyond recognition by acculturation.

The baker, his partner, and their daughter left Austria to live together—both adults were still legally married to their first spouses. Although a desire to leave their established families prompted their migration, they quickly reverted to traditional spheres: he went into working-class politics, and she into homemaking. Whenever he was blacklisted, however, the sales of her home-produced knitting tided them over. In his first job as "master mechanic" in a sewing-machine factory, the former baker relied on the better-trained women working below his supervision to teach him their skills. When he tried to organize workers by distributing leaflets, he was arrested; the same would have happened under the Habsburg monarchy in Austria, but in the United States he was merely fined for littering the streets and not subjected to a political trial, which would have resulted in both a higher sentence and in publicity for the cause. In Cleveland, workers from several Slavic ethnicities decided in a show of working-class solidarity to strike together; to avoid ethnic friction, each group punished its own strikebreakers. When the baker joined the Communist Party, immigration authorities put pressure on the family to leave the United States. They returned to Austria as political emigrants, and their American-born children had to become acculturated there.[56]

In the nineteenth-century struggle for better working conditions, during the strikes of 1919, and in the labor organizations of the 1930s, immigrant workers came to terms with the system and the system with them. Americanization or Canadianization from the bottom up also involved institutional accommodation from the top down. However, neither U.S. society as a whole nor labor unions confronted their own racism. Afro-American workers remained segregated and were rarely if ever admitted to immigrant or native-born working-class organizations.[57]

A North American migration region emerged and expanded. American planters with capital moved to Cuba and elsewhere. From 1820 to 1930, 85.4 percent of U.S. immigrants came from Europe; others came from Canada, Mexico, and the West Indies. Although only about 150,000 Canadian-born immigrants lived in the United States in 1850, Canada became a transit country for European migrants: 2.6 million moved from there to the United States between 1871 and 1930.[58] Perhaps one million French-Canadians migrated to textile mills in New England or moved further into the United States. Between 300,000 and 400,000 resided there from the 1890s to the 1920s, with considerable back-and-forth fluctuations, depending on economic prospects and family requirements. English-Canadians settled in Michigan and on the prairies as well as in the state of Washington. The small community of Afro-Canadians had grown with the arrival of fugitive slaves via the "underground railroad"; it declined as a result of migration to the northern industrial cities of the United States after 1900. After visa requirements were introduced in 1924, immigration from Canada declined steadily. In the early twentieth century, Canadian agents recruited settlers from south of the border but excluded Afro-Americans.[59]

In the south, the future reservoirs of labor, Mexico and the Caribbean, remained separate partly because of color prejudices in White-dominated North America. Mexico, a country with little immigration, had lost its northern territories and peoples to the United States in 1848. Northward cross-border migration consisted of a trickle of labor migrants to California and turn-of-century recruitment of *braceros*. In the interwar years of the 1920s and 1930s, migration, still viewed with apprehension because of its "racial composition," was encouraged by employers in search of cheap labor after European exclusion from the immigration flows. Mexican immigrants settled, worked, and commuted mostly along a border belt with Los Angeles as the largest community. In the 1920s, their migrations expanded northward to the steel centers of Pennsylvania and of Gary, Indiana, as well as to Chicago. In that decade almost half a million came—11 percent of total immigration—but during the Great Depression return migration increased and was enforced.[60] Migration from the Caribbean increased parallel to U.S. investment in the islands; the figures jumped from a total of 35,600 in the 1890s to 183,000 in the first decade of the twentieth century. Havana cigar makers moved to Ybor City, Florida, or vice versa; other Caribbean migrants selected East Coast cities as destinations. Some went as far north as Toronto. New York's Caribbean colony had grown to over 100,000 by the time immigration restrictions took effect in 1924.

Within the United States, interregional migrations involved more and more Afro-Americans. In the 1870s, freed families left the South to work in agriculture in Kansas and moved to urban areas in small numbers. Pushed by lynch-mob pogroms, political disenfranchisement, and land-tenure arrangements, the children of ex-slaves increasingly migrated to northern urban jobs from the 1890s onward (about 100,000 net from 1890 to 1900). Some employers hired such migrants as strikebreakers. When immigration from Europe came to a sudden stop in 1914, the departures from the South developed into a new proletarian mass migration. From 1916 to 1920, 0.7 million Afro-Americans moved north, and 0.25 million westward: in the "Great Migration," almost 10 percent of the 10.4 million Black second-class citizens moved away from the South within a span of five years.[61] In centers of investment and metropolitan areas with war-related labor shortages, the Black working-class population grew by leaps and bounds. Single men and women aged twenty to twenty-four made up the largest segment of the migrants; widowed and divorced women came with their children because of educational opportunities. Black professionals followed as Black communities in the North developed a need for doctors, teachers, and journalists. The migrants used nearly religious terms in their letters to describe the "promised land" to their kin and friends in the South. By 1925 Black culture had its center in Harlem in New York City, and Black music began to exert an influence on White audiences.[62] Because Black Americans remained segregated in the North, which resisted the blending found in Latin American societies, a small but vocal "Back to Africa" movement emerged in the 1920s.[63]

In the 1920s, low cotton prices pushed both Blacks and Whites out of the southern rural economy. Drought and dustbowl in the southern and central states and in Saskatchewan deepened the impact of the Great Depression, and both factors uprooted families: White (and some Black) farmers fled the dustbowl and went to California and British Columbia; southern Blacks continued to migrate; the unemployed of many cultures and colors rode the rails to pursue illusory job opportunities; first-generation immigrants returned to their European family networks to tide them over; first-generation Mexican *braceros* were deported; and other Chicanos departed. Straitened economic circumstances and social pressures compelled hundreds of thousands to be on the move.[64]

In the U.S. and Canadian West (as in Russia's Siberian East), Chinese workers had joined the proletariat. So did Japanese and Indian workers along the whole of the Pacific coast of the Americas, some as free merchants and artisans, many as temporarily bound laborers. The working-class diasporas from Europe and Asia overlapped in North and South America, where they joined forces or competed with free Black and White labor (chaps. 15.5, 15.6).

Migration to Dependent Economies in Latin America

Most of the nominally independent Central and South American polities remained politically and economically dependent, first on Europe and then on North America (chap. 8.6). In the first decades after independence hostility toward the ruling ethnicities, the Portuguese and the Spanish, reduced immigration; but over time settler migration from Southern Europe resumed, and laborers began to arrive in large numbers. Of the 50–55 million European migrants, about one-fifth went to Latin America, as compared to more than 70 percent to North America. The number of arrivals grew from 1850 to 1885, then rose rapidly to 1914, stagnated in the interwar years, and resumed after 1945 for one decade (map 14.4). Migration to countries where new peoples were formed by descendants of Natives, African-origin forced migrants, and European-origin free migrants provided opportunities not available in colonies where White administrators and capitalists exploited subjugated Colored populations. In the Latin American color gradation, working-class immigrants from Europe, considered more White, held a competitive advantage over local workers of mixed origin, considered more Colored.[65]

Labor regimes, patterns of migration, and societal composition changed when slavery was abolished (last in Brazil), and the Afro-Atlantic Migration System—but not Black Atlantic culture—ended. Into the 1870s slaves had still been brought in; thereafter, a small number of Afro–Latin Americans returned to West Africa, and manumitted slaves and free Afro–South and –North Americans migrated between societies of the Americas. The Euro-Atlantic System changed around 1900, when Italian migration reached South and North America and thus integrated its dual Mediterranean- and Atlantic-European branches. The United States replaced European states as dominant political power in Latin America. Migrations internal to Latin America increased when ex-slave families left plantations, first in a villagization process and then in medium-distance rural-to-urban migrations. Plantation owners and the governments dominated by them experimented with labor recruitment schemes before they settled on bringing in free migrants from Europe.[66]

Migrants to the Latin or Afro-Native-Latin societies continued to originate in Mediterranean cultures. From the 1850s to 1924, 38 percent came from Italy, 28 percent from Spain, 11 percent from Portugal, and the rest from Russia (Jews), Germany, and France. Argentina and Brazil received almost four-fifths of the newcomers,

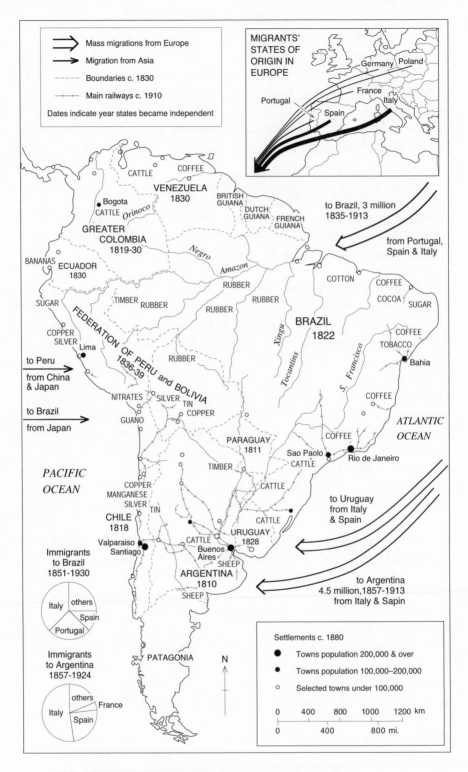

14.4 (In)dependent Latin America: Migration, Intervention, Investment

46 percent and 33 percent respectively, Cuba 14 percent, and Uruguay and Mexico a mere 3–4 percent each. Among the smaller groups, Portuguese Canary Islanders continued their chain migration; Syrians and Lebanese, called "Turks," acculturated easily; Eastern European immigrants moved toward the mainstream over generations; some settlers in tightly knit colonies, especially Germans, a few Swiss, and French people, remained isolated from the surrounding society. Return migrants to Southern Europe were called "Indianos" rather than "Americanos."

The societies of the Caribbean, the Guianas, and the Pacific coast also included contract laborers and free migrants from Asia. Some intermarried locally, while others, who could afford it, brought in women from their culture of origin. After exclusion from North America, Japanese immigrants came to Brazil and Peru, often as families (chap. 15.5).

In the Latin American economies, which developed more slowly than those of the northern cores, acculturation was easier for Mediterranean migrants than in northern White anglophone societies. Wages were favorable relative to transportation costs and to living expenses in the cultures of origin, but harsh working conditions on plantations resulted in secondary rural-to-urban migrations and high rates of return. The self-selection of migrants channeled people according to their social profiles and the receiving society's economies. For example, unmarried men from Portuguese Terceira in the Azores who were between fourteen and twenty-five years of age and had no prior migratory experience moved to the United States; married men from the same place of origin who did have previous migratory experience and skills or property moved to Brazil.[67]

Argentina pursued a policy of encouraging the immigration of both agricultural and industrial labor. From 1869 to 1914, about 6.0 million Europeans arrived, and 2.7 million returned home; the country's population more than quadrupled from 1.7 million in 1869 to 7.9 million in 1914, when 58 percent of all Argentinians were foreign-born or the children of immigrants. Before the 1890s, agrarian settlement resembled that of plains elsewhere in the world: flat, semi-arid land from which the native Araucanians had been expelled became accessible by railways underwritten by British capital and constructed by heavily subsidized private companies with immigrant labor forces. The overwhelming predominance of settlers and harvest laborers of northern Italian origin conflicted with the large landholders' policy of relying on sharecroppers and an agrarian proletariat. After the mid-1890s, even hard-working families could no longer rise to independent landownership.

Migrants reached an economy of "expansion without development"—that is, a society experiencing urbanization without industrialization. Argentina had no frontier; it had one city, Buenos Aires, with a Spanish elite, Italian bourgeois and lower middle-classes, and multiethnic shantytowns (chap. 8.6). For six decades, 70 percent or more of the population of the city were foreign-born; by 1914 the share had declined to 30 percent, "twice the proportion ever reached in the United States." Half of the immigrants were Italian; one-third were Spanish and 5 percent French, including people of Basque origin; other ethnicities—Swiss, Poles, Germans, and Jews—accounted for less than 2 percent. Steamship fare from Italy to Buenos Aires, which was about $50, made the trip profitable even for seasonally commuting harvest laborers. The sex ratio, 2.5 to 1 among Italian migrants, was more balanced among the resident population because few women returned home.

The so-called old-stock Argentinian landed elite, perhaps similar to some segments of Europe's nobilities, remained in cattle raising as a status-providing source of income. They also dominated politics. In contrast to rural settlers, urban immigrant families experienced intergenerational upward mobility. Italian-Argentinians who invested their savings instead of transmitting funds home were able to rise from the status of workers and employees to that of proprietors. Immigrants were underrepresented only among artisans and domestics. They could participate easily in political life because even without being naturalized citizens they enjoyed all rights except the vote. Italians were active in the development of the labor movement and of socialist parties. They dominated cultural life, partly because the native-born elites held Italian civilization in high regard. Modest cities of 50,000 inhabitants offered several weeks of opera in the winter by bringing in Italian troupes on tour. Urban and rural life remained more strongly separated than almost anywhere else in the Americas and Europe.[68]

In Brazil, the first postindependence phase of European immigration lasted from the 1820s to the 1860s. German, Italian, and Polish settlers came to the coffee plantations of Rio Grande do Sul, where planters had relocated because of soil exhaustion north of Rio de Janeiro. The politically powerful planters promoted a program to assist the migration of families from northern Italy, who were settled on land or were employed in numbers as large as those of slaves had been before—5,000 on the largest coffee plantation alone. Many fled the miserable working conditions, "unsettling" in a literal sense, as Nugent puts it. This made Brazil different from any other country in the Americas. Unassisted young men—mainly from Portugal, but also from Italy and Spain—stayed in the cities. The second phase of European immigration brought a quarter million in the 1870s, half a million in the 1880s, more than a million in the 1890s, or a total of 3.4 million from 1870 to 1920, of whom 860,000 returned to Europe or moved elsewhere.[69]

After the end of slavery in 1888, Afro-Brazilians could blend into the multicolored population rather than face U.S.-type segregation. They migrated to jobs or sharecropping opportunities, and some returned as seasonal laborers to plantations. In prospering regions and cities, European labor displaced free Africans, who had to migrate to stagnating regions or take the most menial jobs. By contrast, Italian immigrants experienced good opportunities for upward mobility and, as in Argentina, joined the middle classes. Entrepreneurs brought capital and skills. Given Brazil's population size, the ratio of immigrants to the native-born was always lower than in other receiving states in the Americas.[70]

The Brazilian Euro-Creole elites engaged in a nation-building process conceived in European terms and relying on contemporary concepts of race to prevent Indio and Black peoples from accessing political resources. At first, Indios and Blacks were said to be mentally incapable of participation. Since this stance cast aspersions on the country's ability to join the Atlantic World on an equal footing, notions of improving the "population stock" by "crossbreeding" and "Whitening" emerged in a second phase. After 1900, a third approach positioned the old elites, which refused to consider innovations, against the new rising technocrats and specialists who were seeking to gain political influence. General improvements in physical and mental health, they argued, could be achieved through inoculation, cleanliness, and health services. Similar arguments were common in the United States, where social workers advocated cleanliness among germ-carrying immigrants and where Henry Ford's famous five-dollar wage was predicated on a social worker's certificate that the household of the respective factory worker was clean and, in a way, Americanized.[71]

In the Caribbean, migration after the end of slavery was limited to the circum-Caribbean zone in the nineteenth century, with only a few sailors, whalers, and people aspiring to be entrepreneurs going further afield. In the early twentieth century, the building sites of the Panama Canal became a major destination, attracting some 40,000 free and some 20,000 contracted Barbadian migrants, 80,000 Jamaicans, and men shipped from Guadeloupe and Martinique. The death rates were high. Wage remittances induced others to migrate to U.S. investments in the 1920s, in particular to banana plantations in the Greater Antilles and in Cuba, Costa Rica, and Nicaragua. Others moved seasonally to the Dominican Republic, where in 1937 some 15,000–20,000 Haitian migrant sugar estate workers were murdered in the "Trujillo massacre." By that time, the plantation regime had become a political regime of "banana republics" run by multinational robber-baron corporations, such as United Fruit. Over time, there emerged the search for an "authentic" Caribbean culture, a common cultural experience or "nationalism," and a widespread awareness of deprivation (compared, for example, to the situation of immigrants in New York).[72] Migration from the British possessions to North America remained possible because British-Caribbean migrants, regardless of skin color, qualified for the unfilled British quota when the United States enacted national-origin legislation in the early 1920s. It remained on the books until the 1952 Immigration Act was passed.

14.3 Transcultural Identities and Acculturation in the Age of Nation-States

The nineteenth-century homogenization of various groups of subjects in a state's citizenry and a nation's culture changed demands for and processes of acculturation. In medieval and early modern times, traveling merchants and settled broker communities, placed in walled-in compounds in the Baltic and Mediterranean Worlds and in separate quarters in Africa and Asia, had retained their distinctiveness. In the mercantilist and statist seventeenth and eighteenth centuries, religious refugees had been settled in privileged urban positions, and culturally defined agriculturalists in privileged and separate rural colonies. In bourgeois-democratic societies of the nineteenth century no privileged status could be negotiated. If all people were equal, none could claim special status—and none could be different from the nation. In fact, most states were not based on one cultural group, the "nation," but rather on dynastic territorial aspirations and the state's administrative homogenization of different regional cultures. Thus nation-states were usually state-nations. The consequences for immigrants were far-reaching. To begin with, newcomers could no longer negotiate special status, and those who still held privileges, like Mennonites in Russia, lost them. Second, immigrants were not to organize as cultural groups because equality and participation were individual rights. Thus newcomers were expected to shed cultural distinctiveness, now labeled clannishness, and to assimilate.

While immigrants lost the option of positive discrimination or privileges, they, like resident minorities, could not escape negative discrimination, ethnic labeling, and inferior class positions. The middle class, particularly its male section, defined itself as the "nation" and developed rules of respectability that excluded intermarriage across class and racial boundaries. The constitutional construction of citizens, equal before the law and before institutions of political systems based on natural rights, neither incorporated cultural differences nor abolished exclusion because of class and gender. Yet nineteenth-century migrants continued to transport regional and local cultural loyalties. German-speakers in New York, for example, still organized by region as Mecklenburgers or Swabians, as Hungarian-Germans or Saxons. English, Irish, and Scottish immigrants held loyalties to home counties. As English-speakers, they could more easily join the composite American or Canadian mainstream, just as Italians could enter the Argentinian mainstream, or Portuguese the Brazilian one. Thus specific cultural capital rather than skills facilitated entry. Nation-states assigned social slots by ethnocultural belonging in contravention to the founding principle of equality. The ruling ethnic group assigned to itself the top slot, the status of "nation," a privileged position with gatekeeper functions. It relegated all other resident cultural groups to minority status and newcomers to the status of "foreigners" or "immigrants."[73]

The dress codes of medieval times had not survived the development of new societies, and labels—like the yellow star—had not yet been introduced. Skin color came to serve as a marker not just for colonized peoples (chaps. 11.1, 11.3). British, French, and Spanish peoples and Germans respectively had primary status as Whites, while peoples from the periphery, except Scandinavians or "Nordic" peoples, were not White: Italians were "swarthy" or "olive"; Eastern Europeans were termed "dark"; and the Irish had yet to become White. If a self-styled "Britisher" in North America called an immigrant (for example, a Jewish man) "a real White man," he wanted to recognize some particular achievement that was unusual for a person "normally" deemed racially inferior (as determined by the majority population).[74]

But simple markers—Black or Negro, Yellow or Oriental, Red or Indian—were not the only barriers. The construction of inferiority resulted in the stereotyping of character traits: Irish men were seen as drunkards, and Irish women as inferior domestics—though compared to England, Ireland since 1831 had had a better education system. French-Canadians in New England were labeled "the Chinese of the East."

Even though the power of exploitation lay with the oft-analyzed capitalist middle classes, the power of definition lay with the cultural middle class, the intellectuals or gatekeepers. To be defined as being of inferior status circumscribed how much a working immigrant or native-born family could eat after a day of labor. One result was that working-class ethnocultural groups sharing hegemonic labeling often struggled against each other; the definition of the "Other" by cultural background and skin color overrode common interests.

The migrants' interest in finding jobs without delay coincided temporarily with the interest of the receiving political economy in human labor regardless of culture, as long as it was cheap. Immediately after arrival, migrants confined by their self-perceived interest to a survival economy had to come to terms with conditions in the labor market segment of the receiving society that they wanted to enter. They shed cultural customs that obstructed ways of earning a living.[75] Migrants were not committed to a particular culture because they had left a world of "known impossibilities" (thanks to exploitation by landowners, dowry constraints, pogroms, anti-worker police control, unbearable gender hierarchies, impoverishing procreation and inheritance systems) and now were entering a world of "unknown possibilities."[76]

In this situation, but only under these constraints, subsistence wages were acceptable. Once migrants acquired sufficient knowledge about patterns of work, hiring processes, and living expenses that enabled them to explore options, they embarked on a quest for better working and living conditions and for a status more equal to that of workers born into the society they had entered. In the process, they used their cultural resources strategically. The formation of ethnic group structures from the bottom up occurred in reaction to the formation of hegemonic cultural group structures from the top down. In societies hostile to the integration of newcomers, immigrant groups had to develop "institutional completeness" to survive without having recourse to social services or institutional provisions of the host societies.[77]

Ethnic communities with organizational structures and with children for whom a future had to be charted came into being only when sojourner status changed to permanent residence and when the migrants' sex ratio became balanced. Once a community (social capital) had been established as a resource, the pace of acculturation and its direction could become self-determined. Communities provided protection against derision from members of the receiving culture and support for emotional and material security. Individual experiences in community contexts—the actual use of human and social capital—thus depended on structural options and societal ascription by the receiving culture and state.

Both the receiving society and the migrants adjusted to some degree. The former shaped jobs, one aspect of the nation's economy, to suit cheap immigrant labor with limited communication potential (unless the immigrants spoke the receiving society's language), while the latter abandoned parts of their cultural heritage to achieve material advance. Immediate insertion and long-term acculturation involved cultural interaction along cultural borderlines that provided options or generated friction. Migrants continuously had to make decisions about how to re-act until, once better established, they could decide how to "pro-act."[78] In closed or racist societies, interaction might be limited to being pushed around. In open societies, borderlines expanded into borderlands in which cultural change was negotiated and experienced. Closed societies forced migrants ready to acculturate back into ethnic niches, a process called secondary minority formation. Acculturation was retarded because the receiving societies provided no entry gates except via exploitative labor relations.[79]

Argentina provided better access to institutions (at least for Italian immigrants) than did the United States; Poles preferred ethnic communities in France or North America to the restrictive German society, but they needed premigration economic resources to cross the Atlantic. Immigrant laborers of a skin color other than White were segregated and often were restricted to extremely limited labor market segments and urban social spaces.

Because cultural differences—values and memories, in particular—were invisible (at least to the undiscerning eyes of host society populations), the specific regional characteristics of immigrants were not recognized by members of the receiving society. Men and women from the environs of Dublin or the province of Munster were equally labeled Irish. The self-homogenization as "Italians" of people from the vast variety of cultures in geographic Italy, stretching from Lombardy to Calabria, helped them to achieve economic or political influence. Men from different provinces of China or from the diaspora became "the" Chinese, or "John Chinaman." The "nationalization" of regional specifics thus occurred after migration: immigrants from many different cultures within or bordering Germany became "Germans" (or, in particular periods, "Krauts") or "Poles." From this perspective, migrants' lives became transnational. Rather than feeling deficient, uprooted, or dislocated, migrants carefully established continuities between their societies of origin and of arrival in order to prevent disruptions in their identities; they knew how to function in two cultures.

Migrants from specific regional cultures, however, organized along lines of cultural affinity, of first socialization. During childhood and schooling, local and family identity emerges first and mostly unconsciously. Shared and unquestioned, seemingly "natural" norms and values shape lifetime identities. Parental economic status and the chances of adolescents in accessible regional labor markets involve a second step: young people acquire a regional identity when they evaluate their chances in job markets or in agriculture. Schoolteachers may also teach them distinctiveness from people of neighboring regions. The top-level national identity is acquired last. After migration, ethnic communities thus form as ethno-local communities in which international political borders or feelings of national belonging matter little. Migrants thus lead transcultural lives and acquire transcultural identities. Societies that respect such multiple identities become multicultural rather than multinational, as was the case under the Habsburg monarchy.

Over time in South and North America, the descendants of newcomers had to come to terms with the stereotypes in which the surrounding society packaged them; they had to deal with the culture ascribed to them. Even in pluralist societies, active, complex, and subtle ways of everyday life became simplified markers concentrating on visual elements: embroidered ceremonial dresses were seen as "Japanese", Oktoberfests as "German", and colored Easter eggs as "Ukrainian." To the undiscerning eyes of the receiving society as well as to the children of immigrants reared outside the "original" culture, the signs lost their specific regional, sacred, or festive meanings. Thus the ethnic culture that immigrant groups sought to maintain was no longer the culture of origin. It was—and is—a combination of a memory of the past at the time of departure (frozen in time) modified by experiences in the new society (gained under socioeconomic pressures) expressed in signs. Ethnic culture becomes a "symbolic culture" distinct from but also part of a larger lived, everyday culture.[80]

15

The Asian Contract Labor System (1830s to 1920s)

and Transpacific Migration

The intrusion of Europeans into the Indic trade emporia (chap. 7) changed labor demands, on a modest scale at first, in larger proportions under Dutch rule, and massively under nineteenth-century British imperialism and that of other empires. Steamships, beginning in the 1830s, and the Suez Canal, opened in 1869, changed Asia's geographical position in the world economy. In the 1850s, when English, French, and German capital established Łódź as a textile center in Russian Poland, a Parsee opened a cotton mill in Mumbai/Bombay, and a regional migration system developed and brought peasants to the mill. Distant politics had an impact on local economies. When Manchester mills substituted Indian cotton for American imports during the U.S. Civil War, for example, exports increased tenfold, but then the boom collapsed in 1866. For family economies, boom or bust translated into endless working hours or undernourishment, into migration and dislocation. When the African Slave Migration System was slowly abolished between 1807 and the 1870s, plantation regimes from Java to Cuba, mine owners in Malaya and South Africa, and guano pit entrepreneurs in Peru demanded new manageable workers with low reproduction costs. European labor migrants, however, selected destinations in temperate zones with free wage labor and democratic-capitalist institutions.

Colonial administrators therefore imposed a system of indentured labor, also called a "second slavery," on Asian men and women. Parallel to the voluntary and self-bound migrations in the Atlantic System, the migrations of "the other fifty million" involved a minority of free migrants, large numbers of self-bound migrants, and forced moves. The system that began informally in British India in the 1820s was buttressed by legislation from 1834 to 1917. It began earlier and lasted longer in the Chinese orbit.[1] Estimates of total numbers vary widely. In the case of the Chinese from 1800 to 1914, one estimate arrived at 2.5 million migrants within Asia and 0.7 million to other continents; another estimate was as high as 6.75 million from 1876 to 1907. With regard to India from 1834 to 1937, Kingsley Davis estimated 30.2 million migrants and 23.9 million returnees, or a net emigration of 6.3 million. A recent summary of data arrived at only 9.0 million pre-1917 migrants. Indian migration grew continuously after 1900. Out of a population of 281 million, 1.4 million left between

1901 and 1905, and 3.3 million between 1926 and 1930, with about 7 in 8 migrants re-turning. Free migrations are not included in most estimates (map 15.1). The decisive break in patterns of migration came with Japanese aggression in China in 1937 and in Burma in 1942. After 1945 new regional systems emerged (chaps. 19.5, 19.6).[2]

Among White capitalists and working-class organizations alike, the term "coolie" for self-indentured or kidnapped laborers came to be synonymous with cheap and despised men and women. It meant "bitter strength" in Chinese and "wage for menial work" in Tamil. Originally, it signified members of the Kuli tribe, described as "degenerate and inferior" in Gujarati.[3] The workers, assumed to be of peasant origin, were more often recruited from among urban underclasses. In India, men of higher castes signed up because of the misrepresentation of the work to be done. Employers imposed a labor regime of brute force or of sadistically elaborate systems of penalties. The coolies' destinations within Asia were Burma, Thailand, Malaya (including the Straits Settlements), some Pacific islands, and "White Asia" (Australia and New Zea-land). Those who traveled across the Indian Ocean were destined for East and South Africa, and those who traveled across the Pacific were headed for the western coasts of the two Americas and the Caribbean.[4]

Five peoples with manifold internal ethnic divisions were involved. Based on centuries of emigration, a thriving diaspora of Chinese merchants, capitalists, arti-sans, and workers was connected to the commercial and power centers of the colo-nizers. In India, where emigration or temporary labor migration had been negligible, the British administration developed a contract system of migration.[5] In Java, the Dutch recruited workers, as did several colonizing powers in the Pacific Islands. Though the numbers of colonizers were small, their impact on local societies was large and was exacerbated by the introduction of Indian contract laborers.[6] Men from Meiji Japan began to migrate in the late 1850s. Lastly, Filipinos migrated to the United States after their country became a U.S. colony in 1898.

15.1   Traditional and New Patterns of Bondage

Bondage in many Asian societies rested on family economies and hierarchies—chil-dren could be alienated by the decision of their parents—and on socioeconomic power structures that permitted the servitude of the poorer social groups. In India's Bihar, the *kamiuti* system secured loans to the poor in exchange for a right to their services and that of their children. Subsequent generations remained *kamias*, to be sold, leased, mortgaged, or transferred with land until debts were repaid. In Madras, rural laborers and servants became virtual serfs of landlords when they were unable to repay loans. Such systems intensified under British rule, and according to some authors subinfeudation occurred in indigo cultivation or on tea plantations.[7]

In Southeast Asia and the Indonesian archipelago, the customs related to slavery, debt bondage, and the forced labor of war captives were as varied as the societies. In the seventeenth-century sultanate of Mataram, Java, the aristocracy lived off the forced labor of the common people and the taxes imposed on them. Islamic coastal

15.1 Principal Overseas Migrations, 1830s–1919, of Asian Indentured and Free Migrants

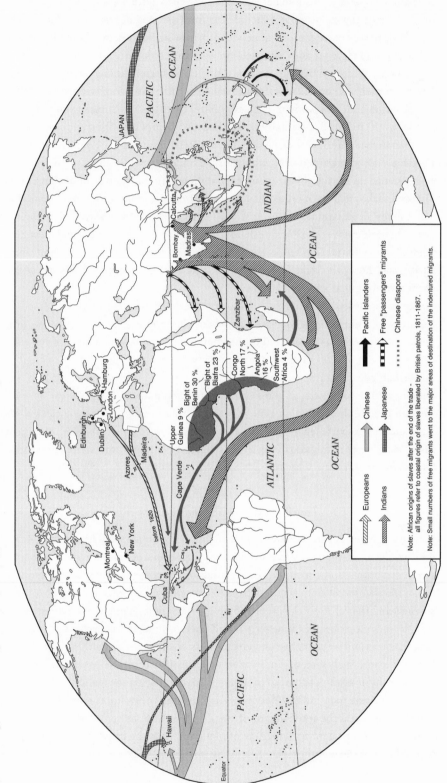

Legend:

Europeans
Indians
Chinese
Japanese
Pacific Islanders
Free "passengers" migrants
Chinese diaspora

Note: African origins of slaves after the end of the trade –
all figures refer to coastal origin of slaves liberated by British patrols, 1811-1867.

Note: Small numbers of free migrants went to the major areas of destination of the indentured migrants.

Place labels on map: JAPAN, PACIFIC OCEAN, INDIAN OCEAN, ATLANTIC OCEAN, PACIFIC OCEAN, Equator, Edinburgh, Dublin, London, Hamburg, Azores, Madeira, Cape Verde, Montreal, New York, Cuba, Hawaii, before 1820, Bombay, Calcutta, Madras, Zanzibar, Upper Guinea 9 %, Bight of Benin 30 %, Bight of Biafra 23 %, Congo North 17 %, Angola 16 %, Southwest Africa 4 %

people like the Makassarese and the Sumbawans held large numbers of slaves. In a mountain region of central Celebes, a hereditary slave class existed. In North Borneo, on the other hand, bound laborers cultivated gardens and fields for their own benefit and shared their earnings from trade or crafts with their masters. Rather than chattel, they were a restricted underclass. After contact, European merchants' trade networks supplied some rulers or ruling classes with slaves—for example, from the famine-stricken Coromandel Coast of India.[8] In Manchu China, tenants in northern regions were liberated from labor duties and life in landlord-assigned lodgings, though slavery did continue to exist in small pockets. The peasantry enjoyed greater personal independence than serfs did in Europe.[9]

At first, the European powers changed little. They and their joint stock companies relied on the enslavement and immobilization of local labor (chap. 7.4). But resident populations could refuse to enter wage or bound labor and could use their resources—knowledge of the terrain and supportive networks—for resistance. Imported bound labor lacked such resources and thus was more easily controlled and immobilized at the point of arrival. While the Spanish operated only a small-scale slave trade from the Philippines to Spanish America (chaps. 7.3, 8.4), the Dutch East India Company used enslavement as punishment of populations who resisted its monopolistic strategies. Enslavement practices involved the sale of war captives for profit, plantation slavery, bound domestic labor, and the use of bound servants to signal status and for display in rituals of power. Governors-general in Batavia had their carriages accompanied by "train[s] of richly dressed outriders and guards," and officials on the Coromandel Coast appeared with "standard bearers, trumpeters, musicians, twenty armed attendants and a swarm of coolies, besides a bodyguard of twelve Dutch soldiers." In colonial Dutch households, slave nurses socialized the children. Buginese women from Celebes were enslaved as concubines because Dutch men valued their beauty. Productive slavery involved Chinese laborers in settler agriculture in Java and the Cape Colony and in the Company's plantation system. The kind of regional system of forced labor put into practice by the Dutch became globalized in the British Empire. Mauritian planters recruited contract workers in India, and a British-Caribbean planter transferred the practice to the West Indies. Existing local migration systems were intensified or new ones created wherever migrant European owners of capital and power-wielding administrators arrived.[10]

Internal and Colonizer-Imposed Causes of Migration in Three Societies

In pre-1850s imperial China, socioeconomic decline, political unrest, ethnic antagonism, population growth, and natural disasters—all exacerbated by Euro-imperialist penetration—caused massive dislocation and stimulated emigration. First, the imperial government imposed heavy taxation, and corrupt local magistrates misused funds allocated for maintenance of irrigation and road systems. Minor uprisings throughout the 1840s, the Taiping rebellion of 1850–64, and the Hui rebellion of

1855–73, as well as their repression, involved nativist resistance against the "foreign" Manchu, of native-born or *pen-ti* against the "guest" settlers, the Hakka from Jianxi and other provinces, and of Han Chinese miners in Yunnan against Muslim Hui miners, even though intermarriage had made the groups almost indistinguishable. Second, rapid population growth from 300 million in 1790 to 420 million in 1850 aggravated subsistence problems. Sichuan's population grew from 8.4 to 44.2 million (1776–1850), and that of Hubei from 18.6 to 33.7 million (1786–1850). The price of rice, the main food staple, increased tenfold before 1850, and agriculture stagnated thereafter because of internal warfare. At the same time, inflation reduced incomes, and the government-imposed devaluation of copper (the circulating medium) in relation to silver (the taxpaying medium) further undercut peasant families' precarious living conditions. As in Europe, the "peasant question" remained unsolved, or, more accurately, their exploitation continued and reformers were exiled. A vast reservoir of potential migrants existed.

With regard to cultural interchange, imperial ideology placed the Celestial Dynasty in the center and relegated other peoples and states to lesser positions. Neighboring southern peoples—the Burmese, Thai, and Vietnamese—were considered subservient. The nomad warriors of the north and the northwestern frontiers had been "pacified," and Mongol notables lived in Beijing; daughters of the emperors were married off to princes in Mongolia. The court regulated foreigners in the empire. Caravan traders and traveling merchants were permitted to exchange goods, but they had to depart at the end of each trading season.

In nineteenth-century European-Chinese relations, neither side resorted to the help of intercultural brokers. Only the Portuguese held a trading town, Macao; the British and the United States had yet to insert themselves. China's imperial bureaucrats placed European state-supported merchants in "tributary nation"–status and restricted them to Canton. U.S. interests chose a precapitalist form of penetration by engaging in missionary, medical, and sinological work in southern China. The British—concerned about "the new dignity of Britain as a world power" (Spence)— began a policy of penetration by instigating opium smuggling and prosecuting the Opium War from 1839 to 1842. In the war's aftermath, the European powers extracted privileges of extraterritoriality in five ports. The British occupied Hong Kong and Kowloon, extracted a war "indemnity" that imposed a further burden on Chinese peasants, and enforced the sale of cheap British textiles, which destroyed village production. A British delegation of 1863, led by men "of immense conceit and arrogance," was convinced that "the notion of a gentleman acting under an Asiatic barbarian is preposterous." While European governments propounded racist concepts derived from notions of superiority and "honor," Chinese authorities held foreigners as a group responsible for the misdeeds of particular persons. As in many cultures, the Other was constructed in sexual terms. One ditty of the Boxer Rebellion said of Euro-Americans: "Their men are all immoral; / Their women truly vile. / For the Devils it's mother-son sex / That serves as the breeding style." Economic competition, high-handed attitudes, and the missionaries' impositions brought on popular riots and rebellions. Liberalist economic attitudes and the demand for cheap labor caused rapid economic and population growth in the foreign enclaves. Hong Kong, with a population of 4,000 in 1842 when the British acquired it, housed 24,000 in 1845, 56,000 in 1854, and 126,000 in 1866; it doubled in population again by 1900.[11]

Chinese migrants traditionally came from the *Sam Yup* or Four Districts of the two coastal provinces of Guangdong/Kwangtung (the Cantonese and the Teochiu) and from Xiamen/Amoy and the surrounding area in Fujian/Fukien (the Hokkien) as well as from the island of Hainan (Hailam) and from among the immigrant Hakka. Separated from the rest of the empire by a mountain range, these provinces with little arable land and no natural riches experienced an unusual number of natural disasters from 1830 to 1910. The fast-growing population reached a density of one person per quarter acre. As a consequence of the separation of peasant families from land, a free labor force emerged at a time when capitalist plantation economies and British imperial connections permitted or enforced migration beyond the limits of the traditional diaspora (chap. 7.1). Free and bound men left in ever larger numbers from the 1840s onward (maps 15.2, 15.3).[12]

Chain migration led the Chinese, like all emigrants, to form clusters according to their region of origin at particular locations of their three main destinations: Southeast Asia (the easiest migration route), Latin America (Cuba and Peru, in particular), and the United States and Canada (the most costly destination). Teochiu-speakers from the Shantou/Swatow and Hailam-speakers from Hainan arrived in Thailand. Urban Cantonese and those who used the Cantonese dialect formed networks across the diasporas.

In 1860, the British government imposed the principle of "free emigration" on China, and in 1868 the Chinese government, which until then had totally disregarded emigrants and emigration, ending its policy of disregard for emigrants, regulated the coolie trade and opened consulates abroad. The Chinese government now sought ties to Chinese overseas merchants, whose role as middlemen it had shunned for centuries while all of the Western powers had benefited from their connections. Diaspora Chinese sent remittances to their families, which were so-called emigrant communities consisting only of women, children, and the elderly. Wealthy merchants began to invest in China. However, the Nationality Law of 1909 renationalized emigrants and their descendants through the male line, regardless of where they had been born or now resided. This concept, adopted in Japan earlier and in Germany in 1913, constructed a single resident and diasporic nation. As a consequence, migrants were viewed as foreigners by host governments.[13]

Beginning in the 1870s, increased trade, the expansion of coal mining, and the establishment of shipyards and factories induced the in-migration of skilled labor and technicians. The construction of railways and ports temporarily absorbed surplus labor; but once the new transportation systems became operative, the vast numbers of men engaged in porterage and barge pulling were thrown out of work. The introduction of steam-power caused immensely larger unemployment than existed in economies based on animal-powered transport. Early-twentieth-century railway

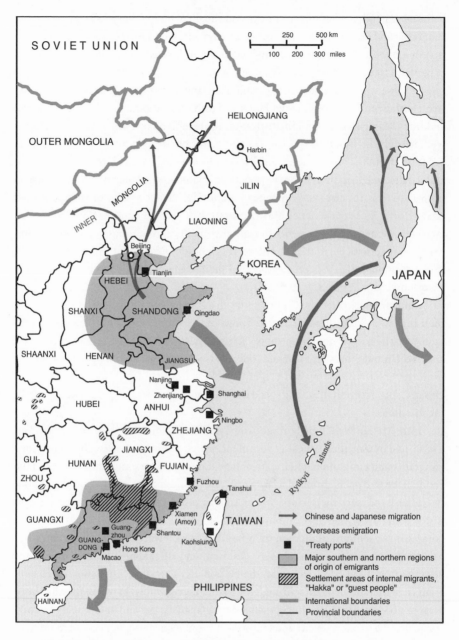

15.2 East Asia: Internal Migration and Emigration, 1840s–1920s

construction in China's northern plains increased the flow of information and permitted outbound transportation of workers from the provinces of Chihli, Shandong, and Henan. In Chihli, climatic conditions and short growing seasons prevented predictable crop yields; in Shandong, where better conditions prevailed, floods were a constant threat. An estimated 9–10 million people died or fled during the drought and famine of 1876–79. When the Treaty of Shimonoseki (1895) opened northern ports to

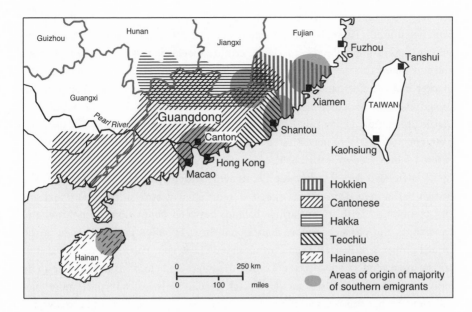

15.3 Peoples of the Southern Chinese Emigration Provinces

European and Japanese imports, cheap machine-spun cotton cloth increased the demand for cash while home production collapsed. The regular cash flow of emigrant remittances or the departure of whole families as a way to survive was possible only for those with the initial means to migrate. As was the case everywhere, the most impoverished could not move; students left temporarily; and schoolteachers and journalists joined the diasporic communities.[14]

In India, the incorporation of increasing sections of the subcontinent into the British Empire mobilized the highly sedentary labor force.[15] The "Permanent Settlement" of 1793 reorganized Bengal, Bihar, and Orissa in the north; in 1812, societies in the south were also reorganized. First, the British institutionalized a variety of land revenue systems, such as of the *zamindar* and *ryotwari* type, and farmed out tax collection to men from local elites. Granted positions that were modeled on those of European landlords, *zamindars* ruthlessly exploited the population. Second, new legislation concerning the ownership of private land permitted the alienation of land, and a new class of exploitative landlords emerged. This new class of middlemen—moneylenders, tax farmers, and landowners—remained dependent on and became allied with the colonial overlords.[16]

Two examples illustrate the new patterns of rural migration and labor. In the tribal lands of the Godavari district in West Central India, the imposed tax and land ownership arrangements provoked revolts. These were quelled, and the local Hill Reddis and Khoyas were forced to migrate to marginal lands to make room for settlers from the plains. Subsequently, the tax districts were auctioned off to men from business castes who encouraged tribal peasants to come with laborers and with service castes to clear forests and cultivate the land. In southeastern India, village weavers

Asian Contract Labor and Transpacific Migration   373

had kept their independence from merchants and owned land, thus deriving income from two sources. This classic arrangement of risk diversification and flexible income substitution in unpredictable markets permitted weavers to work at their pleasure and consumers to benefit from low prices. The entry of European purchasers into the market increased demand, and the weavers' response—a deliberate decision to increase returns, which increased daily hours at the looms—involved entire families in textile production, alienating them from their land. Food purchases as well as wage-payments to hired labor necessitated larger cash flows, and the craft-farming families entered debtor-creditor relationships.[17]

A mere two decades after the Permanent Settlement, the *Fifth Report* to the British Parliament (1812) on its effects noted that it destroyed the traditional village community with its precarious balance between population, agriculture, and handicrafts and produced "more distress and beggary and a greater change in the landed property of Bengal" than ever observed elsewhere. Furthermore, British imports caused gendered dislocation. Locally manufactured cloth "from thread spun by native women of every class" provided "each woman . . . [with an income] more than sufficient for her subsistence" (*Bengal Hurkaru* newspaper in 1835). Imported yarns, superior in quality and cheaper in price, made women's work superfluous and sent families into poverty. Few still had the means to migrate; even the British governor-general noted that "the misery hardly finds a parallel in the history of commerce. The bones of the cotton weavers are bleaching on the plains of India." Trade and tariff policies levied prohibitive taxes on the export of artisanal products but permitted the free entry of British goods. Until 1800 London's Spitalfields weavers had suffered from cheap Indian imports, but by 1850 village production and communalism had been destroyed. This "deindustrialization" of the village handicraft industry and "refeudalization" of land ownership and tax farming resembles in some respects the end of cottage industry in Europe and the alliance of noble landowners and bourgeois capitalists. The "progressive pauperization of the rural population" created an "agricultural proletariat . . . willing to escape to a better place." This was what the Mauritian plantocracy and planters throughout the British Empire desired.[18]

Developments in the Punjab illustrate the extent of the changes, both their positive and their disruptive aspects. A region of stable population and balanced economy, it became a major supplier of British colonial auxiliaries and of labor migrants to North America. "Emigration began in the 1870s, about a generation after the extension of British rule throughout the province." The new railways carried in cheap factory goods and carried off local men for wagework as far away as Calcutta, where they could then leave for Malaya. Improved irrigation systems, "the extension of cultivation, rising agricultural prices, [and] rising land values"—under the British definition of land "as a transferable asset"—and taxation in cash forced or drew villagers into the new money economy. Good crops encouraged borrowing, and poor harvests made it necessary. Middle-level peasants who availed themselves of the opportunities had to invest, and the resulting mortgages after 1900 "made up a large proportion of the vastly increased rural debt." Emigration in pursuit of wage labor, in particular by the

Jat Sikh, a landowning caste and ethnic group, dispersed men, with women remaining behind. Sikh men, like men from Nepal, were recruited for service in the British army. "In Hong Kong, Singapore, and Malaya, Sikhs were used as policemen, watchmen, caretakers, and in Malaya as dairymen, cart drivers, and mine laborers." They thus came to know other parts of India and of the British Empire, such as Australia and Canada, and initiated self-sustaining migrations.[19]

A decade after the Opium War had opened China, Japan, which had closed itself to foreigners in the 1640s (chap. 7.1), was forced by a U.S. fleet to admit European and American merchants. Choosing a strategy different from Chinese bureaucratic stagnation, Japan's new emperor and the imperial party embarked on a program of modernization (the "Meiji restoration," 1868–1912) that provided for education but taxed and uprooted agrarian populations. By the 1890s, newly powerful Japan succeeded in abrogating the extraterritorial provisions of the inequitable treaties made with foreign powers, and foreign merchants in Yokohama became subject to Japanese jurisdiction. An army of commoners with British military officers as advisers replaced the samurai warrior class. American engineers and missionaries provided technical assistance as well as entryways for American industry; they improved education and helped Westernize society. Consulting with German- and Harvard-trained advisers, the Japanese government embarked on imperialist expansion that was spurred by the doctrine of genetic superiority and xenophobic chauvinism. An antiforeigner party drew on eighteenth-century scholars who had asserted that ancient Japanese culture had been corrupted by foreign Buddhist and Confucian doctrines. Japanese masculine vigor was constructed as superior to Chinese wickedness and craftiness.[20]

In a first step in the 1870s, the Japanese government established settlements on the nearly unpopulated and chilly island of Hokkaido and on the densely populated subtropical Ryúkyú Islands, including Okinawa. Hokkaido's Japanese population increased from 60,000 in 1860 to 2.4 million in 1920. Okinawans, on the other hand, migrated in small numbers to Japan proper and later to newly acquired colonies. Natives on the islands as well as Japanese colonists were never considered equal to the "Japanese proper," just as North American colonists had never been accepted as equals by the British core. In the 1870s, a second move was directed against long-secluded Korea. In 1867 Western troops had attempted to plunder the Korean royal tombs, which were said to be made of gold. Even in the age of industrialization, the myth of gold remained powerful. The Chinese and Russian governments also attempted to gain influence over the Koreans, who in 1894 rioted against the foreigners.

Industrialization in Japan generated considerable internal migration, although as late as 1920—with the exception of Hokkaido's agricultural frontier—93 percent of the rural population was still locally born. However, high-volume short-distance moves brought people into towns and urban agglomerations; and after the liberalization of emigration regulations, Japanese established themselves in Hawai'i and along the Pacific coast of the Americas (chap. 15.5). Contract laborers, like French and English indentured servants of earlier times, were recruited from urban areas, including Tokyo and Yokohama, rather than from among rural populations. But emigration remained limited: in 1937, fewer than half a million Japanese lived in other Asian states (40,000), in Hawai'i and North America (207,000), and in Latin America (227,000). The government attempted to protect Japanese contract laborers abroad or, if this proved not to be feasible, to prevent others from emigrating as contract laborers. It protested anti-Asian racism in North America, anti-alien legislation in California in 1913, and U.S. exclusion in 1924. Around 1900, Japanese emigrants shifted their direction to Peru and Brazil.

As elsewhere in the world, Japanese emigrants became part of the government's project to extend Japan's influence abroad: "[We] should direct our people to one area and avail ourselves of their collective strength." After 1910, this type of colonization targeted Korea and Manchuria and, within Japan, served as a strategy to reduce unrest among the ex-samurai demoted to commoners. Thus, Japanese migrations were part of an imperialist strategy rather the result of colonizer-imposed labor mobility (chap. 17.4).[21]

15.2 The Asian Contract Labor System

Regardless of their culture of origin, the recruitment of contract laborers involved deception and force: idealized descriptions of conditions at the destination, the deliberate creation of debt-bondage (as in the case of Malaya-bound Indians), agent-induced gambling in China, and self-pawning or clan fights, after which the captors sold their prisoners. The term "to be shanghaied," commonly used by sailors when they were enlisted against their will, derives from this practice of kidnapping. In southern China, private middlemen controlled recruitment; in India, the colonizing British mobilized migrants and, after much abuse by recruiting agents and plantation owners, appointed "protectors" of emigrants; in Japan, the government attempted to recruit suitable workers and prevent exploitation similar to that of Chinese bound laborers.[22]

The voyage to the ports began with exhausting trips on foot and continued by railway, often over hundreds of kilometers. Recruited Chinese laborers were fed at special inns and housed in port-city prisonlike depots or "pig pens" to hamper any agency on their part, especially to prevent escape or "desertion." During the trip, in processes similar to rites of passage, village and family social ties were replaced by the control imposed by labor agents. At the same time, a process of deculturation began, stripping away a person's regional culture to create the generic bound worker. For survivors, the process may have included aspects of liberation because in the mixed groups of migrants the categories of caste, class, and custom lost their validity.

Junks transported migrants to destinations within Asia; sailing ships took them on transoceanic voyages. The Calcutta-Caribbean trip lasted on average six months. The Chinese on British and Spanish ships bound for the Americas suffered mortality rates of 12 percent before the 1850s. Legal regulations, such as the British government's Chinese Passenger Act of 1855, and the introduction of ocean-going steamships in 1865 lowered mortality. The concomitant reduction of fares and travel time resulted in vastly increased migration flows, often self-directed rather than under contract.[23]

The blanket designation "coolie" for Chinese migrants veils their complex composition. Of the 2.5 million Chinese who left for Asian destinations in the nineteenth century, no more than 11–12 percent were indentured laborers narrowly defined. A second group was made up of "free" migrants under the "credit-ticket-system"—similar to indentured migration from Europe—which bound them to kin, previous migrants, or merchants who had advanced the cost of the voyage. Combined with diasporic networks, voluntary migration permitted a choice of destinations—within the limitations imposed by financial means. Migrants went to Burma, Malaya, the Dutch East Indies, Siam, French Indochina, the Philippines, and the Pacific Islands. About 700,000 left the Asian migration orbit: just under 100,000 were destined for Australia; 270,000 for Cuba, Peru, and other Latin American economies; and 330,000 for North America. The majority of these people paid their own way; only contract laborers bound for Cuba and Peru became de facto slaves.

The mass of India's transoceanic migrants[24] came from a northern belt extending from Bengal through Bihar to Uttar Pradesh (United Provinces), and from a southeastern coastal belt extending from Orissa to Madras. Up to the mid-1850s, recruitment was mainly among non-Hindu aboriginal tribes of the Chota Nagpur district in southern Bihar ("Dhangars," "Kols," "Hill Coolies"), among the poor of the emigration ports (often recent in-migrants), and among the lowest castes, who lived in conditions "of slavery or semislavery." Famine victims with no prospects of reinsertion into labor markets or social positions loomed large as a reservoir for labor across the British Empire (map 15.4). Most left via Calcutta and Madras; in Bombay, local labor demand and the local government's unsympathetic attitude reduced out-migration.[25] Migrants were diverse by faith: Hindu, Muslim, Sikh, Jain, and Christian (not taking into account the internal subdivisions and the lack of central unifying institutions among Hindus). They differed by language—Urdu, Hindi, Bengali, Tamil, Telugu, Punjabi, and Gujarati—which necessitated the "creation of a creolised South Asian language or usage of a non-South Asian lingua franca" or the assimilation of emigrants into the largest language group at a particular destination.

Recruitment by employers or self-recruitment followed patterns of ethnicity and assigned skill.

> [In Burma] Bengalis provided clerical workers and some mechanics; sweepers came from Nellore; North Indians were peons and watchmen; middle class Tamils worked as clerks in railways and for the government; Telugus from the Coromandel coast provided the bulk of labour in the mills and factories and were rickshaw pullers; Riyas from Ganyam district provided railway labour and other industrial work; while the Tamil low castes worked in agriculture and the rice mills.[26]

After migration "some degree of homogeneity" emerged among South Asian emigrants: caste in particular lost its role.[27]

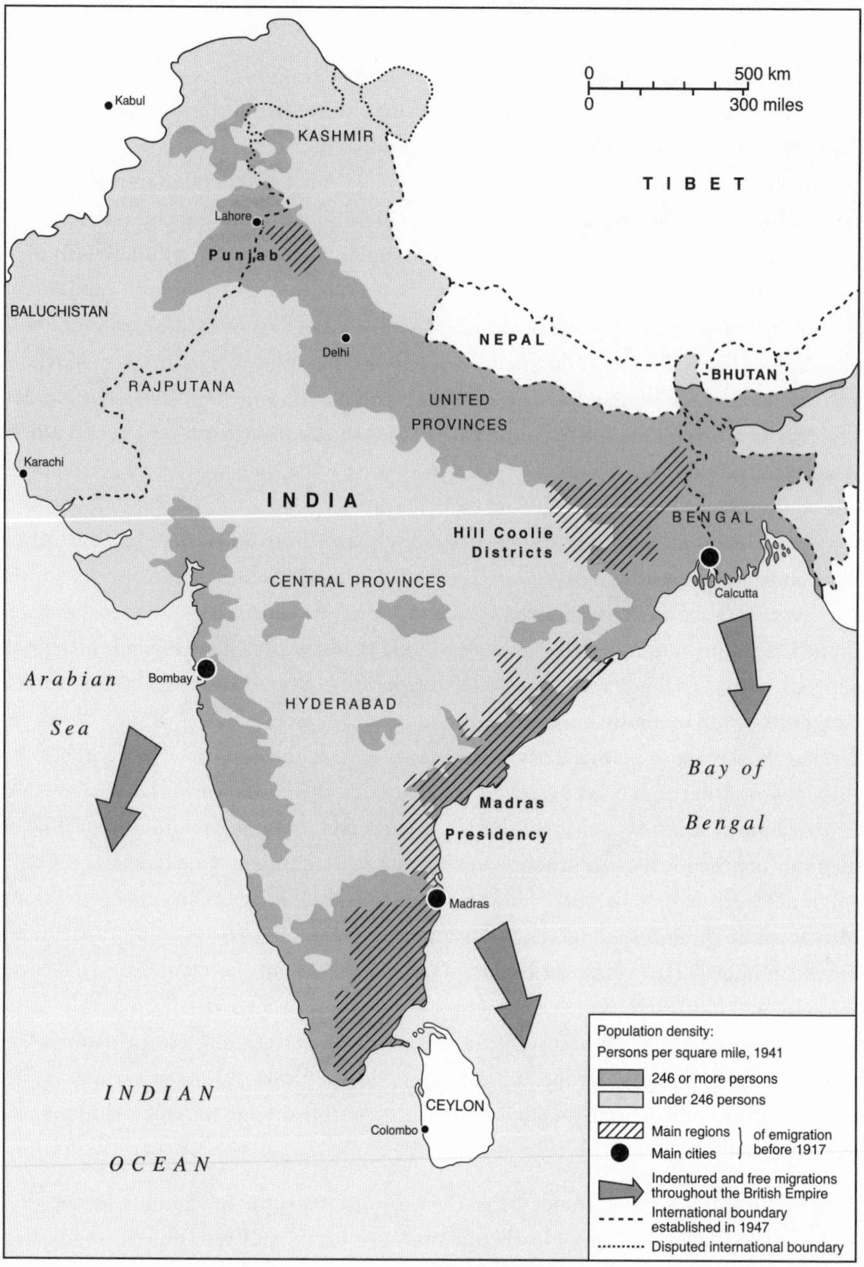

0
500 km
0
300 miles
Kabul
KASHMIR
TIBET
Lahore
Punjab
BALUCHISTAN
Delhi
NEPAL
BHUTAN
RAJPUTANA
UNITED
PROVINCES
Karachi
INDIA
BENGAL
Hill Coolie
Districts
Calcutta
CENTRAL PROVINCES
Arabian
Sea
Bombay
HYDERABAD
Bay of
Bengal
Madras
Presidency
Madras
CEYLON
Colombo
INDIAN
OCEAN
Population density:
Persons per square mile, 1941
246 or more persons
under 246 persons
Main regions
Main cities
of emigration
before 1917
Indentured and free migrations
throughout the British Empire
International boundary
established in 1947
Disputed international boundary

15.4 South Asia: Population Density and Emigration

Of the four outbound migration routes, the first involved 1.5 million contract workers with destinations outside Asia from 1834 to 1916 (as compared to the 1.9 million slaves exported from Africa to destinations in the Americas from 1811 to 1870). One-third went to Mauritius; another third to the Caribbean; 10 percent to Natal; the rest to East Africa and Indian Ocean or Pacific islands. The second route involved the migrations of six million under the *maistry* and *kangani* systems to Burma, Malaya, and Ceylon, most of whom returned. The third route involved small numbers of merchants, who migrated to traditional centers of trade in East Africa and to new diasporic settlements. By the fourth route, the British brought Indians as "imperial auxiliaries" to Malaya (where they served as administrators), to Hong Kong (where they served as policemen), and to many other possessions.

After 1870, migrants from the north moved to the sugar colonies of the Caribbean; Punjabis went to Fiji, and Tamils to Ceylon; emigrants from Madras had as their destination the tea, coffee, and rubber plantations in Malaya or Ceylon and the rice plantations and rice mills in Burma. New groups were mobilized: Rajputs from Ajmere, men from Gwalior and Jaipur, and workers from Bhopal. Men from higher castes migrated to serve as overseers.[28]

The majority of Asian contract migrants were healthy young men, exploitable in the prime of their strength. The migration of women depended on restrictions in the societies of origin as well as at the destination. The ratio of women was lowest among the Chinese: among those destined for Latin America a mere 1 percent on average; only in British Guiana did it briefly reach 16 percent. Attempts to increase the ratio to 15–20 percent never succeeded. Among Indian migrants, the percentage declined from 31.6 percent (1891–95) to 13 percent (1921–24), despite a government-set quota of 25 percent. All Asian societies placed restrictions on free female migration through systems of family values and gendered power hierarchies. In India, the recruitment of women involved coercion and often concentrated on women in desperate straits. Among poor families in China, the tradition of selling daughters into prostitution was adapted, and being sold into labor migration often meant going into sex labor. Sons, on the other hand, were expected to return; to bind them to the family, parents kept their daughters-in-law at home. Among migrants, multiple family formation involved rational economic considerations. When migrating men established two or more families, the sedentary wives in their respective locations attended to business or tilled the land. Migrant Chinese men had to leave wives or children in their family's place of birth since religion mandated that after their death their bones had to be buried with the ancestors regardless of where they had lived and died.

Attitudes toward the recruitment of women depended on labor force requirements in the receiving economies. Where men were encouraged to stay, women were viewed as a stabilizing factor. Authorities in Trinidad, for example, successfully offered a special bounty for wives to join their husbands. The Australian government, on the other hand, excluded Pacific Islander women and children to make men's stays temporary. At many destinations, female migrants were admitted in small numbers only to permit sexual gratification to men in stable or prostitutional relationships, since—according to employers—this made men less unruly. In general, migrant women were stigmatized as being of loose morals.[29]

Some women departed on their own and relied on their enterprising spirit; others, ostracized in their communities, had few options but to leave; for still others, migration permitted escape from low social positions as unmarried daughters or widows. Recruitment for work was multifaceted and not necessarily well informed. Australian government officials recruited men from Melanesia for agricultural work, even though in their home societies agriculture was women's work. Women were imported for domestic labor at a very young age. Of Chinese girls recruited for the Philippines, 40 percent were less than fourteen years old, while only 5 percent of the men migrated at that young an age. A woman's role as a house servant often included serving as a concubine. In most overseas immigrant societies in which men intended to stay, women came to number 10–30 percent; in Malaya's Indian and Fujian-Chinese settlements of long standing, the respective representation of women was 48 percent and 62 percent at the end of the 1920s. The slow pace of community formation among indentured laborers was related to the low rate at which women arrived and settled.[30]

15.3   Internal Labor Migration: The Example of India under British Rule

In South Asia, middle- and long-distance internal free and contract migration was small in proportion to total population and in comparison to Europe or North America. According to the 1891 census, which did not include international migrations under indenture, 89 percent of the population resided in the district of birth, 97 percent in the province of birth. Even industrialized Bengal immigrants were less than 1 percent among its population of 69 million in 1881. In 1931, 3.6 percent, or 12 million men and women out of 353 million, lived outside their province or state of birth. Investments in directly ruled British India did not increase attractiveness for migrants as compared to indirectly ruled princely states. Agriculture, village crafts, the caste system, early marriage, and joint family living arrangements, as well as the division of land among all inheriting sons, contributed to low out-migration rates.

Nonetheless, four major internal migration systems emerged: 1) medium-distance northeastward migrations to Calcutta's jute mills and other industries, to Bengal's coal mines, to Assam's tea plantations, and to Bihar's indigo plantations and factories; 2) migration to urban Mumbai/Bombay from a circle stretching some 300 kilometers (180 miles) in each direction; 3) in-migration from surrounding areas to Delhi, and from the same areas of the United Provinces westward to newly irrigated lands of the Punjab; 4) northward migrations from Madras into Mysore and Hyderabad as well as westward into the estate agriculture of the Ghats. In addition, numerous smaller movements crisscrossed the subcontinent; others targeted plantations in Ceylon.[31]

Women migrated in distinct patterns, sometimes to independent job opportunities in textile factories; but most out-bound mobility was related to marriage. In the tightly knit Hindu communities, fellow-villagers considered each other quasi-relatives; in addition, in most communities potential partners were few since men and women commonly married within their caste or subcaste. Marriage-ancillary migration involved servants who accompanied brides from wealthy families; alternatively, in the case of brides from poor families, it involved needy female kin, like aunts or grandmothers. Birth migration, the custom of women in many South Asian cultures to return to their parents' home for the first child's birth, added to mobility and increased the continuity of relationships. In some instances, marriage migration followed patterns of male labor migration.

Of the three types of settlement and labor migrations—agricultural, to mines, and cityward—peasants, often in family units, migrated to Assam and the Canal Colonies. The valleys of Assam offered fertile land that needed to be cleared. After 1900, Bengal peasants, in particular from the densely populated Mymensingh district, moved into the Brahmaputra valley; some 200,000 did so from 1911 to 1921, and more in the next decade. Local peasants considered them "foreign" and acceptance and acculturation developed only slowly. Others moved to the Punjab, where the Lower Chenab Canal (1901) and the Triple Canal Project (1920) more than quadrupled the acreage of irrigated land. Families of the same faith and caste settled close to each other, and the in-migration of young couples meant high natural population increases.

Indentured estate laborers migrated to tea, coffee, rubber, and cardamom plantations.[32] The largest movement was directed to the northeastern estates of Assam, Jalpaiguri, and Darjeeling, where tea cultivation had been introduced in 1840 and the importation of labor had begun in the 1850s (map 15.5). Local peasants refused to work on the estates, and few landless laborers were available. From 1911 to 1921, 770,000 coolies entered Assam. Their strikes and riots of 1921 resulted in improved working conditions. A slump in the market, due to declining exports to civil-war-torn Russia, reduced the number of workers in the early 1920s. In the southwestern estate belt of Madras, Mysore, and Travancore, some 80,000 migrant workers were counted around 1930.

Under the *kangani* recruiting system, employers sent one laborer to his home village to hire a new gang among his acquaintances. Recruitment for internal migration, less supervised than for overseas jobs, had been devised by experts from Mauritian and other slave societies. In the internal indenture system, contracts lasted for a maximum of five years and regulated minimum rates of pay, housing, and food rations. Since seasons lasted ten months on tea plantations and six to seven months on rubber or coffee plantations, planters expected workers to return to their villages for two to five months. Whereas entire families worked on coffee and tea plantations, single males worked on rubber plantations. The working hours lasted from sunrise to sunset, and corporal punishment and sexual harassment were common. The planters' private power of arrest was abolished as late as 1908. Employers could forcibly

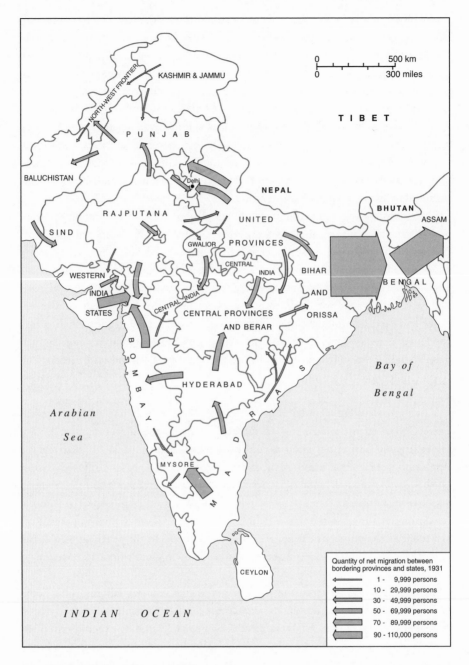

15.5   South Asia: Inter-Provincial Migration, 1931

capture "absconding" coolies, and, in the case of debts, which were often transferred from hereditary landholders to labor agents, wages could be withheld. Where plantation owners granted plots as an inducement to stay, a class of independent small peasant families emerged. From the point of view of planters, this meant the acquisition of women's and children's labor. By the 1930s, one-sixth of Assam's population were immigrants.[33]

Mine workers at the Raniganj coalfield in West Bengal were recruited from the nearby hills beginning in the 1870s. As long as women's labor in mines was not prohibited, whole families migrated. Under the British *zamindary* system, owners of large mines acquired rights over neighboring villages and pressured the population into mine labor. They created a semifeudal labor supply by land grants combined with an obligation to work a stipulated number of days in the mines (*nokarni* system).[34]

In all of South Asia, rural-urban migrations in 1931, which involved larger distances than rural-rural ones, accounted for nearly half of the total internal moves. The male-female ratio amounted to 1.5:1. On average, 37 percent of urban populations were in-migrants, and Bombay topped the list with 75 percent. Neighborhoods were fragmented by the diversity of cultures of origin and of languages, and particular factories—like plantations and mines—were connected to particular recruitment areas. Demand for labor was high because of the low predisposition of villagers to migrate and because people remained wedded to caste-assigned trades. Catastrophes, like the plague epidemic of 1911, still caused the quick, if temporary, return to villages. By the early twentieth century, rural-urban moves integrated the northeast—Bihar, Bengal, and Arakan (coastal Burma)—"in a single system of interlocking labour migration" (Royal Commission on Labor in India, 1931).

Calcutta, which grew slowly, counted 57 percent in-migrants in its population of 680,000 in 1891, and 64 percent of nearly 900,000 in 1911. About half of the migrants came from within Bengal, the others from further away. Workers submitted to factory discipline according to premigration life-patterns. Those from nearby districts frequently returned for short visits to their villages; up-country migrants left the factories during the hot season, which was the planting season in their more agreeable home climate. Because of their shorter work year, they preferred longer daily hours, while the more regularly working short-distance migrants preferred limited hours. Workers with family landholdings did not have to submit to undesirable factory conditions: the scarcity of labor in agriculture and, in comparison to the situation in other states, the higher incomes to be gained from agricultural work offered alternatives. Free migrant laborers replaced indentured workers; information flows replaced employer-dominated recruitment. Elite migration included *zamindars*, who wanted to be close to the British administration, their children, who wanted to attend urban schools, and merchants. Migrations of high and low became intertwined when the servants of elite migrants became anchor points for low-caste chain migrations.

Internal migration occurred parallel to, rather than interlinked with, transoceanic migration, except in the case of laborers who were recruited but then rejected in the ports of embarkation. They hired on for internal indenture.[35]

The interlinked worlds of the Indian Ocean and the South China Sea facilitated migration. In the west of this world, the planters of Mauritius sought Indian indentured labor early on; a free merchant community existed in Zanzibar; colonies from East Africa via Natal to the Cape became destinations for free and contract migrants. Workers from China, where recruitment had shifted from the southern emigration provinces to the north, reached South Africa after 1900. In Southeast Asia, the traditional Overseas Chinese colonies in urban, mining, and agrarian economies expanded and were supplemented by settlement of Indian contract laborers on plantations as well as by the routes taken by free migrants. On the Malay Peninsula a multiethnic Malay-Chinese-Indian people emerged, while Burma's resident population was superstratified by Indian businessmen and urban workers.

The free "passenger" migrants came with their own means and for their own purposes. They explored opportunities for self-directed economic activities, supplied their indentured countrymen and women, and attracted time-expired indentured laborers into their communities. For the last of those, opportunities for community-formation remained low in plantation camps, and subsequent self-organization depended on the respective colonies' political economy: permission to stay after the end of their term, pressures to reindenture, or mandatory return. Notwithstanding their dependency relationship to employers, indentured workers developed labor militancy but could hardly form families.[36]

Labor and Community in East and South Africa

In the 1790s, planters in Mauritius "took advantage of marketing opportunities created in Continental Europe by the collapse of Antillean sugar production following the slave revolts" to initiate coerced Indian labor migration. After the end of slavery, freed families established a smallholding agriculture, and the planter-dominated government turned to the recruiting opportunities of imperial British rule. Convicts, including the political prisoners from the Indian "mutiny," were sent. Voluntary contract labor became "a blatant system of forced labour" under which 450,000 Indians came from 1834 to 1907. Less than one-third returned since taxation was designed to force laborers to reindenture and since vagrancy laws and licensing regulations reduced opportunities outside the plantation sector. This labor regime, cemented by the so-called slave code of 1867, lasted with only minor improvements until 1922. However, as a result of the centralization of sugar milling after 1881, many migrated internally from estates to rural towns. Labor militancy was punishable; labor combinations were outlawed till 1937.[37]

While Mauritius's political economy represented the new Western capitalist plantations, the traditional West India–East Africa connections remained operative in Zanzibar's Indian trader enclave (chap. 6.1), which consisted of 5,000–6,000 Hindus and Muslims, mainly from Kutch and Jamnagar, in 1859. Given local hostility, the merchants did not intermingle with the Zanzibari population but brought in wives, instead. Thus a full-fledged community emerged, which was fragmented, however, in ethno-religious terms: Baluchi soldiers of the Omani sultan, Memons from Sind in shipping and fishing, Parsees, Hindu trading castes—Banias, Bhatias, Lohanas— and Muslim Shia sects, as well as Daudi Bohoras, Ismaili Khojas, Isthnasteris, and Goan Catholics. Hindus returned when they had accumulated wealth, while Muslims stayed with their families. Return also depended on the world economy, which grew when American cloth undersold Indian cloth and when the British enforced the ban on the slave trade after 1873. The Omani sultanate, which protected the "merchant frontiersmen," did not realize that the community became a conduit for British influence and, over time, ascendancy. Vertical links of each of the several South Asian ethno-religious groups to the British in Bombay hindered horizontal Indian homogenization of the community until Bombay's commercial expansion resulted in rural Gujarati in-migration and Gujarati became the community's lingua franca. The privileged status granted by the Omani sultanate prevented "indigenisation." The immigrants "remained a 'fragment' of India in East Africa" and, under the lead of the Ismaili Khoja, the community pursued a strategy of Westernization.[38]

In Natal, after 1860, immigrants from India established a full-fledged community.[39] Local labor was difficult to recruit for the newly established sugarcane economy: land set aside for Africans retarded their proletarianization, and European prejudices prevented recruitment drives. At first, the British pursued a policy of segregation: Africans were to follow "tribal" ways; Europeans to control the economy; and an inserted and partially bound Indian laboring class was to do the plantation and railway work. After returnees complained about their treatment and the "Coolie Commission" reviewed the poor working conditions, a law of 1872 appointed a "Protector of Indian Immigrants" and improved medical services. Planters briefly turned to hiring free and enslaved Africans from Zanzibar; but since they needed experienced workers, indentured Indians came again in 1874. Whereas early migrants had come from Madras, in the 1870s most sailed from Calcutta. Men and women arriving in 1860 were distributed along the coastal belt depending on demand. The volume of labor imports depended on economic cycles in the sugar industry, on particular railway construction projects, and on general depressions, such as the one that lasted from 1866 to 1874.[40]

Indian workers "made it possible to build up a plantation culture not unlike the civilization of the planters of Virginia and South Carolina in the slave days," and a British sugarocracy emerged. In the mid-1870s, 42 percent of the 13,000 cane-field workers were Indians, and 58 percent were Africans. By 1909 the numbers had increased to 26,600 Africans, 19,000 Indians (including 1,400 who were free), and 1,000 Europeans. When it emerged that, contrary to the planters' demands, around 30 percent of the migrants were women, they were hired only at half the men's wages and half the men's food rations. Children were paid according to age. Women had to endure multiple abuses. Many planters denied women and children food if they did not work, and in 1895 the deputy protector of Indian immigrants was besieged by starving women asking for help. Women had to endure sexual harassment by employers, were murdered by husbands because other men "shared" them, and committed suicide after having been abused. Legal marriage involved a £5 fee, which was out of reach for indentured men and women. In 1911, the ratio of men to women stood at 100:66; but their competition over men for partners gave women little bargaining power, and some resisted exploitation by "desertion"—that is, they joined African communities.[41]

In coal mining in Natal, in which Indians had worked since the 1880s, they accounted for 40 percent of the labor force after 1900. Many reindentured as "free" workers. Women worked on the surface in picking and sorting coal. To prevent men from departing, "wives" were sold by management, some repeatedly. In 1906, men and women went on strike. The protector of emigrants in Madras noted that nowhere was there more labor unrest than among the mineworkers. In railway construction, from Witwatersrand to the coast of Natal, no work was available for women, and thus no rations were allocated to them. Men who had come with their wives had to send them back or repudiate them because of the lack of sufficient sustenance. Railway workers often came with skills acquired in construction work on the Indian subcontinent and, after their time under contract expired, moved to railway work in the Belgian Congo and Angola.

At the same time, free Indians came as traders: in the eyes of the Natal British, they were "yellow men" in "yellow trades" whose competition "white" traders feared. However, since plantation owners had to rely on free immigrant traders to supply their Indian workers with food and fabrics, shopkeepers dispersed and settled in coastal cities, plantation camps, country towns, and villages. The government culled from the immigrant community nonproductive as well as politically active members. The sickly, infirm, and elderly were repatriated at government expense to reduce the dependency ratio; men and women not willing to accept the labor regime were sent home to reduce the potential for militancy.

In Durban and Pietermaritzburg, the free Indian population, including independent women, survived in economic niches—in barter for skins with Africans, as waiters or domestics, as gardeners and storekeepers. Sandbars prevented vessels from entering Durban's port, and boatmen from Madras with special Masulah boats and catamarans were brought in. They reached the outer anchorage in any weather. Free Indian mechanics, masons, blacksmiths, and carpenters were brought in from Mauritius for skilled and unskilled work. Ex-indentured servants and enterprising immigrant families established truck farming near Durban and began to operate small tea or sugarcane plantations. Indian and African fishermen developed a virtual monopoly on supplying Durban with fresh fish. Free and indentured Indians were hired for lowly municipal services. But opportunities declined, and returnees to India, under conditions of depression and intentionally exploitative taxation, took home ever smaller amounts of savings. The free community suffered, and reindentures increased.[42]

In the other South African colonies, by contrast, African labor had been mobilized or immobilized for almost a century before Indian and Chinese contract laborers were introduced. Indian labor came to the Cape in the 1860s but was barred from Rhodesia. Supported by a "sympathetic if not pliant government" and eager to offer a "reasonable rate of interest" to European investors, the gold-mining capital of Transvaal was burdened by the Anglo-Boer War (1899–1902), the ravaging of the infrastructure, the dispersal of the prewar labor force, a precipitous fall in gold prices on world markets, and increasingly low-grade ore. To minimize wage costs, management refused to offer wages that would attract African labor from Transvaal's competitive labor market and tapped four other reservoirs. African labor, including recruits from Portuguese Mozambique, remained insufficient. The supply of convict labor was even more limited. White unskilled labor demanded higher wages, organized trade unions, and required investment in mechanization to justify wage expenses. This left the recruitment of Asian contract workers.

Under the Labor Importation Ordinance of 1903 and the Anglo-Chinese Labour Convention of 1904, 64,000 Chinese coolies came as "captive" workers before 1906. Health inspection before departure permitted selection of the fittest in the interests of capital. Recruitment was contracted out to a firm that also supplied coolie labor to Russian employers in Vladivostok and whose agents did not speak the dialects of northern China, where the bound workers came from. They hired labor for "gold digging" with no indication that it involved deep shaft-mining. Some recruits were trained to police their coworkers. To prevent competition for labor between employers and to forestall migrants' initiatives in seeking better jobs, the government restricted the Chinese to mine labor: "There can be no doubt of the benefit which we derive from British institutions," a spokesperson for capital noted. South African agricultural capital acquiesced in recruitment when Chinese were prohibited from independent market gardening; artisans and workers were pacified by a "racial definition of skilled trades." To achieve maximum exploitation, the government criminalized leaving a job ("desertion"), slow work ("loafing"), and inefficient work.[43] Migrants who fled this forced labor regime became outlaws and had to survive by robbery; as a result, a stereotype of the criminal Chinese emerged.[44] Racism brought about an end to recruitment after only three years, and the government decided to repatriate all Chinese coolies at the end of their contracts.

From among the 200,000 South Asian men and women who entered the South African colonies from 1860 to 1911, some 75 percent stayed permanently, nearly two-fifths of them women. In 1911, when 44 percent of the community of 150,000 were African-born, only 10,000 had been able to enter commerce, and a mere 729 the professions. After 1911 acculturation proceeded rapidly; no "old-world" influx from India supported the retention of culture.

In East Africa, where, with the exception of Zanzibar and Mozambique, European penetration began only in the 1880s, British and German interests competed. East African populations, which were mixed in 1500 (chap. 6.2), remained multiethnic in 1900, but European and Asian immigrants were few. When construction of the Uganda railway from Mombasa to Nairobi began in 1896, the "base camp" consisted of a mere 107 Europeans, 6,000 Indians, and 17,400 Swahili-speakers. Among the Europeans were two German businessmen, six Greek and two Romanian hotel-keepers and contractors, and four people categorized as "miscellaneous"; the Indians included 4,800 Punjabi Muslim coolies, 300 soldiers, and 1,100 Baluchi and Arab merchants; Africans were divided into 14,600 free persons, 2,650 slaves, and 150 prisoners. Over the next years, some 35,000 indentured workers were imported mainly from the commercially related villages and towns along the Gulf of Cambay. Only a few hundred Indians lived in German East Africa and the Italian possessions.[45] In British East Africa, passenger Indians from Mauritius joined the workers as teachers, catechists, and interpreters; clerks and shopkeepers followed the conquerors into the interior. A "Chotara" community emerged, "a half-caste breed between the Indian and Swahili" (Sanderson Report of 1909). In distinction to the Ismaili in Zanzibar, Indian and African Sunni Muslims merged easily. Asian immigrants in East Africa amounted to 54,400 by 1921. Denied the right to acquire land, they entered the trades.[46]

Compared to the East African population, immigrants from Asia remained few (1.5 percent), and the Europeans were a minuscule group (0.5 percent). To increase the number of "Whites," the British government offered land to refugees from the South African War, to settlers from Britain, to Finns and, to decrease tensions in Palestine, to Jews (chap. 18.2). However, it rejected a request of the Aga Khan to permit Westernized Ismailis to acquire land in Kenya's fertile highlands. Racism made Europeans unable to even distinguish between Indians, "Mauritians," and Arabs, especially when Indians were Muslims. While settlers in Kenya—like those in British Columbia who rejected the immigration of Sikhs in 1908—refused to admit persons of color, British policy-makers were divided about the position of South Asians in the empire. One London official commented that it was dishonest to squeeze out Indians from the very opportunities they created, and the British viceroy in India supported their demands for equal rights; but the British colonial secretary opposed letting Indians have access to land in Kenya.[47]

Colonial economies and cultures in the migration region of the western Indian Ocean varied from the monoculture in Mauritius to the diversification found in Natal, from British-Kenyan landowners to French-Mauritian planters. The lifestyles of Euro-African upper classes contrasted with the rice- and salt fish–based ones of indigenous and imported peoples. European plantation owners, who opposed state expenditures for workers and deprived the children of indentured laboring families of an education, clamored for tax money when natural disasters wrought havoc with their properties: "Indian immigrants thus paid for the largesse extended by the colonial state to the sugar industry." While the textile industry had been an indicator of relations between capital and—often migrant—labor in the core, the sugar industry was an indicator of the development of relations between migrant capital and migrant labor in a hierarchically structured world economy.[48]

Free Migrants, Indentured Workers, and Imperial
Auxiliaries in Southeast Asia

Just as Gujarati merchants had traded with and settled in East Africa for centuries, so Malabar Coast merchants had traded with Siam and the Malay Peninsula for a millennium and a half. Chinese and Indian immigrants took advantage of the mining and agricultural opportunities of the thinly inhabited peninsula. In the 1830s the population amounted to less than half a million. In 1824 the British merged Penang, Singapore, and the formerly Dutch Malacca into the Straits Settlements (until 1867 part of India), which from the 1870s on included indirect rule of the western Malay states. Within four decades, Singapore's population increased from 11,500 to 90,700 in 1864, of whom 58,000 were Chinese, 13,500 Malays, and 12,700 Indians. Penang, in the same four decades, grew from 48,500 to 127,000, including 55,000 Malays, 39,000 Chinese, and 14,000 Indian merchants and Tamil laborers. Most of the British penetration—or, in European parlance, the establishment of protectorates—was achieved by negotiation. When military action was involved, Indian sepoys fought; Sikh military police acted as an occupation force; and convicts built roads and forts.

Chinese laborers came on their own and worked in tin mining, and Chinese entrepreneurs provided the capital. Others opened up the river valleys of Johore for commercial agriculture. Workers, traders, and shopkeepers of different dialects and cultural practices had to interact with each other. Organizations of the increasingly locally born peninsular Chinese provided protection but also permitted control by domineering Chinese immigrant capitalists. The almost exclusively male immigrants settled earlier than Indian sojourners. In the 1880s Chinese annual arrivals at Singapore and Penang increased from 78,000 to 147,000. Each year just over 20,000 came as indentured "unpaid passengers" or with credit tickets as "little pigs." Depending on investment, demand, and productivity, the size of Chinese mining populations fluctuated greatly. In Perak, for example, their number decreased through the 1870s to 9,000, but after 1877 it jumped to 50,000 within five years. The contracts bound men to work off passage money within a year; overtime pay went into their own pockets. The one-year contracts and the fluctuating demand as well as the large number of small employers permitted workers to use their own discretion in finding the most remunerative jobs. From the point of view of observers, laborers ran "away"; from their own perspective, they moved "toward" better living conditions. Around 1900 most miners worked in open pits; as yet no capital for underground operations was needed. A total of 5.67 million arrived in the Straits Settlements between 1881 and 1915, and a much smaller number in the Federated Malay States. In 1911, when the Chinese population totaled 900,000, the sex ratio had improved to 4 to 1. Men brought in wives and women migrated independently. When in 1930 the British enforced quotas on Chinese men, women (married or single) continued to come, often going into wage labor.

Whenever segments of the Indic World, which were fragmented after three centuries under the rule of competing European powers, were reintegrated into the new whole of the British Empire, comparative labor costs induced capitalists and administrators to move labor from the colonial population core, India, to peripheral regions. Just one year after the establishment of British rule at Penang in 1789, the local administrator requested "artificers" from India since he considered cost of labor in Penang too high. From 1840 to 1910, laborers came under indentures; thereafter, until 1938, they came under the *kangani* system. Free migrants came as independent workers and businessmen, with economic resources like the Tamil Chettyar merchants and bankers, for example, or with training and education. Ninety percent of the migrants originated from southern Tamil-speaking peoples, the rest from Telugu districts and the Malayalam districts of the Malabar Coast.

European plantation owners had at first attempted to recruit Malay people as laborers. They could live off their land and refused to submit to the indignities of wagework under foreign masters. Some British Residents (that is, the masters of local rulers) forced Malay men to work on roads, punishing refusal by penal taxation. While Chinese investors were able to attract workers without government support, European capitalists demanded government action to import labor. Indian indentured workers, already used in coffee and sugar as well as in tapioca and coconut plantations, numbered 120,000 in 1901. When, after 1900, rubber plantations expanded elevenfold within a decade and oil palm cultivation increased, the demand for labor skyrocketed. Javanese, for whom indenture legislation remained in force until 1932, also migrated to the peninsula.

In 1921 the population of Singapore and Malaya of 3.3 million included 1.6 million Malays, 1.2 million Chinese, 0.5 million Indians, and some 60,000 others. Ethnic ascription in this multiethnic society was as common as in other parts of the world. Malays often considered Chinese dangerous but looked upon Indians as "small people." Migration stagnated only briefly during World War I, but the overproduction of natural rubber and the worldwide economic depression of 1928–29 combined to induce British administrators to reduce Indian in-migration to 27,000 in 1932; return migration and shipping-off by concerned authorities amounted to 100,000 as early as 1930. In 1934 planters' protests led to a reversal of the official position, and 102,000 coolies were imported: admission depended on whether planters or administrators determined policy-making.

In the adjoining Dutch colonies and independent British-advised Siam (after 1949, Thailand) people followed multiple smaller migration routes. In the Dutch East Indies, Javanese planters imported labor, but authorities also forced Javanese to migrate to the "outer" islands and to the Caribbean. In Sumatra, coolies worked in tobacco cultivation. In 1934 more than half of the 1.25 million Chinese immigrants lived in the outer islands; of the quarter-million European immigrants, 80 percent lived in Java, where connections to the European metropole were best.[49]

In Siam, the Thai state had been able to withstand European advice until in the 1850s the preying French "crocodile" and British "whale" induced the European-educated King Mongkut to embark on a policy of Westernization. Though a treaty with the "whale" was signed in 1855, Siam could afford to have as independent a policy as Japan owing to its strong economy. As part of the rice-producing region from the Mekong Delta to Burma, Siam became an exporter of rice to feed the rice-eating labor forces spread by the British across considerable parts of the globe. Commercial cultivation in the Central Plain relied on the in-migration of colonists, as was the case in the (British) Burmese Irrawaddy and the (French) Indochinese Mekong Deltas. Seasonal laborers came from the subsistence agricultures of the Siamese periphery, the Northeast in particular. Chinese became involved in the export trade. As in many other regions, development within the capitalist-colonial framework increased regional disparities.[50] The migrant- and bulk-carrying steamships were manned by Asian labor.[51]

When Burma, after several wars, became part of British India, it was mainly Indian troops who had fought the battles, and Indian immigrants then became administrators for the British. "Colonial auxiliaries" of many South Asian ethnicities were "a vital component of British control and development." In 1891, 0.25 million Indians lived in Burma, and, in 1921, nearly 1.0 million out of a total population of 13.2 million. From 1908 to 1929, some 6.5 million Indians came and left. By contrast, Europeans and Eurasians in 1941 numbered only 30,000. In the Burmese construction of foreigners, Chinese, of whom few came, were "cousins," but the Indians and British were "black men." The British viewed the Burmese as "happy-go-lucky people," constructing them along well-known lines as "the Irish of the East." Since the British were few in number, the Indians felt the brunt of Burmese national self-construction and nationalism.

The Burmese, in self-sufficient agriculture and under a pre-British regime of redistribution that ensured sufficient food, enjoyed a higher standard of living than potential migrants in India and saw no need to labor in the interest of the British. Thus farm families continued to be Burmese, but migrants staffed the transport system and the port facilities.

Lower Burma, a sparsely populated land of jungles and creeks, became an integral part of the imperial world economy with the growth of export opportunities for rice. Large-scale Indian immigration began in the mid-1800s, in the wake of soldiers who had reconnoitered the opportunities during the British campaigns; and, after the opening of the Suez Canal, rice exports increased phenomenally. In the decade after 1885 rice paddy cultivation quintupled to five million acres. Peasant families from Upper Burma immigrated and worked as family economic units. Richer peasants employed Indian harvest gangs. Among mill-owners, only the large ones were European; middling ones were Indian, small ones Burmese. Under the colonial regime, their relative economic standing declined.

The first British capital, Moulmein, had a population that was two-thirds Indian during the 1820s. When Rangoon was occupied in 1886, the resident Burmese dominated numerically, but they were pushed into the cheaper suburbs. By the 1920s, two-thirds of Rangoon's population were Indian. Labor markets remained segmented. Telugus from the Coromandel Coast came as factory workers and porters; Oriyas worked in road construction; Tamils from southern Madras arrived as middle-class clerks and as unskilled rural workers; and immigrants from Hindustan in northern India became petty vendors or watchmen.[52] Most Bengalis were government clerks, and Punjabis came in smaller numbers as artisans. Some Oriyas and Tamils also entered the rice-mill labor force. The multiple ethnicities from India were generic Indians in Burmese opinion. The male-female proportion amounted to four to one, and many migrants formed families locally and settled. Intermarriage or common-law unions of Indian men and Burmese women were frequent, and, given that most Burmese men at one time in their lives joined a *sangha*-Buddhist monastery, they were usually in the interest of both sexes. When the men returned to India, they usually left the families behind. Burmese nationalist leaders, in search of a clearly definable nation, complained that the "Burmese nation ha[d] become half-caste" and was headed for "gradual extinction."

Non-Burmese controlled the educational and financial systems. Rangoon University was staffed mainly by British and Indian scholars, whose power of definition included the teaching of history and culture—the teaching of British history was a disaster even in "White" dominions like Canada and Australia. These teachers were not cosmopolitan-minded but imperially trained. Banking was in the hands of the ubiquitous Chettyars. Burmese rice-growing families borrowed from them, and they lost their land to these immigrant Others when repayment became impossible during economic crises. During the Great Depression after 1929, when the Chettyar bankers seized land, Indian workers called an anti-British general strike to protest Gandhi's arrest in May 1930. Burmese workers refused to join, and the strike collapsed. The British, who considered their auxiliaries as physically more enduring than the Burmese, discharged the strikebreakers, and a massive riot resulted. Seven thousand Indians fled Rangoon, and 33,000 returned to India within a month. Further rioting followed in the next years. Because of the hierarchies between colonial peoples, real and constructed, no joint opposition to the British masters developed. Burmese nationalist leaders expressed respect for Indian culture and for Gandhi in particular, a respect accorded to distant, ideal Indians. The real Indians whom they encountered in Burma—the coolies, moneylenders, and rice merchants—were detested.[53]

The export crisis after 1930 created havoc among Burmese farming families, Indian workers, and British institutions. The Indian presence in Burma ended in two refugee movements. When Japanese armies invaded Burma in December 1941 and took Rangoon in March 1942, about half a million Indians fled, and perhaps 10,000–50,000 died en route (chap. 17.4). Two decades later, in 1962, the military government labeled all foreigners, including technical experts, harmful to the nation. By May 1964, 300,000 officially recognized refugees, who were compelled to leave all valuables behind, had arrived in India.[54] Another decade later, the East African Indians were forced into flight. They could not melt into the Black population, whereas Indians who remained in Burma made themselves invisible: they wore Burmese dress, spoke Burmese, and shared the lowly occupations of the Rangoon working classes.

As distinct from the South Asian diaspora of colonial auxiliaries, free migrants, and cheap contract workers, the Chinese diaspora never became an integral part of the British Empire or other colonial empires.[55] In traditional and new diasporic territories, merchants came first, and artisans followed. Both might despise coolies, who nevertheless catered to their needs and increased the volume of trade and profits. In the case of migrants from India, with no previous diaspora, the migration of traders followed that of indentured laborers, and communities developed subsequently. The Chinese experience in Southeast Asia during the colonial period varied from the ghettos of Batavia and Manila to easy intermarriage and the emergence of the Philippine Mestizos and Indonesian Peranakans. When the number of women increased, community-formation and a re-Sinicization began in the Southeast Asian World, *Nanyang;* return migration decreased. The ethnic Chinese's middleman position or even complete control over particular sectors of the economy was to result repeatedly in anti-Sinicism and violence.[56]

15.5 The Second Pacific Migration System

After the first phase of the Pacific Migration System, which had connected the Philippines with New Spain from the 1570s to the mid-seventeenth century, commercial connections continued but involved almost no migration during a two-century-long hiatus (chap. 8.4). In the eighteenth century, free migrants and Hispanicized Chinese participated in the colonization of the North American Pacific coast. In California, individual Chinese lived and worked among the 4,000–5,000 settlers in 1821 who relied on Amerindian agricultural labor. To compete with the Spanish transpacific connection from Asia to Mexico as well as with the Hudson's Bay Company, the British East India Company (EIC) sent some seventy Guangdong craftsmen and sailors to Vancouver Island in 1788. While the English remained sojourners, many of the Chinese settled, mixing with Native people. On a trial basis, a first few indentured laborers were sent to the Caribbean world in the early 1800s, 200 Chinese from Portuguese Macao to British Trinidad in 1806, and several hundred indentured workers to Portuguese Brazil in 1810. The second phase evolved in connection with intra-Asian migrations and thus resembled the initial stages of the Atlantic System. Merchants, prospectors, and free labor developed small communities in Hawai'i and along the Pacific coast of the Americas. Beginning in the 1840s, indentured Chinese and Indian laborers came to the Caribbean and South America, and free and subsequently indentured migrants came to North America. In the 1880s and later, Japanese, Koreans, and Filipinos migrated, too. Exclusion curtailed this phase until a third phase, directed toward North America only, began in the 1940s (chap. 19.5).

Migration to Hawai'i

Halfway across the Pacific, the Polynesian-settled Hawai'ian Islands, Sandalwood Hills in Chinese, became the destination of early migrants from Asia and a port of call for vessels bound for the Americas. Free Chinese came before 1800, and, when cane cultivation was introduced, a Chinese entrepreneur built the first sugar mill in 1802. Both Chinese and Western capital-owning immigrants established plantations, but by midcentury the demand for sugar in California gave U.S. immigrant planters a competitive advantage. They used their influence to reduce the power of Hawai'ian rulers and chiefs to introduce western-style landownership and marginalize Chinese planters in the process. The latter developed rice cultivation as an economic niche.

Into the 1870s, Hawai'ians made up the largest segment of the labor force, but their declining numbers became insufficient to fill the demand for labor. In addition to indentured Chinese laborers and domestic servants, including some 1,500 women, among those recruited, starting in 1852, were South Sea Islander, Japanese, Norwegian and German workers; and after 1878 Portuguese came from Madeira. Because of the harsh working conditions, many of the people from Madeira moved on to the Macao- or Sino-Portuguese communities in California. After the United States annexed Hawai'i in 1898, the exclusion laws applied there, too, and the two major communities stabilized. The Chinese, once numbering 56,000, formed a permanent settlement of 20,000–30,000 with institutions and ethnic enterprises. From marriage with Chinese women—numbering 1,500—or local women, a mixed second generation emerged that expanded the economic base from rice cultivation to market gardening. The Japanese community, which dated from the late 1850s, grew to 61,000 and continued to expand. By 1930 about 40 percent of the population were of Japanese descent (140,000). Independent farming families leased land; workers concentrated in villages adjoining European and U.S.-owned plantations. The latter struck for better working conditions in 1909, but the Chinese, Filipino, and Portuguese working-class diasporas did not yet support them (chap. 16.5). From 1903 to 1907, a fictitious "Territorial Bureau of Immigration," financed by U.S. planters, induced some 7,000 Koreans (gender ratio 10:1) to immigrate. Thus an internationally mixed labor force and a differently mixed entrepreneurial class emerged.[57]

Contract Labor in the Caribbean and South America

At the turn to the nineteenth century, colonial Mexican, Caribbean, and other South American economies experienced slave revolts and achieved independence. However, mass transportation and free migrations began only after the end of slavery in the British Empire in 1834. By midcentury, changes in British imperial economies, in particular the abolition of protective duties for West Indian sugar, sent prices tumbling, and the British financial crisis of 1847–48 cut wage-levels. Thus ended the "old order" plantation system and labor regime (chap. 8).

Planters across the colonial worlds feared massive labor shortages and began to experiment with laborers of various skin colors, cultures, and degrees of controllability. Of the three possible strategies—improved wages and working conditions to attract free labor, concerted price increases to cover costs for noncoerced labor forces, and new forms of coercion—the first two received only cursory attention. Planter regimes, regardless of empire and colony, opted for controllable and exploitable labor from reservoirs sufficiently large to replenish "stock" when transport, un-healthy climates, or overworking depleted those imported earlier. Thus the rising wages of the freed Black population in the Caribbean could be checked. Planters, who were self-styled private entrepreneurs, fought tenaciously for government handouts in the form of publicly assisted passage. The collusion between capital and govern-ment, often simply ascribed to an abstract "capitalist system," may be traced in detail to the influence of planters in colonial legislatures and on administrations of the core. If plantation economies were to collapse for lack of labor, the government in London would face declining colonial revenues and be forced to impose additional taxes at home—where some taxpayers were enfranchised.

Postslavery developments varied from island to island, depending on whether agricultural land was available to which the freed Afro-Caribbean families could migrate. Planters first experimented with the continued bondage of some Afro-Caribbean labor as well as with free Caribbean and African labor. The "great experi-ment" of the postemancipation societies was "the attempt to transform masses of African and creole slaves into law-abiding, thrifty, hard-working, Christianized wage laborers" according to the planters' ideologies. In this type of "Protestant work ethic," the Whites had the ethic, and the Blacks the work—and the cost of modernization was transferred to the workers. Second, the planters tried to enlarge the reservoir of Black labor by indenturing Africans freed from slave ships and by bringing in U.S. or African Africans (chap. 10.4). Third, Yucatán Amerindian prisoners and their wives, as well as peons sold by *hacendados*, were carried to Cuba, in all fewer than 2,000 from 1848 to 1861. Fourth, European labor was induced to migrate with government assistance. Ex-periments with "White" labor began in the mid-1830s but assumed larger proportions in the 1840s: Irish, English, and French people, Germans, Maltese, and some 40,000 Portuguese came before 1882. The latter included Madeirans, descendants of Protes-tant refugees, and people from the Azores. Under prevailing working conditions, the multiethnic "Portuguese" abandoned plantation labor as soon as possible and turned to small trading, often in competition and conflict with local Afro-Caribbeans.[58]

In 1838, when South Asians indentured for five years were shipped to British Guiana, changed public attitudes in the core would not accept planters' demands for longer indentures: the similarity to slavery would have been all too obvious. Ten years after the abolition of slavery, a new imperial system of labor allocation was functioning. Some 20,000 coolies were requested by the British Caribbean posses-sions in 1847, and subsequently a guaranteed loan from London facilitated defrayal of the passage costs.[59] An Anglo-French convention with the government of China ended recruitment in 1866, and in the British colonies Indian coolies constituted the main labor supply. French planters in Guadeloupe, Martinique, and French Guiana imported several hundred laborers from French-controlled Indochina. In a process called "redemption," they also bought, from 1857 to 1862, 17,000 slaves in the Congo and East Africa, who had to work for up to seven years to redeem the cost of their lib-eration. The Surinamese Dutch recruited 33,000 Javanese workers. A total of around 1.75 million migrants and enslaved workers reached the Caribbean from 1811 to 1916:

perhaps 800,000 slaves still came, as did 550,000 Asian Indians, of whom less than one-third returned, and 150,000 Chinese were sent to Spanish Cuba and Puerto Rico. Sixty thousand or fewer free Africans and 200,000 Europeans arrived.[60]

Of the 536,000 migrants to Britain's island and mainland possessions, 80 percent came from India and 3.5 percent from China, the rest from other origins. British Guiana, Trinidad, and Jamaica (with 56, 29.5, and 10 percent respectively) were the largest recipients. Over 5 percent of the arrivals refused to work because they had been deceived by agents. Second-time indentured migrants ("return" migrants) moved between labor markets in the Caribbean and other parts of the British Empire. Among Indian laborers, 33 (later 40) percent had to be women—according to a quota set by the British Colonial Office in 1868. Since women were reluctant to go, orders for men were not always filled, or whole families were sent together. Indentured workers often fled from the plantations, but without existing communities of free Indians they had little support. The enforcement of contracts on exploited workers relied on the coercive apparatus of the state: civil agreements were subject to criminal sanctions, a hybrid legal arrangement—but not a rare one—between private employers and public institutions. This legal apparatus resembled early modern vagrancy laws in Europe. Contract workers resisted exploitation, struck for better working conditions, rioted against foremen, and fought off the sexual exploitation of women by overseers.

Migrants from Madras spoke Tamil, while those from Bengal were of higher caste and spoke Bengali: the incidence of intermarriage was low. Free communities emerged by the 1870s, and the salience of caste declined among second-generation West Indian East Indians. Indian laborers had a better chance for community formation than the Chinese because of the greater presence of women. Settled South Asians became peasant proprietors, migrated to cocoa plantations in Venezuela, or combined small-scale agriculture with temporary wage-labor on plantations. Diversification of economic activities created segmented labor markets. An affluent urban elite emerged, bringing family members and brides from India. By the early twentieth century, the first Indian-Caribbeans had been elected to legislatures.[61]

Chinese were recruited for Cuba starting in 1847 and for Jamaica in the mid-1850s. Teochiu and Hokkien people came from peasant backgrounds, whereas Cantonese came from the artisanal and urban lower classes. In Trinidad and Guiana, their wages were below subsistence level; accompanying women had to ask for wage-work, and some were repudiated by husbands who could not feed them. Recruiters also sent some criminal elements who formed small gangs after arrival—and created widespread anti-Chinese stereotypes. Many Chinese became reindentured, whereas others dispersed to wherever they perceived opportunities, be it in vegetable farming, oyster fishing, or retailing. Elite men opened larger trading establishments or owned cocoa estates. The Trinidad community, down to 800 members in 1900, was reinvigorated in the twentieth century by contacts with California Chinese. In Guiana upward mobility was slow; but in the 1880s some men had become wholesalers, and their children received higher education. The acculturation of Asian migrants to the

Euro-African-Amerindian heterogeneity proceeded by a gradual change of language, intermarriage or liaisons, and the emergence of a community of mixed ancestry.[62]

Spanish Cuba, where 600,000 slaves toiled in 1860 and where some 150,000 Chinese arrived from 1853 to 1874, formed an exception to the pattern of slow acculturation. Spanish merchants, engaged in the contraband slave trade, attempted to cut their losses by shifting to coolies. Family recruitment was considered desirable, with children like women contractually bound to work alongside slaves and be treated similarly. The traffic, mostly through Macao, was stopped by Portugal in 1873. When traders demanded indemnity for lost profits—a shipment of 900 coolies involved costs of 150,000 pesos and receipts of 450,000—an international French and American commission under a Chinese chairman investigated the conditions of coolie life in Cuba with the assent of the Spanish government: recruiting firms carried off most coolies by force, imprisoned them before embarkation, and transported them in "devil-ships"; buyers brutally examined the men and women after their arrival in Havana; eight-year contracts with twelve-hour workdays guaranteed planters low wage costs and the immobility of labor; coolies were subject to corporal punishment and could marry only with their employer's permission. Mortality, including suicides at a rate said to be the highest in the world, was estimated at 10 percent per year by planters, and higher by other sources. Without guaranteed return passage and without money to bribe officials for a passport permitting departure, the survivors became perpetual contract laborers. The commission charged European and Chinese traders with criminal conduct, but it also accused coolies of being stupid or naive. By 1872, 14,000 Chinese had managed to gain their freedom. They sold their labor in self-organized work-gangs or became marginal traders, artisans, and domestics. A Chinese quarter emerged in Havana, and immigrant U.S.-Chinese merchants provided an infusion of capital—but by 1900 the extreme death rates had reduced the Chinese community to a mere 15,000. In the war of independence, some 3,000 Chinese participated.[63]

While the Spanish government feared a strengthening of the Euro-Creole population and its nationalist movement, railway contractors brought their own "White" labor from Spain (Catalonia and Galicia), the United States, and the Canary Islands. Between 1882 and 1895, about 80,000 free Spaniards were recruited for agriculture but refused to accept the working conditions and moved to the cities. When the United States took control of Cuba in 1898, 70 percent of the agricultural labor force was White.

A few South American economies—Peru, Nicaragua, Brazil—also recruited Cantonese, Hawai'ian, and Japanese laborers. In Peru, which attracted investors from Britain, America, Germany, and Italy, working conditions resembled those found in Cuba. After the emancipation of the 25,000 African-origin slaves in 1854, laboring on plantations and in internal improvement programs and digging bird manure (guano) for export became the lot of Hawai'ians and Japanese, who "died like flies"—a "deliverance" from mistreatment, as contemporaries noted. During the economic crisis of the mid-1870s, the coolie trade ended, but free migrants continued to arrive: before 1923, 17,800 were Japanese, about one-third of them women. Hostility against the Chinese was transferred to the Japanese but abated when Japanese men fought in the Peruvian army during a boundary dispute with Ecuador. A thriving community emerged.[64]

Toward the end of the century, colonial cane sugar had to compete with beet sugar grown in the European core by seasonal labor migrants from Europe's periphery. The Colonial Office in London refused to continue indenture after the Sanderson Report of 1909 had documented the abuses of the system. Sufficient free labor could be obtained—if the planter paid competitive wages. In the circum-Caribbean polities, which came under increasing U.S. domination, U.S. capital introduced other plantation products, bananas in particular. The islands had become pluralist societies, which were conflictual at first. The Indian- and Chinese-Caribbean communities became stratified, the former by immigration and the internal accumulation of merchants, the latter by the arrival of California-Chinese merchants. Like the slave communities, the free and term-expired migrant communities became part of the populations and cultural history of the Americas.[65]

Free and Bound Migrations to North America

With the beginning of the transatlantic U.S.-China trade from the 1780s to the 1840s, a few Chinese men came, as did a woman as a model of chinoiserie fashion and some college students. Transpacific arrivals were not registered because the western territories became part of the United States only in the 1840s. One Chinese woman's experience reflects economic constraints, gender roles, and individual initiative across cultures. When her family planned to sell her into slavery, she fled to Macao, converted to Catholicism, and married a Portuguese sailor. He failed to return, and she entered the service of an American merchant, who brought her to San Francisco in 1848.

Sizable migrations of free Chinese from the southern provinces and the diaspora began with the gold rushes: in California in 1848, British Columbia in 1858, and Alaska thereafter.[66] As was true of Europeans, the Chinese were mesmerized by images of immense riches that made the destination seem to be a "Gold Mountain." But the California gold rush ended as early as 1852, and some of the frustrated 58,000 Euro-American miners scapegoated the "alien" Chinese and Mexican prospectors, inducing the state legislature to impose a "foreign miners' head tax" on them. Chinese immigrants moved to wherever gold strikes occurred: Oregon, Idaho, the Black Hills. Free California Chinese prospectors, merchants, and service workers joined the Fraser River gold rush, and within a year a direct shipping route from Hong Kong to Vancouver was opened. The choice of opportunities in this nascent community was larger than in the "established" ten-year-old gold-rush community in California. In 1860, when the transpacific trip took thirty to sixty days, 1,175 Chinese lived in the Fraser valley, and 35,000—including 1,800 women—resided in California. In the early period, women, who under Confucian precepts ranked low, were often exploited under semi-enslaved conditions as prostitutes. However, in the whole of San Francisco's population, the gender ratio stood at 7:1. Involuntary prostitution or self-willed sexual work and entrepreneurship was common among all groups.[67]

The free immigrant entrepreneurs, adventurers, and service workers formed the nucleus for the labor migration of credit-ticket migrants and contract laborers. Their legal position resembled that of eighteenth-century European indentured labor, but their economic position was the opposite. Instead of agricultural labor in family households with subsequent independence, they experienced unfree gang labor in transcontinental railway construction. When such work ended, many settled in railway towns, while others moved to ethnic neighborhoods, so-called Chinatowns, in metropolitan areas. Since cheap labor remained in great demand, the Burlingame Treaty of 1868 granted Chinese the right to immigrate to the United States.

Chinese worked in industries in California and British Columbia, in independent market gardening, or as sharecroppers; along the coast and in the Rockies as miners, in fishing, and in canneries; and in specialized niches, such as abalone fishing. They accounted for one-third of California's truck farmers in 1880. Some moved to the fisheries along Louisiana and in the Gulf of Mexico; some were hired to replace slaves on southern plantations after 1865; and some traveled to eastern factories, where, however, the depression of 1873 almost ended employment. The hostility of resident workers grew when Chinese-American workers were imported by New England's textile mill management as strikebreakers. Chinese-Canadian migrants established restaurants in mining camps, prairie towns, and northern Ontario's lumber region. Racist sentiment and job competition resulted in anti-Chinese and anti-Asian agitation and riots: for example, the San Francisco riots in 1877 and the rejection of Chinese labor for employment in fields and factories in Tennessee.[68]

The Chinese-American communities, with their highly developed cultural and organizational life, were as integrative as Euro-American immigrant ones and ethnic settlements everywhere. Among the multiethnic Chinese, various dialects, different food habits, and other regional specifics had to be homogenized. Ethnic organization was based on locality associations (huiguan), which were comparable to the German Landsmannschaften. The self-help institutions were labeled "secret societies" by Western observers, who did not speak any of the Chinese dialects. Since the wealthy also occupied positions as ethnic leaders and middlemen in the coolie trade, exploitation could be reinforced through such organizations. These, however, also provided social benefits and protection against the hostile Caucasian-American community. By 1900–1901, the Chinese population in California was 45,800 and in British Columbia 14,900; no other state or province counted more than 3,000 Chinese immigrants.[69]

The small U.S. Japanese community of 3,000 expanded rapidly after 1890. The Japanese immigrants, like the Chinese, settled mostly in California and British Columbia and found jobs in farming, fishing, logging, and mining, in shipyards and truck agriculture, and as male domestic servants. After 1907, when anti-Asian riots in

Vancouver and racism in California led to a curtailment of entry from Japan and prevented male workers from sojourning and rotating, those in the country decided to stay and bring in families. Contrary to political intentions, communities stabilized. Industry supported continued immigration in opposition to labor unions and governments. In the fisheries of British Columbia, Japanese and Haida men cooperated, and Japanese, European, and Amerindian women worked alongside each other in the canneries. Ethnic business from boardinghouses to shops developed.[70]

Filipinos and (East) Indians became part of this second Pacific Migration System. Both societies of origin were connected to North America through the new U.S. empire and the old British one. The United States, after waging war on Spain under the guise of supporting independence movements in Cuba and the Philippines in 1898, kept control over Cuba and annexed the Philippines. The people of the Philippines were many-cultured: the ethnic Chinese, in the 1850s, amounted to 50,000–100,000 (chap. 7.3), and there were also unskilled Japanese migrants. Filipinos, denied both independence and citizenship, were not covered by exclusion laws, and migrants, at first mainly men, went to California for work in agriculture.[71]

As part of the British Empire, Canada became the destination of South Asian migrants. Sikh colonial auxiliaries, who had traveled through Canada, returned after 1904 when their regiment was disbanded in Hong Kong—much as disbanded European soldiers had settled along the Habsburg-Ottoman frontier. Other Sikhs, called "Hindu" at the time, followed and worked as unskilled labor in logging, lumbering, and agriculture. In 1908, when 5,000 had arrived, half of whom moved to the United States, the Canadian government ended the immigration of "colored" people from the Empire. A famous test case, the arrival of the *Komagata Maru* in Vancouver in 1914 with 376 Indians on board, ended with their involuntary return. Canadian attempts to send those who had arrived earlier to British Honduras failed. In the United States, where South Asian men could not send for their wives, many intermarried with Mexican women.[72]

From 1850 to 1920, total immigration from the eastern Pacific Rim to the Pacific coast of the United States amounted to 320,000 Chinese, 240,000 Japanese, 30,000 from "other Asia," and 10,000 Pacific Islanders (plus 44,000 immigrants from Australia and New Zealand). These figures include multiple migrations. In Canada, the census of 1921 listed 39,600 Chinese and 15,900 Japanese (23,500 and 15,100 respectively in British Columbia) and 10,500 "East Indians." Compared to European migration in the Atlantic System, the numbers were small. Because the demand for cheap labor remained high when Asian workers were excluded, the recruitment of "Latinos" in Mexico began even before 1900.

15.6   Racism and Exclusion

Only twenty years after Britain imposed free emigration on the reluctant imperial government of China, racist agitation from North America to Australia demanded the exclusion of Asian immigrants and suggested that the Chinese government be ordered to prohibit emigration. Restrictive legislation was passed in North America in the 1880s, in Australia as well as South and East Africa around 1900, and in Latin America in the 1920s and 1930s. Only in Asia itself did migration continue and increase up to the beginning of the Great Depression.

Anglo attitudes lumped together all immigrant Asian workers as "Orientals." They were labeled as clannish because of their self-help organizations, as criminal because of British-induced opium smoking, as inscrutable because host populations did not understand their languages. Racist opinion was intimately connected to economic interest. "White" workers were afraid of competition from "cheap labor," and "White" middle classes found threatening the self-insertion of free Asian immigrants as a lower middle class. The Chinese, with no powerful state to back them, were usually excluded first. Anti-Japanese measures had to be negotiated with the comparatively strong Japanese government. Indian migration within the British Empire was difficult to curtail since citizenship extended across the empire, a provision based on the assumption that Colored colonials would migrate neither to Britain nor to the White colonies.

The second phase of the Pacific Migration System was cut short when the United States imposed the right to "regulate, limit or suspend" the entry of Chinese laborers: the Chinese Exclusion Act in 1882, the exclusion of Overseas Chinese after 1884, and further restrictions in 1888. Canada passed its first anti-Chinese law immediately after the completion of the transcontinental railroad in 1885: immigrants had to pay a head-tax of $50, which was raised to a prohibitive $500 in 1903. A California statute of 1913, based on a federal law of 1790 that restricted naturalization to "free white persons," deprived aliens "ineligible for citizenship" of the right to own agricultural property. Under exclusion, however, Chinese from the United States on visits to China could return if they had family in the United States or owned property worth $1,000 or more; merchants could bring in wives and children; and students from Asia could attend colleges. While Chinese people were unwanted, commerce and the spread of Western ideas among them were to continue.

To counter the elaborate measures of exclusion, the Chinese developed equally elaborate methods of conceiving "paper" children to create eligibility slots for immigration. Between 14,000 and 30,000 reached the United States in each decade from the 1890s to the 1930s and locally born children became ipso facto citizens. Canada's Asian-origin community also grew. Only with the second U.S. Quota Act of 1924 and Canada's Chinese exclusion law of 1923 was immigration reduced to a fraction of its previous volume. Among sections of the Chinese-American community, the slogan "go west, young man, across the Pacific to China" expressed the emotional damage experienced in North America as well as continuing pride in Chinese culture.[73]

Though Japanese never accounted for more than 1 percent of California's population and less in British Columbia, nativists turned to their presence after restrictions on Chinese had been secured. The "White" United States imposed "gentlemen's agreements," more accurately described as "thug-victim agreements," on the Japanese government. Literacy tests became mandatory, although fewer Japanese arrived annually on the West Coast than poorly educated Europeans *daily* on the East Coast. When Japanese immigration, particularly that of ex-servicemen, increased after Japan's victory over Russia in 1905, the United States imposed restrictions in 1907–08, and exclusion from Canada followed.[74] Because the exclusion of South Asians would have violated imperial law, Canada's government engaged in an administrative subterfuge in 1908 by requiring a "continuous journey" from the country of origin as the condition for admission, a requirement impossible to meet by coal-powered ships from India. A British observer noted the double-dealing: Sikh immigrants, treated "with silent contempt by most of the 'superior race'" in Vancouver, had "rendered valiant service to the Empire," of which they were citizens. Thus, during "exclusion," migration continued under humiliating regulations.[75]

North American exclusion induced enterprising Japanese migrants to turn to Brazil and Peru as host countries in the 1890s. In reaction to North American racism, the Japanese government improved trade relations with South American states and provided aid to emigrants, whom it considered to be commercial pioneers. From 1908 to 1934, 142,500 Japanese reached Brazil, and migration to Brazil continued into the 1950s; in Peru it was curtailed in 1936 (chap. 19.6).[76]

In the colonial world of the British Empire, campaigns against "Coloured" immigration from Asia began in the 1890s. In the Australian colonies, Tasmania, and New Zealand, the immigration of Asian labor had increased after the mid-nineteenth century, and regulatory acts protected the migrants from over-exploitation. But as early as 1861 Queensland's Alien Act prevented Asian and African immigrants from becoming naturalized unless they were married, accompanied by their wives, and residents for three years. Labor leaders charged the Chinese with defying the law and taking jobs "by which Europeans derived a livelihood." When the Australasian Intercolonial Conference of 1880–81 attempted to pass restrictions, Queensland, South Australia, and Tasmania kept the door ajar to satisfy agricultural and mining interests. But the 1888 Intercolonial Conference excluded Chinese. Japanese immigrants, who began to arrive in the 1890s, were excluded in 1901. The racist "White Australia" policy came to determine legislation, and an act of 1903 prohibited the naturalization of immigrants from Asia.[77]

The South Africa Act of 1910, which created the Union of South Africa out of the several colonies there, also unified anti-Asian sentiments. After responsible government had been granted to Natal in 1893 and to Transvaal in 1906, Natal-Indians were deprived of the franchise, and Indians in Transvaal had to submit to an "Asiatic registration bill." Debilitating head taxes were imposed on Natal-Indians, in particular on those who were free or not indentured. A family of four needed one person's annual wage just to pay the tax. Transvaal-Indian traders were reduced to particular "locations and bazaars." In 1890 the Orange Free State barred Indians from entry altogether. After the Anglo-Boer War, a deep depression lasting to 1910, a long drought, and the floods of 1905 increased economic problems. In 1911 the South African Parliament restricted immigration from Asia and in 1913 imposed restrictions on resident

Indians and Chinese.[78] In response, the Indian population, among them a young lawyer named Gandhi, began a campaign of passive resistance that was to merge with Indian national consciousness.[79]

In East Africa, the racial-occupational position of Indians above Africans explains their continued immigration even during the Great Depression. Some 100,000 lived there by 1939, and 350,000 in 1960 (chap. 19.8). Mauritian planters, after the end of the Indian indenture system, proved suddenly willing to recruit laborers from Pondoland and Mozambique—they made up about 40 percent of the labor force in 1939. The economic base, cheap and sufficient labor, was more important than ideological pronouncements about inferior skin colors.

In Europe and North America, racist attitudes designated Jews, Poles, and other Eastern Europeans as inferior and of "dark" skin. When migrant Polish laborers sought better working conditions in North America, German Junkers demanded the importation of Asian workers for their East Elbian estates. Labor movements and political elites bitterly polemicized against the "inferior" Asians and refused admission of the "yellow races." Communities of Asian seamen and African migrants in British port cities faced increasing restrictions and involuntary return. In North America, Madison Grant, fearful of "less-than-White" peoples of European origin, lamented in *The Passing of the Great Race* (1916) the fatal dilution of Anglo-Saxon stock; ten years later, Henry Pratt Fairchild took up a similar cry of alarm in *The Melting Pot Mistake.* The exclusion of Southern and Eastern Europeans in the United States in 1917 and 1924 reduced the immigration of peoples who for lack of distinguishing skin color could not be segregated. The continuing demand for industrial labor was then filled by a south-north migration of Afro-Americans, whose visible racial background permitted the enforcement of socioeconomic restrictions. "White" societies in the core and the colonies were split. Industrial and agricultural employers demanded cheap workers regardless of skin color.[80]

Racism and exclusion in labor-importing "White" countries was countered by a growing national consciousness in the "non-White" labor-exporting colonies/countries. The Japanese government had provided some protection to emigrant workers, but the impact of Chinese governmental measures remained low. In India, the discrimination against a people of the British Empire, which contradicted imperial rhetoric, fanned nationalism. Having first called for improved working conditions, Indian leaders soon demanded the abolition of the "second slavery." Britain reacted only when the support of Indians was needed during World War I. South Asian societies supplied 1.2 million men as soldiers and laborers to the British war effort, and about 100,000 Chinese coolies labored in northern France. As a result, the system of indenture was abolished in 1917, with the last contracts ending in 1921.[81]

In 1922 the Indian Emigration Act established control over the recruitment of assisted migrants and provided protection for emigrants to other parts of the British Empire. Chinese labor migration still expanded in the interwar years, in particular from the new northern emigration region. However, improved laws were countered by economic factors. Anti-Asian violence erupted or was fanned in societies from the Americas to Japan during the Great Depression. Siam-Chinese were labeled "the Jews of the Orient." Again hit hardest, Chinese migrants returned home, more than a quarter million in 1933 alone. The civil war there precluded large-scale aid. After 1937, Japanese imperial warfare ended the century-long traditions of Asian migration forever.[82]

16

Imperial Interest Groups and Subaltern

Cultural Assertion

Imperialism, from the view of labor needs of capital and of laboring people of many colors, is a considerably more complex phenomenon than indicated by political history approaches or economic analyses. How was the concept of a civilizing mission of White peoples related to the sending off of ne'er-do-well or simply noninheriting sons to the colonies? Why did labor and labor migration for imperial profit or politics, and for the building of societies, not entitle workers to the status of citizens? Death in war did, over time, provide entitlements; death in guano mines never did. Why has research long shunned the question of cultures in contact as epitomized by the children of imperial men and colonial women?

By the early nineteenth century, colonizer expansion had established four regional patterns of migration and labor regimes. First, merchants, sailors, soldiers, and administrators accessed local labor forces through the respective society's ruler in Africa, India, and Southeast Asia. Second, in Central and Andean America, by contrast, *conquistadores*, land "owners," administrators, and merchants ruled directly over local labor. Third, the same groups in Brazil, the Caribbean, and southeastern North America imported African slaves. When the British Empire and plantation economies globalized while the old-order plantation regime and African slavery declined, regional traditions of Asian labor regimes were globalized by the colonizers as "coolie" contract labor. Finally, in French and British North America and in South Africa, settler immigrants—often with the help of European indentured servants—tilled or raised cattle on land cleared of its inhabitants. Imperial worlds were as global as the hierarchies of rulers and subalterns.

When African societies lost their function of supplying labor to capitalist mass production in the fields, the "dark continent" appeared to the European vision to be in need of en-lightening, and the nineteenth-century imperialist discourse constructed a civilizing mission of out-migrating imperial men and women serving as masters of childlike "Negroes." Stereotypes continued to mediate the views that European and Euro-Creole colonizers held of Asian, African, American, or other peoples who had replaced the non-Christian, non-European generic Others—"the Turks" of earlier centuries. To give verisimilitude to the views, selected "Natives" had been transported to Europe after each conquest to be viewed by decision-makers at the courts. Where colonial populations had been decimated and European domination had been asserted, ideologues of the core constructed the image of the Noble Savage as the inverse of European commercialization and materialism. With the late-nineteenth-century democratization of Western societies, specimens of the Others were exhibited for general viewing: for example, at the Chicago world's fair in 1893, or in zoological gardens, such as Hagenbeck in Germany, or in Buffalo Bill's Wild West show and similar extravaganzas.[1]

The focus on colonial peoples as victims exhibited in shows of the White World diverts attention from the colonizers' unwitting self-exhibition. A British couple traveling in Nigeria in the early twentieth century staged itself as an outpost of the rational, cultured, white World:

> Every night, we tied up at the edge of a sandbank, [dressed for dinner,] and dined—we would not have used a less formal word. . . . Between the two of us we had obeyed our code and had upheld our own and our country's dignity. . . . When you are alone, among thousands of unknown, unpredictable people, dazed by unaccustomed sights and sounds, bemused by strange ways of life and thought, you need to remember who you are, where you come from, what your standards are.[2]

Unfortunately, no African ethnologist left an analysis of this strange staging of alien customs.

In the colonies, the self-described "superior Whites" of the North Atlantic World faced resident subaltern majorities who had little or no reason to consider their cultures and themselves inferior. Imperial elites also faced subaltern migrant working classes, whether self-moved or transported by strategies of profit-accumulation. The dialectic of capital and labor resulted in migrant workers' circumventive or militant strategies to avoid or reduce exploitation; the dialectic of lighter and darker colors of skin resulted in struggles of resistance or for self-determination. The colonized were keenly aware of imposed domination and hegemony.

While African societies were colonized, the descendants of the forced African migrants in the Americas established a distinct cultural sphere, asserted their identities, and came to form an Atlantic African diaspora. Caribbean-African societies, in particular, contributed to the creation of the Black Atlantic. The multicolored societies with a strong input of peoples from the Andes and the pampas contributed to "Latin American" culture.

The focus on subaltern cultures and capitalist penetration detracts from a sociology of imperialism. Imperial migrants pursued family and intergenerational strategies and struggled over gender relations.

Of the 70 million Africans in 1800, some ten million lived north of the Sahara, the others—with the exception of 1.5 million Malagasy—in "Black Africa." European-ruled territories remained few: French Senegal, the British Gold Coast, Portuguese Angola and Mozambique, and the Cape, which had the largest concentration of Europeans, some 16,000 Boers and a few thousand British people. European visitors' and intruders' "exploration" of "unknown" spaces relied on well-informed local African guides. Trade and production of luxury goods was in the hands of African peoples, as was the formation of societies and polities.[3] In Mediterranean Africa, the influence of the Ottoman Empire and its still multiethnic administrators—Turks, Mamluks, Albanians, Circassians, and others—declined gradually but persistently.

Direct European intervention in Africa increased after 1830; territorial acquisitions multiplied after 1870; and at the Berlin conference of 1885 the dividing powers recognized each other's spheres of influence. In the intervening half-century, European merchants with *condottiere*-type private armies or European states' small squadrons of regular troops supported by hired African regiments carved up the continent and its peoples. In the north, four regions emerged. Egypt and the Omani state asserted influence over Arabia. Algeria and Tunisia were the object of French conquest after 1830, while Morocco remained independent until 1912. Ethiopia, coveted by the English and French, was militarily colonized by Italy after 1882. The Nilotic Sudan remained contested ground as a catchment area for slaves (map 16.1).

In 1830s Egypt, French Saint-Simonians and British and French entrepreneurs infused concepts of Western-type "modernization" as well as capital for the construction of the Suez Canal. By midcentury, investors and technical experts had established a network of connections for capital transfer, job acquisition, and innovation—as well as a young or middle-aged immigrant men's career network. In the early 1870s, when the slave trade from the upper Nile region was officially abolished, vast infrastructural projects as well as cotton cultivation mobilized workers. A nationalist movement among the rising elites and antiforeigner riots among urban populations countered European impositions or the pace of change. As in India, the British hegemon underestimated both the cultural traditions and the future-oriented project for self-determination.[4]

In Algeria, the coastal cities had lost trade to European-Mediterranean merchants, and their inhabitants emigrated. The population of Algiers had declined from 100,000 in the early eighteenth century to 30,000 by 1830. As the hub of the Tunisian and Saharan trade, the Algerian city of Constantine also housed 30,000. From the mountains, agricultural people, unable to increase their subsistence base, migrated to the plains for seasonal work. The Ottoman presence consisted of administrators and some 15,000 Turkish soldiers; Kouloughlis, the sons of Turkish fathers and Algerian mothers, dominated the economy; descendants of Andalusian Muslim refugees lived in separate quarters. These groups' commercial and cultural urbanity evoked attacks from orthodox clerics. White Christian slaves, a mere 2,000 by 1800, served in

16.1 Africa, c. 1880 and c. 1914

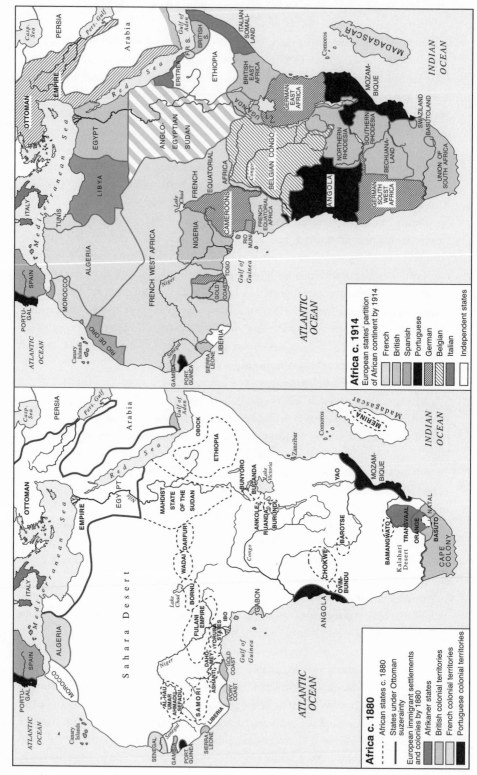

Africa c. 1914

European states' partition
of African continent by 1914

- French
- British
- Spanish
- Portuguese
- German
- Belgian
- Italian
- Independent states

Africa c. 1880

- – – – African states c. 1880
- —— States under Ottoman
  suzerainty
- European immigrant settlements
  and colonies by 1880
- Afrikaner states
- British colonial territories
- French colonial territories
- Portuguese colonial territories

domestic employ and managed the government-owned taverns, a subterfuge to circumvent the Koran's prohibition on alcohol; a similar number of Black slaves worked as manual laborers. The lively freed African community engaged in skilled crafts. The cities of the Tell housed immigrants from the interior: Mzabis owned shops (chap. 6.2), Biskris labored as water carriers and porters, and Kabyles in unskilled or semi-skilled jobs. These *barraniyun* ("strangers") remained distinct by religious practice and economic pursuit. Life followed the Islamic-Ottoman mode of self-contained ethnic and craft quarters. Islamic and Jewish traditions of ritual personal hygiene and public baths explain the relatively healthy environment, as compared to conditions in European cities.

The Jewish community consisted of impoverished descendants of the late-fifteenth-century Hispanic and Balearic refugees. Eighteenth-century immigrant French and Italian merchants, who were called *juifs francs*, a generic designation comparable to the medieval "Christian Franks," became middlemen in the European trade. When fiscal exactions by Ottoman administrators and Native elites resulted in crisis for the cultivators and their oppression, Jewish merchants and bankers immigrated with their families from Livorno. After one of them was murdered by a janissary in 1805 with approval by an *ulama*, a riot in Algiers took the lives of 200 Jews.[5]

When French conquest began in 1830, Algeria's population of about three million consisted of rural landholders, sharecroppers, and mainly Berber-origin landless laborers (about 50 percent), nomads (44 percent), and urban dwellers (less than 6 percent). In the 1840s, French capital and European settlers, intending to change Arab low-yield cultivation to an agriculture of plenty, produced a crop of some 300 how-to books and pamphlets, alienated Arab-settled land, and suppressed civil liberties for the benefit of about 110,000 immigrants of French (43 percent) as well as of Spanish, Italian, Maltese, Swiss, Prussian, Bavarian, and Hessian background. In France, agrarian restructuring, improved transport, and national market integration had resulted in massive rural-urban migrations. In-migrants numbering 25,000 to 35,000 joined the Parisian population of one million annually. Fearful of these *classes dangereuses*, the revolutionary government of 1848 planned to transport some 100,000 of them to Algeria. Of the 15,000 who were shipped within a year under army supervision to villages not yet built, one-third died, and another third fled back to France or to Algerian cities.

A reclassification of land in the 1870s reduced Muslim land rights, and additional European *colons*, including many French Jews, came. Some 630,000 Europeans lived in Algeria by 1901. Arab and Berber migration to *colon*-owned land or to the cities involved dispossessed peasants, nomads, as well as mountain and oasis peoples. A Native Code regulated and restricted local migration in the interests of the colonizers. Plans to recruit either Sudanese or Irish labor came to nothing; epidemics, famines, and natural disasters reduced native North African populations.

Of the other regions in North Africa, Tunis became a joint Italian-French sphere of influence and received Italian migrants. In Morocco, France imposed a protectorate in 1912. Its Roman Empire–inspired planners developed a myth of a North African granary. They dispossessed Moroccan peasants but could attract a mere 6,000 immigrants rather than masses of cultivators. Only the Moroccan elite benefited from the concentration of landownership. After wheat production failed, a "California-style" citrus fruit and vegetable agriculture became the new panacea. Western observers of 1930 found "the European," in fact 1.25 million of them, "perfectly acclimated," but they overlooked the fact that the many cultures of 1830s North Africa had become culturally more homogeneous, ready to demand equal rights (chap. 18.3).[6]

At the other end of Africa, the Dutch settler colony on the Cape (chap. 9.5) became British in 1806. In contrast to the homogenizing settlers in Algeria, the Cape's two groups remained antagonistic. Whereas the constitution of 1853 granted the franchise to male British subjects, White or Black, who had a minimum of property or income, ethnically diverse African men and women worked under ethnically diverse European overseers. While Dutch and British capital fought for control over resources, settlers fought over the color of and control over the labor force. The resulting segmented society formed a contrast to Latin American ethnogenesis.

Within two decades after the discovery of diamonds between the Vaal and Orange Rivers in 1866, diamonds worth £39 million had been extracted, and in 1886 gold was discovered in the Witwatersrand region of southern Transvaal. Minor investments created large amounts of capital for the core and an ethnic niche economy for Dutch-Jewish diamond experts and for diamond cutters in Amsterdam. Kimberly, founded in 1871, counted a population of 10,000 by 1874; and Johannesburg's population grew from zero in 1886 to 100,000 men and women from across southern Africa and 50,000 from Europe by 1899. To prevent illicit diamond trading and to protect workers from the money-consuming temptations of city life, diamond mine owners housed them in closed compounds. At first, the system helped workers to carry wages home, and, as a consequence, the mines could rely on self-recruitment.

In agriculture farmers imposed restrictions on the Khoi, and after 1846 the government imposed segregation on Native peoples. A spiritual movement of resistance among the Xhosa ended in tragedy: expecting help from supernatural powers or historical heroes, they slaughtered their cattle, but starvation ensued and two-thirds died. After 1860 the colonizers imported indentured workers from India's peoples and Chinese from the northern provinces. Throughout the century, population dislocation followed from British and Afrikaner competition, from Europeans' encroachment on Zulu land and the resistance they met, and from strife between African peoples. To counter established Whites, immigrant Whites in Transvaal organized an *uitlander* party. The labor militancy of Africans and community-establishment of Indian immigrants added to the political spectrum. To reduce Dutch-Afrikaner influence, the British passed an Aliens Expulsion Act and an Aliens Immigration Restriction Act in Transvaal in 1896; the Transvaal Afrikaner (Boer) government in turn refused to enfranchise immigrants of five years' residence, who happened to be mainly British subjects. In the subsequent war, the British Empire brought in some 300,000 soldiers and deported some 120,000 Afrikaner women and children to camps. Deportation as an imperial strategy had been used against French-speaking Acadians in the

Canadian colonies in the 1750s and was to be used against Kikuyu and Kabaka rulers in East Africa in the 1950s. After the Union of South Africa was established in 1910, migrant labor from Asia was excluded (chap. 15.6).

Since the 1860s, African men from Mozambique and other neighboring colonies had traveled by foot to jobs in the mines. At that time, Portuguese Angola and Mozambique held only a small Euro-immigrant population of about 3,000; thereafter, some 7,500 Asian immigrants settled in Mozambique. A mixed-origin population emerged. In the process of African labor migration, ethnic identities were reshaped by interaction, but male and female cultures evolved separately. Rather than being "total institutions," mines brought forth new eth-class interaction among the 300,000 migrant workers of the 1930s (chap. 18.4).[7]

Heterogeneity also characterized East and West Africa. In the east, the British inserted themselves through influence on Zanzibar; the Germans and the British established mainland settler colonies. In the west, the British held a zone of influence after 1807. The French, coming later, faced the resistance of the Mandinka state (1870–98) of some twenty tribal kingdoms. French rule after 1898 relied on traditional chiefs and on competition between them rather than on the integrative Islamic religious structures. The British, by contrast, sent costly administrative personnel from the core. Both systems succeeded in dividing African peoples into Francoized or Anglicized elites and traditional-culture urban lower classes and hinterland dwellers. Regardless of European origin, officials surrounded themselves with the pomp and circumstance of what they considered civilization. When touring their districts with their entourage, they needed upward of fifteen porters per person at sixty pounds per headload to transport tents, food, and clothing.[8]

In their view, lifestyles without property made "the African"—meaning men and women of multiple cultures and states—"inferior, shiftless, leisure-loving, lazy," whose "elasticity of demand for income, once his target income had been achieved, approached zero." Since labor was difficult to recruit, "missionaries" came to teach the value of work and opened training institutions for skilled craftsmen and "orderly" housewives. To exact forced labor, the empires "shored up the authority of chiefs," or, in societies without chiefs, they "hand-picked individuals." From the Gold Coast to Nigeria, the British—with regional variations—demanded compulsory work from men aged 15–50 and women aged 15–45. Wage incentives, if offered at all, were low. In West Africa, army carriers' "wages" provided 25 percent less income than independent farming; East African Kikuyu received wages that amounted to one-tenth of their farming income. In 1907 Kenya's provincial commissioner expressed the interest of the British state-industrial complex: "There will be no real progress until the people are weaned from this principle [of livestock as the medium of exchange] and taught to buy a multitude of perishable commodities which will eventually become so necessary to them that they will be forced year by year to work more and more to satisfy their needs."[9]

The early labor migrations of the Soninke, a Mande-speaking West African group, indicate that itinerant traders, perceiving demand for labor, relayed information back to other members of their groups. The self-willed Soninke migrations were to extend to France after independence. Colonizer-appointed chiefs shifted the burden of compulsory labor to weaker members of a society. In the German- and Portuguese-controlled territories of Southwest Africa, indigenous rulers and their male supporters, who traditionally had raided weaker peoples for cattle, held colonizers at some distance by becoming their extended arms. They raided villages for labor and helped to force their subjects or neighbors into the colonial system.

In the fragile ecology of many African regions, peoples who were impoverished by drought or other natural disasters migrated first. Migrants were caught in a web of power relationships between wage-appropriating local rulers and exploitative immigrant employers. By the 1920s, as working-class militancy and collective action emerged, the preference for and the distance of migrations grew.[10] Mentalities changed. Once established, labor migration could become one of several strategies to obtain cash income, independent of an actual need or coercion to depart. The arrival of Asian-origin immigrant or traditional African traders in hinterlands resulted in new expectations. Market values came to be reckoned in cash rather than in goats or sheep. Centrifugal forces began their impact on communities and families. On the level of individuals, escape from oppressive parents or societies, rejection of a marriage proposal, and increase in prestige might induce outbound mobility. Life-cycle patterns and family relations changed. Men were able to pay bride-price earlier and do so independently of parents. On the other hand, since migration usually was seasonal or multiannual, centripetal forces remained strong. The women and children of families remained behind; rural ways of life were stabilized by the infusion of cash. Jobs within walking distance kept migrants within their own systems of orientation. Some authors suggest psychological reasons for migration: a substitute for traditional rites of passage to manhood, a desire to venture far afield out of a sense of adventure. African labor migration resembles labor migration elsewhere in the world.[11]

Regional patterns of migration involved Ovambo men in Southwest African harbor and railroad work. In Kenya, the number of migrant laborers grew from 5,000 in 1903, when the colonial state began to alienate Kikuyu land, to 120,000 in 1923. Since migrants worked seasonally, the actual annual volume of migration was at least twice as high. Kikuyus and others developed a market agriculture by growing coffee and other cash crops whose cultivation did not permit economies of scale. In traditional market-oriented economies, such as groundnut production in Senegal, migratory patterns existed previous to and independent of colonial rule.[12] Gendered patterns of labor kept women—for example, in the Ngoni and Ngonde societies of the Great Lakes area—in bondage, and in the 1880s and 1890s Bemba raids and "entrepreneurial brigandage" generated "a flow of women and children who were often kept in villages, their disposability obscured until such time as they were needed and found themselves handed over to traders in exchange for goods" (chap. 6.5). But women ran away, attempting to return to their people or to migrate independently.

Women's position as independent laborers was undercut by missionaries' concepts of marriage but strengthened by postmigration loose forms of urban cohabitation, which permitted partners to leave each other quickly. Some African women used colonial courts and missionary precepts to pursue strategies of liberation from customary subservience. Unmarried cohabitation was condemned as licentious by the colonizers' gatekeepers, even though colonial administrators lived with Native women and left them when ending their tours of duty. Women who followed their own interests were castigated as "runaways," while male departure from unsatisfactory labor relations would be termed resistance. In territories with high male out-migration for wage labor, sex ratios rose to 2:1 "in favor of" women. This meant additional work to feed children and elders. To keep women in their assigned place, some colonial administrations subjected women to gender-specific pass-laws, forcing them to carry a marriage certificate or apply for a pass.[13]

At the beginning of the twentieth century, the European presence in Africa was politically all-powerful, economically intrusive with regard to labor relations, of cultural consequence with regard to elites, but numerically weak. Settlement clusters were limited to 0.75 million in Algeria (less than 14 percent of the population), 1.25 million in South Africa and Rhodesia (22 percent of 6 million), and 24,000 in Angola and Mozambique. Among African workers and soldiers, contact led to eth-class consciousness. French-Guinean soldiers, who fought in Europe in World War I and carried back socialist ideas, engaged in the Conakry dockworkers' strikes in 1918 and 1919. Francophone elites, who developed an Afro-French culture and literature, moved from advocating *négritude* to demanding self-rule and independence. Decolonization was only a few decades away (chap. 19.8).

16.2   From the African Diaspora to the Black Atlantic

While societies in Africa were forced to reconstitute themselves under external rule and new economic relations, the subaltern Afro-Atlantic diaspora contested labor regimes and created cultures (chap. 6.2). Africans sustained the cultures of the Americas: as an Anglo-African self-sustaining plantation population in the United States and as majorities in the Caribbean, in the Afro-European-origin culture of Brazil, and in Indio-African-European-origin cultures in Central America and the Andean states. The many local worlds the slaves created became a diaspora (map 16.2).[14]

Just as the appearance of "the Indian"—the American Native—in the European view had recast the debate on the foundations of societies and states (chap. 11.1), so the debate over bondage or liberty juxtaposed individual rights and the quest for profits. A political economy of what Inikori and Engerman have called the politics of profits and power emerged. In view of the cost of military conquest and the size of actual and potential colonial populations, mercantilist dynastic states and nineteenth-century capitalist nation-states had to conceive of themselves as a—White—unity. Up to the 1870s, "Such European solidarity was essential to the success of the slave trade. After all, the Europeans shared a sense of their tenuousness on the African coast."[15]

To reduce the cost of external control in the plantation economies, Europeans/Whites aimed at self-control of the children/Blacks. If exploited peoples' social orga-

16.2   Empires and Diasporas

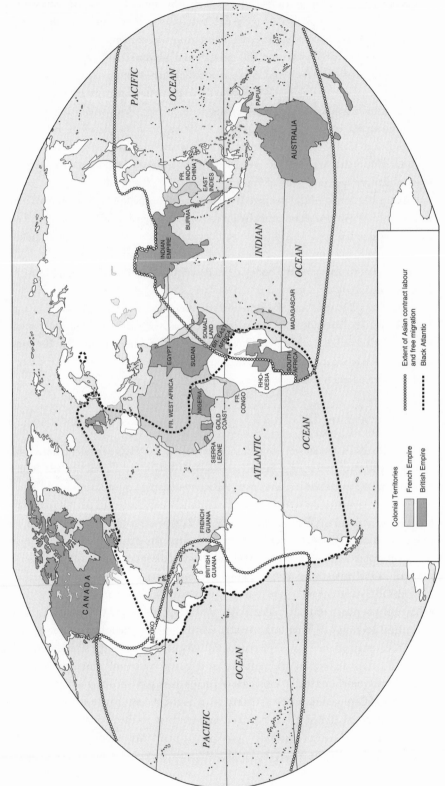

PACIFIC OCEAN

PAPUA

AUSTRALIA

FR. INDO-CHINA

EAST INDIES

BURMA

INDIAN EMPIRE

INDIAN OCEAN

MADAGASCAR

SOMALI LAND

BR. EAST AFRICA

EGYPT

SUDAN

SOUTH AFRICA

RHO-DESIA

FR. CONGO

FR. WEST AFRICA

NIGERIA

GOLD COAST

SIERRA LEONE

ATLANTIC OCEAN

FRENCH GUIANA

BRITISH GUIANA

MEXICO

CANADA

PACIFIC OCEAN

PACIFIC OCEAN

Colonial Territories

French Empire

British Empire

Extent of Asian contract labour and free migration

Black Atlantic

nization and self-esteem were destroyed, the women and men could be re-socialized to aspire to commodities and to Whiteness. This project was only partly successful, and the White-Black dichotomy was never rigorously maintained. European men consorted with African women, and Euro-African populations emerged along the coast of Africa, in the Americas, and in the Caribbean in particular. Africans, called "Black Portuguese," and mixed-origin Luso-Africans combined commercial knowledge, traveling experience, and language—with *"fale de Guine"* as the lingua franca of the South Atlantic trading world—to establish themselves as "people in the middle," as brokers and independent businessmen along the littorals of the Atlantic Ocean. If they were captured and enslaved by Euro-origin inhabitants of these same littorals, they influenced slave cultures, helped build "Black Indian" Maroon societies, and influenced the cultures of New Orléans (French period) and New Netherland (the Dutch period of New York). In mid-sixteenth-century southwestern Europe, many of the 10,000 African slaves in Lisbon and the 6,000 in Seville were Creoles. This "founding generation" inhabited a genetically fused White-Black world of commercial societies with slaves before the emergence of full-fledged slave societies with plantation economies.[16]

Africans, socialized in Africa or Iberia, reached the Americas as pilots, as *conquistadores*, or as free and bound laborers; into the nineteenth century, more African-origin than European-origin men and women crossed the Atlantic. Slaves were victims, brutally treated, and exploited. Slaves produced the consumer goods and the surplus value for the cores. Slaves carried their cultural baggage with them. They made the worlds in which slaveholders lived. Conquerors, planters, and investors had faced choices. They could have contracted free labor, hired temporarily bound labor, or purchased labor bound for life and generations; they could select workers from their own or from distant cultures. They chose commodified over contracted labor and used the state—since the Enlightenment a public institution—to enforce their side of private-law contracts by public-law criminal statutes.

The Africa-to-America exchange of commodified producers (and reproducers) was one important aspect of capital accumulation in England in particular, although misguided investments, economic cycles, and elite consumption patterns complicated the patterns of accumulation. It permitted "immense opportunities for the development of a division of labor across diverse regions of the world, all linked together by the Atlantic Ocean." This intercontinental specialization within nations "brought peasant crafts and the products that replaced them increasingly into the market-place."[17] New England's textile industry provides one example of interrelations between slavery, capital formation, and multiple migrations. The original investor-merchants had accumulated capital in slavery-related maritime commerce. A regional advantage, waterpower, and nation-state-mediated slave-produced cotton made factories profitable. Planters bought factory-produced textiles and shoes for their slaves. To staff the factories, women were mobilized in short-distance migrations from the declining agriculture of the region. When they rebelled against working conditions, French-Canadians from the large families of the St. Lawrence valley and postfamine colonial Irish people replaced them. When these workers rebelled, capital shifted production to the southern states and relied on free Black and White labor under strict paternalistic control. Across the Americas, enslaved and free Black underclasses did the backbreaking work. Exclusion from access to resources and political institutions cemented their race-class position: "Scientific racism interpreted these characteristics in genetic terms."[18]

In addition to their part in building the economies of the Americas, Africans and their descendants shaped the culture of the Atlantic World. The emergence of the Black Atlantic involved self-homogenization out of many ethnocultural origins into regional variations of African Americans, out of many languages into Black American English and Creole-Spanish. In the first generations, slaves from a particular ethnicity who were sufficiently numerous in one locality could also re-form their premigration cultural group. Families transmitted pre- and postmigration cultural patterns. Social life involved self-organization, mock elections, and other rituals. The inferiorized and racialized men and women reasserted and adapted identities, developed strategies of resistance, and influenced White culture. Each self-assertion demanded a decision from the master class whether to tolerate subaltern peoples' expression in hopes of keeping the labor force contented or to incur the costs of repression and potential revolt. The master race, permanently watchful, had to negotiate and compromise or to militarize society.[19]

The nineteenth-century return migration of free and freed Afro-Americans and of Afro-Europeans increased cultural and political interaction between the societies of the Americas and of West Africa. Freed slaves who had escaped to Britain and men and women from Canada's Halifax community returned to Sierra Leone, to which the British shipped Maroons whom they were unable to control in Jamaica. With the Nova Scotians came ideas of revolutionary America, and with the Jamaicans ideas of Caribbean rebellions. Both could connect to indigenous concepts of self-organization —or they could be set against each other. The British could use the Maroons, probably of Ashanti origin, against the Atlantic-African Nova Scotians. Some 60,000 enslaved men and women from many ethnicities captured from illegal slave-trading ships were deposited in Sierra Leone after the 1840s, and in Freetown a "polyglot community" of Krios (from the term "Creoles") emerged. Some tried to make their way back to their people; others became missionaries among nonconverted peoples; some lived like Black Englishmen. Freed slaves of many cultural backgrounds, some 16,000 by midcentury, returned or were returned to Africa and settled in Liberia, founded by U.S. "charity" in 1821. Later, Black Brazilians came and engaged in politics or founded mercantile companies.[20]

The cosmopolitan group of European thinkers and revolutionaries (chap. 12.4) had an equivalent in the Atlantic World's Black intelligentsia. British radicals included Black and Creole "sailors, moving to and fro between nations, crossing borders in modern machines that were themselves micro-systems of linguistic and political hybridity," as Paul Gilroy has noted. In the Age of Revolution, perhaps one-quarter of "the British navy was composed of Africans for whom the experience of slavery was a powerful orientation to the ideologies of liberty and justice." Radical Robert Wedderburn, the son of a slave dealer and a slave woman, was freed at birth, brought up in the interstices of the slave and free worlds of Kingston, Jamaica, and migrated to London. Radical Martin Delany, born in Virginia and an active U.S. abolitionist, traveled to Liberia and Europe, and made Canada his home in exile until he returned after the U.S. Civil War and became involved in politics in South Carolina. As early as 1852 he recognized similarities of "nations within nations" regardless of color: Africans in the United States and Poles in tsarist Russia, Hungarians in the Habsburg Empire and Scottish, Irish, and Welsh peoples in the United Kingdom. He searched for both cultural roots and a new future. While White radicals traversed an intellectual route from cosmopolitanism to the concept of nation-states, Black radicals moved through an Atlantic World of three continents. Their world was one of solidarity, imbued with a labor theory of value; it was an "Atlanticist radicalism," albeit a subaltern one.[21]

In the realm of spirituality, African migrants carried their belief systems and religious practices with them. The European and African concepts and structures of clerical mediation between human beings and spiritual worlds stood diametrically opposed: an insecure priesthood, in non-Muslim African cultures often aligned with kings or chiefs, versus the powerful clergy of hierarchical Christian churches, which were aligned with institutionalized states. European migrants transported dissenting traditions to North America, while African migrants brought a multiplicity of beliefs: out of their fusion new denominations with weak hierarchies emerged. The seemingly monolithic Catholic Church had to compromise when attempting to take Africans into its fold. New forms of religious expression—the gospel song, for example, or sectarian worship, such as the Voodoo cult—permeated societies. From different cosmologies, functions of priesthood, and gender roles in church affairs, a hybrid practice of religion emerged.[22]

Of the many expressions of Afro-Atlantic popular culture—in dress, objects of adornment, and aesthetic principles—music and dance achieved the greatest impact. Gatekeepers of White racial supremacy devalued this contribution as "sexually explicit," unharmonious "nigger music." They overlooked the fact that slave lives were not harmonious and that White men were sexually explicit in their attitudes toward Colored women. Eighteenth-century Euro-Creole planters adapted to Afro-Creole women's cultural worlds. The late- nineteenth-century lower classes in Anglo-America and Europe readily picked up on Afro-Caribbean music and "Latin" dance. By the 1930s the opposition to jazz and "dirty" dancing had lost out. In North America, "Negro" music from New Orleans and the plantations was transported to urban Euro-America by Chicago's white big bands. Latin music merged Amerindian songs and instruments with African rhythms and Euro-Christian hymns, regionally specific to Bahia or Martinique, Buenos Aires or Cuba, Trinidad or Peru.

Migrants "atlanticized" some of these tonal and dance expressions. The tango, according to one source, emerged in the poor sections of Buenos Aires and Montevideo among immigrant packinghouse workers from the Iberian Peninsula or Italy and among prostitutes from many cultures. The music incorporated Neapolitan and

Andalusian love songs about women left behind. Others emphasize gaucho influences, Black music in White parody, and sailors' tunes from mid-nineteenth-century Havana. A playful sexuality of lower-class migrants developed, which was different from the power-imposing sexuality of colonial administrators. Face-to-face dancing became cheek-to-cheek contact and was stylized in the 1890s. The intercultural and lower-class bandonion replaced flutes as main instrument. This amusement of the underclasses remained unacceptable to the middle and upper echelons of Argentine society, but both tango and jazz were transported to cities in Europe and the United States. London, the banking house of the world, was one place of cultural intermixture; the Paris of the 1910s and 1920s was another. Seasonally traveling Argentine intellectuals—Bohemians?—introduced the exotic dancing that became a craze in the metropoles and was then reimported to upper-class social spaces of Buenos Aires, bans by the Catholic Church notwithstanding. Similarly, Chicago jazz was reimported to New Orleans. The samba, of Bantu origins, emerged from the poor quarters of Rio de Janeiro and reached the high society of Europe. The European-origin and Mulatto higher classes in Rio had opposed it and had sent police to control the lower-class *sambistas*. Race and class merged—the forces of control lost their hold on the minds of the multiracial lower classes.

Each transfer between cultures, classes, and continents involved adaptations and changes. Musicians and dancers lived transnationally; national cultures incorporated the dance styles into their repertoires and projected the nationalized, sometimes "sanitized" versions back onto cultures of origin or an internationalized Atlantic world. Exchange gained in speed first with cheap transatlantic migrant steamship tickets and, subsequently, with inexpensive records. Symphony orchestras and grand opera competed with backstreet-bar piano players and slave or working-class bands in a cultural mix that would be taken up both by "pure" race labels and chamber music but could never be segmented into nations, colors, classes. The orchestrated masses along assembly lines and on the stage of the fun-palaces connected the economic and the cultural, matching, in effect, time-and-motion studies with choreography: the musical as a clockwork-like mass dance on stage reflected the synchronized movements of mass laborers in fields and factories.[23]

The White Atlantic, the Black Atlantic, and the Amerindian Atlantic made up a world structured by power relationships and color hierarchies. Its dialectics of subaltern and hegemonic cultures incorporated trade and commodities from Asia; Indian and Chinese indentured laborers and free migrants reached out from their enclaves and added to the mixture. The seemingly high and mighty colonizer migrants, too, had to negotiate positions and interactions. They pursued their strategies and were as heterogeneous or, if need be, as homogeneous as the subaltern co-inhabitants of the globalized imperial worlds.

The Black Atlantic's two major sides, backbreaking, profit-generating labor and culture-creating community-building, are usually discussed separately. Similarly, the White imperial World is usually discussed only from the single perspective of economic domination and exploitation.[24] But imperial strategies involve migration projects of many interest groups.

The interpretation of imperialism in terms of capital and profits needs to be expanded first by a sociology of commercial elites, administrative classes, cultural gatekeepers, and their family and career interests. Second, imperial expansion provided elites of the cores concerned with national population development, the British in particular, with an opportunity to export unemployed "superfluous" people and with them the costs of reproduction and lower-class militancy. Third, colonial military men and administrators and the planners of imperial population policies at home spoke of "surplus women" in the core and the lack of "White" women in the colonies. Reverse migration brought administrators used to domestic service by "Colored" boys and girls back home or to the White Dominions—the settler societies of Canada, Australia, and New Zealand. The sons of colonized elites, who did not necessarily view themselves as coming from peripheral peoples, migrated to the educational facilities of the cores. There they learned to speak in terms of the colonizers' frames of reference.

From the point of view of colonized men and women, the diasporas of colonizers appeared as arrogant British, French, Dutch, or Portuguese people in the nineteenth century, and in earlier times as "Germans" in Eastern Europe, as "Franks" in Palestine, as "Spaniards" in the Americas. Positions of power translated themselves into individual identities and group constructions. The imperial newcomers expected the colonial residents to adjust. Engulfed in discourses of superiority and protected by practices of power, these immigrants had no interest in subtle regional differences, everyday lifestyles, or achievements of high cultures. Power reduced cognitive abilities: there was no need to be discerning. Men and women of subaltern peoples and diasporas, on the other hand, had to be highly alert to the whims and wishes of the masters on pain of incurring heavy punishment. They had to be observant and creative to survive.

On their lives a vast "human experiment" was to be imposed. Englishmen like David Livingstone pronounced "Christianity, Commerce and Civilization" to be the goals of expansion. Frenchmen like the engineer and investor Ferdinand de Lesseps considered European migrants sources of inspiration to lesser developed societies. U.S. men like Henry M. Stanley sweepingly demanded the acquisition of "the human communities [in colonized lands], the muscles of whose members have a more immediate and practical value to us. For without these, the flowers, the plants, the gums, the moss, and the dye weeds of the tropical world must ever remain worthless to them and to ourselves." They all agreed that European and North American industrial and commercial conquests would be beneficial to all colonized peoples and classes.[25]

Imperial strategies were pursued by men of all White states. While nineteenth-century Britain and France expanded in Africa and Asia, the latecomers, Germany and the United States, expanded continentally into Central Europe and into Central America and the Caribbean respectively. In both states (and, subsequently, in the Soviet Union), working-class organizations joined the expansionist discourse and self-elevated themselves as entitled to rule over neighboring working classes.[26] Around 1900 Japan joined the imperial powers (chap. 17.4). In all, imperialist states from 1870 to 1900 acquired control over 10 million square miles and 150 million people—a tenth of the world's population. These masses were ruled by tiny numbers of imperial migrants and their more numerous colonial auxiliaries. For example, some 60,000 Whites and 150,000 Native soldiers controlled the Indian subcontinent in 1914.[27]

The relationship between state and economic elites distinguished Atlantic imperialism from other societies. The trade emporia of the Indian Ocean and the Hausa trading circuits had functioned separately from political power; Hanseatic merchants had built their own power base. By contrast, in China (as in seventeenth-century Spain) merchants were hampered by bureaucratic control, and Japan's social order placed merchants at the bottom of the social order. Some societies relied on inserted mercantile communities: Germans in Russia, Jews in Eastern Europe, Chinese in Southeast Asia. In Europe, the establishment of the large chartered companies after 1600 permitted merchants to use state power and states to instrumentalize commercial expansion. Power and honor became entwined. Commercial success was constructed as a matter of national honor; any violation of a merchants' interest somewhere on the globe demanded military retribution from the respective state.

The combination of military and commercial power permitted high rates of accumulation. British planters' profits from sugarcane depended on protective legislation in the empire. Between 1870 and 1883 the Dutch Deli (Java) Company increased its capital sevenfold and, from value created by its coolies' labor, paid profits of on average 73 percent annually. The exchange of goods based on use value, such as beads for furs, did not involve an unfair advantage, it has been argued, since each side bartered for and received what it needed most. This perspective overlooks the consumption-accumulation dichotomy, which permitted imperial merchants to accumulate profits that they then used to exploit the other side. Exchange relationships became power relationships. Paul Kennedy has emphasized the comparative advantage of great powers, and Henri Brunschwig phrased the connection bluntly: "*Free* trade, if it was to be profitable, assumed the existence of an unchallengeable fleet and points of supply on all world routes." The nineteenth-century mass migrations resulted from such power, as did the twentieth-century poverty-induced migrations under unequal terms of trade (chaps. 19, 20).[28]

Imperialism involved a shift from the predominance of commercial capital via industrial capital to the primacy of investment capital. It thus involved competition between sections of each state's economic elites, and an analysis of which particular social groups benefited from the imperialist project is required to understand capital flows and migration. States arose "when a warrior transformed a cohort of young, unmarried men into an armed band."[29] The nineteenth-century European states had emerged from dynastic power apparatuses and their hired migrant soldiers; the North American states from settler societies and their militias; the Caribbean and South American states from buccaneer and *conquistador* acquisitions; and the African states from the slave-trade-induced realignment of power. Under the impact of the rising middle strata, dynastic units were transformed into polities of estates. Under Enlightenment theory, they became public institutions, and the justification for power came to be derived from the residents of the territory, the people. Excluded from the citizenry, however, were men without property and all women.

The White middle classes and ruling elites were internally segmented. Practices of access to state offices and specific cultural practices, defined as generically national, made hierarchies of class and gender an integral part of "democratic" polities, defined as the "nation," the "mother country" or "fatherland," or the "core" or "capitalist center." This constructed homogeneity was intended to benefit particular groups. "It cannot be denied, that if nationalism had not coloured the whole of this period, it would in the long run have been impossible for a small group of profiteers," whether Caribbean planters, Brazilian slave owners, Algerian settlers, or the merchants and financiers of the cores, "to insist on the carrying out of a policy which enormously increased the budget. This is why . . . the 'colonialists' seized every opportunity to repeat the arguments of [scholarly] geographical societies and to beat the patriotic drum" (Brunschwig). The "national interest" mandated the continued exploitation of the Others, constructed as lazy children by a mother or father state. "If we changed the established order, several million Frenchmen would fall into poverty [noted a French imperialist]: and if humanity tells us to improve the lot of the Negroes, reason orders us to confirm their enslavement." Distant imperial and emigrant elites influence the social order of the core.[30]

Who gained advantages by what political means depended on the social customs and political processes of a particular state. To reduce their expenses British families from the gentry and nobility, who could not provide for younger sons' lifestyles in keeping with their aspirations, sent many of them to the colonies to be "self-sufficient" on government salaries paid from public tax revenues. Sons who became colonial officials or officers in armies and navies were expensive. Colonial expansion, according to a contemporary observer, provided "a vast system of outdoor relief." Another noted: "There are thousands of men in the old country who have not been brought up to work of any kind, and who consequently are unable to contribute towards their own support." The most competent men did not leave or were kept at home by their families—just as Russian peasant communes sent their least productive members into the army. Dutch men with incomplete schooling left for the colonies, as did "misfits and black sheep who were either forced by misfortune . . . or were sent . . . by their families." Such abandonment by family-of-birth and life in all-male communities far from the social world of childhood often might lead to mental disease. Contemporary observers acknowledged the prevalence of "acts of bestiality, sexual indulgences, physical torture and murders, together with expressions of megalomania," but blamed them on tropical climates and life among Natives. The uprooted ex-Europeans used power to retain as many cultural traits as possible. "An Englishman beginning his life has great advantages over the citizen of any other country. He has the choice over half-a-dozen splendid countries to live in, of every variety of climate; he may choose according to his fancy, and remain an Englishman always" (Rowan). To keep it that way, schools even in the White Dominions taught children English geography and English institutions. It did not prepare them for life in their own societies.[31]

In France, internal problems of the military and dynastic elite explain the beginning of nineteenth-century expansion.[32] The conquest of Algiers was meant to distract attention from the faltering power of the Bourbons. The new late-nineteenth-century quest for glory occurred in reaction to the defeat by Bismarck's Germany in 1870–71. "France had to reforge her prestige in the community of European nations . . . not on the Rhine, but in Africa." At this point, career opportunities inserted themselves. French male administrators migrated to the colonies to achieve promotion or escape supervision. On the periphery, they "generated their own expansive drives" to satisfy their ambitions and to maneuver themselves to gain more influence. The *officiers soudanais* turned the colony into their own private preserve.[33] The dialectic of colonial rule, according to a French author, "eventually defeats the most obdurate native rebel, and the most progressive and humane of colonists." It involves "the destruction of traditional society and culture" both in the colonies and the cores.[34]

French slaving merchants grew rich, bought offices, and received letters of nobility. Codes of honor changed from fighting and dueling to being a good credit risk. Displays of wealth, and conspicuous consumption in the case of the nobility, became middle-class status-conferring investments, such as in country estates for wine production.

Educated segments of the middle classes—university and school teachers— showed great interest in the other cultures and carved them into academic subjects, thus providing themselves with securely tenured positions. Journalists and authors provided and sold texts and photographic images about the distant "possessions." Scholars in geography, history, languages, and surveying methods formed learned societies to supply practical knowledge. The British Colonial Office instituted a Visual Instruction Committee after 1902. To elevate their contributions and make themselves indispensable, many of these intellectual gatekeepers participated in the construction of "scientific" racism. In an "imaginary ethnography," they viewed other cultures through their own cultural preconceptions, an "orientalist" view in regard to Asia according to Edward Said.[35]

Finally, some colonial ventures depended on the in-migration of large numbers of settlers from the core. In the core states, population bases varied, and who was to migrate depended on class and power relationships. French peasants, secure on their land and enfranchised, did not migrate in sizable numbers, and this "deprived French empire-builders of colonists." British landlords' policies of enclosure supplied colonists "recklessly to the white dominions." Industrial employers, on the other hand, had different interests and opposed emigration to keep a wage-depressing reservoir of labor available. In France, colonial commerce amounted to only a small share of the state's economy; thus "the nation's businessmen had small enthusiasm for colonies," and farmers "were anti-imperialist because imports from colonies often competed with domestic production." In imperial Germany, prospective migrants did not follow governmental exhortations to populate new colonial acquisitions where economic prospects were dim. Workers migrated to industrialized North America rather than to arid African lands. In the wake of World War I, the British government tried to rid itself of the responsibility for demobilized, often disabled soldiers under a scheme styled Empire Settlement. Concepts of citizens as the foundation of democratic polities had not taken hold among governing classes.[36]

A sociology of imperial personnel is thus able to uncover group interests and strategies, a vast project of creating global job opportunities and another of shoveling paupers and others out of home societies.

Colonizer Masculinity

The colonizers' "human experiment" included a savage masculinity. A British colonial official, sympathetic to Buddhist religion as giving solace to the weak, developed this educational project for the "beautiful world God has given us":

> It is our duty to sweep away the cowardly, the inefficient, the weak, who misuse it, and put in their place the strong and useful. The Burman already has too much faith. . . . He must not shrink at the blows of the world and seek seclusion from it, but go out and affront it. . . . He must learn to be savage, if necessary to destroy, to hurt and push aside without scruple. He must learn to be a man.

One of the aims of male migration to Canada was "to become a man." Similarly, French male administrators in West Africa and German colonial officers in Southwest Africa treated those they considered weak with ruthlessness. Particularly aggressive males were considered the material of which empires were made, and imperial men went out into the world to recast men of other societies in their image. Imperialism included a specific ideology of masculinity.[37]

If sections of colonized peoples tried to assert self-determination ("rebelled"), control was ruthlessly reasserted. The British gunned down the sepoys who "mutinied" in India and massacred dervishes in the Sudan; German merchants and military officers committed atrocities in Southwest Africa; an international force repressed the Boxer rebellion in China. When peoples designated as labor forces refused to work, punitive expeditions killed men and women to achieve submission. This "everyday violence" consequent upon male colonizers' migrations took more lives than the colonizers' wars did. But the power of gunpowder receded behind the power of definition and racialization of the peoples of the world. Conversion came to mean enforced submission and loss of identity.

When the most republican of all colonizer societies sent the "Rough Rider" Theodore Roosevelt to defeat the Cuban and Philippine Spanish-Creole-Native armies in 1898, the link between weak and strong men, as well as the connection between skin color and White democratic theory, interpreted by White statesmen, came into the open. Cuba, Puerto Rico, and the Philippines were denied the choice of either independence or statehood within the U.S. federal system. "The prospect of . . . admission of Spanish creoles and negroes of the West India islands and of the Malays and Tagal of the Philippines to participation in the conduct of our government [was] so alarming," commented Carl Schurz, that few were ready to accept it. When Filipino freedom fighters distributed a Spanish translation of the Declaration of Independence, the U.S. Army confiscated the "incendiary document," and U.S. senators branded the declaration that all man are created equal "a living lie." An anti-imperialist journalist countered with republican manliness: "Here we have a star-tling illustration of the depth of shame to which corporate greed and militarism have already brought the Republic. . . . The deadly peril . . . threatens the cause of free government and human rights." Free men, after all, drafted the Declaration of Independence.[38]

Colonial Men: Auxiliaries and Elites

The thin layer of immigrant colonizer bureaucrats and military officers had to forge alliances with local elites who could enforce power relationships on the mass of the peoples. Imperialist armed and police forces were largely staffed by Colored "colonial auxiliaries" (chap. 15.4). British armies in India were recruited from the Gurkhas and other colonials; British administrators relied on Tamil clerks and Sikh-staffed police forces. German troops in East Africa in 1914 comprised 3,500 Whites and 12,000 Black Askari. Toward the end of European colonialism, the French army at Dien Bien Phu in 1953–54 consisted of Frenchmen, North Africans, Black Africans, and mercenaries of many cultural origins. Without colonial auxiliaries and mediating colonial elites who passed off the cost of imperialism to weaker ethnic groups, social strata, or women, European rule would have assumed neither a global reach nor its particular local expressions.

In West Africa, considered a White man's grave, the British government at first used Native men as administrators. Under the impact of growing imperialist sentiment and the increasing availability of quinine, from the 1880s on, experienced African administrators and educators were passed over for superior positions in favor of young Englishmen with "little experience" and fewer qualifications. A university-educated Nigerian inspector of schools in 1910 had "the mortification of seeing young men with defective knowledge of the local situation being appointed over me to depreciate my labour." Two middle-class groups with similar aspirations, who differed by qualification and by power, were pitted against each other. "It will certainly be several generations [noted an Englishman self-servingly in 1900] before the West African native, however carefully he may be, will have gained that force of character which the Englishman now inherits as a sort of birthright and which will fit him to be placed in an independent position of authority, whether in the Service of the Church or the State." In Euro-democratic theory, superior "birthright" had yielded to the rule of the people, but in justification of colonial rule predemocratic nobility-commoner relationships were transposed onto racialized colonizer-colonized relationships.[39]

Racial attitudes were negotiated from location to location. In Calcutta a "caste" of colonial British enforced rigid segregation, but in Mumbai/Bombay Jewish-Indians and Hindu-Indians could interact socially with the British. While the British hid their insane in special lunatic asylums for Whites, so that Natives would not see debilitated Whites and question the image of superiority, they left senile officers in charge of the army. One British general, coming upon a mass meeting of 6,000–10,000 Indian men and women held against his orders, had his soldiers fire into the crowd in what came to be called the Amritsar Massacre (1919). He left 279 dead and some 1,200 wounded without calling for medical help. From London, British-Indian relations seemed to involve a hierarchy of distance and respect marred occasionally by "incidents"; from close-up, those relations seemed to be guided by arrogant ineptitude and exploitative brutality. If Indians expressed their discontent, the British overlords were unable to understand it, since most never learnt the indigenous languages.[40]

A comparison with White Dominions helps place the importance of communication for self-assertion in context. At the time of the Amritsar Massacre and the Nigerian ordinances, high-ranking Europeans visited the Rocky Mountains as tourists—carrying their notions of rank in their cultural baggage. Canadian outfitters and packers, who clearly ranked lower, had little stomach for such pretensions. "An English lord, who on the first evening of his outing, coldly informed the men, 'I am not used to eating with my servants,' was told that he could wait until they had finished." A German officer, who started ordering the men around, was regarded as a lunatic and told to shut up. White men speaking the same language could talk back. Because of the congruity of languages between elites and subalterns in the White Dominions, the English could listen and had to listen.[41]

Although imperial powers sent out superfluous sons and bored administrators, who were visually handicapped because their upbringing literally prevented them from seeing Others as equals, colonial elites often sent their best abroad. Segments of these elites negotiated their way into the colonizers' social space. When in India the old Persian language of record and of the courts was replaced by English in 1837, Native English-speaking administrators began to connect to the political power and capital flows of the core. The measure also displaced Muslim elites in favor of Anglicized Hindu ones, thus causing both vertical and horizontal mobility—as well as fostering Hindu-Muslim conflict. Among the minorities, the Parsees had Anglicized themselves quickly. For sons of the elites, visits to England became part of their education, just as travel to Italy had been for Englishmen in centuries past. As intermediaries with the cultural knowledge that the British lacked, the educated colonized elites occupied profitable positions between Europeans and local economies, but, in their dependency on the colonial rulers, many were blocked in their aspirations. The movement for all-Indian unification began among the Native English-speaking middle classes.[42]

The French version of cultural superiority involved a policy of assimilation, of turning the African and Asian middle-class colonists into Frenchmen by education, administration, military service, and fiscal practices. The project was "naively utopian, sexist and racist" (Aldrich/Connell). Over time assimilation was replaced by association, "separate but equal treatment which favoured the development of male native elites but kept women and the masses at arm's length from legal equality or political power."[43] Men from these core-educated new elites, in demanding independence, provided for their own future careers.

The new colonial middle classes were cosmopolitan. They not only had been educated in the European capitals; but many had lived in or been exiled to hubs of political activity in Europe. Edward Said remembers having lived as a child in Palestine and Egypt among English, French, and Greek people, among Jews of Egyptian, Palestinian, Italian, or British culture, and among Muslims of different religious creeds. Mohandas K. Gandhi, born in 1869, left India as a nineteen-year-old to study law in England and then practiced in South Africa. Revolted by discrimination, he returned to India and in 1920 began a campaign of nonviolence that was to drive the British out of South Asia. A Vietnamese by the name of Ho Chi Minh worked as a mess boy on a French liner and as a kitchen helper in London; and in 1919 he wrote a memorial for the Versailles Peace Conference demanding independence for Vietnam. The future Chinese leader Sun Yat-sen, from a poor rural family in the Guangdong area, joined an elder brother in Hawai'i, received a mission school education, and developed concepts of Western democracy. After he had gone to medical school in Hong Kong, the British did not consider him acceptable for practice in the Dominions, and ranking Chinese snubbed him. He became the spokesman of Chinese nationalism. Ho Chi Minh began his Declaration of Independence of the Democratic Republic of Viet Nam in 1945 with quotes from American revolutionary texts and the French revolutionary Declaration of the Rights of Man. Issues of equality had not been solved by men with the higher birthrights.[44]

16.4   The Anthropology of Empire: Gender, Sex, and Children

The networks of empire and laboring diasporas included women and children as well as men. Male strategists of empire and of profit maximization sent out men, encouraging unions with Native women because concubinal relationships were considered medically less dangerous than prostitutional ones. Population planners sent out "surplus women" as well as "imperial mothers." If Britain exported young men, a surplus of young women had to be accommodated. Wives of colonial administrators were part of ritual displays of power in Dutch Batavia and in Spanish America. White imperial nurses ministered to sick Natives in British possessions. Other women came for their own purposes without asking the strategists' permission. In classic studies of empire, the issues of bodies, sensuality, and sexuality and of childbearing, the rearing of children, and class-specific positioning received only cursory attention. Contemporary accounts discuss masculinity explicitly or as subtexts, often in terms of "European pornographic phantasies."[45] The increasing migration of women permitted community formation among labor migrants and resulted in new gendered racial boundaries between the representatives of empire and the Colored colonized. The "anthropology of empire" involves analysis of the construction of Others in gendered and sexualized terms, gender relations among bound and free laborers as well as between imperial men and women, provision for children, classification of mixed children, gendered education, and identity formation.

"Daughters of the Empire" or "Imperial Mothers"

In late-nineteenth-century Britain, ideologues of empire intensified the drive to send out cultured women and strong men to provide the colonies with people said to be superior to immigrants from other cultures and to provide the younger generation of the British Empire's core with opportunities. Periodicals like the *Imperial Colonist* and *United Empire: The Royal Colonial Institute Journal* were among the most outspoken advocates of the civilizing and empire-building role of "surplus women," those who would not find husbands in England and who could not contribute to national wealth at home, given—we should add—traditional gendered spheres and incomes. An official count in 1911 listed 1.3 million more "females than males" in the United Kingdom and a surplus of 0.8 million males in the self-governing Dominions.[46]

British women reformers "hoped to shape the future development of the nation upon the soundest, most rational and most moral principles. For them, these principles were embodied in the Victorian home. The nation was the home and the home was the woman; all were best British." Chaste homemaking, national character, and imperial expansion merged—in housework and in bed. This arrangement disposed of the issue of wages for homemakers. In some European cultures, middle-class women were considered inviolable Madonnas, but lower-class domestic servant women were regarded as sexually accessible to male household members. This arrangement blurred as well as reinforced class distinctions.[47] Class and gender, emotions and economics merged when Colored women as service providers became concubines or *petites épouses* and accepted the role. It raised them above servant, colonial, or ethnic status without making them equals, and it could result in upward mobility for their children. But the eugenics movements downgraded Colored women.

Organizations like the British Women's Female Emigration Association encouraged and coordinated the migration of young women by promising "genteel" domestic positions and coyly assuming marriage. Childbearing was hardly mentioned. Middle-class women were to civilize colonial society as governesses and nurses, and working-class women were to labor as domestics. Daughters of the impoverished British gentry were to be provided with life-course options. The Association intended to provide protection, help with finding jobs, and "homes of welcome" for cultural insertion, but—within the framework of class and imperial tasks—aspects of control became paramount.[48]

The "daughters of the empire" had to be young. The envisioned career from domestic help to wife of the single male householder and to bearer of children for the British Empire's empty spaces in the White colonies mandated childbearing age. In practice, underpaid domestic or farm labor awaited the emigrants, as two educated British women found when they toured Canada in 1909 and 1911 to gain firsthand experience of working conditions. Both reiterated preconceived notions of class: proletarian women were incapable, and middle-class ones talked "eagerly" about "happy" lives and preferred "this healthy, busy land" to "the hectic life of Paris and London." Some women's—like men's—concepts of empire settlement never overcame the outdated romanticism of "virgin soils" and agricultural lives.[49]

Concepts of "imperial motherhood" were applied in South Africa, where in less-than-empty spaces the presence of the White race had to be increased and where homes were filled by Black houseboys. Imperial strategists had even argued that British women were needed to prevent British men from engaging in miscegenation with Dutch-Boer women. Class strategists demanded that superior women be recruited for men of superior station. Calculations placed the demand for women in 1902 at 60,400, for "Anglicising the country, if we mean to keep it loyal to the mother land. It can only be done by women, through State aid." In homes the first step was to replace Black by White and boys by girls. Women were sent out as "lady companions," "helps," or "family friends," as if no cash nexus existed. But because wages were low, the feminization of domestic labor brought Black women into homes, contrary to what was intended. White women became governesses or chose a path of prostitution, which paid considerably better. Still others structured their own lives independent of notions of race by forming unions with Black houseboys. Neither patriarchal nor colonial ideology had foreseen this type of independence.[50]

Women's organizations envisioned a wider sphere for emigrants, but "their feminism, if it existed, was subordinated to their imperialism and to their bourgeois interests." Those selected for emigration were of strong character and Anglo-Saxon ideals; according to the concepts of eugenics, their offspring would be healthy, and they would build "homes" on which the future of the British Empire rested. To achieve this goal, the imperial women's associations planned to protect emigrants from their (assumed) proclivity to deviate from the path of chastity and from developing too much independence by a system of compulsory government registration and reception centers. "It was not guns and butter that preoccupied these empire builders, but babies— the potential offspring of the female immigrants who were the objects of their reform work." These "actively virtuous" and patriotic women considered women "the stuff of which nations were built." The previous supporters of imperial men, Colored women, came to be considered a degenerating influence.[51]

Intimate Life and the Construction of the Others

Imperial men, whether they were administrators of the Pacific Islands or fur hunters in northern expanses, consorted with local women. Métis and Eurasian children were born, accepted, or rejected. Both in the lonely north and in places densely crowded with Others, some White men went mad (in official parlance, were "driven off balance") from "excessive solitude."[52] While coolie men's madness was not part of imperial or employer responsibility, control over them was—and, according to received wisdom, men with sexual "outlets" were more docile. Ideologues of race constructed colonized men as lusting after White women.

The construction of Others, whether as ethnics or as enemies, frequently referred to sexuality and assumed indecency. It aimed at control over women, one group's men guarding their exclusive access to the sexuality of "their" women. Recriminations were mutual: Natives in Latin America behaved "beastly," said the Europeans; Europeans practiced unnatural sex, said the Chinese. Immigrant Christian observers labeled many traditions of other societies as indecent. Missionary men commented on the nude upper torsos of men and women not yet converted to European or middle-class notions of dress. Some delighted in taking photos of the women in order to send them home as evidence of "heathen" lifeways. The custom of Japanese men of winding money belts around the body and opening their clothes to pay for something was considered indecent. Chinese laborers in Hawai'i, at first commended for being "quiet, able and willing men," were said to exert "a corrupting influence on the native female population" when they lived in consensual unions with Native women. In debates about Asian exclusion, the threat allegedly posed by non-White men to White women played a considerable role. In mid-1890s Australia, lurid stories were told of a Chinese community of 270 males and two women. The San Francisco School Board planned to segregate Japanese boys in "oriental" schools so that they would "cease violating White girls." The intensity of White men's fantasies about the sexuality of men and women of other skin colors was matched by their interest in dependent women's bodies.[53]

Racialized power and profit maximization shaped cohabitation, ascription, and sexual relations. In Malaya, planters overcrowded bunkhouses, "mixing the sexes indiscriminately." "These arrangements, devised with a keen eye to minimising labour costs, were rationalised in terms of the alleged habits and customs of the people." Across the globe, owners of bound labor fantasized about promiscuity among their workers. The high number of suicides among contract laborers at many destinations and the assaults of jealous men on women of their group were not factored into calculations of profit or assessments of morality. Construction of lower-class European sexuality proceeded along similar lines and often reflected class-specific living arrangements. Middle-class incomes permitted the spread of family life across several private rooms, with sexual life and childbirth relegated to a couple's bedroom. Other classes, especially ethnicized or racialized segments of classes, who could not afford privacy, were labeled morally degenerate. However, the men in imperial headquarters did not provide lowly servants or soldiers with privacy. For reasons of cost efficiency, soldiers were prohibited from marrying but were provided with prostitutes. British fortifications housed soldier families in large halls, separated from each other at night only by blankets drawn between the "rooms." Thus the semipublic sexuality of lower-ranking Others—regardless of class, ethnicity, or race—was planned as well as stigmatized.[54]

The childbearing capacities of women, the presence of children, and male sexuality were openly debated as part of the construction of nations when the men in the Canadian House of Commons debated the end of Chinese exclusion in 1947 and the admission of immigrant men to citizenship. The government gave three reasons for the end of exclusion: 1) the United Nations charter clause concerning nondiscrimination, 2) the rising importance of Asia as an economic region and the various forms of competition with the United States, and 3) China's wartime cooperation. Racist opponents of Chinese immigration discussed male "urges" and women's wombs. The British character of British Columbia was to be preserved—but the province's first elite had been Métis, the children of Scottish traders and Native women of several cultures. National homogeneity would be endangered by Chinese women's capacity to give life. If 30,000 women came—some 8,000 could have come according to the bill—the "family feeling" of Chinese men might result in three babies per couple, and 90,000 Chinese would migrate out of women's wombs into British-Canadian society. Thus women's sexuality was necessary for men's urges, but life-giving was a danger to the nation. Exclusion of women under a "life-giving clause" was the opposite of the "death-clause" enabling foreign men to gain citizenship, even posthumously, if they served as soldiers.[55]

Imperial Men, Access to Women, and Children of Mixed Origin

Like religious men in celibate institutions and laboring men shipped by coolie recruiters, the imperial diasporas of soldiers and administrators lived in almost exclusively male communities. Home societies and families of origin, from whom these men had been uprooted, did not desire their return; or return was made impossible by institutional arrangements. Discipline, the cost of replacement, and the duration of a return trip mandated continuous "tours of duty." On the other hand, free migrants, including laboring ones, were quite capable of returning and arranging for partnerships or marriages.

Domestic chores for many of the imperial men, particularly those in the armed services, were carried out by "boys" rather then by women. State-mandated military drafts may have been the economic reason because draftees received no wages. The construction of "the forces" or "the services" as network-providing and offering psychic/emotional rewards was part of a community-construction that refused to reflect a procreative social organization. But sex was reflected, and the lifestyle imposed on soldiers as well as on imperial administrators and plantation managers was considered "unnatural" by the organizers of empire. European-origin plantation staff, not subject to military discipline or national honor, had its reproductive work done by local female housekeepers. Private enterprise did not object to the sexual exploitation of Native domestics or female laborers. Sexual relations with non-White women, while not conforming to concepts of "racial purity," did fit views of maleness. Purity in the "home" societies was maintained by prohibiting men from bringing back their Colored wives/partners and mixed children when employment in the colonies ended.

The construction of Native women's sexuality emerged from all-male communities and power hierarchies. In plantation societies, involuntarily celibate men— if heterosexual—might feel tempted by the mere presence of Native women. Like Catholic clerics' perceptions of European women's sexuality, the perception of colonial women's bodies emerged out of a life of sexual deprivation, an ideology of male sexuality in need of release, a conglomerate of the inviolability of (White) female bodies and the accessibility of (inferior, colonized, Colored) female bodies. The self-denial or institutionally imposed asceticism (perhaps masochistic) might explain the construction of sexually aggressive women and the sadistic punishments of female slaves in Anglo-America and of female plantation workers in Dutch Java. Colonial men projected fantasies onto other classes, ethnicized or racialized groups, or onto the other sex in general as part of their contact with non-European societies labeled primitive.[56]

From involuntary sex, but mostly from love and desire in mixed unions, children were born. Male-staffed imperial governments paid attention to such consequences of sexuality, no matter if the parents were imperial White, imperial mixed, or labor migrant in background. Whether children as part of imperial administrations and labor forces were wanted or rejected depended on the "color mix" of the partners, prevalent ideologies, and class position. Population planners' calculations and moralists' preachings hardly ever paused to consider that mixed relationships may have been affectionate and that the resulting children were wanted even by parents separated by power and color hierarchies. The assumption was simple: men needed outlets for their sexual energies. The other side was complex: women's bodies, their life-giving capacity, complicated racial boundaries and membership categories in nations. The belonging of children of mixed origin could not be determined by single-category minds.

In Western ideology and practice, the cultural belonging of a child followed that of the father, since a wife's ethnicity, if different before marriage, followed that of the husband. In the colonies, arrangements depended on power relationships and on acceptance of a child by either the husband's or the wife's kin and cultural group. The Dutch prohibited mixed couples in the Southeast Asian colonies from returning to the Netherlands. Scottish fur traders of the Hudson's Bay Company left their First Nations wives when they returned. In all cases, the children of White men and

Colored women remained in colonial societies and were defined as Colored in Anglo and Dutch White Protestant or Anglican societies. In Catholic Latin Euro-Creole societies, their color was negotiated. "Skin color was an obstacle to social ascendancy only if the person who aspired to become fully assimilated was not accepted by the dominant social group. On the other hand, it did not count if a colored individual's relatives and friends were powerful enough to acknowledge their ties. . . . Success was the surest means of 'purifying' the blood."[57]

In slave societies, however, property relationships overrode descent through male lineage. Where mothers were the private property of slaveholders, so were the children. This inconsistency in race ideology secured both the sanctity of property relationships and future labor for slaveholders. The labor and bodies (persons?) of children of bound mothers were allocated even before birth. Neither the parents' Christian religion nor the founding principle of Western society that all were born equal saved these children from servitude for life. Individual manumission was an option only if the father of a child was the slave owner himself, but the granting of freedom still depended on societal norms and on the attitudes of particular fathers.

Unlike the attitude toward parental emotions and children's identities, the cost of reproduction was openly debated. When abolition changed property in human labor, the cost of child-care and care for the elderly was shifted from the slaveholder class to the victimized working class. Similarly, the costs of the abolition of serfdom in Europe were borne by land cessions from serfs to owners. Aged slaves were freed before working-age adults and unborn children before their mothers—in Brazil, for example, by the *Lei do Ventre Libre* and the *Lei dos Sexagenários*, which freed unborn children and those over sixty years of age. U.S. planters in legislatures of the slave states discussed the break-even point in the life of slaves to determine a cost-neutral age at which liberation would be economically acceptable. Slaves had to work off the owners' "investment" in feeding them before being granted liberty.[58]

In family economies, too, economic and power relationships could be stacked against children. In some societies, children—often female ones—could be sold into bondage in times of need. In times of famine, such sale could ensure their survival. In African cultures, women and children remained in dependent relationships to men, who kept control over their labor and who could transfer them to other kin groups. In Europe, the children of the poor were sent off to fend for themselves when parents could no longer feed them, or they were bundled off to the White colonies by philanthropic organizations.[59] Artisan families exchanged sons in apprenticeship relations and daughters in domestic service positions. Among free migrants, the departure of married men without their families left the responsibility for feeding children in the hands of women. Generations of children were socialized without fathers or with fathers who were only sporadically or seasonally present. (In the late twentieth century, when women would migrate into domestic labor and men would stay behind, children were being raised by female kin without mothers being present.)

If laborers were needed, peasant or working-class women had to give birth. Plantation owners began slave "breeding"; others provided migrant laborers with small plots of land to induce them to bring in their wives and procreate, or the land afforded to peasant families was calculated at a sufficiently small scale to ensure the wage labor of the children. A landowner in Kenya concisely summarized racialized economic interests, life-cycle mobility, and gendered spaces: "It stands to reason that the more prosperous and contented is the population of a reserve, the less the need or inclination of the young men of the tribe to go out into the field. From the farmers' point of view the ideal reserve is a recruiting ground for labour, a place from which the able-bodied go out to work, returning occasionally to rest and to beget the next generation of labourers."[60] The bodies of children, like those of men and women, were allocated for imperial as well as for private economic purposes.

The Bodies of Laboring Men and Women

Planters and other employers did not hire human beings but rather *"piezas"* or body segments of workers—"hands" and *"braceros."* Suppliers charged workers as commodities, "tobacco, portuguese labourers . . . lumber," or "canvas, Japanese laborers, macaroni, and a Chinaman," or in alphabetical itemization "Fertilizer, Filipinos." On Brazilian coffee plantations families were hired according to the number of "hoes" they could mobilize—one more term for working-age human beings. Muscle power was needed; identities were considered detrimental to employers' interests. In the case of women, designated "wenches" or "girls," more than hands were wanted: reproductive labor for migrant workers, homemaking for middle-class men, sex in both cases. Sexual services may also have been expected from boys, but taboos on homosexuality have consigned such relationships to secrecy. Identity-threatening work made no distinction between persons and their labor power.[61]

Labor migrants perceived the interest in their bodies and occasionally used the term "flesh markets" both for sale of sex by women and labor by men, in particular if workers had to walk the streets or wait on a market square until hired. Child labor was bought on "children's markets" or through debt relationships. Perceptions of bound, free, and sex work merged: chattel slavery, wage slavery, and "white slavery," the involuntary prostitution of White women. In some contexts demeaning treatment by employers violating male workers' identities was called "rape." Both men and women saw themselves as beings with bodies and identities; both knew that they sold their bodies, regardless of which part the purchaser was interested in.

Low wages for productive labor implied lower wages for reproductive labor. Free working-class male migrants could not afford to support female reproductive workers on a one-to-one basis. In Russian *arteli* and North American boardinghouses one woman, only rarely a man, supplied food and cleaning services to several men, usually without sexual services. When employers of bound labor forces arranged maintenance and reproduction, whether food preparation for slaves or camp life for contract workers, they likewise cut costs. The respectable directors of the East India Company or similar enterprises, like the planners of empire, calculated economic and political interests and prohibited marriage of their "servants." Salaries paid to men for whom

Native women performed reproductive work could be lower than if European women did the work. Extremely unbalanced male-female ratios—underlying, for example, the construction of "Chinese debauchery"—were part of Europeans' economic calculations, governmental strategies, and migration practices.

From low wages sexually exploitative male-female relationships resulted. South Asian Kling migrant workers held a "share" in a woman. White Natal mine owners sold Indian women to workers. Railroad and plantation managers in Queensland, Natal, and South America refused to feed women for homemaking and sexual work. They allocated food to women only if they also worked in production, an arrangement that precluded the allocation of rations to women in childbirth. Sharing of persons was not limited to the non-Whites. Middle-class British-Canadians, who could not afford a full-time male domestic, held a "share" in a "Chinaman."[62]

Imperial strategists, the British Colonial Secretary in 1846, for example, discussed "difficulties in the moral order of things" as in the case of Indian contract labor, resulting from the "thin sprinkling of women, whom it has been found practicable to introduce with the large mass of males; the yet rarer occurrence of cases of immigration in families; [and] . . . the separation of men from every natural and domestic relation of life." The secretary's concern focused on duration of contracts and the contradiction between capitalists' labor demands and human nature—that is, male sexuality. Short contracts were too expensive, and overly long ones would prevent men from signing contracts. Men might leave wives or postpone marriage for a number of years, but it seemed unrealistic to assume that men would move for decades into forced celibacy. While male laborers were considered more tractable with women, a male-female 1:1 relationship undercut, it was thought, competitive production costs. Moralists of the empires, on the other hand, labeled sexual relations of other than 1:1 ratios and unstable relations as immoral. Euro-Christian morality clashed with the Euro-capitalist bottom lines of profit. The Colonial Office compromised and after 1853 insisted on "a minimum of one female for every three males" in shipments of Indian workers to Mauritius. After 1868, a female-male migrant ratio of 2:3 was imposed. When, in 1908, a Japanese consul sought to have Australia's rules governing the entry of wives relaxed, White observers admitted "the inhumanity of separating husband and wife." However, if wives were admitted, Asian children born in Australia would be British. They would later take "white wives" or "introduce wives of their own blood from abroad." Exclusion appeared as "a necessity for our very existence" as a race. It was not sex per se but the life-giving consequences that caused racial exclusion.

Of migrant women from India, one-third accompanied husbands; the others sought to escape social and economic oppression, were widowed, had been abandoned by husbands, or had left their partners. Most were societally constructed as promiscuous; many were forced into prostitution. Among Chinese labor and free migrants, wives might accompany merchants, and enslaved women were brought in for purposes of prostitution. Once workers settled, they might bring in wives at their own expense. Of course, women also came on their own.[63]

To "maximise profits," employers refused "the expense and responsibility of maintaining the unproductive units of small children and the elderly." Since only healthy and working-age men and women migrated, labor-supplying societies underwrote the costs of raising the young and feeding the old. Where labor migrants returned temporarily to recuperate from overwork, even the cost of maintaining them was passed back to families, communities, and societies of origin. This was the case for Potosí mineworkers. Coolies sent back from Malaya to India were called "sucked oranges." European workers returned from North America to their societies of origin during economic recessions.[64]

In urban contexts in which migrant men accounted for large parts of the population, "prostitution" might be a form of migrant domestic labor, as, for example, among clerics in Rome. One of the few studies written from women's perspectives analyzed immigrant prostitutes in Nairobi. Their work "replenishes—supports, feeds, idealizes, entertains, appreciates, reinforces, and relaxes, in some combination—men who work." Imperial men needed "home comforts," and so did workers. Migrant young Kikuyu women, for example, worked as self-employed laborers. The extent of interaction, whether limited to street contact or to homes, depended less on choice than on access to housing, a scarce resource in immigrant cities across the globe. Some forms of "prostitution" mimicked or copied married life on a *pro tempore* basis. Such homemaking was a direct result of wages and a new economic regime.[65]

Even if class position, wage level, or economic status permitted a one-to-one relationship of productive to reproductive labor, economic considerations remained part of marriage negotiations. Where women's work was considered less valuable than men's, brides, or their parents, had to pay their way into marriage by offering a dowry to the groom or his family. In societies in which women's work was valued more highly, as in Africa, men had to pay a bride-price to acquire a partner and worker. Dowries among common people also served to provide the young couple and their expected children with the basic furnishings of the household. To acquire household utensils, women migrated into wage labor before marriage, or men did so after marriage. Migrating men with sufficient income to support a full reproductive worker chose marriage, common law unions, or concubinage. Women in such unions acted as cultural brokers, providing men with opportunities to tie into social networks beyond male camaraderie. They tutored men in overcoming Otherness, taught them the language of the receiving culture, and provided access to the social capital of their family of birth. Partnership involved an increase of social and human capital.

Imperial missionaries' insistence on monogamous marriage overlooked the multiple interests involved in consorting. European-style monogamy was an economic arrangement to pass titles, offices, and property down a particular line: it was inheritance-oriented. Among Spanish-Americans, widows inherited, but custom demanded that they remarry, whether they liked it or not. African relational arrangements meant that a woman whose husband/partner had died would live with a kinsman for protective and subsistence reasons. In some agricultural and trading economies, polygamy was an economically rational arrangement. With few exceptions, men held the power. But Mulatto women in some Caribbean societies and trading women in Senegal could negotiate relative independence from their European-origin male partners.

16.5   Global Perspectives: Subaltern Cultures and Racialized Diasporas

Issues of control over laboring classes were paramount in the cores and the colonies. The powerful of Europe and the United States defined the internal underclasses as "fellows without fatherland" (Germany), as people "superfluous at home" (Britain), or as "three-fifths" disenfranchised slaves (the United States). Below the diasporas of imperial administrators ranked non-national communities like the Overseas Chinese or the Jewish diaspora. At the bottom were the peasant populations who migrated on their own or were mobilized. Laboring diasporas of many ethnicities and skin colors consisted of former peasants, rural laborers, urban unskilled workers, and displaced artisanal and skilled workers. From the 1820s to the 1930s, more than one-half of the European populations moved internally. Untold millions moved within Africa; a large share in South America; 50–55 million in the Atlantic World; some 30 million or more in the Asian World; and more than two million from Africa to the Americas.

The slave migrations bound the continents of the Atlantic World together; migrations of contract laborers connected the continents of the Pacific World; labor migrations that were free within economic constraints linked Europe and the Americas as well as South Asia and East Africa. Institutionalized ties bound masters to slaves, imperial administrators and plantation owners to contract laborers, and industrialists to wage labor forces of many ethnicities. The powerful moved for the sake of power, profit, and control over labor forces, independent small people moved to acquire "virgin, rich land; the powerless as near-slaves, . . . and power, more often than not, has a racial basis."[66] Before the age of bourgeois revolution had made nations out of Europe's heterogeneous populations, they had spawned diasporas across the globe. Migrant men and women reached the diasporas with local or regional identities, such as Welsh or Hokkien. They were nationalized or continentalized into Britons or Asians by post-migration labeling.

To observers in receiving societies, newcomers looked alike and were reclassified into large groups. Peoples from many parts of Africa were seen as "slaves," with the Ibo or Masai generically designated as "Africans"; men and women from cultures of Asia became "coolie laborers" or "opium-addicted merchants"; Tamils and Gujarati were labeled "Indians." Migrants from diverse regional ways of life and from two distinct economic systems along the length of the Apennines became "Italians." Territorial and political-unit ascriptions or labor-regime classifications were superimposed on widely differing ethnocultural identities at all social levels. Plantation society in Java consisted of planters, overseers, and bound laborers. The planters were typically considered Dutch—but at one location on the eastern coast of Java in 1884 there were 390 Dutchmen, 123 Prussians, Bavarians, and men from other German principalities, eighty-eight Britons, forty Swiss, twelve Frenchmen, eleven Austrians, and twenty-four men from seven other nationalities. Clerks and overseers included Overseas Chinese, Euro-Chinese, and *Sinjos* (of mixed origin). The workers included Chinese who were Hailokhong, Keh, or from Macao; Indians who were Klings and Bengalese; Siamese, Tamils, and Malays from the multiethnic Straits Settlements; Bataks from Sumatra and Malayan Gajoes, Alas, and Mandailingers; Beweanese and Bandjeranasin from other islands—in addition to local peoples. Colonial societies were multicultural and hierarchical.

Communication up and down hierarchies was hampered by arrogance, stratification, and speechlessness. Planters were genteel, clerks just inferior personnel, and coolies "beasts." Those in power lacked knowledge of local languages. In Java, for example, the colonizer elite used broken Malay and accused coolies of stupidity when they misunderstood garbled orders. When a Dutch district officer suggested that communication skills be improved, he was told that planters did not talk to their horses but used whips or spurs, as they did and intended to do with "their" coolies. The power of defining who was superior helped the colonizers to stay on top of their coolies.[67]

New Laborers and Racialized Diasporas

Migrant mass workers often numbered several thousand on a single plantation or in a single factory. A Peruvian coastal plantation used 2,000 workers; a German machinery and armaments factory grew from seventy-two workers in 1848 to 12,000 twenty-five years later. These "new laborers" (Eric Wolf) of the nineteenth-century capitalist mode of production had to move over ever larger distances to ever larger concentrations and could often be replaced easily with cheaper or more docile labor. According to Breman, "the extremely active official interference in the subjugation of labour" was a major characteristic "of the peripheral capitalism." The state apparatus enforced the obligations of workers and supported breaches of contract by employers. In many colonies, planters staffed the "courts"; in others, they were the state.[68]

The class dichotomy interacted with internalized color bars: "White" workers shared racist attitudes. The gatekeepers and labor union leaders were male, and thus gender also undercut class. Within Europe, peoples from the periphery were racialized: a British man commented on "the danger to the Empire arising from the indiscriminate immigration into Canada of Russians and Galician Jews, Greeks, Germans, Dutch, Poles, Hungarians, Italians, and even Syrians and Turks, and other people." He contrasted these "hordes" with the English.[69]

Migrant workers formed communities and coalesced in diasporas, which were characterized by continued contact and interaction of the different segments with each other and with the society of origin. Men and women moved between segments; families were spread over continents. Diasporas were divided by ethnicity and color but overlapped in space. In many regions of the world, including industrialized North America, laboring people from Europe, Latin America, Africa, and Asia— White, Brown, Black, Yellow—faced each other and competed for jobs unless divided into separate labor market segments. Because of internalized color hierarchies, racialized interdiasporic conflict occurred in contested spaces. The European-origin laboring diasporas spread to South Africa and Australia but remained small outside the Atlantic World. In the British Empire, they too had to contend with notions of superiority. French-Canadians moving to textile mills in New England were considered by Massachusetts officials "sordid and low," "the Chinese of the Eastern States." Italians were called "the Chinese of Europe." Racial boundaries were fluid and were reconstructed depending on who defined culture and who was needed as a worker.[70]

Diasporas were internally hierarchical. Foremen and labor recruiters from among colonial peoples aligned themselves with colonizers. Chinese labor bosses deprived Chinese workers of self-determination. Indian colonial auxiliaries did the same with many peoples. Africans, Malays, Burmese, or Trinidadians "saw the Indian as the man in authority" or confronted "an Indian tally-clerk weighing their produce." The European manager "who was really controlling their affairs" remained hidden. At the same time, Indian migrants were also despised as "pariahs," performed "the most menial jobs" to keep cities clean, and "sweated in the docks and on the plantations" doing work the Native "sons of the soil were too proud to do themselves." Indian migrants could thus belong to a working-class, an imperial British, or an inserted middle-class diaspora.[71]

Where White immigrants of means held the power, as in Australia, they manipulated hierarchies of White laborers: permanently employed, long-term indentured, and itinerant contract workers. For a few decades, they admitted Chinese contract laborers without women and had some 3,000 Pacific Islanders kidnapped from 1883 to 1885. All were inserted into "the rigorous caste-structure operating on the large estates." Planters "strove to establish an aristocratic society with themselves at the apex"; the political classes wanted a "wealthy coterie of British aristocrats and members of the bourgeoisie to rule over vast armies of non-European indentured servants who were without any political and civil rights." On the estates, "the various ethnic groups . . . would be designated specific occupational tasks and were also housed separately." As a consequence, "inter-tribal and inter-ethnic hostility was a daily occurrence."[72]

In North America, race riots pitted White and Black against each other in competition for social space, and Latino "greasers" were beaten up. The segregation of diasporas by color and ethnic culture did not preclude cooperation in particular organizations and locations or on shop floors. The cultural dialectics were not fully controlled either by racism or by economic discrimination. Color labeling, however, achieved significance beyond particular societies. The mission "to acquaint the colored workers with the responsibility of employment" was also considered necessary in the cores—in Detroit automobile factories of the 1920s, for example.

Patterns of labor-force composition depended on decisions by employers and migrants. Assam tea plantation owners experimented with Chinese workers; Ceylonese planters discussed the importation of African slaves; and French rubber plantation managers in Indochina initially made use of Javanese coolies. In Hawai'i, after the

Chinese had been excluded, planters worried in 1900 that the "Japs" were "getting too numerous." Thus Puerto Ricans, Italians, Portuguese, and "Negroes from the South [of the United States]" were to be introduced. "We would ask you to let us know at your earliest convenience how many laborers of each nationality you need," one supplier asked a planter. Capitalists used any form of (state-supported) control, but hardly ever inducements, to increase labor forces. From employers' points of view, permission to cultivate small plots of land—granted, for example, to migrants on Assam's tea plantations—resulted in family migration and thus augmented labor forces. Sumatra planters planned land shortages. "[If] the number of settlers increases as a result of having many children, gradually the land granted them will be inadequate to provide their subsistence. In other words, if a kind of over-population and poverty develops, then the surplus will have to seek work on the estates and thus the desideratum will be achieved—a local labour pool." To make labor markets operational in their own interests, employers used the state to deprive people of the resources needed to live or to migrate according to their own strategies. Capitalist market forces still did not mobilize labor; force did.[73]

Proletarian Mass Migrations and Labor Militancies

It was left to workingmen and workingwomen to devise strategies of resistance in order to prevent damage to their identities. Out of assigned roles and existing power hierarchies, gendered strategies of survival, identity-formation, and cultural self-assertion emerged. In this context, employers established relations with laborers that have been viewed as nearly totalitarian, and transitions from independent lives involved a phase of social negation, out of which a desocialized, depersonalized male or female laborer emerged, who was introduced into the community of the master as a nonbeing. Slaves had no existence outside the realm of their master, and the concepts of "coolie," "alienated wage worker," or "wage-slave" have been taken to imply a similar condition of total dependency. Such approaches to the identities of workers, while justly emphasizing aspects of power and imposition, neglect the self-agency that permitted survival, the reestablishment of cultures and communities, and militancy.

The first step toward reassertion of a self-determined identity was cooperation and community-building with other labor migrants of the same or similar cultural customs or at least of similar work experience. Mutual help reduced dependence on owners, masters, or employers. Such self-reconstruction did not establish replicas of an Old World, such as the Russian Empire, colonized Ireland, the African warrior kingdoms, or Indian caste society. Migrants acted within the constraints imposed by receiving societies and economic dependency; they acted outside the restrictions of their culture of origin.

Migrant laboring families often lived between independent agriculture and wage labor, with some of the members, usually the men, absent for long periods of time. Unless living in big cities, migrants engaged in part-time agriculture to improve their diets and supplement their incomes at their destinations. This strategy permitted high levels of labor militancy because the newcomers were not solely dependent on wages. Migrants in North American mining towns kept pigs and grew vegetables, and those in the German Ruhr District raised goats; freed Afro-Cubans moved to small but independent plots of land. Free workers could attempt to organize on a craft or industrial basis, legal restrictions notwithstanding.

Self-organization, cross-cultural cooperation, and militancy suffered from internal divisions. In the Americas, slaves who escaped early on hunted those who escaped more recently; on Java, young Batak men hunted escaped coolies. Skilled workers excluded unskilled immigrant workers, and men excluded women from craft unions. Employers encouraged segmentation by culture and intentionally mixed migrants of different practices and different legal status to prevent united fronts of workers from emerging. States supported capital—in Transvaal, for example, "by restoring industry's power to determine wages at a level insufficient to maintain a worker and his dependants." Africans were kept dependent "on concurrent wage labor and subsistence agricultural production," and Chinese workers were brought in and expelled a few years later. National or international working-class solidarity did not often develop.[74]

Within the European diaspora, the socialist internationals attempted to bridge national differences. Two alternative reactions in the cores were the internal increase in purchasing power and consumption (a consequence of Fordism, that is, mass production and automation) in the United States and "social imperialism" (H.-U. Wehler) in Germany. Out of a fear of social revolution, the state-industrial complex and its supporting classes used imperialist expansion "to regain economic prosperity, and in doing so to maintain the social and political status quo and to block the process of emancipation." Imperialism thus involved class and control in the cores as much as in the colonies.[75]

Labor regimes, the institutional relationships that govern labor relations, include instruments of repression, legal protection for unionization, the informal cultures of workingmen and workingwomen, and the hegemonic cultures of employers. Plantation owners used the state for their purposes, but Indian contract laborers' complaints were sufficiently strong to induce "the Empire," personified by its administrators in India, to appoint "protectors of emigrants." Labor militancy in its simplest form amounted to running away from bondage or to a free job. Maroon communities in the Americas, Chinese escapees in Transvaal, and the high turnover rates among free workers in the Atlantic economies testify to unsatisfactory labor arrangements and to self-directed goal-achievement strategies among migrants. The next level of militancy was spontaneous day-to-day resistance or major strikes, such as the strikes of immigrant workers in North America, Hawai'i, and Malaysia and on plantations or in industries elsewhere. Interethnic support did emerge from shared working conditions. Multiethnic and multiracial militancy developed in particular workplaces and locations rather than internationally. The third level, long-lasting organization, could institutionalize internal working-class discrimination, if it was achieved by a culturally hegemonic group to the disadvantage of the everyday and shop-floor culture of ethnicized or racialized immigrant Others. At the turn of the twentieth century, labor organizations had achieved at least partial legitimacy in the middle-class states of Europe and North America. They were struggling for influence in the Russian Empire. In the colonial world, they were still weak or nonexistent.

In the United States, a nationwide strike of railroad workers in 1877 resulted in countermeasures by the state. In Supreme Court cases about the security of "private" property, corporation lawyers pointed to the dangers of a working-class democracy, "the march of the sixty million." Workers practiced self-government, as in the Homestead, Pennsylvania, strike of 1892: Slovak workers referred to the principles of the Revolution of 1848 in Europe. In the "Uprising of the 20,000" women, New York City's immigrant Jewish and Italian shirtwaist makers in 1909 voted to strike: Jewish workers fused traditional religious practices with militancy in the new industrial order; Sicilian emigrant workers cooperated with emigrant radicals. One union, the Industrial Workers of the World, almost reified mobility in the image of the hobo, the foot-loose rebel against the capitalist order. Christ, the wanderer and rebel, served as one of their persons of reference. After the Russian Revolution, the U.S. government destroyed labor organizations during the "Red Scare," or what more aptly could be called the "White Fear."[76]

In Hawai'i, Asian immigrant workers, together with Portuguese and some Norwegian workers as well as with Mexican migrants, faced a highly repressive labor regime. Though treatment was equally bad for all, cross-cultural solidarity did not emerge before 1920. Resistance at first implied nothing but escape from plantations, resort to identity-numbing drugs (opium or alcohol), or violence against particularly brutal foremen, often of the same ethnicity. One Chinese man, who had been whipped merely because the foreman could not distinguish him from the intended victim, "wanted revenge even to the point of suicide." Identity-affirmation endangered physical survival. Norwegian laborers who "deserted" their contracts were punished as harshly for trying to regain control over their bodies and lives as were Chinese or Japanese laborers. Policemen with revolvers and whips drove them to court like "mules." When women resisted, husbands were fined for the loss of their wives' labor. In 1909, Japanese workers, often families with children, struck for better wages and tried to join "the body politique of Hawaii." They were evicted from their living quarters, arrested, and replaced by migrant workers of other ethnicities. One planter posed the issue squarely, "They'll make intelligent citizens all right enough, but not plantation laborers—and that's what we want." But during an interethnic six-month-long strike of 1920, working families were more successful, and employers could not break their solidarity. The strikers' union became interracial, placing class over ethnicity. The powerful, casting their interests in terms of nation and state, labeled strikers "anti-American . . . alien agitators."[77]

In Malaya, labor militancy began later. British capital used coolies strictly controlled by Chinese contractors as "an inexpensive form of labor control" and compatible with the "racial difference between European and Chinese—Europeans were ignorant of Chinese languages and customs and wished to remain so." Bondage was

increased through drug and opium sales by contractors. On British rubber plantations, workers were whipped to work at the speed required. The labor regime changed
only in the 1930s, when wage incentives replaced the whip, and a struggle over just
wages began. Long-term residence had provided labor migrants with knowledge of
the region and community support. Increasing numbers were literate and educated.
Access to reading material did not come through local middle or upper classes but
from China through the "Proletarian Literature Movement." Malayan-born Chinese
laborers were mobile, and changes in production required skills and autonomy. After
1930 Chinese women were permitted to immigrate without restriction. Gardening
and truck agriculture added to wage incomes and family independence. Common
trade unions developed regardless of regional origin. From 1936 to 1941, militancy
expressed in numerous strikes referred to a "golden past," a historical construction
of more just relationships. At the same time a proletarian culture emerged and supported a communist movement.[78]

Across the globe, the social space inhabited by workers and employers was contested terrain. It was divided by ascription of ethnic or racial "characters" and positioning according to skin color and gender. It was policed by agents of the respective
state paid for by public funds in the interests of some segments of the public.[79] Polities, whether nations or empires, were contested terrain, too. Gatekeepers from hegemonic cultural groups admitted immigrants from selected cultural backgrounds only
to wagework or citizenship. Political economies, on the other hand, needed labor migrants regardless of color or culture as long as they could be controlled. One British
settler in Kenya unequivocally stated that the "white man" was "the master race
and . . . the black men must forever remain cheap labor and slaves."[80] In the dialectics of capital and labor, the power relationships were unequal, but laborers were
not powerless. The citizens of Kenya did gain independence in 1963, but in the 1990s
they were living and laboring in gender hierarchies under unequal terms of trade and
global apartheid.

IV

Twentieth-Century Changes

After the global free and bound "proletarian mass migrations" of the nineteenth century declined, the twentieth century became the "century of refugees." In the interwar years, the Atlantic Migration System stagnated; it dissolved in the 1950s. The Russo-Siberian Migration System lasted into the 1920s, was then warped into forced migration, and also ended in the 1950s. The 1920s and 1930s still witnessed large settlement migrations, especially of Chinese to Manchuria. From the 1930s to the 1950s, first agrarian and then state-building migration of Jewish peoples converged on Palestine/Israel and created Muslim refugees.

The British Empire–imposed Indian contract labor system ended in 1917, but labor migrations in the Asian Migration System accelerated through the 1930s. Japan's victory over Russia in 1905, considered a victory of the "Yellow" over the "White" race in the language of the time, was part of an aggressive expansion that changed the parameters of migration in Asia. The Third German Reich's attempt to establish imperial domination over Eastern European peoples dislocated millions into slave labor. Ethnic un-mixing resulted in transfers of millions of people against their will.

The imperialist reorganization of the world from Great Britain's Opium War against China, the U.S. war against Mexico, and the failure of the European democratic revolutions in the 1840s ended in decolonization in the 1950s. Reverse migrations of administrators, settlers, and colonial auxiliaries initiated a process by which Europe became multicolored. In North America and Australia, the end of the exclusion of non-White immigrants resulted in new Pacific and Latin American migration patterns. As these new migration patterns developed, the charter of the United Nations mandated nondiscrimination.

The military-statist imperial reach of the northern hemisphere was replaced by domination strategies of transnational capital. Income gaps and differences in life-course options between the industrialized and the developing worlds induced migrations to the northern hemisphere, but disparities among peripheral state economies resulted in much larger interregional migrations in the newly independent worlds.

Migration projects of peoples of many colors made multiculturalism a practice of everyday life, whether it was recognized by political institutions or not.

Globalization at the turn of the twenty-first century is simply an adaptation of nineteenth-century patterns of investment and labor migration. Only the speed of communication and travel is new. Around 1900, self-directed information feedback among migrants slowed down or accelerated departures with a time lag of about one year. At the start of the twenty-first century, instant communication flows and plane travel permit migration decisions to be made, changed, or readjusted on short notice. With regard to the division of labor and wealth, the late-nineteenth-century variant of racism has become a global apartheid.

17

Forced Labor and Refugees in the

Northern Hemisphere to the 1950s

Under the influence of natural rights philosophy, the revolutionary principles of popular self-determination, and a new awareness of regional cultures, peoples incorporated into empires with a hegemonic ruling culture sought political self-determination throughout the delayed nineteenth century from 1815 to 1914. The involuntary migrations connected to the demise, first, of the Ottoman realm and, then, of the Habsburg, Hohenzollern, and Romanov empires involved the dislocation and resettlement of some 60–70 million men, women, and children.

After 1918, the newly independent state-nations became the destination of migrations of coethnics who remained outside their often artificial borders. They expelled people of different lifeways. This un-mixing of peoples was sometimes called ethnic cleansing, as if interspersed living were unclean. According to Marrus,

> The growth of the modern nation-state implied not only the naming of certain peoples as enemies of the nation, but also the expulsion of significant groups for whom the state would or could not assume responsibility. With the First World War, the process accelerated powerfully. The war itself schooled the new masters of the state apparatus: civilians could become dangerous enemies; fighting could not stop simply because they were there; on the contrary, it was best to eject unwanted or menacing groups when they threatened to weaken the beleaguered nation.[1]

To bolster national-imperial economies, the forced migration of slave workers became part of Soviet, German, and Japanese state policies. Governments of the democratic states or empires tightened labor regimes.

The two major wars of 1914–18 and 1937–45, begun by military and ideological elites who considered their national race superior, caused some 80 million deaths, and forced women, men, and children to flee before advancing armies. Others, of allegedly inferior nations, were deported or imprisoned in forced labor camps, were exterminated in camps, or murdered locally. After the wars, population shifts dislocated millions to make room for ethnic Others considered either more fitting by governmental population and culture planners or easier to exploit by industry and state economists. The demise of the French and British colonial empires by the late 1950s and the defeat of Japan's late-nineteenth-century imperial expansion, combined with the U.S. penetration into the Colonial Worlds, shifted the struggles for self-rule to the southern hemisphere, where the subsequent formation of state-nations also involved mass expulsions (chap. 19).

17.1 Power Struggles and the Un-Mixing of Peoples

Nineteenth-century republicanism coincided with calls for national unification among Poles, Italians, and Germans. Processes to create nation-states out of empires implied cultural self-assertion on the positive side and cultural-economic oppression on the negative side. The dialectics of liberation and repression in Europe involved, first, the flight of democrats or republicans whenever imperial power structures remained victorious (chaps. 12.5, 13.5). Second, politics and class interacted when "nations" excluded the lower classes from active political participation. The men and women of proletarian mass migrations between 1848 and 1914 selected as their destination the North American states because in addition to jobs they offered more liberties. Working-class struggles continued in the German workers' councils (1918), the strikes in the Atlantic World after 1919, the Kronstadt rebellion (1921), and the Spanish Civil War (1930s). After 1917–18, men and women disenchanted with capitalist rule in Western Europe and North America, and ready to participate in building a workers' republic, migrated to the Soviet Union.[2] Third, women pursued migration strategies to better their position. The state-nations deprived them of political rights as well as of independent ethnocultural status. When a woman married a foreign man, her ethno-national status changed to that of the husband. Nations were male and provided security for (middle-class) property.[3]

Fourth, the attempts to carve out culturally and ethno-racially homogeneous state-nations involved the expulsion of whole groups of "Others" in territories with ethnic checkerboard patterns of settlement.[4] Mixed settlements were common to all borderlands: the Romance language/German mixed areas from Belgium to Alsace, East Central Europe from the Baltic regions via the Polish-Lithuanian-Russian-German areas to the Polish-Ukrainian-Russian territories, and the region extending from the Balkans to Anatolia and the Caucasus. Ten centuries of migrations into and out of these territories had left mosaics of interspersed groups. State-nations, which homogenized populations into the hegemonic group's culture, pursued inclusion as well as exclusion strategies toward internal "minorities" and external coethnics. Governments claimed territories of other states under the pretense that co-nationals lived there—but it was not incidental that such territories often also held valuable mineral resources. The wars of expansion and national unification of the kingdom of Prussia[5] against Austria, Denmark, and France (1860s–71) sent Czechs fleeing, led to the expulsion of 80,000 Germans from France in 1870, and the departure of 130,000 for France when the new German Empire annexed industrial Alsace-Lorraine in 1871. Prussia expelled "foreign" Poles in 1885. Silesia, a coal-mining and industrial region of major strategic importance, was claimed by Habsburg Austria, Hohenzollern Prussia, and, in 1918, by Poland. To Silesians, "nationality" was not a concept. They considered themselves German and spoke a Polish dialect that other Polish-speakers found difficult to understand.[6] The Russification policies in the Romanov Empire sent Jews, Mennonites, and Lutheran and Catholic Germans into westbound migrations (chaps. 13.5–6, 14.1). The definition of groups as minorities and their placement in positions of lesser rights and access to resources forced many individuals and families to consider emigration as an alternative.

The mass migrations of peoples deprived of equality of culture or of political participation by hegemonic administrations caused apprehensions in receiving states wary of ethnic Others and proletarians. The German Reich temporarily closed its borders to transit migrants from the east in 1892, and the United States increased health inspection systems—Eastern European migrants were labeled germ-laden and unclean. Western European Jews helped Eastern European transients out of genuine concern but also to rid themselves of the "backward" Others and to protect their own acculturated status from potentially anti-Semitic reactions. In Britain, which had hosted middle-class intellectual exiles for a long time, the Alien Act of 1905 excluded proletarian masses, often of Jewish religion. An observer commented that refugees found that "ordinary rights" were "withdrawn" from them, that they were being "denationalized" and deprived of their "documents of travel," and that they had to fend for themselves without protection of either the home state or the receiving one. Thus the League of Nations' high commissioner for refugees, Fridtjof Nansen, invented the "Nansen passport" as a non-national travel document, which was approved by international agreement in 1922.[7]

The compact-theory of peoples forming governments had gotten lost along the way. By 1914, a century and a quarter after popular sovereignty had been proclaimed in the French Revolution, the four European empires—Hohenzollern, Habsburg, Romanov, and Ottoman—still denied self-government to the smaller peoples within their territories; governments and gatekeepers of state-nations made and remade peoples. Peoples were shipped to and from "historic" territories, and, as a result of capitalist strategies, unfree mass laborers were shipped to factories. In artistic visions, masses of people were choreographed to move in films like Fritz Lang's *Metropolis*.

The End of Ethnic Coexistence in Ottoman Turkey

In the Ottoman Empire, ethnically, culturally, or religiously defined groups lived in separate social slots (*millet* and *malhalle*) and did not usually intermingle, intermarry, or acculturate. They did interact in the marketplace. Nonethnic administrative elites had once been recruited from many peoples and used a nonethnic language (chap. 5.1). Since the eighteenth century Russia had pushed into the Ottoman realm, and perhaps 1–2 million multiethnic Muslims had fled or migrated from these territories between the 1780s and the 1890s. Circassians and Chechens were resettled to Palestine to protect the military frontier against Bedouin nomads.

In the nineteenth century, when the Ottoman Empire's reach still extended from the Balkans through Palestine, Egypt, and Arabia to Persia, the European powers constructed it as "the weak man of Europe" to pursue their own territorial designs. In the Balkans, the Greeks achieved self-rule in 1832; during the following eight decades, up to 1914, British, French, and Austro-Hungarian intervention, growing Turkish nationalism, and the liberation struggles of many peoples in the empire destroyed traditions of coexistence. Refugees from the island of Chios established themselves in London; Bulgarian rebels and revolutionaries fled into Moldavia and Wallachia; Christian peasants from Bosnia and Herzegovina migrated into Austria or semi-independent Serbia; some 370,000 Christian Macedonians moved into Bulgaria after 1878; the Ottoman retreat in the 1870s left the Balkans' Muslim peasants without protection, and some 177,000 fled or were moved to Anatolia. Refugees of one creed or ethnicity who arrived in mixed settlements vented their bitterness on the respective weaker Others. The multiethnic and multireligious population of Istanbul doubled from the influx of Muslim refugees. In the war of 1912–14 "fighting was as desperate as though extermination were the end sought," said a report of the Carnegie Endowment, and several conventions provided for population exchanges between state-nations. While elites' concepts of a national "home state" frequently did not coincide with the experiences of common people, ethnic strife forced many to consider distant core regions of coethnics their only safe place of residence.[8]

After 1900 the "Young Turk" movement, similar to the national "Young" movements of 1830s Western Europe, called for a national state and repudiated the concept of institutionally graded, protected status for all peoples and cultures. In the new Turkish state, the "National Pact" of September 1919 affirmed the rights of minorities, but two peoples, Armenians and Kurds, were denied independent statehood. Masses of homeless people fled from the genocide committed against Armenians and also emerged from the Greek-Turkish and continued Turkish-Bulgarian population exchanges. A fourth movement, Jewish immigration into Palestine, assumed sizable proportions only in the 1920s (chap. 18.2).

Armenians, divided into settled peasant people and a trading diaspora, had enjoyed cultural autonomy in the Ottoman Empire as a designated "loyal" Christian people under their own patriarch (chap. 7.2). After the defeat of Ottoman forces by the Russian army in 1877–78, they lived on both sides of the border. American Protestant missionaries proselytized among them and established educational, social, and health care services. While the Armenian urban elites sought progress from these missions and protection from Christian states, the Turkish administration feared demands for autonomy; Turkish nationalists massacred some 30,000 Armenians in 1909. An Armenian rebellion provided a brief respite and opportunities for emigration, but in 1915 the Turkish government resumed deportations to Syria and Mesopotamia. Of perhaps 600,000 Armenians sent, some 90,000 survived. In 1918, the new Armenian republic in the Soviet Union was overrun by about half a million refugees, and within a year an estimated 10 percent of the state's population died of starvation and epidemics. By the late 1920s, some 225,000 Armenians lived in diasporic dispersal in several states of the region, in most Western European states, especially in France, and in North America (map 7.5).[9]

The population exchange between Greece and Turkey, legitimized by the Treaty of Lausanne of July 1923, "repatriated" 1.25 million Greeks from Turkey, who received little help from the impoverished state but as skilled artisans and farmers provided economic potential. The 400,000 Turks moved to Turkey were to be augmented to one million by a further "repatriation" plan of 1938, which, however, was not implemented. A Turko-Bulgarian Agreement of 1925 provided for the voluntary emigration of Turks from Bulgaria and Bulgarians from Turkey. In the mid-1930s, 620,000 Turkish-origin citizens were counted in compact settlements in Bulgaria's northeastern territories; another 65,000 resided in southern Dobrudja, which was ceded by Romania in 1940. From 1928 to 1939, 125,000 Turks left Bulgaria for Turkey; between 1950 and 1953, another 250,000 departed; and between 1968 and 1976, an additional 50,000 went to Turkey. Mass emigration resumed in 1989.[10]

In 1934, the Turkish minister of the interior estimated that two million Turks still lived in neighboring states; they were, in his words, descendants of those "who directly participated in the Turkish conquests of the last centuries, who installed themselves in the conquered regions and lived there for centuries as masters." While under multiethnic Ottomanism other ethnicities had participated in the conquests, the construction of the achievements as Turkish suited nationalist elites—viewed from the outside such "achievements" were related to or constructed as oppression. All of the transfers to "un-mix" peoples sprang from projects of the new nationalist governments and their population planners, who viewed ethnocultural and ethnoreligious lifestyles as badges of political allegiance. Those shunted about were descendants of generations of immigrant settlers for whom repatriation (return to the fatherland) meant dislocation to an alien social environment.[11]

Another former Ottoman territory, Palestine, was administered by the British government under a League of Nations' mandate. The Balfour Declaration of November 1917 promised establishment "of a national home for the Jewish people" without infringing on "the civil and religious rights of existing non-Jewish communities." Druse, Christian Assyrian, and Jewish migrations and the competition for resources and self-government among all groups of the region made the multicultured eastern Mediterranean conflict-prone (chap. 18.2).[12] In North Africa the realignment of Arab states in the former Ottoman realm did not involve major population movements. On the Arabian Peninsula, Wahabi forces, a puritanical Muslim sect, formed Saudi Arabia in 1926. In Egypt, declared a protectorate in 1914, the British deported members of its nationalist elites to Malta to prevent them from attending the Versailles Peace Conference in 1919. Pronationalist sentiment had been fanned by the British wartime requisitions of forced laborers. In many Arab states, anti-Semitism became a cause of Arab nationalists in the process of boundary construction and the struggle for "national" self-determination.

From the Caspian Sea to Persia, the British attempted to regain influence in order to safeguard oil interests. Ethnic struggles and anti-Bolshevik policies interacted. The

British, using a "Persian Cossack Brigade" forced the Turks out of Soviet Baku. In Persia (after 1935, Iran) Reza Khan, also relying on Cossacks, engineered a coup in 1921. British engineers and locally mobilized labor completed the Trans-Iranian Railway from the Caspian Sea to the Persian Gulf in 1939.

The new South Slav or Yugoslav state combined Serbs, Montenegrins, Croats, Slovenes, and Dalmatians. In a division established twelve centuries earlier by the Latin and Byzantine Churches, the Orthodox Serbs used Cyrillic script and the Roman Catholic Croats Latin script for the same language. In Romania, Jews, emancipated in 1919, faced anti-Semitism and violence. When Muslims of southern Albania rebelled (1937), ostensibly against a government decree forbidding the veiling of women but in fact expressing a deep-seated discontent, the Italian fascist government intervened and occupied the country.

The core of the former Ottoman Empire became the Turkish nation-state, with numerous minorities. These processes turned some 8.5 million people into refugees. Cultural modernization policies introduced the Latin script and purged the intercultural Turkish language of Arab and Persian words. German refugees from Nazism became village teachers in 1930s Turkey. The Westernization of Turkey would permit Turkish men and women to migrate to jobs in Western Europe in the 1960s. The refusal of cultural and political independence forced Kurds to take the same routes as guest workers or as refugees and forced Armenians to remain divided into a diaspora, now centered in North America, and a resident population in their successor state within the Soviet Union.

War and Expulsion: Central and Eastern Europe

The first twentieth-century European civil war—in Euro-American-centered terminology a "world war"—did not "break out" in 1914 like a volcanic eruption; it was, instead, a calculated strategy. Some 60 million men were mobilized and marched about; women had to take their jobs, or, alternatively, labor markets within a country had to be internationalized by preventing foreign workers from leaving or by recruiting additional ones, often under pressure. In France, for example, the labor force was made up of some 230,000 Spaniards and 135,000 North Africans, Vietnamese, and Chinese, as well as workers from neighboring Belgium or distant Madagascar. After 1917, non-European war zones and powers involved the colonies of the belligerents and the United States. The British mobilized 1.2 million non-European soldiers, mainly in India; the French drafted 0.6 million, mainly in North and West Africa. The German Reich, which had imported a predominantly male corps of workers from Eastern Europe, included among its war aims acquiring control over this reservoir of labor.[13]

When war began in August 1914, around five million Europeans did not live in their state of birth. Overnight, the status of many changed from guest, labor migrant, or immigrant to "hostile alien" or "citizen of an enemy nation." Somewhat less than 10 percent of them were interned at one time or other; others were expelled or repatriated. As evidenced by the anti-German riots in Great Britain, the internment of citizens of neutral states in France as well as the denaturalization of French citizens born in enemy states, and the internment of citizens of the Allies in Germany, nationalist xenophobia was exacerbated by wartime hysteria among military and civilian administrators.[14]

During the war, the civilian populations of, initially, Belgium and then of Poland, the Baltic provinces, and western Russia, as well as those in southeastern Europe, were cast into a nightmare of dislocation, starvation, and death. Armies and displaced civilians preyed on people who were desperately struggling to survive. Within three months after the German attack, one-fifth of the Belgian population of around seven million were refugees in the Netherlands, France, and Great Britain. Of Serbia's population of three million, one-third were refugees, one-tenth in the army, and another tenth in camps in Hungary and Bulgaria, often as forced laborers. Typhus killed 150,000. Several hundred thousand trekked to the Adriatic coast and spread across the Mediterranean islands and Allied countries.

First, men, women, and children all over Europe fled singly or in families the lines of fire or the reach of distant artillery. Second, military administrators and civilian authorities expelled groups whose loyalty they questioned: such as Poles from Germany and Jews with their Yiddish-German dialect and the descendants of German immigrants from Russia. Third, to slow down the advance of German armies, retreating Russian forces pursued a policy of destruction, and by December 1915 Russia counted 2.7 million refugees. Half a year later, the number amounted to five million. Fourth, with the armistice, deserted, wounded, sick Russian soldiers returned, and demobilization sent hundreds of thousands of additional men in search of their families or of shelter. Fifth, by the beginning of the 1920s, some 1.5 million children who had lost their parents by separation or death were said to be wandering about, starving, cold, and close to death. The "American Committee for Relief in the Near East" took charge of 75,000 orphaned or abandoned children in the Armenian territories alone. Sixth, people drafted into the Russian war industries were let go or escaped; those deported from German-occupied territories to forced labor had to find their way back. Seventh, the Russian Revolution of October 1917 sent a stream of political exiles, refugee aristocrats, and bourgeois entrepreneurs into the Axis-occupied regions—Finland and the Baltic countries, for example—and then further to the west (chap. 13.6). Lastly, at the end of the fighting, prisoners of war had to be repatriated: for example, two million Germans from the Allies, forced laborers from the Reich, and Russian prisoners from Austria and Germany.

After the war, the newly independent Baltic and Polish states became the destination of returning prewar emigrants, of peoples displaced by warfare, and of co-nationals from outside the new borderlines. Poland, divided for a century and a half between Russia, Prussia, and Austria, had been devastated by armies from all of the belligerents. In a separate war, in 1920, it fought for an eastern and southeastern extension of its territories. Displaced civilians and demobilized soldiers returned to villages that no longer existed. According to government figures, 1.25 million refugees had returned by 1920; another 700,000 had been resettled by 1923; and a further 300,000 were expected. Within its new borders, Hungary received Magyar ethnics from Romania (140,000), from Czechoslovakia (57,000), and from Yugoslavia (37,000), while it expelled Hungarian-Germans. The new borders, mandated by the peace treaties, forced approximately five million Europeans to change residence between states (map 17.1).

The civil war in the Soviet Union (1918–21), involving royalist-liberal-Bolshevik struggles as well as Ukrainian and other national liberation movements, forced defeated troops and politicians with their families to flee northward to Finland and the Baltic states, southward to Istanbul, Syria, and Palestine, and westward (to France, in particular). Wherever the refugees were deposited, some stayed, acculturated, and intermarried, and others died without children. In East Asia, the Chinese cities of, first, Harbin and, later, Shanghai became centers of anti-Bolshevik exiles, some 60,000 according to international relief organizations. A decade and a half later, both cities were to shelter Jewish refugees from Nazi Germany. Colonies of émigrés also existed in Turkistan, Manchuria, and Mongolia.[15]

The Austro-Hungarian dual monarchy had exported vast numbers of male and female labor migrants to North America, particularly from the empire's peripheries, where no investments had been made to stimulate industrialization (chap. 14). The migrants supported the independence movements of the East Central European peoples with funds, with printed materials in languages suppressed by imperial authorities at home, and with political lobbying in Washington. None of the new states was monocultural: borders were drawn without regard for mosaics of settlement; people who stayed put found themselves in ethnically different states. National gatekeepers were certain about historic ethnic territories, a certainty that was often related to natural resources in the areas claimed. The postwar establishment of these "nation-states" left more than 20 million men, women, and children outside the states of their ethnocultural cousins. Several possibilities might determine the fate of such people: 1) "minorities," who in their compact but small territories formed the majority, could attempt to stay; 2) small groups could "opt" for the recently created "home" nation and leave; 3) those who did not fit the constructed nations could be expelled or exchanged for others considered more suitable; and 4) those deemed unacceptable by any state became "stateless," trapped wherever they had happened to lose their citizen status. Multiple identities were considered threatening to the ideology of homogeneous nation-states, and nationhood complicated the lives of culturally reconfigured men and women. In the Polish-Russian-Baltic borderlands, for example, many considered themselves simply "local ones" rather than ethnics or nationals. Borderlines between groups were fuzzy; people along such boundaries were often multilingual in a rudimentary way.[16]

In the interwar years, thousands of migrants from North America returned to help build political institutions and to invest in the economy of "their" states, while tens of thousands left the devastated lands for the Americas. Population planners in Great Britain sent unemployed and demobilized soldiers in a last "empire mi-

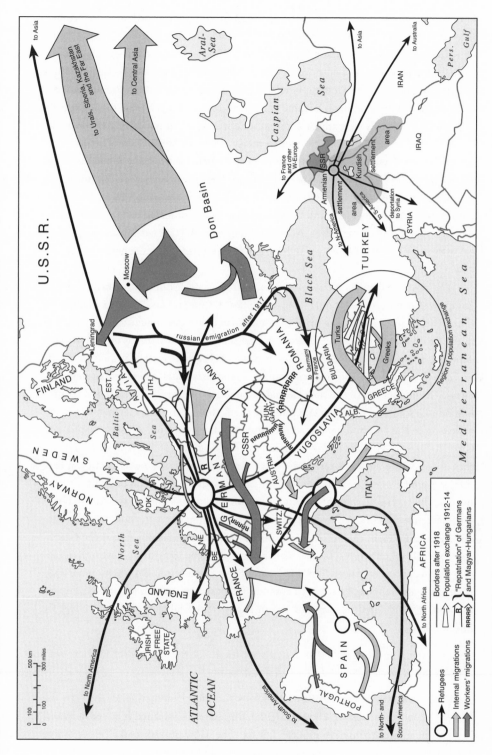

17.1 Population Transfer, Migration, and Flight in Europe, 1912–1939

gration" scheme to Canada or Australia—men to marginal farm lands and women into domestic service. After the workers' surrender in the British General Strike of 1926, miners' families emigrated to Canada. To prevent further ethnic antagonism, some states improved minority rights, and others pursued homogenization policies. In Belgium, the Flemish language was placed on a par with French in 1922, and in Switzerland Romansh became the fourth official language in 1937. Catalans in Spain successfully demanded some autonomy. By contrast, Italy's government pursued a policy of Italianization in formerly Austrian South Tyrol/Trentino. In Alsace-Lorraine, where German-speakers faced Francoization, Italian laborers arriving in the mining towns added another culture. The two newly created multiethnic independent cities—Fiume, settled by Austrians, Slovenians, and Italians, and Danzig/Gdansk, settled by Poles and Germans—remained contested between neighboring states. Of the former empires, Austria became a small state without further political pretensions, while Germany and Turkey had to retrench but schemed to regain power.[17]

The postwar displacement and settlement of Eastern European German-origin groups was as politically troublesome as the post-Ottoman population exchanges. In the official terminology of the time, the German people were divided into those living in the Reich (Reichsdeutsche), those living adjacent to the Reich but outside its borders (Grenzdeutsche), and those living further east or southeast (Auslandsdeutsche or Volksdeutsche)—in addition, of course, to the Austrians and German-language Swiss. The population of the new German Republic of 62.4 million included 1.5 million non-Germans, 1.1 million Poles among them, and 1.3 million German-origin expellees from the east and people who voluntarily departed from Alsace, Poland, and Gdansk/Danzig. Volksdeutsche migrated in large numbers to the Americas and further afield, while adjacent territories with Grenzdeutsche were eyed with annexationist aspirations. After it had annexed Austria, with a population of eight million, in 1938, the Nazi government counted 10 million Germans outside the Reich. When the Sudeten region of Czechoslovakia, with a population of 3.5 million, was incorporated into the Reich, the Polish government, using the occasion, seized the Czech-controlled Teschen region (240,000 inhabitants), and the Hungarian government appropriated parts of southern Slovakia (one million inhabitants). On 1 September 1939 Nazi Germany launched its war to conquer Lebensraum, to gain added living space for what it considered its superior Aryan people and a labor reservoir of allegedly inferior Slavs.[18]

Peoples in the Soviet Union: Empire and Autonomy

Wartime devastation resulted in a disastrous decline of food supplies even in the Soviet Union's breadbasket, Ukraine. Hunger migrations assumed mass proportions in a famine unprecedented in modern Europe. The badly provisioned cities emptied, and from 1918 to 1921 five million or more people died. Out-migration was facilitated by the continuing links of urban workers to their villages of origin. After the great famine, malnutrition forced people to move from northern to southern Siberia and from there westward. With the resumption of transport and levies of forced supplies for cities under the New Economic Policy of 1921–27, agricultural output increased, migratory directions reversed, and industrial production resumed. But a second flight from starvation was to occur when the expropriation of property owned by well-to-do peasants (*kulaks*) disrupted agricultural production after 1928 (chap. 17.2).[19]

The struggles for decolonization and governmentally granted autonomy for many peoples involved complex free und coerced migrations. The Soviet Union established autonomous socialist republics for many peoples, the Armenian republic among them. Birobidzhan in the Soviet Far East became a Jewish enclave. Decolonization from Ukraine to the trans-Caspian territories involved non-Russian peoples, such as the Uzbeks and Kirghiz, who had used the tsarist empire's wartime loss of control to expel immigrant Russians settlers. The refugees turned to land emptied through starvation. In Kazakhstan, where tsarist-government-supported Russian settlers had displaced nomads, the communist authorities reduced landholdings, and Kazakhs and Kirghiz returned with their flocks from China to where they had fled after their unsuccessful revolt of 1916. When new Russian settlers "spontaneously" alienated lands officially closed to immigrants, the Kazakh Soviet restricted Russian landownership. The government of the Soviet Union reacted in 1928 by opening Kazakhstan, as it had Siberia and the Far East, to settlers. As was true under tsarism, the ethnically Russian Bolshevik state apparatus, the Office of Colonization, ruled over other nationalities and labeled the Kazakhs' defense of their rights a "nationalistic deviation." The nomad population was reduced from 2–3 million families before 1917 to fewer than 0.5 million in 1935. When displaced families slaughtered their herds, food shortages increased mortality among them and reduced supplies for urban populations. The Constitution of 1936 redrew boundaries to reduce the self-determination of non-Russian peoples.

In the Russian Far East, Chinese, Koreans, and Japanese immigrants competed with Russian ones (chap. 13.4), and grain imports from recently settled Manchuria caused a decline in prices that unsettled peasant economies (chap. 18.1). Because immigrant Russians were far from their home base, Chinese merchants and Japanese fishermen held a competitive advantage. By 1915, some 90,000 Koreans, expropriated by the Japanese Society for Eastern Colonization to make room for large rice plantations, had arrived. The 1926 census counted 168,000 Koreans, half of whom had acquired Russian citizenship (chap. 17.4). Other sources put the number as high as 250,000. One-fifth of the Russian Far East's population was of East Asian origin.

After its decline in the years 1917 to 1923, the Soviet population began to grow rapidly. Massive rural-urban migrations changed the relative size of ethnic groups, and the Jewish population, no longer confined to the Pale of Settlement, dispersed. Population growth in agricultural Ukraine was below average; in the Russian industrialized cities and new industrial regions, it was far above average. Between 1926 and 1939, approximately five million eastbound migrants crossed the Urals or moved southeastward into Kazakhstan and the Central Asian Uzbek, Tadzhik, Turkmen, and Kirghiz Soviet Socialist Republics. Of these, less than one-sixth were peasant settlers; the others were labor migrants moving to industrial and mining frontiers. When such opportunities in industry led to labor shortages in logging, peat digging, and construction, the state introduced a system of forced labor (chap. 17.2).[20]

Political Emigration and Jewish Flight under Fascism

Before refugees from the war of 1914–18 were fully integrated, fascist governments in several countries caused renewed flight. The replacement of democratic governments forced previous elites and labor leaders into exile, but the totalitarian regimes aimed at the intellectual decapitation of their societies and of subjected peoples. Those fleeing had few options. Even before the advent of fascism, the Western World had erected barriers against immigrants from racist ideologies out of a fear of acquiring impoverished masses. With its restrictive immigration laws of 1917, 1921, and 1924, the United States allowed for only small quotas of Eastern Europeans and barred entry to any people who were likely to become public charges; Canada excluded radicals and Jews. Except for the Italian exiles of the 1920s, all refugees entered depression economies. They found for a brief time strong sympathy for their opposition to fascism but could not get jobs; when their sojourns became extended, support for them dwindled. Jews fleeing for political and intellectual reasons as well as from racist persecution found even less help. The increasingly powerful Third German Reich pressured neighboring governments not to admit refugees.[21]

In quick succession, fascist regimes sent political opponents into flight: Italy beginning in 1922, Germany after early 1933, Spain from 1936–39 onward, Portugal starting in 1933–36, Austria after 1933, then Hungary, southeastern Europe, and the annexed Sudeten and Czech territories. Fascist terrorism in Italy began in the early 1920s. Émigrés from the liberal elites, militant unions, and socialist or anarchist parties, as well as artists and intellectuals, were derisively called *fuorusciti* (foreign fellows), just as German socialists had once been labeled *vaterlandslose Gesellen* (fellows without a fatherland). Before 1926, 1.5 million Italian workers continued prewar patterns of migration (chap 14.1); then the Italian fascist movement criminalized emigration undertaken without permission. The émigrés could join working-class diasporas in France, Switzerland, Spain, Belgium, Argentina, and North America. The diasporic *prominenti*, however, often supported fascism. Paris became the center of the antifascists: some 900,000 Italians lived in France until their vibrant culture was destroyed after 1939.[22]

In Nazi Germany, the *Ermächtigungsgesetz* of March 1933 began a boycott of Jewish businesses and professionals. Some 10,000–20,000 Eastern European Jews were expelled, and some 65,000 Jewish and Christian bourgeois notables and cultural leaders fled the Brownshirts' terror in 1933. The 1935 Nuremberg Laws deprived German Jews of citizenship. By law, a "Jew" was now constructed as someone with two Jewish parents, and a "half Jew" as a person with one Jewish parent; to be "quarter Jewish" meant having one Jewish grandparent. Intermarriage between Jews and

Aryans was forbidden. After the "pogrom night" (*Kristallnacht*) of 9 November 1938, Jews could no longer earn a living. Since only about 1 percent of the German population—some 600,000 people—were "non-Aryan," German racism has been called anti-Semitism without Jews. By 1938, 150,000 Jewish and some 50,000 non-Jewish men, women, and children had fled. Ever more restrictive Nazi emigration policies prevented the transfer of assets. Thus refugees would arrive impoverished in host societies, which could ill afford and were unwilling to support them. Increasing numbers went overseas or, if Jewish, to Palestine.[23]

On the Iberian Peninsula, Spain's "army existed for the exclusive purposes of supporting 20,000 commissioned officers" (Kulischer). Without colonies or enemies, but in search of a cause, military officers in Morocco rebelled, pitting against each other the two Spains: the modernizing coastal and northern areas and the elites of the stagnant, reactionary agricultural areas. The fascist generals sent African ("Moorish") soldiers to fight the Republicans, and an image of atrocity-committing North Africans emerged. Some 45,000 radicals and democrats from all over Europe and North America as well as advisers from the Soviet Union came to defend the Spanish Republic. "Volunteers" sent by the German and Italian governments supported the insurgents. By August 1938, two million refugees from fascist-controlled areas had reached Republican Spain. After the Republic's collapse, some 200,000 soldiers and about 250,000 civilians fled across the Pyrenees to France, where they faced ideological, emotional, and economic biases. French authorities sent back men of military age, who according to nation-state ideology were "deserters." French people, who with some 388,000 refugees from Nazi Germany and its occupied areas in 1939 accommodated the largest concentration of refugees in the Western world, felt overburdened and reacted with fear. For lack of funds and sympathy, refugees were placed in makeshift camps with insufficient food and mail censorship. Still intent on sending refugees back to fascist Spain, the conservative French government seized the gold reserves of the legitimate Spanish Republic to pay the insurgent fascists to accept the refugees. Those who could avoid return joined the French army or resistance; some 20,000 went to Mexico: about 4,000 communists went into Soviet exile, followed by some 5,000 orphaned children. In 1951, 112,000 Spanish refugees still lived in France.[24]

France, as a traditional immigration country, had attracted migrants in the 1920s to make up for wartime population losses. In 1931, when three million Poles, Belgians, Italians, and Polish-Germans resided in the country, soaring unemployment rates caused the Right to mount a campaign of xenophobia. When German refugees began to arrive, the Ministry of the Interior tightened admission regulations, turned back refugees at the borders, and expelled clandestine entrants. The conservative Daladier government, which moved against workers and labeled refugees spies, could not turn the tide in 1939: exiles came from occupied Czechoslovakia, and some 40,000 refugees from Greater Germany. Britain received 50,000 people in flight from the Reich in the period 1933–39 and 6,000 refugees from Czech lands. Switzerland, also a haven for nineteenth-century political exiles, had admitted 110,000 French civilian refugees during World War I. But under the impact of the Great Depression, in the face of pressure from the German Reich, and in a mood of vaguely anti-Semitic complacency, the government permitted the entry of Jews only for transit to permanent resettlement elsewhere. When large numbers of Austrians came after annexation, smug officials rejected pre-*Anschluß* passports as invalid. In the words of its top police officer, Switzerland was not to be "saturated with Jews." Sent back to Nazi Greater Germany, such returning refugees often ended up in labor or death camps.[25]

The refugee-generating fascist states were surrounded by refugee-refusing democratic states. This left the Soviet Union as a country of refuge. But of the thousands of communist and trade union militants who went there many were to perish during the Stalinist purges. Thus few doors remained open. Turkey accepted refugees, as did some Eastern European states and China.[26]

Jewish citizens of Europe, as well as Gypsies and homosexuals within the reach of the German administrators, suffered most. After emancipation, the Jewish people had acculturated to their respective societies. "Emancipated, bourgeois Germans of Mosaic Persuasion . . . considered themselves secure and safe in their homeland"; the wealthy Sephardic community and the recently arrived Ashkenazim were well integrated in the Netherlands; so was the multiple-origin Jewish population of France. Nevertheless, anti-Semites were active: the reactionary general staff of the French army had instigated the Dreyfus affair; the British government passed the anti-alien law of 1905. Most Eastern European Jews, on the other hand, were impoverished and segregated. In Russia, a wave of pogroms since the 1880s was encouraged by the Orthodox Church's chief procurator, who envisioned a nation without Jews: one-third would convert, one-third would emigrate, and another third would perish. In Romania, Jewish artisans around 1900 cried out: "We want to live like human beings, and if this is impossible here we shall live elsewhere. We want both, liberty and bread!" To draw international attention to their plight, thousands walked some 1,500 kilometers (900 miles) to Hamburg to set sail for North America. Like pilgrims of old, these *"fusgeyers"* walked in sandals, with staffs, clad in a distinctive garment. In Poland, public opinion favored "the elimination of the Jew from economic life" and the "Polonization" of commerce (chaps. 13.5, 14.1).[27] In the immigrant receiving countries of North America, Jews, like all Eastern and Southern European immigrants, were considered racially inferior. When Jewish men, women, and children could still leave Nazi Germany, under great difficulties and suffering terrible humiliation, the United States admitted only 8,600 under its quota legislation, down from 243,000 in 1929, and Canadian immigration bureaucrats closed the doors to refugees and exiles, commenting that "none is too many."[28]

In 1930, 3.3 million Jews lived in Poland, about 757,000 in Romania, 445,000 in Hungary, and 3.0 million in Russia. In Germany, 525,000 Jews were counted; of Austria's 180,000, 165,000 lived in Vienna. When the persecution of Jewish people intensified in 1938 and German armies advanced eastward and westward in 1939, a second wave of flight carried those who had taken refuge in neighboring countries further afield, to North Africa or Turkey, for example. The *Reichsfluchtsteuer*, a tax on those leaving the Reich, confiscated German Jews' property. Some Jewish aid organizations accepted the inevitable. Under the Ha'avara (Hebrew: "transfer") Agreement, the Nazi government contracted to exchange Jewish human beings for foreign currency and access to international markets. The central German Bank proposed permission for 150,000 Jews to emigrate in return for capital transfers. From April 1938 to August 1939, 126,500 Jews managed to flee Greater Germany. Some 20,000 Polish Jews, expelled from Austria/Germany, were deprived of their citizenship by the Polish government, and the semifascist Romanian government denationalized one-third of the country's citizens of Jewish faith. In August 1938, the Italian government ordered Jews who had arrived in the country after 1919 to depart within six months. It barred Jewish teachers and students from educational institutions and prohibited marriages between Italians and non-Aryans. In May 1939, Hungary placed restrictions on Jews in the professions and in business, expelled them from government service, and ordered them to emigrate within five years. In the Netherlands, Anne Frank and her family, hidden in Amsterdam, were betrayed by an informer.[29]

Though it became apparent that the volume of refugees would accelerate, authorities across Europe slowed down entry and were obsessed with the administrative orderliness of admission. At the July 1938 refugee conference in Evian, France, U.S. diplomats insisted on establishing an Inter-Governmental Committee on Refugees to negotiate an end to the chaos of expulsions and establish procedures for property transfer. The latter would free receiving societies from the cost of support. When in May 1939 the German steamer *St. Louis* reached Cuba with 930 refugees, the authorities refused to accept the previously granted entry documents. Neither Latin American governments nor the United States and Canada would admit the desperate men and women. Others chose the eastward route to Harbin in Manchuria and to cosmopolitan Shanghai. Among the latter's population of four million Chinese, some 100,000 Japanese, Russians, British people, Germans, Austrians, and Americans lived in the International Settlement, Frenchtown, and Little Tokyo. Its Jewish community consisted mainly of exiles from Poland and Russia who arrived in 1917–18. An estimated 18,000 refugees, including 13,500 men and women of Jewish faith, had arrived by 1939.[30]

Democratic and fascist governments alike concurred that Jews might be removed to some "unsettled territory where an organized community life in the modern sense does not yet exist," as U.S. journalist Walter Lippmann phrased it in 1939. The most frequently named destination was tropical French Madagascar, with a population of 3.8 million Natives and 36,000 Europeans; others included North Borneo (where the British proponent of the idea had economic interests), the Dominican Republic, British Guiana, Cyprus, the Philippines, the Belgian Congo, Ecuador, Haiti, Mexico, Surinam, and southwestern Ethiopia. According to Marrus:

> Meeting the preconceptions of the time, government leaders and civil servants warmed to the image of young Jews tilling the soil of sunny, distant lands, improving their own lives immeasurably in the process. In reality,

three quarters of the Jews in Germany were over forty, most lived in large cities, only 2 percent knew anything about agriculture, and over one half were involved in trade and commerce. One can only conclude that the projects were seldom designed with Jews clearly in mind at all.

Thus Palestine remained the only destination. There, however, the local Arab population was being displaced, and the British, holders of the territorial mandate, feared for their relations with Arab governments. Arab citizens had revolted before the British reduced immigration to 10,500 in 1937. Even Jewish supporters of a Zion in Palestine expressed concern that the community of 400,000, engaged in tilling the land and building a nation, would be overwhelmed by mass arrival of refugees from fascism. Understanding that the choice was between immediate rescue or death, "New Zionists" unsuccessfully suggested a transfer of 1.5 million Jews to Palestine over ten years. The Jewish "Aliyah Bet" movement and the underground military Haganah smuggled some 18,100 into the territory from 1938 to 1941.

After September 1939, German Jews were first transported to Polish territories as an inferior laboring population. In a second phase, the resettlement area was to be made *judenrein:* human beings of Mosaic religion were to be cleaned out. Thus the deportees were deported again, this time to the ghettos of Polish cities. Overcrowding and planned starvation resulted in epidemics and phenomenal death rates. The third deportation, or "final solution," transported men, women, and children to camps were they were to be worked to death in war-related factories run by German industry and the ss and financed by German banks, resulting in "natural diminution" in the terminology of the times—as opposed to elimination in the gas chambers of the death camps and the killing fields of the *Wehrmacht,* the ss *Einsatzgruppen,* and their local supporting Baltic or Ukrainian fascists. In the Holocaust, between five and six million were exterminated. Of the slave workers, those unable to work were sent to the gas chambers, too. At Babi Yar, a ravine near Kiev, more than 33,000 were massacred. More than a million were exterminated in Auschwitz/Oswiecim, as sportsmen used the rising hot air above the smokestacks for their glider planes. Since the British secret service had deciphered German codes in 1942, the Allies were able to tape the "success" reports sent from massacre sites.

Survival in occupied Eastern Europe was possible only by retreating into the woods and wetlands impenetrable to occupation forces. An estimated 200,000–350,000 Jews reached the nonoccupied Soviet Union. In addition, individual officials, for whom humanity, Christian duty, or common decency was more important than their national government's policy, provided Jewish and political refugees with visas and escape routes or blinked at the activities of clandestine aid organizations. About 100,000 left through Italy, Spain, and Portugal, the fascist governments of which for various reasons did not follow extermination policies. The Spanish government, in fact, sheltered Sephardic Jews, descendants of those expelled in 1492, who by whatever logic were considered Spain's "lost children." Among neutral countries, Turkey became the most important transit route, and Istanbul housed tens of thousands of refugees. Sweden admitted Norwegian refugees and Danish Jews as well as others, a total of 237,000 during the war years. Its Berlin mission negotiated the release of concentration camp inmates and supported rescue missions for Eastern European Jews.[31] In the end, the representatives of one branch of the German-language family, Yiddish-speakers, were almost completely exterminated.[32]

17.2   The New Labor Regimentation

In the 1920s and the Great Depression years, governments increasingly restricted geographical mobility of workers across the northern hemisphere. Immigration controls reduced international working-class migration; in many countries unemployed men and, sometimes, women were sent to relief camps; North American and Western European governments deported labor activists and the unemployed. Forced labor—whether in the form of slavery, temporary confinement to camps, or involuntary contract ("coolie") labor—ended, according to most interpretations, from the 1880s (African slavery in the Americas) to about 1920 (the contract labor system in the British Empire). Yet, from the 1890s to the 1930s international organizations battled against continuations of restrictive labor regimentation with various pacts: the Brussels Agreement of 1890 to prohibit slavery, the Convention of Saint-Germain of 1919 to outlaw its veiled forms, the League of Nations' Anti-Slavery Convention of 1926, the Geneva-based International Labour Office's Forced Labour Convention of 1930–31, and the Convention on the Fraudulent Recruiting of Indigenous Workers of 1936.[33]

Nationalist, class, gender, and (semi-)fascist ideologies determined the regulation of labor and migration in 1920s Europe. France, after the postwar depression and a temporary closing of the borders, became the most important destination of labor migrants with almost two million arriving. This mobility was encouraged since 1.35 million French soldiers—10 percent of the adult male population—had been killed in World War I or were listed as missing in action. France had to replenish its male labor force. On the other hand, to reserve national soil for an "undiluted" French nation, nationalists prohibited Italian peasant immigration to southwestern France in 1926, where land prices were one-fifth to one-tenth of those in the northern Italian plains. Italian fascists restricted emigration to avoid "denationalization" and ordered pregnant emigrant women to return to give birth on Italian soil—fatherland or mother country? Emigration to the African acquisitions was encouraged to denationalize the Native inhabitants, and in the Ethiopian colony children of mixed parentage were recognized as Italian as long as the father was Italian: men's sperm and women's wombs were part of imperial projects.

To reduce self-organization by class, fascist Spain outlawed unions and workers' parties. In the 1920s, 200,000 (net figures) underemployed laborers from northern and eastern regions went to France, to the Department of the Pyrenees, in particular; then internal migration from the interior grain-producing economy to the cities of Madrid, Barcelona, and other coastal industrial areas reduced emigration. Fascism and its control over workers lasted until the system's demise in 1975. In France, employer recruitment of Polish workers left them with no right to change jobs or move to better working conditions.[34]

In the Americas, the U.S. government deported labor organizers and radicals, men and women, to the Soviet Union after 1917 and deported Mexican workers to Mexico in the 1930s. Although outlawed after 1867, peonage—forced labor based on (alleged) debt—continued to be imposed on Afro-American and Mexican-American laborers. Prison farm officials arbitrarily arrested labor migrants. In the 1930s, the congressional Wickersham Commission had to investigate "lawlessness in law enforcement." Some states—Georgia, for example—made it illegal to offer out-of-state employment to employed servants, "croppers," or farm laborers. Forms of involuntary labor were also common in U.S. colonies, such as the Philippines, or in zones of influence, including Cuba and Guatemala.[35] In 1920s Canada, male harvest laborers and female domestics were sent to their destinations under police guard to work off assisted passage contracts. In camps for the unemployed during the Great Depression, administered by the military, men received minimal wages. Immigrants did not dare apply for relief for fear of deportation. Free immigrant workers were not free to organize, to demand better wages, or to receive assistance when impoverished. In the interior of South America, the peonage system resembled slavery, and landowners had rights to the part-time labor of "Natives."[36]

In several African states, slavery continued to exist. In Saudi Arabia, for which traders sometimes recruited Black and White slaves under the guise of a pilgrimage to Mecca, the government imposed restrictions in 1936. Most Muslim states from Morocco to Afghanistan abolished slavery in the interwar years, as did Christian Ethiopia, but such practices continued, leading the League of Nations to establish an Advisory Committee on Slavery in 1938. Types of indentured labor remained operative in the Congo and Sierra Leone; contract labor in Southeast Asia and the sale of children in China continued. Experts estimated that in 1930 three million workers were in bondage worldwide.[37]

Forced laborers could be used in places to which free workers would not migrate on their own. They could be shifted by authorities or employers/owners to wherever the need for them arose. No preparation for accommodation was necessary, since they had to construct their own camps. In economies with insufficient consumer goods, an increase in camp labor decreased consumption. If knowledge about forced labor was public, the system could be used to intimidate free workers. From the viewpoint of efficiency, however, aspects of unsatisfactory performance included the inability of labor slaves to handle (or be entrusted with) complex machinery, low productivity owing to passive resistance or to starvation, and the costs of control. Urban slavery in Brazil, industrial serfdom in tsarist Russia, and experiments with industrial slavery in the United States had been successful because incentives permitted some self-determination, savings, and perhaps the purchase of freedom. While chattel slaves were private property and protected as such, forced laborers from large reservoirs under the control of the user state represented no economic value. Since slave laborers could easily be replaced, they were often worked to death, whether in the

Soviet Union, Nazi Germany, or militarist Japan (chap. 17.4). South Africa developed a particularly harsh system of bondage that lasted into the 1980s (chap. 18.4).[38]

Free Migration and Forced Labor in the USSR

Before the international and civil wars beginning in 1914, Russia had ranked fifth among the world's industrial powers (chap. 13.5–6). At the time of the October Revolution in 1917, the legacies of tsarist rule included memories of serfdom, deportation, and the involuntary labor of soldiers. Wartime destruction in 1914–18, revolutionary dislocation after 1917, and civil war until 1921 explain why production reached prewar levels only in 1928. In addition, the Soviet economy faced issues of industrialization that had beset resident and migrant workers in the economies of the Atlantic World before 1914: the high demand for labor, high rates of accumulation and correspondingly high levels of exploitation of labor, the priority of investment over consumption, strong international competition, and low status in international power hierarchies. Poor working and living conditions increased the propensity to migrate.

Up to 1928, Stalin's "Great Turning Point," migrations were voluntary—within constraints akin to those faced by East Elbian rural workers a few decades before and by British textile workers a century earlier. Russia's rural populations were as unskilled for industrial work as many of the transatlantic migrants were. Neither employers nor the state favored a one-to-one relationship of productive to reproductive migrant labor, and workers could not afford such a ratio (chap. 13.3). Forced collectivization and industrialization changed the Russo-Siberian Migration System (chap. 17.1): rural-urban migrations assumed unprecedented proportions, and the five-year plans from 1929 to 1942 achieved a tripling of the industrial labor force. One million migrants came to the cities annually before 1926, 2.6 million annually from 1927 to 1930, and 4.3 million in 1931. The government attempted to slow down migration by putting pressure on remaining family members. Migrants reacted to overcrowding in urban Moscow and Leningrad by deflecting their destinations to the new eastern industrial cities. From 1921 to 1939 the urban population more than doubled and became "ruralized": two-fifths had arrived from the countryside within the last twelve years. This was the first of five phases of migration.

During the second phase, collectivization—rather than emphasizing the commune-*kolkhoz* continuity—destroyed village communes in favor of reservoirs of individualized laborers. The new *kolkhozes* were to supply food to urban populations through state levies without rewards or incentives and to supply industry with workers without training institutions in place. During the destruction of the traditional peasant economy, *kulaks* left in search of new lands, fled to industrial work, or were shipped off to labor camps, often therefore to death. Flight from the resulting famine, the second in a decade, resulted in the death of millions, particularly in Ukraine, and food shortages in the cities caused another exodus. When experienced workers left, industry lost its trained labor force. Migration policies were contradictory. Collectivization reduced the need for rural labor, but *kolkhoz* administrators granted families with migrants in the cities fewer assignments and thus less rural income. This rationale, intended to spread work, resulted in a slowdown of temporary migration. Negative information about urban living conditions filtered back and further reduced migration, and urban bureaucrats prohibited rural migrants from taking employment to prevent the infiltration of the (ideologically constructed) working class by "class-alien elements."

During the third phase, that of consolidation, some 250,000 skilled factory workers were sent to rural areas before 1938 to introduce mechanization. Rural electrification projects paralleled programs of the same nature in the United States. Urban administrators were sent into *kolkhoz* management. In a vast campaign of increasing literacy and of inculcation of a new consciousness—parallel to but different from the modernization campaign in Turkey—communist and educational cadres moved from urban to rural areas. Millions of surplus peasants moved as unskilled workers to the expanding industries or as navvies to road and railway construction. Within five years, 12.5 million new wage-workers were drawn into the urban labor forces. To alleviate rural labor shortages during harvest and to change mentalities, communist youths were sent to *kolkhozes,* 241,000 in 1933. While the disasters of rural reorganization shaped popular memory, the buoyant spirit of the youth movement departing toward a new future became a dominant image of Soviet publicized discourse.

Village out-migration no longer involved male heads of families on seasonal journeys. Men and women of all ages, the young in particular, came and did not intend to return. The composition of the working class changed from second- or third-generation skilled urban laboring families to young, enthusiastic, often single men and women without traditions of industrial work and labor organization. To alleviate the demand for skilled workers and technicians, men came from across the Western world to the seemingly unlimited opportunities in the Soviet Union (chap. 13.6). Finns, Russians, and others returned from the United States, as did children of Jewish emigrants. Radical Finnish-Americans and -Canadians, under government surveillance because of their communist leanings, left for lumbering work in Soviet (formerly Finnish) Karelia. Technical experts came from the United States and Germany; political refugees came from the Seattle general strike, the Italian Fiat Workers' Council, and Bulgaria. When cotton cultivation was introduced in Kazakhstan and experts were needed, Black Americans came from the racist and depression-ridden United States to start new lives. When the Communist Party decided to admit foreign engineers, foremen, and skilled workers, reportedly more than 400,000 people applied—Germans, Austrians, and Americans, as well as Czechs, Italians, people of English and French origin, Spaniards, Swedes, and, in the Far East, Japanese. Of the 42,500 admitted, Finns worked in lumbering, Japanese in fishing, most others in the industrializing Urals, Ukraine, and Kuzbass. Toward the end of the 1930s, the arrival of political refugees from the Spanish Civil War and Germany increased. But admission was restricted; English engineers were accused of sabotage; the immigrants' hopes and political beliefs came apart quickly.[39]

Labor relations had been regulated by the General Labor Code of 1922, but when free migration and labor recruitment failed to fill demand, a decree of February 1930 terminated unemployment benefits and permitted assignment to jobs regardless of previous training, working conditions, or distance. In 1932 an internal passport system was put in place to control the mobility of urban laboring men and women sixteen years of age and over. Although a new clause in the criminal code made workers' breach of contract a punishable offense, employers/state administrators could act at will (Asian contract workers in the British Empire had been treated similarly). In the Constitution of 1936, the right-to-work clause enshrined secure subsistence as a basic right but also made work a civic duty. The combining of government and "economic organs" (with control over employment) in one organization, the Communist Party, created a state-industrial complex that rigorously subjected workers to dogmatic planning processes and volatile Party lines, to Taylorist ideologies of scientific management, and to bureaucratic ineptitude.[40]

After 1930, in the fourth phase of labor migration, recruitment from rural areas continued, but the allocation to job sites was chaotic. Some *kolkhoz* boards refused to send men, while others levied a share of the migrants' wages, making migration unprofitable to individuals and families. Factories and industrial complexes recruited thousands of workers without providing even minimal amenities. Cautious villagers, who sent scouts to check out recruiters' promises, often were warned not to depart. Among workers, the gap between experienced actual working conditions and those perceived elsewhere was large. The turnover rate reached 25 percent per month in some factories, and a "floating" laboring population emerged.

By 1931, formalized linkages between rural labor recruitment and the supply of agricultural machinery and between particular industrial complexes and particular collective farms were operative. As a result, *kolkhoz* workers could be sent to industrial work against their will, and factory mechanics came to farms voluntarily or involuntarily to operate the new machinery and train peasant *kolkhoz* workers. Immigrant foreign workers, often class-conscious advocates of workers' rights, developed an ambivalent relationship with their Russian comrades. They looked down on "slacking" Russians until they understood that a lack of industriousness was a survival technique. Their pay permitted a higher standard of living and relationships with voluntary female partners, prostitutes, or hired maids. No foreign women came as skilled workers; a few arrived as political refugees. All of these immigrant men and women were subject to political surveillance, and many ended up in political prisons or forced labor camps.[41]

In the fifth phase, beginning in the mid-1930s, labor recruitment mobilized urban reserves of men, women, and youths to increase supply without the need for additional housing and food. New communal eating and child-care arrangements reduced housework, and the resulting opportunities induced women to seek employment in numbers far beyond the plan's target and far beyond labor force participation in capitalist societies. They worked in jobs designated as women's careers as well as in heavy industry and mining. The activation of juvenile labor undercut the 1920s prohibition of child labor and alleviated the high levels of youth unemployment. In the 1930s, young men and women, willing or not, were to receive vocational training and continuous employment.

The construction of the "Magnitogorsk Giant" steel complex provides an illustration of the frontier spirit, industrialization, hopes, mass migration, and abominable living conditions of the Stalinist era. In March 1929, an advance party of twenty-five reached Magnetic Mountain, about 60 kilometers (40 miles) east of the southern Urals, with fabulous, easily accessible ore deposits. Labor recruiting officials shared a vision, printed posters, made promises, and spread success stories of earth moved and concrete poured. Three-and-a-half years later, a quarter-million Russian workers, engineers with their families, and a few hundred foreign technicians and European political refugees lived in a tent city with insufficient water and food supplies. In May 1931, 40,000 *kulak* families dispatched in boxcars found no housing available. Many fled. Others came of their own free will and tried to fulfill their own hopes.

In 1938 the authorities tightened the passport system by introducing workbooks in which workers had to document their hiring and discharge histories. Workers were not permitted to move without a regular discharge, and employers could refuse discharges. In June 1940, the eight-hour workday and the seven-day workweek were introduced, and self-determined geographical mobility became a criminal offense punishable by forced labor. In October 1940, the compulsory mobilization of young male workers coupled with compulsory vocational training began. Skilled workers, technicians, and administrators could be transferred to wherever they were needed, including the Siberian east. Labor allocation was shifted from the People's Commissariats of Agriculture and Labor to the Commissariat of the Interior—that is, to the police. This "military-type mobilization of the workers," as authors justly critical of the system point out, was meant to ensure the country's survival when the German armies attacked in 1941.[42]

During World War II, migrations were related to the eastward shift of industry beyond the Urals and the opening of new mines in Siberia. The populations of West Siberia, East Siberia, the Soviet Far East, and Kazakhstan increased from a total of 21.8 million in 1939 to 30.8 million in 1959. This relocation and expansion increased the demand for raw materials from the frozen north, to which free labor would hardly choose to migrate. Thus captive labor worked in lumbering and road and railroad construction. The transfer of whole factories before the German advance necessitated the construction of cities in places devoid of human habitation and infrastructure. The labor camps (*gulags*) were controlled by the general administration of police (the NKVD) (map 17.2).

Estimates of the number of forced workers during the peak of the system varied from 2.3 million to 20 million in 1941 (about 10 percent of the total labor force). Post-1989 research indicates that there were 2.9–3.5 million forced laborers in 1941, about one-tenth of them women, and at least 0.75 million Polish and other deportees. Also involved were men and women legally deported without prior judicial proceedings for up to five years and workers rounded up in the streets. Although criminals con-

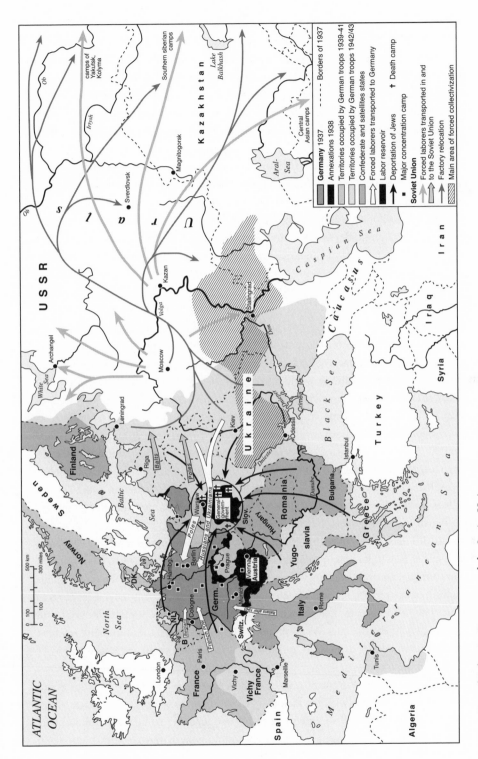

17.2   Forced Labor in Germany and the Soviet Union, 1930s–1940s

stituted only a small minority, people deemed "offenders against the socialist mode of life," including corrupt public officials, formed a larger group. Political "offenders" included peasants, in particular of Ukrainian background or from national minorities who were striving for independence, as well as Jews, refugee communists from Western Europe, and persons persecuted for their religious beliefs. The forced labor system also served ethno-political goals in occupied eastern Poland and the Baltic republics. Deportees (often whole families) faced extremely high death rates. Some 420,000 men were released on condition that they join the army. In the war economy, the economic importance of the system increased. Only in the late 1940s, according to some studies, did the standard of living improve. When the system was exposed in 1956, the camps were abolished within eighteen months. Some survivors returned to their homes; others' homes no longer existed; a few joined emigrant families. Deported in 1940, the Polish Kojder family counted twenty-two dead during their transport by boxcar, labor in a *gulag,* and departure before reaching Canada in 1947.[43]

From Forced Labor to Slave Labor in Wartime Germany

Since the 1880s, the labor regime of the German Reich relied on external recruitment combined with harsh internal controls. The East Elbian latifundia faced large-scale emigration owing to a lack of land, the increasing seasonality of work in response to structural changes, declining world market prices for wheat, and the inferior social status of laborers. Between 1871 and 1900, 2.7 million emigrated; more migrated internally. The Prussian-occupied Polish territories became a reservoir of labor for eastern agriculture and western mining and industry. Comparatively higher wages also brought Catholic Russian and Austrian-Polish migrants into the country (chap. 14.1). The German government's hostility to Catholicism and to Polish demands for independence had resulted in the expulsion of 40,000 "foreign Poles" in 1885. The expellees included women who had lost their German nationality/ethnicity by marrying Polish men. Employers, however, demanded the readmission of cheap labor. The authorities rejected a suggestion that Chinese coolies be imported into the Prussian east, just as free Italian labor migrants—"the Chinese of Europe"—had been brought into southern German states with liberal admission policies. When the government readmitted eastern foreign workers in 1890, though only on a seasonal basis, 433,000 came. The Reich soon ranked second among labor-importing countries. Russian and Austrian Poles, Ruthenians (Ukrainians), Italians, and, in smaller numbers, workers of other nationalities came: 1.26 million by 1910, among them 543,000 women (43 percent of the total).

To enter, Eastern European workers had to have a job, and after 1903 they could be expelled immediately if they lacked a "legitimizing pass" from the *Deutsche Arbeiterzentrale.* They had to agree not to change jobs and to behave submissively. (The rules were applied flexibly to workers from northern and Western Europe and from Switzerland.) Some settled and formed communities; others, such as Italian brickmakers and construction workers, returned home in the winter, which delayed community-formation. Most German states admitted only single male and female foreign Polish workers. Lithuanian and Czech migrants were not permitted to work in ethnically mixed border provinces, and after the Russian revolution of 1905 the migration of Russian Jews was restricted. Foreign Polish migrants—that is, those from Russia and Austria—were forced to depart during a "closure period" each winter, a regulation that incidentally freed employers from paying wages in winter. Thus seasonal foreign laborers were immobilized when in the Reich and involuntarily mobilized for their return home each winter. The Reich's authorities rejected any attempts by the Austrian, Hungarian, and Russian governments to improve the status of their migrating subjects.[44]

This first phase had operated for twenty-five years and established the principle of a rotating labor force for reasons of nationalist ideology and cultural purity. The second phase involved forced labor. When war was declared during harvest time in August 1914, the Prussian Ministry of War prohibited agricultural workers from enemy countries and "hostile aliens" in industry from leaving. While more than 300,000 Russian Poles were compelled to remain, draft-age workers from allied Austria-Hungary were sent home, and Italians were expelled. Initially, the forced laborers were to be expelled as enemy aliens after the harvest, but the impact of early military defeats led to a reversal of policy. The prewar authoritarian labor regime became in wartime a forced labor regime: compulsory seasonal rotation was transformed into compulsory immobility. In addition, some 90 percent of the 2.5 million prisoners of war (POWs) were utilized as a labor reservoir—"Western" POWs in industry, "Slavic" POWs in agriculture, and both in mining. Under a decree of October 1916 aimed at "Combating Unwillingness to Work," the military compelled 500,000–600,000 men, women, and children in occupied Eastern Europe to sign contracts to work in the Reich. Since they allegedly deprived the German army and people of food, "working classes of non-German nationality" were given rations kept at starvation levels. Belgians were deported from the west to the Reich; others "volunteered." One of the Reich's war aims was to acquire eastern territories that would permanently provide the economy with cheap and docile workers. Defeat intervened, and the forced laborers were repatriated.[45]

Other European states introduced wartime labor regimes, too. France relied on colonial labor and forcibly drafted African soldiers for the European war. Britain also imposed compulsory labor on colonial populations—the *kasanvu* system in Uganda, for example. Coolies from China and Vietnamese workers were sent to Britain and France (chap. 15.6).[46]

The third phase of foreign labor in the 1920s involved relatively few people, with a peak of 236,000 workers in 1928. The Weimar Republic's "governmentalization" of the labor market mandated equal pay for Native and foreign workers as well as improved residence conditions; on the other hand, it limited foreigners to jobs shunned by Germans. When the political spectrum shifted to the right in the late 1920s, "antisocial" elements among German workers were sent to camps. The Weimar Republic's right-wing commissioner of foreign labor remained in office under Nazi rule, and its

Ordinance on Foreign Workers, which centralized a restrictive admission and control policy, was implemented by fascist bureaucrats.

In a fourth phase after 1933, the new Nazi government restricted Germans' freedom of movement. "Racially fit" young men and women had to serve in agriculture, which was characterized in formal terms as voluntary work, but in fact the refusal to enlist meant the loss of unemployment benefits; a change of jobs would result in punitive wage deductions. The program channeled labor to sectors with low wages and poor working conditions, and lodging and food on the farms was often substandard. At first, this *Arbeitsdienst* was seen as an escape from unemployment, and a public works program was perceived as better than the handing-out of scanty relief payments. But employment offices were transformed into institutions of labor allocation, and workbooks, compulsory after 1936, provided complete control over mobility. The construction of freeways—which happened to be eastbound—and armament programs soon demanded "man-power" beyond the availability of men. Women were pressured to register for workbooks, and child-care was delegated or relegated to municipalities.

Political prisoners were assigned to forced labor, as were Jews, whose construction as "racially unfit" had excluded them from most employment before then. The ideological concepts of racial purity precluded the introduction of foreign labor, but economic interest overrode ideology. By 1936, the Nazi government negotiated with Poland, where unemployment stood at 40 percent, for agricultural laborers. The numbers of imported workers grew quickly, as did the variety of sending countries. In 1939, an estimated 90,000 Poles, 37,000 Italians, and 36,000 Yugoslavs, Hungarians, Bulgarians, and Dutch people worked in German agriculture. The *Anschluss* of Austria and the annexation of Czechoslovakia in 1938 permitted the conscription of another 200,000 workers. Security police and "protective custody" enforced work obligations. The militarization of the German labor force and the racialized inclusion of non-Germans created a continuous process from a corporatist regime to Nazi rule and from the prewar era to the war years.[47]

Immediately after the occupation of Poland in September 1939, the fifth phase in the transformation of the German labor regime resulted in some 300,000 POWs and civilian prisoners being transferred to Germany for compulsory labor, mainly in agriculture. In early 1940, the German governor-general in Poland imposed a levy of one million workers, half of them to be women. People were rounded up in the streets, in cinemas, or, when girls were needed as household help, after school. Eastern Europe's allegedly "subhuman" peoples became essential for the Aryan war economy. By the summer of 1940, some 700,000 Poles worked in the Reich, visibly separated by a "P" insignia on their clothing; they were housed in camps and fed miserably. They could not use public transport or public pools; nor could they attend church. They were barred from changing jobs and their district of residence. Since not all Germans subscribed to the racialization, ever-increasing control was needed to prevent fraternization, friendly treatment, and emotional attachments (map 17.2).

From Western Europe, French POWs were conscripted for labor, some 1.2 million within a year. They could be relieved if their family or home community sent a replacement. Civilian foreign workers included Italians, Belgians, and Yugoslavs. The 2.1 million civilian foreigners and 1.2 million POWs accounted for 9 percent of the Reich's labor force in 1941. After the attack on the Soviet Union in June 1941, its citizens were constructed as racially below all others. Some 60 million Russians, Belorussians, Ukrainians, and men and women from many other ethnicities came under German rule. Employment was forbidden, a *Vernichtungskrieg* (war of extermination) was being waged: "Many tens of millions have become superfluous in this entire area and will die or have to emigrate to Siberia." Of 3.35 million Russian POWs at the end of 1941, 60 percent died of starvation and disease, a death toll regretted by labor authorities.[48]

The self-styled Aryan industrialists and population planners, who had envisioned quick victory in and hegemony over Central and Eastern Europe with a reservoir of slave labor, realized in 1942 that they had succumbed to self-delusion. Because a long war of attrition lay ahead, policy was reversed. In addition to POWs, 40,000 forced Russian civilian workers per week were transported to Germany, men and women in equal numbers and children as young as twelve years of age. Housed in barbed-wire camps with primitive barracks, segregated by sex and fed with near-starvation rations, they had to wear badges that read "OST," for *Ostarbeiter*, meaning inferior Slavic workers. Disobedience, slow work, attempts to escape, and fraternization with Germans were punishable by death. Their survival was of no importance: new workers could always be rounded up.

Parallel to the westbound transport of slave labor, Jewish Germans were shipped eastward to concentration camps, first for work, then to be exterminated. While weakened Russian slave workers were sent back, the elderly, the children, and the pregnant women among the Jewish captives were sent to the gas chambers immediately.

Racial hierarchies began with French civilian workers at the top; next came other western workers, southern workers from allied or dependent countries, then Czechs and Poles, and, at the bottom, the expendable Russian workers. After Mussolini's downfall in 1943, 600,000 Italians were deported to work in the Reich. Only when large parts of the German population began to question the war effort and secretly to defect from the regime did resistance and mass flight become possible. By 1943, 33,000 foreign workers on average fled each month. At the end of the war, in May 1945, some 1.9 million POWs and 5.7 million civilian foreign workers, about one-third of them women, slaved in Germany, as did 600,000 concentration camp inmates. Together, they accounted for 20 percent of the labor force.[49]

By May 1945, the alleged German superiority lay in ruins. Repatriation began. French and others from the west walked home; many of the eastern workers were shipped back to destroyed societies and, in the case of Stalinist Russia, to charges of collaboration. Others could emigrate to Britain, North America, or Australia, while some remained in Germany. A few months later, Allied victory ended the forced labor regime in Japan (chap. 17.4).

In the less than six years of European war, unprecedented millions were forced into flight or relocation camps. The war in Asia had begun two years before both wars merged after Pearl Harbor in December 1941 (chap. 17.4). Under the guise of national purity and loyalty, government population planners, who had shifted masses of human beings around as laboring or surplus populations, now shifted them around as "human material." Concepts of population reserves, once developed by colonizers for "Natives" of North America, Africa, and Australia, came to be applied in Europe and Asia after 1939.

The peculiar construction of allegiance and duty to a nation in wartime made dissenters and pacifists persecuted citizens even in democratic states. The Canadian government, for example, had interned conscientious objectors in camps administered by the military during World War I. When the fascist states began their wars of conquest, their nationals abroad—including refugees from fascism as well as descendants of immigrants—were labeled enemy aliens, and many were interned. Few distinctions were made. British tribunals, for example, processed political refugees, German Jews, and German-British Nazis indiscriminately. Of those rounded up, Jews and Nazis were quartered in the same barracks, but three-quarters turned out to be genuine refugees.[50]

On the continent, wartime dislocation began with uncoordinated mass flight. After the German and Soviet attack on Poland, hundreds of thousands fled, at first toward Warsaw. The unit of measure, "hundreds of thousands," would soon change to "millions"; directions became haphazard, and distances ever larger. Some Poles succeeded in crossing the Baltic Sea, and about 140,000 fled through Hungary or Rumania to be evacuated via the Middle Eastern British zone of influence to England and France. Men joined the government-in-exile's Polish Legions and fought with the Allies. Information about anti-Jewish atrocities by the German occupiers sent Jews fleeing across the lines of the Soviet army. After the Nazi-Soviet pact, Soviet authorities returned communist German exiles to the Reich. When the Soviet Union attacked Finland and occupied Karelia in November 1939, most of the 420,000–450,000 Karelian Finns were deported to Finland; 11 percent of the Finnish population were refugees. Some 265,000 men and women returned when Finnish troops retook Karelia in 1941, only to flee again before the renewed Soviet advance in 1944. In France, both the northern Nazi and southern Vichy administrations rounded up Jews. Vichy placed foreign Jews in camps, but some could flee to Portugal and others to Mexico. Danish people in one night ferried the country's 7,500 Jews to neutral Sweden. At the end of the first few months of western warfare, two million French, two million Belgian, 70,000 Luxembourger, and 50,000 Dutch refugees in France were near destitution according to Red Cross estimates. Tens of thousands of orphaned, abandoned, or misplaced children roamed the streets and countryside.[51]

According to Nazi planning, inferior West Slavic peoples were to be pushed eastward. Their lands were to become "living space" (*Lebensraum*) for Aryan Germans and Nordic races. Further east, lesser peoples were to cooperate with the Third Reich for their own advantage or be used as cheap labor. The "General Plan East" ordered "resettlement" of 80–85 percent of all Poles, 75 percent of the Belorussians, 65 percent of the Ukrainians, and 50 percent of the Czechs in Russia or Siberia.

Overextended from the beginning, the German military needed "colonial auxiliaries" and resorted to population transfers or the local regimentation of labor. Plans to transport Danish soldiers and police as agents of control to other parts of Europe were not implemented, but Baltic and Ukrainian units were used or volunteered to fight against other nationalities; and segments of the political apparatus of several states cooperated with Nazi Germany. In the Soviet Union, after two famines and collectivization, large numbers of Ukrainians, for example, saw the advancing German armies as liberators. But in the Nazis' plans, Ukraininan peasants were to produce food for the *Herrenmenschen,* and the urban population was to be starved to death. Refugees from peoples whose elites cooperated with the Nazis were compromised when they reached the Soviet Union. As designated enemy aliens, many were assigned to forced labor in camps or in the army. Tens of thousands perished through bureaucratic and military ineptitude as well as wartime shortages and suffering.[52]

The Nazis intended to expand the contiguous German-settled territories to a line 500 kilometers east of the Polish-German prewar border. Thus occupied Poland was divided into an area to be resettled with Germans (*Reichsgaue* or provinces) and a Polish-settled labor camp, the *Generalgouvernement.* "Operation Tannenberg" emptied the *Reichsgaue* of 750,000 Poles at a rate of 10,000 a day. The total grew to 1.2 million subsequently. Many of those deported had been resettled after 1918 from territories of the new Russian and Ukrainian Socialist Republics. Under the decapitation concept, intellectuals and political leaders were interned or killed. Often families were torn apart: women were transported eastward; men were sent west to labor camps; and children were taken away for "Germanization" programs. In the Polish territories occupied by the USSR, more than one million, perhaps as many as 1.8 million, were deported to forced labor camps. Half of them died within a year. At the end of the war, 18 percent of the Polish population, or nearly one in five Poles, were dead.[53]

As a dumping ground for "undesirables," the *Generalgouvernement* received about one million people—Jews from the Reich and Austria and deported Poles. To increase the German race, Nazi bureaucrats divided the Polish population into "potential Germans," inferior Slavs, and biologically defective or politically unwanted people. The latter were sent to concentration camps. Some six million, classified as Slavic Poles, were to be deprived of education and remain a laboring population without legal rights. "Potential Germans," after genetic, medical, and cultural examination, were divided into four groups. Groups 1 and 2, perhaps 1.7 million, received German citizenship. Those in Group 3 were made provisional Germans, and the men could prove their Germanness by enlisting in the German army, which many did—under conditions of starvation they secured better food rations. Group 4 consisted of "Polonized Germans."

Diasporic Germans from southern and Eastern Europe were to be resettled in the *Reichsgaue*. Over the centuries, some of the German emigrants, those in rural colonies in particular, had considered themselves distinct and separate, or even culturally superior to the people among whom they lived. But since the 1880s they had lost their special status under a regime of bureaucratic rationalization and nationalization. While some had migrated to North America, those who stayed, whether third- or tenth-generation ethnics, remained wedged between premigration customs frozen in time and economic interaction with the modern host societies. Some, like a vocal segment of the Sudeten-Germans, supported the Nazi regime or were induced to do so. Resettlement began in October 1939 when the Reich had all German-origin people from Lithuania, Latvia, and Estonia released from their citizenship and ordered them to trek westward to the annexed Polish lands. In the south, German-language South Tyrolians were moved to North Tyrol and Carniola to expand the Austrian-German borderlands. After the Sudeten-German Nazis' clamor for annexation, other states were eager to rid themselves of potential secessionists. The Soviet Union acceded to the Reich's demands to permit German-origin people from its Polish, Belorussian, and Ukrainian regions to depart. While some were willing to leave, many were forced to march westward by Nazi *Umsiedlungskommandos*, operating by permission in the USSR. Only in Yugoslavia did Nazi Yugoslav-German opinion successfully oppose the removal of "valuable German stock," which allegedly was needed to provide the lesser peoples of the region with a standard of quality. In one of the deadly ironies of race-and-purity population planning, the supposedly superior German stock was ordered to trek on foot or in horse-drawn wagons, while an efficient railway transport system was created to transport "undesirables" eastward to resettlement or death camps.

Within a year, 500,000 German-origin settlers from the Baltic states to Bessarabia were uprooted. Another 750,000 trekked westward in the next years. The government of Greater Germany was as indifferent to their life-course projects as it had been to the humanity of the "inferior peoples" shipped out. Of the "German stock," only half a million were resettled; the others remained in camps, and the program ended in disaster. In 1944, when Soviet troops approached the *Reichsgaue*, these uprooted, German-origin people commenced another trek westward, which was often interrupted by fast advancing Soviet troops and then ended in deportation eastward.[54]

Soviet bureaucrats, equally unconcerned about life-courses, considered many non-Russian peoples "unreliable" because of the avowed Nazi sympathies of their elite segments or because of their minority status in the Soviet Empire. Many were deported toward the interior of Russia and further East, including peoples from the recently occupied Baltic and Polish states, refugees from the territories occupied by German armies, the 1.4 million German-origin people in Russia (as counted in the census of 1939), as well as the peoples of the Caucasus, Crimea, Transcaucasia, and the Caspian steppes. There was neither food nor clothing and shelter for the uprooted (map 17.3).

When Poland was divided up, the government-in-exile was permitted to recruit army units, and these soldiers with some 40,000 civilian dependents were permitted to leave Russia. After the war they were resettled in the British Empire: 16,000 in East Africa, 3,000 in Rhodesia, 4,000 in India, and 7,000 in the Middle East. Others settled in Britain or migrated to Canada and the United States as displaced persons.[55]

In the USSR in 1941–42, a massive program of transplanting industry toward and beyond the Ural Mountains secured self-defense in the "Great Patriotic War." For relocated workers and their families, however, working conditions were abominable, living conditions worse, the mortality rates high (chap. 17.2). There were few alternatives: 350,000 civilians had to be evacuated before the German armies encircled Odessa in August 1941, and hundreds of thousands fled in October 1941, when the government evacuated Moscow. From Leningrad, blockaded by the German army for seventeen months, half a million men and women escaped starvation across frozen Lake Ladoga, and nearly one million died—out of a total of just under three million. The German forces debated whether to starve the whole population, to transport survivors to the Russian interior, or, for propagandistic purposes, to permit a "humanitarian" rescue by the Red Cross for transportation to the United States or elsewhere.[56]

In southeastern Europe, where the Reich, Italy, Hungary, and Bulgaria had divided Yugoslavia among themselves, in 1941 20,000 (Slavic) Slovenians from Austrian-settled southern Syria were exchanged for 18,000 German-origin people from Croatia. Serbs were expelled from dispersed settlements to their core territories and subjected to a reign of terror and massacres by the Croatian Ustasha. When the Bulgarian military administration expelled Macedonians or Bulgarianized them, some 300,000 fled. Romania had annexed Bukovina, Bessarabia, and the southeastern Ukraine but ceded southern Dobrudja; the planned resettlement in annexed regions of "pure" Romanians from distant diasporic villages as well as some 250–300,000 Romanian and other Jews was stymied when the German *Einsatzgruppe D*, after having finished off the Ukrainian Jews, arrived to continue its deadly work. Later in the war, the advance of Soviet armies meant further relocations.

The mobilization of men for nation-state armies and their internment as prisoners of war in other nation-states are factors not usually considered in analyses of population transfers. In World War II, however, mobilization and internment involved involuntary mobility and interaction. Prisoners of war, forced to work in the war industries and agriculture of the capturing power, interacted with local populations. Attitudes toward and stereotypes about "Others" emerged. Germans, who worked alongside forced laborers until 1945, a mere decade later labored alongside guest workers. Were attitudes transferred? German civilians and Allied prisoners of war faced the same air raids—how did local people react when Nazi authorities refused air-raid shelter to the aliens? Prisoners of war from many nationalities were spread through Germany to labor in agriculture, mining, or factories. German POWs labored in France and Russia; after the war, some 30,000 were assigned to Belgian coal

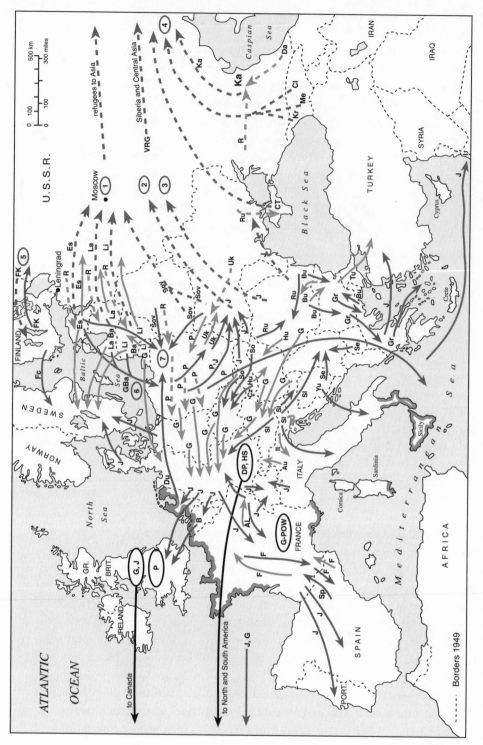

17.3   European Flight, Deportations, and Resettlement, 1939–1949

Movements in Central, Western, and Southeastern Europe before 1945

▨ Coastal zones from which civilian population was evacuated

↑ Refugees, deportees, transferred, "repatriated"

- - ↑ **Movements in the East before 1945**

① Fleeing, evacuated, and deported Estonians, Latvians, Lithuanians, Poles, Jews

② Refugees and evacuees from occupied Soviet territory

③ Jewish refugees

④ Deported Caucasus nationalities and others

⑤ Evacuated Karelians

⑥ Germans from the Baltic states transferred westward under Nazi-Soviet Pact, 1940

⑦ Baltic states' and Soviet citizens from German-occupied territories fleeing westward from Stalin's regime

Movements, 1945 - 1949

↑ Refugees, expellees, transferred, "repatriated"

- - ↑ Replacement migrants

(DP, HS) **DP**-Displaced Persons, **HS**-Holocaust Survivors

(G-POW) **G**erman **p**risoners-**o**f-**w**ar who stayed in France

(G, J) **G**erman and **J**ewish refugees, interned as enemy aliens and deported to Canada

(P) Demobilized Polish army

AL-Alsace-Lorrainers, **A**ustrians, **B**elgians, **B**altic peoples, **B**ulgarians, **CI**-Chechen-Ingush, **CT**-Crimean Tatars, **C**zechs, **D**agestani, **D**utch, **E**stonians, **F**rench, **Fc**-Finnish children, **FK**-Finnish-Karelians, **G**ermans, **GBa**-Germans from the Baltic states, **G**reeks, **H**ungarians (Magyar and other ethnicities), **J**ews, **K**almyks, **K**arachai, **L**atvians, **L**ithuanians, **M**eskhetians, **P**oles, ethnic Russians, **R**umanians, **S**erbs, **S**lovenians, **S**lovaks, **S**oviet citizens regardless of ethnicity, **S**panish, **T**urks, **U**krainians, **VRG**-Volga Russian-Germans, **Y**ugoslavs regardless of ethnicity

The map does not indicate flight ahead of advancing armies, evacuation and flight from bombed cities, returning POWs.

mines, and 1.75 million were put to work in France. When return became possible in April 1947, 20 percent of those in France decided on a kind of retroactive voluntary migration by opting to stay.[57] At a time when no Allied shipping tonnage was said to be available to transport refugee Jews out of Europe, 400,000 German POWs were shipped to the United States. Most returned; some emigrated subsequently.

When in February 1943 the retreat of the German armies began, collaborators from among Ukrainians and other nationalities as well as anti-Soviet Cossacks fled. *Herrenmenschen* in uniform and standard-bearing Aryans trudged westward. When the Soviet army reached the prewar German borders, they had moved past tens of millions of refugees and many millions tried to stay ahead of them.

Flight, Expulsion, and Migration in Postwar Europe

In 1945, the total number of refugees in Europe was estimated to be 30 million; 55–60 million people had died. But governments, willing to transfer surplus populations in the past, were not ready to receive refugees in need. The British government feared a "flooding" by "alien immigrants"; the Canadian government refused to host a conference to examine the restrictive immigration policies of the free world. The Inter-Governmental Committee on Refugees was revived without powers. The Allies committed themselves to create conditions that "will enable all, of whatever nationality, to return to their homes"—a subterfuge to avoid an open admission that people be sent back (principle of *refoulement*), thus depriving refugees of the ability to choose where to begin their lives anew.[58]

Behind the Soviet armies' westward advance, some 2.5 million refugee Poles and Czechs returned to their homelands; in front of the Soviet-Western demarcation line, the western Allies began to repatriate the 7.6 million mainly Eastern European slave laborers from Germany. The program was motivated less by compassion than by food shortages and by Soviet claims to "their" citizens or "human material." Russians shipped back, often against their will, were treated as potential subversives and re-interned; among those "repatriated" were non-Russians who had fought for their own people's independence on the German side.

Civilian refugees, forced laborers, and Jewish survivors from the death camps were called "displaced persons" (DPs) to distinguish them from POWs and demobilized or straggling soldiers. Hundreds of thousands were resettled in immigration countries before the end of 1951, but the perhaps 200,000 "hard-core cases" who remained in West Germany were deprived of their nationality but were not granted German citizenship and thus became "stateless" persons.[59] The perhaps one million surviving Jews in Europe—in Poland 80,000 of 3.3 million or one in forty—were treated like other DPs, with no regard for their particular needs. Palestine remained closed to them because Britain continued to fear Arab hostility. The emotional damage and the destruction of identities suffered by refugees were often not immediately visible and received no attention. In Poland, indigenous anti-Semitism remained rampant, and in the summer of 1946 more than forty members of Kielce's community of 250

Jews were killed in a pogrom by their neighbors. At the end of 1946, 170,000 eastern Jewish survivors had fled to territories administered by the western Allies. Their hopes for admission to North America foundered in the quota limitations; "repatriation" to Palestine emerged only slowly as an option. The callous British request that the USSR settle Jews in Birobidzhan, the Jewish autonomous region in the Soviet Far East, elicited merely a query about empty spaces in the British Empire (chap. 18.2).

Some 12.5 million refugees and expellees of diverse variants of eastern German and diasporic German emigrant cultures and dialects reached the four German zones between 1945 and 1949. Their "insertion" initially involved de facto segregation; integration was achieved only over time and under government pressure. After 1949, West Germany continued to receive migrants descended from East Central and Eastern European German immigrants of previous centuries, whose bloodlines gained them the legal designation of "ethnic Germans" or *Deutschstämmige*.[60]

Settling east of the new German border were 4.5 million Poles dislocated by German occupation forces and then driven to flee from eastern Polish lands incorporated into the USSR. In the Polish territories, some 25 million resettlement and deportation moves took place between 1939 and 1949, with many people being moved more than once.

In the south of the Soviet Union, segments of the Ukrainian and Transcaucasian populations had repeated their attempt in World War I to gain independence. Once Soviet rule was reestablished, this made them traitors, and the autonomous republics of the Crimean Tatars, the Kalmyks, and the Chechen and Ingush peoples were abolished. Some 0.6–1 million people were deported: Central Asian ethnicities, Georgians, Armenians, Turks, Volga and Crimean Tatars, Moutaineer people, Kalmyks and Cossacks. Immigrant Russian ethnics profited economically, and new Russian and Ukrainian peasants were brought in to cultivate vacated lands. The newly acquired western territories from (Finnish) Karelia along the Polish-Belorussian-Ukrainian borderlands to (Romanian) Bessarabia lost parts of their populations by flight or transfer and were resettled by Russian immigrants. In the Far East, the southern Sakhalin Island, taken from Japan, was settled by immigrant farmers and fishermen. Much of the migration was governmentally enforced, but perceived opportunities and a lively and mobile youth movement contributed to the reallocation of peoples.

In southeastern Europe, Hungarians fled when Transylvania was incorporated into redesigned Romania. In the fall of 1949, Greece, wracked by civil war, counted some 700,000 refugees in a population of seven million. Men and women of the Yugoslav peoples fled each other. Sections of the population of Venezia-Giulia and Trieste, an area of mixed settlement contested between Italy and Yugoslavia, also left. When Italian-occupied Dalmatia was reincorporated into Yugoslavia, some 300,000 ethnic Italians out of a population of 0.9 million left. Tunisians and Ethiopians of Italian origin returned from Africa. Aid to refugees, at first provided by the UN Relief and Rehabilitation Administration, was coordinated after December 1946 by the International Refugee Organization.[61]

In the aftermath of war, the establishment of communist rule in East Central Europe caused new refugee movements; to escape poor economic—and thus poor life-course—prospects, western and southern Europeans emigrated to North America into the mid-1950s. The Dutch government supported emigration for fear of "overpopulation," while the West German government retarded it to keep a labor force for reconstruction; the conservative Italian government encouraged departure to rid itself of radical and unemployed working-class voters. Net out-migration from Europe from 1946 to 1955 amounted to 4.5 million people, including the DPs, most of whom went to Canada, the United States, South America (from southern Europe), and Australia, as well as to Israel; most were admitted outside the regular quotas. Britain settled Polish and other European volunteer workers.[62]

Much of the refugee migration was family migration, with women often the heads of families because men were soldiers, prisoners of war, or dead. A special form of women's postwar emigration was departure as war brides. The United States, to take the major recipient state as an example, had sent 16 million men for combat or war-related activities in fifty-seven countries. Nonfraternization policies toward enemy populations were quickly undercut by human relations. From 1942 to 1952, an estimated one million married, and hundreds of thousands of war brides reached the United States; only occasionally did a man remain in his wife's country. Some 41,000 Canadian soldiers were married overseas, mostly to British women. At first, Japanese brides could not hope for lasting unions because the exclusion laws prevented them from immigrating. American and Canadian public opinion accepted the foreign women, albeit with reservations. Politically mandated national hierarchies were undercut by everyday contact or because of principles of humanity. The war brides were to become the ethnic nuclei of postwar migrations.[63]

17.4   Imperialism, Forced Labor, and Relocation in Asia

The second major European war of the twentieth century was preceded by Japanese imperialist warfare since 1937; it was a "world war" from the perspective of military efforts and political alliances, but population movements in Asia remained separate. In elite migrations, however, European and American military advisers had gone to China and Japan since the turn of the century. In both countries, bureaucrats and intellectual gatekeepers had constructed themselves and their peoples as superior. From the end of the nineteenth century onward, Japan could back its claims with concentrated military power, but rebellion, warlords, and a corrupt bureaucracy burdened China. Both countries had to deal with impositions from the colonial powers of the northern hemisphere. During the war of 1914–18, South Asia as well as other parts of the colonial empires had supplied men and materials to the Allies—that is, their colonial overlords—and as a consequence could accelerate their process of self-liberation. China and Vietnam supplied workers to the Allies but did not reap political benefits. The French had 80,000 Vietnamese working for them, and the British recruited some 100,000 workers in Shandong province. The latter were disinfected like cattle and had serial numbers riveted resembling dog tags around their wrists. Most labored under dangerous conditions and lived in unsanitary accommodations in northern France. In recompense for supplying the Allied forces in Europe with munitions, Japan received Germany's possessions in China and the South Sea Islands ("Nan'yo" in Micronesia). It extracted from China special rights to Manchuria and Inner Mongolia in 1917.[64]

Imperial Japan and Civil-War China to the 1930s

After the Russian Empire incorporated the Far East into its territories (chap. 13.4), Sakhalin, Korea, and Manchuria became contested territories with considerable potential for in-migration. To gain access to what it saw as its markets, Japan attacked China and in 1895 annexed Taiwan and the Pescadores (P'eng-hu or Hoko) Islands and "leased" the northern territories (renamed Kantoshu), encompassing Port Arthur and Dalian (Lü-shun and Lüda). In 1905, it defeated Russia and annexed South Sakhalin (renamed Karafuto). Korea, first a "protectorate," was annexed in 1910. Under the influence of Western imperialist thought, Japan began to assume the "burden" of extending the benefits of its civilization to its lesser neighboring peoples (map 17.4).

Taiwan, like Korea an agricultural appendage to Japan, became a laboratory for agricultural, social, and fiscal improvements. Japanese administrators established the security of landholdings and, in contradistinction to Western colonizers, did not introduce the plantation mode of production. Their policies facilitated economic development from which small- and middle-level Taiwanese producers benefited. In Korea, on the other hand, agricultural modernization came as a "ruthless developmental shock," marked by the enforced cultivation of export crops, especially rice for Japan, and the confiscation of land for Japanese settlers. When local populations had to revert to inferior grains like barley and millet, many emigrated to Manchuria or Russian Siberia. The Korean "peninsulars," considered racially similar, had Japanese citizenship imposed on them. The population, which had been stable before 1905, began to increase rapidly under modernization, especially as a result of improved health care. By contrast, South Sakhalin/Karafuto was valued because of its natural resources and—like the Ryúkyú Islands—for its strategic location. Its Japanese population of 12,000 in 1906 grew to over 400,000 four decades later; the Japanese there worked in manufacturing, commerce, and transportation.

"Surplus" people, a population concept shared by imperial elites regardless of culture, were to migrate from Japan to the newly acquired "living space," where the population density was severely underestimated: two million were sent to Taiwan, and 10 million to Korea. Instead of sturdy agricultural pioneers, the staple of imperialist pamphleteers, peddlers, small traders and artisans, shopkeepers, and adventurous merchants were the people who migrated. All looked for profits rather than field labor; most gravitated to the cities; some became landlords. Migration was a male middle- and lower-middle-class project. A few Japanese women went abroad as wives, midwives, and prostitutes. By choosing Brazil, Peru, Hawai'i, and the Philip-

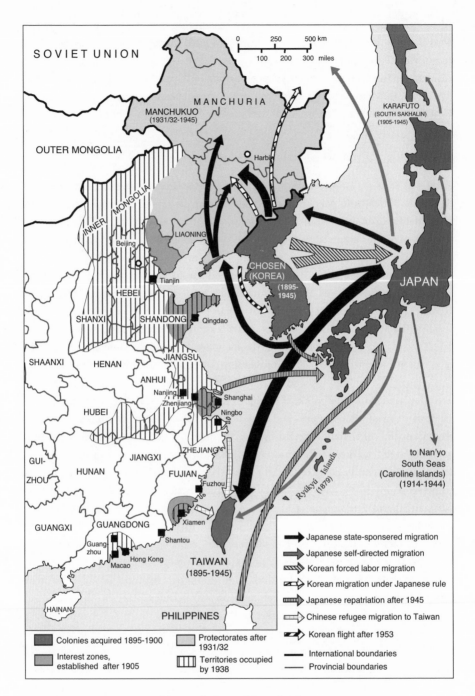

17.4 East Asia: Expansion of Japan, Flight, and Forced Labor

pines as destinations, agricultural migrants undercut the government's rural settlement project. In Nan'yo, the Japanese government introduced sugar cultivation, education, and modernization.

Japanization was meant to bond the colonized to the colonizers. Administrative personnel sent from Japan prevented the emergence of local administrators with distinct interests. Taiwanese and Korean middle classes took advantage of the imperial connection—for example, by sending students to Japanese universities. A Japanese-inspired youth movement in Korea capitalized on generational differences and the mobility of adolescents. But the majority of the colonial populations remained agriculturalists and unskilled urban workers. Japanization by mass immigration remained a planners' scheme. A mere 165,000 Japanese resided among 3.5 million Chinese and 24,000 Natives in Taiwan in 1920 (in 1940, 315,000 among 5.5 million); less than half a million Japanese lived among the Korean population of 19.5 million in 1925 (in 1940, 700,000 among 23.5 million).[65]

In China, competing nationalist warlords as well as the war between nationalists and communists disrupted a society burdened by an ossified bureaucracy and Western imperialist interference. Led by Sun Yat-sen, who had lived in exile in Japan and Europe, and by Chiang Kai-shek, who had been trained in Japan, the nationalist Kuomintang staffed its war academy with German and, until 1927, Russian instructors. Japan, following models of European imperialist penetration, established for itself a special status in Manchuria and Inner Mongolia and, in 1919, took over Shandong. The United States, pursuing a different approach, in 1924 transferred the outstanding $6 million debt from the Boxer Rebellion "indemnity" to a new China Foundation for Promotion of Education and Culture, a form of peaceful penetration. In the civil war, a communist-organized army of the landless in Jiangxi and Fujian, after defeat by the nationalists, embarked on the long march through Guizhou and Sichuan to northern Shaanxi.

Forced Labor, War, Refugees

In 1926, Japan's modernization program became militaristic. The state, with a population of 56 million in 1920, could rely on the labor of 21 million in Sakhalin, Taiwan, and Korea. Concern over population growth led to a dual strategy of expansion into China and of export-oriented industrialization at home. Colonization, targeting five million people for Manchukuo, once again failed, attracting only 50,000 from 1931 to 1939. Policies to serve Japan's economic interests, masked as a "Greater East Asia Co-Prosperity Sphere," established an inner sphere of Japanese territory, with the master people required to maintain purity of blood, ringed by an outer sphere of assumedly friendly and racially akin peoples as well as of a further sphere of allegedly lesser peoples.[66]

Next to Nazi Germany and Stalinist Russia, Japan's empire became the third region of forced labor. Japanese labor unions were weak, and their international connections were at best intermittent. State bureaucrats and employer organizations determined labor relations. Militancy from the bottom up was hampered by the continuing rural connections of workers who, as late as the Great Depression, would rely on help from rural families rather than resort to strikes. The National Essence Society and the Harmonization Society advocated the corporatist cooperation of capital and labor; the nearly fascist "New Order for Labor" and "Industrial Patriotic Association" emerged, the influence of which was mitigated by wartime welfare legislation.

The colonies were forced to produce industrial and military supplies under the control of a "directive minority" of imported Japanese managerial personnel with capital from the core (Taeuber). Korean peasants were uprooted to form an urban industrial, low-skill, mobile proletariat. People from the southern populous, rice-producing provinces in Korea were forced to move internally or to Japan, where a mere 800 had lived in 1910. They were assigned to menial jobs shunned by Japanese, and anti-Korean riots in 1923 marginalized them even further. From 1917 to 1929, 1.2 million Koreans arrived, and 0.85 million returned. In 1940, 1.2 million lived in Japan; forced laborers increased the number to 1.9 million in 1944. By 1945, more than 10 percent of the Korean population worked outside Korea; another 20 percent had been drafted for urban work or were otherwise uprooted. Manpower shortages in Korea led to the promotion of Koreans to middle-rank positions, but, to counter potentially nationalist activities, the repression of the colonized was intensified.

After several forays into northern China and in need of a market for its industrial products, especially textiles, Japan accelerated its military expansion in Manchuria (1931–32), which under the name Manchukuo became an independent state/Japanese protectorate. The Japanese military organized heavy industry close to the Manchurian mines in the midst of an agricultural subsistence economy sustained by recent immigrants (chap. 18.1). High wages and, under depression conditions, an abundant labor supply resulted in free labor markets, except that ethnicized immigration policies kept Chinese immigration low while encouraging Korean and Japanese workers to come. By 1940, 1.4 million workers were imported from Korea's north. Factories suffered from a lack of trained personnel because the colonizers made no effort to expand the educational system. The two-tiered employment system, in which all better-paying positions were reserved for Japanese while poorly paid and dirty jobs were left to immigrant workers of other ethnicities, resulted in high turnover rates and production shortages when the military machine geared up for war.

Full-scale war began in 1937 when Japanese armies took Shanghai and seized larger parts of China. After the fall of Nanjing, the nationalists' capital, in December 1937, tens of thousands of Chinese were massacred, and large numbers of women were raped; the city was looted and partly destroyed. Peasants were driven out of their homes in scorched-earth campaigns. By 1939, an estimated 12 million refugee Chinese had arrived in the western provinces of Yunnan, Guizhou, and Sichuan. The International Refugee Organization evacuated Europeans from China, but Jewish refugees continued to arrive. China mobilized some 13 million soldiers and suffered (according to Japanese figures) 2.7 million or (according to Chinese figures) 1.7 million casualties in the war.

In Japan, policy-makers allocated labor according to the military's priorities, both by exerting more stringent control and by offering—unkept—assurances that living conditions would not deteriorate. Starting in 1941, labor reserves were managed centrally; in 1942 skilled workers and technicians were prohibited from changing jobs, and employers were enjoined from "stealing" technicians from other factories with wage incentives.[67] In the occupied territories, civilian and POW labor was conscripted: for example, a "sweat army" of British, Australian, Dutch, Tamil, and Indian captives was compelled to build the Siam or "Death" Railway.[68] Forced labor, according to one estimate, cost 60,000 lives among Indians alone; Chinese revolted at least on one occasion. Another type of identity-destroying labor forced Korean women into "comfort stations" as prostitutes for Japanese soldiers. Estimates of the number of women involved vary between 100,000 and more than 200,000.[69]

In December 1941, Japan attacked the U.S. fleet at Pearl Harbor, Hawai'i, along with U.S. bases in the Philippines and British forces in Hong Kong and Malaya. By 1942, it occupied much of China, French Indochina, British Burma, Dutch Indonesia, and most of the Pacific Islands. Indian free migrants, laborers, and colonial auxiliaries of the British fled Burma en masse (chap. 15.4). Japan's bombing raids resulted in urban flight as far as Calcutta. Japanese city dwellers were ordered to move to the countryside to escape Allied bombs and to produce food. The Western Allies and China forced Japanese armies into a slow retreat after mid-1942; in 1945 U.S. troops landed on Okinawa; in August nuclear bombs on Hiroshima and Nagasaki ended the war, annihilating the cities' people, including tens of thousands of Korean forced workers.

The internment and repatriation of the 6.5 million Japanese abroad began. The population of South Sakhalin/Karafuto was 93 percent Japanese; of Nan'yo's population of 132,000, 81,000 were Japanese. In the Chinese occupation zones, Japanese had remained few in number: 200,000 were in the Leased Territory; Japanese constituted 6 percent of the 6.4 million inhabitants of Taiwan and 2.9 percent (1942 figures) of the 26.4 million inhabitants of Korea. Repatriation was completed by the end of 1946.[70]

Over one million men, women, and children were repatriated from Japan to South Korea; the North Korean government's repatriation campaign brought home another 100,000. Those remaining were designated "third-country nationals"— neither Japanese nor Allied citizens. They had to hide their ethnicity because of continuing discrimination, but many intermarried. Official Japanese figures listed 611,100 Koreans in 1958—a mixture of displaced persons, guest workers, immigrants, and descendants of immigrants. In 1965 a Japanese–South Korean treaty granted them permanent resident–status, but with the humiliating requirements of fingerprinting and mandatory identification papers.[71]

One group of former inhabitants of Japan suffered from the war a continent away. When the state of Japan attacked Pearl Harbor, Japanese-American and Japanese-Canadian immigrants and citizens were perceived as a military threat by some. Under racist prodding and often to the profit of their European-origin neighbors, the Canadian government had all Japanese and Japanese-Canadians living within 100 miles of the coast removed to the interior. Despite government assurances, all confiscated properties were sold by a federal agency. Of the 125,000 men and women of Japanese birth or ancestry in the United States and the 150,000 in Hawai'i, 110,000 were detained in desert concentration camps. According to a report of the U.S. government four decades later, the decision "was not justified by military necessity" but rather by "race prejudice, war hysteria, and a failure of political leadership."[72]

In postwar Asia, the Euro-American belligerent colonial powers promised various forms of partnership or independence to India (1940), Burma (1945), the Philippines (1946), and other colonies. As in postwar Europe, the emergence of new states was accompanied by power struggles between stronger and weaker polities and the expulsion and flight of large populations. In many states, nationalist or reformist rebellions, often involving peasant masses, and conflicts pitting Muslims against people of different faiths were frequent, and the Cold War ideology of the West labeled them "communist"-inspired. Depending on the degree of industrialization and the demand for labor, new postcolonial intra-Asian migration patterns emerged, and, with the abolishment of Asian exclusion by the two North America states, the third phase of the Pacific Migration System began.

In postwar Korea, a moderate, prewar collaborationist elite stood opposed to an anticolonial, leftist-oriented elite, which returned from underground activities and exile. The former was aging and established; the latter young and dynamic. The prosecution of collaborators implied partial elite displacement. The country was divided into a northern political entity, with a population of nine million, and a southern polity, with a population of 21 million. Before the beginning of the Korean War in June 1950, 1.8 million fled southward. In 1960 some four million refugees from the north amounted to more than one-third of the southern population.[73]

The Chinese civil war ended in 1949, when the nationalist armies and government, an estimated two million people in all, withdrew to Taiwan. This occupation-type arrival destroyed part of the island's economic system. Some 340,000 Chinese refugees, landowners and students in particular, headed for neighboring countries, almost half of them going to Burma. A few thousand moved to northern Laos, and 14,000 went to Portuguese Macao. The largest number of Chinese refugees entered British Hong Kong; the population there doubled from 1931 to 1941, reaching 1.64 million, and then doubled again to 3.2 million by 1961. Refugees arriving in Southeast Asian countries received help from the Chinese diaspora, often from distant family members. By mid-1953, the "Overseas Chinese" numbered 13.4 million in sixteen countries or enclaves in Southeast Asia, and another 300,000 were located in the Americas, Oceania, Africa, and Europe.[74]

In South Asia, Hindu-Muslim relations involved socioeconomic hierarchies. With the early, modest successes of the independence movement, tensions increased as competing leaderships sought to shape an institutional future. The tripartite British-Hindu-Muslim negotiations in 1947 divided the country into (Hindu) India and "the land of the pure," (Muslim) West and East Pakistan.[75] The subcontinent's

389 million people spoke fifteen official, twenty-four regional, and twenty-three local languages as well as some 700 dialects; "Indian" as an ethnic or cultural description remained a creation of outside observers. Cultural identities were defined by ethnicity, language, religion, caste, and other factors whose relative importance varied from region to region. Ethnic Bengalis, whether Muslims or Hindus, had more in common across religious boundaries with Muslims of Pathan ethnicity or with Hindus of Tamil ethnicity. Religious designations—Hindu, Muslim, Sikh, Buddhist, Jain, Christian—refer to lifestyles and social hierarchies, to communities rather than mere creeds. The bulk of the Muslims, 22 percent of the population, were agriculturalists; the 68 percent of the population who were Hindus were shopkeepers and moneylenders or worked in cloth and other factories.

The division of the subcontinent was to involve a projected four million people in moves from one part to another. In October 1947, a forty-five-mile-long column of 800,000 Hindus and Sikhs trekked from Pakistan to India. Rumored and actual persecution, rape, and murder increased fear and flight. In the Punjab, where Muslims, Sikhs, and Hindus settled interspersed, massacres and atrocities occurred. From Karachi, long free of intercommunal violence, almost one-third of the population departed—mainly Hindus in commerce. In the exchange between West and East Bengal (India and East Pakistan), 1.2 million people out of a population of 20 million Hindus and 8 million Muslims moved eastbound, while 4.8 million of 32 million Muslims and 10 million Hindus headed westward. Governments and armies, originally reluctant to support the population exchanges, started to speed up the east- and westbound movements to reduce the danger of epidemics and to resettle people in time for sowing and harvesting in order to lessen the threat of famine. Many moved to places inhabited by relatives and friends; a Ministry of Relief and Rehabilitation in India resettled refugees. By the end of 1947, 7.3 million men, women, and children had been exchanged between the two religion-based states. An estimated one million died during the treks; women were particularly liable to attack and robbery because they carried their traditional marriage gifts of gold and jewelry. By 1951, refugee numbers had increased to 14.5 million.[76] In 1961, as compared with the distribution of people in 1931, regional populations were more homogeneous by religion. But cultural and linguistic heterogeneity remained. Only 370 million out of a total population of 548 million (1961) spoke one of India's fifteen languages scheduled in the Constitution.[77]

In Burma, which achieved independence in 1948, Chinese technicians filled the vacancies left by the flight of British Indians in 1942. They faced riots in reaction to the alleged support of the People's Republic of China for "minority" peoples in Burma. Within the multiethnic population, the Karen people in the east-central region unsuccessfully attempted to form a separate state in the late 1940s, and the Mon people opposed the central government in the 1950s. In Malaya a small nationalist-communist uprising was quelled by British troops in 1950, but about 500,000 Chinese agriculturalists were forced to resettle in order to starve the insurgents. Siam/Thailand, which survived the war years before 1945 as an ally of Japan, became a refugee-receiving country during the Vietnam War in the 1960s.

When France reestablished colonial rule in Indochina (later Cambodia, Laos, and Vietnam), a war of independence began. When the 1954 cease-fire divided the country into a nationalist-communist north and a Buddhist, Catholic-ruled, U.S.-dependent south, 140,000 civilians opted to move to North Vietnam, with a population of 16 million, while 860,000 moved south, with a population of 11.5 million, before May 1955. Of the latter, the vast majority were Catholics (71 percent); most of the others were Buddhists, and the remainder were tribal peoples like the Nungs.[78]

The Netherlands East Indies declared independence two days after Japan's surrender. British and Dutch troops, sent to intern Japanese troops, instead fought the Indonesian People's Army, but the state achieved independence in 1949. Of the 240,000 European residents, more than four-fifths were of Dutch origin (figures of 1930). However, the designation "Europeans" veiled the other, Asian, side since 70 percent were "Indos," the offspring of intermarriages. Before independence, families from the highest social strata had left; after independence, some 15 percent of the Indos opted for Indonesian citizenship, while about 100,000 colonial auxiliaries, midlevel officials, and military men with their families were evacuated to the Netherlands. Most of them had never been in the Netherlands before; some did not speak Dutch; and most—the Ambonese, for example—were non-White. In 1957, Indonesia expelled the remaining Dutch nationals and expropriated Dutch agricultural properties.[79]

Japan's attempt to establish a colonial empire and the Allied intervention, combined with Europe's internal warfare at the same time, left the colonial system in shambles. French, Dutch, and U.S. attempts to reestablish colonial rule or zones of influence prolonged the processes of dislocation. China, as a new imperial power, annexed Tibet, causing mass flight into India, Nepal, and Bhutan. After independence, the new nationalist elites, confronted with multiethnic populations, pursued models of state formation that placed one cultural group in a hegemonic position. Industrial growth, rural-urban migrations, or the mass export of workers, often of women for domestic labor, characterize the decades from the 1960s onward. Migrants carried the cultures of Asia, which had survived colonialism, into the metropoles (chap. 19.5–6).

18

Between the Old and the New,

1920s to 1950s

In the interwar years, several regional migration systems, in particular in the Asian world, continued to function. Migration from India to East Africa, Burma, and the Malay Peninsula and from China to Malaya continued. Continuity meant the stabilization of communities, with increasing numbers of women among migrants and of locally born "ethnics" as opposed to newcomers. The Southeast Asian Migration Subsystem ended with the Japanese invasion in 1937, and the Indo-African Subsystem came to a halt after the East African states gained their independence (chaps. 15.4, 17.5).

Four major migratory movements characterize the 1920s to 1950s: 1) Peasants, searching for land, migrated to a "settlement belt" or "pioneer fringe" that girded the northern hemisphere. White farmers moved to islands of settlement in Africa and Latin America, and Chinese farmers went in much larger numbers to Manchuria. At the same time, severe droughts turned fertile lands into dust bowls and sent families fleeing. 2) Large-scale Jewish migrations to Palestine, subsequently Israel, established a new society that combined settlement with state-building—and generated Palestinian refugees in the process. 3) An enhanced national consciousness among most colonial peoples and the wars in the Atlantic and Pacific Worlds from 1937 to 1945 destabilized the imperial position of both Europe and the United States. Decolonization caused "reverse migrations" of descendants of "White" settlers and investors to their ancestors' countries of origin, the return of colonial administrators and soldiers, and the flight of usually non-White colonial auxiliaries. Imperialism survived under the guise of unequal terms of trade. 4) South Africa's coerced resettlement and temporary migration system received its institutionalized underpinnings from the 1920s to the 1940s.

In the Atlantic System, the post-1945 exodus from the war-devastated European countries brought about a last surge of North American–bound migrations. With Europe's economic recovery in the mid-fifties, this migration almost came to a standstill, except in the case of Italians and Portuguese. In its place, two continental south-north migration systems emerged (chap. 19.2–3). The Russo-Siberian Migration System, which changed deeply during the industrialization and urbanization of the

Soviet Union, ended in the 1950s. The socialist region remained separate from the capitalist region until 1989 (chap. 19.9). Under the impact of exclusion and worldwide depression, the Pacific Migration System remained limited to merchants and small numbers of other migrants.

18.1   Peasant Settlement from Canada to Manchuria

By the second decade of the twentieth century, most agriculturally usable lands across the globe had been settled by immigrants from Europe or internal migrants. In some regions, as in Assam, India, fertile land was still available. But, in general, settler migrants had to content themselves with ever more marginal lands and tenuous links to markets. Canada's Peace River District, for example, was separated from settled areas by 150–200 miles of muskeg and timberlands. In 1930, its population stood at a mere 40,000, and homesteaders' diaries reveal the unremitting hard work and loneliness they had to endure. The experience of "making do," of bare survival or outright defeat, contrasted starkly with Canadian poets' paeans to the golden wheat. Nevertheless, the quest for land and larger crops continued in the 1920s and 1930s: the agricultural sciences developed new strains of grain for short northern summers and new dry-farming techniques. Irrigation permitted the cultivation of semiarid lands.

Five zones of new settlement included the High Plains from the Texas Panhandle to Alberta, via Montana, and west to central Oregon; a global northern belt from Canada's plains and Peace River District as well as southern Alaska via the lowland plains of Manchuria and Mongolia to southern Siberia; in Latin America a south-north belt along the eastern foothills of the Andes; a similar African belt extending along the cool subtropical highlands from Transvaal to Kenya; and sections of Australia, Tasmania, and New Zealand. Scholars of the "Pioneer Settlement Study" rhapsodized about men and women on the "pioneer fringe" across the globe and about independent lives: "Virgin soil is being put under the plow, houses are built to shelter pioneer families, and the web of frontier civilization is being woven." But the study was published three years after the onset of the Great Depression (map 18.1).

Settlement, from the perspective of Euro-American scholars from the 1920s to the 1950s, involved issues of race and virility. They explored temperate zones for "White," European settlers and looked for strong, healthy men. Reflecting the eugenics movement, they commented that "slack" workers and "sickly people (especially women)" tended not to last (Joerg). In Australia, the exclusion of Asian immigrants retarded the filling of the land and meant that the country's economic potential was underutilized, but, noted one study, Australia's "leaders" recognized the implications of power and race: vacant lands might become a source of danger by attracting "another kind of people" in search of land. "A white Australian policy has definite, if distant, political objectives, but it also has social objectives of the highest order."[1]

In technologically advanced societies, the short 1920s between postwar recession and post-1929 unemployment did provide opportunities. Farmers' and new settlers'

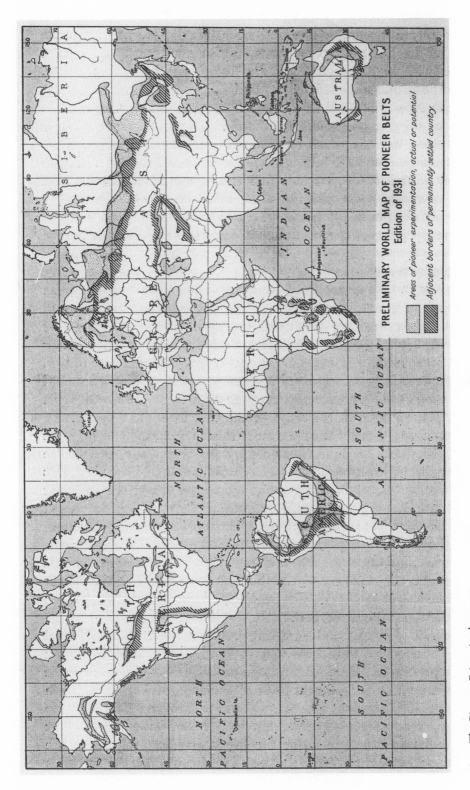

PRELIMINARY WORLD MAP OF PIONEER BELTS
Edition of 1931

Areas of pioneer experimentation, actual or potential

Adjacent borders of permanently settled country

18.1 The Pioneer Fringe in the 1930s

rising expectations grew with rural electrification programs in the United States and the USSR. Wireless sets, telephones, and even cars connected isolated settlers to the next urban center, but viable economies only developed in some regions, thanks to the introduction of new crops or because of railroad connections to larger markets. Most settler migrants had to fashion lives from meager surroundings. Recurring droughts, dust storms, and depression sent hopeful men and women into seasonal labor elsewhere. Desertification processes were worse: "Man is fleeing, not advancing," having lost once fertile and prosperous areas. The Gobi Desert advanced because of deforestation by earlier settlers and nomads, and in North America dustbowl families trekked across the continent to become underpaid seasonal harvest laborers in California or British Columbia. Steinbeck's *Grapes of Wrath* and Dorothea Lange's and Margaret Bourke-White's photos documented the trek of the dispirited and their lost hopes and futures. Manchurian settlement was accelerated by a severe drought in Shandong; Chingizî Aytmatov depicted different experiences yet similar life-stories in the inner Asian Soviet Union.[2]

When the Depression of 1929 began, hopes for the future became reminiscences of the past. Families on the margins of settlement, whom racial ideologues would call "pioneers," like families on urban fringes, who would be labeled "scum," worked hard—survival was an achievement and success not an option. Whenever soil or sources of supplementary income gave out, families had to move on to alternative ways of subsistence; rural settlers had to be as mobile as casual workers. "When one's neighbor leaves, one is also inclined to go. It is a self-stimulating process." In 1950s North America, the aging pioneer men and women of the 1920s drifted back to cities that provided comfort, and so did their children, drawn by social life, amusements, and jobs.[3]

In Africa, the north from Morocco to Egypt counted more than one million "White settlers," while the southern tip supported 1.7 million. A third region, ranging from Transvaal to Kenya, attracted European settlers in the interwar years. In the temperate and fertile highlands, with "black labor near at hand" (Bowman) and easy market access, White settlers with capital were to produce raw materials and buy "agricultural machinery and other material necessities" from the cores. Indian free migrants and former contract laborers provided trading links between coastal cities and inland White settlers. According to White population planners, development and innovation were characteristic of the "white man's system of land use," whereas in southern Rhodesia, for example, "the natives can be cared for under their present cultural system on about 37 percent of the territory." The subdivision of land among the children of White settlers, however, blurred White-Black economic differences and distinctions; "the poor white" lived hardly above the level of a Native family.

In racialized labor regimes, such as in Kenya, the European governments sold land to White settlers and then labeled the original inhabitants "squatters." Among the latter, White landowners would select families to retain as a labor force and eject all others, who would have to migrate to a new landlord or find a place on a Reserve or gravitate toward an urban area. In South Africa after 1913, Native tenants had to "enter into agreement" with a White landlord "whereby in return for the right to live on his farm they [would] give him three months' labor free of wages." For others, so White scholars argued, the "glamour of urban life" and "the superior conditions of employment" would encourage cityward migration, but White governments excluded Black families from the cities. Labor analysts advocated contractual relationships in industry and mining, a kind of improved master-servant relationship under which settlers would gradually accede to demands by African workers for improved standards of living and education. But the settler-controlled political system in South Africa imposed apartheid in 1948 (chap. 18.4). In Nigeria, on the other hand, "where vacant land was abundant" but the climate not to the liking of Whites, an internal population shift occurred from the more developed regions south of the Niger and Benue Rivers to the central region north of the rivers. Self-determined migration of Africans was limited to areas marginal to White interests.[4]

In Latin America, the eastern Andean border valleys and the Bolivian plateau provided few opportunities. Settlers could not easily draw on local labor and were distant from markets; in the nineteenth century, they had faced decline when areas of intensive agriculture in proximity to mines or administrations lost population to new economic centers. From Colombia's *llanos*, the grass-covered Orinoco-drained plains, for example, cattle raising had shifted to coastal regions. Workers, whether independent or hired, migrated to the quinine-bark-collection economy of 1872–87 and the subsequent rubber-collection economy of 1887–1912. When the market failed in 1912, large-scale emigration was the only choice. Thousands of men had migrated from the Moyobamba region, in northern Peru, expecting to amass fortunes in the Amazon forests. But after the boom's end, the base town lost 7,000 of its 12,000 inhabitants. From Argentina to Brazil, the Matto Grosso and Gran Chaco region had benefited from the opening of meatpacking plants in São Paulo: internal migrants came; Japanese immigrants settled; Russian Mennonites established colonies. Natives resisted the entry of Whites and their "occasional demands" for *peonada*, forced labor. The collapse of Brazil's coffee economy enforced rural mobility. People who chose not to follow the main, cityward migration, moved to the Paraná Plateau, west of São Paulo, and other agricultural frontier regions; some 1.2 million did so in the 1940s and 1950s. Patagonia, southern Chile, and Argentina had been settled decades earlier, after the military campaigns of 1879–84 had subdued the Native peoples. Migrants converged southward from the pampas, northward from Punta Arenas, and eastward from Chile; in addition, Welsh immigrants had come. A class of small landowners had emerged in Peru's coastal valleys. Migration in many regions was an escape from decline rather than a move toward opportunities. A 1920s assessment of Latin America as "the land of the future" missed the actual story.[5]

In Asia, Japanese had settled annexed neighboring islands in the later nineteenth century; migration stimulated by imperialist and military expansion involved only small numbers of peasant settlers. Administrators exploited or dislocated local populations, particularly in Korea (chap. 17.4). The Dutch, in their Indonesian colony, relocated 230,000 people from Java and other islands to the southern half of Sumatra as farmers, a program that was to be continued by the government of independent Indonesia (chap. 19.6).

Of all the varieties of interwar peasant migrations, that of Chinese northward was the most important. People from the southern provinces had traditionally left for overseas destinations. North of the Amur, the settlement of Russian migrants and their interaction with indigenous peoples had developed over two centuries (chaps. 7.1, 13.4). About 10 percent of China's fast growing population were minority peoples of more than fifty nationalities: Muslim Turkic-speaking peoples from the Uighurs to the Kazakhs in Central Asia, Mongolian and Tibetan peoples in Mongolia and the Himalayas, Koreans and Manchu in the north. Beijing accommodated small communities or seasonal market populations of maritime Arab Muslim traders, Turkic Muslims from Samarkand, and nomad Mongol traders. Commercial connections reached far into the interior: the Muslims of Sinhaw, Inner Mongolia, for example, grew tobacco for the British American Tobacco Company.

Under the impact of Western imperial penetration, vast labor reserves were dislocated in the northern provinces, and Mongolia was colonized with the Chinese government's support in the 1920s. Younger sons of peasant families came. In the new villages, "elders" were men in their thirties. Women either migrated with the men or came with their children after the first crop had been planted. Because of limited means, men often migrated seasonally to distant wage labor. Irrigation projects— for example, south of Saratsi in 1929–31—needed between 1,000 and 5,000 migrant laborers depending on the season. Single men formed temporary alliances with local women: children were raised as Mongols if they stayed with their mothers or as Chinese when they entered immigrant communities. Children of poor families were no longer sold but were hired out, instead, to herd the flocks of Mongol villages. As adolescents, they were to return to their families. But alienation, the experience of mobility, and bilingualism induced many to migrate into towns to work as interpreters. The cattle drives organized by Chinese traders brought meat on the hoof to new railway terminals for sale in Beijing or other markets, thus connecting nomad and pioneer economies to the core.[6]

Migration to Manchuria was vastly larger. By the mid-nineteenth century, Chinese from the northern provinces moved first to the Liao River valley and then to regions north of Mukden (Shenyang) and Harbin, along the Sungari (Songhua) River. Many had been dislocated by the Taiping and Muslim rebellions; more came because of population growth and the economically debilitating corruption of officialdom. The construction of the eastbound railroad from Beijing to Suiyuan and of the northbound line to Harbin provided mass transportation. Impoverished families, however, had to walk hundreds of miles and build modest homes "of sun-dried mud bricks or of pounded earth, with a mud roof laid over a mattress of reeds or brush. There are commonly two rooms, one with a crude mud stove. . . . Wood is scarce, and its use restricted to the roof beams, doors, and windows."[7] In the North American prairies, sod houses were equally small in the first years of settlement.

Manchuria's population doubled from 15 million in 1911 to 30 million in 1931.[8]

Up to the 1920s, the government encouraged and assisted migration; private companies or administrative bodies held and sold land. Until 1925, three-quarters of the 500,000 seasonal workers returned each year to their families in Shandong or Chihli. From 1927 to 1930, railway-stimulated in-migration increased to an average of about one million people per year. Only two-fifths still came seasonally, and the share of women and children grew substantially. Most migrants came of their own accord from Shandong province, motivated by continued droughts, famine, and civil war. The mass migration to "Manchukuo," the region's name under Japanese rule after 1931–32, provided Japanese-run coalmines, railway construction, and cities with unskilled workers.

While in Mongolia cultural interaction was the rule, by sheer numbers the Chinese immigrants in Manchuria absorbed the local Manchu people. By 1926, some 300,000 Korean rice farmers, displaced by Japan's imperialist penetration, reached Manchuria. But the nationalist Chinese society under control of the Kuomintang government was afforded little opportunity to move beyond subsistence farming. Chinese formed classic urban immigrant communities in which families from the same region or village of origin settled close to each other, founded mutual aid societies, banded together in vigilante-type groups to keep order under frontier conditions, and established credit arrangements to avoid moneylenders. Since settlement was compact, the frontier moved ahead slowly. New railroads, banks, and market crops facilitated migration, but the traditional Confucian concepts of the family, of ancestral spirits related to the land, and of the role of sons retarded change.[9]

By 1940, Manchuria's 43.2 million people consisted of 36.8 million Chinese, 2.7 million Manchus, 1.1 million Mongols, 1.45 million Koreans, 0.85 million Japanese, and smaller numbers of Russians and other ethnicities. Inner Mongolia had a population of five million, of which only one-fifth were Mongols (Lattimore's estimate). Outer Mongolia remained Mongol, with small pockets of Russians. Chinese Turkistan was home to Central Asian Turkish people, Muslim Chinese, Manchus, and smaller minorities. Some 450 million people lived in historic China, and 45 million in the territories outside, including Tibet. As was true everywhere else, ethnic identity was constructed: settled Mongols were Chinese, and itinerant Chinese traders became Mongols. The ubiquitous population planners estimated that Mongolia could still absorb one million immigrants, and Manchuria 30 million.[10]

Across the globe, peasant colonists—whether singly or in families, hoped for independent lives, but insurmountable challenges forced many to give up. Observers described colonization projects as worlds of men, and one scholar offered the opinion that loneliness resulted in "not a few tragedies" for women. He noted at the same time: "Many older women [in Rhodesia and Nyasaland], in the event of the death of their husbands, carry on alone. One of the arguments used in England in favor of women's suffrage was the fact that a woman held the record for yield of cotton per acre.... But despite these new interests many women are temperamentally incapable of leading such a life."[11] Patterns of women's roles differed, of course, between lonely farms in North America, compact villages in China, and estates in Africa, but nowhere was peasant colonization a male preserve. In most regions, it placed migrants over Natives, White over Black, Chinese over Manchu.

18.2 Diaspora to Homeland and Vice Versa: Jewish Migrants, Arab Refugees

Since the 1880s, the mass exodus of Russian Jews from the tsarist empire had linked the Russo-Siberian to the Atlantic Migration System (chaps. 13.5, 14.1). With the growing anti-Semitism and nationalism in the Atlantic World, Theodor Herzl, in 1903, negotiated with Egypt—then under British control—a lease of the Sinai Peninsula for Jewish settlements. After the dissolution of the Ottoman Empire in 1918, the British government as the League of Nations' mandatory power in Palestine promised settlements to Jewish immigrants as well as security of landownership to Arab residents. Before 1914, however, only 60,000 of 2.75 million Jewish migrants worldwide went to Palestine, and in the interwar years only a small minority of Jewish refugees chose to settle there. Jewish migrants to Palestine were part of the interwar agricultural settlement migration; local Muslim peasants migrated to cities, and some emigrated as far away as the Canadian prairies. From 1919 to 1939, 345,000 Jewish men, women, and children immigrated to Palestine; from 1940 to 1944, another 45,000 came as refugees from fascism. The way to Palestine was *aliyah,* a process of ascending to a special place, a spiritual project.

The United Nations November 1947 partition of Palestine envisaged a Jewish state with an Arab minority of just under 400,000 or 42.5 percent of the population.[12] The surrounding Arab states countered with immediate intervention, "a war of extermination" in the words of the Arab League's secretary general. However, the offensive failed. The proclamation of Israel's statehood in 1948 and the several Arab-Israel military campaigns generated further waves of refugees: some 250,000 Arab residents fled from the coastal Plain of Sharon; Jaffa emptied; when truce negotiations failed, Haifa's Arab population left within a day. In some areas, only a few thousand Christian Arabs were left, and a total of only 142,000 Arabs remained.

In 1948 the UN's mediator estimated refugees to number 330,000, including 50,000 in Jewish-controlled territories. In the camps of the UN Relief and Works Agency for Palestinian Refugees (UNRWA) the numbers tripled to some 0.9–1.2 million when the poor from other areas joined soup lines and resettlement programs. After Israel agreed to resettle 100,000 refugees, the number of Arabs in the state grew to 250,000. The Arab governments, hoping to reverse the political situation, showed little inclination to settle Palestinian refugees, who became pawns of the Arab-Israeli power struggles. In 1950 the UNRWA reported that its work was sabotaged.

For the refugees, only migration was left as an alternative. By 1952, some 20,000 had been absorbed into Kuwait and Saudi Arabia as technical experts in government or for the Aramco oil company; others were accepted by states from Libya to the Gulf area, often with the support of UNRWA training programs or small loans to establish economically sound ventures. Still others fled to assigned reserves, such as the Gaza

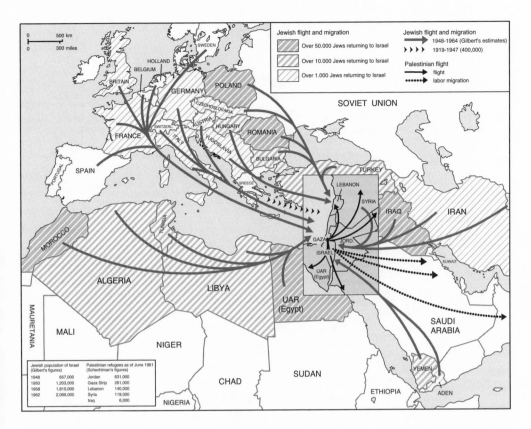

Jewish population of Israel (Gilbert's figures)		Palestinian refugees as of June 1961 (Schechtman's figures)	
1948	657,000	Jordan	631,000
1950	1,203,000	Gaza Strip	261,000
1958	1,810,000	Lebanon	140,000
1962	2,069,000	Syria	119,000
		Iraq	6,000

18.2 Jewish and Palestinian Flight and Migrations to 1964

Strip. Only Jordan granted citizenship to the refugees; it began an agricultural settlement program at a time when many refugees had acquired training and economic independence by their own efforts. In Syria Palestinians began to settle semi-arid lands
in need of irrigation. By 1961, 140,000 had been accommodated in Lebanon, 119,000
in Syria, 6,000 in Iraq, 631,000 in Jordan, and 261,000 in the Gaza Strip—a total of
1.2 million. To regain some measure of self-determination, ever larger numbers of
the Palestinian Arab refugees became migrant workers far beyond the Arab states;
many saw high achievements in education as a way to escape the camps; militant
Palestinian groups unsuccessfully tried to take over power in Jordan in 1970 and in
Lebanon after 1975 (chap. 19.7).

Parallel to the Arab exodus, a mass immigration of Jews from many countries
and cultures filled the land (map 18.2). From 1945 to 1960, three-quarters of all Jewish migrants chose Palestine/Israel as their destination. In a comparative perspective,
new arrivals amounted to 266 per 1,000 population in 1949, 154 per 1,000 in 1950,
and 133 per 1,000 in 1951, whereas in the peak year of U.S. immigration, 1907, all
foreign-born amounted to a mere 15 per 1,000 population; in Canada and Argentina
in 1913, there were 38 foreign-born per 1,000; and in India during the refugee crisis
of 1947, the number was 22 per 1,000.[13] Israel's Law of Return entitled every Jew to

citizenship upon arrival. Cultural heterogeneity led to intra-Jewish conflict: 51 percent came from Muslim countries, 41 percent from Eastern and Central Europe, and a mere 88,000 (8 percent) from Western counties. Newcomers hailed from thirty-two countries, and Palestinian Arabs were dispersed in as many.

The first wave of refugee arrivals up to December 1948 mainly brought Holocaust survivors: 80,000 from Poland, 38,000 each from Romania and Bulgaria, a mere 5,000 from Czechoslovakia and Hungary, and 24,000 internees who had escaped from fascism but had been held as "illegal immigrants" by the British on Cyprus. To these 150,000 Europeans of Jewish faith, a second wave added another 200,000—estimates vary—from North Africa, the Arabian Peninsula, and Iraq. They, too, were a culturally diverse group. Iraqi Jews, for example, were mostly middlemen and urban people, whereas the Yemeni Jews had lived secluded, backward lives. A third wave, a new exodus from Eastern Europe in 1950–51, brought 425,000. After a hiatus of just three years, apprehensions gripped Jewish communities in Morocco and Libya, though no threat to lives or property existed. In fact, the Moroccan monarch had protected the Jewish community when the protectorate's overlord, the French Vichy government, had delivered Jews to German forces. The Arabization of the school system threatened the Jewish affinity to French language and culture, and both sophisticated urban "Casablans" and "the more primitive" Jews from the mountains began to depart. Although in June 1956 the government barred departure, because the heavy loss of skills and capital caused economic problems, 300,000 left Morocco in the next years. In the wake of the British-French Suez aggression in 1956, a further exodus from North Africa (extending from Algeria to Egypt) paralleled the Hungarian refugee crisis. Algeria's Jewish community of 135,000 dwindled to a mere 10,000 in 1963. This exodus ended 450 years of coexistence dating from the mass arrival after the Iberian expulsions (chap. 4).[14]

The Israeli state, like all other states with high levels of flight, seized abandoned property to accommodate newcomers. Western observers voiced concern about the absence of mechanisms for property transfers from the country of flight to the country of destination. Their views proceeded from abstract notions of the security of property, not from a concern for self-determined life-courses. A human-centered approach would at least have discussed the need for "starting capital" or household utensils at the destination. Immigrant refugees in Israel, like Palestinians in Arab states, received shelter in tent colonies located wherever space was available, without regard to access to labor markets or land. As a consequence, each new wave of arrivals—as well as those bypassed by placement agencies staffed by Jews of different ethnicity—was relegated to life on the fringes of society.

After a decade of mass arrivals, the right of access to Israel for all men, women, and children of Jewish faith was restricted to those who suffered from immediate danger to life and liberty in the society of origin. As in other immigration countries, no family was eligible that did not have one breadwinner under the age of forty-five; no family with mentally deficient, handicapped, or tuberculosis-infected members could enter unless space was available in Israel's health-care facilities; no family liable to become a burden to the state would be allowed to settle. Policies changed from immediate rescue to manageable resettlement.

A report of 1964 juxtaposed the Euro-American "first Israel" including the Eastern European Ashkenzim and a "second Israel" of Afro-Asian Jews, ranging from the Iberian Sephardim to North African and Turkish Jews, as well as including Yemeni, Iraqi, and other Oriental Jews. This was also a distinction between White and Colored. The two communities lacked mutual understanding and were unwilling to work for mutual respect. Little intermarriage occurred between the two immigrant groups, and by the 1990s a third group, the recently arrived Russian Orthodox Jews, practiced endogamy.

Jews from across the world have continued to settle in Israel, despite continuing warfare, external hostility, and internal racism. In 1972, only 8.5 percent of the Jewish population had been born in Israel; 44 percent were born in Europe, America, or Oceania, 24.5 percent in Asia, and 23 percent in Africa. The Jewish nation-state that Herzl had envisioned around 1900, including its Arab Muslim population, turned out to be pluralist in terms of regional origin, customs, and religious practices.[15]

18.3   Decolonization and Reverse Migrations

In many parts of the colonial worlds, movements for self-government accelerated in the interwar years. In the Eastern Mediterranean–Red Sea–Persian Gulf region, Britain granted formal independence to Egypt in 1922 and to Iraq in 1930. On the other hand, France ended a Druse uprising in its Syrian mandate in 1925 by bombing the rebels, and Italy invaded Ethiopia in 1935. After World War II, colonial regimes collapsed, inducing 1) reverse migrations of descendants of colonizer personnel and settlers, 2) migrations to the core of colonial auxiliaries or "collaborators" facing retribution from those they had controlled, and 3) replacement migrations to vacated farmland or urban jobs, with the formerly colonized fanning out from the social or geographical "reserves" to which they had been relegated.

A survey of Europeans in the colonies reveals their limited numerical presence, despite all of the economic and political power they brought to bear. By 1914, Germany had merely 15,000 settlers in Southwest Africa, fewer in East Africa. In the 1920s, 164,000 British people, 45,000 women among them, lived in India. In 1930, Portuguese Angola and Mozambique held European-origin populations of only 40,000 and 18,000 respectively.[16] Italians, reluctant to migrate to Libya, including Tripolitania and Cyrenaica, numbered fewer than 30,000 in the new African colonies by 1938. Fascist mobilization sent another 90,000 to Africa and projected that the Somalian highlands would become the home of five million Italians. Defeat intervened. The British central African colonies counted 300,000 Europeans in 1945, and French Morocco, Algeria, and Tunisia had 1.25 million in 1930; a negligible number lived in West Africa. South African Whites amounted to 2.6 million in a population of 12.7 million in 1951.[17]

Decolonization ended, first, the temporary assignments of administrators and soldiers in colonies of exploitation and, second, the privileged position of long-term settler families in colonies of settlement. Like "Loyalists" following the beginning of the American War of Independence in 1776, many would emigrate, some in immediate flight, others over time. They saw their political power crumble, their economic calculations collapse, their life-styles vanish, and "their" subaltern Native labor rise to citizenship. Most were locally born ("Creoles") and had never known the society of origin. Third, colonial auxiliaries had to leave, whether recruited locally as in French Algeria, distributed across an empire as in the case of the Sikhs, or pitted against majority populations as in the case of the Hmong in Indochina. Their former policing role made them liable to retribution and punishment by the newly sovereign people. Fourth, men, women, and children of genetically mixed ancestry as well as elites with a cultural affinity to the core found themselves in a precarious position. The withdrawal of elites in possession of capital, skills, and knowledge could create havoc in the new economies.[18]

Wars for independence or the transition to it resulted in multiple refugee streams. At first, colonizers on the defensive shifted populations: in the 1950s, the British resettled half a million Chinese in Malaya, tens of thousands of Kikuyu from Nairobi, and the ruling Kabaka elders from Buganda; the French uprooted Algerian peasants. Second, wars for independence dislocated people of whole regions. For example, 100,000 fled Portuguese Guinea-Bissau for Senegal and Guinea-Conakry before independence in 1974. Third, in postindependence societies, factional wars between different political groups, as in Angola and Mozambique, or between divided parts of divided societies, as in Vietnam and Korea, displaced millions. Conflicts exacerbated by the intervention of superpowers or former colonial overlords led to the highest death tolls and created the largest refugee movements (see map 19.2).

In some of the newly independent states, dominant majorities displaced resident or immigrant minorities. East African South Asians had to leave Kenya and Uganda by the early 1970s. Again, the issue of men's control over and access to women was raised. Throughout their presence, immigrant men from India had married African women; after independence, immigrant Indian women were told by some East African politicians to be available for African men.[19] The issue of self-determination of immigrant minorities of long standing undercut the new states' institutional hegemony. Tamils in Ceylon/Sri Lanka, who were perceived as a threat by the Sinhalese majority, demanded autonomy and began an armed struggle. According to an agreement with India, which many had immigrated from in the previous century and a half, some 525,000 were "repatriated" in 1964; several 100,000 more were to receive Sri Lankan citizenship. Karen people left Burma/Myanmar. A third issue involved status or class and class-consciousness rather than ethnicity. In China and Vietnam, for example, landowners were deported. This ideologically motivated recomposition of society also followed an economic rationale: structural changes and mechanization favored larger agricultural units and forced farm families everywhere to abandon their land. In capitalist societies, laissez-faire liberalism sent families packing; in social-democratic societies, financial incentives permitted a transition to urban life. In formerly colonial areas, the rural-urban migrations began late and have lasted to the present. These intra- and interregional migrations in the immediate aftermath of decolonization were much larger than reverse migrations to the cores.

In the metropoles, however, the latter received the bulk of the often hostile attention. They involved the arrival of some 5.5 to 8.5 million Italian, French, British, Belgian, Dutch, and other White colonials and of non-White auxiliaries before 1975. Metropolitan populations saw no reason to have their taxes allocated to the support of settler and planter "returnees"; mixed-origin families and their children faced racism; "Colored" auxiliaries often ended up in camps or substandard housing. Home governments assumed that refugee auxiliaries would stay only temporarily until conditions in their states of origin would permit their return. In most cases, however, return never became an option; the Others were in the cores to stay. The "color problem" changed from a distant colonial issue to one of immediate home concern: "The empire strikes back" noted critics of colonialism gleefully.

The European colonizing powers did not seize the opportunity offered by the defeat of Japanese imperialism to negotiate an end to their own imperialism. Wars for independence began in the populous colonies of Asia, Dutch Indonesia, and French Indochina. By the 1960s, Britain, France, the Netherlands, Italy, and Belgium had had to relinquish most of their colonies worldwide; Portugal held out until the mid-1970s. Its tiny enclaves in the Indic and East Asian Worlds contained only small European-origin populations. On the other hand, the Portuguese African territories, to which sizable numbers of migrants had been directed only in the 1940s, held an estimated 400,000 European-origin people in Angola (7 percent of the population) and 200,000 in Mozambique (3 percent) in 1970. After the belated granting of independence to Angola and Mozambique in 1975, half a million Portuguese were repatriated. The even later implementation of independence in British Rhodesia/Zimbabwe (1965–80) and in Namibia (1990) resulted in reverse migrations of 250,000 and 43,000 respectively. In the British and other colonial worlds, migrants also moved between colonies: for example, from the formerly Belgian Congo after its independence to what was still colonial British Kenya, from India to East Africa, and from many non-White colonies to the White Dominions of Australia, New Zealand, or Canada. Such displaced settlers often felt that they had left their rightful homes and the achievements of their hard work behind. But, by leaving, they also stepped off the backs of exploited and dispossessed "Natives," like the Kikuyu in Kenya. This aspect, which did not become part of White memory, formed the basis of a new national consciousness of those liberated from the colonizers' yoke.[20]

The Netherlands combined a tradition of free immigration of people from neighboring European states with restrictions on the return of mixed couples from the colonies (chaps. 7.4, 12.2). The Dutch government, which had refused to accept a unilateral declaration of independence by the leaders of the Indonesian liberation movement after the defeat of the Japanese occupation, was forced in 1949 to accept decolonization. From 1946 to 1962, some 300,000 Dutch citizens of European or Euro-Asian origin "returned" to where most had never lived before. In addition,

12,500 Moluccan soldiers were evacuated. The former became citizens and were integrated; the latter were housed in compounds and remained marginalized. When an independent Moluccan Republic failed to develop, thus making return impossible, the second-generation "sojourners" violently protested for better living conditions. In an act of self-criticism, the Dutch government and society responded positively. With Surinamese independence (1973–75) and Antillean/Aruban political change, some 240,000 and 80,000 colonials respectively migrated to the Netherlands by 1992. They, too, were integrated—though tensions remain.[21]

In the British Commonwealth, citizenship had been granted to all residents in the colonies, but except for sailors few had migrated to England permanently before the end of World War II. Demobilized Jamaican soldiers, unable to find work in Jamaica, came to the United Kingdom in 1948; uprooted Hindu, Sikh, and Muslim refugees from India and Pakistan came soon after, as did migrants from other West Indies islands. By 1961 some 336,000 non-White immigrants resided in the United Kingdom. After the government passed in November 1961 a restriction bill divorcing citizenship rights from immigration rights, almost 100,000 New Commonwealth residents arrived before the act took effect on 1 July 1962. The act stopped the increase of migration but not migration itself. In each of the next two decades, about 450,000 arrived, their composition changing from single male workers to families. In a second restriction bill of 1968, the entry of East African Asians with British passports was restricted; the racist British politician Enoch Powell delivered his infamous "Rivers of Blood" speech, the keynote of a new racism in Europe against the peoples it had exploited for centuries (chaps. 10, 15, 16). Each new wave of non-White British citizens arriving in the "home" country induced further restrictions, but a multiracial society had emerged—albeit stratified and racialized.[22]

French Algeria, which gained independence in a war lasting from 1954 to 1962, serves as an example of decolonization-related flight, population transfer, and migration. France, a haven for refugees and an immigration country since the nineteenth century, also attracted students from its colonies in a program to spread French culture and language to African and Indochinese elites. Though unwanted, labor migrants and small entrepreneurs arrived in small numbers, including 49,000 North and West Africans from 1921 to 1936. In the next three years, 25,000 circumvented formal restrictions. Their communities, totaling 100,000 by 1939, would provide support networks to the arrivals of the 1950s and 1960s.

In the early 1950s, colonial "*rapatriés*," who left before formal independence and official repatriation programs were instituted, reached France en masse. The liquidation of France's colonial empire began with defeat in Vietnam in 1954: 70,000 men, women, and children returned. When Guinea seceded from the *communauté*, 10,000 came. By 1962, 310,000 of 450,000 French citizens had arrived from the former protectorates of Tunisia and Morocco, both of which became independent in 1956. Some 15,000 fled or were expelled from Egypt after the 1956 Anglo-French Suez aggression. A Secretariat for Repatriation managed the placement of the so-called national refugees. Jews were strongly represented: starting in 1956, some 25,000 came from

Morocco, 30,000 from Tunisia, and 100,000, including 3,000 Arab-speaking Saharan Jews, from Algeria.[23]

With impending Algerian independence, the European-origin minority of one million, 80 percent of them Algerian-born, were caught between the terrorist Secret Army Organization's attempts to prevent their exodus and French derogatory attitudes to the *pieds noirs*. They left slowly before 1962 and in mass flight thereafter; by March 1963, 850,000 had reached France. Early reverse migrants could transfer assets, as had been the case for Vietnamese middle-class families who left before the collapse of the U.S. war in their country in 1975. Some 90 percent of the Algerian-French had relatives to turn to. After 1962 mainly "poor Whites" fled, and massive government aid and labor market programs became necessary. Refugees often remained in overcrowded Marseille, the port of entry, on the—mistaken—assumption of quick return. Thousands refused to accept dock work, which was "Arab work" in their view. Some fled from government-enforced regional distribution programs for fear of having to suffer "Siberian"-type climatic conditions in northern France. Others, used to Arab service and domestic help, now passively waited for government services and help. Still others took the initiative and migrated to perceived opportunities in Spain and elsewhere. The relationship between the metropolitan French and the Algerian-French grew tense. Culturally, the Euro-Algerians were of many backgrounds: Spanish, Italian, and Maltese. The 300,000 Algerian Muslims in France in 1962 were augmented within six months by an additional 100,000, mostly *harkis*, who had served French authorities as policemen, political agents, and soldiers. Only 6,000 of them were evacuated officially, but by mid-1963 those left behind fled at a rate of 5,000 daily.

The other side, independent Algeria, had to deal with problems that dwarfed those of French society. The savage war had devastated the countryside and displaced 3.5 million, or 50 percent, of the rural population. Where peasants supplied many of the guerilla fighters, the French army imposed free-fire zones and scorched villages. Expelled families were concentrated in army-built *centres de regroupement* characterized by primitive facilities and poor administration. A "thousand new villages" program of 1959, imposed by the French civilian authorities, provided unsuitable prefabricated housing, designed by urban engineers. Little regard was paid to rural Muslim lifestyles, and shantytowns adjacent to existing settlements housed other refugees. About 250,000 Algerians fled to Morocco and Tunisia before their return began in mid-1962.

The postindependence government pursued a policy of creating *villages de reconstruction* and self-managed cooperatives for veteran guerilas and displaced rural people. But many of the wartime compounds and villages became permanent settlements. Economic problems resulted in an exodus toward the cities. Left to fall into a dilapidated state by absentee Algerian-French owners, industrial plants, businesses, and farms were confiscated. A program to recruit new educational and administrative personnel from France to replace refugee-expertise proved stillborn—fear prevented French experts from coming.

In the 1970s and 1980s, a construction program of socialist villages provided access to utilities and services. Criticized for its aspects of social engineering, the program resembled planned resettlement from thinly settled regions elsewhere in the world, which was aimed at making social service institutions available and viable. Increasingly, Algerian villages and urban neighborhoods sent laborers to France in multi-year migrations. Remittances permitted survival in marginalized regions that were no longer economically viable without subventions.[24]

Across the globe, the colonizers indelibly shaped colonial social space. But the resulting patterns were not simply French, British, or Dutch in nature; they were negotiated with, appropriated, rejected, or transformed by resident peoples. The colonized peoples, in turn, adapted lifestyles, cash economies, and political views. Migrants and refugees transplanted colonial experiences and mentalities into metropolitan societies. When people of a skin color other than White and reverse migrants of mixed origins (with some European ancestry) reached White Europe, the host societies— France, the Netherlands, and Britain, in particular—became many-colored against their will. While France and Britain attempted to reduce migration by restrictive legislation, the Dutch and the Swedish began to reconstruct themselves in a conscious, but not unopposed, process of change. Having been immigration countries in the past, they adopted policies similar to those of immigration states in North America and Australasia, which had abolished Asian exclusion and reduced discrimination in the 1960s. Since the 1960s, racist ideology has lost its homogeneity, although obstinate attitudes of White superiority remain rampant in sections of the northern societies. White European and Euro-origin North American societies were remade by immigrants of many colors with few means and against considerable odds.

18.4   Aftermath or Continuity: Racialized Labor Mobility in South Africa

In the 1950s the UN strengthened the League of Nations' 1926 resolution against slavery, and its Forced Labour Committee in Geneva heard evidence concerning the U.S. South, Eastern European countries, the Soviet Union, colonies of the major Western nations, and other parts of the world. The labor practices and legislation of South Africa provided the most blatant case of coercion of migrant labor.[25]

Between 1902 and 1940, the increasingly interventionist Euro-segment of the South African state first expelled Chinese contract workers and restricted Indian ones (chap. 15.4) and then imposed a system of labor controls and pass laws on Africans. The restriction to reserves, "Homelands" or "Bantustans," since 1913, which was consolidated in the Bantu Self-Government Act of 1959, involved the involuntary relocation of two to three million people from "White" territories. In 1948, partly in reaction to labor militancy, the Population Registration Act institutionalized apartheid under the "white supremacy" doctrine: there was no place for "the Bantu" above the level of menial labor. All aspects of life were racialized: mixed marriages were prohibited (1949), interracial sexual contacts outlawed (1950), and identity checks established (1952). The Pass Law required Native persons to carry booklets with information about their physical features and place of origin, their residence, and their employment status.

The three elements of the regimentation of labor resources included the strong coercive and administrative involvement of the state and the bureaucratization of labor markets, a concomitant expansion of labor recruitment on a subcontinental scale, and administrative and elite interests in the supplier states that permitted a perpetuation of the system. The labor regime forced Africans to work for European-origin employers, to migrate seasonally or over extended periods of time, and to leave families behind and live in camps. By government regulation, only about 1 percent of the African male labor force were permitted to bring families and live in family housing. Thus the powerful mining core drew its labor from a marginal countryside, and utility companies often pursued similar strategies. The state guaranteed industry's labor system (map 18.3).

In 1960, Mozambique, Malawi, Zimbabwe, Zambia, Tanzania, and Angola supplied 155,000 workers. Labor recruitment north of South Africa supplied 28.9 percent of the gold-mining labor in 1936 and 53.6 percent in 1972. Neighboring colonial and, subsequently, independent governments acquiesced to temporary migration, but they prohibited permanent departures in order to appropriate part of the migrants' remittances for their own use. Contracts, often only of a few months' duration, permitted immediate reengagement. In the mining labor force of 627,000 in 1969, White workers—10 percent of the total—held all of the supervisory and administrative positions.

In farm labor and domestic service, with 1.7 million workers in 1969, 0.9 million were seasonal migrants. Among migrants, more than half were women, who came on their own or as part of families; of the regular employees, only one-sixth were women. To alleviate labor shortages caused by the restrictions on mobility, farmers could build prisons and be allocated long-term (Black) inmates. Did the legal system restrict itself to punishing offenders, or did it seek to ensure a regular supply of labor, whether or not those who were put to work had committed offenses?

Residency and departure obligations imposed on Africans varied by regional economy. In the rural Western Cape, the apartheid system divided Africans into four categories. "Article 10 Bantu," who had been born in the region or had lived there for fifteen years or had worked for ten years with the same employer, had a right to stay. "Long-term Bantu" of two or more years' residence were sent back with their families to Homelands if they became unemployed. Rotating labor forces, the "12-months men" and the "4–8-months seasonal laborers," formed the third and fourth categories. Farmers opposed the government-mandated rotation of the "12-months men" because of the time needed to familiarize them with a particular farm and because of the possibly necessary investment in their training. The debate hinged on sex and women's bodies: men, argued the farmers, had to be permitted to return to their families, for "they are men." To avoid such loss of time, they should be permitted to bring their families. Women, argued the government when rejecting the demand,

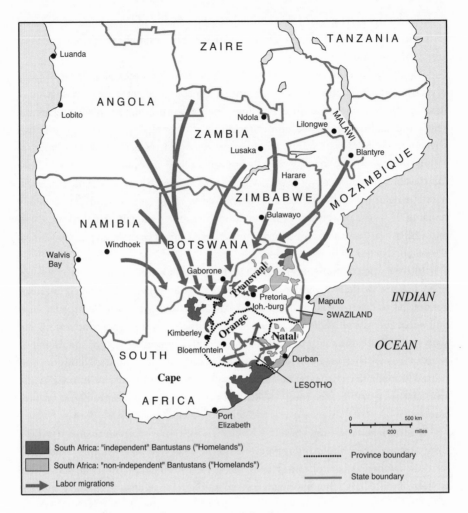

18.3   Labor Segregation in and Migration to South Africa, 1970s

were "incubators of labour," of children, who if born in the territory where the men worked would have a right to stay permanently.[26]

For urban labor, hostels provided mass accommodation, which instead of beds often offered just concrete slabs or bare floors. Corrugated iron "tents" afforded the worst housing. Where governmental influx control did permit whole families to come, all members lost their right to housing when the breadwinner was discharged or left on his own will or died in a work accident. Men and women were segregated into separate compounds with no right of access to the opposite sex's units. Suburbs, like Johannesburg's Soweto and the separately administered Alexandra, became slums through overcrowding. Soweto's suburban homes deteriorated when no additional housing could be built, but the increasing numbers of in-migrants waiting for a place in a hostel had to be accommodated as lodgers. In Alexandra, the White government violated Black homeowners' property rights when it decided to shift the whole population to a newly created township. After ten years of relocation and of segregation of women into hostels, Alexandra's population had grown from 60,000 to between 80,000 and 100,000.

The African labor reservoir was as cheap as forced labor: it built its own housing or, under the restrictions on acquiring land, crowded itself ever closer. Recognizable by skin color, it did not have to wear insignia like "OST" or the yellow Star of David. The disruption of trans-border labor migration from 1974 to 1976—the years of transition to independence in the Portuguese colonies—was offset by an internal mobilization of some 300,000 African workers. Death squads of police officers terrorized the internationalized labor force from as far away as Tanzania and Zambia, from Malawi and Portuguese Mozambique.[27]

South African society was divided into Europeans (as of 1994, 14 percent), Coloured of mixed ethnic background, including Asian descendants of the small Chinese community and of Indian contract and free migrants (12 percent), and Africans of Zulu, Tsonga, Sotho, Xhosa and Pondo (Mpondo), Venda, Tswana, Ndebele, or Herero ethnicity. Ranked by number of speakers, the many mother tongues included Zulu, Afrikaans, North Sotho, English, five other African languages, and five South Asian ones. Early in the century, the Indian community had opposed the system of segregation. In 1973 the widespread protests and industrial actions of Black workers, which were to culminate in the Soweto uprising of 1976, were harbingers of change. The African National Congress and the Communist Party, both underground or in exile, organized internal resistance. The 1980 Lusaka Declaration of the neighboring states and an international boycott of South African products supported the liberation movement externally. In 1986 the pass laws were abolished, and apartheid was brought to an end between 1989 and 1994. The will to live decent lives had finally toppled the system, and new forms of migration developed.[28]

19

New Migration Systems since the 1960s

.

Starting in the 1960s, labor migrations assumed new regional and transcontinental patterns; refugee generation shifted from Europe to Latin America, Africa, and Asia; merit-based admission systems encouraged migrations of highly trained people; and family reunion became a major issue in policy formulation. Interaction and intermarriage decreased racialization in some societies, and exclusionist movements gained strength in others. Sensationalist reports about the new migrations in Europe and North America have repeatedly centered on crime: Latin drug syndicates, Russian mafias, Chinese triads, or arms-dealing Albanians. The robbery of human beings from Africa in the past by Euro–North American traders and the terms of trade that rob the 4.4 billion people in the developing countries of the rewards of their labor in the present have never been discussed in terms of thievery or a disregard for security of property.[1]

The postcolonial world may be interpreted in terms of "global apartheid," in which low-wage jobs and low standards of living are assigned to people outside North America, Europe, and Australasia. Thus the color barrier, abolished in North American admission procedures and reduced in Europe by colonial reverse migrations, re-emerges as globalized racialization. The postimperialist world is characterized by economic power structures imposed by capitalist financial markets and institutions. Ever more multinational or non-national companies (MNCs) operate outside political boundaries and control. As a consequence, two million men and women—sometimes with their children—migrate annually to richer countries worldwide, be it to Nigeria, Japan, or the Euro–North American World (chap. 19.1).

In the 1960s, reverse colonial and labor migrations reintegrated Western and West Central Europe with the Mediterranean World of North Africa and with Turkey in Asia. In the Americas, the attracting cores of the United States/Canada, Venezuela, and Argentina are increasingly integrated into one hemispheric migration region. In Asia, the classic four regions of South, Southeast, East Asia, and Japan remain separate in terms of migration; the Chinese diaspora experiences nationalist pressures from host societies. The region from the Maghreb in North Africa to Arabia and to the Iranian Highlands forms a fragmented West Asian/Arab/Islamic World, its western section connected by labor migration to Europe and its eastern one to the oil-economies of the Persian Gulf. Sub-Saharan Africa's regional migration systems include rural-to-urban, postindependence and post–civil war resettlement, and massive refugee migrations. The end of the socialist system reintegrated Eastern Europe and the former Soviet Union into worldwide patterns of migration. No overall interpretation fits all patterns, all regions, all cultural groups, all economic regimes (chaps. 19.2–19.9).

19.1 Migrant Strategies and Root Causes

While voluntary migrants attempt to shape their lives by self-determined decisions, the increasing number of refugees from wars, environmental disasters, and development displacement face severely constrained options. Anthony Richmond has questioned the juxtaposition of voluntary and involuntary migrants and suggests a continuum from proactive to reactive migrants. Proactive migrants, facing potentially flight-inducing situations, leave as long as they can chose between options; reactive ones flee when no other options are left. Proactive refugees' transfer of assets from low-standard-of-living to high-standard-of-living societies devalues their assets, and such economic-before-becoming-refugee migrants often suffer a status decline from middle-class to self-employed or self-exploiting. Since asylum law based on the Geneva Convention recognizes only reactive migrants, the initiative of proactive migrants is often derogatorily labeled "shopping for asylum" in receiving states. Men and women who find neither desirable life-course options in their society of origin nor admission elsewhere may migrate without asking permission and thus become undocumented or, from administrations' views, illegal migrants.

Next to labor migrants, refugees form the largest group of movers. Smaller in number but more influential are skilled and elite migrants. Patterns of refugee generation and labor market demands have resulted in a feminization of migration. In several societies humanitarian concepts have resulted in family reunion under special clauses. Intergenerational imbalances due to population growth force young people to leave less developed countries (LDCs). On the other hand, no longer self-reproducing and consequently aging populations in industrialized countries, which often pursue restrictive immigration policies, may soon need to recruit young immigrants for intergenerational transfer payments in their social security systems.[2]

Voluntary Migrants

Cores attracting voluntary labor migrants have increased to four major ones: Western Europe, North America, the Persian Gulf, and several Southeast and East Asian economies. Smaller regional systems include Argentina, Venezuela, South Africa, Nigeria and Zaire/Congo among others (map 19.1). Some of these political economies discard migrant/immigrant workers during recessions, while others, like Japan, pursue a policy of rigorous exclusion. The three main labor-exporting regions com-

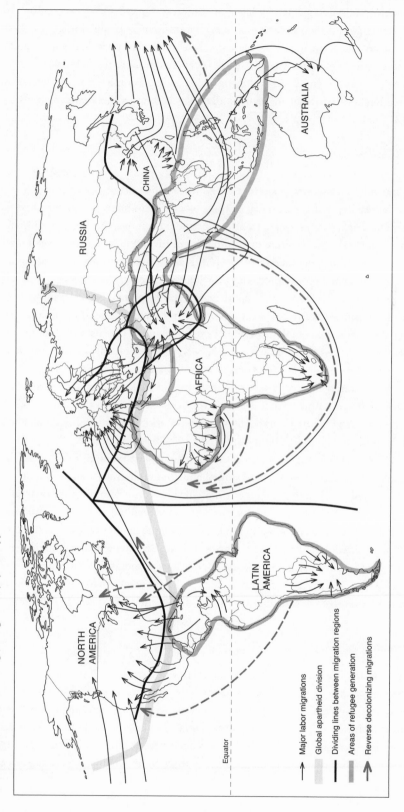

19.1 Major Labor and Refugee Migrations, 1960s–1990s

↑ Major labor migrations

   Global apartheid division

| Dividing lines between migration regions

   Areas of refugee generation

↑ Reverse decolonizing migrations

NORTH
AMERICA

LATIN
AMERICA

AFRICA

RUSSIA

CHINA

AUSTRALIA

Equator

prise the societies of the Mediterranean, Southeast Asia, and the Caribbean/Central America. Thus comparatively less developed sending regions raise and educate workers for the highly developed world in "a form of development aid given by the poor countries to the rich" (Castles and Kosack). Remittances of savings by migrant men and women may partially counterbalance the flow of human capital.[3]

As under proto-industrial regimes in which raw or semifinished materials were moved to village producers with the necessary tools and machinery, production is again being shifted outward: in the case of the clothing industry, for example, to the *maquiladora* zone in Mexico south of the U.S. border, to the southern provinces of China, or to small textile factories in Tunisia. However, producers no longer own the means of production; rather, so-called free enterprise zones protect capital from any risks or loss of profitability stemming from working-class militancy or state-mandated contributions to social security systems.

Rural-urban migrations have accelerated in the developing world of Latin America, Africa, and Asia. In industrialized states, a partial reversal in the form of a vast suburbanization and the establishment of "industrial parks" outside big cities may be discerned. Capital often locates new production facilities in regions known for low levels of unionization and labor militancy, in the U.S. South or Southeast Asia, for example. Receiving economies continue to be characterized by stratified labor markets with regionally differentiated access. Oil-based economies, for example, attract technicians and administrative personnel from the Atlantic World, male skilled and unskilled labor from Palestine, Egypt, and India, and female domestic workers from Southeast Asia.

A new type of migration involves temporary moves from middle-class status in low-wage countries to working-class status in high-wage countries. For instance, Polish and Mexican teachers migrate seasonally to harvest work in Western Europe or North America, where they can earn more in a few weeks than in several months at home while continuing to take advantage of the low cost of living in their society of origin. Global economic disparities are increasing while commuting between societies has become easier and faster unless hindered by entry-regulations.

Forms of labor immobilization and of forced migrations of bound labor continue to exist. The South African labor regime has been the most visible example (chap. 18.4). Slaves are still being captured in Nilotic Sudan and sold from there, even though slavery was abolished in Saudi Arabia in 1962 and in Mauritania in 1981. In South Asia, debt bondage immobilizes workers. India's abolition act of 1976 notwithstanding, two million agricultural laborers (5 percent of the agricultural labor force), mostly from lower Hindu castes and from the hill tribes, were still bonded in 1978. In the 1990s Asian child laborers were still being transported to factories for carpet weaving and brick making.[4] Forced labor on plantations of multinational food corporations in Central America, on large estates in Brazil, and on sugar plantations in the Dominican Republic (involving Haitians sent by the Duvalier family) is documented. As was true under slavery, flight becomes self-liberation.[5] Finally, women from low-wage societies are transported against their will to sexual service jobs.[6]

Elite migration, once a domain of merchants, engineers, and highly skilled arti-sans, has become a migration of highly skilled technical personnel and young people with university training. An early, oft-cited, but minor case was the run on Nazi Germany's rocket scientists after May 1945. The "brain drain" migration of Third World students to First World universities and employment opportunities, on the other hand, became a mass phenomenon that deprived developing economies of exper-tise. The North American immigration reform—the point system of the 1960s—put a premium on education—years of schooling, professional training, linguistic capa-bilities—and helped cement the technological and research lead of these advanced societies.[7]

Humanitarian precepts counter such selectivity since family reunion is not lim-ited to rationales of the point system. Chains of families had migrated in the nine-teenth century from India or from Europe. Flight in Europe before 1945 tore families apart, but bonds lasted; in the 1990s separated families still were attempting to re-unite with the help of search agencies. Refugees of the 1990s have faced the same pre-dicament. The admission regulations of some resettlement countries permit family reunion in sequential migrations. Thus the selection of refugees who fit the labor market criteria of the receiving society is counterbalanced by admission of families regardless of qualifications and of the point system. For elite migrants, the admission of family members is often available immediately.

Undocumented migrants, whose numbers have sometimes been widely in-flated for xenophobic reasons, choose to ignore admission regulations that bar them from developing life-course strategies. Their numbers rose in the late 1970s when recession-hit receiving countries tightened entry regulations. The scope of the issue can be seen in the regularization programs in Argentina, France, Italy, and the United States in 1987–89; the policies of the oil-exporting states; the diplomatic pressures of Hong Kong on neighboring states; and the increase of external border controls in the European Union. Governments attempt to negotiate compromises between the interests of migrants and the society of destination by offering special programs of temporary admission for contract workers, trainees, or students. In times of political tensions, however, as happened during the 1990–91 Persian Gulf War or the Nige-rian recession in 1983, governments expel or illegalize regular migrants. Regardless of the political framework, undocumented migrant families often work in the informal economy and thus contribute to the gross national product of the receiving societies.[8]

A core-periphery dichotomy of labor-importing industrialized and labor-exporting low-income societies hides the complexity of labor migrations and eco-nomic regimes. Migrants make their decisions in a distinct cultural subsystem, whether it be a Philippine island, Tamil India, Palestinian camps, Italian villages, or Colombian cities. Men and women move according to economic linkages, informa-tion flows, and cultural affinities. Algerians would hardly select England or South Asians France as a destination because colonial legacies, human capital, and cultural practices gave Algerians French and South Asians English as a language and system of signification. In the 1950s, skilled Philippine migrants joined communities in the

United States rather than establish new ones in societies alien to them. Capitalists, state political elites, and cultural gatekeepers interact with culturally and economically defined migrant groups and these with individuals in family economies in a framework of multiple interests, rationalities, strategies, and identities.[9]

Refugees and Root Causes

In addition to internal and interstate wars, the root causes of refugee generation include regional political, class, ethnic, religious, and gender tensions; the global division of power; global economic disparities in resource distribution and labor market demands; natural or—in gendered perspective—men-made disasters; population growth; and development policies that displace the powerless. In 1995 the United Nations High Commissioner for Refugees (UNHCR) counted 27.4 million "refugees and other persons of concern"; nongovernmental organizations (NGOs) estimated people not under UNHCR mandate but forced to move because of environmental, sociopolitical, or other causes at some 80 million; the World Bank estimated "development-induced displacement" at 90–100 million in a single decade (chap. 20.2).[10]

The twentieth-century mass generation of refugees by expansionist warfare and ethnic displacement began in Europe and expanded under Japanese imperialism to East Asia and, after 1945, because of Hindu-Muslim tensions, to South Asia. In the 1950s it began to shift under internal or superpower-induced conflict to the newly independent states of Asia and Africa and rightist regimes in Latin America; and in the early 1990s, with the dismemberment of Yugoslavia, back to Europe again (map 19.2).[11]

Most refugees remain within the larger regions of origin. Resettlement offered by developed societies or obtained by individual refugees' own initiatives have expanded the range of destinations for very limited numbers only. European refugees were settled by the respective states of coethnics (under the "nationality concept") or resettled in "White" Euro-Creole states in the Americas or Australasia. During the Cold War, the Western belligerents accepted men and women fleeing the Eastern sphere. But under the regime of global apartheid, the admission of refugees from the LDCs, who crossed borders to rich countries and crossed color lines in the process, was restricted in the mid-1980s. Asylum applications in Europe increased from 60,000 in 1983 to almost 700,000 in 1992. In reaction, airlines transporting refugees without visas were penalized; in Europe, Poland and the Czech Republic were paid by neighboring states to the west to create a *cordon sanitaire*; in North America, a barbed wire fence closed off much of the U.S. border to Mexico.[12]

Policy-generated refugees, those persecuted "for reasons of race, religion, nationality, membership of a particular social groups or political opinion," have a right to asylum under the terms of the Geneva Convention of 1951 and the 1967 Protocol. Persecution because of gender was added in 1990. This definition, based on the political theory of sovereign states, does not cover civil wars and dictatorial regimes

19.2 Major Refugee Migrations in the 1970s

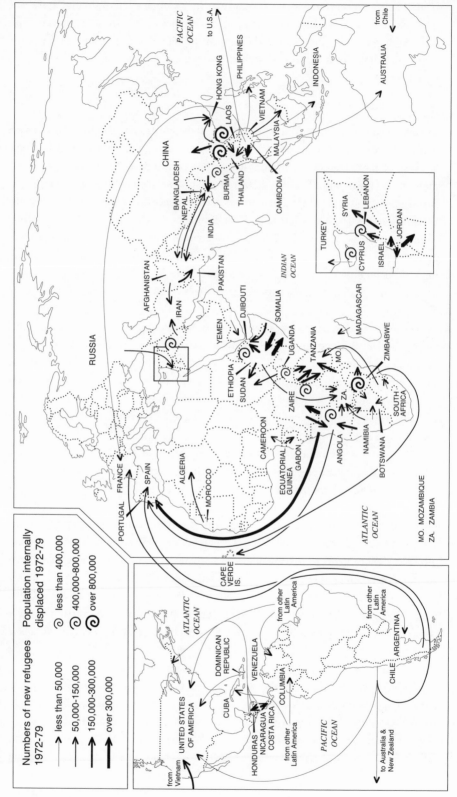

Numbers of new refugees 1972-79

→ less than 50,000
→ 50,000-150,000
➡ 150,000-300,000
➡ over 300,000

Population internally displaced 1972-79

@ less than 400,000
@ 400,000-800,000
@ over 800,000

during which whole state apparatuses lose the trust of the territory's people. Major policy-generated refugee streams may be summarized under seven headings: 1) the creation of new societies and the displacement of religious, ethnic, and political "enemies," as in Palestine/Israel and in China/Hong Kong/Taiwan; 2) the decolonization-induced reverse migration of imperial settlers and colonial auxiliaries, refugee movements across colonizer-shaped political boundaries, and impoverishment through core-imposed export economies; 3) postdecolonization armed conflicts among competing Native elites involving concepts of social order, as in Mozambique and in Angola, or between superpower-supported warlords, as in Somalia, or between ideological systems, as in Vietnam, or struggles connected to the interests of a hegemonic core state and multinational capital, as in Zaire, Haiti, or Nigeria; 4) nonelective rule, differentiated into personal, clan, or group "kleptocracies" (Zucker and Zucker), as in the case of the Marcos and Duvalier regimes in the Philippines and Haiti; 5) genocidal regimes, as in Cambodia or in Rwanda, and politically exacerbated famines, as in Ethiopia, Sudan, and North Korea; 6) fundamentalist rule or raiding, as in Islamic Afghanistan, Iran, and Algeria; 7) the rule of right-wing elite segments, as in many Latin American societies. In such conflicts, a specific interest—purity of religion, male domination of women, power spheres of capitalism or of Russian socialism, profits for ruling elites—is imposed on the commonweal of society, reducing opportunities or threatening survival. Thus refugees may originate from minorities as well as from majorities with structurally restricted access to institutional remedies, political power, and economic resources.[13]

Most conflicts in Latin America involved class-based right-wing regimes; some positioned Euro-Creole populations against Indio peoples, as in Guatemala. Political refugees faced exclusion from asylum-granting societies because refugee-generating and -receiving governments were aligned with each other. Thus Salvadoran and Haitian refugees—but not Cuban warrior-refugees and bourgeois from the Batista era—were excluded from the United States. In Asia, people fled from Tibet, Vietnam, Cambodia, Laos, Burma/Myanmar, Sri Lanka, Iran, and Afghanistan. Refugee-generation by regimes in Africa involved outside-directed capitalist interests, as in Zaire; factional fights, as in Sierra Leone and Liberia; conflict about territorial rule and mineral resources, as in the West Saharan region; ethno-religious conflict, exacerbated by drought and/or warlordism, as in Sudan, Eritrea, Ethiopia, and Somalia; socioethnic conflict, supported by French and U.S. interests, as in Rwanda and Burundi; and ideological strife, as in Angola and Mozambique. East of the Mediterranean, denial of statehood to the Kurdish and Armenian people, factional fighting in Lebanon, and ethnopolitical struggles in Cyprus sent people fleeing. During the dissolution of the USSR and the subsequent decolonization of its southern territories, 1.5 million Armenians, Azerbaijanis, and Georgians were displaced, as were peoples in the Central Asian states. The dissolution of multiethnic Yugoslavia into "nations" resulted in about four million refugees, two-thirds of them from the traditionally mixed settlements of Bosnia and Herzegovina.[14] In 1995, refugee distribution across continents amounted to 53.2 percent in Africa, 28.4 percent in Asia, 9.8 percent in Europe, 3.7

percent in North America, 3.5 percent in the area of the former USSR, and 1.1 percent in Latin America.

Disparities of global economic power as reflected in the terms of trade formulated by theorists of economic liberalism are not matched by a concomitant liberalist theory of admission policies toward economic refugees. The UN *Human Development Report* of 1995 noted that the richest 20 percent of the world population are almost sixty times wealthier than the poorest 20 percent, a gap that has doubled since 1960 and continues to grow. Although, according to the World Bank, the average annual per capita gross national product (GNP) amounted to US$380 in low-income countries as compared to US$23,090 in high-income economies in 1993, there is, because of cultural factors, "no direct correlation between income and development differentials on the one hand and international migration on the other." South Africa's GNP is thirty-three times higher than that of Mozambique, Malaysia's fourteen times higher than that of Bangladesh, and Argentina's ten times that of Bolivia, but people do not leave en masse. According to World Bank estimates, import restrictions by industrialized countries reduce the LDCs' GNP by more than they receive in development aid. In the mid-1990s, a net capital transfer from the poor to the rich states was registered.[15] In human terms, every day 40,000 human beings die of hunger, and at the same time half a million dollars are transferred to rich countries. Pets in industrialized countries are fed better than the children in poor countries. For centuries, parents have opted for migration under similar circumstances.[16]

Ecological deterioration results from natural climatic shifts, from man-made pollution and greenhouse emissions, and from population increase and the use of particular lands beyond their "carrying capacity." In 1995, environmental migrants amounted to an estimated 25 million; 135 million people were threatened by severe desertification; 550 million lived with chronic water shortages. Global warming, fueled by emissions from individual human and collective industrial activities, will displace tens of millions because of the rising sea level. Among spectacular cases of men-made displacement, one can point to the French and American nuclear tests on Pacific islands and the Russian nuclear disaster at Chernobyl.[17]

As factors of migration, population growth and malnourishment or outright starvation are closely connected to cultural factors, internal class hierarchies, and international terms of trade. The world's population of six billion, as of the year 2000, continues to grow, even if at declining rates. To reduce the potential of hunger migrations, birth control is advocated by population planners from "White" countries, which have sent migrants and ruler-investors across the globe since the sixteenth century. To avoid hypocrisy in calling for such measures, studies of "population load" beyond local "carrying capacities" need to be matched by political strategies implementing conservation-oriented lifestyles in the industrialized world.

Over 800 million people, or one in seven worldwide, "are chronically undernourished, eating too little to meet minimal energy requirements. Millions more suffer acute malnutrition during transitory or seasonal food insecurity." The lack of initiative ascribed to the hungry of the 1990s by the well-fed was and is neither innate nor class-specific but stems from nutritional deficiencies. Globally, "an average of about 2,700 calories of food per person per day—enough to meet anyone's energy requirements"—is available, but world market prices and the substitution of export for subsistence crops, driven by demands of multinational capital, have raised the local cost of food beyond the reach of the poor. Levels of undernourishment have declined rapidly in East Asia. They have remained stable in North Africa and the Middle East at 10 percent of the population, in Latin America at 14 percent, and in South Asia at 18 percent. But the level has risen dramatically, to 41 percent, in sub-Saharan Africa, where in the 1980s drought forced 10 million farmers to abandon their land and where food production per person has declined consistently since 1970.[18]

Development displacement occurs when infrastructural projects like dams and water reservoirs, open-pit mines, and transport networks are imposed on densely settled people by economic planners, governments, or international agencies, or when urban fringes expand rapidly into neighboring rural areas. Populations benefiting from such often well-intentioned projects usually have better access to resources than those who are displaced, whose marginalization is, in effect, increased. As reported by the World Bank, displacement and on-site resistance have been intensive and costly. The development of industries without proper safety standards has also dislocated people worldwide, whether in Italy (at Seveso), in India (at Bhopal), or in the former Soviet Union (at Chernobyl).[19]

The number of refugees from environmental disasters is increasing, and the food-providing "green revolution" is being eroded by MNC control over seed cultivation. While calls for "sustainable development," ecological conservation, punishment of crimes against humanity, and easier refugee admission have multiplied, migration remains for many the only immediate remedy under the intra-state and global power relationships that now prevail.[20]

The Feminization of Migration

In the most literal sense, women often flee "men-made" war, social hierarchies, bad agricultural planning, and young males' cultures of violence—often encouraged by political elites. Stagnating economies and First World arms sales provide underemployed young men with easy access to light weaponry and even to heavy armament. Fundamentalist or rightist regimes, whether in Chile under Pinochet or in Afghanistan under the Taliban or in Bosnia-Herzegovina under the rule of a Serb clique, have curtailed women's rights and personal integrity. Other forms of violence against women range from the genital mutilation of female children to intra-familial male domination and to the structural exclusion of female participation in public spheres. In reacting against "Western" impositions, rigid fundamentalist and rightist regimes have romanticized women's oppressed status in the name of cultural or national identity. If family men flee, remaining women and children often face retributive violence; fleeing women are constrained by having to keep the rest of the family together; in refugee camps staffed by men, women are particularly vulnerable. In the mid-1980s, when the European Parliament and UNHCR recognized women "as a particular social group," 90 percent of the Ethiopian refugees in Somalia were children under fifteen and women; women headed 80 percent of the Kampuchean refugee households along the Thai border; over half of the households of Palestinian exiles were headed by women, as were those of Guatemalans in Mexico and Salvadorans in Nicaragua.[21]

The "flesh markets" in which potential migrant workers were inspected for health and physical stamina before being transported to join distant unskilled labor forces have been and are being supplemented by the trade in and forced migration of cheap and docile wives and sex workers as well as by the trade in "body parts" for organ transplants, UN conventions notwithstanding.[22] First, women from low-income societies like the Philippines, Sri Lanka, Poland, and Russia emigrate—or are exported by international marriage agencies—to countries with higher GNPs, such as Japan and Germany, where native-born women's out-migration from rural and peripheral areas has resulted in an undersupply of cheap labor and of partners for men remaining in agriculture. This had been the experience of European mail-order and Asian picture brides going to nineteenth-century North America.[23] Second, as was true under imperialism (chap. 16.4), "international power relations are expressed by the bodies of women." In the past, the United States imported, via a small "White slave trade," European women for sexual services; in China, the sale of girls for debt, consensual concubinage, and colonizers' exploitation was common. However, women also migrated on their own.[24] In Japan, women from the poorer classes in the south were carried off as prostitutes to Southeast Asian colonies and Manchukuo, and the Japanese army used Korean women in army brothels across the empire. During the 1960s and 1970s, the abuse of women continued with U.S. involvement in Southeast Asia; in one "entertainment area" adjoining a U.S. military base in Thailand, the population increased from 40,000 to 70,000 in a decade, and the number of prostitutes rose fivefold. Women came or were brought in from rural regions as "entertainers." After the departure of U.S. forces, 3,000 Amerasian children were left in town. A piece of graffiti expressed the entwined personal and global economic relationships and migration dreams: "Yankee go home . . . but take me with you." Recruitment reservoirs in Southeast Asia include the eldest daughters of poor families, who are expected to support parents or the education of siblings; divorced women, in particular from the Catholic Philippines; or unmarried women with children, if they are stigmatized in their home societies. The construction of the "Other" has turned Southeast Asian women in general into prostitutes, but the Western immigrant entrepreneurs who often manage the sex business are not labeled "pimps."[25]

Labor migrations bring women into underpaid segments of labor markets as nurses in hospitals, caregivers, and domestic labor with irregular work hours. The global recession after 1973 prevented young men, the classic demographic reservoir of labor migrants, from entering local or distant labor markets.[26] Migration into domestic service and caregiving is directed toward societies in which native-born women can enter the labor force at better-paid and status-carrying levels without the reallo-

cation of house and family labor between genders. Special entry provisions attract domestic workers to North America, Singapore, and Persian Gulf states yet place them
in precarious legal positions. In Europe, the socioeconomic developments have gone
in a similar direction, but the color barrier has prevented recruitment of non-White
caregivers. Eastern European women, however, are recruited or migrate on their own,
as is true of Latin American women with North America as their destination.[27] The
employment of immigrant women in child-care has changed state strategies aimed at
having mothers inculcate national virtues into their children. In fact, child-care jobs
have opened the way for single immigrant women to gain citizenship but not economic advancement.[28] Particular routes of women's migration—to industrial labor or
as part of family migration—will be discussed below.

19.2   Western and Southern Europe: Labor Migrants as Guest Workers and Foreigners

Western Europe's population, reduced by tens of millions during World War II, grew
with the arrival of several million Eastern European German refugees and expellees,
the settlement of displaced Poles and Ukrainians as "European Volunteer Workers" in
Britain,[29] and the return of a few million reverse migrants from the colonies to France,
Britain, Belgium, the Netherlands, and mid-1970s Portugal (chaps. 17, 18.3). In several
postcolonial independent states, internal conflicts led to further departures of Euro-
colonials. Intra-European refugee movements ended in the early 1950s, and in the
1960s governments imposed stringent restrictions on the entry of men and women
from the former colonies. In terms of overseas migration, however, Europe's migration balance was negative by 2.7 million in the decade after 1950, came out even in
the 1960s, and was positive after 1970. From the 1960s on, Western Europe's migration
experience was one of labor migration.

Postwar reconstruction notwithstanding, the emigration of Europeans continued since the labor demands of national economies and multinational companies
did not match individuals' aspirations. Into the late 1950s, Germans left the destroyed
and Holocaust-tarnished society, even though policy-makers constructed a "community of fate" morally bound to rebuild the country. In West Germany, the ubiquitous
population planners, however, did permit surplus women and eastern refugee farmers
to emigrate. After the wartime carnage, women without the prospect of finding husbands as well as farmers without land might form a reservoir of protest. Portugal's
corporatist regime encouraged its population "surplus" to populate the African colonies. Up to the early 1980s, more people left Great Britain than immigrated, and at
the end of the conservative era of Thatcherist economic restructuring, one-third of
the Britons were ready to depart.[30]

Intra-European labor migration continued. From the traditional labor-exporting
periphery, Irish people still migrated to Britain, Italians to France, and Spaniards to
France and Germany. But in northern Europe, Sweden began to attract labor, and
Finns, especially Swedish-Finns, came. Eastern Europe was cut off by the "iron cur-

tain," and internal German east-west migrations ended with the Berlin Wall in 1961. Though exit rules were liberalized in Poland and less so in Hungary, the two Europes, Yugoslavia excepted, remained separate till 1989. Thus Mediterranean Europe was the only labor reservoir left. In the 1950s Italy's conservative government initiated a labor migration program to rid itself of the unemployed and to deprive the socialist and communist parties of potential voters. Men and women from the Iberian Peninsula, Italy, Yugoslavia, and Greece, and finally from Turkey migrated to northwestern Europe. In France they mixed with migrants from the North African colonies. South-north mobility, encouraged and managed by intergovernmental agreements, followed the classic patterns of job availability, formation of cultural communities, and sequential moves. Historic links—cultural, economic, and/or political—and power relationships influenced decisions about destinations. Migrants from former colonies went to the "mother countries," ethnic Germans to Germany, Finns to Sweden, Irish men and women to Britain. In addition, Italian and Portuguese men and women continued to cross the Atlantic to join ethnic communities in North America (map 19.3).[31]

The receiving countries' recruitment policies, aimed at importing temporary workers during labor shortages and returning them during periods of recession, were designed to "cushion" economic cycles by preventing wage increases in boom periods and high unemployment during economic downturns. To avoid the "foreign worker"–label, used in Nazi Germany, as well as the rights-conferring term "immigrant," the newcomers were called guest workers. At first, they filled shortages in skilled or semiskilled industrial sectors, and they subsequently did so in the service sector. With continuous economic growth and the availability of jobs that native workers no longer accepted in view of wages and working conditions, migrants became structurally indispensable.

A second policy rationale assumed that benefits would accrue to sending states. Less-skilled migrants would receive training and upon return transfer these new skills or invest savings into small-scale business. As early as 1973, however, Baučič showed that skilled workers were leaving Yugoslavia, draining the economy of a trained labor force. They underwent deskilling experiences while earning higher wages and, upon their return, transferred neither skills nor capital for investment.[32]

When government-driven labor recruitment ended after the oil-price shock of 1973, migrants initiated a family reunion–phase that ran contrary to administrators' projections of return. To the migrants, it made no sense to go back to crisis-ridden societies of origin. Humanitarian concerns in receiving societies prevented involuntary repatriation. The structural difference vis-à-vis depression migrants in 1930s North America lay in a status change: by taking paid labor in Western Europe, migrants enrolled in social security systems. Entitled to benefits, they did not have to rely on family support at "home"—in fact, it had become unclear where home was. Transculturally competent migrants joined labor movements and participated in strikes; in some industries they had higher rates of unionization than native-born workers. Since the late 1970s, some 14–15 million "foreigners" have resided in the

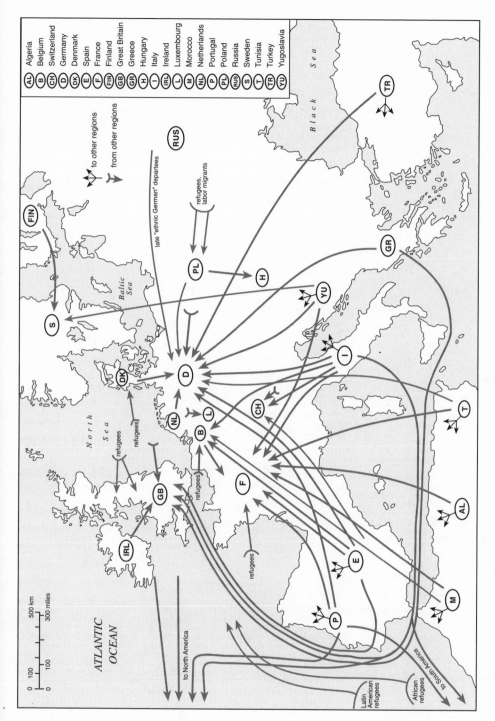

19.3 European and Transatlantic Migrations

Western European countries, ranging from 3.3 percent of the population in Great Britain—via a middle range of 6.5–9 percent in France, Germany, and Belgium—to 16 percent in Switzerland in 1989.

While European governments, unwilling to accept immigration, built barriers, immigrants built communities, sent children to school, developed entrepreneurial niches, and were indispensable in numerous labor market segments. In Hawai'i around 1910, planters had categorically stated that immigrant Asians were to be workers but not citizens (chap. 16.5); in the 1980s, several European governments took the same position. Talking heads in governments pushed return incentives; skinheads engaged in anti-immigrant violence; gray-headed elderly formed exclusionist movements. However, the Dutch and Swedish governments shifted to political innovation and began to pursue policies of integration and multiculturalism, and the French and British governments developed step-by-step measures, though in this regard they often did too little too late. Germany and Austria experienced multicultural lifestyles in the cities, but national governments rejected policy initiatives. Naturalization was easier in Austria than in Germany, perhaps reflecting Austria's past as a state of many peoples. Switzerland insisted on rotation policies.[33]

Cultural interaction through foodways (chap. 11) remained important and differed from nineteenth-century North American acculturation patterns, in which immigrants hid their "Old World" ways of preparing food in the privacy of their homes. In the present, mainstream men and women frequent ethnic restaurants, if at first only because of low prices owing to immigrant self-exploitation. In West Germany, where Italian guest workers were called "spaghetti munchers" and Turkish newcomers "garlic chewers," spaghetti and garlic became part of the standard cuisine. Acceptance of foreign eating habits is related to power hierarchies: U.S. soldiers introduced ketchup without being labeled "tomato mush snouts." Interactive foodways involved gendered skill adaptation. German women experienced the ketchup-innovation as deskilling but learned to introduce Italian ingredients into their cuisine. Ethnic chefs and native-born clienteles negotiated adaptations: Cantonese or Sichuan cuisine became generic Chinese food in Swedish, German, or French variants. Though often considered superficial, such changes involved the redefinition of aspects of national everyday cultures. Once adapted, contributions of this kind are no longer credited to newcomers but become part of the Self.[34]

Migration patterns in Western Europe changed in the mid-1980s when refugee arrivals and undocumented immigration, in particular from Africa, assumed larger proportions. Earlier, only West Africans and Antilleans had integrated France into their migratory circuits, as Jamaicans and South Asians had done with Britain. In southern Europe, employers hired undocumented North African migrants in preference to native-borns or regular immigrants in order to evade contributions to social security funds. Racist reaction came from National Front–type political parties. After a fifty-year hiatus, east-west migrations, often in the form of seasonal labor or under the guise of training programs, resumed in 1989. Multinational German-based construction conglomerates hired undocumented Eastern European workers. Some of the reconnected Eastern European sending states in turn became hosts to labor and trader migrants from further east (chap. 19.9).[35]

In the 1990s, multiple migrations in, to, and from Western and Southern Europe included internal south-north and east-west movements, as well as streams of new-comers from culturally related African, South Asian, and Indochinese societies. Yugo-slav refugees arrived in the early 1990s. What distinguishes "Fortress Europe" from North America is the European Union's lack of positive policy responses, including the restrictive Schengen agreement of 1985 and the Dublin convention of 1990. During the 1988–91 peak of migrant and refugee arrivals, Germany as the main destination received no more migrants per 1,000 of population than Canada had accepted regularly for almost a decade. Migration within the European Union, freed from restrictions by the Maastricht Agreement of 1993, has not increased substantially.[36]

19.3 Multicultured and Multicolored Immigration to North America

European immigrants had supplied the unskilled labor to the North American economies before 1917. In the interwar years, the United States reduced immigration by quota legislation, while Canada continued to attract migrants. From 1945 to 1952, the United States admitted just under 450,000 displaced persons and 190,000 other refugees, and Canada took in 186,000—almost exclusively European-origin people. These immigrants could connect to communities across the continent, while those from Asia connected to pre-depression-era communities in the Pacific coast states or were sponsored by war brides.[37] The two major streams of voluntary newcomers, from Italy and Portugal, sent many people into construction in Canada's eastern cities. Britons continued to arrive in Canada, and Eastern European refugees came as a result of the several uprisings in the Soviet zone of influence (chap. 19.9). Canada also accepted politically motivated British migrants during the Suez crisis in 1956 and half a million Americans during the Vietnam War. It lost workers and professionals to the United States, who were attracted by higher wages. The struggle of non-Anglophone European immigrant groups for equal rights with the hegemonic first-comers led to slow structural integration. In contrast to Europe, the North American states gave access to citizenship and political office to immigrants, who could thus participate in the shaping of institutions and policies. Once barriers to citizenship had been removed for non-White peoples, immigrants of other origins strove for the same inclusion.[38]

The United States and Canada changed immigration policies in the 1940s, ending Chinese exclusion but imposing minuscule quotas. There was no anticipation of a possible third phase of the Pacific Migration System. In other respects, policies remained traditional: the United States turned to Mexican labor to alleviate wartime shortages; the Canadian government, while acknowledging the need for further immigration and for a comprehensive policy in 1947, intended to rely on traditional Anglo-European reservoirs. Massive changes in hemispheric as well as Pacific patterns of migration caused both states to revamp their legal frameworks in the 1960s.

They not only abolished preferences by region of origin but also introduced pluralist or multicultural policies internally. Migrants were admitted because of skills, as highly qualified professionals or business investors, under programs for family reunion, or as refugees for humanitarian reasons. These criteria matched the aspirations of well-trained young people across Third World sending regions and resulted in a "brain drain" in Asia, Latin America, and Africa. In view of worldwide power hierarchies, demands for compensation to the countries of origin, discussed at the Geneva-based International Labour Organization, came, not surprisingly, to naught. On the whole, the new laws resulted in a fundamental change in immigration to North America. The share of Europeans fell to below one-half in the United States in 1961, in Canada in the period 1975–79; to below one-third in the United States in 1970 and in Canada in 1985–89; and to less than one-eighth in the United States in the 1980s.

With regard to labor migration, the relationship of the United States to Mexico was not altogether different from that of West Central Europe to Poland. Poland had been divided in 1795; parts of Mexico divided off between 1826 and 1852. The German-Slavic cultural borderlands had an equivalent in the Anglo-Hispanic zone from Texas to California. Like Poles, Mexicans were to come as temporary workers: "While they are not easily assimilated, this is of no very great importance as long as most of them return to their native land. In the case of the Mexican, he is less desirable as a citizen than as a laborer" (Dillingham Commission, 1911). Southwestern "growers," the equivalent of colonial plantation owners or East Elbian Junkers, recruited *braceros* under an exemption from the literacy test instituted for all immigrants in 1917. In the 1920s, Mexicans could collect one-fifth of their seasonal pay only upon departure at the border; during the depression thirties, many were deported—or, in officialese, "repatriated." With the next war came the next recruitment program: some five million Mexican workers arrived from 1942 to 1964. Government agencies, like those of nineteenth-century British India, acceded to all demands from planters and ranchers, including occasional round-ups of "illegal" Mexicans, deported in Operation Wetback. Once official recruitment ended, relationships between workers and planters lasted, and migrants—documented or undocumented—continued to come and be hired. As in other parts of the world, laborers struggled for better working conditions.[39]

By the late 1970s and early 1980s, Mexico and the Caribbean became the largest source of legal immigrants to the United States. Most went into seasonal field labor but increasingly also into permanent urban enclaves across the country (chap. 14.2). The Caribbean islands became a source of migrants to Canadian cities, with English-speaking migrants heading for Ontario and French-speaking Haitians going to Montreal. About one-fifth of U.S.-bound migrants came with white-collar skills, but both countries also imported women for domestic labor and care-giving. The Caribbean communities grew rapidly to 315,000 foreign-born in the United States and 210,000 in Canada in 1980. The United States admitted Cuban refugees but siphoned off Haitians on the high seas. The Cuban refugees, who arrived in four waves from 1959 to

1994, including a legal boatlift of 125,000 "Marielitos" in 1980, number more than one million.[40] From Puerto Rico, a U.S.-held territory, middle-class and subsequently working-class people began to depart when industrialization strategies attempted to alleviate unemployment but mobilized laborers beyond the limitations of the semi-colonial economy. Over two million Puerto Ricans net had migrated to the United States by 1980. Spanish-speaking Cubans clustered in Florida, and Puerto Ricans in the New York City area; both struggled for bilingual education and institutions. The two regions became to some degree culturally Hispanicized. Changes in New York's manufacturing sector, development in Puerto Rico, and economic opportunities else-where in the United States led to return migration and a dispersal of Puerto Ricans to other locations. Cubans, on the other hand, remained highly concentrated in Florida and, as refugees from Castroism, enjoyed official support. The increasingly fortified border between the United States and Mexico was breached by a new guest-worker program under the Reagan administration. While the presence even of undocumented Latin American migrants forces institutions—schools and hospitals, for example—to change from the bottom up, these newcomers have not achieved parity with other immigrant groups in terms of earnings and structural integration. Developments like subcontracting increase the demand for small-scale immigrant entrepreneurs from Latin American middle classes, but they keep them in economically precarious posi-tions. When the U.S. Immigration Reform and Control Act of 1986 permitted the legalization of undocumented migrants, three million applied, more than two-thirds of them Mexicans. In the 1990s, border controls and exclusionist propositions, in-cluding the expulsion of migrant children from schools, gained ground.[41]

With regard to refugee admission, both countries admitted people for humani-tarian reasons beyond the definitions of the Geneva Convention. Canada, as a coun-try of resettlement, selects individuals with high insertion capabilities. Once estab-lished, they may sponsor relatives regardless of economic suitability and help friends to come. U.S. involvement in Vietnam, Somalia, and Latin America led to large num-bers of people of colors other than White to arrive as refugees under sponsorship clauses. Canada also recruited temporary female labor for domestic work and child-care from the Caribbean and Southeast Asia. Subsequent legislation permitted adjust-ment of their status to that of immigrants. While most positions in the service sector available to immigrants remain dead-end jobs, as they have been through the ages, global apartheid has relegated whole societies of origin to dead-end economies. As a consequence, immigration from Third World countries to Canada increased from 8 percent of the total in the early 1960s to 50 percent by 1975.[42]

In the early 1990s, Canada's annual immigrant admissions reached a quarter mil-lion; per 1,000 of population, immigration to Canada has been higher than it has been to the United States; 16 percent (4.3 million) of the Canadian population were foreign-born in 1991. The massive non-European immigration changed the color com-position of the North American societies. Since color-of-skin classifications were in-creasingly difficult to maintain, a "Hispanic-origin, of all races" category was intro-duced into U.S. census schedules, and the "multiple origin" category includes people of mixed colors. Critical voices have warned of the "Browning" or "Asianization" of America, but opinion polls show widespread acceptance of the development. Young people have decided to intermarry; Toronto's population reached a non-European-origin majority in 2000. In the United States in 1990, 20 percent of the population was of a "race" other than European, and 9 percent were of Hispanic origin. While the continent integrated to some degree into one hemispheric migration region, the North American Free Trade Agreement of 1992 changed once again the parameters of migration and the demand for cheap labor, forcing families to adjust their income-generating and emotional strategies. The agreement, in contrast to transnational protocols of the European Union, does not permit the free movement of people.[43]

U.S. immigration legislation always combined an official policy with a "back door" for cheap labor (Zolberg); "capital has always been clearly at the controls" (Papademetriou).[44] Whereas in the nineteenth century Asian workers also entered through the back door, the third phase of the Pacific Migration System since the 1960s has been directed to the front door and has involved large numbers of middle-class migrants (chap. 19.5). (See map 19.4.)

19.4 Migration in and from Dependent Economies: The Caribbean, Central America, and South America

Latin America's export-oriented economies have remained on the periphery of capitalist economic development. In some states, multinational food corporations continued the plantation regime; in others, landless and smallholding rural people, mobilized by internal and foreign investment and mechanization, moved to cities. Millions fled dictatorial regimes. Six distinct migration regions have emerged: the Caribbean; Mexico, with its northbound outflow and transit migration from further south; Central America, with its refugee-generating societies; Venezuela, as an immigrant-attracting country; Brazil, characterized by internal migrations; and Argentina, as the core of the southern cone. In socioeconomic terms, the poor tend to migrate internally; skilled and subsequently unskilled urban and small-town workers have moved to neighboring economies; middle-class men and women are more likely to leave for overseas destinations in the former colonial European cores or, more often, the North American capitalist cores. All have often been displaced by foreign investors who, supported by governmental elites, tap cheap, internally migrating labor forces but bring their own managerial personnel and supply networks.[45]

The Caribbean, in the orbit of European colonial powers and by the late nineteenth century an area of U.S. investment strategies, became a region of inter-island labor migrations after the end of slavery (chap. 14.2); the Dutch islands of Curaçao and Aruba attracted migrants when oil refineries were built in 1918 and 1929. Northbound migration was limited before 1880 when some 9,000–14,000 migrants reached the United States per decade. The numbers tripled in the next two decades and tripled again in the period 1911–20, to 123,500. In the next decade, the first migrants reached Canada, and Marcus Garvey transferred the Universal Negro Improvement Associa-

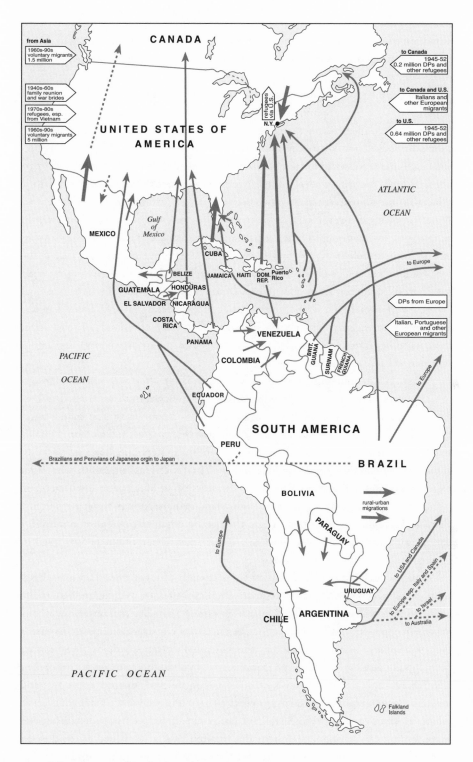

from Asia

1960s-90s
voluntary migrants
1.5 million

1940s-60s
family reunion
and war brides

1970s-80s
refugees, esp.
from Vietnam

1960s-90s
voluntary migrants
5 million

CANADA

to Canada
1945-52
0.2 million DPs and
other refugees

to Canada and U.S.
Italians and
other European
migrants

to U.S.
1945-52
0.64 million DPs and
other refugees

UNITED STATES OF
AMERICA

*Gulf
of
Mexico*

MEXICO

refugees
via U.S.

N.Y.

ATLANTIC

OCEAN

CUBA

BELIZE

JAMAICA   HAITI   DOM.   Puerto
REP.   Rico

GUATEMALA   HONDURAS

EL SALVADOR   NICARAGUA

COSTA
RICA

PANAMA

VENEZUELA

to Europe

DPs from Europe

Italian, Portuguese
and other
European migrants

COLOMBIA

BRIT.
GUIANA

SURINAM

FRENCH
GUIANA

PACIFIC

OCEAN

ECUADOR

to Europe

SOUTH AMERICA

PERU

Brazilians and Peruvians of Japanese orgin to Japan

B R A Z I L

BOLIVIA

rural-urban
migrations

to USA and Canada

PARAGUAY

to Europe

to Europe esp. Italy and Spain

to Israel

URUGUAY

to Australia

PACIFIC OCEAN

CHILE   ARGENTINA

08 Falkland
Islands

19.4   Migration to and in the Americas

tion from Jamaica to the United States in 1916. The Immigration Act of 1924 reduced migration to a trickle. Inter-island migration stagnated in the depression thirties but resumed during World War II, with U.S. military bases rather than cane fields as destinations.

Afro-Caribbean eastbound transatlantic migrations in the 1960s resulted from imperial British, French, and Dutch connections as well as from the end of colonial rule. Before 1961, during the period of de facto exclusion from the United States, 230,000–280,000 non-White Caribbeans arrived in Britain, providing labor for postwar economic reconstruction and draining island economies of skilled workers, particularly in the building trades. A limited number of women migrated independently. When the Commonwealth Immigrants [Exclusion] Act curtailed migration from non-White countries in 1962, migrants opted for family reunion and community stabilization. As a destination for French Antilleans and French Guianans in the late 1950s and for larger numbers of men and women from Martinique and Guadeloupe in the 1970s and 1980s, France could count 190,000 Caribbean-born residents in 1982 (census figures). Migration from continental Dutch Surinam, especially of Indian- and Javanese-origin men and women, began after independence in 1975. Some 200,000 Surinamese and 30,000 Dutch Antilleans resided in the Netherlands in 1990. In all three receiving states, labor market insertion has been at the bottom level, residential segregation high, and racism evident.

When U.S.-bound migration became lawful again after 1965, diverse groups of Caribbean labor migrants and refugees established communities. In addition to Cuban refugees and Puerto Rican migrants, some 800,000 left or fled the Dominican Republic, and another 600,000 came from the British West Indies, from Jamaica in particular. In voluntary moves—from the Dominican Republic, for example—proactive middle-class migrants left first, followed by lower-class migrants, who often were undocumented. Refugees from the dictatorship of Haiti were not welcomed —thus perhaps as many as 800,000 came clandestinely. Others moved to French Canada, especially to Montreal, where they could connect to small communities dating from before World War II. Some 350,000 Caribbean-origin people lived in Canada at the beginning of the 1990s.

Inter-island labor migration is directed seasonally to sugarcane economies, long-term to the oil economies, and to industries across the region. Women migrate to the oil economies—as well as to the United States and Canada—as domestic workers. When job opportunities for men decline at the end of construction booms, women's domestic labor remains in demand by the new middle classes. Industrial and tourist development attracted Cubans and Dominicans to Puerto Rico, and migration of Haitian laborers to the Dominican Republic has continued. Jamaican domestics and Western financial money-laundering operators have migrated to the Cayman Islands, where, as white experts or black laborers, both can gain only a precarious status. Migrant remittances have bolstered the consumption side of the island economies. In some societies, rivalry between African-origin and Asian-origin inhabitants is evident; in others—Trinidad and Jamaica, for example—Black Power and Indian-origin movements have made their mark. In cultural terms, the islands continue to radiate outward as a vibrant part of the Black Atlantic, but economically the region remains under the influence of the United States[46]

In Mexico, connected for a century by emigration and seasonal migration to the United States, a comprehensive immigration law of 1886 established the right of free entry and exit. While only a few settlers came to its northern rural areas, the role of foreigners in the state's elite was one of the causes for the Mexican Revolution in 1910. The nationalist Constitution of 1917 regulated the entry of foreigners and the exit of nationals. Populationist policies to encourage return from the United States as well as immigration were unsuccessful. However, when the depression hit in 1929–30, half a million returned. Mexico was and is a country of refuge, attracting left-wing Russian exiles after 1917, Spanish Republicans from fascism, U.S. exiles under McCarthyism, Chileans and Argentines from military rule, and Guatemalans, Salvadorans, and Hondurans from recent right-wing regimes. This sheltering role in the shadow of the United States has received little recognition. Labor migrants arrive as seasonal agricultural workers from Guatemala; a few immigrants have come from Spain and the United States. The latter, may, however, be of Mexican origin or Chicano-cultured.

With regard to U.S.-bound labor migration, the United States recruited *braceros* without even asking the consent of the Mexican government in 1954. After the end of recruitment in 1964, migrants continued to come without documents; their mobility was "more sensitive to laws of supply and demand of international labor markets than to immigration legislation." The percentages of urban-origin migrants, of well-educated ones, and of women going to large U.S. cities grew, reflecting both changed labor demands and the changed interests and strategies of migrants. In 1980, some 2.5 million Mexican-born men, women, and children resided in the United States (census figures), but a mere 3,100 in Canada. It must be noted, however, that the rate of Mexican migration to the north is less intense than the flow of departures from Europe was in the early twentieth century.[47]

In South America, European immigration stagnated in the interwar and depression years. Some countries accepted refugees from Europe or harbored undocumented ones, including fugitive fascists and war criminals after 1945. In the early postwar years, assisted migration helped some of Europe's displaced persons to come—until economic recovery in Europe ended the flow and induced many to return. In the 1960s only Italians continued to migrate to Argentina, as they did to Canada and northern Europe.

In Brazil, sometimes considered a powerful capitalist subcenter, more than 810,000 immigrants arrived between 1942 and 1963 from Portugal (40.6 percent), Spain (14.9 percent), Italy (14.2 percent), Japan (6.7 percent), and elsewhere. At the same time, a native-born unskilled labor force migrated to the cities—some 10 percent of the rural population or a net total of three million in the 1940s and seven million in the 1950s. They increasingly met demand. Both leftist (1955–61) and conservative governments (including the military coup in 1964) favored industrial development, the mechanization of agriculture, and improved transportation facilities. The result was increased self-displacement over greater distances and the emergence of shantytowns (*favelas*) on the urban fringes. Migrant men, women, and children, rather than leading deprived, victimized lives, possessed considerable human capital, adapted to economic changes better than the established central-city urban working classes, and established burgeoning tertiary or informal sectors. Rural-to-rural migrations had been directed to the Paraná Plateau or the Central Zone (chap. 18.1); during the 1970s, migration to the Amazon region remained limited. Nevertheless, slash-and-burn forest clearance annihilated secluded Indio peoples and destroyed the ecosystem. Road construction and the relocation of the capital, from Rio de Janeiro to Brasilia, mobilized hundreds of thousands of men, and urban service attracted even larger numbers of women. At first many moved back and forth between rural and city labor.[48]

Venezuela's oil-based economy created a new regional labor migration system involving mainly Colombians and, in smaller numbers, Dominicans and Jamaicans. The registered foreign population tripled to almost 600,000 between 1950 and 1971, to which perhaps as many undocumented workers have to be added. Refugees from political repression in the southern cone also arrived. Few found employment in the oil industry; most worked in construction, which was fueled by the revenue boom. Skill selectivity connected particular regions of origin to particular labor markets at destination: "Informal, fragmented information is perceived and built up by a largely illiterate mass of people into a coherent and fairly accurate appraisal of reality." In Colombia, the government reduced the need for emigration by planned "development within the country." Highland families adapted life-course strategies to long-range economic and cultural change, and internal migrations reversed the two-thirds/one-third rural-urban population ratio between 1950 and 1980. In the 1970s urban professional migrants, including many women, left for Florida and New York; the Venezuelan economic crisis in 1983 pushed immigrant workers, in particular undocumented ones, into more marginal positions.[49]

Argentina became the center of a second new labor migration system. Its pre-1930s "grand policy" had "aimed at incorporating citizens into the national society and not just workers into the economy," but in the interwar decades pro-natalist policies replaced open-door attitudes. Basques and Jews, both without the support of a state, as well as Poles were excluded. Political refugees from Paraguay came after 1947. Postwar European immigration, including half a million Italians, was cut short by a depression in the early 1950s. Subsequently, the neighboring countries of Paraguay, Bolivia, and Chile became the major suppliers of labor, at first informally and then under bilateral agreements. Traditionally, migrants had moved internally and then crossed borders into adjoining regions; by the 1960s they explored opportunities in the whole of Argentina. Inhabitants of the coastal cities of Argentina, Uruguay, and Brazil engaged in inter-urban circular migrations depending on regional economic performance. Internal migration converged on Buenos Aires. According to census results, by 1970 a tenth of Paraguay's population of 2.5 million lived in Argentina — according to estimates of scholars, a fifth did. Mostly young people with above-average education or skills migrated in an almost balanced sex ratio. Return rates were high. Uruguay became an emigration country for political and economic reasons in the early 1960s. Repeated regularization programs have brought Argentina's immigration policy into line with life-course strategies of migrant families.

In Latin America as a whole, most rural-urban migrations involved more women than men, and in societies with few cities, like Peru, women accounted for the majority of the long-distance migrations. In Argentina, immigrant women's participation in the paid labor force varied by cultural group, position in the migration sequence, and labor market possibilities. Women from Bolivia, who mostly followed their husbands, had low participation rates; when they did work, they were often engaged in petty trade. For most other immigrant women, domestic service was the major sector of employment. Internally migrating Argentine women also went into factory work. Women's labor market participation may be underestimated and, in census data, undercounted because of the "virtual absence of recognition for the role women play in smallholder agriculture."[50] The sequential migration of families, the separate but often parallel mobility of single men and women with postmigration or postreturn family formation, and long-term separation demand highly adaptable family structures and flexibility in intrafamily labor allocation.[51]

Some migrations involve ethnic clustering of First Nations people, as in the case of the Tilantoqueño Indians in Mexico City, Guatemalan Indians in agricultural regions, or Aymara Indians in government-sponsored settlements in Bolivia. In Guatemala, the nineteenth-century tradition of forcing highland Indios into seasonal plantation labor was continued into the late twentieth century. Military resettlement programs in response to revolutionary activities displaced over 10 percent of the total population, in particular highland Indios. Owing to political repression and violence as well as to comparatively slow development, Latin America became an emigration region in the 1960s.[52]

Political refugees have been another important group on the move. Faced with right-wing death squads and government *violencia,* such refugees left Paraguay after 1947, Brazil after 1964, and Chile, Uruguay and Argentina in the period 1973–76 and later. Political refugees from Chile numbered some 200,000; those uprooted in El Salvador, Nicaragua, and Guatemala between 1.8 and 2.8 million in the 1980s. Displacement in Honduras, on the other hand, was small. Intergovernmental cooperation often barred refugees fleeing rightist terror from entering the United States until the Refugee Act of 1980 granted "temporary protected status." Canada accepted refugees for resettlement, and subsequent migrations enlarged these communities. While most refugees remained in neighboring countries, those sent into exile by the 1973 Chilean coup dispersed worldwide.

In some civil wars, ethnic groups faced displacement, as happened to the Miskito Indians in Nicaragua; sometimes corrupt elites fled, as occurred after the Cuban revolution; sometimes women were singled out for particularly harsh treatment, as in Chile, when their rights were curtailed, or in Argentina, where the military murdered imprisoned pregnant "suspects" after they had given birth. Women in their roles as mothers or grandmothers organized highly visible protest activities.[53]

By the 1990s, refugee repatriation and a continuous voluntary northward migration characterized most of Latin America. The multiple migrations in the Caribbean region, including return from North America and from inter-island moves, have fostered an emergent common Caribbean identity. The concentration of Colombians in Venezuela and Bolivians in Argentina may contribute to changed perceptions about national ideologies and transnational practices.

19.5 From Asia Outward: The Third Phase of Pacific Migrations

In Asia, the defeat of Japanese imperialism (chap. 17.4), the independence of most colonies established by Europeans, and the wars in Korea and Vietnam changed the parameters of migration. So did subsequent industrialization in Japan and South Korea, the highly restrictive emigration policy of the People's Republic of China, middle-class educational achievements in India, and lack of employment in Southeast Asian societies. Development and urbanization characterized all societies—though delayed in Vietnam and aborted by internal genocide in Kampuchea/ Cambodia.

On the receiving side, South America, with the exception of Brazil, did not attract migrants in the post-1940s phase. The Japan-to-Brazil link was reversed in the 1990s when many returned (chap. 19.6). In North America, a decisive change in attitudes and policies began with the wartime alliance with China against Japan, with visions of postwar investment opportunities in Asia, and with a decline of anti-Asian racism internally. Nevertheless, change in the legal framework was slow. Chinese were legally admitted to the United States in a quota of merely 105 persons annually as of 1943; the same was true in Canada as of 1947. Exclusion was followed by two decades of tiny quotas[54] until the U.S. Immigration Act of 1965 and the Canadian immigration regulations of 1967 effected basic changes. Since then, the vast majority of the transpacific migrants, including Pacific Islanders, have been destined for North America. However, a new region of destination emerged with the economic takeoff in the South Pacific region led by Australia.[55]

The third phase of transpacific migrations followed, as we have seen, an initial phase instigated by Spanish colonial interests and a second phase characterized by free and contract labor migration. The postexclusion phase of North America–bound transpacific migrations can be divided into three distinct periods: 1) family-reunion and exempted migration before the mid-1960s; 2) the migration of refugees from "the three Chinas"—the People's Republic (PRC), Taiwan, and Hong Kong—and from Overseas Chinese communities, as well as from the Cold War–era conflicts in Korea, Vietnam, Laos, and Cambodia; and 3) subsequent voluntary mass migration.

Family reunion strategies mainly involved Chinese migrants because Japanese men had sent for their wives and formed families in the early phase of restrictions, from 1907 to the 1920s. U.S. military involvement, ranging from a liberating role in World War II to its later imperial reach, resulted in a second type of family migration. Six thousand Chinese war brides reached the United States in 1945; from 1952 to 1962, 48,000 Japanese, 16,000 Philippine, and 8,000 Korean women arrived as wives of servicemen. Under family sponsorship clauses, they could bring in near relatives. Few skilled labor migrants came in these decades because postwar reconstruction in Asia provided jobs.

The cultural agenda of the United States, which had as a goal the development of educational systems in Asian states, involved the admission of students to its universities. Graduate returnees introduced U.S. concepts, teaching materials, and ideologies to acquaintances and students in an intended multiplier effect. The intensification of cultural and economic relations was paralleled by U.S.-centered migration strategies of individuals or families from the educated middle classes.[56]

With regard to refugees, a mere 18,500 Indochinese—including Vietnamese brides of U.S. soldiers—settled in the United States between 1945 and 1974, whereas in France, the original colonizing power, a Vietnamese community was well established. A first peak of refugee arrivals followed the U.S. withdrawal from Vietnam in 1975, and a second, higher one, involving "boat people," occurred in the period 1979–82. Some 760,000 refugees, just over one-half of the total, were resettled in the United States under the Indochina Migration and Refugee Assistance Act of 1975 and the Refugee Act of 1980 (as well as 43,000 immigrants in the same period). Australia, Canada, and France accepted about 100,000 refugees each. In the United States, refugees from Vietnam and neighboring countries were administratively distributed to sites across the country, but in secondary migrations clusters emerged—of Vietnamese in California and highland tribal Lao (Hmong) in Minneapolis, for example. In the early 1980s, refugee flows from Asia became self-sustaining. This influx of "boat people" coincided with "boat lifts" from Cuba and the increasing incidence of flight from Haiti by boat; at the same time, U.S. authorities became concerned about the arrival of potentially large numbers of "feet people"—those who might try to walk across the land border rather than arrive by boat—from right-wing regimes in Central America. In reaction, drastic screening measures were introduced.[57]

Voluntary migration skyrocketed after 1965, and by 1990 Asian-origin people accounted for just under half of the annual immigration. By 1998 more than five million Asian newcomers had reached the United States, and more than 1.5 million had arrived in Canada. Because of independent migration strategies, family reunion clauses, and labor market demands, women account for a slight majority of the Asian immigrants entering North America since 1945. U.S. postcolonial or military involvements in the Philippines, South Korea, and Vietnam explain the arrival of 1.1 million Filipinas and Filipinos by 1992, of 0.7 million Koreans and an equal number of Vietnamese, and of 0.55 million Laotians, Cambodians, and Thais (including refugees). Also to be counted are 0.9 million Chinese and 0.55 million Indians. Migration from Japan, given its sound pre-1998 economy, remained a small factor. The south and central Pacific Islander migrants, who numbered 110,000 from 1961 to 1983, originated primarily in Hawai'i (which was admitted to statehood in 1959) and the connected territories of Guam and Samoa. In Canada, before 1991, just under one million migrants arrived from East and Southeast Asia, and just under half a million from South Asia. California and Toronto have attracted the largest number of Asian immigrants. Predominantly middle-class and well-educated migrants have entered all segments of the economy; families that run small and mid-sized businesses have become transnationally mobile, and their children have above-average levels of college education.[58]

Migration to Australasia, in the nineteenth century part of the Asia-outward migrations to "White" countries, now occurs in the South Pacific region, which has emerged as an economic force since the mid-1940s. Australia and New Zealand are developing positions independent from traditional British and more recent North American linkages in order to become part of the Asian economies.[59] Both states modified their entry policies after 1949, when Australia admitted nationalist Chinese refugees and subsequently Anglo-Asians. Shifts in Australia's immigration illustrate the changes in economic relations and cultural attitudes. Following World War II, displaced persons from Europe predominated; northwestern Europeans were part of the main immigration flow in the 1950s, and southern Europeans figured prominently in the 1950s and 1960s. But by the early 1970s, when "White" policies and preferential treatment for Europeans had been abolished, voluntary migrations from Asia increased.[60]

Australia's in-between position vis-à-vis White Western and Asian societies is highlighted by its having been a preferred destination for Euro-Asian migrants during decolonization: of the 178,000 resident Asia-born immigrants in 1976, less than one-half were of Asian ethnicity. In the next five years, the volume increased, and the ethnic balance changed: of the 303,000 Asia-born newcomers, two-thirds were ethnic Asians. Australia opened its doors in response to refugee-generating conflicts, such as the Indonesia/Timor crisis of 1975 and the expulsion of the Ugandan Asians. A century after the recruitment of South Pacific contract laborers against their will, Tongans, Fijians, and Somoans are arriving as voluntary labor migrants and establishing a South Pacific diaspora. Australian and New Zealand professionals, in turn, staff managerial and administrative offices in the island states. The new South Pacific Migration System retains only distant links to Europe.[61]

Hong Kong, too, occupies an in-between position. It grew extremely fast before the 1930s (chap. 15.1), was emptied of half of its population of 1.6 million under the Japanese occupation, and grew again when hundreds of thousands of refugees from the PRC arrived after the nationalists' defeat in 1949. Connected to the old financial center, London, as well as increasingly to the new centers in New York and, subsequently, in Toronto, its economy expanded. However, when Vietnamese boat people arrived, laborers were no longer needed because factory production was being shifted to the surrounding provinces of the PRC. They were kept in camps and repatriated against their will. The end of the British lease of Hong Kong in 1997 prompted a precautionary exodus of employees of multinational corporations and the proactive migration of independent middle-class families. Their migration to the South Pacific region or to North America is intentionally transnational. Hong Kong remains the economic base, while Australia, New Zealand, Canada or the United States provide passports and a base for parts of the family. In glib modernist terms, astronaut migrants with lifelines attached orbit around their original base; they drop their parachute kids at North American or international private educational institutions. From an analytical perspective, migrant families have traditionally kept a base while migrating over great distances, and their children have often been sent far from home for education and training. What is new is not only the amount of funds transferred but also the economic integration of the Pacific World.

Westbound transpacific migration and travel brought businessmen to Hong Kong, Singapore, Manila, and Japan, and millions of American, other Western, and Australian men were stationed in Asia during the several postcolonial wars. The peaceful consequences include new mixed ethnic groups; American-Thai, American-Vietnamese, American-Philippine, and other children of part-Asian extraction; the emigration of women as wives; and the settling of some of the men as husbands. Such emotional conversion may be viewed as a self-determined extension of the economic and power nexus of intimate relations under imperialism. On the other hand, "Western" men's spending power for sex labor brought forth a transnational economy of "imperial sons and national pimps," and the patterns of women's employment were combined with sexual harassment (chaps. 16.4, 19.1). Global power relationships continue to be reflected in personal relations.[62]

In economic terms, the shift to the Pacific World has been located in 1984 when the balance of transoceanic commerce tipped in favor of the Pacific. Culturally, the shift became noticeable in North America in the 1980s; the former colonial cores in Europe—France, Britain, and the Netherlands—are connected through Vietnamese neighborhoods, South Asian enclaves, or Indonesian food. Pacific migration results in intercivilizational exchange and conversion, which makes the Pacific World comparable to the twelfth-century Mediterranean and nineteenth-century Atlantic worlds.

The new "Pacific Rim" concept implies an orientalist view, a projection of a Euro-American perspective on Asia, as Arif Dirlik has argued, unless the Asian and Australian perspective with the Americas as a rim is incorporated. The nineteenth-century imperial British poet, Rudyard Kipling, rhapsodized that "East is East and West is West, and never the twain shall meet." Like any certainty, this view was particularist and narrow, its global pretension notwithstanding. Wing Tek Lum, a Chinese-Hawai'ian poet of American citizenship, reflected the complexities of multiple viewpoints:

> O
> East is East
> and
> West is West.
> but

I never did
understand
why
in Geography class
the East was west
and
the West was east
and that no
one ever
cared
about the difference.[63]

As long as the Atlantic was the core of the global political economy and of knowledge distribution, it was clear to hegemonic gatekeepers where east and west were.
But the ethnocultural composition of the gatekeepers is changing.

19.6   Intra-Asian Migrations and Diasporas

In Asia, post-1945 refugee migrations preceded new patterns of labor migration (map
19.5). Reverse migrations of colonizer personnel involved the loss of expertise and
opened opportunities for new middle classes. The major economic regions/states remained separate, and migrations continued to be internal (chaps. 15, 17.4, 18.1, 18.3).
During the postwar reconstruction boom little need for economic emigration existed,
but—as in nineteenth-century Europe—the construction of "nations" turned groups
with negotiated status into people without citizenship. New immigration controls
excluded migrants who would augment internal "minorities."[64]

Of the several diasporas, most Indian contract laborers and colonial auxiliaries
returned, some settled as citizens of new states. Japanese imperial migrants had
been shipped back by the allies. However, some diasporic communities of Indians
or Japanese of prewar origin remained. The 16 million Overseas Chinese in 1962,
who had survived war and decolonization-induced economic change, found themselves in new states as minorities among hegemonic peoples: Thailand (3.8 million),
Indonesia (2.5 million), Malaya (2.4 million), Singapore (1.3 million), and Vietnam (1.0
million) among others. They came to form a majority in Singapore and live in "large
minority societies" in Malaysia and Hawai'i and in "minority societies" in most of
Asia and much of the Americas.[65] They held economic elite positions or assumed
middlemen roles between elites and populations. Their material and educational advance—partly due to a cultural choice of hard work, partly because of trade connections and skills—caused envy, invited projections, or resulted in economic power
over Natives. Thus conflicts were ethnicized and exploited by political elites. Some
Western-aligned states considered Overseas Chinese to be communist agents, particularly after the PRC government encouraged them to participate in social revo-

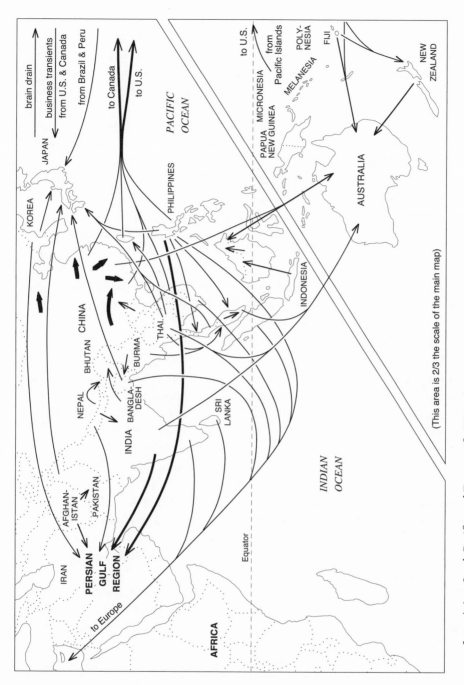

19.5   Intra-Asian, South Pacific, and Transpacific Migrations

lutionary activities. As individuals and as communities, the Chinese diaspora had to define its position in relation to the new states, to economic indigenization policies, as well as to the PRC, a process in which Taiwan remained marginal. Its choices included joining pluralist societies, entering into legally defined minority status, embarking on assimilationist courses like Indonesianization, or even engaging in return migration.[66]

Emigration from Asian states began with the U.S.-bound "brain drain"—the departure of women as servicemen's brides was not viewed as a resource drain. In the 1970s, North America, Australia/New Zealand, and the oil-exporting West Asian and Arab states became the three major destinations, while Britain, France, and other regions remained minor receiving areas. By the mid-1970s, more than half a million migrants were arriving annually in the United States, Canada, Australia, and New Zealand. Migration strategies and the numbers of people involved depended on economic development. South Korea, for example, having sent emigrants for two decades, became an immigration country in the 1980s. North America–bound migrants originate from the strata of the economically well-off and/or highly educated. In opposite direction, transient experts and commercial personnel from investor states migrate to Asian Newly Industrialized Countries (NICs).[67]

Refugee-generation followed internal and superpower-driven conflicts in Korea and Vietnam and the imposition of nonindigenous rule in Tibet in 1959 and in Timor in 1975. It also resulted from the unequal internal distribution of power (as in West and East Pakistan), from investment and cultural strategies that disadvantaged minorities (as in Burma/Myanmar), or from internal upheaval (as in the PRC during the Great Leap Forward and the Cultural Revolution).[68] Middlemen minorities, revolutionaries, and people suspected of communist loyalties were driven out, as in the case of the approximately 200,000 Chinese (out of 2.2 million) forced to leave Indonesia in 1965–66,[69] or they fled, as Chinese businesspeople did from Vietnam and Cambodia after 1975. Large developmental programs displaced people in subaltern positions. In India, for example, an estimated 40 percent of the 23 million people victimized by "national" development were "tribals" who accounted for only 8 percent of the total population. In the late 1990s, the Narmada valley dam project threatened to displace tens of millions.[70]

Rural settlement or labor migrations have declined. The Indonesian government encouraged farmers to migrate to the "open spaces" of Sumatra from "overpopulated Java" (chap. 18.1); Batak from the island of Samosir on Lake Toba, Sumatra, have migrated to surrounding agricultural sites. These migrations and religio-economic Christian-Muslim tensions caused local violence in the 1990s. In marginal regions, "residual emigrant societies" emerge in which the elderly predominate, fertility declines, and intergenerational relations come apart. The migration of married men without their families may change patrilocal residence patterns, as when their wives left behind prefer to live with their own families of origin. In cases in which these women's brothers have emigrated, such choice is encouraged by their parents who have been deprived of care-providing daughters-in-law for old age. Cityward emigration of marriage-age women has led to the importation of "replacement women" from neighboring poorer states.[71]

Vast rural-urban migrations transform all Asian societies. About 25 percent of the population lived in cities in 1980, 33 percent in 1990, and 41 percent in 2000. Global economic strategies—whether they involve the placement of electronics factories, garment shops, or office work linked by telecommunications—provide jobs that are often filled by independently migrating women, although at exploitative wages and working conditions. In the 1970s, more women than men migrated to cities in Thailand, the Philippines, and Korea, while men formed the majority of migrants in Japan, Singapore, Malaysia, and Iran. Mobilization varied according to the roles assigned to women in Buddhist and Islamic societies, labor markets at destinations, and educational opportunities. Warrior-clerics have increased restrictions on women's mobility in West Asia, especially in Iran and Afghanistan. As in European and Russian migration history, the initial stage of cityward migration in Asia involves commuting between village and city. As in Latin America and Africa, most migrants enter the informal sector or urban economies, which according to UN experts is "one of the few processes operating . . . to correct social and economic inequalities."[72]

No matter whether they occur in socialist, capitalist, or corporatist states, intra-Asian migrations involve structural adaptation from primarily agricultural to primarily industrial production and to investments by MNCs in search of cheap and nonunionized labor forces. Governments supply underemployed labor reserves to internationally mobile capital, with at best only limited protection of their rights.

In the PRC, the commune system of rural production and the exit and entry permit system of 1958 curbed or even blocked internal migration.[73] In 1978, when 82.4 percent of the population lived in rural areas, the "reforms and opening" policy continued to assign landholding to the communes but left production decisions and the sale of surpluses to families. In 1984 market mechanisms were strengthened, and in 1988 migration was deregulated: farmers could move to the cities provided they could feed themselves and possessed sufficient capital to run an independent small business. Regional disparities between increasing agricultural incomes in the vicinity of eastern cities and stagnating incomes in hilly and arid western regions added incentives to migrate. The cost of migration is high, however, since families lose their rights in land and the income from it, and thus they cannot acquire a starting capital to cover the expense of travel and economic reinsertion.

The government-sponsored creation of nonagricultural employment in towns and villages reduced long-distance cityward migration in the PRC. But in the 1980s, temporary labor migrants began to move in masses to urban labor markets, where housing was scarce. They took advantage of information flows and connections established by urban youths sent to the countryside to spread new ideas and ideologies. The traditional return to villages at the lunar new year in early spring and subsequent new migration to urban jobs—which involved some 50 million moves in 1992—taxed the transport system and led to temporary labor shortages in industries and personnel-employing urban households. The total "floating population," estimated officially at 60 million in 1992, may be as high as 100 million; in addition, planners in 1995 estimated an "overstock" of rural people in the range of 270 million. However, China's agricultural output has kept pace with population growth.[74]

Out-migration goes mainly west to east, from Tibet to Sichuan and from Sichuan to Beijing, Shanghai, and Guangzhou. Coastal cities are linked by ever larger inter-urban migrations. The Special Economic Zones of Guangdong province, an emigration region for centuries, had attracted more than 10 million in-migrants by 1994. In Beijing sojourners were estimated to number 0.9 million in 1984, with one-quarter in construction, one-quarter in search of jobs, and 5 percent in domestic labor. By 1994 their number amounted to 5 million. Migrants cluster by ethnicity or, if Chinese, by language and region of origin; they engage in particular trades and reside in distinct neighborhoods. Some 6.7 percent of the population (55 million people) belong to "minorities," and Chinese speak nine languages in addition to Mandarin. "Chinatowns in Beijing" emerge with strange dialects, "exotic" markets, and different restaurants and eating habits. Migration is expected to accelerate: in northeastern China long-lasting drought has exacerbated rural problems; the Three Gorges dam project on the Yangtze will displace about 1.3 million peasants; the reduction of state-owned industrial complexes will cause unemployment among urban laboring families. Under these conditions, undocumented workers move to Taiwan and North America, often in bondage to work off the debt incurred to the new traders in human cargo. Legal migrants move in many directions. After 1989, small numbers of laborers and entrepreneurs migrated to Russia, to Moscow in particular.[75]

In Japan, the legal framework of 1894 had defined any resident non-Japanese or immigrant as a "foreigner" and permitted movement only under strict controls and obligatory "certificates of alien registration"; it remained part of the Immigration Control Act of 1951 but was drastically reformed in 1990. The regulations applied to Chinese who came after the annexation of Taiwan in 1895 and in the 1920s, to Filipino migrants of the 1920s, and to Korean laborers under imperialist recruitment. Of the last, an estimated 600,000 remained in 1950, while some 80,000 were repatriated to the People's Republic of Korea. In 1990, less than 1 percent of Japan's population of 123 million was "foreign," including 830,000 mostly second- or third-generation Koreans.

During the high growth rates of the 1960s, internal migration of school graduates from rural to urban areas was encouraged. With regard to migration from outside, the official "no guest worker" policy was breached as early as the 1960s to recruit nurses from South Korea, Singapore, and the Philippines; since the 1970s Southeast Asian women have arrived in search of jobs in "service trades" and entertainment. In-migration from Southeast Asia increased in relation to the slowdown of migration to the oil economies after the Persian Gulf War of 1990. Japan, with a per capita GNP of US$21,020 in 1988, attracts men and women from low-income Asian societies, such as South Korea ($3,600 per capita GNP), the Philippines ($630, or 3 percent of the Japanese level), and Bangladesh ($170, a per capita GNP 125 times lower than Japan's). Since the mid-1980s, "working tourists" (estimated to number 300,000 in 1993) have come from Thailand, South Korea, China, the Philippines, Malaysia, Bangladesh, Taiwan, Pakistan, and Myanmar, as well as from Iran and Peru, and have overstayed their visas. About one-fifth of them are women. Migrant strategies respond to international financial strategies: after the yen was permitted in 1985 to float and rise against the dollar in order to help the stagnating U.S. economy, the value of wage remittances doubled by 1987.[76]

The 1990 passport law permitted descendants of Japanese emigrants to return as citizens. The admission of "ethnic Japanese" is an attempt to reduce labor shortages without recourse to hiring foreign workers. From among the 1.2 million Japanese-origin Brazilians, 80,000 Peruvians, and 120,000 other Latin Americans (1990 figures), this "U-turn migration of Nikkei," as journalists have called it, involved some 160,000 from Brazil and 28,000 from Peru by 1993. Since intermarriage with Brazilian partners makes returnees physically discernable, racist hiring practices place them below Japanese. In the late 1990s, critics of Japanese ethnocentrism have demanded an amnesty program for undocumented immigrants and a policy change toward an "open nation" by providing for "guest worker" admission. In 1999 the governmental economic planning agency noted that, at present birthrates, the Japanese population of 126 million will decrease by 0.6 million annually without immigration.[77]

In Malaya/Malaysia and Singapore (chap. 15.4), immigrants and their children came to outnumber Malays by the 1930s. In 1941, Indians and Indonesians each accounted for 14 percent of the population, and Chinese for about 40 percent. The hard-working and permanently settled Chinese accumulated property on the spot while sojourning Indians sent back savings and thus were less visibly rich. At the time of state-formation after independence in 1957, return migration reduced the Indian presence, but since 1949 this had no longer been an option for most Chinese. But out of resentment against arrogant Westerners, the locally born Chinese middle classes adhered to a Chinese nationalism and stood juxtaposed to the English-educated Malay elite and its construction of nationhood. The Federation of Malaysia that was established in 1963 as a multiethnic state for purposes of ethnocultural hegemony, invited predominantly Chinese Singapore to withdraw from the federation when it became fully independent in 1965. Although riots between Chinese and Malays occurred repeatedly and ethno-economic hierarchies persisted, Singapore's society also served as a model of integration into the early 1990s. Educational attainment led to external and internal migration, including upward mobility, and rapid industrialization and poor working conditions on plantations led to the importation of workers from Indonesia and of undocumented laborers from southern Thailand and the southern Philippines.[78]

Industrializing Singapore attracted workers from Malaysia into the 1960s, but in the 1980s it exported skilled workers and professionals to Malaysia. Its 1983 population consisted of Chinese (76 percent), Malays (15 percent), and Indians (6 percent); thus nationhood in Singapore came to be the opposite of Malaysian consciousness: a segment of the Chinese diaspora segment turned into a city-nation. When birthrates declined among the Chinese, who were upper- and middle-class professionals, while the Malay population—that is, the working classes—continued to grow, the patriarchal founding father and prime minister, Lee Kuan Yew, demanded on the anniversary of the state's birth in 1983 that educated women revert to having more children.

In 1998 Singapore's affluent bourgeoisie, with many women in highly qualified positions, employed 100,000 maids mainly from the Philippines and Indonesia but also from Myanmar and Sri Lanka. Employers have experimented with worker selection: "fair" servants are preferred to dark-skinned ones; agencies advertise domestic workers as "obedient"; some receive no days off to prevent them from congregating with other maids and organizing. The immigrant women, often with husbands and children left behind, are bound by contracts, work without regulated hours, and are "regularly screened for pregnancy as well as for venereal and other diseases." In the late 1990s, Singapore's labor force was 15 percent foreign with migrants locked into guest-worker status. The state "has developed policies to maximize the benefits of foreign labor while minimizing its social and economic costs."[79]

In the single year of 1987, emigration from the Philippines involved 450,000 men and women going temporarily to jobs in eighty countries and another 113,000 leaving permanently (official figures). In 1998, six million Filipinos and Filipinas were working in over 120 countries. Rural families, aware of their powerlessness with regard to weather conditions and world-market-driven prices for their products, have achieved risk-diversification by sending family members into wage labor in nearby provincial towns, into inter-island migrations often bound for distant Manila, or into employment in overseas economies ranging from the United States to the Persian Gulf states. Regional development has increased the propensity to migrate (for example, from Ilocos in the north of Luzon outward); because aspirations rise, migration for survival becomes migration to achieve improved status. Migrants remain part of dispersed family economies; for example, migrant children postpone marriage because the family of birth still relies on their income. And identities become transcultural across rural-urban boundaries: migrant saleswomen are neither peasants in the city nor salesladies during visits home.[80]

As in many Asian states, international migration is governmentally supervised. The Philippine Overseas Employment Administration connects family lives, international investments, and the exploitation of domestic labor. The equivalent importing agency in Malaysia announced in 1997 that it would reduce its recruitment of Philippine women for domestic labor in favor of cheaper Bangladeshi and Sri Lankan women. The Philippine government exemplifies the willingness of developing states to deliver low-cost labor to MNCs without social accountability. After the Korean War boom of the 1950s, the government created an "Export Processing Zone" for cheap labor, which was ringed by barbed wire. Officials wanted foreign jobs for men, while plant managers hired internally migrating women assumed to be immune to unionization. However, working conditions and below-subsistence wages led to militancy emanating "not from notions of rights" but from humiliation, the exigencies of moral economies, and the need to feed families. This type of exploitation indicates that constraints placed on family economies under global pressures differ from options for self-willed mobility to internationally accessible labor market segments far away. In response to labor militancy, companies easily shift assembly units to other neocolonial regions that are in competition with the Philippines, such as Korea and Brazil. International capital, which "repatriates" profits, turns away from "high-bulk, low-value commodities"—the classic raw materials—to "lighter goods, such as computer chips, that can be profitably air-freighted halfway around the world." Local middle classes often benefit at least temporarily from MNC investment strategies.[81]

In South Asia, after independence and the postpartition population exchange, populations have remained diverse because state borders do not conform to cultures, and migration between linguistic regions increases heterogeneity (chaps. 15.3, 17.4). Women's marriage migration has remained high; students' educational migrations have increased; and migration specific to ethnic groups, such as the migration of Punjabi Sikhs into the Indian armed forces, has continued. Settlement migration has been directed to wastelands made arable, newly irrigated dry lands, malarial areas opened through mosquito control, and illegally deforested lands. Rural "footloose labour" remains "neo-bonded." Seasonal in-migration—of perhaps 150,000 laborers in the Bardoli district, east of Surat, for example—results in a three-layered hierarchy of landowners, local laborers, and migrants (who in the Bardoli district are controlled by employer-imported "Sindhi" strongmen). Impoverished women increasingly leave villages for domestic or textile jobs in urban agglomerations. In this "multi-ethnic low-income society" migration grew in the 1960s and 1970s: a "low-skilled labor force" moved from the countryside to the city or between urban areas.

Interurban moves involve middle-class men in search of employment and entrepreneurial migrations to government projects or market opportunities. "In India's largest cities, the major industrial enterprises are almost all owned by 'outsiders,' not Europeans, but Marwaris from Rajasthan, Parsis from Bombay/Mumbai, and Gujaratis, Punjabis, and Sindhis." Office workers, too, "are aliens in the area in which they work."

Every city and town in India is dotted with ethnic enclaves of migrant origin with specialized economic functions. In Madurai, the weavers originate from Saurashtra; in Bombay, the city's milk is delivered by migrants from Uttar Pradesh, the port laborers are from Andhra Pradesh, the clerical personnel are from Tamil Nadu, the construction workers are from Rajasthan; in the famous Chandhi Chauk bazar of old Delhi each specialized section of the bazar (one selling gold jewelry, another Banaras silks, a third brassware, a fourth wedding ornaments, a fifth leathergoods) is run by a caste whose members come from and continue to be linked to other bazars in towns of northern India.

Indian cities do not follow melting-pot patterns: "They are polyglot centers in which substantial numbers of both migrants and natives have acquired each other's language or learned to communicate through a third tongue."[82]

Diversity is counteracted by urban (multi-)linguistic homogeneity. Of Mumbai/Bombay's 4.2 million inhabitants in 1961, 43.8 percent were Marathi, and 19.1 percent Gujarati; of Delhi's 2.4 million, 74.7 percent were Hindi, and 13.3 percent Punjabi; of Calcutta/Kolkata's 2.9 million, 63.8 percent were Bengali, and 19.3 percent Hindi-speaking; and of Madras/Chennai's 1.7 million, 71.0 percent were Tamil-speaking, and 14.1 percent Telugu-speaking. In 1971 nearly 40 percent of the urban population of 108.6 million were internal, often interstate migrants. This percentage is lower than that of nineteenth-century European cities. Labor migrants have to add the language of residence to their language of birth; middle-class migrants need Hindi as a cultural link between language groups and English as the language of technology and scholarship. Among unskilled factory labor, caste declines in importance, while ethnic clustering is important for recruiting networks.

In the 1960s, competition for land or jobs led to anti-immigrant movements in the northeastern state of Assam, the western part of Andhra Pradesh, the southernmost districts of Bihar, and in Bombay and Bangalore. Native-born "sons of the soil," whether peasants or educated urbanites, demanded the exclusion of ethnoculturally different citizens. Myron Weiner has discussed the use of political power by the indigenous "to overcome their fears of economic defeat and cultural subordination by more enterprising, more skilled, better educated migrant communities."[83]

External migration began with return of (multi-)ethnic Indians after the demise of the British Empire and with arrival of Tibetan, Bihari Muslim, and Sri Lankan Tamil refugees. In Pakistan, "refugee warriors," victims of war, and women arrived from Afghanistan, first from the Soviet intervention, then from the fundamentalist wars, a total of 3 million in the early 1990s. Iranian refugees also settled. Muslims from Bihar and Uttar Pradesh had migrated to East Pakistan after partition in 1947, but they opted for West Pakistan after the independence of Bangladesh in 1971. Some 300,000 assembled for "repatriation" in camps, but the two governments never agreed on a transfer. Labor migrants arrived in India from Nepal and Bhutan, from Pakistan and Bangladesh, and from Sri Lanka. Nepal had exported agricultural products from the plains and manpower from the hills since the nineteenth century. Some served in the British army (Gurkhas), while others migrated to Assam, Sikkim, Bhutan, and Indian cities. By 1961, one million Nepali and hill-language speakers were counted in India. In 1988 Bhutan decided to illegalize long-term and recent Nepali immigrants. Called for road and construction work in the 1960s, they were forced to use Bhutan's official language and, though living in the warm plain, wear the mountain people's warm dress, which was styled the "national" garb. By mid-1994, 85,000 were living in UNHRC camps.[84]

Sri Lanka's multiethnic and multireligious population of 8.1 million in 1953 consisted of Low Country Sinhalese (3.5 million), Kandyan Sinhalese (2.2 million), Indian Tamils (1.0 million), Ceylon Tamils (0.9 million), Ceylon Muslims or "Moors" (0.5

million), and others. In 1981 the Sri Lankan and Indian Tamils, concentrated in the north, accounted for 12.6 and 5.6 percent of the population, Muslims and others for 7.8 percent. The original Tamil community had been resident for almost two centuries; others had come as contract laborers to British-owned plantations since the 1820s. Educated Tamils were overrepresented in the administration and in business. In postindependence Sri Lanka, rising Tamil ethno-nationalism and Sinhalese demands for equal representation in administrative posts clashed. Insurrection and ethnic rioting produced India-bound and global refugee movements of Tamils and Muslims. An agreement of 1964 provided for repatriation of 525,000 Indian-origin inhabitants (1968–79) and citizenship for the 300,000 other Indian-origin inhabitants. In subsequent years, the Tamil language was granted special status, and further repatriation agreements concerned Tamil plantation workers. By 1995, about 1.5 million had left; some 200,000 reached Europe, 100,000 or more North America, and some 10,000 Southeast Asia and Australia. For humanitarian reasons and because of a shortage of labor in the hotel and catering sectors, Swiss officials were induced to admit 42,000 Tamils in the 1980s, an influx that continued until the early 1990s recession slowed the economy down while refugee arrivals from Yugoslavia, the Middle East, and Africa increased.[85]

Postpartition emigration from India, Pakistan, and Bangladesh involved semi- and unskilled workers who migrated to "declining" industries in Great Britain and professionals destined for Great Britain, North America, and Australia. In Britain the Commonwealth Immigration [Restriction] Act of 1962 ended this "citizen migration" (Gilani), but communities had been established. Because of family reunion, the South Asian community as a whole counted 750,000 members in Britain in 1981 and 80,000 in other West European countries. Second, mid-1970s "guest-worker migration" was directed to the oil-exporting states of West Asia and the Arabian Peninsula. Indian merchants had traded in the region for centuries; migrant Baluchi mercenaries had settled; and in the 1930s Indians had migrated to the early oil-exploration areas under the British mandate. In 1981, 1.2 million Pakistanis, 0.8 million Indians, 160,000 Bangladeshis, and 130,000 Sri Lankans resided in these economies, usually with two-year renewable contracts. In the late 1980s migrants sent home US$3,000 million a year, a sum sufficient to cover all of India's balance-of-trade deficit. Third, the North American immigrant community, established in the mid-1960s, was augmented by the recruitment of computer software specialists in the 1980s and 1990s. Total emigration from India, as low as 4,200 in 1976, stabilized around 240,000 annually in the early 1980s; it thus remained smaller than the Philippine and Chinese migrations.[86]

In the whole of the Asian region, Japan and the NICS—South Korea, Taiwan, Hong Kong, and Singapore—became importers of labor in the 1980s. The Philippines, the South Asian states, and Iran remain exporters. Asian labor migrants substratify native-born working classes or enter regions without reservoirs of labor, as in the Arab Gulf states. Middle classes from several states and from the Overseas Chinese send highly educated migrants able to enter receiving societies at elevated levels. Undocumented migrant men have to take so-called "3-D" jobs—dangerous, difficult, and dirty—while women are channeled into the "3-s" jobs—sewing, service, and sex. Travel cost and "fees" have to be worked off under conditions of debt-bondage, such as one finds, for example, in New York sweatshops. Most migrants leave low standards of living. Iranians depart from a functioning economy burdened by an oppressive religious regime, and Afghans seek refuge from a country destroyed by armed male clerics.[87]

19.7   Labor Migration to the Oil Economies of the Persian Gulf

The area designated the "Near East" from one Western viewpoint, and the "Middle East" from another, encompasses northeastern Africa, the Arabian Peninsula, West Asia, and the "linking states" between Europe and Asia, including Lebanon, Syria, Israel, and Jordan. Peoples defined by ethno-religious belonging come from many ethnicities and varieties of faith—including multiple Muslim persuasions; orthodox, liberal, and secular Jewish enclaves; and diverse Christian communities—and live in interspersed settlements that continue the Ottoman *millet* in modernized form. The region, once the hinge between the Mediterranean and Indic Worlds, received slaves from Sudan, East Africa, and Central Asia (chaps. 2, 6.4). For centuries pearl divers migrated seasonally to the Persian Gulf and, when in the late 1920s Japanese cultured pearls flooded the market, sought employment in the gradually expanding industry of oil production and processing. By 1950 personnel of the French and British mandate powers and of the Italian fascist period had left, while Greek, Italian, and South Asian merchants remained in the cities.

Pilgrimages annually brought about one million men and women to Mecca and Medina in the 1980s. From among the Islamic populations of Libya, Lebanon, Jordan, and Yemen, about one out of every 100 persons undertakes the journey per year; fewer from the distant Asian and sub-Saharan faithful participate. The region's Muslims are divided into Sunnis (as of 1990, 185 million), Shiites (11 million in Iraq, Lebanon, Kuwait, Bahrain), Zaydis (4 million in North Yemen), as well as small groups of Alawites, Kharijites (or Ibadis) and Ismailis. Druses, a further Muslim group, are now usually considered distinct from Islam. The Yazidis in northern Iraq form a religiocultural group of their own. Power struggles and hierarchized access to state resources have led to inter- and intradenominational warfare, generating refugees, for example, in Lebanon, southern Iraq, and Kuwait. Diasporas of Armenians, Kurds, Palestinians, and Lebanese exist and spread beyond the region, while parts of the Jewish diaspora have contracted and are now centered on the state of Israel.[88]

Emigration and internal migration in the region and in North Africa as a whole are multidirectional, despite the recent predominance of the oil economy (map 19.6). Emigration from Lebanon dates back to the Maronite-Druse war in 1860 and a crisis in silkworm breeding. By 1914, some 300,000 Lebanese or "Syrians" had reached the Americas; after the civil war of 1975–76, the Lebanese diaspora scattered to South America (750,000 people), North America (500,000), the Gulf states (300,000), Africa

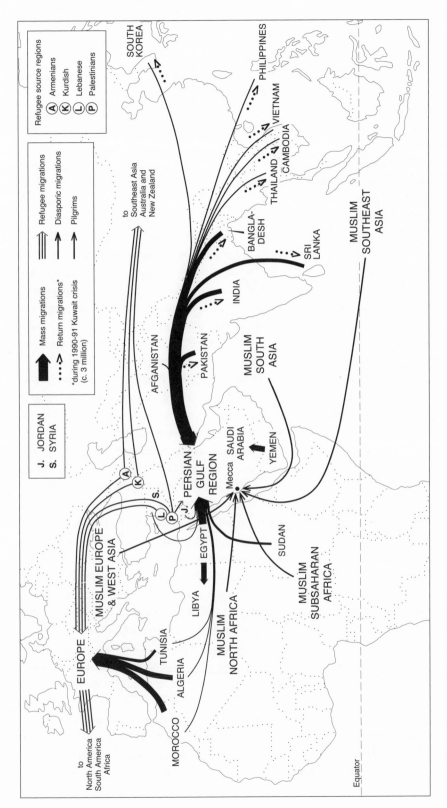

19.6 North African and Persian Gulf Migrations

(150,000), Australia (60,000), and Europe (50,000). Since the 1950s, Palestinians spread across the Arab states and into Southeast Asia, forming an involuntary diaspora more literate than the host populations except in Lebanon, Israel, and Jordan. Education provides exit opportunities from the refugee camps (chap. 18.2). The North African diasporas are concentrated in France (as of 1989, 2 million) and Iran (1.4 million), followed by those in the United States (0.7 million) and Turkey (0.7 million) and smaller communities elsewhere. The host-society label "Arab" hides heterogeneous populations that include mountain Berbers and Bedouin nomads, settled peasants and cosmopolitan traders. Merchants with capital left Lebanon; skilled workers and professionals began the out-migration flows from Egypt, followed by unskilled workers after the mid-1970s.[89]

In Egypt, the process of making nomads in the northwestern coastal region sedentary contrasted with displacement migration of agriculturalists from areas flooded by the Aswan Dam. The government-sponsored migration of Egyptian peasant families to "underpopulated Iraq with its oil wealth, and its relatively unexploited agricultural resources," was stopped for political reasons by the Iraqi government in 1977. The migrants, clustered by regional origin, considered other Egyptians "strangers" and regarded neighboring Iraqi communities as alien because of their different religious life-patterns. Family economies, gender roles, and intergenerational relations changed under the impact of new crops, new attitudes about contraception, and parents' tradition-driven attempts to control their daughters' and sons' spouse selection. Literacy levels had no impact on household performance—agricultural skills and the development of family strategies never depended on reading or writing abilities. Many illiterate migrants are highly capable in accounting.[90]

In the Gulf economies, government contracts with Western oil companies stipulated employment of local labor, and in 1950 less than one-sixth of the industry's 140,000 employees came from outside the region, including British and U.S. technical personnel and Indian clerks, skilled workers, and artisans. Intraregional migration—at first from Aden, Asmara (Ethiopia), Sudan, and Persia, and then from Lebanon, Egypt, Syria, and South Yemen—grew quickly. Palestinians with high educational capital settled and brought in families. By 1972, some 650,000 workers from states without mineral resources had arrived as labor engaged in infrastructural improvements and public services. The trebling of the price of oil in 1973 and expansion without domestic labor reserves made the Gulf oil economies the third-largest labor-importing region in the world after North America and Western Europe: an estimated 1.7 million guest workers were employed by 1975, and 3.0 million were by 1980. Since mobilization in the region's populous societies was slower than the industry's expansion, some 30,000 mobile South and Southeast Asians took advantage of employment opportunities in 1975. South Asians could link to the traditional Indian communities in coastal cities of the region. Of the eight million guest workers (51 percent of the labor force) in 1985, 3.7 million came from Arab countries, 2.2 million from India and Pakistan, and 2.2 million from other, mainly Southeast Asian countries. Migration from Asian states declined after 1983. In that year 93 percent of the workers leaving South Korea and 85 percent of those leaving the Philippines headed for the Gulf. During the oil-price slump of the late 1980s, Saudi Arabia replaced expensive Western experts with cheaper technical personnel from South and East Asia and the Palestinian diaspora.[91]

Egypt became the largest regional labor exporter, with university graduates, teachers, engineers, and skilled workers departing first. Next unskilled workers moved to Libya; but when political tensions and expulsion curtailed options, the majority turned to Iraq, where an estimated one million resided in the 1980s. During the prolonged Iraq-Iran war, the military draft depleted Iraq's internal male labor force, and the Iraqi government waived visa and work-permit rules, although Egyptians had to travel via "neutral" Jordan owing to Iraq-Egypt discord about Arab policies toward Israel. Egyptians continued their transnational mobility even when internal labor shortages developed, thus reducing internal migration from the densely populated Nile valley to the Cairo conurbation. In Egypt, wage levels rose; remittances improved standards of living; and investments in motorized pumps for irrigation increased agricultural output. Women who stayed behind managed family economies, including financial affairs. Return migrants invested in local small business, transport, and crafts—viable enterprises in the densely settled regions.

In North Yemen, by contrast, different socio-religious norms, combined with income from labor migration, restricted women's roles. Under British imperial rule, male Yemeni workers had moved to Aden and East Africa; and after the overthrow of the regime of imams in 1962, men left the extremely poor society en masse. By 1980, one-third of the Yemen Arab Republic's gainfully employed male population worked in Saudi Arabia, and another third were returnees. Remittances quickly improved standards of living and facilitated the switch in agricultural production from labor-intensive subsistence crops to high-grade produce. As a consequence, women's labor in agriculture ended; propane stoves made the collection of firewood superfluous; the tending of livestock was rendered unnecessary by the ability to purchase imported foods; and improved water supplies reduced time spent with other women while carrying water home. Women's lives changed from hard labor in public to invisibility in homes. This new seclusion of women increased a family's reputation for religiosity and its social standing.[92]

Southeast Asian women increasingly work as domestics in the Gulf states. Live-in positions demand insertion into the private sphere of a different culture; unregulated working conditions create high strain. Well-educated Catholic Filipinas, for example, have to adjust to Muslim family life and submission to illiterate upper-class Kuwaiti Muslim women. Women also migrate as trained personnel, as nurses and engaged in other social services, for example. In sending societies, social relations are changing. In Bangladesh remittances are invested in hiring female help and thus increase opportunities of paid labor for women. In Pakistan, the prestige-carrying jobs of intellectuals, government officials, and clerks pay less than manual labor in oil economies; the middle classes cannot match ostentatious working-class consumption based on remittances.[93]

The recruitment of migrant labor is organized through government agencies or regulated private ones, although some irregular and often extortionate hiring as well as irregular overstays continue. The formalization of recruitment permits laborers to remain part of the home society's social security system, as in the case of the Philippines, or the careful selection of qualified labor, as in the case of South Korea. Such institutional arrangements are premised on the return of migrants. However, the guest-worker status tends to acquire permanency when socioeconomic advance in the receiving society is possible or when economic conditions in the countries of origin remain unfavorable to reinsertion. Sequential migration and permanent settlement balances male-female ratios: 50:50 among Palestinians in Kuwait, 60:40 among Egyptians in Saudi Arabia, but only 80:20 among Yemenis in Saudi Arabia. In most Gulf states, migrants with high incomes were permitted from the start to bring in families, and Indians developed a full community life because of long-established settlement clusters and because of the presence of professional migrants.[94]

This migration system was thrown into havoc in August 1990 when the Iraqi ruler's troops invaded Kuwait. Some 800,000–900,000 migrants fled, and another 50,000 did so after the Allied intervention in January 1991. Saudi Arabia expelled almost one million Yemenis because of the pro-Iraq stance of unified Yemen, and Iraq expelled some 0.7 million Egyptian workers when Egypt joined the Allies. The post-defeat internal Iraqi war on Kurds in the north and Shiites in the south generated another three million refugees. In terms of individual lives, the majority of the guest-worker refugees lost all their possessions and remained in camps for months. Recently arrived migrants who had not yet paid off their fare and fees were saddled with debts beyond redemption unless they could migrate again—doubling the debt in the process. In terms of sending societies, governments recognized the vulnerability of their citizens turned foreign workers because of the absence of internationally binding protective legislation, and the home economies faced the need to absorb returnees at a time when emigrant remittances dropped precipitously.

In late 1991 migration resumed, but the patterns changed. Shifts in the relative volume of recruitment were politically induced, by hostility toward Jordan, for example, because of its transit-economy-driven pro-Iraq stand, or economically induced, as in the replacement of Filipinos by Bangladeshis with less education and lower wage demands. The migration of highly educated individuals, on the other hand, has continued unabated because of the Gulf states' policy of creating social service institutions without hiring local personnel. Because training would involve women and change gender relations, schools, hospitals, and municipal services are mainly staffed by immigrants. The Gulf societies have become structurally dependent on migrants in all sectors of their economies.[95]

19.8 Intra-African Labor and Refugee Migrations

Under decolonization in the 1960s 1) borders shaped by the accidents of colonial rule resulted in migrations without regard for "official" boundaries; 2) population composition was "nationalized" by new governments; 3) land redistribution implied population redistribution; 4) urbanization continued; 5) clan rule, dictatorships, ethnosocial antagonism, and continued former colonizer and new superpower involvement generated millions of refugees. Amin has argued that, as in Europe, politicians and administrators in Africa became professional statists who defended institutional and territorial arrangements left by the colonizers even if they bore no relation to cultural boundaries and were not economically viable. The new states repeated the European model of elevating one particular culture to "national" hegemonic dominance over heterogeneous populations (chap. 17.1), a process that in Britain, for example, had involved centuries of English and mercenary warfare against the Scots, the Irish, and the Welsh. African labor migration systems evolved from regionally disparate economic development (map 19.7).

In the wake of colonizer withdrawal, 1.4 million non-Muslim citizens left the North African societies from Morocco to Libya, including French-Algerians, Jewish-French-Algerians, Moroccan Jews, Italians, and Afro-Italians. Egypt's nationalization policies, under which only one-tenth of a firm's staff could be aliens, sent the old and prosperous Greek and Cypriot community of about 140,000 people into emigration. The independence of Rwanda and Burundi in 1961–62 involved an uprising of (agricultural) Bantu-speaking Hutu, who constituted 84 percent of the population, against the (pastoral) Tutsi elites. Tens of thousands fled to Uganda and Tanganyika, while Rwanda, in 1968, became a haven for fugitive white mercenaries from Congo. In Portugal's colonies, where a crisis in forced labor–based cotton and sugar production led to a withdrawal of capital, government-encouraged settlers arrived in the 1950s, only to depart after independence was granted in the mid-1970s.[96]

Because national boundaries in Africa reflect the former colonizers' staking-out of territories, seasonal and short-term migrant workers who cross international borders often remain in their own cultural space. For example, Mende and Kpelle live both in Liberia and Sierra Leone; Yoruba in Nigeria and Benin; Ewe in Togo and Ghana, Makonde in Mozambique and Tanzania; and Kakwa in Uganda, Sudan, and Zaire. Traditional regional mobility became undocumented interstate migration when the new governments imposed control over boundaries and population composition. Subsequently, the now-defunct East African Community and the Economic Community of West African States began to restore free movement.

Self-determination involved, first, elite reconstitution: colonizer personnel left, and colonial auxiliaries and independent imperial migrants were expelled. When exiles repatriated themselves spontaneously and as refugees from wars of liberation returned, programs of reinsertion had to be developed. Colonizer-encouraged migrations were reversed, as in the case of the forced out-migration of the descendants of French-speaking Dahomeans, whose forebears were brought into Togo to replace German-trained Togolese when France took the colony from German rule. Second, after Africanization, the "nationalization" of bureaucracies and economies involved the expulsion of non-nationals: Voltaics from Ghana, Ghanaians from Sierra Leone, Nigerians from Ghana, Dahomeans from Upper Volta. This nationalist elite "cleans-

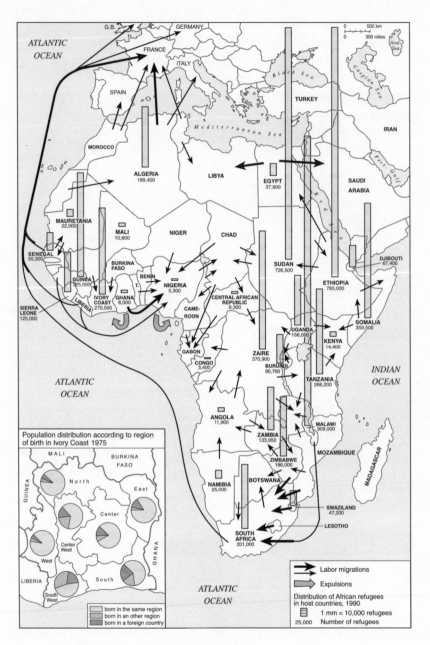

19.7 Intra-African Labor and Refugee Migrations

ing" broke up encrusted hierarchies; but shortages of new trained personnel cut services, and the repatriation of capital by expelled entrepreneurs caused economic stagnation. Third, poor living conditions and, in some states, dictatorial regimes depleted elites and caused brain-drain migration. By 1987, 30 percent of the highly skilled manpower—some 70,000 scientists, professionals, and educators—had left sub-Saharan Africa.[97]

Rapid postcolonial urbanization brought masses of young rural migrants to cities without housing and amenities. They entered construction, casual labor, or the informal sector rather than industries. The consequences of this for regions of origin cover a broad spectrum from stagnation to continued town-village connections, to elite replacement and economic change through return migration, and to communally planned development through "improvement unions" to allocate remittances. In recent decades, interurban migrations have increased.[98]

African women, "autonomous" rather than "associational migrants," migrate to attain "greater control over their productive resources" through education, labor market entry, or self-employment. Depending on government and elite interests, regulations either tie women to land or push them out of rural cash economies. Whereas in Kenya, for example, single female household heads and married women without sons may not own land, the South African system of labor recruitment has feminized smallholder agriculture. In some regions of Lesotho, three-quarters of the households are female-headed, in northern Zambia 50–70 percent, and in the central province of Kenya 90 percent. "Male absenteeism," declining soil quality, and the increasing cultivation of cash crops push women off the land. In West Africa trading women have continued their traditional independent migrations. Trained and educated urban women may enter long-distance migration, as when Saudi Arabia, after expelling its Yemeni labor force, recruited 5,000 nurses and midwives and 260 doctors in Port Harcourt, Nigeria.[99]

Drought and environmental degradation in Africa's vulnerable ecology displace agricultural and pastoralist peoples. The natural fragility of ecosystems is aggravated by "ecocidal" war tactics, such as the burning of crops, the mining of fields, and the killing of animals. Some leave "just in time" to avoid impoverishment; others flee starvation. A long-term decline in rainfall displaced people in the Sahelian zone (late 1960s), in Mauritania (1970s, 1980s), in Ethiopia (1984–85), and in Sudan (1988, 1998). In some states—Ethiopia and Sudan, for example—drought was exacerbated by government policies and civil war; elsewhere, internal warfare of factions of the new societies—warlords with male militias or government and military elites—dislocated the state's populations. People become pawns in the power struggles that take place in privatized states. In 1988, 1.5 to 2.0 million Sudanese out of a total population of 24 million had to flee warfare and starvation. Large refugee camps and shantytowns emerged around Khartoum and around Addis Ababa in the east and Nouakchott in the west. Those displaced by drought, political regimes, and factional warfare in "one of the poorest regions of the world . . . seek refuge in equally poor countries within the region": 3.4 million internally displaced civilians in 1987, 6.7 million in 1995 (according to UNHCR definitions), and 16.8 million in 1993. An estimated 60 percent of the refugees move to where kin or coethnics reside, and thus the burden of support rests on family and neighbors. In the Horn of Africa, most refugee-generating polities are also refugee-hosting societies; in West Africa's Sierra Leone and Liberia, peacekeeping forces from neighboring states have tried to reduce the bloodshed and protect their own migrant nationals in the process.[100] The reestablishment of stable governments since the late 1980s has resulted in refugee returns to Uganda, Ethiopia, Zimbabwe, Namibia, and Mozambique, for example.[101]

From a regional perspective, Libya, which has received workers from both Egypt and Tunisia, divides the continent's north into an eastern area connected to the labor markets of the Persian Gulf and a western area connected to Europe. The sub-Saharan region contains the West and the South African labor migration systems and smaller ones centered on Kenya and Malawi, as well as refugee-generating governments in the formerly Portuguese belt (Angola and Mozambique) and from Rwanda/Burundi to Sudan.

In the North African states from Libya to Mauritania, sizable Berber minorities, some 14 million in a total population of 60 million (1990), include the Mzab community in Algeria (chaps. 6.2, 16.1) and the Tuaregs in the south. From their mountain settlements, many migrate to the opportunities of the Arab-dominated cities, and their children attend schools in which Arabic is spoken. The mechanization of agriculture in Libya, Tunisia, and Algeria, as well as in the Middle East, causes out-migration from family farms. Rural incomes remain low; women—particularly in Tunisia—supplement agricultural income with wage-work in small European-owned rural textile factories. Rural-urban migration has increased, as has trans-Mediterranean labor migration from western North Africa to France and other European destinations. The 2.5 million Arab/Berber people in Europe in 1990 formed underclasses, while those going from eastern North Africa to the Gulf economies (chap. 19.7) formed a new working class inserted between nomadic Bedouins and resident wealthy Arab populations. When European governments reduced the recruitment of laborers in the 1970s, commuter migrations were replaced by family reunion and community stabilization; Tangier and other North African ports became embarkation points for undocumented migrants.[102]

In West Africa (chap 16.1), mid-nineteenth-century migration related to the groundnut trade made immigrant farmers (*navetanes* or strangers) from the interior sharecroppers on surplus land in return for labor. The volume of migration increased with the cultivation of export-oriented cocoa and coffee; its patterns changed under a regime of colonizer investment and forced mobilization. The century-old rural labor migration system of the Soninke from southwestern Mauritania, eastern Mali, and western Senegal shifted in the 1930s to rural-urban migrations, which made connections to France through sailors shipping out from Dakar. In Marseille they joined the sailors' labor union and, in a cultural-economic move, fought competition from the "Arabes anglais" from Aden but acquiesced in the hiring of sailors from the French Côte des Somalis (Djibouti). More recently, Sarakole men have migrated to French automobile factories. Accelerated intraregional migrations from countries of the interior (Burkina Faso, Mali, Niger, Chad) to coastal regions continue traditional patterns westward to Senegambia and southward to Ghana and Ivory Coast. The settlement of seasonal migrants shifted the population balance between savannah and coastal regions from 50:50 to 33:66 and increased the population of coastal cities from 0.2 million to 4.5 million (including natural increase) during the period from 1920 to

1970. Since then, migration from the drought-stricken Sahelian zone has added to the influx.[103]

In Nigeria, multiple migratory flows connect the southern coastal, the agrarian central, and the densely settled northern regions. Colonizing rural migrations to new lands accounted for much of the migration until 1950 (chap. 18.1); then the migration of skilled laborers from the south to the north became part of urbanization and proletarianization processes. Yoruba and Hausa moved as merchants and traders, the latter also as unskilled workers, while Ibo migrants went into skilled labor, mining, and domestic service. The arrival of well-educated migrants—Ibo, for example—has created antagonism resulting in massive violence and civil war. Regional and ethnic differences in educational systems and attainments as well as liberal capitalist policies have exacerbated traditional inequalities.

Usually founded by middle-class professionals and businessmen, postmigration ethnic associations—whether Ibo, Yoruba, Urhobo, Ijaw, or Ibibio—provide protection against discrimination, give credit when European-owned banks refuse loans, and attempt to improve each group's social standing. The associations established backward links from the cities of Lagos and Port Harcourt to the regions of origin. Often in competition with traditional chiefs, they pursue political-cultural agendas in order to combine tribal, village, and kin identities into larger ethnic ones; they superimpose a "culture of modernity" on non-cash-based ways of life; they improve roads, hospitals, electricity, and postal offices. Women's associations support maternity and child welfare clinics. The associations, having first established their own language-based educational institutions, also served to organize voters for ethnic leaders in postindependence politics. Political competition bred ethnic rivalry, and the associations became "instruments for personal and regional aggrandizement."[104]

By 1975, approximately 2.8 million men and women worked in West African states not of their nationality. In Ghana the 830,000 migrants amounted to 12.3 percent of the population. When groundnut prices dropped sharply in 1969–70, the state expelled 214,000 foreigners. In Nigeria, under the impact of the oil boom, two million to three million mainly male migrants arrived from Ghana, Chad, Cameroon, Togo, and Benin between 1975 and 1983. They included a "brain drain" of teachers, professionals, and technicians. After the oil-price drop in 1983, the government expelled between one and two million. Government-induced or -tolerated discrimination against low-status migrants may become self-defeating when destructive internal violence results. Reformers have suggested a pan–West African approach and nondiscrimination in the multiethnic urban societies, in which the ten principal languages of the region had become the linguae francae for 90 percent of the people by 1970.[105]

Central Africa is connected to Nigeria by labor out-migration and to Ghana by in-migration and the semipermanent settlement of fishermen. From the northern Muslim regions, pilgrims travel to Mecca and Medina; before air transport was commonly available, they stopped along the way to earn money for the next part of the journey. Mineral-rich Gabon and Zaire/Congo have attracted investments from France, Portugal, and the United States; the plantation economies of São Tomé and

Príncipe are also foreign-owned. Investors send European and North American managerial personnel, whose migrations are usually culturally and economically related to former colonial rule. Independent migrants include wholesale traders of Indian, Pakistani, and Lebanese extraction, small merchants from West African trading ethnicities, and unskilled sojourning laborers. The predominantly male migration of unskilled laborers causes imbalanced sex ratios in sending and receiving regions. Only in Zaire have family reunion and independent female migration balanced the ratio.[106]

In southern Africa (chaps. 16.1, 18.4), the internal warfare of competing elite and ideological groups in formerly Portuguese Angola and Mozambique, armed by the two superpowers, had displaced two million civilians internally in each state by 1990; others fled to South Africa, Malawi, and Zimbabwe. After the peace agreement of October 1992, 1.7 million refugees had returned to Mozambique from neighboring countries by 1995, but in Angola internal and external repatriation ended when conflict reescalated in mid-1998. In South Africa, migrant workers' hostels and camps became centers for organization and resistance while capitalists either disconnected whole regions from access to jobs or hired workers who had circumvented the influx control system to cut recruiting expenses. Ever more male workers, single women, and families evaded confinement to the homelands, and in 1986 the government abolished the Influx Control Act—the legal framework that kept one-third of the African laboring population in temporary migrant status thereby collapsed. After the end of apartheid, South African society faces massive immigration pressures from neighboring peoples because of its comparatively high standard of living, high unemployment notwithstanding. Thus the regional migration system continues to function while changing.[107]

In East Africa the colonizers had relied on migrant laborers (chaps. 15.4, 16.1) and changed the gendered allocation of work in the process. Road maintenance was allocated to African communities in which men who worked as artisans assigned it to women who traditionally worked the earth. Large-scale cotton growing after 1904 involved the mobilization of women's labor on the plantations and of male porters in long-distance transport. This enforced mobility became a drift toward cities, and the incipient money economy increased demand for wage-paying jobs. Women in nonmonetarized agriculture demanded a share of their husbands' cash incomes; men revised their attitudes concerning agricultural income and pushed women out when world-market-oriented cultivation of cotton, rubber, and coffee paid wages. The landowning Ganda, as independent producers with multiple goals, could react to price fluctuations in the world market faster than large absentee-owned and highly capitalized units geared to the single goal of profit-generation. Thus they could withdraw from the colonizer-controlled labor market or migrate only seasonally and over short distances. The labor migration of nonlandowning ethnicities reached into Ruanda-Urundi, Tanganyika, and the Congo.

Patterns of internal and external migration changed when Kenya, Tanzania, and Uganda achieved independence in 1961–63. The resettlement of Africans to Kenya's former "scheduled areas," which had been reserved for Europeans, remained limited, whereas the volume of migration "between the impoverished and land-hungry periphery and the rapidly growing urban areas and commercial farms" was large. In 1960, Uganda's population of just under 17 million included some 11,000 European and 70,000 Asian immigrants. The African working class was or had to be highly mobile. Only one-fifth of Kampala's labor force—in a population of 47,000 in 1960—had resided in the city five years and longer. The patterns of seasonal migration depended on the crops cultivated: women stayed behind when crops required regular tending; both men and women migrated from grain-growing regions because fieldwork was limited to sowing and harvesting. Wages and the accumulation of savings depended on cultural practices and economic position. The majority of resident Ganda earned more than 150 shillings per month, but many migrant workers took in less than 70. Ganda workers aimed for self-employment and education, but their status-conscious consumption expenditures made the accumulation of capital difficult. No relocation of industrial production across the countries of East Africa was achieved, and the labor-importing centers of the colonial period remained the postcolonial cores.[108]

The East African independence movements had been strongly supported by the state of India but less so by Indian-origin East Africans. Solidarity among Third World peoples foundered on the rocks of imperial/postcolonial race-class hierarchies. The British-induced racialization of society, which made East African Indians civil servants, traders, and merchants, was countered by an "indigenization" policy to promote Africans. In Zanzibar the African population overthrew the Arab-origin government in 1964. Asian and Arab immigrants and ethnics faced confiscation of their property; Ismailis, who had remained institutionally distinct, became targets of violence. After the Arusha Declaration of 1967, which promoted African self-reliance, Indian-owned banks and firms were nationalized, and minority groups were denied trading licenses. To promote a multiracial society and to reverse ethno-racial hierarchies in marriage patterns, Arab and Indian men were prevented from marrying African women, while the women were told to marry African men. East African Asian refugees first moved locally and regionally from villages to towns and port cities, from Zanzibar to Dar es Salaam, from Tanzania to Kenya. Encountering further restrictions, families with little property returned to India, and those with means emigrated to Britain and North America. The Indians' imperial middle-class position and their cultural preferences for higher education proved to be useful human capital during flight and reinsertion. The Ugandan Bhindi family, for example, was spread across the former British Empire, with a grandmother in the home village in India and one daughter in England. Its skills, at the time of expulsion in 1972, fitted Canadian refugee admission criteria. Subsequent diasporic connections involved the marriage of one son with a Kenyan-Asian woman and a loan to start a business in Canada from a friend in England.[109]

In 1979, the Amin regime was toppled by the Uganda Liberation Army. Many of the quarter-million external Ugandan refugees had established themselves securely in Sudan. Return would not have been immediate had not internal war in

Sudan involved attacks on refugees. The Ugandan power struggles and resulting economic collapse, administrative decentralization and attempts to socialize agriculture in Tanzania, and the expulsion of foreign African workers from Uganda in the wake of the expulsion of Asians interrupted traditional regional patterns of migration; nationalism and eth-class struggles ended traditional Indic connections. Male preponderance among migrants in all three countries was challenged by women; Kenya's upper-class women "combined British models and Islamic aims to form institutes and associations that would equip them with skills they perceived to be essential for living in a transformed Mombasa."[110] New ethnic and gender relations, urbanization and long-distance, South Africa–bound migration, as well as the emergence of Nyasaland/Malawi as a labor-importing economy, characterize contemporary labor migrations. So do political structures and polity-encouraged capital flows. The liberated Ugandan economy received capital from previously expelled East African Indians and the government's economic policies achieved high growth rates, while the Kenyan dictatorship of President Daniel arap Moi impoverished the people.

Mass refugee-generation is occurring in Sudan, Ethiopia and Eritrea, and the Horn of Africa under the combined impact of long-term drought, ecological decline, a rigidly Marxist regime in Ethiopia, a separatist one in Eritrea, warlordism in Somalia, Arab-African and Muslim-Christian and ethnic antagonisms in Sudan, and elite Tutsi-Hutu political and class antagonism in Rwanda and Burundi. Elites and clan leaders pit their armies against each other while populations flee. Drought prevents help from relatives; starvation reigns unless international agencies provide food. In the extremist Hutu uprising of 1994, about one million Tutsi and moderate Hutu were killed. In Sudan, where a small-scale slave trade continues to this day, north-south Muslim-Christian antagonism has resulted in partial genocide. The state's nineteen ethnocultural groups speak about 100 languages; Arabs are the predominant population group (as of 1989, 9.5 million), followed by Fur (3.2 million) and Dinka (3 million). Historically, the region had been one of coexistence of peoples of Christian, Muslim, Jewish, and Animist beliefs. The Christian community once had achieved statehood and had hosted a Jewish community. Commercial exchange through Ethiopia had paralleled routes through the Persian Gulf.[111]

In the present, emigration from sub-Saharan Africa remains limited notwithstanding the developmental lag and poverty due to unequal worldwide terms of trade: limited West African migration to France, an even smaller flow from East Africa to Britain, and a negligible one to North America, with connections to Portugal and visa-overstaying or refugee migration to Western Europe and "internationalist exchange" moves to the Soviet Union. Immigration restrictions prevented continuous labor or trader migrations. It was only in the 1990s that refugee communities—from Somalia, for example—succeeded in establishing communities in North America, that sequential and often undocumented trader and refugee migrants settled in Europe outside of France and Britain, and that undocumented migrants inserted themselves in Mediterranean Europe. In North America, the culture of Afro-Americans differs from that of the Caribbean-centered Black Atlantic, which, as yet, has not coalesced with lifestyles of recent migrants from Africa or connected to modern multiethnic African cultures.[112]

19.9   Eastern Europe: Internal Migrations and Post-1989 Changes

Subsequent to the World War II–related population dislocations and the forced labor regimes of the Cold War era (chap. 17.2), migrations in East Central Europe and the Soviet Union (the Commonwealth of Independent States [CIS] as of 1991) fell into two phases: a period of closed boundaries that varied from state to state, and the opening-up that began in 1989. Before 1989 the communist governments championed the rights of the proletariat while curtailing its freedom of movement; after 1989 Western governments that had previously championed freedom of movement restricted the entry of Eastern Europeans, who came as labor migrants rather than as refugees from oppression. Fences exuberantly torn down along the West-East "iron curtain" in 1989 were rebuilt to keep migrants out.

Under the regime of closed borders, relatively few migrants left secretly or, from some countries, legally. The last possibility of mass departure—from the German Democratic Republic—was ended by the Berlin Wall in 1961. During and after the uprising in Hungary in 1956, the "Prague Spring" in 1968, and the coup in Poland in 1981, perhaps 200,000 or more migrants left each country. The Soviet Union expelled a few dissidents, and permitted Jews to leave in the 1970s. Ethnic Turks emigrated or were forced to emigrate from Bulgaria, and Germans and Jews left or were compelled to leave Romania. From the mid-1970s on, German-origin people could emigrate in small numbers from Poland and the Soviet Union. Some technical personnel migrated to construction projects supported by their governments, in Egypt or Cuba, for example (map 19.8).

The exception to the pattern was Yugoslavia, which under Tito followed its own distinctive variant of socialism and ethnic integration. With regard to migration, the free exit of labor migrants was permitted after the early 1950s, making Yugoslavia in effect part of Europe's southern zone rather than of the "Communist Bloc." The number of Yugoslav workers in Europe increased to 850,000 in 1973 and remained above 500,000 after the mid-1970s recession. While at first more men and women departed than returned, circulation and return were high thereafter. Yugoslavia also became a transit country for guest workers from further east, Greeks in particular.[113]

Immigration to Eastern Europe was minuscule: only a few returnees came from the communities of descendants of the nineteenth-century labor migrants (chap. 14.2). After Poland's liberal period of 1956 ended, only about 10,000–20,000 retiree migrants from the labor diaspora arrived annually to enjoy their hard-currency pensions, given the low cost of living. Armenians returned to their areas of settlement in the Soviet Union, and Russian refugees came back from China. Under the principle of socialist internationalism, workers or trainees from Third World countries—Cuba, Angola, and Mozambique, for example—formed a kind of segregated guest-worker group; students from Africa and Asia received scholarships and support.

19.8   Eastern European Migrations, esp. after 1989

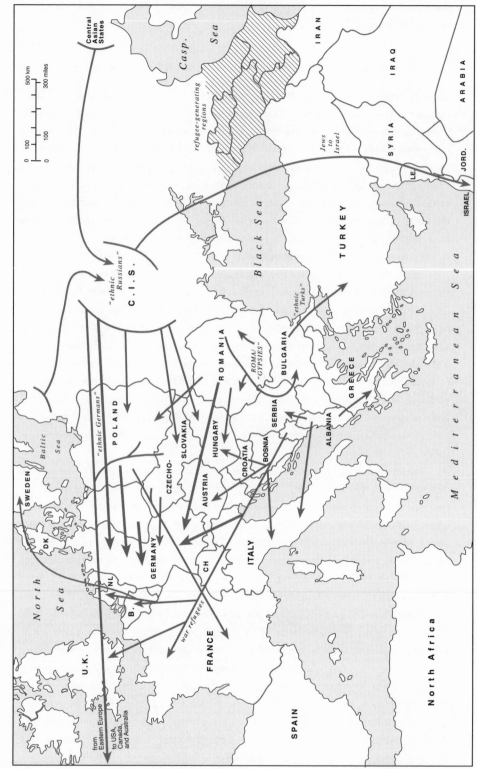

Interstate migrations, too, were small in number. East Germany, whose population declined owing to flight before 1961 and to low birthrates, attracted Hungarian and Czech workers; later, Poles, Slovaks, and others migrated to Hungary, and Bulgarian workers went to the Soviet Union. But each of these migrations involved at most some 20,000, and thus, taken together, they were in no way comparable to guest-worker, oil-economy, or *bracero* migrations.

Internal migration during postwar reconstruction was governmentally regulated up to the late 1960s. Thereafter, voluminous interregional flows, often rural-urban, emerged from economic disparities and individual aspirations. Contrary to widespread Western assumptions, "the individual [was] essentially free to make his own migration decisions within a framework provided by economic and social policy — such as siting of new towns, provision of housing, agricultural policy." In the advanced East Central European economies, internal migration declined from the 1950s (as of 1955, 4.0 million migrants) to the early 1970s (as of 1970, 2.1 million), or to a rate of between twenty and thirty per thousand. In Czechoslovakia and East Germany, whose industrialization predated the war period, rural-urban migrations remained comparatively low. In Poland, on the other hand, where small farms remained private but because of government-regulated prices for produce were economically not viable, rural-urban migrations continued at high levels into the 1980s. Most migration was short- and medium-distance; only Warsaw and Kraków attracted migrants from across the state. While unskilled workers migrated to industrial centers, educated, skilled, or trained migrants left the cities for new developments in smaller towns. Marriage often involved inter-village migration or town-to-village return. In other multiethnic countries, the migration of young working-age "ethnics" of both sexes from traditional territories to job opportunities elsewhere involved ethnoregional dispersal.[114]

In the Soviet Union, the balance of inter-republic migrations changed depending on the relative state of economic development. The eastward migration to Siberia was reversed as early as the 1970s, and the southward migration to non-Russian territories only in the 1990s. Incentives encouraged internal migration to increase or even maintain labor forces in the less-developed regions. On the one hand, migrants were freed from such obligations as debts and compulsory deliveries of agricultural produce; they were also permitted to retain property in their place of origin, were exempted from military draft, and were granted low-cost transportation for persons or goods. On the other hand, supplementary incomes, additional vacations, and support for traveling expenses made residence on the margins of the empire bearable. Youth campaigns and moral suasion sent young men and women to construction labor in Siberia and elsewhere. In the central regions, interurban migration replaced rural-urban moves. From 1926 to 1970, the net urban gain had amounted to nearly 60 million people; by the 1960s, 60–65 percent of urban in-migration came from other cities.[115]

After 1989, the patterns of migration changed, most intensively in the four years to 1992. According to Ardittis, five major types of east-west migrations developed:

1) labor migration (whether of a temporary or permanent nature, of a legal or illegal character), resulting from economic restructuring and rising unemployment; 2) refugee migrations as a consequence of ethnic tensions, civil war, and wars of separation; 3) ethnic emigration, in particular of the descendants of German immigrants of previous centuries and of citizens of Jewish faith; 4) return migration to states and cultural regions of origin, often of Russians who had lost their privileged positions; and 5) temporary migration or emigration to Western Europe, North America, and elsewhere.[116]

In Poland, the liberalization of emigration predated the policy changes of 1989. The diaspora in the United States (chap. 14.1) provided networks of support, and the West German economy offered seasonal jobs. Perhaps one million left in the 1980s, often temporarily and repeatedly. In 1988, for example, a total of 1.7 million moves were counted. (By contrast, the Hungarian refugees of 1956 were unable to connect to emigrant communities in North America because of differences in politics, interests, and social status.) According to opinion polls in Poland, large-scale temporary migrations, in particular of people with secondary education, will continue. Poland, in turn, is becoming a destination for trader migrants or construction workers from the CIS.

Ethnic disengagement combined with hopes for economic improvement motivates the migration of German-origin people from Poland, Russia, and Romania. As everywhere ethnic belonging is a construct; the number of people describing themselves as Russian-Germans entitled to admission to Germany grew when opportunities to actually migrate increased. Between 1950 and 1987, 1.4 million came; but after *glasnost*, from 1989 to 1993, another 1.5 million arrived. Thereafter, entry was administratively slowed down to 225,000 per year. At the turn of the twenty-first century, few of the immigrants deemed to be German ethnics still spoke German, and hostility toward "the Russians" among their German neighbors further decreased inmigration.

Ethnic Hungarians returned to Hungary under less than voluntary conditions from Romania, especially from Transylvania, which before 1918 was part of historic Hungary, where ethnic stratification had placed Magyars above Romanians. Almost 350,000 ethnic Turks left politically unstable Bulgaria for Turkey in the period 1989–92. Bulgarians also began to migrate to Western Europe. Refugees from the dissolution of Yugoslavia fled to all parts of East Central and Western Europe. By 1993—before the violence in Kosovo—some five million were already displaced.[117] (Proactive migrants, those departing before the actual beginning of armed conflict or expulsion, are usually young men in quest of better life-courses.)

Ethnic migrations from the USSR and within the CIS have assumed massive proportions since 1989. In addition to the departure of German-origin people, some 330,000 Jews left for Israel, and another 120,000 went to the United States within the first four years. In the Caucasus region and in Russia's southern Central Asian periphery, local wars resulted in ethnic un-mixing and refugee-generation. The federal structure of the USSR and rights granted to minorities did not prevent struggles for independence after 1989 because no substantial redistribution of power had been achieved. Of the more than 25 million privileged Russian immigrants and their descendants outside Russia proper—where about 120 million ethnic Russians live—many began to leave their regions of residence after 1989. Reverse migrations have flowed from the newly independent Baltic states, where standards of living are higher and birthrates low, and from Armenia, Georgia, and Azerbaijan in the Caucasus region. In the Central Asian federal states, Russian immigrants had taken industrial jobs while local people preferred traditional rural or pastoral ways of life in agriculture. However, tsarist settlement policies and Bolshevik collectivization had dispossessed many of fertile lands (chaps. 13.2, 17.2). Educated Russian ethnics from the non-Russian territories have few migration options except for return because, in contrast to Ukrainians and Poles, they cannot rely on worldwide diasporic communities to help with insertion in other foreign lands. They may perhaps be compared to reverse migrants from the colonies in 1960s Western Europe.[118]

Ethnic disengagement—"un-mixing" or "ethnic cleansing"—has reversed centuries of interspersed living, sometimes mediated by Jewish brokers, Chinese traders, or German-origin urban artisans in craft production. The reasons for this trend include ethnic hierarchies emerging both from investment patterns and lifestyle choices, such as attitudes about work and about consumption in particular, as well as from cultural traits ascribed by ethnic or national elites who, as cultural gatekeepers, strengthen their own position in the process. The term "cleansing" implies that cultural interaction has to be cleaned up. Socioeconomic changes that liberate ethnic or religious groups from traditional or assigned positions within societal power structures and permit individual or group mobility involve a change from hierarchized coexistence to competitive social advance (or decline). Such developments as Scottish devolution and Tamil-Sinhalese antagonism indicate that cultural-economic self-determination has been a potent force in conflicts of the late twentieth century and the years following. Such conflict has been viewed as one group's bid for "liberation" from another when it is directed against a dominant group; but once liberators have assumed self-determination and power, they often do not accord rights to smaller ethnoculturally distinct groups in the same region or in the new polity. Although many-colored immigrants have been accepted into White societies, resident non-White populations—whether they be Black citizens of the United States, Aboriginals in Australia, Maoris in New Zealand, or First Nations in Canada—have not gained full equality, despite the emergence of an Afro-American middle class and the mandating of Maori rights and political participation. New "seasonal migrations" involve global mass tourism, which results in local migration to service jobs as well as in the "touristification" of cultures, new life-cycle mobility, and the retirement migration of the relatively wealthy to agreeable climates.[119]

20

Intercultural Strategies and Closed

Doors in the 1990s

"Migration is primarily a human phenomenon and its outcome depends on the responses of the participating migrants and their households" (Gunatilleke). The micro-level decision making occurs in both the policy framework and institutions of the labor-supplying or refugee-generating countries and the admission regulations of receiving states. Over the centuries and across societies "there are as many migrations as there are historical situations" (Manchuelle). This is why all "laws of migration" remain devoid of meaning and why even a general frame of interpretation is difficult to develop. To take the example of emigrant remittances, those of nineteenth-century transatlantic migrants had only a minor impact on most societies of origin, whereas those of late twentieth-century Gulf state workers are changing economies and social structures. Explanations of migration based on economic rationales led one scholar to conclude "with a clarion call to put man before money. Remittances are flowing in, but the men [and women] who are toiling for the money should hold the centrepiece of any policy regarding migration."[1] The combination of a "systems approach" with a human-agency approach proposed in this study attempts to link the level of states and continents to migrant-sending families and migrating individuals via the mesolevel of the regions out of which migrants come and into which they seek to go.

The scope of the task may be indicated by a brief recapitulation of some aspects of the volume of migration. In the mid-1990s, an estimated 125 million people, or 2 percent of the world's population, resided abroad, a figure to which naturalized and undocumented migrants, multiple moves, and internal mobility in states the size of China have to be added. In some states, one-third of the residents are foreign-born, and even such net figures hide the huge amount of gross moves.[2] Tens of millions of labor migrants have moved to Europe, North America, and the Gulf states since the 1960s. Some 25 million refugees and other "people of concern" to the UNHCR live in transition. Within a single decade, 90–100 million men, women, and children have been displaced in the developing world by "normal" infrastructural measures. Several hundreds of millions live on the edge of departure in ecologically endangered environments.[3]

Most of the displaced and the not yet displaced are too poor to migrate far. They lack access to political processes to challenge governments and institutions involved in displacing them. The starving villagers of southern Sudan, 2.4 million in July 1998, could only try to reach the next "feeding center." Those with some means will move to new life-course projects over considerable distances. Of two Tamil brothers in Toronto, one migrated via Montreal, the other via an industrial job in southern Germany. Fluent in Tamil, English, French, and German, they operated a small store. Middle-class and elite migrants have easy access to information sources. Depending on information flows and connections to acquaintances and kin, refugee Somalis from the middle class may choose destinations as different as France, Canada, Italy, or the United States. "Brain brokers" or "body shoppers" export talent: for example, computer experts from India to North America. Most are able to develop their resources; some drop by the roadside. Somalia's first woman jazz singer, Maryam Mursal, fled with her five children through desert lands for months before ending up in Denmark in 1992. A resourceful Joyce Fraser, reaching Canada from Guyana in the 1970s, began as a visa overstayer but could legalize her status and bring in her children.[4]

To achieve a perspective on both dislocations and intentionally chartered transnational life-courses, the place of people in states and the changing status of migrants over the past centuries will first be retraced. Second, we will discuss present-day labor and refugee migration in terms of economic and political power and outline approaches to prevent the uprooting of peoples. Third, we will examine actual admission regulations as well as apartheid-style exclusion. Finally, we will again focus on the migrants in terms of their identities and strategies. Governmental approaches to "managing diversity," "channeling refugee streams," and "admission control" have an impact on the migrants' lives but do not illuminate the complex emotional, spiritual, and material lives of the men, women, and children involved.

20.1   From Multiethnic Polities to the Un-Mixing of Peoples into Nation-States and Decolonization

Across time and space, societies combine many cultures, whether defined by religion, ethnicity, family or clan lineage. With the possible exception of small tribal units, cultures have been internally differentiated by status or class and gender. The twelfth-century Mediterranean World involved three continents and six civilizations; the fifteenth-century Chinese and Inca states encompassed many peoples under centralized rule; in the Indic World, states and trade emporia coexisted, as did in Europe the Hanseatic, Urban Italian, and Urban Dutch mercantile regions with dynastic states. Civilizations, trading regions, and states included peoples of many religions, languages, and cultures.

State administrators, groups of merchants, and religious elites developed patterns of interaction. These patterns—like the exertion of authority over resident populations—had to be consensual, even if hierarchical, in order to produce benefits without high costs. Rulers accommodated migrants at their pleasure and according to their interest: merchants from different cultures might be accorded privileges; immigrant peasants might be settled on sparsely populated land. Migrants received support from or faced the hostility of resident neighbors. Interethnic dependency relationships, like intraethnic social hierarchies, often included labor or tribute services.

Conflictual expansions of power or wealth—or quests for control over neighboring populations or religious denominations—produced high levels of mobility, as in the case of the Christian crusades aimed at Palestine and the proselytizing by Muslims in West and South Asia. Doctrinal differences within a creed or between creeds could result in mass flight. In Europe's Latin Christendom,[5] wars after the early sixteenth-century reformations annihilated up to one-third of a region's peoples. Belief systems, dynastic states, and regions of commerce struggled for hegemony and access to the resources of populations. People were defined by their religion, as Muslims, Christians, or Jews, or by generic regional origins and cultural practices, as Germans, Wends, or Franks.

The patterns of intercultural contact in sub-Saharan Africa involved the merging of peoples through migration, rule, and intermarriage as well as through the subservient status of humans as pawns or slaves. In China, conquering Manchu and resident Han peoples had to come to terms with each other after 1644, and both with peoples of non-Chinese ethnicity. The Chinese diaspora and the merchants of the Indian Ocean trade emporia negotiated status, self-administration, and intercultural brokerage with local rulers. Any negotiated arrangement could be unilaterally ended, however, through the imposition of power, as in the expulsion of the Jews and Moriscos from the Iberian states or of Chinese traders from Southeast Asian societies. The expulsion of middlemen minorities or brokers has usually meant massive disruption of the respective society's economic development.

In the sixteenth century, global power hierarchies changed. Europe's states and merchants, the clients of West African gold-producing and Asian luxury goods–producing societies, repudiated negotiation in favor of imposition. They began to establish themselves over their suppliers and defined them: in terms of religion as pagans; in terms of color of skin as Black, Red, or Yellow; or in terms of rule as commercial, dynastic, or religious enemies. The sixteenth-century ascendancy of Europe and the nineteenth-century ascendancy of the northern hemisphere has influenced migration patterns up to the present.

A decisive change in the relationship of segments of elites with each other and to the populations of a polity was the conceptual shift from the state as family fief of a dynasty to territorial unit. States, which had been established or divided according to the power and family politics of particular dynasties, became distinct territorial entities according to the model set forth in the Peace of Westphalia (1648). The inhabitants of such entities were theorized by Hobbes as inherently violent and anarchic, thus needing a distinct institution, the state, to impose order. The administrators of such order could protect separate groups—Jews, for example—or expel and uproot unwanted population groups. Locke, starting from a positive view of human nature, developed a notion of the commonweal, politically organized into commonwealths, with civil rights for "Pagan, Mahometan, Jew." But the Westphalian model only permitted dissenters to leave rather than be persecuted.[6]

States in other parts of the world had developed patterns of coexistence earlier, always interrupted by powerful rulers, local strongmen, or new hegemonic migrants. In the Islamic World from southeastern Europe via Palestine to North Africa, Ottoman administrators constructed a political system with the three religions of the book—Islam, Judaism, and Christianity—placed in a nonconflictual, albeit hierarchical, relationship; acting on concepts of toleration and economic interest, they admitted migrants—Iberian Jews, for example. They ordered merchants or agricultural producers to resettle when the empire's economy and regional populations benefited from such moves.

In Europe, commercial regions, religious institutions, and political rule became geographically congruent, while populations remained heterogeneous. The political economy of these states, under the doctrine of mercantilism, was based on the legal and economic practices of the early modern corporatist towns and Urban Worlds and on those of migrating Jewish and Lombard financiers. In the Age of Revolution, from 1776 to 1849, the populations of colonies in the Americas and of the Bourbon state in Europe redefined themselves as sovereign peoples, rather than as subjects, and assumed control. In some cultures, discourse stressed the role of men (English*men*), in others it was seemingly gender-neutral (Americans), in again others participation of both sexes was emphasized (French *citoyens* and *citoyennes*). The new concept of the "nation" made people a unit of culture or descent rather than of a vague common regional origin, as in the medieval *natio*. This homogenization of inhabitants of many cultures relegated some to a minority status with lesser political, economic, and cultural rights. Individuals and families of these constructed "minorities" often decided to emigrate to better conditions. The concept of nation-states has continued to influence the position of migrants to the present.

These new mercantilist territorial units and the subsequent state-nations were and are premised on three conflicting theorems, each of limited analytical value: that of the state, of the nation, and of the political economy. Common people, whether resident or migrant, appear in the mercantilist concept as producers and in the nation-state concept as a unifying myth—and states demand loyalty from their citizens. Groups of different cultures, if of assumed disloyalty, could and can be expelled, as in the twentieth-century un-mixing of peoples. Although Euro–North American rule of the colonial worlds ended, its political thought continues to exert its hegemonic hold. The Westphalian state model of 1648, nation-state concepts of 1789, and twentieth-century bureaucratic rule were globalized and with it constructions of a people's pure origins and the subversive role of Others.

As it developed in practice, the "state" referred neither to peoples nor to cultures. Bureaucrats organized in state apparatuses delimited territorial boundaries first on the basis of haphazard dynastic and noblemen's acquisitions and later on the basis of how colonies were formed, without regard to cultural region or, in other words, principles of ethnicity. Such boundaries were legitimized somehow at some arbitrary historical point in time by one of the Churches, by tradition and lineage, by sheer power over territories, or by the fear of destructive warfare resulting from different dynasties' claims to the same piece of territory.

When the newly powerful middle classes—administrators, intellectuals, and mercantilists or industrialists—had to distance themselves from the trans-European nobility (later from colonizer personnel), intellectual gatekeeper elites constructed regional folk cultures into the "true" origins of nations and defined which cultural groups were part of a nation and which were to be assigned to minority status. Administrators established entry and exit rules for migrants and legislated hierarchies of access to resources for hegemonic and subaltern residents; they decided who could vote and who was excluded from political participation by gender, class, age, or culture. The commercial and capital-owing segments of the middle classes used the state apparatus for the protection of their interests, both internally against the lower classes and externally against demands from colonized peoples. Contemporary rulers and diplomats were aware of the implications. The Congress of Vienna in 1815, after ratifying the annexation of Poland by the neighboring empires, included an explicit protection for Poles as an ethno-national minority—but economic marginalization within the empires would force Poles into economic migrations at the end of the nineteenth century. Many-cultured populations were homogenized through common legal frameworks (in schools, in military service, and so on) as well as through prescriptions about women's role in child-rearing. The heterogeneous populations interacted in marketplaces and neighborhoods. From the late nineteenth century onward, state-mandated social security systems legislated migrants' access to services.[7]

The third premise of territorial states—their cohesion as political economies —changed a dynasty's subjects, alienable through inheritance and in personalized dependency relationships as service-rendering and tithe-paying resident or migrant populations, to taxpaying producers of wealth and assets of states in the mercantilist period. Productive people were connected to territorially based economies; unproductive military men were hired from among low-wage foreigners, as in the case of the Netherlands and the Swedish states. The Ching, Ottoman, and Habsburg dynasties reduced state expenses by settling self-provisioning, internally migrating or immigrant soldiers in contested borderlands. In nation-states, military service became a national duty for men. The new concept of the congruity of state and economy replaced merchant brokership with state power in the quest for raw materials and finished goods not available inside a state's territory. Groups of producers or traders were sometimes resettled internally according to the state's or the dynastic court's interests. New migration policies attracted people to enhance productive capacities and prohibited the emigration of men whose skills were in short supply.

The shift from mercantilism to liberal capitalism and industrial production changed the laboring population's status to a factor of production and to surplus population in times of oversupply. States still prohibited the emigration of economic assets, such as specialized mechanics or factory workers, but shipped out those considered a burden—for example, designated criminals to Australia and the poor as indentured servants to North America. People designated as "surplus" at home might be made "useful" elsewhere. Migrants admitted into a state were no longer placed in a special negotiated status, as the Huguenots had been in Europe or trade communities had been in the port cities of the Indian Ocean; the new migrants were expected to acculturate themselves as individuals to the nation's practices, norms, and values or were admitted as temporary workers only.

In the late nineteenth century, under imperialism and national chauvinism, the inclusion of subaltern colonial peoples and the exclusion of minorities within state-nations assumed new importance. All those excluded from equal participation in nations or empires had the option to depart or were forced to leave by economic circumstances. First, aided by improved transport facilities, the new industrial working classes became internationally mobile. Their states of birth limited their access to institutions, to the surplus value they produced, or to middle-class "national" cultures. Second, regional so-called minority populations were marginalized culturally and economically. For those distant from markets and monetarized relationships, geographical and occupational mobility often remained low until penetration by or inclusion into larger market networks induced regional developmental change and opened new perspectives for or imposed new constraints on earning a living. After migration, working-class immigrants found (and find) themselves in positions of lesser rights in some states. International capital and multinational companies, on the other hand, began to evade state control from the late nineteenth century onward.

Hegemonic peoples occupied positions close to markets and money economies and had access to other parts of the globe. A colonizer state's expansion from a commercial enclave to a plantation territory demanded the sending out of administrators, settlers, and laborers. Colonial peoples were defined as subaltern and made available for exploitation strategies, often with the help of indigenous elites. Local laborers were forced to migrate to produce crops or dig minerals for export. Upon their arrival, some labor migrants were immobilized by slave or contract-labor regimes. The acquisition of colonial territories by the United States, whose political elites were committed to not repeating European models, resulted in public debates about the colonial and citizenship status of the annexed Puerto Rican and Philippine peoples. The racist ideology of monochrome European elites became contested ground in the Americas.[8]

In Europe, the contest between hegemonic cultures, self-defined as nations, and "minorities" demanding self-rule ended in 1918 with the division of empires into somewhat arbitrarily established national territories that even under the best of intentions could never have done justice to interspersed settlement—a process that was to repeat itself after decolonization in other parts of the world. People outside the newly delimited borders were resettled; mosaics of settlement were "un-mixed" by deportation. Although the Versailles Peace treaty included safeguards for minorities in Europe, the demands of self-determination by colonial peoples were rejected. In the Americas, the descendants of the first inhabitants continued to be restricted to reserves in the north and to highlands in the south. A debate about self-determination began only in the 1970s under the slogan of "Red Power." In India and China, the ruling cultures had relegated indigenous minorities to "tribal" status.

The conflation of state, political economy, territory, nation, and ethnic culture precluded a negotiating of positions. As happened after the European war of 1914–18, colonized people were "un-mixed" to fit into territories after decolonization. Resident people of many cultures and multiple religions were sorted into or forced out of territories: Muslims into Pakistan, Hindus into India, Ghanaians out of Nigeria, Senegalese out of Ghana, Chinese into minority status in Indonesia, Indians out of East Africa. Groups who could not or would not migrate were massacred. Most migrants and diasporic people could and did negotiate allegiances; only some turned against their society of residence and supported their distant state of origin during local or larger conflicts. In nineteenth- and twentieth-century state formation, most cultural groups were denied independent statehood—in the 1990s, some 5,000 ethno-cultural groups were living in 190 states. Neither political philosophers nor political theorists and social scientists—nor population planners—have ever been able to arrive at a definition of a nation.[9]

In the postcolonial states, national homogenization and ethnic un-mixing included the resistance of Berber peoples in North Africa to Arabization and the clandestine migration of West African men and women into states that designated them as non-nationals. Looking at traditionally many-cultured Malaysia, one scholar noted:

> Nation-building is essentially a synthetic process engineered by intellectual minorities. States that were a direct consequence of colonization were imposed on peoples whose leaders, on independence, were left the infrastructure of a state but not the unifying nationality. . . . Nation-state formation facilitates the process of ethnicization. Ethnic identities become the basis of political group formation in an open and competitive political system.[10]

Economically, a new international division of labor changed state attitudes toward migrants once again. Color lines, breached by reverse migrations from the colonies to the cores, broke down when they did not fit the investment strategies of global capital and the demand for cheap female domestic labor by middle classes in the White northern hemisphere. When (White) women of the core were admitted into better-paying labor market segments, their "natural" and thus unpaid role of rearing children to become virtuous citizens was delegated (or relegated) to women of color from cheap-labor states. On the positive side, new attitudes about race, nondiscrimination, refugee admission, and migrant-family formation resulted in changed admission regulations in some of the former colonizer states and in North America. They permitted the entry of people who were not White. Where open admission was restricted, as in Britain, mobile groups of migrants stabilized; where restrictions remained paramount, migrants entered as undocumented workers in increasing numbers. Across the world, the human rights principle of freedom of movement had never been implemented. A right to exit was nowhere matched by a right to enter, to immigrate.[11]

Capital had left the constraints of territorial borders and constructed national interests for more than a century. In the second half of the twentieth century, one segment, the multinational companies, consolidated their global investment strategies and transferred profits from the labor of workers in a particular society to wherever returns on investment were considered better. As a result of such strategies, once-industrialized zones—like the northeastern United States—were turned into "rust belts" with high emigration, whereas "free enterprise zones" in the Philippines or South China became regions of immigration.[12]

In some societies, struggles from the bottom up, enlightened policies, or public opinion have brought forth a reconstruction of the social fabric, from monocultural to pluralist or multicultural. Short of mass expulsions or genocidal policies, the many-cultured composition of peoples may not be turned back to some mythic "pure" past or cast into a gatekeeper-designed national future. Borders may still be closed to human beings, however, to prevent "Colored" Third World or other immigrants from coming. Restrictionist sentiment is strong in Europe and Japan as well as in parts of India and elsewhere. Since 1500, perhaps 75 million Europeans have spread over the world; from the late nineteenth century on, hundreds of thousands of Japanese have done so, too. None of the involuntary recipient societies could exclude these migrants.[13] In the 1990s, migration from the southern hemisphere to Europe has differed from migration out of Europe in past centuries: the new migrants do not come with firepower, capital, and superiority complexes. "We are here because you were there," is the retort of postcolonial migrants knocking at the door of former "mother countries." Globalization occurred several centuries ago.

According to republican and democratic theory, human beings are born equal, but they are socialized into local and regional cultures, into unequal power relationships, and into particular polities. Whether they stay in the social and geographic space conferred to them by birth depends on local possibilities for earning a living, on information flows and migration traditions, and on options for access to other economies/polities, as well as on an evaluation of the emotional cost of migration, the loss of cultural traditions and relationships, and the openness of receiving societies.

20.2 Economic Power or Global Justice: Modern Migrations[14]

The dominant movements of the last third of the twentieth century involve labor and refugee migrations from poor countries to rich ones or between Lesser Developed Countries (LDCs). They have been analyzed in terms of a socioeconomic approach to root causes (chap. 19.1), in terms of a policy approach to refugee-generating governments, and in terms of a theoretical-philosophical approach to global justice. In northern hemisphere politics, such migrants are labeled a "refugee problem" once they arrive at Heathrow or Chicago O'Hare Airport, on Mediterranean beaches or at the Rio Grande, or at Australian points of arrival. In LDCs they are considered a problem as dwellers on the urban fringes. According to Balán, "Often what passes as a migration policy designed to control the inflow of poor, uneducated migrants to capital cities [and whole societies] is just a mechanism for preserving the way of life for the privileged few, which runs counter to the demand for labour."[15]

Global inequalities in power relationships and in access to capital are recognized as mobilizing factors, but few initiatives are being taken to redress such imbalances. Industrialized states, whose economies have long received development aid from the surplus value produced by each and every plantation laborer and from the colonies' natural assets, provide aid to LDCs at below the UN-advocated minimum rate of 1 percent of their gross national products. Interest payments and strings attached to aid resulted in net capital transfer from poor to rich states in the 1990s. The "free trade" panacea as a corrective to imbalances conveniently skirts the power factor in global economic relations, whether exerted by superpowers, the capitalist core, or multinational companies. Free trade, as analysts of imperialism showed, favored states that positioned their navies across the oceans of the world. Economic liberalism, theorized by Adam Smith more than two centuries ago, was premised on early manufacturing and urban societies, in which labor, capital, and entrepreneurs and businessmen on a relatively equal footing reacted to each other in the market on the basis of equal power, comprehensive information, and enlightened self-interest. Smith's project was neither procapitalist nor social Darwinist in orientation, but rather antibureaucratic.[16]

One approach to the root causes of departure from low-wage countries targets economic power and speculative international transfer payments or, alternatively, support for local economies and lifestyles. Economist James Tobin proposed a 0.5 percent tax on international capital transfers, which would end the "vagabondage" of capital under the rule of financial freebooters who place the interests of the few, "shareholder value," above the lives of the many, "stakeholder value," in the terminology of the late 1990s. The revenue, estimated to amount to US$1.8 billion daily, NGOs suggested, should be invested in LDCs by international institutions. James Goldsmith, on the other hand, observed that while neither the movement of capital nor that of human beings can be controlled successfully by states, the transport of products has always been controlled. Goods should be sold in the region where they are produced to force investors to take note of local standards of living, cultural norms, and political frameworks. This "communitarian preference" would foster local economic growth, whereas the power-based free-market ideology of the General Agreement on Tariffs and Trade (GATT) increases global inequalities.[17]

A second approach, a polity-and-peace strategy, targets refugee-generating violent conflict between or within states as well as arms sales. While customary discourse about "international" or "civil" war implies that societies or people are at war and that wars "break out," political elites declare war in the name of a state or fight each other within states. A focus on "refugee-generation" permits an analysis of political actors, while studies of "waves of refugees" concentrate on the tail end of the process. Preventive diplomatic, policing, or military peacekeeping missions, directed against governments of rapacious or monoethnic elites, clans, or dictators not legitimated by popular will, might reduce human suffering and mass flight. However, nonmilitary economic sanctions place burdens on populations at large, and military intervention may be undertaken in the interests of one or more of the intervening powers. The differential response of "the West" to aggression against oil-rich Kuwait and resource-poor Bosnia demonstrates the problem. Furthermore, arms-producing and -providing First World states are requested to agree to nonproliferation agreements for some or any types of weaponry. This would involve radical changes in the political economies of arms-producing states. Polity-centered strategies highlight the shortcomings of political theory and raise several issues: Who is the sovereign to be respected in the case of intervention—a people, particular classes, a state apparatus, or a particular government? Does (perceived) oppression give minorities a right to secede? May governments premised on security of property close down arms production and trade? At issue are peace and protection as well as equal access to power and material resources for all members of a polity regardless of gender, age, class, and color of skin.[18]

Internal wars about resource distribution and wars of liberation conducted by subaltern peoples against titular nations—"transnational internal" wars—frequently receive support from labor and exile diasporas (Tamil, Palestinian, or Kurdish, for example). In the past, German social democracy survived the Bismarckian repression of 1878–90, owing to the financial aid provided by emigrants from North America; the liberation of East Central European peoples from the tsarist, Ottoman, Hohenzollern, and Habsburg empires was achieved in part through the influence of emigrants on U.S. policy at the time of the Versailles Peace Conference in 1918–19. Liberation movements and struggles in cultures of origin may also benefit from emigrants' mediating capacities, as in the case of African colonial elites steeped in a Paris-centered *francophonie* during decolonization. Political exclusion and economic marginalization, as in the cases of Indian immigrants in South Africa around 1900 and of Kurds in European states in the 1990s, prevents brokerage. Politically articulate and empowered migrants may have a problem-solving impact, but those excluded from political processes turn to weaponry-supplying roles.

A third, ecological approach to root causes involves changes in lifestyle in the developed world and of pollution-generating economic growth in LDCs. The 1992 recommendations of the World Ecology Conference in Brazil have not been acted upon, however. A fourth approach targets population development—both rapid growth in the developing countries and gradual decline in the industrialized ones. To reduce growth rates, the UN advocates a strategy centered on women, the world's "wasted asset," by empowering them through education, income-providing employment, and family planning information.[19]

To improve living conditions in emigration regions, bottom-up strategies rather than top-down planning have proved successful. Loans from the World Bank and other, comparable sources reach the macrolevel, powerful institutions and those groups that have access to them, and follow a capital-centered strategy. In a microlevel or human-centered approach, the UN Development Programme emphasizes seed money for self-help, in particular for women and for community organizations. For example, the Grameen Bank in Bangladesh provides small loans to women who establish themselves in farming or business. Local needs may involve global connections: ownership of one cell phone in a village permits villagers to stay in touch with their labor migrant kin in Malaysia or Dubai as well as with regional markets. Small-scale capital infusion also aids rural-urban migrants in Asian, African, or Latin American societies, who generally do not move to industrial jobs but into a self-directed informal sector. Such bottom-up strategies strengthen the flexible and productive tertiary sector of new state economies and avoid the mass displacement resulting from many top-down mega-projects.[20]

Global justice theory mandates the implementation of human rights and justice for each and every living person. It extends the principles of democratic political theory, equal political rights and equality before the law, to class and economic status.[21] By contrast, a localized "communitarian" approach, which suggests community self-determination, postulates the right of privileged communities to exclude newcomers from disadvantaged societies but does not shield exploited communities from penetration by more powerful ones.[22] Though based on European-origin political thought and human rights doctrine, concepts of global justice have been accepted by UN member states across the globe and have been used to criticize the power and exploitation strategies of the capitalist world. They may build on moral economies that have developed in most local societies even when questioning built-in patterns of deference and hierarchy. The implementation of human rights will have to negotiate compromises in values, customs, and legal codes from culture to culture.

As long as opportunities and outcomes are unequally distributed across states and continents, rational women and men will seek to improve their or their children's chances by migration (or internal reform or revolt). Around 1900, a U.S.-bound migrant from southern Italy commented that he would have been dishonest to his family had he not pursued a strategy of taking advantage of job opportunities and resources that were far from home. While liberalist ideology restricts itself to economics, liberalist theory explains migrants' strategies for improving their and their children's lives. Their decisions to relocate involve intiative, self-help, and entrepreneurship—that is, voluntarism and free enterprise. Their rational decision making may take into account multiple factors: economic considerations, intergenerational improvements, change of gender restrictions. Migration may be considered a survival strategy under a worst-case scenario, but more often it can be seen as an investment strategy meant to increase human and social capital for life-course projects.

20.3   Citizenship in a Postnational World versus Global Apartheid[23]

The incorporation of migrant Others into nation-state political systems has been contested terrain. In between admission and exclusion, diaspora status permits partial negotiated or customary inclusion over many generations, as in the case of trader groups such as the Overseas Chinese, the Hausa, or the Amsterdam Portuguese Jews. Immigration countries—Australia and Canada, for example—grant citizenship easily after residence. Other states admit foreigners as temporary laborers, for example in Europe after the 1880s or West Africa since the 1960s; as racialized contract laborers, for example in the British Empire in the past or Singapore in the present; or as temporary "guests," for example in European and Gulf states in the 1990s. Nonimmigration countries erect obstacles to the acquisition of citizenship; their procedures are discretionary, and minimum periods of residence may extend to twelve years.

The 1990s debates about immigrant and refugee admission as well as about cultural homogeneity or diversity are still premised on the concepts of the nation-state and the equality of individuals before the law. Recognition of ethnic groups is said to contravene universalist "first principles" of democratic theory. Differentiation into cultural groups, or "diversity," is an integral part of all societies, however, and not something imported from without by migrants, who may be stigmatized for the "divisiveness" they ostensibly create. The equality of citizens is constantly challenged by the social practices of exclusion and by the self-organization of interest groups. Custom, class, and status divide residents of a polity with regard to their access to societal resources, such as education, labor markets, capital resources, courts, and legislative institutions. Citizens, according to legal codification and in public opinion, are positioned as men or women or children, or as members of business associations or of labor unions. Established gatekeeper groups use their power of definition to fragment societies into White over Black, the well-to-do over welfare clients or *favela* inhabitants, into Tutsi elites over lower-ranking Hutu majorities, into privileged members of the *nomenklatura* over common socialist workers. Groups may either define themselves or be defined from the outside by cultural practices.

Switzerland, the model democracy, and the United Kingdom, the model nation, incorporate four regional ethnic cultures each. The model multicultural state in 1980s Asia, Malaysia, incorporates many peoples. Political borders include hundreds of language and dialect groups within one state, as in India, or divide language-groups. Co-resident groups are reduced to "minority" status, as in the case of Japan's Hokkaido and Ryūkyū peoples or France's Basques, Bretons, and Alsatians. Such territorial groups are usually concentrated in a particular region where they form the majority in contrast to nonterritorial peoples, such as Gypsies, Jews, Overseas Chinese, or African trading communities, and immigrant minorities. Those discriminated against may react by engaging in struggles within the system, resorting to rebellion, or migrating to another society and to what are perceived as better cultural or economic ways of life. Demands for ethno-regional autonomy demonstrate that hegemonic groups have not accommodated diversity in order to form one nation, a statewide legal and institutional overlay notwithstanding. Thus migrants also have no "national" model to acculturate to. In some states, diversity is enshrined constitutionally in concepts of federalism, and tolerance is accommodated in concepts of pluralism or multiculturalism.

The spectrum of political enfranchisement ranges from the integrative-multicultural type (open admission to citizenship on the basis of *ius soli*, shared political practices through birth in a state's territory); via the integrative-assimilationist type (predicated on the demand for cultural homogenization); to the exclusionist type (based on *ius sanguinis* or the lineage principle, privileging birth into an ethnoculturally similar group with little possibility for "naturalization"). The concept of "naturalization" illustrates the irrational or biological aspects underlying membership in polities: are noncitizens unnatural? Lineage-concepts, which derive from tribal practices or the position of a (noble) class in a particular historical period, have been adopted by some middle-class states to defend an allegedly pure nation. Subject status in dynastic states was based on residence in a territory and loyalty to a ruler; citizen status, as defined in the French Revolution, is based both on residence and on acceptance of the republican system. Thus a residency period of a few years and a certain competency at dealing with the admitting society's institutions and official language are required in many states. From the point of view of both migrant human rights and democratic political theory, the standards for admission to citizenship need to be more or less universal.

States that conflate citizenship with membership in a national culture or with a descent group reject dual or multiple citizenship, thus discriminating against the very transnational migrants whom they often need to recruit. Multiple citizenship distinguishes between active and dormant citizenships: migrants (but not tourists or other short-term travelers) may hold more than one citizenship, and residence in a given place determines which is operative. Operative citizenship entails obligations from the payment of taxes and law-abiding conduct to military service. Provisions for multiple citizenship reflect postnational concepts of states and societies in an age of high mobility.[24]

Historically, journeymen artisans carried travel carnets (notebooks) in which their stopovers, periods of work, and entitlement to temporary support were listed (chap. 3.3). This self-management provided flexibility beyond that permitted by territorially based administrations. Adapted to modern passport systems, a migrant by choosing residency also opts for concurrent obligations and entitlements. He or she may transfer entitlements across borders and has to fulfill personal obligations regardless of state of residence, such as support payments for dependents.[25] Multiple citizenship with access to different social security systems would end the compartmentalization of transnational migrants' entitlements and obligations.

In societies with social security systems, migrants no longer have to rely on self-help and ethnic or working-class mutual aid associations; legal labor-market entry mandates inclusion into the support systems of unemployment benefits, medical care, and old-age pension funds. Thus, documented migrants are in a position equal to native-born workers and employees. Such systems protect native-born populations from economic competition based on undercutting standards of living, and they protect migrants from exploitation. If such inclusion is paralleled by exclusion from political participation, migrants achieve denizen status rather than citizen status, and in many states such a status allows for only insecure rights of residence.[26]

Further research is needed to assess the degree to which migrants seek citizenship. From the 1830s to the 1920s, immigrants in Canada showed little interest in citizenship because they were satisfied with the institutional framework of an immigration society and the options for economic insertion. Rather than with the state, they identified with the region selected for settlement or with a craft, and their children received citizenship at birth. Immigrant letters indicate that continuity of family relations and options for return—transnational identities—were more important than political participation. Migrants in postnational states need citizenship to fight discrimination or to participate in proactive politics; they do not need it for access to labor markets and social security. Citizenship is a protection against loss of status in times of recession, as demonstrated by the expulsions of non-nationals by West African states.[27]

The debate about inclusion in some immigrant societies of the 1990s was eclipsed by gatekeeper rhetoric, sometimes based on imagined future migrations, about the arrival of undesirables and the disuniting of societies. The specter of separate and alien cultural groups was raised in the northern hemisphere, inspired by, among others, economic and ecological refugees from the Third World, imagined Russian masses fleeing postcommunist social inequalities, or Balkan ethnics in actual flight from the Yugoslav civil wars.[28] The prejudices of "sons of the soil" concerned immigrant outsiders in Assam, Andhra Pradesh, and Bihar; in Japan the same sort of hostility was directed at Korean labor migrants. Conservatives in Canada attacked the policy of multiculturalism; their counterparts in the United States blamed pluralism for whatever problems society experienced. In France, the National Front made North African immigrants the object of fear and loathing; in Germany, "Ausländerfeindlichkeit" found fault with all Others.[29] Ideological superstructures, from honor to racial superiority, often lead to anti-alien hostility, discrimination, and violence. It is easier to beat up an immigrant than to beat a recession, to chase a newcomer out of the country than to oust a politician feeding on ethnic strife from office. If the culture and morality of the allegedly superior majority people in a state are assumed to be threatened by the presence of a much smaller group of immigrants—of, for example, Whiteman by Coloredwoman—then the value system must be brittle. The economics and the pathology of racism and the psychology of projection of feared shortcomings from the Self onto the Other need researchers' attention.

Anti-immigrant hostility and governmental exclusion policies may be understood by borrowing from economist John K. Galbraith's concept of a "culture of contentment": wealthy societies remain unconcerned about poverty in their midst; industrialized states have become democracies of the well-fed and contented without compassion for and a desire to aid people in LDCs. The nineteenth-century chauvinism of national culture has become a chauvinism of wealth. Anthony Richmond has conceptualized worldwide exploitative relationships as "global apartheid" (chap.

19.1). Migrants who understand the economic interests behind cultural facades react by circumventing restrictions, by crossing borders without documents. Individually, they attempt to equalize life-course opportunities. "Illegal" immigrants question the legitimacy of inequality and the morality of global apartheid.[30]

20.4 *Multiple Identities and Transcultural Everyday Lives*

Migrants leave their complex societies as well as intricate family relationships in order to chart independent life-courses. The reasons that influence the decision to depart also influence a migrant's interactions with the receiving society, whether it is regarded as a temporary haven from which to instigate the overthrow of an oppressive regime at home, or viewed as a long-term work environment, or thought of as a permanent place of residence for family formation or entrepreneurial opportunities. Migrants carry their ways of life as "cultural baggage" unless they are moved across borders at a young age by parents. Within the frame of norms and practices of this primary socialization, migrants come to terms with the host society in a secondary socialization process.[31]

Viewed from a perspective of national cultures, bifurcated or hyphenated identities emerge from this interaction: Chinese-Americans or Italian-Australians, or, with more segregation, Koreans in Japan, Asians in Uganda, Turks in Germany. With the exception of voluntary self-segregation, as in the case of Mennonites, for example, cultural adaptation over two or three generations changes newcomers or ethnics into members of the receiving society's mainstream. This was the experience of Huguenots in German lands and of Indians in Trinidad. The receiving society's mainstream also changes: in Malaya/Malaysia, resident Malays and immigrant Chinese developed a new society; in Siberia, a Russian-Native culture emerged; in the United States in the late nineteenth century, the Taylorization of production was given impetus by the arrival of immigrant unskilled workers, thereby establishing a new factory mode of work; in Manchuria, immigrants and industrialization engulfed the resident people.

Migrants "live simultaneously in home and host societies": they lead transcultural lives.[32] Men and women and children of the nineteenth-century labor and settler diasporas—such as the Black Atlantic, the Overseas Chinese, and peasant migrants in North America and South Russia—made homes and created communities wherever they put down roots. They lived in networks extending over continents rather than in inter-national suspension between boundary-separated states. Although the concepts of bourgeois cosmopolitanism and working-class internationalism may overemphasize class cultures and class solidarity across state and national boundaries, the concept of "culture shock" overemphasizes disruption. Migrants attempt to select social spaces in the receiving society that correspond to their skills and interests. Problems emerge from racism rather than from migration. A 1990s Bangladeshi immigrant in London's racialized Isle of Dogs, commented: "I can surf around the world on the Internet, I have family who phone me from America and Australia but I am afraid to go outside my own front door in Cubitt Town."[33] Diasporic exchanges have accelerated with the accessibility of air travel and telecommunication, but they are not new. The concept of the "global village" and the notion that "migration is a one-way trip, there is no home to go back to" neglect cultural specifics and memories of the past in migrants' minds.[34] Migrants tend not to be simply uprooted: they follow strategies of flexible adjustment, and they arrive at their destinations with individual worldviews, values, and customs.

Migrants' first step in receiving societies is entry into a labor market segment or another economic activity. Individuals and families need immediate income for physical survival since receiving societies are unwilling to provide assistance, and co-ethnics, if willing to offer financial support, usually have only limited means of doing so. Economic insertion was part of refugee experiences after the second twentieth-century European war, Japan's imperial expansion, and the Pakistan-India partition. Only with refugee-generation in Africa and Asia did camp life become the rule because of the lack of jobs in the regions of settlement and because of the refusal of industrialized societies to admit the dislocated. Constricted insertion or full participation depended on economic cycles, open or segregated labor markets, and migrants' social and job skills. This was as true for migrants of the past as it is for Mediterranean, Caribbean, Polish, or Philippine "guest workers" and "guest domestics" of the present.

Regulations regarding entry into labor markets, an achievement of nineteenth-century labor movements, and the governmentally mandated professionalization of many jobs have raised barriers for migrants, whose insertion traditionally was predicated on flexibility without formal job qualifications, on a willingness to accept low-paying jobs, and on independent family labor. In states with protective labor and safety legislation, migrants lack low-level entryways and the "right" to self- and family exploitation; consumer protection may increase initial investments and general production costs in small businesses to levels that are prohibitive for recent immigrants. Thus, some select undocumented entry and uncontrolled marginal work; others are smuggled into illegal economies, as in the case of bound Chinese workers brought into New York textile factories during the 1990s.[35] In Europe, Canada, and Australia, high productivity and skills needed to operate expensive machinery are required for better-paying jobs.

Once migrants have secured their economic basis, they turn to cultural reproduction. They face statewide cultures with common norms and institutions as well as widely differing regional or class implementations of those norms, which undergo constant evolution. Culture, a process not a status, is interactive. Since identities are interactive constructs, they assume multiple expressions and redefinitions over time. Depending on whom she is communicating with, an immigrant Muslim woman with one child may define herself by ethnicity, religion, motherhood, gender, single-parent role, age, culture of origin, or postmigration nationality.

Migrants often congregate in ethnic quarters to limit the amount of cultural change they experience, as was true of medieval European merchants in China, Portuguese Jews in the Netherlands, rural settlers in the North American plains or Manchuria, and casual workers in late-twentieth-century African cities. Residents of receiving societies who decry ethnic-group cohesion often construct groups of outsiders at the same time: "the women," "the welfare cheaters," "the Turks," "the Asians" (or "the Orientals"). Labeling divides societies and forces migrants and the resident disadvantaged alike to seek protection in their own group or in separate political organizations.

Ethnocultural group formation and the protection of deeply ingrained cultural practices permit a self-determined transition into the new society's everyday life without damage to identities. The theoretical contradiction between the corporate and liberal constructions of societies, between group and individual rights, is bridged in lived experience by societal pluralism and individual choice. Mainstream "nationals" or minority ethnics may leave their group of birth, choose between cultural identities, or convert from one creed to another. The universalist principle overrides group construction and cohesion when individual men, women, and children decide about their belonging and cultural identity.

Cultural identity is both an individual and a group process taking place within a family, an urban neighborhood or a village, a region, a state, a religion, and other supra-state entities. Cultural environment defines people as Bengalis or Punjabis, as Californians or Bostonians. National construction and homogenization across regional boundaries turns these groups into Indians or Americans with practiced and ascribed identities, with complex, many-layered loyalties. When identities are developed or constructed in interaction with others, similarities may be emphasized or boundaries drawn, thus bringing together or separating out groups with different practices, customs, norms, and values. The power of self-definition is part of identity-creation, but the power to impose definitions on Others often serves as an instrument of discrimination.[36]

Concerns about the divisiveness of multicultural patterns of living at the turn of the twenty-first century reflect the construction of the Other as alien or dangerous. Cultural differences are exploited by elite interest groups or among neighbors, as in the case of the former Yugoslavia or of Rwanda and Burundi. Traditions of pluralism do not prevent expressions of racism, as the anti-immigration positions of segments in the population of California or Assam show. The expulsion of the Ugandan and other African Asians in 1972 and the secession of non-Russian peoples from the Commonwealth of Independent States show that cultural differences and economic hierarchies continue to motivate conflict.

While highly visible conflict enters history texts, the everyday patterns of interaction defy categorization. Having to trade or negotiate across cultural differences or to work and communicate alongside each other, Natives and newcomers come to terms with each other's ways, customs, and norms, at least to a degree that exchange becomes mutually advantageous. Foreign merchants of five hundred years ago, locked into *funduqs* and *Höfe*, decided to stay where they were and open businesses locally; they fell in love and married women from the indigenous culture.

Sons and daughters of medieval noble families were betrothed over great distances and, after meeting, learned to get along with each other and find a common language —not necessarily either partner's native tongue; the in-migrating bride or groom brought servants, advisers, and confidantes who formed a foreign nucleus in the courtly world, an ethnic group. The nineteenth-century climate of anti-Semitism notwithstanding, Germans and Jews intermarried; so did twentieth-century Orthodox Serbs and Muslim Bosnians. Patterns of immigration, cultural exchange or conversion, and intermarriage created new cultures and new peoples in the past and do so in the present, as the "Browning" of North American peoples shows. The concept of "visible minorities," introduced in Canada to quantify discrimination and to pass affirmative action policies, has become redundant in the case of highly educated Chinese immigrants: the members of the group do not consider themselves visible—that is, visibly different—nor are they perceived as such by Others.[37]

The "horizontal" acculturation of everyday life—private and public—has to be accompanied by "vertical" or structural acculturation in the economic and institutional sphere, with access to positions in business and government on all levels. Structural acculturation not only reflects an immigrant group's adaptation; it also reflects the receiving society's openness to admit newcomers and change itself. Discriminatory societies lock newcomers (or residents) into particular social slots or strata, be they class- or caste-based. A "vertical mosaic" develops, to use a Canadian term that might also be applied to Singapore, in which immigrant groups cannot move upward in social hierarchies.[38]

Although some prophets of a coming apocalypse assume that mass migrations will "inundate" rich societies, potential migrants do not merely move because of wage differentials or consumer choice. People are tied to their origins by ways of life instilled in early childhood, by kin and friendship networks, and by limited economic means. Once they are ready to chart a life-course on their own as adolescents or are pushed out as adults by political regimes, economic decline, or environmental degradation, they assess options. Whether they are located in nearby urban areas or farther away, societies that permit survival, present options, or allow improvements will be attractive—but may also be identity-threatening. Men and women move to cash incomes and less rigorous norms. Monetarization, often criticized as commodifying values, provides options for deciding how to obtain a disposable income. Retention and change are arenas of contest in individual minds, in family economies, and in social groups. Clinging to a particular spiritual culture in the face of the material improvement of neighbors of a different persuasion, or despite images of distant wealthy societies, demands an individual decision to reject material gain. Similarly, the question whether women as mothers should raise children and imbue them with national virtues or should have access to labor markets and hire children caregivers from a different culture will change intimate relationships, domestic hierarchies, and socialization into a culture—and pit traditionalists against modernizers. According to Stolcke, "Genuine tolerance for cultural diversity can flourish without entailing disadvantages only where society and polity are democratic and egalitarian enough to enable people to resist discrimination (whether as immigrants, foreigners, women, Blacks) and develop differences without jeopardizing themselves and solidarity among them."[39]

Research has concentrated on adaptation and the human and social capital necessary to achieve transitions, multiple identities, and transcultural patterns of living. Migration and acculturation have been recognized as basic human conditions. It is time to ask why some people can neither accept the mobility of others nor deal with diversity. Their dead-end cultures may indeed be eclipsed by flexible, transcultural migrants.

A family of Overseas Chinese owned a business on the island of Penang in Malaysia, but like all diaspora dwellers they had de-territorialized and left nation and state constructs behind. When they migrated to Auckland, New Zealand, they chose to hold both New Zealand and Malaysian citizenship. The parents reduced their material assets in Kuala Lumpur in order to invest in a university education for two of their three children, whose gain in human capital, through learning English and obtaining an advanced education, was to open the way to other economies and social spaces, the United States in particular. The parents kept their Malaysian citizenship, and the father explained their reasoning by asking: "Why should a person who can walk on either of two roads cut himself off from one—and leave only one? What if that single one is cut off as well?"[40]

Notes

Contexts: An Introductory Note to Readers

1. J. B. Harley and David Woodward, *Cartography in Prehistoric, Ancient, and Medieval Europe and the Mediterranean* (Chicago, 1987), 4; Greg Dening, "An Imprinted Land," *Australian's Review of Books* 4, 7 (Aug. 1999), 11–13.

1 Worlds in Motion, Cultures in Contact

1. David Herlihy has argued that gender relations in Europe changed from the tenth century on, recasting power and property relations between men and women. *Medieval Households* (Cambridge, Mass., 1985), 79–111.
2. William H. McNeill, *Europe's Steppe Frontier, 1500–1800* (Chicago, 1964), 56–59.
3. Robert Bartlett and Angus MacKay, eds., *Medieval Frontier Societies* (Oxford, 1989).
4. Nina Glick Schiller, Linda Basch, and Cristina Blanc-Szanton, *Towards a Transnational Perspective on Migration: Race, Class, Ethnicity and Nationalism Reconsidered* (New York, 1992), 1–24; Anthony H. Richmond, *Global Apartheid: Refugees, Racism and the New World Order* (Toronto, 1994).
5. Frank Thistlethwaite, "Migration from Europe Overseas in the Nineteenth and Twentieth Centuries," XI Congrès International des Sciences Historiques, *Rapports*, vol. 5 (Stockholm, 1960), 32–60; Rolando Mellafe, "The Importance of Migration in the Viceroyalty of Peru," in Paul Deprez, ed., *Population and Economics: Proceedings of Section V of the Fourth Congress of the International Economic History Association* (Winnipeg, 1970), 303–13; Samir Amin, "Migrations in Contemporary Africa: A Retrospective View," in Jonathan Baker and Tade A. Aina, eds., *The Migration Experience in Africa* (Uppsala, 1995), 29–40; Charles Tilly, "Migration in Modern European History," in William H. McNeill and Ruth S. Adams, eds., *Human Migration: Patterns and Politics* (Bloomington, 1978), 48–72; Klaus J. Bade, *Europa in Bewegung: Migration vom späten 18. Jahrhundert bis zur Gegenwart* (München, 2000).
6. Of the Chicago School, the studies of Robert E. Park, William I. Thomas/Florian Znaniecki, and Ernest W. Burgess were of particular relevance. The women associated with this line of thought—social reformers and authors Edith and Grace Abbott, Jane Addams, Sophonisba P. Breckenridge, Margaret Byington, Frances A. Kellor, and others—have received limited at-

tention. See Stow Persons, *Ethnic Studies at Chicago, 1905-45* (Chicago, 1987); Milton M. Gordon, *Assimilation in American Life: The Role of Race, Religion, and National Origins* (New York, 1964); Everett C. Hughes, "The Study of Ethnic Relations," *Dalhousie Review* 24 (1948): 477–82; and Hughes and Helen MacGill Hughes, *Where Peoples Meet: Racial and Ethnic Frontiers* (Glencoe, Ill., 1952); and Fredrik Barth, ed., *Ethnic Groups and Boundaries: The Social Organization of Culture Difference* (Boston, 1969).

7   Richmond, *Global Apartheid*, 3–116.

8   Douglas S. Massey et al., "Theories of International Migration: Review and Appraisal," *Population and Development Review* 19 (Sept. 1993): 431–66, and "International Migration Theory: The North American Case," *Population and Development Review* 20 (Dec. 1994): 699–752; Dirk Hoerder, "Changing Paradigms in Migration History: From 'To America' to Worldwide Systems," *Canadian Review of American Studies* 24, 2 (spring 1994): 105–26.

9   See, for example, Peter R. Shergold, *Working-Class Life: The "American Standard" in Comparative Perspective, 1899–1913* (Pittsburgh, 1982).

10 Bartlett and MacKay, *Medieval Frontier Societies*; Walter Nugent, *Crossings: The Great Transatlantic Migrations, 1870-1914* (Bloomington, Ind., 1992); Dirk Hoerder, "Labour Migrants' Views of 'America,'" *Renaissance and Modern Studies* 35 (1992): 1–17.

11 Massey et al., "Theories," 439.

12 Edna Bonacich, "A Theory of Ethnic Antagonism: The Split Labor Market," *American Sociological Review* 37 (1972): 547–59; Clark Kerr, *Markets and Other Essays* (Berkeley, 1977); Michael J. Piore, *Birds of Passage: Migrant Labor and Industrial Societies* (New York, 1979); Walter Licht, "Labor Economics and the Labor Historian," *International Labor and Working Class History* 21 (1982): 52–62.

13 Janet L. Abu-Lughod, *Before European Hegemony: The World System A.D. 1250-1350* (New York, 1989); Alan K. Smith, *Creating a World Economy: Merchant Capital, Colonialism, and World Trade, 1400-1825* (Boulder, 1991); Immanuel M. Wallerstein, *The Modern World-System*, 3 vols. (New York and San Diego, 1974–89); Andre G. Frank and Barry K. Gills, eds., *The World Systems: Five Hundred Years or Five Thousand?* (London, 1993); Eric R. Wolf, *Europe and the People without History* (Berkeley, 1982); Philip D. Curtin, *Cross-Cultural Trade in World History* (New York, 1984).

14 John Berry et al., eds., *State of the Art Review of Research on Canada's Multicultural Society* (Ottawa, 1993); Rudolph J. Vecoli, "The *Contadini* in Chicago: A Critique of [Handlin's] *The Uprooted*," *Journal of American History* 51 (1964): 404–17. Lucie Cheng and Edna Bonacich, eds., *Labor Migration under Capitalism: Asian Workers in the United States before World War II* (Berkeley, 1984); Camille Guerin-Gonzales and Carl Strikwerda, eds., *The Politics of Immigrant Workers: Labor Activism and Migration in the World Economy since 1830* (New York, 1993). Paul E. Lovejoy, ed., *Africans in Bondage: Studies in Slavery and the Slave Trade* (Madison, 1986); Lovejoy and Nicholas Rogers, eds., *Unfree Labour in the Development of the Atlantic World* (Ilford, 1994); Joseph Inkori and Stanley L. Engerman, eds., *The Atlantic Slave Trade: Effects on Economies, Societies, and Peoples in Africa, the Americas, and Europe* (Durham, N.C., 1992); Joseph E. Harris, ed., *Global Dimensions of the African Diaspora* (Washington, D.C., 1982).

15 Dirk Hoerder, ed., *Labor Migration in the Atlantic Economies: The European and North American Working Classes during the Period of Industrialization* (Westport, Conn., 1985); Leslie P. Moch, *Moving Europeans: Migration in Western Europe since 1650* (Bloomington, Ind., 1992); Barbara A. Anderson, *Internal Migration during Modernization in Late*

Nineteenth-Century Russia (Princeton, 1980); Donald W. Treadgold, *The Great Siberian Migration: Government and Peasant in Resettlement from Emancipation to the First World War* (Princeton, 1957).

16 Mark Wyman, *Round-Trip to America: The Immigrants Return to Europe, 1880–1930* (Ithaca, 1993); Samuel L. Baily, "Cross-Cultural Comparison and the Writing of Migration History: Some Thoughts on How to Study Italians in the New World," in Virginia Yans-McLaughlin, ed., *Immigration Reconsidered: History, Sociology, and Politics* (New York, 1990), 241–53; Nugent, *Crossings.* Essay collections introducing the revisions include Ira Glazier and Luigi de Rosa, eds., *Migration across Time and Nations: Population Mobility in Historical Contexts* (New York, 1986); Yans-McLaughlin, *Immigration Reconsidered* (1990); Rudolph J. Vecoli and Suzanne M. Sinke, eds., *A Century of European Migrations, 1830–1930* (Urbana, Ill., 1991); Dirk Hoerder and Leslie P. Moch, eds., *European Migrants: Global and Local Perspectives* (Boston, 1996); Jan Lucassen and Leo Lucassen, eds., *Migration, Migration History, History: Old Paradigms and New Perspectives* (Bern, 1997).

17 Cheng and Bonacich, *Labor Migration under Capitalism;* Colin Clarke, Ceri Peach, and Steven Vertovec, eds., *South Asians Overseas: Migration and Ethnicity* (Cambridge, 1990), esp. Hugh Tinker, "Indians in Southeast Asia: Imperial Auxiliaries," 39–56; Michael Adas, ed., *Islamic and European Expansion: The Forging of a Global Order* (Philadelphia, 1993); Surendra Bhana and Joy B. Brain, *Setting Down Roots: Indian Migrants in South Africa, 1860–1911* (Johannesburg, 1990); U. Bissoondoyal and S. B. C. Servansing, eds., *Indian Labor Immigration* (Moka, Mauritius, 1986).

18 Guerin-Gonzales and Strikwerda, *Politics of Immigrant Workers;* Sinnappah Arasaratnam, *Indians in Malaysia and Singapore* (rev. ed., Kuala Lumpur, 1979); N. Gerald Barrier and Verne A. Dusenbery, eds., *The Sikh Diaspora: Migration and Experience beyond Punjab* (Delhi, 1989); Piet C. Emmer, ed., *Colonialism and Migration: Indentured Labor before and after Slavery* (Dordrecht, 1986).

19 Walter F. Willcox and Imre Ferenczi, eds., *International Migrations*, 2 vols. (New York, 1929 and 1931); E. P. Thompson, "The Moral Economy of the English Crowd," *Past and Present* 50 (Feb. 1971): 76–135; Dirk Hoerder, ed., *"Struggle a Hard Battle"—Essays on Working Class Immigrants* (DeKalb, Ill., 1986). Migration-related studies of labor economists are published by the Geneva-based International Labor Organization among others.

20 Saskia Sassen-Koob, *The Mobility of Labor and Capital* (London, 1988); Robin Cohen, *The New Helots: Migrants in the International Division of Labor* (Aldershot, 1987); Lydia Potts, *The World Labor Market: A History of Migration* (German orig., 1988; London, 1990); Stephen Castles and Mark J. Miller, *The Age of Migration: International Population Movements in the Modern World* (New York, 1993); Guerin-Gonzales and Strikwerda, *The Politics of Immigrant Workers.*

21 Arthur M. Schlesinger Jr., *The Disuniting of America: Reflections on a Multicultural Society* (New York, 1991); Christoph Butterwegge and Siegfried Jäger, eds., *Europa gegen den Rest der Welt: Flüchtlingsbewegungen–Einwanderung–Asylpolitik* (Cologne, 1993); Myron Weiner, *Sons of the Soil: Migration and Ethnic Conflict in India* (Princeton, 1978); Robert Miles, *Racism* (London, 1950; 2d ed., 1989).

22 Anthony D. Smith, *National Identity* (Reno, 1991) and *The Ethnic Origins of Nations* (Oxford, 1987); Eric Hobsbawm and Terence Ranger, eds., *The Invention of Tradition* (Cambridge, 1983). See also Benedict Anderson, *Imagined Communities: Reflections on the Origin and Spread of Nationalism* (1983; 3d ed., London, 1986).

23 Louise A. Tilly and Joan W. Scott, *Women, Work and Family* (New York, 1978); Rita J. Simon and Caroline B. Brettell, *International Migration: The Female Experience* (Totowa, N.J., 1986); Jean Burnet, ed., *Looking into My Sister's Eyes: An Exploration in Women's History* (Toronto, 1986); Barbara Bush, *Slave Women in Caribbean Society, 1650–1838* (Bloomington, Ind., 1990); Claire C. Robertson and Martin A. Klein, eds., *Women and Slavery in Africa* (Madison, 1983).

24 R. Paul Shaw, *Migration Theory and Fact: A Review and Bibliography of Current Literature* (Philadelphia, 1975); Samuel L. Baily, "The Village-Outward Approach to the Study of Social Networks: A Case Study of the Agnonesi Diaspora Abroad, 1885–1989," *Studi Emigrazione* (Rome) 19, 105 (Mar. 1992): 43–67. An individual perspective is also adopted in Caroline B. Brettell, *We Have Already Cried Many Tears: The Stories of Three Portuguese Migrant Women* (Cambridge, Mass., 1982).

25 Philip D. Curtin, *The Atlantic Slave Trade: A Census* (Madison, 1969); Willemina Kloosterboer, *Involuntary Labour since the Abolition of Slavery: A Survey of Compulsory Labour throughout the World* (Leiden, 1960); Tom Bass and Marcel van der Linden, eds., *Free and Unfree Labour: The Debate Continues* (Bern, 1997).

26 This section has benefited from comments by Nancy Green and François Weil, École des Hautes Études en Sciences Sociales, Paris, and Jack Veugelers, University of Toronto. James H. Jackson Jr., and Leslie P. Moch, "Migration and the Social History of Modern Europe," *Historical Methods* 22 (1989): 27–36; Mary M. Kritz, Lin L. Lim, and Hania Zlotnik, eds., *International Migration Systems: A Global Approach* (Oxford, 1992), 1–16; Robert J. Kleiner et al., "International Migration and Internal Migration: A Comprehensive Theoretical Approach," in Glazier and de Rosa, *Migration*, 305–17; Ronald Skeldon, *Population Mobility in Developing Countries: A Reinterpretation* (New York 1990), 27–46; A. L. Mabogunje, "Systems Approach to a Theory of Rural-Urban Migration," *Geographical Analysis* 2, 1 (1970): 1–18; J. J. Mangolam and H. K. Schwarzweller, "General Theory in the Study of Migration: Current Needs and Difficulties," *International Migration Review* 3 (1968): 3–18; M. P. Todaro, *Internal Migration in Developing Countries: A Review of Theory, Evidence, Methodology and Research Priorities* (Geneva, 1976); James T. Fawcett and Fred Arnold, "Explaining Diversity: Asian and Pacific Immigration Systems," in Fawcett and Benjamin V. Cariño, eds., *Pacific Bridges: The New Immigration from Asia and the Pacific Islands* (Staten Island, N.Y., 1987), 453–73; J. A. Jackson, ed., *Migration* (Cambridge, 1969); Mike Parnwell, *Population Movements and the Third World* (London, 1993).

27 These processes are discussed in greater detail in Dirk Hoerder, "From Migrants to Ethnics: Acculturation in a Societal Framework," in Hoerder and Moch, *European Migrants*, 211–62.

28 Christopher McDowell, ed., *Understanding Impoverishment: The Consequences of Development-Induced Displacement* (Providence, 1996), 1–9.

29 Christiane Harzig, ed., *Peasant Maids, City Women: From the European Countryside to Chicago* (Ithaca, 1997).

30 Aristide Zolberg, "International Migration Policies in a Changing World System," in McNeill and Adams, *Human Migration*, 241–86; Nugent, *Crossings*, 7–10; essays in Lucassen and Lucassen, *Migration History*.

31 Nancy L. Green, "The Comparative Method and Poststructural Structuralism: New Perspectives for Migration Studies," in Lucassen and Lucassen, *Migration History*, 57–72; Dirk Hoerder, "Segmented Macrosystems and Networking Individuals: The Balancing Functions of Migration Processes," in ibid., 73–84.

32 This section is based on Hoerder, "Labour Markets, Community, Family: A Gendered Analysis of the Process of Insertion and Acculturation," in Wsevolod Isajiw, ed., *Multiculturalism in North America and Europe: Comparative Perspectives on Interethnic Relations and Social Incorporation* (Toronto, 1997), 155–83; the same article appears in Spanish in *Estudios Migratorios Latinoamericanos* 30 (1995): 249–76.

33 Leslie P. Moch's *Moving Europeans: Migration in Europe since 1650* (Bloomington, 1992) concerns village people whose lives emerge out of the overlay of regional structures. Samuel Baily's "village-outward" approach reconstructs the socialization and distant options of families. Donna R. Gabaccia uses this approach in her survey of European, Asian, and Latin American women's migration, *From the Other Side: Women, Gender and Immigrant Life in the U.S., 1820–1990* (Bloomington, 1994).

34 The assumption that immigrant letters paint a rosy picture does not hold up under critical examination. Migrants encouraged by success stories expect help from the letter-writer upon arrival—a built-in corrective that prevents earlier migrants from inflating their achievements. Walter D. Kamphoefner, Wolfgang Helbich, and Ulrike Sommer, eds., *News from the Land of Freedom: German Immigrants Write Home*, trans. Susan C. Vogel (German orig., 1988; Ithaca, 1991), introduction.

35 The classic formulation of this approach is Tilly and Scott, *Women, Work and Family*, 12ff.; Hoerder, "From Migrants to Ethnics," 211–62.

36 This process is described in "From Lithuania to the Chicago Stockyards—An Autobiography: Antanas Kaztauskis," first published in 1904, repr. in David M. Katzman and William M. Tuttle Jr., eds., *Plain Folk: The Life Stories of Undistinguished Americans* (Urbana, 1982), 104–5; Donna R. Gabaccia, *Militants and Migrants: Rural Sicilians Become American Workers* (New Brunswick, 1988), 80. Hasia R. Diner argues that in Ireland the post-famine "rearrangement of family life" caused out-migration; see *Erin's Daughters in America: Irish Immigrant Women in the Nineteenth Century* (Baltimore, 1983), 31–32.

37 Hoerder, "From Migrants to Ethnics"; Harzig, *Peasant Maids, City Women*.

2 Antecedents: Migration and Population Changes in the Mediterranean-Asian Worlds

1 Jerry H. Bentley, *Old World Encounters: Cross-Cultural Contacts and Exchanges in Pre-Modern Times* (New York, 1993), 9; Janet L. Abu-Lughod, *Before European Hegemony: The World System A.D. 1250–1350* (New York, 1989), 3–40. Abu-Lughod emphasizes politics when she contrasts states supportive of mercantile endeavor with others that constrained it. Andre G. Frank dates the world system's origins as far back as 1000 C.E., Frank and Barry K. Gills, eds., *The World System: Five Hundred Years or Five Thousand?* (London, 1993); Peter Gran, *Islamic Roots of Capitalism: Egypt, 1760–1840* (Syracuse, 1998); Fernand Braudel, *Civilisation matérielle, économie, et capitalisme, XVe–XVIIIe siècle*, 3 vols. (Paris, 1979), English: *Civilization and Capitalism, 15th to 18th Century*, 3 vols., trans. Siân Reynolds (New York, 1981–84), introduction.

2 S. D. Goitein, *A Mediterranean Society: The Jewish Communities of the Arab World as Portrayed in the Documents of the Cairo Geniza*, 5 vols. (Berkeley, 1967–93); Edward Burman, *The World before Columbus, 1100–1492* (London, 1989); Martin Bernal, *Black Athena: The Afroasiatic Roots of Classical Civilization* (New Brunswick, 1987); Ross E. Dunn, *The Adventures of Ibn Battuta: A Muslim Traveler of the 14th Century* (Berkeley, 1986), quotes on

124–25, 188–89; H. A. R. Gibb, ed. and trans., *The Travels of Ibn Battūta, A.D. 1325–1354,* sev. vols. (Cambridge: Hakluyt Society, since 1958).

3 Thomas A. Brady Jr., Heiko A. Oberman, and James D. Tracy, eds., *Handbook of European History, 1400–1600: Late Middle Ages, Renaissance, and Reformation,* 2 vols. (Leiden, 1994), 1:155, 159; Matthias Puhle, *DieVitalienbrüder: Klaus Störtebeker und die Seeräuber der Hansezeit* (Frankfurt/Main, 1994), 65–67.

4 Abu-Lughod, *Before European Hegemony,* quote on 8–9, 58–59, 352–64; UNESCO, *The Silk Roads: Highways of Culture and Commerce,* ed. Vadime Elisseef (New York, 1999).

5 Robert S. Lopez and Irving W. Raymond, eds., *Medieval Trade in the Mediterranean World: Illustrated Documents Translated with Introductions and Notes* (New York, 1955), 29–38, 51–54.

6 Unity ended after the death of Khan Mongka in 1259. But only the rule of Timur (1370–1405) and the fourteenth-century decline of trade ended travel. The term "silk route" was coined in 1877. L. Carrington Goodrich, "Trade Routes to China from Ancient Time to the Age of European Expansion," in Jean Labatut and Wheaton Lane, eds., *Highways in Our National Life* (Princeton, 1950), 16–32; Stephan Conermann and Jan Kusber, eds., *Die Mongolen in Asien und Europa* (Frankfurt/Main, 1997); Reuven Amitai-Preiss and David O. Morgan, eds., *The Mongol Empire and Its Legacy* (Leiden, 1999).

7 Michael Brett, "Ifriqiya as a Market for Saharan Trade from the Tenth to the Twelfth Century A.D.," *Journal of African History* 10 (1969): 347–64; Richard W. Bulliet, *The Camel and the Wheel* (Cambridge, Mass., 1975).

8 Burman, *World before Columbus,* 18–23, 103–30; Bernard Lewis, *The Muslim Discovery of Europe* (New York, 1982), 185.

9 *The Itinerary of Benjamin of Tudela,* trans. and ed. M. N. Adler (New York, 1907). George F. Hourani, *Arab Seafaring in the Indian Ocean in Ancient and Early Medieval Times* (Princeton, 1951); Louis I. Rabinowitz, *Jewish Merchant Adventurers: A Study of the Radanites* (London, 1948). When the Austrian Georg Christoph Fernberger traveled a similar route more than four centuries later, from 1588 to 1593, he had read Benjamin of Tudela's account and commented on the many cultured men in cities from Constantinople to Pegu; *Reisetagebuch (1588–1593): Sinai, Babylon, Indien, Heiliges Land, Osteuropa,* trans. and ed. Ronald Burger and Robert Wallisch (Frankfurt/Main, 1999), 90.

10 Henry H. Hart, *Marco Polo: Venetian Adventurer* (Norman, Okla., 1967), 43; Marco Polo, *The Travels of Marco Polo* (London, 1908); Louis Hambis, "Le Voyage de Marco Polo en Haute Asie," in E. Balazs et al., *Oriente Poliano: Studi e conferenze tenute all'Is. M.E.O. in occasione del VII centenario della nascita di Marco Polo, 1254–1954* (Rome, 1957), 173–91; Leonardo Olschki, *Marco Polo's Precursors* (Baltimore, 1943), and Olschki, *Marco Polo's Asia* (Berkeley, 1960); Dunn, *Ibn Battuta,* 1–12; Abu-Lughod, *Before European Hegemony,* 28–30, 163–67, 316–51.

11 Bentley, *Old World Encounters,* 152–160, quote on 156. RenéGrousset, *The Empire of the Steppes: A History of Central Asia,* trans. N. Walford (French orig.; New Brunswick, 1970); Abu-Lughod, *Before European Hegemony,* 153–84.

12 Wang Li, as quoted in Bentley, *Old World Encounters,* 111, from Chen Yüan, *Western and Central Asians in China under the Mongols: Their Transformation into Chinese* (Los Angeles, 1966).

13 Teobaldo Filesi, *China and Africa in the Middle Ages,* trans. D. L. Morison (London, 1972),

quote on 1–2, 8–65; Jeannette Mirsky, ed., *The Great Chinese Travelers: An Anthology* (Chicago, 1974), 175–202, 242; Louise Levathes, *When China Ruled the Seas: The Treasure Fleet of the Dragon Throne, 1405–1433* (New York, 1995); Bentley, *Old World Encounters*, 158–63; Abu-Lughod, *Before European Hegemony*, 172–73.

14 André Miquel, "L'Europe occidentale dans la relation arabe d'Ibrâhîm b. Yacub (Xe s.)," *Annales: Économies, sociétés, civilisations* 21 (1966): 1048–64; Dunn, *Ibn Battuta*, 39, 207–27, 295–307. The *rihla* literature hardly mentions women.

15 Baron von Meyendorff, "Trade and Communication in Eastern Europe, A.D. 800–1200," in Arthur P. Newton, ed., *Travel and Travellers of the Middle Ages* (London, 1926); Archibald R. Lewis, *Nomads and Crusaders, A.D. 1000–1368* (Bloomington, 1988), 56–58; Jonathan Riley-Smith, ed., *The Atlas of the Crusades* (London, 1991), 84–85, 100–101.

16 Abu-Lughod, *Before European Hegemony*, 175–82, 189–97; Philip D. Curtin, *Cross-Cultural Trade in World History* (Cambridge, 1984), chaps. 5–6; Lewis, *Nomads and Crusaders*, 22–26, 110–12, 121, 134.

17 Malcolm Letts, *Sir John Mandeville: The Man and His Book* (London, 1949), and Letts, ed., *Mandeville's Travels*, 2 vols. (London, 1953). See also Chaucer's *Canterbury Tales*, perhaps the travel account (albeit fictional) with the most lasting impact. Richard Hakluyt, *The Principall Navigations, Voiages and Discoveries of the English Nation* (1589); David B. Quinn, ed., *The Hakluyt Handbook* (London, 1974). Already in 1154 King Roger II of Sicily had ordered Arab experts to question pilgrims' and merchants' and to compile their stories in *Book of Roger, or the Delight of Whoso Loves to Make the Circuit of the World*.

18 Fritz Kramer, *Verkehrte Welten: Zur imaginären Ethnographie des 19. Jahrhunderts* (2d ed., Frankfurt/Main, 1981); Burman, *World before Columbus*, 50–61.

19 Quote translated from Jeanne Vielliard, ed., *Le guide du Pèlerin de Saint-Jacques de Compostelle* (3d ed., Mâcon, 1963), in Alan Kendall, *Medieval Pilgrims* (London, 1970), 43, see also 51–58, 107; Sidney Heath, *In the Steps of Pilgrims* (1st ed., 1911; rev. and enlarged ed., New York, 1951), 134; Fredric Jameson, "Of Islands and Trenches: Neutralization and the Production of Utopian Discourse," *Diacritics* 7, 2 (June 1977), quote on 16.

20 Lewis, *Nomads and Crusaders*, 35–38; Goitein, *Mediterranean Society*, 1:273–352. Pilgrims described the multilingual commerce on Cyprus.

21 Lewis, *Muslim Discovery of Europe*, quote on 185. The state of historiography is summarized in Brady et al., *Handbook of European History*.

22 The split of the Christian Church between Byzantium and Rome occurred in 1054. Other denominations included Nestorians and Chaldeans, Maronites, Jacobites or Syriacs, Copts, and Armenians.

23 Subhi Y. Labib, *Handelsgeschichte Ägyptens im Spätmittelalter (1171–1517)* (Wiesbaden, 1965), 1–121.

24 Abu-Lughod, *Before European Hegemony*, 78–134, 131n; Armando Sapori, *The Italian Merchant in the Middle Ages*, trans. Patricia A. Kennen (French orig.; New York, 1970), 71–91; *The Cambridge Economic History of Europe*, vol. 3: M. M. Postan, E. E. Rich, Edward Miller, eds., "Economic Organization and Policies in the Middle Ages" (Cambridge, 1963), 3–41; Thomas W. Robisheaux, "The World of the Village," in Brady et al., *Handbook of European History*, quote on 1:83.

25 *Cambridge Economic History*, 3:119–53, esp. 123.

26 For migrations in the other civilizations, see chaps. 6–9.

27 The best summaries are Charles Verlinden, *L'esclavage dans l'Europe médiévale*, 2 vols. (Bruges, 1955–77), and Jacques Heers, *Esclaves et domestiques au Moyen Âge dans le monde méditerranéen* (Paris, 1981). For slavery in Islam, see Bernard Lewis, *Race and Slavery in the Middle East: An Historical Enquiry* (New York, 1990). Goitein, *Mediterranean Society*, 1:130–47.

28 These areas were depopulated by Crimean Tatars to a degree that they had to be repopulated by eighteenth-century migrations within and into the tsarist empire (chap. 13.2).

29 Contemporary notions of skin color occasionally designated North Africans as White, sub-Saharan Africans as Black.

30 Stephen P. Bensch, "From Prizes of War to Domestic Merchandise: The Changing Face of Slavery in Catalonia and Aragon, 1000–1300," *Viator* 25 (1994): 63–93; Philip K. Hitti, *History of the Arabs* (8th ed.; London, 1963), 514; Verlinden, *L'esclavage*, 286–88; Aziz Ahmad, *A History of Islamic Sicily* (Edinburgh, 1975), 105–6; Ian F. Hancock, *The Pariah Syndrome: An Account of Gypsy Slavery and Persecution* (2d rev. ed., Ann Arbor, 1987).

31 Islamic law did not provide this protection to female slaves. Goitein, *Mediterranean Society*, 1:130–47; Lewis, *Race and Slavery*, 38–39.

32 Benjamin Z. Kedar, "The Genoese Notaries of 1382: The Anatomy of an Urban Occupational Group," in Harry Miskimin, David Herlihy, and A. L. Udovitch, eds., *The Medieval City* (New Haven 1977), 75, 92–94; Heers, *Esclaves et domestiques*, 286–87 (quote translated by D. H.); Susan M. Stuard, *A State of Deference: Ragusa/Dubrovnik in the Medieval Centuries* (Philadelphia, 1992), 118–53; Verlinden, *L'esclavage*, 394, 519; Lewis, *Race and Slavery*, 37–49.

33 Agus argues that rustic Judeans were not expelled and that expelled elites constituted a select group capable of developing unmatched techniques of survival under the persecutions. Irving A. Agus, *Urban Civilization in Pre-Crusade Europe: A Study of Organized Town-Life in Northwestern Europe during the Tenth and Eleventh Centuries Based on the Responsa Literature*, 2 vols. (New York, 1965), 1:11–15. Jews lived in areas of Sunni Islam; the Shiite creed was more hostile. Haim H. Ben-Sasson et al., eds., *A History of the Jewish People* (Hebrew orig., 1969; Cambridge, Mass., 1976), 385–560.

34 The best account of Jews in Muslim society is Bernard Lewis, *Cultures in Conflict: Christians, Muslims, and Jews in the Age of Discovery* (New York, 1995); see also Mark R. Cohen, *Under Crescent and Cross: The Jews in the Middle Ages* (Princeton, 1994).

35 The modern generic term "ghetto" for Jewish quarters originated when part of the Jewish community of Venice was moved in 1516 into the *getto*, meaning "foundry," a fortresslike building with a single entrance that could be guarded at night. Brian Pullan, *Rich and Poor in Renaissance Venice: The Social Institutions of a Catholic State, to 1620* (Oxford, 1971), 476–509.

36 Quoted in Ben-Sasson et al., *Jewish People*, 463. Note the time lag of one generation in the acculturation process. Agus, *Urban Civilization*, 1:30.

37 Harry C. Schnur, "Jüdische Ehe und Familie im Mittelalter," in Willy van Hoecke and Andries Welkenhuysen, eds., *Love and Marriage in the Twelfth Century* (Leuven, 1981), 88–101; according to Schnur, women usually migrated with their husbands but could not be forced to move to a country with a different language (89). Goitein, *Mediterranean Society*, 1:42–59, 273–352, 3:336–41.

38 An example of distances and cultures traversed is the life of the savant Moses Maimonides (1138–1204). His family first fled to Fez in Morocco and probably lived disguised as con-

verts; then to the crusaders' Palestine, which was inhospitable for Jews; and then to Muslim Egypt.

39 Angus MacKay, *Spain in the Middle Ages: From Frontier to Empire, 1000-1500* (London, 1977), 79-94; Ben-Sasson et al., *Jewish People*, 466-67, 488.

40 In the region between the Black and Caspian Seas, the ruling groups of the Khazar kingdom had adopted Judaism as their religion. Ben-Sasson et al., *Jewish People*, 462-63; Kenneth R. Stow, *Alienated Minority: The Jews of Medieval Latin Europe* (Cambridge, Mass., 1992), 2.

41 Viking raids had disturbed populations along the North Sea and Atlantic littorals and deep into river estuaries. Vikings were the first ethnicity to establish a northern trading system. Other groups moved to Iceland and to Greenland and Newfoundland. Settlement in the latter was temporary, and the Greenland villages were abandoned as climatic conditions deteriorated.

42 Lucien Musset, "L'aristocratie normande au XIe siècle," in Philippe Contamine, ed., *La noblesse au Moyen Âge XIe-XVe siècles: Essais à la mémoire de Robert Boutruche* (Paris, 1976), 71-96; David Walker, *The Normans in Britain* (Oxford, 1995).

43 Concerning their subsequent enslavement, see the section "Mediterranean Slavery" earlier in this chapter.

44 Ahmad, *Islamic Sicily*, 37-41, 52-75, 82-96; David Abulafia, *Frederick II: A Medieval Emperor* (London, 1988), 25-53, 144-71; Norman Daniel, *The Arabs and Mediaeval Europe* (1975; 2d ed., London, 1975), 142-68; Clifford R. Backman, *The Decline and Fall of Medieval Sicily: Politics, Religion, and Economy in the Reign of Frederick III, 1296-1337* (Cambridge, 1995); Steven Runciman, *The Sicilian Vespers: A History of the Mediterranean World in the Later Thirteenth Century* (1st ed., 1958; repr. Cambridge, 1982). In 1266, during the wars for Angevin control, Saracen archers, German horsemen, and Italian mercenaries fought side by side. Ibid., 92-93.

45 The "Age of the Crusades" often refers to the conquest of Palestine only. Crusades were also undertaken, however, against dissenting Christians, such as the Albigensians in southern France, against Christian lay powers, and against Slavic or other "heathen" peoples. Even the fifteenth-century Portuguese expansion into Africa was styled as a crusade. Norman Housley, *The Italian Crusades: The Papal-Angevin Alliance and the Crusades against Christian Lay Powers, 1254-1343* (Oxford, 1982); Pierre Belperron, *La croisade contre les Albigeois et l'union du Languedoc à la France (1209-1249)* (Paris, 1945); Michael Costen, *The Cathars and the Albigensian Crusade* (Manchester, 1997). A broad approach is taken in Riley-Smith, *Atlas of the Crusades*, and in Kenneth M. Setton, ed., *A History of the Crusades*, 6 vols. (Madison, 1955-89); on the historiography, see Christopher Tyerman, *The Invention of the Crusades* (Toronto, 1998).

46 William L. Langer, ed., *An Encyclopedia of World History* (London, 1987), quote on 274. A dated reference work, *Raum und Bevölkerung in der Weltgeschichte (Bevölkerungs-Ploetz)*, 2 vols. (1955), gives 1.1 million departures from Europe with 0.5 million arrivals in Palestine (2:18). Josiah C. Russell, "The Population of the Crusader States," in Setton, *Crusades*, 5:295-314. On the little-studied social impact of the crusades, see Simon Lloyd, *English Society and the Crusades, 1216-1307* (Oxford, 1988).

47 Although only men are mentioned specifically, this figure no doubt included women. Information from Schiffahrts-Museum, Regensburg. Fernand Braudel, *The Mediterranean and the Mediterranean World in the Age of Philip II*, 2 vols. trans. Siân Reynolds (French orig., 1949; 2d rev. ed., Paris, 1966; New York, 1972), 1:146-47, 2:1081.

48 Edwin Pears, *The Fall of Constantinople: Being the Story of the Fourth Crusade* (1885; repr., New York, 1975), 380; Lewis, *Nomads and Crusaders*, 127; Riley-Smith, *Atlas of the Crusades*, 84–85; Abu-Lughod, *Before European Hegemony*, 109–11.

49 Riley-Smith, *Atlas of the Crusades*, 82, 88; Philippe Contamine, *War in the Middle Ages*, trans. Michael Jones (French orig., 1980; Oxford, 1984), 74–77; Lewis, *Nomads and Crusaders*, 101–6, 126; James A. Brundage, "Prostitution, Miscegenation, and Sexual Purity in the First Crusade," in Peter W. Edbury, ed., *Crusade and Settlement: Papers Read at the First Conference of the Society for the Study of Crusades and the Latin East and Presented to R. C. Smail* (Cardiff, 1985), 57–65; Régine Pernoud, *La femme au temps des croisades* (Paris, 1990); Amin Maalouf, *The Crusades through Arab Eyes*, trans. Jon Rothschild (French orig., Paris, 1983; London, 1984), 19.

50 The conquerors and the conquered—the exploiters and the exploited—are contrasted in Joshua Prawer, *The Latin Kingdom of Jerusalem: European Colonialism in the Middle Ages* (London, 1972), 506; Carlo M. Cipolla, *Before the Industrial Revolution: European Society and Economy, 1000–1700* (2d ed., New York, 1980), 206; Abu-Lughod, *Before European Hegemony*, 105–8.

51 Prawer, *Latin Kingdom*, 48–63, 68–70, 233–51; Maalouf, *Crusades through Arab Eyes*, 50–51, 196–200; Riley-Smith, *Atlas of the Crusades*, 29–30, 40–41; Burman, *World before Columbus*, quote on 28; William of Tyre, *A History of Deeds Done beyond the Sea*, trans. from the French by Emily A. Babcock and A. C. Krey, 2 vols. (Latin orig.; New York, 1943), 1:507–8; Meron Benvenisti, *The Crusaders in the Holy Land*, trans. Pamela Fitton (Hebrew orig.; Jerusalem, 1970), 17–21. Peasants rose against the Franks in 1113 and 1182–83.

52 Aziz S. Atiya, *Crusade, Commerce and Culture* (Bloomington, Ind., 1962); Vladimir P. Goss and Christine V. Bornstein, eds., *The Meeting of Two Worlds: Cultural Exchange between East and West during the Period of the Crusades* (Kalamazoo, Mich., 1986); R. C. Smail, *Crusading Warfare (1097–1193)* (Cambridge, 1956), chap. 3. The analysis of acculturation was penned by William, born in 1130 and archbishop of Tyre from 1175 onward, who spoke French, Latin, Greek, Arabic, and, perhaps, Hebrew and Persian. He consulted Arab sources for his history of Syria and had an understanding of Islamic customs and religion. Burman, *World before Columbus*, 28–29. Hans E. Mayer, ed., *Die Kreuzfahrerstaaten als multikulturelle Gesellschaft: Einwanderer und Minderheiten im 12. und 13. Jahrhundert* (Munich, 1997).

53 Burman, *World before Columbus*, quote on 30–31; Prawer, *Latin Kingdom*, 513; Labib, *Handelsgeschichte Ägyptens*, 64–121.

54 F. E. Peters, *Jerusalem and Mecca: The Typology of the Holy City in the Near East* (New York, 1986), 44–45 (quoting a Muslim account); D. J. Hall, *English Mediaeval Pilgrimage* (London, 1965), 17; Heath, *In the Steps*, 26; Burman, *World before Columbus*, 28; Dunn, *Ibn Battuta*, 70–71, 106.

55 Riley-Smith, *Atlas of the Crusades*, 54, 74, 102; Burman, *World before Columbus*, 32–33; Lewis, *Muslim Discovery of Europe*, 195–98. For the other end of the Mediterranean world, see David Waines, "The Culinary Culture of al-Andalus," in Salma K. Jayyusi, ed., *The Legacy of Muslim Spain*, 2 vols. (2d ed., Leiden, 1994), 2:725–38.

56 Iris Origo, "The Domestic Enemy: Eastern Slaves in Tuscany in the Fourteenth and Fifteenth Centuries," *Speculum* 30 (1955): 321–66, quote on 325; P. Lambrechts, "Le commerce des Syriens en Gaule," *L'antiquité classique* 6 (1937): 35–62; Yves Lequin, ed., *La mosaïque*

France: Histoire des étrangers et de l'immigration (Paris, 1988), 104; Jayyusi, *Legacy*, 1:3–87, 2:679–708, 2:741–58.

57 Lee Anne Durham Seminario, *The History of the Blacks, the Jews and the Moors in Spain* (Madrid, 1975), 73–78; Evariste Lévi-Provençal, *La civilisation arabe en Espagne* (3d edition, Paris, 1961).

58 Hermann Kellenbenz, ed., *Handbuch der europäischen Wirtschafts- und Sozialgeschichte*, 6 vols. (Stuttgart, 1980), 2:342; Jayyusi, *Legacy*, 1:14–15, and Expiración García Sánchez, "Agriculture in Muslim Spain," in Jayyusi, *Legacy*, 2:987–99; L. P. Harvey, *Islamic Spain, 1250 to 1500* (Chicago, 1990), 5–14.

59 Harvey, *Islamic Spain*, 1–5; see the essays by Mikel de Epalza, Margarita López Gómez, L. P. Harvey, and Raymond P. Scheindlin in Jayyusi, *Legacy*, 1:149–234. Cross-religious political and military alliances were possible, as when Muslim governors called for aid to Charlemagne against the Muslim caliph.

60 María J. Viguera, "On the Social Status of Andalusi Women," in Jayyusi, *Legacy*, 2:709–24; Durham Seminario, *Blacks, Jews and Moors*, 79–80.

61 Other texts mention 23,000 families.

62 This number probably included peasant families outside the city. After the Christian conquest in 1226, the city became nearly vacant. By 1530 it had perhaps 150,000 inhabitants. John Edwards, *Christian Córdoba: The City and Its Region in the Late Middle Ages* (Cambridge, 1982), 6–10.

63 Robert Hillenbrand, "'The Ornament of the World': Medieval Córdoba as a Cultural Center," in Jayyusi, *Legacy*, 1:112–35, and the section "Art and Architecture," in Jayyusi, *Legacy*, 2:583–676; Daniel, *Arabs and Mediaeval Europe*, 80–112. Berber raids reduced much of the grandeur as early as the eleventh century; Kellenbenz, *Handbuch*, 2:24–30.

64 Pierre Guichard, "The Social History of Muslim Spain," in Jayyusi, *Legacy*, 2:679–708.

65 Some estimates are as high as eleven million in the eighth century and fifteen million in the tenth century. Harvey, *Islamic Spain*, 5–9, 14.

66 The Almoravids came at the end of the eleventh century; Almohads in the mid-twelfth century.

67 Opposition to the policy came from Alfonso's wife, Queen Constance, and Archbishop Bernard, among others. Both were immigrants from France, as contemporaries noted with disdain: religious and other conflicts were ethnicized.

68 Charles H. Haskins, "The Renaissance of the Twelfth Century," in Archibald R. Lewis, ed., *The Islamic World and the West*, A.D. 622–1492 (New York, 1970), 78–86; Burman, *World before Columbus*, 26, 38–41; Abu-Lughod, *Before European Hegemony*, 20–24.

69 Harvey, *Islamic Spain*, 14–15. On the city of Granada, see James Dickie, "Granada: A Case Study of Arab Urbanism in Muslim Spain," in Jayyusi, *Legacy*, 1:88–111.

70 MacKay, *Spain in the Middle Ages*, 15–18, 45–57, 211.

71 John D. Latham, "Towards a Study of Andalusian Immigration and Its Place in Tunisian History," *Cahiers de Tunisie* 5 (1957): 203–52; Harvey, *Islamic Spain*, 55–63, 118–37; Robert I. Burns, "The Language Barrier: The Problem of Bilingualism and Muslim-Christian Interchange in the Medieval Kingdom of Valencia," in Mario Vassallo, ed., *Contributions to Mediterranean Studies* (Valletta, Malta, 1977), 116–36, and Burns, "Societies in Symbiosis: The Mujedar-Crusader Experience in Thirteenth-Century Spain," *International History Review* 2 (1980): 349–85, and Burns, "Immigrants from Islam: The Crusaders' Use of Mus-

lims as Settlers in Thirteenth-Century Spain," *American Historical Review* 80 (1975): 21–42; Thomas F. Glick and Oriol P. Sunyer, "Acculturation as an Explanatory Concept in Spanish History," *Comparative Studies in Society and History* 11 (1969): 136–54; Braudel, *The Mediterranean,* 2:780–92; MacKay, *Spain in the Middle Ages,* 36–45.

72 Harvey, *Islamic Spain,* 15–16.

73 MacKay, *Spain in the Middle Ages,* 40.

74 Ibid., 36–45, 58–70; Michael R. Weisser, *The Peasants of the Montes: The Roots of Rural Rebellion in Spain* (Chicago, 1976), 4–5; Hermann Kellenbenz, ed., *Fremde Kaufleute auf der iberischen Halbinsel* (Cologne, 1970). The *repartimiento* decrees dividing the spoils permit a reconstruction of some of the population shifts.

75 Walter Schlesinger has discussed the ideological components of the historiography of the eastward moves in "Die geschichtliche Stellung der mittelalterlichen deutschen Ostbewegung," *Historische Zeitschrift* 183 (1957): 517–42. Walter Kuhn, "Die deutsche Ostsiedlung vom Mittelalter bis zum 18. Jahrhundert" in Göttinger Arbeitskreis, ed., *Das östliche Deutschland: Ein Handbuch* (Würzburg, 1959), 165–283; Charles Higounet, *Die deutsche Ostsiedlung im Mittelalter* (Berlin, 1986).

76 Michael Burleigh, *Prussian Society and the German Order: An Aristocratic Corporation in Crisis, 1410–1466* (Cambridge, 1984); Eric Christiansen, *The Northern Crusades: The Baltic and Catholic Frontier, 1100–1525* (London, 1980); Helen Nicholson, *Templars, Hospitallers, and Teutonic Knights: Images of the Military Orders, 1128–1291* (Leicester, N.Y., 1993); Werner Paravicini, "L'Ordre teutonique et les courants migratoires en Europe centrale, XIIIe–XIVe siècles," in Simonetta Cavaciocchi, ed., *Le migrazioni in Europa secc. XIII–XVIII* (Florence, 1994), 311–24.

77 Jacques Le Goff, *Das Hochmittelalter* (Fischer Weltgeschichte, vol. 11; Frankfurt/Main, 1965), 56–59. In the southern Balkans and on the Russian plains, further eastward migrations followed upon retraction of the Ottoman Empire after 1600 (chap. 13.2).

78 Depending on the ethnic composition of new settlements, holdings were measured in Frankish or Flemish *Hufen.* On Flemish emigrations, see Jan A. van Houtte, *An Economic History of the Low Countries, 800–1800* (London, 1977), 61. Klaus J. Bade, ed., *Deutsche im Ausland — Fremde in Deutschland: Migration in Geschichte und Gegenwart* (Munich, 1992), 29ff.; Carl Göllner, ed., *Geschichte der Deutschen auf dem Gebiete Rumäniens,* vol. 1: *12. Jahrhundert bis 1848* (Bucharest, 1979); Ernst Wagner, *Geschichte der Siebenbürger Sachsen: Ein Überblick* (3d ed., Innsbruck, 1963); Immo Eberl, ed., *Die Donauschwaben: Deutsche Siedlungen in Südosteuropa* (Stuttgart, 1983). See Bade, *Deutsche,* 466ff., for further literature.

79 *Cambridge Economic History of Europe,* vol. 1: M. M. Postan and H. J. Habakkuk, eds., *The Agrarian Life of the Middle Ages* (2d ed., Cambridge, 1966), 449–86; Kellenbenz, *Handbuch,* 2:27–28, 510–15. A third group of newcomers were miners who concentrated in the Sudeten and Carpathian mountains, in Upper (Slovakian) and Lower Hungarian mining towns (chap. 3.3). Ethnic strife occurred between Czechs and Germans during the Hussite wars at the beginning of the fifteenth century (chap. 4). The German influence lasted into the nineteenth century. Dirk Hoerder with Inge Blank, "Ethnic and National Consciousness from the Enlightenment to the 1880s," in Hoerder and Blank, eds., *Roots of the Transplanted,* 2 vols. (New York, 1994), 1:37–110.

80 In terms of population history, "Europe" excludes the Russian territories beginning at an imaginary boundary that approximates the post-1945 western border of the Soviet Union.

81 Since population records for the whole of Europe are not available, all estimates are based on regional or local sources. Jan de Vries, "Population," in Brady et al., *Handbook of European History*, 1:1–50. J. C. Russell, "Population in Europe 500–1500," in Carlo M. Cipolla, ed., *The Fontana Economic History of Europe*, 6 vols. (London, 1972), 1:40, 45, 50; David B. Grigg, *Population Growth and Agrarian Change: An Historical Perspective* (Cambridge, 1980), 54–61; Thomas McKeown, *The Modern Rise of Population* (New York, 1976), 1–5.

82 Brady et al., *Handbook of European History*, 1:15–17, 342.

83 De Vries, "Population," 18–37. Biologically and medically, the impact of breastfeeding has not been substantiated. The impact of spacing is obvious for survival of children because each infant can receive more care.

84 Merry E. Wiesner, "Family, Household, and Community," in Brady et al., *Handbook of European History*, 1:55–68; Edith Ennen, *Frauen im Mittelalter* (Munich, 1984).

85 Russell, "Population," 40–41, 51–54. Warm spells—for example, around 1200—permitted the growing of olive trees in England and fig trees in Germany, but they also permitted malaria to reach France. The concept of a "Little Ice Age," developed by G. Utterström, has been criticized by Emmanuel Le Roy Ladurie (*Histoire du climat depuis l'an mil*, Paris, 1967), who argues that the cold periods extended from 1215 to 1350 and from 1590 to 1850. Patrick R. Galloway, "Long-Term Fluctuations in Climate and Population in the Preindustrial Era," *Population and Development Review* 12, 1 (1986): 1–24.

86 John Walter and Roger Schofield, eds., *Famine, Disease and the Social Order in Early Modern Society* (Cambridge, 1989), 27–28, 123–24; Brian Pullan, "Wage Earners and the Venetian Economy, 1550–1630," *Economic History Review*, 2d ser., 16 (1964), reprinted in Pullan, ed., *Crisis and Change in the Venetian Economy in the Sixteenth and Seventeenth Centuries* (London, 1968), 146–74, esp. 161.

87 David Herlihy, *The Black Death and the Transformation of the West*, ed. Samuel K. Cohn Jr. (Cambridge, Mass., 1997). See, for example, for the French case, the essays by Henri Dubois, "La dépression (XIVe et XVe siècles)," and by Arlette Higounet-Nadal, "Le relèvement," in Jacques Dupâquier et al., *Histoire de la population française*, vol. 1: *Des origines à la Renaissance* (Paris, 1988), 313–420; Russell, "Population," 41, 55.

3 Continuities: Mobility and Migration from the Eleventh to the Sixteenth Century

1 *Viator: Medieval and Renaissance Studies* 1 (1970): quote from preface. For important introductions to medieval migrations, see Gerhard Jaritz and Albert Müller, eds., *Migration in der Feudalgesellschaft* (Frankfurt/Main, 1988), and Simonetta Cavaciocchi, ed., *Le migrazioni in Europa secc. XIII–XVIII* (Florence, 1994).

2 Ernst Schubert, "Fremde im mittelalterlichen Deutschland," *IMIS-Beiträge* (Univ. Osnabrück) 7 (1998): 7–33; Peter Laslett, Karla Oosterveen, and Richard M. Smith, eds., *Bastardy and Its Comparative History* (Cambridge, Mass., 1980); Archibald R. Lewis, *Nomads and Crusaders, A.D. 1000–1368* (Bloomington, Ind., 1988), 113–93.

3 Antoni Maczak, *Travel in Early Modern Europe*, trans. Ursula Phillips (Polish orig., 1980; Oxford, 1994); J. J. Jusserand, *English Wayfaring Life in the Middle Ages (XIVth Century)*, trans. Lucy T. Smith (London, 1889; 2d ed., 1920), 24–138; Norbert Ohler, *The Medieval Traveller*, trans. Caroline Hillier (German orig., 1986; Woodbridge, U.K., 1989); Margaret W. Labarge, *Medieval Travellers: The Rich and Restless* (London, 1982); Xenja von Ertzdorff

and Dieter Neukirch, eds., *Reisen und Reiseliteratur im Mittelalter und in der frühen Neuzeit* (Amsterdam, 1992); Lorenzo Camusso, *Travel Guide to Europe 1492: Ten Itineraries in the Old World*, trans. Jay Hyams and Sarah Hilditch (Italian orig., 1990; New York, 1992); Irene Erfen and Karl-Heinz Spieß, eds., *Fremdheit und Reisen im Mittelalter* (Stuttgart, 1997); Christopher Dyer, *Standards of Living in the Later Middle Ages: Social Change in England c.1200-1520* (Cambridge, 1989), 54, 73; J. R. Hale, *Renaissance Europe: Individual and Society, 1480-1520* (1st ed., 1971; Berkeley, 1977), 115.

4 Shulamith Shahar, *The Fourth Estate: A History of Women in the Middle Ages*, trans. Chaya Galai (Hebrew orig., 1981; London, 1983), 126-73; Dyer, *Standards of Living*, 50-54, 99; Labarge, *Medieval Travellers*, 52-67.

5 During the Hundred Years' War (1338-1453), the invasion of Normandy in 1346 involved 100,000 troops. To call it an "English-French" war imposes the terminology of an era of nation-states onto dynastic states. Guy Llewelyn Thompson, *Paris and Its People under English Rule: The Anglo-Burgundian Regime, 1420-1436* (Oxford, 1991), 206-24.

6 John W. Bernhardt, *Itinerant Kingship and Royal Monasteries in Early Medieval Germany, c.936-1075* (Cambridge, 1993); Elsbeth Andre, *Ein Königshof auf Reisen: Der Kontinentalaufenthalt Eduards III. von England 1338-1340* (Vienna, 1996); Antonio Rumeu de Armas, *Itinerario de los Reyes Católicos 1474-1516* (Madrid, 1974). For princes and bishops visiting Vienna, see Ferdinand Opll, *Nachrichten aus dem mittelalterlichen Wien: Zeitgenossen berichten* (Vienna, 1995). Labarge, *Medieval Travellers*, 33-51.

7 Carol Neel, "The Origins of the Beguines," in Judith M. Bennett et al., eds., *Sisters and Workers in the Middle Ages* (Chicago, 1989), 240-60; C. H. Lawrence, *The Friars: The Impact of the Early Mendicant Movement on Western Society* (London, 1994).

8 Benjamin Z. Kedar, "The Genoese Notaries of 1382: The Anatomy of an Urban Occupational Group," in Harry A. Miskimin, David Herlihy, and A. L. Udovitch, eds., *The Medieval City* (New Haven, 1977), 73-94.

9 For compelled migrations during the Hundred Years' War, see Jacques Dupâquier et al., *Histoire de la population française*, vol. 1: *Des origines à la Renaissance* (Paris, 1988), 407-9; Christopher Allmand, *The Hundred Years War: England and France at War c.1300-c.1450* (Cambridge, 1988), 58, 73; Nicholas Wright, *Knights and Peasants: The Hundred Years War in the French Countryside* (Woodbridge, U.K., 1998); Michael Mallett, *Mercenaries and Their Masters: Warfare in Renaissance Italy* (London, 1974), 207-30.

10 Fritz Redlich contrasted an early "sedentary type" of mercenary, who returned home regularly, with a sixteenth-century "uprooted" type. *The German Military Enterpriser and His Work Force: A Study in European Economic and Social History*, 2 vols. (Wiesbaden, 1964-65), 1:115-41, 454-532, 2:170-277; Richard A. Preston, Alex Roland, and Sydney F. Wise, *Men in Arms: A History of Warfare and Its Interrelationships with Western Society* (5th ed., Fort Worth, 1991), 92; Philippe Contamine, *War in the Middle Ages*, trans. Michael Jones (French orig., 1980; Oxford, 1984), 239-42; Fernand Braudel, *The Mediterranean and the Mediterranean World in the Age of Philip II*, 2 vols., trans. Siân Reynolds (French orig., 1949; 2d rev. French ed., 1966; New York, 1972), 1:1051. Supernumerary sons of the Mecklenburg lower gentry became buccaneers on the Baltic Sea harassing Hansa merchants. André Corvisier, *Armies and Societies in Europe, 1494-1789*, trans. Abigail T. Siddall (French orig., 1976; Bloomington, Ind., 1979), 143-48, 174-76, discusses recruitment patterns as regards gender, class, and regional origin.

11 *Raum und Bevölkerung in der Weltgeschichte (Bevölkerungs-Ploetz)*, 4 vols. (Würzburg,

1965–68), 2:42–43. The Swiss population increased from 0.8 million in 1500 to 1.2 million in 1700; a remnant of the tradition of pikemen leaving Swiss cantons can be found in today's Swiss Guard of the Vatican. Walter Schaufelberger, *Der alte Schweizer und sein Krieg: Studien zur Kriegsführung vornehmlich im 15. Jahrhundert* (Zurich, 1952); Contamine, *War in the Middle Ages*, 135, 158–61, 242–49; Preston et al., *Men in Arms*, 75–82, 90–91; Michael Howard, *War in European History* (London, 1976), 38–41; Thompson, *Paris and Its People under English Rule*, 206–24.

12 Gilbert J. Millar, *Tudor Mercenaries and Auxiliaries, 1485–1547* (Charlottesville, 1980), 19–20, 45–47, 193, quote on 145; Jonathan Israel, *The Dutch Republic: Its Rise, Greatness, and Fall, 1477–1806* (Oxford, 1995), 267–71; Robert C. Davis, *Shipbuilders of the Venetian Arsenal: Workers and Workplace in the Preindustrial City* (Baltimore, 1991), 89, 109; Geoffrey Parker, *The Army of Flanders and the Spanish Road, 1567–1659: The Logistics of Spanish Victory and Defeat in the Low Countries' Wars* (Cambridge, 1972), 25–59, 84–85, 197; Gráinne Henry, *The Irish Military Community in Spanish Flanders, 1586–1621* (Dublin, 1992); John McGurk, "Wild Geese: The Irish in European Armies (16th to 18th Centuries)," in Patrick O'Sullivan, ed., *The Irish World Wide: History, Heritage, Identity*, 6 vols., vol. 1: *Patterns of Migration* (London, 1992), 36–62.

13 Hermann Kellenbenz, ed., *Handbuch der europäischen Wirtschafts- und Sozialgeschichte*, 6 vols. (Stuttgart, 1980), 2:106–18; Carlo M. Cipolla, *Before the Industrial Revolution: European Society and Economy, 1000–1700* (2d ed., New York, 1980), 75–78; *Cambridge Economic History of Europe*, vol. 1: M. M. Postan, ed., *The Agrarian Life of the Middle Ages* (2d ed., Cambridge, 1966), 334–39 (subsequent citations to Postan volume are cited as vol. 1 of *Cambridge Economic History*).

14 Georges Duby, "Medieval Agriculture 900–1500," in Carlo M. Cipolla, ed., *The Fontana Economic History of Europe*, 6 vols. (Hassocks, U.K, 1976), 1:175–220; Werner Rösener, *The Peasantry of Europe*, trans. Thomas M. Barker (German orig., 1993; Oxford, 1994), and Rösener, *Peasants in the Middle Ages*, trans. Alexander Stützer (German orig., 1985; Urbana, Ill., 1992); Aaron J. Gurjewitsch, *Stumme Zeugen des Mittelalters: Weltbild und Kultur der einfachen Menschen*, trans. Ulrike Fromm (Russian orig., n.d.; Vienna, 1997); Wilhelm Abel, *Agricultural Fluctuations in Europe: From the Thirteenth to the Twentieth Centuries*, trans. Olive Ordish (3d rev. German ed., 1978; London, 1980), 111–12; J. A. Chartres, *Internal Trade in England 1500–1700* (London, 1977), 20ff.; Zs. P. Pach, "The Shifting of International Trade Routes in the 15th–17th Centuries," *Acta Historica Academiae Scientarium Hungaricae* 14 (1968): 302–8; *Cambridge Economic History*, 1:48; *Cambridge Economic History*, vol. 2: M. M. Postan and Edward Miller, eds., *Trade and Industry in the Middle Ages*, (2d ed., Cambridge, 1987), 357; *Cambridge Economic History*, vol. 3: M. M. Postan, E. E. Rich, and Edward Miller, eds., *Economic Organization and Policies in the Middle Ages* (Cambridge, 1963), 101–8; N. J. G. Pounds, *An Historical Geography of Europe* (Cambridge, 1990), 233.

15 Jonathan Riley-Smith, *Atlas of the Crusades* (London, 1991), 32–33, 40–41; *Cambridge Economic History*, 1:294–96.

16 *Cambridge Economic History*, 1:66–91; Michel Mollat, *Les pauvres au Moyen Âge: Étude sociale* (Paris, 1978), 205–8; Ian D. Whyte, "Migration in Early-Modern Scotland and England: A Comparative Perspective," in Colin G. Pooley and Whyte, eds., *Migrants, Emigrants, and Immigrants: A Social History of Migration* (London, 1991), 87–105.

17 *Cambridge Economic History*, 1:308–19, 322–34. Sir Thomas More, *Utopia* (Harmondsworth, 1965), 44–47.

18 David Herlihy and Christiane Klapisch-Zuber, *Tuscans and Their Families: A Study of the Florentine Catasto of 1427* (French orig., 1978; New Haven, 1985), 115–20; *Cambridge Economic History*, 1:342–48, 353–61; Braudel, *Mediterranean*, 1:416.

19 Christopher Dyer, *Everyday Life in Medieval England* (London, 1994), 2–42, 78, quotes on xiii–xiv. See also R. H. Hilton, *Bond Men Made Free: Medieval Peasant Movements and the English Rising of 1381* (London, 1973); John A. F. Thomson, *The Transformation of Medieval England, 1370–1529* (London, 1983), 40–46; E. Le Roy Ladurie, *Montaillou: Village occitan de 1294 à 1324* (Paris, 1975). Peasant decision making within the constraints of smallholdings, social values, and market forces is analyzed in Aleksandr V. Chayanov, *The Theory of Peasant Economy*, ed. Daniel Thorner, Basile Kerblay, and R. E. F. Smith (Russian orig., 1925; Homewood, Ill., 1966), and Witold Kula, *An Economic Theory of the Feudal System: Towards a Model of the Polish Economy, 1500–1800*, trans. Lawrence Garner (Polish orig., 1962; London, 1976). Georges Duby, *Rural Economy and Country Life in the Medieval West*, trans. Cynthia Postan (French orig., 1962; Columbia, S.C., 1968); Shahar, *The Fourth Estate*, 220–50.

20 Braudel, *Mediterranean*, 2:734–39; *Cambridge Economic History*, 1:695–740.

21 Andraés Kubinyi, "Horizontale Mobilität im spätmittelalterlichen Königreich Ungarn," in Jaritz and Müller, *Migration*, 113–39, esp. 120–31.

22 Jusserand, *Wayfaring*, quote on 265.

23 "Rolls of Parliament," ii. p. 340, C.E. 1376, quoted in Jusserand, *Wayfaring*, 269.

24 A. L. Beier, "Vagrants and the Social Order in Elizabethan England," *Past and Present* 64 (Aug. 1974): 14–17. For the European continent, see E. Perroy, "Wage Labour in France in the Later Middle Ages," and F. Graus, "The Late Medieval Poor in Town and Countryside," in Sylvia L. Thrupp, ed., *Change in Medieval Society: Europe North of the Alps, 1050–1500* (New York, 1964), 237–47 and 314–24; *Cambridge Economic History*, 1:654, 732; Abel, *Agricultural Fluctuations in Europe*, 156.

25 The literature is legion. Robert Vivier, "La grande ordonnance de Fevrier 1352: Les mesures anticorporatives et la liberté du travail," *Revue historique* 46 (1921): 201–14; Helen Robbins, "A Comparison of the Effects of the Black Death on the Economic Organization of France and England," *Journal of Political Economy* 36 (1928): 447–79; Jacques Le Goff, "Le temps du travail dans la crise du XIVe siècle," *Moyen Âge* 69 (1963): 597–613; William M. Bowsky, "The Impact of the Black Death upon Sienese [Italy] Government and Society," *Speculum* 39 (1964): 1–34, esp. 24.

26 Robert W. Scribner, "Mobility: Voluntary or Enforced? Vagrants in Württemberg in the Sixteenth Century," in Jaritz and Müller, *Migration*, 65–88; A. L. Beier, *Masterless Men: The Vagrancy Problem in England, 1560–1640* (London, 1985), 3–13 (the Beier volume is also about "masterless women"); John Pound, *Poverty and Vagrancy in Tudor England* (1971; 2d ed., London, 1986), 42–55. Brian Pullan, *Rich and Poor in Renaissance Venice: The Social Institutions of a Catholic State, to 1620* (Oxford, 1971), 239–326; Duby, *Rural Economy*, 293–311.

27 14 Eliz. ch. v. "Statutes," vol. iv. part i. pp. 590ff., quoted in Jusserand, *Wayfaring*, 236. Paul Slack, *The English Poor Law, 1531–1782* (Cambridge, 1995).

28 Scribner, "Mobility," 67–69. See also Bernd Roeck, *Außenseiter, Randgruppen, Minderheiten: Fremde im Deutschland der fühen Neuzeit* (Göttingen, 1993), 66–80, 119–31; Beier, *Masterless Men*, 123–45.

29 Beier, *Masterless Men*, quote on 3, 14–28. Esther Cohen, "Le vagabondage à Paris au XIVe

siècle," *Moyen Âge* 88 (1982): 293–313. On poor migrants in Lyon, see Natalie Zemon Davis, *Society and Culture in Early Modern France: Eight Essays* (Stanford, 1975), 49–51.

30 Pound, *Poverty and Vagrancy*, 1–22, also discusses inflation, harvest failures, and the disso-lution of monasteries; Patrick Fitzgerald, " 'Like Crickets to the Crevice of a Brew-house': Poor Irish Migrants in England, 1560–1640," in O'Sullivan, *The Irish World Wide*, 1:13–35.

31 Braudel, *Mediterranean*, 2:739–43; Beier, *Masterless Men*, 29–48. Noah Gordon's novel *The Physician* (New York, 1986) describes the world of traveling healers.

32 Tessa Watt, *Cheap Print and Popular Piety, 1550–1640* (Cambridge, 1991), 11–23; Beier, *Masterless Men*, 86–106; Gerald Strauss, *Nuremberg in the Sixteenth Century* (New York, 1966), 210.

33 Beier, "Vagrants," 18–19; Bronislaw Geremek, *The Margins of Society in Late Medieval Paris*, trans. Jean Birrell (Polish orig., 1971; New York, 1987), 29–43, 135–60, 242–55. For subse-quent centuries, see Arlette Farge, *Vivre dans la rue à Paris au XVIIIe siècle* (Paris, 1979); Robert Jütte, *Poverty and Deviance in Early Modern Europe* (Cambridge, 1994), 146–50.

34 Peter Laslett, *Family Life and Illicit Love in Earlier Generations: Essays in Historical Soci-ology* (Cambridge, 1977), 68–83, 98–101; Robert Fossier, *La terre et les hommes en Picardie jusqu' à la fin du XIIIe siècle*, 2 vols. (Paris, 1968), 1:275–96, 2: 571–602; Jean-Marie Con-stant, *Nobles et paysans en Beauce aux XVIe et XVIIe siècles* (Lille, 1981), 74–103; Kellen-benz, *Wirtschafts- und Sozialgeschichte*, 2:26–27. Venetian unskilled workers came in chain migrations from Bergamo province across a distance of around 200 kilometers. Brian Pullan, "Wage Earners and the Venetian Economy, 1550–1630," (1964), repr. in Pullan, ed., *Crisis and Change in the Venetian Economy in the Sixteenth and Seventeenth Centuries* (London, 1968), 159; Jean P. Poussou, "De l'intérêt de l'étude historique des mouvements migratoires européens du milieu du Moyen Âge à la fin du XIXe siècle," in Cavaciocchi, *Migrazioni in Europa*, 33; Sune Åkerman, Hans C. Johansen, and Robert Ostergren, "Long-Distance Migration in Scandinavia, 1500–1900," paper for the 17th International Congress of the Historical Sciences (Madrid, 1990), quote on 53.

35 Paul M. Hohenberg and Lynn Hollen Lees, *The Making of Urban Europe, 1000–1950* (Cam-bridge, Mass., 1985), 74–98; Pounds, *Historical Geography*, 220–28; Robert S. Lopez, *The Commercial Revolution of the Middle Ages, 950–1350* (London, 1971), 60–136; Pach, "Inter-national Trade Routes," 287–321; *Cambridge Economic History*, vol. 3, esp. R. de Roover, "The Organization of Trade"; O. Verlinden, "Markets and Fairs"; and Sylvia Thrupp, "The Guilds." Cipolla, *Fontana Economic History of Europe*, 1:32–34.

36 Purchases by a Lyon noblewoman included goods from the whole of the Eurasian economic network; Hale, *Renaissance Europe*, 35–36. Leipzig merchants had correspondents across the continent. Fritz Lendenmann, *Schweizer Handelsleute in Leipzig* (Bern, 1978), 3–18; Nils Brübach, *Die Reichsmessen von Frankfurt am Main, Leipzig und Braunschweig (14. bis 18. Jahrhundert)* (Stuttgart, 1994); F. W. Carter, *Trade and Urban Development in Poland: An Economic Geography of Cracow, from Its Origins to 1795* (Cambridge, 1994), 53–55, 126–28.

37 Susan M. Stuard, *A State of Deference: Ragusa/Dubrovnik in the Medieval Centuries* (Phila-delphia, 1992), 172–73; Riccardo Calimani, *The Ghetto of Venice*, trans. K. S. Wolfthal (Ital-ian orig., 1985; New York 1987); *Cambridge Economic History*, quotes on 2:347.

38 Jacques Le Goff, "The Town as an Agent of Civilization, 1200–1500," in Cipolla, *Fontana Economic History of Europe*, 1:76–79; Frédéric Mauro, "Merchant Communities, 1350–1750," in James D. Tracy, ed., *The Rise of Merchant Empires: Long-Distance Trade in the Early Modern World, 1350–1750* (Cambridge, 1990), 255–86; J. A. Goris, *Étude sur les colonies*

marchandes méridionales à Anvers, 1477–1567 (Louvain, 1925); Subhi Y. Labib, *Handels-geschichte Ägyptens im Spätmittelalter (1171–1517)* (Wiesbaden, 1965), 163–233, 286–336.

39 *Cambridge Economic History*, 2:351; Janet L. Abu-Lughod, *Before European Hegemony: The World System A.D. 1250–1350* (New York, 1989), 108–9.

40 Klaus Friedland, *Die Hanse* (Stuttgart, 1991); Philippe Dollinger, *La Hanse (XIIe–XVIIe siècles)* (Paris, 1964); Volker Henn and Arnved Nedkvitne, eds., *Norwegen und die Hanse* (Frankfurt/Main, 1994); T. H. Lloyd, *England and the German Hanse, 1157–1611* (Cambridge, 1991); Wilhelm Koppe, *Lübeck-Stockholmer Handelsgeschichte im 14. Jahrhundert* (Neu-münster, 1933), 104–8, 242–64.

41 S. R. Epstein, "Regional Fairs, Institutional Innovation, and Economic Growth in Late Medi-eval Europe," *Economic History Review* 47 (1994): 459–83; *Cambridge Economic History*, 2:357, 3:101–5, 108.

42 Baron von Meyendorff, "Trade and Communication in Eastern Europe, A.D. 800–1200," in Arthur P. Newton, ed., *Travel and Travellers of the Middle Ages* (London, 1926); Paul Bush-kovitch, *The Merchants of Moscow, 1580–1680* (Cambridge, 1980), 6–69; Henrik Birnbaum, "On Some Evidence of Jewish Life and Anti-Jewish Sentiments in Medieval Russia," *Viator* 4 (1973): 225–55.

43 *Cambridge Economic History*, 3:119–53; Abu-Lughod, *Before European Hegemony*, 55–75. For fifteenth- and sixteenth-century Spain, see Hermann Kellenbenz, ed., *Fremde Kaufleute auf der iberischen Halbinsel* (Cologne, 1970).

44 *Cambridge Economic History*, 3:72, 98, 100–101, 357–59; Michael E. Mallett, *The Floren-tine Galleys in the Fifteenth Century* (Oxford, 1967), 29–57; *Cambridge Economic History*, 2:354.

45 George D. Ramsay, *English Overseas Trade during the Centuries of Emergence* (London, 1957); Kenneth R. Andrews, *Trade, Plunder and Settlement: Maritime Enterprise and the Genesis of the British Empire, 1480–1630* (Cambridge, 1984), 41–100; Mary Prior, "Women and the Urban Economy: Oxford 1500–1800," in Prior, ed., *Women in English Society, 1500–1800* (London, 1985), 98–105; quote from Mary Ashraf, ed., *Political Verse and Song from Britain and Ireland* (Berlin, 1975), 40; Sylvia L. Thrupp, *The Merchant Class of Medieval London, 1300–1500* (Chicago, 1948), quote p. 208.

46 Kubinyi, "Horizontale Mobilität," 120–31.

47 Stuard, *Ragusa/Dubrovnik*, 102–3.

48 Herlihy and Klapisch-Zuber, *Tuscans*, 108–20, 136, 151–57, 201, 224. Linda Martz, *Poverty and Welfare in Habsburg Spain: The Example of Toledo* (Cambridge, 1983), 4–5, 12–13; Michael R. Weisser, *The Peasants of the Montes: The Roots of Rural Rebellion in Spain* (Chi-cago, 1976), 78–80.

49 Diane O. Hughes, "Kinsmen and Neighbors in Medieval Genoa," in Miskimin et al., *Medi-eval City*, 95–111; Richard A. Goldthwaite, *The Building of Renaissance Florence: An Eco-nomic and Social History* (Baltimore, 1980), 242–86, 363, 386.

50 Braudel, *Mediterranean*, 1:334–41, quote p. 336.

51 In the eighteenth century, craftsmen and merchants were mostly of German origin; workers and marginal artisans were of Bosnian background. Nineteenth-century industrialization brought Moravian, Bohemian, Carniolan (Krainian), Styrian, Serbian, Croatian, Tyrolean, Carinthian, Italian, and German workers. Catholic Croatian Bosnians, Bunjeci from the Voj-vodina, and Germans from Swabia had settled in rural colonies nearby. Gyözö Bezerédy, *Pécs* (Pécs, 1986).

52 Herlihy and Klapisch-Zuber, *Tuscans*, 13, 136, 151–52.

53 Mollat, *Les pauvres au Moyen Âge*, 205–20; Robert A. Schneider, *Public Life in Tou-louse, 1463–1789: From Municipal Republic to Cosmopolitan City* (Ithaca, 1989), 296–97; Erich Maschke and Jürgen Sydow, eds., *Gesellschaftliche Unterschichten in den südwest-deutschen Städten* (Stuttgart, 1967), 1–74; Thomas Fischer, *Städtische Armut und Armen-fürsorge im 15. und 16. Jahrhundert* (Göttingen, 1979), 155–75; Sherrill Cohen, "Asylums for Women in Counter-Reformation Italy," in Sherrin Marshall, ed., *Women in Reformation and Counter-Reformation Europe: Private and Public Worlds* (Bloomington, 1989), 166–88. Pullan, *Rich and Poor*, 243–48.

54 Extremely useful is Wilfried Reininghaus, *Die Entstehung der Gesellengilden im Spät-mittelalter* (Wiesbaden, 1981). See also his essay in Jaritz and Müller, *Migration*, 179–215, and his "Die Migration der Handwerksgesellen," *Vierteljahrschrift für Sozial- und Wirtschaftsgeschichte* 68 (1981): 1–21. Kurt Wesoly, *Lehrlinge und Handwerksgesellen am Mittelrhein* (Frankfurt/Main, 1985); Knut Schulz, *Handwerksgesellen und Lohnarbeiter* (Sigmaringen, 1985); Helmut Bräuer, "Probleme der Migration von Handwerkern und Ge-sellen während des Spätmittelalters und in der frühen Neuzeit," *Beiträge zur historischen Sozialforschung* 19 (1989): 78–84; Rainer S. Elkar, ed., *Deutsches Handwerk in Spätmittel-alter und Früher Neuzeit* (Göttingen, 1983); Alfred Doren, *Deutsche Handwerker und Hand-werkerbruderschaften im mittelalterlichen Italien* (Berlin, 1903), 85.

55 The only constant seems to have been that whatever happened to be women's work at a particular time, it was considered unskilled. Merry E. Wiesner, "Guilds, Male Bonding and Women's Work in Early Modern Germany," *Gender and History* 1 (1989): 125–37, and, Wies-ner, "*Wandervogels* and Women: Journeymen's Concepts of Masculinity in Early Modern Germany," *Journal of Social History* 24 (1990): 767–82.

56 J. C. Russell, "Population in Europe 500–1500," in Cipolla, *Fontana Economic History of Europe*, 1:50. Susan Bridgen, "Youth and English Reformation," and Steven R. Smith, "The London Apprentices as Seventeenth-Century Adolescents," in Paul Slack, ed., *Rebellion, Popular Protest and the Social Order in Early Modern England* (Cambridge, 1984), 83–87 and 219–31.

57 Margret Wensky, *Die Stellung der Frau in der stadtkölnischen Wirtschaft im Spätmittel-alter* (Vienna, 1980), 113–62; Schulz, *Handwerksgesellen*, 39, 45, 282; Reininghaus, *Entste-hung*, 218–22, 225; Grethe Jacobsen, "Female Migration in the Late Medieval Town," in Jaritz and Müller, *Migration*, 43–55, quote on 52; Kurt Wesoly, "Der weibliche Bevölker-ungsanteil in spätmittelalterlichen und frühneuzeitlichen Städten und die Betätigung von Frauen im zünftigen Handwerk," *Zeitschrift für die Geschichte des Oberrheins* 128 (1980): 69–117. See also Perroy, "Wage Labour in France," 237–47.

58 In later centuries, the obligation to migrate became a requirement. The oversupply of labor was to be kept on the move, and journeymen were to be prevented from settling down and competing with guild-organized masters.

59 Jan A. van Houtte, *An Economic History of the Low Countries, 800–1800* (London, 1977), 61; Reininghaus, *Entstehung*, 49–50, 108–12, 158–61; Davis, *Society and Culture*, 21, 69; Cynthia M. Truant, "Solidarity and Symbolism among Journeymen Artisans: The Case of Compagnonnage," *Comparative Studies in Society and History* 21 (1979): 214–26.

60 By contrast, the Latin term *prostituere* means to offer oneself publicly. Jacques Rossiaud, "Prostitution, jeunesse et société dans les villes du Sud-Est au XVe siècle," *Annales: Écono-mies, sociétés, civilisation* 31 (1976): 303; Shahar, *The Fourth Estate*, 205–10.

61 Most of these songs date from the eighteenth and nineteenth centuries; only some have been traced to the sixteenth century. Oskar Schade, ed., *Deutsche Handwerkslieder* (Leipzig, 1865; repr., Wiesbaden, 1970), 105–88; Wolfgang Steinitz, ed., *Deutsche Volkslieder demokratischen Charakters aus sechs Jahrhunderten*, 2 vols. (Berlin, 1955–62), 1:191–225.

62 John Ashton, ed., *Real Sailor Songs* (London, 1891; repr., 1973), 31–32, 39, 55–56, 60. These songs also refer to forced migration by navy impressment (30–31). One song (39) takes up high mobility, construction of the Other, and the topic of female servants' dowries. Suzanne J. Stark, *Female Tars: Women Aboard Ship in the Age of Sail* (London, 1998); Margaret S. Creighton and Lisa Norling, eds., *Iron Men, Wooden Women: Gender and Seafaring in the Atlantic World, 1700–1920* (Baltimore, 1996).

63 Reininghaus, "Migration," 9–14; Schulz, *Handwerksgesellen*, 282–86. Since travel routes cannot be determined from the sources available, all distances given are as the crow flies. It is not clear whether journeymen stopped for work in between and moved in stages.

64 Braudel, *Mediterranean*, 433–35; George Unwin, *The Guilds and Companies of London* (London, 1908; repr., 1963), 2–5, 32–34, 243–55; Steven A. Epstein, *Wage Labor and Guilds in Medieval Europe* (Chapel Hill, 1991), 168–72, 232–47.

65 Schulz, *Handwerksgesellen*, 42, 357–61.

66 The secrets of their craft—that is, their expertise—and the rites of initiation brought forth a lore about what came to be called freemasonry. Scottish masons' lodges were probably at the origin of the history; English lodges developed a mythical trade history, the "Old Charges." The initiation of men from the middle classes changed the character of freemasonry, which spread to other countries.

67 Mathematical knowledge of skilled masons working on cathedral projects, for example, far surpassed that of students at Oxford or other universities. Reinhard Bentmann and Heinrich Lickes, *Kirchen des Mittelalters* (Wiesbaden, 1978), 60–114; Martin Warnke, *Bau und Überbau: Soziologie der mittelalterlichen Architektur* (Frankfurt/Main, 1976), 20–62; Georges Duby, *Le temps des cathédrales: L'art et la société, 980–1420* (Paris, 1976); Jean Gimpel, *The Cathedral Builders*, trans. Teresa Waugh (French orig., 1980; Engl. ed., 1988); Frances Gies and Joseph Gies, *Cathedral, Forge, and Waterwheel: Technology and Invention in the Middle Ages* (New York, 1994), 82–104, on the connection to Asian and Arab technology.

68 *Cambridge Economic History*, 2:768–87; R. A. Leeson, *Travelling Brothers: The Six Centuries' Road from Craft Fellowship to Trade Unionism* (London, 1979), 23–57, 74; Nicola Coldstream, *Masons and Sculptors* (Toronto, 1991), 15–20. For a detailed study of one region, see Donald Woodward, *Men at Work: Labourers and Building Craftsmen in the Towns of Northern England, 1450–1750* (Cambridge, 1995).

69 *Cambridge Economic History*, 2:691–761. The best survey is Karl-Heinz Ludwig and Raffaelo Vergani, "Mobilität und Migrationen der Bergleute vom 13. bis zum 17. Jahrhundert," in Cavaciocchi, *Migrazioni in Europa*, 595–96. See also the illustrated survey by Helmut Wilsdorf, *Kulturgeschichte des Bergbaus: Ein illustrierter Streifzug durch Zeiten und Kontinente* (Essen, 1987), 105, 161, plates 60–61. For the British Isles, see Bryan Earl, *Cornish Mining* (London, 1968), and Raphael Samuel, *Miners, Quarrymen, and Saltworkers* (London, 1977); Hans-Joachim Braun, *Technologische Beziehungen zwischen Deutschland und England von der Mitte des 17. bis zum Ausgang des 18. Jahrhunderts* (Düsseldorf, 1974), 14–16; Susan C. Karant-Nunn, "The Women of the Saxon Silver Mines," in Marshall, *Women in Reformation and Counter-Reformation Europe*, 29–46; Israel, *The Dutch Republic*, 271–75.

70 Constantin J. Jirecek, *Die Handelsstraßen und Bergwerke von Serbien und Bosnien während des Mittelalters* (Prague, 1879), 43–61; G. Baudisch, "Deutsche Bergbausiedlungen auf dem Balkan," *Südostdeutsches Archiv* 12 (1969): 32–61.

71 The number of active miners in the central German Mansfeld region, for example, fell from 2,000 to twenty-six.

72 According to a rule from earlier, prediasporic times, Jews were to visit Jerusalem at Passover, Shavuot, and Sukkot, whereas Muslims had to visit Mecca once in a lifetime. Surinder M. Bhardwaj and Gisbert Rinschede, eds., *Pilgrimage in World Religions* (Berlin, 1988); Dale F. Eickelman and James Piscatori, eds., *Muslim Travellers: Pilgrimage, Migration, and the Religious Imagination* (Berkeley, 1990); Susan Naquin and Chün-fang Yü, eds., *Pilgrims and Sacred Sites in China* (Berkeley, 1992); E. Alan Morinis, *Pilgrimage in the Hindu Tradition: A Case Study of West Bengal* (Delhi, 1984); Carol Iancu, "Les pèlerinages dans le judaïsme après 70 et dans Israel aujourd'hui," in Jean Chélini and Henry Branthomme, eds., *Les Chemins de Dieu: Histoire des pèlerinages chrétiens des origines à nos jours* (Paris, 1982), 345–64.

73 Victor W. Turner, "Pilgrimages as Social Processes," in Turner, ed., *Dramas, Fields, and Metaphors: Symbolic Action in Human Society* (Ithaca, 1974), 166–230; Victor W. Turner and Edith Turner, *Image and Pilgrimage in Christian Culture: Anthropological Perspectives* (New York, 1978). See also Mircea Eliade, *The Sacred and the Profane: The Nature of Religion*, trans. Willard R. Trask (French orig.; New York, 1959). Christian K. Zacher, *Curiosity and Pilgrimage: The Literature of Discovery in Fourteenth-Century England* (Baltimore, 1976).

74 Ludwig Schmugge, "Kollektive und individuelle Motivstrukturen im mittelalterlichen Pilgerwesen," in Jaritz and Müller, *Migration*, 268–69; Alan Kendall, *Medieval Pilgrims* (London, 1970), 12–15; F. E. Peters, *Jerusalem and Mecca: The Typology of the Holy City in the Near East* (New York, 1986), 40–41.

75 Hedwig Röckelein, Claudia Opitz, and Dieter R. Bauer, eds., *Maria, Abbild oder Vorbild? Zur Sozialgeschichte mittelalterlicher Marienverehrung* (Tübingen, 1990), 12–15; Peter Brown, *The Cult of the Saints: Its Rise and Function in Latin Christianity* (Chicago, 1981); Werner Freitag, *Volks- und Elitenfrömmigkeit in der frühen Neuzeit: Marienwallfahrten im Fürstbistum Münster* (Paderborn, 1991), 260; D. J. Hall, *English Mediaeval Pilgrimage* (London, 1965), 6–10.

76 While for Jerusalem the pilgrim traffic remained the mainstay, Mecca was situated on "a major overland trade route [once linking] eastern producers and Roman consumers in the urban markets of the Mediterranean." Peters, *Jerusalem and Mecca*, 31–32, 48, 52–55. A.-M. Armelin, "Pèlerins de Saint-Jacques," in R. de la Coste-Messelière, ed., *Pèlerins et chemins de St. Jacques en France et en Europe du Xe siècle à nos jours* (Paris, 1965), 71–84; Ludwig Schmugge, "Die Entstehung des organisierten Pilgerverkehrs," *Quellen und Forschungen aus italienischen Archiven und Bibliotheken* 64 (1984): 1–83.

77 F. Rapp, "Les Pèlerinages dans la vie religieuse de l'occident médiéval aux XIVe et XVe siècles," in F. Raphaël et al., *Les Pèlerinages de l'antiquité biblique et classique à l'occident médiéval* (Paris, 1973), 117–60, see 120ff.; George B. Parks, *The English Traveller to Italy* (Rome, 1954); *New Catholic Encyclopedia*, 18 vols., (New York, 1967–79), 11:362; Kendall, *Pilgrims*, 54–58; Sara Warneke, *Images of the Educational Traveller in Early Modern England* (Leiden, 1995), 18–19.

78 Exaggerated hopes of nineteenth-century migrants to America suggest a "secularization of hope." Dirk Hoerder, "Labour Migrants' Views of 'America,'" *Renaissance and Modern Studies* 35 (1992): 1–17.

79 Fabri's life exemplifies geographical mobility: born in Zurich c.1434, he moved with his mother after his father's death to a village near Schaffhausen, then to Winterthur. In 1452 he entered a convent in Basel, relocated to a convent in Ulm, Germany, traveled to Pforzheim (1457), Aix-la-Chapelle (1467), and Rome (1476). His two pilgrimages to Jerusalem lasted seven and nine months respectively. During the second, he continued on to Egypt in a caravan of about forty-five persons employing among others seven camel and six donkey drivers, two Arab guides, two translators, and one Ethiopian slave. *Voyage en Égypte de Felix Fabri, 1483*, trans. Jacques Masson (Cairo, 1975), introduction; *The Book of the Wanderings of Brother Felix Fabri*, trans. A. Stewart (London, 1892), is an English version. Werner Paravicini, ed., *Europäische Reiseberichte des späten Mittelalters: Eine analytische Bibliographie*, Teil 1 [Part 1]: "Deutsche Reiseberichte," ed. Christian Halm (Frankfurt/Main, 1994), 210–20.

80 *Informacion for Pylgrymes* (c.1498; repr., 1515; 3d ed., 1524), quoted in Sidney Heath, *In the Steps of the Pilgrims* (1911; rev. and enlarged ed., New York, 1951), 138–40; Michel Balard, "Les transports vers les colonies du Levant au Moyen Âge," 3–26, and Jean Richard, "Le transport outre-mer des croisés et des pèlerins," in Klaus Friedland, ed., *Maritime Aspects of Migration* (Cologne, 1989), 27–44.

81 Stefan Baumgartner, *Reise zum Heiligen Grab 1498 mit Herzog Heinrich dem Frommen von Sachsen*, ed. Thomas Kraus (Göppingen, 1986); Riley-Smith, *Atlas of the Crusades*, 44.

82 *The Book of Margery Kempe*, ed. W. Butler-Bowden (New York, 1944), is a vivid dictated memoir. Ellen Ross, "Diversities of Divine Presence: Women's Geography in Christian Tradition," in Jamie Scott and Paul Simpson-Housley, eds., *Sacred Places and Profane Spaces: Essays in the Geographics of Judaism, Christianity and Islam* (New York, 1991), 93–114; H. F. M. Prescott, *Le voyage de Jérusalem au XVe siècle* (Paris, 1959), 79, 117–23, 152.

83 Baumgartner, *Reise*, 5, quote on 24; Freitag, *Marienwallfahrten*, 221; Hall, *Pilgrimage*, 7; Heath, *In the Steps*, quote on 13.

84 According to a contemporary chronicler, the Council of Constance (1414–18) was attended by 72,460 clerics, secular rulers, doctors of law, and their staff and servants. Other sources give lower figures—but still in the five-digit range.

85 See, for example, on Germans, Clifford W. Maas, *The German Community in Renaissance Rome, 1378–1523* (Madison, 1971).

86 Monica Kurzel-Runtscheiner, *Töchter der Venus: Die Kurtisanen Roms im 16. Jahrhundert* (Munich, 1995), 9–35, 259–61.

87 Rapp, "Pèlerinages," 140; Kendall, *Pilgrims*, 12; Schmugge, "Motivstrukturen," 276–77; *Cambridge Economic History of Europe*, 1:75; *New Catholic Encyclopedia*, 9:924–74.

4   The End of Intercivilizational Contact and the Economics of Religious Expulsions

1 Benjamin Z. Kedar, "Expulsion as an Issue of World History," *Journal of World History* 7 (1996): 165–80, provides a typology of expulsions and argues that their specific character developed in medieval Europe. Jean P. Poussou, "De l'intérêt de l'étude historique des mouvements migratoires européens du milieu du Moyen Âge à la fin du XIXe siècle," and Jacques

Dupâquier, "Macro-migrations en Europe (XVIe–XVIIIe siècles)," in Simonetta Cavaciocchi, ed., *Le migrazioni in Europa secc. XIII–XVIII* (Florence, 1994), 21–46, 65–90.

2 Hermann Kellenbenz, ed., *Handbuch der europäischen Wirtschafts- und Sozialgeschichte*, 6 vols. (Stuttgart, 1980), 2:355, 374.

3 Henry C. Lea, *The Moriscos of Spain: Their Conversion and Expulsion* (Philadelphia, 1901; repr., New York, 1968), 1–24; L. P. Harvey, *Islamic Spain, 1250 to 1500* (Chicago, 1990), 329; Julio Caro Baroja, *Los Moriscos del reino de Granada: Ensayo de historia social* (Madrid, 1957); Anwar G. Chejne, *Islam and the West: The Moriscos, a Cultural and Social History* (Albany, 1983); Antonio Domínguez Ortiz and Bernard Vincent, *Historia de los Moriscos* (Madrid, 1978).

4 Harvey, *Islamic Spain*, 331–35, quote on 338; Lea, *Moriscos of Spain*, 25–56, 82–110, 213–70. See also Peggy K. Liss, *Isabel the Queen: Life and Times* (New York, 1992), 149–233.

5 Military action was delayed since most of the Spanish troops were fighting in the Netherlands and reinforcements from garrisons in Italy had to be shipped in.

6 Lea, *Moriscos of Spain*, 126–29, 187–88, 379–80; James Casey, "Moriscos and the Depopulation of Valencia," *Past and Present* 50 (1971): 19–40; Chejne, *Islam and the West*, 1–30; A. C. de C. M. Saunders, *A Social History of Black Slaves and Freedmen in Portugal, 1441–1555* (Cambridge, 1982), 42; Henri Lapeye, *Géographie de l'Espagne morisque* (Paris, 1959).

7 Lea, *Moriscos of Spain*, 292–365; Andrew C. Hess, *The Forgotten Frontier: A History of the Sixteenth-Century Ibero-African Frontier* (Chicago, 1978), 174.

8 Paloma Díaz-Mas, *Sephardim: The Jews from Spain*, trans. George K. Zucker (Spanish orig., 1986; Chicago, 1992), outlines the history and migrations of the Sephardim into the twentieth century. Gérard Chaliand and Jean-Pierre Rageau, *The Penguin Atlas of Diasporas*, trans. A. M. Berrett (French orig., Paris, 1991; New York, 1995), 1–71.

9 According to Stow, Jews did not decline from being allies of kings to a group of lesser class standing; rather, a defined legal and constitutional status remained important in medieval society. Kenneth R. Stow, *Alienated Minority: The Jews of Medieval Latin Europe* (Cambridge, Mass., 1992), 3–4. John Edwards, ed., *The Jews in Western Europe, 1400–1600* (Manchester, 1994); Jeremy Cohen, *The Friars and the Jews: The Evolution of Medieval Anti-Judaism* (Ithaca, 1982), and, Cohen, "Recent Historiography on the Medieval Church and the Decline of European Jewry," in James R. Sweeney and Stanley Chodorow, *Popes, Teachers, and Canon Law in the Middle Ages* (Ithaca, 1982), 251–62; Haim H. Ben-Sasson, ed., *A History of the Jewish People* (Hebrew orig., 1969; Cambridge, Mass., 1976), 482, 485–86, 505.

10 Robert Chazan, *European Jewry and the First Crusade* (Berkeley, 1987); Peter Elman, "The Economic Causes of the Expulsion of the Jews in 1290," *Economic History Review*, ser. 1, 7 (1937): 145–52; David S. Katz, *Philosemitism and the Readmission of the Jews into England, 1603–1655* (Oxford, 1982); Simon Schwarzfuchs, "The Expulsion of the Jews from France (1306)," in Abraham A. Neuman and Soloman Zeitlin, eds., *Seventy-Fifth Anniversary of the Jewish Quarterly Review* (Philadelphia, 1967), 482–89.

11 Alfred Haverkamp, "Zur Geschichte der Juden im Deutschland des späten Mittelalters und der frühen Neuzeit," in Haverkamp, ed., *Zur Geschichte der Juden im Deutschland des späten Mittelalters und der frühen Neuzeit* (Stuttgart, 1981), 27–93; Elman, "Economic Causes of the Expulsion of the Jews," 145–52; Markus J. Wenniger, *Man bedarf keiner Juden mehr: Ursachen und Hintergründe ihrer Vertreibung aus den deutschen Reichsstädten im 15. Jahrhundert* (Cologne, 1981); Ben-Sasson, *History of the Jewish People*, 462–693; Robert [Roberto] Bonfil, *Jewish Life in Renaissance Italy*, trans. Anthony Oldcorn (Italian orig.,

n.d.; Berkeley, 1994), and Bonfil, "Aliens Within: The Jews and Antijudaism," in Thomas A. Brady Jr., Heiko A. Oberman, and James D. Tracy, eds., *Handbook of European History, 1400-1600: Late Middle Ages, Renaissance, and Reformation*, 2 vols. (Leiden, 1994), 1:263–302; Brian S. Pullan, *The Jews of Europe and the Inquisition of Venice, 1550-1670* (New York, 1983); Benjamin Ravid, "The Socio-Economic Background of the Expulsion and Readmission of the Venetian Jews, 1571-1573," in Frances Malino, ed., *Essays in Modern Jewish History: A Tribute to Ben Halpern* (Rutherford, 1982).

12 John Edwards, *Christian Córdoba: The City and Its Region in the Late Middle Ages* (Cambridge, 1982), 181–88; Philippe Wolf, "The 1391 Pogrom in Spain: Social Crisis or Not?" *Past and Present* 50 (Feb. 1971): 4–18; Angus MacKay, "Popular Movements and Pogroms in Fifteenth-Century Castile," *Past and Present* 55 (May 1972): 33–67.

13 Jane S. Gerber, *The Jews of Spain: A History of the Sephardic Experience* (New York, 1992), provides a survey of subsequent developments and migrations. Isidore Loeb, "Le nombre des Juifs de Castille et d'Espagne," *Revue des études juives* 14 (1887): 162–83; Cecil Roth, *A History of the Marranos* (Philadelphia, 1932); Benzion Netanyahu, *The Marranos of Spain, from the Late XIVth to the Early XVIth Century* (New York, 1973); Yitzhak Baer, *A History of the Jews in Christian Spain*, trans. Louis Schoffman, 2 vols. (Hebrew orig.; Philadelphia, 1961–66); Henry Kamen, "The Mediterranean and the Expulsion of Spanish Jews in 1492," *Past and Present* 119 (1988): 3–55. Kamen reduces the number of expellees further. While much of his argument is nuanced, his final assessment of the 1492 expulsion as "painless surgery" (51) is callous. See also Antonio Domínguez Ortiz, *Los judeoconversos en Espana y América* (Madrid, 1971). Liss, *Isabel the Queen*, 263–78, 165, on Jewish ancestors of the "Catholic Monarchs."

14 John D. Latham, "Towards a Study of Andalusian Immigration and Its Place in Tunisian History," *Cahiers de Tunisie* 5 (1957): 203–52; Jacques Berque, "Des 'Marranos' musulmans à Fès?" in *Mélanges en l'honneur de Fernand Braudel*, 2 vols. (Toulouse, 1973), 1:123–35. See also the docu-fiction by Amin Maalouf, *Léon l'Africain* (Paris, 1986). Mark A. Epstein, *The Ottoman Jewish Communities and Their Role in the Fifteenth and Sixteenth Centuries* (Freiburg, 1980); Avigdor Levy, *The Sephardim in the Ottoman Empire* (Princeton, 1992); Esther Benbassa, *Juifs des Balkans: Espaces judéo-ibériques, XIVe–XXe siècles* (Paris, 1993); Stanford J. Shaw, *The Jews of the Ottoman Empire and the Turkish Republic* (New York, 1991), quote on 33–34.

15 Benzion Netanyahu, *The Origins of the Inquisition in Fifteenth-Century Spain* (New York, 1995), argues that race and not religion was the root of the Inquisition. Michael R. Weisser, *The Peasants of the Montes: The Roots of Rural Rebellion in Spain* (Chicago, 1976), quote on 82.

16 Lea, *Moriscos of Spain*, 134–35.

17 Frederick A. Norwood, *Strangers and Exiles: A History of Religious Refugees*, 2 vols. (Nashville, 1965–69); Margaret Spufford, ed., *The World of Rural Dissenters, 1520-1725* (Cambridge, 1995).

18 Kathryn M. Karrer, *Millennial Activities in Late Thirteenth-Century Albi, France* (New York, 1996).

19 Jarold K. Zeman, *The Anabaptists and the Czech Brethren in Moravia, 1526-1628: A Study of Origins and Contacts* (The Hague, 1969), esp. 72–82; Karl Bosl, ed., *Handbuch der Geschichte der böhmischen Länder*, 4 vols. (Stuttgart, 1967–74), 1:498–536; Rudolf Rícan, *The History of the Unity of Brethren: A Protestant Hussite Church in Bohemia and Moravia,*

trans. C. D. Crews (Czech orig., 1957; Bethlehem, Pa., 1992); Eduard Winter, *Die tschechische und slowakische Emigration in Deutschland im 17. und 18. Jahrhundert* (Berlin, 1955); Tobias Giretschek quoted in *Dem Kelch zuliebe Exulant: 250 Jahre Böhmisches Dorf in Berlin-Neukölln* (Berlin, 1987), 14 (trans. D. H.). Berlin included some 4,500 Bohemian Brethren in a population of 60,000 in the 1780s.

20 Internal reform of the Catholic Church was achieved by the Council of Trent (1545–63).

21 Zwingli had experienced the usual family and career migrations (Basel, Bern, Glarus, Einsiedeln, Zurich) and had participated in several military campaigns, reaching into Italy. Among Catholic theologians, too, conflicts with the Inquisition could lead to migration. The reform-minded Ignatius of Loyola (1491–1556), who studied theology in Salamanca, had to move to the Sorbonne in Paris. He also undertook a pilgrimage to Jerusalem. For the leading woman among the Catholic reformers, the mystical author Teresa de Jesús (Teresa of Avila), geographical mobility was limited to travel between Carmelite convents.

22 Jacques Le Goff, ed., *Hérésies et sociétés dans l'Europe pré-industrielle, 11e–18e siècles* (Paris, 1968). The literature on these groups is legion. See, for example, Bernd G. Längin, *Die Hutterer: Gefangene der Vergangenheit, Pilger der Gegenwart, Propheten der Zukunft* (Hamburg, 1986); Lee C. Hopple, "Religious-Geographical History of the Hutterian Brethren in Europe and Russia, 1523–1879," *Pennsylvania Folklife* 42, 3 (spring 1993): 135–45.

23 At the Second Diet of Speyer (1529), the evangelical states "protested" against a resolution proposed by the Catholic party; hence the name "Protestants."

24 Frederick A. Norwood, *The Reformation Refugees as an Economic Force* (Chicago, 1942), 78–82, 108–12; Charles R. Boxer, *The Dutch Seaborne Empire, 1600–1800* (London, 1965), 137–39.

25 Mary Prior, "Reviled and Crucified Marriages: The Position of Tudor Bishops' Wives," and Marie B. Rowlands, "Recusant Women, 1560–1640," in Prior, ed., *Women in English Society, 1500–1800* (London, 1985), 118–48, 149–80; Patrick McGrath, *Papists and Puritans under Elizabeth I* (London, 1967). The Visitation nuns capitulated to male demands for enclosure in 1610, the Ursuline sisters in 1612, those of Notre Dame in 1615. By 1631, ten houses of the English sisters were closed, 300 women having been sent home to their families.

26 Andrew N. Porter, ed., *Atlas of British Overseas Expansion* (London, 1991), 22–24; Michael Perceval-Maxwell, *The Scottish Migration to Ulster in the Reign of James I* (London, 1973); Karl S. Bottigheimer, *English Money and Irish Land: The "Adventurers" in the Cromwellian Settlement of Ireland* (Oxford, 1971), and, Bottigheimer, "Kingdom and Colony: Ireland in the Westward Enterprise, 1536–1660," in K. R. Andrews et al., eds., *The Westward Enterprise: English Activities in Ireland, the Atlantic and America, 1480–1650* (Liverpool, 1978), 45–64; C. E. J. Caldicott et al., eds., *The Huguenots and Ireland: Anatomy of an Emigration* (Dublin, 1987); James E. Handley, *The Irish in Scotland, 1798–1845* (Cork, 1943).

27 Jeremy D. Bangs, ed., *The Pilgrims in the Netherlands: Recent Research* (Leiden, 1985); Keith L. Sprunger, *Dutch Puritanism: A History of English and Scottish Churches of the Netherlands in the Sixteenth and Seventeenth Centuries* (Leiden, 1982). For the Puritans in New England, see, for example, Virginia D. Anderson, *New England's Generation: The Great Migration and the Formation of Society and Culture in the Seventeenth Century* (Cambridge, 1991); Allen French, *Charles I and the Puritan Upheaval: A Study of the Causes of the Great Migration* (London, 1955).

28 The older figure of half a million refugees is now generally considered too high.

29 Liliane Mottu-Weber, *Économie et refuge à Genève au siècle de la Réforme: La draperie*

et la soierie (1540–1630) (Geneva, 1987); Walter Bodmer, *Der Einfluß der Refugiantenein-wanderung von 1550–1700 auf die schweizerische Wirtschaft* (Zurich, 1946). J. A. H. Bots and G. H. M. Posthumus Meyjes, *La Révocation de l'Edit de Nantes et les Provinces-Unies, 1685* (Amsterdam, 1986). Irene Scouloudi, ed., *Huguenots in Britain and Their French Background, 1550–1800* (London, 1987); Bernard Cottret, *The Huguenots in England: Immigration and Settlement, c.1550–1700,* trans. Peregrine and Adriana Stevenson (French orig., 1985; Cambridge, 1991); Robin D. Gwynn, *Huguenot Heritage: The History and Contribution of the Huguenots in Britain* (London, 1985). Ingrid Mittenzwei, ed., *Hugenotten in Brandenburg-Preußen* (Berlin, 1987); Thomas Klingebiel, *Weserfranzosen: Studien zur Geschichte der Hugenottengemeinschaft in Hameln (1690–1757)* (Göttingen, 1992); Heinz Schilling, *Niederländische Exulanten im 16. Jahrhundert: Ihre Stellung im Sozialgefüge und im religiösen Leben deutscher und englischer Städte* (Gütersloh, 1972); Jon Butler, *The Huguenots in America: A Refugee People in New World Society* (Cambridge, Mass., 1983); Abraham D. Lavender, *French Huguenots: From Mediterranean Catholics to White Anglo-Saxon Protestants* (New York, 1990); Charles W. Baird, *History of the Huguenot Emigration to America,* 2 vols. (New York, 1885; repr., Baltimore, 1966).

30 Gaston Tournier, *Les galères de France et les galériens protestants des XVIIe et XVIIIe siècles,* 2 vols. (Paris, 1943–49), 1: 57–218. Albert Girard, *Le commerce français a Séville et Cadix aux temps des Habsbourg* (Paris, 1932), 547–48.

31 Beate Magen, *Die Wallonengemeinde in Canterbury von ihrer Gründung bis zum Jahre 1635* (Frankfurt/Main, 1973), 31–58, 171–81; Andrew Pettegree, *Foreign Protestant Communities in Sixteenth-Century London* (Oxford, 1986), 77–214; Ronald Mayo, *The Huguenots in Bristol* (Bristol, 1985); Ole P. Grell, *Dutch Calvinists in Early Stuart London* (Leiden, 1989); Laura H. Yungblut, *"Strangers Settled Here amongst Us": Policies, Perceptions, and the Presence of Aliens in Elizabethan England* (London, 1996).

32 Andrew Pettegree, *Emden and the Dutch Revolt: Exile and the Development of Reformed Protestantism* (New York, 1992). Emden, a small town at the German-Dutch border, hosted Dutch Reformists, Anabaptists, and English and French Reformed Church members after the mid-sixteenth century. Herman Van der Wee and Jan Materné, "Antwerp as a World Market in the Sixteenth and Seventeenth Centuries," in Jan Van der Stock, ed., *Antwerp, Story of a Metropolis: 16th–17th Century* (Ghent, 1993), 19–31; J. Briels, *Zuid-Nederlanders in de Republiek 1572–1630: Een demografische en cultuurhistorische studie* (Saint-Niklaas, 1985); Sherrin Marshall, "Protestant, Catholic, and Jewish Women in the Early Modern Netherlands," in Marshall, ed., *Women in Reformation and Counter-Reformation Europe: Private and Public Worlds* (Bloomington, 1989), 120–39.

5 Ottoman Society, Europe, and the Beginnings of Colonial Contact

1 Bennassar and Pierre Chaunu, eds., *L'ouverture du monde, XIVe–XVIe siècles* (Paris, 1977), 175ff.; William McNeill, *Europe's Steppe Frontier, 1500–1800* (Chicago, 1964), 33–36.

2 The term "Gypsy"—perhaps referring to people coming from Egypt—has been criticized because of its derogatory and racist connotations. No generally accepted new term is available. Here it is used as an ethnic designation for several culturally related groups, Roma and Sinti, for example.

3 The decision of the Imperial Diet of the Holy Roman Empire of 1496–97 was adopted across

Europe. Angus Fraser, *The Gypsies* (Oxford, 1992); Reimar Gilsenbach, *Weltchronik der Zigeuner*, 1 vol. to date (Frankfurt/Main, 1994); Andreas Hundsalz, *Stand der Forschung über Zigeuner und Landfahrer: Eine Literaturanalyse* (Stuttgart, 1978), 24–27, 84–89. See chap. 12.1 for later developments.

4 Speros Vryonis Jr., *The Decline of Medieval Hellenism in Asia Minor and the Process of Islamization from the Eleventh through the Fifteenth Century* (Berkeley, 1971), 25–30, 42–65; see also Peter Charanis, *Studies on the Demography of the Byzantine Empire: Collected Studies* (London, 1972), essays 1–7.

5 The name derives from Osman (r. c.1290–1326), ruler of a Turkoman principality in Anatolia.

6 For new views, see Halil Berktay and Suraiya Faroqhi, eds., *New Approaches to State and Peasants in Ottoman History* (London, 1992); Halil Inalcik, *The Ottoman Empire: The Classical Age, 1300–1600*, trans. Colin Imber and Norman Itzkowitz (Turkish orig., n.d.; London, 1973); Inalcik and Donald Quataert, eds., *An Economic and Social History of the Ottoman Empire, 1300–1914* (Cambridge, 1994).

7 Edward Said, *Orientalism* (London, 1978); Albert Mas, *Les Turcs dans la littérature espagnole du siècle or*, 2 vols. (Paris, 1967), 1:11, 109, 2:295–300, 416–68; Kiril Petkov, *Infidels, Turks, and Women: The South Slavs in the German Mind, ca. 1400–1600* (New York, 1997); Rosario Villari, *The Revolt of Naples*, trans. James Newell (Italian orig., 1967; Oxford, 1993), quote on 31.

8 The advance was stalled briefly by the Mongol incursions under Timur from 1400 to 1420. Halil Inalcik, "The Policy of Mehmed II toward the Greek Population of Istanbul and the Byzantine Buildings of the City," *Dumbarton Oaks Papers* 23/24 (1969/70): 229–49; Leften S. Stavrianos, *The Balkans since 1453* (New York, 1958), 96–115, 171–77; Peter F. Sugar, *Southeastern Europe under Ottoman Rule, 1354–1804* (Seattle, 1977); Jonathan Riley-Smith, ed., *Atlas of the Crusades* (London, 1991), 150, 164, 166; McNeill, *Europe's Steppe Frontier*, 43–44.

9 Ömer L. Barkan, "Les déportations comme méthode de peuplement et de colonisation dans l'empire ottoman," *Revue de la Faculté des Sciences Economiques de l'Université d'Istanbul* 11 (1946): 524–69, 13 (1948): 56–79, 15 (1950): 209–329.

10 Vryonis, *Decline of Medieval Hellenism*, 30–33.

11 Kemal H. Karpat, "*Millets* and Nationality: The Roots of the Incongruity of Nation and State in the Post-Ottoman Era," in Benjamin Braude and Bernard Lewis, eds., *Christians and Jews in the Ottoman Empire: The Functioning of a Plural Society*, 2 vols. (London, 1982), 1:141–69; see also the essay by Braude, in Braude and Lewis, *Christians and* Jews, 69–88, which is critical of the standard interpretation of the *millet* system; Vryonis, *Decline of Medieval Hellenism*, 143–350.

12 Each local group fleeing from pogroms established its own synagogue, and its members continued to live close to each other. Mark A. Epstein, *The Ottoman Jewish Communities and Their Role in the Fifteenth and Sixteenth Centuries* (Freiburg, 1980), 28. Stanford J. Shaw, *The Jews of the Ottoman Empire and the Turkish Republic* (New York, 1991), 25–108. When the position of Jews deteriorated in Arabic Islam's Middle Ages after 1250, Ottoman conquest became a liberating experience for them, too. The position of Jews in Ottoman society declined as the empire itself declined after 1600 (Shaw, *Jews of the Ottoman Empire*, 109–46). Norman A. Stillman, *The Jews of Arab Lands: A History and Sourcebook* (Philadelphia, 1979). Studies of the special situation of Jews abound.

13 Robert Mantran, *La vie quotidienne à Constantinople au siècle de Soliman le Magnifique* (Paris, 1965), 60–74, 159–89, and Mantran, "Foreign Merchants and the Minorities in Istanbul during the Sixteenth and Seventeenth Centuries," in Braude and Lewis, *Christians and Jews*, 1:127–37; Inalcik, *Ottoman Empire*, 140–45; Paul M. Strässle, *Der internationale Schwarzmeerhandel und Konstantinopel 1261–1484 im Spiegel der sowjetischen Forschung* (Bern, 1990).

14 Inalcik, *Ottoman Empire*, 121–39, 146–50; Gilles Veinstein, "Some Views on Provisioning in the Hungarian Campaigns of Suleyman the Magnificent," and Michael Rogers, "Ottoman Luxury Trades and Their Regulation," in Hans G. Majer, ed., *Osmanistische Studien zur Wirtschafts- und Sozialgeschichte* (Wiesbaden, 1986), 177–85 and 135–55. According to Rogers, among slaves and prisoners of war working for Bursa silk weavers the following ethnic groups were listed: Bosnians, Russians, Greeks, Italians, Vlachs, Çerkes, Albanians, Hungarians, and Croats (142). Andrew C. Hess, "The Evolution of the Ottoman Seaborne Empire in the Age of the Oceanic Discoveries, 1453–1525," *American Historical Review* 75 (1970): 1882–1919.

15 Inalcik, *Ottoman Empire*, 13, 35–52, 66–68, 70–73, quote on 7; Sugar, *Southeastern Europe*, 274–75. Michael R. Hickok, *Ottoman Military Administration in Eighteenth-Century Bosnia* (Leiden, 1997).

16 Inalcik, *Ottoman Empire*, 150–62; Sugar, *Southeastern Europe*, 75; Armin Hetzer, "Gesellschaftliche Modernisierung und Sprachreform," *Balkan-Archiv*, n.s., 17/18 (1992/93): 255–416.

17 B. D. Papoulia, *Ursprung und Wesen der "Knabenlese" im osmanischen Reich* (Munich, 1963); Inalcik, *Ottoman Empire*, 78–79; Sugar, *Southeastern Europe*, 56–59; Suraiya Faroqhi, "Political Initiatives 'From the Bottom Up' in the Sixteenth- and Seventeenth-Century Ottoman Empire," in Majer, *Osmanistische Studien*, 24–33.

18 Sugar, *Southeastern Europe*, 273. The slave system began to disintegrate in the last quarter of the sixteenth century. The decline of the empire has been related to the emergence of ethnic cliques, to the influence of the janissaries in politics, and to the influence of favorites from among the wealthy on sultans—but not to the men in power.

19 Leslie P. Peirce, *The Imperial Harem: Women and Sovereignty in the Ottoman Empire* (Oxford, 1993), 3–12, 30–31, revises the two classic Western-Christian notions of the *harem* as a retreat for profligate sultans and of the empire's decline when women assumed a larger role in politics.

20 As in the Christian Church, calls to restrict the role of women came mostly from the all-male *ulemas*, the religious establishment. The segregation of gender-spheres in the palace was related to social status. Among the poorer classes, women participated in everyday chores outside of the walled sphere of the house. In this short summary, changes in gender-roles over time cannot be discussed. Cf. Inalcik, *Ottoman Empire*, 85–87. See also Gavin R. G. Hambly, ed., *Women in the Medieval Islamic World: Power, Patronage and Piety* (New York, 1998).

21 Berktay and Faroqhi, *New Approaches*; M. A. Cook, *Population Pressure in Rural Anatolia, 1450–1600* (London, 1972), 37–41; Leila Erder, "The Measurement of Preindustrial Population Changes: The Ottoman Empire from the 15th to the 17th Century," *Middle Eastern Studies* 11 (1975): 284–301, and Erder and Suraiya Faroqhi, "Population Rise and Fall in Anatolia, 1550–1620," *Middle Eastern Studies* 15 (1979): 322–45; Inalcik, *Ottoman Empire*, 145.

22 Norman Daniel, *Islam and the West: The Making of an Image* (Edinburgh, 1960), and Daniel,

The Arabs and Mediaeval Europe (1975; 2d ed., London, 1979), 267–302. Edward Burman, *The World before Columbus, 1100-1492* (London, 1989), 15–17; S. D. Goitein, *A Mediterranean Society: The Jewish Communities of the Arab World as Portrayed in the Documents of the Cairo Geniza,* 5 vols. (Berkeley, 1967–93), 1:51–56.

23 Jacques Verger, "Noblesse et savoir: Étudiants nobles aux universités d'Avignon, Cahors, Montpellier et Toulouse (fin du XIVe siècle)," in Philippe Contamine, ed., *La noblesse au Moyen Âge, XIe-XVe siècles* (Paris, 1976), 289-314; Michael H. Shank, "A Female University Student in Late Medieval Crakow," in Sherrin Marshall, ed., *Women in Reformation and Counter-Reformation Europe: Private and Public Worlds* (Bloomington, 1989), 190–97; Charles R. Boxer, *The Dutch Seaborne Empire, 1600-1800* (London, 1965), 176–77.

24 The best summary is Hilde de Ridder-Symoens's article "Mobility" in her edited volume *A History of the University in Europe,* vol. 1 (Cambridge, 1992), 280–85, and Ridder-Symoens, "La migration académique des hommes et des idées en Europe, XIIIe–XVIIIe siècles," *Université et cité: A la recherche du passé* (Geneva, 1983), 69–78; Sven Bagge, "Nordic Students at Foreign Universities until 1660," *Scandinavian Journal of History* 9 (1983): 287–318; Rainer C. Schwinges, *Deutsche Universitätsbesucher im 14. und 15. Jahrhundert* (Wiesbaden, 1986); Norbert Ohler, *The Medieval Traveller,* trans. Caroline Hillier (German orig., 1986; Woodbridge, U.K., 1989), 223–25; Hein Retter, comp., *Fahrende Schüler zu Beginn der Neuzeit: Selbstzeugnisse aus dem 16. Jahrhundert* (Heidenheim, 1972).

25 Ingrid Matschinegg, "Ausländer in Italien: Überlegungen zu den Italienbesuchern im 15. und 16. Jahrhundert," *Beiträge zur historischen Sozialforschung* 19 (1989): 73–77. On out-migration from Italy, I am indebted to research in progress by Donna Gabaccia and her *Italy's Many Diasporas* (London, 2000). Fernand Braudel, *The Mediterranean and the Mediterranean World in the Age of Philip II,* 2 vols., trans. Siân Reynolds (French orig., 1949; 2d rev. French ed., 1966; New York, 1972), 1:201, 222; J. R. Hale, *Renaissance Europe: Individual and Society, 1480-1520* (1st ed., 1971; Berkeley, 1977), 38–39.

26 Sara Warneke, *Images of the Educational Traveller in Early Modern England* (Leiden, 1995); Malcolm Letts, "Some Sixteenth-Century Travellers in Naples," *English Historical Review* 33 (1918): 176–96.

27 *Cambridge Economic History of Europe,* vol. 3: M. M. Postan, E. E. Rich, and Edward Miller, eds., *Economic Organization and Policies in the Middle Ages* (Cambridge, 1963), 102; Ridder-Symoens, "Mobility," 280–82.

28 Bernard Chevalier, "France from Charles VII to Henry IV," in Thomas A. Brady Jr., Heiko A. Oberman, and James D. Tracy, eds., *Handbook of European History, 1400-1600: Late Middle Ages, Renaissance, and Reformation,* 2 vols. (Leiden, 1994), 1:371, 385.

29 First published in 1701; reprinted in James T. Boulton, ed., *Selected Writings of Daniel Defoe* (Cambridge, 1975), 51–81.

30 Robert-Henri Bautier, "Le 'Melting Pot' de la Gaule du Haut Moyen Âge," in Jacques Dupâquier et al., *Histoire de la population française,* 4 vols. (Paris, 1988), 1:123–70, 409–15; Gérard Noiriel, *Le Creuset français: Histoire de l'immigration XIXe-XXe siècles* (Paris, 1988), English: *The French Melting Pot: Immigration, Citizenship, and National Identity,* trans. Geoffroy de Laforcade (Minneapolis, 1996).

31 Richard Wermser, *Statistische Studien zur Entwicklung des englischen Wortschatzes* (Bern, 1976), 56–70; Karl Brunner, *Die englische Sprache: Ihre geschichtliche Entwicklung,* 2 vols. (1950/51; rev. ed. Tübingen, 1960/62).

32 Guy Llewelyn Thompson, *Paris and Its People under English Rule: The Anglo-Burgundian*

Regime, 1420-1436 (Oxford, 1991), 47-145; Sarah Hanley, "Engendering the State: Family Formation and State Building in Early Modern France," *French Historical Studies* 16 (1989): 4-27.

33 Thomas Robisheaux, *Rural Society and the Search for Order in Early Modern Germany* (Cambridge, 1989), 147ff., quotes on 161, 170.

34 The religious impetus was supplemented by the search for Prester John's (mythical) Christian kingdom somewhere in the south. When the Christian kingdom of Ethiopia was reached in 1494, it proved to be doctrinally different (Coptic rather than Latin Church) and neither rich nor powerful.

35 Gunpowder had been a Chinese invention, but the Europeans were able to construct ships with cannon on board. C. G. F. Simkin, *The Traditional Trade of Asia* (Oxford, 1968), 260-62.

36 The Atlantic islands were divided between Castile and Portugal by the treaty of 1479. The Azores and Madeira became Portuguese colonies; Castile held the Canaries.

37 John H. Parry, *The Age of Reconnaissance, Discovery, Exploration and Settlement, 1450-1650* (London, 1963); Charles R. Boxer, *The Portuguese Seaborne Empire, 1415-1825* (London, 1969), 18, 31; Felipe Fernández-Armesto, *Before Columbus: Exploration and Colonisation from the Mediterranean to the Atlantic, 1229-1492* (London, 1987), 151-222; David Watts, *The West Indies: Patterns of Development, Culture, and Environmental Change since 1492* (Cambridge, 1987), 80-86.

38 Sir John Hawkins began England's penetration into the slave trade; from the 1590s onward, Dutch sea power cut into the trade, and by the 1630s the Dutch had seized several of the Portuguese trading posts on the West African coast.

39 Philip D. Curtin, *The Atlantic Slave Trade: A Census* (Madison, 1969), 18, and, Curtin, "Major Trends," in Eugene D. Genovese, ed., *The Slave Economies*, 2 vols. (New York, 1973), 1:73-80; higher numbers are given in A. C. de C. M. Saunders, *A Social History of Black Slaves and Freedmen in Portugal, 1441-1555* (Cambridge, 1982), 11-27, 47-61.

40 Antonio Domínguez Ortiz, *The Golden Age of Spain, 1516-1669*, trans. James Casey (Spanish orig., n.d.; London, 1971), 164. See also José Antonio Saco, *Historia de la esclavitud desde los tiempos más remotos hasta nuestros días*, 5 vols. (2d ed., Havana, 1937); Saunders, *Black Slaves and Freedmen*, 52-88, 113-37.

41 Saunders, *Black Slaves and Freedmen*, 47-50, 50-61, 134-48, quote on 1; Lee Anne Durham Seminario, *The History of the Blacks, the Jews, and the Moors in Spain* (Madrid, 1975), 26-28.

42 Saunders, *Black Slaves and Freedmen*, 89-112; Basil Davidson, *Black Mother: The Years of the African Slave Trade* (Toronto, 1961), 203; Seminario, *History*, 29-34.

43 Frédéric Mauco, "Merchant Communities, 1350-1750," and Irfan Habib, "Merchant Communities in Precolonial India," in James D. Tracy, ed., *The Rise of Merchant Empires: Long-Distance Trade in the Early Modern World, 1350-1750* (Cambridge, 1990), 278-79 and 371-99.

44 Wolfgang Reinhard, *Geschichte der europäischen Expansion*, 4 vols. (Stuttgart, 1983-90); Eberhard Schmitt, *Die Anfänge der europäischen Expansion* (Idstein, Ger., 1991); Janet L. Abu-Lughod, *Before European Hegemony: The World System, A.D. 1250-1350* (New York, 1989), 19-20; Inalcik, *Ottoman Empire*, 38, 51-52; Subhi Y. Labib, *Handelsgeschichte Ägyptens im Spätmittelalter 1171-1517* (Wiesbaden, 1965), 441-80; Helmut Wilsdorf, *Kulturgeschichte des Bergbaus* (Essen, 1987), 143-44, 201-4; Mauco, "Merchant Communities," 276-

77; Salih Özbaran, "The Ottoman Turks and the Portuguese in the Persian Gulf, 1534–1581," *Journal of Asian History* 6 (1972): 45–87.

45 Schmitt, *Anfänge*, quote on 56–57 (trans. D. H.).

46 Ibid., 60–73.

47 Mark Kurlansky, *Cod: A Biography of the Fish That Changed the World* (Toronto, 1997), 19–153.

48 John Merson, *Straßen nach Xanadu* (English orig., 1989; Hamburg, 1989); Laurette Séjourné, *Altamerikanische Kulturen* (Frankfurt/Main, 1971), 19; Watts, *West Indies*, 79–80; St. Clair Drake, "Diaspora Studies and Pan-Africanism," in Joseph E. Harris, *Global Dimensions of the African Diaspora* (Washington, D.C., 1982), 372. A recent study also suggests early Chinese contacts: Jim Bailey, *Sailing to Paradise: The Discovery of the Americas by 7000 B.C.* (New York, 1996).

49 Ruth Pike, *Enterprise and Adventure: The Genoese in Seville and the Opening of the New World* (Ithaca, 1966); Edmundo O'Gorman, *The Invention of America: An Inquiry into the Historical Nature of the New World and the Meaning of History* (Bloomington, 1961); Huguette Chaunu and Pierre Chaunu, *Seville et l'Atlantique, 1504–1560*, 8 vols. (Paris, 1955–59), cited in Schmitt, *Anfänge*, 67.

50 Schmitt, *Anfänge*, quote on 35; William H. McNeill, "The Age of Gunpowder Empires, 1450–1800," in Michael Adas, ed., *Islamic and European Expansion: The Forging of a Global Order* (Philadelphia, 1993), 103–39; Tzvetan Todorov, *The Conquest of America: The Question of the Other*, trans. by Richard Howard (French orig., Paris, 1982; New York, 1985), 14–50.

6   Africa and the Slave Migration Systems

1 The savannah belt was called "Sudan," meaning "land of the Blacks." Thus historic Sudan, as distinct from the modern state, consisted of Nilotic, Central, and Western Sudan.

2 Kevin Shillington, *History of Africa* (New York, 1989), 157–64; Yvan Debbasch, *La nation française en Tunisie, 1577–1835* (Paris, 1957); Kenneth R. Andrews, *Trade, Plunder and Settlement: Maritime Enterprise and the Genesis of the British Empire, 1480–1630* (Cambridge, 1984), 5; Pierre Chaunu, *Conquête et exploitation des Nouveaux Mondes, XVIe siècle* (Paris, 1969); Philip D. Curtin, *Cross-Cultural Trade in World History* (Cambridge, 1984), 132, 38–39; Alan K. Smith, *Creating a World Economy: Merchant Capital, Colonialism, and World Trade, 1400–1825* (Boulder, 1991).

3 William Y. Adams, *Nubia: Corridor to Africa* (Princeton, 1977); Basil Davidson, *A History of East and Central Africa to the Late Nineteenth Century* (Garden City, N.Y., 1969), 34ff.; Paul Bohannan and Philip Curtin, *Africa and Africans* (4th ed., Prospect Heights, Ill., 1995), 165–78. On cultural dispersion northward to Egypt as well as to Asian societies, see Graham W. Irwin, ed., *Africans Abroad: A Documentary History of the Black Diaspora in Asia, Latin America, and the Caribbean during the Age of Slavery* (New York, 1977), 3–176.

4 J. H. Greenberg, *Languages of Africa* (The Hague, 1963); "L'Afrique noire avant la traite," in Bartolomé Bennassar and Pierre Chaunu, eds., *L'ouverture du monde, XIVe–XVIe siècles* (Paris, 1977), 76–84; Joseph Ki-Zerbo, *Histoire de l'Afrique noire d'hier à demain* (Paris, 1978), 129–96; Pierre Alexandre, *Les Africains: Initiation à une longue histoire et à de vieilles civilisations* (Paris, 1981), 234–413; Philip Curtin, Steven Feierman, Leonard Thomp-

son, and Jan Vansina, *African History* (Boston, 1978), 26–29, 95–101; Elias N. Saad, *Social History of Timbuktu: The Role of Muslim Scholars and Notables, 1400–1900* (Cambridge, 1983), 3.

5 A Greek-language guide to the culture and trade of Azania at the Tana River dates from the first century C.E.

6 H. Neville Chittick, "The 'Shirazi' Colonization of East Africa," *Journal of African History* 6 (1965): 275–94.

7 The Indonesians must have arrived before 400 C.E., as the absence of Sanskrit words in the Malgache language indicates emigration before Indian penetration of Indonesia. It is closely related to one of the languages of Borneo.

8 Extract from ibn Baṭṭūṭah in Basil Davidson, ed., *The African Past: Chronicles from Antiquity to Modern Times* (London, 1964), 116–17; Shillington, *Africa*, 122–30, 146–53.

9 Shillington, *Africa*, 138–46; Curtin et al., *African History*, 118; John Iliffe, *Africans: The History of a Continent* (Cambridge, 1995).

10 Basil Davidson, *Black Mother: The Years of the African Slave Trade* (Toronto, 1961), 229–37; Davidson, *East and Central Africa*, 34–72, quotes on 100, 108; Kilwa Chronicle cited in Davidson, *African Past*, 119; H. Neville Chittick, "East Africa and the Orient: Ports and Trade before the Arrival of the Portuguese," in UNESCO, *Historical Relations across the Indian Ocean* (Paris, 1980), 13–22; Chittick and Robert I. Rotberg, eds., *East Africa and the Orient* (New York, 1975); Vitorino Magalhães-Godinho, "Portuguese Emigration from the Fifteenth to the Twentieth Century: Constants and Changes," in Piet C. Emmer and Magnus Mörner, eds., *European Expansion and Migration: Essays on the Intercontinental Migration from Africa, Asia, and Europe* (New York, 1992), 23–25; Robert W. July, *A History of the African People* (New York, 1970), 76–100.

11 Curtin, *Cross-Cultural Trade*, 24–37; Bohannan and Curtin, *Africa and Africans*, 175–76; Bennassar and Chaunu, *L'ouverture du monde*, 71–89.

12 Later, in the eighteenth and nineteenth centuries, puritanical, sometimes nomadic Muslim sects, when powerful and proselytizing, wrought havoc on wealthy merchant communities. When small and in search of an economic base, they inserted themselves into commercial niches.

13 Curtin, *Cross-Cultural Trade*, 49–53. Donald C. Holsinger, "Migration, Commerce and Community: The Mīzābīs in Eighteenth- and Nineteenth-Century Algeria," *Journal of African History* 21 (1980): 61–74; L. Vigourous, "L'émigration mazabite dans les villes du Tell algérien," *Travaux de l'institut de recherches sahariennes* 3 (1945): 87–102. Similarly, the Sanusiyya order manned and controlled the trans-Saharan caravan trade from Cyrenaica (eastern Libya) after the 1840s.

14 Enid Schildkraut, *People of the Zongo: The Transformation of Ethnic Identities in Ghana* (Cambridge, 1978); Abner Cohen, *Custom and Politics in Urban Africa: A Study of Hausa Migrants in Yoruba Towns* (Berkeley, 1969); Ralph A. Austen and Jonathan Derrick, *Middlemen of the Cameroons Rivers: The Duala and Their Hinterland, c.1600–c.1960* (New York, 1999). For later migrations, see Harold Olofson, "The Hausa Wanderer and Structural Outsiderhood [1970–71]: An Emic and Etic Analysis," in R. Mansell Prothero and Murray Chapman, eds., *Circulation in Third World Countries* (London, 1985), 55–74.

15 Curtin, *Cross-Cultural Trade*, quotes on 33, 53–59; Allen F. Isaacman, *Mozambique: The Africanization of a European Institution; the Zambezi Prazos, 1750–1902* (Madison, 1972); Bohannan and Curtin, *Africa and Africans*, quotes on 176, 178; Davidson, *East and Cen-*

tral Africa, quotes on 100, 108; Michael N. Peearson, *Port Cities and Intruders: The Swahili Coast, India, and Portugal in the Early Modern Era* (Baltimore, 1998). In the mid-twentieth century some 30 million people used the Swahili language.

16 Slavery has often been studied from the United States backward. David B. Davis's comparative approach and Latin American historians' contributions show the limitations of this perspective. Furthermore, few English-language historians take note of French-language publications, whether French or African. Martin A. Klein has pointed to the "heated response from Senegalese and French historians" to research as masterful as that of Philip D. Curtin. All sides argue from issues persisting to the present, the moral blemish associated with slavery and the continuity of Africa's economic backwardness. Martin A. Klein, "The Impact of the Atlantic Slave Trade on the Societies of the Western Sudan," in Joseph E. Inikori and Stanley L. Engerman, *The Atlantic Slave Trade: Effects on Economies, Societies, and Peoples in Africa, the Americas, and Europe* (Durham, N.C., 1992), 25–47.

17 Toyin Falola and Paul E. Lovejoy, "Pawnship in Historical Perspective," in Falola and Lovejoy, eds., *Pawnship in Africa: Debt Bondage in Historical Perspective* (Boulder, 1994), 1–26, and essays by Fred Morton, Robin Law, Gareth Austin, Martin A. Klein, and Richard Roberts, ibid.

18 Nathan I. Huggins, *Black Odyssey: The Afro-American Ordeal in Slavery* (1st ed., 1977; New York, 1979), quote on 5; *The Interesting Narrative of the Life of Olaudah Equiano, or Gustavus Vasa, the African* (6th ed., London, 1793), excerpted in David Northrup, ed., *The Atlantic Slave Trade* (Lexington, Mass., 1994), 74–80; Claude Meillassoux, *Anthropologie de l'esclavage: Le ventre de fer et d'argent* (Paris, 1986), is sensitive to all aspects of depersonalization, while Orlando Patterson, *Slavery and Social Death* (Cambridge, 1982), neglects aspects of gender.

19 Paul E. Lovejoy, *Transformations in Slavery: A History of Slavery in Africa* (Cambridge, 1983); Michèle Duchet, "Reactions to the Problem of the Slave Trade: An Historical and Ideological Study," in UNESCO, *The African Slave Trade from the Fifteenth to Nineteenth Century* (Paris, 1979), 31–54.

20 Philip D. Curtin, *The Atlantic Slave Trade: A Census* (Madison, 1969), 119, 216, 235. Curtin's margin of error is in the 10 percent range. Paul E. Lovejoy, "The Volume of the Atlantic Slave Trade: A Synthesis," *Journal of African History* 23 (1982): 473–502. Of the numerous studies on this subject, only Joseph E. Inikori, "Discussion: Measuring the Atlantic Slave Trade," *Journal of African History* 17 (1976): 595–627, has arrived at substantially higher figures (15.4 million exported, 13.4 million imported); Inikori and Engerman, "Introduction: Gainers and Losers in the Atlantic Slave Trade," in Inikori and Engerman, *Atlantic Slave Trade*, 5–6; A. M. H. Sheriff, "The Slave Mode of Production along the East African Coast, 1810–1873," in John R. Willis, ed., *Slaves and Slavery in Muslim Africa*, 2 vols. (London, 1985), 2:161–81.

21 Jean Bazin, "Etat guerrier et guerres d'état," in Bazin and Emmanuel Terray, eds., *Guerres de lignages et guerres d'états en Afrique* (Paris, 1982), 319–74, quote on 362.

22 John Thornton, *Africa and Africans in the Making of the Atlantic World, 1400–1680* (Cambridge, 1992), 184–92; Philip D. Curtin, *Economic Change in Precolonial Africa: Senegambia in the Era of the Slave Trade*, 2 vols. (Madison, 1975); Boubacar Barry, *La Sénégambie du dix-cinquième au dix-neuvième siècle: Traite négrière, Islam et conquête coloniale* (Paris, 1988).

23 Parick Manning, *Slavery and African Life: Occidental, Oriental, and African Slave Trades*

(Cambridge, 1990), 170–71, and review by Martin Klein, "Simulating the African Slave Trade," *Canadian Journal of African Studies* 28 (1994): 296–99, and Klein, "The Demography of Slavery in Western Sudan: The Late Nineteenth Century," in Dennis Cordell and Joel Gregory, eds., *African Population and Capitalism: Historic Perspectives* (Boulder, 1987), 50–61.

24 Roger Anstey, *The Atlantic Slave Trade and British Abolition, 1760–1810* (London, 1975), 60–86; Joseph C. Miller, "The Significance of Drought, Disease, and Famine in the Agriculturally Marginal Zones of West-Central Africa," *Journal of African History* 23 (1982): 17–61, and Miller, *Way of Death: Merchant Capitalism and the Angolan Slave Trade, 1730–1830* (Madison, 1988); John Fage, "Slavery and the Slave Trade in the Context of West African History," *Journal of African History* 10 (1969): 393–404; Northrup, *Atlantic Slave Trade*, 80–95; Walter Rodney, *A History of the Upper Guinea Coast, 1545–1800* (Oxford, 1970), 275–78; Klein, "The Impact," 32–41.

25 William [Willem] Bosman, *A New and Accurate Description of the Coast of Guinea, Divided into the Gold, the Slave, and the Ivory Coasts* (Dutch orig.; 2d ed., London, 1721), quoted in Northrup, *Atlantic Slave Trade*, 71–74; Anstey, *Atlantic Slave Trade*, 17–21.

26 Richard B. Sheridan, "Slave Demography in the British West Indies and the Abolition of the Slave Trade," in David Eltis and James Walvin, eds., *The Abolition of the Atlantic Slave Trade: Origins and Effects in Europe, Africa, and the Americas* (Madison, 1981), quote on 262; Curtin, *Atlantic Slave Trade*, 268, table on 77; Northrup, *Atlantic Slave Trade*, graph on 45.

27 Philip D. Curtin, *The Tropical Atlantic in the Age of the Slave Trade* (Washington, D.C., 1991), 2–4, quote on 13; Eric E. Williams, *Capitalism and Slavery* (1964; Chapel Hill, N.C., 1994); Barbara J. Solow, *Slavery and the Rise of the Atlantic System* (Cambridge, Mass., 1991); Inikori and Engerman, "Gainers and Losers," 8–10; Paul E. Lovejoy and David Richardson, "Trust, Pawnship, and Atlantic History: The Institutional Foundations of the Old Calabar Slave Trade," *American Historical Review* 104 (1999): 333–55.

28 Davidson, *East and Central Africa*, 162–64, 194–96, 220–80; Davidson, *Black Mother*, 238–55, quote on 242; Anstey, *Atlantic Slave Trade*, 57; Edward A. Alpers, *Ivory and Slaves in East Central Africa: Changing Patterns of International Trade to the Later Nineteenth Century* (London, 1975); Robert L. Stein, *The French Slave Trade in the Eighteenth Century: An Old Regime Business* (Madison, 1979); Johannes M. Postma, *The Dutch in the Atlantic Slave Trade* (Cambridge, 1990).

29 Davidson, *Black Mother*, 180 (Chinese report); Basil Davidson, *Africa in History: Themes and Outlines* (1st ed., 1966; rev. ed., New York, 1991), 206; John Laffin, *The Arabs as Master Slavers* (Englewood, N.J., 1982); Bernard Lewis, *Race and Slavery in the Middle East: An Historical Enquiry* (Oxford, 1990); Murray Gordon, *Slavery in the Arab World* (French orig., 1987; New York, 1989).

30 Gordon, *Slavery in the Arab World*, 18–47.

31 Late-nineteenth-century Arab and Indian Muslim intellectual leaders and reformers stressed equality and emphasized those passages of the Koran that encouraged manumission.

32 Willis, *Slaves and Slavery*, 1:4.

33 Ralph A. Austen, "From the Atlantic to the Indian Ocean: European Abolition, the African Slave Trade, and Asian Economic Structures," in Eltis and Walvin, *Abolition*, 199–200; Patrick Manning, "The Slave Trade: The Formal Demography of a Global System," in Inikori

and Engerman, *Atlantic Slave Trade*, 121, and Manning, *Slavery and African Life*; Lewis, *Race and Slavery in the Middle East*, quote on 101.

34 Abdul Sheriff, *Slaves, Spices and Ivory in Zanzibar* (Athens, Ohio, 1987).

35 Lovejoy, *Transformations*, 25, 44 passim; Manning, *Slavery and African Life*, and "Slave Trade," 117–41, esp. 118–20, has estimated death rates of 15 percent in the intra-African trade and of 30 percent in both oceanic circuits. Most authors summarily assume 15–20 percent. On a very thin data base, Ralph A. Austen estimated as many as 17 million slaves traded. "The Trans-Saharan Slave Trade: A Tentative Census," in Henry A. Gemery and Jan S. Hogendorn, eds., *The Uncommon Market: Essays in the Economic History of the Atlantic Slave Trade* (New York, 1979), 23–76, and Austen, "From the Atlantic to the Indian Ocean," 117–39; Raymond W. Beachey, *The Slave Trade of Eastern Africa* (London, 1976); W. Gervase Clarence-Smith, *The Economics of the Indian Ocean Slave Trade in the Nineteenth Century* (London, 1989); Janet J. Ewald, "Slavery in Africa and the Slave Trades from Africa," *American Historical Review* 97 (1992): 465–85, quote on 467.

36 Lovejoy, *Transformations*, 1–22, 66–87; Martin A. Klein, "The Study of Slavery in Africa: A Review Article," *Journal of African History* 19 (1978): 599–609; Suzanne Miers and Igor Kopytoff, eds., *Slavery in Africa: Historical and Anthropological Perspectives* (Madison, 1977).

37 Miers and Kopytoff, *Slavery in Africa*, 12–39; Claude Meillassoux, ed., *Esclavage en Afrique précoloniale* (Paris, 1975).

38 Klein, "The Impact," quote on 33; Davidson, *Africa in History*, 212; Huggins, *Black Odyssey*, 8–21.

39 Martin Klein, "The Demography of Slavery in Western Sudan," 50–61; Claire C. Robertson and Martin A. Klein, eds., *Women and Slavery in Africa* (Madison, 1983), quote on 3; "Foreword" by Suzanne Miers, ix; Klein, "Women in Slavery in Western Sudan"; and Marcia Wright, "Bwanikwa: Consciousness and Protest among Slave Women in Central Africa, 1886–1911," in Robertson and Klein, *Women and Slavery*, 67–92 and 246–67. On manhood, see Orlando Patterson, "On Slavery and Slave Formations," *New Left Review* 117 (1979): 31–67.

40 Manning, "Slave Trade," 138–39; Suzanne Miers and Richard Roberts, eds., *The End of Slavery in Africa* (Madison, 1988).

41 Ewald, "Slavery in Africa," 470–71.

7 Trade-Posts and Colonies in the World of the Indian Ocean

1 Historical migrations in the four Asian regions have not been synthesized either regionally or continent-wide except for studies of particular cities. Much of the information in this chapter has been culled from the sophisticated economic histories of the trade emporia. Only for the nineteenth century, especially with regard to the contract labor migration, does a voluminous and high-quality historiography exist.

2 Ashin Das Gupta, *Merchants of Maritime India, 1500–1800* (Aldershot, U.K., 1994), 7:153; Edi Sedyawati, "'Fremdes' und 'Eigenes' in Kunst und Kultur Indonesiens," *Versunkene Königreiche Indonesiens* (Mainz, 1995), 193–204.

3 Joseph E. Schwartzberg, ed., *A Historical Atlas of South Asia* (Chicago, 1978; 2d rev. ed., Oxford, 1992), 33–35, 191–99; Kirti N. Chaudhuri, *Trade and Civilization in the Indian*

Ocean: An Economic History from the Rise of Islam to 1750 (Cambridge, 1985), 9–62; Richard M. Eaton, "Islamic History as Global History," in Michael Adas, ed., *Islamic and European Expansion: The Forging of a Global Order* (Philadelphia, 1993), 1–36; Jamal Malik, *Islamische Gelehrtenkultur in Nordindien: Entwicklungsgeschichte und Tendenzen am Beispiel von Lucknow* (Leiden, 1997).

4   Schwartzberg, *Atlas of South Asia*, 196, 199–200.

5   The reintroduction of the tax and the prohibition of the Hindu faith caused major rebellions and dislocations in 1669.

6   Philip D. Curtin, *Cross-Cultural Trade in World History* (Cambridge, 1984), chap. 6; Schwartzberg, *Atlas of South Asia*, 194; C. G. F. Simkin, *The Traditional Trade of Asia* (Oxford, 1968), 168–70; Jagadish N. Sarkar, *Studies in Economic Life in Mughal India* (Delhi, 1975), 204–29, 230–57; Kirti N. Chaudhuri, *Asia Before Europe: Economy and Civilization of the Indian Ocean from the Rise of Islam to 1750* (Cambridge, 1990); Judith Tucker, "Gender and Islamic History," in Adas, *Islamic and European Expansion*, 37–73.

7   Maria A. P. Meilink-Roelofsz, *Asian Trade and European Influence in the Indonesian Archipelago between 1500 and about 1630* (The Hague, 1962), 13–26, 89–115.

8   Meilink-Roelofsz, *Asian Trade*, 36–59, quote on 59, 67; Simkin, *Traditional Trade*, 163–167; Curtin, *Cross-Cultural Trade*, 128–35; Das Gupta, *Merchants of Maritime India*, essay VII: 152–55; K. A. Nilakanta Sastri, *South Indian Influences in the Far East* (Bombay, 1949); Widjojo Nitisastro, *Population Trends in Indonesia* (Ithaca, N.Y., 1970), 10, 38–40, 87–90; Ruth T. McVey, ed., *Indonesia* (New Haven, 1963), 20–23.

9   G. M. Dening, "The Geographical Knowledge of the Polynesians and the Nature of Inter-Island Contact," in Jack Golson, ed., *Polynesian Navigation* (3d ed., Wellington, N.Z., 1972), 102–53, quotes on 103 and 112–13.

10 Ping-ti Ho, *Studies on the Population of China, 1368–1953* (Cambridge, Mass., 1959), 136–39.

11 Dorothy Ko, *Teachers of the Inner Chambers: Women and Culture in Seventeenth-Century China* (Stanford, 1994).

12 Ho, *Population of China*, 139–53.

13 John R. Shephard, *Statecraft and Political Economy on the Taiwan Frontier, 1600–1800* (Stanford, 1993). On the treatment of the aboriginal inhabitants, see Government of Formosa, *Report on the Control of Aborigines in Formosa* (Taihoku, 1911), and Janet B. M. McGovern, *Among the Head-Hunters of Formosa* (London, 1922). As late as 1930, survivors of the Native peoples in the mountains of Central Taiwan rebelled against Japanese troops (Musha Rebellion).

14 Michael R. Godley, "China's Policy Towards Migrants, 1842–1949," in Christine Inglis et al., eds., *Asians in Australia: The Dynamics of Migration and Settlement* (Singapore, 1992), 1–21.

15 Jonathan D. Spence, *The Search for Modern China* (New York, 1990), 12–116; Ho, *Population of China*, 187–92, 281–82. All population figures are just estimates.

16 The term "Overseas Chinese" came into use only in the second half of the nineteenth century.

17 Charles R. Boxer, *The Christian Century in Japan, 1549–1650* (Berkeley, 1951), 101 passim.

18 In the mid-fifteenth century, Portuguese migrants jointly with Muslim ones fought as mercenaries in the Vijayanagaran army, bringing knowledge about improved firearms and war mounts with them.

19 For example, in 1327, the northern Indian sultanate's capital was transferred from Delhi to

Devagiri, and the population had to move there. The capital Ahmadabad was built in 1411–42, and the Taj Mahal was under construction from 1632 to 1657.

20 Lynn Pan, ed., *The Encyclopedia of the Chinese Overseas* (Richmond, U.K., 1999); Wang Gungwu, *The Chinese Overseas: From Earthbound China to the Quest for Autonomy* (Cambridge, Mass., 2000); Chaudhuri, *Trade and Civilization*, 32–33, 100–107; Simkin, *Traditional Trade*, 174, 176; Meilink-Roelofsz, *Asian Trade*, 66–68.

21 Curtin, *Cross-Cultural Trade*, 167–72; Simkin, *Traditional Trade*, 203–205, 217–20; T'ien Ju-K'ang, "The Chinese Junk Trade: Merchants, Entrepreneurs, and Coolies, 1600–1850," in Klaus Friedland, ed., *Maritime Aspects of Migration* (Cologne, 1989), 381–90.

22 Simkin, *Traditional Trade*, 213; G. William Skinner, *Chinese Society in Thailand: An Analytical History* (Ithaca, N.Y., 1957); Alfonso Felix Jr., ed., *The Chinese in the Philippines*, 2 vols. (Manila, 1966–69); Victor Purcell, *The Chinese in Southeast Asia* (2d rev. ed., London, 1965); Yen Ching-hwang, "Ch'ing Changing Images of Overseas Chinese (1644–1912)," *Modern Asian Studies* 15 (1981): 261–85; Shih-shan H. Tsai, "Preserving the Dragon Seeds: The Evolution of Ching Emigration Policy," *Asian Profile* 7 (1979): 497–506.

23 An Egyptian-Indian fleet was destroyed by the Portuguese in 1509, and Diu was fortified after 1535 as protection against Ottoman fleets; but by midcentury the trade via Alexandria and Cairo to Venice was functioning again.

24 Chaudhuri, *Trade and Civilization*, 51–62.

25 The term, which originally referred to Jews from Mesopotamia, came to include Jews from Syria, the Ottoman Empire, Aden, and Yemen, as well as non-Arab-speaking ones from Persia and Afghanistan.

26 Joan G. Roland, *Jews in British India: Identity in a Colonial Era* (Hanover, N.H., 1989), 1–28; Charles R. Boxer, *The Dutch Seaborne Empire, 1600–1800* (London, 1965), 144–46.

27 Gérard Chaliand and Jean-Pierre Rageau, *The Penguin Atlas of Diasporas*, trans. A. M. Berrett (French orig., Paris, 1991; New York, 1995), 73–93. For an earlier, political role, see Seta B. Dadoyan, *The Fatimid Armenians: Cultural and Political Interaction in the Near East* (Leiden, 1997).

28 David M. Lang, *Armenia: Cradle of Civilization*, 2 vols. (rev. ed., London, 1978); Curtin, *Cross-Cultural Trade*, 182–85; Frederic Macler, "Les Arméniens de Galicie," *Revue des études arméniennes* 6 (1926): 7–17; Silvio van Rooy, "Armenian Merchant Habits as Mirrored in the 17th–18th-Century Amsterdam Documents," *Revue des études arméniennes*, n.s., 12 (1966): 347–558; C. D. Telekian, "Marseille, La Provence, et les Arméniens," *Mémoirs de l'Institut Historique de Provence* 5 (1929): 5–65.

29 Niels Steensgaard, *The Asian Trade of the Seventeenth Century: The East India Companies and the Decline of the Caravan Trade* (Chicago, 1973), 26, 50; Frédéric Mauro, "Merchant Communities, 1350–1750," in James D. Tracy, ed., *The Rise of Merchant Empires: Long Distance Trade in the Early Modern World, 1350–1750* (Cambridge, 1990), 270–74; Keram Kévonian, "Marchands arméniens au XVIIe siècle," *Cahiers du monde russe et soviétique* 16 (1975): 199–24; Michel Aghassian and Keram Kévonian, "Le commerce arménien dans l'océan Indien aux XVIIe et XVIIIe siècles," in Denys Lombard and Jean Aubin, eds., *Marchands et hommes d'affaires asiatiques dans l'Océan Indien et la mer de Chine, 13e-20e siècles* (Paris, 1988), 155–82; Lvon Khachikian, "The Ledger of the Merchant Hovannes Joughayetsi," *Journal of the Asiatic Society* (Calcutta) 8 (1966): 153–86.

30 Stephen F. Dale, *Islamic Society on the South Asian Frontier: The Mappilas of Malabar, 1498-1922* (New York, 1980); Genevieve Bouchon, "Les musulmans du Kerala à l'époque de

la découverte portugaise," in Jean Aubin, ed., *Mare Luso-Indicum*, 4 vols. (Geneva, 1971–1980), 2:3–59. See also as a literary rendering Amitav Ghosh's novel *In an Antique Land* (New Delhi, 1992).

31 Chaudhuri, *Trade and Civilization*, 121–37; Curtin, *Cross-Cultural Trade*, chap. 7; Trevor Cairns, *Europe Finds the World* (9th ed., Cambridge, 1987), 28–39; Ibrahim Khoury, "Les aspects maritimes des migrations humaines dans le monde musulman des origines au début du XVIe siècle," in Friedland, *Maritime Aspects of Migration*, 357–80.

32 Simkin, *Traditional Trade*, 176–78; Curtin, *Cross-Cultural Trade*, 137–39; Chaudhuri, *Trade and Civilization*, 63–79; Kenneth R. Andrews, *Trade, Plunder and Settlement: Maritime Enterprise and the Genesis of the British Empire, 1480-1630* (Cambridge, 1984), 30–32, citing Hakluyt.

33 Boxer, *Dutch Seaborne Empire*, 212; Curtin, *Cross-Cultural Trade*, 145.

34 Frank Perlin, "Proto-Industrialization and Pre-Colonial South Asia," *Past and Present* 98 (Feb. 1983): 30–95, quote on 89; Richard von Glahn, *Fountain of Fortune: Money and Monetary Policy in China, 1000-1700* (Berkeley, 1996), 6.

35 Rafael Bernal, "The Chinese Colony in Manila, 1570–1670," in Felix, *Chinese in the Philippines*, quote on 1:60; William L. Schurz, *The Manila Galleon* (New York, 1939, repr., 1959), 40–41, 49; Francis E. Hyde, *Far Eastern Trade, 1860-1914* (London, 1973), 2.

36 The Spanish crown prohibited enslavement after 1594.

37 Milagros C. Guerrero, "The Chinese in the Philippines, 1570–1670," and Rafael Bernal, "The Chinese Colony in Manila, 1670–1770," and Alberto Santamaria, "The Chinese Parian (El Parian de los Sangleyes)," in Felix, *Chinese in the Philippines*, 1:15–39, 40–66, 67–118, and the section "Chinese Mestizo," 2:45–74; Antonio S. Tan, *The Chinese in the Philippines, 1898-1935: A Study of Their National Awakening* (Quezon City, 1972), 16–30; Shubert C. C. Liao, ed., *Chinese Participation in Philippine Culture and Economy* (Manila, 1964), 2–32; Edgar Wickberg, *The Chinese in Philippine Life, 1850-1898* (New Haven, 1965), 3–41.

38 T. B. Duncan, "Navigation between Portugal and Asia in the Sixteenth and Seventeenth Centuries," in C. Pullapilly and E. J. Van Kley, eds., *Asia and the West: Encounters and Exchanges from the Age of Explorations* (Notre Dame, 1986), 3–25; Simkin, *Traditional Trade*, 182: "There were never more than 10,000 Portuguese in Asia." Vitorino Magalhães-Godinho, "Portuguese Emigration from the Fifteenth to the Twentieth Century," in Piet C. Emmer and Magnus Mörner, eds., *European Expansion and Migration: Essays on the Intercontinental Migration from Africa, Asia, and Europe* (New York, 1992), 16–19; A. J. R. Russell-Wood, *The World on the Move: The Portuguese in Africa, Asia, and America, 1415-1808* (New York, 1992), 58–122; Schwartzberg, *Atlas of South Asia*, 199–200.

39 Chaudhuri, *Trade and Civilization*, 64, 76–77; Boxer, *The Christian Century in Japan*, 101–2, 190–91, 236–37; Boxer, *Dutch Seaborne Empire*, quote on 109–10, 128–29, 149, 156, quote of an eighteenth-century Surinam governor on 169, 159–60; Boxer (170) reports that a black slave, taken to Holland in 1728, became free and Rev. Jacobus Capitein as a *predikant*. The one people that accepted Christianity in large numbers, the Ambonese, had to leave their homes and emigrate to the Netherlands after Indonesia's independence in 1949.

40 Schwartzberg, *Atlas of South Asia*, 203; Chaudhuri, *Trade and Civilization*, quote on 78–79, 176.

41 Curtin, *Cross-Cultural Trade*, 131; "Plunder is an effective, but potentially very expensive way to acquire wealth" (ibid., 157); Boxer, *Dutch Seaborne Empire*, quote on 217.

42 Simkin, *Traditional Trade*, 194–98, 224–35; Boxer, *Dutch Seaborne Empire*, 111–12, 211,

244–25; Chaudhuri, *Trade and Civilization*, 83, 203–20. After 1900, the Dutch initiated population transfers from Java to less populated islands. Spontaneous interisland migration also developed.

43 Jean G. Taylor, *The Social World of Batavia: European and Eurasian in Dutch Asia* (Madison, 1983), 3–51; Boxer, *Dutch Seaborne Empire*, 241–66; Leonard Blussé, *Strange Company: Chinese Settlers, Mestizo Women, and the Dutch in VOC Batavia* (Dordrecht, 1986).

44 Frank Spooner, "Batavia 1673–1790: A City of Colonial Growth and Migration," in Ira A. Glazier and Luigi de Rosa, eds., *Migration across Time and Nations: Population Mobility in Historical Contexts* (New York, 1986), 30–57; Simkin, *Traditional Trade*, 232; A. van Marle, "De groep der Europeanen in Nederlands-Indie," *Indonesie* 5 (1951/52): 97–121, 314–41, 483–507. Ann Stoler, "Sexual Affronts and Racial Frontiers: European Identities and the Cultural Politics of Exclusion in Colonial Southeast Asia," in Geoff Eley and Ronald G. Suny, eds., *Becoming National: A Reader* (New York, 1996), 286–322.

45 Jan Lucassen, "The Netherlands, the Dutch, and Long-Distance Migration, in the Late Sixteenth to Early Nineteenth Centuries," in Nicholas Canny, ed., *Europeans on the Move: Studies on European Migration, 1500–1800* (Oxford, 1994), 169–80, esp. 172–73; Jonathan I. Israel, *The Dutch Republic: Its Rise, Greatness, and Fall, 1477–1806* (Oxford, 1995), 622–24. The topic of migration was part of contemporary literature. Heinrich von Kleist in his *Der zerbrochne Krug* (1808) referred to the high death rates of migration to the East Indies.

46 Contemporary observers charged that the VOC treated soldiers and sailors worse than slaves because they could be replaced more cheaply. Boxer, *Dutch Seaborne Empire*, 76–93, 121–22, 238–40, 245–46, 314–15; Jaap R. Bruijn et al., *Dutch-Asiatic Shipping in the 17th and 18th Centuries*, 3 vols. (The Hague, 1987), 1:143–72, and Bruijn and Femme S. Gaastra, eds., *Ships, Sailors and Spices: East India Companies and Their Shipping* (Amsterdam, 1993); Martin Bossenbroek, *Volk voor Indië: De werving van Europese militairen voor de Nederlandse koloniale dienst, 1814–1909* (Amsterdam, 1992), and Bossenbroek, *Van Holland naar Indië Het transport van koloniale troepen voor het Oost-Indische Leger, 1815–1909* (Amsterdam, 1986). The Netherlands government dissolved the VOC in 1799.

47 Boxer, *Dutch Seaborne Empire*, 186–87, 191–95.

48 Christopher Bayly, *Rulers, Townsmen and Bazaars: North Indian Society in the Age of British Expansion, 1770–1870* (Cambridge, 1983); Kumkum Chatterjee, *Merchants, Politics and Society in Early Modern India: Bihar, 1733–1820* (Leiden, 1996); Sudipta Sen, *Empire of Free Trade: The East India Company and the Making of the Colonial Marketplace* (Philadelphia, 1998). See the notes to chap. 16 for literature on British India.

49 Lionel F. Frost, "Coming Full Circle: A Long-Term Perspective on the Pacific Rim," in Sally M. Miller, A. J. H. Latham, and Dennis O. Flynn, eds., *Studies in the Economic History of the Pacific Rim* (London, 1998), 45–62, quote on 52.

8   Latin America: Population Collapse and Resettlement

1 For precontact Indian migration and settlement, see David Watts, *The West Indies: Patterns of Development, Culture, and Environmental Change since 1492* (Cambridge, 1987), 44–53. Piet C. Emmer, "European Expansion and Migration: The European Colonial Past and Intercontinental Migration–an Overview," in Emmer and Magnus Mörner, eds., *European Expansion and Migration: Essays on the Intercontinental Migration from Africa, Asia, and Europe* (New York, 1992), 3; Nicolás Sánchez-Albornoz, "The Population of Spanish

America," and Maria L. Marcílio, "The Population of Colonial Brazil," in Leslie Bethell, ed., *The Cambridge History of Latin America* (Cambridge, 1984), 2:15–19 and 2:45–52 (hereafter *CHLA*). With regard to slave imports, Curtin's figures will be used.

2   Watts, *West Indies*, 53–71, quote on 41.

3   Noble David Cook, "Migration in Colonial Peru: An Overview," in David J. Robinson, ed., *Migration in Colonial Spanish America* (Cambridge, 1990), 44–46; Rolando Mellafe, "The Importance of Migration in the Viceroyalty of Peru," in Paul Deprez, ed., *Population and Economics: Proceedings of Section V of the Fourth Congress of the International Economic History Association, 1968* (Winnipeg, 1970), 303–13.

4   William L. Sherman, *Forced Native Labor in Sixteenth-Century Central America* (Lincoln, Nebr., 1979), 15–19.

5   Helen H. Tanner et al., eds., *The Settling of North America: The Atlas of the Great Migrations into North America from the Ice Age to the Present* (New York, 1995), 30–43; Alvin M. Josephy Jr., *The Indian Heritage of America* (New York, 1968), and Josephy, ed., *America in 1492: The World of the Indian Peoples before the Arrival of Columbus* (New York, 1992).

6   Watts, *West Indies*, 71–75; Noble David Cook, *Demographic Collapse: Indian Peru, 1520–1620* (Cambridge, 1981).

7   Alfred W. Crosby, *Ecological Imperialism: The Biological Expansion of Europe, 900–1900* (Cambridge, 1986), 195–216, and Crosby, "The Columbian Voyages, the Columbian Exchange, and Their Historians," in Michael Adas, ed., *Islamic and European Expansion: The Forging of a Global Order* (Philadelphia, 1993), 141–64; Tzvetan Todorov, *The Conquest of America: The Question of the Other*, trans. Richard Howard (French orig., Paris, 1982; New York, 1984), 53–123.

8   Magnus Mörner, ed., *The Expulsion of the Jesuits from Latin America* (New York, 1965), 3–30, quote on 7; John L. Phelan, *The Millennial Kingdom of the Franciscans in the New World* (1956; rev. ed., Berkeley, 1970); Gilberto Freyre, *The Masters and the Slaves (Casa-grande y senzala): A Study in the Development of Brazilian Civilization*, trans. Samuel Putnam (Portuguese orig., 4th ed., 1943, Rio de Janeiro; rev. ed., New York, 1956), 109.

9   Gibson, "Indian Societies under Spanish Rule," in *CHLA* 2:383–84; Nancy M. Farriss, "The Cosmic Order in Crisis," in Alan L. Karras and John R. McNeill, eds., *Atlantic American Societies: From Columbus through Abolition, 1492–1888* (London, 1992), 99–143; Edward G. Gray and Norman Fiering, eds., *The Language Encounter in the Americas, 1492–1800: A Collection of Essays* (Oxford, 2000).

10   Ida Altman, *Emigrants and Society: Extremadura and America in the Sixteenth Century* (Berkeley, 1989), 165.

11   Peter Boyd-Bowman, "Spanish Emigrants to the Indies, 1595–98: A Profile," in Fredi Chiappelli et al., eds., *First Images of America: The Impact of the New World on the Old*, 2 vols. (Berkeley, 1976), 2:723–35, quote on 732; Altman, *Emigrants*, 4, 173–89; Annie Molinié-Bertrand, *Au siècle d'or—l'Espagne et ses hommes: La population du Royaume de Castille au XVIe siècle* (Paris, 1985), 377–91. Destinations in the Americas competed with Italy or the Netherlands, both part of the Habsburgs' holdings.

12   Vitorino Magalhães-Godinho, "Portuguese Emigration from the Fifteenth to the Twentieth Century: Constants and Changes," in Emmer and Mörner, *European Expansion*, 13–48, esp. 24–26.

13   The different estimates, some as high as 750,000 by 1700 or as low as 500,000 for the whole period, are discussed in Nicolás Sánchez-Albornoz, "The First Transatlantic Transfer: Span-

ish Migration to the New World, 1493–1810," in Nicholas Canny, ed., *Europeans on the Move: Studies on European Migration, 1500–1800* (Oxford, 1994), 26–36. Magnus Mörner, *Adventurers and Proletarians: The Story of Migrants in Latin America* (Pittsburgh, 1985), and, Mörner, "Immigration into Latin America, especially Argentina and Chile," in Emmer and Mörner, *European Expansion*, 211–43; Woodrow Borah, "The Mixing of Populations," in Chiappelli, *First Images*, 2:707–22; Magnus Mörner, "A Bibliography on Spanish Migration," ibid., 797–804, especially for Spanish-language titles. Nicolás Sánchez-Albornoz, *The Population of Latin America: A History*, trans. W. A. R. Richardson (Spanish orig., n.d.; Berkeley, 1974), 66–67.

14 Magnus Mörner, "Spanish Migration to the New World prior to 1810: A Report on the State of Research," in Chiappelli, *First Images*, 2:752, 753, quote on 758; Auke P. Jacobs, "Legal and Illegal Emigration from Seville, 1550–1650," in Ida Altman and James Horn, eds., *"To Make America": European Emigration in the Early Modern Period* (Berkeley, 1991), 59–84; J. J. Parsons, "The Migration of Canary Islanders to the Americas: An Unbroken Current since Columbus," *The Americas* 39 (1983): 447–81.

15 James Lockhart, "Letters and People to Spain," in Chiappelli, *First Images*, 2:783–96.

16 Enrique Otte, "Die europäischen Siedler und die Probleme der Neuen Welt," *Jahrbuch für die Geschichte von Staat, Wirtschaft und Gesellschaft Lateinamerikas* 6 (1969): 1–40; Altman, *Emigrants*, 247–74; Godinho, "Portuguese Emigration," 30–32.

17 George M. Foster, *Culture and Conquest: America's Spanish Heritage* (Chicago, 1960); Ida Altman, "Emigrants and Society: An Approach to the Background of Colonial Spanish America," *Comparative Studies in Society and History* 30 (1988): 170–90.

18 Mörner, "Spanish Migration," 744–46; Peter Boyd-Bowman, "Patterns of Spanish Emigration to the Indies until 1600," *Hispanic American Historical Review* 56 (1976): 580–604; Norman F. Martin, *Los vagabundos en la Nueva España, siglo XVI* (Mexico, 1957); Peter Stern and Robert Jackson, "*Vagabundaje* and Settlement Patterns in Colonial Northern Sonora," *The Americas* 44 (1988): 461–78; Julia Hirschberg, "Transients in Early Colonial Society: Puebla de los Angeles, 1531–1560," *Biblioteca Americana* 1 (1983): 1–33; Cynthia Radding, *Wandering Peoples: Colonialism, Ethnic Spaces, and Ecological Frontiers in Northwestern Mexico, 1700–1850* (Durham, N.C., 1997).

19 James M. Lockhart, *Spanish Peru, 1532–1560: A Colonial Society* (Madison, 1968), 114–40; Leon G. Campbell, "The Foreigners in Peruvian Society during the Eighteenth Century," *Revista de Historia de América* 73/74 (1972): 153–63; Inge Wolff, "Zur Geschichte der Ausländer im spanischen Amerika: Die Stellung des *extranjero* in der Stadt Potosí vom 16. bis zum 18. Jahrhundert," in *Europa und Übersee* (Hamburg, 1962), 78–108; Seymour B. Liebman, "The Jews of Colonial Mexico," *Hispanic American Historical Review* 43 (1963): 95–108; Charles F. Nunn, *Foreign Immigrants in Early Bourbon Mexico, 1700–1760* (Cambridge, 1979).

20 Mörner, "Spanish Migration," 737–49.

21 Laurette Séjourné, *Altamerikanische Kulturen* (Frankfurt/Main, 1971), 19–26; Watts, *West Indies*, 53–71; Sherman, *Forced Native Labor*, 87–88; María T. Molino García, *La encomienda en el nuevo reino de Granada durante el siglo XVIII* (Sevilla, 1976), 61–62, 103–8.

22 Altman, *Emigrants*, 221–25, quote on 224; Watts, *West Indies*, 98–117; Silvio A. Zavala, *La encomienda indiana* (Madrid, 1935; rev. ed., Mexico, 1973), 18, 26–32.

23 Richard M. Morse, "The Urban Development of Colonial Spanish America," in *CHLA* 2:67–103, esp. 81–90.

24 Pierre Chaumu, *European Expansion in the Later Middle Ages* (Amsterdam, 1979); Kris E. Lane, *Pillaging the Empire: Piracy in the Americas, 1500-1750* (Armonk, N.Y., 1998); Robert L. Stein, *The French Slave Trade in the Eighteenth Century: An Old Regime Business* (Madison, 1979), 3-6, quote on 6.

25 Jointly with Dutch organizers, Sweden established in 1638 a colony on the Delaware, which lasted until 1655. The Dutch in Brazil occupied Bahia in 1624-25 and Recife and Olinda from 1630 to 1654. Jan Lucassen, "The Netherlands, the Dutch, and Long-Distance Migration, in the Late Sixteenth to Early Nineteenth Centuries," in Canny, *Europeans on the Move*, 169-80; Watts, *West Indies*, 135-41; R. A. J. van Lier, *Frontier Society: A Social Analysis of the History of Surinam* (The Hague, 1971); Paolo Bernardini and Norman Fiering, eds., *The Jews and the Expansion of Europe to the West, 1400-1800* (Oxford, 2000).

26 Watts, *West Indies*, 143-73, 156-60, 176-231; Carl Bridenbaugh and Roberta Bridenbaugh, *No Peace beyond the Line: The English in the Caribbean 1624-1690* (New York, 1972), 9-34; Borah, "Mixing of Populations," 704-22.

27 As in the case of the Atlantic crossing, where fishermen probably preceded the state-sponsored explorers, transpacific contacts may have been established earlier by Chinese sailors and by South Sea voyagers on rafts.

28 William L. Schurz, *The Manila Galleon* (New York, 1959), 5-50; Dennis O. Flynn and Arturo Giráldez, "Introduction: The Pacific Rim's Past Deserves a Future," in Sally M. Miller, A. J. H. Latham, and Dennis O. Flynn, eds., *Studies in the Economic History of the Pacific Rim* (London, 1998), 1-18; John M. Liu, "A Comparative View of Asian Immigration to the USA," in Robin Cohen, ed., *The Cambridge Survey of World Migration* (Cambridge, 1995), 253-59; Evelyn Hu-DeHart, "Latin America in Asia-Pacific Perspective," in Arif Dirlik, ed., *What Is in a Rim? Critical Perspectives on the Pacific Region Idea* (1993; 2d ed., Lanham, Md., 1998), 251-82; Clarence E. Glick, *Sojourners and Settlers: Chinese Migrants in Hawaii* (Honolulu, 1980).

29 Gibson, "Indian Societies under Spanish Rule," 412-14.

30 Spanish-America: approximately 300,000; Portuguese-America: 560,000; British, French, Dutch, and Danish Caribbean: 460,000; Anglo-American mainland: approximately 30,000.

31 Regulations to correct the imbalance required that one-third of the slaves imported should be female. Philip D. Curtin, *The Atlantic Slave Trade: A Census* (Madison, 1969), 95-126; Sánchez-Albornoz, *Population of Latin America*, 75.

32 Sánchez-Albornoz, *Population of Latin America*, 130-34; Borah, "Mixing of Populations," 708-10; David A. Brading, *Miners and Merchants in Bourbon Mexico, 1763-1810* (Cambridge, 1971). On the interaction of race, ethnicity, and culture and concomitant ideologies, see Robert M. Levine, *Race and Ethnic Relations in Latin America and the Caribbean: Dictionary and Bibliography* (Metuchen, N.J., 1980); Magnus Mörner, *Race Mixture in the History of Latin America* (Boston, 1967), 58; Marvin Harris, *Patterns of Race in the Americas* (New York, 1964); Robert B. Toplin, ed., *Slavery and Race Relations in Latin America* (Westport, Conn., 1974); Carl Degler, *Neither Black nor White: Slavery and Race Relations in Brazil and the United States* (Madison, 1971).

33 Careri had left Naples five years earlier for North Africa and had traveled through Asia Minor via India to the Philippines and arrived in Mexico via Acapulco. Nunn, *Foreign Immigrants*, 5-8.

34 Oakah L. Jones, *Los Paisanos: Spanish Settlers on the Northern Frontier of New Spain* (Norman, Okla., 1979), 6-11.

35   Philip D. Curtin, *Cross-Cultural Trade in World History* (Cambridge, 1984), 180–82; Richard M. Morse, *The Bandeirantes: The Historical Role of the Brazilian Pathfinders* (New York, 1965); Clodomir V. Moog, *Bandeirantes and Pioneers,* trans. L. L. Barrett (Portuguese orig., Rio de Janeiro, 1954; New York, 1964).

36   Godinho, "Portuguese Emigration," 24; A. J. R. Russell-Wood, "Ports of Colonial Brazil," in Karras and McNeill, *Atlantic American Societies,* 174–211; Bolivar Lamounier et al., *La Population du Brésil* (São Paulo, 1975), 7–30, 100–107; Laird W. Bergad, "Demographic Change in a Post-Export Boom Society: The Population of Minas Gerais, Brazil, 1776–1821," *Journal of Social History* 29 (1996): 895–932; Herbert S. Klein and Clotilde A. Paiva, "Freedman in a Slave Economy: Minas Gerais in 1831," *Journal of Social History* 29 (1996): 933–62.

37   Inter-Caribbean migrations depending on relative economic opportunities have been discussed above (chap. 8.3); internal migration in the United States and Canada will be treated below (see chaps. 9 and 14.2).

38   Robinson, *Migration,* 1–17; Cook, "Migration in Colonial Peru," 53–61; Oliver Marshall, comp., *European Immigration and Ethnicity in Latin America: A Bibliography* (London, 1991).

39   George Lovell and William R. Swezey, "Indian Migration and Community Formation: An Analysis of *Congregación* in Colonial Guatemala," and Rodney Watson, "Informal Settlement and Fugitive Migration amongst Indians of Late-Colonial Chiapas, Mexico," in Robinson, *Migration,* 18–40 and 238–78.

40   Frederick P. Bowser, *The African Slave in Colonial Peru, 1524–1650* (Stanford, 1974); Michael M. Swann, "Migration, Mobility, and the Mining Towns of Colonial Northern Mexico," in Robinson, *Migration,* 143–181; Peter Bakewell, *Miners of the Red Mountain: Indian Labor in Potosí, 1545–1650* (Albuquerque, 1984).

41   Catherine Delamarre and Bertrand Sallard, *La femme au temps des conquistadores* (Paris, 1992); Juan F. Maura, *Women in the Conquest of the Americas,* trans. John F. Deredita (Spanish orig., n.d.; New York, 1997). See also the older Luis Martín, *Daughters of the Conquistadores: Women of the Viceroyalty of Peru* (Albuquerque, 1983).

42   David J. Robinson, "Migration in Eighteenth-Century Mexico: Case Studies from Michoacán," *Journal of Historical Geography* 15 (1989): 55–68, quote on 60–61.

43   Irene Silverblatt, "Andean Women in the Inca Empire," *Feminist Studies* 4 (1978): 37–59, and Silverblatt, "Andean Women under Spanish Rule," in Mona Etienne and Eleanor Leacock, eds., *Women and Colonization: Anthropological Perspectives* (New York, 1980), 149–85; Asunción Lavrin, "Women in Spanish American Colonial History," in *CHLA* 3:321–55; Ann Wrightman, "'. . . residente en esa ciudad . . .': Urban Migrants in Colonial Cuzco," in Robinson, *Migration,* 86–111, quote on 111. For New Spain, see John Kicza, "Migration to Major Metropoles in Colonial Mexico," in Robinson, *Migration,* 193–211.

44   Robinson, "Migration in Michoacán," 55–68, quote on 63–64; Rosemary D. F. Bromley, "Disasters and Population Change in Central Highland Ecuador, 1778–1825," in David J. Robinson, ed., *Social Fabric and Spatial Structure in Colonial Latin America* (Ann Arbor, 1979), 85–116.

45   Brading, *Miners and Merchants,* 6–14, 106–14 on merchants and Mexico City, 146–49, 164–65, 248–60 on mining.

46   Lyman L. Johnson and Susan M. Socolow, "Population and Space in Eighteenth Century Buenos Aires," in Robinson, *Social Fabric,* 339–68, quotes on 350–52. Foreign immigrants came mainly from Italy but also from Ireland. Patrick McKenna, "Irish Migration to Argen-

tina," in Patrick O'Sullivan, ed., *The Irish World Wide: History, Heritage, Identity*, 6 vols., vol. 1: *Patterns of Migration* (London, 1992), 63–83.

47   Hilary McF. Beckles, "The Colours of Property: Brown, White and Black Chattels and Their Responses on the Caribbean Frontier," in Paul E. Lovejoy and Nicholas Rogers, eds., *Unfree Labour in the Development of the Atlantic World* (Ilford, U.K., 1994), 36–51. Essays by Carmen Castañeda, Elsa Malvido, Robert McCaa in Robinson, *Migration*. Kenneth J. Andrien and Rolena Adorno, eds., *Transatlantic Encounters: Europeans and Andeans in the Sixteenth Century* (Berkeley, 1991).

48   Richard Price, ed., *Maroon Societies: Rebel Slave Communities in the Americas* (Baltimore, 1979); Pedro D. Chapeaux, "Cimarrones Urbanos," *Revista de la Biblioteca Nacional José Martí* 2 (1969): 145–64; Gabriel Debien, "Le marronage aux Antilles Françaises au XVIIIe siècle," *Caribbean Studies* 6 (1966): 3–44; Mavis C. Campbell, "The Maroons of Jamaica: Imperium in Imperio?" *Pan-African Journal* 6 (1973): 45–55; Jane Landers, "Cimarrón Ethnicity and Cultural Adaptation in the Spanish Domains of the Circum-Caribbean, 1503–1763," in Paul E. Lovejoy, ed., *Identity in the Shadow of Slavery* (London, 2000), 30–54; Gad Heuman, ed., *Out of the House of Bondage: Runaways, Resistance and Marronage in Africa and the New World* (London, 1985); Barbara Kopytoff, "The Development of Jamaican Maroon Ethnicity," *Caribbean Quarterly* 22 (1976): 33–50; Flávio dos Santos Gomes, *Histórias de quilombolas: Mocambos e comunidades de senzalas no Rio de Janeiro—século século XIX* (Rio de Janeiro, 1995); Franklin W. Knight, *The Caribbean: The Genesis of a Fragmented Nationalism* (Oxford, 1978), 69–79; Jerome S. Handler, "Slave Revolts and Conspiracies in Seventeenth-Century Barbados," *Nieuwe West-Indische Gids* 65, 1–2 (1982): 5–42.

9   Fur Empires and Colonies of Agricultural Settlement

1   This interpretation reflects Atlantic ideology. In Russia, the Siberian frontier assumed the central place in the rhetoric of "exploration."

2   F. A. Golder, *Russian Expansion on the Pacific, 1641–1850: An Account of the Earliest and Later Expeditions Made by the Russians along the Pacific Coast of Asia and North America, including Some Related Expeditions to the Arctic Regions* (1914; repr., New York, 1971); S. B. Okun, *The Russian-American Company*, ed. B. D. Grekov, trans Carl Ginsburg (Russian orig., Moscow, 1939; Cambridge, Mass., 1951).

3   James Forsyth, *A History of the Peoples of Siberia: Russia's North Asian Colony, 1581–1990* (Cambridge, 1992); Marc Raeff, *Siberia and the Reforms of 1822* (Seattle, 1956); Günther Stökl, *Die Entstehung des Kosakentums* (Munich, 1953); Philip Longworth, *The Cossacks* (London, 1969). Cossacks temporarily established a state of their own. Their mid-seventeenth-century uprising under Bogdan Chmielnicki involved atrocities against the Jewish population.

4   The upstream Mississippi route was hardly used. Philip D. Curtin, *Cross-Cultural Trade in World History* (Cambridge, 1984), 188–229. Conrad E. Heidenreich and Arthur J. Ray, *The Early Fur Trades: A Study in Cultural Interaction* (Toronto, 1976); William J. Eccles, "The Fur Trade and Eighteenth-Century Imperialism," repr. in Alan L. Karras and John R. McNeill, eds., *Atlantic American Societies: From Columbus through Abolition, 1492–1888* (London, 1992), 212–41, and Eccles, *France in America* (East Lansing, 1990); Philip P. Boucher, *Les Nouvelles Frances: France in America, 1500–1815, an Imperial Perspective* (Provi-

dence, 1989); Oliver A. Rink, *Holland on the Hudson: An Economic and Social History of Dutch New York* (Ithaca, 1986).

5 Edmund S. Morgan, "The Labor Problem at Jamestown," *American Historical Review* 76 (1971): 595–611; K. G. Davies, *The North Atlantic World in the Seventeenth Century* (Minneapolis, 1974), 79; Almon W. Lauber, *Indian Slavery in Colonial Times within the Present Limits of the United States* (New York, 1913); Marc Egnal, *Divergent Paths: How Culture and Institutions Have Shaped North American Growth* (Oxford, 1996).

6 Helen H. Tanner et al., eds., *The Settling of North America: The Atlas of the Great Migrations into North America from the Ice Age to the Present* (New York, 1995), 42–43, 54–55; Gary B. Nash, *Red, White, and Black: The Peoples of Early America* (Englewood Cliffs, N.J., 1974); A. Irving Hallowell, "The Backwash of the Frontier: The Impact of the Indian on American Culture," in Walker D. Wyman and Clifton B. Kroeber, eds., *The Frontier in Perspective* (Madison, 1957), 229–58.

7 J. Norman Heard, *White into Red: A Study of the Assimilation of White Persons Captured by Indians* (Metuchen, N.J., 1973); James Axtell, "The White Indians of Colonial America," *William and Mary Quarterly* 3, 32 (1975): 55–88; Wilcomb E. Washburn, ed., *The Indian and the White Man* (Garden City, N.Y., 1964); James W. Covington, *The Seminoles of Florida* (Gainesville, Fla., 1993).

8 Tanner, *Settling*, 74–77, 90–91, 126–27; Helen H. Jackson, *A Century of Dishonor: A Sketch of the United States Government's Dealings with Some of the Indian Tribes* (New York, 1881); Walter H. Blumenthal, *American Indians Dispossessed: Fraud in Land Cessions Forced upon the Tribes* (Philadelphia, 1955); Louis Filler and Allen Guttman, eds., *The Removal of the Cherokee Nation: Manifest Destiny or National Dishonor?* (Boston, 1962); Robert F. Berkhofer Jr., *The White Man's Indian: Images of the American Indian from Columbus to the Present* (New York, 1978).

9 Ruth Pike, *Penal Servitude in Early Modern Spain* (Madison, 1983); Virginia Thompson and Richard Adloff, *The French Pacific Islands: French Polynesia and New Caledonia* (Berkeley, 1971); Martyn Lyons, *The Totem and the Tricolour: A Short History of New Caledonia since 1774* (Kensington, Austral., 1986); Franz von Holtzendorff, *Die Deportation als Strafmittel in alter und neuer Zeit und die Verbrechercolonien der Engländer und Franzosen in ihrer geschichtlichen Entwicklung und criminalpolitischen Bedeutung* (Leipzig, 1859).

10 A. Roger Ekirch, *Bound for America: The Transportation of British Convicts to the Colonies, 1718–1775* (Oxford, 1987); Ian Duffield and James Bradley, eds., *Representing Convicts: New Perspectives on Convict Forced Labour Migration* (Leicester, 1997).

11 Robert J. Steinfeld, *The Invention of Free Labor: The Employment Relation in English and American Law and Culture, 1350–1870* (Chapel Hill, 1991); David W. Galenson, "Labor Market Behavior in Colonial America: Servitude, Slavery, and Free Labor," in Galenson, ed., *Markets in History: Economic Studies of the Past* (Cambridge, 1989), 93–94; Edmund S. Morgan, *American Slavery, American Freedom: The Ordeal of Colonial Virginia* (New York, 1975), 79–97; Paul Craven and Douglas Hay, "The Criminalization of 'Free' Labour: Master and Servant in Comparative Perspective," in Paul E. Lovejoy and Nicholas Rogers, eds., *Unfree Labour in the Development of the Atlantic World* (Ilford, U.K., 1994), 71–101.

12 Abbot E. Smith, *Colonists in Bondage:. White Servitude and Convict Labor in America, 1607–1776* (Chapel Hill, 1947), 336; David W. Galenson, *White Servitude in Colonial America: An Economic Analysis* (Cambridge, 1981); Farley Grubb, "The Incidence of Servi-

tude in Trans-Atlantic Migration, 1771–1801," *Explorations in Economic History* 22 (1985): 316–39. The essays in Piet C. Emmer, ed., *Colonialism and Migration: Indentured Labour before and after Slavery* (Dordrecht, 1986), provide a summary of research on English, Dutch, French, and German indentured servants, as well as on the absence of indenture in Spanish America.

13 D. W. Meinig, *The Shaping of America: A Geographical Perspective on 500 Years of History*, 3 vols., vol. 1: "Atlantic America, 1492–1800" (New Haven, 1986), provides a survey of internal migration and settlement patterns.

14 In eighteenth-century Bordeaux, 40 percent of the grooms and 25 percent of the brides were migrants to the city. Peter Moogk, "Manon's Fellow Exiles: Emigration from France to North America before 1763," in Nicholas Canny, ed., *Europeans on the Move: Studies on European Migration, 1500–1800* (Oxford, 1994), 241. Among colonial soldiers the country-town relationship was more balanced (ibid., 256–57). Leslie Choquette, *Frenchmen into Peasants: Modernity and Tradition in the Peopling of French Canada* (Cambridge, Mass., 1997).

15 Gabriel Debien, *Les engagés pour les Antilles (1634–1715)* (Paris, 1952); Leslie Choquette, "Recruitment of French Emigrants to Canada," and Christian Huetz de Lemps, "Indentured Servants Bound for the French Antilles," in Ida Altman and James Horn, eds., *"To Make America": European Emigration in the Early Modern Period* (Berkeley, 1991), 131–71 and 172–203; Frédéric Mauro, "French Indentured Servants for America, 1500–1800," in Emmer, *Colonialism and Migration*, 83–104; Moogk, "Emigration from France," 244–45; Silvio Dumas, *Les filles du roi en Nouvelle-France: Étude historique avec répertoire biographique* (Quebec, 1972); Yves Landry, *Orphelines en France, pionnières au Canada: Les filles du roi au XVIIe siècle, suivi d'un répertoire biographique des filles du roi* (Ottawa, 1992); Christian Dessureault et al., "Living Standards of Norman and Canadian Peasants," in Anton J. Schuurman and Lorena S. Walsh, eds., *Material Culture: Consumption, Life-Style, Standard of Living, 1500–1900* (Milan, 1994), 95–112.

16 Marianne Wokeck, "Harnessing the Lure of the 'Best Poor Man's Country': The Dynamics of German-Speaking Immigration to British North America, 1683–1783," in Altman and Horn, *"To Make America,"* 204–43; Georg Fertig, "Migration from the German-Speaking Parts of Central Europe," in Canny, *Europeans on the Move*, 210–18, quote on 213; Hans Fenske, "International Migration: Germany in the Eighteenth Century," *Central European History* 13 (1980): 332–47; Farley Grubb, "The Market for Indentured Immigrants: Evidence on the Efficiency of Forward-Labor Contracting in Philadelphia, 1745–1773," *Journal of Economic History* 45 (1985): 855–68; Günter Moltmann, "The Migration of German Redemptioners to North America, 1720–1820," in Emmer, *Colonialism and Migration*, 105–22; William I. Hull, *William Penn and the Dutch Quaker Migration to Pennsylvania* (Swarthmore, Pa., 1935); Wolfgang von Hippel, *Auswanderung aus Südwestdeutschland: Studien zur württembergischen Auswanderung und Auswanderungspolitik im 18. und 19. Jahrhundert* (Stuttgart, 1984). Caricature reprinted in Hermann von Freeden und Georg Smolka, eds., *Auswanderer: Bilder und Skizzen aus der Geschichte der deutschen Auswanderung* (Leipzig, 1937), following p. 24.

17 Total "English Atlantic migration" of 530,500 includes 180,000 migrants to Ireland, and across the ocean: 190,000 to the West Indies, 116,000 to the Chesapeake, 23,500 to the Middle Atlantic region, and 21,000 to New England. In the eighteenth century, a mere

80,000 moved to mainland North America (50,000), the West Indies (20,000), and Ireland (10,000). See Nicholas Canny's excellent summary of the recent literature, "English Migration into and across the Atlantic during the Seventeenth and Eighteenth Centuries," in Canny, *Europeans on the Move*, 39–75, table on 64.

18 For a concise survey of British emigration worldwide, see Hugh Tinker, "The British Colonies of Settlement," in Robin Cohen, ed., *The Cambridge Survey of World Migration* (Cambridge, 1995), 14–20. David Cressy, *Coming Over: Migration and Communication between England and New England in the Seventeenth Century* (Cambridge, 1987); Mildred Campbell, "Social Origins of Some Early Americans," in James M. Smith, ed., *Seventeenth-Century America: Essays in Colonial History* (Chapel Hill, 1959), 63–89; Henry A. Gemery, "Markets for Migrants: English Indentured Servitude and Emigration in the Seventeenth and Eighteenth Centuries," in Emmer, *Colonialism and Migration*, 33–54; Virginia D. Anderson, *New England's Generation: The Great Migration and the Formation of Society and Culture in the Seventeenth Century* (Cambridge, 1993), 89–130; James Horn, "Domestic Standards of Living in England and the Chesapeake, 1650–1700," and Lois G. Carr, "Emigration and the Standard of Living: The Eighteenth-Century Chesapeake," in Schuurman and Walsh, *Material Culture*, 71–82 and 83–94.

19 T. C. Smout, N. C. Landsman, and T. M. Devine, "Scottish Emigration in the 17th and 18th Centuries," in Canny, *Europeans on the Move*, 76–112; Elsa B. Grage, "Scottish Merchants in Gothenburg, 1621–1850," in T. C. Smout, ed., *Scotland and Europe 1200–1850* (Edinburgh, 1986), 112–27; A. Åberg, "Scottish Soldiers in the Swedish Armies in the 16th and 17th Centuries," in Grant G. Simpson, ed., *Scotland and Scandinavia, 800–1800* (Edinburgh, 1990), 90–99. Ian Charles Cargill Graham, *Colonists from Scotland: Emigration to North America, 1707–1783* (Ithaca, 1956); David S. Macmillan, "Scottish Mercantile and Shipping Operations in the North American Colonies, 1760–1825," in Macmillan, ed., *Canadian Business History: Selected Studies, 1947–1971* (Toronto, 1972), 44–103; J. M. Bumsted, *The People's Clearance: Highland Emigration to British North America, 1770–1815* (Edinburgh, 1982).

20 L. M. Cullen, "The Irish Diaspora of the 17th and 18th Centuries," in Canny, *Europeans on the Move*, 113–48; Joyce Lorimer, *English and Irish Settlement on the River Amazon, 1550–1646* (London, 1989); Henry Gráinne, *The Irish Military Community in Spanish Flanders, 1586–1621* (Dublin, 1992); Audrey Lockhart, *Some Aspects of Emigration from Ireland to the North American Colonies between 1660 and 1775* (New York, 1976); R. J. Dickson, *Ulster Emigration to Colonial America, 1718–1775* (London, 1966); Bruce S. Elliott, *Irish Migrants in the Canadas: A New Approach* (Montreal, 1988); Wayland F. Dunaway, *The Scotch-Irish of Colonial Pennsylvania* (Chapel Hill, 1944); Thomas Power, ed., *The Irish in Atlantic Canada, 1780–1900* (Fredericton, N.B., 1991); John J. Silke, "The Irish Abroad in the Age of the Counter-Reformation," and J. G. Simms, "The Irish on the Continent, 1691–1800," in T. W. Moody et al., eds., *A New History of Ireland* (Oxford, 1976), 3:587–633 and 4:629–56.

21 Terry G. Jordan and Matti Kaups, *The American Backwoods Frontier: An Ethnic and Ecological Interpretation* (Baltimore, 1989), 135–210; Karl Scherer, ed., *Pfälzer—Palatines: Beiträge zur pfälzischen Ein- und Auswanderung sowie zur Volkskunde und Mundartforschung der Pfalz und der Zielländer pfälzischer Auswanderer im 18. und 19. Jahrhundert* (Kaiserslautern, 1981). Some of the Palatines migrated first to England: Daniel Statt, *Foreigners and Englishmen: The Controversy over Immigration and Population, 1660–1760* (Newark, Del., 1995),121–65.

22   Bernard Bailyn, *The Peopling of British North America: An Introduction* (New York, 1986), 9–20, quote on 13, and Bailyn, *Voyagers to the West: A Passage in the Peopling of America on the Eve of the Revolution* (New York, 1986).

23   Roger Daniels, *Coming to America: A History of Immigration and Ethnicity in American Life* (New York, 1990), 67–68.

24   Thomas Dublin, *Women at Work: The Transformation of Work and Community in Lowell, Massachusetts, 1826–1860* (New York, 1979); Philip S. Foner, ed., *The Factory Girls: A Collection of Writings on Life and Struggles in the New England Factories of the 1840's* (Urbana, Ill., 1977).

25   Daniels, *Coming to America*, 124–25; Ingrid Schöberl, *Amerikanische Einwandererwerbung in Deutschland, 1845–1914* (Stuttgart, 1990); Thomas J. Archdeacon, *Becoming American: An Ethnic History* (New York, 1983), 27–56; Bruno Ramirez, *Crossing the 49th Parallel: Migration from Canada to the United States, 1900–1930* (Ithaca, 2001).

26   Dirk Hoerder, "Labour Migrants' Views of 'America,'" *Renaissance and Modern Studies* 35 (1992): 1–17; Hoerder and Horst Rößler, eds., *Distant Magnets: Expectations and Realities in the Immigrant Experience, 1840–1930* (New York, 1993).

27   Leopold Marquard, *The Story of South Africa* (London, 1955); T. R. H. Davenport, *South Africa: A Modern History* (2d ed., Johannesburg, 1981).

28   Charles R. Boxer, *The Dutch Seaborne Empire, 1600–1800* (London, 1965), 273–89; Elizabeth A. Eldredge and Fred Morton, eds., *Slavery in South Africa: Captive Labor on the Dutch Frontier* (Boulder, 1994), quote on 2; for the First Nations, see the essays in Richard Elphick and Hermann Giliomee, eds., *The Shaping of South African Society, 1652–1840* (Middletown, Conn., 1989).

29   Boxer, *Dutch Seaborne Empire*, 280–93; Basil Davidson, *A History of East and Central Africa to the Late Nineteenth Century* (Garden City, N.Y., 1969), 281–87; Vivian Bickford-Smith, *Ethnic Pride and Racial Prejudice in Victorian Cape Town: Group Identity and Social Practice, 1875–1902* (Cambridge, 1995); Elizabeth Elbourne, "Freedom at Issue: Vagrancy Legislation and the Meaning of Freedom in Britain and the Cape Colony, 1799 to 1842," in Lovejoy and Rogers, *Unfree Labour*, 114–29.

30   "Aboriginal Australia" (map) in David Horton, ed., *The Encyclopaedia of Aboriginal Australia*, 2 vols. (Canberra, 1994); Anne Salmond, *Between Worlds: Early Exchanges between Maori and Europeans, 1773–1815* (Honolulu, 1997).

31   Stephen Nicholas and Peter R. Shergold reassess the historiography of the deportations and place the Australian experience in a global context, Stephen Nicholas, ed., *Convict Workers: Reinterpreting Australia's Past* (Cambridge, 1988), 3–39. L. L. Robson, *The Convict Settlers of Australia* (Melbourne, 1965); Alan G. L. Shaw, *Convicts and the Colonies: A Study of Penal Transportation from Great Britain and Ireland to Australia and Other Parts of the British Empire* (London, 1966); Anne Conlon, "'Mine Is a Sad yet True Story': Convict Narratives, 1818–1850," *Journal of the Royal Australian Historical Society* 55 (1969): 43–82; Robert Evans Jr., "Some Notes on Coerced Labor," *Journal of Economic History* 30 (1970): 861–66; Lloyd Evans and Paul Nicholls, *Convicts and Colonial Society, 1788–1853* (Stanmore, Austral., 1976); George Rudé, *Protest and Punishment: The Story of the Social and Political Protesters Transported to Australia, 1788–1868* (Melbourne, 1978). I am grateful to Anna Hoerder for help in accessing Australian libraries.

32   Anne Summers, *Damned Whores and God's Police: The Colonization of Women in Australia* (Ringwood, Austral., 1976); Michael Sturma, "Eye of the Beholder: The Stereotype of

Women Convicts, 1788–1852," *Labour History* [Australia] 34 (1978): 3–10; Monica Perrott, *A Tolerable Good Success: Economic Opportunities for Women in New South Wales, 1788–1830* (Sydney, 1983); Annette Salt, *These Outcast Women: The Parramatta Female Factory 1821–1848* (Sydney, 1984); Deborah Oxley, "Who Were the Female Convicts?" *Journal of the Australian Population Association* 4 (1987): 56–71, quote on 69.

33 Ian Duffield, "From Slave Colonies to Penal Colonies: The West Indian Convict Transportees to Australia," *Slavery and Abolition* 7 (1986): 25–45.

34 Robin F. Haines, *Emigration and the Labouring Poor: Australian Recruitment in Britain and Ireland, 1831–60* (New York, 1997); Eric Richards, "Migration to Colonial Australia: Paradigms and Disjunctions," in Jan Lucassen and Leo Lucassen, eds., *Migration, Migration History, History: Old Paradigms and New Perspectives* (Bern, 1997), 151–76, and Richards, "Voices of British and Irish Migrants in Nineteenth-Century Australia," in Colin G. Pooley and Ian D. Whyte, eds., *Migrants, Emigrants, and Immigrants: A Social History of Migration* (London, 1991), 19–41; Renate Vollmer, *Auswanderungspolitik und soziale Frage im 19. Jahrhundert: Staatlich geförderte Auswanderung aus der Berghauptmannschaft Clausthal nach Südaustralien, Nord- und Südamerika, 1848–1854* (Frankfurt/Main, 1995); Patrick O'Farrell, ed., *Letters from Irish Australia, 1825–1929* (Sydney, 1984); Helen R. Woolcock, *Rights of Passage: Emigration to Australia in the Nineteenth Century* (London, 1986).

10   Forced Labor Migration in and to the Americas

I am grateful to Gabriele Intemann for accessing and summarizing the Spanish-language and Portuguese-language research for this topic.

1 C. G. F. Simkin, *The Traditional Trade of Asia* (Oxford, 1968), 231–32; S. Manickan, *Slavery in Tamil Country: A Historical Overview* (Madras, 1982); Leopold Marquard, *The Story of South Africa* (London, 1954), 99–101.

2 Andreas Venzke, *Christoph Kolumbus mit Selbstzeugnissen und Bilddokumenten* (Reinbek, 1992), 92; Alfonso F. Silva, *La esclavitud en Sevilla y su tierra a fines de la Edad Media* (Seville, 1979), 149.

3 Silvio A. Zavala, *Los esclavos indios en Nueva España* (Mexico, 1968), 12; William L. Sherman, *Forced Native Labor in Sixteenth-Century Central America* (Lincoln, Nebr., 1979), 47; O. Nigel Bolland, "Colonization and Slavery in Central America," in Paul E. Lovejoy and Nicholas Rogers, eds., *Unfree Labour in the Development of the Atlantic World* (Ilford, U.K., 1994), 11–25.

4 Zavala, *Los esclavos indios*, 30–41, 107, 170–309; Sherman, *Forced Native Labor*, 56–57; P. J. Bakewell, *Silver Mining and Society in Colonial Mexico: Zacatecas, 1546–1700* (Cambridge, 1971), 122. Bartolomé de las Casas, "Brevísima relación de la destrución de las Indias," and "Historia de las Indias."

5 Silvio A. Zavala, *La encomienda indiana* (Madrid, 1935; rev. ed., Mexico, 1973), and Zavala, *New Viewpoints on the Spanish Colonization of America* (Philadelphia, 1943; repr. New York, 1968), and Zavala, *Los esclavos indios*; José A. Saco, *Historia de la esclavitud de los indios en el Nuevo Mundo, seguida de la historia de los repartimientos y encomiendas*, 2 vols. (Havana, 1932); Néstor Miranda Ontaneda, *Klientelismus und koloniale Abhängigkeit: Eine ethnosoziologische Analyse des Repartimiento-Encomienda-Systems auf den Antillen (1492–1525)* (doctoral diss., Univ. of Heidelberg, 1968); Lesley B. Simpson, *The Encomienda in New Spain: The Beginning of Spanish Mexico* (rev. ed., Berkeley, 1950; repr.,

1966, with new appendix), and Simpson, *Studies in the Administration of the Indians in New Spain*, 4 vols. (Berkeley,1934–40); Sherman, *Forced Native Labor*. Regional studies include Salvador Rodríguez Becerra, *Encomienda y conquista: Los indios de la colonización en Guatemala* (Seville, 1977); Maria T. Molino García, *La encomienda en el nuevo reino de Granada durante el siglo XVIII* (Seville, 1976); Thomas Gomez, *L'envers de l'Eldorado: Économie coloniale et travail indigène dans la Colombie du XVIème siècle* (Toulouse, 1984).

6 Sherman, *Forced Native Labor*, 82; Murdo J. MacLeod, *Spanish Central America: A Socioeconomic History, 1520–1720* (Berkeley, 1973), 52; Frances V. Scholes, *The Spanish Conquerer as a Business Man* (Albuquerque, 1957), 18; Bolland, "Colonization and Slavery," 15.

7 Frederick P. Bowser, *The African Slave in Colonial Peru, 1524–1650* (Stanford, 1974), 5–7; James Lockhart, *Spanish Peru, 1532–1560: A Colonial Society* (Madison, 1968); Zavala, *Los esclavos indios*, 6–20, 66; Simpson, *The Encomienda in New Spain*, 18–28, 214–29; Sherman, *Forced Native Labor*, quote on 41, 54–60, 68–70; Rodríguez Becerra, *Encomienda y conquista*, 66; David H. Randell, "The Indian Slave Trade and Population of Nicaragua during the Sixteenth Century," in William M. Denevan, ed., *The Native Population of the Americas in 1492* (Madison, 1976), 67–76; Linda Newson, *The Cost of Conquest: Indian Decline in Honduras under Spanish Rule* (Boulder, 1986).

8 Simpson, *The Encomienda in New Spain*, xiii, 10, 39–55; Sherman, *Forced Native Labor*, 193; Zavala, *La encomienda indiana*, 23–24; Elinor G. K. Melville, "Land-Labour Relations in Sixteenth-Century Mexico: The Formation of Grazing Haciendas," in Lovejoy and Rogers, *Unfree Labour*, 26–35.

9 Zavala, *Los esclavos indios*, 48; Simpson, *The Encomienda in New Spain*, 218; Sherman, *Forced Native Labor*, 40, 77, 193–203; Hilary McF. Beckles, "The Colours of Property: Brown, White and Black Chattels and their Responses on the Caribbean Frontier," in Lovejoy and Rogers, *Unfree Labour*, 36–51

10 Zavala, *La encomienda indiana*, 212–14; for the territory of modern Bolivia: Nicolás Sánchez-Albornoz, "The Population of Spanish America," in Leslie Bethell, ed., *The Cambridge History of Latin America* (Cambridge, 1984), 2:6–7 (hereafter cited as *CHLA*).

11 Bowser, *African Slave*, 5–7, quoting Lockhard on 7; Sherman, *Forced Native Labor*, 103–4, 112–22, 218–25; Ann Zulawski, "Frontier Workers and Social Change: Pilaya y Paspaya (Bolivia) in the Early Eighteenth Century," in David J. Robinson, ed., *Migration in Colonial Spanish America* (Cambridge, 1990), 116.

12 Its Mexican equivalent, the *cuatequil* system, had less of an impact.

13 Charles Gibson "Indian Societies under Spanish Rule," in *CHLA*, quote on 2:404; Peter Bakewell, *Miners of the Red Mountain: Indian Labor in Potosí, 1545–1650* (Albuquerque, 1984), and Bakewell, "Mining in Colonial Spanish America," in *CHLA*, 2:125; Jeffrey A. Cole, *The Potosí Mita, 1573–1700: Compulsory Indian Labor in the Andes* (Stanford, 1985); Bowser, *African Slave*, 18–20. In 1718 the Council of the Indies recommended abolition of the *mita*, but only the liberal Cortes (National Assembly) of Cadíz (in 1812) passed the measure.

14 Bakewell, *Silver Mining*, 124–29, quote on 128; David A. Brading and Harry E. Cross, "Colonial Silver Mining: Mexico and Peru," *Hispanic American Historical Review* 52 (1972): 545–79.

15 Similar to the study of forced Indio labor, research on Latin American slavery started late. Magnus Mörner, "African Slavery in Spanish and Portuguese America: Some Remarks on Historiography and the Present State of Research," in Wolfgang Binder, ed., *Slavery in the*

Americas (Würzburg, 1993), 57–87; Richard Graham, "Brazilian Slavery Reexamined: A Review Article," *Journal of Social History* 3 (1970): 431–53. For surveys, see Rolando Mellafe, *Negro Slavery in Latin America* (Berkeley, 1975); Herbert S. Klein, *African Slavery in Latin America and the Caribbean* (New York, 1986); Vincent B. Thompson, *The Making of the African Diaspora in the Americas, 1441–1900* (Harlow, U.K., 1987); Hugh Thomas, *The Slave Trade: The Story of the Atlantic Trade, 1440–1870* (New York, 1997); Robin Blackburn, *The Making of New World Slavery: From the Baroque to the Modern, 1492–1800* (London, 1997).

16 Klein, *African Slavery*, 23; Franklin W. Knight, "The Atlantic Slave Trade and the Development of Afro-American Culture," in David Eltis and James Walvin, eds., *The Abolition of the Atlantic Slave Trade: Origins and Effects in Europe, Africa, and the Americas* (Madison, 1981), 287–300.

17 Bowser, *African Slave*, 50–51, quote on 362; Mellafe, *Negro Slavery*, 40–41, 76; Enriqueta Vila Vilar, "Das spanische Handelsmonopol und seine inneren Widersprüche," in Walther L. Bernecker et al., eds., *Handbuch der Geschichte Lateinamerikas*, 3 vols. (Stuttgart, 1992–96), 1:692–719.

18 Other authors have arrived at higher figures: 5.5 million for the Caribbean (P. C. Emmer), 5 million for Brazil (R. E. Conrad), and 3 million for Spanish America (R. Mellafe).

19 Philip D. Curtin, *The Atlantic Slave Trade: A Census* (Madison, 1969), 47–49, 268, table on 77; Robert E. Conrad, *World of Sorrow: The African Slave Trade to Brazil* (Baton Rouge, 1986), 34; Mellafe, *Negro Slavery*, 73; Piet C. Emmer, "Immigration into the Caribbean: The Introduction of Chinese and East Indian Indentured Laborers between 1839–1917," in Emmer and Magnus Mörner, eds., *European Expansion and Migration: Essays on the Intercontinental Migration from Africa, Asia, and Europe* (New York, 1992), 245–76, esp. 245–47.

20 Curtin, *Atlantic Slave Trade*, 119; Mellafe, *Negro Slavery*, 75–76, 83; Sánchez-Albornoz, "Population of Latin America," 74–84; Vila Vilar, "Das spanische Handelsmonopol," 714–15; Fredrick P. Bowser, "Africans in Spanish American Colonial Society," in *CHLA*, 2:361–65, and Bowser, *African Slave*, 57–65; Renate Pieper, "Die demographische Entwicklung," in Bernecker, *Handbuch der Geschichte Lateinamerikas*, 1:313–28; Klein, *African Slavery*, 29, 83–84, 95; David Eltis, "The Nineteenth-Century Transatlantic Slave Trade: An Annual Time Series of Importers into the Americas Broken Down by Region," *Hispanic American Historical Review* 67 (1987): 109–38.

21 Bowser, "Africans in Spanish American Colonial Society," 366, quote on 367, and *African Slave*, 5–103; Klein, *African Slavery*, quote on 29–30, 84–85; Mellafe, *Negro Slavery*, quote on 89–90, 95–96; Inge Wolff, "Negersklaverei und Negerhandel in Hochperu, 1545–1640," *Jahrbuch für Geschichte von Staat, Wirtschaft und Gesellschaft Lateinamerikas* 1 (1964): 157–86; William F. Sharp, *Slavery on the Spanish Frontier: The Colombian Chocó 1680–1810* (Norman, Okla., 1976).

22 Frank Tannenbaum, *Slave and Citizen: The Negro in the Americas* (New York, 1946), 43ff., 97–98; Mieko Nishida, "Manumission and Ethnicity in Urban Slavery: Salvador, Brazil, 1808–1888," *Hispanic American Historical Review* 73 (1993): 361–91, esp. 374–86; R. K. Kent, "African Revolt in Bahia: 15–24 January 1835," *Journal of Social History* 3 (1969/70): 334–56; Kátia M. de Queirós Mattoso, *To Be a Slave in Brazil, 1550–1880* (4th ed., New Brunswick, 1994), 164–65; Bowser, "Africans in Spanish American Colonial Society," 374–78, quote on 378.

23 Miguel Acosta Saignes, *Vida de los esclavos negros en Venezuela* (Caracas, 1967); Robert J. Ferry, "Encomienda, African Slavery, and Agriculture in Seventeenth-Century Caracas,"

Hispanic American Historical Review 61 (1981): 609–35; Mellafe, *Negro Slavery*, 27. See the important essays in David B. Gaspar and Darlene Clark Hine, eds., *More Than Chattel: Black Women and Slavery in the Americas* (Bloomington, 1996).

24 Alexander Marchant, *From Barter to Slavery: The Economic Relations of Portuguese and Indians in the Settlement of Brazil, 1500-1580* (Baltimore, 1942); Urs Höner, *Die Versklavung der brasilianischen Indianer* (Zurich, 1980); John Hemming, *Red Gold: The Conquest of the Brazilian Indians* (London, 1978); Stuart B. Schwartz, "Indian Labor and New World Plantations: European Demands and Indian Responses in Northern Brazil," *American Historical Review* 81 (1978): 43–79; Georg Thomas, *Die portugiesische Indianerpolitik in Brasilien 1500-1640* (Berlin, 1968), 203–4. For Guiana, see Mary N. Menezes, *British Policy towards the Amerindians in British Guiana, 1803-1873* (Oxford, 1977).

25 Bennassar, "Les conquérants du Brésil," *L'Histoire* 101 (June 1987): 8–17; Conrad, *World of Sorrow*; Kent, "African Revolt in Bahia," 340–41; Gilberto Freyre, *The Masters and the Slaves (Casa-grande & senzala): A Study in the Development of Brazilian Civilization*, trans. Samuel Putnam (Portuguese orig., 4th ed., 1943, Rio de Janeiro; rev. ed., New York, 1956); Mattoso, *To Be a Slave in Brazil*, 33–69; Chirly dos Santos-Stubby, "Formen der weiblichen afrikanischen Sklaverei in Brasilien," and Hannes Stubbe, "Über die Kindheit der afrobrasilianischen Sklaven," in Rüdiger Zoller, ed., *Amerikaner wider Willen: Beiträge zur Sklaverei in Lateinamerika und ihren Folgen* (Frankfurt/Main, 1994), 175–202, 203–30; Sylviane A. Diouf, *Servants of Allah: African Muslims Enslaved in the Americas* (New York, 1998).

26 The summary designation "Africans" prevents an understanding of customs and identities on which resistance was based. Paul E. Lovejoy, "Background to Rebellion: The Origins of Muslim Slaves in Bahia," in Lovejoy and Rogers, *Unfree Labour*, 151–80; Mattoso, *To Be a Slave in Brazil*, 12–26; Nishida, "Manumission and Ethnicity," quote on 374; Herbert S. Klein, *The Middle Passage: Comparative Studies in the Atlantic Slave Trade* (Princeton, 1978), 25–27; Pierre Verger, *Flux et reflux de la traite des nègres entre le Golfe de Bénin et Bahia de Todos os Santos du XVIIe au XIVe siècle* (Paris, 1968).

27 Ana Maria Barros dos Santos, *Die Sklaverei in Brasilien und ihre sozialen und wirtschaftlichen Folgen: Dargestellt am Beispiel Pernambuco 1840-1889* (Munich, 1985), and Barros dos Santos, "Quilombos: Sklavenaufstände im Brasilien des 17. Jahrhunderts," in Zoller, *Amerikaner wider Willen*, 161–73; A. J. R. Russell-Wood, *The Black Man in Slavery and Freedom in Colonial Brazil* (New York, 1982), 105–8, 124–25, and Russell-Wood, "The Gold Cycle," in Leslie Bethell, ed., *Colonial Brazil* (Cambridge, 1987), 190–243; Jürgen Hell, *Sklavenmanufaktur und Sklavenemanzipation in Brasilien 1500-1888* (Berlin, 1986), 108–26.

28 Kent, "African Revolt in Bahia," 335; Carl N. Degler, *Neither Black nor White: Slavery and Race Relations in Brazil and the United States* (New York, 1971); Detlev Schelsky, "Die 'questão racial' in Brasilien," in Zoller, *Amerikaner wider Willen*, 257–87; Stuart B. Schwartz, "Resistance and Accommodation in Eighteenth Century Brazil: The Slaves' View of Slavery," *Hispanic American Historical Review* 57 (1977): 69–81; Mattoso, *To Be a Slave in Brazil*, 157, quote on 200; Nishida, "Manumission and Ethnicity," 374–85. Barros dos Santos, "Quilombos: Sklavenaufstände"; R. K. Kent, "Palmares: An African State in Brazil," *Journal of African History* 3 (1965): 161–75.

29 Verger, *Flux et reflux*, 532–33 and the chap. "Formation d'une société brésilienne au Golfe de Bénin" (599–635); Conrad, *World of Sorrow*, 126–53.

30 Noël Deerr, *The History of Sugar*, 2 vols. (London, 1949–50); Sidney W. Mintz, *Sweetness and Power: The Place of Sugar in Modern History* (New York, 1985), and Mintz, ed., *Slavery, Colonialism, and Racism: Essays* (New York, 1974); Sidney M. Greenfield, "Plantations, Sugar Cane and Slavery," in Michael Craton, ed., *Roots and Branches: Current Directions in Slave Studies* (Toronto, 1979), 85–119, and Greenfield, "Madeira and the Beginning of New World Sugar Cane Cultivation and Plantation Slavery," in Vera D. Rubin and A. Tuden, eds., *Comparative Perspectives on Slavery in New World Plantation Societies* (New York, 1977), 536–52; J. H. Galloway, "The Mediterranean Sugar Industry, " *Geographical Review* 67 (1977): 177–94; Stuart B. Schwartz, *Sugar Plantations in the Formation of the Brazilian Society: Bahia, 1550–1835* (Cambridge, 1985), 3–27.

31 Franklin W. Knight, *The Caribbean: The Genesis of a Fragmented Nationalism* (New York, 1978), 23–49, quote on 28.

32 Robert L. Stein, *The French Slave Trade in the Eighteenth Century: An Old Regime Business* (Madison, 1979), 5–7; Knight, *The Caribbean*, 51–57.

33 Richard S. Dunn, *Sugar and Slaves: The Rise of the Planter Class in the English West Indies, 1624–1713* (Chapel Hill, N.C., 1972); Carl Bridenbaugh and Roberta Bridenbaugh, *No Peace beyond the Line: The English in the Caribbean, 1624–1690* (New York, 1972); Knight, *The Caribbean*, 90–91, 96–97, 110.

34 Richard B. Sheridan, "Slave Demography in the British West Indies and the Abolition of the Slave Trade," in Eltis and Walvin, *Abolition of the Atlantic Slave Trade*, 259–85. John Thornton, *Africa and Africans in the Making of the Atlantic World, 1400–1680* (Cambridge, 1992), 167–68.

35 The juxtaposition is taken from Eugene D. Genovese's studies of U.S. slavery, *The World the Slaveholders Made: Two Essays in Interpretation* (New York, 1969) and *Roll, Jordan, Roll: The World the Slaves Made* (1972; repr., New York, 1976); Jerome S. Handler, *The Unappropriated People: Freedmen in the Slave Society in Barbados* (Baltimore, 1974); Barry W. Higman, *Slave Populations of the British Caribbean, 1807–1834* (Baltimore, 1984).

36 Barbara Bush, *Slave Women in Caribbean Society, 1650–1838* (Bloomington, 1990), 1–22, 34, 46–50, 151–67, quote on 15; Knight, *The Caribbean*, 93–120.

37 Knight, *The Caribbean*, 105–7. During the French-American alliance in the American War of Independence, a French battalion of Black soldiers from Saint Domingue fought on the American side.

38 David Geggus, "The Haitian Revolution," in Franklin W. Knight and Colin A. Palmer, eds., *The Modern Caribbean* (Chapel Hill, N.C., 1989), 21–50, quotes on 34, 35; Yves Bénot, *La Révolution française et la fin des colonies: Essai* (Paris, 1988); C. L. R. James, *The Black Jacobins: Toussaint L'Ouverture and the San Domingo Revolution* (London, 1938); Gwendolyn M. Hall, *Social Control in Slave Plantation Societies: A Comparison of St. Domingue and Cuba* (Baltimore, 1971); Thomas O. Ott, *The Haitian Revolution, 1789–1804* (Knoxville, 1973); David B. Davis, *The Problem of Slavery in the Age of Revolution, 1770–1823* (Ithaca, N.Y., 1975), remains the best comparative analysis.

39 Knight, *The Caribbean*, 96–97; Klein, *African Slavery*, 89–94; Franklin W. Knight, *Slave Society in Cuba during the Nineteenth Century* (Madison, 1970); Arthur F. Corwin, *Spain and the Abolition of Slavery in Cuba, 1817–1886* (Austin, Tex., 1967); Elizabeth M. Petras, *Jamaican Labor Migration: White Capital and Black Labor, 1850–1930* (Boulder, 1988).

40 Monica Schuler, *"Alas, Alas, Kongo": A Social History of Indentured African Immigration into Jamaica, 1841–1865* (Baltimore, 1980), and Schuler, "Kru Emigration to British and

French Guiana, 1841–1857," in Paul E. Lovejoy, ed., *Africans in Bondage: Studies in Slavery and the Slave Trade* (Madison, 1986), 155–201, and Schuler, "The Recruitment of African Indentured Labourers for European Colonies in the Nineteenth Century," in Piet C. Emmer, ed., *Colonialism and Migration: Indentured Labour before and after Slavery* (Dordrecht, 1986), 125–61; Knight, *The Caribbean*, quote on 121; David Northrup, *Indentured Labor in the Age of Imperialism, 1834–1922* (Cambridge, 1995), 20–21, 33.

41 Howard Temperly, "Regionalismus, Bürgerkrieg und die Wiedereingliederung des Südens," in Willi Paul Adams, ed., *Die Vereinigten Staaten von Amerika* (Frankfurt/Main, 1977), 78, 107; Peter Wood, *Black Majority: Negroes in Colonial South Carolina from 1670 through the Stono Rebellion [1739]* (New York, 1974); Philip D. Curtin, "The Tropical Atlantic in the Age of Slave Trade," in Michael Adas, ed., *Islamic and European Expansion: The Forging of a Global Order* (Philadelphia, 1993), 165–97; John Hope Franklin, *From Slavery to Freedom: A History of Negro Americans* (1947; rev. 3d ed., New York, 1967), 60–70; Betty Wood, *The Origins of American Slavery: Freedom and Bondage in the English Colonies* (New York, 1997).

42 The literature on slavery is legion. Franklin, *From Slavery to Freedom*, provided a valuable, repeatedly updated synthesis early on. The older interpretations, slavery as a school for a civilized life (U. B. Phillips) and slavery as a "total institution" that infantilized personalities (Stanley Elkins), have long been abandoned in favor of control and exploitation of labor (Kenneth Stampp) and of Black community and family formation (Eugene Genovese, Herbert G. Gutman, George P. Rawick). Ira Berlin, *Many Thousands Gone: The First Two Centuries of Slavery in North America* (Cambridge, Mass., 1998).

43 Herbert Aptheker, *American Negro Slave Revolts* (1943; anniversary ed., New York, 1993), and Aptheker, "Maroons within the Present Limits of the United States," *Journal of Negro History* 24 (1939): 167–84; Alice H. Bauer and Raymond A. Bauer, "Day to Day Resistance to Slavery," *Journal of Negro History* 27 (1942): 388–419; Eugene D. Genovese, *From Rebellion to Revolution: Afro-American Slave Revolts in the Making of the Modern World* (Baton Rouge, 1979); Bolland, "Colonization and Slavery," 20.

44 John W. Blassingame, *The Slave Community: Plantation Life in the Antebellum South* (rev. ed., New York, 1979); Elizabeth Fox-Genovese, *Within the Plantation Household: Black and White Women of the Old South* (Chapel Hill, N.C., 1988); Herbert G. Gutman, *The Black Family in Slavery and Freedom, 1750–1925* (New York, 1976); Jacqueline Jones, *Labor of Love, Labor of Sorrow: Black Women, Work, and the Family from Slavery to the Present* (New York, 1985); Lawrence W. Levine, *Black Culture and Black Consciousness: Afro-American Folk Thought from Slavery to Freedom* (New York, 1977).

45 Alfred N. Hunt, *Haiti's Influence on Antebellum America: Slumbering Volcano in the Caribbean* (Baton Rouge, 1988); Franklin, *From Slavery to Freedom*, 150–51, 175–217; Daniel F. Littlefield, *Africans and Seminoles: From Removal to Emancipation* (Westport, Conn., 1977).

46 Klein, *African Slavery*, 243–71; David Eltis, *Economic Growth and the Ending of the Transatlantic Slave Trade* (New York, 1987); Martin A. Klein, "Slavery, the International Labour Market and the Emancipation of Slaves in the Nineteenth Century," in Lovejoy and Rogers, *Unfree Labour*, 197–220; Seymour Drescher, "Brasilian Abolition in Comparative Perspective," *Hispanic American Historical Review* 68 (1988): 429–60, and Drescher, "The Ending of the Slave Trade and the Evolution of European Scientific Racism," in Joseph E. Inikori and Stanley L. Engerman, eds., *The Atlantic Slave Trade: Effects on Economies, Societies, and Peoples in Africa, the Americas, and Europe* (Durham, N.C., 1992), 361–96; Peter Blanchard,

Slavery and Abolition in Early Republican Peru (Wilmington, Del., 1992); Robin Blackburn, *The Overthrow of Colonial Slavery, 1776–1848* (London, 1988).

11   Migration and Conversion: Worldviews, Material Culture, Racial Hierarchies

1   Kenneth R. Andrews, *Trade, Plunder and Settlement: Maritime Enterprise and the Genesis of the British Empire, 1480–1630* (Cambridge, 1984), 5; Pierre Chaunu, *Conquête et exploitation des nouveaux mondes, XVIe siècle* (Paris, 1969); Philip D. Curtin, *The Tropical Atlantic in the Age of the Slave Trade* (Washington, D.C., 1991), quote on 13.

2   Anthony Pagden, *European Encounters with the New World: From Renaissance to Romanticism* (New Haven, 1993), quote on 52, and Pagden, *The Fall of Natural Man: The American Indian and the Origins of Comparative Ethnology* (Cambridge, 1982); Lewis Hanke, *All Mankind Is One: A Study of the Disputation between Bartolomé de Las Casas and Juan Ginés de Sepúlveda in 1550 on the Intellectual and Religious Capacity of the American Indians* (DeKalb, Ill., 1974), 84–85, 93–94; Wolfgang Haase and Reinhold Meyer, eds., *The Classical Tradition and the Americas*, 2 vols. (Berlin, 1994), vol. 1: "European Images of the Americas and the Classical Tradition"; Peter Mason, "Classical Ethnography and Its Influence on the European Perception of the Peoples of the New World," in Haase and Meyer, *European Images*, 1:135–72. Helmut Reinicke, *Wilde Kälten 1492: Die Entdeckung Europas* (Frankfurt/Main, 1992); Peter Hulme and Neil L. Whitehead, eds., *Wild Majesty: Encounters with Caribs from Columbus to the Present Day: An Anthology* (Oxford, 1992).

3   Pagden, *Fall of Natural Man*, 44, 52–53, 88; Lewis Hanke, *The First Social Experiments in America: A Study in the Development of Spanish Indian Policy in the Sixteenth Century* (Gloucester, Mass., 1964), 51; Peter Mason, *Deconstructing America: Representations of the Other* (London, 1990), 110–11; Thomas Lange, "Soutanenkaserne oder heiliges Experiment? Die Jesuitenreduktionen in Paraguay im europäischen Urteil," in Karl-Heinz Kohl, ed., *Mythen der Neuen Welt: Zur Entdeckungsgeschichte Lateinamerikas* (Berlin, 1982), 210–23; Richard C. Trexler, *Sex and Conquest: Gendered Violence, Political Order, and the European Conquest of the Americas* (Ithaca, 1995).

4   In their reification of private property, these Latin-speaking theorists overlooked the fact that the verb *privare*, in classical Latin, meant "to rob."

5   John Locke, *Two Treatises of Government*, ed. Thomas I. Cook (New York, 1966), 121–32.

6   Beate Jahn, "The Cultural Foundations of IR Theory, or The Blind Spot in the Mirror," unpublished paper, Bremen, Nov. 1997; Beate Jahn, *The Cultural Construction of International Relations: The Invention of the State of Nature* (Basingstoke, U.K., 2000).

7   Tzvetan Todorov, *The Conquest of America: The Question of the Other*, trans. Richard Howard (French orig., Paris, 1982; New York, 1984), 38; Olive P. Dickason, *The Myth of the Savage: And the Beginnings of French Colonialism in the Americas* (Edmonton, 1984), and Dickason, "Old World Law, New World Peoples, and Concepts of Sovereignty," in Stanley H. Palmer and Dennis Reinhartz, eds., *Essays on the History of North American Discovery and Exploration* (College Station, Tex., 1988), 52–78; Anthony Pagden, *Spanish Imperialism and the Political Imagination: Studies in European and Spanish-American Social and Political Theory, 1513–1830* (New Haven, 1990); Joachim Moebus, "Über die Bestimmung des Wilden und die Entwicklung des Verwertungsstandpunkts bei Kolumbus," and Birgit Scharlau, "Beschreiben und Beherrschen: Die Informationspolitik der spanischen Krone im 15. und 16.

Jahrhundert," in Kohl, *Mythen der Neuen Welt*, 49–56 and 92–100; David S. Landes, *The Wealth and Poverty of Nations: Why Some Are So Rich and Some So Poor* (New York, 1998).

8 Gary Nash, *Red, White, and Black: The Peoples of Early America* (Englewood Cliffs, N.J., 1974).

9 Stephen Greenblatt, *Marvelous Possessions: The Wonder of the New World* (Oxford, 1991); Woodrow Borah, "Mixing of Populations," in Fredi Chiappelli et al., eds., *First Images of America: The Impact of the New World on the Old*, 2 vols. (Berkeley, 1976), 2:707–22, esp. 715–18; Frauke Gewecke, *Wie die neue Welt in die alte kam* (Stuttgart, 1986), esp. 72–87.

10 Robert F. Berkhofer Jr., *The White Man's Indian: Images of the American Indian from Columbus to the Present* (New York, 1978), esp. 86–111; Roy H. Pearce, "The Significance of the Captivity Narrative," *American Literature* 19 (1947–48): 1–20.

11 David B. Quinn, ed., *The Hakluyt Handbook* (London, 1974). Rijksmuseum, Amsterdam, seventeenth-century section. Photographers' publications include Clark Worswick and Ainslie Embree, *The Last Empire: Photography in British India, 1855–1911* (Millerton, N.Y., 1976); Bernard Smith, *European Vision and the South Pacific, 1768–1850: A Study in the History of Art and Ideas* (London, 1960); Thomas Theye, "Ferne Länder—Fremde Bilder: Das Bild Asiens in der Photographie des 19. Jahrhunderts," in Klaus Pohl, ed., *Ansichten der Ferne: Reisephotographie 1850 bis heute* (Gießen, 1983), 59–95; Pascal Blanchard et al., *L'autre et nous: "Scènes et types"* (Paris, 1995); Elizabeth Edwards, ed., *Anthropology and Photography, 1860–1920* (New Haven, 1992). Exotic female nudity is discussed in Ricabeth Steiger and Martin Taureg, "Körperphantasien auf Reisen: Anmerkungen zum ethnographischen Akt," in Michael Köhler and Gisela Barche, eds., *Das Aktfoto: Ansichten vom Körper im fotografischen Zeitalter: Ästhetik, Geschichte, Ideologie* (2d rev. ed., Munich, 1986), 120–40. Albert Friedenthal, *Das Weib im Leben der Völker*, 2 vols. (2d rev. ed., Berlin, 1910), did not get beyond eastern and southeastern Europe.

12 Montesquieu, *Lettres persanes* (1721, expanded 1754), quoted in Borah, "Mixing of Populations," 2:714–15. Magnus Mörner, "Spanish Migration to the New World prior to 1810: A Report on the State of Research," in Chiappelli, *First Images*, 2:737–82, esp. 758–61.

13 Lester D. Langley, *The Americas in the Age of Revolution, 1750–1850* (New Haven, 1996); R. A. Humphreys and John Lynch, eds., *The Origins of the Latin American Revolutions, 1808–1826* (New York, 1965); Caroline Robbins, *The Eighteenth-Century Commonwealthman: Studies in the Transmission, Development, and Circumstance of English Liberal Thought from the Restoration of Charles II until the War with the Thirteen Colonies* (Cambridge, Mass., 1959).

14 Andrews, *Trade, Plunder and Settlement*, 4, 24–30, quote on 27; Charles R. Boxer, *The Dutch Seaborne Empire, 1600–1800* (London, 1965), 73–89.

15 Charles H. Talbot, "America and the European Drug Trade," in Chiappelli, *First Images*, 2:833–44, quotes on 834, 837; Joseph Ewan, "The Columbian Discoveries and the Growth of Botanical Ideas," ibid., 2:807–12; Jonathan D. Sauer, "Changing Perception and Exploitation of New World Plants in Europe, 1492–1800," ibid., 2:813–32, esp. 818–20. For botanical research in Dutch Asia, see Boxer, *Dutch Seaborne Empire*, 202–5. Chinese medical knowledge, contrary to most of China's other achievements, never became part of European medical practice. Annotation in this section will not include the large body of literature on agriculture, plant introduction, and foodways.

16 Boxer, *Dutch Seaborne Empire*, 180–86. Real porcelain began to be produced a century later, from 1709 on, at the manufactory in Meissen, Saxony (ibid., 194–96).

17 Beverly Lemire, *Fashion's Favourite: The Cotton Trade and the Consumer in Britain, 1660–1880* (Oxford, 1991), 3–42, quote on 12; Boxer, *Dutch Seaborne Empire*, 196–97.

18 Earl J. Hamilton, "What the New World Gave the Economy of the Old," in Chiappelli, *First Images*, 2:861–65; J. Sermet, "Acclimatation: Les jardins botaniques espagnols au XVIIIe siècle et la tropicalisation de l'Andalousie," in *Mélanges en l'honneur de Fernand Braudel*, 2 vols. (Toulouse, 1973), 1:555–582.

19 C. H. H. Wake, "The Changing Pattern of Europe's Pepper and Spice Imports, ca. 1400–1700," *Journal of European Economic History* 8 (1979): 361–403, esp. 392–93; Boxer, *Dutch Seaborne Empire*, 222; Sauer, "Changing Perception and Exploitation," 817.

20 Sidney W. Mintz, "Time, Sugar, and Sweetness," *Marxist Perspectives* 2 (1979): 56–73, and Mintz, *Tasting Food, Tasting Freedom: Excursions into Eating, Culture, and the Past* (Boston, 1996), 17–32 ("Food and Its Relationship to Concepts of Power"); Hamilton, "What the New World Gave," 859–60, 868–69.

21 Boxer, *Dutch Seaborne Empire*, 197–98, 223; Hans G. Adrian et al., *Das Teebuch: Geschichte und Geschichten, Anbau, Herstellung und Rezepte* (Munich, 1983), 7–59, 105–28.

22 David Watts, *The West Indies: Patterns of Development, Culture, and Environmental Change since 1492* (Cambridge, 1987), 55–57; Hamilton, "What the New World Gave," 854–56, 860; Redcliffe N. Salaman, *The History and Social Influence of the Potato* [in Britain], ed. J.G. Hawkes (1949; rev. ed., Cambridge, 1985).

23 Eric R. Wolf, *Europe and the People without History* (Berkeley, 1982), 319–321, 330; Hugh Tinker, *A New System of Slavery: The Export of Indian Labour Overseas, 1830-1920* (London 1974).

24 Magnus Mörner, *Race Mixture in the History of Latin America* (Boston, 1967; Span. trans., Buenos Aires, 1969); Maria C. García Sáiz, "Die Rassenmischung in Amerika und ihr Niederschlag in der Kunst," in *Gold und Macht: Spanien in der Neuen Welt: Eine Ausstellung anläßlich des 500. Jahrestages der Entdeckung Amerikas* (Vienna, 1986), 132–36; anonymous, "Serie de Mestizajes: Cobres Anónimos, Siglo XVIII," Museo de América, Madrid; J. Hector St. John de Crèvecoeur, *Letters from an American Farmer* (London, 1782); Jacqueline Peterson and Jennifer S. H. Brown, eds., *The New Peoples: Being and Becoming Métis in North America* (Winnipeg, 1985); Bruce Alden Cox, ed., *Native People, Native Lands: Canadian Indians, Inuit and Métis* (Ottawa, 1991); Sylvia Van Kirk, *"Many Tender Ties": Women in Fur-Trade Society in Western Canada, 1670-1870* (Winnipeg, 1980); Adele Perry, *On the Edge of Empire: Gender, Race, and the Making of British Columbia, 1849-1871* (Toronto, 2000); Sharon M. Lee, "Racial Classification in the U.S. Census: 1890-1990," *Ethnic and Racial Studies* 16, 1 (Jan. 1993): 75–94.

25 David Eltis, "Free and Coerced Transatlantic Migrations: Some Comparisons," *American Historical Review* 88 (1983): 251–80; Stanley L. Engerman, "Slavery and Emancipation in Comparative Perspective: A New Look at Some Recent Debates," *Journal of Economic History* 46 (1986): 317–39, esp. 318–22; Watts, *West Indies*, 143–231; Franklin W. Knight, "The Atlantic Slave Trade and the Development of Afro-American Culture," in Joseph E. Inikori and Stanley L. Engerman, eds., *The Atlantic Slave Trade: Effects on Economies, Societies, and Peoples in Africa, the Americas, and Europe* (Durham, N.C., 1992), 287–300; Patrick Manning, "The Slave Trade: The Formal Demography of a Global System," ibid., 117–41, quote on 121.

26 Thomas F. Gossett, *Race: The History of an Idea in America* (New York, 1965), 3–31, quotes on 12, 19–20; Robert Miles, *Racism* (London, 1989), 14–19, quotes on 18, 21, 102, 103.

27 At the turn of the twenty-first century, scholarly opinion has swung back. Though the development of human beings occurred in several distinct places, the humans of today all seem to be descended from African ancestors. The lineages of other ancestors died out.

28 Gossett, *Race*, 32–83, quotes on 47, 65 (Nott); Winthrop D. Jordan, *White over Black: American Attitudes toward the Negro, 1550–1812* (Chapel Hill, 1968); Jacques Barzun, *Race: A Study in Modern Superstition* (New York, 1937); George M. Fredrickson, *The Black Image in the White Mind: The Debate on Afro-American Character and Destiny, 1817–1914* (New York, 1971); Miles, *Racism*, quote on 104.

29 Seymour Drescher, "The Ending of the Slave Trade and the Evolution of European Scientific Racism," in Inikori and Engerman, *Atlantic Slave Trade*, 361–96, quote on 369; James Walvin, *England, Slaves, and Freedom, 1776–1838* (Basingstoke, U.K., 1986); Herbert S. Klein, *African Slavery in Latin America and the Caribbean* (New York, 1986), 243–71; Gordon W. Allport, *The Nature of Prejudice* (Cambridge, Mass., 1954); Michael P. Banton, *White and Coloured: The Behaviour of British People towards Coloured Immigrants* (London, 1959).

12   Europe: Internal Migrations from the Seventeenth to the Nineteenth Century

1 Klaus J. Bade, *Europa in Bewegung: Migration vom späten 18. Jahrhundert bis zur Gegenwart* (Munich, 2000).

2 Jan Lucassen, "The Netherlands, the Dutch, and Long-Distance Migration in the Late Sixteenth to Early Nineteenth Centuries," in Nicholas Canny, ed., *Europeans on the Move: Studies on European Migration, 1500–1800* (Oxford, 1994), 152–91, quote on 153. Dirk Hoerder and Horst Rössler, eds., *Distant Magnets: Expectations and Realities in the Immigrant Experience* (New York, 1993), and Hoerder, "Labour Migrants' Views of 'America,'" *Renaissance and Modern Studies* 35 (1992): 1–17; Hugo Soly, "Social Aspects of Structural Changes in the Urban Industries of Eighteenth-Century Brabant and Flanders," in Herman Van der Wee, ed., *The Rise and Decline of Urban Industries in Italy and in the Low Countries (Late Middle Ages–Early Modern Times)* (Leuven, 1988), 241–60.

3 In the thinly settled United States, on the other hand, administrative circuit riding continued into the nineteenth century.

4 Frederick William I of Prussia (r. 1713–40) "collected" "tall boys" (*lange Kerls*) from across Europe. Court historians have discussed neither the recruiting expenses nor the possible sexual preferences involved. Günter Barudio, *Das Zeitalter des Absolutismus und der Aufklärung 1648–1779* (Frankfurt/Main, 1981), 228; André Corvisier, *Armies and Societies in Europe, 1494–1789*, trans. Abigail T. Siddall (French orig., 1976; Bloomington, 1979), 116–48, and Corvisier, "Service militaire et mobilité géographique au XVIIIe," *Annales de démographie historique* (1970), 185–204; Canny, *Europeans on the Move*, 84, 105, 121–126.

5 István Deák, *Beyond Nationalism: A Social and Political History of the Habsburg Officer Corps, 1848–1918* (New York, 1990), and Deák, "The Ethnic Question in the Multinational Habsburg Army, 1848–1918," in N. F. Dreisziger, ed., *Ethnic Armies: Polyethnic Armed Forces from the Time of the Habsburgs to the Age of the Superpowers* (Waterloo, Ont., 1990), 21–49; Gregory Hanlon, *The Twilight of a Military Tradition: Italian Aristocrats and European Conflicts, 1560–1800* (New York, 1998).

6 Peter H. Wilson, "The German 'Soldier Trade' of the Seventeenth and Eighteenth Centuries:

A Reassessment," *International History Review* 18 (1996): 757–92; "Uniforms," in *Encyclopedia Britannica*, 11th ed. (Cambridge, 1910–11), 27:582–93. For ethnicity and armed forces in the nineteenth century, see Dreisziger, *Ethnic Armies*. In the twentieth century, victorious armies brought home voluntary war brides, a new facet of international marriage markets and migration.

7 Stanford J. Shaw, "The Ottoman Census System and Population, 1831–1914," *International Journal of Middle East Studies* 9 (1978): 325–38; Moses Avigdor Shulvass, *From East to West: The Westward Migration of Jews from Eastern Europe during the Seventeenth and Eighteenth Centuries* (Detroit, 1971); Jane S. Gerber, *The Jews of Spain: A History of the Sephardic Experience* (New York, 1992), 181–211; Jonathan I. Israel, *European Jewry in the Age of Mercantilism, 1550–1750* (Oxford, 1985), 53–69, 123–236; Rob van Engelsdorp Gastelaars, Jacqueline Vijgen, and Michiel Wagenaar, "Jewish Amsterdam 1600–1940: From 'Ghetto' to 'Neighborhoods,'" in Étienne François, ed., *Immigration et société urbaine en Europe occidentale, XVIe–XXe siècle* (Paris, 1985),127–42. Joan G. Roland, *Jews in British India: Identity in a Colonial Era* (Hanover, N.H., 1989), 16–17; Rudolf Asveer Jacob van Lier, *Frontier Society: A Social Analysis of the History of Surinam* (The Hague, 1971), 85–95; Avraham Barkai, "German-Jewish Migration in the Nineteenth Century, 1820–1910," in Ira A. Glazier and Luigi De Rosa, eds., *Migration across Time and Nations: Population Mobility in Historical Contexts* (New York, 1986), 202–19; Frances Malino and David Sorkin, eds., *Profiles in Diversity: Jews in a Changing Europe, 1750–1870* (Detroit, 1998).

8 In contrast to research on Jewish history, little attention has been paid to the history of the Gypsies. Leo Lucassen, "A Blind Spot: Migratory and Travelling Groups in Western European Historiography," *International Review of Social History* 38 (1993): 209–35, quote on 227; Leo Lucassen, Wim Willems, and Annemarie Cottaar, *Gypsies and Other Itinerant Groups: A Socio-Historical Approach* (Basingstoke, 1998); David Mayall, *Gypsy-Travellers in Nineteenth-Century Society* (Cambridge, 1988). Gérard Chaliand and Jean-Pierre Rageau, *The Penguin Atlas of Diasporas* (French orig., Paris, 1991; New York, 1995), 95–111.

9 Andrew Wilton and Ilaria Bignamini, eds., *Grand Tour: The Lure of Italy in the Eighteenth Century* (London, 1986); Shearer West, ed., *Italian Culture in Northern Europe in the Eighteenth Century* (New York, 1999). Gustav Otruba, "Englische Fabrikanten und Maschinisten zur Zeit Maria Theresias und Josephs II. in Österreich," *Tradition* 12 (1967): 265–77; Martin Schumacher, *Auslandsreisen deutscher Unternehmer 1750 bis 1851 unter besonderer Berücksichtigung von Rheinland und Westfalen* (Cologne, 1968); David J. Jeremy, *Transatlantic Industrial Revolution: The Diffusion of Textile Technologies between Britain and America, 1790–1914* (Cambridge, Mass., 1981), and Jeremy, ed., *International Technology Transfer: Europe, Japan, and the USA, 1700–1914* (Brookfield, Vt., 1991); John R. Harris, "Industrial Espionage in the Eighteenth Century," *Industrial Archeology Review* 7 (1985): 127–38. Dolf Kaiser, *Fast ein Volk von Zuckerbäckern? Bündner Konditoren, Cafetiers und Hoteliers in europäischen Ländern bis zum ersten Weltkrieg: Ein wirtschaftsgeschichtlicher Beitrag* (Zurich, 1985). Otto Moericke, "Eine Reise badischer Bauern nach England im 18. Jahrhundert," *Zeitschrift für die Geschichte des Oberrheins*, n.s., 22 (1907): 657–22; Hans-Heinrich Müller, "Christopher Brown, An English Farmer in Brandenburg-Prussia in the Eighteenth Century," *Agricultural History Review* 17 (1969): 120–35.

10 See, for example, Richard L. Kagan, *Students and Society in Early Modern Spain* (Baltimore, 1974).

11 Sarah C. Maza, *Servants and Masters in Eighteenth-Century France: The Uses of Loyalty*

(Princeton, 1983); Abel Chatelain, "Migrations et domesticité feminine urbaine en France, XVIIIe-XXe siècles," *Revue d'histoire économique et sociale* 4 (1969): 506–28; Jacques Dupâquier, "Geographic and Social Mobility in France in the Nineteenth and Twentieth Centuries," in Glazier and de Rosa, *Migration across Time and Nations*, 356–64; Barbara Henkes, *Heimat in Holland: Deutsche Dienstmädchen 1920-1950*, trans. Maria Csollány (Dutch orig., 1995; Straelen, 1998); David I. Kertzer, *Sacrificed for Honor: Italian Infant Abandonment and the Politics of Reproductive Control* (Boston 1993), 38–70, "Policing Women."

12 J. Jean Hecht, *The Domestic Servant Class in Eighteenth-Century England* (London, 1956), 14–15; Keith Wrightson and David Levine, *Poverty and Piety in an English Village: Terling, 1525-1700* (New York, 1979), 4–5, 64–82; Eric Kerridge, *Agrarian Problems in the Sixteenth Century and After* (London, 1969), 65–93. Thorkild Kjaergaard discusses changing labor needs, land use, population size, soil fertilization, and regulation of labor in *The Danish Revolution, 1500-1800: An Ecohistorical Interpretation* (Cambridge, 1994), 145–78.

13 Pierre Goubert, *L'Ancien Régime*, 2 vols. (Paris, 1969–73), vol.1; Abel Châtelain, *Les Migrants temporaires en France de 1800 à 1914: Histoire économique et sociale des migrants temporaires des campagnes françaises au XIXe siècle et au début du XXe siècle*, 2 vols. (Villeneuve-d'Ascq, 1976); Jean-Pierre Poussou, "Les Mouvements migratoires en France et à partir de la France de la fin du XVe siècle au début du XIXe siècle: approches pour une synthèse," *Annales de démographie historique* (1970), 11–78; Peter Clark, "Migration in England during the Late Seventeenth and Early Eighteenth Centuries," *Past and Present* 83 (1979): 57–90; Georg Fertig, "Transatlantic Migration from the German-Speaking Parts of Central Europe, 1600–1800: Proportions, Structures and Explanations," in Canny, *Europeans on the Move*, 195. Differences in estimated mobility are partly due to different methods, lack of data for short-term migration, and varying time-spans (migration per year or migration during lifetime).

14 Béla Gunda, *Ethnographica Carpatho-Balcanica* (Budapest, 1979), 220–24, 409–12.

15 Julius Klein, *The Mesta: A Study in Spanish Economic History, 1273-1836* (orig. 1920; repr., Port Washington, N.Y., 1964), 17–60.

16 Arnold Beuermann, *Fernweidewirtschaft in Südosteuropa: Ein Beitrag zur Kulturgeographie des östlichen Mittelmeergebietes* (Braunschweig, 1967); Armin Hetzer, "Der Balkansprachenbund als Forschungsproblem," *Südost-Forschungen* [Munich] 48 (1989): 177–94.

17 Richard van Dülmen, *Entstehung des frühneuzeitlichen Europa 1550-1648* (Frankfurt/Main, 1982), 19–101. On the general economic framework, see Peter Kriedte, Hans Medick, and Jürgen Schlumbohm, *Industrialization before Industrialization: Rural Industry in the Genesis of Capitalism*, trans. Beate Schempp (German orig., 1977; Cambridge, 1981). Only rarely were the skills of uprooted cottage workers in demand at the place of arrival.

18 Werner Rösener, *The Peasantry of Europe*, trans. Thomas M. Barker (German orig., 1993; Oxford, 1994), 125–41, map on 128; Daniel Häberle, *Auswanderung und Koloniegründungen der Pfälzer im 18. Jahrhundert: Zur 200jährigen Erinnerung an die Massenauswanderung der Pfälzer 1709 und an den pfälzischen Bauerngeneral Nikolaus Herchheimer, den Helden von Oriskany 6. August 1777* (Kaiserslautern, 1909), 51–60, 139–44, 153–61; Richard Hayes, "The German Colony in County Limerick," *North Munster Antiquarian Journal* 1 (1937): 45–53.

19 Michael Drake, *Population and Society in Norway 1735-1865* (Cambridge, 1969), 86–87; Eric De Geer, *Migration och influensfält: Studier av emigration och intern migration i Fin-*

land och Sverige 1816–1972 (Uppsala, 1977), 112; Sune Åkerman, Hans Christian Johansen, and Robert Ostergren, *Long-Distance Migration in Scandinavia 1500–1900*, XVIIe Congrès International des Sciences Historiques, Madrid 26/8–2/9 1990 (Umeå, 1990).

20 Iain R. Munro, *Immigration* (Toronto, 1978), quote 41; Karl Lilienthal, *Jürgen Christian Findorffs Erbe: Ein Beitrag zur Darstellung der kolonisatorischen und kulturellen Entwicklung der Moore des alten Herzogtums Bremen* (1931; repr., Lilienthal, 1982), 122. The proverb was also used by German settlers in eighteenth-century Russia. Jan De Vries, *European Urbanization, 1500–1800* (Cambridge, Mass., 1984), 106, 194–95, 262.

21 Mack Walker, *The Salzburg Transaction: Expulsion and Redemption in Eighteenth-Century Germany* (Ithaca, 1992); Gerhard Florey, *Geschichte der Salzburger Protestanten und ihrer Emigration 1731–32* (Vienna, 1977); Max Beheim-Schwarzbach, *Hohenzollernsche Colonisationen* (Leipzig, 1874), 265–444; Gustav Schmoller, "Die preußischen Kolonisationen des 17. und 18. Jahrhunderts," *Schriften des Vereins für Socialpolitik* 32 (1886): 1–43; Emil J. Meilicke, *Leaves from the Life of a Pioneer: Being the Autobiography of Sometime Senator Emil Julius Meilicke* (Vancouver, 1948).

22 For previous religious, colonial, and imperial war and settlement in the case of Ireland, see chap. 4.3.

23 The Orthodox Romanian peasantry and Armenian refugees were exempted from the right to practice their religion. The Romanian peasantry began to struggle against the better-placed German-speaking local populations in the nineteenth century.

24 Charles W. Ingrao, *The Habsburg Monarchy, 1618–1815* (Cambridge, 1994), 53–104; Robert A. Kann, *A History of the Habsburg Empire, 1526–1918* (Berkeley, 1974), 54–155; John R. Lampe and Marvin R. Jackson, *Balkan Economic History, 1550–1950: From Imperial Borderlands to Developing Nations* (Bloomington, 1982), 61–71; Kiril Petkov, *Infidels, Turks, and Women: The South Slavs in the German Mind, ca. 1400–1600* (New York, 1997); Fertig, "Migration from the German-Speaking Parts," 62–64, 209; Peter F. Sugar, *Southeastern Europe under Ottoman Rule, 1354–1804* (Seattle, 1977), 106–7; Gunther Erich Rothenberg, *The Austrian Military Border in Croatia, 1522–1747* (Urbana, Ill., 1960).

25 Historic Hungary, home to numerous ethnic groups, negotiated self-administration in 1867. The ethnically dominant Magyars imposed assimilatory policies on the other groups and established independent modern Hungary, which still accommodated "minorities," in 1918.

26 Lampe and Jackson, *Balkan Economic History*, 66–71; Robert A. Kann and Zdenek V. David, *The Peoples of the Eastern Habsburg Lands, 1526–1918* (Seattle, 1984); Barbara Jelavich, *History of the Balkans*, 2 vols. (Cambridge, 1983); Dirk Hoerder with Inge Blank, "Ethnic and National Consciousness from the Enlightenment to the 1880s," in Hoerder, Horst Rössler, and Blank, eds., *Roots of the Transplanted*, 2 vols. (New York, 1994), 1:37–110; Armin Hetzer and Dirk Hoerder, "Linguistic Fragmentation or Multilingualism among Labor Migrants in North America," in Hoerder and Christiane Harzig, eds., *The Immigrant Labor Press in North America, 1840s–1970s: An Annotated Bibliography*, 3 vols. (New York, 1987), 2:29–52.

27 An undated illustration in Philip Longworth, *The Cossacks* (London, 1969), 85, shows "Cossack women helping their menfolk at the siege of Azov" in 1637.

28 Hans Auerbach, *Die Besiedlung der Südukraine in den Jahren 1774–1787* (Wiesbaden, 1965), 40–126; Marc Raeff, *Understanding Imperial Russia: State and Society in the Old Regime*, trans. Arthur Goldhammer (French orig., 1982; New York, 1984), 89–111.

29 Paul J. Hauben, "The First Decade of an Agrarian Experiment in Bourbon Spain: The 'New

Towns' of Sierra Morena and Andalusia, 1766–75," *Agricultural History* 39, 1 (Jan. 1965): 34–40, quote on 37; Rudolf Leonhard, *Agrarpolitik und Agarreform in Spanien unter Carl III.* (Munich, 1909), 284–95.

30 Antonio Eiras Roel, "Estructura demográfica, diversidad regional y tendencias migratorias de la población española a finales del Antiguo Régimen," in Simonetta Cavaciocchi, ed., *Le Migrazioni in Europa secc. XIII–XVIII* (Florence, 1994), 199–231.

31 J. M. Neeson, *Commoners: Common Right, Enclosure and Social Change in Common-Field England, 1700–1820* (New York, 1993), 4–5, 13–47, quote on 27. See also E. A. Wrigley and R. S. Schofield, *The Population History of England, 1541–1871: A Reconstruction* (1981; rev. ed., Cambridge, 1989), 219. Pauline Gregg, *Black Death to Industrial Revolution: A Social and Economic History of England* (London, 1976), 258–67; C. G. A. Clay, *Economic Expansion and Social Change: England 1500–1700*, 2 vols. (Cambridge, 1984), 1:1–28, 67–77, 165–213; Richard Brown, *Society and Economy in Modern Britain, 1700–1850* (London, 1991), 44–46, 126–59, 226–48, 362–65, 395–429; Ivy Pinchbeck, *Women Workers and the Industrial Revolution 1750–1850* (1930; repr., London, 1969); Nicholas Rogers, "Vagrancy, Impressment and the Regulation of Labour in Eighteenth-Century Britain," in Paul E. Lovejoy and Rogers, eds., *Unfree Labour in the Development of the Atlantic World* (Ilford, U.K., 1994), 102–13. For Germany, see Fertig, "Migration from the German-Speaking Parts," 207.

32 Neeson, *Commoners*, 58–59, 188–220, 223, 254–58; K. D. M. Snell, *Annals of the Labouring Poor: Social Change and Agrarian England, 1660–1900* (Cambridge, 1985), 15–66, 123, 138–227.

33 Hecht, *Domestic Servant Class*, 1–9, 19–23, quote on 16 (from *The London Chronicle*, 1763); Johann Wilhelm von Archenholz, *A Picture of England: Containing a Description of the Laws, Customs, and Manners of England* (Dublin, 1791), 191, quote on 13; Snell, *Labouring Poor*, 67–103, 228–69, and concerning female apprentices, 270–319.

34 Hecht, *Domestic Servant Class*, 25–29, 33–34, 208; Vivien B. Elliott, "Single Women in the London Marriage Market: Age, Status, and Mobility," in R. B. Outhwaite, ed., *Marriage and Society: Studies in the Social History of Marriage* (London, 1981), 81–100.

35 Leslie Page Moch and Gary D. Stark, eds., *Essays on the Family and Historical Change* (College Station, Tex., 1983), esp. the essays by David Levine, "Proto-Industrialization and Demographic Upheaval," 9–34, Moch, "Infirmities of the Body and Vices of the Soul: Migrants, Family, and Urban Life in Turn-of-the-Century France," 35–64, and Louise A. Tilly, "Rich and Poor in a French Textile City," 65–90; Jack M. Potter, May N. Diaz, and George M. Foster, eds., *Peasant Society: A Reader* (Boston, 1967).

36 Many immigrants of Jewish background were "New Christians," converts from Judaism. Because conversions were mostly involuntary and because Catholicism was viewed with suspicion by the Dutch, many returned to the faith of their ancestors.

37 William Petty quoted in Lucassen, "The Netherlands, the Dutch, and Long-Distance Migration," 182–83.

38 Peter van Kessel and Elisja Schulte, eds., *Rome, Amsterdam: Two Growing Cities in Seventeenth-Century Europe* (Amsterdam, 1997); C. R. Boxer, *The Dutch Seaborne Empire, 1600–1800* (London, 1965), quote on 21; Jonathan Israel, *The Dutch Republic: Its Rise, Greatness, and Fall, 1477–1806* (Oxford, 1995), 619–36. Amsterdam attracted travelers in such numbers that a Dutch-language visitor's guide appeared in 1663, followed in 1664 by one in German. Philipp von Zesen, *Europas Erster Baedeker: Filip von Zesens Amsterdam, 1664,* ed. Christian Gellinek (New York, 1988). Juliette Roding and Lex Heerma van Voss, eds.,

The North Sea and Culture (1550-1800): Proceedings of the International Conference Held at Leiden 21-22 April 1995 (Hilversum, 1996).

39 Boxer, *Dutch Seaborne Empire,* 60-71, quote on 60.

40 Lucassen, "The Netherlands, the Dutch, and Long-Distance Migration," 159-81; Lucassen, *Dutch Long Distance Migration: A Concise History 1600-1900* (Amsterdam, 1993); Lucassen and Rinus Penninx, *Newcomers: Immigrants and Their Decendants in the Netherlands 1550-1995,* trans. Michael Wintle (Dutch orig., 1985; rev. ed., Amsterdam, 1997); Sölvi Sogner, "Young in Europe about 1700: Norwegian Sailors and Servant-Girls Seeking Employment in Amsterdam," in Jean-Pierre Bardet, François Lebrun, and René Le Mée, eds., *Mesurer et comprendre: Mélanges offerts à Jacques Dupâquier* (Paris, 1993), 514-32. G. V. Scammell, "Manning the English Merchant Service in the Sixteenth Century," *Mariner's Mirror* 56 (1970): 131-54, argues that, although they predominated, English sailors formed "cosmopolitan crews" with Dutchmen, Flemings, Italians, Greeks, and "Negroes"; English sailors also went into service on Portuguese and Spanish ships.

41 Immigration policy became restrictive during a period of unemployment and emerging nationalism. Under a first "foreigners law" of 1849, admission depended on the country's economic and foreign policy interests. Further restrictions were passed in 1918 and 1920. Marij Leenders, *Ongenode gasten: Van traditioneel asielrecht naar immigratiebeleid, 1815-1938* (Hilversum, 1993). I am grateful to Christiane Harzig and her research group for translations from the Dutch.

42 Leslie Page Moch, *Moving Europeans: Migration in Western Europe since 1650* (Bloomington, 1992), chap. 2, provides an excellent analysis of migration in Western Europe, 1650-1750.

43 Hermann Kellenbenz, ed., *Fremde Kaufleute auf der iberischen Halbinsel* (Cologne, 1970), esp. 265-376. For internal migration, see Michael R. Weisser, *The Peasants of the Montes: The Roots of Rural Rebellion in Spain* (Chicago, 1976), 42-70.

44 Abel Poitrineau, *Les Espagnols de l'Auvergne et du Limousin du XVIIe au XIXe siècle* (Aurillac, 1985); Albert Girard, *Le Commerce français a Séville et Cadix aux temps des Habsbourg: Contribution à l'étude du commerce étranger en Espagne aux XVIe et XVIIIe siècles* (Bordeaux, 1932), "La Colonie française d'Andalousie," 538-90; Georges Nadal and É. Giralt, *La Population catalane de 1553 à 1717: L'Immigration française et les autres facteurs de son développement* (Paris, 1960).

45 Michael Roberts, ed., *Sweden's Age of Greatness, 1632-1718* (London, 1973), 58-131; Claude J. Nordmann, *Grandeur et liberté de la Suède (1660-1792)* (Paris, 1971), 285-326; Maria Bogucka, "Les Migrations baltiques et Gdansk au seuil de l'ère moderne, XVIe-XVIIIe siècles," in Klaus Friedland, ed., *Maritime Aspects of Migration* (Cologne, 1989), 107-24; S. Montelius, "Recruitment and Conditions of Life of Swedish Ironworkers during the Eighteenth and Nineteenth Centuries," *Scandinavian Economic History Review* 14 (1966): 1-17; Göran Rosander, *Herrarbete: Dalfolkets säsongvisa arbetsvandringar i jämförande belysning* (Uppsala, 1967); Hans Norman and Harald Runblom, "Migration Patterns in the Nordic Countries," in Dirk Hoerder, ed., *Labor Migration in the Atlantic Economies: The European and North American Working Classes during the Period of Industrialization* (Westport, Conn., 1985), 35-68.

46 This system dated from the Middle Ages. Jacques Dupâquier et al., *Histoire de la population française,* vol. 1: "Des origines à la Renaissance" (Paris, 1988), 406-7; Olwen H. Hufton, *The Poor of Eighteenth-Century France, 1750-1789* (Oxford, 1974), 67-127; Louis Chevalier,

Les classes laborieuses et classes dangereuses à Paris pendant la première moitié du XIXe siècle (Paris, 1958), 267–308, on immigration.

47 Domenico Sella, "Au dossier du migrations montagnards: L'Example de la Lombardie au XVIIe siècle," in *Mélanges en l'honneur de Fernand Braudel*, 2 vols. (Toulouse, 1973), 1:547–54; Fernand Braudel, *Civilisation matérielle et capitalisme* (Paris, 1967), English: *Capitalism and Material Life, 1400–1800*, trans. Miriam Kochan (New York, 1973), 314–29; Marcelo J. Borges, "Moving Algarvians: Migratory Systems in Southern Portugal, 1800–1900," paper presented at the European Social Science Historical Conference, Amsterdam, Mar. 1998.

48 Jan Lucassen, *Migrant Labour in Europe, 1600–1900: The Drift to the North Sea*, trans. Donald A Bloch (Dutch orig., 1984; London, 1987), chap. 6 and appendix 2, esp. pp.108–13.

49 Jerzy Wyrozumski, "La géographie des migrations en Europe centrale et orientale du Moyen Âge au début des temps modernes," in Cavaciocchi, *Le Migrazioni in Europa*, 191–98; Alain Ducellier, "Albanais dans les Balkans et en Italie à la fin du Moyen Âge: Courants migratoires et connivences socio-culturelles," in Cavaciocchi, *Le Migrazioni in Europa*, 233–69.

50 Kazimierz Slaski, *Tysiaclecie polsko-skandynawskich stosunków kulturalnych* [The millenium of Polish-Scandinavian cultural relations (970–1970)] (Wrocław, 1977), 104–270; A. J. S. Gibson and T. C. Smout, *Prices, Food, and Wages in Scotland, 1550–1780* (Cambridge, 1995), 165ff.

51 François, *Immigration et société urbaine*; Olwen H. Hufton, "Women and the Family Economy in Eighteenth-Century France," *French Historical Studies* 9 (1975): 1–22; Antoinette Fauve-Chamoux, "Les Femmes qui migrent au loin (1500–1900): Vie nouvelle ou guillotine sèche?" in Bardet, Lebrun, and Le Mée, *Mesurer et comprendre*, 195–206.

52 Charles Tilly, "Demographic Origins of the European Proletariat," in David Levine, ed., *Proletarianization and Family History* (Orlando, 1984), 1–61, and Tilly, *Coercion, Capital and European States, AD 990–1990* (Cambridge, Mass., 1990); De Vries, *European Urbanization*, 212–56; Horst Matzerath, "Grundstrukturen städtischer Bevölkerungsentwicklung in Mitteleuropa im 19. Jahrhundert", in Wilhelm Rausch, ed., *Die Städte Mitteleuropas im 19. Jahrhundert* (Linz, 1983), 25–46.

53 Hans-Joachim Braun, *Technologische Beziehungen zwischen Deutschland und England von der Mitte des 17. bis zum Ausgang des 18. Jahrhunderts* (Düsseldorf, 1974), 15–17; De Vries, *European Urbanization*, 108–113; Van der Wee, *Rise and Decline of Urban Industries*, 241–245.

54 See chap. 4.3 for references. Rudolf von Thadden and Michelle Magdelaine, eds., *Die Hugenotten, 1685–1985* (Munich 1985; French ed., Paris, 1985); CNRS, ed., *Le Refuge huguenot en Allemagne: Table ronde des 23 et 24 mars 1981* (Paris, 1981); Gerhard Fischer, *Die Hugenotten in Berlin* (Berlin, 1988); essays in Bezirksamt Neukölln von Berlin, ed., *Dem Kelch zuliebe Exulant: 250 Jahre Böhmisches Dorf in Berlin-Neukölln*, 2 vols. (Berlin, 1987); Stefi Jersch-Wenzel, "Der Einfluß zugewanderter Minoritäten," in Otto Büsch, ed., *Untersuchungen zur Geschichte der frühen Industrialisierung, vornehmlich im Wirtschaftsraum Berlin/Brandenburg* (Berlin, 1971), 193–223, and "Minderheiten in der preußischen Gesellschaft," in Otto Büsch and Wolfgang Neugebauer, eds., *Moderne Preußische Geschichte, 1648–1947: Eine Anthologie* (Berlin, 1981), 486–506, and "Preußen als Einwanderungsland," in Manfred Schlenke, ed., *Preußen Beiträge zu einer politischen Kultur*, 2 vols. (Reinbek, 1981), 2:136–61.

55 Stefi Jersch-Wenzel, "Minderheitenrecht im Vergleich," and Kaspar Struckmann, "Identi-

tät und Böhmische Sprache," in *Das Böhmische Dorf in Berlin-Neukölln, 1737-1987* (Berlin, 1987), 105-11, 217-29.

56 Daniel Statt, *Foreigners and Englishmen: The Controversy over Immigration and Population, 1660-1760* (Newark, Del., 1995).

57 Arija Zeida, "Das Wandern der Gesellen und seine Bedeutung für Riga vom 14. bis zum 18. Jahrhundert," in Konrad Fritze, ed., *Bürgertum—Handelskapital—Städtebünde* (Weimar, 1975), 233-51.

58 Knut Schulz, *Handwerksgesellen und Lohnarbeiter: Untersuchungen zur oberrheinischen und oberdeutschen Stadtgeschichte des 14. bis 17. Jahrhunderts* (Sigmaringen, 1985), 270ff., surveys developments since 1600; Helmut Lahrkamp, "Wanderbewegungen im 18. Jahrhundert: Tiroler Maurer, skandinavische Hutmacher, reisende Buchdrucker, böhmische Glashändler und italienische Kaminfeger in Münster," *Westfälische Forschungen* 26 (1974): 123-32; Klaus J. Bade, "Altes Handwerk, Wanderzwang und Gute Policey: Gesellenwanderung zwischen Zunftökonomie und Gewerbereform," *Vierteljahrschrift für Sozial- und Wirtschaftsgeschichte* 69 (1982): 1-37. William H. Sewell Jr., *Work and Revolution in France: The Language of Labor from the Old Regime to 1848* (Cambridge, 1980); Cynthia M. Truant, "Solidarity and Symbolism among Journeymen Artisans: The Case of Compagnonnage," *Comparative Studies in Society and History* 21 (1979): 214-26; Ulrich-Christian Pallach, "Fonctions de la mobilité artisanale et ouvrière," *Francia* 11 (1983): 365-406, esp. 381-82. Fritz Valjavec, *Geschichte der deutschen Kulturbeziehungen zu Südosteuropa*, 3 vols. (rev. ed., Munich, 1970), 3:76f. Claudius Helmut Riegler, *Emigration und Arbeitswanderung aus Schweden nach Norddeutschland 1868-1914* (Neumünster, 1985), and Riegler, "Labor Migration of Skilled Workers, Artisans and Technicians and Technology Transfer between Sweden and Germany before World War I," in Hoerder, *Labor Migration in the Atlantic Economies*, 163-88, and "Scandinavian Migrants' Images and the Americanization of the Work Process," in Hoerder and Rössler, *Distant Magnets*, 160-79.

59 Braun, *Technologische Beziehungen*, 17-30.

60 Italian chimneysweeps and sellers of citrus fruits were part of street life in many Central European towns. See, for example, Gustav Wulz, "Italienische Kaminkehrer und Südfrüchtehändler in Nördlingen," *Schwäbische Blätter für Heimatpflege und Volksbildung* 10 (1959): 122-28; Johannes Augel, *Italienische Einwanderung und Wirtschaftstätigkeit in rheinischen Städten des 17. und 18. Jahrhunderts* (Bonn, 1971), 155-68, 238-50, 282-306. Herbert Lüthy, *Die Tätigkeit der Schweizer Kaufleute und Gewerbetreibenden in Frankreich unter Ludwig XIV und der Regentschaft* (Aarau, CH, 1943); Adelheid Simsch, *Die Handelsbeziehungen zwischen Nürnberg und Posen im europäischen Wirtschaftsverkehr des 15. und 16. Jahrhunderts* (Wiesbaden, 1970); Gigliola Pagano De Divitiis, *English Merchants in Seventeenth-Century Italy* (New York, 1997).

61 Wilfried Reininghaus, ed., *Wanderhandel in Europa: Beiträge zur wissenschaftlichen Tagung in Ibbenbüren, Mettingen, Recke und Hepsten vom 9.-11. Oktober 1992* (Dortmund, 1993); Jean-Pierre Filippini, "Les Juifs d'Afrique du Nord et la communauté de Livourne au XVIIIe siècle," in J. L. Miege, ed. *Les Relations intercommunautaires juives en Méditerranèe occidentale, XVIIIe–Xxe siècles: Actes du colloque international de l'Institut d'Histoire des Pays d'Outre-Mer et du Centre de Recherches sur les Juifs d'Africque du Nord, Abbaye de Sénanque, mai 1982* (Paris, 1984), 60-69; David Hancock, *Citizens of the World: London Merchants and the Integration of the British Atlantic Community, 1735-1785* (Cambridge, 1995); James D. Tracy, ed., *The Rise of Merchant Empires: Long-Distance Trade in the Early*

Modern World, 1350–1750 (Cambridge, 1990), 311–50; Morris Rossabi, "The 'Decline' of the Central Asian Caravan Trade," in Tracy, *Rise of Merchant Empires*, 351–70; Stephen Frederic Dale, *Indian Merchants and Eurasian Trade, 1600–1750* (Cambridge, 1994), 78–127.

62 F. W. Carter, *Trade and Urban Development in Poland: An Economic Geography of Cracow, from Its Origins to 1795* (Cambridge, 1994), 218–19, 244–47, 356–59.

63 Christopher R. Friedrichs, *Urban Society in an Age of War: Nördlingen, 1580–1720* (Princeton, 1979), 54–70.

64 Studies of cities with reference to migration are legion. See, for example, Paul Bairoch, Jean Batou, and Pierre Chèvre, *La Population des villes européennes: Banque de données et analyse sommaire des résultats, 800–1850* (Geneva, 1988); François, *Immigration et société urbaine*; Hugo Soly and Alfons K. L. Thijs, *Minorities in Western European Cities (Sixteenth–Twentieth Centuries)* (Brussels, 1995).

65 Friedrich Bothe, *Geschichte der Stadt Frankfurt am Main* (Frankfurt/Main, 1966), 359–84; Franz Lerner, "Eine Statistik der Handwerksgesellen zu Frankfurt a.M. vom Jahre 1762," *Vierteljahrschrift für Sozial- und Wirtschaftsgeschichte* 22 (1929): 174–93. Paul M. Hohenberg and Lynn Hollen Lees, *The Making of Urban Europe, 1000–1950* (Cambridge, Mass., 1985), chap. 3, esp. 90–98. From early modern times to the seventeenth century, Amsterdam grew from 35,000 inhabitants in 1557 to more than 100,000 in 1622, and Paris from 200,000 inhabitants in 1590 to 412,000 in 1637. Carlo M. Cipolla, ed., *The Fontana Economic History of Europe*, 6 vols. (London 1972), vol. 2 (chap.1 by Roger Mols) and vol. 3 (chap.1 by André Armengaud); Richard van Dülmen, *Entstehung des frühneuzeitlichen Europa*, 19–28.

66 Marco Della Pina, "Andamento e distribuzione della popolazione," in *Livorno et Pisa: Due città e un territorio nella politica dei Medici* (Pisa, 1980), 25–29; Mario Lopes Pegna, *L'Origine di Livorno* (Firenze, 1967); Michele Cassandro, *Aspetti della storia economica e sociale degli Ebrei di Livorno nel Seicento* (Milan, 1983).

67 Ralph Scander, *Karl X's Göteborg på hisingen: En holländsk koloni med svenskt medborgarskap* (Göteborg, 1975), and Scander, "Holländarnas Göteborg." *Fataburen: Nordiska museets och Skansens årsbok*, 1981, 91–114; Helge Almquist, *Göteborgs historia: Grundläggningen och de första hundra åren* (Göteborg, 1929); Stewart P. Oakley, *A Short History of Sweden* (New York, 1966), 85–86, 127–29; Franklin D. Scott, *Sweden: The Nation's History* (Minneapolis, 1977), 189–90. I am grateful to Ulysse deRungs for translations from Swedish.

68 Gilbert Rozman, *Urban Networks in Russia, 1750–1800, and Premodern Periodization* (Princeton, 1976), 146–48; James H. Bater, *St Petersburg: Industrialization and Change* (London, 1976), 17–84, quotes on 49–51. Igor Kopytoff and Suzanne Miers, "African 'Slavery' as an Institution of Marginality," in Miers and Kopytoff, eds., *Slavery in Africa: Historical and Anthropological Perspectives* (Madison, 1977), 40; *A Black Woman's Odyssey through Russia and Jamaica: The Narrative of Nancy Prince* (1850; New York, 1990). See chap. 13.3 for nineteenth-century internal migration to St. Petersburg.

69 Bronislawa Kopczynska-Jaworska, "Lodz—Zur Geschichte der Stadt und zur Kultur des Arbeitermilieus (von den Anfängen bis 1939)," in Monika Glettler, Heiko Haumann, and Gottfried Schramm, eds., *Zentrale Städte und ihr Umland: Wechselwirkungen während der Industrialisierungsperiode in Mitteleuropa* (St. Katharinen, 1985), 45–59; Otto Heike, *Aufbau und Entwicklung der Lodzer Textilindustrie: Eine Arbeit deutscher Einwanderer in Polen für Europa* (Mönchengladbach, 1971), and, Heike, "Polnische Forschungen und Darstellungen zur Geschichte der Stadt Lodz," *Zeitschrift für Ostforschung* 33 (1984): 393–406. The dichotomy of fabulous riches and harsh exploitation in Łódź is the theme of Andrzej

Wajda's 1974 film *Ziemia obiecana* (*The Promised Land*). In 1994 the city's mayor suggested its multicultural past be used to attract tourists.

70 Daniel Roche, *The People of Paris: An Essay in Popular Culture in the 18th Century,* trans. Marie Evans (French orig., 1981; Leamington Spa, U.K., 1987), 9–35. For further developments, see chap. 14.2.

71 Michael Polanyi, "The Republic of Science," *Minerva* 1 (1962): 54–73; David S. Landes, *The Unbound Prometheus: Technological Change and Industrial Development in Western Europe from 1750 to the Present* (Cambridge, 1969). Braun, *Technologische Beziehungen,* 40–75.

72 On women travelers, see John W. Stoye, *English Travellers Abroad, 1604-1667: Their Influence in English Society and Politics* (London, 1952), 48–69, 136–145. Jeremy Black, "France and the Grand Tour in the Early Eighteenth Century," *Francia* 11 (1983): 407–16.

73 Hans Hubrig, *Die patriotischen Gesellschaften des 18. Jahrhunderts* (Weinheim, 1957); Dirk Hoerder, "Some Connections between Craft Consciousness and Political Thought among Mechanics, 1820s to 1840s," *Amerikastudien* 30 (1985): 327–51.

74 Robert R. Palmer, *The Age of Democratic Revolution: A Political History of Europe and America, 1760-1800,* 2 vols. (Princeton, 1969), 197–206; École française de Rome, ed., *L'Émigration politique en Europe du XIX et XX siècles,* Actes du colloque organisé par l'École française de Rome (Rome, 1991); Paul Weber, *On the Road to Rebellion: The United Irishmen and Hamburg, 1796-1803* (Dublin, 1997); Martin A. Miller, *The Russian Revolutionary Emigres, 1825-1870* (Baltimore, 1986), quote on 11. Wallace Brown, *The King's Friends: The Composition and Motives of the American Loyalist Claimants* (Providence, 1965); Jean R. Burnet with Howard Palmer, *"Coming Canadians": An Introduction to a History of Canada's Peoples* (Toronto, 1988), 15. Margery Weiner, *The French Exiles, 1789-1815* (London, 1960); Donald Greer, *The Incidence of the Emigration during the French Revolution* (Cambridge, Mass., 1951); Sabine Diezinger, *Französische Emigranten und Flüchtlinge in der Markgrafschaft Baden (1789-1800)* (Frankfurt/Main, 1991).

75 At the same time, the Latin American revolutions and struggles for independence sent activists and military leaders into exile.

76 Max Beer, *Allgemeine Geschichte des Sozialismus und der sozialen Kämpfe* (7th rev. ed., Berlin, 1931), 441–63; Robert C. Williams, "European Political Emigrations: A Lost Subject," *Comparative Studies in Society and History* 12 (1970): 140–48. Bernard Porter, "The British Government and Political Refugees, c.1880-1914," in John Slatter, ed., *From the Other Shore: Russian Political Emigrants in Britain, 1880-1917* (London, 1984), 23–45; George Haupt, "Rôle de l'exil dans la diffusion de l'image de l'intelligentsia revolutionnaire," *Cahiers du monde russe et soviétique* 19, 3 (1978): 235–49. Margaret Campbell Walker Wicks, *The Italian Exiles in London, 1816-1848* (Manchester, 1937).

77 "Natalie Herzen's Dream," quoted in Miller, *Russian Revolutionary Émigrés,* 222–24; Eleanor Flexner, *Century of Struggle: The Woman's Rights Movement in the United States* (Cambridge, Mass., 1959), 15, 71–77. Two Russian women became active in the Italian socialist movement; see Claire LaVigna, *Anna Kuliscioff: From Russian Populism to Italian Socialism* (New York, 1991), and Angelica Balabanoff, *My Life as a Rebel* (London, 1938).

78 James H. Billington, *Fire in the Minds of Men: Origins of the Revolutionary Faith* (New York, 1980). Most of the literature deals with German Forty-eighters: Charlotte L. Brancaforte, *The German Forty-eighters in the United States* (New York, 1989); Bruce Levine, *The Spirit of 1848: German Immigrants, Labor Conflict, and the Coming of the Civil War*

(Urbana, Ill., 1992); Herbert Reiter, *Politisches Asyl im 19. Jahrhundert: Die deutschen politischen Flüchtlinge des Vormärz und der Revolution von 1848/49 in Europa und den USA* (Berlin, 1992); Carl Frederick Wittke, *Refugees of Revolution: The German Forty-eighters in America* (Philadelphia, 1952); A. E. Zucker, ed., *The Forty-eighters: Political Refugees of the German Revolution of 1848* (New York, 1950); Martin Henkel and Rolf Taubert, *Das Weib im Conflict mit den Socialen Verhältnissen: Mathilde Franziska Anneke und die erste deutsche Frauenzeitung* (Bochum, 1976).

79 Studies of immigration and labor are legion. Increasingly it is recognized that the European labor movements, too, were multiethnic. Dirk Hoerder, ed., *"Struggle a Hard Battle": Essays on Working-Class Immigrants* (DeKalb, Ill., 1986); Donna R. Gabaccia, *Militants and Migrants: Rural Sicilians Become American Workers* (New Brunswick, 1988).

13 The Russo-Siberian Migration System

1 Jerzy Wyrozumski, "La Géographie des migrations en Europe centrale et orientale du Moyen Age au début des temps modernes," in Simonetta Cavaciocchi, ed., *Le Migrazioni in Europa secc. XIII–XVIII* (Florence, 1994), 191–98; Michael Bibikov, Vladimir M. Kabuzan, and Vladislav D. Nazarov, "Ethno-Demographic Changes in the Region of Northern Pontos-Southern Russia-Ukraine," ibid., 271–97.

2 The Cyrillic alphabet replaced Arab styles only under Soviet rule.

3 Hundreds of thousands of Kazakhs had fled conscription by the tsarist army; more were to flee Soviet collectivization in 1932. Many of the peoples of Central Asia unsuccessfully sought independence in 1917; several formed their own republics within the Soviet Union. Andreas Kappeler, *Russland als Vielvölkerreich: Entstehung, Geschichte, Zerfall* (Munich, 1992), 108–21.

4 Old Believers refused to accept the reform of the Russian Orthodox Church by the tsars.

5 Elzbieta Kaczynska, *Das größte Gefängnis der Welt: Sibirien als Strafkolonie zur Zarenzeit* (Frankfurt/Main, 1994); Martin Gilbert, *Atlas of Russian History* (New York, 1972), 54; Haim H. Ben-Sasson, ed., *A History of the Jewish People* (Hebrew orig., 1969; Cambridge, Mass., 1976), 475–76; Donald W. Treadgold, *The Great Siberian Migration: Government and Peasant in Resettlement from Emancipation to the First World War* (Princeton, 1957), 13–35.

6 For First Peoples of Siberia, see Georges Dupeux, ed., *Les Migrations internationales de la fin du XVIIIe siècle à nos jours* (Paris, 1980), 199–202; Daniel R. Brower and Edward J. Lazzerini, eds., *Russia's Orient: Imperial Borderlands and Peoples, 1700–1917* (Bloomington, 1997).

7 Kappeler, *Vielvölkerreich*, 58–59, on the historiographical debate between Ukrainian and Soviet scholars about the ethnic background of the region's population. W. Kubijowytsch [V. Kubiiovych], *Siedlungsgeschichte, Bevölkerungsverteilung und Bevölkerungsbewegung der Ukraine* (Ukrainian orig., Lvov, 1938; Berlin, 1943), 18–33.

8 Inge Blank, "A Vast Migratory Experience: Eastern Europe in the Pre- and Post-Emancipation Era (1780–1914)," in Dirk Hoerder, Horst Rössler, and Inge Blank, eds., *Roots of the Transplanted*, 2 vols. (Boulder, 1994), 1:201–51; Kappeler, *Vielvölkerreich*, 43–50, 57–98; Roger P. Bartlett, *Human Capital: The Settlement of Foreigners in Russia, 1762–1804* (Cambridge, 1979), 6–8, 16–18, 25–26; Paul Bushkovitch, *The Merchants of Moscow, 1580–1680* (Cambridge, 1980), 30; Clifford M. Foust, *Muscovite and Mandarin: Russia's Trade with China and Its Setting, 1727–1805* (Chapel Hill, 1969); Erik Amburger, *Fremde und Einheim-*

ische im Wirtschafts- und Kulturleben des neuzeitlichen Rußland: Ausgewählte Aufsätze,
ed. Klaus Zernack (Wiesbaden, 1982); Stephen Frederic Dale, *Indian Merchants and Eurasian Trade, 1600-1750* (Cambridge, 1994), 78-127.

9   Hans Auerbach, *Die Besiedlung der Südukraine in den Jahren 1774-1787* (Wiesbaden, 1965); Bartlett, *Human Capital*, quote on 13.

10   For a survey of research on peasant discontent, see V. V. Mavrodin, "Soviet Historical Literature on the Peasant Wars in Russia during the 17th and 18th Centuries," *Soviet Studies in History* 1, 2 (fall 1962): 43-63. Bartlett, *Human Capital*, quote on 11. Auerbach, *Südukraine*, 14-16; William McNeill, *Europe's Steppe Frontier, 1500-1800* (Chicago, 1964), 191.

11   Auerbach, *Südukraine*, 21-54, 97-115; IU. M. Tarasov, *Russkaia krest'ianskaia kolonizatsiia Iuzhnogo Urala, vtoraia polovina XVIII-pervaia polovina XIX v.* [Russian peasant colonization of the southern Urals from 1750 to 1850] (Moscow, 1984); V. M. Kabuzan, *Izmeneniia v razmeshchenii naseleniia Rossii v XVIII-pervoi polovine XIX v (Po materialam revizii)* (Moscow, 1917); Bartlett, *Human Capital*, 8-13. Andreas Kappeler, *Rußlands erste Nationalitäten: Das Zarenreich und die Völker der Mittleren Wolga vom 16. bis 19. Jahrhundert* (Cologne, 1982).

12   Contrary to the common image of Jews as urban migrants, some went into agriculture if permitted to own land.

13   The Volga Germans were the first ethnic group after the establishment of the Soviet Union in 1917 to receive autonomy in 1918. When Nazi Germany invaded the USSR in 1941, the Volga Germans were deported eastward for fear of subversion.

14   The census of 1897 listed 1.8 million German-origin persons. War and emigration reduced the population of 2.4 million German-origin people of 1910, including Mennonites and German-speaking Jews, to 1.2 million in 1926. Karl Stumpp, *Die Auswanderung aus Deutschland nach Rußland in den Jahren 1763 bis 1862* (Tübingen, n.d. [before 1972]), 11-108, is a filiopietistic group history. Ingeborg Fleischhauer, *Die Deutschen im Zarenreich: Zwei Jahrhunderte deutsch-russischer Kulturgemeinschaft* (Stuttgart, 1986), and Fleischhauer and Hugo H. Jedig, eds., *Die Deutschen in der UdSSR in Geschichte und Gegenwart: Ein internationaler Beitrag zur deutsch-sowjetischen Verständigung* (Baden-Baden, 1990); Fred C. Koch, *The Volga Germans: In Russia and America, from 1763 to the Present* (University Park, Pa., 1977). For the whole of the German migrations, see Klaus J. Bade, ed., *Deutsche im Ausland, Fremde in Deutschland: Migration in Geschichte und Gegenwart* (Munich, 1992), 29-134. Bartlett, *Human Capital*, xii-xiv, 28, 57, 108 passim; Gilbert, *Atlas of Russian History*, 39.

15   Blank, "A Vast Migratory Experience," 211-14; Lewis H. Siegelbaum, "The Odessa Grain Trade: A Case Study in Urban Growth and Development in Tsarist Russia," *Journal of European Economic History* 9, 1 (spring 1980): 113-51.

16   Gilbert Rozman, *Urban Networks in Russia, 1750-1800, and Premodern Periodization* (Princeton, 1976), 59-61, 70, 113-16, 144-46; Arne Öhberg, "Russia and the World Market in the Seventeenth Century," *Scandinavian Economic History Review* 3 (1955): 123-62; Barbara Engel, "The Woman's Side: Male Outmigration and the Family Economy in Kostroma Province," in Ben Eklof and Stephen Frank, eds., *The World of the Russian Peasant: Post-Emancipation Culture and Society* (Boston, 1990), 71, 79, see also 172; Rose Glickman, "Peasant Women and Their Work," ibid., 54.

17   James H. Bater, *St. Petersburg: Industrialization and Change* (London, 1976), 64-84.

18   Anders Henriksson, *The Tsar's Loyal Germans: The Riga German Community, Social*

Change and the Nationality Question, 1855–1905 (Boulder, 1983); Raimo Pullat, *Die Stadtbevölkerung Estlands im 18. Jahrhundert* (Mainz, 1997).

19 Erik Amburger, *Die Anwerbung ausländischer Fachkräfte für die Wirtschaft Rußlands vom 15. bis ins 19. Jahrhundert* (Wiesbaden, 1968); Hans Rothe, *Deutsche in Rußland* (Vienna, 1996).

20 Barbara A. Anderson, *Internal Migration during Modernization in Late Nineteenth-Century Russia* (Princeton, 1980), 93.

21 The southernmost regions—that is, those just north of the Azov Sea—had fertile soil but were arid.

22 In Prussia and Austria-Hungary, the consolidation of medium-sized rural holdings decreased the availability of land for smallholders while increasing the demand for seasonal day laborers at below-subsistence annual incomes.

23 Peter Kolchin, *Unfree Labor: American Slavery and Russian Serfdom* (Cambridge, Mass., 1987); David A. J. Macey, *Government and Peasant in Russia, 1861–1906: The Prehistory of the Stolypin Reforms* (DeKalb, Ill., 1987).

24 John Bushnell, "Peasants in Uniform: The Tsarist Army as a Peasant Society," in Eklof and Frank, *Russian Peasant,* 101–14.

25 In the western borderlands, Russian Poland and the Baltic provinces, as in the Hohenzollern and Habsburg empires, redemption payments and taxes were assigned to individuals.

26 Blank, "A Vast Migratory Experience," 225; Boris Mirinov, "The Russian Peasant Commune after the Reforms of the 1860s," in Eklof and Frank, *Russian Peasant,* 7–44; Ben Eklof, "Ways of Seeing: Recent Anglo-American Studies of the Russian Peasant (1861–1914)," *Jahrbücher für Geschichte Osteuropas,* n.s., 36 (1988): 57–79. The classic study is Jerome Blum, *Lord and Peasant in Russia: From the Ninth to the Nineteenth Century* (Princeton, 1961), esp. 277–620; Robert Eugene Johnson, *Peasant and Proletarian: The Working Class of Moscow in the Late Nineteenth Century* (New Brunswick, 1979), 42–50; Jeffrey Burds, *Peasant Dreams and Market Politics: Labor Migration and the Russian Village, 1861–1905* (Pittsburgh, 1998).

27 Franco Ramella, "Between Village and Job Abroad: Italian Migrants in France and Switzerland," in Hoerder, Rössler, and Blank, *Roots of the Transplanted,* 2:271–88; Engel, "The Woman's Side," 66–70; Douglas S. Massey and Kristin E. Espinosa, "What's Driving Mexico-U.S. Migration? A Theoretical, Empirical, and Policy Analysis," unpublished paper, Sept. 1995.

28 Anderson, *Internal Migration,* 3–89; Blank, "A Vast Migratory Experience," 201–51; J. W. Leasure and R. A. Lewis, "Internal Migration in Russia in the Late Nineteenth Century," *Slavic Review* 27 (1968): 379–94; I. D. Koval'chenko and N. B. Selunska, "Labor Rental in the Manorial Economy of European Russia at the End of the 19th Century and the Beginning of the 20th," *Explorations in Economic History* 18 (1981): 1–20.

29 Engel, "The Woman's Side," quote on 69; Robert E. Johnson, "Peasant and Proletariat: Migration, Family Patterns, and Regional Loyalties," in Eklof and Frank, *Russian Peasant,* 81–100, and Johnson, "Family Relations and the Rural-Urban Nexus: Patterns in the Hinterland of Moscow, 1880–1900," in David L. Ransel, ed., *The Family in Imperial Russia: New Lines of Historical Research* (Urbana, 1978), 263–79.

30 Quoted in Glickman, "Peasant Women and Their Work," 45–46, 49; Glickman also quotes D. N. Zhbankov (Kostroma, 1891): "The stronger representatives of the local peasantry [men] have been driven from here by need, and we find ourselves in a mythical kingdom of amazons." Steven L. Hoch, on the other hand, has made a strong argument for husband-and-wife

teams in Russian agriculture in his "Serf Diet in Nineteenth-Century Russia," *Agricultural History* 56 (1982): 319–414.

31 Olga Supek and Jasna Capo, "Effects of Emigration on a Rural Society: Demography, Family Structure and Gender Relations in Croatia," in Hoerder, Rössler, and Blank, *Roots of the Transplanted*, 1:311–40; Danica Simová, Eva Fordinálová, and Anna Stvrtecká, "From Husband's Household to National Activity: The Ambivalent Position of Slovak Women," ibid., 341–58; Mary E. Cygan, "Polish Women and Emigrant Husbands," ibid., 359–74. Johnson, "Peasant and Proletariat," 84–86.

32 Robert E. Johnson, "Peasant Migration and the Russian Working Class: Moscow at the End of the Nineteenth Century," *Slavic Review* 35 (1976): 657; Leasure and Lewis, "Internal Migration," 379–94. Studies of the formation of the Russian working class are numerous; see review essays by Ronald G. Suny, "Russian Labor and Its Historians in the West," *International Labor and Working Class History* 22 (1982): 39–53, and by Michael Richards and Michael B. Share, "Review Essay: The Making and Remaking of the Russian Working Class, 1890–1917," *Journal of Social History* 21 (1988): 781–92.

33 Victoria E. Bonnell, *Roots of Rebellion: Workers' Politics and Organizations in St. Petersburg and Moscow, 1900–1914* (Berkeley, 1983), and Bonnell, ed., *The Russian Worker: Life and Labor under the Tsarist Regime* (Berkeley, 1983); Joseph Bradley, *Muzhik and Muscovite: Urbanization in Late Imperial Russia* (Berkeley, 1985); Rose L. Glickman, *Russian Factory Women: Workplace and Society, 1880–1914* (Berkeley, 1984); Johnson, *Peasant and Proletarian*; Reginald E. Zelnik, *Labor and Society in Tsarist Russia: The Factory Workers of St. Petersburg 1855–1870* (Stanford, 1971), and Zelnik, ed., *A Radical Worker in Tsarist Russia: The Autobiography of Semën Ivanovich Kanatchikov* (Stanford, 1986); Burds, *Peasant Dreams and Market Politics*. See the bibliographies of these publications for Russian-language studies.

34 Quoted in Bradley, *Muzhik and Muscovite*, 206.

35 Mark Bassin discusses the imagery connected to the geographic term "Siberia" in his "Inventing Siberia: Visions of the Russian East in the Early Nineteenth Century," *American History Review* 96 (1991): 763–94.

36 Treadgold, *Great Siberian Migration*, 23–26; John J. Stephan, *The Russian Far East: A History* (Stanford, 1995); Philip Longworth, *The Cossacks* (London, 1969), 243–76; François-Xavier Coquin, *La Sibérie: Peuplement et immigration paysanne au XIXe siècle* (Paris, 1969).

37 Peasants were to receive fifteen *desiatinas* or forty acres of land. Again, comparison with North America is warranted: "Forty acres and a mule" were meant to provide freed Black families with economic independence in the latter half of the 1860s.

38 V.-K. Iatsounski, "Le rôle des migrations et de l'accroissement naturel dans la colonisation des nouvelle régions de la Russie," *Annales de Démographie historique, 1970*, 302–8.

39 Treadgold, *Great Siberian Migration*, 3–9, 13–14. Treadgold began his study of Siberian migration as a comparative venture but then restricted himself to the Russian developments. It is unfortunate that almost no comparative work has been undertaken, thus fostering the misleading notion that one or the other country's history was exceptional. Similarities, obvious to historians of the pre–World War I generation, were forgotten by historians educated under the ideology of an unbridgeable chasm between the East and the West from 1917 to 1989. McNeill's *Europe's Steppe Frontier* provides a comparative treatment.

40 Harmon Tupper, *To the Great Ocean: Siberia and the Trans-Siberian Railway* (Boston, 1965); George Alexander Lensen, ed., *Russia's Eastward Expansion* (Englewood Cliffs, N.J.,

1964); Bassin, "Inventing Siberia," 763; Macey, *Government and Peasant*, 20–21, 33–34 passim; Dirk Hoerder, "The World on the Move," in Helen H. Tanner et al., eds., *The Settling of North America: The Atlas of the Great Migrations into North America from the Ice Age to the Present* (New York, 1995), 112–13.

41 Kubijowytsch [Kubiiovych], *Siedlungsgeschichte*, 62–65. In 1926, after migration had resumed, 23 percent of the Siberian population had not been born there. Treadgold, *Great Siberian Migration*, 32–33, tables 1 and 2, 107–225.

42 Turkistan and the Kirghiz steppe had been conquered in the 1860s. The entire trans-Caspian region was annexed in 1881. George Demko, *The Russian Colonization of Kazakhstan 1896–1916* (Bloomington, 1969); Anderson, *Internal Migration*, 121–53. These territories were to attract experts for irrigation and specialists in cotton growing in the 1930s.

43 Stephan, *The Russian Far East*, 71–80; Lewis H. Siegelbaum, "Another 'Yellow Peril': Chinese Migrants in the Russian Far East and Russian Reaction before 1917," *Modern Asian Studies* 12 (1978): 307–30; for further literature, see chap. 18.1.

44 Like frontier areas everywhere, Mongolia, distant from the seat of power, had been a retreat for Chinese bandits, defeated armies, and demobilized soldiers.

45 For twentieth-century Chinese migrations to Mongolia and Manchuria, see chap. 18.1.

46 Ralph Melville, "Zwischen definitiver Emigration und grenzüberschreitender Migration auf Zeit: Die jüdische, polnische und russische Auswanderung aus dem zaristischen Rußland 1816–1914," *Studia Historiae Oeconomicae* [Poznań] 18 (1985): 79–90.

47 Peter Brock, "Polish Nationalism," in Peter F. Sugar and Ivo J. Lederer, eds., *Nationalism in Eastern Europe* (Seattle, 1969), 310–372; Boguslaw Lesnodorski, *Les Jacobins polonais* (Paris, 1965); Piotr S. Wandycz, *The Lands of Partitioned Poland, 1795–1918* (Seattle, 1974), 117–22.

48 This has been discussed in more detail in Dirk Hoerder and Inge Blank, "Ethnic and National Consciousness from the Enlightenment to the 1880s," in Hoerder, Rössler, and Blank, *Roots of the Transplanted*, 1:37–109.

49 Martin A. Miller, *The Russian Revolutionary Émigrés, 1825–1870* (Baltimore, 1986), 5; see Miller for the Russian-language literature on the emigration of political exiles.

50 Statement of a friend of Herzen, G. N. Vyrubov (1865), quoted in Miller, *Émigrés*, 200.

51 Miller, *Émigrés*, esp. 3–23, 104–34, 199–219. Robert Chadwell Williams, *Culture in Exile: Russian Emigrés in Germany, 1881–1941* (Ithaca, N.Y., 1972), 28; Botho Brachmann, *Russische Sozialdemokraten in Berlin, 1895–1914, mit Berücksichtigung der Studentenbewegung in Preussen und Sachsen* (Berlin, 1962); Alfred Erich Senn, *The Russian Revolution in Switzerland, 1914–1917* (Madison, 1971); Georges Haupt, "Émigration et diffusion des idées socialistes: L'exemple d'Anna Kuliscioff," *Pluriel* 14 (1978): 3–12.

52 The first institutions of higher education for young women had been founded under Catherine II. Daniela Neumann, *Studentinnen aus dem Russischen Reich in der Schweiz (1867–1914)* (Zurich, 1987); Christine Johanson, *Women's Struggle for Higher Education in Russia, 1855–1900* (Kingston, Ont., 1987), 51–58.

53 Per 1,000 students registered, Swiss universities enrolled 516 foreign students, male and female; French universities, 170; Austrian ones, 96; German ones, 80. U.S. lore of scholarship made Germany the most intellectually stimulating environment for higher education, which was emulated at Johns Hopkins University in Baltimore.

54 Additionally, women from the Caucasian and Siberian territories were present but listed as "Asians" in Swiss statistics.

55 Joanna Trollope, *Britannia's Daughters: Women of the British Empire* (London, 1983), 91; Neumann, *Studentinnen*, 11–25, 91, quote on 96, 120–32, and biographies of the women's achievements after completing their degrees, 183–238.

56 Neumann, *Studentinnen*, 117–58; Jan Marinus Meijer, *Knowledge and Revolution: The Russian Colony in Zurich (1870–1873): A Contribution to the Study of Russian Populism* (Assen, Neth., 1955); Claudie Weill, *Étudiants russes en Allemagne, 1900–1914: Quand la Russie frappait aux portes de l'Europe* (Paris, 1996).

57 Developments in the Balkans among Danubian-Germans were similar.

58 Tova Yedlin and Joanna Matejko, eds., *Alberta's Pioneers from Eastern Europe: Reminiscences*, 2 vols. (2d ed., Edmonton, 1978), 75–77.

59 Jerome Davis, *The Russian Immigrant* (New York, 1922), 10–13. The Polish territories received German colonists from 1830 to 1860. In the Prussian-held Polish territories, the *Kulturkampf* was directed against Catholicism as well as against Polishness.

60 Bernard D. Weinryb, *The Jews of Poland: A Social and Economic History of the Jewish Community in Poland from 1100 to 1800* (Philadelphia, 1973), 119–176; John Doyle Klier, *Russia Gathers Her Jews: The Origins of the "Jewish Question" in Russia, 1772–1825* (DeKalb, Ill., 1986), 21–52; Kappeler, *Vielvölkerreich*, 82–87, 220–66.

61 This section is based on Blank, "A Vast Migratory Experience," 201–51, and Melville, "Migration," 79–90. Patricia Herlihy, *Odessa: A History, 1794–1914* (Cambridge, Mass., 1986). Odessa received numerous émigrés from the French Revolution. Count Richelieu, its prefect in 1803, made the town a cultural center of international reputation. Steven J. Zipperstein, *The Jews of Odessa: A Cultural History, 1794–1881* (Stanford, 1986).

62 Much of the scholarship labels this migration the "first" emigration, thus disregarding all flight from tsarist persecution. By this way of counting, the "second" flight occurred after 1945, directed increasingly to the United States.

63 The number of emigrants given in the literature varies widely. Dodenhoeft has summarized the different estimates and accepts the figure of 1.5 to 2.0 million, while the *Cambridge Encyclopedia* arrives at only one million. Bettina Dodenhoeft, *Laßt mich nach Rußland heim: Russische Emigranten in Deutschland von 1918 bis 1945* (Frankfurt/Main, 1993), 8–10; Archie Brown et al., eds., *The Cambridge Encyclopdia of Russia and the Soviet Union* (Cambridge, 1982), 219. The best Russian treatment is L. K. Skarenkov, *Agonija beloj emigracii* [The agony of the White emigration] (1981; 2d ed., Moscow, 1986). Marc Raeff, *Russia Abroad: A Cultural History of the Russian Emigration, 1919–1939* (Oxford, 1990); Jean-Claude Chesnais, "L'émigration soviétique: Passé, présent, avenir," in *Migrations internationales: Le Tournant* (Paris, 1993), 117–25. Elena Chinyaeva, *Russians outside Russia: The Emigré Community in Czechoslovakia, 1918–1930* (Munich, 2001). Ongoing research by Catherine Gousseff in Paris indicates that the numbers have been inflated.

64 Some of the 1.2 million prisoners of war decided not to return because of the changed political regime.

65 Hans-Erich Volkmann, *Die russische Emigration in Deutschland 1919–1929* (Würzburg, 1966); Robert H. Johnston, *New Mecca, New Babylon: Paris and the Russian Exiles, 1920–1945* (Kingston, Ont., 1988), and Johnston, "Paris: Die Hauptstadt der russischen Diaspora," in Karl Schlögel, ed., *Der große Exodus: Die russische Emigration und ihre Zentren 1917 bis 1941* (Munich, 1994), 260–78, and Schlögel, "Berlin: 'Stiefmutter unter den russischen Städten,'" ibid., 234–59; A. Balawyder, "Russian Refugees from Constantinople and Harbin,

Manchuria, Enter Canada (1923–1926)," *Canadian Slavonic Papers* 14 (1972): 15–30; Doden-hoeft, *Russische Emigranten*, 1–36; Trude Maurer, *Ostjuden in Deutschland, 1918–1933* (Hamburg, 1986), 46–103.

66 Raeff, *Russia Abroad*, 202–3.

67 Sean Callahan, ed., *The Photographs of Margaret Bourke-White* (Greenwich, Conn., 1972), 69–89; Christine Hoffmeister, *Heinrich Vogeler: Die Komplexbilder* (Lilienthal, 1980); Otto Heller, *Sibirien: Ein anderes Amerika* (Berlin, 1930); Fridtjof Nansen, *Sibirien: Ein Zukunftsland* (Leipzig, 1914); Jane Burbank, *Intelligentsia and Revolution: Russian Views of Bolshevism, 1917–1922* (New York, 1986), 208–22.

14 The Proletarian Mass Migrations in the Atlantic Economies

1 David B. Davis, *The Problem of Slavery in Western Culture* (Ithaca, N.Y., 1966), 291–482.

2 This holds true for the model democracy, the United States of America. Alexander Keyssar, *The Right to Vote: The Contested History of Democracy in the United States* (New York, 2000).

3 Alfred W. Crosby, *Ecological Imperialism: The Biological Expansion of Europe, 900–1900* (Cambridge, 1986), 5; Aaron Segal, *An Atlas of International Migration* (London, 1993), 16–21; Helen H. Tanner et al., eds., *The Settling of North America: The Atlas of the Great Migrations into North America from the Ice Age to the Present* (New York, 1995). André Armengaud estimated 60 million from 1700 to 1914: Carlo M. Cipolla, ed., *Europäische Wirtschaftsgeschichte*, vol. 3 (Stuttgart 1985), 39. Frankin D. Scott, ed., *World Migration in Modern Times* (Englewood Cliffs, N.J., 1968); Walter F. Willcox and Imre Ferenczi, eds., *International Migrations*, 2 vols. (New York, 1929–31); Dirk Hoerder, "The Traffic of Emigration via Bremen/Bremerhaven: Merchants' Interests, Protective Legislation, and Migrants' Experiences," *Journal of American Ethnic History* 13 (1993): 68–101.

4 Haim H. Ben-Sasson, ed., *A History of the Jewish People* (Hebrew orig., 1969; Cambridge, Mass., 1976), 750–890; Jacques Kornberg, *Theodor Herzl: From Assimilation to Zionism* (Bloomington, 1993); Jacob Barnai, *The Jews in Palestine in the Eighteenth Century: Under the Patronage of the Istanbul Committee of Officials for Palestine*, trans. Naomi Goldblum (Hebrew orig., 1982; Tuscaloosa, Ala., 1992).

5 James D. Tracy, ed., *The Rise of Merchant Empires: Long-Distance Trade in the Early Modern World, 1350–1750* (Cambridge, 1990); Peggy K. Liss, *Atlantic Empires: The Network of Trade and Revolution, 1713–1826* (Baltimore, 1983); Ralph Davis, *The Rise of the Atlantic Economies* (London, 1973, repr., 1982); Charles Verlinden, *Les origines de la civilisation atlantique* (Neuchâtel, 1966); David K. Fieldhouse, *Die Kolonialreiche seit dem 18. Jahrhundert* (Frankfurt/Main, 1965). A more recent perspective includes Africa: Paul Gilroy, *The Black Atlantic: Modernity and Double Consciousness* (Cambridge, Mass., 1993). Alan L. Karras and John R. McNeill, eds., *Atlantic American Societies: From Columbus through Abolition, 1492–1888* (London, 1992), 1–15, 245–68, argue that the Atlantic World was part of the Old Regime. With regard to migration, this view is not convincing.

6 Terry Coleman, *The Railway Navvies: A History of the Men Who Made the Railways* (London, 1965); Runo B. A. Nilsson, *Rallareliv: Arbete, familijemönster och levnadsförhållanden för järnvägsarbetare i Jämtland –1928* (Uppsala, 1982); Peter Kriedte, Hans Medick, and Jürgen Schlumbohm, *Industrialization before Industrialization: Rural Industry in the*

Genesis of Capitalism, trans. Beate Schempp (German orig., 1977; Cambridge, 1981); Eric J. Hobsbawn, *The Age of Capital, 1848–1875* (New York, 1975), 310.

7 Donna Gabaccia, *Militants and Migrants: Rural Sicilians Become American Workers* (New Brunswick, 1988), 20–30.

8 F. C. Valkenburg and A. M. C. Vissers, "Segmentation of the Labour Market: The Theory of the Dual Labour Market: The Case of the Netherlands," *Netherlands Journal of Sociology* 16 (1980): 155–70; Herbert G. Gutman, *Work, Culture, and Society in Industrializing America: Essays in American Working-Class and Social History* (New York, 1976), 23–24.

9 Louise A. Tilly, "Industrialization and Gender Inequality," in Michael Adas, ed., *Islamic and European Expansion: The Forging of a Global Order* (Philadelphia, 1993), 246–69; Peter N. Stearns "Interpreting the Industrial Revolution," ibid., 199–242; Gail C. Brandt, " 'Weaving It Together': Life Cycle and the Industrial Experience of Female Cotton Workers in Quebec, 1910–1950," *Labour/Le Travailleur* 7 (1981): 113–26.

10 Thomas J. Archdeacon, *Becoming American: An Ethnic History* (New York, 1983), 134; Colin G. Pooley and John C. Doherty, "The Longitudinal Study of Migration: Welsh Migration to English Towns in the Nineteenth Century," in Pooley and Ian D. Whyte, eds., *Migrants, Emigrants and Immigrants: A Social History of Migration* (London, 1991), 143–73, and Kate Bartholomew, "Women Migrants in the Mind: Leaving Wales in the Nineteenth and Twentieth Centuries," ibid., 174–87.

11 Charlotte Erickson, "Who Were the English and Scots Immigrants to the United States in the Late Nineteenth Century?" in D. V. Glass and Roger Revelle, eds., *Population and Social Change* (London, 1972), 347–82; Walter Nugent, *Crossings: The Great Transatlantic Migrations, 1870–1914* (Bloomington, 1992), 44–48; Terry Coleman, *Going to America* (New York, 1972).

12 Robin Cohen, ed., *The Cambridge Survey of World Migration* (Cambridge, 1995), p. 11 on Francis Bacon; Stephen Constantine, "Empire Migration and Social Reform 1880–1950," in Pooley and Whyte, *Migrants*, 62–83, and Constantine, ed., *Emigrants and Empire: British Settlement in the Dominions between the Wars* (Manchester, 1990); Joanna Trollope, *Britannia's Daughters: Women of the British Empire* (London, 1983); Rita S. Kranidis, *The Victorian Spinster and Colonial Emigration: Contested Subjects* (New York, 1999); Gillian Wagner, *Children of the Empire* (London, 1982). See also Jonathan Swift, *A Modest Proposal for Preventing the Children of Poor People from Being a Burthen to Their Parents, or the Country, and for Making Them Beneficial to the Publick* (1729), repr. in Carl Van Doren, ed., *The Portable Swift* (New York, 1948), 549–59.

13 Charlotte Erickson, "The Encouragement of Emigration by British Trade Unions, 1850–1900," *Population Studies* 3 (1949–50): 248–73; R. V. Clements, "Trade Unions and Emigration, 1840–80," *Population Studies* 9 (1955–56): 167–80; Pamela Horn, "Agricultural Trade Unionism and Emigration, 1872–1881," *Historical Journal* 15 (1972): 87–102; Howard L. Malchow, "Trade Unions and Emigration in Late Victorian England: A National Lobby for State Aid," *Journal of British Studies* 15, 2 (1976): 92–116; Colin Newbury, "Labour Migration in the Imperial Phase: An Essay in Interpretation," *Journal of Imperial and Commonwealth History* 3 (1975): 234–56.

14 Wolfgang Kaschuba, "Kindermarkt und Kinderarbeit in Oberschwaben im 19. und 20. Jahrhundert," *Sozialwissenschaftliche Informationen für Unterricht und Studium* 85, 1 (1985): 23–34; Otto Uhlig, *Die Schwabenkinder aus Tirol und Vorarlberg* (rev. ed., Stuttgart, 1983);

Michael John and Albert Lichtblau, "Vienna around 1900: Images, Expectations, and Experiences of Labor Migrants," in Dirk Hoerder and Horst Rössler, eds., *Distant Magnets: Expectations and Realities in the Immigrant Experience, 1840-1930* (New York, 1993), 52–81. The sending away of children who could not be fed was a theme of German fairy tales.

15 Wolfgang Köllmann and Peter Marschalck, "German Emigration to the United States," *Perspectives in American History* 7 (1973): 499–544; Günter Moltmann, ed., *Deutsche Amerikaauswanderung im 19. Jahrhundert: Sozialgeschichtliche Beiträge* (Stuttgart, 1976); Kathleen N. Conzen, "Peasant Pioneers: Generational Succession among German Farmers in Frontier Minnesota," in Steven Hahn and Jonathan Prude, eds., *The Countryside in the Age of Capitalist Transformation: Essays in the Social History of Rural America* (Chapel Hill, N.C., 1985), 259–92.

16 The emigration and immigration statistics do not match because of problems of classification: German citizens versus German-speakers.

17 Hartmut Keil and John B. Jentz, eds., *German Workers in Industrial Chicago, 1850-1910: A Comparative Perspective* (DeKalb, Ill., 1983), Keil, ed., *German Workers' Culture in the United States, 1850 to 1920* (Washington, 1988); Christiane Harzig, ed., *Peasant Maids, City Women: From the European Countryside to Urban America* (Ithaca, N.Y., 1997); Walter D. Kamphoefner, *The Westfalians: From Germany to Missouri* (Princeton, 1987); Nugent, *Crossings*, 63–72; Wolfgang Helbich, ed., *"Amerika ist ein freies Land . . .": Auswanderer schreiben nach Deutschland* (Darmstadt, 1985), 130, 132–33, 139–40 passim; Walter D. Kamphoefner, Wolfgang Helbich, and Ulrike Sommer, eds., *News from the Land of Freedom: German Immigrants Write Home*, trans. Susan C. Vogel (German orig., 1988; Ithaca, N.Y., 1991); for similar Swedish letters, see H. Arnold Barton, ed., *Letters from the Promised Land: Swedes in America, 1840-1914* (Minneapolis, 1975), 179.

18 Klaus Bade, ed., *Auswanderer, Wanderarbeiter, Gastarbeiter: Bevölkerung, Arbeitsmarkt und Wanderung in Deutschland seit der Mitte des 19. Jahrhunderts*, 2 vols. (Ostfildern, 1984), esp. Bade's essay "Die deutsche überseeische Massenauswanderung im 19. und frühen 20. Jahrhundert: Bestimmungsfaktoren und Entwicklungsbedingungen."

19 David Fitzpatrick, *Irish Immigration, 1801-1921* (Dublin, 1984); Arthur Redford, *Labour Migration in England, 1800-1850*, rev. by W. H. Chaloner (1st ed., 1926; Manchester, 1964); Cormac O'Gráda, "A Note on Nineteenth-Century Emigration Statistics," *Population Studies* 29 (1975): 143–49; Joel Mokyr, *Why Ireland Starved: A Quantitative and Analytical History of the Irish Economy, 1800-1850* (London, 1983); R. Dudley Edwards and T. Desmond Williams, eds., *The Great Famine: Studies in Irish History, 1845-52* (1957; repr., New York, 1976), esp. 319–88; Frank Neal, *Black '47: Britain and the Famine Irish* (New York, 1998). For potato blight and starvation in the Scottish Highlands, see T. M. Devine and Willie Orr, *The Great Highland Famine: Hunger, Emigration and the Scottish Highlands in the Nineteenth Century* (Edinburgh, 1988).

20 Hasia R. Diner, *Erin's Daughters in America: Irish Immigrant Women in the Nineteenth Century* (Baltimore, 1983); Deirdre Mageean in Harzig, *Peasant Maids*, 57–97, 223–60.

21 Kerby A. Miller, *Emigrants and Exiles: Ireland and the Irish Exodus to North America* (New York, 1985); Cormac O'Gráda, "Demographic Adjustment and Seasonal Migration in Nineteenth-Century Ireland," in Louis M. Cullen and François Furet, eds., *Irlande et France XVIIe-XXe siècles: Pour une histoire rurale comparée* (Paris, 1980), 181–93; Nugent, *Crossings*, 49–54.

22 The ethnically Polish territories have to be considered as a cultural whole. Piotr S. Wandycz,

The Lands of Partitioned Poland, 1795–1918 (Seattle, 1974); Norman Davies, God's Playground: A History of Poland, 2 vols. (New York, 1981); Inge Blank, "A Vast Migratory Experience: Eastern Europe in the Pre- and Post-Emancipation Era (1780–1914)," in Dirk Hoerder and Blank, eds., Roots of the Transplanted, 2 vols. (New York, 1994), 1:201–51, esp. 235–36.

23 Celina Bobinska and Andrzej Pilch, eds., Employment-Seeking Emigrations of the Poles World-Wide, XIX and XX C., trans. Danuta E. Zukowska (Kraków, 1975); Ewa Morawska, "Labor Migrations of Poles in the Atlantic World Economy, 1880–1914", Comparative Studies in Society and History 31 (1989): 237–72. Anna Zarnowska, "Changes in the Occupation and Social Status of Women in Poland since the Industrial Revolution till 1939," Comparative Studies in Society and History 71 (1995): 123–31, and Zarnowska, "Rural Immigrants and Their Adaptations to the Working-Class Community in Warszaw," in Hoerder and Blank, Roots of the Transplanted, 2:289–304; Blank, "A Vast Migratory Experience," 231–47. When independent Poland was reestablished in 1918, return migration increased until economic problems and inflation stopped people from coming back.

24 Nancy L. Green, ed., Jewish Workers in the Modern Diaspora (Berkeley, 1998), and Green, The Pletzl of Paris: Jewish Immigrant Workers in the "Belle Epoque" (New York, 1986); Jonathan Boyarin, Polish Jews in Paris: The Ethnography of Memory (Bloomington, 1991); Jack Wertheimer, Unwelcome Strangers: European Jews in Imperial Germany (Oxford, 1987); Trude Maurer, Ostjuden in Deutschland, 1918–1933 (Hamburg, 1986); William J. Fishman, East End Jewish Radicals, 1875–1914 (London, 1975); Ronald Sanders, Shores of Refuge: A Hundred Years of Jewish Emigration (New York, 1988); Joel Perlmann, "The Geographic Origin of Russian-Jewish Immigrant Arrivals in the United States at the Turn of the [20th] Century," research report, European Social Science History Conference, Noordwijkerhout, Netherlands, 9–11 May 1996. Simon Kuznets, "Immigration of Russian Jews to the United States: Background and Structure," Perspectives in American History 9 (1975): 35–124; Moses Rischin, The Promised City: New York's Jews, 1870–1914 (Cambridge, Mass., 1962); Joseph Brandes, Immigrants to Freedom: Jewish Communities in Rural New Jersey since 1882 (Philadelphia, 1971); Stephen A. Speisman, The Jews of Toronto: A History to 1937 (Toronto, 1979); Susan A. Glenn, Daughters of the Shtetl: Life and Labor in the Immigrant Generation (Ithaca, N.Y., 1990).

25 Anna M. Martellone, "Italian Mass Emigration to the United States, 1876–1930: A Historical Survey," Perspectives in American History, n.s., 1 (1984): 379–423; Dino Cinel, "The Seasonal Emigration of the Italians in the Nineteenth Century: From Internal to International Destinations," Journal of Ethnic Studies 10 (1982–83): 43–68; Nugent, Crossings, 95–100; Gianni Toniolo, An Economic History of Liberal Italy, 1850–1918, trans. Maria Rees (Italian orig., 1988; London, 1990), 73–97.

26 Post–World War I immigration restrictions in the United States and some Latin American countries forced potential migrants to reorient themselves and consider their options in Europe.

27 Nugent, Crossings, quote on 96; Ercole Sori, L'Emigrazione italiana dall'unità alla seconda guerra mondiale (Bologna, 1979), 19–47; Gianfausto Rosoli, ed., Un secolo di emigrazione italiana, 1876–1976 (Rome, 1980), and Rosoli, "Italian Migration to European Countries from Political Unification to World War I," in Dirk Hoerder, ed., Labor Migration in the Atlantic Economies: The European and North American Working Classes during the Period of Industrialization (Westport, Conn., 1985), 95–116; Bruno Bezza, ed., Gli Italiani fuori d'Italia: Gli emigrati italiani nei movimenti operai dei paesi d'adozione (1880–1940) (Milan,

1983); Donna Gabaccia, "The 'Yellow Peril' and the 'Chinese of Europe': Global Perspectives on Race and Labor, 1815–1930," in Jan Lucassen and Leo Lucassen, eds., *Migration, Migration History, History: Old Paradigms and New Perspectives* (Bern, 1997), 177–96.

28 Carl Strikwerda, "Tides of Migration, Currents of History: The State, Economy, and the Transatlantic Movement of Labor in the Nineteenth and Twentieth Centuries," *International Review of Social History* 44 (1999): 367–94; Hoerder, *Labor Migration in the Atlantic Economies*, and Hoerder and Blank, *Roots of the Transplanted*; Nugent, *Crossings*, 101–7.

29 To compare social barriers in other European regions: in Danish and Swedish literature, the earning of 50 öre (14 cents U.S.) was described as almost impossible. Barton, *Letters*, 42, see 256, 285; Martin Anderson Nexø, *Pelle der Eroberer*, 2 vols., trans. Mathilde Mann (Danish orig., 1906–10; German trans., Berlin, 1949), 1:117, 126–29; Astrid Lindgren, "Sammelaugust," 22–31, in *Erzählungen* (Hamburg, 1979).

30 Marie Hall Ets, ed., *Rosa: The Life of an Italian Immigrant* (Minneapolis, 1970), 76–88, 120–22; E. Patricia Tsurumi, *Factory Girls: Women in the Thread Mills of Meiji Japan* (Princeton, 1990); Tilly, "Industrialization and Gender Inequality," 275–81.

31 Ets, *Rosa*, 17–26, 41–42, 113–41, 153–65. Suzanne Sinke, "The International Marriage Market: A Theoretical Essay," in Dirk Hoerder and Jörg Nagler, eds., *People in Transit: German Migrations in a Comparative Perspective, 1820–1930* (Cambridge, 1995), 227–48. Helbich, *Auswanderer schreiben*, 133, 136 ("could you find a girl and send her over as a partner for me"), 137; Barton, *Letters*, 195, 234; *Reports of the Immigration Commission* (Dillingham Commission), 41 vols. (Washington, D.C., 1911), 3:358–59, 362–65.

32 Ets, *Rosa*, 172–75.

33 David M. Gordon, Richard Edwards, and Michael Reich, *Segmented Work, Divided Workers: The Historical Transformation of Labor in the United States* (Cambridge, 1982), analyze production processes but not the segmentation of labor markets.

34 *Reports of the Immigration Commission*, 3:349–54.

35 Clark Kerr, *Labor Markets and Wage Determination: The Balkanization of Labor Markets and Other Essays* (Berkeley, 1977); Michael J. Piore, *Birds of Passage: Migrant Labor and Industrial Societies* (New York, 1979); John B. Jentz, "Skilled Workers and Industrialization: Chicago's German Cabinetmakers and Machinists, 1880–1900," in Keil and Jentz, *German Workers*, 73–85.

36 Edna Bonacich, "A Theory of Ethnic Antagonism: The Split Labor Market," *American Sociological Review* 37 (1972): 547–59; John B. Christiansen, "The Split Labor Market Theory and Filipino Exclusion: 1927–1934," *Phylon* 40 (1979): 66–74; Jeffrey G. Reitz, "Ethnic Concentrations in Labour Markets and Their Implications for Ethnic Inequality," in Raymond Breton et al., *Ethnic Identity and Equality: Varieties of Experience in a Canadian City* (Toronto, 1990), 135–95; Dirk Hoerder, ed., *"Struggle a Hard Battle": Essays on Working-Class Immigrants* (DeKalb, Ill., 1986).

37 Margareta R. Matovic, *Stockholmsäktenskap: Familjebildning och partnerval i Stockholm, 1850–1890* (Stockholm, 1984).

38 Heinz Fassmann, "Emigration, Immigration and Internal Migration in the Austro-Hungarian Monarchy, 1910", in Hoerder and Blank, *Roots of the Transplanted*, 1:253–307.

39 Adna F. Weber, *The Growth of Cities in the Nineteenth Century: A Study in Statistics* (1899; Ithaca, N.Y., 1963), 230–84; Wolfgang Köllmann, "Industrialisierung, Binnenwanderung und soziale Frage", in, ed., *Bevölkerung in der industriellen Revolution* (Göttingen, 1974), 117; V. G. Kiernan, "Britons Old and New," in Colin Holmes, ed., *Immigrants and Minori-*

ties in British Society (London, 1978), 23–59; René Leboutte, "Le rôle des migrations dans la formation des bassins industriels en Europe, 1800–1914," in Antonio Eiras Roel and Ofelia Rey Castelao, eds., *Les Migrations internes et à moyenne distance en Europe, 1500–1900* (Santiago de Compostela, 1994), 443–82.

40 James H. Jackson Jr., *Migration and Urbanization in the Ruhr Valley, 1821–1914* (Atlantic Highlands, N.J., 1997); Steve Hochstadt, *Mobility and Modernity: Migration in Germany, 1820–1989* (Ann Arbor, 1999); Karl M. Barfuß, "Foreign Workers in and around Bremen 1884–1918," in Hoerder and Nagler, *People in Transit*, 201–24, based on Barfuß's book *"Gastarbeiter" in Nordwestdeutschland, 1884–1918* (Bremen, 1986).

41 Heinz Fassmann, "A Survey of Patterns and Structures of Migration in Austria, 1850–1900," in Hoerder, *Labor Migration in the Atlantic Economies*, 79, 87–91; Richard Klucsarits and Friedrich G. Kürbisch, *Arbeiterinnen kämpfen um ihr Recht* (Wuppertal, 1982); Dirk Hoerder, "Labour Migrants' Views of 'America,'" *Renaissance and Modern Studies* 35 (1992): 1–17; John and Lichtblau, "Vienna around 1900."

42 Karl M. Brousek, *Wien und seine Tschechen: Integration und Assimilation einer Minderheit im 20. Jahrhundert* (Vienna, 1980); Monika Glettler, *Die Wiener Tschechen um 1900: Strukturanalyse einer nationalen Minderheit in einer Großstadt* (Vienna, 1980), and Glettler, "The Acculturation of the Czechs in Vienna," in Hoerder, *Labor Migration in the Atlantic Economies*, 297–320.

43 Glettler, "Acculturation," 299, 302–5, 313; Fassmann, "Migration in Austria," 87–89.

44 Christoph Kleßmann, *Polnische Bergarbeiter im Ruhrgebiet, 1870–1945* (Göttingen, 1978), and Kleßmann, "Polish Miners in the Ruhr District: Their Social Situation and Trade Union Activity," in Hoerder, *Labor Migration in the Atlantic Economies*, 253–76; Krystyna Murzynowska, *Die polnischen Erwerbsauswanderer im Ruhrgebiet während der Jahre 1880–1914*, trans. Clara Bedürftig (Polish orig., 1972; Dortmund, 1979).

45 Hans Mommsen, *Die Nationalitätenfrage und die Sozialdemokratie im Habsburgischen Vielvölkerstaat* (Vienna, 1963); Otto Bauer, *Die Nationalitätenfrage und die Sozialdemokratie* (Vienna, 1907); Raimund Löw, *Der Zerfall der "Kleinen Internationale": Nationalitätenkonflikte in der Arbeiterbewegung des alten Österreich (1889–1914)* (Vienna, 1984). Among German socialists, the internationalist position taken by Rosa Luxemburg (of Polish and Jewish origin) was an exception. Ulrich Herbert, *A History of Foreign Labor in Germany, 1880–1980: Seasonal Workers, Forced Laborers, Guest Workers*, trans. William Templer (German orig., 1986; Ann Arbor, 1990), 46–81.

46 The three towns of Buda, Obuda, and Pest became a unified city in 1873. Ildikó Kríza, "Ethnic Identity and National Consciousness of the Hungarian Peasantry during the Age of Dualism," in Hoerder and Blank, *Roots of the Transplanted*, 1:175–97; Peter Sipos, "Migration, Labor Movement, and Workers' Culture in Budapest, 1867–1914," ibid., 2:155–71; Laszlo Katus, "Ethnicity in a Central European Metropolis: Budapest 1850–1914," manuscript, Labor Migration Project, University of Bremen, 1991, 10–19.

47 Abel Châtelain, *Les migrants temporaires en France de 1800 à 1914: Histoire économique et sociale*, 2 vols. (Lille, 1977); Isabelle Bertaux-Wiame, "The Life History Approach to the Study of Internal Migration: How Women and Men Came to Paris between the Wars," in Paul Thompson and Natasha Burchardt, eds., *Our Common History: The Transformation of Europe* (London, 1982), 186–200.

48 Nancy L. Green, "'Filling the Void': Immigration to France before World War I," in Hoerder, *Labor Migration in the Atlantic Economies*, 149, 156–58, and Green, *The Pletzl of Paris*;

Gérard Noiriel, *Le creuset français: Histoire de l'immigration XIXe–XXe siècles* (Paris, 1988); Gary S. Cross, *Immigrant Workers in Industrial France: The Making of a New Laboring Class* (Philadelphia, 1983); Yves Lequin, ed., *Histoire des étrangers et de l'immigration en France* (Paris, 1992), 313–78.

49 Holmes, *Immigrants and Minorities in British Society*, in particular the introduction by the editor and the survey by V. G. Kiernan, quote on 52; Colin Holmes, *John Bull's Island: Immigration and British Society, 1871–1971* (London, 1988), 19–114; Kenneth Lunn, ed., *Hosts, Immigrants and Minorities* (Folkestone, 1980); E. J. Collins, "Migrant Labour in British Agriculture in the Nineteenth Century," *Economic History Review*, ser. 2, 29 (1976): 38–59; Fishman, *East End Jewish Radicals*; Lloyd P. Gartner, *The Jewish Immigrant in England, 1870–1910* (1960; 2d ed., London, 1973); Ng Kwee Choo, *The Chinese in London* (Oxford, 1968); Robin Cohen, "Shaping the Nation, Excluding the Other: The Deportation of Migrants from Britain," in Lucassen and Lucassen, *Migration*, 351–72.

50 Willcox and Ferenczi, *International Migrations*, 2:201–36, with quote on 219 from P. Leroy-Beaulieu (1886): "France is quite as much an immigration country as Argentina or Australia. In good years or bad from 40,000 to 50,000 foreigners go there to settle and found a family." François Weil, *Les Franco-Américains, 1860–1980* (Paris, 1989). Green, " 'Filling the Void,' " 143–61; Georges Mauco, *Les étrangers en France* (Paris, 1932).

51 Klaus J. Bade, " 'Preußengänger' und 'Abwehrpolitik': Ausländerbeschäftigung, Ausländerpolitik und Ausländerkontrolle auf dem Arbeitsmarkt in Preußen vor dem Ersten Weltkrieg," *Archiv für Sozialgeschichte* 24 (1984): 91–283; Herbert, *Foreign Labor*, 9–23; summary of admission regulations in Lothar Elsner and Joachim Lehmann, *Ausländische Arbeiter unter dem deutschen Imperialismus, 1900 bis 1985* (Berlin, 1988), 25–29, 38–56, 370–75. Richard C. Murphy, *Gastarbeiter im Deutschen Reich: Polen in Bottrop 1891–1933* (Wuppertal, 1982); John J. Kulczycki, *The Foreign Worker and the German Labor Movement: Xenophobia and Solidarity in the Coal Fields of the Ruhr, 1871–1914* (Oxford, 1994); René Del Fabbro, *Transalpini: Italienische Arbeiterwanderung nach Süddeutschland im Kaiserreich 1870–1918* (Osnabrück, 1996); Hermann Schäfer, "Italienische 'Gastarbeiter' im Deutschen Kaiserreich (1890–1914)," *Zeitschrift für Unternehmensgeschichte* (1982), 192–214. International conferences to regulate the Central European labor market were held in Berlin in 1909 and in Budapest in 1910. Herbert, *Foreign Labor*, 23–53.

52 Thomas Dublin, *Women at Work: The Transformation of Work and Community in Lowell, Massachusetts, 1826–1860* (New York, 1979). Robert S. Starobin, *Industrial Slavery in the Old South* (New York, 1970); Charles B. Dew, "Black Ironworkers and the Slave Insurrection Panic of 1856," *Journal of Southern History* 41 (1975): 321–38. Floyd S. Fierman, *Guts and Ruts: The Jewish Pioneer on the Trail in the American Southwest* (New York, 1985); Moses Rischin and John Livingston, eds., *Jews of the American West* (Detroit, 1991).

53 Ray A. Billington, *The American Frontier Thesis: Attack and Defense* (Washington, D.C., 1958; repr., 1971); Fred A. Shannon, "A Post-Mortem on the Labor-Safety-Valve Theory," (1945), repr. in Richard Hofstadter and Seymour M. Lipset, eds., *Turner and the Sociology of the Frontier* (New York, 1968), 172–86; Dirk Hoerder, "From Euro- and Afro-Atlantic to Pacific Migration Systems: A Comparative Approach to North American History," in Thomas Bender, ed., *Rethinking American History in a Global Age* (Berkeley, forthcoming).

54 Stephan Thernstrom, Ann Orlov, and Oscar Handlin, eds., *Harvard Encyclopedia of American Ethnic Groups* (Cambridge, Mass., 1980), provide summaries and references to further literature. John Bodnar, *The Transplanted: A History of Immigrants in Urban America*

(Bloomington, 1985); Roger Daniels, *Coming to America: A History of Immigration and Ethnicity in American Life* (New York, 1990); Donna Gabaccia, *From the Other Side: Women, Gender, and Immigrant Life in the U.S., 1820–1990* (Bloomington, 1994); Ronald Takaki, *A Different Mirror: A History of Multicultural America* (Boston, 1993).

55 Studies on Chicago are legion. I have relied on Harzig, *Peasant Maids*, and on James R. Grossman, *Land of Hope: Chicago, Black Southerners, and the Great Migration* (Chicago, 1989).

56 Dirk Hoerder, ed., *Josef N. Jodlbauer, Dreizehn Jahre in Amerika, 1910–1923: Die Autobiographie eines österreichischen Sozialisten* (Vienna, 1996); research on Cleveland, Labor Migration Project, University of Bremen, under the direction of Adam Walaszek.

57 James R. Barrett, "Americanization from the Bottom Up: Immigration and the Remaking of the Working Class in the United States, 1880–1930," *Journal of American History* 7, 3 (Dec. 1992): 996–1020; Catherine Collomp and Marianne Debouzy, "European Migrants and the U.S. Labor Movement, 1880s–1920s," in Hoerder and Blank, *Roots of the Transplanted*, 2:339–81; Donald Avery and Bruno Ramirez, "European Immigrant Workers in Canada: Ethnicity, Militancy and State Repression," ibid., 2:411–40; Donald H. Avery, *Reluctant Host: Canada's Response to Immigrant Workers, 1896–1994* (Toronto, 1995); John Bodnar, *Workers' World: Kinship, Community, and Protest in an Industrial Society, 1900–1940* (Baltimore, 1982); Gisela Bock, *Die andere Arbeiterbewegung in den USA von 1909–1922: The Industrial Workers of the World* (Munich, 1976); Patrick Renshaw, *The Wobblies: The Story of Syndicalism in the United States* (Garden City, N.Y., 1967).

58 Marcus L. Hansen, with John B. Brebner, *The Mingling of the Canadian and American Peoples* (New Haven, 1940); Bruno Ramirez, *On the Move: French-Canadian and Italian Migrants in the North Atlantic Economy, 1860–1914* (Toronto, 1991) and Ramirez, *Crossing the 49th Parallel: Migration from Canada to the United States, 1900–1930* (Ithaca, 2001); John J. Bukowczyk and David R. Smith, eds., topical issue of *Mid-America* (fall 1998) on English-Canadian emigration; R. W. Coats and M. C. MacLean, *The American-Born in Canada* (Toronto, 1943).

59 C. Stewart Doty, ed., *The First Franco-Americans: New England Life Histories from the Federal Writers' Project, 1938–1939* (Orono, Maine, 1985); Jacques Rouillard, *Ah les États: Les Travailleurs canadiens-français dans l'industrie textile de la Nouvelle-Angleterre d'après le témoignange des derniers migrants* (Montreal, 1985); Yves Frenette, "La genèse d'une communauté canadienne-française en Nouvelle-Angleterre: Lewiston, Maine, 1800–1880," *Historical Papers* (Quebec, 1989), 75–99. Dan Hill, "The Blacks in Toronto," in Robert F. Harney, ed., *Gathering Place: Peoples and Neighbourhoods of Toronto, 1834–1945* (Toronto, 1985), 75–105; Robin W. Winks, *The Blacks in Canada: A History* (New Haven, 1971).

60 Maurice R. Davie, *World Immigration with Special Reference to the United States* (New York, 1936), 208–22; Abraham Hoffman, "Stimulus to Repatriation: The 1931 Federal Deportation Drive and the Los Angeles Mexican Community," *Pacific Historical Review* 42 (1973): 205–19; Juan Gómez-Quiñones, "The First Steps: Chicano Labor Conflict and Organizing, 1900–1920," *Aztlan* 3, 1 (1973): 13–50. Immigration across the land borders was fully recorded only from 1908.

61 The preceding westward migration has been analyzed by William L. Katz, *The Black West* (Garden City, N.Y., 1971); Kenneth W. Porter, *The Negro on the American Frontier* (New York, 1971); W. Sherman Savage, *Blacks in the West* (Westport, Conn., 1976).

62 Daniel M. Johnson and Rex R. Campbell, *Black Migration in America: A Social Demo-*

graphic History (Durham, N.C., 1981), provide a concise survey. Nell I. Painter, *Exodusters: Black Migration to Kansas after Reconstruction* (rev. ed., Lawrence, Kans., 1986); Spencer R. Crew, *Field to Factory: Afro-American Migration, 1915–1940* (Washington, D.C., 1987); Florette Henri, *Black Migration: Movement North, 1900–1920* (Garden City, N.Y., 1975); Carole Marks, *Farewell—We're Good and Gone: The Great Black Migration* (Bloomington, 1989); Joe W. Trotter Jr., ed., *The Great Migration in Historical Perspective: New Dimensions of Race, Class, and Gender* (Bloomington, 1991); Milton C. Sernett, *Bound for the Promised Land: African American Religion and the Great Migration* (Durham, 1997); Nicholas Lemann, *The Promised Land: The Great Black Migration and How It Changed America* (New York, 1991), continues the story from 1940 to 1970, a period when five million Black men, women, and children left the rural South, which still lacked democratic institutions as well as jobs.

63 Edwin S. Redkey, *Black Exodus: Black Nationalist and Back-to-Africa Movements, 1890–1910* (New Haven, 1969).

64 Matt S. Meier and Feliciano Rivera, *The Chicanos: A History of Mexican Americans* (New York, 1972), 115–67; Rodolfo Acuña, *Occupied America: A History of Chicanos* (2d ed., New York, 1981), 123–54; María Herrera-Sobek, *Northward Bound: The Mexican Immigrant Experience in Ballad and Song* (Bloomington, 1993), 122–46. Irving Bernstein, *The Lean Years: A History of the American Worker, 1920–1933* (Boston, 1960); Bernard Sternsher, ed., *Hitting Home: The Great Depression in Town and Country* (Chicago, 1970). Raymond A. Mohl and Neil Betten, *Steel City: Urban and Ethnic Patterns in Gary, Indiana, 1906–1950* (New York, 1986), 48–90 on Black segregation, 91–107 on the life of Mexican immigrants.

65 Oliver Marshall, comp., *European Immigration and Ethnicity in Latin America: A Bibliography* (London, 1991); Judith L. Elkin, *Jews of the Latin American Republics* (Chapel Hill, N.C., 1980).

66 Carlos A. Hasenbalg, "Race and Socioeconomic Inequalities in Brazil," in Pierre-Michel Fontaine, ed., *Race, Class and Power in Brazil* (Los Angeles, 1985), 25–41; George R. Andrews, "Black and White Workers: São Paulo Brazil, 1888–1928," *Hispanic American Historical Review* 68 (1988): 491–524; Herbert S. Klein, *The Middle Passage: Comparative Studies in the Atlantic Slave Trade* (Princeton, 1978), 95–120; Francisco V. Luna and Herbert S. Klein, "Slaves and Masters in Early Nineteenth-Century Brazil: São Paulo," *Journal of Interdisciplinary History* 21 (1991): 549–73. Béatrice Ziegler, *Schweizer statt Sklaven: Schweizerische Auswanderer in den Kaffee-Plantagen von São Paulo, 1852–1866* (Stuttgart, 1985).

67 Donald Denoon, *Settler Capitalism: The Dynamics of Dependent Development in the Southern Hemisphere* (Oxford, 1983); Magnus Mörner, "Immigration into Latin America, especially Argentina and Chile," in Piet C. Emmer and M. Mörner, eds., *European Expansion and Migration: Essays on the Intercontinental Migration from Africa, Asia, and Europe* (New York, 1992), 217–31. On particular ethnicities: Martin Nicoulin, *La genèse de Nova Friburgo: Émigration et colonisation suisse au Brésil, 1817–27* (Fribourg, 1973); Jean-Pierre Blancpain, *Les allemands au Chili (1816–1945)* (Cologne, 1974); James J. Parsons, "The Migration of Canary Islanders to the Americas: An Unbroken Current since Columbus," *The Americas* 39 (1983): 447–81; Jean Andreu, Bartolomé Bennassar, and Romain Gaignard, *Les Aveyronnais dans la Pampa: Fondation, développement et vie de la colonie aveyronnaise de Pigüé, Argentine, 1884–1974* (Toulouse, 1977), 5; Glyn Williams, *The Desert and the Dream: A Study of Welsh Colonization in Chubut [Argentina], 1865–1915* (Cardiff, 1975); John Mayo,

"The British Community in Chile before the Nitrate Age [before 1880]," *Historia* 22 (1987): 135–50; Maria I. B. Baganha, "The Role of Information and Networking on Portuguese Migratory Flows," unpublished paper, 11th International Economic History Congress, Milan, Sept. 1994.

68 José C. Moya, *Cousins and Strangers: Spanish Immigrants in Buenos Aires, 1850–1930* (Berkeley, 1998); Samuel Baily, *Immigrants in the Lands of Promise: Italians in Buenos Aires and New York City, 1870–1914* (Ithaca, N.Y., 1999), and Baily, "The Adjustment of Italian Immigrants in Buenos Aires and New York, 1870–1914," *American Historical Review* 82 (1983): 281–305, and Baily and Franco Ramella, eds., *One Family, Two Worlds: An Italian Family's Correspondence across the Atlantic, 1901–1922* (New Brunswick, 1988); Nugent, *Crossings*, 112–21, quotes on 112 and 119; Michael Edelstein, *Overseas Investment in the Age of High Imperialism: The United Kingdom, 1850–1914* (New York, 1982); Gianfausto Rosoli, ed., *Identità degli Italiani in Argentina: Reti sociali—famiglia—lavoro* (Rome, 1993); Fernando J. Devoto and Gianfausto Rosoli, eds., *L'Italia nella società argentina* (Rome, 1988), and Devoto, *Estudios sobre la emigración italiana a la Argentina en la segunda mitad del siglo XIX* (Naples, 1991); Oscar Cornblit, "European Immigrants in Argentine Industry and Politics," in Claudio Veliz, ed., *The Politics of Conformity in Latin America* (Oxford, 1967), 221–48; Mark Jefferson, *Peopling the Argentine Pampa* (New York, 1926).

69 Nugent, *Crossings*, 122–35, quote on 134; David Higgs, ed., *Portuguese Migration in Global Perspective* (Toronto, 1990); João Evangelista, *Um Século de População Portuguesa (1864–1960)* (Lisbon, 1971), 91–161; Frederick C. Luebke, *Germans in the New World: Essays in the History of Immigration* (Urbana, Ill., 1990); Stuart C. Rothwell, *The Old Italian Colonial Zone of Rio Grande do Sul, Brazil* (Porto Allegre, 1959); Bobinska and Pilch, *Employment-Seeking Emigrations of the Poles World-Wide*; Donald Hastings, "Japanese Emigration and Assimilation in Brazil," *International Migration Review* 3 (1969): 32–53; Magnus Mörner, *Adventurers and Proletarians: The Story of Migrants in Latin America* (Pittsburgh, 1985), 111; Thomas H. Holloway, "Creating the Reserve Army: The Immigration Program of São Paulo, 1886–1930," *International Migration Review* 12 (1978): 187–209, and Holloway, *Immigrants on the Land: Coffee and Society in São Paulo, 1886—1934* (Chapel Hill, N.C., 1980); Werner Baer, *The Brazilian Economy: Growth and Development* (3d ed., New York, 1989); Fernando Bastos de Avila, *L'immigration au Brésil: Contribution à une théorie générale de l'immigration* (Rio de Janeiro, 1956); Warren Dean, *Rio Claro: A Brazilian Plantation System, 1820–1920* (Stanford, 1976); Martin T. Katzman, "The Brazilian Frontier in Comparative Perspective," *Comparative Studies in Society and History* 17 (1975): 266–85.

70 *La Popolazione di origine italiana in Brasile,* vol. 3 of Fondazione Giovanni Agnelli, *Euroamericani* (Turin, 1987); Nancy P. Naro, "The Transition from Slavery to Migrant Labour in Rural Brazil," in Paul E. Lovejoy and Nicholas Rogers, eds., *Unfree Labour in the Development of the Atlantic World* (Ilford, U.K., 1994), 183–96.

71 Tania R. de Luca, "Ethnic Progress and Civilization: Challengers to the Nation," unpublished paper, European Social Science History Conference, Amsterdam, Mar. 1998; Alan M. Kraut, *Silent Travelers: Germs, Genes, and the "Immigrant Menace"* (New York, 1994); Stephen Meyer, *The Five Dollar Day: Labor Management and Social Control in the Ford Motor Company, 1908–1921* (New York, 1981); Jeffrey L. Gould, *To Die in This Way: Nicaraguan Indians and the Myth of Mestizaje, 1880–1965* (Durham, N.C., 1998), discusses the construction of a mixed but homogeneous nation in Nicaragua and the "forgotten" indigenous culture.

72 Bonham C. Richardson, *The Caribbean in the Wider World, 1492–1992: A Regional Geography* (Cambridge, 1992), 132–42, and Richardson, "Caribbean Migrations, 1838–1985," and Bridget Brereton, "Society and Culture in the Caribbean: The British and French West Indies, 1870–1980," in Franklin W. Knight and Colin A. Palmer, eds., *The Modern Caribbean* (Chapel Hill, N.C., 1989), 203–28; Alan B. Simmons and Jean Pierre Guengnat, "Caribbean Exodus and the World System," in Mary M. Kritz, Lin L. Lim, and Hania Zlotnik, eds., *International Migration Systems: A Global Approach* (Oxford, 1992), 94–114; Elizabeth M. Petras, *Jamaican Labor Migration: White Capital and Black Labor, 1850–1930* (Boulder, 1988).

73 Anthony D. Smith, *Theories of Nationalism* (London, 1971), and Smith, *The Ethnic Origins of Nations* (Oxford 1986); Benedict Anderson, *Imagined Communities: Reflections on the Origin and Spread of Nationalism* (London, 1983); Eric J. Hobsbawn and Terence Ranger, eds., *The Invention of Tradition* (Cambridge, 1983).

74 Matthew Frye Jacobson, *Whiteness of a Different Color: European Immigrants and the Alchemy of Race* (Cambridge, Mass., 1998); Theodore W. Allen, *The Invention of the White Race*, 2 vols. (New York, 1994–97); Noel Ignatiev, *How the Irish Became White* (New York, 1995); Karen Brodkin, *How Jews Became White Folks and What That Says about Race in America* (New Brunswick, 1998); Kathleen Paul, *Whitewashing Britain: Race and Citizenship in the Postwar Era* (Ithaca, N.Y., 1997). George M. Fredrickson, "Understanding Racism: Reflections of a Comparative Historian," in Fredrickson, *The Comparative Imagination: On the History of Racism, Nationalism, and Social Movements* (Berkeley, 1997), 77–97.

75 Migrants who experienced the psychosocial cost of initial adaptation as exorbitant in relation to the benefits to be gained from the receiving economy quickly returned to their home societies.

76 This phrase was coined by Nugent, *Crossings*, 96.

77 Raymond Breton, "Institutional Completeness of Ethnic Communities and Personal Relations of Immigrants," *American Journal of Sociology* 70 (Sept. 1964): 193–205.

78 Special trajectories of acculturation were chosen by religious separatists, such as the Mennonites, and by cosmopolitan or internationalist individuals, whose communication skills and standing enabled them to gain membership in mainstream societies without a time lag.

79 Dirk Hoerder, "From Migrants to Ethnics: Acculturation in a Societal Framework," in Hoerder and Moch, eds., *European Migrants: Global and Local Perspectives* (Boston, 1996), 211–62, and Hoerder, "Segmented Macrosystems and Networking Individuals: The Balancing Functions of Migration Processes," in Lucassen and Lucassen, *Migration*, 73–84.

80 Kathleen N. Conzen et al., "The Invention of Ethnicity: A Perspective from the USA," *Altreitalie* (Apr. 1990): 37–63; Werner Sollors, ed., *The Invention of Ethnicity* (New York, 1989).

15   *The Asian Contract Labor System (1830s to 1920s)*
and Transpacific Migration

1 Hugh Tinker, *A New System of Slavery: The Export of Indian Labour Overseas, 1830–1920* (London, 1974). David Northrup, *Indentured Labor in the Age of Imperialism, 1834–1922* (Cambridge, 1995), 5–7.

2 High estimates: W. Arthur Lewis, *Growth and Fluctuations, 1870–1913* (London, 1978), 181–88; Philip D. Curtin, "Migration in the Tropical World," in Virginia Yans-McLaughlin, ed., *Immigration Reconsidered: History, Sociology, and Politics* (New York, 1990), 21–36;

Neville Bennett, "Japanese Emigration Policy, 1880–1941," in Christine Inglis et al., eds., *Asians in Australia: The Dynamics of Migration and Settlement* (Singapore, 1992), 23. Low estimates: Colin Clarke, Ceri Peach, and Steven Vertovec, eds., *South Asians Overseas: Migration and Ethnicity* (Cambridge, 1990), 8–10; Northrup, *Indentured Labor*, 155–61. Mary F. Somers Heidhues, *Southeast Asia's Chinese Minorities* (Hawthorn, Vic., 1974), 16; Hugh Tinker, *Separate and Unequal: India and the Indians in the British Commonwealth, 1920–1950* (London, 1976), 36; A. J. H. Latham, "Southeast Asia: A Preliminary Survey, 1800–1914," in Ira A. Glazier and Luigi De Rosa, eds., *Migration across Time and Nations: Population Mobility in Historical Contexts* (New York, 1986), 11–29; Kunniparampil Curien Zachariah, *A Historical Study of Internal Migration in the Indian Subcontinent, 1901–1931* (New York, 1964), 2–3, 139; Kingsley Davis, *The Population of India and Pakistan* (New York, 1951), 99.

3   Joan M. Jensen, *Passage from India: Asian Indian Immigrants in North America* (New Haven, 1988), 9; Jan Breman and E. Valentine Daniel, "The Making of a Coolie," *Journal of Peasant Studies* 19, 3/4 (1992): 268–72.

4   Breman and Daniel, "Making of a Coolie," 272–91, and Breman, *Taming the Coolie Beast: Plantation Society and the Colonial Order in Southeast Asia* (Delhi, 1989), ix–74, and Breman, *Labour Migration and Rural Transformation in Colonial Asia* (Amsterdam, 1990), 60.

5   Persia C. Campbell, *Chinese Coolie Emigration to Countries within the British Empire* (London, 1923; repr. London, 1971); Ta Chen, *Emigrant Communities in South China: A Study of Overseas Migration and Its Influence on Standards of Living and Social Change* (New York, 1940). Indian, Chinese and Pacific Island contract workers were the subject of early research by Campbell (1923), Ta Chen in the 1940s, several studies in the 1960s and early 1970s, and Tinker's massive survey, *New System of Slavery* (1974). Only in connection with the independence of the Southeast Asian states did scholarly attention increase. Of model quality are the sensitive analyses of coolie experiences and identities in Breman and Daniel, "Making of a Coolie" (1992), and Breman, *Taming the Coolie Beast* (1989).

6   H. E. Maude, *Slavers in Paradise: The Peruvian Slave Trade in Polynesia, 1862–1864* (Canberra, 1981); Adrian Graves, "The Nature and Origins of the Pacific Islands Labour Migration to Queensland, 1863–1906," in Shula Marks and Peter Richardson, eds., *International Labour Migration: Historical Perspectives* (London, 1984), 112–39. Kenneth Lowell Gillion, *Fiji's Indian Migrants: A History to the End of Indenture in 1920* (Melbourne, 1962); Terrence Loomis, *Pacific Migrant Labour, Class, and Racism in New Zealand: Fresh off the Boat* (Aldershot, U.K., 1990); Adrian Graves, "Colonialism and Indentured Labour Migration in the Western Pacific, 1840–1915," in Piet C. Emmer, ed., *Colonialism and Migration: Indentured Labour before and after Slavery* (Dordrecht, 1986), 237–59.

7   Kernial Singh Sandhu, *Indians in Malaya: Some Aspects of Their Immigration and Settlement (1786–1957)* (Cambridge, 1969), 40–45; Tinker, *New System of Slavery*, 44, 53; Ranajit Das Gupta, "Plantation Labour in Colonial India," *Journal of Peasant Studies* 19, 3/4 (1992): 173–98.

8   Bruno Lasker, *Human Bondage in Southeast Asia* (Chapel Hill, 1950), 15–206; Widjojo Nitisastro, *Population Trends in Indonesia* (Ithaca, N.Y., 1970), 42–46; Ruth Thomas McVey, ed., *Indonesia* (New Haven, 1963), 61–75; Dharma Kumar, "Colonialism, Bondage and Caste in British India," in Martin A. Klein, ed., *Breaking the Chains: Slavery, Bondage, and Emancipation in Modern Africa and Asia* (Madison, 1993), 112–30.

9   Shi Zhihong, "Changes in Landlord Economy in the Early Qing Period of China, 1644–1840," in A. J. H. Latham and H. Kawakatsu, eds., *The Evolving Structure of the East Asian Eco-*

nomic System since 1700: A Comparative Analysis (Milan, 1994), 31–32; James L. Watson, "Chattel Slavery in Chinese Peasant Society: A Comparative Analysis," *Ethnology* 15 (1976): 361–75, and Watson, ed., *Asian and African Systems of Slavery* (Oxford, 1980).

10 Charles R. Boxer, *The Dutch Seaborne Empire, 1600–1800* (London, 1965), 213, 225–28, 246–57, 268–73; Piet C. Emmer and Magnus Mörner, eds., *European Expansion and Migration: Essays on the Intercontinental Migration from Africa, Asia, and Europe* (New York, 1992).

11 Ping-ti Ho, *Studies on the Population of China, 1368–1953* (Cambridge, 1959), 153–58; Jonathan D. Spence, *The Search for Modern China* (New York, 1990), 201, quote on 232–33; Glenn Melancon, "Honour in Opium? The British Declaration of War on China, 1839–1840," *International History Review* 21 (1999): 855–74; Anne L. Foster, "Prohibition as Superiority: Policing Opium in South-East Asia, 1898–1925," *International History Review* 22 (2000): 253–73.

12 Lynn Pan, ed., *The Encyclopedia of the Chinese Overseas* (Richmond, U.K., 1999), 20–71; Sing-wu Wang, *The Organization of Chinese Emigration, 1848–1888: With Special Reference to Chinese Emigration to Australia* (San Francisco, 1978); Walton Look Lai, *Indentured Labor, Caribbean Sugar: Chinese and Indian Migrants to the British West Indies, 1838–1918* (Baltimore, 1993), 37–41; Sucheng Chan, *This Bittersweet Soil: The Chinese in California Agriculture, 1860–1910* (Berkeley, 1986), 7–26; June Mei, "Socioeconomic Origins of Emigration: Guangdong to California, 1850–1882," in Lucie Cheng and Edna Bonacich, eds., *Labor Immigration under Capitalism: Asian Immigrant Workers in the United States before World War II* (Berkeley, 1984), 219–47.

13 Edgar Wickberg, "The Chinese as Overseas Migrants," in Judith M. Brown and Rosemary Foot, eds., *Migration: The Asian Experience* (New York, 1994), 12–37; Victor Purcell, *The Chinese in Southeast Asia* (Oxford, 1951); Heidhues, *Chinese Minorities,* 13–14; Michael R. Godley, "China's Policy Towards Migrants, 1842–1949," in Inglis et al., *Asians in Australia,* 1–21; Robert L. Irick, *Ch'ing Policy toward the Coolie Trade, 1847–1878* (San Francisco, 1982); Ching-huang Yen, *Coolies and Mandarins: China's Protection of Overseas Chinese during the Late Ch'ing Period (1851–1911)* (Singapore, 1985), 32–36, and Yen, "Ch'ing Changing Images of Overseas Chinese," *Modern Asian Studies* 15 (1981): 261–85.

14 Spence, *Modern China,* 117–268, quote on 122; Pierre-Étienne Will, *Bureaucratie et famine en Chine au 18e siècle* (Paris, 1980).

15 Large-scale famines in several regions in the eighteenth and nineteenth centuries killed millions and dislocated more. Survivors, weakened and lacking migratory traditions and information about destinations, usually did not move.

16 Joseph E. Schwartzberg, ed., *A Historical Atlas of South Asia* (1978; 2d rev. ed., Oxford, 1992), 211; Gail Omvedt, "Migration in Colonial India: The Articulation of Feudalism and Capitalism by the Colonial State," *Journal of Peasant Studies* 7 (1980): 185–212.

17 Sinnappah Arasaratnam, "Weavers, Merchants and Commerce: The Handloom Industry in Southeastern India 1750–1790," in Arasaratnam, *Maritime Trade, Society and European Influence in Southern Asia, 1600–1800* (Aldershot, U.K., 1995), xvi; Beverly Lemire, *Fashion's Favourite: The Cotton Trade and the Consumer in Britain, 1660–1800* (New York, 1991), 3–42; Eric R. Wolf, *Europe and the People without History* (Berkeley, 1982), 267–95; K. N. Chaudhuri, *The Trading World of Asia and the English East India Company, 1660–1760* (Cambridge, 1978), 237–312, esp. 243–58.

18 J. C. Jha, "Early Indian Immigration to Mauritius (1834–1842)," in U. Bissoondoyal and S. B. C. Servansing, eds., *Indian Labour Immigration: Papers Presented at the International Confer-*

ence on Labour Immigration (23–27 October, 1984) Held at the Mahatma Gandhi Institute (Moka, Mauritius, 1986), 9–19, report of 1812 quoted on 10; governor quoted in Lai, *Indentured Labor,* 23–24; Basdeo Mangru, *Benevolent Neutrality: Indian Government Policy and Labour Migration to British Guiana, 1854–1884* (London, 1987), 53–78; M. S. A. Rao, "Migration, Agricultural Development, and Deprivation: A Case Study of a Tribal Situation in India," in Glazier and De Rosa, *Migration across Time and Nations,* 58–75; Omvedt, "Migration in Colonial India."

19 Hugh Johnston, *The East Indians in Canada* (Ottawa, 1984), quotes on 3–5.

20 Ramon H. Myers and Mark R. Peattie, eds., *The Japanese Colonial Empire, 1895–1945* (Princeton, 1984); Peter Nosco, *Remembering Paradise: Nativism and Nostalgia in Eighteenth-Century Japan* (Cambridge, Mass., 1990); H. D. Harootunian, *Things Seen and Unseen: Discourse and Ideology in Tokugawa Nativism* (Chicago, 1988); Edward Beauchamp and Akira Iriye, eds., *Foreign Employees in Nineteenth-Century Japan* (Boulder, 1990); Fumiko Fujita, *American Pioneers and the Japanese Frontier: American Experts in Nineteenth-Century Japan* (Westport, Conn., 1994).

21 Irene B. Taeuber, *The Population of Japan* (Princeton, 1958), 173–90; Bennett, "Japanese Emigration Policy," 23–43; Marius B. Jansen, "Japanese Imperialism: Late Meiji Perspectives," in Myers and Peattie, *Japanese Colonial Empire,* 61–79, quote on 69, cf. p. 141.

22 Tinker, *New System of Slavery,* 66–69, 122–33; Ravindra K. Jain, "South Indian Labour in Malaya, 1840–1920: Asylum, Stability and Involution," in Kay Saunders, ed., *Indentured Labour in the British Empire, 1834–1920* (London, 1984), 168, 171; Brij V. Lal, "Labouring Men and Nothing More: Some Problems of ·Indian Indenture in Fiji," ibid., 128; Graves, "Pacific Islands Labour Migration," 114–20.

23 Sandhu, *Indians in Malaya,* 93; Mangru, *Benevolent Neutrality,* 130–35; G. William Skinner, *Chinese Society in Thailand: An Analytical History* (Ithaca, N.Y., 1957), 32, 48–55; Tinker, *New System of Slavery,* 94, 134–47, 156–72; Peter Richardson, *Chinese Mine Labour in the Transvaal* (London, 1982), 64, 124–25, 151–59; Watt Stewart, *Chinese Bondage in Peru: A History of the Chinese Coolie in Peru, 1849–1874* (Durham, N.C., 1951), 18, 47–69; Lal, "Labouring Men," 131; Hubert Gerbeau, "Engagees and Coolies on Réunion Island: Slavery's Masks and Freedom's Constraints," in Emmer, *Colonialism and Migration,* 209–36, esp. 224.

24 India-Ceylon and India-Burma migrations occurred internal to British India but, in terms of culture, were external moves.

25 Lai, *Indentured Labor,* 29–32, quote on 30; Clarke, Peach, and Vertovec, *South Asians Overseas,* quote on 6; Sanderson Report, "Report of the Committee on Emigration from India to the Crown Colonies and Protectorates," *British Parliamentary Papers,* vol. 27, Cd. 5194 (1910); Lal, "Labouring Men," 130; and Jain, "South Indian Labour," 158–82.

26 Omvedt, "Migration in Colonial India," 199. Recent research from a subaltern studies–approach includes Marina Carter, *Voices from Indenture: Experiences of Indian Migrants in the British Empire* (London, 1997), based on migrant letters from Mauritius; Patrick Peebles, *The Plantation Tamils of Ceylon* (London, 2001).

27 Lai, *Indentured Labor,* 25–28. K. N. Chaudhuri, *Asia before Europe: Economy and Civilisation of the Indian Ocean from the Rise of Islam to 1750* (Cambridge, 1990), 368–72; Mangru, *Benevolent Neutrality,* 53–78; Clarke, Peach, and Vertovec, *South Asians Overseas,* 5–7; S. Arasaratnam, "The Evolution of Malaysian Indian Society: Social and Cultural Aspects of Settlement," in Bissoondoyal and Servansing, *Indian Labour Immigration,* 152–53.

28 The figures follow Clarke, Peach, and Vertovec, *South Asians Overseas,* 8–10; Philip D.

Curtin, *The Atlantic Slave Trade: A Census* (Madison, 1969), 234; Mangru, *Benevolent Neutrality*, 60–65.

29 Skinner, *Chinese Society in Thailand*, 126; Tinker, *New System of Slavery*, 89–90; Breman and Daniel, "Making of a Coolie"; Imre Ferenczi and Walter F. Willcox, *International Migrations*, vol. 1: "Statistics" (New York, 1929), 303–9, 906; Donald Wood, *Trinidad in Transition: The Years after Slavery* (London, 1968), 162–64.

30 Kay Saunders, "The Workers' Paradox: Indentured Labour in the Queensland Sugar Industry to 1920," in Saunders, *Indentured Labour*, 221–22; M. D. North-Coombes, "From Slavery to Indenture: Forced Labour in the Political Economy of Mauritius, 1834–1867," ibid., 98; Edgar Wickberg, *The Chinese in Philippine Life, 1850–1898* (New Haven, 1965), 175; Gillion, *Fiji's Indian Migrants*, 5; Sandhu, *Indians in Malaya*, 185.

31 S. N. Agarwala, ed., *India's Population: Some Problems in Perspective Planning* (Westport, Conn., 1960), 25; Davis, *Population*, 107–10, 123; Dietmar Rothermund, "A Survey of Rural Migration and Land Reclamation in India, 1885," *Journal of Peasant Studies* 4 (1977): 230–42; Anand A. Yang, "Peasants on the Move: A Study of Internal Migration in India," *Journal of Interdisciplinary History* 10 (1979): 37–58. M. D. Morris, *The Emergence of an Industrial Labor Force in India: A Study of the Bombay Cotton Mills, 1854–1947* (Berkeley, 1965); Ranajit Das Gupta, "Factory Labour in Eastern India: Sources of Supply, 1855–1946," *Indian Economic and Social History Review* 13 (1976): 277–330.

32 Indigo cultivation in Bengal's deltaic region represented a special case. European capitalists used *zamindari* taxation to force the local peasantry into debt-bondage, thus immobilizing their labor force.

33 Davis, *Population*, 114–21; Tinker, *New System of Slavery*, 101–3; Das Gupta, "Plantation Labour in Colonial India," 173–98.

34 Tinker, *New System of Slavery*, 51, 135; C. P. Simmons, "Recruiting and Organizing an Industrial Labour Force in Colonial India: The Case of the Coalmining Industry, c.1880–1939," *Indian Economic and Social History Review* 13 (1976): 455–85; Detlef Schwerin, "Control of Land and Labor in Chota Nagpur," in Dietmar Rothermund and D. C. Wadhwa, eds., *Zamindars, Mines, and Peasants: Studies in the History of an Indian Coalfield and Its Rural Hinterland* (New Delhi, 1978), 21–67.

35 Davis, *Population*, 127–37; Arjan de Haan, "Migration on the Border of Free and Unfree Labor: Workers in Calcutta's Jute Industry, 1900–1990," in Jan Lucassen and Leo Lucassen, eds., *Migration, Migration History, History: Old Paradigms and New Perspectives* (Bern, 1997), 197–222, Royal Commission cited on 198.

36 Kenneth McPherson et al., "The Social Expansion of the Maritime World of the Indian Ocean: Passenger Traffic and Community Building, 1815–1939," in Klaus Friedland, ed., *Maritime Aspects of Migration* (Cologne, 1989), 427–40.

37 M. D. North-Coombes, "Indentured Labour in the Sugar Industries of Natal and Mauritius," in Surendra Bhana, ed., *Essays on Indentured Indians in Natal* (Leeds, 1990), 12–87, quotes on 18; Jha, "Indian Immigration," 9–19; J. Manrakhan, "Examination of Certain Aspects of the Slavery-Indenture Continuum of Mauritius," in Bissoondoyal and Servansing, *Indian Labour Immigration*, 39.

38 Michael Twaddle, "East African Asians through a Hundred Years," in Clarke, Peach, and Vertovec, *South Asians Overseas*, 149–63; Jagdish S. Gundara, "Fragments of Indian Society in Zanzibar: Conflict and Change in the 19th Century," *Africa Quarterly* 21, 2–4 (1981): 23–

40, quotes on 25, 37; Surendra Bhana and Joy B. Brain, *Setting Down Roots: Indian Migrants in South Africa, 1860–1911* (Johannesburg, 1990), quote on 34.

39 Natal was unofficially pronounced British by settlers in 1824 and was settled by Dutch-Afrikaners and Zulus in the late 1830s. It was officially declared British in 1843 and became a colony separate from the other south African ones in 1856.

40 The Natal Indian community has been as well studied as European ethnic groups in North America, sometimes with as much filiopietism. Surendra Bhana, "A Historiography of the Indentured Indians in Natal: Review and Prospects," in Bissoondoyal and Servansing, *Indian Labour Immigration*, 309–28; Joy Brain, "Indentured and Free Indians in the Economy of Colonial Natal," in Bill Guest and John M. Sellers, eds., *Enterprise and Exploitation in a Victorian Colony: Aspects of the Economic and Social History of Colonial Natal* (Pietermaritzburg, 1985), 210; Bridglal Pachai, *The International Aspects of the South African Indian Question, 1860–1971* (Cape Town, 1971), 3–5.

41 Edgar H. Brookes and C. de B. Webb, *A History of Natal* (Pietermaritzburg, 1965), 92, quoted in North-Coombes, "Indentured Labour," 24; Bhana and Brain, *Setting Down Roots*, 28–42; Jo Beall "Women under Indenture in Colonial Natal 1860–1911," in Clarke, Peach, and Vertovec, *South Asians Overseas*, 57–74.

42 Bhana and Brain, *Setting Down Roots*, 43–62, 193; Brain, "Indentured and Free Indians in the Economy of Colonial Natal," 199–233; Surendra Bhana, "Indian Trade and Trader in Colonial Natal," in Guest and Sellers, *Enterprise and Exploitation*, 235–63.

43 Richardson, *Chinese Mine Labour*, 12–175, quotes on 14, 28, 30, 31, and Richardson, "Coolies, Peasants and Proletarians: The Origins of Chinese Indentured Labour in South Africa, 1904–1907," in Marks and Richardson, *International Labour Migration*, 167–85; Melanie Yap and Dianne Leong Man, *Colour, Confusion and Concessions: The History of the Chinese in South Africa* (Hong Kong, 1996).

44 The same construction turned Eastern European forced workers after liberation in Germany in 1945 into criminals robbing food.

45 German East Africa came under British administration in 1920. Temporarily departed or expelled German settlers were permitted to return in 1925. Italy acquired Eritrea in 1885, Abyssinia in 1889, and parts of Somalia in 1889.

46 Twaddle, "East African Asians," 149–63; M. F. Hill, *Permanent Way*, 2 vols. (Nairobi, 1950), vol. 1: "The Story of the Kenya and Uganda Railway," 146.

47 Richa Nagar, "The South Asian Diaspora in Tanzania: A History Retold," *Comparative Studies of South Asia, Africa, and the Middle East* 16, 2 (1996): 62–80; Robert G. Gregory, *South Asians in East Africa: An Economic and Social History, 1890–1980* (Boulder, 1993); Lawrence William Hollingsworth, *The Asians of East Africa* (London, 1960); George Delf, *Asians in East Africa* (Oxford, 1963).

48 North-Coombes, "Indentured Labour," 12–87, quote on 36.

49 Maurice R. Davie, *World Immigration with Special Reference to the United States* (New York, 1936), 306–7; Jain, "South Indian Labour," 158–82; Sinnappah Arasaratnam, *Indians in Malaysia and Singapore* (rev. ed., Kuala Lumpur, 1979), 20–39, and Arasaratnam, "The Evolution of Malaysian Indian Society: Social and Cultural Aspects of Settlement," in Bissoondoyal and Servansing, *Indian Labour Immigration*, 152–64; T. E. Smith, "Immigration and Permanent Settlement of Chinese and Indians in Malaya and the Future Growth of the Malay and Chinese Communities," in C. D. Cowan, ed., *The Economic Development of*

South-East Asia: Studies in Economic History and Political Economy (London, 1964), 174–85; Rupert Emerson, Malaysia: A Study in Direct and Indirect Rule (Kuala Lumpur, 1964), 29–57; R. N. Jackson, Immigrant Labour and the Development of Malaya, 1786-1920 (Kuala Lumpur, 1961), 30–108; J. Norman Parmer, Colonial Labor Policy and Administration: A History of Labor in the Rubber Plantation Industry in Malaya, c.1910-1941 (Locust Valley, N.Y., 1960), 2–31, 273; John Ingleson, "Life and Work in Colonial Cities: Harbour Workers in Java in the 1910s and 1920s," Modern Asian Studies 17 (1983): 455–76.

50 Chris Dixon and Michael J. G. Parnwell, "Thailand: The Legacy of Non-Colonial Development in Southeast Asia," in Dixon and Michael Heffernan, eds., Colonialism and Development in the Contemporary World (London, 1991), 204–25.

51 Chinese sailors came to settle in London, Hamburg, and Dutch ports. Ng Kwee Choo, The Chinese in London (London, 1968); Frederik van Heek, Chineesche Immigranten in Nederland (Leiden, 1936).

52 Hindustan is the Arabic word for India; in Western usage, it refers to the northern region of the Indus River.

53 E. Sarkisyanz, Buddhist Backgrounds of the Burmese Revolution (The Hague, 1965), 98–127, 136–48; Hugh Tinker, "Indians in Southeast Asia: Imperial Auxiliaries," in Clarke, Peach, and Vertovec, South Asians Overseas, 39–55, citation on 42; Michael Adas, "Immigrant Asians and the Economic Impact of European Imperialism: The Role of South Indian Chettiars in British Burma," Journal of Asian Studies 33 (1974): 385–401.

54 Additional refugees arrived in 1970 after the Burma-Bangladesh controversy. Because of land shortages, Bangladeshis had emigrated to Assam and Tripura and then to the Akyab district in Burma, where they fostered or were accused of fostering a secessionist movement.

55 On the Chinese, see Linda Y. C. Lim and L. A. Peter Gosling, eds., The Chinese in Southeast Asia, 2 vols. (Singapore, 1983); Tsen-ming Huang, The Legal Status of Chinese Abroad (Taipei, 1954); Ong Siang Song, One Hundred Years' History of the Chinese in Singapore (Singapore, 1967); Donald Earl Willmott, The Chinese of Semarang: A Changing Minority Community in Indonesia (Ithaca, N.Y., 1960); Kenneth Perry Landon, The Chinese in Thailand (London, 1941); Arthur Huck, The Chinese in Australia (Melbourne, 1968); James C. Jackson, Chinese in the West Borneo Goldfields: A Study in Cultural Geography (Hull, 1970).

56 Sandhu, Indians in Malaya, 117–21, 190; Godley, "China's Policy Towards Migrants," 1–21, esp. 16–17.

57 Clarence E. Glick, Sojourners and Settlers: Chinese Migrants in Hawai'i (Honolulu, 1980); Bruno Lasker, Filipino Immigration to Continental United States and to Hawai'i (Chicago, 1931); John M. Liu, "Race, Ethnicity, and the Sugar Plantation System: Asian Labor in Hawai'i, 1850 to 1900," in Cheng and Bonacich, Labor Immigration under Capitalism, 186–209; Ronald Takaki, Pau Hana: Plantation Life and Labor in Hawai'i, 1835-1920 (Honolulu, 1983); Alan Takeo Moriyama, Imingaisha: Japanese Emigration Companies and Hawai'i, 1894-1908 (Honolulu, 1985); C. H. Lowe, The Chinese in Hawai'i: A Bibliographical Survey (Taipei, 1972); Mitsugi Matsuda, The Japanese in Hawai'i, 1868-1967: A Bibliography of the First Hundred Years (Honolulu, 1968).

58 Bridget Brereton, "Society and Culture in the Caribbean: The British and French West Indies, 1870-1980," in Franklin W. Knight and Colin A. Palmer, eds., The Modern Caribbean (Chapel Hill, 1989), 85–110, quote on 86; Francisco A. Scarano, "Labor and Society in the Nineteenth Century," ibid., 51–84; Carl H. Senior, "Robert Kerr Emigrants of 1840: Irish 'Slaves' for Jamaica," Jamaica Journal 42 (1978): 104–16; Lai, Indentured Labor, 1–18;

K. O. Laurence, *Immigration into the West Indies in the 19th Century* (St. Lawrence, Barbados, 1971).

59 Evelyn Hu-DeHart, "Latin America in Asia-Pacific Perspective," in Arif Dirlik, ed., *What Is in a Rim? Critical Perspectives on the Pacific Region Idea* (1993; 2d ed., Lanham, Md., 1998), 251–82, and Hu-DeHart, "Coolies, Shopkeepers, Pioneers: The Chinese of Mexico and Peru, 1849–1930," *Amerasia Journal* 15, 2 (1989): 91–116.

60 John S. Furnivall, *Netherlands India: A Study of a Plural Economy* (Cambridge, 1944); Piet C. Emmer and A. J. Kuijpers, "The Coolie Ships: The Transportation of Indentured Labourers between Calcutta and Paramaribo 1873–1921," in Friedland, *Maritime Aspects of Migration*, 403–26; Emmer, "Immigration into the Caribbean: The Introduction of Chinese and East Indian Indentured Laborers between 1839–1917," in Emmer and Mörner, *European Expansion and Migration*, 245–76, esp. 245–47; David Eltis, "The Traffic in Slaves between the British West Indian Colonies, 1807–1833," *Economic History Review* 25 (1972): 55–64; Franklin W. Knight, "Jamaican Migrants and the Cuban Sugar Industry, 1900–1934," in Manuel Moreno Fraginals, Frank Moya Pons, and Stanley L. Engerman, eds., *Between Slavery and Free Labor: The Spanish-Speaking Caribbean in the Nineteenth Century* (Baltimore, 1985), 94–117; I. M. Cumpston, *Indians Overseas in British Territories, 1834–1854* (London, 1953), 15–35; Mangru, *Benevolent Neutrality*, 13 passim; Curtin, "Migration in the Tropical World," 32.

61 Lai, *Indentured Labor*, 19–70, 107–53, 217–64; Judith Ann Weller, *The East Indian Indenture in Trinidad* (Rio Piedras, Puerto Rico, 1968).

62 Lai, *Indentured Labor*, 87–106, 188–216.

63 *The Cuba Commission Report: A Hidden History of the Chinese in Cuba: The Original English-Language Text of 1876*, introd. by Denise Helly (Baltimore, 1993), 3–30, dispatch of the commission discussed on 32–34; Duvon Clough Corbitt, *A Study of the Chinese in Cuba, 1847–1947* (Wilmore, Ky., 1971); Evelyn Hu-DeHart, "Chinese Labour in Cuba in the Nineteenth Century: Free Labour or Slavery?" *Slavery and Abolition* 14, 1 (1993): 67–86.

64 Stewart, *Chinese Bondage in Peru*, 3–24 passim; Peter Blanchard, *Slavery and Abolition in Early Republican Peru* (Wilmington, Del., 1992), and Blanchard, "Asian Immigrants in Peru, 1899–1923," *North/South* 9 (1979): 60–75; Toraje Irie, "History of Japanese Migration to Peru," trans. William Himel, *Hispanic American Historical Review* 21 (1951): 648–723; Michael J. Gonzales, *Plantation Agriculture and Social Control in Northern Peru, 1875–1933* (Austin, 1985), and Gonzales, "Chinese Plantation Workers and Social Conflict in Peru in the Late Nineteenth Century," *Journal of Latin American Studies* 21 (1989): 385–424, and Gonzales, "Capitalist Agriculture and Labour Contracting in Northern Peru, 188–1905," *Journal of Latin American Studies* 12 (1980): 291–315; Evelyn Hu-DeHart, "Coolies, Shopkeepers, Pioneers: The Chinese of Mexico and Peru, 1849–1930," *Amerasia Journal* 15, 2 (1989): 91–116; Teiiti Suzuki, *The Japanese Immigrant in Brazil*, 2 vols. (Tokyo, 1969).

65 V. Shepherd, "Indians and Blacks in Jamaica in the Nineteenth and Early Twentieth Centuries: A Micro-Study of the Foundation of Race Antagonisms," *Immigrants and Minorities* 7 (1988): 95–112; Laurence, *Immigration into the West Indies*, 76–79.

66 Chinese migration to Australia also began when gold was discovered there in 1851. The New Zealand discoveries in 1861 caused only internal migration and in-migration of Australians and Californians.

67 Judy Yung, *Chinese Women of America: A Pictorial History* (Seattle, 1986), 14ff., and Yung, *Unbound Feet: A Social History of Chinese Women in San Francisco* (Berkeley, 1995).

68 Gunther Paul Barth, *Bitter Strength: A History of Chinese in the United States, 1850–1870* (Cambridge, Mass., 1964), 117–20; Northrup, *Indentured Labor*, 7; Alexander Plaisted Saxton, *The Indispensable Enemy: Labor and the Anti-Chinese Movement in California* (Berkeley, 1971); Elmer Clarence Sandmeyer, *The Anti-Chinese Movement in California* (Urbana, 1939); James W. Loewen, *The Mississippi Chinese: Between Black and White* (1971; 2d ed., Prospect Heights, Ill., 1988).

69 H. M. Lai, "Chinese," in Stephan Thernstrom, Ann Orlov, and Oscar Handlin, eds., *Harvard Encyclopedia of American Ethnic Groups* (Cambridge, Mass., 1980), 217–34; Shih-Shan Henry Tsai, *The Chinese Experience in America* (Bloomington, 1986); Anthony B. Chan, *Gold Mountain: The Chinese in the New World* (Vancouver, 1983); Peter S. Li, *The Chinese in Canada* (Toronto, 1988), 11–40.

70 Harry H. L. Kitano, "Japanese," in Thernstrom, Orlov, and Handlin, *Harvard Encyclopedia of American Ethnic Groups*, 561–71; W. Peter Ward, *The Japanese in Canada* (Ottawa, 1982); Ken Adachi, *The Enemy That Never Was: A History of the Japanese Canadians* (Toronto, 1976), 133–56.

71 Norman G. Owen, "On the Margins of Asia: The Philippines since 1500," in Latham and Kawakatsu, *Evolving Structure*, 69–80; Lasker, *Filipino Immigration*. The term "Filipino" for the multiethnic peoples of the islands came into use only around the turn of the twentieth century.

72 Hugh Johnston, *The Voyage of the Komagata Maru: The Sikh Challenge to Canada's Colour Bar* (Vancouver, 1989); Norman Buchignani, Doreen M. Indra, and Ram Srivastiva, *Continuous Journey: A Social History of South Asians in Canada* (Toronto, 1985), 12–70; N. Gerald Barrier and Verne A. Dusenbery, eds., *The Sikh Diaspora: Migration and Experience beyond Punjab* (Delhi, 1989); Karen Isaksen Leonard, *Making Ethnic Choices: California's Punjabi Mexican Americans* (Philadelphia, 1992).

73 Roger Daniels, *Coming to America: A History of Immigration and Ethnicity in American Life* (New York, 1990), 234–64, and Daniels, *Asian America: Chinese and Japanese in the United States since 1850* (Seattle, 1988), 91–93; K. Scott Wong and Sucheng Chan, eds., *Claiming America: Constructing Chinese American Identities during the Exclusion Era* (Philadelphia, 1998); Howard Palmer, *Patterns of Prejudice: A History of Nativism in Alberta* (Toronto, 1982), 17–60.

74 Roy Lawrence Garis, *Immigration Restriction: A Study of the Opposition to and Regulation of Immigration into the United States* (New York, 1927); Robert C. Brown, "Full Partnership in the Fortunes and in the Future of the Nation," *Nationalism and Ethnic Politics* (fall 1995): 9–25; Bennett, "Japanese Emigration Policy, 1880–1941," 32.

75 C. F. J. Galloway, *The Call of the West: Letters from British Columbia* (London, 1916), 256–58, 276; M. Allendale Grainger, *Woodsmen of the West* (1908; repr., Toronto, 1964), 32, 79.

76 C. Harvey Gardiner, *The Japanese and Peru, 1873–1973* (Albuquerque, 1975), 22–41. A Japanese-Peruvian became president in the 1990s. Donald Hastings, "Japanese Emigration and Assimilation in Brazil," *International Migration Review* 3, 2 (1969): 32–53.

77 C. F. Yong, *The New Gold Mountain: The Chinese in Australia 1901–1921* (Richmond, Austral., 1977); Andrew Markus, *Fear and Hatred: Purifying Australia and California, 1850–1901* (Sydney, 1979); A. T. Yarwood, *Asian Migration to Australia* (Melbourne, 1964); S. Chandrasekhar, ed., *From India to Australia: A Brief History of Immigration, the Dismantling of the "White Australia" Policy, Problems and Prospects of Assimilation* (La Jolla, Calif., 1992); C. Y. Choi, *Chinese Migration and Settlement in Australia* (Sydney, 1975); Charles A.

Price, *The Great White Walls Are Built: Restrictive Immigration to North America and Australia 1836-1888* (Canberra, 1974), 41–48, 96–125, 167–68, quote on 165; Ann Curthoys and Andrew Markus, eds., *Who Are Our Enemies? Racism and the Australian Working Class* (Neutral Bay, Austral., 1978); A. C. Palfreeman, *The Administration of the White Australia Policy* (Melbourne, 1967); Robert A. Huttenback, *Racism and Empire: White Settlers and Colored Immigrants in the British Self-Governing Colonies, 1830-1910* (Ithaca, N.Y., 1976), 277–316.

78 All Chinese contract mine laborers were deported by 1911, by which time the Natal community had lost its economic base.

79 Twaddle, "East African Asians," 149–63; Pachai, *South African Indian Question*; Maureen Swan, *Gandhi: The South African Experience, 1893-1914* (Johannesburg, 1985).

80 John Higham, *Strangers in the Land: Patterns of American Nativism, 1860-1925* (New York, 1963); Klaus J. Bade, "Massenwanderung und Arbeitsmarkt im deutschen Nordosten von 1880 bis zum Ersten Weltkrieg," *Archiv für Sozialgeschichte* 20 (1980): 265–323, esp. 312.

81 Sean Brawley, *White Peril: Foreign Relations and Asian Immigration to Australasia and North America, 1919-78* (Sydney, 1995); John Horne, "Immigrant Workers in France during World War I," *French Historical Studies* 14 (1985): 57–88; Tyler Stovall, "Colour-Blind France? Colonial Workers during the First World War," *Race and Class* 35, 2 (1993): 35–55.

82 After the war, a mass return began; from British Malaya alone, 5,000 arrived per month. The People's Republic set aside wastelands in Anhui province for the—usually urban—returnees. Godley, "China's Policy Towards Migrants," 17–18; Wu Paak-shing, "China's Diplomatic Relations with Mexico," *China Quarterly* 4 (1939): 439–59; Heidhues, *Chinese Minorities*, 30–44; Stephen Fitzgerald, *China and the Overseas Chinese: A Study of Peking's Changing Policy, 1949-1970* (Cambridge, 1972).

16 Imperial Interest Groups and Subaltern Cultural Assertion

1 Richard White and Patricia N. Limerick, *The Frontier in American Culture* (Berkeley, 1994), 17; Nigel T. Rothfels, "Bring 'em Back Alive: Carl Hagenbeck and Exotic Animal and People Trade in Germany, 1848-1914" (Ph.D. diss., Harvard Univ. 1994); Fritz Kramer, *Verkehrte Welten: Zur imaginären Ethnographie des 19. Jahrhunderts* (Frankfurt/Main, 1981).

2 Quoted in Margaret Strobel, *Gender, Sex, and Empire* (Washington, D.C., 1993), 21.

3 Donald H. Simpson, *Dark Companions: The African Contribution to the European Exploration of East Africa* (London, 1975); Roger D. Abrahams and John F. Szwed, *After Africa: Extracts from British Travel Accounts* (New Haven, 1983).

4 Khaled Fahmy, *All the Pasha's Men: Mehmed Ali, His Army, and the Making of Modern Egypt* (New York, 1997).

5 John D. Ruedy, *Modern Algeria: The Origins and Development of a Nation* (Bloomington, 1992), 22–29.

6 Neil MacMaster, "Labour Migration in French North Africa," in Robin Cohen, ed., *The Cambridge Survey of World Migration* (Cambridge, 1995), 190–95; Michael J. Heffernan, "The Parisian Poor and the Colonization of Algeria during the Second Empire," *French History* 3 (1989): 377–403; Heffernan and Keith Sutton, "The Landscape of Colonialism: The Impact of French Colonial Rule in the Algerian Rural Settlement Pattern, 1830-1987," in Chris Dixon and Heffernan, eds., *Colonialism and Development in the Contemporary World* (London, 1991), 121–52; Will D. Swearingen, *Moroccan Mirages: Agrarian Dreams and*

Deceptions, 1912–1986 (London, 1987), 20, 32, 186; Augustin Bernard, "Rural Colonization in North Africa," in W. L. G. Joerg, ed., *Pioneer Settlement: Cooperative Studies by 26 Authors* (New York, 1932), 221–35; Ursula K. Hart, *Two Ladies of Colonial Algeria: The Lives and Times of Aurélie Picard and Isabelle Eberhardt* (Athens, Ohio, 1987), xiii–xvi.

7 Francis Wilson, *Migrant Labour in South Africa* (Johannesburg, 1972), 1–28; Jonathan Crush, Alan Jeeves, and David Yudelman, *South Africa's Labor Empire: A History of Black Migrancy to the Gold Mines* (Boulder, 1991); Patrick Harries, *Work, Culture, and Identity: Migrant Laborers in Mozambique and South Africa, c.1860–1910* (Portsmouth, N.H., 1994); Gervase Clarence-Smith, *The Third Portuguese Empire, 1825–1975: A Study in Economic Imperialism* (Manchester, 1985), 106, 134, 178.

8 Babacar Fall, *Le Travail forcé en Afrique occidentale française (1900–1945)* (Paris, 1993); Sheldon Gellar, *Structural Changes and Colonial Dependence: Senegal, 1885–1945* (Beverly Hills, 1976), 36–48; Jean Ganiage, *L'expansion coloniale de la France sous la Troisième République 1871–1914* (Paris, 1968); Peter M. Slowe, "Colonialism and the African Nation: The Case of Guinea," in Dixon and Heffernan, *Colonialism and Development*, 106–20; Ronald Robinson, John Gallagher, and Alice Denny, *Africa and the Victorians: The Official Mind of Imperialism* (1961; 2d ed., London, 1981); Walter I. Ofonagoro, "An Aspect of British Colonial Policy in Southern Nigeria: The Problems of Forced Labour and Slavery, 1895–1928," in Boniface I. Obichere, *Studies in Southern Nigerian History* (London, 1982), 219–43; Martin A. Klein, *Slavery and Colonial Rule in French West Africa* (New York, 1998).

9 Sharon B. Stichter, *Migrant Labour in Kenya: Capitalism and African Response, 1895–1975* (Harlow, U.K., 1982), quotes on 32.

10 François Manchuelle, *Willing Migrants: Soninke Labor Diasporas, 1848–1960* (Athens, Ohio, 1997); Richard J. B. Moorson, "The Formation of the Contract Labour System in Namibia, 1900–1926," in Abebe Zegeye and Shubi Ishemo, eds., *Forced Labour and Migration: Patterns of Movement within Africa* (London, 1989), 55–108.

11 Tiyambe Zeleza, "Labour, Coercion and Migration in Early Colonial Kenya," in Zegeye and Ishemo, *Forced Labour and Migration*, 159–79; J. Clyde Mitchell, "The Causes of Labour Migration," ibid., 28–54; Shubi L. Ishemo, "Forced Labour, *Mussoco* (Taxation), Famine and Migration in Lower Zambézia, Mozambique, 1870–1915," ibid. 109–58; P. H. Gulliver, "Nyakyusa Labour Migration," *Rhodes-Livingstone Journal* 21 (1957): 32–63, and Gulliver, "Labour Migration in a Rural Economy," in the pamphlet series *East African Studies* 6 (Kampala, 1955); Isaac Schapera, *Migrant Labour and Tribal Life: A Study of Conditions in the Bechuanaland Protectorate* (London, 1947); Nyasaland (= Malawi) Government, *Report of the Committee to Enquire into Emigrant Labour* ("Lacey Report") (Zomba, 1935); Margaret Read, "Migrant Labour in Africa and Its Effects on Tribal Life," *International Labour Review* 45 (1942): 605–31; Audrey I. Richards, ed., *Economic Development and Tribal Change: A Study of Immigrant Labor in Buganda* (1954; rev. ed., Nairobi, 1973).

12 Stichter, *Migrant Labour in Kenya*, 25–68; Babacar Fall and Mohamed Mbodj, "Forced Labor and Migration in Senegal," and Fall, "Manifestations of Forced Labour in Senegal: As Exemplified by the Société des Salins du Sine-Saloum Kaolack 1943–1956," in Zegeye and Ishemo, *Forced Labour and Migration*, 255–88.

13 Marcia Wright, *Strategies of Slaves and Women: Life-Stories from East/Central Africa* (New York, 1993), quotes on 7, 29; Majorie Mbilinyi, "Women's Resistance to 'Customary' Marriage: Tanzania's Runaway Wives," in Zegeye and Ishemo, *Forced Labour and Migration*, 211–54; Luise White, "Domestic Labor in a Colonial City: Prostitution in Nairobi, 1900–

1952," in Sharon B. Stichter and Jane L. Parpart, eds, *Patriarchy and Class: African Women in the Home and the Workforce* (Boulder, 1988), 139–60.

14   T. O. Ranger, ed., *Emerging Themes of African History* (Dar es Salaam, 1968); Engelbert Mveng, ed., *Perspectives nouvelles sur l'histoire africaine* (Paris, 1971). Benjamin Quarles, *The Negro in the Making of America* (New York, 1964); Roger Bastide, *African Civilizations in the New World* (New York, 1971); Martin L. Kilson and Robert I. Rotberg, eds., *The African Diaspora: Interpretive Essays* (Cambridge, Mass., 1976); Joseph E. Harris, ed., *Global Dimensions of the African Diaspora* (Washington, D.C., 1982), esp. Harris's "Introduction," 3–14, and Daniel L. Racine, "Concepts of Diaspora and Alienation as Privileged Themes in Négritude Literature," 94–105; Vincent Bakpetu Thompson, *The Making of the African Diaspora in the Americas, 1441-1900* (Harlow, U.K., 1987); Aubrey W. Bonnett and C. Llewellyn Watson, eds., *Emerging Perspectives on the Black Diaspora* (Lanham, Md., 1990); John Thornton, *Africa and Africans in the Making of the Atlantic World, 1400-1680* (Cambridge, 1992), 13–42; Paul Gilroy, *The Black Atlantic: Modernity and Double Consciousness* (Cambridge, Mass., 1993); Michael L. Conniff and Thomas J. Davis, *Africans in the Americas: A History of the Black Diaspora* (New York, 1994); Ronald Segal, *The Black Diaspora* (London, 1995).

15   Nathan I. Huggins, *Black Odyssey: The Ordeal of Slavery in America* (1st ed., 1977; London, 1979), quote on 46; Paul Lovejoy and Nicholas Rogers, eds., *Unfree Labour in the Development of the Atlantic World* (London, 1994).

16   Ira Berlin, "From Creole to African: Atlantic Creoles and the Origins of African-American Society in Mainland North America," *William and Mary Quarterly* 53 (1996): 251–88.

17   Joseph E. Inikori and Stanley L. Engerman, "Introduction: Gainers and Losers in the Atlantic Slave Trade," in Inikori and Engerman, eds., *The Atlantic Slave Trade: Effects on Economies, Societies, and Peoples in Africa, the Americas, and Europe* (Durham, N.C., 1992), 7–9, quote on 7; Eric Williams, *Capitalism and Slavery* (Chapel Hill, 1944).

18   Ronald Bailey, "The Slave(ry) Trade and the Development of Capitalism in the United States: The Textile Industry in New England," in Inikori and Engerman, *Atlantic Slave Trade*, 205–46; Inikori and Engerman, "Gainers and Losers," quote on 14; Jacqueline D. Hall et al., *Like a Family: The Making of a Southern Cotton Mill World* (Chapel Hill, 1987).

19   Stephan Palmié, ed., *Slave Culture and the Cultures of Slavery* (Knoxville, 1995); Sidney W. Mintz, ed., *Slavery, Colonialism, and Racism* (New York, 1974); Thornton, *Africa and Africans*, 183–205.

20   Marcus Garvey's Universal Negro Improvement Association in North America and the Caribbean encouraged return to Africa. Edwin S. Redkey, *Black Exodus: Black Nationalist and Back-to-Africa Movements, 1890-1910* (New Haven, 1969); Akintola J. G. Wyse, "The Sierra Leone Krios: A Reappraisal from the Perspective of the African Diaspora," in Harris, *Global Dimensions*, 309–37; S. Y. Boadi-Siaw, "Brazilian Returnees of West Africa," ibid., 291–307; Boubacar Barry, "Afro-Americans and Futa Djalon," ibid., 282–90.

21   Gilroy, *Black Atlantic*, 5–28, quotes on 12–13; Iain McCalman, "Anti-Slavery and Ultra Radicalism in Early Nineteenth-Century England: The Case of Robert Wedderburn," *Slavery and Abolition* 7 (1986): 99–117; Peter Linebaugh, "All the Atlantic Mountains Shook," *Labour/Le Travailleur* 10 (1982): 87–121; James Clifford, "Traveling Cultures," in Lawrence Grossberg et al., eds., *Cultural Studies* (New York, 1992), 96–112.

22   Thornton, *Africa and Africans*, 235–71; Melville J. Herskovits, *The Myth of the Negro Past* (1941; Boston, 1990), and Herskovits, *The New World Negro*, ed. Frances Herskovits (Bloom-

ington, 1966); George E. Simpson, *Black Religions and the New World* (New York, 1978). The incorporation of folk beliefs had also occurred when the Church superimposed itself on European ethnicities. Keith Thomas, *Religion and the Decline of Magic: Studies in Popular Belief in Sixteenth and Seventeenth Century England* (London, 1971); William Christian, *Local Religion in Sixteenth-Century Spain* (New York, 1981).

23 Thornton, *Africa and Africans*, 221–34; Gilroy, *Black Atlantic*, 72–110; Isabelle Leymarie, *Du Tango au reggae: Musiques noires d'Amérique latine et des Caraïbes* (Paris, 1996), and Leymarie, *La Musique sud-américain: Rythmes et danses d'un continent* (Paris, 1997); Donald R. Hill, *Calypso Calaloo: Early Carnival Music in Trinidad* (Gainesville, Fla., 1993); Robin Dale Moore, *Nationalizing Blackness: Afrocubanismo and Artistic Revolution in Havana, 1920–1940* (Pittsburgh, 1997).

24 John A. Hobson, *Imperialism: A Study* (1902; 3d ed., London 1938); Vladimir I. Lenin, "Imperialism, the Highest Stage of Capitalism: A Popular Outline" (1917), in *Collected Works*, vol. 19 (New York, 1942).

25 Winfried Baumgart, *Imperialism: The Idea and Reality of British and French Colonial Expansion, 1880–1914* (Oxford, 1982), 14–24, quote on 14; William J. Samarin, *The Black Man's Burden: African Colonial Labor on the Congo and Ubangi Rivers, 1880–1900* (Boulder, 1989), Stanley quote on 1. See also David Hancock, *Citizens of the World: London Merchants and the Integration of the British Atlantic Community, 1735–1785* (Cambridge, 1995).

26 Colonial acquisitions of both were few, and Germany lost its colonies in 1918.

27 Franz Ansprenger, *The Dissolution of the Colonial Empires* (London, 1989), 136–37; Harrison M. Wright, *The "New Imperialism": Analysis of Late-Nineteenth-Century Expansion* (2d ed., Lexington, Mass., 1976), vii.

28 Henri Brunschwig, *French Colonialism, 1871–1914: Myths and Realities*, trans. William G. Brown (French orig., 1960; London, 1966), quote on 6 (emphasis added); Jan C. Breman, *Taming the Coolie Beast: Plantation Society and the Colonial Order in Southeast Asia* (Delhi, 1988), 24–36; Paul Kennedy, *The Rise and Fall of the Great Powers: Economic Change and Military Conflict from 1500 to 2000* (New York, 1987).

29 Janet J. Ewald, *Soldiers, Traders and Slaves: State Formation and Economic Transformation in the Greater Nile Valley, 1700–1885* (Madison, 1990), and Ewald, "Slavery in Africa and the Slave Trades from Africa" [review essay], *American Historical Review* 97 (1992): 465–85, quote on 479.

30 Brunschwig, *French Colonialism*, 151–66, quote on 151; Robert L. Stein, *The French Slave Trade in the Eighteenth Century: An Old Regime Business* (Madison, 1979), quotes on 196, 200; Husselo S. Alatas, *The Myth of the Lazy Native: A Study of the Image of the Malays, Filipinos and Javanese from the 16th to the 20th Century and Its Function in the Ideology of Colonial Capitalism* (London, 1977).

31 Brunschwig, *French Colonialism*, quote on 161; Baumgart, *Imperialism*, 97; John J. Rowan, *The Emigrant and Sportsman in Canada: Some Experiences of an Old Country Settler* (London, 1876), 1–3, quotes on 2 and 9. Lewis H. Gann and Peter Duignan, *The Rulers of British Africa, 1870–1914* (Stanford, 1978), uncritically placed "these pioneers among the creators of modern Africa. They were the new Romans who built the foundations" (ix); Breman, *Taming the Coolie Beast*, quotes on 198; Piet C. Emmer, "European Expansion and Migration: The European Colonial Past and Intercontinental Migration—an Overview," in Emmer and Magnus Mörner, eds., *European Expansion and Migration: Essays on the Intercontinental Migration from Africa, Asia, and Europe* (New York, 1992).

32 The French state had had to abandon its first overseas empire in North America in 1763 and 1803, along with Haiti after its self-liberation in 1804.

33 Christopher M. Andrew and Alexander S. Kanya-Forstner, "Centre and Periphery in the Making of the Second French Colonial Empire, 1815–1920," *Journal of Imperial and Commonwealth History* 16, 3 (1988): 9–34, quote on 9; James J. Cooke, *New French Imperialism, 1880–1910: The Third Republic and Colonial Expansion* (Newton Abbot, U.K., 1973), quote on 11; Robert S. Lee, *France and the Exploitation of China: A Study in Economic Imperialism, 1885–1901* (Oxford, 1989).

34 Martyn Lyons, *The Totem and the Tricolour: A Short History of New Caledonia since 1774* (Kensington, Austral., 1986), quote on x–xi.

35 Stein, *French Slave Trade*, quotes on 188–96; Brunschwig, *French Colonialism*, 24–30; Robert A. Huttenback, *Racism and Empire: White Settlers and Colored Immigrants in the British Self-Governing Colonies, 1830–1910* (Ithaca, 1976); James R. Ryan, *Picturing Empire: Photography and the Visualization of the British Empire* (London, 1997), 175–210; David Spurr, *The Rhetoric of Empire: Colonial Discourse in Journalism, Travel Writing, and Imperial Administration* (Durham, N.C., 1993); Nancy Stepan, *The Idea of Race in Science: Great Britain, 1800–1960* (London, 1982). Syrine Chafic Hout, *Viewing Europe from the Outside: Cultural Encounters and Critiques in the Eighteenth-Century Pseudo-Oriental Travelogue and the Nineteenth-Century "Voyage en Orient"* (New York, 1997); Edward W. Said, *Orientalism* (London, 1978).

36 Brunschwig, *French Colonialism*, introduction by R. E. Robinson, quotes on vii–viii; Hans-Christoph Schröder, *Sozialismus und Imperialismus: Die Auseinandersetzung der deutschen Sozialdemokratie mit dem Imperialismus und der "Weltpolitik" vor 1914* (Hanover, Ger., 1968); Hugh J. M. Johnston, *British Emigration Policy 1815–1830: "Shovelling Out Paupers"* (Oxford, 1972); John A. Schultz, "Finding Homes Fit for Heroes: The Great War and Empire Settlement," *Canadian Journal of History* 18 (1983): 99–110; Stephen Constantine, ed., *Emigrants and Empire: British Settlement in the Dominions between the Wars* (Manchester, 1990); W. A. Carrothers, *Emigration from the British Isles* (London, 1929); Jacques Marseille, *Empire colonial et capitalisme français: Histoire d'un divorce* (Paris, 1984).

37 H. Fielding-Hall, *A People at School* (London, 1906), 150, quoted in E. Sarkiryanz, *Buddhist Backgrounds of the Burmese Revolution* (The Hague, 1965), 138–40; James H. Walker, *A Scotsman in Canada* (Toronto, 1935), 5 passim.

38 Christopher Lasch, "The Anti-Imperialists, the Philippines and the Inequality of Man," *Journal of Southern History* 24 (1958): 319–31, Schurz quote on 327; editorial, *Arena* 27 (May 1902): 538–39; David Hawke, *A Transaction of Free Men: The Birth and Course of the Declaration of Independence* (New York, 1964), 237–46, quotes of imperialists on 232, 234; Henry F. Graff, ed., *American Imperialism and the Philippine Insurrection* (Boston, 1969); David F. Healy, *U.S. Expansionism: The Imperialist Urge in the 1890s* (Madison, 1970).

39 A. J. N. Tremearne, *Niger and the West Sudan* (London, 1900), 75, quoted in Obichere, *Southern Nigerian History*, 179. After riots in the West Indies in 1935 and 1937 because of poverty and suffering, an investigative commission presented such a dark picture of racism, "that the British government refused to publish it so as not to provide propaganda material for use by Nazi Germany." The Second World War and Nazi interest in colonies prompted the British government to pass the Colonial Development and Welfare Funds Act in 1940. Obichere, *Southern Nigerian History*, 186–87.

40 Mrinalini Sinha, *Colonial Masculinity: The "Manly Englishmen" and the "Effeminate Bengali" in the 19th Century* (Manchester, 1995); Waltraud Ernst, *Mad Tales from the Raj: The European Insane in British India, 1800–1858* (London, 1991); Ansprenger, *Dissolution*, 38–39; Penderel Moon, *The British Conquest and Dominion of India* (London, 1989), 673–74; Hugh Tinker, *Separate and Unequal: India and the Indians in the British Commonwealth, 1920–1950* (London, 1976). See also Catherine Hall, *White, Male, and Middle-Class: Explorations in Feminism and History* (London, 1991).

41 Dirk Hoerder, *Creating Societies: Immigrant Lives in Canada* (Montreal, 1999), quote on 208.

42 Hakim Adi, *West Africans in Britain, 1900–1960: Nationalism, Pan-Africanism and Communism* (London, 1998); Antoinette Burton, *At the Heart of the Empire: Indians and the Colonial Encounter in Late Victorian Britain* (Berkeley, 1998); Frederick Cooper and Ann Laura Stoler, eds., *Tensions of Empire: Colonial Cultures in a Bourgeois World* (Berkeley, 1997).

43 Brunschwig, *French Colonialism*, 160–61; Robert Aldrich, *Greater France: A History of French Overseas Expansion* (New York, 1996), and Aldrich and John Connell, *France's Overseas Frontier: Départements et territoires d'outre-mer* (Cambridge, 1992), 12–61, quote on 41; Raymond F. Betts, *Assimilation and Association in French Colonial Theory, 1890–1914* (New York, 1961), vii. Mathew Burrows, "'Mission civilisatrice': French Cultural Policy in the Middle East, 1860–1914," *Historical Journal* 29 (1986): 109–35; M. D. Lewis, "'One Hundred Million Frenchmen': The Assimilation Theory in French Colonial Policy," *Comparative Studies in Society and History* 4 (1961/62): 129–53; Raoul Girardet, *L'Idée coloniale en France de 1871 à 1962* (Paris, 1972), vii. In Britain, adolescents who left for the colonies were told that the experience would make "men" out them. James H. Walker, *A Scotsman in Canada* (Toronto, 1935), 5 passim.

44 Edward W. Said, "Arabs and Jews," in Baha Abu-Laban and Ibrahim Abu-Lughod, eds., *Settler Regimes in Africa and the Arab World: The Illusion of Endurance* (Wilmette, Ill., 1974), 236; Bernard B. Fall, ed., *Ho Chi Minh on Revolution: Selected Writings, 1920–66* (New York, 1967), v–xii, 141–43; Jonathan D. Spence, *The Search for Modern China* (New York, 1990), 227–28.

45 Ann L. Stoler, "Making Empire Respectable: The Politics of Race and Sexual Morality in 20th-Century Colonial Cultures," *American Ethnologist* 16 (1989): 634–60, quote on 635; Strobel, *Gender, Sex, and Empire*; Nupur Chaudhuri and Margaret Strobel, eds., *Western Women and Imperialism: Complicity and Resistance* (Bloomington, 1992); Linda Bryder, "Sex, Race, and Colonialism: An Historiographic Review," *International History Review* 20 (1998): 806–22; Clare Midgley, ed., *Gender and Imperialism* (Manchester, 1998).

46 Keith Williams, "'A Way Out of Our Troubles': The Politics of Empire Settlement," in Constantine, *Emigrants and Empire*, 22–44; Arthur Grimble, "Women as Empire Builders," *United Empire: The Royal Colonial Institute Journal* 13 (1922): 195–99; Dominions Royal Commission, *First Interim Report* (1912), quoted in Jean J. van Helten and Keith Williams, "The Crying Need of South Africa: The Emigration of Single British Women to the Transvaal, 1901–10," *Journal of Southern African Studies* 10 (1983): 17–38.

47 Barbara Roberts, "A Work of Empire: Canadian Reformers and British Female Immigration," in Linda Kealey, ed., *A Not Unreasonable Claim: Women and Reform in Canada, 1880s–1920s* (Toronto, 1979), 185–201, quote on 201; John R. Gillis, "Servants, Sexual Relations, and the Risks of Illegitimacy in London, 1801–1900," *Feminist Studies* 5 (1979): 142–73.

48 Janice Gothard, "'The Healthy, Wholesome British Domestic Girl': Single Female Migration and the Empire Settlement Act, 1922–30," in Constantine, *Emigrants and Empire*, 72–95; Joanna Trollope, *Britannia's Daughters: Women of the British Empire* (London, 1983); Anthony J. Hammerton, *Emigrant Gentlewomen: Genteel Poverty and Female Emigration, 1830–1914* (London, 1979), 187–94; Patricia Clarke, *The Governesses: Letters from the Colonies, 1862–1882* (London, 1985).

49 Marion Cran, *A Woman in Canada* (Toronto, 1912), 10–28, 53 passim; Ella C. Sykes, *A Home Help in Canada* (London, 1912), vii–xv, 41 passim. See also Elizabeth K. Morris, *An Englishwoman in the Canadian West* (Bristol, 1913); Patrick A. Dunae, *Gentlemen Emigrants: From the British Public Schools to the Canadian Frontier* (Vancouver, 1981).

50 Memorandum by Major General Sir John Ardagh, June 1902, quoted in van Helten and Williams, "The Crying Need of South Africa," cited on 24–25; Charles van Onselen, *Studies in the Social and Economic History of the Witwatersrand, 1886–1914*, 2 vols. (London, 1982), vol. 1: "New Babylon."

51 Roberts, "A Work of Empire," 187–88, quote on 187, passim; Veronica Strong-Boag, *Parliament of Women: The National Council of Women of Canada 1893-1929* (Ottawa, 1976), 182, 194.

52 Arthur Grimble, "Women as Empire Builders," *United Empire: The Royal Colonial Institute Journal* 13 (1922): 195–99, esp. 196–97.

53 Neville Bennett, "Japanese Emigration Policy, 1880–1941," in Christine Inglis et al., eds., *Asians in Australia: The Dynamics of Migration and Settlement* (Singapore, 1992), 27–32; Clarence E. Glick, *Sojourners and Settlers: Chinese Migrants in Hawaii* (Honolulu, 1980), 7–9, quotes on 8 and 13.

54 Douglas M. Peers, "Privates off Parade: Regimenting Sexuality in the 19th-Century Indian Empire," *International History Review* 20 (1998): 823–54; Ravindra K. Jain, "South Indian Labour in Malaya, 1840–1920: Asylum, Stability and Involution," in Kay Saunders, ed., *Indentured Labour in the British Empire, 1834–1920* (London, 1984), 158–82; Brij V. Lal, "Labouring Men and Nothing More: Some Problems of Indian Indenture in Fiji," ibid., 126–57, esp. 149.

55 Canadian citizenship was extended to immigrant men from many nations because they had died for the sake of the nation in World War II. House of Commons [Canada], *Debates*, 1946, 502–17, 586–609, 685–726, 795–805 (Citizenship Act), and 1947, 307–45 passim (Immigration Act); R. Craig Brown, "Full Partnership in the Fortunes and in the Future of the Nation," *Nationalism and Ethnic Politics* (fall 1995): 9–25; Reg Whitaker, *Canadian Immigration Policy Since Confederation* (Ottawa, 1991). See, in general, George L. Mosse, *Nationalism and Sexuality: Middle-Class Morality and Sexual Norms in Modern Europe* (Madison, 1985).

56 Ronald Hyam, *Empire and Sexuality: The British Experience* (Manchester, 1990), discussed imperial men's migration out of Victorian Britain in terms of sexual liberation with no regard for women's points of view concerning such liberation. Kenneth Ballhatchet, *Race, Sex and Class under the Raj: Imperial Attitudes and Policies and Their Critics, 1793-1905* (London, 1980); Breman, *Taming the Coolie Beast*, xiii passim; John D. Kelly, "Discourse about Sexuality and the End of Indenture in Fiji: The Making of Counter-Hegemonic Discourse," *History and Anthropology* 5 (1990): 19–61.

57 Kátia M. de Queirós Mattoso, *To Be a Slave in Brazil, 1550-1880*, trans. Arthur Goldhammer (French orig., 1979; 4th ed., New Brunswick, 1994), quote on 197.

58 Stanley L. Engerman and Robert W. Fogel, *Time on the Cross: The Economics of American Negro Slavery* (New York, 1989), 29–37, 155–57.

59 A. G. Scholes, *Education for Empire Settlement: A Study of Juvenile Migration* (London, 1932); Joy Parr, *Labouring Children: British Immigrant Apprentices to Canada, 1869–1924* (London, 1980); Gillian Wagner, *Children of the Empire* (London, 1982); Philip Bean and Joy Melville, *Lost Children of the Empire* (London, 1989).

60 R. L. Tignor, *The Colonial Transformation of Kenya: The Kambu, Kikuyu, and Maasai from 1900 to 1939* (Princeton, 1976), 292, quoted in Robert Miles, *Racism* (London, 1989), 109.

61 Ronald Takaki, *Pau Hana: Plantation Life and Labor in Hawaii, 1835–1920* (Honolulu, 1983), 23–24, citing order receipts of 1889; June Mei, "Socioeconomic Origins of Emigration: Guangdong to California, 1850 to 1882," in Lucie Cheng and Edna Bonacich, eds., *Labor Immigration under Capitalism: Asian Workers in the United States before World War II* (Berkeley, 1984), 219–47; Herbert S. Klein, "European and Asian Migration to Brazil," in Cohen, *Cambridge Survey*, 208–14.

62 Breman, *Taming the Coolie Beast*, 192–94; Hoerder, *Creating Societies*, 224.

63 Kay Saunders, "The Workers' Paradox: Indentured Labour in the Queensland Sugar Industry to 1920," in Saunders, *Indentured Labour*, 221–22; David Northrup, *Indentured Labor in the Age of Imperialism, 1834–1922* (Cambridge, 1995), 75–77.

64 Bennett, "Japanese Emigration Policy," 35.

65 White, "Domestic Labor in a Colonial City," 139–60, quote on 139; Janet M. Burja, "Women 'Entrepreneurs' of Early Nairobi," in Colin Sumner, ed., *Crime, Justice and Underdevelopment* (London, 1982), 122–61.

66 Bennett, "Japanese Emigration Policy," 23–43, quote on 23.

67 Breman, *Taming the Coolie Beast*, 23, 33, 60–63, 77, 197.

68 Eric R. Wolf, *Europe and the People without History* (Berkeley, 1982), 354–83; Jan C. Breman, *Labour Migration and Rural Transformation in Colonial Asia* (Amsterdam, 1990), 54, quotes on 61, 64.

69 Basil Stewart, *The Land of the Maple Leaf: Or, Canada as I Saw It* (London, 1908), quotes on viii and 135; Angela Woollacott, " 'All This Is the Empire, I Told Myself': Australian Women's Voyages 'Home' and the Articulation of Colonial Whiteness," *American Historical Review* 102 (1997): 1003–29.

70 Massachusetts Bureau of the Statistics of Labor, *Twelfth Annual Report, 1881,* quote on 469–70; Donna Gabaccia, "The 'Yellow Peril' and the 'Chinese of Europe': Global Perspectives on Race and Labor, 1815–1930," in Jan Lucassen and Leo Lucassen, eds., *Migrations, Migration History, History: Old Paradigms and New Perspectives* (Bern, 1997), 177–96; John H. M. Laslett, "Challenging American Exceptionalism: Overlapping Diasporas as a Model for Studying American Working Class Formation, 1810–1924," mimeographed, Chicago, 1987.

71 Tinker, *Separate and Unequal*, 9.

72 Saunders, "The Workers' Paradox," 213–59, quotes on 225, 227–28, 231; Charles A. Price, *The Great White Walls Are Built: Restrictive Immigration to North America and Australia, 1836–1888* (Canberra, 1974), 11–17, 40.

73 Ann L. Stoler, *Capitalism and Confrontation in Sumatra's Plantation Belt, 1870–1979* (New Haven, 1985); Breman, *Labour Migration and Rural Transformation,* quote on 19, 46; Takaki, *Pau Hana,* quotes on 22, 25, 26; Stichter, *Migrant Labour in Kenya,* 1–68.

74 Peter Richardson, *Chinese Mine Labour in the Transvaal* (London, 1982), quote on 60;

Basdeo Mangru, *A History of East Indian Resistance on the Guyana Sugar Estates, 1870–1950* (New York, 1996); Gary Y. Okihiro, ed., *In Resistance: Studies in African, Caribbean, and Afro-American History* (Amherst, 1986); H. Haraksingh, "Control and Resistance among Indian Workers: A Study of Labour on the Sugar Plantations of Trinidad, 1875–1917," in D. Dabydeen and B. Samaroo, eds., *India in the Caribbean* (London, 1987).

75 Baumgart, *Imperialism*, 98–144, quote from Wehler, 143–44; Hans-Ulrich Wehler, *Bismarck und der Imperialismus* (Cologne, 1969), and Wehler, ed., *Imperialismus* (3d rev. ed., Königstein/Taunus, 1979); Michael Adas, "'High' Imperialism and the 'New' History," in Adas, ed., *Islamic and European Expansion: The Forging of a Global Order* (Philadelphia, 1993), 311–44. While some nineteenth-century photographers brought pictures of colonial "savages" to Britain, James Greenwood photographed *The Wilds of London* (1874) and *The Wild Man at Home* (London, n.d.). Ryan, *Picturing Empire*, 178.

76 James R. Barrett, "Unity and Fragmentation: Class, Race, and Ethnicity on Chicago's South Side, 1900–1922," in Dirk Hoerder, ed., *"Struggle a Hard Battle": Essays on Working-Class Immigrants* (DeKalb, Ill., 1986), 229–53, introduction 3–15, and essays by Bruce C. Levine, Donna Gabaccia, Paul Krause, Maxine S. Seller, and David Montgomery; Hoerder, "Immigrants, Labor and the Higher Courts from 1877 to the 1920s," *Storia Nordamericana* 4 (1987): 3–29; David R. Roediger, *The Wages of Whiteness: Race and the Making of the American Working Class* (New York, 1991); Herbert G. Gutman, *Work, Culture, and Society in Industrializing America* (New York, 1976).

77 Takaki, *Pau Hana*, 127–76, quotes on 127, 159; Ruth Akamine, "Class, Ethnicity, and the Transformation of Hawaii's Sugar Workers, 1920–1946," in Camille Guerin-Gonzales and Carl Strikwerda, eds., *The Politics of Immigrant Workers: Labor Activism and Migration in the World Economy since 1830* (New York, 1993), 175–95.

78 Donald M. Nomini, "Popular Sources of Chinese Labor Militancy in Colonial Malaya, 1900–1941," in Guerin-Gonzales and Strikwerda, *Politics of Immigrant Workers*, 215–42, quote on 221; R. N. Jackson, *Immigrant Labour and the Development of Malaya, 1786–1920* (Kuala Lumpur, 1961). For labor militancy of Indian workers, see, for example, Sateeanund Peerthum, "Forms of Protest and Resistance of Indian Labourers," in U. Bissoondoyal and S. B. C. Servansing, eds., *Indian Labour Immigration* (Moka, Mauritius, 1986), 88–94, and Peerthum, "Resistance against Slavery," in Bissoondoyal and Servansing, eds., *Slavery in South West Indian Ocean* (Moka, Mauritius, 1989), 124–30; Kusha Haraksingh, "Culture, Religion and Resistance among Indians in the Caribbean," ibid., 223–37.

79 For research on labor organization on a global scale, see International Conference of the Historians of the Labor Movement, ed., *Proceedings*, 31 vols. (Linz, Aus., 1996–).

80 Miles, *Racism*, 102–4, quoting from M. P. K. Sorrenson, *Origins of European Settlement in Kenya* (Nairobi, 1968), 238, 242.

17   Forced Labor and Refugees in the Northern Hemisphere to the 1950s

1 This chapter relies on Michael R. Marrus, *The Unwanted: European Refugees in the Twentieth Century* (Oxford, 1985), quote on 51; a survey is Andrew Bell-Fialkoff's *Ethnic Cleansing* (New York, 1996), 7–49; Richard Marienstras, *Être un peuple en diaspora* (Paris, 1975), 36–37; Franz Ansprenger, *The Dissolution of the Colonial Empires* (London, 1989); Ludger

Kühnhardt, *Die Flüchtlingsfrage als Weltordnungsproblem: Massenzwangswanderungen in Geschichte und Politik* (Vienna, 1984); Dusan Kecmanovic, *The Mass Psychology of Ethnonationalism* (New York, 1996); Dariusz Stola, "Forced Migrations in Central European History," *International Migration Review* 26 (1992): 324–41.

2　See for example William Preston Jr., *Aliens and Dissenters: Federal Suppression of Radicals, 1903–1933* (Cambridge, Mass., 1963); Reino Kero, "The Canadian Finns in Soviet Karelia in the 1930s," in Michael G. Karni, ed., *Finnish Diaspora*, 2 vols. (Toronto, 1981), 1:203–13.

3　George Mosse, *Nationalism and Sexuality: Respectability and Abnormal Sexuality in Modern Europe* (New York, 1985); Donna Gabaccia, "Women of the Mass Migrations: From Minority to Majority, 1820–1930," in Dirk Hoerder and Leslie Page Moch, eds., *European Migrants: Global and Local Perspectives* (Boston, 1996), 90–111, and Gabaccia, *From the Other Side: Women, Gender and Immigrant Life in the U.S., 1820–1990* (Bloomington, 1994). Eric J. Hobsbawn and Terence Ranger, eds., *The Invention of Tradition* (Cambridge, 1983); Benedict Anderson, *Imagined Communities: Reflections on the Origin and Spread of Nationalism* (1983; 3d ed., London, 1986); Peter Alter, *Nationalism*, trans. Stuart McKinnon-Evans (German orig., 1985; London, 1989).

4　In the United States, the northward migration of Afro-Americans also resulted in violence, in the form of riots, to mark territories between Whites and "Negroes." The struggle over who was part of a given "nation" was a global phenomenon. Elliott Rudwick, *Race Riot at East St. Louis, July 2, 1917* (1st ed., 1964; Boston, 1982).

5　The Prussians originally were a Baltic people settled to the northeast of what later became the state of Prussia.

6　German occupation troops in World War Two considered Silesians racially inferior, and after 1945 the Polish government expelled them. Piotr Wróblewski, "National Minorities in Poland and Mechanisms of Their Ethno-National Revival," *Migracijske teme* [Zagreb] 12 (1996): 349–60; Zbigniew Kurcz, *Mniejszóác niemiecka w Polsce* [The German minority in Poland] (Wroclaw, 1995). I am grateful to Piotr Wróblewski for information and translations.

7　Alan M. Kraut, *Silent Travellers: Germs, Genes, and the "Immigrant Menace"* (New York, 1994); Bernard Gainer, *The Alien Invasion: The Origins of the Alien Act of 1905* (London, 1972); Marrus, *The Unwanted*, 14–39, 86–91, 158–66, 177–88; John H. Simpson, *The Refugee Question* (London, 1940), 3.

8　Fikret Adanir and Hilmar Kaiser, "Migration, Deportation, and Nation-Building: The Case of the Ottoman Empire," in René Leboutte, ed., *Migrations and Migrants in Historical Perspective: Permanencies and Innovations* (Brussels, 2000), 273–92; Paul Dumont, "L'émigration des Musulmans de Russie vers l'Empire Ottoman," in Georges Dupeux, ed., *Les migrations internationales de la fin du XVIIIe siècle à nos jours* (Paris, 1980), 212–18; Carnegie Report quoted in Marrus, *The Unwanted*, 45; Robert J. Donia, *Islam under the Double Eagle: The Muslims of Bosnia and Hercegovina, 1878–1914* (Boulder, 1981); see Kühnhardt, *Flüchtlingsfrage*, 39–52, for a survey of flight from 1900 to 1945. In 1922 Istanbul also housed 25,000 Russian, 75,000 Turkish, and 155,000 Greek refugees.

9　Gérard Chaliand and Yves Ternon, *Le génocide des Arméniens* (Brussels, 1980); James L. Barton, *The Story of Near East Relief (1915–1930): An Interpretation* (New York, 1930); Firuz Kazemadeh, *The Struggle for Transcaucasia (1917–1921)* (Oxford, 1951); Anaïs Ter-Minassian, "Migrations des Arméniens en Russie et en Union Soviétique aux XIXe and XXe siècles," in Dupeux, *Migrations*, 222–24; Vahakn N. Dadrian, *The History of the Armenian Genocide: Ethnic Conflict from the Balkans to Anatolia to the Caucasus* (Oxford,

1995); Frederick A. Norwood, *Strangers and Exiles: A History of Religious Refugees*, 2 vols. (Nashville, Tenn., 1965–69), 2:265–68.

10 Daniela Bobeva, "Emigration from and Immigration to Bulgaria," in Heinz Fassmann and Rainer Münz, eds., *European Migration in the Late Twentieth Century: Historical Patterns, Actual Trends, and Social Implications* (Aldershot, U.K., 1994), 221–37; Joseph B. Schechtman, *The Refugee in the World: Displacement and Integration* (New York, 1964), 54–67; Simpson, *Refugee Question*, 7–11; André Wurfbain, *L'Échange greco-bulgare des minorités ethniques* (Lausanne, 1930); Dimitri Kossev et al., "Bulgarie: Les Migrations bulgares de la fin du XVIIIe siècle à la seconde guerre mondiale," in Dupeux, *Migrations*, 555–63; Stephen P. Ladas, *The Exchange of Minorities: Bulgaria, Greece and Turkey* (New York, 1932); Charles B. Eddy, *Greece and the Greek Refugees* (London, 1931).

11 Cited in Schechtman, *The Refugee in the World*, 54.

12 Norwood, *Strangers and Exiles*, 2:268–70; R. S. Stafford, *The Tragedy of the Assyrians* (London, 1935); Kemal H. Karpat, "Ottoman Immigration Policies and Settlement in Palestine," in Baha Abu-Laban and Ibrahim Abu-Lughod, eds., *Settler Regimes in Africa and the Arab World: The Illusion of Endurance* (Wilmette, Ill., 1974), 57–72, and essays by James J. Zogby and Fawaz Turki, ibid.

13 Lothar Elsner, "Foreign Workers and Forced Labor in Germany during the First World War," in Dirk Hoerder, ed., *Labor Migration in the Atlantic Economies: The European and North American Working Classes during the Period of Industrialization* (Westport, Conn., 1985), 189–222; John Horne, "Immigrant Workers in France during World War I," *French Historical Studies* 14 (1985): 57–88.

14 Richard B. Speed, *Prisoners, Diplomats, and the Great War: A Study in the Diplomacy of Captivity* (New York, 1990), 141–53.

15 The openness of Shanghai to refugees was not matched by openness to Chinese working-class immigrants, who were ethnicized by the city's Chinese elites. Emily Honig, *Creating Chinese Ethnicity: Subei People in Shanghai, 1850–1980* (New Haven, 1992).

16 Joseph Schechtman, *European Population Transfers, 1939–1945* (New York, 1946), 6; Marrus, *The Unwanted*, 68–70, 178–79. For cultural and linguistic interaction among Eastern European immigrants in Canada, see Paul Migus, ed., *Sounds Canadian: Languages and Cultures in Multi-Ethnic Society* (Toronto, 1975), 32; Dirk Hoerder, *Creating Societies: Immigrant Lives in Canada* (Montreal, 1999), chaps. 18, 19.

17 The French and British colonial empires were dismantled only after World War II. Ireland, the one colony in Europe, achieved independence in 1920–22.

18 *Statistik des Deutschen Reichs*, vol. 401 (Berlin, 1930), 412–23, 491–92, 623–40; Marrus, *The Unwanted*, 52–61; Meir Buchsweiler, *Volksdeutsche in der Ukraine am Vorabend und Beginn des Zweiten Weltkriegs—ein Fall doppelter Loyalität*, trans. Ruth Achlama (Hebrew orig., 1980; Gerlingen, 1984).

19 Benjamin M. Weissman, *Herbert Hoover and Famine Relief to Soviet Russia, 1921–1923* (Stanford, 1974); Eugene M. Kulischer, *Europe on the Move: War and Population Changes, 1917–47* (New York, 1948), 64–71, 94–99.

20 Kulischer, *Europe on the Move*, 64–88, 99–128.

21 Marrus, *The Unwanted*, 122–35; Norwood, *Strangers and Exiles*, 2:277–96.

22 Nancy L. Green, Laura L. Frader, and Pierre Milza, "Paris: City of Light and Shadow," in Dirk Hoerder and Horst Rössler, eds., *Distant Magnets: Expectations and Realities in the Immigrant Experience, 1840–1930* (New York, 1993), 34–51; Marrus, *The Unwanted*, 124–

28; Roberto A. Ventresca, "'To Right Past Wrongs': Fascism, Antifascism and the Politics of Ethnic Identity in Canada," paper given at the "For Us There Are No Frontiers" symposium, Tampa, Fla., Apr. 1996.

23 Ruth Fabian and Corinna Coulmas, *Die deutsche Emigration in Frankreich nach 1933* (Munich, 1978); David Pike, *German Writers in Soviet Exile, 1933-1945* (Chapel Hill, N.C., 1982); Barbara Vormeier, "Dokumentation zur französischen Emigrantenpolitik (1933-1944)," in Hanna Schramm, ed., *Menschen in Gurs: Erinnerungen an ein französisches Internierungslager, 1940-1941* (Worms, 1977), 157-245; Jarrell C. Jackman and Carla M. Borden, eds., *The Muses Flee Hitler: Cultural Transfer and Adaptation, 1930-1945* (Washington, D.C., 1983), esp. Alan Beyerchen, "Anti-Intellectualism and the Cultural Decapitation of Germany under the Nazis," 29-44; Mitchell G. Ash and Alfons Söllner, eds., *Forced Migration and Scientific Change: Emigré German-Speaking Scientists and Scholars after 1933* (Cambridge, 1996).

24 Louis Stein, *Beyond Death and Exile: The Spanish Republicans in France, 1939-1955* (Cambridge, Mass., 1979); Kulischer, *Europe on the Move*, 227-47; Marrus, *The Unwanted*, 190-94.

25 Moshe Bejski, "The 'Righteous Among the Nations' and Their Part in the Rescue of Jews," in Yisrael Gutman and Efraim Zuroff, eds., *Rescue Attempts during the Holocaust: Proceedings of the Second Yad Vashem International Historical Conference*, trans. Moshe Gottlieb et al. (Jerusalem, 1974), 627-47; Alfred A. Häsler, *The Lifeboat Is Full: Switzerland and the Refugees, 1933-1945*, trans. Charles L. Markmann (German orig., 1967; New York, 1969); Helmut F. Pfanner, "The Role of Switzerland for the Refugees," in Jackman and Borden, *The Muses Flee Hitler*, 235-48; David S. Wyman, *Paper Walls: America and the Refugee Crisis 1938-1941* (Amherst, Mass., 1968); Marrus, *The Unwanted*, 145-58.

26 Marrus, *The Unwanted*, 135-41; Frank Epp, *Mennonite Exodus: The Rescue and Resettlement of Russian Mennonites since the Communist Revolution* (Altona, Man., 1962); Harvey Dyck, "Collectivization, Depression, and Immigration, 1929-30: A Chance Interplay," in Dyck and H. Peter Krosby, eds., *Empire and Nations: Essays in Honour of Frederick H. Soward* (Toronto, 1969), 144-59; Jan Cremer and Horst Przytulla, *Exil Türkei: Deutschsprachige Emigranten in der Türkei 1933-1945* (2d ed., Munich, 1991).

27 Jack Wertheimer, *Unwelcome Strangers: European Jews in Imperial Germany* (Oxford, 1987), quote on 3; Marrus, *The Unwanted*, quotes on 34, 144; Nancy Green, "Jewish Migrations to France in the 19th and 20th Centuries: Community or Communities?" *Studia Rosenthaliana* [special issue] 23 (fall 1989): 135-53, and Green, *The Pletzl of Paris: Jewish Immigrant Workers in the "Belle Epoque"* (French orig., 1985; New York, 1986); Trude Maurer, *Ostjuden in Deutschland, 1918-1933* (Hamburg, 1986); William J. Fishman, *East End Jewish Radicals, 1875-1914* (London, 1975); Ezra Mendelsohn, *The Jews of East Central Europe between the World Wars* (Bloomington, 1983); Lloyd P. Gartner, *The Jewish Immigrant in England, 1870-1914* (London, 1960); Steven E. Aschheim, *Brothers and Strangers: The East European Jew in German and German Jewish Consciousness, 1800-1923* (Madison, 1982).

28 Irving Abella and Harold Troper, *None Is Too Many: Canada and the Jews of Europe, 1933-1948* (Toronto, 1983), ix; E. Thomas Wood and Stanislaw Jankowski, *Karski: How One Man Tried to Stop the Holocaust* (New York, 1994); Richard Breitman, "The Allied War Effort and the Jews, 1942-43," *Journal of Contemporary History* 20 (1985): 135-56, and research in progress on recently released documents of the British National Security Agency.

29 Raul Hilberg, *The Destruction of the European Jews* (Chicago, 1961); Herbert A. Strauss,

"Jewish Emigration from Germany: Nazi Policies and Jewish Responses," *Yearbook of the Leo Baeck Institute* 25 (1980): 313–61, 26 (1981): 323–409; Juliane Wetzel, "Auswanderung aus Deutschland," in Wolfgang Benz, ed., *Die Juden in Deutschland, 1933–1945: Leben unter nationalsozialistischer Herrschaft* (Munich, 1988), 413–98; Marrus, *The Unwanted*, 61–68, 128–31, 166–77, 158–207, 212–19; Helmut Genschel, *Die Verdrängung der Juden aus der Wirtschaft des Dritten Reiches* (Göttingen, 1966); David Yisraeli, "The Third Reich and the Transfer Agreement," *Journal of Contemporary History* 6, 2 (1971): 129–48.

30   Jacques Vernant, *The Refugee in the Post-War World* (London, 1953), 581–82, on restrictions in Latin America; David Kranzler, "The Jewish Refugee Community of Shanghai, 1938–1945," *Wiener Library Bulletin* 26, 3/4 (1972/73): 28–37; Renata Berg-Pan, "Shanghai Chronicle: Nazi Refugees in China," in Jackman and Borden, *The Muses Flee Hitler*, 283–90; Percy Finch, *Shanghai and Beyond* (New York, 1953); Felix Gruenberger, "The Jewish Refugees in Shanghai," *Jewish Social Studies* 12 (1950): 329–48.

31   Marrus, *The Unwanted*, citing Lippman on 184, 246–67, 278–82; Léon Papeleux, *Les Silences de Pie XII* (Brussels, 1980); John F. Morley, *Vatican Diplomacy and the Jews during the Holocaust, 1939–1943* (New York, 1980); Leni Yahil, "Scandinavian Countries to the Rescue of Concentration Camp Prisoners," *Yad Vashem Studies* 6 (1967): 181–220.

32   Hans-Heinrich Nolte, ed., *Deutsche Migrationen* (Münster, 1996), has pointed to the linguistic affinity.

33   With regard to forced labor in penal systems and related to military drafts, see Paul Cornil, "Trends in Penal Methods with Special Reference to Prison Labor," in Marvin E. Wolfgang, ed., *Crime and Culture: Essays in Honor of Thorsten Sellin* (New York, 1968), 387–404; Robert Evans Jr., "The Military Draft as a Slave System: An Economic View," *Social Science Quarterly* 50 (1969): 535–43. For pre-twentieth century deportation of criminals, see chaps. 9.3, 9.5, 13.4.

34   Kulischer, *Europe on the Move*, 206–25 (Italy), 227–39 (Spain); Georges Mauco, *Les Étrangers en France: Leur rôle dans l'activité économique* (Paris, 1932); Robin Cohen, "Shaping the Nation, Excluding the Other: The Deportation of Migrants from Britain," in Jan Lucassen and Leo Lucassen, eds., *Migration, Migration History, History: Old Paradigms and New Perspectives* (Bern, 1997), 351–73.

35   Walter Wilson, *Forced Labor in the United States* (New York, 1933), 28–49, 68–83 passim; Erskine Caldwell and Margaret Bourke-White, *You Have Seen Their Faces* (New York, 1937); Pete Daniel, *The Shadow of Slavery: Peonage in the South, 1901–1969* (Urbana, Ill., 1972), 21; Abraham Hoffman, "Stimulus to Repatriation: The 1931 Federal Deportation Drive and the Los Angeles Mexican Community," *Pacific Historical Review* 42 (1973): 205–19.

36   Donald H. Avery, *Reluctant Host: Canada's Response to Immigrant Workers, 1896–1994* (Toronto, 1995), chaps. 4–5; Isaiah Bowman, *The Pioneer Fringe* (New York, 1931), 297, 314.

37   Bernard Lewis, *Race and Slavery in the Middle East: An Historical Enquiry* (Oxford, 1990), 78–84, 167–69; Raymond L. Buell, *The Native Problem in Africa*, 2 vols. (London, 1928), 1:658–59; essays by Gareth Austin and by Martin A. Klein and Richard Roberts in Toyin Falola and Paul E. Lovejoy, eds., *Pawnship in Africa: Debt Bondage in Historical Perspective* (Boulder, 1994), 119–59, 303–20; Paul E. Lovejoy and Nicholas Rogers, eds., *Unfree Labour in the Development of the Atlantic World* (Ilford, U.K., 1994). Jonathan D. Spence, *The Search for Modern China* (New York, 1990), 14–15, 309, 373.

38   Marcel van der Linden, "Forced Labour and Non-Capitalist Industrialization: The Case of Stalinism (ca. 1929–ca. 1956)," in Tom Brass et al., *Free and Unfree Labour* (Amsterdam,

1993), 19–30, and Brass and van der Linden, eds., *Free and Unfree Labour: The Debate Continues* (Bern, 1997).

39   Reino Kero, "Canadian Finns," 203–14; Lewis H. Siegelbaum and Ronald G. Suny, eds., *Making Workers Soviet: Power, Class, and Identity* (Ithaca, N.Y., 1994), 1–26; Kulischer, *Europe on the Move*, 88–93; Robert A. Lewis and Richard H. Rowland, *Population Redistribution in the USSR: Its Impact on Society, 1897–1977* (New York, 1979), 158–98; Andrea Graziosi, "Foreign Workers in Soviet Russia, 1920–1940: Their Experience and Their Legacy," *International Labor and Working-Class History* 33 (1988): 38–59.

40   Paul Barton, *L'Institution concentrationnaire en Russie, 1930–1957* (Paris, 1959); James Bunyan, *The Origin of Forced Labor in the Soviet State, 1917–1921: Documents and Materials* (Baltimore, 1967); Stanislaw Swianiewicz, *Forced Labour and Economic Development: An Enquiry into the Experience of Soviet Industrialization* (Oxford, 1965).

41   Robert Conquest, *Kolyma: The Arctic Death Camps* (New York, 1978). Numerous memoirs of internees and forced laborers have been published. See, for example, Margarete Buber-Neumann, *Under Two Dictators*, trans. Edward Fitzgerald (German orig., 1949; London, 1949); Elinor Lipper, *Eleven Years in Soviet Prison Camps*, trans. Richard and Clara Winston (German orig., 1950; Chicago, 1951); *Red Goals* [memoirs of women in camps, 1923–32] (London, 1935); Vladimir Tchernavin, *I Speak for the Silent Prisoners of the Soviets*, trans. Nicholas M. Oushakoff (Russian orig., n.d.; Boston, 1935); Moshé Zalcman, *La véridique Histoire de Moshé: Ouvrier juif et communiste au temps de Staline*, trans. Halina Edelstein (Yiddish orig., 1970; Paris, 1977); Walter A. Rukeyser, *Working for the Soviets: An American Engineer in Russia* (New York, 1932).

42   Stephen Kotkin, *Magnetic Mountain: Stalinism as a Civilization* (Berkeley, 1995), 72–105; Arvid Brodersen, *The Soviet Worker: Labor and Government in Soviet Society* (New York, 1966), 40–117, quote on 79; Werner Hofmann, *Die Arbeitsverfassung der Sowjetunion* (Berlin, 1957); Solomon M. Schwarz, *Labor in the Soviet Union* (New York, 1952), 1–199; Donald Filtzer, *Soviet Workers and Stalinist Industrialization: The Formation of Modern Soviet Production Relations, 1928–1941* (London, 1986); Mervyn Matthews, *The Passport Society: Controlling Movement in Russia and the USSR* (Boulder, 1993).

43   David J. Dallin and Boris I. Nicolaevsky, *Forced Labor in Soviet Russia* (New Haven, 1947), 3–48; Steven Rosenfielde, "An Assessment of the Sources and Uses of Gulag Forced Labour 1929–56," *Soviet Studies* 33 (1981): 51–87, and 39 (1897): 292–313, with comments by Robert Conquest, 34 (1982): 434–39, and S. G. Wheatcroft 35 (1983): 223–37. Newly accessible Soviet documents imply that wartime deaths were higher than admitted by the government to the population and that the camp population was lower. Hans-Heinrich Nolte, "Eine sowjetische Liste der Personenverluste im Zweiten Weltkrieg von 1946," *1999: Zeitschrift für Sozialgeschichte des 20. Jahrhunderts* 1 (1999): 126–33; Edwin Bacon, "'Glasnost' and the Gulag: New Information on Soviet Forced Labour around World War II," *Soviet Studies* 44 (1992): 1069–86, and Bacon, *The Gulag at War: Stalin's Forced Labour System in the Light of the Archives* (London, 1994); Apolonja M. Kojder and Barbara Glogowska, *Marynia, Don't Cry: Memoirs of Two Polish-Canadian Families* (Toronto, 1995), 1–138.

44   Klaus J. Bade, "Massenwanderung und Arbeitsmarkt im deutschen Nordosten von 1880 bis zum Ersten Weltkrieg," *Archiv für Sozialgeschichte* 20 (1980): 265–323, and Bade, "'Preußengänger' und 'Abwehrpolitik': Ausländerbeschäftigung, Ausländerpolitik und Ausländerkontrolle auf dem Arbeitsmarkt in Preußen vor dem Ersten Weltkrieg," *Archiv für Sozialgeschichte* 24 (1984): 91–283; Ulrich Herbert, *A History of Foreign Labor in Germany,*

1880–1980: Seasonal Workers, Forced Laborers, Guest Workers, trans. William Templer (German orig., 1986; Ann Arbor, 1990), 9–119; Lothar Elsner and Joachim Lehmann, *Ausländische Arbeiter unter dem deutschen Imperialismus, 1900 bis 1985* (Berlin, 1988); Frieda Wunderlich, *Farm Labor in Germany, 1810–1945: Its Historical Development within the Framework of Agricultural and Social Policy* (Princeton, 1961), 27–30, 159–355.

45 Fritz Fischer, *Griff nach der Weltmacht: Die Kriegszielpolitik des kaiserlichen Deutschland 1914/18* (Düsseldorf, 1961), 128–33, 310–21, 601.

46 Babacar Fall, *Le travail forcé en Afrique Occidentale française 1900–1945* (Paris, 1993), 126–45; Jean Suret-Canale, *French Colonialism in Tropical Africa, 1900–1945,* trans. Till Gottheiner (French orig., 1964; London, 1971), 134–43. Colonial Whites opposed the recruitment of Native peoples for fear that after demobilization the trained soldiers might turn against their colonizers.

47 Herbert, *History of Foreign Labor,* 127–31; Wunderlich, *Farm Labor in Germany,* 292–336; Cesare Bermani, Sergio Bologna, and Brunello Mantelli, *Proletarier der "Achse": Sozialgeschichte der italienischen Fremdarbeiter in NS-Deutschland 1937 bis 1943* (Berlin, 1997).

48 Quoted in Herbert, *History of Foreign Labor,* 143.

49 Ulrich Herbert, "'Ausländer-Einsatz' in der deutschen Kriegswirtschaft, 1939–1945," in Klaus J. Bade, ed., *Deutsche im Ausland, Fremde in Deutschland: Migration in Geschichte und Gegenwart* (Munich, 1992), 354–67; Herbert, *History of Foreign Labor,* 131–84; Edward L. Homze, *Foreign Labor in Nazi Germany* (Princeton, 1967); International Labour Office [John H. E. Fried], *The Exploitation of Foreign Labour by Germany* (Montreal, 1945); Hamburger Stiftung zur Förderung von Wissenschaft und Kultur, *"Deutsche Wirtschaft": Zwangsarbeit von KZ-Häftlingen für Industrie und Behörden* (Hamburg, 1991); Annekatrein Mendel, *Zwangsarbeit im Kinderzimmer: "Ostarbeiterinnen" in deutschen Familien von 1939 bis 1945: Gespräche mit Polinnen und Deutschen* (Frankfurt/Main, 1994); Helga Bories-Sawala, *Franzosen im "Reichseinsatz": Deportation, Zwangsarbeit, Alltag: Erfahrungen und Erinnerungen von Kriegsgefangenen und Zivilarbeitern* (Frankfurt/Main, 1996).

50 Francois Lafitte, *The Internment of Aliens* (London, 1988); Peter Gillman and Leni Gillman, *"Collar the Lot!": How Britain Expelled Its Wartime Refugees* (London, 1980); Miriam Kochan, *Britain's Internees in the Second World War* (London, 1983); Bernard Wasserstein, "Intellectual Emigrés in Britain, 1933–1939," in Jackman and Borden, *The Muses Flee Hitler,* 249–56. See also Richard Bosworth and Romano Ugolini, eds., *War, Internment and Mass Migration: The Italo-Australian Experience, 1940–1990* (Rome, 1992).

51 Schechtman, *European Population Transfers;* Grzegorz Frumkin, *Population Changes in Europe since 1939* (New York, 1951); Malcolm J. Proudfoot, *European Refugees, 1939–52: A Study of Forced Population Movement* (London, 1956); Marrus, *The Unwanted,* 174–75, 194–97, 200–204.

52 Marrus, *The Unwanted,* 235–36; Alexander Dallin, *German Rule in Russia, 1941–1945: A Study of Occupation Policies* (London, 1957); Karel Berkhoff, "'They Must Die Off': The Nazi Campaign to Starve the Cities of Ukraine during World War II," research in progress, University of Toronto, April 1997.

53 Norman Davis, *Heart of Europe: A Short History of Poland* (Oxford, 1986), 63–83; Hellmuth Hecker, *Die Umsiedlungsverträge des Deutschen Reiches während des Zweiten Weltkrieges* (Frankfurt/Main, 1971).

54 Wolfgang Benz, "Fremde in der Heimat: Flucht—Vertreibung—Integration," in Bade,

Deutsche im Ausland, 374–86; Marrus, *The Unwanted*, 219–30; Anthony Komjathy and Rebecca Stockwell, *German Minorities and the Third Reich: Ethnic Germans of East Central Europe between the World Wars* (New York, 1980); G. C. Paikert, *The Danube Swabians: German Populations in Hungary, Rumania and Yugoslavia and Hitler's Impact on Their Patterns* (The Hague, 1967).

55 Schechtman, *The Refugee in the World*, 47–55; Marrus, *The Unwanted*, 194–200, 245–52; Fred C. Koch, *The Volga Germans in Russia and the Americas, from 1763 to the Present* (University Park, Pa., 1977).

56 Marrus, *The Unwanted*, 241–45; Harrison E. Salisbury, *The 900 Days: The Siege of Leningrad* (New York, 1969); Hans-Norbert Burkert and Hans-Jochen Markmann, *900 Tage Blockade Leningrad: Leiden und Wiederstand der Zivilbevölkerung im Krieg*, 3 vols. (Berlin, 1991), 2:70.

57 Johannes-Dieter Steinert, *Migration und Politik: Westdeutschland—Europa—Übersee 1945–1961* (Osnabrück, 1995), 44–58.

58 Proudfoot, *European Refugees*, 158–59.

59 Vernant, *The Refugee in the Post-War World*; G. J. van Heuven Goedhard, "People Adrift," *Journal of International Affairs* 7 (1953): 7–29; Wolfgang Jacobmeyer, *Vom Zwangsarbeiter zum heimatlosen Ausländer: Die Displaced Persons in Westdeutschland, 1945–1951* (Göttingen, 1985), tables on 60, 173, 225, and Jacobmeyer, "The 'Displaced Persons' in West Germany, 1945–1951," in Göran Rystad, ed., *The Uprooted: Forced Migration as an International Problem in the Post-War Era* (Lund, Sweden, 1990), 271–88; Mark R. Elliott, *Pawns of Yalta: Soviet Refugees and America's Role in their Repatriation* (Urbana, Ill., 1982); Nicholas Bethell, *The Last Secret: Forcible Repatriation to Russia, 1944–7* (London, 1974).

60 Hedwig Rudolph, "Dynamics of Immigration into a Nonimmigrant Country: Germany," in Fassmann and Münz, *European Migration*, 113–26, and table 6.2; Marion Frantzioch, *Die Vertriebenen: Hemmnisse, Antriebskräfte und Wege ihrer Integration in der Bundesrepublik Deutschland* (Berlin, 1987).

61 Robert Conquest, *The Nation-Killers: The Soviet Deportation of Nationalities* (New York, 1970); Kulischer, *Europe on the Move*, 298–301; John J. Stephan, *The Russian Far East: A History* (Cambridge, 1994); Davis, *Heart of Europe*, 82; Aleksandr M. Nekrich, *The Punished Peoples: The Deportation and Fate of Soviet Minorities at the End of the Second World War* (New York, 1978); Leszek A. Kosinski, "International Migration of Yugoslavs during and Immediately after World War II," *East European Quarterly* 16 (1982): 183–98; Marrus, *The Unwanted*, 298–317; Schechtman, *The Refugee in the World*, 68–72.

62 Frank G. Boudreau and Clyde V. Kiser, eds., *Selected Studies of Migration since World War II* (New York, 1958), 11–29; Anthony T. Bouscaren, *International Migrations since 1945* (New York, 1963), 2–93; Julius Isaac, *British Post-War Migration* (Cambridge, 1954); B. P. Hofstede, *Thwarted Exodus: Post-War Overseas Migration from the Netherlands* (The Hague, 1964); Steinert, *Migration und Politik*, 25–37.

63 Elfrieda B. Shukert and Barbara S. Scibetta, *War Brides of World War II* (New York, 1988); Joyce Hibbert, *The War Brides* (Toronto, 1978); Yukiko Koshiro, *Trans-Pacific Racisms and the U.S. Occupation of Japan* (New York, 1993).

64 Spence, *Modern China*, 291–92.

65 Peter Duus, "Economic Dimensions of Meiji Imperialism: The Case of Korea, 1895–1910," in Ramon H. Myers and Mark R. Peattie, eds., *The Japanese Colonial Empire, 1895–1945* (Princeton, 1984), 128–71, and Peattie, "The Nan'yo: Japan in the South Pacific, 1885–1945,"

ibid., 194–98. By 1935, 50,000 Japanese lived in Nan'yo; only on some islands was the original population still in the majority. Samuel Pao-San Ho, "Colonialism and Development: Korea, Taiwan, and Kwantung," ibid., 347–98; Chih-ming Ka, *Japanese Colonialism in Taiwan: Land Tenure, Development, and Dependency, 1895–1945* (Boulder, 1995); Gregory Henderson, "Japan's *Chosen:* Immigrants, Ruthlessness and Developmental Shock," in Andrew C. Nahm, ed., *Korea under Japanese Colonial Rule: Studies of the Policy and Techniques of Japanese Colonialism* (Kalamazoo, Mich., 1973), 261–69.

66 Mark R. Peattie, "Japanese Attitudes toward Colonialism, 1895–1945," in Myers and Peattie, *Japanese Colonial Empire,* 80–127; Irene B. Taeuber, *The Population of Japan* (Princeton, 1958), 123–70, 198–203; International Labour Office, *Industrial Labour in Japan* (Geneva, 1933).

67 Louise Young, *Japan's Total Empire: Manchuria and the Culture of Wartime Imperialism* (Berkeley, 1998), 307–411; Joseph B. Schechtman, *Population Transfers in Asia* (New York, 1949); Taeuber, *Population of Japan,* 173–90; Narihiko Ito, "Eine Skizze über Kolonialherrschaft, Invasionskrieg und Arbeiterbewegung unter dem japanischen Imperialismus," in Hans Hautmann, ed., *Internationale Tagung der Historiker der Arbeiterbewegung: 20. Linzer Konferenz 1984* (Vienna, 1989), 436–41; Ehud Harari, *The Politics of Labor Legislation in Japan: National-International Interaction* (Berkeley, 1973), 10–50; Andrew Gordon, *Labor and Imperial Democracy in Prewar Japan* (Berkeley, 1991), 302–42; Ramon H. Myers, *The Japanese Economic Development of Manchuria, 1932 to 1945* (New York, 1982), 158–200.

68 The Chinese defenders connected their army to British India by the 715-mile-long Burma Road, from Kunming across the mountains. Hundreds of thousands of men, women, and children built the road by manual labor. Among this conscripted labor force, death rates were high. Spence, *Modern China,* 458; Sinnappah Arasaratnam, *Indians in Malaysia and Singapore* (rev. ed., Kuala Lumpur, 1979), 30–31.

69 George Hicks, *The Comfort Women: Sex Slaves of the Japanese Imperial Forces* (St. Leonards, Austral., 1995); Ustinia Dolgopol and Snehal Paranjape, *Comfort Women, an Unfinished Ordeal: Report of a Mission* (Geneva, 1994); Keith Howard, ed., *True Stories of the Korean Comfort Women: Testimonies* (London, 1995).

70 Bruno Lasker, *Asia on the Move: Population Pressure, Migration, and Resettlement in Eastern Asia under the Influence of Want and War* (New York, 1945).

71 Simpson, *Refugee Question,* 26; Geoffrey Tyson, *Forgotten Frontier* (Delhi, 1992); Spence, *Modern China,* 448–469; Edward I-te Chen, "The Attempt to Integrate the Empire: Legal Perspectives," in Myers and Peattie, *Japanese Colonial Empire,* 269–74.

72 Commission on Wartime Relocation and Internment of Civilians, *Personal Justice Denied* (Washington, D.C., 1982), quote on 18. Ken Adachi, *The Enemy that Never Was: A History of the Japanese Canadians* (Toronto, 1976), 193–277; Donald Avery, "Canada's Response to European Refugees, 1939–1945: The Security Dimension," in Norman Hillmer, Bohdan Kordan, and Lubomyr Luciuk, eds., *On Guard for Thee: War, Ethnicity, and the Canadian State, 1939–1945* (Ottawa, 1988), 179–216. Roger Daniels, *Concentration Camps USA: Japanese Americans and World War II* (New York, 1972), and Daniels, ed., *American Concentration Camps,* 9 vols. (New York, 1989), and Daniels, Sandra C. Taylor, and Harry H. L. Kitano, eds., *Japanese Americans: From Relocation to Redress* (1986; rev. ed., Seattle, 1991); Yoshiko Uchida, *Desert Exile: The Uprooting of a Japanese American Family* (Seattle, 1982).

73 Bouscaren, *International Migrations,* 122–27; Schechtman, *The Refugee in the World,* 172–81.

74 Schechtman, *The Refugee in the World*, 310–36; Edvard Hambro, *The Problem of Chinese Refugees in Hong Kong*, report submitted to the UNHCR (Leyden, 1955), 190.

75 The idea of separation had been developed at first by Muslim students at Cambridge University, typical gatekeeper and planner elites, who subsequently were not involved in flight.

76 Figures varied, depending on which side counted. Scholarly estimates reach as high as 15 million refugees. William Henderson, "The Refugees in India and Pakistan" *Journal of International Affairs* 7 (1953): 57–65; C. Emdad Haque, "The Dilemma of Nationhood and Religion: A 'State of the Art' Review of Research on Population Displacement Resulting from the Partition of the Subcontinent," mimeographed, York University, Toronto, Center for Refugee Studies, n.d. [copyright 1986]; Stephen L. Keller, *Uprooting and Social Change: The Role of Refugees in Development* (Delhi, 1975), 1–16; Kanti B. Pakrasi, *The Uprooted: A Sociological Study of the Refugees of West Bengal, India* (Calcutta, 1971); R. N. Saksena, *Refugees: A Study in Changing Attitudes* (Bombay, 1961); Norwood, *Strangers and Exiles*, 2:357–68; Victor Kiernan, "The Separation of India and Pakistan," in Robin Cohen, ed., *The Cambridge Survey of World Migration* (Cambridge, 1995), 356–59; Sarah Ansari, "The Movement of Indian Muslims to West Pakistan after 1947," in Judith M. Brown and Rosemary Foot, *Migration: The Asian Experience* (New York, 1994), 149–68; Urvashi Butalia, *The Other Side of Silence: Voices from the Partition of India* (Durham, N.C., 2000).

77 Joseph E. Schwartzberg, ed., *A Historical Atlas of South Asia* (Chicago, 1978; 2d rev. ed., Oxford, 1992), 92, 231; Schechtman, *The Refugee in the World*, 89–160.

78 Schechtman, *The Refugee in the World*, 161–71.

79 Ibid., 301–9.

18 Between the Old and the New, 1920s to 1950s

1 Isaiah Bowman, *The Pioneer Fringe* (New York, 1931), v–vii, 102, quote on 200; W. L. G. Joerg, ed., *Pioneer Settlement: Cooperative Studies by 26 Authors* (New York, 1932), v, 107, quote on 362–63. The studies of Anglo pioneers in the Joerg volume have a French equivalent in the proceedings of the *Congrès de la Colonisation Rurale, Alger, 26–29 mai 1930*, 4 vols. (Algiers, 1931). Vol. 4, titled "La colonisation rurale dans les principaux pays de peuplement," provides a comparative perspective. See also J. B. Condliffe, ed., *Problems of the Pacific, 1929: Proceedings of the Third Conference of the Institute of Pacific Relations, Kyoto, 1929* (Chicago, 1930). Donald Denoon, "The Political Economy of Labour Migration to Settler Societies: Australasia, Southern Africa, and Southern South America, between 1890 and 1914," in Shula Marks and Peter Richardson, eds., *International Labour Migration: Historical Perspectives* (London, 1984), 186–205. In Australia, a sequence of squatters', pastoralists', and, finally, farmers' migrations ended in 1901 when 15 million sheep and 1.5 million cattle perished in a severe drought.

2 Walter J. Stein, *California and the Dust Bowl Migration* (Westport, Conn., 1973); Anne Marie Low, *Dust Bowl Diary* (Lincoln, Nebr., 1984); Charles J. Shindo, *Dust Bowl Migrants in the American Imagination* (Lawrence, Kans., 1997); James N. Gregory, *American Exodus: The Dust Bowl Migration and Okie Culture in California* (New York, 1989).

3 Bowman, *Pioneer Fringe*, 4, 29.

4 Ibid., quotes on 200–212; essays by John H. Wellington, C. T. Loram, Ethel T. Jollie, and H. Clifford Darby in Joerg, *Pioneer Settlement*, 146–220; Leslie Green, "Migration, Urbani-

zation, and National Development in Nigeria," in Samir Amin, ed., *Modern Migrations in Western Africa* (London, 1974), 281–304, esp. 283–85.

5 Essays by Raye R. Platt, W. L. Schurz, and Wellington D. Jones in Joerg, *Pioneer Settlement*, 80–145; Otto Nordenskjöld, *Südamerika: Ein Zukunftsland der Menschheit* (Stuttgart, 1927); George Martine, "Brazil," in Charles B. Nam, William J. Serow, and David F. Sly, eds., *International Handbook on Internal Migration* (New York, 1990), 31–46, esp. 36–37.

6 Owen Lattimore, "Chinese Colonization in Inner Mongolia: Its History and Present Development," in Joerg, *Pioneer Settlement*, 288–312; L. H. Dudley Buxton, "Present Conditions in Inner Mongolia," *Geographical Journal* 61 (1923): 393–413, and Buxton, *The Eastern Road* (London, 1924).

7 George B. Cressey, "Chinese Colonization in Mongolia: A General Survey," in Joerg, *Pioneer Settlement*, 277.

8 The region consists of several distinct settlement areas, which, due to space, cannot be differentiated here.

9 Robert H. G. Lee, *The Manchurian Frontier in Ch'ing History* (Cambridge, Mass., 1970), esp. chap. 5 "The Sinicization of the Manchurian Frontier," 78–115; C. Walter Young, "Chinese Immigration and Colonization in Manchuria," in Joerg, *Pioneer Settlement*, 330–59, and Young, "Chinese Labor Migration to Manchuria," *Chinese Economic Journal* 1 (1927): 613–33; Owen Lattimore, "Chinese Colonization in Manchuria," *Geographical Review* 22 (1932): 177–95; Tim A. Wright, "A Method of Evading Management—Contract Labor in Chinese Coal Mines before 1937," *Comparative Studies in Society and History* 23 (1981): 656–78; Hoon K. Lee, "Korean Migrants in Manchuria," *Geographical Review* 22 (1932): 196–204.

10 Irene B. Taeuber, *The Population of Japan* (Princeton, 1958), 192–95; Owen Lattimore, *Inner Asian Frontiers of China* (1940; Boston, 1962), 10–15; Chu Hsiao, "Manchuria: A Statistical Survey of Its Resources, Industries, Trade, Railways and Immigration," in Condliffe, *Problems of the Pacific*, 380–422; Ching-ch'ao Wu, "Chinese Immigration in the Pacific Area," *Chinese Social and Political Science Review* 12 (1928): 543–60.

11 H. Clifford Darby, "Pioneer Problems in Rhodesia and Nyasaland," in Joerg, *Pioneer Settlement*, 217–18.

12 For the sequence of partition plans, see Rafic Bustani and Philippe Fargues, *The Atlas of the Arab World: Geopolitics and Society* (New York, 1990), 22. Essays by Stephen Halbrook, Walter Lehn, Kemal H. Karpat, and Adnan Abu-Ghazaleh in Baha Abu-Laban and Ibrahim Abu-Lughod, eds., *Settler Regimes in Africa and the Arab World: The Illusion of Endurance* (Wilmette, Ill., 1974), 20–95. Benny Morris, *Righteous Victims: A History of the Zionist-Arab Conflict, 1881–1999* (New York, 1999).

13 Joseph B. Schechtman, *The Refugee in the World: Displacement and Integration* (New York, 1964), 182–261, quote on 184; Lucille W. Pevsner, "The Arab Refugees," *Journal of International Affairs* 7 (1953): 42–50; Aristide Zolberg, Astri Suhrke, and Sergio Aguayo, *Escape from Violence: Conflict and the Refugee Crisis in the Developing World* (Oxford, 1989); Ilja M. Dijour, "Jewish Migration in the Post-War Period," *Jewish Journal of Sociology* 4 (1962): 72–81; Frederick A. Norwood, *Strangers and Exiles: A History of Religious Refugees*, 2 vols. (Nashville, 1965–69), 2:334–56.

14 Schechtman, *The Refugee in the World*, 265–68; Jean-Claude Lasry and Claude Tapia, *Les Juifs du Maghreb: Diasporas contemporaines* (Paris, 1989).

15 Schechtman, *The Refugee in the World*, 262–309; Eliezer Ben-Rafael, *The Emergence of Ethnicity: Cultural Groups and Social Conflict in Israel* (New York, 1982), 21–80, 232.

16　In Portugal, the semifascist Salazar regime continued to direct migrants to Angola after 1945.

17　Bureau of Census and Statistics, *Union Statistics for Fifty Years, 1910–1960* (Pretoria, 1960), table A–3; Harrison M. Wright, *The "New Imperialism": Analysis of Late-Nineteenth-Century Expansion* (Lexington, Mass., 1976), vii.

18　Marc Michel, *Décolonisations et émergence du tiers monde* (Paris, 1993); "Repatriates and Colonial Auxiliaries" (section) in Robin Cohen, ed., *The Cambridge Survey of World Migration* (Cambridge, 1995), 321–52.

19　Richa Nagar, "The South Asian Diaspora in Tanzania: A History Retold," *Comparative Studies of South Asia, Africa and the Middle East* 16, 2 (1996): 62–80, esp. 67–68; P. G. Powesland, "History of the Migration in Uganda," in Audrey I. Richards, ed., *Economic Development and Tribal Change: A Study of Immigrant Labour in Buganda* (rev. ed., Nairobi, 1973).

20　William Mintner, "The Ideological Foundation of Settler Regimes: The Portuguese in Africa," in Abu-Laban and Abu-Lughod, *Settler Regimes*, 31–42; David Simon, "The Ties That Bind: Decolonization and Neo-Colonialism in Southern Africa," in Chris Dixon and Michael J. Heffernan, eds., *Colonialism and Development in the Contemporary World* (London, 1991), 21–45.

21　Jan Lucassen and Rinus Penninx, *Newcomers: Immigrants and Their Descendants in the Netherlands 1550–1995*, trans. Michael Wintle (Dutch orig., 1985; rev. ed., Amsterdam, 1997); Herman Obedijn, "Vers les bords de la mer du Nord: Les Retours aux Pays-Bas induits par la décolonisation," in Colette Dubois and Jean L. Miège, eds., *L'Europe retrouvée: Les Migrations de la décolonisation* (Paris, 1994), 49–74.

22　Julius Isaac, *British Post-War Migration* (Cambridge, 1954); Muhammad Anwar, "'New Commonwealth' Migration to the UK," in Cohen, *Cambridge Survey*, 274–78, and Vaughan Robinson, "The Migration of East African Asians to the UK," ibid., 331–36; Ceri Peach, *West Indian Migration to Britain: A Social Geography* (Oxford, 1968), deals with the 1950s and 1960s.

23　Schechtman, *The Refugee in the World*, 73–86; Eugene M. Kulischer, *Europe on the Move: War and Population Changes, 1917–1947* (New York, 1948), 247.

24　Raymond F. Betts, *France and Decolonisation, 1900–1960* (London, 1991), 78–114; André Dirlik, "The Algerian Response to Settlement," in Abu-Laban and Abu-Lughod, *Settler Regimes*, 73–80; Michael J. Heffernan and Keith Sutton, "The Landscape of Colonialism: The Impact of French Colonial Rule in the Algerian Rural Settlement Pattern, 1830–1987," in Dixon and Heffernan, *Colonialism and Development*, 121–52, esp. 135–43; Ammar Bouhouche, "The Return of Algerian Refugees Following Independence in 1962," in Tim Allen and Hubert Morsink, eds., *When Refugees Go Home: African Experiences* (London, 1994), 71–77.

25　International Labour Office, Ad Hoc Committee on Forced Labour, *Report on Forced Labour* (Geneva, 1953); Murray Gordon, *Slavery in the Arab World* (French orig., 1987; New York, 1989); Abebe Zegeye and Shubi I. Ishemo, eds., *Forced Labour and Migration: Patterns of Movement within Africa* (London, 1989).

26　Jonathan Crush, Alan Jeeves, and David Yudelman, *South Africa's Labor Empire: A History of Black Migrancy to the Gold Mines* (Boulder, 1991); Francis Wilson, *Migrant Labour in South Africa* (Johannesburg, 1972), 4–22, and Wilson, *Labour in the South African Gold Mines 1911–1969* (Cambridge, 1972); Martin Legassick and Francine de Clerq, "Capitalism and Migrant Labour in Southern Africa: The Origins and Nature of the System," in Marks and Richardson, *International Labour Migration*, 140–66; Jonathan Crush, "The Chains of Migrancy and the Southern African Labour Commission," in Dixon and Heffernan, *Colonialism and Development*, 46–71; Julia Wells, "Passes and Bypasses: Freedom of Movement for African Women under the Urban Areas Act of South Africa," in Margaret J. Hay and Marcia Wright, eds., *African Women and the Law: Historical Perspectives* (Boston, 1982), 126–50; Colin Murray, *Families Divided: The Impact of Migrant Labour in Lesotho* (Cambridge, 1981).

27 Wilson, *Migrant Labour*, 29–119. Among the many publications on international migration, see, for example, R. Christiansen and J. Kydd, "The Return of Malawian Labour from South Africa and Zimbabwe," *Journal of Modern African Studies* 21 (1983): 311–26; Duncan Clarke, *Foreign Migrant Labour in Southern Africa: Studies on Accumulation in the Labour Reserves, Demand Determinants and Supply Relationships* (Geneva, 1977); T. Dunbar Moodie, with Vivienne Ndatshe, *Going for Gold: Men, Mines, and Migration* (Berkeley, 1994); for a comparison of Siberia and South Africa, see F. Johnstone, "Rand and Kolyma: Afro-Siberian Hamlet," *South African Sociological Review* 1 (1989): 1–45.

28 Paul Drechsel and Bettina Schmidt, *Südafrika: Chancen für eine pluralistische Gesellschaftsordnung: Geschichte und Perspektiven* (Opladen, 1995), provide an excellent survey of race relations (or non-relations), both in history and since the end of apartheid, and language statistics on 232.

19 New Migration Systems since the 1960s

1 In addition to the scholarly literature cited below, this chapter draws on the German, Canadian, U.S., and French press of the 1990s to August 1998. Gerald L. Posner, *Warlords of Crime: Chinese Secret Societies—the New Mafia* (New York, 1988); UN Development Programme, *Human Development Report* [annual] (New York, 1990–).

2 Anthony H. Richmond, "Reactive Migration: Sociological Aspects of Refugee Movements," *Journal of Refugee Studies* 6, 1 (1993): 7–24, and Richmond, *Global Apartheid: Refugees, Racism, and the New World Order* (Toronto, 1994); Art Hansen and Anthony Oliver-Smith, eds., *Involuntary Migration and Resettlement: The Problems and Responses of Dislocated People* (Boulder, 1982); José Alvarado and John Creedy, *Population Ageing, Migration, and Social Expenditure* (Cheltenham, U.K., 1998).

3 Stephen Castles and Godula Kosack, *Immigrant Workers and Class Structure in Western Europe* (Oxford, 1973), 478; Samir Amin, ed., *Modern Migrations in Western Africa* (London, 1974), 98–110; Mike Parnwell, *Population Movements and the Third World* (London, 1993); B. Singh Bolaria and Rosemary von Elling Bolaria, eds., *International Labour Migrations* (New York, 1997).

4 Jonathan Derrick, *Africa's Slaves Today* (London, 1975); Gandhi Peace Foundation and National Labour Institute, *National Survey on the Incidence of Bonded Labour: Preliminary Report* (New Delhi, 1979), 1–30; J. L. Hamilpurker, *Changing Aspects of Bonded Labour in India* (Bombay, 1989); Anti-Slavery International, *Children in Bondage: Slaves of the Subcontinent* (London, 1991). In view of the 250 million child laborers worldwide, an antichild labor convention was passed by the International Labour Organization, Geneva, in June 1999; Kevin Bales, *Disposable People: New Slavery in the Global Economy* (Berkeley, 1999).

5 Jemera Rone, *The Struggle for Land in Brazil: Rural Violence Continues* (New York, 1992), and Rone, "Forced Labor in Brazil Re-Visited," *Human Rights Watch Short Report* 5, 12 (Nov.

1993); Mary Jane Camejo, *Harvesting Oppression: Forced Haitian Labor in the Dominican Sugar Industry* (New York, 1990); Maurice Lemoine, *Bitter Sugar: Slaves Today in the Caribbean*, trans. Andrea Johnston (French orig., Paris, 1981; London, 1985).

6   Human Rights Watch/Asia and Women's Rights Project, *A Modern Form of Slavery: Trafficking of Burmese Women and Girls into Brothels in Thailand* (New York, 1993).

7   Reginald Appleyard, ed., *The Impact of International Migration on Developing Countries* (Paris, 1989); Jeffrey Henderson and Manuel Castells, eds., *Global Restructuring and Territorial Development* (London, 1987); Allan M. Findlay, "Skilled Transients: The Invisible Phenomenon?" in Robin Cohen, ed., *The Cambridge Survey of World Migration* (Cambridge, 1995), 515–22; Chan Kwok Bun and Ong Jin Hui, "The Many Faces of Immigrant Entrepreneurship," ibid., 523–31; John Salt, "Highly Skilled Migrants, Careers and International Labor Markets," *Geoforum* 19 (1988): 387–99.

8   Mark J. Miller, "Illegal Migration," in Cohen, *Cambridge Survey*, 537–40; Bimal Ghosh, *Huddled Masses and Uncertain Shores: Insights into Irregular Migration* (The Hague, 1998).

9   Castles and Kosack, *Immigrant Workers and Class Structure*; Saskia Sassen-Koob, *The Mobility of Labour and Capital: A Study of International Investment and Labour Flow* (London, 1988); Rosalind E. Boyd, Robin Cohen, and Peter C. W. Gutkind, eds., *International Labour and the Third World: The Making of a New Working Class* (Aldershot, U.K., 1987); Robin Cohen, *The New Helots: Migrants in the International Division of Labour* (Aldershot, U.K., 1987); Lydia Potts, *The World Labour Market: A History of Migration*, trans. Terry Bond (German orig., n.d.; London, 1990); Nigel Harris, *The New Untouchables: Immigration and the New World Worker* (New York, 1995); Christian Mercier, *Les Déracinés du capital: Immigration et accumulation* (Lyon, 1977).

10 Louise W. Holborn, *Refugees, a Problem of our Time: The Work of the United Nations High Commissioner for Refugees, 1951–1972*, 2 vols. (Metuchen, N.J., 1975); Ludger Kühnhardt, *Die Flüchtlingsfrage als Weltordnungsproblem: Massenzwangswanderungen in Geschichte und Politik* (Vienna, 1984); Peter J. Opitz, ed., *Das Weltflüchtlingsproblem: Ursachen und Folgen* (Munich, 1988), and, Opitz, ed., *Der globale Marsch: Flucht und Migration als Weltproblem* (Munich, 1997); UNHCR, *The State of the World's Refugees, 1995: In Search of Solutions* (Oxford, 1995), 19–23, 224–27; U.S. Central Intelligence Agency, Geographic Resources Division, *The Challenge of Ethnic Conflict to National and International Order in the 1990s: Geographic Perspectives* ([Washington, D.C., 1995]); Christopher McDowell, ed., *Understanding Impoverishment: The Consequences of Development-Induced Displacement* (Providence, 1996), 1–3, citing World Bank on 2; *Winning the Human Race? The Report of the Independent Commission on International Humanitarian Issues* (1988; London, 1998).

11 Paul Tabori, *The Anatomy of Exile: A Semantic and Historical Study* (London, 1972); Aristide Zolberg, Astri Suhrke, and Sergio Aguayo, *Escape from Violence: Conflict and Refugee Crisis in the Developing World* (Oxford, 1989), 3–33; Andrew Bell-Fialkoff, *Ethnic Cleansing* (New York, 1996), 119–209.

12 Alan Dowty, *Closed Borders: The Contemporary Assault on Freedom of Movement* (New Haven, 1987); Danièle Joly and Robin Cohen, eds., *Reluctant Hosts: Europe and Its Refugees* (Aldershot, U.K., 1989); Peter H. Koehn, *Refugees from Revolution: U.S. Policy and Third-World Migration* (Boulder, 1991); Gerald Dirks, *Canada's Refugee Policy: Indifference or Opportunism?* (Montreal, 1977).

13 Aristide Zolberg, "The Formation of New States as a Refugee-Generating Process," *Annals*

of the American Academy of Political and Social Science 467 (1983): 24–38; Naomi F. Zucker and Norman L. Zucker, "U.S. Admission Policies towards Cuban and Haitian Migrants," in Cohen, *Cambridge Survey*, 447; U.S. Committee for Refugees, *World Refugee Survey* [annual] (New York, 1980–); Michael S. Teitelbaum and Myron Weiner, eds., *Threatened Peoples, Threatened Borders: World Migration and U.S. Policy* (New York, 1995), 13–38.

14 Opitz, *Das Weltflüchtlingsproblem*, 66–217; UNHCR, *The State of the World's Refugees, 1995*, 12–13, 24–96; François Jean, ed., *Populations in Danger* (London, 1992); Ronald Skeldon, *Migration and Development: A Global Perspective* (Essex, U.K., 1997).

15 Michael P. Todaro, *Internal Migration in Developing Countries: A Review of Theory, Evidence, Methodology and Research Priorities* (Geneva, 1976); UN Economic and Social Commission for Asia and the Pacific, *Migration and Urbanization in Asia and the Pacific: Interrelationships with Socio-Economic Development and Evolving Policy Issues* (New York, 1992), 9, noted that entrepreneurs from Japan, South Korea, and Taiwan were leaving Thailand in the early 1990s for "cheaper labour countries due to increased labour cost and infrastructure bottlenecks." World Bank, *World Development Report 1995: Workers in an Integrating World* (Oxford, 1995); UN Development Programme, *Human Development Report* [annual] (New York, 1990–); Reinhard Lohrmann, "International Migration Dynamics and Immigration Policy in Europe: An International Perspective," in Albrecht Weber, ed., *Einwanderungsland Bundesrepublik Deutschland in der Europäischen Union: Gestaltungsauftrag und Regelungsmöglichkeiten* (Osnabrück, 1997), 31–43, quote on 35–36; Dieter Nohlen and Franz Nuscheler, ed., *Handbuch der Dritten Welt*, 8 vols. (2d rev. ed., Hamburg, 1982–83).

16 Statement of a group of monks and nuns in support of their demand to release LDCs from their debt-load. *Frankfurter Rundschau*, 10 Oct. 1992. At the late 1999 Seattle summit of the World Trade Organization, NGOs and "Third World" countries rebelled against the "agenda of the rich." *Le Monde diplomatique*, Jan. 2000.

17 Norman Myers and Jennifer Kent, *Environmental Exodus: An Emergent Crisis in the Global Arena* (Washington, D.C., 1995); "Environmental Refugees," special issue of *Refuge* 12, 1 (June 1992); Arthur H. Westing, "Population, Desertification, and Migration," *Environmental Conservation* 21 (1994): 110–14; Gerald O. Barney et al., *The Global 2000 Report to the President: Entering the 21st Century*, 2 vols. (Washington, D.C., 1980).

18 Michael S. Teitelbaum and Jay Winter, *A Question of Numbers: High Migration, Low Fertility, and the Politics of National Identity* (New York, 1998); Tony Loftas and Jane Ross, eds., *Dimensions of Need: An Atlas of Food and Agriculture* (Rome, 1995), 14–19; Joni Seager, *The New State of the Earth Atlas* (New York, 1995), maps 2, 3, 6, 15, 18; Michael Kidron and Dan Smith, *The New State of War and Peace: An International Atlas* (New York, 1991); Dan Morgan, *Merchants of Grain* (New York, 1979); Susan George, *How the Other Half Dies: The Real Reasons for World Hunger* (Harmondsworth, 1976); David L. L. Shields, ed., *The Color of Hunger: Race and Hunger in National and International Perspective* (Lanham, Md., 1995); Carrying Capacity Network, *The Carrying Capacity Briefing Book*, 2 vols. (Washington, D.C., 1996); Joel E. Cohen, *How Many People Can the Earth Support?* (New York, 1995).

19 Essays by Anthony Oliver-Smith, Andrew Gray, and Darrell A. Posey, in McDowell, *Understanding Impoverishment*, 77–135; Jeremy Seabrook, *Victims of Development: Resistance and Alternatives* (London, 1993).

20 In July 1998, a treaty for an International Criminal Court to prosecute genocide, crimes against humanity (including "forced pregnancy"), and war crimes was completed.

21 Lucy Bonnerjea, *Shaming the World: The Needs of Women Refugees* (London, 1985), 6; Jacqueline Bhabha, Francesca Klug, and Sue Shutter, *Worlds Apart: Women under Immigration and Nationality Law* (London, 1985); Anders B. Johnsson, "The International Protection of Women Refugees: A Summary of Principal Problems and Issues," *International Journal of Refugee Law* 1, 2 (1989): 221–31; Diana Cammack, "Development and Forced Migration: The Case of Afghan Refugee Women in Pakistan," in Cohen, *Cambridge Survey*, 461–66. Dutch Refugee Association, *International Seminar on Refugee Women* (Amsterdam, 1986); C. E. J. de Neef and S. J. de Ruiter, *Sexual Violence against Women Refugees* (The Hague, 1984); Beatrice N. Hackett, *Pray God and Keep Walking: Stories of Women Refugees* (Jefferson, N.C., 1996).

22 Third World women were used to test newly developed birth-control pills for side effects; then the organ transplant and blood-collection industry turned to Third World countries. UN Department of Economic and Social Affairs, *Study on Traffic in Persons and Prostitution* (New York, 1959). After ten years, the convention had only twenty-five signatory states, none of which were Western industrial states.

23 Kate Young, Carol Wolkowitz, and Roslyn McCullagh, eds., *Of Marriage and the Market: Women's Subordination Internationally and Its Lessons* (London, 1981); Kunio Sato, "Wives for Farmers: A Critical Import," *Japan Quarterly* 35 (1988): 253–59; Ilse Lenz, "Die unsichtbare weibliche Seite des japanischen Aufstiegs: Das Verhältnis von geschlechtlicher Arbeitsteilung und kapitalistischer Entwicklung," in Ulrich Menzel, ed., *Im Schatten des Siegers: Japan*, 4 vols. (Frankfurt/Main, 1989), 3:227–71.

24 See essays by Frank Costigliola, Linda Bryder, Douglas M. Peers, Eileen P. Scully, and Sonya O. Rose in "Sex, Race, and Diplomacy," thematic issue of *International History Review*, 20, 4 (Dec. 1998): 789–919.

25 Kamala Kempadoo and Jo Doezema, eds., *Global Sex Workers: Rights, Resistance, and Redefinition* (London, 1998); Sletske Altink, *Stolen Lives: Trading Women into Sex and Slavery* (London, 1995); Ilse Lenz, "Zwischen fremden Spiegeln . . . Zur Figur der wandernden Prostituierten in ostasiatischen Gesellschaften," *Peripherie* 27 (1987): 51–72, quote on 69; Berit Latza, *Sextourismus in Südostasien* [Philippines and Thailand] (Frankfurt/Main, 1987), 66–89, 233–79; Etsuko Kaji and Jean Inglis, "Sisters against Slavery: A Look at Anti-Prostitution Movements in Japan," *AMPO [Japanese Asia Quarterly Review]* 6, 2 (1974): 19–23; Katharine H. S. Moon, *Sex among Allies: Military Prostitution in U.S.-Korea Relations* (New York, 1997).

26 Annie Phizacklea, ed., *One-Way Ticket: Migration and Female Labour* (London, 1983), and Phizacklea, "Migration and Globalization: A Feminist Perspective," in Khalid Koser and Helma Lutz, eds., *The New Migration in Europe: Social Constructions and Social Realities* (London, 1998), 21–38; Vivian Lin, "Women Electronics Workers in Southeast Asia: The Emergence of a Working Class," in Henderson and Castells, *Global Restructuring*, 112–33; Fred Arnold and Suwanlee Piampiti, "Female Migration in Thailand," and Piampiti, "Female Migrants in Bangkok Metropolis," in James T. Fawcett, Siew-Ean Khoo, and Peter C. Smith, eds., *Women in the Cities of Asia: Migration and Urban Adaptation* (Boulder, 1984), 143–64, 227–46.

27 European Trade Union Confederation, *Women at Work: White Paper on Working Women in Europe* (Brussels, 1976); Ekkehard Launer and Renate Wilke-Launer, eds., *Zum Beispiel: Dienstmädchen* (Göttingen, 1995); Noeleen Heyzer, Geertje Lycklama Nijehold, and Nedra Weerakoon, eds., *The Trade in Domestic Workers: Causes, Mechanisms, and Consequences*

of *International Migration* (Kuala Lumpur, 1994); Nicky Gregson and Michelle Lowe, *Servicing the Middle Classes: Class, Gender and Waged Domestic Labour in Contemporary Britain* (London, 1994); Patricia M. Daenzer, *Regulating Class Privilege: Immigrant Servants in Canada, 1940s-1990s* (Toronto, 1993).

28 Wenona Giles and Sedef Arat-Koç, eds., *Maid in the Market: Women's Paid Domestic Labour* (Halifax, 1994); Abigail B. Bakan and Daiva Stasiulis, eds., *Not One of the Family: Foreign Domestic Workers in Canada* (Toronto, 1997), esp. essays by Sedef Arat-Koç, "From 'Mothers of the Nation' to Migrant Workers," 53–79, and Patricia M. Daenzer, "An Affair between Nations: International Relations and the Movement of Household Service Workers," 81–118.

29 France settled German prisoners of war who stayed voluntarily.

30 "Isle of Despair," *Time*, 15 Mar. 1993, 20–27. Johannes-Dieter Steinert, *Migration und Politik: Westdeutschland—Europa—Übersee, 1945-1961* (Osnabrück, 1995), 28–37, 125–43, 175–89. Steeped in nineteenth-century concepts, population planners considered forming German enclaves by bloc settlement of emigrant farmers.

31 Steinert, *Migration und Politik*, 87–101, 220–38; Castles and Kosack, *Immigrant Workers and Class Structure*; Russell King, ed., *Mass Migration in Europe: The Legacy and the Future* (Chichester, U.K., 1993); David Pinder, ed., *The New Europe: Economy, Society, and Environment* (Chichester, U.K., 1998); Maria A. Roque, ed., *Human Movements in the Western Mediterranean* (Barcelona, 1989). A German-Moroccan recruitment agreement was not implemented owing to reduced labor needs after 1973.

32 Hans C. Buechler and Judith M. Buechler, eds., *Migrants in Europe: The Role of Family, Labor, and Politics* (New York, 1987); Colin Holmes, ed., *Migration in European History*, 2 vols. (Cheltenham, U.K., 1996); Ivo Baučič, "Yugoslavia as a Country of Emigration," *Options méditerranéennes* 5, 22 (1973): 55–66; Nermin Abadan-Unat, "Turkish Migration to Europe," in Cohen, *Cambridge Survey*, 279–84; Daniel Kubat, ed., *The Politics of Return: International Return Migration in Europe* (Rome, 1984); Mirjana Morokvasic, "Cash in Hand for the First Time: The Case of Yugoslav Immigrant Women in Europe," and Czarina Wilpert, "Migrant Women and Their Daughters: Two Generations of Turkish Women in the Federal Republic of Germany," in Reginald T. Appleyard and Charles Stahl, eds., *International Migration Today*, 2 vols. (Paris, 1988), 2:155–67, 168–86.

33 Christoph Butterwegge and Siegfried Jäger, eds., *Europa gegen den Rest der Welt? Flüchtlingsbewegungen, Einwanderung, Asylpolitik* (Cologne, 1993), and Butterwegge and Jäger, eds., *Rassismus in Europa* (Cologne, 1992); Phil Cohen and Harwant S. Bains, eds., *Multi-Racist Britain* (London, 1988); James Donald and Ali Rattansi, eds., *"Race," Culture, and Difference* (London, 1992), 62–103; Rattansi and Sallie Westwood, eds., *Racism, Modernity and Identity* (Cambridge, 1994); Alec G. Hargreaves, *Immigration, "Race" and Ethnicity in Contemporary France* (London, 1995); Maxim Silverman, *Deconstructing the Nation: Immigration, Racism, and Citizenship in Modern France* (London, 1992); John Rex, *Ethnic Minorities in the Modern Nation State* (London, 1996); Ian R. G. Spencer, *British Immigration Policy since 1939: The Making of Multi-Racial Britain* (London, 1997); Hans-Joachim Hoffmann-Nowotny, *Soziologie des Fremdarbeiterproblems: Eine theoretische und empirische Analyse am Beispiel der Schweiz* (Stuttgart, 1973); Didier Lapeyronnie, ed., *Immigrés en Europe: Politiques locales d'intégration* (Paris, 1992).

34 For North America, see Donna Gabaccia, *We Are What We Eat: Ethnic Food and the Making of Americans* (Cambridge, Mass., 1998).

35 Heinz Fassmann and Rainer Münz, eds., *European Migration in the Late Twentieth Cen-*

tury: *Historical Patterns, Actual Trends, and Social Implications* (Aldershot, U.K., 1994); Ronald E. Krane, ed., *International Labor Migration in Europe* (New York, 1979).

36 Philip Rees et al., eds., *Population Migration in the European Union* (Chichester, U.K., 1996); Maria B. Rocha-Trindade, *Recent Migration Trends in Europe: Europe's New Architecture* (Lisbon, 1993); Robert Miles and Dietrich Thränhardt, eds., *Migration and European Integration: The Dynamics of Inclusion and Exclusion* (London, 1995); Silvio Ronzani, *Arbeitskräftewanderung und gesellschaftliche Entwicklung: Erfahrungen in Italien, in der Schweiz und in der Bundesrepublik Deutschland* (Königstein/Taunus, 1980); Russell King and Richard Black, eds., *Southern Europe and the New Immigrations* (Brighton, U.K., 1997); Manuel Castells, "Immigrant Workers and Class Struggles in Advanced Capitalism: The Western European Experience," *Politics and Society* 5 (1975): 33–66.

37 The U.S. quota legislation divided the world into eastern and western hemispheres and still treated the two parts differently. Hania Zlotnik, "Policies and Migration Trends in the North American System," in Simmons, *The Impact of Free Trade*, 81–103; George J. Borjas, and Richard B. Freeman, eds., *Immigration and the Work Force: Economic Consequences for the United States and Source Areas* (Chicago, 1992); Michael C. Thornton, "The Quiet Immigration: Foreign Spouses of U.S. Citizens, 1945–1985," in Maria P. P. Root, ed., *Racially Mixed People in America* (Newbury Park, Calif., 1992), 64–76.

38 Stanley Lieberson and Mary C. Waters, *From Many Strands: Ethnic and Racial Groups in Contemporary America* (New York, 1988); Teitelbaum and Weiner, *Threatened Peoples* (New York, 1995); Rubén G. Rumbaut, "Origins and Destinies: Immigration to the United States since World War II," *Sociological Forum* 9 (1994): 583–621; Frank D. Bean, Robert G. Cushing, and Charles W. Haynes, "The Changing Demography of U.S. Immigration Flows: Patterns, Projections, and Contexts," in Klaus J. Bade and Myron Weiner, eds., *Migration Past, Migration Future: Germany and the United States* (Providence, R.I., 1997), 121–52.

39 Aristide Zolberg, "The Main Gate and the Back Door: The Politics of American Immigration Policy, 1950–76," paper presented at the Council on Foreign Relations, Washington, D.C., Apr. 1978; Kitty Calavita, "Mexican Immigration to the USA: The Contradictions of Border Control," in Cohen, *Cambridge Survey*, 236–44, Dillingham Commission quote on 236.

40 Figures are unreliable: immigrants from the former British possessions may define themselves as British; Caribbean-origin is predominantly African but includes Asian-origin as well as European-origin. Zucker and Zucker, "Cuban and Haitian Migrants," 447–51; Doris M. Meissner, "Political Asylum, Sanctuary and Humanitarian Policy," in Bruce Nichols and Gil Loescher, eds., *The Moral Nation: Humanitarianism and U.S. Foreign Policy Today* (Notre Dame, 1989), 123–43. Sidney W. Mintz, *Worker in the Cane: A Puerto Rican Life History* (1960; rev. ed., New York, 1974).

41 Constance R. Sutton and Elsa M. Chaney, eds., *Caribbean Life in New York City: Sociocultural Dimensions* (New York, 1992); Anthony H. Richmond, *Caribbean Immigrants: A Demo-Economic Analysis* (Ottawa, 1989).

42 Anthony H. Richmond, *Post-War Immigrants in Canada* (Toronto, 1967), and Richmond and Lawrence Lam, "Migration to Canada in the Post-War Period," in Cohen, *Cambridge Survey*, 263–70; D. Chuenyan Lai, "Emigration to Canada: Its Dimensions and Impact on Hong Kong," in Jean Burnet et al., eds., *Migration and the Transformation of Cultures* (Toronto, 1992), 241–52; C. Michael Lanphier, *A Study of Third-World Immigrants* (Ottawa, 1979).

43 G. Reginald Daniel, "Beyond Black and White: The New Multiracial Consciousness," in Root, *Racially Mixed People in America*, 333–41; Reynolds Farley, ed., *State of the Union:*

America in the 1990s, 2 vols. (New York, 1995): essays by Roderick J. Harrison and Claudette E. Bennett, William H. Frey, Barry R. Chiswick and Teresa A. Sullivan, 2:141–336; Richard D. Alba, *Ethnic Identity: The Transformation of White America* (New Haven, 1990); Mary C. Waters, *Ethnic Options: Choosing Identities in America* (Berkeley, 1990); Sharon M. Lee, "Racial Classification in the U.S. Census: 1890–1990," *Ethnic and Racial Studies* 16, 1 (Jan. 1993): 75–94; Angus Reid Group, *Multiculturalism and Canadians: National Attitude Study, 1991* (Ottawa, 1991); Jeffrey G. Reitz and Raymond Breton, *The Illusion of Difference: Realities of Ethnicity in Canada and the United States* (Toronto, 1994); Philip L. Martin, "Trade and Migration: The Case of NAFTA," *Asian and Pacific Migration Journal* 2 (1993): 329–67.

44 Zolberg, "The Main Gate and Back Door"; Demetrios G. Papademetriou, "International Migration in North America and Western Europe: Trends and Consequences," in Appleyard and Stahl, *International Migration Today*, 1:311–79, quote on 320; U.S. President's Commission on Migratory Labor, *Report on Migratory Labor in Agriculture* (Washington, D.C., 1951); Alan B. Simmons, ed., *International Migration, Refugee Flows and Human Rights in North America: The Impact of Free Trade and Restructuring* (New York, 1996), esp. essay by Kathryn Kopinak, "Household, Gender and Migration in Mexican *Maquiladoras:* The Case of Nogales," 214–28.

45 Mary M. Kritz, and Douglas T. Gurak, eds., *International Migration in Latin America*, special issue of *International Migration Review*, vol. 13 (New York, 1979); Aristide Zolberg and Robert C. Smith, *Migration Systems in Comparative Perspective: An Analysis of the Inter-American Migration System with Comparative Reference to the Mediterranean European System* (Washington, D.C., 1996); Jorge Balán, "International Migration in Latin America: Trends and Consequences," in Appleyard and Stahl, *International Migration Today*, 1:210–63.

46 Alan B. Simmons and Jean Pierre Guengnat, "Caribbean Exodus and the World System," in Mary M. Kritz, Lin L. Lim, and Hania Zlotnik, eds., *International Migration Systems: A Global Approach* (Oxford, 1992), 94–114; Bonham C. Richardson, *The Caribbean in the Wider World, 1492–1992: A Regional Geography* (Cambridge, 1992), 142–57; Ransford W. Palmer, ed., *U.S.-Caribbean Relations: Their Impact on Peoples and Culture* (Westport, Conn., 1998); Robert A. Pastor, ed., *Migration and Development in the Caribbean: The Unexplored Connection* (Boulder, 1985); Ceri Peach, *West Indian Migration to Britain: A Social Geography* (Oxford, 1968); Margaret Byron, *Post-War Caribbean Migration to Britain: The Unfinished Cycle* (Aldershot, U.K., 1994); Stuart Hall, "Migration from the English-Speaking Caribbean to the United Kingdom, 1950–80," in Appleyard and Stahl, *International Migration Today*, 1:264–310; Nancy Foner, "West Indians in New York City and London," in Sutton and Chaney, *Caribbean Life*, 108–20; Silvia Pedraza, "Review of Research: Cuba's Revolution and Exodus," *Journal of the International Institute* 5, 2 (winter 1998): 8–9; Juan E. Hernández-Cruz, "Migratory Trends in Puerto Rico: 1950 to the Present," in Cohen, *Cambridge Survey*, 248–52, and Ceri Peach, "Anglophone Caribbean Migration to the USA and Canada," ibid., 245–47; Paula L. Aymer, *Uprooted Women: Migrant Domestics in the Caribbean* (Westport, Conn., 1997); Elsa Chaney and Maria G. Castro, eds., *Muchachas No More: Household Workers in Latin America and the Caribbean* (Philadelphia, 1989).

47 Evelyn Hu-DeHart, "Coolies, Shopkeepers, Pioneers: The Chinese of Mexico and Peru, 1849–1930," *Amerasia Journal* 15, 2 (1989): 91–116; Jacques Vernant, *The Refugee in the Post-War World* (London, 1953), 579–678; Manuel Garcia y Griego, John R. Weeks, and Roberto H.

Chande, "Mexico," in William J. Serow et al., eds., *Handbook on International Migration* (New York, 1990), 205–20, quote on 209; Jorge A. Bustamante, "The Historical Context of the Undocumented Immigration from Mexico to the United States," *Aztlan* 3 (1972): 257–82; Alejandro Portes, ed., *Illegal Mexican Immigrants to the U.S.*, special issue of *International Migration Review* 12 (1978); Julian Samora, with Jorge Bustamante and Gilbert Cardenas, *Los Mojados: The Wetback Story* (Notre Dame, 1971).

48 Teiiti Suzuki, *The Japanese Immigrant in Brazil*, 2 vols. (Tokyo, 1969), 2:11–18; George Martine, "Brazil," in Charles B. Nam, William J. Serow, and David F. Sly, eds., *International Handbook on Internal Migration* (New York, 1990), 31–46; Fernando Bastos de Avila, "Immigration, Development and Industrial Expansion in Brazil," *Migration* 1, 3 (1961): 21–32. Herbert S. Klein, "European and Asian Migration to Brazil," in Cohen, *Cambridge Survey*, 208–14. Ecuador's development was similar to Brazil's: mainly internal cityward migration to the informal sector; Diego Palacios, "Ecuador," in *International Handbook on Internal Migration*, 85–101.

49 Alan B. Simmons, Sergio Diaz-Briquets, and Aprodicio A. Laquian, *Social Change and Internal Migration: A Review of Research Findings from Africa, Asia, and Latin America* (Ottawa, 1977), 89–92, quote on 79; Simmons, "The Emergence of Planning Orientations in a Modernizing Community: Migration, Adaptation, and Family Planning in Highland Colombia" (Ph.D. diss., Cornell Univ., 1970); Gabriel M. Castaño, "Effects of Emigration and Return on Sending Countries: The Case of Colombia"; Luz Marina Díaz, "The Migration of Labour in Colombia," in Cohen, *Cambridge Survey*, 223–25.

50 Elsa M. Chaney and Martha W. Lewis, *Women, Migration and the Decline of Smallholder Agriculture* (Washington, D.C., 1980), quote on 36, cited in Balán, "Latin America," quotes on 118, 232.

51 Balán, "Latin America," 221–227, and Balán, "The Role of Migration Policies and Social Networks in the Development of a Migration System in the Southern Cone," in Kritz et al., *International Migration Systems*, 115–30; Michael Micklin, "Guatemala," in *International Handbook on Internal Migration*, 163–87.

52 Balán, "Latin America," 248–56; Simmons et al., *Social Change and Internal Migration*, 86–88.

53 Studies quoted in Simmons et al., *Social Change and Internal Migration*, 80–81; Elizabeth G. Ferris, *The Central American Refugees* (New York, 1987); Jaime Llambias–Wolff, "Chile's Exiles and Their Return: Two Faces of Expatriation," in Cohen, *Cambridge Survey*, 229–31; *The State of the World's Refugees, 1995*, 50–51, 72, 150–51; Zolberg, Suhrke, and Aguayo, *Escape from Violence*, 180–224.

54 Gloria H. Chun, "'Go West . . . to China': Chinese American Identity in the 1930s," in K. Scott Wong and Sucheng Chan, eds., *Claiming America: Constructing Chinese American Identities during the Exclusion Era* (Philadelphia, 1998), 165–90. The 1952 U.S. immigration law maintained racial discriminatory criteria by establishing an Asia-Pacific triangle from India to Japan to the Pacific Islands with a joint total quota of only 2,000.

55 Evelyn Hu-DeHart, "Latin America in Asia-Pacific Perspective," in Arif Dirlik, ed., *What Is in a Rim? Critical Perspectives on the Pacific Region Idea* (1993; 2d ed., Lanham, Md., 1998), 251–82; Stephen Fitzgerald, *China and the Overseas Chinese: A Study of Peking's Changing Policy, 1949–1970* (Cambridge, 1972); James T. Fawcett and Benjamin V. Cariño, eds., *Pacific Bridges: The New Immigration from Asia and the Pacific Islands* (Staten Island, N.Y., 1987); Daniel Kubat, "Asian Immigrants to Canada," ibid., 29–45, table on 233; Fred

Arnold, Urmil Minocha, and James T. Fawcett, "The Changing Face of Asian Migration to the United States," ibid., 105–52; Bill O. Hing, *Making and Remaking Asian America through Immigration Policy, 1850–1990* (Stanford, 1993), table on 48; Sean Brawley, *The White Peril: Foreign Relations and Asian Immigration to Australasia and North America, 1919–1978* (Sydney, 1995).

56 John M. Liu, "A Comparative View of Asian Immigration to the USA," in Cohen, *Cambridge Survey*, 253–59; John M. Liu, Paul M. Ong, and Carolyn Rosenstein, "Dual Chain Migration: Post-1965 Filipino Immigration to the United States," *International Migration Review* 25 (1991): 487–515.

57 Linda W. Gordon, "Southeast Asian Refugee Migration to the United States," in Fawcett and Cariño, *Pacific Bridges*, 153–73; Bruce Grant, *The Boat People: An "Age" Investigation* (New York, 1980); William Liu, Maryanne Lamanna, and Alice Murata, *Transition to Nowhere: Vietnamese Refugees in America* (Nashville, 1979); Astri Suhrke, "Indochinese Refugees: The Law and Politics of First Asylum," *Annals of the American Academy of Political and Social Science* 467 (1983): 102–15; Jacqueline Desbarats, "Indochinese Resettlement in the United States," *Annals of the Association of American Geographers* 75 (1985): 522–28; Chan Kwok Bun, "The Vietnamese Boat People in Hong Kong," in Cohen, *Cambridge Survey*, 380–85.

58 Ronald T. Takaki, *Strangers from a Different Shore: A History of Asian Americans* (Boston, 1989), 357–491; Sucheng Chan, *Asian Americans: An Interpretative History* (Boston, 1991); Donna Gabaccia, "Women of the Mass Migrations: From Minority to Majority, 1820–1930," in Dirk Hoerder and Leslie P. Moch, eds., *European Migrants: Global and Local Perspectives* (Boston, 1996), 90–111; Monica Boyd, "Female Migrant Labor in North America: Trends and Issues for the 1990s," in Simmons, *Impact of Free Trade*, 193–213, and Boyd, "Immigrant Women in Canada," in Rita J. Simon and Caroline B. Brettell, eds., *International Migration: The Female Experience* (Totowa, N.J., 1986), 45–61; Paul W. Kuznets, "Koreans in America: Recent Migration from South Korea to the United States," in Sidney Klein, ed., *The Economics of Mass Migration in the Twentieth Century* (New York, 1987), 41–69; Elliott R. Barkan, *Asian and Pacific Islander Migration to the United States: A Model of New Global Patterns* (Westport, Conn., 1992); Cathy A. Small, *Voyages: From Tongan Villages to American Suburbs* (Ithaca, 1997).

59 Sally M. Miller, A. J. H. Latham, and Dennis O. Flynn, eds., *Studies in the Economic History of the Pacific Rim* (London, 1998); Dirlik, *What Is in a Rim?*

60 Constance Lever-Tracy and Michael Quinlan, *A Divided Working Class: Ethnic Segmentation and Industrial Conflict in Australia* [1960s–70s] (London, 1988); Werner Senn and Giovanna Capone, eds., *The Making of a Pluralist Australia, 1950–1990: Selected Papers from the Inaugural EASA Conference, 1991* (Bern, 1992); Stephen Castles et al., *Mistaken Identity: Multiculturalism and the Demise of Nationalism in Australia* (Sydney, 1990); Christine Inglis et al., eds., *Asians in Australia: The Dynamics of Migration and Settlement* (Singapore, 1992); Laksiri Jayasuriya, "Immigration Policies and Ethnic Relations in Australia," in O. P. Dwivedi et al., eds., *Canada 2000: Race Relations and Public Policy* (Guelph, 1989).

61 Richard Bedford, "International Migration in the South Pacific Region," in Kritz et al., *International Migration Systems*, 41–62; Epeli Hau'ofa, "The New South Pacific Society: Integration and Independence," in Anthony Hooper et al., eds., *Class and Culture in the South Pacific* (Suva, Fiji, 1987), 1–16; G. Lakshmana Rao, Anthony H. Richmond, and Jerzy Zu-

brzycki, *Immigrants in Canada and Australia* (Toronto, 1984); Huw R. Jones, "Immigration Policy and the New World Order: The Case of Australia," in Gould and Findlay, *Population Migration*, 161–72; Charles A. Price, "The Asian and Pacific Island Peoples of Australia," in Fawcett et al., *Pacific Bridges*, 175–97; Andrew D. Trlin, "New Zealand's Admission of Asians and Pacific Islanders," ibid., 199–227.

62 A. J. H. Latham, "The Reconstruction of Hong Kong Nineteenth-Century Pacific Trade Statistics: The Emergence of Asian Dynamism," in Miller, Latham, and Flynn, *Pacific Rim*, 155–71; Neferti Xina M. Tadiar, "Sexual Economies in the Asia-Pacific Community," in Dirlik, *Critical Perspectives*, 219–48; Leon F. Bouvier and Anthony J. Agresta, "The Future Asian Population of the United States," in Fawcett et al., *Pacific Bridges*, 285–301; Ronald Skeldon, "East Asian Migration and the Changing World Order," in Gould and Findlay, *Population Migration*, 173–93, esp. 182.

63 Essays by Dirlik, Alexander Woodside, Bruce Cumings, and Donald M. Nonini in Dirlik, *Critical Perspectives*, 3–96; Wing Tek Lum, "East/West Poem," (1980), repr. in Rob Wilson, "Blue Hawaii: *Bamboo Ridge* as 'Critical Regionalism,'" ibid., 325–26.

64 Ronald Skeldon, "International Migration within and from the East and Southeast Asian Region: A Review Essay," *Asian and Pacific Migration Journal* 1 (1992): 19–63; Charles W. Stahl, Reginald T. Appleyard, and Toshikazu Nagayama, eds., *International Manpower Flows and Foreign Investment in Asia,* special issue of *Asian and Pacific Migration Journal* 1, 3–4 (1992), esp. Stahl and Appleyard, "International Manpower Flows in Asia: An Overview," 417–76; Appleyard, "Asia and the Pacific," 91.

65 Edgar Wickberg, "The Chinese as Overseas Migrants," in Judith M. Brown and Rosemary Foot, eds., *Migration: The Asian Experience* (New York, 1994), 12–27, relying on official figures places the number of Overseas Chinese as high as 30 million in 1989. Leo Suryadinata, ed., *The Ethnic Chinese in the ASEAN States: Bibliographical Essays* (Singapore, 1989), and Suryadinata, ed., *Political Thinking of the Indonesian Chinese, 1900–1995: A Sourcebook* (2d ed., Singapore, 1997); Lamgen Leon, *Asians in Latin America and the Caribbean: A Bibliography* (Flushing, N.Y., 1990); Donald E. Willmott, "The National Status of the Chinese in Indonesia" (mimeographed; Ithaca, N.Y., 1956); Indira Ramanathan, *China and the Ethnic Chinese in Malaysia and Indonesia, 1949–1992* (New Delhi, 1994).

66 T. Hayase, "Overseas Chinese in Southeast Asia," *Oriental Economist* [Tokyo] 33, 660 (1965): 580–84, cited in Reginald T. Appleyard, "International Migration in Asia and the Pacific," in Appleyard and Stahl, *International Migration Today*, 1:89–167; Wang Gungwu, "Sojourning: The Chinese Experience in Southeast Asia," unpublished Jennifer Cushman Memorial Lecture, 1992, which provides the best discussion of concepts related sojourning and migration; Daniel Chirot and Anthony Reid, eds., *Essential Outsiders? Chinese and Jews in the Modern Transformation of Southeast Asia and Central Europe* (Seattle, 1997).

67 Paul M. Ong, Lucie Cheng, and Leslie Evans, "Migration of Highly Educated Asians and Global Dynamics," *Asian and Pacific Migration Journal* 1 (1992): 543–67; Liisa Cormode, "Japanese Foreign Direct Investment and the Circulation of Personnel from Japan to Canada," in W. T. S. Gould and A. M. Findlay, eds., *Population Migration and the Changing World Order* (Chichester, U.K., 1994), 67–89; John Salt, "Highly Skilled International Migrants, Careers and International Labour Markets," *Geoforum* 19 (1988): 387–99; Appleyard, "Asia and the Pacific," 91–93; Skeldon, "East Asian Migration," 187–88.

68 The Great Leap Forward (1958–61) resulted in a famine during which an estimated 20 million people were relocated from the cities. During the Cultural Revolution, hundreds of

thousands of returned Overseas Chinese were accused of bourgeois mentality. Many fled to Hong Kong or Macao.

69 In 1998, Indonesian Chinese, especially those of Jakarta, were scapegoated during the riots against the corrupt Suharto regime. Gendered violence involved sexual attacks on women.

70 McDowell, *Understanding Impoverishment,* 4; Appleyard, "Asia and the Pacific," 99–100.

71 Muriel Charras and Marc Pain, eds., *Spontaneous Settlements in Indonesia: Agricultural Pioneers in Southern Sumatra* (Paris, 1993), 16–37 passim; Clark E. Cunningham, *The Postwar Migration of the Toba-Bataks to East Sumatra* (New Haven, 1958); essays by Judith Strauch, Veena N. Thadani/Michael P. Todaro, Peter C. Smith/Siew-Ean Khoo, and Stella P. Go in Fawcett et al., *Women in the Cities of Asia,* 15–77.

72 Philip M. Hauser, Daniel B. Suits, and Naohiro Ogawa, eds., *Urbanization and Migration in ASEAN Development* (Tokyo, 1985); UN, *Migration and Urbanization,* 1–9, 25, quote on 9; Lee On-Jook, *Urban-to-Rural Return Migration in Korea* (Seoul, 1984); Ashok K. Dutt et al., eds., *The Asian City: Processes of Development, Characteristics, and Planning* (Dordrecht, 1994), 279–352; Dean K. Forbes, *Asian Metropolis: Urbanisation and the Southeast Asian City* (Melbourne, 1996), 14–26.

73 Between 1949 and the 1970s, millions of urban dwellers were repeatedly forced for ideological reasons or by famine to move to the countryside. An estimated 17 million urban youths were sent to villages after 1968.

74 G. J. R. Linge and D. K. Forbes, eds., *China's Spatial Economy: Recent Developments and Reforms* (Hong Kong, 1990), 129–43, 181–92; Hu Zhenliang and Ye Qingfeng, "Migration of Farm Labour in Today's China: Features, Problems and Policies," paper given at Thirty-first Linz Conference, Sept. 1995; Dennis T. Yang, "Rural-Urban Migration Issues in Contemporary China," paper given at "Capitalist Restructuring and Labor: Asia and Americas" symposium, Duke University, Feb. 1995. Ashwani Saith, *The Re-emergence of the Chinese Peasantry: Aspects of Rural Decollectivisation* (London, 1987), 65–71; Graham E. Clarke, "The Movement of Population to the West of China: Tibet and Qinghai," in Brown and Foot, *Asian Experience,* 221–57.

75 On distribution of ethnic groups: Population Census Office of the State Council of the People's Republic of China and the Institute of Geography of the Chinese Academy of Sciences, *The Population Atlas of China* (Hong Kong, 1987), 26–39; Aihwa Ong and Donald M. Nonini, eds., *Ungrounded Empires: The Cultural Politics of Modern Chinese Transnationalism* (London, 1997). On ethnicity in China, see Nicole Constable, ed., *Guest People: Hakka Identity in China and Abroad* (Seattle, 1996); Colin Mackerras, *China's Minority Cultures: Identities and Integration since 1912* (New York, 1995); Frank Dikötter, ed., *The Construction of Racial Identities in China and Japan: Historical and Contemporary Perspectives* (London, 1997); Leo J. Moser, *The Chinese Mosaic: The Peoples and Provinces of China* (Boulder, 1985). Press reports in January 2000 indicate that one-tenth of the resettlement funds had been misappropriated by corrupt officials.

76 Edward W. Wagner, "The Korean Minority in Japan, 1904–1950" (mimeographed; New York: Institute of Pacific Relations, 1951); Richard H. Mitchell, *The Korean Minority in Japan* (Berkeley, 1967); Wolfgang Herbert, *Foreign Workers and Law Enforcement in Japan* (London, 1996), 3–39; Takashi Oka, *Prying Open the Door: Foreign Workers in Japan* (Washington, D.C., 1994), 1–10; Hiroshi Komai, *Migrant Workers in Japan,* trans. Jens Wilkinson (Japanese orig., n.d.; London, 1995); Yoshio Kawashima, "Japanese Laws and Practices on Indo-Chinese Refugees," *Osaka University Law Review* 38, 2 (1991): 1–12; Toshikazu Naga-

yama, "Clandestine Migrant Workers in Japan," *Asian and Pacific Migration Journal* 1 (1992): 417–76; Yoko Sellek, "Illegal Foreign Migrant Workers in Japan: Change and Challenge to Japanese Society," in Brown and Foot, *Asian Experience*, 169–201; Hiromi Mori, *Immigration Policy and Foreign Workers in Japan* (New York, 1997).

77 Mori, *Immigration Policy and Foreign Workers*; Haruo Shimada, *Japan's "Guest Workers": Issues and Public Policies*, trans. Roger Northridge (Japanese orig., n.d.; Tokyo, 1994).

78 Wang Gungwu, "Migration Patterns in History: Malaysia and the Region," *Journal of the Malaysian Branch of the Royal Asiatic Society* 58 (1985): 43–57; Graeme J. Hugo, "Indonesian Labour Migration to Malaysia: Trends and Policy Implications," *Southeast Asian Journal of Social Science* 21 (1993): 36–70; Siew-Ean Khoo and Peter Pirie, "Female Rural-to-Urban Migration in Peninsular Malaysia," and Jamilah Ariffin, "Migration of Women Workers in Peninsular Malaysia: Impact and Implications," in Fawcett et al., *Women in the Cities of Asia*, 125–42, 213–26; James Nayagam, "Migrant Labor Absorption in Malaysia," *Asian and Pacific Migration Journal* 1 (1992): 477–94; Aihwa Ong, *Spirits of Resistance and Capitalist Discipline: Factory Women in Malaysia* (Albany, 1987).

79 Pang Eng Fong, "Absorbing Temporary Foreign Workers: The Experience of Singapore," *Asian and Pacific Migration Journal* 1 (1992): 495–509, quote on 495; Jasmina Kuzmanovic, "Singapore's Foreign Maids," *Toronto Globe and Mail*, 30 July 1998, quotes; Geraldine Heng and Janadas Devan, "State Fatherhood: The Politics of Nationalism, Sexuality and Race in Singapore," in Andrew Parker et al., eds., *Nationalisms and Sexualities* (New York, 1992), 343–64.

80 Sun-Hee Lee, *Why People Intend to Move: Individual and Community-Level Factors of Out-Migration in the Philippines* (Boulder, 1985); Sally E. Findley, *Rural Development and Migration: A Study of Family Choices in the Philippines* (Boulder, 1987); Lillian Trager, *The City Connection: Migration and Family Interdependence in the Philippines* (Ann Arbor, 1988); Cynthia H. Enloe, "Women Textile Workers in the Militarization of Southeast Asia," in June Nash and María P. Fernández-Kelly, eds., *Women, Men, and the International Division of Labor* (Albany, 1983), 407–25.

81 Norman G. Owen, "On the Margins of Asia: The Philippines since 1500," in A. J. H. Latham and H. Kawakatsu, eds., *The Evolving Structure of the East Asian Economic System since 1700: A Comparative Analysis* (Milan, 1994), 69–80, quote on 77; Elizabeth U. Eviota and Peter C. Smith, "The Migration of Women in the Philippines," in Fawcett et al., *Women in the Cities of Asia*, 165–90; Nicole Constable, *Maid to Order in Hong Kong: Stories of Filipina Workers* (Ithaca, N.Y., 1997); Nona Grandea, *Uneven Gains: Filipina Domestic Workers in Canada* (Ottawa, 1996); Jane A. Margold, "From Assembly Line to Front Line: Transnational Capital and Factory Women in the Philippines," unpublished paper, Duke University, Feb. 1995, quotes on 5, 17; Gary Y. Okihiro, "Comparing Colonialisms and Migrations, Puerto Rico and the Philippines," unpublished paper, Duke University, Feb. 1995; Irene Fernandez, "Multinationals and Women," in Women's International Solidarity Affair in the Philippines, *The Culture of Foreign Domination: Women's Issues, Alternatives and Initiatives* (Manila, 1992), 99–102; Joaquin L. Gonzalez, *Philippine Labour Migration: Critical Dimensions of Public Policy* (Singapore, 1998).

82 Myron Weiner, *Sons of the Soil: Migration and Ethnic Conflict in India* (Princeton, 1978), quotes on 3, 40–52, migration by ethnic group on 62–74; Lok R. Baral, *Regional Migrations, Ethnicity and Security: The South Asian Case* (New Delhi, 1990); Jan C. Breman, *Of Peasants, Migrants, and Paupers: Rural Labour Circulation and Capitalist Production in*

West India (Delhi, 1985), 404–6, 424–25, and Breman and Sudipto Mundle, *Rural Transformation in Asia* (Delhi, 1992), and Breman, *Footloose Labour: Working in India's Informal Economy* (Cambridge, 1997), 49–83, 264; A. M. Shah, "The Rural-Urban Networks in India," *South Asia* 11, 2 (Dec. 1988): 1–27; Andrea M. Singh, "Rural-to-Urban Migration of Women in India: Patterns and Implications," and Nasra M. Shah, "The Female Migrant in Pakistan," in Fawcett et al., *Women in the Cities of Asia*, 81–107, 108–24; Haraprasad Chattopadhyaya, *Internal Migration in India: A Case Study in Bengal* (Calcutta, 1987); Mbjid Husain and M. Hasseena Hashia, *Seasonal Migration of Kashmiri Labour: A Spatio-Temporal Analysis* (New Delhi, 1989).

83 Weiner, *Sons of the Soil*, 19–21, quote on 17; Ashok R. Basu, "Urban Squatters in South Asia," in R. C. Sharma, ed., *South Asian Urban Experience* (New Delhi, 1988), 111–26.

84 Baral, *Regional Migration*, 31–33; Zolberg, Suhrke, Aguayo, *Escape from Violence*, 150–79; David Seddon, "Migration: Nepal and India," in Cohen, *Cambridge Survey*, 367–70; *Newsweek*, 13 June 1994; *Frankfurter Rundschau*, 6 June 1994.

85 Baral, *Regional Migration*, 6–7, 35–30; Christopher McDowell, *A Tamil Asylum Diaspora: Sri Lankan Migration, Settlement and Politics in Switzerland* (Providence, R.I., 1996), 15–23, 69–115; H. P. Chattopadhyaya, *Ethnic Unrest in Modern Sri Lanka: An Account of Tamil-Sinhalese Race Relations* (New Delhi, 1994); Sinnappah Arasaratnam, *Sri Lanka after Independence: Nationalism, Communalism, and Nation Building* (Madras, 1986); Chelvadurai Manogaran, *Ethnic Conflict and Reconciliation in Sri Lanka* (Honolulu, 1987).

86 Appleyard, "Asia and the Pacific," 110–14; Balán, "International Migration," 249; Colin Clarke, Ceri Peach, and Steven Vertovec, eds., *South Asians Overseas: Migration and Ethnicity* (Cambridge, 1990), 17–23; Milton Israel and N. K. Wagle, eds., *Ethnicity, Identity, Migration: The South Asian Context* (Toronto, 1993); Ijaz S. Gilani, *Citizens, Slaves, Guest-Workers: The Dynamics of Labour Migration from South Asia* (Islamabad, 1985), 20–23; Deepak Nayyar, "International Labour Migration from India: A Macro-Economic Analysis," in Rashid Amjad, ed., *To the Gulf and Back: Studies on the Economic Impact of Asian Labour Migration* (New Delhi, 1989), 95–142, 98; Hassan N. Gardezi, *The Political Economy of International Labour Migration* (Montreal, 1995).

87 Constance Lever-Tracy et al., *Asian Entrepreneurs in Australia: Ethnic Small Business in the Chinese and Indian Communities of Brisbane and Sydney* (Canberra, 1991); Melanie Knights, "Migrants as Networkers: The Economies of Bangladeshi Migration to Rome," in King and Black, *Southern Europe and the New Immigrations*, 113–37; R. A. Mahmood, "Bangladeshi Immigrants in the United Kingdom," *Bangladesh Public Administration Journal* 4, 2 (1990): 75–98. Graeme Hugo, "Illegal International Migration in Asia," in Cohen, *Cambridge Survey*, 397–402; Anchalee Singhanetra-Renard, "The Mobilization of Labour Migrants in Thailand: Personal Links and Facilitating Networks," in Kritz et al., *International Migration Systems*, 190–220; Chung-tong Wu and Christine Inglis, "Illegal Immigration to Hong Kong," *Asian and Pacific Migration Journal* 1 (1992): 601–22; Charles W. Stahl, "Labor Migration amongst the ASEAN Countries," in Hauser, Suits, and Ogawa, *Urbanization and Migration*, 109–29; Asian Population and Development Association, *Labor Migration in Asia* (Tokyo, 1992).

88 Ian J. Seccombe, "International Migration in the Middle East: Historical Trends, Contemporary Patterns and Consequences," in Appleyard and Stahl, *International Migration Today*, 1:180–209, esp. 180–96; Günter Meyer, "Labour Migration into the Gulf Region and the Impact of the Latest Gulf War," *Applied Geography and Development* 39 (1992): 106–25; Gilani,

Citizens, 25; Rafic Boustani and Philippe Fargues, *The Atlas of the Arab World: Geopolitics and Society* (New York, 1990), 28–30; Mordechai Nisan, *Minorities in the Middle East: A History of Struggle and Self-Expression* (London, 1991).

89   Boustani and Fargues, *Arab World*, 103–4, 106, 118–19.

90   Laila El-Hamamsy and Jeannie Garrison, eds., *Human Settlements on New Lands: Their Design and Development* (Cairo, 1979), 75–113, quote on 370; Camillia Fawzi El-Solh, "Egyptian Peasant Women in Iraq: Adapting to Migration," in Abebe Zegeye and Shubi Ishemo, eds., *Forced Labour and Migration: Patterns of Movement within Africa* (London, 1989), 370–402; Eare L. Sullivan and Karina Korayem, "Women and Work in the Arab World," *Cairo Papers in Social Science* (1981); Mona Abaza, "The Changing Image of Women in Rural Egypt," *Cairo Papers in Social Science* (1987).

91   J. S. Birks and C. A. Sinclair, *International Migration and Development in the Arab Region* (Geneva, 1980), and Birks et al., "Who Is Migrating Where? An Overview of International Labor Migration in the Arab World," in Alan Richards and Philip L. Martin, eds., *Migration, Mechanization, and Agricultural Labor Markets in Egypt* (Cairo, 1983), 103–116, and Birks et al., "The Demand for Egyptian Labor Abroad," ibid., 117–34; Gilani, *Citizens*, 24–30; Godfrey Gunatilleke, ed., *Migration of Asian Workers to the Arab World* (Tokyo, 1986); Amjad, *To the Gulf and Back*; Myron Weiner, "International Migration and Development: Indians in the Persian Gulf," *Population and Development Review* 8 (1982): 1–36; *Labor Migration in Asia*, 14–15, 25–29; Appleyard, "Asia and the Pacific," 101–105; Meyer, "Labour Migration," 114; Onn Winckler, *Population Growth and Migration in Jordan, 1950–1994* (Brighton, U.K., 1997).

92   Meyer, "Labour Migration," 110–18; Gilani, *Citizens*, 69–70.

93   Muinul Islam, "Bangladeshi Migration: An Impact Study," in Cohen, *Cambridge Survey*, 360–66; Weiner, "Indians in the Persian Gulf," 7; Edita A. Tan and Dante B. Canlas, "Migrant's Saving Remittances and Labour Supply Behaviour: The Philippines Case," in Amjad, *To the Gulf and Back*, 223–54, F. R. Arcinas, "The Philippines," in Gunatilleke, *Migration of Asian Workers*, 259–305, 267, 294–98; Ijaz S. Gilani, "Effects of Emigration and Return on Sending Countries: The Case of Pakistan," in Appleyard and Stahl, *International Migration Today*, 2:204–16. Nurses often migrate to Europe, the United States, or Hong Kong.

94   Boustani and Fargues, *Arab World*, 98, 105; Meyer, "Labour Migration," 120–23; Arcinas, "The Philippines," 282–85; the Asian Population and Development Association's *Labor Migration in Asia* surveys exit programs. Weiner, "Indians in the Persian Gulf," 6, 18–22 passim.

95   Allan M. Findlay, "Return to Yemen: The End of the Old Migration Order in the Arab World," in Gould and Findlay, *Population Migration*, 205–23; Nicholas van Hear, "Displaced People after the Gulf Crisis," in Cohen, *Cambridge Survey*, 424–30; John Connell and Jenny Wang, "Distant Victims? The Impact of the Gulf War on International Migration to the Middle East from Asia," in Kattalai S. Ramachandran, ed., *Gulf War and Environmental Problems* (New Delhi, 1991), 275–318.

96   Amin, *Modern Migrations*, 115–19; Aderanti Adepoju, "Migration in Africa: An Overview," in Jonathan Baker and Tade A. Aina, eds., *The Migration Experience in Africa* (Uppsala, 1995), 87–108; Joseph B. Schechtman, *The Refugee in the World: Displacement and Integration* (New York, 1964), 329–47; Shubi L. Ishemo, "Forced Labour and Migration in Portugal's African Colonies," in Cohen, *Cambridge Survey*, 162–65.

97   G. O. Olusanya, "The Nigerian Civil Service in the Colonial Era: A Study of Imperial Re-

actions to Changing Circumstances," in Boniface I. Obichere, ed., *Studies in Southern Nigerian History* (London, 1982), 175–200; Vaughan Robinson, "The Migration of East African Asians to the UK," in Cohen, *Cambridge Survey*, 331–36; Krishna Ahooja-Patel, "Regulations Governing the Employment of Non-Nationals in West Africa," in Amin, *Modern Migrations*, 170–90; Anthony I. Asiwaju, ed., *Partitioned Africans: Ethnic Relations across Africa's International Boundaries, 1884–1984* (London, 1984).

98 Essays by Aderanti Adepoju, A. Ahianyo-Akakpo, and J. Bugnicourt in Amin, *Modern Migrations*, 127–37, 138–55, 191–214. William J. Hanna and Judith L. Hanna, *Urban Dynamics in Black Africa: An Interdisciplinary Approach* (Chicago, 1971), 27–73, 107–43; Kenneth Little, *Urbanization as a Social Process: An Essay on Movement and Change in Contemporary Africa* (London, 1974), 7–19, 40–54, and Little, *West African Urbanization: A Study of Voluntary Associations in Social Change* (Cambridge, 1965); Josef Gugler and William G. Flanagan, *Urbanization and Social Change in West Africa* (Cambridge, 1978), 50–73; Helmuth Heisler, *Urbanisation and the Government of Migration: The Inter-Relation of Urban and Rural Life in Zambia* (New York, 1974).

99 Adepoju, "Migration in Africa," 94–97; Catherine Coquery-Vidrovitch, *African Women: A Modern History*, trans. Beth G. Raps (French orig., 1994; Boulder, 1997); essays on women in Baker and Aina, *Migration Experience in Africa*, 257–338.

100 In 1995, almost 800,000 Liberians and 240,000 Sierra Leoneans fled to neighboring states, and another 800,000 and 300,000 were internally displaced. *State of the World's Refugees*, quote on 114.

101 Art Hansen and Della E. McMillan, eds., *Food in Sub-Saharan Africa* (London, 1986); Johnathan Bascom, "The New Nomads: An Overview of Involuntary Migration in Africa," in Baker and Aina, *Migration Experience in Africa*, 197–219, esp. 200–201; Boustani and Fargues, *Arab World*, 81; Peter Kohn, "Repatriation of African Exiles: The Decision to Return," in Cohen, *Cambridge Survey*, 347–52; Tim Allen and Hubert Morsink, eds., *When Refugees Go Home: African Experiences* (Geneva, 1994), esp. editors' introduction and essays by John R. Rogge and Barry N. Stein, 1–70; Adepoju, "Migration in Africa," 101–4.

102 Boustani and Fargues, *Arab World*, maps on 98, 102; *Le Monde*, 12 June 1996.

103 Amin, "Migrations in Contemporary Africa: A Retrospective View," in Baker and Aina, *Migration Experience in Africa*, 29–40; Aderanti Adepoju, "International Migration in Africa South of the Sahara," in Appleyard and Stahl, *International Migration Today*, 1:17–88, esp. 60–78; Paulina Makinwa-Adebusoye, "The West African Migration System," in Kritz, Lim, Zlotnik, *International Migration Systems*, 63–79; Elisabeth N'Doye, "Migration des pionniers Mourid wolof vers les terres neuves: Rôle de l'économie et du religieux," and Elizabeth Dussauze-Ingrand, "L'Émigration Sarakollaise du Guidimake vers la France," in Amin, *Modern Migrations*, 239–57, 371–83; Dennis D. Cordell, Joel W. Gregory, and Victor Piché, *Hoe and Wage: A Social History of a Circular Migration System in West Africa* (Boulder, 1996); Manchuelle, *Soninke Labor Diasporas*, 179–211; Michel Samuel, *Le Prolétariat africain noir en France: Témoignages* (Paris, 1978).

104 Moriba Touré and T. O. Fadayomi, eds., *Migrations, Development and Urbanization Policies in Sub-Saharan Africa* (Dakar, 1992), 7–152; Leslie Green, "Migration, Urbanization, and National Development in Nigeria," in Amin, *Modern Migrations*, 281–304; Austin M. Ahanotu, "The Role of Ethnic Unions in the Development of Southern Nigeria: 1916–66," in Obichere, *Southern Nigerian History*, 155–74.

105 Hilda Kuper, ed., *Urbanization and Migration in West Africa* (Berkeley, 1965); J. Adomako-

Sarfoh, "The Effects of Expulsion of Migrant Workers on Ghana's Economy," in Amin, *Modern Migrations*, 138–55.

106 Adepoju, "Africa South of the Sahara," 22–36; Laurent Monnier, *Ethnie et intégration régionale au Congo: Le Kongo Central, 1962–1965* (Paris, 1968).

107 *State of the World's Refugees*, 174–75; K. B. Wilson, "Refugees, Displaced People and Returnees in Southern Africa," in Cohen, *Cambridge Survey*, 434–40; Jonathan Crush, "Cheap Gold: Mine Labour in Southern Africa," ibid., 172–77; Alan H. Jeeves, "Migrant Labour and the State under Apartheid, 1948–1989," ibid., 178–82.

108 P. G. Powesland, "History of the Migration in Uganda," in Audrey I. Richards, ed., *Economic Development and Tribal Change: A Study of Immigrant Labour in Buganda* (rev. ed., Nairobi, 1973), 17–51; Walter Elkan, *Migrants and Proletarians: Urban Labour in the Economic Development of Uganda* (London, 1960), 21–47; W. T. S. Gould, "Mission and Migration in Colonial Kenya," in Chris Dixon and Michael J. Heffernan, eds., *Colonialism and Development in the Contemporary World* (London, 1991), 92–105, quote on 102; Sharon B. Stichter, *Migrant Labour in Kenya: Capitalism and African Response, 1895–1975* (London, 1982); C. M. F. Lwoga, "From Long-Term to Seasonal Labour: Migration in Iringa Region, Tanzania: A Legacy of the Colonial Forced Labour System," in Zegeye and Ishemo, *Forced Labour and Migration*, 180–210.

109 J. S. Mangat, *A History of the Asians in East Africa, c.1886 to 1945* (Oxford, 1969), 132–78; Richa Nagar, "The South Asian Diaspora in Tanzania: A History Retold," *Comparative Studies of South Asia, Africa and the Middle East* 16, 2 (1996): 62–80; Milly Charon, *Between Two Worlds: The Canadian Immigrant Experience* (1983; rev. ed., Montreal, 1988), 303–13. See also the personal account in Thomas P. Melady and Margaret B. Melady, *Uganda: The Asian Exiles* (Maryknoll, N.Y., 1976).

110 Allen and Morsink, *When Refugees Go Home*, 50–54, 96–104; W. T. S. Gould, "Regional Labour Migration Systems in East Africa: Continuity and Change," in Cohen, *Cambridge Survey*, 183–89, and Gould, "Migration and Recent Economic and Environmental Change in East Africa," in Baker and Aina, *Migration Experience in Africa*, 122–45; Adepoju, "Africa South of the Sahara," 36–46; Milline J. Mbonile, "Migration and Urban Development in Tanzania: Internal Responses to Structural Adjustment," in Gould and Findlay, *Population Migration*, 249–71; Margaret Strobel, *Muslim Women in Mombasa 1890–1975* (New Haven, 1979), quote on 220.

111 Johnathan Bascom, "The Dynamics of Refugee Repatriation: The Case of the Eritreans in Eastern Sudan," in Gould and Findlay, *Population Migration*, 225–48; Bruce Nichols, "Rescuing Ethiopia's Black Jews," in Nichols and Loescher, *Moral Nation*, 288–310; Abebe Zegeye, "Hunger, War, and Flight: The Horn of Africa," in Cohen, *Cambridge Survey*, 441–46; Boustani and Fargues, *Arab World*, 34–36.

112 Aderanti Adepoju, "Links between Internal and International Migration: The African Situation," in Appleyard and Stahl, *International Migration Today*, 2:24–45; Laura Bigman, "Contemporary Migration from Africa to the USA," in Cohen, *Cambridge Survey*, 260–62; Robinson, "Migration of East African Asians to the UK," ibid., 331–36; R. Mansell Prothero and Murray Chapman, eds., *Circulation in Third World Countries* (London, 1985).

113 Janez Malacic, "Labor Migration from Former Yugoslavia," in Fassmann and Münz, *European Migration*, 207–219; Vladimir Grecic, "Former Yugoslavia," in Solon Ardittis, ed., *The Politics of East-West Migration* (New York, 1994), 126–35.

114 Paul Compton, "Migration in Eastern Europe," in John Salt and Hugh Clout, eds., *Mi-*

gration in Post-War Europe: Geographical Essays (Oxford, 1976), 168–219, quote on 168; Leszek A. Kosinski, "Urbanization in East-Central Europe after World War II," *Eastern European Quarterly* 8 (1974): 130–53.

115 Andrei Rogers, *Migration and Settlement: A Multiregional Comparative Study* (Dordrecht, 1986), Svetlana Soboleva on the Soviet Union, 284–304; Anatoli Vishnevsky and Zhanna Zayonchkovskaya, "Emigration from the Soviet Union: The Fourth Wave," in Fassmann and Münz, *European Migration*, 239–59; Alexei Polyakov and Igor Ushkalov, "Migrations in Socialist and Post-Socialist Russia," in Cohen, *Cambridge Survey*, 490–95; Tanya Basok and Alexander Benifand, "Soviet Jewish Emigration," ibid., 502–6; Robert H. Rowland, "The Soviet Union," in *International Handbook on Internal Migrations*, 323–43.

116 Solon Ardittis, "East-West Migration: An Overview of Trends and Issues," in Ardittis, *Politics of East-West Migration*, 3–46; and essays in Fassmann and Münz, *European Migration*. After 1989, "how to" studies appeared in the West: how to keep migrants out or at least manage their entry. See, for example, Council of Europe, *People on the Move: New Migration Flows in Europe* (Strasbourg, 1992). Bernd Knabe, "Bilanz und Prognosen der Migrationen aus der bisherigen Sowjetunion und aus dem übrigen Osteuropa in den Westen," in Andreas Demuth, ed., *Neue Ost-West-Wanderungen nach dem Fall des Eisernen Vorhangs?* (Münster, 1994), 73–96.

117 Dövényi and Gabriella Vukovich, "Hungary and International Migration," in Fassmann and Münz, *European Migration*, 187–205, esp. 194–95; Daniela Bobeva, "Emigration from and Immigration to Bulgaria," ibid., 221–37. In 1970, the German Red Cross estimated that 290,000 ethnic Germans remained in Poland; but by 1993 some 850,000 had emigrated and 440,000 were estimated to be still in Poland (see also chap. 17.3). Piotr Korcelli, "Emigration from Poland after 1945," ibid., 171–85.

118 Table 14.5 in Cohen, *Cambridge Survey*, 492. Cristiano Codagnone, "The New Migration in Russia in the 1990s," in Koser and Lutz, *New Migration in Europe*, 39–59; Lothar Mertens, *Alija: Die Emigration der Juden aus der UdSSR/GUS* (2d rev. ed., Bochum, 1993); Dina Siegel, *The Great Immigration: Russian Jews in Israel* (New York, 1998); Lilia Shevtsova, "Post-Soviet Emigration Today and Tomorrow," *International Migration Review* 16 (1992): 241–57; Stephan Kux, "Soviet Federalism," in Rachel Denber, ed., *The Soviet Nationality Reader: The Disintegration in Context* (Boulder, 1992), 597–613.

119 Russell King et al., "International Retirement Migration in Europe," *International Journal of Population Geography* 4, 2 (1998): 91–111; Simone Abram et al., eds., *Tourists and Tourism: Identifying with People and Places* (Oxford, 1997), 51–70.

20 Intercultural Strategies and Closed Doors in the 1990s

1 Godfrey Gunatilleke, ed., *Migration of Asian Workers to the Arab World* (Tokyo, 1986), quote on 21; François Manchuelle, *Willing Migrants: Soninke Labor Diasporas, 1848–1960* (Athens, Ohio, 1997), quote on 226; Muinul Islam, "Bangladeshi Migration: An Impact Study," in Robin Cohen, ed., *The Cambridge Survey of World Migration* (Cambridge, 1995), 360–66, quote on 366; Ijaz S. Gilani, *Citizens, Slaves, Guest-Workers: The Dynamics of Labour Migration from South Asia* (Islamabad, 1985), "Evaluating the Consequences of a Migration Movement," 61–70.

2 In the United Arab Emirates, 90.0 percent are foreign-born; in Kuwait, 71.6 percent; in Hong Kong, 39.99 percent; in Luxembourg, 31.5 percent; in Israel, 30.9 percent. Rein-

hard Lohrmann, "International Migration Dynamics and Immigration Policy in Europe: An International Perspective," in Albrecht Weber, ed., *Einwanderungsland Bundesrepublik Deutschland in der Europäischen Union: Gestaltungsauftrag und Regelungsmöglichkeiten* (Osnabrück, 1997), 31–43, esp. 33.

3 Philip Martin and Jonas Widgren, *International Migration: A Global Challenge* (Washington, D.C., 1996); World Bank, *Resettlement and Development: The Bankwide Review of Projects Involving Involuntary Resettlement, 1986–1993* (Washington, D.C., 1994), cited in Christopher McDowell, ed., *Understanding Impoverishment: The Consequences of Development-Induced Displacement* (Providence, 1996), 2; Fredric Jameson and Masao Miyoshi, eds., *The Cultures of Globalization* (Durham, N.C., 1998); Tomas Hammar, Grete Brochmann, Kristof Tamas, and Thomas Faist, eds., *International Migration, Immobility and Development: Multidisciplinary Perspectives* (Oxford, 1997).

4 Press reports and oral information, 1992–98; Joyce C. Fraser, *Cry of the Illegal Immigrant* (Toronto, 1980); Beatrice N. Hackett, *Pray God and Keep Walking: Stories of Women Refugees* (Jefferson, N.C., 1996).

5 Other Christian denominations had remained marginal after the destruction of the Albigensians and the victory over Byzantine Christendom. Later, eastern Orthodox Christianity assumed new importance.

6 Stephen D. Krasner and Daniel T. Froats, "The Westphalian Model and Minority-Rights Guarantees in Europe," InIIS working paper, 2/96 (University of Bremen, 1996); Art. I of the Final Act of the 1648 peace conference. See chaps. 5.1, 5.2, 11.1, and 14.3 above for particular developments. David Held, *Democracy and the Global Order: From the Modern State to Cosmopolitan Governance* (Stanford, 1995), 29–140.

7 Anthony D. Smith, *National Identity* (Reno, 1991), 14, and Smith, *The Ethnic Origins of Nations* (Oxford, 1986); Miroslav Hroch, *Social Preconditions of National Revival in Europe*, trans. Ben Fowkes (Czech orig., n.d.; Cambridge, 1985); Eric Hobsbawm and Terence Ranger, eds., *The Invention of Tradition* (Cambridge, 1983); Benedict Anderson, *Imagined Communities: Reflections on the Origin and Spread of Nationalism* (1983; 3d ed., London, 1986); Floya Anthias and Nira Yuval-Davis, eds., *Woman, Nation, State* (London, 1989); Theodor Schieder and Otto Dann, eds., *Nationale Bewegung und soziale Organisation* (Munich, 1978); Peter Alter, *Nationalism*, trans. Stewart McKinnon-Evans (German orig., 1985; London, 1989); Dirk Hoerder and Inge Blank, "Ethnic and National Consciousness from the Enlightenment to the 1880s," in Hoerder and Blank, eds., *Roots of the Transplanted*, 2 vols. (New York, 1994), 2:37–109; Robin Cohen, "Fuzzy Frontiers of Identity: The British Case," *Social Identities* 1 (1995): 35–62.

8 Theodore W. Allen, *The Invention of the White Race*, 2 vols. (New York, 1997); Matthew Frye Jacobson, *Whiteness of a Different Color: European Immigrants and the Alchemy of Race* (Cambridge, Mass., 1998); Gary Y. Okihiro, "Comparing Colonialisms and Migrations, Puerto Rico and the Philippines," Duke University, unpublished paper, Feb. 1995.

9 Minority Rights Group International, *World Directory of Minorities* (London, 1997); David Levinson, ed., *Encyclopedia of World Cultures*, 10 vols. (Boston, 1991–96). The literature on minorities is legion; see, for example, A. C. Hepburn, ed., *Minorities in History* (New York, 1979); Antony Alcock, Brian Taylor, and John Welton, eds., *The Future of Cultural Minorities* (London, 1979); Hugh Miall, ed., *Minority Rights in Europe* (London, 1994). Ulrich Schneckener and Dieter Senghaas, "Auf der Suche nach friedlicher Koexistenz: Modelle zur

Bearbeitung ethno-nationaler Konflikte in Europa," InIIS working paper, 8/97 (University of Bremen, 1997).

10 Lian Kwen Fee, "Migration and the Formation of Malaysia and Singapore," in Cohen, *Cambridge Survey*, 392–96, quote on 392.

11 Alan Dowty, *Closed Borders: The Contemporary Assault on Freedom of Movement* (New Haven, 1987); Bertrand Badie and Catherine Wihtol de Wenden, eds., *Le Défi migratoire: Questions de relations internationales* (Paris, 1993); Myron Weiner, "On International Migration and International Relations," *Population and Development Review* 11 (1985): 441–55; José D. Inglés, *Study of Discrimination in Respect of the Right of Everyone to Leave Any Country, Including His Own, and to Return to His Country*, UN Economic and Social Council, Commission on Human Rights, Subcommission on Prevention of Discrimination and Protection of Minorities (E/CN.4/Sub.2/229/Rev. 1, 1963; New York, 1963); Hurst Hannum, *The Right to Leave and Return in International Law and Practice* (Washington, D.C., 1987); Nino Falchi, *International Migration Pressures: Challenges, Policy Response and Operational Measures: An Outline of the Main Features*, International Organization for Migration (Geneva, 1995). The duplicity of Western freedom of movement theory was exposed in U.S.-China negotiations in 1979: faced with demands for a liberal exit policy from China, the Chinese negotiator offered to release as many million Chinese as the United States would admit. Roger Daniels, "Changes in Immigration Law and Nativism since 1924," *American Jewish History* 76 (1986): 159–80, esp. 176.

12 Karl Polanyi, *The Great Transformation* (New York, 1944); Jeffrey Henderson and Manuel Castells, eds., *Global Restructuring and Territorial Development* (London, 1987).

13 Estimates of European out-migration vary from 60 million to 80 million. Aaron Segal, *An Atlas of International Migration* (London, 1993), 10–21.

14 Ronald Skeldon, *Migration and Development: A Global Perspective* (Essex, U.K., 1997); *Winning the Human Race? The Report of the Independent Commission on International Humanitarian Issues* (1st ed., 1988; London, 1998).

15 Cornelis D. de Jong, "The Root Causes Approach," paper given at the conference "Organizing Diversity," Berg-en-Dal, Netherlands, Nov. 1995; Jorge Balán, "International Migration in Latin America: Trends and Consequences," in Reginald T. Appleyard, ed., *International Migration Today*, 2 vols. (Paris, 1988), 1:210–63, quote on 247.

16 Gunnar Myrdal, *The Challenge of World Poverty: A World Anti-Poverty Program in Outline* (New York, 1970); McDowell, *Understanding Impoverishment*; Adam Smith, *An Inquiry into the Nature and Causes of the Wealth of Nations* [1776], ed. R. H. Campbell, A. S. Skinner, and W. B. Todd (Oxford, 1976), 72–81, 376–80, 411–27.

17 The "Tobin tax" would have yielded estimated revenues of US$1.6 trillion annually; it was proposed again by NGOs at the Seattle summit of the World Trade Organization, Dec. 1999. James Goldsmith, *The Trap* (French orig., 1993; New York, 1994), and Goldsmith, *La Réponse à la Commission européenne et aux libre-échanists, premiers responsables du chômage, du déclin de la nation et de l'Europe* (Paris, 1995).

18 Ernst-Otto Czempiel, *Weltpolitik im Umbruch: Das internationale System nach dem Ende des Ost-West-Konflikts* (Munich, 1993); Brian Barry, "Nationalism, Intervention and Redistribution," paper given at the conference "Citizenship and Exclusion," Amsterdam, Apr. 1996; Jonathan Glover, "State Terrorism," in R. G. Frey and Christopher W. Morris, eds., *Violence, Terrorism, and Justice* (Cambridge, 1991), 256–75; Harry Beran, "A Liberal Theory of

Secession," *Political Studies* 32 (1984): 21–31; U.S. Central Intelligence Agency, *The Challenge of Ethnic Conflict to National and International Order in the 1990s: Geographic Perspectives: A Conference Report* (Washington, D.C., 1995); Michael Kidron and Dan Smith, *The New State of War and Peace: An International Atlas* (New York, 1991). According to a report of the Congressional Research Service, the United States, from 1990 to 1998 the largest arms-trading polity, has made such sales "a legitimate instrument of U.S. foreign policy"; *Toronto Globe and Mail*, 5 Aug. 1998, and Duncan L. Clarke, Daniel B. O'Connor, and Jason D. Ellis, *Send Guns and Money: Security Assistance and U.S. Foreign Policy* (Westport, Conn., 1997).

19 World Commission on Environment and Development (Gro Helen Brundtland, chair), *Our Common Future* (Oxford, 1987); UN Population Fund, *Annual Report*, 1992.

20 UN Development Programme, *Human Development Report* [annual] (New York, 1993), 84–99; Mayra Buvini'c, Catherine Gwin, and Lisa M. Bates, *Investing in Women: Progress and Prospects for the World Bank* (Washington, D.C., 1996). Women's organizations in Palestinian self-administered territories, for example, demanded demilitarization of their male children. Chris Rolfe, Clare Rolfe, and Malcolm Harper, *Refugee Enterprise: It Can Be Done* (London, 1987).

21 Veit Bader, ed., *Citizenship and Exclusion* (London, 1997); Verena Stolcke, "Talking Culture: New Boundaries, New Rhetorics of Exclusion in Europe," *Current Anthropology* 36 (1995): 1–24; Will Kymlicka, *Multicultural Citizenship: A Liberal Theory of Minority Rights* (Oxford, 1995), is based on Canadian experience only; Joseph H. Carens, "Who Belongs? Theoretical and Legal Questions about Birthright Citizenship in the United States," *University of Toronto Law Journal* 27 (1987): 413–43, and Carens, "Migration and Morality: A Liberal Egalitarian Perspective," in Brian Barry and Robert E. Goodin, eds., *Free Movement: Ethical Issues in the Transnational Migration of People and of Money* (New York, 1992), 25–47.

22 Michael Walzer, *Spheres of Justice: A Defense of Pluralism and Equality* (New York, 1983); Veit Bader, "Reply to Michael Walzer," and "Citizenship and Exclusion: Radical Democracy, Community, and Justice; or, What Is Wrong with Communitarianism?" *Political Theory* 23 (1995): 211–46, 250–52.

23 This section is influenced by papers and discussions at three international symposia held in 1995–96: "Organizing Diversity: Migration and Refugees: Canada and Europe," Nijmegen, Nov. 1995; "Becoming American/American Becoming: International Migration to the United States," U.S. Social Science Research Council, Sanibel Island, Fla., Jan. 1996; "Citizenship and Exclusion," Amsterdam, Apr. 1996 (published in Bader, *Exclusion and Citizenship*).

24 Rainer Bauböck, ed., *From Aliens to Citizens: Redefining the Legal Status of Immigrants* (Aldershot, U.K., 1994), and Bauböck, *Transnational Citizenship: Membership and Rights in International Migration* (Aldershot, U.K., 1994); Yasemin N. Soysal, *Limits of Citizenship: Migrants and Postnational Membership in Europe* (Chicago, 1994); Stephen Castles and Mark J. Miller, *The Age of Migration: International Population Movements in the Modern World* (New York, 1993), 195–230.

25 Bi- or multinational agreements permit the transfer of social security credits, usually through highly complex and thus expensive and time-consuming bureaucratic procedures.

26 Tomas Hammar, *Democracy and the Nation State: Aliens, Denizens, and Citizens in a World of International Migration* (Aldershot, U.K., 1990).

27 Christiane Harzig, "Immigration Policy and the Creation of the Modern Citizen: A German Perspective," paper given at the annual meeting of the Social Science History Association, Washington, D.C., Oct. 1997; Dirk Hoerder, *Creating Societies: Immigrant Lives in Canada* (Montreal, 1999); studies on Overseas Chinese in Southeast Asia cited in chap. 19, nn. 55, 65, 66, and 86.

28 In Western Europe, estimates of 20 million prospective "Russian" migrants circulated in 1989, even though Russians had no networks of previous migrations, while few noted that, according to opinion polls, after Prime Minister Thatcher's policies had been implemented, one-third of the British were ready to leave their country. Bernd Knabe, "Bilanz und Prognosen der Migrationen aus der bisherigen Sowjetunion und aus dem übrigen Osteuropa in den Westen," in Andreas Demuth, ed., *Neue Ost-West-Wanderungen nach dem Fall des Eisernen Vorhangs?* (Münster, 1994), 73–96; "Isle of Despair," *Time*, 15 Mar. 1993, 20–27.

29 Yasmeen Abu-Laban and Daiva Stasiulis, "Ethnic Pluralism under Siege: Popular and Partisan Opposition to Multiculturalism," *Canadian Public Policy* 18 (1992): 365–86; Christoph Butterwegge and Siegfried Jäger, eds., *Rassismus in Europa* (Cologne, 1992), and Butterwegge and Jäger, eds., *Europa gegen den Rest der Welt: Flüchtlingsbewegungen–Einwanderung–Asylpolitik* (Cologne, 1993); Klaus J. Bade, ed., *Das Manifest der 60: Deutschland und die Einwanderung* (Munich, 1994).

30 John K. Galbraith, *The Culture of Contentment* (Boston, 1992). In 1998, the government of Norway appointed a Commission on Values (Hanne Sophie Greve, chair) to discuss materialism in Norwegian society. Anthony Richmond, *Global Apartheid: Refugees, Racism, and the New World Order* (Toronto, 1994).

31 Dirk Hoerder, "From Migrants to Ethnics: Acculturation in a Societal Framework," in Hoerder and Leslie P. Moch, eds., *European Migrants: Global and Local Perspectives* (Boston, 1985), 211–62, and Hoerder, "Segmented Macrosystems and Networking Individuals: The Balancing Functions of Migration Processes," in Jan Lucassen and Leo Lucassen, eds., *Migrations, Migration History, History: Old Paradigms and New Perspectives* (Bern, 1997), 73–84, and Hoerder, "Labour Markets—Community—Family: A Gendered Analysis of the Process of Insertion and Acculturation," in Wsevolod Isajiw, ed., *Multiculturalism in North America and Europe: Comparative Perspectives on Interethnic Relations and Social Incorporation* (Toronto, 1997), 155–83. Richard Alba has recently argued for retaining the assimilation concept; "The Assimilation of Immigrant Groups: Concept, Theory and Evidence," paper presented at the "Becoming American/American Becoming" conference, Sanibel Island, Fla., Jan. 1996.

32 The term "transnationalism" retains the nationhood paradigm; even first socialization and postmigration connections are regionally limited. On a structural level, the term highlights "political, economic, social, and cultural processes that extend beyond the borders of a particular state but are directly shaped by state policies and by the institutional practices of states." Nina Glick Schiller, "Who Are These Guys? A Transnational Reading of the U.S. Immigrant Experience," unpublished paper presented at the "Becoming American/American Becoming" conference, quote on 2; Nina Glick Schiller, Linda Basch, and Cristina Blanc-Szanton, *Towards a Transnational Perspective on Migration: Race, Class, Ethnicity and Nationalism Reconsidered* (New York, 1992), esp. editors' introduction, 1–24.

33 Phil Cohen et al., proposal for a research project at East London University, "Finding the Way Home: Young People's Models of Community Safety and Racial Danger" (Jan. 1996), quote on 1–2.

34 Iain Chambers, *Migrancy, Culture, Identity* (London, 1994); James Clifford, "Travelling Cultures," in Lawrence Grossberg, Cary Nelson, and Paula Treichler, eds., *Cultural Studies* (London, 1992); Stuart Hall, "Minimal Selves," in L. Appignanesi, ed., *Identity: The Real Me: Post-Modernism and the Question of Identity* (London, 1987), 44.

35 Peter Kwong, *Forbidden Workers: Illegal Chinese Immigrants and American Labor* (New York, 1998); *Newsweek*, international ed., 21 June 1993, 21–24.

36 Wsevolod W. Isajiw, "Definitions and Dimensions of Ethnicity: A Theoretical Framework," in *Challenges of Measuring an Ethnic World: Science, Politics and Reality: Proceedings of the Joint Canada–United States Conference on the Measurement of Ethnicity, April 1–3, 1992* (Ottawa, 1992), 407–27; Danielle Juteau, "The Production of Ethnicity: Material and Ideal Dimensions," paper given at the annual meeting of the American Sociological Association, Cincinnati, Aug. 1991; Dirk Hoerder, "Ethnic Cultures under Multiculturalism: Retention or Change?," in Hans Braun and Wolfgang Klooss, eds., *Multiculturalism in North America and Europe: Social Practices, Literary Visions* (Trier, 1994), 82–102.

37 The concept of "visible minorities" rests on the assumption that while White as a color is not visible, all other skin colors are. J. Paul Grayson, with Tammy Chi and Darla Rhyne, "The Social Construction of 'Visible Minority' for Students of Chinese Origin" (mimeographed, York University, Toronto, 1994).

38 In states with multiple ethnocultural resident groups, high levels of structural integration do not prevent powerful groups from reinvigorating past cultural differences in order to exclude present social groups from high office, from parts of the territory, or even from life-chances, as wars and massacres in the Yugoslav successor states and in Rwanda and Burundi indicate.

39 Stolcke, "Talking Culture," quote on 13.

40 Mr. Ang, cited in Donald M. Nonini, "Shifting Identities, Positioned Imaginaries: Transnational Traversals and Reversals by Malaysian Chinese," in Aihwa Ong and Donald M. Nonini, eds., *Ungrounded Empires: The Cultural Politics of Modern Chinese Transnationalism* (London, 1997), 203–27, quote on 211.

Selected Bibliography

The bibliography contains entries in the languages known to this author—German, English, and French. Some important studies in other European languages have been included. The works cited are categorized as follows:

The titles within the section on migrations from the seventeenth to the nineteenth century are further broken down into their relevance to continent-wide regions.

1 General Works and Atlases

Adas, Michael, ed., *Islamic and European Expansion: The Forging of a Global Order* (Philadelphia, 1993).

Barnard, Alan, and Jonathan Spencer, eds., *Encyclopedia of Social and Cultural Anthropology* (London, 1996).

Ben-Sasson, Haim H., ed., *A History of the Jewish People* (Hebrew orig., 1969; Cambridge, Mass., 1976).

Boustani, Rafic, and Philippe Fargues, *The Atlas of the Arab World: Geopolitics and Society* (New York, 1991).

Bryder, Linda, "Sex, Race, and Colonialism: An Historiographic Review," *International History Review* 20 (1998): 806–22.

Chaliand, Gérard, Michael Jan, and Jean-Pierre Rageau, *Atlas historique des migrations* (Paris, 1994).

Chaliand, Gérard, and Jean-Pierre Rageau, *The Penguin Atlas of Diasporas*, trans. A. M. Berrett (French orig., Paris, 1991; New York, 1995).

Chirot, Daniel, and Anthony Reid, eds., *Essential Outsiders: Chinese and Jews in the Modern Transformation of Southeast Asia and Central Europe* (Seattle, 1997).

Cohen, Robin, ed., *The Cambridge Survey of World Migration* (Cambridge, 1995).

Cohn-Sherbok, Dan, *Atlas of Jewish History* (London, 1994).

Comrie, Bernard, et al., eds., *The Atlas of Languages: The Origin and Development of Languages throughout the World* (New York, 1996).

Curtin, Philip D., *Cross-Cultural Trade in World History* (Cambridge, 1984).

Doeringer, Peter B., and Michael J. Piore, *Internal Labor Markets and Manpower Analysis* (Lexington, Mass., 1971).

Duby, Georges, ed., *Atlas historique: L'histoire du monde en 334 cartes* (2d ed., Paris, 1994).

Dupeux, Georges, ed., *Les migrations internationales de la fin du XVIIIe siècle à nos jours* (Paris, 1980).

Frank, Andre Gunder, "A Plea for World System History," *Journal of World History* 2 (1991): 1–28.

Friedland, Klaus, ed., *Maritime Aspects of Migration* (Cologne, 1989).

Gabaccia, Donna R., *Italy's Many Diasporas* (London, 2000).

Glazier, Ira A., and Luigi De Rosa, eds., *Migration across Time and Nations: Population Mobility in Historical Contexts* (New York, 1986).

Gungwu, Wang, ed., *Global History and Migrations* (Boulder, 1997).

Harley, J. B., and David Woodward, *Cartography in Prehistoric, Ancient, and Medieval Europe and the Mediterranean* (Chicago, 1987).

Hughes, Everett C., and Helen MacGill Hughes, *Where Peoples Meet: Racial and Ethnic Frontiers* (Glencoe, Ill., 1952).

Kidron, Michael, and Ronald Segal, *The State of the World Atlas* (London, 1981).

Kidron, Michael, and Dan Smith, *The New State of War and Peace: An International Atlas* (New York, 1991).

Klein, Martin A., ed., *Breaking the Chains: Slavery, Bondage, and Emancipation in Modern Africa and Asia* (Madison, 1993).

Kloosterboer, Willemina, *Involuntary Labour since the Abolition of Slavery: A Survey of Compulsory Labour throughout the World* (Leiden, 1960).

Kymlicka, Will, *Multicultural Citizenship: A Liberal Theory of Minority Rights* (Oxford, 1995).

Levinson, David, *Ethnic Relations: A Cross-Cultural Encyclopedia* (Santa Barbara, Calif., 1994).

———, ed., *Encyclopedia of World Cultures*, 10 vols. (Boston, 1991–96).

Midgley, Clare, ed., *Gender and Imperialism* (Manchester, 1998).

Miles, Robert, *Capitalism and Unfree Labour: Anomaly or Necessity?* (London, 1987).

———, *Racism* (London, 1989).

Minority Rights Group International, *World Directory of Minorities* (London, 1997).

Pan, Lynn, ed., *The Encyclopedia of the Chinese Overseas* (Richmond, U.K., 1999).

Richmond, Anthony H., *Global Apartheid: Refugees, Racism, and the New World Order* (Toronto, 1994).

Schwartzberg, Joseph E., ed., *A Historical Atlas of South Asia* (Chicago, 1978; 2d rev. ed., Oxford and New York, 1992).

Scott, Franklin D., ed., *World Migration in Modern Times* (Englewood Cliffs, N.J., 1968).

Seager, Joni, ed., *The State of the Earth Atlas* (London and New York, 1990).

Seager, Joni, Clark Reed, and Peter Stott, eds., *The New State of the Earth Atlas* (New York, 1995).

Segal, Aaron, *An Atlas of International Migration* (London, 1993).

Simon, Rita J., and Caroline B. Brettell, *International Migration: The Female Experience* (Totowa, N.J., 1986).

Smith, Alan K., *Creating a World Economy: Merchant Capital, Colonialism, and World Trade, 1400–1825* (Boulder, 1991).

Tanner, Helen H., et al., eds., *The Settling of North America: The Atlas of the Great Migrations into North America from the Ice Age to the Present* (New York, 1995).

Willcox, Walter, and Imre Ferenczi, eds., *International Migrations*, 2 vols. (New York, 1929–31).

2   Theory and Methodology: Recent Approaches

Allen, Theodore W., *The Invention of the White Race*, 2 vols. (New York, 1994–97).

Anderson, Benedict, *Imagined Communities: Reflections on the Origin and Spread of Nationalism* (1983; 3d ed., London, 1986).

Baily, Samuel L., "The Village-Outward Approach to the Study of Social Networks: A Case Study of the Agnonesi Diaspora Abroad, 1885–1989," *Studi Emigrazione* (Rome) 19, 105 (Mar. 1992): 43–67.

Berry, John, et al., eds., *State of the Art Review of Research on Canada's Multicultural Society* (Ottawa, 1993).

Bonacich, Edna, "A Theory of Ethnic Antagonism: The Split Labor Market," *American Sociological Review* 37 (1972): 547–59.

Conzen, Kathleen N., David Gerber, Ewa Morawska, George E. Pozetta, and Rudolph J. Vecoli, "The Invention of Ethnicity: A Perspective from the U.S.A.," *Journal of American Ethnic History* 12 (1992): 3–41.

Fawcett, James T., and Fred Arnold, "Explaining Diversity: Asian and Pacific Immigration Systems," in James T. Fawcett and Benjamin V. Cariño, eds., *Pacific Bridges: The New Immigration from Asia and the Pacific Islands* (Staten Island, N.Y., 1987), 453–73.

Goldlust, John, and Anthony H. Richmond, "A Multivariate Model of Immigrant Adaptation," *International Migration Review* 8 (1974): 193–225.

Hobsbawm, Eric, and Terence Ranger, eds., *The Invention of Tradition* (Cambridge, 1983).

Hoerder, Dirk, "Changing Paradigms in Migration History: From 'To America' to World-Wide Systems," *Canadian Review of American Studies* 24, 2 (spring 1994): 105–26.

———, "From Migrants to Ethnics: Acculturation in a Societal Framework," in Hoerder and Leslie Page Moch, eds., *European Migrants: Global and Local Perspectives* (Boston, 1996), 211–62.

Jackson, James H., Jr., and Leslie Page Moch, "Migration and the Social History of Modern Europe," *Historical Methods* 22 (1989): 27–36.

Jacobson, Matthew F., *Whiteness of a Different Color: European Immigrants and the Alchemy of Race* (Cambridge, Mass., 1998).

Jameson, Fredric, "Of Islands and Trenches: Neutralization and the Production of Utopian Discourse," *Diacritics* 7, 2 (June 1977): 2–21.

Kazal, Russell A., "Revisiting Assimilation: The Rise, Fall, and Reappraisal of a Concept in American Ethnic History," *American Historical Review* 100 (1995): 437–71.

Kleiner, Robert J., et al., "International Migration and Internal Migration: A Comprehensive Theoretical Approach," in Ira A. Glazier and Luigi De Rosa, eds., *Migration across Time and Nations: Population Mobility in Historical Contexts* (New York, 1986), 305–17.

Kramer, Fritz, *Verkehrte Welten: Zur imaginären Ethnographie des 19. Jahrhunderts* (Frankfurt/Main, 1981).

Kritz, Mary M., Lin L. Lim, and Hania Zlotnik, eds., *International Migration Systems: A Global Approach* (Oxford, 1992).

Mabogunje, A. L., "Systems Approach to a Theory of Rural-Urban Migration," *Geographical Analysis* 2, 1 (1970): 1–18.

Mangolam, J. J., and H. K. Schwarzweller, "General Theory in the Study of Migration: Current Needs and Difficulties," *International Migration Review* 3 (1968): 3–18.

Massey, Douglas S., et al., "International Migration Theory: The North American Case," *Population and Development Review* 20 (Dec. 1994): 699–752.

———, "Theories of International Migration: Review and Appraisal," *Population and Development Review* 19 (Sept. 1993): 431–66.

Mazlish, Bruce, and Ralph Buultjens, eds., *Conceptualizing Global History* (Boulder, 1993).

Ohaegbulam, Festus Ugboaja, *Towards an Understanding of the African Experience from Historical and Contemporary Perspectives* (Lanham, Md., 1990).

Parnwell, Mike, *Population Movements and the Third World* (London, 1993).

Richardson, Allen, "A Theory and a Method for the Psychological Study of Assimilation," *International Migration Review* 2, 1 (fall 1967): 3–30.

Said, Edward W., *Orientalism* (London, 1978).

Schiller, Nina Glick, Linda Basch, and Cristina Blanc-Szanton, "From Immigrant to Transmigrant: Theorizing Transnational Migration," *Anthropological Quarterly* 68 (1995): 48–63.

———, *Towards a Transnational Perspective on Migration: Race, Class, Ethnicity and Nationalism Reconsidered* (New York, 1992).

Shaw, R. Paul, *Migration Theory and Fact: A Review and Bibliography of Current Literature* (Philadelphia, 1975).

Skeldon, Ronald, *Population Mobility in Developing Countries: A Reinterpretation* (New York, 1990).

Smith, Anthony D., *The Ethnic Origins of Nations* (Oxford, 1986).

———, *National Identity* (Reno, 1991).

Tilly, Charles, *Coercion, Capital, and European States, A.D. 990–1992* (1st ed., 1990; rev. ed., Oxford, 1992).

———, "Migration in Modern European History," in William H. McNeill and Ruth S. Adams, eds., *Human Migration: Patterns and Politics* (Bloomington, 1978), 48–72.

Tilly, Louise A., and Joan W. Scott, *Women, Work, and Family* (New York, 1978).

Todaro, M. P., *Internal Migration in Developing Countries: A Review of Theory, Evidence, Methodology and Research Priorities* (Geneva, 1976).

Zelinsky, Wilbur, "The Hypothesis of the Mobility Transition," *Geographical Review* 61 (1971): 219–49.

3 Medieval and Early Modern Migrations

Abu-Lughod, Janet L., *Before European Hegemony: The World System A.D. 1250–1350* (New York, 1989).

Amitai-Preiss, Reuven, and David O. Morgan, eds., *The Mongol Empire and Its Legacy* (Leiden, 1999).

Andrews, Kenneth R., *Trade, Plunder and Settlement: Maritime Enterprise and the Genesis of the British Empire, 1480–1630* (Cambridge, 1984).

Atiya, Aziz S., *Crusade, Commerce, and Culture* (Bloomington, 1962).

Bartlett, Robert, and Angus MacKay, eds., *Medieval Frontier Societies* (Oxford, 1989).

Bennassar, Bartolomé, and Pierre Chaunu, eds., *L'ouverture du monde: XIVe–XVIe siècles* (Paris, 1977).

Bentley, Jerry H., *Old World Encounters: Cross-Cultural Contacts and Exchanges in Pre-Modern Times* (New York, 1993).

Bosl, Karl, "On Social Mobility in Medieval Society: Service, Freedom, and Freedom of Movement as Means of Social Ascent," in Sylvia L. Thrupp, ed., *Early Medieval Society* (New York, 1967), 87–102.

Brady, Thomas A., Jr., Heiko A. Oberman, and James D. Tracy, eds., *Handbook of European History, 1400–1600: Late Middle Ages, Renaissance, and Reformation,* 2 vols. (Leiden, 1994).

Braude, Benjamin, and Bernard Lewis, eds., *Christians and Jews in the Ottoman Empire: The Functioning of a Plural Society,* 2 vols. (London, 1982).

Braudel, Fernand, *Civilisation matérielle, économie et capitalisme: XVe–XVIIIe siècle,* 3 vols. (1st ed., 1967; Paris, 1979); English: *Civilization and Capitalism, 15th–18th Century,* 3 vols., trans. Siân Reynolds, (New York, 1982–84).

———, *La Méditerranée et le monde méditerranéen à l'époque de Philippe II* (1st ed., 1949; 2d rev. ed., Paris, 1966); English: *The Mediterranean and the Mediterranean World in the Age of Philip II,* 2 vols., trans. Siân Reynolds, (New York, 1972–73).

Burman, Edward, *The World before Columbus, 1100–1492* (London, 1989).

Carter, F. W., *Trade and Urban Development in Poland: An Economic Geography of Cracow, from its Origins to 1795* (Cambridge, 1994).

Cavaciocchi, Simonetta, ed., *Le migrazioni in Europa secc. XIII-XVIII: Atti dela "Venticinquesima settimana de studi," 3-8 maggio 1993* (Florence, 1994).

Cavalli-Sforza, Luigi Luca, and Francesco Cavalli-Sforza, *The Great Human Diasporas: The History of Diversity and Evolution,* trans. Sarah Thorne (Italian orig., 1993; Reading, Mass., 1995).

Contamine, Philippe, *War in the Middle Ages,* trans. Michael Jones (French orig., 1980; London, 1984).

Corvisier, André, *Armies and Societies in Europe, 1494–1789,* trans. Abigail T. Siddall (French orig., 1976; Bloomington, 1979).

Daniel, Norman, *Islam and the West: The Making of an Image* (Edinburgh, 1960).

Díaz-Mas, Paloma, *Sephardim: The Jews from Spain,* trans. George K. Zucker (Spanish orig., 1986; Chicago, 1992).

Erfen, Irene, and Karl-Heinz Spieß, eds., *Fremdheit und Reisen im Mittelalter* (Stuttgart, 1997).

Ertzdorff, Xenja von, and Dieter Neukirch, eds., *Reisen und Reiseliteratur im Mittelalter und in der frühen Neuzeit* (Amsterdam, 1992).

Fernández-Armesto, Felipe, *Before Columbus: Exploration and Colonisation from the Mediterranean to the Atlantic, 1229–1492* (Basingstoke, 1987).

Filesi, Teobaldo, *China and Africa in the Middle Ages,* trans. David L. Morison (Italian orig., 1962; London, 1972).

Fossier, Robert, *Peasant Life in the Medieval West,* trans. Juliet Vale (French orig., 1984; Oxford, 1988).

Geremek, Bronislaw, *The Margins of Society in Late Medieval Paris,* trans. Jean Birrell (Polish orig., Warsaw, 1971; French ed., Paris, 1976; New York, 1987).

Gies, Frances, and Joseph Gies, *Cathedral, Forge, and Waterwheel: Technology and Invention in the Middle Ages* (New York, 1994).

Gimpel, Jean, *The Cathedral Builders*, trans. Teresa Waugh (French orig., rev. ed., 1980; London, 1998).

Goitein, S. D., *A Mediterranean Society: The Jewish Communities of the Arab World as Portrayed in the Documents of the Cairo Geniza*, 5 vols. (Berkeley, 1967–88).

Goodrich, L. Carrington, "Trade Routes to China from Ancient Time to the Age of European Expansion," in Jean Labatut and Wheaton J. Lane, eds., *Highways in Our National Life* (Princeton, 1950), 16–32.

Goss, Vladimir P., and Christine Verzár Bornstein, eds., *The Meeting of Two Worlds: Cultural Exchange between East and West during the Period of the Crusades* (Kalamazoo, Mich., 1986).

Gran, Peter, *Islamic Roots of Capitalism: Egypt, 1760-1840* (Syracuse, 1998).

Grousset, René, *The Empire of the Steppes: A History of Central Asia*, trans. Naomi Walford (French orig., 1939; New Brunswick, 1970).

Gurjewitsch, Aaron J., *Stumme Zeugen des Mittelalters: Weltbild und Kultur der einfachen Menschen*, trans. Ulrike Fromm (Russian orig., n.d.; Vienna, 1997).

Hanley, Sarah, "Engendering the State: Family Formation and State Building in Early Modern France," *French Historical Studies* 16 (1989): 4–27.

Harvey, L. P., *Islamic Spain, 1250 to 1500* (Chicago, 1990).

Heers, Jacques, *Esclaves et domestiques au Moyen-âge dans le monde méditerranéen* (Paris, 1981).

Hess, Andrew C., "The Evolution of the Ottoman Seaborne Empire in the Age of the Oceanic Discoveries, 1453–1525," *American Historical Review* 75 (1970): 1882–1919.

———, *The Forgotten Frontier: A History of the Sixteenth Century Ibero-African Frontier* (Chicago, 1978).

Higounet, Charles, *Die deutsche Ostsiedlung im Mittelalter* (Berlin, 1986).

Hohenberg, Paul M., and Lynn Hollen Lees, *The Making of Urban Europe, 1000-1950* (Cambridge, Mass., 1985).

Hourani, George F., *Arab Seafaring in the Indian Ocean in Ancient and Early Medieval Times* (Princeton, 1951).

Inalcik, Halil, and Donald Quataert, eds., *An Economic and Social History of the Ottoman Empire, 1300-1914* (Cambridge, 1994).

Jaritz, Gerhard, and Albert Müller, eds., *Migration in der Feudalgesellschaft* (Frankfurt/Main, 1988).

Jayyusi, Salma Khadra, ed., *The Legacy of Muslim Spain*, 2 vols. (Leiden, 1994).

Johanek, Peter and Heinz Stoob, eds., *Europäische Messen und Märktesysteme in Mittelalter und Neuzeit* (Cologne, 1996).

Kedar, Benjamin Z., "Expulsion as an Issue of World History," *Journal of World History* 7 (1996): 165–80.

Kellenbenz, Hermann, ed., *Fremde Kaufleute auf der iberischen Halbinsel* (Cologne, 1970).

Kurzel-Runtscheiner, Monica, *Töchter der Venus: Die Kurtisanen Roms im 16. Jahrhundert* (Munich, 1995).

Labarge, Margaret Wade, *Medieval Travellers: The Rich and Restless* (London, 1982).

Le Goff, Jacques, "Le temps du travail dans la crise du XIVe siecle," *Moyen Âge* 69 (1963): 597–613.

Lewis, Archibald R., *Nomads and Crusaders, A.D. 1000-1368* (Bloomington, 1988).

———, ed., *The Islamic World and the West, A.D. 622-1492* (New York, 1970).

Lewis, Bernard, *Cultures in Conflict: Christians, Muslims, and Jews in the Age of Discovery* (New York, 1995).

————, *The Muslim Discovery of Europe* (New York, 1982).

Ludwig, Karl-Heinz, and Raffaelo Vergani, "Mobilität und Migrationen der Bergleute vom 13. bis zum 17. Jahrhundert," in Simonetta Cavaciocchi, ed., *Le migrazioni in Europa secc. XIII-XVIII: Atti dela "Venticinquesima settimana di studi," 3-8 maggio 1993* (Florence, 1994), 593–622.

Maalouf, Amin, *The Crusades through Arab Eyes*, trans. Jon Rothschild (French orig., 1983; London, 1984).

Mayer, Hans E., ed., *Die Kreuzfahrerstaaten als multikulturelle Gesellschaft: Einwanderer und Minderheiten im 12. und 13. Jahrhundert* (Munich, 1997).

McNeill, William H., *Europe's Steppe Frontier, 1500-1800* (Chicago, 1964).

————, *The Rise of the West: A History of the Human Community* (Chicago, 1963).

Mirsky, Jeannette, ed., *The Great Chinese Travelers: An Anthology* (Chicago, 1974).

Moraw, Peter, ed., *Unterwegssein im Spätmittelalter* (Berlin, 1985).

Morinis, Alan, ed., *Sacred Journeys: The Anthropology of Pilgrimage* (Westport, Conn., 1992).

O'Gorman, Edmundo, *The Invention of America: An Inquiry into the Historical Nature of the New World and the Meaning of Its History* (Bloomington, 1961).

Ohler, Norbert, *The Medieval Traveller*, trans. Caroline Hillier (German orig., 1986; Woodbridge, U.K., 1989).

Parry, J. H., *The Age of Reconnaissance, Discovery, Exploration, and Settlement, 1450-1650* (London, 1963).

————, *The Discovery of the Sea* (London, 1975).

————, *Europe and a Wider World, 1415-1715* (London, 1949).

Peters, F. E., *Jerusalem and Mecca: The Typology of the Holy City in the Near East* (New York, 1986).

Pounds, N. J. G., *An Historical Geography of Europe* (Cambridge, 1990).

Prawer, Joshua, *The Latin Kingdom of Jerusalem: European Colonialism in the Middle Ages* (London, 1972).

Preston, Richard A., Alex Roland, and Sydney F. Wise, *Men in Arms: A History of Warfare and Its Interrelationships with Western Society* (5th ed., Fort Worth, 1991).

Reininghaus, Wilfried, *Die Entstehung der Gesellengilden im Spätmittelalter* (Wiesbaden, 1981).

Ridder-Symoens, Hilde de, "Mobility," in Ridder-Symoens, ed., *A History of the University in Europe*, vol. 1: *Universities in the Middle Ages* (Cambridge, 1992), 280–304.

Riley-Smith, Jonathan, ed., *The Oxford Illustrated History of the Crusades* (Oxford, 1995).

Schlesinger, Walter, "Die geschichtliche Stellung der mittelalterlichen deutschen Ostbewegung," *Historische Zeitschrift* 183 (1957): 517–42.

Schmitt, Eberhard, *Die Anfänge der europäischen Expansion* (Idstein, 1991).

Setton, Kenneth M., ed., *A History of the Crusades*, 6 vols. (Philadelphia and Madison, 1955–89).

Stow, Kenneth R., *Alienated Minority: The Jews of Medieval Latin Europe* (Cambridge, Mass., 1992).

Stuard, Susan Mosher, *A State of Deference: Ragusa/Dubrovnik in the Medieval Centuries* (Philadelphia, 1992).

Thrupp, Sylvia L., ed., *Change in Medieval Society: Europe North of the Alps, 1050-1500* (New York, 1964).

Tracy, James D., ed., *The Rise of Merchant Empires: Long-Distance Trade in the Early Modern World, 1350-1750* (Cambridge, 1990).

Verlinden, Charles, *L'esclavage dans l'Europe médiévale*, 2 vols. (Bruges, 1955–77).

Vogler, Bernard, ed., *Les migrations de l'antiquité à nos jours: Actes du colloque tenu à Stras-bourg les 7 et 8 mars 1994* (Strasbourg, 1996).

Vries, Jan de, "Population," in Thomas A. Brady Jr., Heiko A. Oberman, and James D. Tracy, eds., *Handbook of European History, 1400–1600: Late Middle Ages, Renaissance, and Reforma-tion* (Leiden, 1994), 1:1–50.

Weinryb, Bernard D., *The Jews of Poland: A Social and Economic History of the Jewish Commu-nity in Poland from 1100 to 1800* (Philadelphia, 1973).

Yungblut, Laura H., *Strangers Settled Here amongst Us: Policies, Perceptions, and the Presence of Aliens in Elizabethan England* (London, 1996).

Zacher, Christian K., *Curiosity and Pilgrimage: The Literature of Discovery in Fourteenth-Century England* (Baltimore, 1976).

4 Migrations from the Seventeenth to the Nineteenth Century

General

Adas, Michael, ed., *Islamic and European Expansion: The Forging of a Global Order* (Philadel-phia, 1993).

Aldrich, Robert, *Greater France: A History of French Overseas Expansion* (New York, 1996).

Baumgart, Winfried, *Imperialism: The Idea and Reality of British and French Colonial Expan-sion, 1880–1914* (rev. ed., Oxford, 1982)

Betts, Raymond F., *Assimilation and Association in French Colonial Theory, 1890–1914* (New York, 1961).

Brunschwig, Henri, *French Colonialism, 1871–1914: Myths and Realities,* trans. William Gran-ville Brown (French orig., 1960; London, 1966).

Chaunu, Pierre, *Conquête et exploitation des Nouveaux Mondes, XVIe siècle* (Paris, 1969).

Cooper, Frederick, and Ann Laura Stoler, eds., *Tensions of Empire: Colonial Cultures in a Bour-geois World* (Berkeley, 1997).

Crosby, Alfred W., *Ecological Imperialism: The Biological Expansion of Europe, 900–1900* (Cam-bridge, 1986).

Curtin, Philip D., *Cross-Cultural Trade in World History* (Cambridge, 1984).

———, *Death by Migration: Europe's Encounter with the Tropical World in the Nineteenth Cen-tury* (Cambridge, 1989).

Davies, K. G., *The North Atlantic World in the Seventeenth Century* (Minneapolis, 1974).

Deerr, Noël, *The History of Sugar,* 2 vols. (London, 1949–50).

Dixon, Chris, and Michael Heffernan, eds., *Colonialism and Development in the Contemporary World* (London, 1991).

Emmer, Piet C., ed., *Colonialism and Migration: Indentured Labour before and after Slavery* (Dordrecht, 1986).

Emmer, Piet C., and Magnus Mörner, eds., *European Expansion and Migration: Essays on the Intercontinental Migration from Africa, Asia, and Europe* (New York, 1992).

Fredrickson, George M., *The Black Image in the White Mind: The Debate on Afro-American Character and Destiny, 1817–1914* (New York, 1971).

Green, Nancy L., *Ready-to-Wear and Ready-to-Work: A Century of Industry and Immigrants in Paris and New York* (Durham, N.C., 1997).

———, ed., *Jewish Workers in the Modern Diaspora* (Berkeley, 1998).

Guerin-Gonzales, Camille, and Carl Strikwerda, eds., *The Politics of Immigrant Workers: Labor Activism and Migration in the World Economy since 1830* (New York, 1993).

Karras, Alan L., and John R. McNeill, eds., *Atlantic American Societies: From Columbus through Abolition, 1492-1888* (London, 1992).

Kiernan, Victor G., *The Lords of Human Kind: Black Man, Yellow Man, and White Man in an Age of Empire* (Boston, 1969; repr., New York, 1986).

Leroy-Beaulieu, Paul, *De la colonisation chez les peuples modernes* (1st ed., 1874; 4th rev. ed., Paris, 1898).

Lewis, M. D., "'One Hundred Million Frenchmen': The Assimilation Theory in French Colonial Policy," *Comparative Studies in Society and History* 4 (1961/62): 129-53.

Lovejoy, Paul E., and Nicholas Rogers, eds., *Unfree Labour in the Development of the Atlantic World* (Ilford, U.K., 1994).

Marks, Shula, and Peter Richardson, eds., *International Labour Migration: Historical Perspectives* (Hounslow, U.K., 1984).

Mintz, Sidney W., *Sweetness and Power: The Place of Sugar in Modern History* (New York, 1985).

———, ed., *Slavery, Colonialism, and Racism: Essays* (New York, 1974).

Northrup, David, *Indentured Labor in the Age of Imperialism, 1834-1922* (Cambridge, 1995).

Norwood, Frederick A., *Strangers and Exiles: A History of Religious Refugees*, 2 vols. (Nashville, Tenn., 1965-69).

Nugent, Walter, *Crossings: The Great Transatlantic Migrations, 1870-1914* (Bloomington, 1992).

Pagden, Anthony, *European Encounters with the New World: From Renaissance to Romanticism* (New Haven, 1993).

———, *Spanish Imperialism and the Political Imagination: Studies in European and Spanish-American Social and Political Theory, 1513-1830* (New Haven, 1990).

Piore, Michael J., *Birds of Passage: Migrant Labor and Industrial Societies* (New York, 1979).

Potts, Lydia, *The World Labour Market: A History of Migration*, trans. Terry Bond (German orig., 1988; London, 1990).

Stoler, Ann L., "Making Empire Respectable: The Politics of Race and Sexual Morality in 20th-Century Colonial Cultures," *American Ethnologist* 16 (1989): 634-60.

Strobel, Margaret, *Gender, Sex, and Empire* (Washington, D.C., 1993).

Todorov, Tzvetan, *The Conquest of America: The Question of the Other*, trans. Richard Howard (French orig., Paris, 1982; New York 1984).

Wolf, Eric R., *Europe and the People without History* (Berkeley, 1982).

Africa, including the Slave Trade and the Black Diaspora

Alpers, Edward A., *Ivory and Slaves in East Central Africa: Changing Patterns of International Trade to the Later Nineteenth Century* (London, 1975).

Anstey, Roger, *The Atlantic Slave Trade and British Abolition, 1760-1810* (London, 1975).

Austen, Ralph A., "The Trans-Saharan Slave Trade: A Tentative Census," in Henry A. Gemery and Jan S. Hogendorn, eds., *The Uncommon Market: Essays in the Economic History of the Atlantic Slave Trade* (New York, 1979), 23-76.

Barry, Boubacar, *La Sénégambie du XVe au XIXe siècle: Traite négrière, Islam et conquête coloniale* (Paris, 1988).

Berlin, Ira, "From Creole to African: Atlantic Creoles and the Origins of African-American Society in Mainland North America," *William and Mary Quarterly* 53 (1996): 251-88.

Bhana, Surendra, ed., *Essays on Indentured Indians in Natal* (Leeds, 1990).

Bhana, Surendra, and Joy B. Brain, *Setting Down Roots: Indian Migrants in South Africa, 1860–1911* (Johannesburg, 1990).

Chittick, H. Neville, and Robert I. Rotberg, eds., *East Africa and the Orient: Cultural Synthesis in Pre-Colonial Times* (New York, 1975).

Cohen, Abner, *Custom and Politics in Urban Africa: A Study of Hausa Migrants in Yoruba Towns* (Berkeley, 1969).

Conniff, Michael L., and Thomas J. Davis, *Africans in the Americas: A History of the Black Diaspora* (New York, 1994).

Conrad, Robert Edgar, *World of Sorrow: The African Slave Trade to Brazil* (Baton Rouge, 1986).

Curtin, Philip D., *The Atlantic Slave Trade: A Census* (Madison, 1969).

Davidson, Basil, *A History of East and Central Africa to the Late Nineteenth Century* (Garden City, N.Y., 1969).

Davis, Darién J., ed., *Slavery and Beyond: The African Impact on Latin America and the Caribbean* (Wilmington, Del., 1995).

Davis, David B., *The Problem of Slavery in Western Culture* (Ithaca, N.Y., 1966).

Eltis, David, and James Walvin, eds., *The Abolition of the Atlantic Slave Trade: Origins and Effects in Europe, Africa, and the Americas* (Madison, 1981).

Ewald, Janet J., "Slavery in Africa and the Slave Trades from Africa," *American Historical Review* 97 (1992): 465–85.

———, *Soldiers, Traders, and Slaves: State Formation and Economic Transformation in the Greater Nile Valley, 1700–1885* (Madison, 1990).

Falola, Toyin, and Paul E. Lovejoy, eds., *Pawnship in Africa: Debt Bondage in Historical Perspective* (Boulder, 1994).

Galaty, John G., and Pierre Bonte, eds., *Herders, Warriors, and Traders: Pastoralism in Africa* (Boulder, 1991).

Gilroy, Paul, *The Black Atlantic: Modernity and Double Consciousness* (Cambridge, Mass., 1993).

Harris, Joseph E., ed., *Global Dimensions of the African Diaspora* (Washington, D.C., 1982).

Huggins, Nathan Irvin, *Black Odyssey: The Afro-American Ordeal in Slavery* (1st ed., 1977; New York, 1979).

Inikori, Joseph E., and Stanley L. Engerman, eds., *The Atlantic Slave Trade: Effects on Economies, Societies, and Peoples in Africa, the Americas, and Europe* (Durham, N.C., 1992).

Irwin, Graham W., ed., *Africans Abroad: A Documentary History of the Black Diaspora in Asia, Latin America and the Caribbean during the Age of Slavery* (New York, 1977).

Isaacman, Allen F., *Mozambique: The Africanization of a European Institution; the Zambezi Prazos, 1750–1902* (Madison, 1972).

Kilson, Martin L., and Robert I. Rotberg, eds., *The African Diaspora: Interpretive Essays* (Cambridge, Mass., 1976).

Klein, Herbert S., *The Middle Passage: Comparative Studies in the Atlantic Slave Trade* (Princeton, 1978).

Lovejoy, Paul E., *Transformations in Slavery: A History of Slavery in Africa* (Cambridge, 1983).

———, "The Volume of the Atlantic Slave Trade: A Synthesis," *Journal of African History* 23 (1982): 473–502.

Manchuelle, François, *Willing Migrants: Soninke Labor Diasporas, 1848–1960* (Athens, Ohio, 1997).

Mangat, J. S., *A History of the Asians in East Africa, c.1886 to 1945* (Oxford, 1969).

Manning, Patrick, *Slavery and African Life: Occidental, Oriental, and African Slave Trades* (Cambridge, 1990).

Meillassoux, Claude, *Anthropologie de l'esclavage: Le ventre de fer et d'argent* (Paris, 1986).

———, ed., *Esclavage en Afrique précoloniale* (Paris, 1975).

Miers, Suzanne, and Igor Kopytoff, eds., *Slavery in Africa: Historical and Anthropological Perspectives* (Madison, 1977).

Miers, Suzanne, and Richard Roberts, eds., *The End of Slavery in Africa* (Madison, 1988).

Miller, Joseph C., *Way of Death: Merchant Capitalism and the Angolan Slave Trade, 1730–1830* (Madison, 1988).

Mintz, Sidney W., and Richard Price, *The Birth of African-American Culture: An Anthropological Perspective* (Boston, 1992).

Morton, Fred, *Children of Ham: Freed Slaves and Fugitive Slaves on the Kenya Coast, 1873 to 1907* (Boulder, 1990).

Northrup, David, ed., *The Atlantic Slave Trade* (Lexington, Mass., 1994).

Pachai, Bridglal, *The International Aspects of the South African Indian Question, 1860–1971* (Cape Town, 1971).

Read, Margaret, "Migrant Labour in Africa and Its Effects on Tribal Life," *International Labour Review* 45, 2 (1942): 605–31.

Richardson, Peter, *Chinese Mine Labour in the Transvaal* (London, 1982).

Robertson, Claire C., and Martin A. Klein, eds., *Women and Slavery in Africa* (Madison, 1983).

Samarin, William J., *The Black Man's Burden: African Colonial Labor on the Congo and Ubangi Rivers, 1880–1900* (Boulder, 1989).

Sheriff, Abdul, *Slaves, Spices, and Ivory in Zanzibar: Integration of an East African Commercial Empire into the World Economy, 1770–1873* (Athens, Ohio, 1987).

Simpson, Donald H., *Dark Companions: The African Contribution to the European Exploration of East Africa* (London, 1975).

Solow, Barbara L., ed., *Slavery and the Rise of the Atlantic System* (Cambridge, 1991).

Stichter, Sharon B., *Migrant Labour in Kenya: Capitalism and African Response, 1895–1975* (Harlow, U.K., 1982).

Thompson, Vincent Bakpetu, *The Making of the African Diaspora in the Americas, 1441–1900* (Harlow, U.K., 1987).

Thornton, John, *Africa and Africans in the Making of the Atlantic World, 1400–1680* (Cambridge, 1992).

UNESCO, *The African Slave Trade from the Fifteenth to the Nineteenth Century: Reports and Papers of the Meeting of Experts Organized by UNESCO at Port-au-Prince, Haiti, 1978* (Paris, 1979).

Willis, John Ralph, ed., *Slaves and Slavery in Muslim Africa*, 2 vols. (London, 1985).

Asia, including Contract Labor, West Asia (the Eastern Mediterranean), Hawai'i, and Australasia

Alatas, Hussein Syed, *The Myth of the Lazy Native: A Study of the Image of the Malays, Filipinos and Javanese from the 16th to the 20th Century and Its Function in the Ideology of Colonial Capitalism* (London, 1977).

Arasaratnam, Sinnappah, *Indians in Malaysia and Singapore* (rev. ed., Kuala Lumpur and New York, 1979).

———, *Maritime Trade, Society and European Influence in South Asia, 1600–1800* (Aldershot, U.K., 1995).

Aubin, Jean, ed., *Mare Luso-Indicum: Études et documents sur l'histoire de l'Océan Indien et des pays riverains a l'époque de la domination portugaise*, 4 vols. (Geneva, 1971–80).

Beauchamp, Edward R., and Akira Iriye, eds., *Foreign Employees in Nineteenth-Century Japan* (Boulder, 1990).

Behal, Rana P., and Prabhu P. Mohapatra, "Tea and Money Versus Human Life: The Rise and Fall of the Indenture System in the Assam Tea Plantations, 1840–1908," *Journal of Peasant Studies* 19, 3/4 (1992): 142–72.

Bissoondoyal, Uttama, and S. B. C. Servansing, eds., *Indian Labour Immigration: Papers Presented at the International Conference on Indian Labour Immigration, 23–27 Oct. 1984, Held at the Mahatma Gandhi Institute* (Moka, Mauritius, 1986).

———, eds., *Slavery in the South West Indian Ocean* (Moka, Mauritius, 1989).

Boxer, Charles R., *The Christian Century in Japan, 1549–1650* (Berkeley, 1951; repr. 1974).

———, *The Dutch Seaborne Empire, 1600–1800* (London, 1965).

———, *The Portuguese Seaborne Empire, 1415–1825* (London, 1969).

———, *Race Relations in the Portuguese Empire, 1415–1825* (New York, 1963).

Breman, Jan C., *Labour Migration and Rural Transformation in Colonial Asia* (Amsterdam, 1990).

———, *Taming the Coolie Beast: Plantation Society and the Colonial Order in Southeast Asia* (Delhi and New York, 1987).

Breman, Jan C., and E. Valentine Daniel, "The Making of a Coolie," *Journal of Peasant Studies* 19, 3/4 (1992): 268–95.

Campbell, Persia C., *Chinese Coolie Emigration to Countries within the British Empire* (1923; repr., London, 1971).

Chandrasekhar, S., ed., *From India to Australia: A Brief History of Immigration, the Dismantling of the "White Australia," Policy, Problems and Prospects of Assimilation* (La Jolla, 1992).

Chaudhuri, K. N., *Asia before Europe: Economy and Civilisation of the Indian Ocean from the Rise of Islam to 1750* (Cambridge, 1990).

———, *Trade and Civilisation in the Indian Ocean: An Economic History from the Rise of Islam to 1750* (Cambridge, 1985).

Clarence-Smith, William Gervase, ed., *The Economics of the Indian Ocean Slave Trade in the Nineteenth Century* (London, 1989).

Corris, Peter, *Passage, Port and Plantation: A History of Solomon Islands Labour Migration, 1870–1914* (Melbourne, 1973).

Cumpston, I. M., *Indians Overseas in British Territories, 1834–1854* (London, 1953).

Dale, Stephen Frederic, *Indian Merchants and Eurasian Trade, 1600–1750* (Cambridge, 1994).

Das Gupta, Ashin, *Merchants of Maritime India, 1500–1800* (Aldershot, U.K., 1994).

Das Gupta, Ranajit, "Factory Labour in Eastern India: Sources of Supply, 1855–1946," *Indian Economic and Social History Review* 13 (1976): 277–330.

———, "Plantation Labour in Colonial India," *Journal of Peasant Studies* 19, 3/4 (1992): 173–98.

Davis, Kingsley, *The Population of India and Pakistan* (Princeton, 1951).

Felix, Alfonso, Jr., ed., *The Chinese in the Philippines*, 2 vols. (Manila and New York, 1966–69).

Gillion, K. L., *Fiji's Indian Migrants: A History to the End of Indenture in 1920* (Melbourne, 1962).

Gosling, L. A. Peter, and Linda Y. C. Lim, eds., *The Chinese in Southeast Asia*, 2 vols. (Singapore, 1983).

Heidhues, Mary F. Somers, *Southeast Asia's Chinese Minorities* (Hawthorn, Austral., 1974).

Ho, Ping-ti, *Studies on the Population of China, 1368–1953* (Cambridge, Mass., 1959).

Huck, Arthur, *The Chinese in Australia* (Melbourne, 1968).

Inglis, Christine, et al., eds., *Asians in Australia: The Dynamics of Migration and Settlement* (Singapore, 1992).

Irick, Robert L., *Ch'ing Policy toward the Coolie Trade, 1847–1878* (Taipei, 1982).

Jackson, R. N., *Immigrant Labour and the Development of Malaya, 1786–1920: A Historical Monograph* (Kuala Lumpur, 1961).

Jain, Ravindra K., *South Indians on the Plantation Frontier in Malaya* (New Haven, 1970).

Jensen, Joan M., *Passage from India: Asian Indian Immigrants in North America* (New Haven, 1988).

Jupp, James, ed., *The Australian People: An Encyclopedia of the Nation, Its People, and Their Origins* (North Ryde, NSW, 1988).

Kondapi, C., *Indians Overseas, 1838–1949* (New Delhi, 1951).

Lasker, Bruno, *Human Bondage in Southeast Asia* (Chapel Hill, N.C., 1950).

Lee, Robert H. G., *The Manchurian Frontier in Ch'ing History* (Cambridge, Mass., 1970).

Lewis, Bernhard, *Race and Slavery in the Middle East: An Historical Enquiry* (Oxford, 1990).

Lombard, Denys, and Jean Aubin, eds., *Marchands et hommes d'affaires asiatiques dans l'Océan Indien et la mer de Chine, 13e–20e siècles* (Paris, 1988).

Loomis, Terrence, *Pacific Migrant Labour, Class and Racism in New Zealand* (Aldershot, U.K., 1990).

Mahajani, Usha, *The Role of Indian Minorities in Burma and Malaya* (Bombay, 1960; repr., Westport, Conn., 1973).

Maude, Henry E., *Slavers in Paradise: The Peruvian Labour Trade in Polynesia, 1862–1864* (Suva, Fiji, 1981).

Meilink-Roelofsz, Marie A. P., *Asian Trade and European Influence in the Indonesian Archipelago between 1500 and about 1630* (The Hague, 1962).

Morris, M. D., *The Emergence of an Industrial Labor Force in India: A Study of the Bombay Cotton Mills, 1854–1947* (Berkeley, 1965).

Munro, Doug, "The Labor Trade in Melanesians to Queensland: An Historical Essay," *Journal of Social History* 28 (1995): 609–27.

Nicholas, Stephen, ed., *Convict Workers: Reinterpreting Australia's Past* (Cambridge, 1988).

Nilakanta Sastri, K. A., *South Indian Influences in the Far East* (Bombay, 1949).

Oaten, Edward F., *European Travellers in India during the Fifteenth, Sixteenth, and Seventeenth Centuries* (London, 1909).

Özbaran, Salih, "The Ottoman Turks and the Portuguese in the Persian Gulf, 1534–1581," *Journal of Asian History* 6 (1972): 45–87.

Pearson, M. N., *Merchants and Rulers in Gujarat: The Response to the Portuguese in the Sixteenth Century* (Berkeley, 1976).

Price, Charles A., *The Great White Walls Are Built: Restrictive Immigration to North America and Australasia, 1836–1888* (Canberra, 1974)

Purcell, Victor, *The Chinese in Malaya* (2d rev. ed., Kuala Lumpur and London, 1967).

————, *The Chinese in Southeast Asia* (Oxford, 1951).

Rao, M. S. A., ed., *Studies in Migration: Internal and International Migration in India* (Delhi, 1986).

Roland, Joan G., *Jews in British India: Identity in a Colonial Era* (Hanover, N.H., 1989).

Rothermund, Dietmar, and D. C. Wadhwa, eds., *Zamindars, Mines and Peasants: Studies in the History of an Indian Coalfield and Its Rural Hinterland* (Delhi, 1978).

Saunders, Kay, ed., *Indentured Labour in the British Empire, 1834-1920* (London, 1984).

Simkin, C. G. F., *The Traditional Trade of Asia* (Oxford, 1968).

Sinha, Mrinalini, *Colonial Masculinity: The "Manly Englishmen" and the "Effeminate Bengali" in the Late Nineteenth Century* (Manchester, 1995).

Sopher, David E., *The Sea Nomads: A Study Based on the Literature of the Maritime Boat People of Southeast Asia* (Singapore, 1965).

Stoler, Laura Ann, *Capitalism and Confrontation in Sumatra's Plantation Belt, 1870-1979* (New Haven, 1985).

Takaki, Ronald, *Pau Hana: Plantation Life and Labor in Hawaii, 1835-1920* (Honolulu, 1983).

Tinker, Hugh, *A New System of Slavery: The Export of Indian Labour Overseas, 1830-1920* (London, 1974).

Wickberg, Edgar, *The Chinese in Philippine Life, 1850-1898* (New Haven, 1965).

Yang, Anand A., "Peasants on the Move: A Study of Internal Migration in India," *Journal of Interdisciplinary History* 10 (1979): 37-58.

Yarwood, Alexander T., *Asian Migration to Australia: The Background of Exclusion, 1896-1913* (Melbourne, 1964).

Yen, Ching-Hwang, *Coolies and Mandarins: China's Protection of Overseas Chinese during the Late Ch'ing Period (1851-1911)* (Singapore, 1985).

Latin America and the Americas as a Whole

Altman, Ida, and James Horn, eds., *"To Make America": European Emigration in the Early Modern Period* (Berkeley, 1991).

Andrien, Kenneth J., and Rolena Adorno, eds., *Transatlantic Encounters: Europeans and Andeans in the Sixteenth Century* (Berkeley, 1991).

Avila, Fernando Bastos de, *L'immigration au Brésil: Contribution à une théorie générale de l'immigration* (Rio de Janeiro, 1956).

Baily, Samuel L., *Immigrants in the Land of Promise: Italians in Buenos Aires and New York City, 1870-1914* (Ithaca, N.Y., 1999).

Bakewell, Peter, *Miners of the Red Mountain: Indian Labor in Potosí, 1545-1650* (Albuquerque, 1984).

Bastide, Roger, *African Civilisations in the New World*, trans. Peter Green (French orig., 1967; New York, 1971).

Berlin, Ira, and Philip D. Morgan, eds., *Cultivation and Culture: Labor and the Shaping of Slave Life in the Americas* (Charlottesville, 1993).

Blackburn, Robin, *The Making of New World Slavery: From the Baroque to the Modern, 1492-1800* (London, 1997).

Boyd-Bowman, Peter, *Patterns of Spanish Emigration to the New World (1492-1580)* (Buffalo, 1973).

Bush, Barbara, *Slave Women in Caribbean Society, 1650-1838* (Bloomington, 1990).

Campbell, Leon G., "The Foreigners in Peruvian Society during the Eighteenth Century," *Revista de Historia de América* 73/74 (1972): 153–63.

Carroll, Patrick J., "Recent Literature on Latin American Slavery," *Latin American Research Review* 31 (1996): 135–47.

Chiappelli, Fredi, et al., eds., *First Images of America: The Impact of the New World on the Old*, 2 vols. (Berkeley, 1976).

Cole, Jeffrey A., *The Potosí Mita, 1573–1700: Compulsory Indian Labor in the Andes* (Stanford, 1985).

Cook, Noble David, *Demographic Collapse: Indian Peru, 1520–1620* (Cambridge, 1981).

Cornblit, Oscar, "European Immigrants in Argentine Industry and Politics [1880s–1920s]," in Claudio Veliz, ed., *The Politics of Conformity in Latin America* (Oxford, 1967), 221–48.

Degler, Carl N., *Neither Black nor White: Slavery and Race Relations in Brazil and the United States* (New York, 1971; repr., Madison, 1986).

Denevan, William M., ed., *The Native Population of the Americas in 1492* (Madison, 1976).

Devoto, Fernando J., *Le migrazioni italiane in Argentina: Un saggio interpretativo* (Naples, 1994).

Dobyns, Henry F., "Estimating Aboriginal American Population: An Appraisal of Techniques with a New Hemispheric Estimate," *Current Anthropology* 7 (1966): 395–449.

Fraginals, Manuel Moreno, Frank Moya Pons, and Stanley L. Engerman, eds., *Between Slavery and Free Labor: The Spanish-Speaking Caribbean in the Nineteenth Century* (Baltimore, 1985).

Galenson, David W., *White Servitude in Colonial America: An Economic Analysis* (Cambridge, 1981).

Gardiner, C. Harvey, *The Japanese and Peru, 1873–1973* (Albuquerque, 1975).

Gaspar, David Barry, and Darlene Clark Hine, eds., *More Than Chattel: Black Women and Slavery in the Americas* (Bloomington, 1996).

Holloway, Thomas H., *Immigrants on the Land: Coffee and Society in São Paulo, 1886–1934* (Chapel Hill, N.C., 1980).

Kent, R. K., "Palmares: An African State in Brazil," *Journal of African History* 3 (1965): 161–75.

Lai, Walton Look, *Indentured Labor, Caribbean Sugar: Chinese and Indian Migrants to the British West Indies, 1838–1918* (Baltimore, 1993).

Laurence, K. O., *Immigration into the West Indies in the 19th Century* (Barbados, 1971).

Liebman, Seymour B., "The Jews of Colonial Mexico," *Hispanic American Historical Review* 43 (1963): 95–108.

Lier, R. A. J. van, *Frontier Society: A Social Analysis of the History of Surinam*, trans. M. J. L. van Yperen (Dutch orig., 2d ed., Deventer, 1971; The Hague, 1971).

Mellafe, Rolando, "The Importance of Migration in the Viceroyalty of Peru," in Paul Deprez, ed., *Population and Economics: Proceedings of Section V* [Historical Demography Section] *of the Fourth Congress of the Economic History Association, 1968* (Winnipeg, 1970), 303–13.

Mörner, Magnus, *Adventurers and Proletarians: The Story of Migrants in Latin America* (Pittsburgh, 1985).

———, *Race Mixture in the History of Latin America* (Boston, 1967).

Moya, José C., *Cousins and Strangers: Spanish Immigrants in Buenos Aires, 1850–1930* (Berkeley, 1998).

Mullin, Michael, *Africa in America: Slave Acculturation and Resistance in the American South and the British Caribbean, 1736–1831* (Urbana, Ill., 1992).

Nunn, Charles F., *Foreign Immigrants in Early Bourbon Mexico, 1700–1760* (Cambridge, 1979).

Petras, Elizabeth McLean, *Jamaican Labor Migration: White Capital and Black Labor, 1850–1930* (Boulder, 1988).

Pike, Ruth, *Penal Servitude in Early Modern Spain* (Madison, 1983).

Radding Murrieta, Cynthia, *Wandering Peoples: Colonialism, Ethnic Spaces, and Ecological Frontiers in Northwestern Mexico, 1700–1850* (Durham, N.C., 1997).

Richardson, Bonham C., *The Caribbean in the Wider World, 1492–1992: A Regional Geography* (Cambridge, 1992).

——, "Caribbean Migrations, 1838–1985," in Franklin W. Knight and Colin A. Palmer, eds., *The Modern Caribbean* (Chapel Hill, N.C., 1989), 203–28.

Robinson, David J., ed., *Migration in Colonial Spanish America* (Cambridge, 1990).

Rosenstiel, Annette, *Red and White: Indian Views of the White Man, 1492–1982* (New York, 1983).

Rosoli, Gianfausto, ed., *Identità degli Italiani in Argentina: Reti sociali—famiglia—lavoro* (Rome, 1993).

Sánchez-Albornóz, Nicolás, *The Population of Latin America: A History*, trans. W. A. R. Richardson (Spanish orig., 1968; Berkeley, 1974).

Schuler, Monica, *"Alas, Alas, Kongo": A Social History of Indentured African Immigration into Jamaica, 1841–1865* (Baltimore, 1980).

Schurz, William L., *The Manila Galleon* (New York, 1939, repr., 1959).

Schwartz, Stuart B., *Sugar Plantations in the Formation of Brazilian Society: Bahia, 1550–1835* (Cambridge, 1985).

Sheridan, Richard B., *Sugar and Slavery: An Economic History of the British West Indies, 1623–1775* (Baltimore, 1974).

Sherman, William L., *Forced Native Labor in Sixteenth-Century Central America* (Lincoln, Nebr., 1979).

Solberg, Carl, *Immigration and Nationalism: Argentina and Chile, 1890–1914* (Austin, Tex., 1970).

Suzuki, Teiiti, *The Japanese Immigrant in Brazil*, 2 vols. (Tokyo, 1969).

Watts, David, *The West Indies: Patterns of Development, Culture, and Environmental Change since 1492* (Cambridge, 1987).

Zavala, Silvio, *Los esclavos indios en Nueva España* (Mexico, 1968).

Zoller, Rüdiger, ed., *Amerikaner wider Willen: Beiträge zur Sklaverei in Lateinamerika und ihren Folgen* (Frankfurt/Main, 1994).

Anglo America

Archdeacon, Thomas J., *Becoming American: An Ethnic History* (New York, 1983).

Avery, Donald H., *Reluctant Host: Canada's Response to Immigrant Workers, 1896–1994* (Toronto, 1995).

Baganha, Maria Ioannis Benis, *Portuguese Emigration to the United States, 1820–1930* (New York, 1990).

Bailyn, Bernard, *The Peopling of British North America: An Introduction* (New York, 1986).

——, *Voyagers to the West: A Passage in the Peopling of America on the Eve of the Revolution* (New York, 1986).

Barrett, James R., "Americanization from the Bottom Up: Immigration and the Remaking of the

Working Class in the United States, 1880–1930," *Journal of American History* 80 (1992): 997–1020.

Barton, Josef J., *Peasants and Strangers: Italians, Rumanians, and Slovaks in an American City, 1890–1950* (Cambridge, Mass., 1975).

Berkhofer, Robert F., Jr., *The White Man's Indian: Images of the American Indian from Columbus to the Present* (New York, 1978).

Bodnar, John, *The Transplanted: A History of Immigrants in Urban America* (Bloomington, 1985).

Brancaforte, Charlotte L., *The German Forty-Eighters in the United States* (New York, 1989).

Brodkin, Karen, *How Jews Became White Folks and What That Says about Race in America* (New Brunswick, 1998).

Bukowczyk, John J., and Nora Faires, "Immigration History in the United States, 1965–1990: A Selective Critical Appraisal," *Canadian Ethnic Studies* 33, 2 (1991): 1–23.

Burnet, Jean R., with Howard Palmer, *"Coming Canadians": An Introduction to a History of Canada's Peoples* (Toronto, 1988).

Chan, Sucheng, *This Bittersweet Soil: The Chinese in California Agriculture, 1860–1910* (Berkeley, 1986).

Cheng, Lucie, and Edna Bonacich, eds., *Labor Immigration under Capitalism: Asian Workers in the United States before World War II* (Berkeley, 1984).

Choquette, Leslie, *Frenchmen into Peasants: Modernity and Tradition in the Peopling of French Canada* (Cambridge, Mass., 1997).

Coleman, Terry, *Going to America* (New York, 1972).

Crew, Spencer R., *Field to Factory: Afro-American Migration, 1915–1940* (Washington, D.C., 1987).

Daniels, Roger, *Asian America: Chinese and Japanese in the United States since 1850* (Seattle, 1988).

———, *Coming to America: A History of Immigration and Ethnicity in American Life* (New York, 1990).

Debouzy, Marianne, ed., *In the Shadow of the Statue of Liberty: Immigrants, Workers and Citizens in the American Republic, 1880–1920* (French orig., Saint-Denis, 1988; Urbana, Ill., 1992).

Diner, Hasia R., *Erin's Daughters in America: Irish Immigrant Women in the Nineteenth Century* (Baltimore, 1983).

Dirlik, Arif, ed., *Chinese on the American Frontier* (Lanham, Md., 1997).

Friedman-Kasaba, Kathie, *Memories of Migration: Gender, Ethnicity, and Work in the Lives of Jewish and Italian Women in New York, 1870–1924* (Albany, N.Y., 1996).

Gabaccia, Donna R., *From the Other Side: Women, Gender, and Immigrant Life in the U.S., 1820–1990* (Bloomington, 1994).

———, *Militants and Migrants: Rural Sicilians Become American Workers* (New Brunswick, 1988).

Glazer, Nathan, and Daniel Patrick Moynihan, *Beyond the Melting Pot: The Negroes, Puerto Ricans, Jews, Italians, and Irish of New York City* (Cambridge, Mass., 1963).

Glenn, Susan A., *Daughters of the Shtetl: Life and Labor in the Immigrant Generation* (Ithaca, N.Y., 1990).

Gordon, Milton M., *Assimilation in American Life: The Role of Race, Religion, and National Origins* (New York, 1964).

Grossman, James R., *Land of Hope: Chicago, Black Southerners, and the Great Migration* (Chicago, 1989).

Gurock, Jeffrey S., ed., *American Jewish History*, 8 vols. (New York, 1997–98).

Handlin, Oscar, *The Uprooted: The Epic Story of the Great Migrations That Made the American People* (Boston, 1951).

Hansen, Marcus Lee, with John Bartlett Brebner, *The Mingling of the Canadian and American Peoples* (New Haven, 1940).

Harzig, Christiane, ed., *Peasant Maids, City Women: From the European Countryside to Urban America* (Ithaca, N.Y., 1997).

Hawkins, Freda, *Canada and Immigration: Public Policy and Public Concern* (2d ed., Kingston, Ont., 1988).

Henri, Florette, *Black Migration: Movement North, 1900-1920* (Garden City, N.Y., 1975).

Highham, John, *Strangers in the Land: Patterns of American Nativism, 1860-1925* (New York, 1963).

Hing, Bill Ong, *Making and Remaking Asian America through Immigration Policy, 1850-1990* (Stanford, 1993).

Hoerder, Dirk, ed., *"Struggle a Hard Battle": Essays on Working-Class Immigrants* (DeKalb, Ill., 1986).

Iacovetta, Franca, Paula Draper, and Robert Ventresca, eds., *A Nation of Immigrants: Women, Workers, and Communities in Canadian History, 1840s-1960s* (Toronto, 1998).

Ichioka, Yuji, *The Issei: The World of the First Generation Japanese Immigrants, 1885-1924* (New York, 1988).

Jacobson, David, ed., *The Immigration Reader: America in a Multidisciplinary Perspective* (Oxford, 1998).

Jacobson, Matthew Frye, *Special Sorrows: The Diasporic Imagination of Irish, Polish, and Jewish Immigrants in the United States* (Cambridge, Mass., 1995).

———, *Whiteness of a Different Color: European Immigrants and the Alchemy of Race* (Cambridge, Mass., 1998).

Jensen, Joan M., *Passage from India: Asian Indian Immigrants in North America* (New Haven, 1988).

Johnson, Daniel M., and Rex R. Campbell, *Black Migration in America: A Social Demographic History* (Durham, N.C., 1981).

Kamphoefner, Walter D., Wolfgang Helbich, and Ulrike Sommer, eds., *News from the Land of Freedom: German Immigrants Write Home*, trans. Susan C. Vogel (German orig., 1988; Ithaca, N.Y., 1991).

Keil, Hartmut, and John B. Jentz, eds., *German Workers in Industrial Chicago, 1850-1910: A Comparative Perspective* (DeKalb, Ill., 1983).

Korman, Gerd, *Industrialization, Immigrants, and Americanizers: The View from Milwaukee, 1866-1921* (Madison, 1967).

Kraut, Alan M., *Silent Travelers: Germs, Genes, and the "Immigrant Menace"* (New York, 1994).

Lemann, Nicholas, *The Promised Land: The Great Black Migration and How It Changed America* (New York, 1991).

McCaffrey, Lawrence J., *The Irish Catholic Diaspora in America* (rev. ed., Washington, D.C., 1997).

Marks, Carole, *Farewell—We're Good and Gone: The Great Black Migration* (Bloomington, 1989).

Meier, Matt S., and Feliciano Ribera, *Mexican Americans, American Mexicans: From Conquistadors to Chicanos* (rev. ed., New York, 1993)

Meinig, D. W., *The Shaping of America: A Geographical Perspective on 500 Years of History*, vol. 1: *Atlantic America, 1492–1800* (New Haven, 1986).

Miller, Kerby A., *Emigrants and Exiles: Ireland and the Irish Exodus to North America* (New York, 1985).

Palmié, Stephan, ed., *Slave Cultures and the Cultures of Slavery* (Knoxville, 1995).

Pedraza, Silvia, and Rubén G. Rumbaut, eds., *Origins and Destinies: Immigration, Race, and Ethnicity in America* (Belmont, Calif., 1996).

Porter, John, *The Vertical Mosaic: An Analysis of Social Class and Power in Canada* (Toronto, 1965).

Portes, Alejandro, and Rubén G. Rumbaut, *Immigrant America: A Portrait* (Berkeley, 1990).

Pozetta, George E., ed., *Ethnicity and Gender: The Immigrant Woman* (New York, 1991).

Ramirez, Bruno, *On the Move: French-Canadian and Italian Migrants in the North Atlantic Economy, 1860–1914* (Toronto, 1991); French ed.: *Par monts et par vaux: Migrants canadiens-français et italiens dans l'économie nord-atlantique, 1860–1914* (Quebec, 1991).

Redkey, Edwin S., *Black Exodus: Black Nationalist and Back-to-Africa Movements, 1890–1910* (New Haven, 1969).

Rischin, Moses, and John Livingston, eds., *Jews of the American West* (Detroit, 1991).

Smith, Abbot E., *Colonists in Bondage: White Servitude and Convict Labor in America, 1607–1776* (Chapel Hill, N.C., 1947).

Sollors, Werner, ed., *The Invention of Ethnicity* (New York, 1989).

Strikwerda, Carl, "Tides of Migration, Currents of History: The State, Economy, and the Transatlantic Movement of Labor in the Nineteenth and Twentieth Centuries," *International Review of Social History* 44 (1999): 367–94.

Takaki, Ronald, *Strangers from a Different Shore: A History of Asian Americans* (Boston, 1989).

Thernstrom, Stephan, Ann Orlov, and Oscar Handlin, eds., *Harvard Encyclopedia of American Ethnic Groups* (Cambridge, Mass., 1980).

Thomas, William I., and Florian Znaniecki, *The Polish Peasant in Europe and America: Monograph of an Immigrant Group*, 5 vols. (Chicago, 1918–20).

Vecoli, Rudolph J., "The *Contadini* in Chicago: A Critique of *The Uprooted*," *Journal of American History* 51 (1964): 404–17.

Vecoli, Rudolph J., and Suzanne M. Sinke, eds., *A Century of European Migrations, 1830–1930* (Urbana, Ill., 1991).

Weil, François, *Les Franco-Américains, 1860–1980* (Paris, 1989).

Wong, K. Scott, and Sucheng Chan, eds., *Claiming America: Constructing Chinese American Identities during the Exclusion Era* (Philadelphia, 1998).

Wyman, Mark, *Round-Trip to America: The Immigrants Return to Europe, 1880–1930* (Ithaca, N.Y., 1993).

Yans-McLaughlin, Virginia, ed., *Immigration Reconsidered: History, Sociology, and Politics* (New York, 1990).

Europe, including Russia

Amburger, Erik, *Die Anwerbung ausländischer Fachkräfte für die Wirtschaft Rußlands vom 15. bis ins 19. Jahrhundert* (Wiesbaden, 1968).

Anderson, Barbara A., *Internal Migration during Modernization in Late Nineteenth-Century Russia* (Princeton, 1980).

Bade, Klaus J., *Kontinent in Bewegung: Europa und die Migration im 19. und 20 Jahrhundert* (Munich, 2000).

———, ed., *Deutsche im Ausland, Fremde in Deutschland: Migration in Geschichte und Gegenwart* (Munich, 1992).

Baines, Dudley, *Migration in a Mature Economy: Emigration and Internal Migration in England and Wales, 1861–1900* (New York, 1985).

Bairoch, Paul, Jean Batou, and Pierre Chèvre, *La population des villes européennes 800–1850: Banque de données et analyse sommaire des résultats* (Geneva, 1988).

Bartlett, Roger P., *Human Capital: The Settlement of Foreigners in Russia, 1762–1804* (Cambridge, 1979).

Bassin, Mark, "Inventing Siberia: Visions of the Russian East in the Early Nineteenth Century," *American Historical Review* 96 (1991): 763–94.

Bater, James H., *St Petersburg: Industrialization and Change* (London, 1976).

Bezza, Bruno, ed., *Gli Italiani fuori d'Italia: Gli emigrati italiani nei movimenti operai dei paesi d'adozione, 1880–1940* (Milan, 1983).

Blank, Inge, "A Vast Migratory Experience: Eastern Europe in the Pre- and Post-Emancipation Era (1780–1914)," in Dirk Hoerder and Inge Blank, eds., *Roots of the Transplanted* (New York, 1994), 1:201–51.

Bobinska, Celina, and Andrzej Pilch, eds., *Employment-Seeking Emigrations of the Poles World-Wide, XIX and XX C.*, trans. Danuta E. Zukowska (Polish orig.; Krakow, 1975).

Bradley, Joseph, *Muzhik and Muscovite: Urbanization in Late Imperial Russia* (Berkeley, 1985).

Brady, Ciaran, and Raymond Gillespie, eds., *Natives and Newcomers: Essays on the Making of Irish Colonial Society, 1534–1641* (Dublin, 1986).

Brower, Daniel R., and Edward J. Lazzerini, eds., *Russia's Orient: Imperial Borderlands and Peoples, 1700–1917* (Bloomington, 1997).

Burds, Jeffrey, *Peasant Dreams and Market Politics: Labor Migration and the Russian Village, 1861–1905* (Pittsburgh, 1998).

Bushkovitch, Paul, *The Merchants of Moscow, 1580–1680* (Cambridge, 1980).

Canny, Nicholas P., *The Elizabethan Conquest of Ireland: A Pattern Established, 1565–76* (Hassocks, U.K., 1976).

———, ed., *Europeans on the Move: Studies on European Migration, 1500–1800* (Oxford, 1994).

Châtelain, Abel, *Les migrants temporaires en France de 1800 à 1914*, 2 vols. (Villeneuve-d'Asque, 1976).

Chevalier, Louis, "L'émigration française au XIXe siècle," *Études d'Histoire Moderne et Contemporaine* 1 (1947): 127–71.

Clark, Peter, and David Souden, eds., *Migration and Society in Early Modern England* (London, 1987).

Coquin, François-Xavier, *La Sibérie peuplement et immigration paysanne au XIXe siècle* (Paris, 1969).

Dodenhoeft, Bettina, *"Laßt mich nach Rußland heim": Russische Emigranten in Deutschland von 1918 bis 1945* (Frankfurt/Main, 1993).

Eiras Roel, Antonio, and Ofelia Rey Castelao, eds., *Les migrations internes et à moyenne distance en Europe, 1500–1900* (Santiago de Compostela, 1994).

Elsner, Lothar, "Foreign Workers and Forced Labor in Germany during the First World War," in

Dirk Hoerder, ed., *Labor Migration in the Atlantic Economies: The European and North American Working Classes during the Period of Industrialization* (Westport, Conn., 1985), 189–222.

L'émigration politique en Europe aux XIXe au XXe siècles: Actes du colloque organisé par l'École française de Rome (Rome, 1991).

Emmer, Piet C., and Magnus Mörner, eds., *European Expansion and Migration: Essays on the Intercontinental Migration from Africa, Asia, and Europe* (New York, 1992).

Erickson, Charlotte, *Invisible Immigrants: The Adaption of English and Scottish Immigrants in Nineteenth-Century America* (Coral Gables, Fla., 1972).

Fassmann, Heinz, *Einwanderungsland Österreich? Historische Migrationsmuster, aktuelle Trends und politische Maßnahmen* (Vienna, 1995).

Fenske, Hans, "International Migration: Germany in the Eighteenth Century," *Central European History* 13 (1980): 332–47.

Fischer, Wolfram, "Rural Industrialization and Population Change," *Comparative Studies in Society and History* 15 (1973): 158–70.

François, Etienne, ed., *Immigration et société urbaine en Europe occidentale, XVIe-XXe siècle* (Paris, 1985).

Green, Nancy L., *The Pletzl of Paris: Jewish Immigrant Workers in the "Belle Epoque"* (French orig., 1985; New York, 1986).

Hancock, David, *Citizens of the World: London Merchants and the Integration of the British Atlantic Community, 1735-1785* (Cambridge, 1995).

Haupt, George, "Rôle de l'exil dans la diffusion de l'image de l'intelligentsia révolutionnaire," *Cahiers du monde russe et soviétique* 19 (1978): 235–49.

Higgs, David, ed., *Portuguese Migration in Global Perspective* (Toronto, 1990).

Hochstadt, Steve, *Mobility and Modernity: Migration in Germany, 1820-1989* (Ann Arbor, 1999).

Hoerder, Dirk, ed., *Labor Migration in the Atlantic Economies: The European and North American Working Classes during the Period of Industrialization* (Westport, Conn., 1985).

Hoerder, Dirk, and Inge Blank, eds., *Roots of the Transplanted*, 2 vols. (New York, 1994).

Hoerder, Dirk, and Leslie Page Moch, eds., *European Migrants: Global and Local Perspectives* (Boston, 1996).

Hoerder, Dirk, and Jörg Nagler, eds., *People in Transit: German Migrations in a Comparative Perspective, 1820-1930* (Cambridge, 1995).

Holmes, Colin, *John Bull's Island: Immigration and British Society, 1871-1971* (London, 1988).

Hvidt, Kristian, *Flight to America: The Social Background of 300,000 Danish Emigrants* (New York, 1975).

Israel, Jonathan I., *European Jewry in the Age of Mercantilism, 1550-1750* (Oxford, 1985).

Johnson, Robert Eugene, *Peasant and Proletarian: The Working Class of Moscow in the Late Nineteenth Century* (New Brunswick, 1979).

Kappeler, Andreas, *Rußland als Vielvölkerreich: Entstehung—Geschichte—Zerfall* (Munich, 1992).

Karpat, Kemal H., *The Gecekondu: Rural Migration and Urbanization in the Ottoman Empire* (Cambridge, 1976).

Klier, John Doyle, *Russia Gathers Her Jews: The Origins of the "Jewish Question" in Russia, 1772-1825* (DeKalb, Ill., 1986).

Kulczycki, John J., *The Foreign Worker and the German Labor Movement: Xenophobia and Solidarity in the Coal Fields of the Ruhr, 1871-1914* (Oxford, 1994).

Lequin, Yves, ed., *Histoire des étrangers et de l'immigration en France* (Paris, 1992; revision of *La mosaïque France*).

———, ed., *La mosaïque France: Histoire des étrangers et de l'immigration* (Paris, 1988).

Lucassen, Jan, *Migrant Labour in Europe, 1600-1900: The Drift to the North Sea*, trans. Donald A. Bloch (Dutch orig., 1985; London, 1987).

Lucassen, Jan, and Leo Lucassen, eds., *Migration, Migration History, History: Old Paradigms and New Perspectives* (Bern, 1997).

Lucassen, Jan, and Rinus Penninx, *Newcomers: Immigrants and Their Descendants in the Netherlands 1550-1995* (Dutch orig., 1985; rev. ed., Amsterdam, 1997).

Lucassen, Leo, "A Blind Spot: Migratory and Travelling Groups in Western European Historiography," *International Review of Social History* 38 (1993): 209–35.

Lunn, Kenneth, ed., *Hosts, Immigrants and Minorities* (Folkestone, 1980).

Marschalck, Peter, *Deutsche Überseewanderung im 19. Jahrhundert: Ein Beitrag zur soziologischen Theorie der Bevölkerung* (Stuttgart, 1973).

Martellone, Anna Maria, "Italian Mass Emigration to the United States, 1876-1930: A Historical Survey," *Perspectives in American History*, n.s., 1 (1984): 379–423.

Miller, Martin A., *The Russian Revolutionary Émigrés, 1825-1870* (Baltimore, 1986).

Moch, Leslie Page, *Moving Europeans: Migration in Western Europe since 1650* (Bloomington, 1992).

Morawska, Ewa, "Labor Migrations of Poles in the Atlantic World Economy, 1880-1914," *Comparative Studies in Society and History* 31 (1989): 237–72.

O'Sullivan, Patrick, ed., *The Irish World Wide: History, Heritage, Identity*, 6 vols., vol. 1: *Patterns of Migration* (London, 1992).

Panayi, Panikos, *Immigration, Ethnicity, and Racism in Britain, 1815-1945* (Manchester, 1994).

———, *Outsiders: A History of European Minorities* (London, 1999).

Pooley, Colin G., and Ian D. Whyte, eds., *Migrants, Emigrants, and Immigrants: A Social History of Migration* (London, 1991).

Poussou, Jean-Pierre, "Les mouvements migratoires en France et à partir de la France de la fin du XVe siècle au début du XIXe siècle: Approches pour une synthèse," *Annales de démographie historique* (1970): 11–78.

Puskás, Julianna, *From Hungary to the United States (1880-1914)*, trans. Maria Bales (Hungarian orig.; Budapest, 1982).

Raeff, Marc, *Russia Abroad: A Cultural History of the Russian Emigration, 1919-1939* (New York and Oxford, 1990).

Rosoli, Gianfausto, ed., *Un secolo di emigrazione italiana, 1876-1976* (Rome, 1978).

Runblom, Harald, and Hans Norman, eds., *From Sweden to America: A History of the Migration* (Minneapolis, 1976).

Semmingsen, Ingrid, *Norway to America: A History of the Migration*, trans. Einar Haugen (Norwegian orig., 1975; Minneapolis, 1978).

Shulvass, Moses A., *From East to West: The Westward Migration of Jews from Eastern Europe during the Seventeenth and Eighteenth Centuries* (Detroit, 1971).

Simpson, Grant G., ed., *Scotland and Scandinavia, 800-1800* (Edinburgh, 1990).

Soly, Hugo, and Alfons K. L. Thijs, *Minorities in Western European Cities (Sixteenth-Twentieth Centuries)* (Brussels, 1995).

Sori, Ercole, *L'emigrazione italiana dall'unità alla seconda guerra mondiale* (Bologna, 1979).

Statt, Daniel, *Foreigners and Englishmen: The Controversy over Immigration and Population, 1660–1760* (Newark, Del., 1995).

Thistlethwaite, Frank, "Migration from Europe Overseas in the 19th and 20th Centuries," in *XIe Congrès International des Sciences Historiques: Rapports*, vol. 5, (Uppsala, 1960), 32–60.

Thomas, Brinley, *Migration and Economic Growth: A Study of Great Britain and the Atlantic Economy* (Cambridge, 1954).

Treadgold, Donald W., *The Great Siberian Migration: Government and Peasant in Resettlement from Emancipation to the First World War* (Princeton, 1957).

Wertheimer, Jack, *Unwelcome Strangers: European Jews in Imperial Germany* (New York and Oxford, 1987).

5 Twentieth-Century Migrations to the 1950s

Anderson, Alan B., and James S. Frideres, *Ethnicity in Canada: Theoretical Perspectives* (Toronto, 1981).

Anglade, Jean, *La vie quotidienne des immigrés en France de 1919 à nos jours* (Paris, 1976).

Asiwaju, Anthony I., ed., *Partitioned Africans: Ethnic Relations across Africa's International Boundaries, 1884–1984* (Lagos, 1984; London, 1985).

Barrier, N. Gerald, and Verne A. Dusenbery, eds., *The Sikh Diaspora: Migration and the Experience beyond Punjab* (Delhi, 1989).

Bowman, Isaiah, *The Pioneer Fringe* (New York, 1931).

Brass, Tom, and Marcel van der Linden, eds., *Free and Unfree Labour: The Debate Continues* (Bern, 1997).

Brawley, Sean, *The White Peril: Foreign Relations and Asian Immigration to Australasia and North America, 1919–1978* (Sydney, 1995).

Breman, Jan, and Sudipto Mundle, *Rural Transformation in Asia* (Delhi and New York, 1992).

Chaliand, Gérard, and Yves Ternon, *Le génocide des Arméniens* (Brussels, 1980).

Chan, Sucheng, ed., *Entry Denied: Exclusion and the Chinese Community in America, 1882–1943* (Philadelphia, 1991).

Conquest, Robert, *The Nation Killers: The Soviet Deportation of Nationalities* (New York, 1970).

Crush, Jonathan, Alan Jeeves, and David Yudelman, *South Africa's Labor Empire: A History of Black Migrancy to the Gold Mines* (Boulder, 1991).

Dallin, David J., and Boris I. Nicolaevsky, *Forced Labor in Soviet Russia* (New Haven, 1947).

Fall, Babacar, *Le travail forcé en Afrique-Occidentale française 1900–1945* (Paris, 1993).

Genizi, Haim, *America's Fair Share: The Admission and Resettlement of Displaced Persons, 1945–1952* (Detroit, 1993).

Graziosi, Andrea, "Foreign Workers in Soviet Russia, 1920–1940: Their Experience and Their Legacy," *International Labor and Working-Class History* 33 (spring 1988): 38–59.

Henderson, William, "The Refugees in India and Pakistan" *Journal of International Affairs* 7 (1953): 57–65.

Herbert, Ulrich, *A History of Foreign Labor in Germany, 1880–1980: Seasonal Workers, Forced Laborers, Guest Workers*, trans. William Templer (German orig., 1986; Ann Arbor, 1990).

Jackman, Jarrell C., and Carla M. Borden, eds., *The Muses Flee Hitler: Cultural Transfer and Adaptation, 1930–1945* (Washington, D.C., 1983).

Jacobmeyer, Wolfgang, *Vom Zwangsarbeiter zum heimatlosen Ausländer: Die Displaced Persons in Westdeutschland, 1945–1951* (Göttingen, 1985).

Joerg, W. L. G., ed., *Pioneer Settlement: Cooperative Studies by 26 Authors* (New York, 1932).

Keller, Stephen L., *Uprooting and Social Change: The Role of Refugees in Development* (Delhi, 1975).

Kitano, Harry H. L., and Roger Daniels, *Asian Americans: Emerging Minorities* (2d ed., Englewood Cliffs, N.J., 1995).

Kulischer, Eugene M., *Europe on the Move: War and Population Changes, 1917–47* (New York, 1948).

Lewis, Robert A., and Richard H. Rowland, *Population Redistribution in the USSR: Its Impact on Society, 1897–1977* (New York, 1979).

Marrus, Michael R., *The Unwanted: European Refugees in the Twentieth Century* (Oxford, 1985).

Matthews, Mervyn, *The Passport Society: Controlling Movement in Russia and the USSR* (Boulder, 1993).

Myers, Ramon H., and Mark R. Peattie, eds., *The Japanese Colonial Empire, 1895–1945* (Princeton, 1984).

Ng, Kwee Choo, *The Chinese in London* (London, 1968).

Paikert, G. C., *The Danube Swabians: German Populations in Hungary, Rumania and Yugoslavia and Hitler's Impact on Their Patterns* (The Hague, 1967).

Proudfoot, Malcolm J., *European Refugees, 1939–52: A Study of Forced Population Movement* (London, 1956).

Rosenfielde, Steven, "An Assessment of the Sources and Uses of Gulag Forced Labour 1929–56," *Soviet Studies* 33 (1981): 51–87, and 39 (1897): 292–313, with comments by Robert Conquest, 34 (1982): 434–39, and S. G. Wheatcroft, 35 (1983): 223–37.

Rystad, Göran, ed., *The Uprooted: Forced Migration as an International Problem in the Post-War Era* (Lund, Sweden, 1990).

Saksena, R. N., *Refugees: A Study in Changing Attitudes* (New York and Bombay, 1961).

Schechtman, Joseph B., *Population Transfers in Asia* (New York, 1949).

———, *Postwar Population Transfers in Europe, 1945–1955* (Philadelphia, 1962).

———, *The Refugee in the World: Displacement and Integration* (New York, 1964).

Scruggs, Otey M., *Braceros, "Wetbacks," and the Farm Labor Problem: A History of Mexican Agricultural Labor in the United States 1942–1954* (New York, 1988).

Shukert, Elfrieda B., and Barbara S. Scibetta, *War Brides of World War II* (New York, 1989).

Siegelbaum, Lewis H., and Ronald G. Suny, eds., *Making Workers Soviet: Power, Class, and Identity* (Ithaca, N.Y., 1994).

Simpson, John Hope, *The Refugee Question* (Oxford, 1940).

Tinker, Hugh, *Separate and Unequal: India and the Indians in the British Commonwealth, 1920–1950* (London, 1976).

van Onselen, Charles, *Chibaro: African Mine Labor in Southern Rhodesia, 1900–1933* (London, 1976).

Vernant, Jacques, *The Refugee in the Post-War World* (London, 1953).

Williams, Robert C., *Culture in Exile: Russian Émigrés in Germany, 1881–1941* (Ithaca, N.Y., 1972).

Young, Louise, *Japan's Total Empire: Manchuria and the Culture of Wartime Imperialism* (Berkeley, 1998).

Abu-Laban, Baha, and Ibrahim Abu-Lughod, eds., *Settler Regimes in Africa and the Arab World: The Illusion of Endurance* (Wilmette, Ill., 1974).

Abu-Laban, Yasmeen, and Daiva Stasiulis, "Ethnic Pluralism under Siege: Popular and Partisan Opposition to Multiculturalism," *Canadian Public Policy* 18 (1992): 365–86.

Adelman, Howard, ed., *Refugee Policy: Canada and the United States* (Toronto, 1991).

Adelman, Howard, and John Sorenson, eds., *African Refugees: Development Aid and Repatriation* (Boulder, 1994).

Alba, Richard D., *Ethnic Identity: The Transformation of White America* (New Haven, 1990).

Allen, Tim, and Hubert Morsink, eds., *When Refugees Go Home: African Experiences* (London, 1994).

Amin, Samir, ed., *Modern Migrations in Western Africa: Studies Presented and Discussed at the Eleventh International African Seminar, Dakar, April 1972* (London, 1974).

Anderson, Karen, *Changing Woman: A History of Racial Ethnic Women in Modern America* (New York, 1996).

Anthias, Floya, and Nira Yuval-Davis, *Racialized Boundaries: Race, Nation, Gender, Colour, and Class and the Anti-Racist Struggle* (London, 1992).

Appleyard, Reginald T., ed., *International Migration Today*, 2 vols. (Paris, 1988).

Ardittis, Solon, ed., *The Politics of East-West Migration* (New York, 1994).

Bade, Klaus J., and Myron Weiner, eds., *Migration Past, Migration Future: Germany and the United States* (Providence, 1997).

Bader, Veit M., ed., *Citizenship and Exclusion: Crossing Boundaries of Disciplines and Countries* (New York, 1997).

Badie, Bertrand, and Catherine Wihtol de Wenden, eds., *Le Défi migratoire: Questions de relations internationales* (Paris, 1993).

Bakan, Abigail B., and Daiva Stasiulis, eds., *Not One of the Family: Foreign Domestic Workers in Canada* (Toronto, 1997).

Baker, Jonathan, and Tade A. Aina, eds., *The Migration Experience in Africa* (Uppsala, 1995).

Barkan, Elliott R., *Asian and Pacific Islander Migration to the United States: A Model of New Global Patterns* (Westport, Conn., 1992).

———, ed., *A Nation of Peoples: A Sourcebook on America's Multicultural Heritage* (Westport, Conn., 1999).

Barry, Brian, and Robert E. Goodin, eds., *Free Movement: Ethical Issues in the Transnational Migration of People and of Money* (New York, 1992).

Bauböck, Rainer, *Transnational Citizenship: Membership and Rights in International Migration* (Aldershot, U.K., 1994).

Bauböck, Rainer, Agnes Heller, and Aristide R. Zolberg, eds., *The Challenge of Diversity: Integration and Pluralism in Societies of Immigration* (Aldershot, U.K., 1996).

Bell-Fialkoff, Andrew, *Ethnic Cleansing* (New York, 1996).

Bhabha, Jacqueline, Francesca Klug, and Sue Shutter, *Worlds Apart: Women under Immigration and Nationality Law* (London, 1985).

Birks, J. S., and C. A. Sinclair, *International Migration and Development in the Arab Region* (Geneva, 1980).

Böröcz, József, *Leisure Migration: A Sociological Study in Tourism* (Oxford, 1996).

Bonacich, Edna, et al., eds., *Global Production: The Apparel Industry in the Pacific Rim* (Philadelphia, 1994).

Bonnerjea, Lucy, *Shaming the World: The Needs of Women Refugees* (London, 1985).

Borrie, Wilfred D., et al., *The Cultural Integration of Immigrants: A Survey Based upon the Papers and Proceedings of the UNESCO Conference Held in Havana, April 1956* (Paris, 1959).

Boyd, Rosalind E., Robin Cohen, and Peter C. W. Gutkind, eds., *International Labour and the Third World: The Making of a New Working Class* (Aldershot, U.K., 1987).

Breman, Jan C., *Footloose Labour: Working in India's Informal Economy* (Cambridge, 1997).

Brown, Judith M., and Rosemary Foot, *Migration, the Asian Experience* (New York, 1994).

Buechler, Hans C., and Judith-Maria Buechler, eds., *Migrants in Europe: The Role of Family, Labor, and Politics* (New York, 1987).

Burnet, Jean, Danielle Juteau, Enoch Padolsky, Anthony Rasporich, and Antoine Sirois, eds., *Migration and the Transformation of Cultures: A Project of the Unesco World Decade for Cultural Development* (Toronto, 1992).

Butterwegge, Christoph, and Siegfried Jäger, eds., *Europa gegen den Rest der Welt? Flüchtlingsbewegungen—Einwanderung—Asylpolitik* (Cologne, 1993).

———, eds., *Rassismus in Europa* (Cologne, 1992).

Carens, Joseph H., "Who Belongs? Theoretical and Legal Questions about Birthright Citizenship in the United States," *University of Toronto Law Journal* 27 (1987): 413–43.

Castells, Manuel, "Immigrant Workers and Class Struggles in Advanced Capitalism: The Western European Experience," *Politics and Society* 5 (1975): 33–66.

Castles, Stephen, and Godula Kosack, *Immigrant Workers and Class Structure in Western Europe* (2d ed., Oxford, 1985).

Castles, Stephen, and Mark J. Miller, *The Age of Migration: International Population Movements in the Modern World* (New York, 1993).

Clarke, Colin, Ceri Peach, and Steven Vertovec, eds., *South Asians Overseas: Migration and Ethnicity* (Cambridge, 1990).

Cohen, Philip, and Harwant S. Bains, eds., *Multi-Racist Britain* (Basingstoke, 1988).

Cohen, Robin, *Frontiers of Identity: The British and the Others* (London, 1994).

———, *The New Helots: Migrants in the International Division of Labour* (Aldershot, U.K., 1987).

Constable, Nicole, ed., *Guest People: Hakka Identity in China and Abroad* (Seattle, 1996).

Cooper, Frederick, *Decolonization and African Society: The Labor Question in French and British Africa* (New York, 1996).

Cornelius, Wayne A., Philip L. Martin, and James F. Hollifield, eds., *Controlling Immigration: A Global Perspective* (Stanford, 1994).

Cushman, Jennifer W., and Wang Gungwu, eds., *Changing Identities of the Southeast Asian Chinese since World War II* (Hong Kong, 1988).

Demuth, Andreas, ed., *Neue Ost-West-Wanderungen nach dem Fall des Eisernen Vorhangs?* (Münster, 1994).

Dirlik, Arif, ed., *What Is in a Rim? Critical Perspectives on the Pacific Region Idea* (Boulder, 1993; 2d ed., Lanham, Md., 1998).

Donald, James, and Ali Rattansi, eds., *"Race," Culture, and Difference* (London, 1992).

Dowty, Alan, *Closed Borders: The Contemporary Assault on Freedom of Movement* (New Haven, 1987).

Fassmann, Heinz, and Rainer Münz, eds., *European Migration in the Late Twentieth Century: Historical Patterns, Actual Trends, and Social Implications* (Aldershot, U.K., 1994).

Fawcett, James T., and Benjamin V. Cariño, eds., *Pacific Bridges: The New Immigration from Asia and the Pacific Islands* (Staten Island, N.Y., 1987).

Fawcett, James T., Siew-Ean Khoo, and Peter C. Smith, *Women in the Cities of Asia: Migration and Urban Adaptation* (Boulder, 1984).

Forbes, Dean K., *Asian Metropolis: Urbanisation and the Southeast Asian City* (Melbourne, 1996).

Gilani, Ijaz S., *Citizens, Slaves, Guest-Workers: The Dynamics of Labour Migration from South Asia* (Islamabad, 1985).

Giles, Wenona, and Sedef Arat-Koç, eds., *Maid in the Market: Women's Paid Domestic Labour* (Halifax, 1994).

Gordon, Avery F., and Christopher Newfield, eds., *Mapping Multiculturalism* (Minneapolis, 1996).

Gould, W. T. S., and A. M. Findlay, eds., *Population Migration and the Changing World Order* (Chichester, U.K., 1994).

Gunatilleke, Godfrey, ed., *Migration of Asian Workers to the Arab World* (Tokyo, 1986).

Hammar, Tomas, *Democracy and the Nation State: Aliens, Denizens, and Citizens in a World of International Migration* (Aldershot, U.K., 1990).

Hammar, Tomas, Grete Brochmann, Kristof Tamas, and Thomas Faist, eds., *International Migration, Immobility, and Development: Multidisciplinary Perspectives* (Oxford, 1997).

Harris, Nigel, *New Untouchables: Immigration and the New World Worker* (New York, 1995).

Independent Commission on International Humanitarian Issues, *Winning the Human Race? The Report of the Independent Commission on International Humanitarian Issues* (1st ed., 1988; London, 1998).

Isajiw, Wsevolod W., *Understanding Diversity: Ethnicity and Race in the Canadian Context* (Toronto, 1999).

Jameson, Fredric, and Masao Miyoshi, eds., *The Cultures of Globalization* (Durham, N.C., 1998).

Joly, Danièle, and Robin Cohen, *Reluctant Hosts: Europe and Its Refugees* (Aldershot, U.K., 1989).

Kallen, Evelyn, *Ethnicity and Human Rights in Canada* (2d ed., Toronto, 1995).

Kempadoo, Kamala, and Jo Doezema, eds., *Global Sex Workers: Rights, Resistance, and Redefinition* (London, 1998).

King, Russell, ed., *Mass Migration in Europe: The Legacy and the Future* (Chichester, U.K., 1993).

King, Russell, and Richard Black, eds., *Southern Europe and the New Immigrations* (Brighton, U.K., 1997).

Komai, Hiroshi, *Migrant Workers in Japan*, trans. Jens Wilkinson (Japanese orig., 1993; London, 1995).

Koser, Khalid, and Helma Lutz, eds., *The New Migration in Europe: Social Constructions and Social Realities* (London, 1998).

Kovacs, Martin L., ed., *Ethnic Canadians: Culture and Education* (Regina, 1978).

Kritz, Mary M., and Douglas T. Gurak, eds., *International Migration in Latin America*, special issue of *International Migration Review*, vol. 13 (1979).

Kühnhardt, Ludger, *Die Flüchtlingsfrage als Weltordnungsproblem: Massenzwangswanderungen in Geschichte und Politik* (Vienna, 1984).

Lewis, Bernard, and Dominique Schnapper, eds., *Musulmans en Europe: Changement social en Europe occidentale* (Arles, 1992).

Li, Peter S., ed., *Race and Ethnic Relations in Canada* (Toronto, 1990).

Liebkind, Karmela, ed., *New Identities in Europe: Immigrant Ancestry and the Ethnic Identity of Youth* (Aldershot, U.K., 1989).

Little, Kenneth, *Urbanization as a Social Process: An Essay on Movement and Change in Contemporary Africa* (London, 1974).

Loomis, Terrence, *Pacific Migrant Labour, Class, and Racism in New Zealand: Fresh off the Boat* (Aldershot, U.K., 1990).

Mackerras, Colin, *China's Minority Cultures: Identities and Integration since 1912* (New York, 1995).

Martin, Philip, and Jonas Widgren, *International Migration: A Global Challenge* (Washington, D.C., 1996).

McDowell, Christopher, ed., *Understanding Impoverishment: The Consequences of Development-Induced Displacement* (Providence, 1996).

Mercier, Christian, *Les déracinés du capital: Immigration et accumulation* (Lyon, 1977).

Michel, Marc, *Décolonisations et émergence du tiers monde* (Paris, 1993).

Miles, Robert, and Dietrich Thränhardt, eds., *Migration and European Integration: The Dynamics of Inclusion and Exclusion* (London, 1995).

Moodie, T. Dunbar, with Vivienne Ndatshe, *Going for Gold: Men, Mines, and Migration* (Berkeley, 1994).

Mori, Hiromi, *Immigration Policy and Foreign Workers in Japan* (New York, 1997).

Myers, Norman, and Jennifer Kent, *Environmental Exodus: An Emerging Crisis in the Global Arena* (Washington, D.C., 1995).

Nam, Charles B., William J. Serow, and David F. Sly, eds., *International Handbook on Internal Migration* (New York, 1990).

Nash, June, and María P. Fernández-Kelly, eds., *Women, Men, and the International Division of Labor* (Albany, 1983).

Nisan, Mordechai, *Minorities in the Middle East: A History of Struggle and Self-Expression* (London and Jefferson, N.C., 1991).

Ong, Aihwa, and Donald M. Nonini, eds., *Ungrounded Empires: The Cultural Politics of Modern Chinese Transnationalism* (London, 1997).

Opitz, Peter, J., *Das Weltflüchtlingsproblem: Ursachen und Folgen* (Munich, 1988).

Pastor, Robert A., ed., *Migration and Development in the Caribbean: The Unexplored Connection* (Boulder, 1985).

Phizacklea, Annie, ed., *One-Way Ticket: Migration and Female Labour* (London, 1983).

Pinder, David, ed., *The New Europe: Economy, Society, and Environment* (Chichester, U.K., 1998).

Portes, Alejandro, ed., *The Economic Sociology of Immigration: Essays on Networks, Ethnicity, and Entrepreneurship* (New York, 1995).

Portes, Alejandro, and John Walton, *Labor, Class, and the International System* (New York, 1981).

Prothero, R. Mansell, and Murray Chapman, eds., *Circulation in Third World Countries* (London, 1985).

Ramanathan, Indira, *China and the Ethnic Chinese in Malaysia and Indonesia, 1949–1992* (New Delhi, 1994).

Rattansi, Ali, and Sallie Westwood, eds., *Racism, Modernity and Identity: On the Western Front* (Cambridge, 1994).

Rees, Philip, et al., eds., *Population Migration in the European Union* (Chichester, U.K., 1996).

Reimers, David M., *Unwelcome Strangers: American Identity and the Turn against Immigration* (New York, 1998).

Reitz, Jeffrey G., and Raymond Breton, *The Illusion of Difference: Realities of Ethnicity in Canada and the United States* (Toronto, 1994).

Richmond, Anthony H., *Post-War Immigrants in Canada* (Toronto, 1967).

Rose, Peter I., *Tempest-Tost: Race, Immigration, and the Dilemmas of Diversity* (New York, 1997).

Rudolph, Hedwig, and Mirjana Morokvasic, eds., *Bridging States and Markets: International Migration in the Early 1990s* (Berlin, 1993).

Rumbaut, Rubén G., "Origins and Destinies: Immigration to the United States since World War II," *Sociological Forum* 9 (1994): 583–621.

Salt, John, and Hugh Clout, eds., *Migration in Post-War Europe: Geographical Essays* (Oxford, 1976).

Sassen, Saskia, *Transnational Economies and National Migration Policies* (Amsterdam, 1996).

Schnapper, Dominique, *L'Europe des immigrés: Essai sur les politiques d'immigration* (Paris, 1992).

Serow, William J., Charles B. Nam, David F. Sly, and Robert H. Weller, eds., *Handbook on International Migration* (New York, 1990).

Silverman, Maxim, *Deconstructing the Nation: Immigration, Racism, and Citizenship in Modern France* (London, 1992).

Simmons, Alan B., ed., *International Migration, Refugee Flows and Human Rights in North America: The Impact of Free Trade and Restructuring* (New York, 1996).

Simmons, Alan B., Sergio Diaz-Briquets, and Aprodicio A. Laquian, *Social Change and Internal Migration: A Review of Research Findings from Africa, Asia, and Latin America: A Report of the Migration Review Task Force of the International Development Research Centre* (Ottawa, 1977).

Skeldon, Ronald, "International Migration within and from the East and Southeast Asian Region: A Review Essay," *Asian and Pacific Migration Journal* 1 (1992): 19–63.

———, *Migration and Development: A Global Perspective* (Essex, U.K., 1997).

Soysal, Yasemin N., *Limits of Citizenship: Migrants and Postnational Membership in Europe* (Chicago, 1994).

Stahl, Charles W., Reginald T. Appleyard, and Toshikazu Nagayama, eds., *International Manpower Flows and Foreign Investment in Asia*, special issue of *Asian and Pacific Migration Journal* 1, 3/4 (1992).

Teitelbaum, Michael S., and Jay Winter, *A Question of Numbers: High Migration, Low Fertility, and the Politics of National Identity* (New York, 1998).

Touré, Moriba, and T. O. Fadayomi, eds., *Migrations, Development, and Urbanization Policies in Sub-Saharan Africa* (Dakar, 1992).

United Nations Development Programme, *Human Development Report* [annual] (New York: Oxford, 1990–).

U.S. Committee for Refugees, *World Refugee Survey* [annual] (New York, 1980–).

Weiner, Myron, *The Global Migration Crisis: Challenge to States and to Human Rights* (New York, 1995).

———, *Sons of the Soil: Migration and Ethnic Conflict in India* (Princeton, 1978).

Wihtol de Wenden, Catherine, and Bertrand Badie, eds., *Migrations et relations transnationales*, topical issue of *Études internationales* 24, 1 (Mar. 1993).

Zegeye, Abebe, and Shubi Ishemo, eds., *Forced Labour and Migration: Patterns of Movement within Africa* (London, 1989).

Zolberg, Aristide, "The Formation of New States as a Refugee-Generating Process," *Annals of the American Academy of Political and Social Science* 467 (1983): 24–38.

Zolberg, Aristide, Astri Suhrke, and Sergio Aguayo, *Escape from Violence: Conflict and the Refugee Crisis in the Developing World* (Oxford, 1989).

Sources for Maps and Figures

Maps

1.1 Perspectives: Euro-, American-, Asian-Centeredness

2.1 Cultural Regions, 12th Century. Adapted from Archibald R. Lewis, *Nomads and Crusaders, A.D. 1000–1368* (Bloomington, 1988), 169; Haim H. Ben-Sasson, ed., *A History of the Jewish People* (Cambridge, Mass., 1976), map 1.

2.2 Circuits of the 13th-Century World System. Adapted from Janet L. Abu-Lughod, *Before European Hegemony: The World System A.D. 1250–1350* (New York, 1989), 34.

2.3 Afro-Eurasian Trade Routes, 12th–15th Centuries I

2.4 Afro-Eurasian Trade Routes, 12th–15th Centuries II. Adapted from Janet L. Abu-Lughod, *Before European Hegemony: The World System A.D. 1250–1350* (New York, 1989), 48, 96, 123, 138–40, 143, 202; *The Anchor Atlas of World History*, 2 vols. (Harmondsworth, 1974–1978), 1:214; Geoffrey Barraclough, ed., *The Times Concise Atlas of World History* (London, 1982), 58–59; Irene M. Franck and David M. Brownstone, *The Silk Road: A History* (New York, 1986), 218; Jonathan Riley-Smith, ed., *Atlas of the Crusades* (London, 1991), 100, 105; Yves Lequin, ed., *La Mosaïque France: Histoire des étrangers et de l'immigration* (Paris, 1988), 104; Ross E. Dunn, *The Adventures of Ibn Battuta: A Muslim Traveler of the 14th Century* (Berkeley, 1986), 42, 82, 107, 138, 175, 184, 188–89, 246, 277.

2.5 Migrations of Dispersal, State-Building, and Colonization before 1347. Adapted from Georges Duby, ed., *Atlas historique: L'histoire du monde en 334 cartes* (2d ed., Paris, 1994), 41, 56–57; *Putzger Historischer Weltatlas* (100th ed., Berlin, 1980), 50–51; Dan Cohn-Sherbok, *Atlas of Jewish History* (London, 1994), 87; Janet L. Abu-Lughod, *Before European Hegemony: The World System A.D. 1250–1350* (New York, 1989), 142.

3.1 Warfaring Mercenaries and Armies. Adapted from Geoffrey Parker, *The Army of Flanders and the Spanish Road, 1567–1659: The Logistics of Spanish Victory and Defeat in the Low Countries' Wars* (Cambridge, 1975), 84–85, and Fernand Braudel, *The Mediterranean and the Mediterranean World in the Age of Philip II*, 2 vols., trans. Siân Reynolds (New York, 1972–73), 838; *History Atlas of the World* (1962; repr. 1981), map 51.

3.2 Peasant Mobility and Market Connections. Adapted from Christopher Dyer, *Everyday Life in Medieval England* (London, 1994), 259, 272; Andrew Pettegree, *Foreign Protestant Communities in Sixteenth-Century London* (Oxford, 1986), 21; Robert Fossier, *La terre et les hommes en Picardie jusqu'à la fin du XIIIe siècle*, 2 vols. (Paris, 1968), 599.

3.3 Selected 15th-Century Artisans' Migrations. Adapted from Knut Schulz, *Handwerksgesellen und Lohnarbeiter: Untersuchungen zur oberrheinischen und oberdeutschen Stadtgeschichte des 14. bis 17. Jahrhunderts* (Sigmaringen, 1985), 283 and 284.

3.4 Long-Distance Pilgrimage to Santiago de Compostela, 15th and 16th Centuries. Adapted from A.-M. Armelin, "Pèlerins de St. Jacques," 71–84 in R. de la Coste-Messelière, ed., *Pèlerins et chemins de Saint-Jacques en France et en Europe du Xe siècle à nos jours* (Paris, 1965), 48–49; Jean Chélini and Henry Branthomme, eds., *Chemins de Dieu: Histoire des pèlerinages chrétiens des origines à nos jours* (Paris, 1982), 166.

4.1 Moriscos and Christians in Valencia between 1565 and 1609. Reprinted from Fernand Braudel, *The Mediterranean and the Mediterranean World in the Age of Philip II*, 2 vols., trans. Siân Reynolds (New York, 1972–73), 782.

4.2 Jewish Expulsions, 11th–15th Centuries, and Gypsy Migrations, 9th–15th Centuries. Adapted from Dan Cohn-Sherbok, *Atlas of Jewish History* (London, 1994), 83, 91, 116; Andrew C. Hess, *The Forgotten Frontier: A History of the Sixteenth-Century Ibero-African Frontier* (Chicago, 1978), fig. 5; Andreas Hundsalz, *Stand der Forschung über Zigeuner und Landfahrer: Eine Literaturanalyse unter vorwiegend sozialwissenschaftlichen Gesichtspunkten* (Stuttgart, 1978), 25; Gérard Chaliand and Jean-Pierre Rageau, *The Penguin Atlas of Diasporas*, trans. A. M. Berrett (New York, 1995), 96, 108.

4.3 Christian Flight and Migrations. Adapted from Frederick A. Norwood, *Strangers and Exiles: A History of Religious Refugees*, 2 vols. (Nashville, Tenn., 1965–69), 56, 265; Robin D. Gwynn, *Huguenot Heritage: The History and Contribution of the Huguenots in Britain* (London, 1985), 24, 37; *Dem Kelch zuliebe Exulant: 250 Jahre Böhmisches Dorf in Berlin-Neukölln* (Berlin, 1987), 75; Bernd G. Längin, *Die Hutterer: Gefangene der Vergangenheit, Pilger der Gegenwart* (Hamburg, 1986), end map.

5.1 Migration and the Ottoman Empire, 1300–1683. Adapted from *The Anchor Atlas of World History*, 2 vols. (Harmondsworth, 1974–78), 1:208; Leften S. Stavrianos, *The Balkans since 1453* (New York, 1958), 68; Georges Duby, ed., *Atlas historique: L'histoire du monde en 334 cartes* (2d ed., Paris, 1994), 70.

5.2 Europe: Universities, 13th–15th Centuries, and Major Political Regions, 1550. Adapted from *The Anchor Atlas of World History*, 2 vols. (Harmondsworth, 1974–78), 1:180; *Putzger Historischer Weltatlas* (100th ed., Berlin, 1980), 66–67.

5.3 "Europe Finds the Larger World," 15th to Early 16th Centuries. Adapted from *The Anchor Atlas of World History*, 2 vols. (Harmondsworth, 1974–78), 1:222, 228; *Putzger Historischer Weltatlas* (100th ed., Berlin, 1980), 62–63; Joseph E. Schwartzberg, ed., *A Historical Atlas of South Asia* (Chicago, 1978; 2d rev. ed., Oxford and New York, 1992), plate VI.B.1; Geoffrey Barraclough, ed., *The Times Concise Atlas of World History* (London, 1982), 64–65; Trevor Cairns, *Europe Finds the World* (London, 1987), 81.

6.1 African Peoples in 1400. Adapted from Geoffrey Barraclough, ed., *The Times Concise Atlas of World History* (London, 1982), 60–61; Colin McEvedy, *The Penguin Atlas of African History* (Harmondsworth, 1980), 65; Philip Curtin et al., *African History* (Boston, 1978), 13, 98.

6.2 Trade Routes at the End of the 15th Century. Adapted from Bartolomé Bennassar and Pierre Chaunu, eds., *L'ouverture du monde, XIVe–XVIe siècles* (Paris, 1977), 39, 79;

Philip Curtin et al., *African History* (Boston, 1978), 102; Andrew C. Hess, *The Forgotten Frontier: A History of the Sixteenth-Century Ibero-African Frontier* (Chicago, 1978), 117.

6.3 African Trade and Migration around 1600. Adapted from Colin McEvedy, *The Penguin Atlas of African History* (Harmondsworth, 1980), 77, 79; Johannes M. Postma, *The Dutch in the Atlantic Slave Trade, 1600–1815* (Cambridge, 1990), 58.

6.4 From Many Peoples to Generic Chattel Slaves. Adapted from Philip Curtin et al., *African History* (Boston, 1978), 228, 241, 253; Roger Anstey, *The Atlantic Slave Trade and British Abolition, 1760–1810* (London, 1975), 62, 65, 71; Barbara Bush, *Slave Women in Caribbean Society, 1650–1838* (Bloomington, 1990), 152.

7.1 Indian Hindu and Arab Muslim Contact to Southeast Asia, 10th–17th Centuries. Adapted from Gérard Chaliand and Jean-Pierre Rageau, *The Penguin Atlas of Diasporas*, trans. A. M. Berrett (New York, 1995), 150.

7.2 The Trade Emporia of the Indian Ocean, 1000–1600. Adapted from Kirti N. Chaudhuri, *Trade and Civilization in the Indian Ocean: An Economic History from the Rise of Islam to 1750* (Cambridge, 1985), 35, 38, 41, 70, 96, 115, 168; Philip D. Curtin, *Cross-Cultural Trade in World History* (Cambridge, 1984), maps 7.1, 9.2, 9.3, 9.4, 9.5; Geoffrey Barraclough, ed., *The Times Concise Atlas of World History* (London, 1982), 59.

7.3 Cultures of the Indian Subcontinent. Adapted from Trevor Cairns, *Europe Finds the World* (London, 1987), 33, 86; Kirti N. Chaudhuri, *Trade and Civilization in the Indian Ocean: An Economic History from the Rise of Islam to 1750* (Cambridge, 1985), 48.

7.4 Chinese Migrations and the Chinese Diaspora. Adapted from Lynn Pan, ed., *The Encyclopedia of Chinese Overseas* (Richmond, U.K., 1999), 49; Gérard Chaliand and Jean-Pierre Rageau, *The Penguin Atlas of Diasporas*, trans. A. M. Berrett (New York, 1995), 131; *The Anchor Atlas of World History*, 2 vols. (Harmondsworth, 1974–78), 1:210; Georges Duby, *Atlas historique: L'Histoire du monde en 334 cartes* (2d ed., Paris, 1994), 226; John R. Shephard, *Statecraft and Political Economy on the Taiwan Frontier, 1600–1800* (Stanford, 1993), 144, 174.

7.5 The Armenian Diaspora, 11th–20th Centuries. Adapted from Gérard Chaliand and Jean-Pierre Rageau, *The Penguin Atlas of Diasporas*, trans. A. M. Berrett (New York, 1995), 74–89.

8.1 Peoples of the Americas in the 15th Century. Adapted from Bartolomé Bennassar and Pierre Chaunu, eds., *L'ouverture du monde, XIVe–XVIe siècles* (Paris, 1977), 93; Philip Curtin et al., *African History* (Boston, 1978), 217; *Hammond Atlas of United States History*, 4.

8.2 Mediterranean, Transatlantic, and Transpacific Voyaging. Adapted from Bartolomé Bennassar and Pierre Chaunu, eds., *L'ouverture du monde, XIVe-XVIe siècles* (Paris, 1977), 34; William L. Schurz, *The Manila Galleon: Illustrated with Maps* (New York, 1939; repr., New York, 1959), end map; David Watts, *The West Indies: Patterns of Development, Culture, and Environmental Change since 1492* (Cambridge, 1987), 81, 85; D. W. Meinig, *The Shaping of America: A Geographical Perspective on 500 Years of History*, vol. 1: "Atlantic America, 1492–1800" (New Haven, 1986), map 6.

8.3 Zones of Cultural Conflict and Contact, 18th Century. Adapted from *Rand McNally Atlas of World History* (rev. ed., Chicago, 1987), 37, 38; Georges Duby, *Atlas historique: L'histoire du monde en 334 cartes* (2d ed., Paris, 1994), 280–82.

9.1 The Commercial Fur Empires. Adapted from Geoffrey Barraclough, ed., *The Times*

Concise Atlas of World History (London, 1982), 68–69, 95; Gérard Chaliand, Michael Jan, and Jean-Pierre Rageau, *Atlas historique des migrations* (Paris, 1994), 67.

9.2   From the Euro-Cultural Zones of 1800 to the Dispossession of First Nations, 1890. Adapted from D. W. Meinig, *The Shaping of America: A Geographical Perspective on 500 Years of History,* vol. 1: "Atlantic America, 1492–1800" (New Haven, 1986), map 68; *Hammond Atlas of United States History,* maps 4A–B, 31D.

9.3   Origins: The Eastern Atlantic Rim, 15th–18th Centuries. Adapted from D. W. Meinig, *The Shaping of America: A Geographical Perspective on 500 Years of History,* vol. 1: "Atlantic America, 1492–1800" (New Haven, 1986), map 6; Christian Huetz de Lemps, "Indentured Servants Bound for the French Antilles," in Ida Altman and James Horn, eds., *"To Make America": European Emigration in the Early Modern Period* (Berkeley, 1991), 178, 196; Bernard Bailyn, *Voyagers to the West: A Passage in the Peopling of America on the Eve of the Revolution* (New York, 1986), 109.

9.4   The Western Atlantic Rim: Destinations and Shifting Zones of Encounter to 1800. Adapted from D. W. Meinig, *The Shaping of America: A Geographical Perspective on 500 Years of History,* vol. 1: "Atlantic America, 1492–1800" (New Haven, 1986), maps 40, 51, 62.

9.5   South Africa: Peoples, Cape Colony, Migrations. Adapted from Philip Curtin et al., *African History* (Boston, 1978), 279, 307, 314; Charles R. Boxer, *The Dutch Seaborne Empire, 1600–1800* (1965; repr., London, 1990), 294; Gérard Chaliand, Michael Jan, and Jean-Pierre Rageau, *Atlas historique des migrations* (Paris, 1994), 88–89.

10.1 Latin–African–Native American Migrations. Adapted from Bernhard Brandt, *Südamerika* (Breslau, 1923), 60; Noble D. Cook, "Migration in Colonial Peru: An Overview," in David J. Robinson, ed., *Migration in Colonial Spanish America* (Cambridge, 1990), 48, fig. 3.1, and Cook, *Demographic Collapse: Indian Peru, 1520–1620* (Cambridge, 1981), map 6; Jan Lucassen, "The Netherlands, the Dutch, and Long-Distance Migration, in the Late 16th to Early 19th Centuries," in Nicholas Canny, ed., *Europeans on the Move: Studies on European Migration, 1500–1800* (Oxford, 1994), 174; Charles R. Boxer, *The Dutch in Brazil, 1624–1654* (Oxford, 1957), maps 1, 2; Philip D. Curtin, *Cross-Cultural Trade in World History* (Cambridge, 1984), map 9.1.

10.2 Relative Size of Slave Imports during the Whole Period of the Atlantic Trade by Destination and Selected Ethnic Origins. Adapted from Philip D. Curtin, *The Atlantic Slave Trade: A Census* (Madison, 1969), 90, 111; Gérard Chaliand and Jean-Pierre Rageau, *The Penguin Atlas of Diasporas,* trans. A. M. Berrett (New York, 1995), 114.

11.1 Empires with Colonies and Zones of Encounter/Borderlands, 1775

12.1 European Rural Migrations, 16th–18th Centuries. Adapted from N. J. G. Pounds, *An Historical Geography of Europe* (Cambridge, 1990), 198, 233, 283; Barbara Jelavich, *History of the Balkans: Eighteenth and Nineteenth Centuries,* 2 vols. (Cambridge, 1983), vol. 1, map 14.

12.2 European Labor Migration Systems, 1650–1850. Adapted from Jan Lucassen, *Migrant Labour in Europe, 1600–1900: The Drift to the North Sea,* trans. Donald A. Bloch (London, 1987), 108, 109, 111, 259, 267, and Jan Lucassen, "The Netherlands, the Dutch, and Long-Distance Migration, in the Late 16th to Early 19th Centuries," in Nicholas Canny, ed., *Europeans on the Move: Studies on European Migration, 1500–1800* (Oxford, 1994), 184; Otto Uhlig, *Die Schwabenkinder aus Tirol und Vorarlberg* (2d rev. ed., Stuttgart, 1983), 72.

12.3 Population Density in the Early 19th Century. Adapted from N. J. G. Pounds, *An Historical Geography of Europe* (Cambridge, 1990), 320, 321, 325; Paul Bairoch, Jean Batou, and Pierre Chèvre, *La population des villes européennes, 800–1850: Banque de données et analyse sommaire des résultats* (Geneva, 1988), 245, 250.

12.4 Long-Distance Trade Routes in East Central Europe, Kraków, 1500–1800. Adapted from F. W. Carter, *Trade and Urban Development in Poland: An Economic Geography of Cracow, from Its Origins to 1795* (Cambridge, 1994), maps 48, 52, 54, 56, 58, 60, 62, 66, 76.

13.1 Expansion of Russia, 16th–19th Centuries. Adapted from *The Anchor Atlas of World History*, 2 vols. (Harmondsworth, 1974–78), 1:272; N. J. G. Pounds, *An Historical Geography of Europe* (Cambridge, 1990), 255; Andreas Kappeler, *Rußland als Vielvölkerreich: Entstehung—Geschichte—Zerfall* (Munich, 1992), map 4; Gérard Chaliand, Michael Jan, and Jean-Pierre Rageau, *Atlas historique des migrations* (Paris, 1994), 67; Geoffrey Barraclough, ed., *The Times Concise Atlas of World History* (London, 1982), 84; John J. Stephan, *The Russian Far East: A History* (Cambridge, 1994), 27.

13.2 Migrations of Central Asian Peoples, 16th–18th Centuries. Adapted from Fernand Braudel, *Capitalism and Material Life, 1400–1800*, trans. Miriam Kochan (New York 1973), 59; Georges Duby, *Atlas historique: L'histoire du monde en 334 cartes* (2d ed., Paris, 1994), 172–73; Daniel R. Brower and Edward J. Lazzerini, eds., *Russia's Orient: Imperial Borderlands and Peoples, 1700–1917* (Bloomington, 1997), 136–37; Andreas Kappeler, *Rußland als Vielvölkerreich: Entstehung—Geschichte—Zerfall* (Munich, 1992), map 6.

13.3 Settlement and Origin of Russian-Germans, 1763–1914. Adapted from Karl Stumpp, *Die Auswanderung aus Deutschland nach Rußland in den Jahren 1763–1862* (Tübingen, 1972), map folder; Martin Gilbert, *Atlas of Russian History* (n.p. [U.K.], 1972), 39.

13.4 Siberia, the Russian Far East, and Alaska, 19th Century. Adapted from Martin Gilbert, *Atlas of Russian History* (n.p. [U.K.], 1972), 54, 62, 98; Philip Longworth, *The Cossacks* (London, 1969), 260; John J. Stephan, *The Russian Far East: A History* (Cambridge, 1994), 8, 42, 56, 143; Andreas Kappeler, *Rußland als Vielvölkerreich: Entstehung—Geschichte—Zerfall* (Munich, 1992), map 7.

13.5 Poland and the Jewish Pale of Settlement. Adapted from Martin Gilbert, *Atlas of Russian History* (n.p. [U.K.], 1972), 69, 70; Barbara A. Anderson, *Internal Migration during Modernization in Late Nineteenth-Century Russia* (Princeton, 1980), 168, map 7.1; John D. Klier, *Russia Gathers Her Jews: The Origins of the "Jewish Question" in Russia, 1772–1825* (DeKalb, Ill., 1986), frontispiece, 18; Dan Cohn-Sherbok, *Atlas of Jewish History* (London, 1994), 132, 133, 138, 140, 148.

14.1 Destinations of Migrant Harvest Labor in Central Europe, 1860s–1870s. Reprinted from Ingeborg Weber-Kellermann, *Erntebrauch in der ländlichen Arbeitswelt des 19. Jahrhunderts auf Grund der Mannhardtbefragung in Deutschland von 1865* (Marburg, 1965), map 3.

14.2 Migrations from the European Periphery to the Cores of the Atlantic Economies, 1880s–1914. Adapted from Yves Lequin, ed., *La mosaïque France: Histoire des étrangers et de l'immigration en France* (Paris, 1988), 337; N. J. G. Pounds, *An Historical Geography of Europe* (Cambridge, 1990), 362; Gianfausto Rosoli, ed., *Un secolo di emigrazione italiana, 1876–1976* (Rome, 1978), reprinted in Dirk Hoerder, ed., *Labor Migration in the Atlantic Economies: The European and North American Working Classes during the Period of Industrialization* (Westport, Conn., 1985), 96; Dan Cohn-Sherbok, *Atlas of Jewish History* (London, 1994), 163.

14.3   Migration to North America, 1865–1924, and Bicultural Regions

14.4   (In)dependent Latin America: Migration, Intervention, Investment. Adapted from Geoffrey Barraclough, ed., *The Times Concise Atlas of World History* (London, 1982), 96–97, 111; *Rand McNally Atlas of World History* (rev. ed., Chicago, 1987), 59; Barbara A. Tennenbaum, ed., *Encyclopedia of Latin American History and Culture*, 5 vols. (New York, 1996), 2:240.

15.1   Principal Overseas Migrations, 1830s–1919, of Asian Indentured and Free Migrants. Adapted from David Northrup, *Indentured Labor in the Age of Imperialism, 1834–1922* (Cambridge, 1995), maps 1, 5; Gérard Chaliand, Michael Jan, and Jean-Pierre Rageau, *Atlas historique des migrations* (Paris, 1994), 66.

15.2   East Asia: Internal Migration and Emigration, 1840s–1920s. Adapted from Nicole Constable, ed., *Guest People: Hakka Identity in China and Abroad* (Seattle, 1996), 200.

15.3   Peoples of the Southern Chinese Emigration Provinces. Adapted from Mary F. S. Heidhues, *Southeast Asia's Chinese Minorities* (Victoria, Austral., 1974), map facing p. 1.

15.4   South Asia: Population Density and Emigration. Adapted from Kingsley Davis, *The Population of India and Pakistan* (Princeton, 1951), 20; Gérard Chaliand and Jean-Pierre Rageau, *The Penguin Atlas of Diasporas*, trans. A. M. Berrett (New York, 1995), 151; Hugh Tinker, *A New System of Slavery: The Export of Indian Labour Overseas, 1830–1920* (London, 1974), 40.

15.5   South Asia: Inter-Provincial Migration, 1931. Adapted from Francis Robinson, ed., *The Cambridge Encyclopedia of India, Pakistan, Bangladesh, Sri Lanka, Nepal, Bhutan, and the Maldives* (Cambridge, 1989), 404; Kingsley Davis, *The Population of India and Pakistan* (Princeton, 1951), 109.

16.1   Africa, c.1880 and c.1914. Adapted from Geoffrey Barraclough, ed., *The Times Concise Atlas of World History* (London, 1982), 102-3; *Rand McNally Atlas of World History* (rev. ed., Chicago, 1987), 66; Basil Davidson, *A History of East and Central Africa to the Late Nineteenth Century* (Garden City, N.Y., 1969), 188, 240, 282.

16.2   Empires and Diasporas. Adapted from Geoffrey Barraclough, ed., *The Times Concise Atlas of World History* (London, 1982), 100–101.

17.1   Population Transfer, Migration, and Flight in Europe, 1912–1939. Adapted from Eugene M. Kulischer, *Europe on the Move: War and Population Changes, 1917–47* (New York, 1948), map 1; Peter J. Opitz, *Das Weltflüchtlingsproblem: Ursachen und Folgen* (Munich, 1988), map 2; Gérard-François Dumont, *Les migrations internationales: Les nouvelles logiques migratoires* (Paris, 1995), 120; Dan Cohn-Sherbok, *Atlas of Jewish History* (London, 1994), 172; Gérard Chaliand, Michael Jan, and Jean-Pierre Rageau, *Atlas historique des migrations* (Paris, 1994), 105.

17.2   Forced Labor in Germany and the Soviet Union, 1930s–1940s. Adapted from *Putzger Historischer Weltatlas* (100th ed., Berlin, 1980), 113; David J. Dallin and Boris I. Nicolaevsky, *Forced Labor in Soviet Russia* (New Haven, 1947), 53–73; Martin Gilbert, *Atlas of Russian History* (n.p. [U.K.], 1972), 113; Gérard Chaliand, Michael Jan, and Jean-Pierre Rageau, *Atlas historique des migrations* (Paris, 1994), 107.

17.3 European Flight, Deportations, and Resettlement, 1939–1949. Adapted from Eugene M. Kulischer, *Europe on the Move: War and Population Changes, 1917–47* (New York, 1948), maps 5, 6; Martin Gilbert, *Atlas of Russian History* (n.p. [U.K.], 1972), 131, 132; *Putzger Historischer Weltatlas* (100th ed., Berlin, 1980), 121; Robert Conquest, *The Nation-Killers: The Soviet Deportation of Nationalities* (New York, 1970), 25, 45, 106, 159; Gérard Chaliand, Michael Jan, and Jean-Pierre Rageau, *Atlas historique des migrations* (Paris, 1994), 106, 108–9.

17.4 East Asia: Expansion of Japan, Flight, and Forced Labor. Adapted from Ramon H. Myers and Mark R. Peattie, eds., *The Japanese Colonial Empire, 1895–1945* (Princeton, 1984), map 1; Jonathan D. Spence, *The Search for Modern China* (New York, 1990), 406, 409, 444, 458; Gérard Chaliand, Michael Jan, and Jean-Pierre Rageau, *Atlas historique des migrations* (Paris, 1994), 112.

18.1 The Pioneer Fringe in the 1930s. Reprinted from Isaiah Bowman, *The Pioneer Fringe* (New York, 1931), 50.

18.2 Jewish and Palestinian Flight and Migrations to 1964. Adapted from Martin Gilbert, *The Dent Atlas of Jewish History* (5th ed., London, 1993), 110; Joseph B. Schechtman, *The Refugee in the World: Displacement and Integration* (New York, 1964), 205; Gérard Chaliand, Michael Jan, and Jean-Pierre Rageau, *Atlas historique des migrations* (Paris, 1994), 110–11.

18.3 Labor Segregation in and Migration to South Africa, 1970s. Adapted from Chris Dixon and Michael Heffernan, eds., *Colonialism and Development in the Contemporary World* (London, 1991), 22, 29; Robin Cohen, ed., *The Cambridge Survey of World Migration* (Cambridge, 1995), 173; Anthony Lemon, "Migrant Labour and Frontier Commuters: Reorganizing South Africa's Black Labour Supply," in David M. Smith, ed., *Living under Apartheid: Aspects of Urbanization and Social Change in South Africa* (London, 1983), 70.

19.1 Major Labor and Refugee Migrations, 1960s–1990s

19.2 Major Refugee Migrations in the 1970s. Adapted from Michael Kidron and Ronald Segal, *The State of the World Atlas* (London, 1981), 32.

19.3 European and Transatlantic Migrations. Adapted from Michael Kidron and Ronald Segal, *The State of the World Atlas* (London, 1981), 38.

19.4 Migration to and in the Americas. Adapted from Stephen Castles and Mark J. Miller, *The Age of Migration: International Population Movements in the Modern World* (New York, 1993), map 6.4; Mike Parnwell, *Population Movements and the Third World* (London, 1993), 51.

19.5 Intra-Asian, South Pacific, and Transpacific Migrations. Adapted from Stephen Castles and Mark J. Miller, *The Age of Migration: International Population Movements in the Modern World* (New York, 1993), map 6.5; Reginald T. Appleyard, ed., *International Migration Today*, 2 vols. (Paris, 1988) 1:126; Mike Parnwell, *Population Movements and the Third World* (London, 1993), 46; Gérard Chaliand, Michael Jan, and Jean-Pierre Rageau, *Atlas historique des migrations* (Paris, 1994), 95, 119; Lynn Pan, ed., *The Encyclopedia of Chinese Overseas* (Richmond, U.K., 1999), 47.

19.6 North African and Persian Gulf Migrations. Adapted from Rafic Boustani and Philippe Fargues, *The Atlas of the Arab World: Geopolitics and Society* (New York, 1991), 98, 102, 103, 118; Stephen Castles and Mark J. Miller, *The Age of Migration: International Population Movements in the Modern World* (New York, 1993), map 6.2.

Figures

Index

Agriculture (*continued*)
(*kolkhozes*), 463–65; seasonal labor, 282
map 12.1, 290–94, 505, 511, 554, 645 n.41,
652 n.22; and women, 161, 162, 245, 318,
553, 652 n.30. *See also* Coffee; Cotton;
Ecology; Famine; Foods; Slaves/slavery;
Sugarcane cultivation; Tea cultivation;
Tobacco cultivation

Algeria: France in, 407–9, 422, 503; independence and European-origin minorities, 503;
Jewish community in, 409, 497 map 18.2,
498, 503; migration patterns of, 407, 502,
514 map 19.2, 521 map 19.3, 552 map 19.7;
population patterns in, 148, 407, 408 map
16.1, 409, 413, 499, 500, 503–4; religious
fundamentalism in, 515; slave trade in, 159,
407–9

Andalusia, 41, 191–93, 207, 417–18

Angola, 202, 227, 413, 499, 500–501, 505 map
18.3, 514 map 19.2, 515, 552 map 19.7, 554

Antilles: labor supply and sugarcane cultivation in, 196, 201 map 8.3, 246; migration
patterns of, 502, 527 map 19.4, 528; slavery
in, 242 map 10.2, 250

Anti-Semitism: and Arab states, 449; in Eastern Europe, 341, 450, 458, 459; expulsions
of Jews, 97–99; in France, 458; in Nazi Germany, 457–60; pogroms, 100, 113, 341, 458.
See also Israel; Jews

Anti-Slavery Convention, 461

Arabs: cultural influences of, 28, 38, 85, 149;
and Jewish settlement in Palestine, 496,
497 map 18.2; mercantile interests of,
130–31, 163–65. *See also* Islam; Muslims

Arawaks, 187, 188 map 8.1, 195, 235, 259, 260

Argentina: cattle raising in, 360, 493; civil
war in, 531–32; grasslands of, 187, 204;
gross national product (GNP) of, 516; immigration policies of, 359, 512, 530; Italian
diaspora in, 453, map 17.1, 456; migration
patterns of, 337 map 14.2, 338, 342, 358
map 14.4, 510 map 19.1, 514 map 19.2,
527–31; population patterns in, 359–60,
479; slave imports of, 241, 242 map 10.2;
women in, 531, 532

Armenians: fur trade, 214; languages of, 175–
76; migrations of, 175–76, 177 map 7.5,
450, 476 map 17.3, 479, 547 map 19.6; in

Ottoman Empire, 175–76, 448; in Soviet
Union/Russia, 307, 515, 559, 560 map
19.8; statehood for, 175, 448, 515; Turkish
massacre of, 448, 453 map 17.1

Artisans, 35; in Americas, 194, 201 map 8.3,
206; in British colonial Africa, 411; in
building trades, 61, 84–85, 301; and China,
169, 200; ethnicity of, 80, 83, 600 n.51; in
India, 164, 173–74, 618 n.19; marital status
of, 75, 77; in masonry, 84–85, 602 nn.66,
67; and mechanization, 333; migrations of,
50, 65, 82, 120, 194, 201 map 8.3, 222–23,
280, 298–303, 344, 600 n.51; mining, 84–
86, 602 n.66, 603 n.71; in Ottoman Empire,
111, 164; and slaves, 243; tea chest manufacture, 268; travel carnets of, 576; weavers,
50, 53, 373–74; women as, 56, 82

Asia: African slaves as status symbol in, 157;
anti-immigration movements in South
Asia, 544; East-Central Asian relations,
310 map 13.2, 321, 322 map 13.1; ethnic enclaves in South Asia, 543–44; and Europe,
131, 173; labor in, 6, 193, 366, 511; land
ownership in, 543–44; maritime commerce
in, 135–36; mercenaries in, 173; newly industrialized countries (NICs) in, 538, 545;
oil industry in West Asia, 545; Portuguese
population of (c. 1800), 193; Spain's abolition of slavery in, 200; Uzbeks in, 308 map
13.1, 309, 310 map 13.2, 453 map 17.1, 455

Assam, 380, 382 map 15.5, 544, 577

Australia: Aboriginal peoples in, 228, 231;
Argentinian migrations to, 527 map 19.4;
British Empire in, 414 map 16.2; convict
shipments to, 231, 232; coolie labor in,
367; deportations to, 216, 231; European
migrations to, 227, 340, 453 map 17.1, 454,
476 map 17.3, 480, 560 map 19.8; gold in,
232; immigration policies of, 401, 402, 534;
and intercolonial migrations, 501; labor
supply strategies for, 231–32; Palestinian
migration to, 547 map 19.6; population of,
232, 453 map 17.1; racism in, 232–33; South
Pacific laborers in, 534, 537 map 19.5, 545;
women in, 231, 379–80

Austria, 350, 448, 453 map 17.1, 454

Aztecs, 187, 188 map 8.1, 190

Britain (*continued*)

30, 234, 387, 410; and Israel, 496, 497 map 18.2; Vietnamese workers in, 480–81. *See also* India; South Africa

British Columbia, 232, 393, 399, 400

Buddhism, 166, 172, 539

Bulgaria, 448, 449, 453 map 17.1, 497 map 18.2, 498, 559, 560 map 19.8, 562

Burkina Faso, 552 map 19.7, 554

Burma/Myanmar: British in, 391–92; Chettyars' presence in, 392; Chinese settlement in, 486, 487; education in, 392; ethnic composition of labor force, 391–92; Japan in, 392, 485; Karen people's migration from, 500; and labor migrations, 367, 542; refugee-generation from, 515, 538; rice cultivation in, 391, 392

Burundi, 515, 552 map 19.7, 554

Calcutta, 380, 382 map 15.5

California, 217 map 9.2, 227, 232, 393–94, 398–402, 534

Cambodia, 174, 515, 533, 538, 547 map 19.6

Canada: Africans in, 254; Asian migrations to, 400, 401, 430, 532, 533, 537 map 19.5, 538; and Black Atlantic, 254; and Britain, 414 map 16.2, 453 map 17.1, 454, 523; Caribbean community in, 524, 526–28, 531; and European migrations, 325, 464, 475, 476 map 17.3, 480, 527 map 19.4, 560 map 19.8; immigration policies of, 6, 401, 402, 430, 456, 458, 523–25, 525; internment of pacifists during World War I in, 472; Irish immigration to, 224, 340, 527 map 19.4; Italian immigration to, 523, 527 map 19.4, 529; Japanese community in, 402, 485–86; labor in, 352, 400, 423, 462, 523–25, 528; Métis in, 215–16, 270; migration patterns of, 216, 337 map 14.2, 338, 501, 523, 525, 527 map 19.4, 528, 534; population of, 479, 526, 529; and United States, 226, 355, 523, 527 map 19.4; women laborers in, 525, 528. *See also* British Columbia

Cape Verde Islands, 126, 127 map 5.3, 148, 202

Castes, 5, 166, 375, 377, 378 map 15.4, 383, 425

Castile, 94, 100, 191, 192, 194, 218 map 9.3

Catholic Church: in Africa, 417; and Anglican Church, 104–5; Armenian Christians, 175, 176; Cistercian Order in, 53, 68–69; conversions to, 45, 48, 94, 95, 96 map 4.1, 180, 195; and Council of Trent, 607 n.20; denominational schisms in, 101–7, 113, 224; and First Peoples, 190–91, 235, 237–38, 259; Franciscan Order in, 34, 72, 82, 148, 190; in Iberian Peninsula, 23, 24 map 2.1, 38, 52–53; Inquisition, 48, 94, 95, 96 map 4.1, 175, 292; and Ireland, 104–5; and Islam, 37, 41, 48–49, 50, 51, 52, 94, 95, 96 map 4.1; monasteries and convents of, 62, 80, 86–87, 104; in Ottoman Empire, 113–14; pilgrimages to holy shrines of, 24, 87–89, 603 n.72; slavery in, 160; and women, 87, 89, 102, 105–6, 265, 607 nn.21, 25. *See also* Jesuits

Cattle raising: in Africa, 162, 230; ecological impact of cattle, 144; in Latin America, 237, 358 map 14.4, 360, 493; and railroad transportation, 494; and slaves, 245; transhumance, 67–68, 281–83; and wealth and polygamy, 144

Ceylon, 173, 380, 382 map 15.5

Chad, 552 map 19.7, 554, 555

Chechens, 447, 476–77 map 17.3, 479

Cheng Ho, 35, 131, 143

Childbirth: birth control, 56, 116, 124, 238, 250, 340, 516; and colonization, 428, 430; family size, 3, 13, 221–22, 344; gender balance and reproduction, 204, 208, 255; and slaves, 154, 157, 161–62

Children: abandonment of Amerasian children, 518; and Africans in United States, 254; boys as tithes to nobility, 70; in British colonies, 185; caregivers for, 288, 570; education of, 287, 421–22, 525; ethnic/racial identity of, 35, 159, 164, 214, 494; and Iberian social hierarchies in Latin America, 202–3; immigration and identity formation of, 59, 364–65; infant mortality, 56, 75; Jewish children, 327; as labor supply, 161, 195, 237, 239, 283, 287, 295, 385–86, 433–34, 465–66, 511, 695 n.4; land inheritance of, 66–67, 221; in monasteries and convents,

86–87; sale of female children as debt relief, 169, 432, 518; slave breeding on plantations, 432–33; and slavery, 41, 42, 81, 150, 157–61, 252, 431–32, 463; in World War I, 451. *See also* Family; Marriage; Women

Chile, 203–4, 493, 514 map 19.2, 517, 527 map 19.4, 529–31

China: agriculture in, 171; artisans in, 169; Boxer Rebellion in, 423; British relations with, 370–71; Buddhism in, 172; Chinese diasporas, 5, 170 map 7.4, 173, 174, 200, 258 map 11.1, 367, 371, 393–94, 438, 486, 500, 536, 618 n.16, 704 n.68; conscript labor in, 691 n.68; contract labor in, 376; credit management in, 495; deportation of landowners in, 500; Dutch settlement in, 174; eighteenth-century emancipation of commoners, 172; famine in, 372; food from Americas in, 173; foreign military advisers in, 480, 483; imperialism of, 171, 172; indentured labor in, 366, 368 map 15.1; Indian Ocean passage, 32 map 2.3, 131–32, 165 map 7.2, 168–69; Islam in, 172; and Japan, 173, 481, 482 map 17.4, 484–85; Jesuits, expulsion of, 172; Jews in, 484–85; Kuomintang government, 495; labor militancy in, 442; migration patterns of, 34, 369–73, 377, 453 map 17.1, 457, 482 map 17.4, 484–85, 515, 539–40; mutual aid societies in, 495; opium in, 173, 370; and Polo family (Venice), 32, 34; population in, 171–72, 494; Portuguese settlement in, 174; proselytizing in, 87; religious tolerance in, 34; and Russia, 172, 559, 560 map 19.8; slavery in, 157; and Southeast Asia, 163, 389, 391; and trade, 136, 172; travel narratives of, 31; U.S. relations with, 370, 532, 537 map 19.5; women in, 171, 379. *See also* Beijing; People's Republic of China (PRC); Shanghai; Taiwan

Citizenship: and Asian immigrants in Hawai'i, 522; British citizenship and colonial residents, 7, 502; and Canadian immigrants, 577; democracy, 304; of displaced persons, 478; and immigrants to North America, 523; and immigration policy, 7, 296–97; and inclusivity, 574–76; Israel's

Law of Return, 497–98; of Jews in Nazi Germany, 456, 459; of Korean nationals in Japan, 481; multiple citizenships, 576, 582; and resident alien status, 472

Class: and British migration, 222–23; burgher class in Dutch Cape Colony, 230; and deportations, 231, 232, 500; English servant class, 288; mercenaries, social classes of, 63, 64 map 3.1; middle class as Victorian ideal, 427–29; multiethnicity of working class, 12; and racism, 252, 437; and sexuality, 429–30; and value of migration, 263–64. *See also* Castes; Ethnicity; Otherness; Race and racism; Slaves/slavery

Coffee, 151, 156, 204, 236 map 10.1, 245–46, 267, 358 map 14.4, 381–82, 412, 493, 554

Cold War, 486, 513, 559

Colombia, 358 map 14.4, 493, 527 map 19.4, 530

Colonialism: and agriculture, 194, 409–10; arrogance of, 418–19; of Britain, 185, 199, 201 map 8.3, 411, 426–28, 501, 502, 519; and competition with domestic goods, 423; and consumerism, 411; decolonization, 515, 551; depopulation of Native peoples and slave importation, 196, 197 map 8.2, 238; Dutch in Indies, 182–84; *encomiendas* as, 195, 237; of France, 68, 199, 201 map 8.3, 411, 488, 501; indigenous rulers' support of, 412; and marriage, 427–30, 433; of Portugal, 126, 127 map 5.3, 612 n.36; and racism, 424–26; and religion, 53, 68–69, 105; and savage masculinity, 375, 423–24; of United States, 102, 103 map 4.3, 222, 424, 569; and women, 427–29, 431, 495–96

Columbus, Christopher, 131–33, 187, 194, 235, 260

Commonwealth of Independent States (CIS). *See* Soviet Union

Communications: communication networks of building trades, 85; Incan mail and courier systems, 188; migrants as informants, 17, 19–20, 59–60, 62, 278, 587 n.34; monetary transactions as, 30; printed and written information as, 91; and railroads, 5, 225, 312, 319–20, 359, 371–72, 374, 388, 412, 441, 450, 494–95; travel narratives, 31,

Communications (*continued*)
34, 36, 37, 263, 576. *See also* Languages;
Ships; Travel

Compagnie des Indes Orientales, 181

Compagnie des Îles d'Amérique, 248

Concubines, 28, 42, 116–17, 151, 158, 251, 369, 380, 427, 518

Constantinople (Istanbul), 35, 46, 77, 113–14

Conversion: *aldeias* settlements, 245; Amerindians conversion to Christianity (*requerimiento*, c. 1513), 195; Christianity in Indic World, 180; of clergy during Reformation, 104; emigration as alternative to, 104; of First Peoples, 237; of foreigners in Spanish Americas, 194; in Islam, 116, 164, 166, 307; of Jews, 100, 107; *muladís*, 48, 50; and Muslims, 48, 50, 94, 107, 145–46, 164, 307, 614 n.12; Muwallads, 173; of slaves, 42, 116. See also *Moriscos*

Cotton, 29, 205, 245, 266, 358 map 14.4, 373, 374, 464, 556

Creoles, 1, 190, 202, 207, 244, 270, 500

Crusades, 23, 38, 46, 47, 87–88, 95, 163, 566, 591 nn.45–47

Cuba: boat people, 533; civil war in, 531; East European labor in, 559, 560 map 19.8; economic development in, 251; involuntary labor in, 394–95, 462; massacre of Afro-Caribbean leadership (1844), 252; migration patterns of, 342, 524–25, 528; population in, 251; and refugees, 459, 515, 533; slavery in, 250, 256, 394–95; sugarcane cultivation in, 151, 196, 197 map 8.2, 201 map 8.3; and United States, 355, 424, 515, 524–25, 533

Cultural Revolution (PRC), 538, 704 n.68

Curtin, Philip, 136, 145, 150, 151, 157, 202, 241

Cuzco, 188–89, 206, 236 map 10.1

Czechoslovakia, 453 map 17.1, 457, 497 map 18.2, 498, 515, 560 map 19.8, 561

Davidson, Basil, 142, 149, 157

Debt bondage, 149, 160, 169, 367–68, 432, 462–63, 511, 518, 546, 579

Denmark, 216, 241, 341, 472, 521 map 19.3

Depression (1930s), 6, 19, 356, 461, 462, 492, 529

Dervishes, 114, 423

Diasporas: Armenian diaspora in North America, 450; Chinese diasporas, 5, 170 map 7.4, 173, 174, 200, 258 map 11.1, 367, 371, 372 map 15.2, 373 map 15.3, 438, 486, 536–38, 618 n.16, 704 n.68; diaspora support for war, 573; Italian diasporas, 453 map 17.1, 456; Jewish diasporas, 43–44, 590 n.36

Domestic service: in Iberian Peninsula, 235; slaves in, 158, 243, 246; in South Africa, 505; women in, 18, 24, 56, 81, 349, 428, 518–19, 528, 542, 549. *See also* Labor supply; Slaves/slavery

Dominican Republic, 511, 527 map 19.4, 528, 530

Dutch Deli (Java) Company, 420

Dutch East India Company (VOC), 131, 172, 180–84, 228, 230, 369, 621 n.46

East Africa: Britain in, 414 map 16.2, 552 map 19.7, 558; capitalist production in, 159; China's Indian Ocean trade with, 168–69; cotton cultivation in, 556; currency in, 143; German colonial population in (c. 1914), 499; independence movement in, 557; Indian migration to, 403, 501, 557; inmigration to, 28, 227; labor migrations, 387–88, 552 map 19.7, 556; migration to Britain, 552 map 19.7, 558; Polish migration to, 475; Portugal in, 148–49; railroad construction in, 388; slave trade in, 150; South Asian immigrants in, 388, 392; Swahili culture, 143, 149; White migration to, 388; women's employment in, 556

East India Company (EIC), 180, 184–85, 215, 223, 227, 393

Ecology: in Africa, 552 map 19.7, 553, 558; climate, 4, 56, 136, 199, 243, 269, 356; ecocidal war, 553; forest reduction, 68, 171, 187, 188 map 8.1, 269, 530; impact of cattle on, 144; land reclamation in South Asia, 543; migrations influenced by, 516–17; World Ecology Conference, 573

Education: brain drain, 512, 524, 538, 552; in Burma, 392; of children, 287, 421–22, 525; in Europe, 61, 74, 118–19, 280, 303, 323, 325, 654 n.53; gentlemen travelers, 120, 303; as human capital for reinsertion,

557; and literacy, 38, 50, 246, 247, 525, 548; multiculturalism in, 422; of Palestinians, 497, 548; in Russia, 319, 340, 464; scholarly migrations, 108, 118–19; teaching of geography and imperialism, 421–22; in United States, 525, 533, 534; universities, 61, 74, 118–19, 323, 324, 654 n.53; of women, 171, 322, 325

Egypt: Aswan Dam construction, 548; and Berbers, 139; Britain in, 407, 408 map 16.1, 414 map 16.2, 449, 453 map 17.1; French citizens in, 502, 510 map 19.1; and Jewish migrations, 496–98; labor in, 551, 552 map 19.7, 559, 560 map 19.8; migration patterns of, 35–36, 547–49, 552 map 19.7; nationalist movement in, 407; slave trade in, 158, 159; women's economic involvement in, 549

Electrification programs, 492

Elites/nobility: in Argentina, 360; depictions of New World as aspirations of, 262; and indigenous peoples, 405–6, 416, 569; in Japan, 173; land holdings of, 68–70; marriages of, 60–61; merchant elite network in Europe, 299–300 map 12.4; mobility of, 27–28; "old immigration," superiority of, 336; in Ottoman Empire, 111; and peasants, 69–72; in Philippines, 180; and public office, 115–16, 123; of Renaissance Europe, 122; and slavery, 128, 151, 161; sons as colonial officials, 421–22, 425; spice consumption of, 29, 410; technical personnel migration, 512; tribute collection in Latin America, 202

Encomiendas, 195, 237–38

England. See Britain

Equiano, Olaudah, 150, 155

Eritrea, 515, 552 map 19.7, 558

Ethiopia: famine in, 515; and Italy, 407, 408 map 16.1, 453 map 17.1, 461, 499; migration to and from, 552 map 19.7, 554; and refugees, 515, 518, 552 map 19.7, 553, 558; repatriation in, 476 map 17.3, 479, 510 map 19.1

Ethnicity: in Africa, 507, 551, 552 map 19.7, 557; of Caribbean slave population, 241, 242 map 10.2; and citizenship, 574–76; and construction of inferiority, 362–63; of Cossacks, 212–14, 286, 307, 626 n.3; credit

arrangements, ethnicization of, 78, 97, 99; ethnic cleansing, 563; ethnic diversity in South Asia, 543–44; ethnicization of negative experience, 65, 78, 97, 101, 110, 120; ethnogenesis, 200–204, 246, 247, 270, 415, 535, 624 n.31; in European borderlands, post–World War I, 452; of German-origin people in Eastern Europe, 562; in India, 377, 486–87; in Ireland, 105; of labor force in postslavery era, 395–98; and land-brokers, 148; in Manchuria, 495; migration and changing urban ethnic composition, 71; in Mongol China, 34; multiethnicity of armies, 52, 416–17; multiethnic populations, interactions in, 349; and mutual aid associations, 479, 495, 555, 576–77; and nationalism, 13; of New Spain's transient population, 194; of nobility, 60; Portuguese trading communities, ethnic diversity of, 130; and religious identity, 311, 486–87; slaves, ethnic stereotypes of, 128; and tolerance in Ottoman Empire, 115–16

Eugenics, 360–61, 375, 416, 490

Factories: Argentine women in, 531; assembly lines, 344; Calcutta jute mills, 380, 382 map 15.5; and family labor, 269, 334, 511; in Hong Kong, 534; and mass production, 298, 344; in Russia, 464; sweatshops, 546, 579. See also Taylorism; Textile manufacture

Families: African slave trade's impact on, 160; Asian labor recruitment of, 379–80; and Chinese diaspora, 371; elder care, 13, 334, 538–39; family formation, 12, 56, 76, 79–80, 215, 254, 339–40, 346, 531; gender balance and reproduction, 204, 208, 255; in Jewish communities, 38, 44, 327; and labor migrations to South Africa, 505–6; as labor supply, 160–61, 269, 288, 334, 579; and migrant decision making, 16–21, 206–7, 345, 512–13, 578; in out-migration from Europe (1945–55), 480; and polygamy, 158, 160; reunions and migrations of, 527 map 19.4, 528, 532–33, 545; in rise of urban bourgeoisie, 75; settlement recruitment of, 283–87; and slavery, 154, 155, 250–51; in Spanish Caribbean migrations, 249. See also Children; Marriage; Women

Famine: in Africa, 412, 553; in Asia, 174, 372, 377, 515; in Europe, 56–57, 124–25, 169, 224, 339–40, 454–55; in Latin America, 188, 245; politically exacerbated famines, 515; and population growth in twenty-first century, 516

Finland, 452, 453 map 17.1, 519, 521 map 19.3

Foods: American crops in China, 173; canned foods, 354; Chibcha (Colombia) trade in, 188; cocoa, 243, 554; and dietary changes, 36, 132, 162, 173, 196, 266–68; ethnic foods and acculturation, 269, 522; and European urbanization, 295–96; maize, 162, 173, 268; potatoes, 268, 339; rice, 269, 292, 334, 341, 370, 391, 481, 495; salt, 29, 135, 142; spices, 29, 131, 159, 182, 266–67; tea, 267–68, 380, 381–82, 382 map 15.5; and warfare, 149. *See also* Agriculture; Coffee; Grain; Sugarcane cultivation

Forasteros, 238

Forced labor: and army recruitment, 278–79, 316, 468; in British colonial Africa, 411; in construction projects, 59, 466, 467 map 17.2, 691 n.68; control of, 462–63; coolies, 367, 372 map 15.2, 373 map 15.3, 377, 469; debt bondage, 149, 160, 169, 367–68, 432, 462–63, 511, 518, 546, 579; Forced Labour Convention, 461; in France, 469; in Germany, 445, 460, 467 map 17.2, 469–74; human porterage, 169, 198, 238–39, 243, 268, 371, 556; indentured labor, 216–20, 366–67, 368 map 15.1, 375–76, 381–83, 390, 395–98; Indios in Guatemala, 531; in Japan, 445, 483–84; and Jesuits, 245; *mita* labor, 239–40; Nepali laborers in Bhutan, 544; peonage, 462; prisoners of war as, 469, 475–77, 476 map 17.3, 485; in South Africa, 504–7; in Soviet Union, 445, 464–65, 467 map 17.2; in Uganda (*kasanvu* system), 469. *See also* Bound labor; Labor supply

Formosa. *See* Taiwan

France: and Africa, 241, 248, 414 map 16.2, 469, 548, 552 map 19.7, 555, 558; in Algeria, 407, 408 map 16.1, 409, 414 map 16.2, 422, 503; artisan migration from, 292; Asian migration to, 537 map 19.5, 538; Atlantic slave trade, 151, 156; Caribbean migrations to, 527 map 19.4, 528; and colonialism, 61, 68, 69, 199, 201 map 8.3, 488, 501; cultural superiority and education in, 426; and Druse community in Syria, 499; Eastern European migrations to, 341, 560 map 19.8; and England, 215, 251; fur empires of, 213 map 9.1; in Guiana, 216, 217 map 9.2, 414 map 16.2, 527 map 19.4, 528; immigration restrictions in, 453 map 17.1, 457, 512; Jews in, 98 map 4.2, 99, 458; and labor migrations, 450, 453 map 17.1, 456, 461, 471, 519, 554; as mercenary source, 63, 64 map 3.1; migration patterns in, 221, 337 map 14.2, 502, 521 map 19.3; in Morocco, 409–10, 552 map 19.7; National Front, 522, 577; in North Africa, 407, 408 map 16.1, 409, 414 map 16.2; nuclear testing by, 516; population patterns in, 304, 322, 350, 451–53 map 17.1, 457, 502, 522, 662 n.50; religious tolerance in, 106; Russian émigrés in, 329; St. Lawrence settlements, 213 map 9.1, 214, 218 map 9.3, 221, 353 map 14.3, 415–16; in Vietnam, 480, 502, 533. *See also* Marseille; Paris

Fugger family, 38, 78, 265

Fur trade, 181, 213 map 9.1, 214–15, 218 map 9.3

Gabon, 552 map 19.7, 555

Gama, Vasco da, 129–30, 136–37, 144–45

Garvey, Marcus, 526–28, 677 n.20

Gaza Strip, 496–97

Geneva Convention, 509, 513–15, 525

Germany: Eastern European migrations to, 469, 560 map 19.8, 561; Huguenots in, 106, 608 n.32; immigration restrictions in, 447, 476 map 17.3, 479; industrialization in, 339; Jews in, 457–60; labor supply in, 334, 336, 450, 467 map 17.2, 469, 471, 476 map 17.3, 479; Lombardy-to-Flanders trade route, 77; as mercenary source, 63, 64 map 3.1; migration patterns from, 337 map 14.2, 338, 339, 353 map 14.3, 521 map 19.3; Nazism in, 453 map 17.1, 456–60, 467 map 17.2; northern fens, colonization of, 283–84; Polish migrations to, 341, 560 map 19.8, 562; population of, 301, 348–51, 454, 499, 522–23; postwar reconstruction of, 519; Protestantism in, 104, 107; and refugee mi-

from, 62–63, 64 map 3.1; migration patterns of, 194, 290 n.12.2, 293–94, 337–38, 341–42, 358 map 14.4, 521 map 19.3, 527 map 19.4, 529, 530; population changes in, 342; Rome, 75, 87, 88, 89–90; taxation of working class in, 341–42; undocumented migrants in, 512; urban growth in, 70

Itinerancy, 61–62, 72–74, 80–81, 117, 303, 324, 334, 335 map 14.1, 654 n.53

Ivory, 143, 145

Ivory Coast, 552 map 19.7, 554

Jamaica: British in, 248; labor supply and sugarcane cultivation, 196, 197 map 8.2; migration patterns of, 527 map 19.4, 528, 530; population of, 251, 528–29; slavery in, 250, 252; sugarcane cultivation in, 250

Japan: agricultural modernization in Korea and Taiwan, 481; annexation of Taiwan and Pescadores Islands, 481, 482 map 17.4; and Canada, 402, 485–86; and China, 173, 481, 482 map 17.4, 484–85; foreigners in, 173, 174, 375, 480; Greater East Asia Co-Prosperity Sphere, 483; health-care guest workers in, 540, 541; imperialism of, 375–76, 420; invasion of Burma, 392; Japanese settlement in Brazil, 376, 402, 481–83, 527 map 19.4, 529, 532, 537 map 19.5, 541; Jesuits in, 173, 180; Karafuto (South Sakhalin) annexed by, 481, 482 map 17.4, 483; and Korea, 173, 372 map 15.2, 481–85, 540, 577; links to Pacific coast labor markets, 353 map 14.3, 357, 372 map 15.2, 375, 399–400, 401–2; in Manchuria, 482 map 17.4, 484, 518; migration patterns of, 7, 173–74, 358 map 14.4, 372 map 15.2, 375–76, 481–83, 532, 537 map 19.5, 539–41; in Nan'yo (Caroline Islands), 482 map 17.4, 483; and Okinawa, 372 map 15.2, 375; population in, 173, 540, 541; and Russia, 329, 481; and United States, 375, 401–2, 485; university education in, 483; working tourists in, 541

Japanese Society for Eastern Colonization, 455

Java, 166, 168, 367, 493–94, 538

Jazz, 417–18

Jerusalem: acculturation of Franks in, 47, 592 n.52; pilgrimages to, 24, 87–89, 603 n.72; reconquest of, 47; repopulation of, 46–47

Jesuits, 172, 173, 180, 190–91, 244, 245

Jews: in Algeria, 409; Ashkenazim, 96–100, 258 map 11.1; in Baghdad, 42–43; in Birobidzhan, 453 map 17.1, 455, 479; in Caribbean, 198, 241; and Christian crusades, 97–98; in diamond industry, 410; Eastern Europe population of, 322 map 13.5, 327, 328 fig. 13.2; and education, 325, 327; expulsions of, 42, 97–99, 175, 292, 590 n.33; families of, 38, 39 map 2.5, 44, 279, 327; as financial agents, 97, 175, 289, 567, 605 n.9; guilds, exclusion from, 97; in Holocaust, 459, 467 map 17.2, 471–72; in Iberian Peninsula, 23, 24 map 2.1, 43–44, 48–49, 100, 590 n.38; in India, 175; and Islam, 43–44, 590 n.38; in Nazi Germany, 457–60; in Netherlands, 101, 175, 289, 458, 459, 580; in Ottoman Empire, 95, 98 map 4.2, 111, 113–14, 567, 609 n.12; in Pale of Settlement, 326 map 13.5, 325–26, 328 fig. 13.2, 341; in Palestine, 496, 497 map 18.2; pogroms against, 113, 341; in Russia/Soviet Union, 327, 451, 453 map 17.1, 559, 560 map 19.8, 562; and slavery, 42; as U.S.-bound migrants, 325, 341, 560 map 19.8, 562. See also Anti-Semitism; Israel

Jordan, 496–97, 514 map 19.2, 546, 547 map 19.6, 548, 549

Journeymen, 24, 81–84 map 3.3, 602 nn.61, 62

Kaffa, 41, 111, 117

Kalmyks, 476 map 17.3, 479

Kantoshu, 481, 482 map 17.4

Karafuto (South Sakhalin), 481, 482 map 17.4, 483, 485

Karelia, 476 map 17.3, 479

Kazakhstan, 453 map 17.1, 455, 464, 466, 467 map 17.2

Kazaks, 212–14, 626 n.3

Kenya, 227, 492–93, 500, 501, 552–57

Kikuyu, 411, 412, 500, 501

Kilwa, 143, 145, 148

Korea: agricultural modernization in, 481; factional war in, 500; invasions of, 375;

Korea (*continued*)

Japan in, 173, 372 map 15.2, 481–85, 540, 577; labor shortages in, 484; migration patterns of, 481, 482 map 17.4, 486, 533, 537–39, 547 map 19.6, 549; refugee-generation from, 538

Kowloon, 370, 372 map 15.2

Kraków, 99, 109, 299–300 map 12.4, 324, 561

Kurds, 448, 453 map 17.1, 515

Kuwait, 496, 497 map 18.2, 549, 550

Labor activism, 386, 392, 441, 511, 520

Labor supply: of Africans in U.S. South, 254, 636 n.42; *asiento* licensing system, 241; of children, 161, 195, 237, 239, 283, 287, 295, 433–34, 465–66, 511, 695 n.4; and Chinese colonization of Mongolia, 494; of Chinese workers in Pacific coast markets, 353 map 14.3, 357, 393, 398–401; for clothing industry, 266, 511; for contract labor, 6, 158, 234, 376, 462; of coolies, 268, 367, 377; ethnic composition of, 437–39; families as, 160–61, 269, 288, 334, 579; importation of male labor in Germany, 450, 467 map 17.2; in India, 374–75, 378 map 15.4, 379, 382 map 15.5, 544; internationalization of labor markets, 344–45; and Korean out-migration, 482 map 17.4, 484; living arrangements of male workers, 345, 506; in Manchuria (Manchukuo), 484, 518; Mexican migrations to United States, 353 map 14.3, 355–56, 513, 523, 524, 527 map 19.4, 529; migrants and job professionalization, 579; for mining of precious minerals, 242; *mita* labor, 239–40; for New England textile mills, 225, 226, 415–16; for oil industry, 530, 545, 546, 547 map 19.6, 548, 552 map 19.7, 555; and Palestinian migrations, 496–97 map 18.2, 547 map 19.6; and Panama Canal, 361; railroads' impact on, 371–72 map 15.2, 374; recruitment of, 192, 282–87, 296–97, 381–83, 390, 517–18, 524, 529; *repartimiento de indios*, 238; in Russia, 314–15, 316–18, 320, 322 map 13.1, 463, 652 n.30; seasonal labor, 282 map 12.1, 290–94, 290 map 12.2, 505, 511, 645 n.41, 652 n.22; for South Africa, 505, 506 map 18.3; South Pacific laborers in Australia, 534; of undocumented mi-

grants, 512, 522–23, 525, 526, 528, 529, 530, 554; of Vietnamese workers in Europe, 480–81; of women, 85, 195, 225, 237–38, 379–81, 386, 450, 465–66, 517–18, 525; during World War I, 450. *See also* Forced labor; Guest workers; Migration headings; Slaves/slavery

Lamaism, 172, 321

Land holdings: in Africa, 553, 556; colonization, 59, 61, 105, 283–84; *estancias* in Spanish Americas, 195; homesteading in Russia, 312, 313 map 13.2, 319, 653 nn.37, 39; in Latin America, 203, 235; in North American colonies, 215; Russian land-ownership in Kazakhstan, 453 map 17.1, 455; settlement recruitment, 192, 282–87; and slaves in Islamic world, 158; in South Asia, 500, 543–44; and women, 553

Languages: in Africa, 136–37, 144; Berber language, 141 map 6.1, 148; Chinese, 171, 371; dialects, 122; English, 122, 425–26; German as lingua franca, 285, 315; Gullah, 254; of Iberian Peninsula, 95, 191; of Indian emigrants, 377; indigenous languages and historical research, 191; Malay, 168; and migration destinations, 524, 528, 565; multilingualism, 30, 50, 51, 61–62, 286, 544; of Ottoman administration, 115; pidginization of, 136, 254; slave trade languages, 153, 155; in South Africa, 507; Swahili, 137, 143, 149; Tamil, 166, 545; Telugu, 166; text translations, 28, 47, 52, 102, 592 n.52; in trade, 76, 77; Turkish language purged of Arab and Persian, 450; Yiddish, 44, 461

Laos, 486, 515, 533

Las Casas, Bartolomé de, 192, 235, 260

Lebanon: migrations from, 546–48; Muslim pilgrimage to Mecca, 546, 547 map 19.6; out-migration of merchants, 548; Palestinian settlement in, 497 map 18.2, 514 map 19.2, 548; refugee-generation from, 515

Legislation, migration: anti-immigration, 401, 402–3, 415, 430; in Britain, 502, 528, 545; Canadian immigration regulations (1967), 532; in China, 484–85; Dublin convention (1990), 523; freedom of movement and right of entrance, 570–71, 713 n.11; in

India, 403–4; integration policies in Sweden and Netherlands, 522; Israel's Law of Return, 496, 497 map 18.2, 498; in Japan, 540; Maastricht Agreement (1993), 523; Schengen Agreement (1985), 523; in United States, 523–26, 528, 532, 533, 700 n.37

Legislation, slave, 243–44, 250

Less developed countries (LDCs), 509, 513, 516, 571–72, 697 n.16

Liberia, 416, 515, 551, 552 map 19.7, 553

Libya: Egyptian labor migration to, 549; Jewish migration to Israel, 497 map 18.2, 498; labor migrations, 552 map 19.7, 554; migration patterns in, 552 map 19.7, 554; Muslim pilgrimage to Mecca, 546, 547 map 19.6; Palestinian refugees in, 496, 497 map 18.2; trans-Saharan slave trade, 159

Lima, 206, 236 map 10.1, 241, 242 map 10.2, 243

Łódź, 302, 315, 341, 366

Macao, 130, 174, 370, 372 map 15.2, 373 map 15.3, 482 map 17.4, 486

Magnitogorsk Giant, 466, 467 map 17.2

Magyars, 38, 39 map 2.5, 562

Malacca, 130, 166–69, 174

Malawi, 505, 506 map 18.3, 507, 552 map 19.7, 554, 558

Malaysia (Malaya): coolie labor in, 367; cultural incorporation in, 575; Filipino migration to, 537 map 19.5, 541; gender ratios in migrations to, 539; gross national product of, 516; labor militancy in, 441–42; population patterns in, 390, 487, 500, 536, 541; and refugee migrations, 514 map 19.2; statehood of, 541

Mali, 552 map 19.7, 554

Malta, 449, 453 map 17.1

Mamluks, 40, 139, 140

Manchuria (Manchukuo), 172–73, 452–53 map 17.1, 481–84, 492, 494–95, 518

Manila, 169, 178, 179, 200

Manumission: in Brazil, 247; contraband slave trade, 162; of slaves in Islamic world, 158, 159, 616 n.31; of slaves of color, 243–44, 247; of U.S. slaves, 254, 255

Maritime trade, 163, 165 map 7.2, 166–68, 228, 229 map 9.5

Maroons, 208, 209, 416

Marriage: and acculturation, 44, 115, 244; of Anglican clergy, 105; of cacique family princesses to Spanish men, 202, 203, 262; versus celibacy, 59, 75, 77, 339; in colonial Africa, 413; of *conversos* to Spanish nobility, 100; as debt payment, 149; in Dutch colonies in Indies, 182–84; dynastic marriages of elites, 60–61; gender ratios in New Spain, 193–94; international marriage agencies, 518; in Jewish communities, 43, 327, 457, 590 n.37; *limpieza de sangre*, 101, 262, 270, 271, 606 n.15; mercantile marriages, 43, 75, 76, 79, 136; and migration, 3, 12, 13, 14, 43, 280, 343; of North American colonists, 215; patterns in thirteenth-century Europe, 56; polygamy, 144, 158, 160; postponement and birth-family support, 542; restrictions on, 124, 238, 480, 557; of slaves, 154, 158, 244; and social mobility, 79, 81, 83; of sugarcane workers, 386; and women, 4, 13, 43, 50, 79, 158, 446, 518, 590 n.37. *See also* Men and masculinity; Women

Marrus, Michael, 445, 459–60

Marseille, 79–80, 503

Martinique, 199, 221, 251, 527 map 19.4, 528

Mauritania, 511, 554

Mauritius, 150, 384, 386, 403

McNeill, William, 109

Mecca, 47, 87, 140, 546, 547 map 19.6, 555, 603 nn.72, 76

Medina, 546, 555

Men and masculinity: celibacy, 59, 75, 77, 339; living arrangements of male workers, 345, 506; and male dominance in European migration, 202, 624 n.31; male labor supply in Germany, 450, 467 map 17.2; and migration, 423, 464, 490, 511, 518, 538–39, 545–46, 556; savage masculinity, 375, 423–24; sexuality and sexual practices, 46, 260, 271, 417, 429–34, 518. *See also* Marriage; Women

Mennonites, 104, 286, 297

Mercenaries: in Asia, 166, 168, 173, 618 n.18; in colonial armies, 424; in Europe, 61, 62–65, 106, 223–24, 278; Jewish mercenaries,

Mercenaries (*continued*)
175; women as, 63, 64 map 3.1. *See also* Soldiers; Wars

Merchants: African free men as, 243; in China's trading diasporas, 34–35, 168–69; coastal mercantile communities in China, 172; diasporic communities of, 168–69; Dutch merchants in Caribbean, 249; enclaves, 76; ethnic composition of Caribbean slave traders, 241–42; indentured laborers' transport, 217; in Indonesia, 168; Japanese merchants, 173; kinship of slaves in merchant families, 158; merchant companies, 123; merchant elite network in Europe, 299–300 map 12.4; migration to Spanish America (c. 1700), 194; piracy, 166, 179, 194, 198; *Schedelsche Weltchronik*, 108; slaves as domestic servants, 158, 243; trade fairs and street vendors, 32 map 2.3, 37, 38, 60, 61, 176. *See also* Banking and commerce; Labor supply; Trade

Métis, 215–16, 270

Mexico: and American identity, 209; Caribbean migration to, 527 map 19.4, 529; immigration legislation in, 525, 529; and Latin American migrations, 529; *maquiladoras* in, 511; Mexican Revolution, 529; mining in, 206, 207, 240; population of, 206, 207, 243; slave trade routes to, 236 map 10.1, 237, 242 map 10.2; Spanish Civil War refugees in, 453 map 17.1, 457; Spanish slave transports to, 200, 201 map 8.3; and United States, 353 map 14.3, 355–56, 513, 523, 524, 527 map 19.4, 529; women as heads of refugee families in, 518

Middle class: and Asian entrepreneurship, 534; and British migration, 222–23; as domestic ideal, 427–29; and Dominican voluntary migrations, 528; ethnicity of, 60; expulsion from Iberian Peninsula, 292; mobility of, 280; and mutual aid associations, 555; Protestant ethic of, 104; Shirazis and commerce, 159; and state building, 362, 421

Migrant decision making, 16–21, 206–7, 345, 512–13, 578

Migrants, undocumented, 512, 522–23, 525, 526, 528, 529, 530, 554

Migration, forced: Algerian war, 503, 514 map 19.2; and Catholic Church, 190, 237–38; in China, 371–73, 482 map 17.4, 484; of tsarist supporters ("second migration"), 328–29, 655 nn.62, 63, 64; deportations, 45, 216, 231–32, 327, 410, 411, 460, 476 map 17.3, 479, 569; development displacement, 516–17; of Egyptians from Iraq, 550; and famine, 339–40, 454–55, 516–17; and France, 409, 453 map 17.1, 457; of Hindus and Sikhs, 487; of indentured laborers, 216–20, 366–68 map 15.1, 375–76, 381–83, 390, 395–98; Ireland from, 224, 339–40; of Jews, 42, 97–99, 100, 175, 292, 326 map 13.5, 327–28, 341, 453 map 17.1, 456–57, 459–60, 590 n.33; of Koreans by Japanese, 481–85; of Kurds from Iraq, 550; and land enclosure, 286–88; of *Mozárabes*, 49–50; of Muslims, 48, 50, 93–95, 292, 447, 448, 550; of Native Americans, 215–16, 217 map 9.2, 225; in Ottoman Empire, 111, 112 map 5.1, 113–14, 117; from Poland, 324; of political refugees, 500, 531; of Puritans, 105; in Russia, 314, 326 map 13.5, 327–28 fig. 13.2, 329, 447; of soldiers, 278–79; in South Africa, 230–31, 504–6 map 18.3; in United States, 215–17, 225, 255, 492; of Yemenis from Saudi Arabia, 550

Migration, internal: of Arab-Islamic merchants, 163; in Caribbean, 205, 526; in Europe, 519; India, 380–81, 382 map 15.5; and Japanese industrialization, 375; under *kangani* recruiting system, 381–83, 390; in Korea, 486; of laborers in Germany, 468–69; in Latin America, 205; of Mongols, 163; in North America, 205; in People's Republic of China, 539–40; in Spain, 453 map 17.1, 461; Turks, 163

Migration, return: of African Americans, 416; of Afro-Europeans, 416; of American-educated nationals, 533; of colonial populations, 499–501; from colonies to Western Europe, 519; and Dutch government, 501–2; to Eastern Europe, 559, 560 map 19.8; to Egypt, 549; and entrepreneurship, 520; during Great Depression, 6, 19, 356, 461, 492, 529; impact on metropolitan areas of, 501; of Indian workers, 392; from North

America, 339, 452–53; and independence, 500–503; of Puerto Ricans from United States, 525; and reinvestment in Iberian Peninsula, 193; to South Asia, 547 map 19.6; to Soviet Union, 464, 559, 560 map 19.8, 563; from United States, 344, 363, 666 nn.75, 78

Migration, rural-to-urban, 283; in Africa, 553; in Brazil, 527 map 19.4, 529–30; in Eastern Europe, 560 map 19.8, 561; ethnic composition of, 296; in Europe, 56; in former colonial areas, 500–501, 553; in Godavari district (West Central India), 373; of Incas, 189; of Japanese peasants, 173; and land enclosure, 287–88; in People's Republic of China, 539–40; South Asia, 383; in Soviet Union, 453 map 17.1, 455; in Stalinist Russia, 463; in Tunisia, 554

Migration, voluntary 509–13; of Asians to North America, 533; and brain drains, 512, 524, 538, 552; of Bulgarians from Turkey, 449, 453 map 17.1; to Caribbean plantations, 253; and China, 372 map 15.2, 373 map 15.3, 377; colonization of Russia as, 311–13 map 13.2; during crusades, 23, 38, 46, 47, 87–88, 95, 97–98 map 4.2, 163, 566, 591 nn.45, 46, 47; from Dominican Republic, 527 map 19.4; of Eastern European women, 317–18, 519; European labor migrations, 519–20; to Australia, 232; of peasants, 2; of Puritans, 105; to Siberia, 319; from social-democratic societies, 500–501; of South Pacific laborers to Australia, 534; of Turks from Bulgaria, 449, 453 map 17.1

Migration strategies, 16–20, 70, 206–7, 345, 512–13, 520

Minas Gerais, 204, 236 map 10.1, 245, 246

Mining: in Bengal, 380, 382 map 15.5, 383, 670 n.32; of diamonds in Cape Colony, 410; German POWs in Belgian coal mines, 475, 476 map 17.3; labor for, 24, 84–86, 187, 188 map 8.1, 205, 236 map 10.1, 246, 386, 602 n.66, 603 n.71; in Manchuria (Manchukuo), 484; in Mexico, 206, 207, 240; in Minas Gerais, 204, 236 map 10.1, 245, 246; and *mita* labor, 239–40; in Mozambique, 411; under *nokarni* labor system, 383; in Potosí, 187, 236 map 10.1; in Russia, 311;

and slavery, 204, 207, 236 map 10.1, 237, 242–43, 245, 246; in South Africa, 505, 506 map 18.3; and tin, 173, 389; in Zimbabwe, 130, 143. *See also* Gold; Silver

Miskito population, 237, 531

Missionaries, 411; Americans as, 370; and *cumbes* settlement, 244; Franciscans, 34, 72; Jesuits, 34, 172, 173, 190–91, 244, 245

Moluccas, 168, 180, 216, 502

Mongolia, 172, 173; Chinese migrations to, 322–22, 322 map 13.1, 495; Muslim trade in, 321; population of, 495; World War I refugees in, 452, 453 map 17.1

Mongols: conversion to Islam, 164, 307; and cultural exchange, 164; internal migration of, 163; and Kazakhs, 307–9, 310 map 13.2; military conquest by, 164; and missionaries, 34; invaders of trade routes, 58; in multiethnic Ch'ing dynasty administration, 169; plagues in, 58; and slavery, 164

Moriscos, 48, 94, 95, 96 map 4.1, 194

Morocco: Arabization of education system in, 498; European-origin population in (1930), 499; France in, 408 map 16.1, 409–10, 552 map 19.7; Jews in, 497 map 18.2, 498, 503; migration patterns in, 139, 521 map 19.3, 547 map 19.6, 552 map 19.7; repatriation of French citizens from, 502, 510 map 19.1; slavery in, 159, 462

Mortality: in contact populations of Americas, 189–90; and diseases, 75, 155, 189–90, 195–96, 214, 376–77; of Irish immigrants, 339; and malnutrition, 56–57, 516–17; of *mita* in Potosí, 239–40; and pathogens transmitted by Europeans, 189–90; and plagues, 3, 24, 55, 57–58, 71; of sailors in Asian trade areas, 184; of slaves, 155, 156, 158, 159, 196, 235, 246, 247, 376–77

Mozambique, 130; Asian immigration to, 411; ethnic groups in, 551, 552 map 19.7; European population in, 413, 499, 501; family emigrations from Atlantic islands to, 193; gross national product of, 516; labor recruitment for South Africa in, 505, 506 map 18.3, 507; migration patterns in, 552 map 19.7, 554; Portuguese migration to, 227, 501; and refugee migrations, 515, 552

Mozambique (*continued*)
map 19.7; war in, post-independence, 500, 514 map 19.2, 515

Mozárabes, 49–50

Mulattoes: manumission of, 244; in migration to Spanish Americas, 194; in Puerto Rico, 251; in Saint Domingue, 251–52

Multinational corporations (MNCs), 511, 517, 526, 539, 542–43

Muscovy Empire, 109, 181, 608 n.1

Muslims: in Balkans, 448, 453 map 17.1; Christianity's relations with, 52, 91, 92–94, 109, 180; coexistence patterns among, 91; in Constantinople (Istanbul), 114; as displaced refugees, 513, 514 map 19.2; Hindu relations with, 486; Ibadi, 148; in Iberian Peninsula, 23, 24 map 2.1, 48, 49, 51, 93, 161, 265, 292; in independent Algeria, 503; intermarriage of, 93–94, 115, 166; Jewish relations with, 48–49; in merchant settlement in Ayutthaya, Siam, 174; in Mongolian trade, 326; in North Africa, 45, 503; out-migration to Britain, 502; pilgrimages of, 47, 87, 140, 546, 547 map 19.6, 555, 603 n.72, 603 nn.72, 76; pluralism in societies of, 43; as slaves, 246; as soldiers, 46, 166, 618 n.18; South Asian migrations of, 544, 545; Sufism, 166; and Turks, 110

Mutual aid associations, 479, 495, 555, 576–77

Mzabis, 148, 409

Namibia, 501, 506 map 18.3, 552 map 19.7, 554

Nansen, Fridtjof, 447

Nan'yo (Caroline Islands), 482 map 17.4, 483, 485

Nepal, 488, 537 map 19.5

Netherlands: and abolition, 256; and American colonies, 198, 201 map 8.3, 624 n.25; artists of, 184; and Atlantic slave trade, 151, 156, 241; and diamond industry, 410; end of economic prominence of, 184; fur empire of, 213 map 9.1; and independence movements, 488, 501–2; Indic World settlements, 181–82; integration policies in, 182, 522; Jews in, 101, 175, 289, 458, 459, 580;

labor policies of, 350; migration patterns of, 198, 216, 289, 290 map 12.2, 476 map 17.3, 479, 501–2, 519, 521 map 19.3, 527 map 19.4, 528, 560 map 19.8; peat colonies in, 284; and Portugal, 131, 181; Protestants in, 105–7, 180; as refuge during World War I, 451; in South Africa, 228–30. *See also* Dutch East India Company (VOC)

New York: Black culture in Harlem, 356; Colombian migrations to, 530; Dominican community in, 527 map 19.4; New Netherland, 198, 201 map 8.3; Puerto Rican community in, 525, 527 map 19.4; religious refugees in, 224; Russian émigrés in, 326, 329; sweatshops in, 546, 579

New Zealand: Asian migrants in, 534, 537 map 19.5, 538; coolie labor in, 367; European diaspora in, 227; exploitation of native peoples in, 228; gold, 232; and intra-colonial migration, 501; Irish migration to, 340; Maori in, 231; migration patterns of, 537 map 19.5; Palestinian migration to, 547 map 19.6

Nicaragua, 189, 237, 518, 527 map 19.4, 531

Nigeria, 414 map 16.2, 510 map 19.1, 515, 551, 552 map 19.7, 555

Nobility. *See* Elites/nobility

Nongovernmental organizations (NGOs), 513, 572, 713 n.17

Norman society, 38, 39 map 2.5, 44–45

North America: African migration to, 552 map 19.7, 558–59; Americanness, emphasis of, 209–10; Armenian diaspora in, 450; Asian migrations to, 486; Caribbean-Mexican migration, 7, 201 map 8.3, 353 map 14.3; Chinese migration to, 217 map 9.2, 227; citizenship for immigrants, 523; colonies in, 102, 103 map 4.3, 185, 198, 201 map 8.3, 222, 224, 225, 624 n.25; cultural autonomy in, 199, 352; domestic worker migration to, 519; European migrations to, 322, 337 map 14.2, 452, 453 map 17.1, 489; immigrant dependence on indigenous people, 212; internal migration in, 205; Irish migration to, 105, 218 map 9.3, 223–24; Italian migration to, 342, 453 map 17.1, 456, 489; Japanese migration to, 217 map

by, 130; silver as currency in, 178; and slave trade, 126–29, 150–53, 159, 612 n.38; and Spain in New World, 32; strategic settlements of, 130; system of domination of, 178; trade dispute with Ottoman Empire, 148; trade-posts, 178; Treaty of Tordesillas, 241

Potemkin villages, 286

Potosí, 239–43, 358 map 14.4

Prague, 109, 328–29, 655 nn.62, 63, 64

Prostitution: of courtesans, 82–83, 90, 601 n.60; of Korean women (comfort women), 485, 518; and male migrants, 433–35; and migration, 74, 192; as slavery, 379, 485, 511, 518; and soldiers, 430

Protestantism, 101–7, 113, 222, 448, 607 n.23

Prussia, 222, 278, 282 map 12.1, 284, 340, 652 n.22

Puerto Rico, 196, 197 map 8.2, 251, 424, 525, 527 map 19.4, 528, 569

Punjab, 374–75, 378 map 15.4, 379, 382 map 15.5, 487

Puritans, 103 map 4.3, 105, 222

Pushkin, Alexander, 302, 309

Quakers, 104, 222

Race and racism: anti-immigration legislation, 401–4, 504; in Australia, 232–33; Chinese workers, discrimination against, 321; class, 437; colonial returnees in metropolitan areas, 501; coolies, image of, 268, 367, 377; Creoles, 1, 190, 202, 207, 244, 270, 500; in East Africa, 388, 558; eugenics, 360–61, 375, 416, 490; in France, 522, 577; freedom of movement and right of entrance, 570–71, 713 n.11; and genetic differences, 336; global apartheid, 525, 577–78; Gypsies, 109, 608 n.2; and interracial marriages, 244, 247; *limpieza de sangre*, 101, 262, 270, 271, 606 n.15; and minority migration to Britain, 502; Mulattoes in Mexico, 203; in Nazi Germany, 453 map 17.1, 456–57, 467 map 17.2, 469–74; racial superiority theories, 272–73; and sexual fantasies, 429–30; and slave manumission, 244, 247; in South Africa, 493, 504–7, 556; in United States, 6, 7, 162, 254, 255, 438,

518, 636 n.42; in West Indies, 424, 679 n.39. *See also* Legislation; Migration (various headings); Skin color; Slaves/slavery; Whiteness

Railroads, 5, 225, 312, 319–20, 359, 371–72, 374, 388, 412, 441, 450, 494–95

Refugees: Armenian, 448–49, 453 map 17.1; displaced persons, 476 map 17.3, 478; economic impact of, in Reformation, 104; environmental, 516–17, 558; heretical sects as, 101–2, 103 map 4.3; Huguenots as, 106, 297; from Iberian Jewish persecution, 100; Inter-Governmental Committee on Refugees, 459; labor recruitment of, 296–97; and nation building, 296–97; and Pakistan-India migrations, 487; Palestinians as, 496–97, 514 map 19.2; from Poland, 323, 324; political asylum of, 515, 533; political refugees, 304–5, 322–25; population of (1945), 478; repatriation of, 371, 476 map 17.3, 478, 479, 482 map 17.4, 485, 501, 541; during Spanish Civil War, 457; of Thirty Years' War, 222; in United States, 222, 224; during World War I, 451–52, 453 map 17.1

Rhodesia, 387, 413, 475, 501

Richmond, Anthony, 8, 509, 577–78

Romania, 450, 453 map 17.1, 458, 497 map 18.2, 498, 559, 560 map 19.8

Rome, 75, 87, 88, 89–90

Royal African Company, 181, 248

Rubber industry, 269, 358 map 14.4, 493

Russia: African Americans in, 302; agriculture in, 302, 317–18, 652 n.30; census of (1897), 315; and China, 172, 559, 560 map 19.8; Chinese population of, 321, 323 map 13.1; collectivization in, 463–64; draft-based army recruitment in, 278–79, 317; homesteading in, 312, 313 map 13.2, 319, 653 nn.37, 39; industrialization in, 463; Japanese conquest of, 481, 482 map 17.4; Jews in, 326 map 13.5, 325–28 fig. 13.2, 341, 451, 453 map 17.1, 455, 458, 479; labor supply in, 314–15, 316–18, 321, 322 map 13.1, 463, 652 n.30; migration patterns of, 222, 294, 302, 316–17, 341, 521 map 19.3, 652 n.30; *narodniki* in, 324; northwesterly trade route, 77; pogroms in, 113, 341, 458; religious discrimination in, 325; rural

395–98; Indios enslavement, 235–36; and Jews, 40; kidnapping, 150, 155, 245, 376; and legislation, 243–44, 504; male slaves, 41–42, 162, 250; manumission of, 42, 116–17, 128, 158, 159, 162, 243–44, 247, 254, 255, 616 n.31; Maroons, 208, 209; in mining, 204, 207, 236 map 10.1, 237, 242–43, 245, 246; Mongols, 164; mortality of, 155, 156, 158, 159, 196, 197 map 8.2, 235, 246, 247, 376–77; Muslims and Islam, 49, 116–17, 150, 157, 158, 159, 258 map 11.1, 616 n.31; opposition to, 461, 504; and Portugal, 126–29, 150–53, 159, 612 n.38; prostitution as, 485, 511, 518; revolts of, 151, 158, 235, 238, 247, 248, 251; self-determination, 250–51; slave breeding on plantations, 432–33; slave narratives, 150, 155; slave raids, 189, 190, 196, 197 map 8.2, 230, 236 map 10.1, 245; slave retinues, 62, 157–59, 239, 243, 288, 369; in South Africa, 230, 504–5, 511; and Spain, 161, 199–200; in sugarcane cultivation, 47, 150–51, 156, 196–97 map 8.2, 199, 205, 245, 250, 379, 511; in United States, 162, 254, 353 map 14.3, 518, 636 n.42; war captives as, 369; White population's perception of slaves, 250. *See also* Black Atlantic; Bound labor; Forced labor; Serfdom

Soldiers: in British army, 424, 425, 450, 544; demobilization of, 423, 451; draft-based recruitment of, 278–79, 316, 468; exploitation of Native Peoples by, 190; Irish settlement of, 105, 218 map 9.3; janissaries, 40–41, 116, 117; journeymen as, 82; and labor migrations to France, 453 map 17.1, 461; migrations of, 278–79; military service in Ottoman Empire, 115–16; multiethnicity of, 52; private merchant armies in Africa, 407; Scottish migrations of, 223; as slave brokers, 162; slaves as, 158; standing armies, 65, 596 n.10; Turks as slave soldiers in Muslim armies, 110; vagrancy of, 73; yeomen-warriors, 166

Somalia, 515, 518, 525, 552 map 19.7, 565

South Africa: anti-immigration legislation in, 402–3; apartheid in, 493, 505, 507, 556; Bantus, 504–6 map 18.3; Boers, 228–31, 410–11; and Britain, 228–30, 234, 387, 410; ethnic composition of, 507; European population in, 413, 493, 499; gold mining in, 387, 505; gross national product of, 516; Influx Control Act, 556; Khoi peoples, 228–30, 234, 410; labor in, 387, 504–6, 552 map 19.7, 554; migration patterns of, 230–31, 387, 504–5, 506 map 19.7, 552 map 19.7, 558; and Netherlands, 228–30; political parties in, 507; slavery in, 504–5, 511; women and agriculture in, 553

Soviet Union: African Americans and Soviet cotton production, 464; Armenian Republic, 448; autonomous socialist republics in, 455; Chernobyl nuclear disaster, 516–17; electrification programs in, 493; expulsions from, 559, 560 map 19.8; Georgia, 476 map 17.3, 479, 515; independence movements in, 562–63; and Jews, 460, 464, 472, 559, 560 map 19.8; *kolkhozes*, 463–65, 467 map 17.2; migration patterns of, 329–30, 453 map 17.1, 455, 457, 464, 482 map 17.4, 518, 552 map 19.7, 558, 559, 560 map 19.8, 563; Spanish Civil War refugees in, 453 map 17.1, 457; and United States, 227, 320 map 13.4, 326; working conditions in, 465–67 map 17.2

Spain: Algerian-French community in, 503; Argentinian migrations to, 527 map 19.4; Asian slavery abolished by, 200; *asiento* licensing system in, 241; Catalan autonomy in, 454; deportations from, 216; economic crisis (1600s), 193; expulsion of Jesuits, 190; fascism in, 456; fur trade and expansionism, 213 map 9.1; horses taken to New World, 215; immigration patterns of (c. 1800), 290 map 12.2, 293; indolence of Spanish settlers, 179; Italian diaspora in, 453 map 17.1, 456; Jews in, 92, 95–98 map 4.2, 99–100, 113, 175, 292, 460, 605 n.9; and labor migrations, 192, 336, 519; lack of merchandise for commercial exchange, 178; and Latin America migrations, 358 map 14.4, 527 map 19.4, 529; in Manila, 178, 179, 200; migration of foreigners to colonies, 194, 201 map 8.3; migration patterns in, 521 map 19.3; Muslims in, 93–95, 292; and Native peoples, 196, 197 map 8.2, 235, 238; and Portugal in New World, 32; re-creation of Castilian society in New

Taylorism, 344, 465

Tea cultivation, 267–68, 380, 381–82, 382 map 15.5

Textile manufacture: British textiles in China, 370; cloth and clothing production, 50, 207, 266, 373–74, 511; Huguenots in, 106; lace making, 296; in Łódź, 341; New England textile mills, 225, 226, 353 map 14.3, 355, 399, 415–16; and Scottish migrations, 223; in southern Germany, 29; in sweatshops, 546, 579; Tunisian women in, 554; and urban populations, 296, 302; and U.S. Civil War, 366

Thailand: Chinese population of, 536; coolie labor in, 367; gender ratios in migrations to, 539; migration patterns of, 533, 537 map 19.5, 547 map 19.6; prostitution in, 518; and Vietnam War, 487

Tibet, 172, 488, 495, 515

Tobacco cultivation, 199, 215, 243, 267, 358 map 14.4, 390

Togo, 551, 552 map 19.7, 555

Tourism, 528, 541, 563

Trade: Chinese merchants, 371, 536, 541; commodity trading and slavery, 156–57; in diamonds, 204, 410; free trade, 572, 713 n.17; gross national product (GNP), 516, 540–41, 697 nn.15, 16; Hudson Bay Company, 213 map 9.1, 214, 393; and Hundred Years' War, 37–38, 74, 161; Iberian dominance in, 125, 612 n.34; and Kongolese Nzabi societies, 145; in luxury items, 36–37, 47, 89, 142, 179; maritime trade, 163, 165 map 7.2, 166–68, 228, 229 map 9.5; Muslims as traders, 145–48, 614 n.12; newly industrialized countries, 538; in Ottoman Empire, 114; and piracy, 166, 179, 194, 198; and population stability, 75; Portuguese competition with Holland, 181; remote operational basis for, 76; in silk, 31, 309; in spices, 29, 131, 266–67; trade connections and merchants' sons, 40; trade fairs and street vendors, 32 map 2.3, 37, 38, 60, 61, 176; women in flesh markets, 433, 518; in wool, 78, 281–83

Trade routes: in Asia, 29 map 2.2, 126, 127 map 5.3, 163; from Cairo, 43; freight carriers on, 114, 142; for fur trade, 214; land routes, 30–31, 32 map 2.3, 33 map 2.4, 34–36; and lodging places, 31, 59, 62, 90, 114; Lombardy-to-Flanders, 77; Mongol invasions of, 58; to New World, 131–32; Ottoman-Egyptian-Arab route through Indian Ocean region, 174, 619 n.23; and slavery, 40–41, 236 map 10.1, 248. *See also* Railroads; Ships

Transhumance, 78, 205, 281–83, 309

Travel: African guides, 407; gentlemen travelers, 120; lodging places, 31, 59, 62, 90, 114; road construction, 59, 114; and transnational identity, 579, 715 n.32; travel narratives, 31, 34, 36, 37, 263, 576. *See also* Pilgrimages

Treaty of Tordesillas (1494), 241

Treaty of Utrecht (1713), 184

Treaty of Westphalia (1648), 104, 566–67

Trinidad, 249, 379, 528–29

Tunisia: European-origin population in (1930), 499; France in, 407, 408 map 16.1, 414 map 16.2; Jewish repatriation to France from, 503; migration patterns of, 521 map 19.3, 552 map 19.7, 554; repatriation of French citizens from, 502; repatriation of Tunisians, 479; in trans-Saharan slave trade, 159; women's employment in, 554

Turkey: Armenian Genocide, 448; tsarist supporters ("second migration") in, 328–29, 655 nn.62, 63, 64; and Greece, 449, 453 map 17.1; Jews in, 458; migration patterns of, 449, 452, 453 map 17.1, 457–58, 460–61, 521 map 19.3

Tutsi, 230, 558

Uganda, 500, 551, 552 map 19.7, 554, 556–58

Ukraine, 343, 353 map 14.3, 453 map 17.1, 454–55, 463, 519

United Kingdom. *See* Britain

United Nations: *Human Development Report* (1995), 516; partition of Palestine (1947), 496, 497 map 18.2

United Nations High Commissioner for Refugees (UNHCR), 513, 518, 544, 552 map 19.7, 553

United Nations Relief and Works Agency for Palestinian Refugees (UNRWA), 496

United States: abolitionist movement in, 255–56, 272; African Americans in, 6, 202, 226, 254, 353 map 14.3, 355, 356, 462, 636 n.42, 663 n.62; Alaska, 217 map 9.2, 227; and Canada, 226, 523; Caribbean community in, 524–28, 528, 531, 533; Chicago, 354–55; and China, 370, 483, 532, 537 map 19.5; colonialism of, 424, 569; deportations from, 356–57, 462; electrification programs in, 492; and European migration, 216, 221, 337 map 14.2, 338, 340, 476 map 17.3, 480, 524, 560 map 19.8; First Peoples in, 188 map 8.1, 215, 216, 217 map 9.2; Florida, 224, 248, 255, 525, 530; immigration restrictions in, 6, 7, 401, 456, 458; Indochinese migrations to, 533, 537 map 19.5; internment of Japanese-Americans in, 485–86; and investment in Africa mineral resources, 555; and Japan, 375, 401–2, 485; Jewish immigration to, 324, 341, 560 map 19.8, 562; labor activism in, 441, 511; labor and refugee migrations to, 510 map 19.1; Laotian migrations to, 533; Latin American migrations to, 527 map 19.4, 530; legislation and quotas for immigration, 255, 458, 523–26, 528, 532–33, 700 n.37; Mexican migrations to, 353 map 14.3, 355–56, 513, 523, 524, 527 map 19.4, 529; migration and perceptions of America, 226; migration of Free Blacks from, 253; Pacific Islander migrations to, 533–34, 537 map 19.5; Panamanian migrations to, 527 map 19.4; Pennsylvania, 217, 222, 224, 326; in Philippines, 424, 533, 569; Polish migration to, 341, 475, 560 map 19.8, 562; political asylum in, 515, 533; population of, 225, 479, 526, 527 map 19.4; port cities and immigration, 225–26; and Puerto Rico, 424, 525, 527 map 19.4, 569; return migration from, 339; slavery in, 162, 254, 353 map 14.3, 518, 636 n.42; South Korean migrations to, 533; and Soviet Union, 227, 316 map 13.4, 325, 464; Tamil migration to, 545; undocumented migrants in, 512, 526, 529; Vietnamese settlement in, 525, 527 map 19.4, 533; War of Independence, 635 n.37; and women immigrants for domestic service, 528. *See also* New York

Universal Negro Improvement Association, 526–28

Ural Mountains, 453 map 17.1, 455, 466, 467 map 17.2, 475

Uruguay, 342, 358 map 14.4, 359, 527 map 19.4, 531

U.S. Immigration Reform and Control Act (1986), 525

Uzbeks, 308 map 13.1, 309, 310 map 13.2, 453 map 17.1, 455

Vagrancy, 61–62, 72–74, 80–81, 117, 303, 324, 334–35 map 14.1, 654 n.53

Venezuela: *cimarrones* in, 244; foreign-born population in, 530; labor supply and sugarcane cultivation on islands of, 196, 197 map 8.2, 201 map 8.3; leasing of, to Welser, 194; migrations to, 342, 510 map 19.1, 527 map 19.4, 530; oil industry in, 530; slave imports in, 241, 242 map 10.2; Venice, 46, 76–77, 80, 174, 619 n.23

Versailles Peace Conference, 449, 569, 573

Vietnam: and China, 536, 538; deportation of landowners in, 500; factional war in, 500, 514 map 19.2; and France, 480, 502, 533; migration patterns of, 480–81, 487, 525, 527 map 19.4, 533, 547 map 19.6; refugee-generation from, 515, 538

Vietnam War, 523, 527 map 19.4, 533

Wages: cash payments as, 69, 72, 373, 374; and labor supply, 12, 81, 366, 374–75; and remittances, 545, 549

Wallerstein, Immanuel, 27, 30, 158

Wars: diaspora support for, 573; ecocidal war, 553; of expansion, 446–47, 453 map 17.1; and Huguenot forced emigration, 106; Hundred Years' War, 37–38, 74, 161; Incas and war captives, 189; for independence, 488, 496, 500–501; Iraqi invasion of Kuwait, 550; "just wars" theory (Aquinas), 195, 272; and labor, 86, 450; military instructors, migration of, 278; multiethnicity of armies, 52; against Native Americans, 215; nuclear technology, 485, 516; and pacifism, 472; peasant conscription in Mongolian conflict, 212; population displacements by, 472, 531–32; prisoners of war, 199–200,

Dirk Hoerder is Professor of History at the Universitat Bremen in
Germany. He has written and edited numerous books. He is coeditor
of *European Migrants: Global and Local Perspectives; The Settling
of North America: The Atlas of the Great Migrations into North
America from the Ice Age to the Present; People in Transit: German
Migrations in Comparative Perspective, 1820–1930; Roots of the
Transplanted;* and *Distant Magnets: Expectations and Realities
in the Immigrant Experience, 1840–1930.*

Library of Congress Cataloging-in-Publication Data
Hoerder, Dirk.
Cultures in contact : world migrations in the second millennium /
Dirk Hoerder.
p. cm. — (Comparative and international working-class history)
Includes bibliographical references and index.
ISBN 0-8223-2834-8 (cloth: alk. paper)
1. Human beings—Migrations.   2. Migrations of nations—History.
3. Acculturation—History.   I. Title: World migrations in the second
millennium.   II. Title.   III. Series.
GN370 .H64   2002   304.8—dc21   2002002594